Water-Soluble Vitamins							Minerals					
Vitamin C (mg)	Thiamin (mg)	Ribo-flavin (mg)	Niacin (mg NE)§	Vitamin B$_6$ (mg)	Folacin$^{\|}$ (μg)	Vitamin B$_{12}$ (μg)	Calcium (mg)	Phos-phorus (mg)	Mag-nesium (mg)	Iron (mg)	Zinc (mg)	Iodine (μg)
35	0.3	0.4	6	0.3	30	0.5¶	360	240	50	10	3	40
35	0.5	0.6	8	0.6	45	1.5	540	360	70	15	5	50
45	0.7	0.8	9	0.9	100	2.0	800	800	150	15	10	70
45	0.9	1.0	11	1.3	200	2.5	800	800	200	10	10	90
45	1.2	1.4	16	1.6	300	3.0	800	800	250	10	10	120
50	1.4	1.6	18	1.8	400	3.0	1,200	1,200	350	18	15	150
60	1.4	1.7	18	2.0	400	3.0	1,200	1,200	400	18	15	150
60	1.5	1.7	19	2.2	400	3.0	800	800	350	10	15	150
60	1.4	1.6	18	2.2	400	3.0	800	800	350	10	15	150
60	1.2	1.4	16	2.2	400	3.0	800	800	350	10	15	150
50	1.1	1.3	15	1.8	400	3.0	1,200	1,200	300	18	15	150
60	1.1	1.3	14	2.0	400	3.0	1,200	1,200	300	18	15	150
60	1.1	1.3	14	2.0	400	3.0	800	800	300	18	15	150
60	1.0	1.2	13	2.0	400	3.0	800	800	300	18	15	150
60	1.0	1.2	13	2.0	400	3.0	800	800	300	10	15	150
+20	+0.4	+0.3	+2	+0.6	+400	+1.0	+400	+400	+150	#	+5	+25
+40	+0.5	+0.5	+5	+0.5	+100	+1.0	+400	+400	+150	#	+10	+50

$^{\|}$ The folacin allowances refer to dietary sources as determined by *Lactobacillus casei* assay after treatment with enzymes (conjugases) to make polyglutamyl forms of the vitamin available to the test organism.

¶ The recommended dietary allowance for vitamin B$_{12}$ in infants is based on average concentration of the vitamin in human milk. The allowances after weaning are based on energy intake (as recommended by the American Academy of Pediatrics) and consideration of other factors, such as intestinal absorption.

The increased requirement during pregnancy cannot be met by the iron content of habitual American diets nor by the existing iron stores of many women; therefore the use of 30 to 60 mg of supplemental iron is recommended. Iron needs during lactation are not substantially different from those of nonpregnant women, but continued supplementation of the mother for 2 to 3 months after parturition is advisable in order to replenish stores depleted by pregnancy.

HUMAN NUTRITION
AND DIET THERAPY

HUMAN NUTRITION AND DIET THERAPY

Y. H. Hui, Ph.D.

Humboldt State University
Arcata, California

Wadsworth Health Sciences Division
Monterey, California
A Division of Wadsworth, Inc.

Wadsworth Health Sciences Division
A Division of Wadsworth, Inc.

Subject Editor: James Keating

Production: Greg Hubit Bookworks, Larkspur, California

Interior Design: Marilyn Langfeld

Cover Design: Albert Burkhardt

Copy Editor: Paul Monsour

Illustrations: Li Greiner

Chapter-opening photos: George B. Fry III

Typesetting: G&S Typesetters, Inc., Austin, Texas

Production Services Manager: Stacey C. Sawyer

Library of Congress Cataloging in Publication Data

Hui, Yiu H.
  Human nutrition and diet therapy.

  Bibliography: p.
  Includes index.
  1. Diet therapy. 2. Nutrition. 3. Nursing.
I. Title. [DNLM: 1. Nutrition. 2. Diet therapy.
QU 145 H899h]
RM216.H877 1983   615.8′54   82-20136

ISBN 0-534-01336-8

CONTENTS

PART II APPLIED NUTRITION

APPENDICES

CASE STUDIES

PREFACE

ALL OF US want good health, and good nutrition is a major prerequisite to good health. The fact that there is a complex relationship between nutrition and health is now emerging, and it is becoming apparent that this relationship is at least twofold. First, it has long been known that, in a number of pathological conditions, patients can benefit substantially if they are provided with knowledgeable and carefully planned dietary care. Second, recent evidence leads scientists to suspect that many human diseases may be prevented by following good nutritional habits throughout life.

A number of college textbooks that discuss the role of nutrition in health and diseases are now available. These are used mainly by students preparing for careers in the health field. The texts differ from one another in three fundamental ways: levels of sophistication, directly related to the scientific and technical background training of the students; extent of information coverage, which reflects the specific needs of the students; and structural organization and writing style.

The main objective of this book is to provide students in nursing, dietetics, nutrition, and allied health fields with some basic information relating to normal and therapeutic nutrition in humans. With this background knowledge, these health professionals should be able to educate the general public about sound nutritional practices and to provide proper nutritional and dietary care to patients with specific diseases.

With reference to sophistication, coverage, and writing style, a background in biology and chemistry will enable the student to gain a more in-depth understanding of the chemical and biological basis of the information presented throughout the book. However, the lack of this knowledge will not be a handicap in following most of the basic facts and principles discussed in Parts I and II. But some elementary training in biology, human physiology, and chemistry is necessary to follow the contents of Part III. Information coverage in this book is comprehensive at the level of expected student competency. A number of currently important subjects are included even though they may not yet be well understood, were considered unimportant in the past, or are simply new discoveries. Such topics include terminology for fiber, methods of weight reduction, food additives, total parenteral nutrition, insulin pump, high density lipoprotein, and others. Every attempt has been made to assure that the material is easy to read and understand.

The book is organized into three parts. Part I, "Principles of Nutrition," provides three sets of information. The major discussion relates to nutrients, as indicated in Figure 1 (numbers in parentheses refer to chapters). In addition, Chapter 2 discusses energy and body composition. Because these two subjects contain integrated materials, they may be taught before or after a student has become familiar with the role of nutrients. Chapter 9, "Fluids, Electrolytes, and Acid-Base Balance," is of mixed significance in human nutrition (basic, applied, and clinical). Although it is usually taught in human physiol-

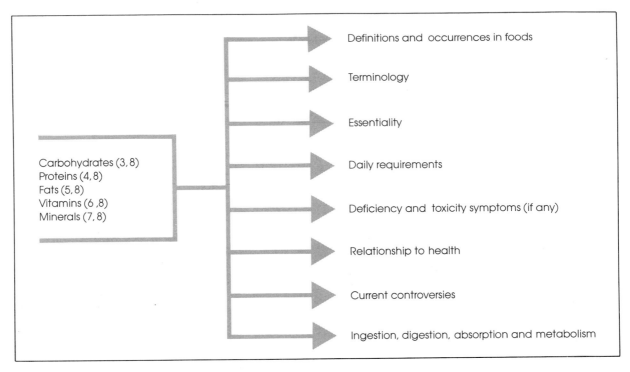

Carbohydrates (3,8)
Proteins (4,8)
Fats (5,8)
Vitamins (6,8)
Minerals (7,8)

Definitions and occurrences in foods

Terminology

Essentiality

Daily requirements

Deficiency and toxicity symptoms (if any)

Relationship to health

Current controversies

Ingestion, digestion, absorption and metabolism

FIGURE 1

ogy, its discussion in Part I serves two purposes: It emphasizes nutritionally related clinical situations, and it serves as a reference source for the study of diet therapy in Part III.

Part II, "Applied Nutrition," offers three approaches to the study of normal nutrition. First, one important and popular topic of discussion in nutritional sciences is the role of nutrition in the life cycle, as illustrated in Figure 2. Part II analyzes this life cycle by discussing the nutritional needs and requirements, nutritional status, and nutrition-related health problems and controversial issues of each stage.

Second, Part II relates nutrition to our environment, as indicated in Figure 3. Cultural, ethnic, and geographical backgrounds have always played an important part in our preferences for certain foods. Now scientists believe that some of our eating practices benefit our health, while others have a negative impact. Similarly, nutritionists believe that many degenerative diseases in our old age result from bad eating habits adopted since childhood, habits which may be corrected through nutrition education. Our concern for food safety has always empha-

sized biological food poisoning. However, the public has recently begun to express alarm about food and color additives and accidental chemical contamination of our food supply. Part II attempts to explore these complicated relationships between our nutritional well being and our environment.

Third, Part II also discusses drugs (16), obesity (12), undernutrition (11), and community nutrition (19). This information is of significance in both applied nutrition and diet therapy. For example, overweight and starvation are considered diseases by many health professionals, whereas some instructors consider them topics for clinical programs. These chapters can be taught separately or integrated into Part III.

Part III, "Diet Therapy," is devoted entirely to the nutrition and dietary care of patients with clinical disorders, as indicated in Figure 4. A careful study of this diagram illustrates how the pertinent chapters in Parts I and II serve Part III. For ease of reference, a number of clinical disorders are presented in Chapter 31: the nutrition and dietary care of immobilized, mental, elderly, or rehabilitating patients, and patients

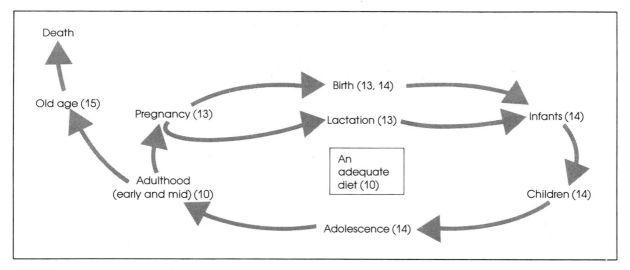

FIGURE 2

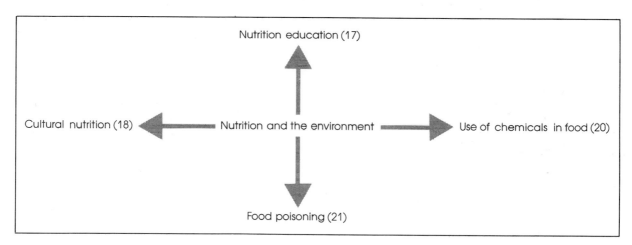

FIGURE 3

with food allergy, anorexia nervosa, or infection.

A textbook of this nature has an inherent limitation—size. Thus, certain subjects are either not discussed or covered only briefly. For example, Part III does not include the role of nutrition and diet in some metabolic diseases, diseases of the musculoskeletal system, the causation of cancer, some childhood diseases (e.g., epilepsy), and physical handicaps. Diet therapy for infection, mental illness, anorexia nervosa, and food allergy are discussed only briefly. However, the extensive list of references in Appendix F provides an opportunity for students who may

be interested in more details to explore further. This presentation strategy permits the inclusion in Part III of additional basic and applied materials in patient care. For example, detailed discussions are provided for commercial nutritional products, techniques of improving patient compliance with a therapeutic diet, food selection systems, meal and menu plans, clinical management procedures, and patient education. It is hoped that these in-depth analyses will provide students in nursing, dietetics, and nutrition a larger frame of reference in patient care.

The information presented in this book has

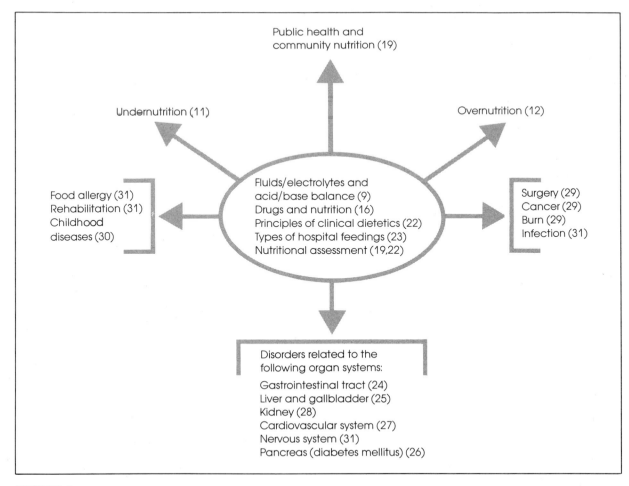

FIGURE 4

been derived mainly from the latest books, journal articles, conferences, and symposia on the subject matter. These references are included in Appendix F. Standard citations for specific references are also provided in the text itself.

To help students relate the information in the text to real-life situations, several special features are offered. To provide both students and teachers with an overview of the latest developments in nutritional sciences, Chapter 1 includes an authoritative analysis by a well-known nutritionist and physician, Dr. J. Hirsch of Rockefeller University in New York. To permit students to see the immediate application of the information in the text, Chapters 2, 3, and 6 include pertinent clinical cases or field practices from current literature. In Chapters 22 to 31, applicable case studies are provided, relating directly to the clinical

disorders discussed. Most of these case studies have been prepared by the author from actual case histories, although the identities of the patients have been changed or modified.

Three other features of the book should be emphasized:

1. Part III provides more than six types of food exchange lists for different clinical conditions: diabetes, sodium restriction (hypertension, congestive heart failure), sodium and potassium restriction (kidney diseases), calcium restriction (hypercalcemia), phenylalanine restriction (phenylketonuria), and hyperlipoproteinemia.

2. Appendices A through E present 25 tables of major reference data, including food composition tables, growth curves, blood and

urine analyses, and Recommended Daily Dietary Allowances. These tables serve two important purposes: They assist a student in completing classroom assignments and, together with the text materials, they serve as a useful reference source for health professionals who may be directly or indirectly responsible for the nutritional and dietary care of a patient.

3. A teaching aid in the form of an instructor's manual contains a variety of materials designed to familiarize the instructor with the objectives of the book. Other features include activities, discussions, and projects; a test bank of essay questions, matching quizzes, and multiple-choice questions; and a list of audiovisual and journal resources keyed to each chapter. The instructor's manual is intended to supplement the knowledge and experience each teacher brings to the subject of nutrition and diet therapy.

ACKNOWLEDGMENTS

Many persons have contributed their efforts in helping me to complete this book. It would be impossible to name them all here, and I take this opportunity to thank those not individually mentioned.

James Keating, the sponsoring editor for this book, has been the main driving force from conception of this project to completion of the manuscript. Without his foresight, encouragement, support, and friendship, I would not have succeeded in bringing this work to completion. I am unable to fully express my appreciation in words —all I can say is *thank you*.

Because this is my first experience in writing for an undergraduate audience, I was assisted by Mary Pat Fisher, a professional writer and the author of several books of her own. Ms. Fisher transformed my original 2,000 manuscript pages into their present form. The reader is the best judge of her expertise and professionalism. However, I assume full responsibility for the final result, since the rewritten materials were subject to my final approval and further modification.

Mary Farr and Dorothy Bissell are two friends who have stood by me since September 1971. They have complete faith in my endeavors and help me in all aspects of my research and writing whenever they can. They spent many hours reviewing this book in manuscript form. I will always be grateful to them.

The entire staff of reference librarians at Humboldt State University is always there to provide assistance whenever I need it. They have my sincere appreciation. Darlena Blucher of this university has been a great friend and helper. She contributed something to practically every chapter of the manuscript. Other professors at this university have helped to review some of the chapters. These wonderful individuals are Bill Allen, Gary Brusca, John De Martini, Joseph Leeper, Dick Meyer, Joan Pierson, Denis Potter, and James Waters. I am grateful to Evelyn Wunderlich of the University of California Extension Service for her special contribution to Chapter 17. Many students have helped with my research and writing, and I thank them all, especially Patricia Radcliff, Patricia Novak, Kathy McConnell, Ann Fischer, Debbie Hague, and Karen Nelson.

A group of local dietitians have critically evaluated different chapters of the manuscript. I am grateful to Karen Anderson, Joan McCartney, Barbara Magladry, Kathy Munoz, and Eileen Stocum. I am indebted to Vicky Smith, a consulting dietitian in Humboldt County. In spite of her job and family, she is always there to share her time, knowledge, and expertise whenever I need it. She has contributed to many facets of this project, and I hope someday I can reciprocate.

This book has been produced under the management of Greg Hubit Bookworks of Larkspur, California. The excellent quality and professionalism of its work is self-evident. I would also like to thank all authors who have permitted me to reproduce their work.

Finally, I am deeply grateful to my family for their indispensable and long-enduring patience and support.

Y. H. H.

HUMAN NUTRITION
AND DIET THERAPY

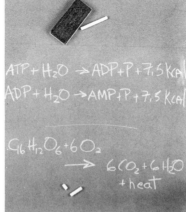

$$ATP + H_2O \rightarrow ADP + P + 7.5 \, kcal$$
$$ADP + H_2O \rightarrow AMP + P + 7.5 \, kcal$$

$$C_6H_{12}O_6 + 6O_2 \rightarrow 6CO_2 + 6H_2O + heat$$

PART I

PRINCIPLES OF NUTRITION

Chapter 1

Nutrition, Diet, and the American People

TODAY, MANY PEOPLE are paying considerable attention to what they eat, with the idea that food intake is closely related to health and a sense of well-being. In some cases, this concern is exaggerated: Some people tend to link every dietary factor with some form of human disease, without good scientific evidence. Nevertheless, knowing how nutrition influences our well-being can help us to decide what kind of lifestyles to lead.

This chapter will review some controversial nutritional issues that are of major concern to health professionals and the American people: the relationship between health and diet, health foods, food safety, adding nutrients to foods, the relationship of exercise to health, and world hunger. We will also provide a brief analysis of how health professionals with a background in foods, nutrition, diet therapy, and related fields fit into the American health care system. First, however, we will look briefly at what *nutrition* means.

THE MEANING OF NUTRITION *

According to Webster's *Third International Dictionary*, *nutrition* is "the sum of the processes by which an animal or plant takes in and utilizes food substances . . . typically involving ingestion, digestion, absorption, and assimilation." The Council on Foods and Nutrition of the American Medical Association defines *nutrition* as "the science of food, the nutrients and other substances therein, their action, interaction, and balance in relation to health and disease and the processes by which the organism ingests, absorbs, transports, utilizes and excretes food substances." These definitions outline the areas covered in this text.

A relatively new science, nutrition evolved from the basic sciences of chemistry and physiology. Early investigators, primarily Europeans, initiated nutrition studies as they attempted to understand the physiological utilization of food

in supporting the essential processes of life, including growth, reproduction, and lactation. The saga of human nutrition and the improvement of human health in the United States is reflected in the efforts of those scientists who have believed that human performance and well-being—both mental and physical—depend primarily on what one eats.

During the last 100 years, the science of nutrition has progressed from a meager understanding to the point that most of the essential nutrients appear to have been identified. Most nutrients have been isolated in purified form, and the biological functions of many are now reasonably well understood. Nutritionists have speculated that life could be sustained, although probably not enjoyed, by a supply of purified nutrients.

Nutritional deficiency diseases that were common in the past, such as scurvy, rickets, goiter, and pellagra—have been either eliminated or greatly reduced in incidence. Another measure of the progress made in the field of nutrition: The life expectancy of the average American has increased from around 40 years at the turn of the century to almost 70 at the present time—an increase that can be at least partially attributed to improvements in nutritional knowledge. Newborn babies have profited from advances in nutrition, and methods for preventing and managing such disorders as anemia have provided a better chance for children to experience normal growth and to develop their full physical and mental potential. Tremendous progress has been made in agriculture as well as in food science and technology to assure a safe, wholesome food supply for the American people. But the search for even more knowledge about nutrition continues.

"EAT RIGHT AND BE HEALTHY" *

Much of the research now under way concerns the relationship between food choices and health. Data from scientific studies have led

---

*Part of this section has been adapted from Ritchey, S. J. 1975. *Agricultural Yearbook 1975* (Washington, D.C.: U.S. Department of Agriculture), p. 289.

*Adapted from *Home and Garden Bulletin No. 228* (Washington, D.C.: U.S. Department of Agriculture).

many scientists to conclude that the average American diet contributes to some of the chronic diseases that affect older Americans. These scientists believe that reducing dietary calories, fat (especially animal and other saturated fats), cholesterol, sugar, and salt and eating more whole grains, fruits, and vegetables are positive steps toward reducing heart disease, certain cancers, and strokes. Other scientists believe just as strongly that the evidence does not support these conclusions.

In addition to the conflicting opinions of experts, individuals may be confused by the tremendous variety of foods available: More than 10,000 food products confront a shopper at an average American supermarket. Conflicting claims as to which of these foods are good and bad abound. Staying within a food budget presents an additional dilemma, as do family members' differing time schedules and attempts to gain or lose weight.

Although the great abundance of tempting displays in a supermarket makes food choices somewhat confusing, this variety is potentially beneficial. Research indicates that our nutrient and energy needs are best met if we eat a variety of foods. We are therefore indeed fortunate to have a food supply that is both abundant and varied, and to have this food provided in a range of prices. Foods can be purchased fresh, frozen, canned, or dried; they may be partially prepared, completely prepared, or fortified with nutrients. They may even be fabricated foods, such as fruit-flavored beverages with vitamin C added.

We can eat any food we like if we know how to combine it with other foods to provide a desirable diet. Scientists have established human requirements for some nutrients and calories and made recommendations for the amounts to be consumed by people of various ages. As we will see in Chapter 10, nutritionists have translated these recommendations into kinds and amounts of foods needed for a good nutritional foundation. These translations are known as food guides. If followed, they provide an easy way to make desirable food choices.

It is not necessary that everyone makes the same food choices. Life-styles, national origins, religious beliefs, individual tastes, prices, and shopping and preparation time all influence the choices we make. But it is to our advantage to learn to select foods and eat a diet that is both enjoyable and healthful. Good nutrition not only adds to the enjoyment of living: but also affects how we look, how we feel, and how well we can work and play.

HEALTH FOODS *

Are health foods the best food choices? The advantages claimed for health foods over conventionally grown and marketed products are now being hotly debated. Advocates of health, organic, and natural foods—terms whose meanings vary greatly—frequently proclaim that such products are safer and more nutritious than others.

The growing interest of consumers in the safety and nutritional quality of the American diet is a welcome development. However, much of this interest has been sparked by alarmists who imply that the American food supply is unsafe or inadequate in meeting our nutritional needs. Although most of these claims are not supported by scientific evidence, the preponderance of written material available makes it difficult for the general public to separate fact from fiction. As a result, claims that certain health foods or diets prevent or cure disease or provide other benefits to health have become dispersed among sound bits of information and form the basis for folklore and outright fabrication.

Almost daily the public is besieged by claims for new "anticancer" foods, "no-aging" diets, "nonhunger" breads, new vitamins, and other wonder foods. We have reports that natural vitamins are superior to synthetic ones, that the soil in this country is depleted, and that organic fertilizers produce better crops than manufactured fertilizers. We also have many minor myths: that organic (fertilized) eggs are nutritionally superior to infertile eggs, that raw milk is better than pasteurized milk, and the like.

One thing that all health, organic, and natural food products seem to have in common is that

---

*Adapted from Stephenson, M. 1978. *FDA Consumer* 12:18.

Medicine in the '80s: Nutrition*

A look at this past year's *New York Times Christmas Book Review* reveals that Nos. 2 and 6 on the nonfiction Best Seller List deal with human nutrition; and the matter of how to stay healthy and thin by better eating is by no means restricted to the lay public. Governmental agencies have been extremely concerned with clinical nutrition during the late 1970s. These governmental concerns do not appear to have originated from any fundamental or revolutionary discoveries in the biologic sciences that have yielded new information which would then have to be communicated to the public. Rather, there is a growing awareness that nutrition may be an essential ingredient in the prevention of disease. The public at large—whether from a current anti-intellectual bias or a general return to a do-it-yourself attitude in these days of perceived inadequacy of central government and technocracy—has turned to folk wisdom and self-medication to prevent and/or cure disease. Herbal teas, special exercise regimens, and new techniques of interpersonal encounter and meditation are now popular modes for trying to keep fit in body and soul. Needless to say, in this atmosphere, what you eat and how you eat it, matters which involve personal choices at least two or three times per day, are very much in the public eye.

Federal agencies became involved partly in response to public interest, but also as a result of the recognition that national health costs continue to mount and threaten to climb even more steeply. Given this situation, and the governmental commitment to continued and increasing subsidization of the cost of health care, disease prevention has become more attractive. And, the moment one mentions prevention, the question of *what to eat* to keep fit becomes a central issue.

Thus, I view the public as well as the government as the major forces that will bring

Source: J. Hirsch, *Drug Therapy* 10 (1980): 119–138.

clinical nutrition into increasing prominence in the 1980s. At this moment, new biologic insights, or pressures from the biomedical research community, do not seem to be major forces in the promotion of clinical nutrition.

Role of Clinical Nutrition

The foregoing description of the current avid interest in the relationship between food and health is in no way meant to imply that in past years the science of nutrition was unimportant. Apart from its obvious deep roots in home economics and food technology and processing, it must be noted that a number of distinguished departments of nutrition established earlier in this century laid the groundwork for the scientific study of energy and intermediary metabolism, and uncovered the basic nutritional principles needed for the use of animals as experimental tools. Indeed, much of the modern science of biochemistry has deep roots in the science of nutrition. It is also interesting to note than an important impetus to the development of the National Institutes of Health (NIH) was the great success of one of the first laboratories of the United States Public Health Service, manned by Goldberger and his colleagues and dedicated to problems of human clinical nutrition.

Growth of biomedical research

After World War II, the discipline of biomedicine burgeoned in the United States. The NIH, as a source of funds for extramural research and/or as a role model in its intramural programs, catalyzed an immense leap forward in the establishment of biomedical research laboratories throughout the nation and in the growth of new information on biochemistry and metabolism. At this time, clinical nutrition appeared to have already passed its Golden Age. The discovery of the necessary role of vitamins and other micronutrients had already been well established for the diets of humans and animals. No special discipline of clinical nutrition seemed necessary to facilitate closer investigative scrutiny of cellular components and chemical processes, which were becoming the area of most intense scientific interest. In fact, the new biomedical scientists were deeply involved with two principles which appeared to render further investigations of a traditional nutritional nature unnecessary or even invalid.

Dynamic state of body constituents

The utilization of isotope tracers for the labeling of body constituents gave clear evidence for the rapid turnover of tissues, cells, and subcellular components. This being the case, interest naturally focused on the nature of the machinery that permitted these extraordinary changes in body constituents to occur. If, in fact, all parts of our body are "born again," with half-lives of hours, days—or at the most months—then there is little reason to believe that long-term dietary practices can have permanent and lasting impact; by this reasoning, dietary insults or nutritional inadequacies early in life, or at other critical times, should have abundant opportunities to be compensated for in later turnovers. The enzymatic machinery and the genetic endowment providing the blueprint for the development of this machinery, were obviously of more interest than problems engendered by long-term feeding practices.

Doctrine of interconvertibility

It was, of course, known that certain chemical compounds, such as the essential amino acids, vitamins, and other micronutrients, could not be synthesized by the body. Beyond this, however, whether more or less protein, fat, or carbohydrate were ingested daily, and what the particular quality of the fat or carbohydrate might be was considered of little consequence. The offices of clinical investigators were adorned with the

most exquisitely intricate metabolic maps. It appeared that one could take any carbon skeleton and find a pathway for either shortening or elongating it and for adding or deleting whatever group of chemical radicals one would like. This being the case, why indeed should there be a difference in the health of an organism if more or less fat or carbohydrate is eaten? The carbon skeletons of whatever origin were shown by elegant studies to have a common fate in acetyl CoA and thence to be burned or used for synthesis of only a few chemically alike substances for the storage of energy. The number of enzymes (which were beginning to be characterized) seemed infinite, and thus the chemical potential for interconvertibility for foodstuffs almost endless. With this conceptual orientation, the research focus became far removed from the more fundamental approaches of clinical nutrition, or the effect of diets in the promotion of health or prevention of disease. While food selection always interested the American public and biomedical scientists through the 1950s and '60s, it was often not from a health-oriented point of view, but rather because of the keen interest in the bounty of ethnic food possibilities and our appetite for cosmopolitanism. This was, of course, not considered to be a serious or scientific matter. Whether one burns cedar wood, pine, or oak may be of considerable concern to the fireside aesthete, but is of no concern to the stoker who maintains the municipal furnace, providing the energy that does the job.

Enzyme defects

Yet, through these years of focus on the cellular and subcellular nature of human disease, the impact of food and diet on health and disease could not be forgotten. Perhaps the best examples of how clinical nutrition intersected with the new biomedicine are instances in which it was discovered that genetic alterations leading to specific enzymatic defects could be ameliorated by diet. Two cases in point are phenylketonuria (PKU) and lactase deficiency. There are, of course, many others. These instances began to again demonstrate how clinical nutrition investigations and approaches could be useful even within the conceptual framework of inter-convertibility of foodstuffs and dynamic turnover of body constituents. It was clear that the enzymatic apparatus assuring inter-convertibility could, at times, fail, necessitating the dietary introduction or elimination of specific foodstuffs. Either "short-term" nutritional interventions or nutritional "repair" of this type did not violate the orientations of the new breed of biomedical scientists, and their consideration of what constituted valid treatment for disease. But, long-term dietary choice and disease prevention was another matter.

Diet and Disease

In contrast to the views of the new breed of biomedical scientists, long-term nutritional impact never ceased to intrigue epidemiologists and public-health-oriented scientists. The increasing internationalization of the scientific community made possible detailed nutritional observations and reports of populations throughout the world. Although known before the 1950s and '60s, it became especially evident during this period that different populations in different geographic areas suffer from different illnesses. Furthermore, such differences could not be attributed exclusively to genetic factors, since there was abundant experimental proof that, along with the mobility of populations, came changing disease patterns. For example, as the Bantu moved into the city and the rural Japanese moved into urban areas (or to Hawaii or the United States) their patterns of illness altered. Increase in mortality from coronary artery disease, alterations in the incidence of certain types of cancer, and so forth suggested the influence of environment in provoking human disease. Environmental effects other than food intake were implicated, but dietary alterations were al-

ways of paramount concern. The finding that victims of famine in early childhood had permanent alterations not only in body size and fat stores but also in behavior suggested that early nutritional events could have life-long effects. Some observations did not fit with the prevailing interests of biochemistry and cell biology, and thus they were not studied in detail.

Future Outlook

The 1980s are almost certain to be a period during which all of these matters will be carefully examined. Many of the epidemiologic observations relating nutrition to health will, hopefully, be placed on a sounder biologic footing. The pathogenetic sequence whereby lifelong dietary choices can alter disease prevalence will be reexamined. Great strides should also be made in developing methodology and more precise indications for acute clinical nutritional interventions.

Acute nutritional interventions

Trauma, surgery, and severe infections are often accompanied by profound catabolism and generally little or no intake of nutrients. Whether anorexia or inability to eat during such states is part of the "wisdom of the body" or should be completely repaired by aggressive measures such as total parenteral nutrition is yet to be evaluated in a completely satisfactory way. Total parenteral nutrition also offers a valuable adjunctive therapy for chronic inflammatory disease of the bowel. The role of TPN in such disorders will no doubt receive careful clinical evaluation in the next decade. The safest techniques for performing this important therapy and the precise indications will be ascertained. From an investigative standpoint, total parenteral nutrition has also been of interest. The possibility of maintaining alimentation immediately after surgery or trauma permits a variety of studies—not to mention patient benefits—which were heretofore impossible. One byproduct has been the clear demonstration that essential fatty acid deficiency can and does occur in human adults. If there ever was doubt about this, it is now clear that the absence of polyunsaturated fatty acids, combined with a high-carbohydrate diet, can provoke skin lesions which vanish when essential fatty acids are reintroduced. More important, interest has focused on immunologic deficits in patients who are inappropriately nourished after surgery and trauma. It may well be that wound healing and other aspects of recovery from trauma can be assisted by better nutrition. The mechanism of these immunologic changes—whether via humoral antibodies or cell-mediated immunity—is just beginning to receive the intensive study that it demands. In the 1980s, these matters will undoubtedly be frontiers of investigation.

Drug/diet interactions.   Since the 1950s, we have witnessed the development and wide-scale use of increasingly powerful pharmacologic agents. Many of these alter nutrient requirements or the mode of absorption of dietary constituents. Active investigation will be conducted in this area to ascertain appropriate nutritional information for patients on various drugs. The usual prescription for "tid ac" or "tid pc," which indicates awareness that there can be an important relationship of drug ingestion and meals, will be supplemented with more precise information as to what the diet should be. The special vitamin needs of patients receiving such drugs as isoniazid or penicillamine (Cuprimine, Depen), or the avoidance of some vitamin supplements when treating patients with drugs such as levodopa, will receive increasing attention as well.

Effects of dietary constituents on behavior.   It has been clear for several years that essential amino acids such as phenylalanine, tyrosine, and tryptophan are precursors of neurotransmitters and that a continuous supply of these is required. However, the concept that dietary alterations may effect acute changes in brain function is of more

recent origin. The manipulation of dietary amino acids as well as choline, and the careful observation of the effects on behavior and brain function, are important frontiers of the examination of short-term nutritional effects on health and disease.

Long-term nutritional intervention

As for the long-term effects of nutrition on mental functioning, the 1980s will bring increasing scrutiny to the concept of nutritional "critical periods." There is evidence from both animal and human studies that severe deprivation at key times in early life can lead to permanent abnormalities in brain development. Estimates of brain cell size and number have been determined histologically as well as by measurements of DNA and RNA. A series of animal and human behavioral studies suggests that deficiencies of calories, proteins, or essential minerals such as iron may lead to longstanding, if not permanent, behavioral changes. The issue of whether overfeeding early in infancy can provoke either childhood or adult obesity remains under consideration. Since this represents a major research interest to the author, I am hopeful that the 1980s will be active years in the elucidation of this problem.

Development of eating habits.   Very little study has been devoted to critical periods for the development of behaviors that will influence later dietary practices. This, in my estimation, will be an important area for investigation in the 1980s and beyond. Dietary practices seem to be rather inflexible once developed. It seems incredibly difficult to alter diet even when sound information on proper diet is available. For example, behavior modification has had only a slight and usually impermanent effect on calorie intake in human obesity. This suggests that these habits or behaviors may begin very early in life and, if not immutable, are at least extraordinarily resistant to change. The study, therefore, of the ontogenesis of taste and dietary preference will be of extreme importance. The demonstration that the neonate has either an inborn or an almost instantaneously acquired preference for sweet taste that varies from infant to infant will be of increasing concern to the nutritional investigator of the '80s. The modification of dietary preferences by early feeding experiences, and the significance of such early experiences for later diet choice and health outcome, will be key areas of investigation.

Adult diet.   Finally, the matter of adult diet and its significance for health and disease will be explored. There is already more than just suspicion that whether one eats a high-fat or low-fat diet, whether the fat is saturated or unsaturated, whether the diet contains large amounts of fiber, or refined sugar, can have important consequences for fitness, health, and disease. In a recent symposium sponsored by the American Society of Clinical Nutrition, a consensus was expressed that the two diet/disease risk linkages for which there was the most indisputable scientific basis were the relationship between refined sugars and caries and that between excessive caloric intake or obesity and a series of chronic disabilities, including diabetes and hypertension. The relationship of salt intake to hypertension, of cholesterol and saturated fats to heart disease, and of fiber or lack of fiber to malignancy are matters which must be studied further.

Open questions

It is my hope that in the 1980s studies will focus increasingly on the variability of nutritional needs among subgroups of the American population. It is clear, for example, that approximately 17% of Americans are at risk for hypertension. Presumably this is the group that should pay special attention to salt intake. Are there ways to identify these 17% early enough in life to establish reduction in salt intake and other lifelong dietary practices of particular relevance to this group? Does everyone respond to high-cholesterol diet by serum cholesterol elevation and an increased likelihood of atherosclerosis? The likelihood is that the answer to this question would be "no." There may be those who react adversely and those who do not to a high-cholesterol diet. Rather than suggesting nationwide changes in food intake, a rational approach for the 1980s may be the detailed study of individual differences to determine those who are indeed sensitive to certain special nutritional constituents. The concept of a recommended daily allowance for all may be sharply altered if major subgroups of the population are found to have needs that differ sharply from others.

Some of the answers to these important questions may come from an extension of modern cell biology and molecular biology. Unquestionably, these disciplines will remain an integral part of medical science. I believe, however, that other approaches, which feature blends of clinical investigation and behavioral observations, may be central in the further development of clinical nutritional research.

Clinical nutrition did not fare very well in the first few decades of the rapid growth of biomedical science (1950 to 1960). Indeed, the intriguing and highly productive reductionist approaches of recent years seemed to bypass clinical nutrition. Now, however, we are witnessing special pressure from the public and government agencies for a rebirth of research in clinical nutrition. Hopefully, from some of the problems and approaches touched on in this essay will arise the scientific issues that will prompt a renaissance in clinical nutrition. This may be the harbinger of new investigative waves in medicine, as clinical investigation, epidemiology, and behavioral science forge new approaches to the solution of the problems of human disease.

they cost more than conventional foods. Surveys have indicated that health foods can cost 1 to 5 times more at the supermarket than regular foods.

Use of these foods often is tied to the desire for a simpler, pretechnology life-style. But users are often misled if they believe such foods can maintain health and provide better nutritional quality than conventional foods or that they are safer. There is real cause for concern if consumers, particularly those with limited incomes, distrust the regular food supply and buy expensive health foods.

Organically grown foods, once they are removed from the field, cannot be distinguished from commercially fertilized plants. Since plant roots absorb nutrients in an inorganic form, regardless of the source, there is no scientific basis for claiming that organic foods are more nutritious than conventional foods. Instead, differences in the nutrient content of food from plants of the same species depend on their genetic nature, the climate, the nutrients available for growth, and the stage of maturity at which they were harvested. For example, wide variation in the vitamin A content has been found in different varieties of carrots as well as in Valencia oranges grown in different geographical areas.

One of the alleged advantages of organically grown foods is that they are supposedly free from pesticides. However, some chemicals used for a previous crop may remain in the soil and provide small amounts of contaminants for years after the last application of the pesticide. In addition, drifting sprays and debris (e.g., dust) from rainfall runoff from nearby farms may deposit residues in areas where there had been no direct spraying. As a result, traces of pesticides may be found in both organic and conventional foods, but these residues are normally within federal tolerance levels, which are set low enough to protect consumers.

Since most chemically and organically grown foods do not differ in looks, taste, or chemical analysis, the possibility for fraud exists when the consumer does not know if the storekeeper is honest, when the storekeeper cannot tell if the distributor is honest, and when the distributor does not know if its suppliers are living up to their promises. Because of this and the premium prices placed on organic foods, it is not surprising that conventional foods at times have been substituted for organic foods. Nevertheless, many health food operators truly believe in health foods and are sincere in trying to provide consumers with the "real" thing. Some distributors and growers supply affidavits or certificates for foods grown and handled according to organic and natural precepts. It is therefore unfair to assume that all elements of the health food industry engage in unscrupulous marketing practices.

In addition to the possibility of fraudulent claims, many commonly used foods, whether sold as health or conventional foods, actually contain low levels of toxic substances. Some herb teas, favored by many health food advocates, contain chemicals that can cause diarrhea. Kelp tablets, a food supplement commonly sold in health food stores, may contain high levels of arsenic, as do many other products from the sea. As we will see in Chapters 7 and 21, oxalic acid is present in several vegetables, including spinach. Carrots, lettuce, and celery leaves contain natural nitrate and nitrite compounds. This does not mean that we need to be fearful of using these foods. The best thing to do is to exercise care and common sense by eating a balanced diet from a wide variety of foods and by practicing moderation in eating any single food.

FOOD SAFETY*

Since the late 1960s, American consumers have expressed increasing concern about the safety of our food supply. Are the food and color additives added to foods and beverages safe? Do they cause cancer in humans? Does our drinking water contain carcinogens? Is drinking coffee bad for a pregnant woman or even for the general public? Should we or should we not use artificial sweeteners? Why are farmers allowed to use hor-

*Adapted from Lecos, C. 1981. *FDA Consumer* 15:8.

mones to raise cattle? Will there be hormonal residues in the meat we eat and the milk we drink? What will these hormonal chemicals do to our body? One reason why the health food industry has prospered may be traced to the confusion of the general public over these unsettling questions. At present, we do not have straightforward scientific answers to these questions. It is believed that the usage of any chemical in food must be evaluated according to the risks, benefits, and costs involved (see Chapter 20).

In the United States, the federal government has two major regulatory agencies charged with safeguarding the public from potentially dangerous foods. The Department of Agriculture is concerned mainly with meat and poultry products, while the Food and Drug Administration (FDA) is responsible for practically all other edible items. However, the work of the FDA is hampered by factors such as public pressure, vague laws, and inconclusive scientific research. The history of attempts to control the use of saccharin is a classic example of the kinds of difficulties that may arise.

Saccharin is the leading artificial sweetener on the market today. Many dieters use artificial sweeteners as sugar substitutes because they have no calories, and many diabetics use them because they do not influence blood sugar levels.

In 1981 saccharin alone was used fairly regularly by 50 to 70 million Americans, including an estimated one-third of all children under the age of 10. Diet sodas account for most of the 6 million pounds of saccharin consumed each year, followed by sales of the substance as a sugar substitute.

In the United States, saccharin is manufactured by only one corporation, the Sherwin-Williams Paint Company, from petroleum materials. It has no food value. Opponents of its use are not disturbed so much by the fact that it is nonnutritive as by research suggesting that it may cause cancer. In 1977 a Canadian study showing that saccharin could cause bladder tumors in rats eventually prompted the FDA to ban most uses of saccharin. But the saccharin-using public objected so strongly that Congress voted a moratorium on any saccharin ban. This moratorium is still in effect.

Prior to the FDA's thwarted attempt to ban saccharin, this sweetener had been sold amid a maze of conflicting reports and changing legal statuses. In 1958 Congress passed the Food Additives Amendment to the Food, Drug, and Cosmetic Act. This piece of legislation generally placed the burden of proving the safety of new products on their producers. It did not, however, apply to substances already in use and "generally recognized as safe." Saccharin had been in use since 1879; when warned in 1907 about its possible dangers, President Theodore Roosevelt retorted, "My doctor gives it to me every day. Anybody who says saccharin is injurious to health is an idiot."

Despite the complacent attitude of many such users, scientists continued to test the sweetener's safety. Some studies suggested a significant incidence of bladder tumors in saccharin-fed rats. These results were considered inconclusive until a major research project in Canada proved that the cancer-causing agent was not an impurity in the saccharin but the saccharin itself. Canada subsequently banned the use of saccharin except as a sugar substitute to be sold in drug stores with a warning label. The FDA tried to follow suit. But as indicated earlier, its 1977 attempt to ban most uses of saccharin met with such opposition from the public that Congress postponed the ban by passing the Saccharin Study and Labeling Act, funding further research into both the dangers of saccharin as well as possible benefits of its use that might outweigh the risks.

Results of saccharin research since 1977 have been contradictory. The National Academy of Sciences has concluded from its research that saccharin is a weak carcinogen in animals, a potential carcinogen in humans and perhaps a potentiator of cancer-causing effects of other carcinogens. On the other hand, epidemiological studies of humans by the National Cancer Institute have indicated that saccharin use increases the risk of cancer in only certain subgroups: heavy saccharin users and heavy-smoking heavy saccharin users. Two other epidemiological studies failed to link saccharin use with an increased risk of cancer for any users. Some possible explanations for these contradictory findings: (1) Saccharin may be carcinogenic for rats but not for humans; (2) saccharin's carcinogenic effect is so weak as to be almost imperceptible; (3) humans have not been heavily using artificial sweeteners long enough for their long-range effects to show up; and (4) epidemiological studies, which seek to measure cancer-causing effects of a substance by comparing the incidence of cancer in people who do and don't use the substance, may not be sensitive enough to accurately judge the risk to humans.

These and other research problems—plus controversies over what constitutes safety in a food and how rigidly the government should try to legislate safety for its citizens—have complicated efforts to police the food supply. Attempts to make this effort more systematic are discussed in Chapters 20 and 21.

ADDING NUTRIENTS TO FOODS*

Whereas artificial sweeteners have no nutritive value, many foods are now being "enriched" by the addition of nutrients that might have been lost as the original foods were processed, stored, and distributed, or "fortified" by the addition of nutrients that were not in the original foods. Although enrichment and fortification are designed to improve the nutritional quality of foods, some observers question the safety of these practices.

In the past, enrichment and fortification were intended to prevent deficiencies. Salt has been iodizined since 1924 to prevent goiter. Vitamin D has been added to milk since 1933 to help prevent rickets. When World War II military examinations revealed numerous deficiency problems stemming from inadequate childhood nutrition, the enrichment of grain products with niacin, thiamin, riboflavin, iron, and calcium began. These additives continue to be used, and

*Adapted from Reidy, K. 1981. *National Food Situation* Winter: 29 (Washington, D.C.: U.S. Department of Agriculture).

many once major nutritional deficiency conditions—beriberi, pellagra, goiter, and rickets—have almost disappeared in the United States.

Some nutritionists now want to increase the use of nutrient addition to further improve public health. They point out that people in the United States are now eating less, potentially shortchanging themselves on nutrients unless they eat a good variety of nutrient-dense foods. These proponents are skeptical about people's willingness to change their poor food habits, even after a quarter century of public nutrition education. According to this argument, why not try to make the foods people do eat—including "junk foods"—more nutrient dense?

Other nutritionists and scientists feel that extending enrichment and fortification programs would not be simple or altogether desirable. One objection stems from varying individual needs and eating patterns. How much we need of each nutrient depends on factors such as our age, sex, metabolic rate, body size, body composition, physical activity, personal body chemistry, health, and the drugs we may take. Individuals whose needs for a certain nutrient are low or who are likely to ingest large amounts of a particular kind of food might ingest more of a nutrient than their body can safely handle. For instance, since our bodies store vitamins A and D, long-term high intakes of these vitamins could cause toxic accumulation. And our needs for trace minerals are so miniscule that even one dose of a trace mineral several times larger than the needed amount can be toxic.

Another major problem is insufficient information about eating patterns, the food supply, and nutrients themselves. Although great advances have been made in the science of nutrition, it is still a new and growing science. Certain issues—such as how much protein individuals actually need to lead a long and healthy life—are subject to changing opinions. If, as is currently thought, most Americans already consume enough protein everyday, fortifying junk foods with protein would be pointless and perhaps even have negative long-term results. Questions such as which foods should be fortified and with which nutrients involve value judgments that we may not yet be wise enough to make. And if foods are fortified with certain nutrients known to be essential to health but not with others, we run the risk of creating chemical imbalances in our bodies, since many nutrients must apparently interact at appropriate levels to create optimal health.

An additional set of problems involves the technology of enrichment and fortification. If nutrients are added to foods, they must be in a form that the body can use and that will not detract from the taste, appearance, or freshness of the food. And the food chosen must not contain elements that interfere with the body's use of the added nutrient. For instance, the oxalic acid in the bran of cereal can block the absorption of some mineral elements such as calcium. To choose whole-grain bakery products as a carrier for calcium and certain other minerals would therefore be pointless. On the other hand, certain food ingredients actually aid the body's utilization of certain nutrients. Choosing good carriers for food additives will require detailed knowledge of such interrelationships.

To avoid random enrichment and fortification by food manufacturers that might lead to excessive or inadequate nutrient intakes or to the deception of consumers, government agencies have established some guidelines. The FDA has established a fortification policy, guidelines for nutritional quality, and labeling regulations requiring that the nutritional contents of foods be listed to which nutrients have been added. FDA policies also seek to prevent unnecessary fortification of foods. The Federal Trade Commission oversees the "truth in advertising" of foods for which enrichment or fortification claims are made.

In general, the government encourages food manufacturers to: (1) correct nutritional deficiencies that scientists generally recognize; (2) restore foods to nutrient levels present before processing, storage, and handling; (3) balance the vitamin, mineral, and protein content of a food by adding these nutrients in proportion to the total caloric content of the food; and (4) make substitute foods nutritionally equivalent to the food for which they substitute. (For example, infant formula replaces breast milk in many households. The manufacturers try to insure that the nutritional contributions of infant formulas are at least equal to those of breast milk.)

EXERCISE AND DIET*

Health cannot be fully legislated, however. We all continue to make our own food choices as well as life-style choices that affect our general health. Many of us have chosen foods and lifestyles that have made obesity a national problem. To solve it, we must look at both overeating and underexercising.

Our sedentary life-style with its emphasis on the automobile, electric appliances, and "easy living" has decreased the caloric expenditure of the average American, while at the same time our reliance on high-caloric, fattening, and often highly processed foods has increased. To get rid of the extra pounds, many of us depend on crash diets. Crash diets are a serious health hazard, although every new weight loss scheme attracts many followers.

The United States currently enjoys an overabundance of food. As a result of this and possibly other factors, the average American's caloric intake is over the approximately 2,000 kilocalories that will be expended through everyday activity. The result of this is weight gain in the form of fat deposits. It takes 3,500 kilocalories to gain or lose a pound. If a person is consuming 3,200 kilocalories per day and only burning up 2,000, he or she will be 3½ lb heavier each month.

As our everyday activity has decreased, there has been some increase in interest in physical exercise and sports, but in many cases these still tend to be spectator sports. During leisure time, half of our population prefers to sit around and relax, and a quarter go to bars, restaurants, or movies.

On the other hand, half of all Americans exercise regularly to keep in shape. Vigorous exer-

*Part of this section has been adapted from Lloyd, D. S. 1979. *New England Conference in Food, Nutrition, and Health*, Boston.

cising can assist in weight control. According to the President's Council on Physical Fitness and Sports, running and jogging, bicycling, swimming, handball, and squash ranked highest in providing benefits to weight loss through the burning of additional calories. If a person who is 20 lb overweight begins to jog one half-hour per day, four days per week, with no change in caloric input, that person will theoretically lose this excess weight in nine months. In fact, weight loss may be quicker if exercising takes place before a meal, since the person's appetite may be dulled and less food eaten. The calorie-burning intensity of vigorous exercise often persists afterward as well. For instance, a person who runs for 28 minutes may continue to burn up to twice as many calories as usual for as much as 6 hours following the run. In addition, as we become more physically fit, our eating pattern usually changes. We may feel less need to overeat, and the desire for unnecessary foods appears to decrease.

Weight loss is not the only health benefit from regular exercise. When people exercise regularly they say they feel better, have more energy, and sometimes need less sleep. Along with improvements in muscle strength and flexibility, they may feel better about themselves and less depressed and anxious. Many find that exercising inspires them to stop unhealthy habits such as smoking and excessive drinking and to choose more nutritious foods.

Research indicates that exercise has impressive preventive benefits to body systems as well. Those people who exercise regularly are one-and-a-half to two times less likely to develop cardiovascular disease as those who don't. Aerobic exercise—vigorous activities requiring a high intake of oxygen for energy, such as swimming, running, and fast walking—is the kind most beneficial for the heart. Regular sustained exercise may also lower blood pressure and serum cholesterol and raise the level of beneficial high-density lipoproteins. People with lung problems can improve their respiratory capacity by exercising, diabetes can decrease their blood sugar levels, and overweight people who have become diabetic can often free themselves of this condition if they regain their normal weight by exer-

cising and dieting. For these health benefits, spending 15 to 30 minutes three times a week in sustained exercise is a reasonable minimal goal.

WORLD HUNGER *

Affluent people in developed countries have to find artificial ways of burning off the excess calories they eat and of keeping their bodies in shape. These are not problems faced by most of the world's people. Although many Americans are overweight, there are some who go to bed hungry every night. However, the extent of undernutrition in the United States is definitely not as severe as that in many underdeveloped countries. Severe malnutrition is especially common among the peoples of the third world.

The Picture of Hunger

The usual image suggested by the term *world hunger* is one of famine—a local lack of food caused by war or crop failure, sometimes leading to starvation unless food is brought in from other areas. Famines have always been with us. During the famine of 1876 to 1879, for instance, 9 to 13 million people starved to death in China. Thanks to the increasing concern and aid from individuals and countries with greater resources, death tolls from famines are going down. With proper national and international planning, the disastrous effects of famines can sometimes be totally avoided.

Less dramatic but more widespread than famine is the invisible crisis of *chronic undernutrition*. According to the World Bank, one-quarter of the people in the world are chronically undernourished. That is, they habitually or seasonally eat less protein and calories than they need to be active and healthy. Even more suffer nutritional deficiencies because they do not consume adequate quantities of vitamins and minerals. In underdeveloped countries, for instance, iron-

---

*Adapted from *Overcoming World Hunger: The Challenge Ahead*, Presidential Commission on World Hunger, 1980.

deficiency anemia depletes many people's energy and capacity for muscular work. These forms of malnutrution cause high infant mortality rates and decreased resistance to infectious diseases. Epidemics of gastrointestinal and respiratory diseases may be deadly for undernourished peoples. Evidence strongly suggests that undernutrition also limits concentration, motivation, and learning ability, posing grave problems for developing nations whose people are often incapable of realizing their full potential.

Despite its tragic effects on individuals and nations, world hunger usually does not claim public attention unless it is acute and catastrophic. The ongoing problem of chronic malnutrition is less visible and its victims have little power to force changes. Most live on the Indian subcontinent, in Southeast Asia, or in sub-Saharan Africa; chronic malnutrition is also common in parts of the Middle East and Latin America and in low-income pockets within developed nations. Over half of the malnourished are children under 5, and far more women are malnourished than men.

Alleviating World Hunger

The plight of the hungry has not gone altogether unnoticed, however. Many industrialized Western countries are trying to solve the problems of world hunger. In the United States, mounting public and congressional concern over the continuing deterioration of the world food situation led President Carter to appoint a Presidential Commission on World Hunger. The commission's mandate was to identify the basic causes of domestic and international hunger and malnutrition, assess past and present national programs and policies that affect hunger and malnutrition, review existing studies and research on hunger, recommend to the president and Congress specific actions to create a coherent national food and hunger policy, and help implement those recommendations and focus public attention on food and hunger issues. On March 25, 1980, the commission issued a detailed report, *Overcoming World Hunger: The Challenge Ahead.*

The report concluded that chronic undernutrition is the major world hunger problem today. It is getting worse, and by the year 2000 the world is likely to face a major food supply crisis unless steps are taken now to significantly increase food production in developing nations.

Gains in productivity, though crucial, will not in themselves end world hunger, however. For all people to have fair access to food, the interrelated reasons why they now lack access to food must be attacked. These include political maneuverings, poverty, population growth, food production, food distribution, employment, and income issues. For instance, emergency food relief for starvation victims of armed conflicts is often channeled to soldiers rather than women and children. Often intended food relief is blocked by the nations involved or turned into money for guns, making hunger a weapon of war or repression. Even without such distribution problems, food production is limited by the earth's finite resources and by technological shortcomings. The central cause of hunger, however, is poverty, a condition deeply rooted in political, economic, and social realities.

Attempts to deal with world hunger must attack all these interrelated issues, with sensitive attention to how they vary in each country. As the commission pointed out, "There is no ideal food, no perfect diet, no universally acceptable agricultural system waiting to be transplanted from one geographic, climatic, and cultural setting to another."

Despite the complexity of these problems, efforts to alleviate hunger can succeed. Increased public awareness, appropriate government programs, and increased income and productivity have substantially reduced poverty and hunger in some countries. In the United States, for example, federal feeding programs such as school lunches; aid to women, infants, and children; and food stamps have been very successful in reducing hunger and malnutrition. But inflation and cutbacks in government spending threaten the advances that have been made, and some segments of the population—particularly Native Americans, migrant workers, and elderly people—still suffer hunger and disease from malnourishment.

The commission notes that since the United States is the largest producer, consumer, and trader of food in the world, it has a major role and responsibility in alleviating world hunger. Its wholehearted participation is essential to any progress against hunger. But the commission notes that the United States cannot and should not try to shape international efforts single-handedly. Although help from industrialized nations is crucial, so are efforts by developing countries to make their food systems more effective. Since the problems behind food shortages are often manmade, determined human efforts can change them. As the commission concludes, "The outcome of the war on hunger, by the year 2000 and beyond, will be determined not by forces beyond human control, but by decisions and actions well within the capability of nations and people working individually and together."

Because the foreign and domestic policies of the United States government and private activities have sometimes hindered rather than helped attempts to eradicate world hunger, the broad-based plan of action recommended by the commission calls for a major reordering of U.S. national priorities. For such a marked shift in established policies and practices to occur, public support must be mobilized. The American public is only dimly aware of what America as well as other nations could gain if people in all nations could affort to feed themselves. A successful effort to end hunger will require long-term economic and political support, and this support can only exist if the American public understands the realities of world hunger. A long-term nationwide education effort is required to develop public awareness and marshal support to conquer hunger, both in this country and other nations.

NUTRITION EDUCATION

In addition to educating the public about the problems of hunger, we need to educate individuals about the importance of nutrition to their own health. Today people want to make informed choices, and it is our job in the health field to help them. One way to educate the public is at places of work or education. For example, weight charts, food values, and nutrition awareness messages can be displayed in company cafeterias. Employees can be encouraged to achieve and maintain ideal weight by incentives such as paid holidays and job advancements. In public school systems, curricula can be modified so that elementary school teachers are required to have a minimal knowledge of food, nutrition, and diet, while children themselves are taught more about their bodies and the effects of nutrients in food.

Recent studies have confirmed that even many health professionals themselves do not have an adequate background in the area of food and nutrition. Health authorities currently believe that physicians, nurses, and dentists should be encouraged to acquire more knowledge in food and nutrition, especially knowledge relating to prevention. Their professions offer unique opportunities to educate the public about nutrition, diet, and health. Whereas health professionals often have little nutritional training, those in other helping professions such as social workers, physical and recreational therapists, counselors, and psychologists usually have no formal training in the elements of food and nutrition. Nevertheless, they are in a good position to influence people's eating patterns because of their professional relationship with the public. The important role of proper nutrition in physical and mental well-being should not be disregarded by people in the helping professions. To educate those they aid, they need to first educate themselves about the relationships between diet and health.

It is currently believed that an improper diet and a sedentary life are two of the major risk factors leading to diseases and early death. In addition to advising proper eating and frequent exercise, health professionals must also pay attention to other major public health concerns such as dental care (fluoridation of drinking water, oral hygiene, etc.), blood pressure control, reduction of alcohol consumption, quitting smoking, avoidance of drug abuse, and maternal and child care. The health profession's role in nutrition-related preventive medicine—nutrition education and public health and community nutrition—will be explored in Chapters 17, 19, and 22.

NUTRITION IN HEALTH CARE

Nutrition is one of the youngest branches of medical science. Its role in achieving and maintaining good health is both preventive and therapeutic. For nearly a century, experience in clinical medicine has shown that nutrition and diet therapy can positively influence the course of recovery in patients with certain pathological conditions. Rapid advances in nutritional science have increased the role of diet therapy in patient care in the last decade. Part III of this book discusses in detail the principles and application of diet therapy.

As more information becomes available for particular diseases, their management by diet therapy becomes more scientific, exact, and unique. This trend is leading to specialization in both specific dietary care and patient management. Together with an increasing patient population, specialization has increased the frequency of team approaches to in-patient, out-patient, and community health care. By coordinating the knowledge and experience of members, the team can provide better diagnosis, treatment, and overall patient care. Many experienced clinicians firmly believe that a health team treats the whole person rather than the disease or the symptoms.

In a health team approach, several professionals share responsibility for therapeutic feeding. Traditionally the physician diagnoses the patient's condition and prescribes a diet order, the dietitian develops detailed meal plans for the patient, and the nurse serves the foods and monitors the patient's responses.

The dietitian and the nurse both play an important role in the feeding care of a patient. The dietitian works with the patient and his or her family to develop a dietary plan that fits into the clinical management program of the health team. The dietitian works closely with the nurse, who, in the current health care system, has a direct role in making sure that the patient is fed and that the team is fully informed of the patient's eating patterns. With the introduction of total parenteral nutrition, a nurse is assuming more responsibilities in the nutritional care of patients. The nurse is in a unique position to educate the patient about food and nutrition and to lead the patient toward wholesome eating habits after discharge.

Those who work closely with patients everyday have especially good opportunities to tailor meals to varying individual tastes and needs. Eating is a highly personal activity, capable of creating feelings ranging from extreme pleasure to disgust or pain. Whether the nutritional focus is on prevention or therapy, health care professionals must see their clients as individual people with unique feelings about eating, rather than as insensitive food-ingesting machines.

The issues raised in this chapter will be explored to varying extents throughout this book. To begin with, we need a good background in the basic principles of nutrition, to be discussed in the next nine chapters.

Chapter 2

Energy and Body Composition

SEEN FROM AN inglorious chemical perspective, the human body is simply a conglomeration of water, fat, and cell mass. To empower this "lump of clay" to move and think and breathe—to carry on the myriad voluntary and involuntary activities of which it is capable—we need energy. We draw this energy from the foods we eat.

In this chapter we will look at how energy is defined and measured, which kinds of foods are our main sources of energy, and how much food energy we need to support our body processes and our physical activities. We will also examine the major chemical components of the human body: what they are, how they can be measured, and how their proportions change as we age. This information will be useful in understanding nutritional needs at all stages of the life cycle and under normal and pathological conditions. Throughout this book, refer to this chapter during any discussion involving a change in body composition.

MEASURING ENERGY INTAKE

Every day we take in energy from foods and expend energy in our activities. This section will examine the unit measurement for energy, sources of our dietary energy, and how to determine energy levels in food.

Unit Measurement

Energy is defined as the capacity to do work. One unit of energy measurement is the *calorie*, which is the amount of heat energy required to raise the temperature of 1 g of water from 15 °C to 16 °C. Many nutritionists currently prefer to work with a larger unit, the *kilocalorie* (= 1,000 calories). Various forms and abbreviations of these terms are in current use:

calorie*: cal
kilocalorie*: Kilocalorie, Calorie, kcal, Cal

---

*Although the kilocalorie is the preferred unit of measurement, many nutritionists simply refer to it as "calorie" or

Another system of energy measurement is increasingly used. Unlike the calorie system, which is based on heat energy, this system is based on mechanical energy. The basic unit in this system is the *joule*, or *Joule*. One Joule (= 1,000 joules) is the amount of mechanical energy required when a force of 1 newton (N) moves 1 kilogram (kg) by a distance of 1 meter (m). Forms of these terms in current use are:

joule = j
Joule = kilojoule, Kilojoule, kJ, KJ

Although the joule system has been advocated, the familiar calorie units are still widely used in the field. This book uses calorie units throughout, although joule units are also given whenever necessary. To convert calories to joules, multiply calorie units by the equivalency factor of 4.18*:

1 calorie   = 4.18 joule
1 kilocalorie = 4.18 Joule

Sources of Food Energy

The primary sources of food energy are the nutrients protein, carbohydrate, fat, and, for some people, alcohol. The percentages that each of these contributes to the total daily caloric intake vary from person to person and from country to country.

For people in the United States, approximately 10% to 15% of the total daily caloric intake comes from protein, 50% to 60% from carbohydrate, 35% to 45% from fat, and anywhere from 0% to 50% from alcohol. Although alcohol is not a *nutrient* (defined as a nourishing substance in foods) in the strict sense, alcohol does contain calories. In beverages such as beer, it also contains some vitamins. As the 0%-to-50% range suggests, some individuals consume a large percentage of their daily calories from alcoholic beverages, frequently at the expense of nutrients from other food sources.

Some nutritionists now feel that Americans

"cal" instead of "Calorie" or "Cal." This practice is convenient and traditional.

*The equivalency factor is actually 4.186, but a factor of 4.18 or 4.2 suffices for most purposes.

get too many of their daily calories from fat. As we shall see in Chapters 5 and 27, a high intake of fat, especially animal fat, may increase the risk of heart diseases. However, definitive evidence of cause and effect is lacking; how our bodies use the fats we eat depends on a complex set of inter-related factors.

Estimating Energy in Foods

Scientists determine how much energy people consume by analyzing the caloric content of the different foods they eat. This process is compli-cated by differences in the ways laboratory de-vices and human bodies release and use the en-ergy stored in foods.

In the laboratory, a food sample is *oxidized*, or burned, under controlled conditions to estimate its energy content. A sample of the food is placed inside a *bomb calorimeter* (see Figure 2-1). A small electric spark ignites the sample in the presence of oxygen and a catalyst such as platinum. One way of measuring the heat energy released by the complete oxidation of the sample is to note the rise in water temperature. The amount of heat released depends on the relative contents of car-bon and oxygen in the sample; the chemical transformation is shown below.

Carbohydrate, protein, or fat + oxygen $\xrightarrow{\text{catalyst}}$
   heat energy + water + carbon dioxide

A similar process takes place in the human body, especially in the muscle and liver. Once ab-sorbed from the intestine, carbohydrates, pro-teins, or fats provide the body with energy in a comparable chemical mechanism, but with a ma-jor difference in efficiency: The human body al-ways derives less energy than the bomb calorime-ter from a given amount of food. There are three reasons for this difference. First, part of the in-gested food is digested and absorbed, part elimi-nated as fecal waste, and the remaining kept as residue in the bowel. Second, some of the food energy is spent on the work of ingesting, digest-ing, and absorbing food. Finally, part of the ab-sorbed nutrient is not completely oxidized. The body's utilization of ingested protein complicates comparisons between laboratory analysis and ac-tual human use of food energy. One complica-tion is that protein is not completely oxidized in

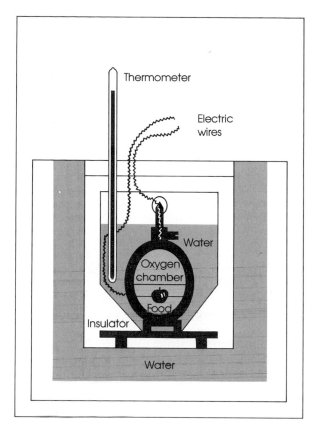

FIGURE 2-1   A simplified diagram of a bomb calo-rimeter.

TABLE 2-1   Energy Values of Food and Alcohol

Substance (1 g)	Energy Content		
	In bomb calorimeter	In human body	
	kcal	kcal	kJ*
Protein	5.65	4	17
Carbohydrate	4.1	4	17
Fat	9.45	9	38
Alcohol (ethanol)	7.1	7	29

*The numbers are rounded for easy reference.

the body, a fact that limits the energy released and leads to the formation of by-products such as urea and uric acid.

The mathematical differences between labo-ratory and human utilization of food energy are presented in Table 2-1. As shown in the table, 1 g of ingested protein will provide 4 kcal of energy for the body, 1 g of carbohydrate 4 kcal, and 1 g of fat 9 kcal.

By using these approximate energy values, the energy content of a food sample can be determined indirectly from the protein, carbohydrate, and fat contents in a sample. These nutrient contents can be obtained either by a direct laboratory analysis or by referring to food composition tables, most of which are published by federal government agencies (see Chapter 10 and the appendices for more information). The contents of protein, carbohydrate, and fat in grams can then be multiplied by the appropriate factors (4, 4, and 9, respectively), and the results totaled. Table 2-2 lists the energy contents of some representative foods. Most food composition tables, however, include the caloric content of the food items listed here.

INDIVIDUAL ENERGY REQUIREMENTS

How much food energy do we need each day? The amount varies considerably, depending on the energy we each expend in a resting state and the energy we expend to power our physical activities. The sum of these figures gives our total individual energy requirement.

Estimating Energy Expenditures

There are two methods of determining how much energy we expend: direct and indirect calorimetry.

The *direct calorimetry* method is similar to that used in measuring food energy in a bomb calorimeter. A person is placed in a chamber that is specially insulated and equipped to detect any slight rise in temperature due to heat released by the person. This rise is usually gauged by the temperature change in water circulating around the chamber (see Figure 2-2) or by an electrical device wired to the walls.

In the direct calorimetry method, the amount of heat released by the person indicates the approximate energy expenditure. This information is usually accompanied by a measurement of the amount of oxygen consumed and

TABLE 2-2 The Caloric Contents of Some Common American Foods*

Food Item	Serving Size	kcal
Cheese, natural blue	1 oz	100
Milk, fluid, whole	1 c	150
Egg, scrambled in butter, milk added	1	95
Butter	1 pat	35
Beef, rib roast, lean and fat	3 oz	375
Salmon, pink, canned, solids and liquid	3 oz	120
Banana	1	100
Raisins, seedless	1 c	420
Bread, French, enriched	1 sl	100
Rice, white, cooked, long-grain	1 c	225
Beans, lima, dry, cooked, drained	1 c	260
Peas, split, dry, cooked	1 c	230
Honey, strained or extracted	1 T	65
Sugar, white, granulated	1 T	45
Broccoli, raw, cooked, drained	1 stalk	45
Potato, baked	1	145
Vegetables, mixed, frozen, cooked	1 c	115
Beer	12 fl oz	150
Cola beverage	12 fl oz	145
Yeast, brewer's, dry	1 T	25

*Adapted from *Nutritive Value of Foods*, Home and Garden Bulletin No. 72 (Washington, D.C.: U.S. Department of Agriculture, 1981).

carbon dioxide released before and after the experiment. These additional data give a general idea of what kinds of fuel the body is burning:

Respiratory quotient (RQ) =
$$\frac{\text{amount of carbon dioxide released}}{\text{amount of oxygen used up}}$$

If the body is burning carbohydrate, then

$$RQ = 1.0$$

If the body is burning fat, then

$$RQ = 0.71$$

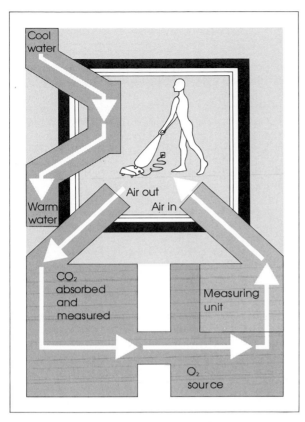

FIGURE 2-2   Measuring the human body's heat production by direct calorimetry.

TABLE 2-3   Effect of Specific Dynamic Action of Food on BMR

Status of Basal Metabolism	Hypothetical Value of Basal Metabolism (kcal)	Increase over Normal (%)
After an overnight fast (i.e., normal basal metabolism)	1,500	0
Within 7 hr after eating a meal	1,575–1,950	5–30

calculated easily from the known relationship that 1 L of oxygen used represents 4.82 kcal of energy released.

Basal Metabolism

The above methods may be used to calculate energy used when the body is either resting or physically active. The former is known as the *basal metabolic rate* (BMR)—the least amount of energy required by the resting human body to keep the most important life processes functioning properly. Such processes include heart beat, brain activity, respiration, hormonal coordination, and the workings of the muscular and nervous systems. This body basal metabolism figure excludes the absorption and digestion of food.

Energy expended in basal metabolism differs among individuals. It can only be determined when the subject is at complete physical and mental rest, free from worry and emotional excitement, and in normal health. The BMR is measured after the subject has not eaten for 12 hours. Preferably the person is awake and lying down in a comfortable room at standard humidity and temperature when the BMR is measured.

After a meal is eaten, the basal metabolic rate increases 5% to 30%. This increase is known as *specific dynamic action*. Its effect is shown in Table 2-3. Although the potential range is large, an average meal produces an average rise of about 10% within 5 hours of eating; this increase drops to about 0% to 5% above BMR 24 hours after eating.

If the body is burning protein, then

$$RQ = 0.81$$

If the body is burning a mixture of the three nutrients, intermediate values are obtained. For instance, under laboratory controlled conditions, the RQ is usually 0.8 to 0.85.

The *indirect calorimetry* method is less costly and involves only a simple measurement of the amount of oxygen consumed by the person over a defined period. One way to measure this is by fitting the subject with a respirometer so that he or she breathes pure oxygen from one special container and exhales carbon dioxide into another. The exact amount of oxygen inhaled can be ascertained in this closed-circuit system. In an open-circuit system, the amount of oxygen in a room is calculated before and after the subject has spent a defined period in the room. The amount of energy spent by the individual can be

---

Alcohol: Nutrient and Poison*

Throw all the beer and spirits into the Irish Channel, the English Channel, and the North Sea for a year and people in England would be infinitely better. It would certainly solve all the problems with which the philanthropist, the physicians and politicians have to deal.—Sir William Osler, 1906

Doctor Osler overstated the case when he said *all* problems would be solved by eliminating alcohol. Nonetheless alcoholism is perhaps the most costly disease with which the medical profession has to deal. Ethanol is a nutrient that when habitually taken in excess causes illness, disability, and death. . . .

Atwater and Benedict used the human calorimeter to first prove that modest amounts of alcohol (75 ml [2½ oz] or 72 g daily) could be substituted for carbohydrate and fat as a source of energy in nonalcoholic humans. Seventy-two grams of alcohol, 63.5 g of butter, and 128 g of sugar were equivalent sources of energy. These meticulous experiments also proved ethanol to be as effective as fat or carbohydrate in sparing nitrogen.

The caloric density of ethanol is 7.1 kcal/g, intermediate between fat (9 kcal/g) and protein and carbohydrate (4 kcal/g);

*Source: C. R. Fleming and J. A. Higgins, *Annals of Internal Medicine* 87 (1977):492.

therefore it is important that physicians and dieticians taking diet histories inquire about alcohol consumption. If one can get an accurate estimate of the number of ounces and concentration of ethanol drunk, one can apply the formula to derive alcohol calories: 0.8 × proof × ounces = kilocalories, or in a metric unit for volume, 0.0267 × proof × millilitres = kilocalories. If as in the case of beer or wine the strength of the alcoholic beverage is specified in terms of percentage, proof is derived by doubling the percentage.

Alcoholic persons may take 30% to 60% of their total calories as ethanol. Twenty ounces (600 ml) of 86-proof liquor represents about 1400 kilocalories, about one half of the normal daily caloric requirement. Malnutrition can result in chronic alcoholic persons because ethanol replaces dietary nutrients, particularly carbohydrates and vitamins, and because malabsorption and maldigestion can result from alcohol—induced hepatic, pancreatic, and small bowel dysfunction. Ethanol is directly or indirectly responsible for impaired intestinal transport of selected vitamins and minerals; decreased hepatocyte uptake and storage of absorbed nutrients; diminished conversion of foodstuffs into active metabolites (for example, thiamine); and excessive loss of nutrients during anabolic and catabolic phases of liver injury (for example, zinc, folic acid). . . .

The exact reason for the rise in BMR after eating is not fully known. However, part of the rise is traceable to the work and energy used in ingesting, digesting, absorbing, and oxidizing food. A high-protein diet is mainly responsible for the large increases (15% to 30%) in BMR after eating. It is suspected that the amino acids of protein can stimulate metabolism, and that the breaking down of the amino groups of amino acids (deamination) is energy consuming. The formation of uric acid and urea from protein also uses a lot of energy.

In addition to changes in basal metabolism after eating, BMRs vary considerably among individuals. The basal metabolic rate of an "average" adult is about 1 kcal/kg body weight/hr. This figure does not apply to very obese or lean individuals or athletes undergoing intensive training. Factors determining individual variations in BMR are summarized below.

1. *Age*. The BMR of a person varies from birth through adulthood, as shown in Table 2-4. The fluctuation is the same for males and

TABLE 2-4 Changes in BMR with Age

Age Range (yr)	BMR
0–2	Increases
2–puberty	Drops
Puberty–20	Rises slowly
21–old age	Falls

Age (yr)	Average BMR (kcal/m²/h)*
6	53
20	41
60	34

*Basal metabolic rate is more accurately reflected in the kilocalories needed per square meter of body surface area per hour than in kilocalories needed per kilogram body weight per hour.

females, unless pregnancy and lactation are involved. After the age of 21, the need for energy for growth decreases.

2. *Pregnancy.* The BMR of a woman increases throughout pregnancy, with the highest value at the end of pregnancy. The average rise is about 20%. This increase is the direct result of high metabolic activity of the fetus, placenta, and maternal tissues.

3. *Undernourishment.* When a person is undernourished, as in starvation, the BMR decreases and may remain lowered until the body is replenished. This drop results from the body's response to a reduction in caloric intake.

4. *Body composition.* Muscle mass has a higher metabolism than body fat. A person with high muscle mass will have a higher BMR than a person of equivalent weight but with more body fat.

5. *Sexual difference.* Because females have less muscle and more body fat, their BMR is about 5% lower than that of males.

6. *Hormones.* Thyroid hormones have important effects on body metabolism. A person with hypothyroidism and thus less body thyroid hormones will have a decreased BMR; a person with hyperthyroidism typically has a higher BMR. Hypothyroidism may be remedied by oral doses of thyroid extract. Surgical removal of part of the thyroid may be

indicated for a person with hyperthyroidism, though the common practice is to use radioactive iodine.

Adrenal hormones also affect BMR. The adrenals are small glands located on the top of the kidneys. When stimulated, as in fright or excitement, they secrete epinephrine, which can cause a temporary but intense increase in BMR.

7. *Body temperature.* When body temperature rises, as in fever, the BMR increases. For each degree Fahrenheit rise, BMR increases by 7%.

8. *Environmental temperature.* The BMR also responds to changes in environmental temperature. As the ambient temperature increases, the normal BMR of a person increases. As the ambient temperature decreases, the body BMR initially decreases. Without warming devices such as clothes or a heater, the process of shivering takes over and the BMR goes up. Since this process cannot continue indefinitely, some warming remedies must eventually be available.

Energy Requirements for Physical Activities

In addition to basal metabolic energy requirements, each person's energy need is also affected by physical activity. An active person needs more energy than a nonactive person, but the extra energy need varies with the type of activity, body build, and the intensity and duration of the activities performed.

Table 2-5 describes the *approximate* energy cost of different forms of activity for a man weighing 70 kg. For convenience, human activities can be divided into four types according to the amount of energy spent: very light, light, moderate, and heavy. Very light activities—such as ironing or sewing clothes, painting the inside of a house, driving a car, or walking slowly—will increase a person's total energy need to 130% of his or her BMR. Light activities—such as waiting on tables, fixing cars, or working on an assembly line—will increase energy need to 150% of the BMR. Moderate activities—such as gardening, dancing, riding a bicycle, or heavy housework such as scrubbing the floor or bathtub—will in-

TABLE 2-5 Approximate Energy Cost of Different Forms of Activities for a 70-kg Man*

Activity	kcal/min
Basketball	9.0–10.0
Boxing	9.0–10.0
Cleaning	4.0– 4.5
Coal mining	6.0– 8.0
Cooking	3.0– 3.5
Dancing	3.5–12.5
Eating	1.0– 2.0
Fishing	4.0– 5.0
Gardening	3.5– 9.0
Horse riding	3.0–10.0
Painting	2.0– 6.0
Piano playing	2.5– 3.0
Running	9.0–21.0
Scrubbing floors	7.0– 8.0
Standing	1.5– 2.0
Swimming	4.0–12.0
Typing, electric	1.5– 2.0
Walking	1.5– 6.0
Writing	2.0– 2.5

*The data in this table have been collected from many sources. Because of large variations among the results of different investigators, ranges of values are used so as to give a general idea of the relationship between types of activity and the energy cost.

crease energy need to 175%. And heavy activities—such as playing basketball or football, chopping wood, or moving pianos—will increase energy need to 200% or more of the BMR.

Total Energy Needs

Our total energy needs depend on both our BMR and our level of physical activities. Together, they influence our total energy needs in several general ways.

Age

During infancy and childhood, both basal metabolism and rigorous activity result in a high energy requirement relative to body size. As the person grows older, physical activity decreases; thus, the total energy need of the adult is less than that of a child. The drop in physical activity is also accompanied by a decrease in the BMR.

Body size

Clearly, a larger person requires more energy to move, work, and so on. Such a person's combined BMR and activity energy need is therefore greater than that of a smaller person.

Climate

When exposed to an ambient temperature of less than 20 °C/68 °F (normal room temperature), a person needs more energy, since shivering and extra clothing increase basal metabolic requirements. When the ambient temperature is hot, a person theoretically needs slightly more energy to do the same work than at a comfortable room temperature. However, since most people reduce the amount of work done in a hot climate, the total energy need may actually decrease.

Pregnancy and lactation

A woman needs more energy when she is pregnant because her BMR increases and she needs more energy to power her larger body's physical activities. A nursing mother needs more energy because part of it is transferred to the infant. Chapter 13 deals with these increased energy needs in greater detail.

Using all the factors discussed above, we can derive certain reference figures. For instance, to calculate the average energy need for a man or woman, we can stipulate that the "standard" person is 23 years old and moderately active in an environmental temperature of 20 °C/68 °F. This reference person's total daily energy need would be:

Person	Weight		Daily Caloric Need (kcal)
	lb	kg	
Man	154	70	2,700
Woman	128	58	2,000

The above reference standards have been established by the National Research Council of the National Academy of Sciences. More information on individual caloric needs is presented in Part 2 of this book.

HUMAN BODY COMPOSITION

As noted above, the muscle content of the body is one factor that determines energy need. In addition, our body composition is related to our dietary needs, nutritional status, and growth and development. The following sections give basic information about human body composition. Like knowledge about varying energy needs, this information will be useful in understanding individuals' varying requirements for the nutrients discussed in the chapters that follow.

General Descriptions of Body Composition

There are many scientific ways to describe body composition, depending on what one wants to emphasize. Most nutritionists prefer to use the following common descriptions as reference points:

1. Functionally and physiologically, we can divide the body into extracellular and intracellular components. The former include bones and extracellular fluids such as blood plasma, lymph, and fluid that bathes cells. The latter include fat and organ cell mass, such as kidney, muscle, heart, and so on. In clinical medicine, this division is probably one of the most important considerations in patient care. It is the major frame of reference in our discussion of fluids, electrolytes, and acid–base balance in Chapter 9, and treating shock and fluid loss in a burn patient (Chapter 29).

2. Structurally, we can partition the body into water, fat, and cell mass solids. Scientists specializing in developmental nutrition recognize the importance of water, fat, and cell mass distribution in the fetus and in pregnant women. This way of describing body composition helps nutritionists to understand the causes of obesity (Chapter 12).

3. Metabolically, the ingredients of the body may be separated into two categories: body fat and lean body mass. The *lean body mass*, also known as the "fat-free body" or the "body cell mass," is what is left after the weight of body fat is subtracted from the total body weight. According to one argument, this way of describing body composition works better in theory than in fact, since some fat may be hidden in muscle and bone cells. At any rate, the lean body mass does all the work of keeping the body functioning. This metabolic division of body components is used extensively in many facets of nutritional sciences. Losing weight (Chapter 12), cachexia in a cancer patient (Chapter 29), and undernutrition (Chapter 11) are much better understood when we consider the body to be made up of fat and lean body mass.

4. Nutritionally or chemically, the body is made up of protein, fat, carbohydrate, water, and ash (minerals). This is an important principle in understanding body metabolism (Chapter 8) and growth (see below and Chapter 14).

These four ways of describing body composition will be explored to varying degrees throughout this book. Although an in-depth analysis is beyond the scope of this book, these descriptions allow some well known but unrelated observations that have a direct bearing on body composition from a nutritional point of view. They are briefly mentioned below.

When a person's body weight changes, the change may involve body water, body fat, or body cell mass. Muscle cells contain about 75% water; red blood cells and cells of the brain, tendons, and connective tissues contain less. Fluids outside body cells (*extracellular fluids*) contain mainly sodium and chloride; fluids inside the cells (*intracellular fluids*) contain mainly potassium, phosphates, protein, and organic acids. The electrolytes and minerals must be balanced within and without the cells and be kept at a constant physiological equilibrium. The balance must be maintained even when the body is at rest.

In a normal, healthy individual, the total body water usually remains constant. But with *overhydration* (edema) there will usually be a gain in body water and/or a loss in body cell mass; with *underhydration* (dehydration) there will usually be a loss of body water or a gain in body cell mass relative to total body weight.

TABLE 2-6 Approximate Body Composition of a 25-Year-Old Male (70 kg) and Female (58 kg)

Body Component	Body Weight			
	Man		Woman	
	kg	% of total	kg	% of total
Protein	11.90	17.0	4.93	8.5
Fat	9.45	13.5	12.76	22.0
Carbohydrate	1.05	1.5	0.87	1.5
Water	43.40	62.0	35.96	62.0
Ash (minerals)	4.20	6.0	3.48	6.0
Total	70.00	100.0	58.00	100.0

Nutritionally, the carbohydrate content of the body is the most easily depleted because it is the main body fuel. Fat and protein are very difficult to deplete in most people, though there are exceptions. Unlike the average individual, an athlete may lose weight and gain cell mass (muscle) with a decrease in body fat. Under conditions such as partial or total starvation, protein and fat will be degraded to provide calories after all available carbohydrate is depleted.

Table 2-6 indicates the approximate body compositions of a man (70 kg/154 lb) and a woman (58 kg/127.6 lb) by chemical components. These data should be used only as general guides, for individuals vary considerably, and body composition changes with age, conditioning, diet, and disease.

Methods of Determining Body Composition

Biologists and medical scientists have tried for many years to devise an acceptable method of determining the actual body composition of individuals directly. Brief descriptions of some available techniques are provided below.

Cadaver analysis

Chemical analysis of dead bodies is the most direct technique of measuring body composition and one of the oldest used. However, this method has many disadvantages, such as the limited number of bodies available; the limited availability of bodies of different ages, races, and sex; the formidable task of analyzing the massive amount of fat, protein, and bones; and the need for extensive space, equipment, and training. Most important, the basic differences between a dead body and a live one have been the center of controversy for many years. Obvious complications of using a dead body include the varying causes of death, dehydration, pathological deterioration, damage from accidental death, and the length of time stored in preserving fluid. However, the chemical analysis of a dead body does provide some general ideas of the approximate composition of fat, protein, carbohydrate, and ash in the human body.

Anthropometric measurements

Another of the oldest techniques is measuring the following characteristics of a living person: height, weight, and body measurements (such as the thickness of triceps and subscapular skin folds). These data, together with knowledge of the race and sex of the individual, can be compared with standard tables to estimate the person's body fat, body water, and so forth. This technique is used extensively by clinical, community, and public health nutritionists. More details are presented in Chapter 19.

Body density or specific gravity measurement

The body density method derives from the fact that the buoyancy of a body depends on how much fat it has. Basically, Archimedes' principle is used. By weighing the person inside and outside of water and approximating how much air is trapped in the body, one can obtain certain essential data: body weight in air, body weight in water, volume of water that is equivalent to the volume of the body, and volume of gas or air space within the gastrointestinal and respiratory tract. This information is then incorporated into a formula from which one can calculate the approximate fat content in the body. In general, the more fat a person has, the lower the specific gravity or density (weight per volume).

Potassium isotopes measurement

The mineral element potassium has two natural radioactive isotopes, ^{40}K and ^{42}K. One technique directly estimates the amount of body potassium. Radioactive ^{40}K (found in foods as well as body tissues) occurs in a constant proportion in relation to "natural" potassium and emits gamma radiation measurable by placing the person in a whole-body counter. Since we know the approximate concentration of potassium in the lean body mass, we can estimate lean body mass if we know the relative contents of ^{40}K and "natural" potassium. Another technique using ^{42}K, called *isotopic dilution*, measures the amount of exchangeable potassium in the body. Again, if total body potassium is known, the lean body mass can be calculated.

After determining the lean body mass of the person, one can calculate the amount of fat in his or her body by subtracting the lean body mass from the body weight.

Body water measurement

Using the dilution principle, one can also measure the total amount of water in the human body. Water contains hydrogen atoms, which can be replaced by isotopic hydrogen, tritium, or deuterium. This "hot" water can either be injected into body fluid or administered orally. It will dissolve in and penetrate all the available water in the body without itself being metabolized. After a period of stabilization, a small amount of body fluid can be withdrawn and analyzed to determine how much water the body contains. From this information one can calculate the lean body mass. Subtracting the lean body mass from the body weight gives the approximate amount of fat in the body.

Other chemicals such as antipyrine and n-acetyl-4-aminopyrine have recently been used rather than radioactive water for this dilution technique.

Fat analysis

Chemicals such as cyclopropane can penetrate directly into body fat, a sample of which can be analyzed after a period of stabilization to determine how much body fat the person has.

X-ray studies

New X-ray techniques permit body fat, bone mass, muscle mass, and so on, to be estimated.

Changes in Body Composition with Age

In addition to measuring body composition by the above techniques, we can make some general assumptions about how individuals vary in body composition. The relative content of each component varies with age, sex, exercise, dietary intake, disease, and other environmental conditions. For example, the body's water content decreases with age; a woman has more fat than a man. A decrease in caloric intake causes weight loss, usually as a loss of fat, whereas an inadequate dietary intake of calcium causes bone loss.

The chemical composition of the human body changes during its entire life cycle. The values presented previously in Table 2-6 apply only to 25-year-old persons. It is difficult and unrealistic to provide similar reference approximations for the young and old, since they are extremely variable. However, to provide some general ideas of the changes in water, fat, and lean body mass that occur at different stages of life, a brief analysis is presented below.

Body water

It is well established that a newborn is made up of a large amount of water. Table 2-7 depicts changes in body composition from birth to the end of the first year. The large decline in body water during the first year of life occurs mainly in the extracellular fluids (see also Chapter 9). This

TABLE 2-7   Approximate Body Composition in Newborns and 1-Year-Olds

	% of Body Weight	
Component	Newborn	1-year-old
Protein	11.5	14.3
Water	74.3	59.1
Fat	11.5	21.9
Ash	2.7	4.7

Food and Water Restriction in the Wrestler *

The American Medical Association strongly and emphatically declares its formal opposition to the common practice of rapid and substantial weight loss among amateur wrestlers in age groups where rapid growth is taking place. The AMA is aware that some coaches advise growing boys to obtain and maintain, during wrestling season, certified weights that are considerably below optimum standards. Crash diets and dehydration are used to retain eligibility at certain weights.

The AMA Committee on Medical Aspects of Sports has established some guidelines: (1) Seven percent to 10% body fat is desirable in the wrestler. (2) The wrestler should participate in a six-week intensive training and conditioning program with no regard for his weight. (3) His weight at the end of this period is to be his minimum effective weight for competition as well as for certification purposes. (4) Any effort to maintain a weight level below this would work a hardship on the boy.

Weight Loss and Body Fat

In their study Tipton and Tcheng demonstrated that wrestlers lost substantial amounts of weight prior to certification, certification being the lowest weight class in which each would be permitted to wrestle. During a 17-day period before the certification date, the average weight loss was 3.1 kg, while the average weight gain after the season was 6.2 kg. This suggests that the wrestlers lost considerable weight before entering the certification period.

Zambraski et al supported this suggestion. Their wrestlers lost 9% to 13% of their body weight before certification, most of it just prior to weigh-in. However, other wrestlers lose as much as 20% of their body

weight during the 16-day certification period. Because competing wrestlers usually participate in the practice of losing weight before the certification period, the program has been of little value.

The body composition of high school wrestlers was studied using skin-fold and girth measurements. The percentage of body fat increased with the weight category (the 44-kg group averaged 4.2% and the 94-kg group averaged 15.5%).

Tcheng and Tipton projected a minimal body weight for wrestlers. Their basic assumption was that the finalists in the Iowa State Wrestling Tournament were the quintessential example of well-conditioned athletes who effectively compete at minimum body weights. The study concluded that many of these wrestlers were "lean" before the season started. It also recommended that the lowest possible body weight includes at least 5% body fat. This is well below the 7% to 10% recommended by the AMA. Because there are so many wrestlers whose weights are between 54 kg to 63 kg, it might be desirable to permit more than one wrestler per class to compete, to have more weight classes than the existing 12, and to promote body composition assessments preseasonally to minimize "making weight."

Zambraski et al have raised some question as to the usefulness of the Tcheng-Tipton equation because, for one class of wrestlers an optimum weight of 69.2 kg was projected; however, this was not achieved until the peak of the season. Two of the wrestlers did not reach this weight by dietary means but by fluid restriction and dehydration. Thus, the formula permitted weights that were too low.

Body Composition

Clarke did a field study of the Tcheng-Tipton method of projecting certified weights of young wrestlers. He made the same assumption that Tcheng and Tipton

Source: L. M. Hursh, *Journal of the American Medical Association* 241 (1979):915–916. Copyright *1979*, American Medical Association.
Note: Also see Chapter 19.

made, that the body composition of the state wrestling finalists reflected the minimum proportion of body fat to permit effective performance and that the certified weight should match the minimal effective weight. However, he made one important contribution to the Tcheng-Tipton formula. He added the factor of body composition: skin-fold thickness of five sites—scapula, triceps, thigh, iliac crest, and abdomen. No effort is made to convert the sum of the skin-fold thickness to percentage of body fat; rather, the sum is used directly.

Clarke's wrestlers lost 15% of their skin-fold thickness during the course of the season. Since fat loss was greater in conference losers than in those who lost in state finals, Clarke suggested that if weight loss is not excessive, it can contribute to effectiveness. Even the effective weight of the heavyweight is related to body composition, because the heavyweight state finalists had much thinner skin folds than the conference wrestlers.

The sum of the skin-fold measurements is linearly related to body weight. Thus, the skin-fold measurement is a refinement of the Tcheng-Tipton method.

Why is there all this concern about wrestlers' making weight? What about their performance? When weight reduction is carried to an extreme, it is hazardous to the health of a growing young man. Food restriction, fluid deprivation, and dehydration produce the following: (1) reduction in muscular strength, (2) decrease in work performance, (3) lowered plasma and blood volumes, (4) reduced cardiac function, (5) lowered oxygen consumption, (6) impaired thermoregu-

latory processes, (7) decreased kidney blood flow, (8) depletion of liver glycogen stores, and (9) increased loss of electrolytes. Many wrestlers think they can overcome all these effects by eating and drinking during the five-hour period between weigh-in and competition. However, this is not so.

A Measure of Performance

Urinary profiles of wrestlers studied show them to be dehydrated at the time of weigh-in. The specific gravity of the wrestlers' urine averaged 1.027. The urine of nonwrestlers averaged 1.023.

At the Illinois State High School Wrestling Tournament in 1975, an effort was made to correlate the specific gravity of the urine as a measure of hydration and performance. More than 300 participants were tested. The average specific gravity of the urine of the first- and second-place winners was 1.015. The average of all others was 1.020, which again suggested that the better-hydrated wrestlers performed better.

The modified Tcheng-Tipton-Clarke method reasonably places the wrestler in a proper weight class to control his food restriction. If one wishes to require a minimum of 7% body fat, the slope line of the Clarke formula can be raised. One other addition that will control dehydration is that the wrestler must produce a urine sample with a specific gravity of 1.015 at weigh-in. This will ensure that the wrestler is fully hydrated at the time of the match. Specific gravity can be measured more quickly than weight by using a hydrometer with a floating ball.

decrease is usually accompanied by an increase in fat and lean tissue mass (mainly protein). Water accounts for about 80% to 85% of the lean body mass at birth and about 77% to 79% at 1 year of age.

The percentage of total body water at the age of 1 remains fairly constant until the adult stage, when body water makes up 70% to 75% of lean

body mass, with the rest distributed in fat.

From the age of 25 to 85, a person's body water gradually decreases, both in absolute and relative amounts. This reduction varies from individual to individual, depending on body size and build. However, it has been established that the loss of body water takes place within the intracellular mass. A person "shrinks" somewhat with age because of this loss of body water, and the skin becomes dry from the combined effects of a loss of turgor from reduced intracellular fluids and a decrease of oil secretion.

Body fat

As indicated in Table 2-7, the amount of body fat doubles from birth to the end of the first year. Sex-related differences begin to appear in infancy: Female infants tend to deposit a greater percentage of body weight as fat than do males.

Sex differences in body fat continue throughout the life cycle. In the female, body fat increases continuously until about 3 years of age, when the increase slows down somewhat. During the prepubescent ages of 8 to 13, the female's body fat continues to rise at a much faster rate, reaching a peak shortly after 14. This rise is then followed by a drop in body fat until the age of 16.5, when body fat content again rises steadily.

The pattern of fat deposition in a male is similar to that of a female until about 3 years of age, when there is a plateau or actual loss of body fat until about 7.5 to 8 years. The male prepubescent period of 8 to 12 is characterized by a rise in body fat, though the difference at this time between the male and female body fat is already very great. For example, at the age of 12, the female averages about 25% to 30% more body fat than the male. In the male, there is another drop in body fat between the ages of 12 and 14, so that by the age of 14.5, the female generally has 70% to 80% more body fat than the male. After the age of 14, the male's body fat rises until the age of 16.5 to 17, when the body fat starts to drop again. During the 18-to-25 age period, the differences between male and female body compositions may be appreciated by studying the values shown in Table 2-6.

As the person ages from 25 to 85 years, body fat continues to rise in both the male and female. Because the female generally keeps her higher level of body fat from adulthood, the female usually has more fat throughout life.

Lean body mass

Since potassium is found predominately within the cells of lean tissue, measuring its concentration gives an estimate of lean body mass.

The concentration of potassium in the lean body mass of a newborn is less than in the adult and increases during infancy and early childhood. It reaches a peak at 8 or 9 years of age, followed by a sharp decline, after which sex differences become apparent.

In the male, body potassium shows a second increase between 14 and 16 years, reaching a peak by the 19th year, followed by another decline. In the female, body potassium continues to decline during adolescence, indicating a decline in the percentage of lean body mass.

In the male, body weight due to lean body mass increases rapidly after the age of 13 to 14, reaching a maximum at 18 to 19 years, after which there is a slow fall. As indicated earlier, in a male 12 to 14 years old, body fat drops, followed by a rise until 16.5 years of age. At this age there is an abrupt fall, after which body fat shows a slow and sustained rise through middle age. The muscular appearance in the male during late adolescence is explained by the simultaneous decrease in body fat and rapid rise in lean body mass.

The increase in lean body mass in females is slower than in males. In 15-year-olds, it reaches its maximum, about 75% of that of a male's maximum. However, as discussed earlier, a female's body fat generally rises between the ages of 8 and 17. She therefore gains fat at the expense of lean body mass, which contains mainly muscle (that is, protein). A comparison of the 25-year-old adult male and female lean body mass or body protein is found in Table 2-6.

As one ages from 25 to 50, the body shows an average decrease of 0.11 kg of cell mass annually. As indicated earlier, since the decrease in body water during old age occurs within the cells, the decrease reflects a definite reduction in body cell mass. Another documented observation is the progressive decline of total body potassium as one gets older. The average amount of potassium per kilogram of body weight falls steadily during adulthood. But since the amount of potassium per kilogram of lean body mass is higher in the adult than in the newborn infant, less lean body mass is actually lost than absolute levels of potassium would suggest.

In summary, from the period of 25 years to death, the body changes in a predictable pattern:

Body fat continues to increase while body cell mass and water content continue to decrease relative to total body weight. For instance, if a man weighs the same at ages 25 and 65, more of that weight will probably be body fat and less will be lean body mass at 65. This pattern is the same for women, only more so: Women have more body fat and less cell mass and water content than men throughout their life spans.

What is the significance of this change with aging? For one thing, since the lean body mass is the metabolically active part of the body, its continuous decline as one gets older is one major clinical problem with geriatric patients. In addition, since drugs and nutrients are destined for this metabolically active part of the body, the estimation of appropriate drug dosages and nutrient requirements should be based on the quantity of lean body mass rather than total body weight.

STUDY QUESTIONS

1. What is one calorie? One joule?
2. How is the energy in food samples measured in the laboratory? How does this method differ from the actual utilization of food energy in the body? What numerical values are used to account for this difference?
3. Discuss the two methods of determining individual energy expenditure.
4. Define basal metabolic rate (BMR). What is the average BMR? What variables influence individual differences in BMR? How?
5. How is a person's total energy need calculated?
6. Discuss the four ways of describing body composition and at least four methods of determining the composition of a particular person's body.
7. How do relative amounts of body water, body fat, and lean body mass change as a person ages?

Chapter 3

Carbohydrates

CARBOHYDRATES ARE A major source of food energy for most people. At present, Americans obtain approximately half of their energy requirement from carbohydrates. Since carbohydrates are generally an inexpensive source of food energy, the consumption of carbohydrates is inversely related to income. In poorer countries, 80% to 90% of people's food energy may come from carbohydrates.

The final sections of this chapter will review conflicting opinions of how much carbohydrate—if any—our bodies actually need for survival and how the amount and types of carbohydrates we consume affect our health. First, however, we will look at what carbohydrates are, how their many forms can be classified, and how our bodies use them. The digestion, absorption, and metabolism of ingested carbohydrates will be explained in detail in Chapter 8.

Percentage	Food sources
10%	Milk and other dairy products
30%	Regular table sugar including that used in pastries, desserts, candies, and beverages. Items such as syrup are included.
60%	Starchy foods such as grains, cereal products, starchy vegetables, and fruits.

FIGURE 3-1   Relative contribution of digestible carbohydrates by different food sources in the American diet.

FORMS OF CARBOHYDRATES

As a whole, the human body derives the major portion of its energy needs from plant carbohydrates, the most abundant organic substances on earth. By means of photosynthesis, all green plants convert carbon dioxide and water, with the assistance of sunlight, into carbohydrates and oxygen. Plant carbohydrates exist in two forms: the wood structure or cellulose, and the plant's sugar and starch storages. The relative amounts of sugar and starch stored in plant foods depend on the plant's maturity (as in the ripeness of a fruit) and environmental conditions, such as temperature, humidity, acidity, moisture, fertility, contamination, and storage conditions. For example, recall how the sweet taste of fruits changes after a period of storage.

We ingest most of our carbohydrates from sugar and the starchy grains, vegetables, and fruits, though some carbohydrates are also available in milk and dairy products (see Figure 3-1). Whether it comes from a plant or the milk of a dairy animal that has eaten green plants, a carbohydrate is always made up of carbon, hydrogen, and oxygen in the ratio of 1:2:1. Because there are two molecules of hydrogen to one of oxygen, as in water, the term *carbohydrate* literally means "hydrated carbon" (that is, water attached to carbon).

Chemically, there are many different kinds of carbohydrates. Table 3-1 classifies carbohydrates and gives some common examples. The major categories are monosaccharides, oligosaccharides, polysaccharides, and organic acids. *Monosaccharides* are considered to be the simplest carbohydrate molecules, for they cannot be hydrolyzed, or "split," into simpler forms. When a carbohydrate contains many units and each unit is made up of two to ten monosaccharides chemically joined, it is called an *oligosaccharide*. In *polysaccharides*, the repeating units contain hundreds to thousands of monosaccharides. Either in the laboratory or in the intestine, the individual units of oligosaccharides can be hydrolyzed so that all the monosaccharides are released and exist in their free forms.

Organic acids are also carbohydrates, since their carbon, hydrogen, and oxygen units exist in the ratio of 1:2:1. However, most consumers are not aware of this form of carbohydrate. For example, citric acid, tartaric acid, and others are common organic acids occurring in many foods we eat. Though this chapter will not discuss organic acids further, detailed information may

TABLE 3-1 Classification and Common Examples of Carbohydrates

A. Monosaccharides
1. 6-carbon sugars: glucose, fructose, galactose, mannose
2. 5-carbon sugars: D-ribose, D-2-deoxyribose, L-arabinose, D-xylose
3. 6-carbon sugar alcohols: sorbitol, mannitol, dulcitol, inositol
4. 5-carbon sugar alcohols: xylitol

B. Oligosaccharides
1. Disaccharides: sucrose, lactose, maltose, trehalose
2. Trisaccharides: raffinose
3. Tetrasaccharides: stachyose

C. Polysaccharides
1. Homopolysaccharides: starch, cellulose, dextrans, glycogen, dextrins, inulin
2. Heteropolysaccharides: mucopolysaccharides, glycolipids, glycoprotein

D. Organic acids
Acetic acid, citric acid, tartaric acid, and others

be obtained from a standard textbook on food science.

A general discussion of how these four types of carbohydrates are digested and metabolized by the body will be found in Chapter 8. The sections that follow will present the unique properties of many common carbohydrates.

Monosaccharides

The most common monosaccharides are six-carbon sugars (hexoses), such as glucose, fructose, galactose, and mannose. Other monosaccharides include five-carbon sugars (pentoses), six-carbon sugar alcohols, and five-carbon sugar alcohols. The intestine of a healthy person can absorb all of them, though the extent and rate of absorption vary. Monosaccharides also vary in known importance to human health.

Glucose

Glucose is the only known six-carbon monosaccharide existing in a fair amount in the human body. It is found mainly in the blood, where

it serves as an important and readily available energy fuel. When needed, the glucose in a cell is oxidized to form water, carbon dioxide, and energy. Normally, there are about 70 to 100 mg of glucose per 100 mL of blood; a person with this range is considered *normoglycemic*. *Hyperglycemia* and *hypoglycemia* refer to high and low blood glucose levels, respectively. Diabetes is associated with hyperglycemia; one preliminary test for the disease is confirmation of glucose in the urine. However, ingesting a large amount of certain chemicals such as vitamin C can complicate this method of identification: Since vitamin C is similar to glucose in its chemical-reducing property, the vitamin C in the urine may be mistakenly identified as glucose.

Glucose has many other names: D-glucose, fruit sugar, corn sugar, and, commercially, dextrose. It is about 70% as sweet as table sugar. Free glucose is found in very few other foods. Some health food stores carry various brands of free glucose commercially prepared from starch. In clinical medicine, dextrose is sometimes used intravenously to feed hospitalized patients.

Commercially, glucose is made from starch or corn by the action of heat, acids, or enzymes, all of which can hydrolyze a polysaccharide into its component monosaccharides. The glucose thus obtained exists in two forms. Anhydrous dextrose contains less than 0.5% water, and dextrose hydrate contains about 9% by weight of water of crystallization. Dextrose hydrate, used frequently in food processing, is generally not available for home use.

In table sugar, milk sugar, and starch, glucose occurs as a chemical component in combination with other monosaccharides. Glucose contents of selected foods are shown in Table 3-2, and the physiological properties of glucose in the human body are comprehensively reviewed in Chapter 26.

Fructose

Fructose, also known as fruit sugar or levulose, is commonly found in many fruits, honey, and plant saps. Like glucose (also a fruit sugar), it contains six carbons, but its chemical structure is different. Its fate in the body, however, is fairly similar to that of glucose. Fructose consumed with other foods will eventually be

TABLE 3-2 Approximate Contents of Glucose, Fructose, and Sucrose in Selected Fruits and Vegetables*

Food Item	% of Fresh Weight		
	Glucose	Fructose	Sucrose
Asparagus	1	1.4	0.3
Celery	0.5	0.5	0.4
Onion	2	1.2	0.9
Tomato	1.1	1.4	0.01
Swiss corn	0.35	0.35	2.9
Apple	1.2	6.2	4
Grape	6	6	2
Pear	1	6.5	1.5
Plum	3.2	1.5	4.5
Strawberry	2	2.2	1.5
Lima bean	0.03	0.1	2.5
Cowpea	0.1	0.05	1.6

*These data are the average values obtained from the results of different investigators. The contents of these monosaccharides vary widely in different plant products. This table is intended to serve as a guide only.

changed to glucose in the liver or broken down into carbon dioxide, water, and energy.

Fructose is one of the two monosaccharides forming the disaccharide sucrose (table sugar). Commercial fructose is intensely sweet—much sweeter than glucose. At present, fructose is used extensively in the pharmaceutical industry and is beginning to be used in food processing.

Clinically, fructose has been explored for a number of potentially useful applications. One well-known advantage of fructose is its ability to speed up alcohol metabolism, although the effectiveness seems to vary with the individual. Clinical and experimental studies have suggested the use of fructose by diabetic patients, because the ingestion of fructose does not induce drastic changes in blood glucose level. Fructose has also been used as an intravenous nutrient, though its rapid infusion can result in the accumulation of a large amount of lactic acid, which can adversely affect the acid-base balance of the body. Further, experimental and clinical studies have indicated that fructose is not as likely to cause dental cavities as sucrose.

Some researchers have suggested that consuming too much fructose can increase blood fatty chemicals and thus enhance the risk of heart disease. This remains a very controversial topic.

Table 3-2 lists the fructose contents of a number of common food items.

Galactose and mannose

The six-carbon monosaccharide *galactose* does not exist as a free sugar. It usually occurs as one of the two components of the disaccharide found in milk. In the body, it can be converted to glucose and vice versa. Abnormality in the metabolism of this chemical in the human body has been implicated in cataract formation.

Small amounts of the six-carbon monosaccharide *mannose* exist as a free sugar in peaches, apples, oranges, and the food manna, from which it takes its name. The cell walls of baker's yeast also contain some mannose, as do certain plant saps. Mannose is also an important component of a number of heteropolysaccharides, such as the vegetable gums. Like galactose, mannose can be converted in the liver to glucose and vice versa.

Five-carbon sugars

The five-carbon sugars, also called *pentoses*, are of little or no importance as a source of energy for the human body. Yet they are synthesized by humans and animals and are present in a small amount in all cells, including bacteria. For example, D-xylose and L-arabinose are widely distributed in vegetable roots and fruits. D-ribose and D-2-deoxyribose are important components of each cell's nucleic acids, which are the chemical components of chromosomes. D-ribose is also one component of riboflavin (vitamin B_2). Because some pentoses are components of the nucleotides in nucleic acids, they play an important role in releasing and forming energy in the body, though they are *not* sources of energy.

When pentoses are ingested in the free form, most are not utilized; instead, they are eliminated in the urine and feces. Because of this characteristic, D-xylose has been used as a "marker" to detect the proper absorptive function of the human intestine. If the normal amount excreted in the urine and feces by a per-

Dietetic Food Diarrhea*

Report of a Case

A 29-year-old healthy man had diarrhea of two weeks' duration. Attempting to reduce weight by dieting, he found it difficult to adhere to the diet and resorted to daily intake of dietetic foodstuffs to aid in his dieting and weight reduction. Within a few days, he noted the onset of diarrhea, defined as five to six watery stools per day, associated with low abdominal cramps but no other symptoms. His usual bowel habit consisted of formed stools without associated abdominal complaints.

History was negative for other probable pathogenetic factors for diarrhea. Results of physical examination, stool cultures, and proctoscopic examination were normal. A general health examination conducted elsewhere before starting his weight reduction

program yielded normal results for complete blood cell count; urinalysis; stool cultures for ova, parasite, and occult blood; biochemical profile; and barium contrast roentgenograms of the gastrointestinal tract. Dietary history disclosed that the patient was consuming the following sugarless foods on a daily basis: two packs of sugarless gum (5 sticks per pack, 1.2 g of sorbitol per stick); two rolls of sugarless mints (11 tablets per roll, 1.4 g of sorbitol per tablet); two dietetic candy bars (5 to 7 g of hexitols per bar); and two dietetic wafers (ranging from 2.8 g of hexitols to 4.4 g of sorbitol per wafer, depending on wafer flavor). The total hexitol ingestion from these products in our patient ranged from 50.9 to 55.1 g/day. Discontinuation of dietetic food intake produced complete cessation of diarrhea and cramps. The patient has since remained free of symptoms. . . .

*Source: M. J. R. Ravry, *Journal of the American Medical Association* 244 (1980): 270. Copyright *1980*, American Medical Association.

son with an intact and healthy intestine is known, the defective absorptive rate can be easily detected.

Six-carbon sugar alcohols

Sorbitol, the most common six-carbon sugar alcohol, is found naturally in fruits such as apples, cherries, pears, plums, and rowanberries. It tastes sweet, though less so than sucrose or table sugar. Commercially, it is made by chemically adding hydrogen atoms (hydrogenation) to glucose, and it is a major ingredient in many dietetic foods. Since the absorption and utilization of sorbitol in the human body has little effect on blood glucose level, sorbitol is used in the manufacture of "diabetic" jams, marmalade, canned fruits, fruit drinks, chocolate, and other items. However, the body does not absorb sorbitol well, and when the ingested amount exceeds 50 g, diarrhea may result.

When mannose and galactose are hydroge-

nated, they form the six-carbon sugar alcohols *mannitol* and *dulcitol*, respectively. Both occur naturally and can also be prepared commercially; for example, mannitol may be obtained from a certain seaweed. Both substances are used as food additives in food processing (mannitol, for instance, is used in sugarless chewing gum). They are also used occasionally in testing for the normality of kidney clearance.

Inositol occurs naturally in different foods, especially cereal brans. The chemical arrangement of this six-carbon sugar alcohol is cyclic. When the alcohol groups of an inositol are attached to "phosphates" chemically, a molecule of phytic acid or its salt, phytate, is formed. Phytic acid is found in whole wheat flour and oatmeal and is suspected to interfere with the absorption of calcium, iron, and zinc.

Though inositol is suspected to be at least partially essential for mice, its need by humans is doubtful. Although it has been labeled as a vitamin for humans, this claim has not been scientifically substantiated. For more information on inositol and phytic acid, refer to Chapters 6 and 7, respectively.

Five-carbon sugar alcohols

Xylitol is a naturally occurring five-carbon sugar alcohol found in many berries. In addition, xylitol may be extracted from wood and farm crop residues such as unused hulls, straw, and stalks of farm crops. Bulk supplies are now available, usually obtained from chemical reaction of birch wood. Xylitol is also synthesized by the human body, mainly from the five-carbon sugar xylose, and commercial production is also possible. The substance is sweeter than table sugar.

Because of its sweet taste and its inability to affect blood glucose level after ingestion, xylitol is suitable as a sugar substitute for diabetic patients and patients with liver problems. In addition, preliminary clinical studies indicate that it may protect teeth from cavities. In Germany and Japan, it is sometimes used in intravenous feeding. Because of possible toxic effects, this use is not currently permitted in the United States. However, under certain conditions of administration, this substance is fairly well tolerated by patients, and it is still being considered for possible use in this country.

Oligosaccharides

The most well known of the oligosaccharides (carbohydrates containing many individual units, each of which is made up of two to ten monosaccharides) are the *disaccharides*. Each of the many units in a disaccharide contains two monosaccharides chemically joined together. Similarly, trisaccharides and tetrasaccharides contain three and four monosaccharides, respectively. This section will describe three common disaccharides: sucrose, lactose, and maltose.

Sucrose

Probably the most well-known disaccharide is *sucrose*, regular table sugar, sometimes called white or refined sugar. Household sugar is obtained mainly from sugar beets or sugar cane.

Sucrose is made up of many repeating units, each of which is a chemical combination of glucose and fructose. In a laboratory, heat, enzymes, or acids can split each unit into its constituents, glucose and fructose. In the human and animal intestine, sucrose must be degraded to its components by the intestinal enzyme sucrase before absorption.

Sucrose is used extensively in cooking and commercial food processing. Pharmaceutically, it is used as an ingredient in the production of tablets because of its sweetness, digestibility, and other properties. One good example is its use in buccal and sublingual tablets, designed to release the active ingredient over a period of 15 to 30 minutes.

The relationship of table sugar to human health is currently the subject of intense debate in both the public and scientific sectors. Analyses of the issues involved are presented throughout this book.

Lactose

The monosaccharides within the disaccharide *lactose* are glucose and galactose. Lactose is also called milk sugar because it is found in the milk of all mammals except the whale and hippopotamus. It is very insoluble in water and not very sweet.

It is well known that lactose can facilitate the absorption of calcium in the human intestine. Since breast milk has more lactose than does homogenized cow's milk, an infant is expected to receive more calcium when breast fed. However, lactose is now added to many commercial infant formulas. At present, lactose is also used in food processing and pharmaceutical preparations.

The enzyme that can digest lactose in the intestine is called *lactase*. Among members of some ethnic groups and under other conditions, the enzyme may disappear at a certain stage in life. This may happen anytime from childhood to adulthood. Such individuals develop adverse symptoms when drinking milk because the undigested and unabsorbed lactose is passed on and fermented by colon bacteria, releasing gas and acid. Symptoms include cramps, bloating, and gas. The clinical management of such patients is discussed in Chapter 24.

TABLE 3-3   The Relative Sweetening Power of Selected Carbohydrates and Carbohydrate-Rich Foods

Carbohydrate or Food	Relative Sweetening Power
Sucrose (table sugar)	100
Fructose	140–170
Honey	120–170
Molasses	110
Glucose	75
Corn syrup	60
Sorbitol	60
Mannitol	50
Galactose	30
Maltose	30
Lactose	15

Maltose

Although the disaccharide *maltose* is also called "malt sugar," it is not very sweet, as indicated in Table 3-3, a comparison of the sweetness of certain carbohydrates. As its name implies, maltose may be obtained by the malting of barley, as occurs in beer production. Commercially, it is obtained by the enzymatic degradation of starch by yeasts. Each unit within maltose is made up of two molecules of glucose. Commercial preparations, which usually contain a mixture of maltose and dextrose (glucose), are used in instant foods and in bakery products.

Polysaccharides

The *polysaccharides* are carbohydrates made up of more than ten monosaccharides. Those that contain carbohydrates only are called *homopolysaccharides*; the examples discussed in this section include starch, glycogen, cellulose, dextrins, dextrans, and inulin. Those polysaccharides that contain carbohydrate and noncarbohydrate substances are called *heteropolysaccharides*, some of which are seaweed extracts, heparin, pectin, and others.

Starch

Starch is a polysaccharide of many units, each of which contains hundreds or thousands of glucose molecules that are chemically joined. Starch is stored in granules within plant seeds and roots such as grains, cereals, beans, and rice. As the major energy storage of a plant, starch is made up of two types of polysaccharides: amylose and amylopectin.

About 15% to 20% of starch is made up of *amylose*, which consists of many glucose units joined linearly without branching. When starch is put in water and then iodine added, the intense blue color is caused by the water-soluble amylose. Certain varieties of maize and rice do not contain amylose, however.

About 75% to 80% of starch is made up of *amylopectin*, which is composed of many glucose units joined in branched configurations. If amylopectin is separated from amylose, it gives a brownish violet color when iodine is added. Since amylopectin, which occurs in flour, is insoluble in water, it is responsible for the thickening of gravy when flour is heated in water, fat, and other ingredients.

When starch granules are first obtained from plants, they hardly dissolve in water. Heat produces a solution of starch, which jells on cooling. Starch granules in a vegetable are actually confined within the plant cell walls in clusters. Solubility produced by heating swells the granules and eventually ruptures the cell walls. Cooking therefore increases the digestibility of a starch food; starch that is only semisolible (for instance, because of poor preparation) may cause indigestion after a meal.

Within the digestive system, starch is hydrolyzed into simpler carbohydrates such as the disaccharide maltose and eventually into the individual molecules of glucose. The simple process of heating starch at 100 °C can also release the glucose molecules and make it taste slightly sweet. The frying or grilling of starchy food or the malting of barley may release glucose and maltose from the polysaccharides to produce a mild, sweet flavor.

Glycogen

Glycogen, sometimes called *animal starch*, is the form in which energy is stored in an animal. It occurs in a small amount in the muscles and livers of land animals and in a more significant quantity in shellfish, especially oysters and scallops. Chemical substances similar to glycogen are also found in algae, yeasts, fungi, tapeworm, and golden bantam sweet corn.

Glycogen resembles the amylopectin of starch, though glycogen is more branched. It contains about 30 to 60 thousand glucose molecules with many branches, each of which is made up of 10 to 18 glucose molecules. Glycogen also differs from amylopectin in another respect: It is fairly soluble in water, forming a very attractive opalescent solution. When iodine is added to a glycogen solution, it forms a deep red color. The chemical linkage between the individual glucose molecules is the same as that in starch. The size of glycogen molecules varies with the animal and its metabolic status. Land animals—such as beef cattle, chickens, lambs, and sheep—do not contain sufficient glycogen to be significant dietary sources of this carbohydrate. During the process of slaughtering, the glycogen in land animal muscles and livers is so degraded that the meat and fowl sold in the grocery stores contain very little glycogen.

Even though the foods we eat may not be rich in glycogen, we can make this compound from other carbohydrates we eat. In the body, glucose and other monosaccharides are converted to glycogen in the liver and muscles. Such stored glycogen is an important and readily available source of glucose. When needed, the glycogen releases glucose, which can be metabolized to form energy and eventually carbon dioxide and water. Glycogen is therefore especially important for people undergoing strenuous activity. Human muscles contain about 5 to 6 oz (150–180 g) of glycogen; the human liver contains 2 to 3 oz (60–90 g). In the digestive system, glycogen can be split by alimentary enzymes to form the individual glucose molecules, which can then be absorbed.

In a number of popular cooked shellfish, such as oysters, lobsters, and scallops, the glycogen content is partially responsible for the delicate sweet flavor. Heat degradation of glycogen releases glucose, which is sweet. For example, about 6% of the wet weight of an oyster is made up of glycogen.

Cellulose

Cellulose is a polysaccharide made up of many glucose molecules that are chemically joined. In the past, the term *cellulose* usually referred to dietary fiber, residue, or roughage in general; its content in foods was found by using the "fiber" values given in food composition tables. However, because of renewed interest in dietary fiber, its definition has recently been subjected to intense debate. Figure 3-2 provides a description of the tentative terminology used for dietary fiber and other carbohydrates. All terms used will likely be standardized in the near future.

The fiber values given in food composition tables are actually less than actual fiber contents. Figure 3-2 lists six other groups of undigestible substances in addition to cellulose: hemicellulose A, hemicellulose B, pectin, lignin, mucilages, and gums. *Hemicellulose A* is a polymer, each unit of which is composed of xylose, galactose, glucose, mannose, and arabinose. *Hemicellulose B* is also a polymer, each unit of which has the components xylose, galactose, glucose, mannose, arabinose, and uronic acid derivatives. *Pectin* is a polymer of a methylester of galacturonic acid and other sugars. *Lignin* is a noncarbohydrate made up of phenylpropane units; lignin levels increase with the age of the plant. *Mucilages* and *gums*, which have varying contents of heteropolysaccharides, are not digested and absorbed to any significant extent by the human small intestine.

Another cause of confusion is the lack of an accurate method for determining available versus unavailable carbohydrate in food (see Figure 3-2). Traditionally, the weight of carbohydrates in a food sample has been obtained by subtracting from the total weight the different weights of protein, fat, ash, and water, all of which are obtained independently by other methods (see Chapter 10). The obvious question is, How does the value so obtained compare with our actual carbohydrate intake?

Dietary fiber serves different uses in the body. It provides bulk in the diet, thus increasing

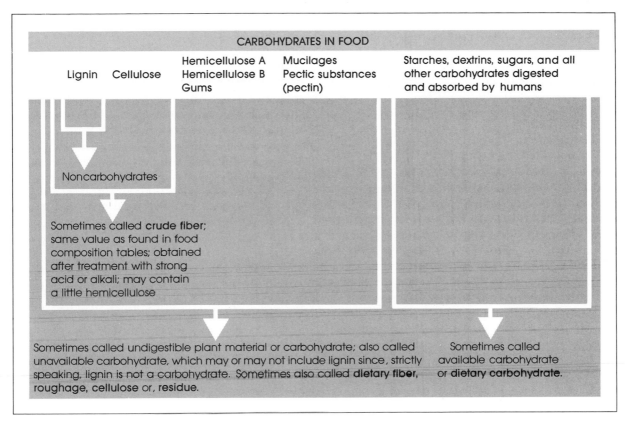

FIGURE 3-2   Terminology for "dietary" carbohydrates.

the satiety value of foods. It maintains good intestinal motility, establishes regular bowel movements, and prevents constipation. The human small bowel does not have the necessary enzymes to digest dietary fiber; fiber is passed on to the large intestine where it is fermented.

Because of technological processing of food, Western populations have decreased their daily consumption of dietary roughage. According to current speculation, this may have increased the risk of developing the following diseases and clinical problems: hiatus hernia, appendicitis, diverticular diseases, irritable bowel syndrome, constipation, hemorrhoids, cancer of the colon, gallstones, varicose veins, obesity, dental caries, diabetes mellitus, and cardiovascular diseases.

Dextrins

Dextrins are small polysaccharides with five to six glucose units. They could therefore be classified as oligosaccharides, but units of more than ten monosaccharides may be present.

In nature, dextrins may be located in the leaves of starch-forming plants. Within the human alimentary tract, dextrins are the products of starch digestion. That is, the long chains of glucose (as in starch) are broken down to a smaller number of glucose units (as in dextrins) per molecule. Another source of dextrins is the crust and toast of bread; they contain a fair amount of dextrins produced by the degradation of starch by moist heat.

Commercially, dextrins are very important. They are sweeter than starch but not as sweet as glucose. When corn is processed to make corn syrup, corn starch is hydrolyzed to form dextrins, which are present in corn syrup. Some dextrins are also formed during the malting of beer. However, processors can now remove the dextrins during the brewing process. Such beer is sold on the market as a low-carbohydrate "light" beer, which provides only 50% to 70% of the energy or calories of regular beer.

In clinical use, the important nutritional supplement "liquid glucose" is actually a mixture of dextrins, maltose, glucose, and water. It is given to hospitalized patients who are unable to digest regular carbohydrate food. Some health food stores carry such dextrin supplements and advocate their usage without a doctor's advice.

Dextrans

Like starch, glycogen, cellulose, and dextrins, *dextrans* are another polysaccharide made up of many glucose molecules chemically joined by characteristic linkages. In nature, this substance can be found in yeast and bacteria. When certain microorganisms are put on a rich sugar medium, they grow and produce dextrans, which make up the slime we normally associate with bacteria or other contaminated or moldy surfaces.

This substance is being studied intensively to explore its potential use as a blood plasma substitute or extender. Dextrans are easily manufactured by growing the bacteria *Leuconostoc mesenteroides* in a sucrose medium. Some clinicians have recommended injecting a solution of dextrans into a patient with blood loss, because dextrans can increase blood volume and prevent shock. Though the safety of dextrans for humans is not yet established, no harm is expected if the number of injections is limited.

Dextrans have been implicated in the development of dental cavities. Bacteria such as *Streptococcus mutans* and *Streptococcus sanguis* are present in our mouths and can change some basic carbohydrate molecules such as sucrose, glucose, and fructose into dextrans, which are the slimy substances on or near teeth edges and surfaces. As a result, the bacteria in the plaque acquire a "home" in which they can ferment other available carbohydrates to form lactic acid, which can produce cavities. In addition to providing a home for bacteria, the dextrans surround the plaque, preventing the alkaline saliva from neutralizing the acid formed.

Inulin

Inulin, also called fructans, is a polysaccharide with many fructose units that are chemically joined. It is found in the roots of the Jerusalem artichoke, dandelion, chicory, dahlia tubers, garlic, and onion bulbs. Cereals and grasses also contain a large amount of inulin.

It is not known if inulin can be digested by the human intestinal tract. However, inulin has three important clinical usages. First, because the kidney can selectively secrete inulin, it has been used extensively to ascertain the urine clearance capacity of the kidney. Second, because inulin can distribute itself mainly in the extracellular fluid when injected into the body, it is occasionally used in clinical studies of fluid and electrolyte distribution. After inulin is labeled with a radioactive isotope and injected into the body, an appropriate fluid analysis and measurement can be used to estimate the volume of the extracellular fluid in the body. Third, inulin has been recommended for use by diabetic patients, on the assumption that the fructose molecules contributed by hydrolyzed inulin will not affect blood glucose level after absorption. Since the digestive physiology of inulin is unknown, such use is now being questioned.

Other polysaccharides and related substances

Heteropolysaccharides are made up of carbohydrate polymers and other chemical substances. Many marine products, such as agar, alginic acid, algin, carrageenan (red seaweed), Irish moss, and vegetable gums (gum arabic, gum ghatti, gum tragacanth, and locust bean gum) are heteropolysaccharides. Many of them are used in the food industry to thicken, emulsify, and stabilize processed food products. In the United States, they are legally classified as food additives; however, people of many other countries consume many of them regularly as food. For example, the Japanese and other Orientals use seaweed as a staple food. Agar, because it is not digested by the human intestine, is also used as a laxative to treat constipation.

Another group of heteropolysaccharides is *mucopolysaccharides.* One of these substances is *heparin,* a very common blood anticoagulant used in clinical medicine.

Pectin is not exactly a polysaccharide, but it does contain some monosaccharides and other chemical substances. It is found in fruits, such as in orange peel. In home food preparation, pectin serves one important purpose: the gelling of food products.

A *glycolipid* contains a sugar and fatty chemicals. Glycolipids are important structural components of the nervous tissues of brain and the spinal cord.

CARBOHYDRATE REQUIREMENTS

Current evidence does not indicate that carbohydrate is an essential nutrient for the human body. For instance, two Arctic explorers once survived without any plant carbohydrate food for at least one year by subsisting mainly on animal meat and fat. They did have some body distress such as bowel discomfort, however, and the amounts of uric acid and acetone in their urine and of triglyceride and cholesterol in their blood were elevated.

Anthropological and medical studies have shown that a number of herdsmen and tribesmen survive well on animal meats and fats without consuming any carbohydrate from plant foods. Many Eskimos subsist on little or no carbohydrate, obtaining less than 20% of their daily energy requirement from plant carbohydrate. Eskimos eat a lot of meat and fat without suffering from any disease directly traceable to the lack of the nutrient. However, it is currently suspected that Eskimos actually consume more carbohydrates than most nutritionists have assumed. Because Eskimos frequently eat their meat raw and frozen, they take in more glycogen than a person purchasing meat with a lower glycogen content in a grocery store. The Eskimo practice of preserving a whole seal or bird carcass under an intact skin with a thick layer of blubber also permits some proteins to ferment into carbohydrates.

Although normal human adults can seemingly survive without carbohydrates, many nutritionists favor the daily consumption of a minimum quantity of this nutrient. Carbohydrate is the main source of energy fuel for the body, chiefly in the form of glucose. Although fat and protein can provide glucose and thus energy, dietary glucose is obviously the more readily available form. If little or no carbohydrate is consumed, the body derives its energy mainly from protein and fat in the diet or from the body (as in the case of starvation). The process takes place mainly in the liver. When protein is degraded for energy, an important nutrient is wasted that could build muscles and bones. Physiologically, carbohydrate thus "spares" protein.

Excessive degradation of fat and protein for energy also results in the formation and accumulation of an undesirable quantity of ketoacids, ketones, acetone, and similar intermediate byproducts. This can create the condition of *ketosis*, which can disrupt the acid balance of the body. This does not seem to pose a problem for a normal, healthy, male adult within a certain period of time (e.g., two years), as observed in the two Arctic explorers. However, ketosis is considered harmful to pregnant women. Also, if an excessive amount of body protein is degraded because of a lack of carbohydrate, the loss of body tissues and muscles is accompanied by a loss of water and electrolytes such as sodium, calcium, potassium, magnesium, and phosphorus. It is argued that a daily intake of 100 g of carbohydrates will prevent ketosis and conserve water and electrolytes.

Excessive consumption of meat protein and animal fat in lieu of carbohydrates will also raise blood cholesterol and triglyceride levels, predisposing the individual to heart disease, as discussed in Chapter 27. In addition, the increase of uric acid in blood and urine may predispose the person to gout and urinary calculi.

Although fat and protein can be degraded for energy, if necessary, carbohydrates may have some functions that other nutrients cannot perform. For instance, brain cells and cells of the eye lens and nervous tissues depend specifically on glucose as a main source of energy. Occasionally they may be able to use ketone bodies for this purpose. Under certain conditions, an extremely low blood glucose level may affect the brain and result in drowsiness, coma, and death, in that order. Carbohydrates also play a very important role in body metabolic processes, such as the conversion of carbohydrates into protein (amino acids), as discussed in Chapter 8. Certain carbohydrate molecules combine with other chemicals to form specific structural components of cells, tissues, and organs. And the indigestible parts of dietary carbohydrates such as roughage or fiber serve special purposes in the body.

Eating carbohydrates often supplies us with other essential nutrients as well. Apart from

Nutrition for Top Sports Performance*

High-Carbohydrate Diets

In a normal mixed diet, carbohydrates provide about 45% of the calories; in a carbohydrate-rich diet, as much as 70% of the calories may ·come from carbohydrates. Such diets are superior to normal- or low-carbohydrate diets in sustaining physical performance for long periods. During prolonged exercise at less than full (submaximal) effort (e.g., distance running or cycling), most energy comes from the oxidation of fat. As the duration or intensity of exercise increases, the athlete's metabolism changes from predominantly aerobic to anaerobic. This shift, combined with other complex metabolic signals, causes the body to oxidize carbohydrates more and fats less. At this point, fatigue becomes imminent.

The onset of exhaustion is thought to reflect depletion of glycogen stored in the muscles and liver. Unlike stores of fat, glycogen stores are limited. A 70-kg man of average build has approximately 50,000 to 100,000 Cal of energy stored as fat but only 1000 to 1400 Cal stored as carbohydrate, in the form of muscle and liver glycogen. When muscle glycogen is depleted, muscular contraction fails. Liver glycogen becomes depleted along with muscle glycogen. When liver glycogen is depleted, the blood glucose level falls, causing exercise-induced hypoglycemia, which impairs the functioning of the nervous system, muscular tissue, and red blood cells.

Since muscle and liver glycogen are essential for endurance, glycogen stores must be maximized before competition. Athletes use three methods to achieve glycogen repletion. The first approach restores muscle and liver glycogen to normal levels before competition; the other two raise tissue glycogen to above-normal concentrations.

Glycogen repletion. The intensity of practice is reduced for at least 3 days before the day of the event, and a normal diet (45% to 50% carbohydrate) is consumed during this period. Depending on the individual's rate of restoration of muscle glycogen, several days may be required to replenish glycogen levels in exhausted muscles. Liver glycogen, on the other hand, can be replenished with only one or two meals containing 50 to 100 g of carbohydrate. The disadvantage with this approach is that an athlete may not achieve normal muscle glycogen by the day of the event.

Repletion of muscle glycogen depends on the intensity of the exercise that preceded the tapering-off period and on the amount of carbohydrate ingested while tapering off. Even when carbohydrates provide 90% of the calories, 46 to 48 hours are required to restore muscle glycogen to pre-exercise levels after exhaustive exercise. Restoration rates vary: Some athletes may not restore muscle glycogen on a high-carbohydrate diet, even after a 5-day rest.

Carbohydrate loading. A low-carbohydrate diet is combined with 2 to 3 days of exhaustive exercise, setting the stage for a "rebound" of muscle glycogen to above-normal levels when a high-carbohydrate diet is consumed during lighter training for 2 to 3 days before competition. The sudden availability of excess carbohydrate causes muscle glycogen stores to rebound, sometimes to as much as 100% above normal levels. Many athletes find this method demanding and choose it only occasionally.

A less rigorous approach, termed "modified" carbohydrate loading, combines 3 days of exhaustive exercise with a normal diet, then specifies a high-carbohydrate diet during the 2- to 3-day tapering-off period. Re-

*Source: Reprinted with permission from E. W. Askew, "Nutrition for Top Sports Performance," *Dietetic Currents* 8 (1981):12−15. Published by Ross Laboratories, Columbus, Ohio 43216.

sulting muscle glycogen levels will be only 65% to 75% of those achieved in full loading. In both methods, exhaustive exercise must precede the high-carbohydrate diet; without it, muscle glycogen gains will be small.

Does carbohydrate loading work? Most athletes think so. Because loss of glycogen is closely related to the onset of exhaustion, large muscle glycogen stores can forestall exhaustion significantly, depending on the degree of glycogen supercompensation. However, carbohydrate loading changes the body's metabolic and nutritional profiles severely and may be stressful. Such diets should be used only occasionally and are not recommended for children or adolescents. Isolated reports of irregular cardiac function following carbohydrate loading also give pause.

table sugar, honey, and syrup, very few foods are made up of carbohydrates alone. Foods such as potatoes, rice, corn, and bread are high-carbohydrate foods, but they also carry other nutrients, such as vitamins, minerals, and minimal amounts of usable though usually incomplete protein.

Many population groups and countries have one or more staple foods that are high in carbohydrates. As an agricultural product, plant carbohydrate is a good return from the investment of soil, fertilizers, and labor. It is cheap and sustains many people in undeveloped countries. And carbohydrate-rich foods are practically the only ones that can be stored for a reasonably long period without deterioration.

Finally, the color, flavor, and texture of carbohydrate-rich foods make them attractive and palatable. Many people find it difficult to prepare a complete and attractive meal without carbohydrates, and many find that eating just meat and fat does not satisfy their appetites.

CARBOHYDRATES, HEALTH, AND DISEASES

Although we need a certain level of carbohydrates for optimal health, how carbohydrate intake relates to health and diseases is currently one of the most debated topics in the field of nutrition. Numerous issues are involved.

Many popular items with high carbohydrate content, such as soft drinks, candies, potato chips, and french fries, are considered to contain only "empty" calories with no nutritive value. Many consumer groups hold such foods responsible for a number of human diseases, especially among children. Although excessive consumption of such foods will make a child lose interest in other more nutritious items, no scientific evidence indicates that those particular foods are disease causing. However, the relationship between sugars and the development of dental cavities has been established. Sucrose in table sugar, bakery products, candies, and other sweetened foods is identified as one major factor causing dental cavities, especially among children.

How sucrose intake may be responsible for other human diseases is still undetermined. For instance, diabetes mellitus is a disease related to the body's failure to metabolize glucose properly because of a disturbed insulin physiology. For many years it has been suggested that consuming many carbohydrates, especially sucrose, may predispose an individual to the disease. This association has not been scientifically proven, however.

For years, dietary carbohydrates, such as potatoes, rice, spaghetti, sugar, bread, and pastries, have been regarded as a group of foods that makes us fat. It is true that excess consumption of such carbohydrate-rich foods will increase fat deposition in the body. However, dietary fat provides nearly twice as many calories per unit weight. Carbohydrates by themselves do not cause obesity; it is the bad habit of overeating these foods (or any food) that produces the large weight gain.

Long-term use of oral contraceptive pills may predispose some individuals to react to dietary glucose, apparently increasing their tendency toward diabetes. Certain health problems may stem from individual intolerances to specific carbohydrates. As discussed earlier and in Chapter 24, some people cannot tolerate milk lactose.

As indicated in the previous section, carbohydrates are important to many body processes, which may not function optimally in their absence. For instance, a lack of dietary fiber may be a causative factor in certain diseases, though this correlation is still very controversial. In some situations, a high intake of carbohydrates may actually be beneficial. For instance, saturation of muscles with glycogen can improve the performance of an athlete engaged in an endurance event such as long-distance running. Also, consuming a large amount of carbohydrates can often help relieve the headaches that frequently occur at high altitudes in some individuals. Certain forms of carbohydrates, such as fructose and xylitol, may also be used in intravenous feeding. This clinical application is presently being explored, and, as more information becomes available, the use of carbohydrates in artificial feeding may be expanded.

STRUCTURAL FORMULAS

Glucose   Fructose   Galactose   Mannose

STUDY QUESTIONS

1. What are our major sources of carbohydrate? What is the basic chemical composition of all carbohydrates? Which foods provide most of the carbohydrates in the American diet?

2. Define monosaccharide. Describe the main functions and sources of glucose, fructose, galactose, and mannose.

3. What are the pentoses? Identify some six-carbon and five-carbon sugar alcohols.

4. Define oligosaccharide. What are the scientific names for table sugar, milk sugar, and

malt sugar? What are the two sweetest carbohydrates?

5. Define polysaccharide. Discuss the characteristics and sources of at least five polysaccharides.

6. What functions does dietary fiber serve in the body? What is the current confusion regarding the amount of fiber or roughage we ingest?

7. Is carbohydrate an essential nutrient? What happens in the body when insufficient carbohydrates are consumed? Are there disadvantages with an excessive carbohydrate intake? If yes, what are they? Be specific.

Chapter 4

Proteins

THE WORD *PROTEIN* is derived from the Greek word *protos*, which means "holding first place" or "primary." All living substances, including viruses and plants, contain protein. About 18% to 20% of a living person is made of protein, which is distributed through the blood, fat tissues, skin, bones, and muscles, as shown in Table 4-1. Our bodies can make protein in a predictable and systematic manner. This body protein undergoes constant turnover, being degraded and resynthesized. Certain basic ingredients from which protein substances are made, however, cannot be synthesized by the body—instead, they must be obtained from the foods we eat.

This chapter begins with a discussion of the elements of protein biochemistry: essential and nonessential amino acids, the components of protein, and the relationship between nitrogen and protein. Following an analysis of the body functions of protein, the chapter examines current thinking on how much protein we need to eat each day and which protein foods are of greatest value to body processes. The digestion, absorption, and metabolism of protein will be examined in Chapter 8; protein malnutrition in Chapter 11; protein intakes of vegetarians in Chapter 18; and a diet adequate in protein in Chapter 10.

ELEMENTS OF PROTEIN BIOCHEMISTRY

All protein substances contain carbon, hydrogen, oxygen, and nitrogen; some also contain sulfur, phosphorus, iron, zinc, and/or copper. The body contains many types of protein. Each protein substance may contain many chains of molecules, each made up of many individual units called *amino acids*. There are 20 to 25 amino acids in nature. If a protein molecule contains 200 units of amino acids, some of the amino acids will obviously occur many times.

Essential and Nonessential Amino Acids

The human body can systematically synthesize most amino acids from raw ingredients such as carbohydrates, fats, a nitrogen source, energy,

TABLE 4-1   Distribution of Protein in the Body*

Tissue	% of Body Protein (approx.)
Blood proteins (albumin and hemoglobin)	10
Fat cells of adipose tissues	3–4
Body skin	9–9.5
Bones	18–19
Muscles	46–47

*The values have been obtained from different investigators and are presented in ranges to emphasize their variability in human bodies.

and other substances. The remaining eight to ten amino acids that we cannot manufacture must be consumed in the diet and are therefore known as *essential amino acids*, since their deficiencies will result in impaired body functions. In general, the term *essential* is applied to any nutrient that the body needs but is unable to synthesize from ordinarily ingested ingredients. Instead, it must depend on dietary sources for these substances. By contrast, *nonessential amino acids* can be made by the body, provided that the necessary "building blocks" are available.

To be of use to the human body, the eight to ten essential amino acids must be present in the diet in a specific proportion. They can then be utilized by the body for repair and maintenance if the nonessential amino acids are there to provide sufficient *nitrogen sources*. However, if any of the essential amino acids occur in insufficient concentration, it will be utilized with other essential amino acids in the body in an appropriate ratio until it is exhausted. This pattern invariably means that a fair amount of the other essential amino acids is not used up. This biological phenomenon of the "right" ratio or pattern of ingested essential amino acids explains why so much importance is placed on the question of dietary protein sources. Proteins that do not contain the amino acids in this ratio are not as desirable as those that do.

The terms *essential* and *nonessential* must be interpreted with caution. Both are actually necessary to protein manufacture and use. Even though nonessential amino acids can be synthesized by the body from ingested nutrients, they

TABLE 4-2   Amino Acids Occurring in Nature

Essential for Adults and Infants	Essential for Infants Only	Nonessential	Questionable[†]
Isoleucine	Arginine*	Alanine	Hydroxyproline
Leucine	Histidine*	Asparagine	Norleucine
Lysine		Aspartic acid	Thyroxine
Methionine		Cysteine	
Phenylalanine		Cystine	
Threonine		Glutamic acid	
Tryptophan		Glutamine	
Valine		Glycine	
		Proline	
		Serine	
		Tyrosine	

*Preliminary evidence suggests that histidine is also an essential amino acid for adults. Some scientists question the essentiality of arginine.

[†]These substances are sometimes called amino acids.

must be present in the proper proportion to the essential ones to permit the efficient metabolism and manufacture of protein molecules in the body. Two physiological conditions are therefore important for normal body protein metabolism: (1) the presence of dietary essential amino acids and (2) the ready availability of nonessential ones from the body pool or foods ingested. Clinical evidence indicates that a patient's body can deteriorate when fed only essential amino acids. In addition to the pool of nitrogen from amino acids, protein metabolism in the body can be facilitated by the availability of other sources of nitrogen, such as purines, creatine, and trimethylamines.

Table 4-2 lists the amino acids that occur in nature, both essential and nonessential. All adults need the same essential amino acids, though females may require slightly smaller quantities than males. Scientists presently believe that the two amino acids *arginine* and *histidine* are essential for infants and children only, though recent preliminary evidence suggests that adults need histidine, too.

According to Table 4-2, *cystine* and *tyrosine* are classified as nonessential amino acids. This is not exactly accurate, for the body cannot make them from carbohydrates, fats, and a nitrogen source. Instead, cystine and tyrosine are derived from the essential amino acids methionine and phe-

nylalanine, respectively. Theoretically, if cystine and tyrosine are adequately supplied in the diet, our needs for methionine and phenylalanine will be reduced by 90% and 35%, respectively.

Protein Components

Whether built from dietary amino acids or synthesized by the body, protein substances vary very much in shape, size, and molecular weight. When amino acids exist singly or in free form, they are known as *free amino acids*. When they exist in chemically joined units of two, each unit of two amino acids is known as a *dipeptide*. The names tripeptide, tetrapeptide, and so on, similarly specify the number of amino acids in each set. The term *polypeptide* applies to the occurrence of 50 to 100 amino acids chemically joined in a unit. Larger molecules with a larger number of amino acids linked together are known as *proteins*.

Though the human intestine can absorb all these substances, it is most efficient in absorbing free amino acids. This means that all peptides and protein molecules must be digested, or *hydrolyzed*, to the free amino acid forms for maximal absorption. Substances that do the digestion are called *enzymes*, which are released from the intestinal wall. Sometimes, if chemical conditions

TABLE 4-3   Functional Contributions by Different Sources of Nitrogen to the Human Body

Nitrogen Source	Functional Contribution
Essential amino acids (protein and nonprotein substances)	Most needed by the human body both quantitatively and qualitatively.
Nonessential amino acids (protein and nonprotein substances)	Needed by the human body in quantity. No specific need for any of the particular amino acids.
Other nonprotein substances	Because the body can make them, they are not needed for any specific function. However, when present in a normal and nonpathological condition, they may facilitate different aspects of body metabolism.

are appropriate, heat or acid may hydrolyze protein molecules to free amino acids. The amino acid solutions used in enteral and parenteral feeding (see Chapter 23) are obtained in this manner.

Protein substances also differ in the following ways: (1) the number of amino acids present, (2) the specific amino acids present, (3) the frequency of appearance of each of the existing natural amino acids, (4) the frequency in which two specific amino acids are juxtaposed (if we assume the existence of 20 natural amino acids, then the possible combinations are enormous: 20 × 20), and (5) the shape of the protein molecule: jointed, spiraled, coiled, bent, folded, or straight.

Nitrogen and Proteins

Unlike fats and carbohydrates, protein molecules contain nitrogen. One common method of estimating the level of protein in foods is to measure the amount of nitrogen.* Food contains protein, which is made up of amino acids, and each amino acid contains nitrogen. Within certain limits, the level of nitrogen directly reflects the quantity of protein present. Thus, by estimating the amount of nitrogen in a food sample, we obtain an approximation of the amount of protein available. However, we now know that this technique has one major drawback: Many nonprotein substances in food contain nitrogen. For example, free amino acids and peptides con-

tain nitrogen but are not protein. The same is true of purines (a structural component in all cells), trimethylamine (a substance found mainly in seafoods), and ammonia, urea, and creatine (by-products of protein metabolism).

Food and body nitrogen sources may therefore be grouped as follows:

1. Protein nitrogen
2. Nonprotein nitrogen
   a. Free amino acids
   b. Peptides
   c. Urea, creatine, creatinine, ammonia, ammonium salts, purines, pyrimidine base, nucleoproteins, chromosomes, trimethylamines, and others

The functional contributions of these protein and nonprotein nitrogen sources are summarized in Table 4-3.

Even though nitrogen in a food or body tissue sample may be part of some nonprotein compound, nitrogen estimation is still widely used to estimate the quantity of protein present. The protein in milk, cereals, and nuts is composed of about 15%, 17%, and 18% nitrogen, respectively. To facilitate calculation and analysis, it is generally assumed that about 16% (obtained from the range of 15% to 17%) of the protein in a food or tissue sample is nitrogen. The conversion factor is therefore 6.25:

$$\frac{16}{100} \times \text{g of protein} = \text{g of nitrogen}$$
$$\text{g of protein} = \text{g of nitrogen} \times \frac{100}{16}$$
$$\text{g of protein} = \text{g of nitrogen} \times 6.25$$

---

*The same method is used for measuring protein in human tissue (for example, blood, liver, and muscle).

If we know how many grams of nitrogen are in a food sample, multiplying by 6.25 provides us with an approximation of how many grams of protein are in the same sample. Table 4-4 lists the approximate protein content of some common foods.

FUNCTIONS OF PROTEINS

Proteins serve many essential purposes in the body. First, protein is the structural component of many important substances: hormones, plasma proteins, antibodies, chromosomes, and others. For example, insulin is a hormone, a protein, and a very important substance that controls the physiological usage of glucose. All enzymes are protein, although the reverse is not true. The enzymes present in the body participate in vital life processes, such as the metabolism of oxygen and the release of carbon dioxide. Plasma proteins include such substances as hemoglobin and albumin, which maintain proper blood chemistry. Most antibodies are proteins, and the important relationship between protein nurture and infection is currently one of the most controversial subjects in human nutrition.

Tryptophan, an essential amino acid, is also a precursor of the vitamin niacin. Chromosomes are made of nucleic acids, and proteins form an important partner in the substance nucleoprotein. Nucleic acids such as DNA (deoxyribonucleic acid) and RNA (ribonucleic acid) direct the types of protein to be made by the body and at the same time predetermine the pattern of amino acids in each protein molecule.

A second major function of protein is its role in body development. Protein is essential for the growth, repair, and maintenance of most body structures. In a child, the absence of protein arrests growth.

Third, protein participates in body metabolism in two direct ways. As enzymes, proteins catalyze many biological and chemical reactions. In some of these reactions, proteins are also the participants, reactants, or substrates. The metabolism of proteins is discussed in detail in Chapter 8.

A fourth function of proteins involves the maintenance of body fluids and acid-base balance.

TABLE 4-4 Protein Content of Some Common American Foods*

Food Product	Serving Size	Protein (g)
Cheese, natural, cheddar	1 oz	7
Milk, whole, 3.3% fat	1 c	28
Ice cream, regular, hardened	1 c	5
Egg, cooked in any form	1	6
Butter	1 T	trace
Beef, ground, lean, broiled	3 oz	18
Tuna, canned in oil, drained	3 oz	24
Apple	1	trace
Grapefruit	½	1
Bread, white, enriched	1 sl	2
Breakfast cereal, hot, cooked (oatmeal or rolled oats)	1 c	5
Spaghetti, tomato sauce with cheese	1 c	6
Beans, cooked, drained	1 c	15
Peanut butter	1 T	4
Walnuts, English, chopped	1 c	18
Cabbage, raw, shredded	1 c	1
Corn, canned, cream style	1 c	5
Potatoes, cooked, baked (2/lb)	1	4
Beer	12 fl oz	1
Gelatin, dry	7 oz	6
Yeast, brewer's, dry	1 T	3

*Adapted from *Nutritive Value of Foods*, Home and Garden Bulletin No. 72 (Washington, D.C.: U.S. Department of Agriculture, 1981).

ance. The presence of proteins in different compartments of the body maintains the equilibrium of osmotic pressure on each side of the partitions. When protein is deficient, blood volume decreases, fluid moves out of blood vessels into the interstitial space, and the person becomes swollen with water (edema). The feeding of protein reverses the process. Protein molecules also serve as a very effective buffer system, controlling body acid-base balance.

Fifth, protein serves as an energy source. Part of the protein we eat contributes to our caloric intake. If it is completely oxidized, 1 g of protein provides 4 kcal.

Finally, protein helps to regulate body detoxification. Many detoxification processes are performed by enzymes that are proteins. When protein intake is low, the body's ability to detoxify ingested foreign substances decreases.

DIETARY REQUIREMENTS FOR PROTEIN

Protein is clearly vital to our health, but how much do we need to eat daily? At present, there is really no consensus about the exact amount required. The National Research Council of the National Academy of Sciences proposes about 0.8 g/kg of body weight per day as the allowance for mixed proteins (those of both animal and plant origin). Thus, the allowance for a 55-kg woman is 44 g of protein per day, and for a 70-kg man 56 g. Table 4-5 lists the daily protein need given in the 1980 Recommended Dietary Allowances (RDA).

As indicated earlier, when we speak of protein need, we mean the adequate intake of eight to ten essential amino acids, a good source of nitrogen, and sufficient calories. Thus, according to the National Academy of Sciences, humans require the minimum daily intake of the essential amino acids given in Table 4-6. Dietary amino acids seldom come in the quantities shown, however. Rather, we tend to eat slightly higher amounts. It is therefore assumed that we eat more than the minimum of each essential amino acid.

Tests of Protein Need

In addition to the reference values provided in Table 4-5, scientists (especially nutritionists) use certain techniques for determining whether a person's protein intake is adequate. For children, the test is based on growth measurements such as height and weight changes. When children are given a certain amount of protein daily, they grow. If their growth pattern is within the standard percentile, they probably consume protein of sufficient quality and quantity.

TABLE 4-5 1980 Recommended Daily Allowance (RDA) for Protein for Different Age Groups and During Pregnancy and Lactation

Age (years) or Condition	RDA (g protein/day)
0.0–0.5	body weight (kg) × 2.2
0.5–1.0	body weight (kg) × 2.0
1–3	23
4–6	30
7–10	34
11–14, male	45
15–51+, male	56
11–18, female	46
19–51+, female	44
Pregnancy	+30
Lactation	+20

An adult's protein need is usually determined by a technique known as *nitrogen balance study*. This technique measures the amounts of nitrogen both consumed and excreted in the urine, feces, perspiration, skin sloughing, hair loss, and menstruation. A person is in *positive nitrogen balance* if his nitrogen intake exceeds the losses and in a *negative nitrogen balance* if the reverse is true. *Nitrogen equilibrium* means that the intake equals the loss. If an otherwise normal and healthy adult is in nitrogen equilibrium, the amount of protein he is eating is appropriate for his individual needs. Table 4-7 provides some hypothetical examples of the results of nitrogen balance studies.

Sometimes a person's type of nitrogen balance can be determined without taking nitrogen measurements. Table 4-8 presents some common clues to nitrogen balance.

Despite the general usefulness of nitrogen balance studies, they must be interpreted with certain qualifications in mind. For one thing, this technique assumes that measuring nitrogen reflects the amount of protein in a food, an assumption that is not totally accurate, as we have seen. Second, the factor of 16% or 6.25 in converting grams of nitrogen to grams of protein available is only an approximation. Third, a good balance study requires a reasonable period

TABLE 4-6   Estimated Amino Acid Requirements of Man*

| Amino Acid | Requirement, mg/kg Body Weight/Day | | | Amino Acid Pattern for High-Quality Proteins, mg/g of Protein[†] |
	Infant (4–6 months)	Child (10–12 years)	Adult	
Histidine	33	?	?	17
Isoleucine	83	28	12	42
Leucine	135	42	16	70
Lysine	99	44	12	51
Total *S*-containing amino acids (methionine and cystine)	49	22	10	26
Total aromatic amino acids (phenylalanine and tyrosine)	141	22	16	73
Threonine	68	28	8	35
Tryptophan	21	4	3	11
Valine	92	25	14	48

*Source: *Recommended Dietary Allowances* (Washington, D.C.: Food and Nutrition Board, National Research Council, National Academy of Sciences, 1980). The essentiality of arginine is undetermined.
[†]2 g/kg/day of protein of the quality listed will meet the amino acid needs of infants.

TABLE 4-7   Hypothetical Examples of Nitrogen Balance in the Human after Ingesting 90–95 g Protein

| Nitrogen Status | Example | | | | |
	1	2	3	4	5
Nitrogen ingested (g)	15	15	15	15	15
Nitrogen in feces (g)	1.5	2.0	1.5	1.5	1.8
Nitrogen in urine (g)	10	16	13.8	13.5	13.0
Nitrogen retained by body (g)	3.5	0	0	0	0.2
Total nitrogen lost by body (g)	0	3.0	0.3	0	0
Nitrogen balance	Positive	Negative	Equilibrium	Equilibrium	Equilibrium

Note. All values are approximations.

of stabilization in the person. That is, if a person is suddenly placed in such a study without some standard adjustments in eating, sleeping, and so forth, the result may not reflect actual body nitrogen utilization. Such stabilization is not attained in many nitrogen balance studies. Finally, actual protein need is not always reflected by nitrogen balance, since the human body is capable of arriving at nitrogen equilibrium at any level of protein intake that is above the minimal requirement.

Individual Factors

As revealed by nitrogen balance studies, an individual's need for dietary protein may differ from the RDA average. A number of factors determine these variations:

1. *Body size.* For two healthy, nonathletic persons of different body size, the need for protein per unit body weight will be fairly similar. The

TABLE 4-8   Some Common Examples for the Different Types of Nitrogen Balance

Nitrogen Balance	Most Likely Situation	Remark
Positive	Growing child Pregnant woman Person recovering from an illness Person's diet changed from low to high protein	Growth and development
Negative	Person receiving surgery or crush injury Person suffering starvation Person immobilized Person receiving a low fat and carbohydrate diet Person's diet changed from high to low protein Elderly*	Body wasting
In equilibrium	A normal, health adult 21–40 years old[†] Subject in a human nitrogen balance experiment	Maintenance; repair of body

*This is not necessarily true in all elderly individuals.
[†]This is theoretically true and the exact age limit is not yet defined.

total protein need of the larger person will therefore be greater.

2. *Age.* During the growing years, protein need per unit body weight is two to three times higher than during the adult years. The increased need for protein stabilizes during puberty. The need for protein during old age is about the same as that for a 25-year-old adult, although some clinical evidence indicates that old people tend to retain nitrogen less efficiently. The possibility that an older person may therefore need to eat more protein than a younger adult is controversial, however.

3. *Sex.* For a man and woman of the same age and weight, the male's requirement for protein per unit weight is slightly higher. This condition is reflected by the greater body fat and less muscle mass in the woman, because protein is essential for the maintenance of the muscle or lean body mass. However, in practice, the requirement of 0.8 g of protein per kilogram body weight applies to both adult men and women.

4. *Nutritional status.* Starvation, wasting, undernutrition, weight loss, and any form of substandard nutrition increase a person's protein need.

5. *Pregnancy and lactation.* A pregnant woman needs more protein for the developing fetus, in-

creased hemoglobin formation, and other physiological adjustments. A nursing mother requires more protein to make milk protein. See Table 4-5 and Chapter 13 for more information.

6. *Climate.* Low ambient temperature means that the body will need more energy, not more protein. By contrast, high ambient temperature may cause sweating, and excess perspiration means that a significant amount of nitrogen (that is, protein) will be lost. In this case, more dietary protein is needed.

7. *Activity.* Unless it causes profuse sweating, heavy physical activity does not require additional protein, though the need for calories is higher. However, inactivity over a prolonged period—as in lengthy confinement to bed—may require more protein to repair atrophied muscle mass.

8. *Conditioning.* Conditioning may affect body protein requirement in different ways. If a person is provided with a subnormal amount of essential amino acids (as in semistarvation), the body may adjust to the lower supply and eventually decrease the protein requirement for maintenance, repairs, and life processes. On the other hand, when a person starts athletic training, such as in football or weight lifting, an increased amount of protein is needed to build up the muscles for constant repairs, maintenance, and development. However, an *established* athlete needs only a normal amount of protein for repairs and maintenance and any additional amount will not provide extra benefits.

9. *Dietary components.* If people have access to only low-quality protein, their quantitative need for such protein sources will be very high. The relative amount of carbohydrate and fat in the diet is also very important in protein requirements. If these nutrients are present in subnormal amounts, the body will have to divert part of the ingested protein as an energy source, and some other body functions will suffer.

10. *Emotional stability.* Preliminary evidence indicates that stresses such as fear, anxiety, and depression may predispose the body to excrete more nitrogen, thus increasing body protein need. This increased need may be the result of changes in body hormonal profile.

11. *Diseases.* Illness generally increases the need for protein for a number of reasons. Any form of physical injury that involves tissue loss obviously requires protein replacement. Since the susceptibility to infection is increased during illness, more protein is needed for manufacturing antibodies, and some special diseases such as cancer call for additional protein intake. Body temperature commonly increases during illness with two effects: Increased basal metabolism may increase the need for protein for repairs, and insensible loss due to perspiration will increase nitrogen loss.

Certain nonspecific hormonal responses in the body during illness may increase the need for protein. For example, the increased synthesis and release of adrenal hormones during sickness may increase breakdown of body muscle mass, which in turn increases protein need. Bed confinement, fractures, and other forms of illness may immobilize the patient, forcing the muscles to atrophy. An increase in body protein is needed for their regeneration. Finally, a person with parasites will suffer a great disadvantage, since many parasites such as worms can consume so much of the protein ingested by the patient that he or she may be "starving in times of plenty."

EVALUATION OF PROTEIN QUALITY

Quality as well as quantity is important to our protein requirement. For a long time, scientists have tried to develop a method for determining the quality of a protein substance for humans. The three most common techniques are described below, followed by generalizations about the value of varying kinds of proteins we eat.

Biological Value

One method of assaying protein quality is to measure its *biological value*, which determines if the protein contains all the essential amino acids in the appropriate proportions needed by the body. In a protein with good biological value, most of the nitrogen is retained after its ingestion, because the protein contains all the essential amino acids in the right ratio for body utilization.

As an illustration, assume that the nitrogen content of a food item is known, and that this nitrogen content actually reflects its protein content. After a person eats this food product, a specific amount of nitrogen will be excreted in the feces and the urine. The biological value of the protein is defined as the following:

$$\frac{\text{Amount of nitrogen retained by the body}}{\text{Amount of nitrogen absorbed by the body}} \times 100\%$$

$$= \frac{\begin{array}{c}\text{nitrogen}\\\text{content}\\\text{in food}\end{array} - \begin{array}{c}\text{nitrogen}\\\text{content}\\\text{in feces}\end{array} - \begin{array}{c}\text{nitrogen}\\\text{content}\\\text{in urine}\end{array}}{\begin{array}{c}\text{nitrogen}\\\text{content}\\\text{in food}\end{array} - \begin{array}{c}\text{nitrogen}\\\text{content}\\\text{in feces}\end{array}} \times 100\%$$

When the biological value of a protein product is greater than 70%, it means that about 70% of the protein eaten is retained by the body. A protein product with a biological value of 70% or more will support growth in a child if sufficient calories are consumed at the same time. Table 4-9 shows the biological values of a number of protein

TABLE 4-9   Biological Value, Net Protein Utilization, and Protein Efficiency Ratio of Various Food Products*

Food Category	Example	Biological Value (%)	Net Protein Utilization (%)	Protein Efficiency Ratio (Using Rats)
Meat and equivalent	Beef, Fish	70–75	70–75	2.1–2.5
		80–85	80–85	3.3–3.7
Dairy products	Milk	80–85	80–85	2.8–3.4
Egg	Egg	90–95	90–95	3.7–4.1
Grains	Whole wheat	60–65	55–60	1.5–2.0
Beans	Soybeans	70–75	65–70	2.1–2.5
Nuts	Peanuts	50–55	45–50	1.4–1.8

*These data have been obtained from the results of a number of investigators. Because of highly variable results, ranges are provided to serve as a general guide only.

foods. It should be noted that the biological value of a protein food does not take digestibility into account. Some proteins are more digestible than others.

Net Protein Utilization

To take digestibility into account, the method of *net protein utilization* has been developed. Net protein utilization is defined as:

$$\frac{\text{Amount of nitrogen retained by the body}}{\text{Amount of nitrogen eaten}}$$

$$= \text{biological value} \times \text{digestibility}$$

$$= \text{biological value} \times \frac{\text{amount of nitrogen absorbed}}{\text{amount of nitrogen eaten}}$$

Table 4-9 provides the net protein utilization of some common foods. Comparing these values with the biological values of the same foods indicates the varying digestibility of these protein foods.

Protein Efficiency Ratio

The simplest method of determining protein quality is the *protein efficiency ratio*. Unlike biological value and net protein utilization, this method does not require any chemical analyses. Instead, the technique involves feeding a specific amount of protein food to a group of animals daily and observing their growth over a defined period of time. The animals are also provided with adequate essential nutrients and calories. The protein efficiency ratio of a particular protein food is the gram of body weight gained by the animals per gram of protein food eaten. Examples for some food products are shown in Table 4-9. This technique is discussed in greater detail in Chapter 10.

Defining Protein Quality

What, then, is a good-quality protein? A good-quality protein is one in which the eight to ten essential amino acids exist in a proportion that reflects our minimal needs. Such a protein is usually made up of half essential and half nonessential amino acids. Most animal products or protein (with the exception of the animal by-product gelatin, which lacks the amino acids tryptophan and lysine) are therefore good-quality protein. When fed to animals, animal products support growth and maintenance. Such a protein usually has a high biological value. By contrast, most vegetables such as wheat (low in the amino acid lysine) and corn (low in the amino acids lysine and tryptophan) will not support growth or maintenance of an animal when fed as the only protein source. Terms used for this contrast in both scientific and

TABLE 4-10 Limiting Amino Acids in Categories of Vegetable Protein Foods

Category	Limiting Amino Acid(s)
Most grain products	Lysine, threonine (sometimes tryptophan)
Most legumes or pulses	Methionine, tryptophan
Nuts and oil seeds	Lysine
Green leafy vegetables	Methionine
Leaves and grasses	Methionine

life processes, and growth. However, if the lack or deficiency is not too severe, life processes, body repairs, and maintenance will be normal, though growth may be arrested. Sometimes the deficient or missing amino acids in vegetable proteins are known as *limiting amino acids*, for their low contents limit or determine how much other essential amino acids can be used. Table 4-10 indicates the different categories of vegetable proteins and the amino acid(s) that are most likely to be low or deficient in them.

Because Americans eat a lot of animal proteins, protein deficiency in the United States is insignificant compared with that in many undeveloped countries. However, insufficient protein intake occurs among many low-income individuals, especially elderly and ethnic populations. And the increasing trend toward vegetarianism has caused concern among health professionals, since many vegetable proteins lack certain essential amino acids. However, all the essential amino acids can be obtained in a vegetarian diet if two or more "complementary" kinds of vegetable proteins are consumed together. If the two products lack different essential amino acids, then the combination will compensate for the deficient amino acids. More detailed discussions of vegetarianism are provided in Chapters 10 and 18.

lay literature are *good* versus *bad*, *complete* versus *incomplete*, *high* versus *low biological value*, and *high-* versus *low-quality protein*.

The term *incomplete* protein usually refers to a protein in which one or more of the eight to ten essential amino acids exist in low or deficient quantity. Eating such proteins may cause nutritional inadequacies, especially in children. If a protein is grossly deficient in one or more of the amino acids, a child who has no better source of protein may suffer in body maintenance, repairs,

STRUCTURAL FORMULAS

Alanine, Glycine, Isoleucine, Leucine, Serine

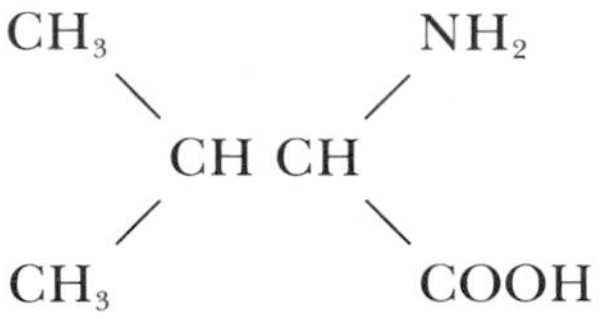

$$CH_3 \quad NH_2$$
$$CH\ CH$$
$$CH_3 \quad COOH$$

Valine

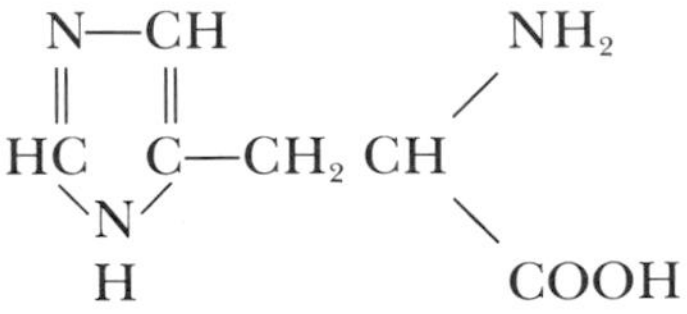

$$N{-}CH \qquad NH_2$$
$$HC \quad C{-}CH_2\ CH$$
$$N \qquad COOH$$
$$H$$

Histidine

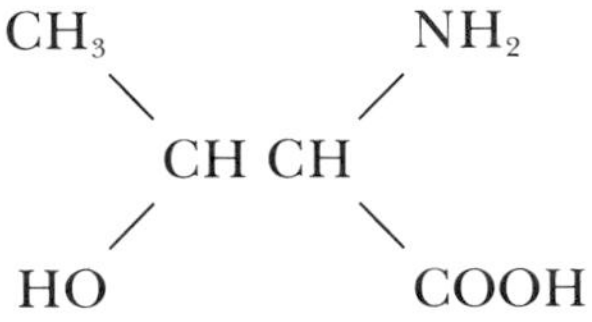

$$CH_3 \qquad NH_2$$
$$CH\ CH$$
$$HO \qquad COOH$$

Threonine

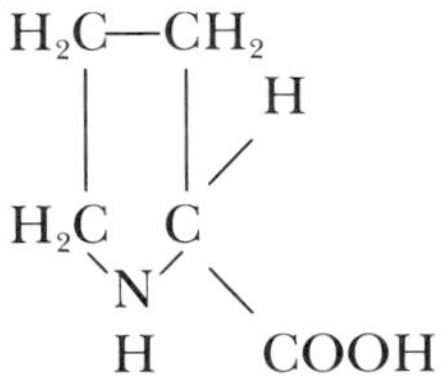

$$H_2C{-}CH_2$$
$$\qquad\qquad H$$
$$H_2C \quad C$$
$$N$$
$$H \quad COOH$$

Proline

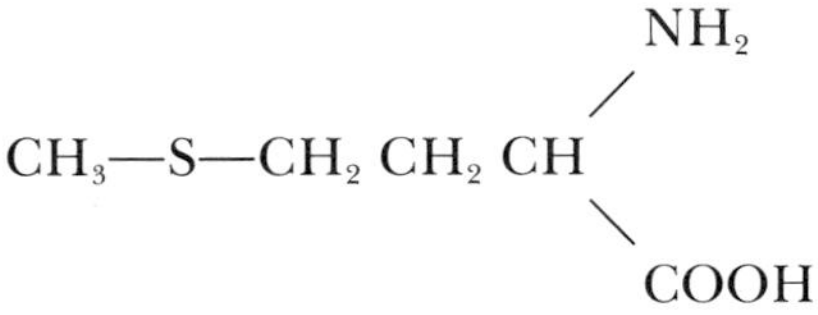

$$NH_2$$
$$CH_3{-}S{-}CH_2\ CH_2\ CH$$
$$COOH$$

Methionine

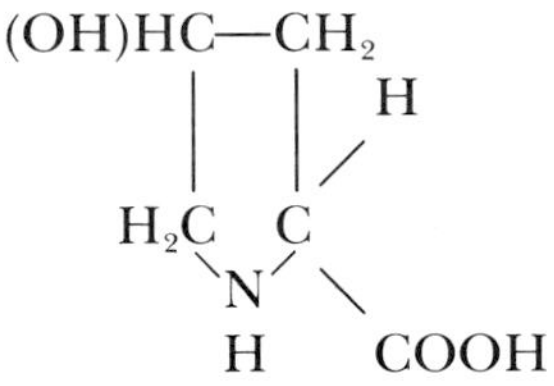

$$(OH)HC{-}CH_2$$
$$\qquad\qquad H$$
$$H_2C \quad C$$
$$N$$
$$H \quad COOH$$

Hydroxyproline

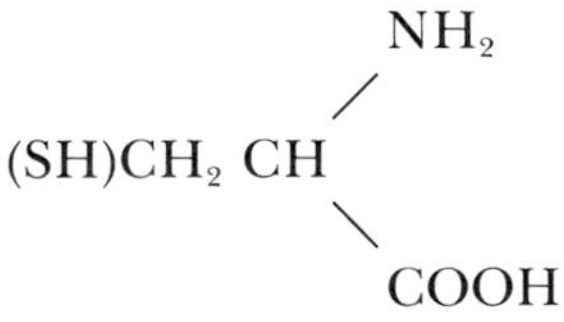

$$NH_2$$
$$(SH)CH_2\ CH$$
$$COOH$$

Cysteine

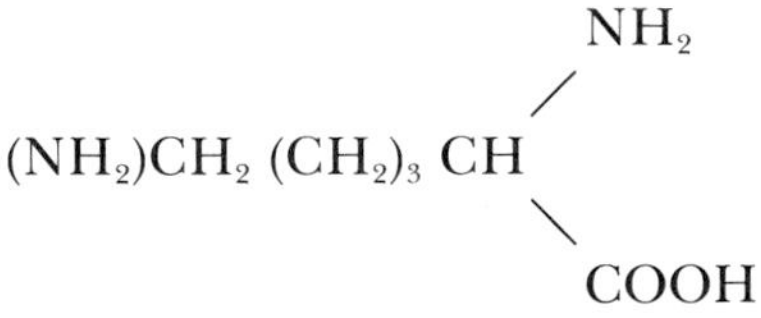

$$NH_2$$
$$(NH_2)CH_2\ (CH_2)_3\ CH$$
$$COOH$$

Lysine

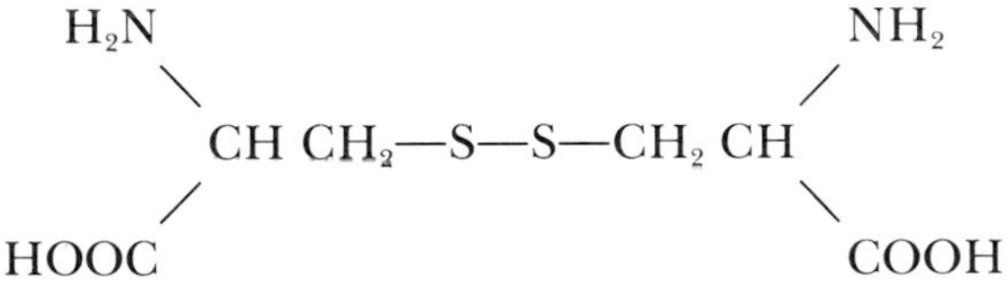

$$H_2N \qquad\qquad\qquad NH_2$$
$$CH\ CH_2{-}S{-}S{-}CH_2\ CH$$
$$HOOC \qquad\qquad COOH$$

Cystine

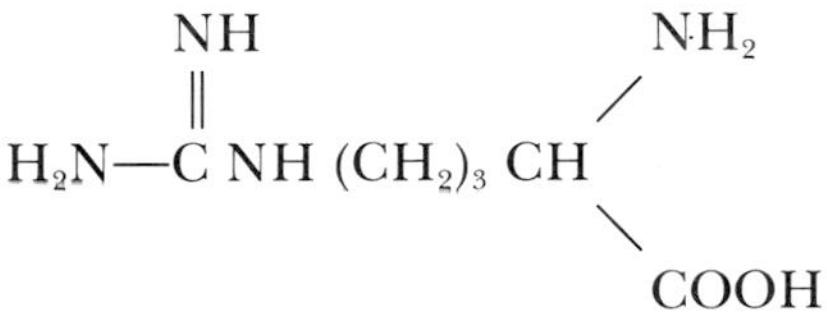

$$NH \qquad NH_2$$
$$H_2N{-}C\ NH\ (CH_2)_3\ CH$$
$$COOH$$

Arginine

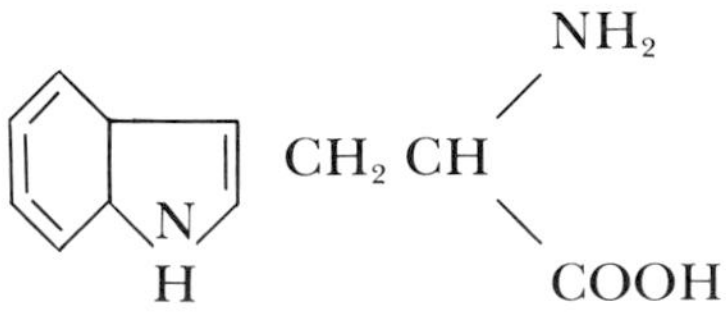

$$NH_2$$
$$CH_2\ CH$$
$$N \qquad COOH$$
$$H$$

Tryptophan

$$NH_2$$
$$HOOC{-}CH_2\ CH$$
$$COOH$$

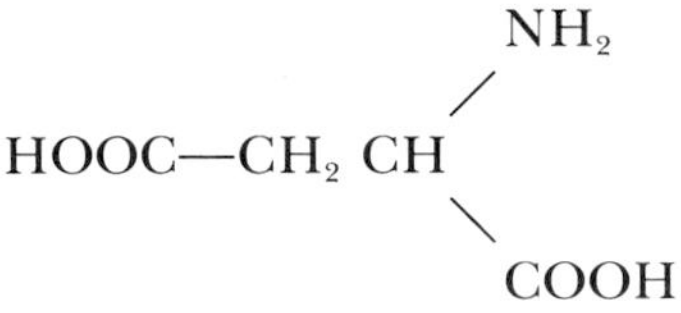

Aspartic acid

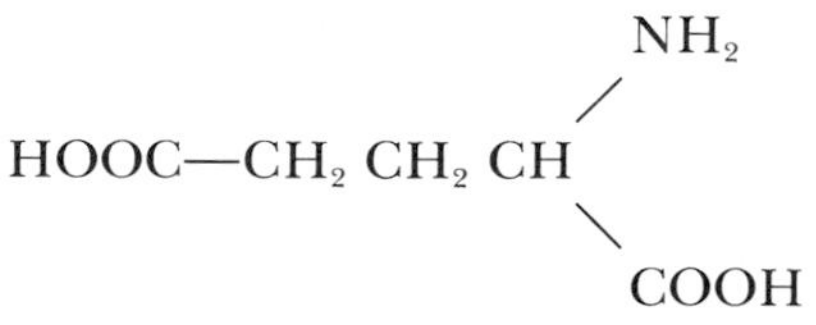

$$HOOC-CH_2\,CH_2\,CH \overset{\displaystyle NH_2}{\underset{\displaystyle COOH}{\big<}}$$

Glutamic acid

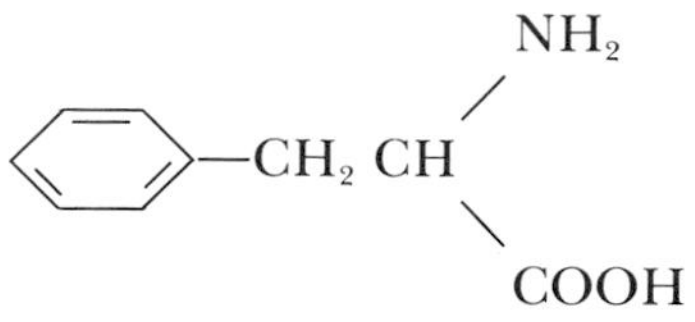

Phenylalanine

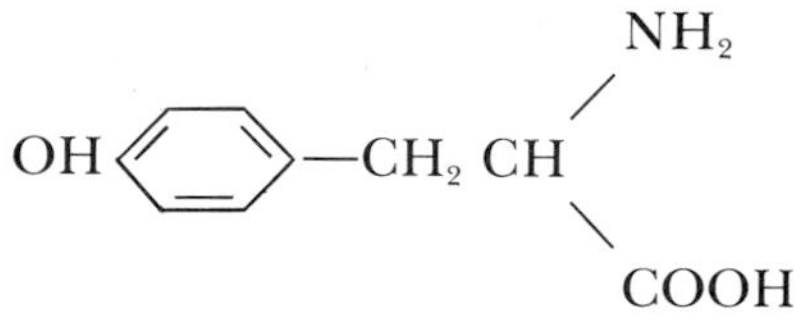

Tyrosine

STUDY QUESTIONS

1. What are the four major elements found in all proteins?
2. Define amino acid, essential amino acid, and nonessential amino acid. Why is regular consumption of nonessential amino acids important?
3. What are free amino acids? How are they involved in the digestion and absorption of proteins?
4. Why is nitrogen content used as an indication of protein level in foods? How is nitrogen level equated mathematically to protein level? What is the drawback of this method?
5. Discuss at least five important functions of protein.

6. When we talk of protein need, we imply three important premises. What are they?
7. Define nitrogen balance study, positive nitrogen balance, negative nitrogen balance, and nitrogen equilibrium. Give an example of each.
8. Discuss at least eight factors involved in determining individual need for protein.
9. What are the three most common methods of determining the quality of proteins? Which kinds of foods are considered complete proteins? Incomplete proteins? What are complementary protein foods?

Chapter 5

Fats

LIKE CARBOHYDRATES AND proteins, fats are made up of carbon, hydrogen, and oxygen, but in different ratios. Compared with carbohydrates and proteins, fat provides more than twice as many calories per molecule, because of fat's lower ratio of oxygen to carbon and hydrogen. Fats are insoluble in water but soluble in organic or fat solvents, such as chloroform, ether, petroleum, and tetrachloride.

Although some foods are almost pure fat—such as butter and oils—in most other common foods fat exists with other nutrients such as protein, carbohydrate, fiber, and other dietary factors. Our major sources of fat are animal fats and vegetable oils. The fat in foods may be visible (as in marbled or fatty meats) or hidden (as in cheese, avocados, olives, nuts, bakery products, and gravies). Table 5-1 shows the fat content of representative foods; refer to Table 6 in the appendix for more information on the level of fats in other common foods.

Although fat's contribution to health and disease is controversial, many nutritionists feel that we eat too much fat or too much of certain kinds of fat. In this chapter we will look at the general functions of fat in our bodies, types of fat, and the possible relationship of fat intake to certain health problems.

THE FUNCTIONS OF FAT

Although the excessive intake of fat may contribute to health problems, we do need some fat in our diet. Fat is an essential nutrient that serves a number of important functions. For one thing, fats are carriers of essential nutrients. The fats we eat normally contain important nutrients, such as essential fatty acids and fat-soluble vitamins (A, D, E, and K).

TABLE 5-1   Fat Content of Representative Foods*

Food	Serving Size	Fat (g)
Cottage cheese, creamed, large curd	1 c	10
Milk, whole	1 c	8
Ice cream, regular	1 c	14
Eggs, whole	1	6
Butter	1 T	12
Mayonnaise, regular	1 T	6
Fish sticks, breaded, cooked	1 fish stick	3
Ground beef, lean	3 oz	10
Chicken breast, fried	2.8 oz	5
White bread, enriched	1 sl	3
Rice, enriched	1 c	trace
Almonds, shelled	1 c	70
Peanut butter	1 T	8
Honey	1 T	0
Green beans, cooked	1 c	trace
Carrots, cooked	1 c	trace
Tomato, raw	1	trace
Apple, raw	1	1
Grapefruit, raw	½	trace
Beer	12 fl oz	0
Chocolate, baking	1 oz	15
Soup, cream of mushroom	1 c	10

*Adapted from *Nutritive Value of Foods*, Home and Garden Bulletin No. 72 (Washington, D.C.: U.S. Department of Agriculture, 1981).

Second, fats are concentrated sources of energy. They can provide 9 kcal per gram compared to 4 for carbohydrate and protein. Although glucose is the direct source of energy for most organs of the human body, the resting muscles and heart can metabolize fatty acids to obtain energy. Stored body fat is a permanent source of energy, especially valuable in times of need such as starvation and illness.

Third, fats can protect us from cold and injury. Stored body fat acts as thermal insulation that protects us from cool temperatures. And, as "padding" around vital parts, such as the heart, kidney, mammary glands, and ovaries, and on places such as the soles of our feet, palms of our hands, buttocks, and cheeks, stored fat provides good protection against injury or trauma.

A fourth important function of fats is their biochemical interrelationship with protein and carbohydrate. The unique metabolism of fatty acids enables fat to be converted to protein. Although the conversion of fat to glucose is not of importance, its ability to provide energy can spare carbohydrate. Chapter 8 provides more information on fat metabolism.

Fifth, fats increase the *satiety value* of foods, the satisfying feeling of being full. It has been suggested that fats do so by causing a prolonged distention of the stomach after eating.

Finally, fats make foods more desirable. They make food taste better and increase its palatability and attractiveness. Many people like the smoothness and richness of fatty food.

CHEMICAL CLASSIFICATION OF FATS

The common word *fats* is used interchangeably with the chemical term *lipids*. In chemical classifications, fats or lipids are divided into three types: simple, compound, and derived. Simple lipids include *fatty acids* (containing only carbon, hydrogen, and oxygen) and *glycerides* (esters of fatty acids and glycerol). Compound lipids include *phospholipids* (compounds of fatty acids and phosphoric acid with a nitrogenous base) and *lipoproteins* (lipids combined with proteins). Derived lipids include *sterols* (such as cholesterol and steroid hormones) and *fat-soluble vitamins* (vitamins A, D, E, and K). The following sections provide discussions of fatty acids, the triglycerides, cholesterol, phospholipids, and lipoproteins; other lipids mentioned above are discussed in other parts of this book.

Fatty Acids and Triglycerides

A *fatty acid* is made up of a linear chain of carbon atoms with hydrogen atoms attached to it. One end of this chain is a carboxyl group that is acidic (able to donate hydrogen ions) and contains oxygen; the other end of the chain is a methyl group. The characteristics of each fatty acid are regulated by the number of carbon atoms in the chain and the number of hydrogen atoms that the chain can hold.

Visible fats or oils, such as beef fat, lard, and corn oil, are made up mostly of triglycerides with a small amount of di- and monoglycerides. A *triglyceride*, sometimes called a *neutral fat*, is made up of glycerol and three fatty acids. If the glyceride contains two molecules of fatty acids, it is called a *diglyceride*, while a *monoglyceride* contains only one fatty acid.

Glycerol is a neutral substance, but a fatty acid is a highly active one. The chemical property of simple fat is thus determined by the characteristics of its fatty acids. These characteristics determine whether a fat is long chain or short chain and "saturated" or "unsaturated," factors which in turn determine whether the fat is hard or liquid at room temperature and how easily it can be absorbed by the body.

Saturated vs. unsaturated fatty acids

When a fatty acid is *saturated*, each carbon joins with four other atoms. All linkages of the carbon atoms are therefore "saturated," because, except for the carbons at the end of the chain of a fatty acid, each carbon in the chain has two hydrogen atoms attached to it—the maximum it can hold. If the fatty acid is *unsaturated*, one or more pairs of adjacent carbon atoms may form a double bond instead of a single bond between each other. As a result, each of the pair of neighboring carbon atoms will carry only one hydrogen atom. Thus, an unsaturated fatty acid usually has two or multiples of two hydrogen atoms less than a corresponding saturated one. If a double bond occurs in two or more places in the chain, the resulting fatty acid is called a *polyunsaturated fatty acid* (PUFA). Those unsaturated fatty acids with one double bond are sometimes called *monounsaturated fatty acids.*

Table 5-2 lists the most common fatty acids—saturated, monounsaturated, and polyunsaturated. It is currently believed that about 40 fatty acids occur naturally with between 2 and 24 carbon atoms. Most have an even number of carbon atoms; fatty acids with an odd number of carbon atoms occur in relatively few living organisms, such as fish and bacteria.

Solubility, melting point, and absorption

The nature of the fats we eat is partly related to their chemical characteristics, which are determined by their component fatty acids. For one thing, fatty acids with very short chains (a small number of carbon atoms) are fairly soluble in water, unlike those with longer chains.

Second, glycerides with more short-chain (fewer than eight carbons) or unsaturated fatty acids will be soft fats or oils (liquid at room temperature, with a low melting point), while fats with long-chain fatty acids are hard fats (solid at room temperature, with a higher melting point). In addition, those lipids containing mostly oleic, linoleic, and other unsaturated fatty acids will be liquid at room temperature. Fats containing mostly palmitic and stearic saturated fatty acids are solid at room temperature. Fats that melt at temperatures above 50 °C (122 °F) are utilized poorly by the body.

Third, it is easier to oxidize unsaturated fatty acids than saturated ones. Thus, cooked fats or oils with a higher content of unsaturated fatty acids have a higher tendency to become rancid (from oxidation).

Finally, short- or medium-chain fatty acids are also easier to absorb. Similarly, fats with PUFAs are absorbed more efficiently than saturated fats with the same number of carbon chains.

The above observations explain why ordinary fats can be solid or liquid and why some fats become rancid faster than others. The ease of

TABLE 5-2 Common Fatty Acids

Name	No. of Carbons	No. of Double Bonds
Saturated fatty acids		
Butyric acid	4	
Caproic acid	6	
Caprylic acid	8	
Capric acid	10	
Lauric acid	12	
Myristic acid	14	
Palmitic acid	16	
Stearic acid	18	
Arachidonic acid	20	
Behenic acid	22	
Monounsaturated fatty acids		
Palmitoleic acid	16	1
Oleic acid	18	1
Erucic acid	22	1
Polyunsaturated fatty acids		
Linoleic acid	18	2
Linolenic acid	18	3
Arachidonic acid	20	4

absorption of certain fatty acids is important under certain clinical conditions as discussed later.

Essential fatty acids

Though the human body is capable of synthesizing a few PUFAs, it cannot make two important ones: linoleic acid and linolenic acid (both of which have 18 carbons, as shown in Table 5-2). These are therefore called *essential fatty acids*, for they must be ingested in the diet. Actually, the body also needs arachidonic acid (20 carbons), but it can synthesize this substance from available linoleic acid if vitamin B_6 is present.

Physiologically, essential fatty acids have several specific functions: (1) regulating cholesterol metabolism, including transportation, conversion to other metabolites, storage, and excretion; (2) maintaining the functions and integrity of cell membranes; and (3) serving as precursors for body synthesis of prostaglandins, thromboxanes, and prostacyclins, all of which are hormonelike substances.

In 1929, researchers found that, when de-

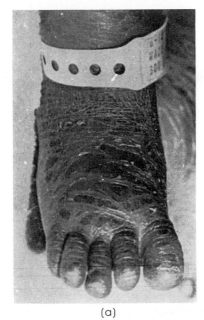

(a)

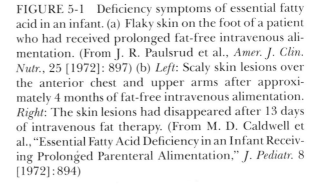

FIGURE 5-1   Deficiency symptoms of essential fatty acid in an infant. (a) Flaky skin on the foot of a patient who had received prolonged fat-free intravenous alimentation. (From J. R. Paulsrud et al., *Amer. J. Clin. Nutr.*, 25 [1972]: 897) (b) *Left*: Scaly skin lesions over the anterior chest and upper arms after approximately 4 months of fat-free intravenous alimentation. *Right*: The skin lesions had disappeared after 13 days of intravenous fat therapy. (From M. D. Caldwell et al., "Essential Fatty Acid Deficiency in an Infant Receiving Prolonged Parenteral Alimentation," *J. Pediatr.* 8 [1972]:894)

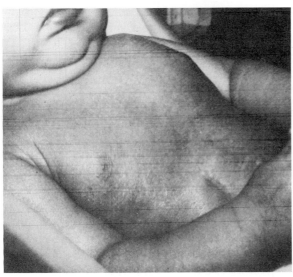

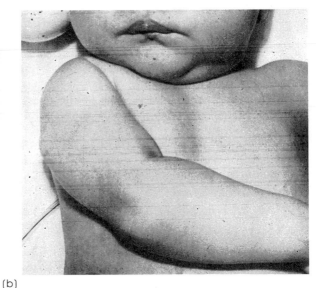

(b)

prived of PUFAs (linoleic acid in particular), rats developed skin and kidney lesions. Other animals such as mice, dogs, calves, pigs, poultry, and insects are also susceptible to essential fatty acid deficiency, but to a lesser extent. In general, linoleic acid can cure all deficiency symptoms, though linolenic and arachidonic acid can also relieve some symptoms.

In humans, infants can develop essential fatty acid deficiency if they are fed nonfat milk for a long period. Figure 5-1 shows the classic symptom of deficiency: eczematous dermatitis, which responds to linoleic acid and/or arachidonic acid therapy. In these patients, the development of skin lesions is characterized by decreasing levels of essential fatty acids in the blood. It is more difficult to induce essential fatty acid deficiency in adults because their body storage of fat is high. Figure 5-2 shows the classic deficiency symptoms in an adult after a prolonged period of intravenous feeding without fat and therefore without essential fatty acids. The symptoms are relieved by administering linoleic acid orally, topically, or intravenously. For oral

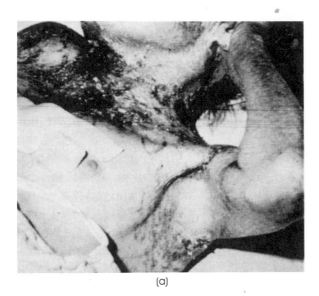
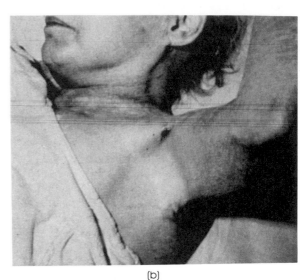

(a)   (b)

FIGURE 5-2   Relief of dermal symptoms of essential fatty acid deficiency
that had been induced by fat-free intravenous alimentation by administration of intravenous fat emulsion. (From M. C. Riella et al., *Annals of Internal
Medicine* 83 [1975]: 786)

and topical applications, any vegetable oil containing an adequate level of linoleic acid is effective. Intravenous lipid solutions are now legally
permitted in the United States (see Chapter 23).

The question of how much dietary *fat* we
need every day should be phrased, How much
essential fatty acids do we need daily? This is
because one major reason we need fat in our diet
is our requirement for essential fatty acids. The
experimental deficiency symptoms induced in infants disappear when they are fed over 1.3% of
their total calories as linoleic acid. It is estimated
that 3% to 4% of dietary calories from linoleic acid
is adequate to prevent deficiency and satisfy an
infant's requirements. Breast milk therefore contains adequate linoleic acid for a baby, since the
acid accounts for 6% to 9% of the milk's caloric
content. It has been shown that the younger the
animal, the greater the essential fatty acid requirement. A high intake of saturated fatty acids
and cholesterol also increases the requirement.

For adults, a diet of 1% to 2% calories from
linoleic acid is adequate, a requirement easily
met by the standard American diet. The typical
American diet, which has 25% to 50% calories as
fat, will provide 5% to 10% of the calories as
linoleic acid. The U.S. Department of Agriculture estimates that about 23 g of linoleic acid (or
about 6% of total dietary energy) are available
per person per day in the current U.S. food supply. About 10% of dietary fat is linoleic acid, and
a diet with 15 to 25 g of the appropriate fatty
foods meets the basic essential fatty acid need.

Dietary sources of fatty acids

In the standard American diet, the fatty
acids most commonly consumed are the unsaturated fatty acids linoleic and oleic acids and the
saturated fatty acids stearic and palmitic acids.
For example, palmitic acid contributes from 10%
to 15% of the total fatty acids in any diet, while
oleic acid contributes 30% or more. An estimated
90% of the daily fatty acids consumed in an
American diet consists of these four fatty acids.

We consume fatty acids from two major
sources: animal fats and plant oils. In general,
animal fats tend to be saturated and plant oils
unsaturated. However, some animal fats contain
a fair amount of unsaturated fats, and some vegetable oils contain a fair amount of saturated fats.
Table 5-3 gives a breakdown of the amounts and
ratios of saturated and unsaturated fatty acids in
common foods.

TABLE 5-3   Fat Content and Major Fatty Acid Composition of Selected Foods*

Food	Total fat (%)	Saturated (%)‡	Unsaturated Oleic (%)	Unsaturated Linoleic (%)	P/S§
Salad and cooking oils					
Safflower	100	10	13	74	7.4/1.0
Sunflower	100	11	14	70	6.4/1.0
Corn	100	13	26	55	4.2/1.0
Cottonseed	100	23	17	54	2.3/1.0
Soybean‖	100	14	25	50	3.6/1.0
Sesame	100	14	38	42	3.0/1.0
Soybean, special processed	100	11	29	31	2.8/1.0
Peanut	100	18	47	29	1.6/1.0
Olive	100	11	76	7	0.6/1.0
Coconut	100	80	5	1	0.2/1.0
Margarine, first ingredient on label¶					
Safflower oil (liquid)—tub	80	11	18	48	4.4/1.0
Soybean oil (liquid)—tub#	80	15	31	33	2.2/1.0
Butter	81	46	27	2	0.4/1.0
Animal fats					
Poultry	100	30	40	20	0.67/1.0
Beef, lamb, pork	100	45	44	2–6	0.04–0.13/1.0
Fish, raw					
Salmon	9	2	2	4	2.0/1.0
Mackerel	13	5	3	4	0.8/1.0
Herring, Pacific	13	4	2	3	0.75/1.0
Tuna	5	2	1	2	1.0/1.0
Nuts					
Walnuts, English	64	4	10	40	10.0/1
Walnuts, black	60	4	21	28	7.0/1
Brazil	67	13	32	17	1.3/1
Peanuts or peanut butter	51	9	25	14	1.6/1
Egg yolk	31	10	13	2	0.2/1
Avocado	16	3	7	2	0.67/1

*Adapted from *Fats in Food and Diet*, U.S. Department of Agriculture Information Bulletin No. 361.

†Total is not expected to equal total fat.

‡Includes fatty acids with chains containing from 8 to 18 carbon atoms.

§P/S = Linoleic acid content/saturated fatty acid content.

‖Suitable as salad oil.

¶Mean values of selected samples, which may vary with brand name and date of manufacture. Includes small amounts of monounsaturated and diunsaturated fatty acids that are not oleic or linoleic.

#Linoleic acid includes higher polyunsaturated fatty acids.

Although the average American receives an adequate amount of linoleic acid or PUFAs, a recent controversy questions the quantity of unsaturated fats ingested in relation to saturated fats. Some scientists believe that we eat more saturated than unsaturated fats and that this practice is undesirable. They propose that we should ingest more unsaturated fatty acids, such as linoleic acid, by using vegetable seed oils extensively in our diet. However, other scientists believe that there is not enough evidence to support this claim. A more detailed analysis is provided at the end of this chapter.

As indicated above, most oils of land plant seeds contain relatively more linoleic acid than do animal fats. Nevertheless, these vegetable oils contain mostly oleic and palmitic acids, followed by linoleic acid; most seed oils also contain some linolenic acids. Olive and coconut oils are exceptions. Olive oil has little linoleic acid but a large amount of oleic acid, while coconut oil contains little linoleic and oleic acids, with a large amount of short-chain, saturated fatty acids. Vegetable oils contain practically no arachidonic acid, but it can be easily synthesized from linoleic acid in an animal's body.

In food preparation and serving, sometimes neither fats nor oils serve certain intended purposes. For example, neither solid nor liquid fats or oils are suitable for certain baking processes, preparing certain dishes, or spreading cheeses, sauces, or the like on breads and crackers. The food industry has developed "hydrogenated" fats and oils to fill this need. *Hydrogenation* is a process whereby oils with a high concentration of unsaturated fatty acids can be turned into a fat with a texture ranging from soft to hard. The actual chemical change centers on saturating the unsaturated bonds with hydrogen. Current technology allows degrees of partial or complete hydrogenation so the final product can be of any texture desired. Hydrogenation also reduces the oils' potential for oxidation and thus rancidity, so that the oils may be safely stored even at room temperature. The three major hydrogenated products we are familiar with are shortening, margarine, and spreads (such as cheese, butter, or cream).

Partially hydrogenated margarines may contain up to 50% PUFAs, making them acceptable for heart patients advised to increase their PUFA intake (see later discussion). Hydrogenated oil can be made from corn, soybean, cottonseed, safflower, peanut, or olive oil. Some vegetable oils, such as soybean oil, are hydrogenated slightly to inhibit rancidity or poor flavor. In peanut butter, a small amount of hydrogenated oil prevents separation of the peanut oil.

The characteristics of animal fats depend partly on whether the animal lived on the land or in the water. Many land animal fats contain 16- to 26-carbon-atom fatty acids, predominantly oleic and palmitic acids. These animal fats are hard, since 20% to 30% of the fatty acids are saturated palmitic acids. Fats from cattle and other ruminants are even harder, for they have more saturated stearic acid instead of unsaturated oleic acid. Milk fats such as butter differ from all other land animal fats in that they contain some fatty acids with only 4 to 12 carbons (butyric and myristic acids).

Freshwater animal fats contain predominantly 16-, 18-, 20-, and 22-carbon fatty acids, although the extent of saturation and relative content vary. Palmitic acid is most common, accounting for 10% to 18% of the total fatty acids in these foods. Among saltwater animals, the most predominant fatty acids have 20 to 22 carbon atoms with up to six double bonds, making them polyunsaturated. Fish that live both in salt water and freshwater, such as trout and salmon, demonstrate the fatty acid pattern of marine animals.

This difference in fat chemistry between land and water animals has sparked debate among scientists, especially nutritionists. Why this difference? Which is better, meat fat or fish oil? At present only one point is clear. If a doctor wants a patient to avoid red meat because of its high content of saturated fat, the nurse and dietician will most likely ask the patient to eat more poultry and certain species of fish, since they contain a relatively higher amount of unsaturated fatty acids.

Medium-chain triglycerides in diet therapy

One form of triglycerides deserves special mention: *medium-chain triglycerides* (MCTs). Containing only fatty acids with 6 to 12 carbon atoms, they are rare in nature but have been frac-

TABLE 5-4 Cholesterol Content of Selected Foods*

Food	Amount	Cholesterol (mg)
Milk, skim, fluid or reconstituted	1 c	5
Cottage cheese, uncreamed	½ c	7
Lard	1 T	12
Cream, light table	1 fl oz	20
Cottage cheese, creamed	½ c	24
Cream, half and half	¼ c	26
Ice cream, regular, approximately 10% fat	½ c	27
Cheese, cheddar	1 oz	28
Milk, whole	1 c	34
Butter	1 T	35
Oysters, salmon; cooked	3 oz	40
Clams, halibut, tuna; cooked	3 oz	55
Chicken, turkey; light meat, cooked	3 oz	67
Beef, pork, lobster; chicken, turkey, dark meat; cooked	3 oz	75
Lamb, veal, crab; cooked	3 oz	85
Shrimp, cooked	3 oz	130
Heart, beef, cooked	3 oz	230
Egg	1 yolk or 1 egg	250
Liver (beef, calf, hog, lamb), cooked	3 oz	370
Kidney, cooked	3 oz	680
Brains, raw	3 oz	1,700+

*Adapted from R. M. Feeley et al., "Cholesterol Content of Foods," *J. Amer. Dietet. Assoc.* 61 (1972):134.

tionated from coconut oil. MCTs are composed of 75% caprylic acid (8 carbons), 22% to 23% capric acid (10 carbons), 1% caproic acid (6 carbons), and 1% lauric acid (12 carbons), with traces of other fatty acids such as linoleic, stearic, and palmitic acids.

MCTs are important in diet therapy because of their special characteristics. They are liquid at room temperature because of their short chain length and low melting points, and are more soluble in water than natural glycerides. MCTs are easily digested by pancreatic lipase and do not require bile salts for absorption. Once absorbed, they enter the portal vein into the liver as fatty acids and do not go through the lacteal system.

Synthetic MCTs are popular in the treatment of intestinal diseases, especially malabsorption, such as steatorrhea, sprue, and pancreatic insufficiency. They provide the patients with a ready source of energy and prevent starvation from a lack of absorbed calories. More information about this special dietary product is presented in Chapters 23 and 24.

Cholesterol

Another type of fat occurring both in plants and animals is *sterols*, mostly unsaturated solid alcohols of the steroid group found in plant and animal fatty tissues. It is currently believed that plant sterols are not absorbed to any significant extent by the human body. However, the animal sterol *cholesterol* has been the subject of controversy for more than two decades because of its possible relationship to heart disease. Cholesterol is found only in animal products, such as beef fats, organ meats, and eggs. Table 5-4 describes the cholesterol content of selected foods.

Cholesterol is a normal constituent of blood and tissues, especially bile and nerves. Some of the cholesterol in human blood and tissues is synthesized by the body, mainly the intestinal mucosa and liver, and some is supplied by the diet. The body makes about two or three times more cholesterol than that consumed. The average Western diet contains about 500 to 1,000 mg/day of cholesterol, while the body makes about 1 to 3 g/day. How much cholesterol each of us actually ingests varies greatly, depending on the kind and amount of foods eaten.

Since we can make cholesterol, the substance is not essential in our diet. However, in our body, cholesterol performs a number of important functions. It is one of the basic ingredients from which bile salts, vitamin D, and certain hormones (adrenal steroid and sex) are formed. Second, the absorption of fatty acids is facilitated by cholesterol, which can be esterified with the acids. Third, cholesterol esters transport fatty acids in the blood circulation.

Do we need cholesterol in the diet? Increasing numbers of health professionals believe that reducing our dietary intake of cholesterol decreases our risk of heart diseases. The major concern is the potential elevation of blood cholesterol from ingested cholesterol. The relationship between blood cholesterol level and the amount of cholesterol ingested in the diet or synthesized by the body is complicated and currently under intense debate. Current thinking on cholesterol's link to heart disease is reviewed in Chapter 27.

Phospholipids

Phospholipids are a class of fats containing phosphorus (a derived lipid). Each phospholipid has a glycerol plus two fatty acids plus a phosphate plus a variable chemical (which differs for each phospholipid). This type of fat primarily serves as a structural component of cell membranes. Because of its semipolar to nonpolar nature, it can mix with fat- and water-soluble ingredients. It is therefore a useful medium in mixing and transport, especially in helping both water- and fat-soluble substances to cross membrane barriers. This function is so important that even if an animal is starved, phospholipids in its cell membranes will not be degraded to provide energy.

Practically everything we eat contains phospholipids, since they occur in all cell membranes. However, our digestive system prevents phospholipids from being absorbed intact. Any ingested phospholipids are hydrolyzed in the small intestine into their chemical components: glycerol, fatty acids, phosphate, and another chemi-

cal. To provide this important group of chemicals for body function and maintenance, some of our organs can synthesize them from the individual components. Consequently, we do not need phospholipids in our diet.

Probably the major commercial usage of phospholipids occurs in the food-processing industry. A good example is the employment of phospholipids in salad dressings such as mayonnaise to mix the fat and water ingredients so that they will not separate.

For many years, there has been a claim that one particular phospholipid, lecithin, can influence blood cholesterol level and thus prevent heart disease. As a result, many health food stores sell lecithin, emphasizing its therapeutic value. This claim cannot be accepted if we recall that most, if not all, of the ingested phospholipids are hydrolyzed into their chemical components in the small intestine. Very few, if any, phospholipids can be absorbed intact.

Lipoproteins

Another derived lipid or fat is *lipoprotein*, which contains a fat component and a protein component. Similar to phospholipids, any ingested lipoprotein is hydrolyzed to its fat and protein components; a lipoprotein cannot be absorbed intact. Our body synthesizes lipoproteins in the intestinal walls and liver. Lipoproteins serve the important function of transporting fat and protein in our circulation. According to current speculation, this derived fat may play an important role in the risk of heart disease, both in men and women. More details are presented in Chapter 27.

FATS AND HEALTH

How is dietary fat related to our health? As discussed earlier, dietary fats serve many uses, and so many factors must be considered to answer this question. Factors involved include how fats are cooked and stored, individual variations in fat need and intake, interrelationships between fat and other foods we heat, and unresolved questions about the link between cholesterol, saturated and unsaturated fats, and risk of heart disease.

Cooking and Storage of Fats

Food is often prepared by frying with fats or oils. However, careful temperature control and preliminary food preparation are essential for proper frying, deep fat or otherwise. If the temperature is too high, the fat may smoke, forming acrolein (which has been shown to be toxic to animals when fed in large doses) and giving the food an unpleasant flavor from the hydrocarbon. Otherwise, frying an oil normally does not reduce its nutritional value.

Storage of fats also demands special care, because fat can be easily oxidized by oxygen, especially if a good catalyst is present. This "spoiled" fat has an off flavor, popularly described as *rancid*. In addition to rancidity, nutrients such as vitamins A and E in fats may be destroyed during the oxidation process. In general, cooked fats or oils should be put in the refrigerator to retard oxidation. The food industry has tried to reduce or prevent rancidity by various methods. The use of antioxidants such as BHA (butylated hydroxyanisole), BHT (butylated hydroxytoluene), and propyl gallate has been very successful, although there is much controversy surrounding the use of BHA and BHT. Another popular technique is to employ special packaging, such as replacing the air in the space above food with nitrogen, using vacuum pack, or incorporating antioxidant in package linings. Some foods contain natural antioxidants, such as the vitamin E in wheat germ.

Individual Variations

Eating too much fat may lead to obesity or perhaps heart disease, but individuals vary greatly in their ability to use fats. Many factors are involved.

Variations in the endocrine system—in the hormonal processes of the thyroid, adrenals, pituitary, ovaries, pancreas, and other organs—play a big part in how well or poorly a body uses fats. So does activity level, for exercise increases the oxygen supply to tissues, improves circulation, and relieves stress, thus enhancing our metabolic processes. Similarly, one's emotional nature and degree of personal involvement with today's fast-paced social and business world influence all facets of our body metabolism and presumably affect body utilization of fat.

Aging has a lot to do with use of fats, too. As we age, our physiological processes slow down, our enzyme mechanisms become less able to handle the foods we eat, and certain body tissues become less active. What we have eaten throughout our life and our present nutritional status also profoundly influence our use of fats.

In addition, some of us have specific diseases that interfere with the absorption and metabolism of fats. And some of us seem to have inherited a tendency to cardiovascular disease, which may be exacerbated by fat intake. This does not mean that those with this tendency will necessarily develop heart disease or that those of us who apparently lack this tendency will never develop cardiovascular problems.

Relationships of Fats to Other Foods Eaten

In addition to considerable individual differences in how our bodies use fats, our utilization of fats is affected by the other foods we eat—by all the nutrients we ingest and the interactions between them.

Researchers have proved that diets high in fat can create abnormally high amounts of fatty chemicals, such as fatty acids, glycerides, and cholesterol, in the body. Some feel that a high level of fats in the blood—particularly cholesterol and triglycerides—is related to atherosclerosis. Evidence that excessive fat intake causes atherosclerosis has not been conclusive, however. Nevertheless, as indicated in Chapter 27, some physicians recommend that cardiovascular patients increase the ratio of polyunsaturated fats to saturated fats ingested to minimize the risk of the disease. If up to 13% or 15% of the total calories in a diet are supplied by polyunsaturated fats, elevated blood cholesterol levels frequently drop.

In addition to the effects of overall fat intake, most other nutrients are important in fat utilization, particularly calcium, magnesium, chromium, zinc, vanadium, niacin, biotin, pantothenic acid, vitamin B_6, and vitamin E. Although we know that these nutrients are involved in fat metabolism, exactly how they act and how much of each is needed for effective fat metabolism are not fully understood. Requirements are probably relative rather than absolute. For instance, when the proportion of polyunsaturated oils relative to other fats eaten increases, the need for vitamin E also increases.

There is evidence that the kind of carbohydrate in the diet influences fat metabolism. For instance, some studies with laboratory animals and humans have shown that a high sucrose intake can produce elevated levels of lipid in the blood. But some investigators think that the tissue changes seen when high amounts of sucrose are fed are not those characteristic of atherosclerosis.

answered. For one thing, the body processes involved in handling fats obtained from foods and from synthesis within the body are not well understood. For another, we do not yet know enough about how these body processes are affected by what we eat and by other factors such as our emotions and the pressures of modern life. Finally, no one can yet say with any certainty what the upper and lower limits of polyunsaturated fats, cholesterol, and total fats should be in diets.

Despite these gray areas, the U.S. Senate has tried to help Americans improve their health through nutrition by issuing "Dietary Goals." One of the recommendations concerns the regulation of fat intake. These recommendations have triggered considerable controversy; the issues are briefly discussed in Chapter 19.

Unanswered Questions

Although nutritional scientists are finding some clues to how the fats we eat affect our health—or lack of it—some major questions are still un-

STRUCTURAL FORMULAS

Glycerides

Glycerol   3 fatty acids   Fat (triglyceride)   3 H_2O (water)

*R = radical (rest of molecule)

H | H—C—OH | H—C—OH | H—C—O—FA₁ | H

Monoglyceride

H | H—C—OH | H—C—O—FA₁ | H—C—O—FA₂ | H

Diglyceride

H | H—C—O—FA₁ | H—C—O—FA₂ | H—C—O—FA₃ | H

Mixed triglyceride

Types of Fatty Acids

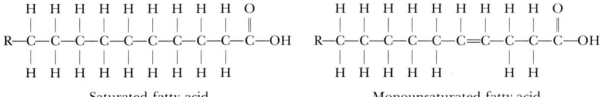

Saturated fatty acid　　　　　　　Monounsaturated fatty acid

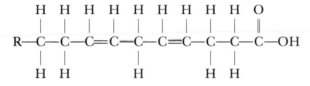

Polyunsaturated fatty acid

Structures and Melting Points of Some Common Fatty Acids

No. of Carbon Atoms	Fatty Acid	Chemical Formula	Melting Point (°C)
Saturated			
4	Butyric	C_3H_7COOH	−7.9
6	Caproic	$C_5H_{11}COOH$	−3.4
10	Capric	$C_9H_{19}COOH$	31.6
16	Palmitic	$C_{15}H_{34}COOH$	62.9
18	Stearic	$C_{17}H_{35}COOH$	69.6
Unsaturated			
18	Oleic	$CH_3(CH_2)_7CH=CH(CH_2)_7COOH$	16.3
18	Linoleic	$CH_3(CH_2)_4CH=CHCH_2CH=$ $CH(CH_2)_7COOH$	−5.0
18	Linolenic	$CH_3CH_2CH=CHCH_2CH=$ $CHCH_2CH=CH(CH_2)_7COOH$	−11.0
20	Arachidonic	$CH_3(CH_2)_4(CH=CHCH_2)_4(CH_2)_2COOH$	−49.5

STUDY QUESTIONS

1. How are fats chemically similar to carbohydrates and proteins? How do they differ chemically and calorically?
2. Discuss at least four important functions of fats in the body.
3. What is a fatty acid? Distinguish between saturated and unsaturated fatty acids. In general, which kind is found mostly in animal fats? In plant oils? Discuss some exceptions to these generalizations.
4. Which fatty acids are considered essential? What are their functions? Discuss the symptoms of essential fatty acid deficiency. Which four fatty acids are most common in the American diet?
5. What is hydrogenation?
6. Define medium-chain triglycerides. Why are they used in diet therapy?
7. What are the origins and functions of body cholesterol?
8. Define phospholipids and lipoproteins.
9. How can cooking and storage affect the nutritional value of fats?
10. In what ways do individuals vary in the ability to use fats? How do intakes of other nutrients affect the body's use of fats?

Chapter 6

Vitamins

LIKE CARBOHYDRATES, PROTEINS, and fats, vitamins are *organic compounds*—substances containing carbon and hydrogen, and often oxygen, nitrogen, and/or sulfur. But unlike these other organic compounds, which must be present in fairly large quantities in the diet, *vitamins* are required in very small amounts to perform the functions essential for life. We do not know much about the biochemical functions of vitamins except for their roles as coenzymes in biological reactions. Although the human body can synthesize at least 3 of the 13 known vitamins (excluding contribution of intestinal flora), the amount produced varies with circumstances. All known vitamins are therefore considered essential nutrients and must be supplied to the body as needed.

In this chapter we will first present an overview of differences between vitamins, considerations in ingesting vitamin supplements and vitamin-enriched foods, and tests for vitamin deficiencies. We will then examine individual vitamins in greater detail. The chapter ends with information on nonessential dietary factors associated with vitamins.

CLASSIFICATIONS

Individual vitamins differ in biochemical and physiological functions and usually in chemical structure. Since each vitamin has unique characteristics, any broad definition must be applied to

TABLE 6-1   A General Comparison of Water- and Fat-Soluble Vitamins

Criteria	Vitamins	
	Water soluble	Fat soluble
1. Medium in which soluble	Aqueous, such as water	Nonpolar, organic, such as oil, fat, or ether
2. Number known to be essential to man	9	4
3. Number human body can synthesize if precursors are provided	1	2
4. Body storage capacity	Minimal	High
5. Body handling of excess intake	Mainly excreted; low toxicity to body	Optimal amount stored, rest excreted; toxicity to body high for two vitamins
6. Means of body disposal	Urine	Bile; if conjugated, urine
7. Urgency of dietary intake	At short intervals, e.g., daily	At longer intervals, e.g., weekly or monthly
8. Rapidity of symptom appearance if deficient	Fast	Slow
9. Chemical constituents	C, H, and O; S, N, and Co in some vitamins	C, H, and O only

each individual chemical with caution. Nevertheless, certain vitamins are similar to each other in several ways.

For one thing, vitamins can be conveniently divided into two groups according to their solubility in aqueous or organic media, as indicated in Table 6-1. The major characteristics of the water-soluble vitamins are summarized in Table 6-2, and those of the fat-soluble ones in Table 6-3. These tables are for general reference purposes only; more information on each vitamin will be presented later.

Three vitamins—vitamin D, vitamin A, and niacin—are similar in that they can be synthesized by the body if the appropriate ingredients are available. These unique examples are as follows:

1. 7-Dehydrocholesterol $\xrightarrow[\text{UV or visible rays of sunlight}]{\text{skin}}$ vitamin D (fat soluble)

2. Carotene $\xrightarrow{\text{intestinal walls}}$ vitamin A (fat soluble)

3. Tryptophan $\xrightarrow{\text{liver}}$ niacin (water soluble)

In this *conversion* process, the starting materials 7-dehydrocholesterol, carotene, and tryptophan are called *precursors* or provitamins. When the three vitamins (D, A, and niacin) are ingested as food instead of being synthesized from precursors by the body, they are called *preformed* vitamins.

Another unique characteristic associated with the metabolism of certain vitamins is the process of *activation*. At this time, at least two known vitamins have been found to remain biologically inactive until activated: vitamin D and folic acid. The activation processes involved are as follows:

1. Vitamin D (ingested or from sunlight synthesis) $\xrightarrow{\text{liver, kidney}}$ vitamin D (active)

2. Folic acid (ingested) $\xrightarrow{\text{cells}}$ Folic acid (active)

TABLE 6-2   Major Characteristics of Water-Soluble Vitamins*

Vitamin	Human Deficiency Symptoms	Major Functions	Food Sources	RDA[†] Established	Remarks
Vitamin C	Scurvy: loose teeth, bleeding gums, painful joints, bruising, skin hemorrhage.	Healing wounds, collagen formation, utilization of other nutrients, body metabolism.	Citrus fruits, strawberries, cantaloupes, kale, broccoli, sweet peppers, parsley, turnip greens, potatoes.	Yes	Undesirable effects from excess dose. Very unstable substance.
Vitamin B$_1$	Beriberi: fatigue, mental depression, poor appetite, polyneuritis, decreased muscle tone.	As coenzyme. Metabolism of carbohydrate, fat, and protein.	Pork, liver and other organ meats, grain (whole or enriched), nuts, legumes, milk, eggs.	Yes	Unstable in food processing.
Vitamin B$_2$	Cheilosis: cracked lips, scaly skin, burning/itching eyes. Glossitis: smooth, red, sore tongue, with atrophy.	As coenzyme. Metabolism of fat, carbohydrate, and protein.	Liver, milk, meat, eggs, enriched cereal products, green leafy vegetables.	Yes	Very susceptible to UV or visible rays of sunlight.
Vitamin B$_6$	In infants: convulsion, irritability. In adults: microcytic hypochromic anemia, irritability, skin lesions, and other nonspecific signs.	As coenzyme. Metabolism of protein.	Pork, beef, liver, bananas, ham, egg yolks.	Yes	Pharmacological dose occasionally relieves morning sickness.
Niacin	Pellagra (the 4 D's): dermatitis, diarrhea, dementia, death. Also sore mouth, delirium, darkened teeth and skin. Hyperpigmentation.	As a coenzyme in the metabolism of fat, carbohydrate, and protein.	Meat, fish, liver, poultry, dark green leafy vegetables, whole or enriched grain products.	Yes	May be synthesized from tryptophan in body.
Folic acid	Megaloblastic anemia.	Formation of nucleic acids (DNA, RNA). Metabolism of methyl (CH$_3$) groups. Rapid turnover of cells, e.g., red blood cells.	Pork, liver and other organ meats, peanuts, green leafy vegetables, yeast, orange juice.	Yes	Deficiency probably most prevalent in Western societies.

TABLE 6-2   (continued)

Vitamin	Human Deficiency Symptoms	Major Functions	Food Sources	RDA[†] Established	Remarks
Vitamin B$_{12}$	Megaloblastic anemia; neurodegeneration.	Same as above.	Animal products: meat, poultry, fish, eggs, etc. Not found in edible plant products.	Yes	Pernicious anemia infers a lack of the intrinsic factor (see text).
Pantothenic acid	Nonspecific symptoms: weight loss, irritability, intestinal disturbances, nervous disorders, burning sensation of feet.	As a coenzyme in the metabolism of fat, protein, and carbohydrate.	Widespread in nature. Meat, poultry, fish, grains, some fruits and vegetables.	No	Sensitive to dry heat.
Biotin	In infants: dermatitis. In adults: anorexia, nausea, muscle pain, depression, anemia, dermatitis, and other nonspecific symptoms.	As a coenzyme in metabolism of fat, carbohydrate, and protein.	Organ meats (liver, kidney), egg yolk, milk, cheese.	No	Antagonist, avidin, found in egg white.

*Only an overview is provided. For details and explanations, consult the sections on the individual vitamins in text.
[†]RDA = Recommended Dietary Allowance, established by the National Research Council of the National Academy of Sciences.

Another group of synthetic or natural substances, *vitamin antagonists* (also known as *antivitamins*, *antimetabolites*, or *pseudovitamins*), are related to vitamins in a very unique fashion. Antivitamins, which may or may not be chemically related to the active vitamin, affect the action of vitamins in two adverse ways. If present in food or the body, these substances can either destroy or displace vitamins. As a result, the vitamins are unable to serve their functions and/or to remain in their normal position in a cell or structure.

To displace a vitamin, the antagonist is usually present in a large quantity—what is known as a "pharmacological dose." When a person ingests a mixture of a vitamin and its antagonists, the body cells, tissues, and organs cannot distinguish between the two and will permit both to participate in regular metabolism, transport, storage, and so forth. When the number of molecules of an antagonist outnumbers that of the related vitamin, the antagonist displaces the vitamin and interferes with its function in catalyzing a chemical reaction or its role as part of a structural component. Indirectly the antagonist thus causes a failure in a body function or collapse of a structural part. Once the antagonist is permitted to participate in body metabolism, especially if it is present in a large amount, its adverse effects will continue. This is because after the antagonist has occupied the position originally belonging to the genuine vitamin, it cannot be easily displaced or removed. The only remedy is to reverse the situation by saturating the subject with a pharmacological dose of the vitamin.

If an antagonist occurs naturally in a food, ill effects may result when enough of the food is eaten to provide a harmful dose. The consequence is a simple case of vitamin deficiency. These natural vitamin antagonists, which may operate by either displacement or destruction of active vitamins, are obviously undesirable under normal circumstances. Luckily, most are susceptible to heat treatment. The Western practice of

TABLE 6-3 Major Characteristics of Fat-Soluble Vitamins*

Vitamin	Human Deficiency Symptoms	Major Functions	Food Sources	RDA† Estab- lished	Remarks
Vitamin A	Eye: night blindness, Bitot's spot, partial and total blindness. Skin: dryness, scaliness, hardening and epithelial changes (affecting body surface), mucosa along respiratory, gastrointestinal, and genitourinary tracts.	In the eye: synthesis of rhodopsin, visual pigment. In the epithelium: differentiation. In the bones and teeth: proper development.	Carotene: dark green and yellow leafy vegetables. Dark yellow fruits. Vitamin A: liver, butter, whole-milk and other fortified dairy products.	Yes	Large doses may be toxic.
Vitamin D	Infancy and childhood: rickets. Adults: osteomalacia.	Calcium metabolism, especially its absorption from the intestine and mobilization from bones.	Fish, especially liver and oil; liver and fortified whole milk.	Yes	Large doses may be toxic.
Vitamin E	Uncommon in adults. Infants (especially premature): RBC susceptibility to hemolysis.	Not known. An antioxidant in food industry.	Wheat germ, vegetable oils, nuts, legumes, green leafy vegetables.	Yes	Therapeutic effects of large doses not substantiated.
Vitamin K	Prolonged blood-clotting time. Hemorrhage. Delayed wound healings.	Responsible for prothrombin synthesis in liver.	Dark green leafy vegetables; alfalfa.	No	Synthesized by intestinal bacteria.

*Only an overview is provided. For details and explanations, consult the sections on the individual vitamins in text.
†RDA = Recommended Dietary Allowance, established by the National Research Council of the National Academy of Sciences.

cooking foods reduces the risk of ingestion, but cases of poisoning by these natural "toxicants" have been documented. Such antagonists can be found in fish, egg whites, and certain vegetables; they are discussed in Chapter 21.

Although the consequences of ingesting antivitamins are usually undesirable, synthetic vitamin antagonists (which usually act by displacement) have been used clinically for two important purposes. For one thing, they are used to produce an experimental vitamin deficiency in animals and humans when it is difficult to eliminate the vitamin from the diet. The difficulty in creat-ing a vitamin deficiency may be due to the wide occurrence of the particular vitamin in food or to bacterial synthesis of the vitamin in the intestine or the environment. Second, synthetic vitamin antagonists are used extensively to manage a number of clinical disorders. Patients with cancer, psoriasis, tuberculosis, blood clots, and a few other diseases have benefited from vitamin antagonists given in large doses. In clinical medicine, this is one type of chemotherapy. Presumably, the antagonists deprive some undesirable organs or cells of the appropriate vitamin for survival. Invariably, however, the healthy parts of the body also suffer some ill effects. The risk-to-benefit ratio of such therapy must therefore be carefully evaluated.

VITAMIN SOURCES

Under normal circumstances, we ingest vitamins from many foods and synthesize a small amount of them in our bodies. How nearly we meet our daily requirements depends on what foods we eat, how well our bodies synthesize vitamins, and how great our individual needs are. These variable factors are hard to pin down. For instance, many vitamins often occur in both active and inactive forms in food; food processing and preparation may release the inactive form. Since our knowledge about the status of active and inactive forms of different vitamins is currently limited, the values of some food vitamin contents given in food composition tables (see Chapter 10) may prove inaccurate as more information becomes available. The retention of vitamins in commercially processed food products is also a highly complex matter varying with the type of food, processing, and storage. Even fresh foods vary widely in vitamin content.

In addition to unknowns in calculating the availability of vitamins in the foods we eat, we vary in our ability to absorb (and synthesize) the vitamins we need. All of us harbor bacteria in our large intestine, the colon, although the numbers and types of bacteria vary with each person within a population group and between population groups. In addition to other factors, diet probably plays a major role in determining the nature of the intestinal flora. These bacteria can, to varying degrees, synthesize different vitamins and contribute to the host's requirement, assuming the vitamins are transported to the appropriate parts of the intestine for absorption. However, if a vitamin is absorbed only by the small intestine, its synthesis in the colon may not permit any significant absorption if transportation is unsatisfactory. Also, certain dietary factors may destroy the bacteria or inhibit their vitamin synthesis; drugs such as antibiotics can also reduce the contribution of this source of vitamins.

Despite these unknowns, many people are increasing the quantity of vitamins they ingest by eating foods with vitamins added and taking vitamin supplements. Because of social, economic, and legislative changes, food companies are increasingly enriching or fortifying food products with vitamins. As indicated in Chapter 1, the general public may be taking in more vitamins than they need, although the pros and cons of this practice are not yet decided. Attempts to establish safe guidelines for enrichment and fortification are in progress.

Vitamin supplements have been used for many years. Before the 1970s, water-soluble vitamins were available as powder or tablets, while fat-soluble vitamins were offered in oil form. The oil was not popular because of its odor, its taste, and the possibility that it will spill either from the bottle or the mouth (when it is given to young children) and soil clothes. Infants can also inhale vitamin oils into the respiratory tract. However, technology has developed water-dispersible, water-soluble, or water-miscible powders and tablets of the fat-soluble vitamins.

A controversial distinction has been made between "natural" and "synthetic" vitamin preparations. At present, if a vitamin preparation is labeled as *natural*, this term implies that the nutrient has been obtained from a natural source such as food. In that sense, B vitamins extracted from liver, vitamin C from rose hips, and fat-soluble vitamins from fish oil are considered and treated as natural. On the other hand, vitamins obtained from bacteria or laboratory synthesis are generally regarded as *synthetic*. Although there are actual chemical differences between some natural and synthetic vitamins, they are sometimes subtle and difficult to interpret if one is not knowledgeable in organic chemistry.

In the 1940s and 1950s, many commercial vitamin supplements were prepared from natural, mainly edible, sources. However, economic and technological changes made the cost of this preparation prohibitive. Currently many of the vitamin supplements on the market are derived from bacteria. Recently, it has been suggested that vitamins obtained from natural sources are superior to those from bacteria or laboratory synthesis.

However, questions have been raised about

the practical application and genuine natural-ness of some of these food-based products. For instance, if we dry 1 lb (454 g) of fresh (wet) liver, we obtain about 8 oz of dry solid containing about 18 mg of vitamin B_2 (plus other nutrients). This amount of vitamin B_2 equals an adult's re-quirement for about 2 weeks. If a bottle of natu-ral vitamin powder (made from liver) claims to provide enough vitamin B_2 for an adult for 4 months, it should contain 64 oz (4 lb) of powder derived from 8 lb of fresh liver. The cost can be high for 8 lb of fresh liver, not to mention the volume of 4 lb of processed powder. Thus, the price and weight of liver powder involved make it unrealistic to use the powder as a source of vitamin B_2. Another practice is to grind the liver powder and soak it in water. The liquid filtered from the mixture is eventually vaporized to ob-tain crystals of the vitamin. The Food and Drug Administration considers a product obtained in this manner to be synthetic and similar to those obtained in a laboratory or from bacteria. In ad-dition, since a large amount of liver is needed to obtain the desired potency of vitamin powder, no matter what method of extraction is used, the cost can be staggering. As a result, there is in-creasing evidence that some natural vitamin tab-lets have synthetic products added to enhance the potency. Apart from the legality of such a practice, a moral issue is involved.

Do natural and synthetic vitamins differ in chemical structure, biological activities, and clini-cal responses? Chemically, the natural and syn-thetic forms of *most* vitamins are similar, al-though some are not. To use the best-known examples, vitamins C and E extracted from foods are chemically different from those obtained from bacteria or laboratory synthesis. The dif-ference is caused by stereoisomerisms or the presence of stereoisomers (that is, compounds with the same structural formula but different in spatial arrangement). However, this difference is eliminated in modern pharmaceutical practices if the biological activity of a vitamin is consid-ered. The potency described on the label of a synthetic vitamin supplement accurately reflects the tablet's contents, although the synthetic sup-plement may weigh more than an equivalent po-tency of the vitamin found in a natural food source. A number of studies have confirmed that the clinical responses of the host are the same whether the vitamin is synthetic or from a food source.

In general, users of vitamin tablets must take into consideration the fact that each tablet has only a small amount of actual vitamin in it. The bulk of the tablet contains inert material: bees-wax, paraffin or carnauba wax, chalk, shellac, sugar, sugar syrup, gelatin, and/or starch. Indi-viduals who take many tablets a day also consume a lot of inert materials, most of which are not absorbed. The concentration of some vitamins in some supplements is greater than that in others, depending on the form of the supplement, the coating, the inert materials used, and the intesti-nal condition of the person.

Recently there has been much dispute over the consumption of a large amount of vitamins to prevent or cure disease. While the benefits of this practice are being debated, one must be careful about the consequences of consuming a large dose of any chemical compound, which may pose hazards.

SYMPTOMS OF VITAMIN DEFICIENCY

Some people take vitamin supplements to cor-rect any deficiencies that may exist or to prevent future deficiencies. However, this is a rather un-realistic approach that may actually lead to im-balances in some nutrients. Pinpointing actual deficiencies is not easy, though.

Individual requirements for specific vita-mins depend on many factors. The most likely causes of human vitamin deficiency are inade-quate intake; malabsorption due to conditions such as lack of bile salts, steatorrhea, insufficient intrinsic factor, or damaged mucosal walls; and increased need due to stress, drugs, or excess excretion.

At present, there is relatively little informa-tion about how different vitamins interact and how drugs react with vitamins. We do not know much about the biochemical functions of vita-mins either except for their role as coenzymes in biological reactions. As discussed in Chapter 8, a coenzyme is made up of a cofactor (a vitamin) and an apoenzyme (a protein). Without the vitamin, the coenzyme does not exist and the reaction fails to proceed. Some metabolites will accumulate and partially or completely cause some of the deficiency symptoms observed.

Although the causes of vitamin deficiencies may be complex and the results not yet well understood, a combination of methods can be used to confirm diagnosis of vitamin deficiency. One is attention to *clinical manifestations*: The attending physician attempts to correlate clinical observations with the deficiency of a specific vitamin. A second is *blood and urine analyses*: The levels of the vitamin and any accumulated metabolites in the blood and urine are fair to accurate indicators of any specific vitamin deficiency. Blood analyses usually identify the level of a test substance per 100 mL of blood. Urinary analyses usually identify the level of a test substance per 24-hour urine collection or per unit of creatinine (see Chapter 8) in the urine. The third and perhaps most popular method of determining vitamin deficiencies is the *administration of a large amount of a vitamin*. A normal person will then show increased levels of the vitamin and its metabolites in the blood and urine, but a person deficient in the vitamin will usually show decreased levels. Occasionally, however, the results are the reverse: Certain metabolites may increase when there is a deficiency and decrease in normal people when a large dose is given.

WATER-SOLUBLE VITAMINS

The water-soluble vitamins are known as vitamins C, B_1, B_2, and B_6, niacin, folic acid, vitamin B_{12}, pantothenic acid, and biotin. The term *vitamin B complex* usually includes all known water-soluble vitamins except C. Although each vitamin has many names, this book uses the most popular ones. For convenience, the symbols for vitamins with accepted numerical origins are used, such as vitamin B_1. The abbreviation RDA refers to the Recommended Dietary Allowance established by the National Research Council of the National Academy of Sciences (see Chapter 10).

The symptoms of deficiency in specific vitamins to be discussed are those found mainly in

humans. Whenever possible, only characteristic and specific symptoms are emphasized. This is an attempt to correlate unique clinical manifestations with specific vitamin lack. For example, hair loss and blindness are characteristic and specific symptoms, while restlessness, weight loss, and weakness are considered nonspecific and noncharacteristic symptoms; that is, there may be many reasons for weight loss, while causative factors for blindness are limited.

Vitamin C

The chemically active form of vitamin C is L-ascorbic acid, a six-carbon substance resembling a monosaccharide. It was discovered and isolated in 1932 and synthesized in 1934, although its importance was recognized much earlier in association with scurvy and the lack of citrus fruits among British sailors. It is a white crystal, stable in acid but sensitive to heat, air, and alkali. In general, it is fairly stable in light. However, the vitamin is destroyed somewhat in solution, especially if copper is present. When a vitamin can be destroyed easily, it is said to be labile.

The vitamin is readily absorbed by the small intestine, mainly in the upper section. Within limits, the blood level of vitamin C reflects recent intake, for the body does not have an extensive storage. The highest concentration of vitamin C is found in the adrenal cortex (60 mg/100 g tissue). The human body contains about 1 to 4 g of the vitamin, permitting the host to live normally without a dietary intake for 90 days. After this period symptoms of scurvy appear. Any excess in the body is normally excreted in the urine, although the kidney reabsorbs the vitamin to a certain extent. Part of the excess vitamin in the body is converted to oxalic acid, which is also excreted. Excretion and utilization of the vitamin can be influenced by the presence of drugs, such as oral contraceptive pills (see Chapter 16).

Functions

Vitamin C plays an important role in many body processes. Although some of its biochemical functions are unknown, it is the most active reducing agent in living substances and therefore serves important functions in food processing. The acidity of vitamin C keeps iron in ferrous form, increasing the absorption of iron. Similarly, vitamin C facilitates calcium absorption. Without vitamin C, the dentin of the teeth does not form properly and the teeth are weak because of defective calcification. Vitamin C is also needed to synthesize two neurotransmitters that are essential for transferring nerve impulses between cells. If these neurotransmitters are missing, the fatigue and weakness characteristic of vitamin C deficiency result. Vitamin C is essential to activate folic acid from its inactive form.

Vitamin C is also important for the synthesis of corticosterone and 17-hydroxycorticosterone. This fact explains the high level of vitamin C in the adrenal cortex and its disappearance during stress when cortical hormone activity is high.

The role of vitamin C in collagen synthesis is of major importance. Connective tissue holds cells together; it is made up of insoluble proteins in a matrix called ground substance. One of the insoluble proteins is collagen, which is found in skin, cartilage, tendons, ligaments, bone, teeth, and blood vessels. Collagen holds the cells and tissues together in an organized fashion. Two major amino acids in collagen are hydroxyproline and hydroxylysine, derived from proline and lysine, respectively, with the help of vitamin C. When vitamin C is lacking, the chemical process of hydroxylation fails, and proline and lysine are not converted to hydroxyproline and hydroxylysine. This failure results in defective collagen, causing the many clinical manifestations of scurvy indicated below.

Requirements and deficiency symptoms

Many species of animals can synthesize ascorbic acid. Their bodies have the appropriate enzyme to convert glucose or galactose to L-ascorbic acid, so it is not essential in their diet. By contrast, humans, primates, guinea pigs, red-vented bulbul birds, and Indian fruit-eating bats cannot synthesize the vitamin and must consume it in their diets. Fish such as trout and carp also need dietary vitamin C. Table 6-4 shows the 1980 RDA of vitamin C for humans of varying age groups.

In humans, vitamin C deficiency causes the syndrome known as *scurvy*. Blood vessels become fragile, especially capillaries, which bruise easily, causing rupture and diffuse tissue bleeding, pin-

TABLE 6-4   1980 RDA for Vitamin C for Different Age Groups and During Pregnancy and Lactation

Population Group	Vitamin C RDA (mg)
Infants	
0–12 months	35
Children	
1–10	45
11–14 years	50
Males and females	
15+ years	60
Pregnancy	+20
Lactation	+40

point (petechial) hemorrhage, and bleeding in the joints and gums. Since skin is made largely of collagen, the lack of vitamin C may influence wound healing. At least in animals, vitamin C deficiency causes delayed wound healing and malformation of scar tissues. Many clinicians recommend the use of vitamin C (100 to 300 mg) before and after an operation to improve wound healing, though others believe this to be unnecessary. Victims suffering scurvy, especially children, develop bone fractures and malformations, since bone contains collagen.

Between 1960 and 1970, scurvy among infants was directly related to the use of cow's milk. Sterilization (pasteurization) of milk and the lack of orange juice or vitamin C supplement result in a deficiency that is uncommon among breast-fed infants, although it has been documented that maternal deficiency can affect the milk. It is currently believed that an excess intake of the vitamin during pregnancy in the form of juice or supplement can condition the unborn to a higher need, thus precipitating scurvy in the newborn even if its intake is normal. In general, it takes about 3 to 12 months for the child to develop vitamin C deficiency due to inadequate intake. One preventive measure is to avoid using unfortified formula as the only food for a prolonged period.

Adults do not develop scurvy easily. Circumstances such as chronic alcoholism, diarrhea, or eating a very restricted diet because of living alone or other reasons may precipitate scurvy. After trauma and surgery, the body's vitamin C may be diverted to the wounds, thereby increasing the person's likelihood of developing scurvy. Among the elderly, poor appetite, decreased mobility, and a fixed income may lead to a borderline intake of vitamin C.

Infant scurvy. At present, the incidence of scurvy has decreased dramatically among infants since most commercial formulas are properly fortified. The early symptoms of scurvy in a child are poor appetite, irritability, arrested growth, tenderness of hips and lower legs, mild paralysis, sore gums, and occasionally skin bleeding. The rapid onset of symptoms is followed by early death if not properly treated. On the other hand, recovery is rapid once vitamin C is administered.

For a child with advanced scurvy, the legs are tender and incapable of moving, a condition resembling paralysis. The child lies quietly on its back, flexing the legs at the knees with flexed and externally rotated hips. Any moving or touching causes the child to cry. Mild to severe hemorrhage appears on many parts of its body—skin, bone joints, mucous membranes, and gums. The child bruises easily. Its gums are swollen and bleed easily, usually during teeth eruption, and loose teeth fall out when ulceration and infection occur. The coughing of blood and passing of bloody urine or feces are common. Other signs of advanced scurvy include malaise, fever, and microcytic hypochromic and macrocytic normochromic anemias, which are usually due to a combination of vitamin C and folic acid deficiency. Cow's milk does not relieve this condition, because it is low in both of these vitamins. The chemistry and architecture of bones also show distinct changes under radiographic examination.

A child with scurvy is given 25 mg of vitamin C, which is usually added to milk, four times a day. Some pediatricians prescribe 50 to 100 mg four times daily; after 1 week on this regimen, the dose may be reduced to 30 mg per day, which may be obtained from orange juice or a supplement.

TABLE 6-5 Rate of Symptom Appearance after Vitamin C Deficiency under One Experimental Study

Days on Deficient Diet	Urinary Vitamin C Level	Extent of Scurvy Symptoms*
29	0	Petechial or pinpoint hemorrhage
90	0	Most of the known symptoms from mild to severe

*In this one study, symptoms are reversed when patient is given 6.5, 66.5, or 130 mg of vitamin C.

Adult scurvy. In adults, scurvy is uncommon except among alcoholics, mental patients, and individuals who avoid vegetables and fruits for some reason. Normally it takes 3 to 7 months for a healthy adult to develop scurvy after dietary depletion. Table 6-5 relates dietary vitamin C intake and symptoms under experimental conditions.

The early symptoms of scurvy in an adult are loss of appetite, tiredness, irritability, muscle and joint pain, weight loss, and skin lesions (dry skin, bruises, and reddish blue spots) on buttocks, legs, thighs, backs, and arms. The victim coughs frequently and becomes feverish.

Advanced symptoms include the following: (1) There is a great tendency toward hemorrhage in skin, muscles, and gums, sometimes accompanied by edema. Bleeding areas may develop ulcers. (2) Wound healings are delayed and old scars may swell and break down. (3) Infection may invade hemorrhaged areas. (4) Bone joints are painful and become hot and swollen, with limited motion. (5) As the disease progresses, the mucous membranes of the intestinal, genital, urinary, and/or respiratory tracts bleed. The gums become red, spongy, and swollen and bleed easily, followed by ulceration, sloughing, and loose teeth falling out. (6) Anemias of both types (microcytic versus macrocytic) may occur. (7) Numerous small hemorrhage petechia may appear under the skin. A slight injury or mechanical trauma causes large bruises and bleeding into

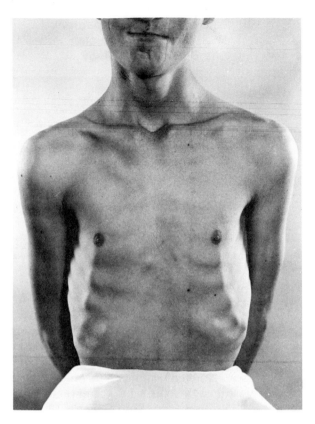

FIGURE 6-1   Healed scorbutic rosary in a boy who had had scurvy off and on since infancy. The sharp edges of the costochondral junctions are easily visible. (From R. W. Vilter, "Effect of Ascorbic Acid in Man," in *The Vitamins: Chemistry, Physiology, Pathology, Methods*, ed. W. H. Sebrell and R. S. Harris [New York: Academic Press, 1967, p. 468]. With permission of Academic Press.)

cavities, with swollen knee or hip joints. (8) Sudden death or heart failure may result from internal hemorrhage. See Figures 6-1, 6-2, and 6-3.

An adult patient with scurvy is given 250 mg of vitamin C four times a day for 1 or 2 weeks. The dose is then reduced to between 50 and 100 mg a few times a day until healing is completed, after which the patient is placed on a balanced diet.

Before surgery if a patient shows less than 8 mg of vitamin C per 100 g of the whole-cell platelets, the attending physician may give extra vitamin C to accelerate the rate of wound healing.

There are many ways to confirm vitamin C deficiency. The blood level of the vitamin is not very helpful, since symptoms do not appear until the blood level is zero. The best technique is the saturation test. For example, when a child is given 200 mg of vitamin C intramuscularly, blood level shows 0.2 mg of the vitamin per 100 mL 4 hours later. Scurvy does not develop until the tissues are less than 20% saturated. Although frank deficiency is easily recognized, borderline cases require clinical experience.

Food sources

The richest sources for vitamin C are citrus fruits and tomatoes; green vegetables are also good sources. Potatoes and root vegetables, although low in vitamin C content, contribute to the American intake because of the large amount consumed. Animal products are not good sources since the vitamin is destroyed during food preparation. In the average American diet, fruits and vegetables contribute more than 90% of the total daily vitamin C intake, dairy products 5%, and meats, poultry, fish and eggs less than 1%. Table 6-6 lists the vitamin C content of some representative foods. More data are provided in Table 6 of the appendix.

Vitamin C is one of the most unstable vitamins. During food preparation, it is important to remember that vitamin C is sensitive to air, cooking temperature, pressure, and light and that it can be leached by water. For example, normal home cooking processes can destroy 50% to 90% of the vitamin C in foods.

Even in raw fruits and vegetables, vitamin C is easily oxidized because of the presence of the enzyme ascorbic acid oxidase. Bruising, cutting, drying, or any procedure that exposes or damages the leaves, fruits, or other part of the plant activates the oxidase. In general, refrigerator temperature, high humidity, and little air movement will minimize vitamin C loss. If during harvest, shipping, and store display there is minimal air exposure and low temperature, very little vitamin C is lost.

Vitamin C content of plant products depends not only on handling, storage, and cooking but also on the types and parts of the plant and their maturity. The longer fruits are permitted to reach maturity, the higher the vitamin C content. On the other hand, the more immature

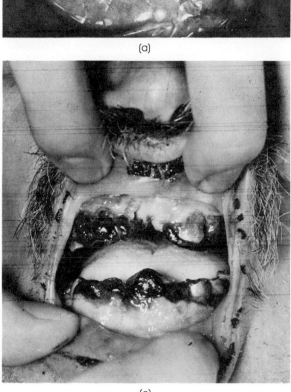

FIGURE 6-2   (a) Scorbutic gingivitis. (From S. Dreizen, *Geriatrics* 29 [1974]: 97. By permission of *Geriatrics*) (b) Scorbutic gingival lesion around a solitary tooth snag. The edentulous gum was normal. (c) Infarcted gangrenous interdental papillae and gingival margins in a patient with severe scurvy. (d) Swollen blue-red lesions in a patient with severe scurvy. (From R. W. Vilter, "Effect of Ascorbic Acid in Man," in *The Vitamins: Chemistry, Physiology, Pathology, Methods*, ed. W. H. Sebrell and R. S. Harris [New York: Academic Press, 1967, pp. 465–466]. With permission of Academic Press.)

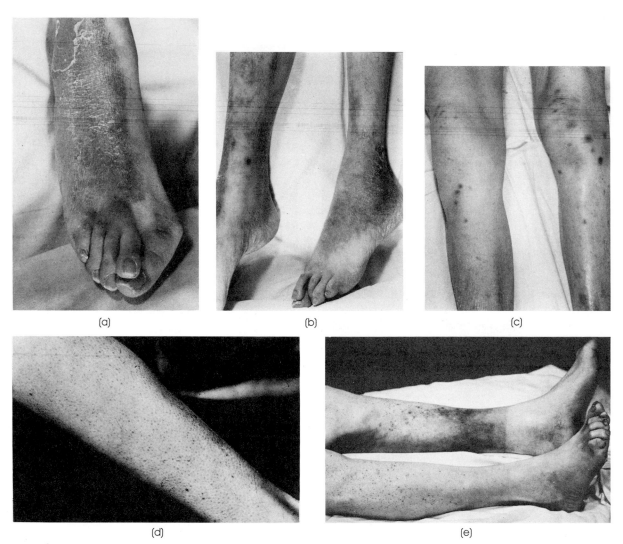

FIGURE 6-3   (a, b) Extensive subcutaneous hemorrhage around both ankles extending laterally in the long dorsum of both feet in a patient with subclinical scurvy. (c) Perifollicular hemorrhages in the exterior surface of both knees in a patient with subclinical scurvy. (From J. B. Booth and G. B. Todd, *Brit. J. Hosp. Med.*, October 1970, p. 513) (d) Perifollicular hemorrhages in the leg due to scurvy. (From R. W. Vilter, "Effect of Ascorbic Acid in Man," in *The Vitamins: Chemistry, Physiology, Pathology, Methods*, ed. W. H. Sebrell and R. S. Harris [New York: Academic Press, 1967, p. 462]. With permission of Academic Press.) (e) Ecchymosis and petechiae from vitamin C deficiency. (From S. Driezen, *Geriatrics* 29 [1974]: 97. By permission of *Geriatrics*.)

TABLE 6-6   Vitamin C Contents of Representative Foods*

Foods	Serving Size	Amount of Vitamin C (mg)
Dairy products		
Cheese, cheddar	1 oz	0
Milk, whole, fluid	1 c	2
Egg, whole	1	0
Meat and equivalents		
Tuna	1 c	2
Beef, roast	3 oz	0
Liver, beef	3 oz	23
Chicken, fried	3 oz	0
Grain products		
Bread, rye	1 sl	0
Macaroni, enriched	1 c	0
Bran, flakes, enriched	1 c	12
Fruits		
Apple	1	6
Avocado	1	30
Cantaloupe	½	90
Orange, fresh	1	66
Orange, juice, fresh	1 c	360
Strawberries, fresh	1 c	88
Vegetables		
Asparagus, canned	4 spears	12
Broccoli, raw, chopped	1 c	140
Lettuce, iceberg	1 c	3
Potato, baked	1	31
Spinach, fresh, cooked	1 c	50
Tomato, raw	1	28
Legumes, nuts, seeds		
Beans, kidney, red	1 c	0
Walnuts, English, chopped	1 c	2
Miscellaneous		
Sugar	1 c	trace
Fats, oils	1 c	0

*Adapted from *Nutritive Value of Foods*, Home and Garden Bulletin No. 72 (Washington, D.C.: U.S. Department of Agriculture, 1981).

seeds are (such as peas and beans), the higher their vitamin C content. Sprouting of beans or peas results in a higher level of vitamin C.

Commercial uses

Tons of vitamin C are manufactured daily in the United States for use as a nutrient supplement and a food additive. In food processing, the biologically inactive (but chemically active) D-ascorbic acid is sometimes used. In food processing, vitamin C serves as: (1) an addition to juices, to enhance the vitamin C content; (2) a color stabilizer in fruit cocktails; (3) an acidifying agent in frozen desserts; (4) a dough conditioner in white flour; (5) a preservative in jams and jellies; and (6) a preservative for color and flavor in alcoholic beverages, such as wine and beer.

This extensive usage of vitamin C in commercial foods considerably increases the American intake.

Pharmacological doses

In the past decade, large doses of vitamin C have been proposed as a therapeutic agent for many clinical disorders, especially respiratory illnesses such as colds. At present no conclusion has been reached regarding these claims. However, the safety of consuming large doses of vitamin C has been subjected to intensive discussion in the last few years. Although vitamin C is water soluble and is thought to be excreted in the urine when an excessive amount is ingested, it is believed that the practice can pose a number of risks.

For one thing, the risk of "conditioning" to a large intake of vitamin C has been documented. If a person becomes accustomed to a large intake of the vitamin over a long period, his or her requirement may become so abnormally high that any sudden transition to a lower intake of the vitamin precipitates scurvy.

Second, the ingestion of large doses of vitamin C may interfere with the effectiveness of certain therapeutic drugs such as anticoagulants.

Third, each time one takes a tablet of vitamin C, one is also unknowingly consuming two other ingredients: inert materials (as carriers) and one mineral, usually sodium (when the vitamin C exists as sodium ascorbate). If a person has high blood pressure or is following a sodium-restricted diet, this source of sodium must be noted. Although the inert materials are harmless, partially digested tablets may cause intestinal obstruction if they are ingested faster than they can be digested and/or absorbed.

The fourth risk involves the partial metabolism of vitamin C to oxalic acid. The normally small amount present in the body increases proportionately if the amount of vitamin C ingested increases. This may increase the risk of stones (calcium oxalate) in the bladder and kidneys.

Fifth, a daily intake of more than 500 mg of vitamin C for a week or more produces an acidic urine, which can eliminate acid-sensitive bacteria and/or encourage the growth of alkaline-sensitive ones. The health implication of this change presumably depends on the type of bacteria inhabiting the genitourinary tract. In clinical practice, doctors prescribe ascorbic acid if it is beneficial for the patient to have an acidic urine.

Sixth, vitamin C is chemically similar to glucose. Thus, if a patient is ingesting a large amount of vitamin C, any laboratory test for urinary glucose may be misinterpreted. For example, the urine may give a false positive diabetic test. Excessive vitamin C intake can also interfere with other blood and urine analyses.

A seventh risk is the diarrhea caused by a large dose of vitamin C or other drugs (many drugs have a laxative effect when consumed in large doses). If the diarrhea is prolonged, nutrients may be lost.

Finally, if a pregnant woman consumes a large amount of vitamin C, the newborn infant may have a higher requirement for the vitamin. More detailed discussion of these potential risks may be found in references listed at the end of this book.

Vitamin B_1

The original chemical name for vitamin B_1 was thiamin or thiamine. It was discovered in 1921, isolated in 1926, and synthesized in 1936. This white, crystalline substance (thiamin hydrochloride) is water soluble and highly unstable to oxidation and temperatures above 100 °C, especially in the presence of alkali.

Functions

Biochemically, thiamin plays an essential role in metabolism by serving as thiamin pyrophosphate, a coenzyme that regulates the formation of acetyl-CoA, decarboxylation of amino acids, and transformation of tryptophan to niacin. The vitamin is especially important in carbohydrate metabolism. Thiamin triphosphate is important in the nerve cell membrane for transmitting high-frequency impulses. If thiamin is deficient, the body accumulates pyruvate and α-ketoglutaric acid and makes less ribose. Some of the clinical symptoms of thiamin deficiency may be direct manifestations of these biochemical abnormalities.

TABLE 6-7   1980 RDA for Vitamin B₁ for Different Age Groups and During Pregnancy and Lactation

Population Group	Thiamin RDA (mg)
Infants	
0– 6 months	0.3
6–12 months	0.5
Children	
1– 3 years	0.7
7–10 years	1.2
Adolescent (11–18 years)	
Male	1.4
Female	1.1
Adults	
Male	
19–22 years	1.5
23–50 years	1.4
51+ years	1.2
Female	
19–22 years	1.1
23+ years	1.0
Pregnancy	+0.4
Lactation	+0.5

Requirements

A person's requirement for vitamin B_1 is directly related to caloric intake. That is, the more carbohydrate one eats, the more thiamin is needed. Table 6-7 provides the average 1980 RDA for different age groups. An excess intake of thiamin is relatively nontoxic, since adults and individuals given 500 mg daily for 1 month suffer no ill effects, although an intravenous dose can elicit allergic reactions in some. A normal person readily absorbs as much as 2 to 5 mg per day of the vitamin, mainly in the duodenum. The body stores very little thiamin; most of it is located in heart and brain tissues, and any excess intake is excreted in the urine.

The substance *alliin* in garlic and onion oil, frequently used by the Orientals, can complex with thiamin to form alliithiamin to facilitate the absorption of the vitamin. Presumably this helps to combat the high incidence of B_1 deficiency among people in Southeast Asia, which results from their high intake of polished rice.

Deficiency

Thiamin deficiency can be caused by a number of factors: (1) low intake of thiamin-rich foods; (2) low caloric intake (too little carbohydrate and fat); (3) folic acid deficiency; (4) excess carbohydrate intake; (5) intravenous glucose given without vitamin B_1, especially in patients with low thiamin storage; (6) alcoholism (reducing intake and absorption of thiamin, with a low level of B_1 coenzyme in the blood); and (7) clinical stresses (anorexia, vomiting, hypermetabolism, and drug therapy—for instance, diuretics increase B_1 excretion). Thiamin deficiency can also reduce stomach acid, further aggravating the deficiency since less B_1 is released from the dietary B_1 complex in foods for absorption within the intestine.

Moderate to severe B_1 deficiency results in the disease *beriberi* (a Singhalese term meaning "I can't, I can't," a good description of this weakness-inducing syndrome). In the absence of B_1, pyruvate (lactate), a by-product of carbohydrate metabolism, accumulates in the body. As a result, the central nervous system, heart, circulation, and alimentary tract are all damaged.

In the past, beriberi was common in many countries, such as China, Japan, Holland, and the Philippines. In most Oriental countries, in which 80% of the caloric intake comes from rice, beriberi was and still is a result of long-term consumption of highly polished (refined) rice and other cereals, for the B_1 is discarded with the husks. The situation in the Philippines illustrates the typical problems encountered in those countries. Refined rice is preferred by the natives because it keeps longer than unrefined rice. Philippine government health authorities now mandate the enrichment of rice with thiamin but noncompliance, repeated washing of rice, and high cooking temperature continue to reduce the intake of thiamin. Beriberi is still the fourth or fifth leading cause of death in the Philippines, where there are 70 to 80 deaths from beriberi per 100,000 births. Hundreds more suffer mild to severe deficiency symptoms and survive.

B_1 deficiency can be aggravated by a low caloric intake and the practices of eating raw fish and chewing tea leaves, both of which contain a thiamin antagonist. In countries such as Thailand and Japan, selected population groups suffer thiamin deficiency because of these practices.

In the United States, about 20% to 30% of the population show biochemical evidence of low B_1 intake. Alcoholics are probably the people most susceptible to B_1 deficiency (see Chapter 25). In addition, subclinical deficiency of thiamin can be identified in individuals whose attempts to lose weight are frequently associated with a large decrease in the intake of carbohydrate and fat. Carbohydrate foods have a high thiamin content.

Adult beriberi.   Signs of beriberi differ somewhat in adults and young children. Early symptoms of adult beriberi are loss of appetite, tiredness, gastrointestinal trouble (nausea, vomiting, and constipation), irritability, weak and heavy extremities, depression, and disorderly thinking. The patient's legs become numb with slightly swollen ankles; the numbness is characterized by itching and a "pins and needles" feeling. Fast heartbeats and cardiac disturbance are identified at a certain stage in every beriberi patient. Many victims also show an abnormal gait with a loss of motor coordination.

Advanced beriberi in an adult may be either "dry" or "wet." The many characteristic manifestations of dry beriberi resemble polyneuritis (a degenerative disease of the nerves). The patient is unable to walk properly; feet are morbid and numb, and walking is characterized by an uncoordinated gait and wrist or foot drops. The victim is thin and emaciated, with wasting of muscles. Muscles are tender, especially when pressure is applied to areas around the calves, and there is muscular weakness in the feet, calves, and legs. When squatting, the patient cannot get up because of a lack of muscular control. The "squat test" is therefore used frequently for diagnosing dry beriberi, especially in the Orient. If unattended, the patient becomes immobilized and may die from infection.

Wet beriberi is characterized by edema of the face and the lower part of the body. The heart swells in some patients, with overt pulsation of distended neck veins, and a rapid heartbeat is accompanied by chest pain. This enlargement of the heart results from increased circulation, caused by the body's attempt to deliver more thiamin to the tissues. Some patients also develop labored breathing and a rapid, irregular pulse. In some patients, however, the edema may not be accompanied by cardiac problems. The absence of albumin in the urine indicates that the patient does not have congestive heart failure or a defective kidney, although oliguria (reduction in urine excretion) occurs in most wet beriberi patients. If conditions deteriorate, death may follow circulatory shock and cardiac failure.

The term *Wernicke-Korsakoff syndrome* is used for the neurological problems due to B_1 deficiency developed in alcoholics, some pregnant women (from excessive vomiting), and patients deficient in thiamin after an intravenous load of glucose. The patient suffers mental deterioration; loss of memory; abnormal perception of time and objects; loss of appetite, nausea, and vomiting; vision disturbance, such as paralyzed eye muscles and abnormal rotation or rolling movements of the eyeballs; and weakness and unnatural gait. Advanced signs include eyelid ptosis, apathy, confusion, and, eventually, if untreated, delirium. Without therapy, most patients die from sudden heart failure. Brain involvement in thiamin deficiency is a serious consideration. Table 6-8 shows the relationship of observable symptoms with the thiamin level in the brain. Figure 6-4 illustrates the classic symptoms of B_1 deficiency.

Each thiamin deficiency case must be diagnosed and treated whenever feasible to avoid irreversible damage to the brain. A beriberi patient with a heart problem or Wernicke-Korsakoff's syndrome should be given large doses of thiamin—for example, 10 to 20 mg intramuscularly a few times a day. If the patient is critically ill, an intravenous dose of 50 to 100 mg is given. Thereafter, the patient receives the same daily intramuscular dose for a few days, followed by oral therapy. Patients with polyneuropathy require about 5 to 10 mg of thiamin three times daily until maximum benefits are observed. Clinical experience indicates that the patient is usually also deficient in other B vitamins, which

TABLE 6-8 Relationship between Neurological Symptoms of Beriberi and Brain Level of Thiamin

Beriberi Symptom	Brain Level of Thiamin (% of normal)
None	50
Slow and steady gait	30
Severe disturbance of posture equilibrium	20

should be given simultaneously. If preferred, preparations such as yeast (brewer's or extract), rice husk (polishings or bran), liver extract, or wheat germ may be used.

Infantile beriberi. When beriberi occurs in children under 6 months old, it is called infantile beriberi. Although infantile beriberi once occurred in this country, it is no longer common. However, in many developing countries infantile beriberi is still common, especially in breast-fed babies. Cow's milk contains twice as much thiamin as normal breast milk and four times as much thiamin as the breast milk from a woman deficient in B_1. Although a B_1-deficient nursing mother may be asymptomatic, her milk can precipitate beriberi in the infant. Furthermore, the mother's bloodstream may carry a large amount of methyl glyoxal (pyruvic aldehyde), a metabolic by-product of thiamin deficiency. Although harmless to the mother, this substance is toxic to the child.

An infant usually develops beriberi when it is 2 to 6 months old. The infant is pale, restless, and unable to sleep, with a poor appetite and occasional vomiting. If beriberi is severe, the baby may have difficulty breathing, a fast heartbeat, and cyanosis (blueness in the face from low blood hemoglobin). Edema, diarrhea, muscle wasting, and crying weakness are characteristic. Frequently the child starts with a piercing cry that dramatically reduces to an inaudible tone. Very little urine is excreted. Sometimes an acute heart beriberi can be precipitated by infection.

All symptoms in the young patient have a rapid onset, and death from acute heart failure may result in 1 to 2 days after symptoms appear if not treated. On the other hand, treatment with 2.5 mg of B_1 leads to a dramatic improvement in a few hours. If there is severe heart failure with convulsion and coma, a slow initial intravenous dose of 25 to 50 mg of B_1 is followed by daily intramuscular injections until satisfactory improvement is evident.

Tests for beriberi. In most beriberi cases, clinical manifestations represent multiple B vitamin deficiency, making specific diagnosis difficult. Some common confirmatory tests are as follows: (1) The *carbohydrate index* measures the level of pyruvate or lactate in the blood after the patient is given a glucose dose and a standard exercise test. This substance accumulates when the patient is deficient in B_1. (2) In the *saturation test*, after a test dose of vitamin B_1 (the loading test), the patient's blood and urinary level of thiamin is analyzed. (3) In the *methyl glyoxal test*, used when a breast-fed infant develops beriberi, the levels of methyl glyoxal in the mother's blood, urine, and milk are ascertained. (4) In tests of *transketolase activity*, the level of this enzyme in red blood cells reflects the patient's recent dietary intake of thiamin. The test is sensitive to a mild degree of thiamin depletion and provides warning before any clinical manifestation of beriberi appears.

Food sources

The richest sources of thiamin are whole and enriched grains, pork, and legumes. Moderately good food sources are kidney, liver, beef, eggs, fish, milk, green vegetables, and some fruits. Table 6-9 shows the thiamin content of representative foods, and Table 6-10 indicates the approximate contribution of thiamin to the American diet by different categories of food. Mandatory enrichment of bread and flour began in 1941 in the United States, and it has been claimed that the enriched bread has saved many alcoholics from thiamin deficiency.

Although foods such as dried brewer's yeast and wheat germ are rich in thiamin, they are not important sources because of the small quantities

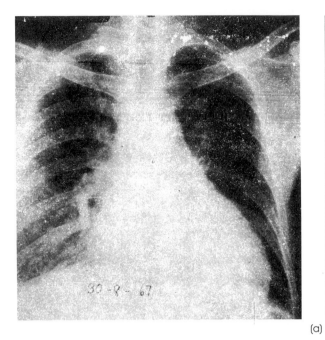
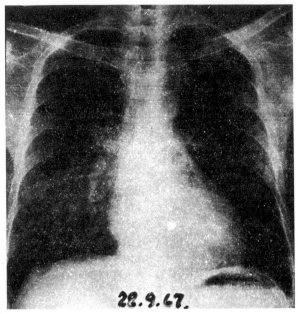

(a)

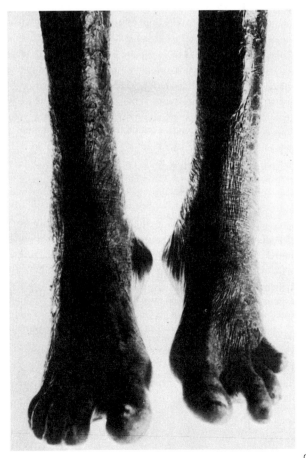
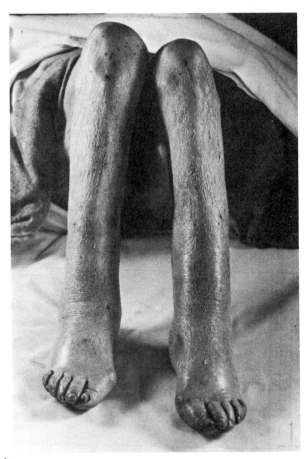

(b)

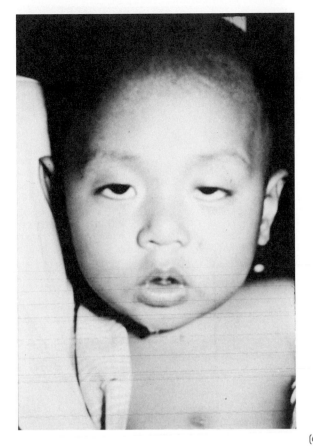
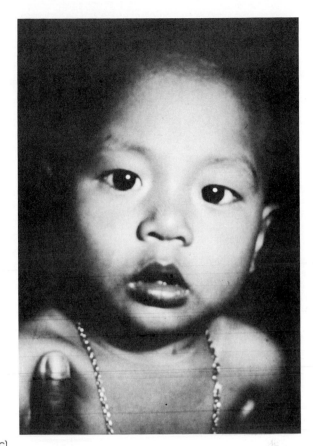

(c)

FIGURE 6-4   (a) Heart in patient with beriberi before (left) and after (right) treatment. Note how swollen heart returns to normal size. (From V. Thongmitr, *J. Med. Assoc. Thailand* 56 [1973]: 703) (b) Wet beriberi with edema of the legs. Left: a young African patient. (Courtesy of World Health Organization) Right: an old American patient. (From S. Dreizen, *Geriatrics* 29 [1974]: 97. By permission of *Geriatrics*) (c) Bilateral ptosis in juvenile beriberi; before (left) and after (right) treatment with thiamin. (From W. Varavithya et al., *Clin. Pediatr.* 14 [1975]: 1083)

usually consumed. A number of foods contain the natural antagonist of vitamin B_1, including fish (especially freshwater fish), some shellfish (mussels, clams, and shrimp), bracken ferns, and tea. The antagonist, thiaminase, is destroyed if the product is cooked. See Chapter 21.

Vitamin B_1 itself is very sensitive to destruction, especially during home food preparation. Since thiamin is destroyed by oxygen, procedures that involve moist heat in the presence of air (such as boiling or stirring) will increase the amount destroyed. The practice of soaking dried beans and other legumes in water for a prolonged period also eliminates a great deal of thiamin unless the liquid is reused. Adding a small amount of baking soda (about ⅕ to ¼ g) reduces the soaking period, but too much alkali also destroys the vitamin. To reduce the loss of thiamin in water, regular rice should not be washed despite instructions to the contrary on package labels.

Although thiamin is sensitive to tempera-

TABLE 6-9 Thiamin Content of Representative Foods*

Food	Serving Size	Amount of Thiamin (mg)
Dairy products		
Cheese, cheddar	1 oz	0.01
Milk, fluid, whole	1 c	0.09
Egg, large, raw, whole	1	0.04
Fish, shellfish, meat, and poultry		
Oysters, raw, meat only	1 c	0.34
Beef, ground, broiled, lean with 10% fat	3 oz	0.08
Lamb, chop, rib, lean only	2 oz	0.09
Fruit and fruit products		
Avocado, raw, whole	1	0.33
Orange juice, from frozen concentrate	1 c	0.23
Cantaloupe, orange fleshed	½	0.11
Grain and grain products		
Bread, whole wheat	1 sl	0.03
Bran, flakes, enriched	1 c	0.58
Noodles, egg, enriched, cooked	1 c	0.22
Legumes, nuts, and seeds		
Beans, dry	1 c	0.27
Cashews, roasted in oil	1 c	0.60
Vegetables and vegetable products		
Asparagus, cooked	1 c	0.23
Corn, sweet, from frozen ear	1 ear	0.18
Lettuce, raw, loose leaf	1 c	0.03
Squash, cooked, summer	1 c	0.11
Miscellaneous		
Sugar, fats, oil	1 c	0
Brewer's yeast, dry	1 T	1.25

*Adapted from *Nutritive Value of Foods*, Home and Garden Bulletin No. 72 (Washington, D.C.: U.S. Department of Agriculture, 1981).

tures higher than 100 °C, certain foods protect the vitamin from heat to various extents. For example, the thiamin in pork is more resistant to heat than that in lamb. Thiamin's sensitivity to alkali also varies. Baking soda used to preserve the bright green color of fresh vegetables during cooling or processing destroys vitamins B_1 and C, although that used to leaven bread has a minimal destructive effect. Sulfite used to preserve foods can destroy thiamin, as can irradiation used experimentally in sterilizing foods.

Vitamin B_2

The yellow-orange crystals of vitamin B_2, or *riboflavin*, are water soluble and stable to heat, acid, and oxidation. But, of all known vitamins, it is probably the most unstable to the ultraviolet or visible rays of sunlight. The vitamin was discovered in 1932, isolated in 1933, and synthesized in 1935. It exhibits a yellow-green fluorescence in water solution.

Vitamin B_2 is readily absorbed by the mucosa of the small intestine, mainly the upper section. Experimental studies have confirmed that about 60% of an ingested vitamin B_2 dose is absorbed in the presence of food, whereas only about 15% is absorbed on an empty stomach. Absorption is slower for a young person than an old one. Thyroid hormone can stimulate B_2 absorption and storage, but the body stores very little of the vitamin, with the liver and kidneys as the main sites. Riboflavin is excreted in the urine, and some that is derived from the bile, mucosal secre-

TABLE 6-10   Approximate Contribution of Thiamin to the American Diet by Different Categories of Food

Food Group	% of Daily Thiamin Intake
Cereal products	30–40
Meat, poultry, fish	25–35
Fruits, vegetables	15–25
Dairy products	5–10
Dry beans, peas, nuts	5–10
Eggs	0– 5

TABLE 6-11   1980 RDA for Riboflavin for Different Age Groups and During Pregnancy and Lactation

Population Group	Riboflavin RDA (mg)
Infants	
0– 6 months	0.4
6–12 months	0.6
Children	
1– 3 years	0.8
7–10 years	1.4
11–14 years	
Male	1.6
Female	1.3
Adolescents (15–18 years)	
Male	1.7
Female	1.3
Adults	
Male	
19–22 years	1.7
23–50 years	1.6
50+ years	1.4
Female	
19–22 years	1.3
23+ years	1.2
Pregnancy	+0.3
Lactation	+0.5

tion, and bacterial synthesis is passed through the bowel. So far, clinical observation indicates that a large dose of B_2 is nontoxic.

Functions

Riboflavin performs a very important function in the body by making many biological reactions possible. As discussed in greater detail in Chapter 8, riboflavin is a component of a coenzyme related to flavoprotein (an enzyme), which functions in the respiratory chain or electron transport system. Riboflavin facilitates the transfer of hydrogen atoms. Metabolically, riboflavin therefore makes the following biological reactions possible: (1) energy metabolism, (2) transformation of folic acid to its coenzyme (as a result, riboflavin indirectly regulates DNA and protein synthesis), (3) degradation of fatty acids, (4) glycogen formation, (5) transformation of tryptophan to niacin, (6) production of red blood cells in bone marrow, and (7) synthesis of corticosteroids in the adrenal gland.

Deficiency

Table 6-11 shows the 1980 RDA for riboflavin according to age group. In the past, riboflavin deficiency was common in many countries including the United States, although it now occurs mainly in underdeveloped countries. However, a sizable portion of the adolescent population of the United States, especially girls, is considered subnormal in riboflavin intake, and chronic alcoholics and many elderly people on a low- or fixed-income suffer overt riboflavin deficiency. In general, the deficiency is usually a combination of the lack of riboflavin and niacin, with mixed clinical manifestations.

The major causes of riboflavin deficiency include inadequate dietary intake, intestinal malabsorption, and clinical stresses (such as liver cirrhosis, surgery, trauma, burns, tuberculosis, rheumatic fever, congestive heart failure, cancer, hyperthyroidism, diabetes, and starvation). Malabsorption may be caused by intestinal diseases such as bowel inflammation or gluten-induced enteropathy. Clinical stresses may increase urinary excretion, reduce riboflavin utilization, or increase requirement of the vitamin.

To study the clinical symptoms of riboflavin deficiency, both spontaneous and induced conditions have been observed. Riboflavin deficiency is induced experimentally by the use of a ribofla-

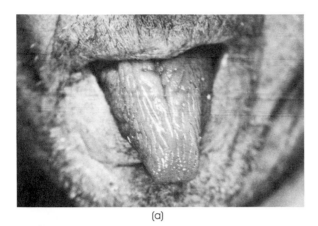

(a)

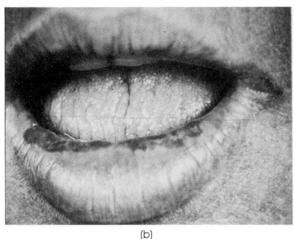

(b)

FIGURE 6-5 Oral lesions in riboflavin deficiency. (From S. Dreizen, *Geriatrics* 29 [1974]: 97. By permission of *Geriatrics*) (a) Glossitis and cheilosis. (b) Cheilosis and cheilitis.

TABLE 6-12 Approximate Contribution of Vitamin B₂ to the American Diet by Different Categories of Food

Food Group	% of Daily Riboflavin Intake
Dairy products	40–45
Meat, poultry, fish, eggs	25–35
Cereal products	10–20
Fruits, vegetables	5–15
Dry beans, peas, nuts	0– 5

with yellow crusts, and red, chapped, and dry lips. Shallow ulcers eventually develop and healed tissues leave scars and atrophic lips. *Glossitis* is characterized by a smooth and red tongue, with flat, swollen, or pebbled papillae. However, these oral changes are not unique to B₂ deficiency; they also usually accompany deficiencies of folic acid, vitamin B₁₂, or niacin to varying degrees. See Figure 6-5.

In some patients with riboflavin deficiency, the skin becomes greasy, scaly, and dry. Areas affected include the base of the nose, the corners and edges of the eyes, ear folds, and the chin; some of these locations are covered with filiform comedones. Such seborrheic dermatitis may also occur around the genital and groin areas.

There are some claims that a patient with riboflavin deficiency may suffer adverse effects on the eye such as cornea vascularization, superficial opacities and ulcerations, inflamed conjunctiva, red and swollen eyelids, and discharges. However, many of these symptoms result from a deficiency of other B vitamins. Some patients with riboflavin deficiency are also known to develop macrocytic anemia.

If a patient shows all of the above symptoms, riboflavin deficiency is easy to diagnose. However, if a patient complains only about sore lips, mouth, and tongue and burning or itching eyes with discharges, specific riboflavin deficiency is difficult to determine and other tests are needed. These include (1) a urine test (the patient is deficient in vitamin B₂ if less than 50 μg of the vitamin are excreted in 24 hours or if there is less than 27 μg/g creatine in the urine), (2) a standard saturation test, and (3) a special test for the

vin antagonist, galactoflavin. If a patient consumes very little of the vitamin for several months, symptoms will also develop. Although riboflavin deficiency produces some unique symptoms, there is no known associated specific disease.

The known clinical manifestations of riboflavin deficiency are both specific and nonspecific. Adult males given less than 0.07 mg of vitamin B₂ per day for 5 to 8 weeks show nonspecific responses such as depression, hysteria, personality changes, weakness, and general malaise. In addition, victims suffering riboflavin deficiency generally show two specific changes in the mouth: cheilosis and glossitis. *Cheilosis* is characterized by cracks or fissures at the corners of the mouth

TABLE 6-13   Vitamin B$_2$ Content of Representative Foods*

Food	Serving Size	Amount of Riboflavin (mg)
Cheese, cheddar, shredded	1 c	0.42
Milk, fluid, whole	1 c	0.40
Ice cream, regular	1 c	0.33
Egg, scrambled in milk and butter	1	0.16
Bluefish, baked with butter	3 oz	0.08
Beef, ground, broiled, lean with 10% fat	3 oz	0.20
Liver, beef, fried	3 oz	3.56
Chicken, breast, fried, bones removed	2.8 oz	0.17
Avocado, raw, whole	1	0.43
Peaches, raw, whole	1	0.05
Orange, whole, peeled	1	0.05
Asparagus, green, cooked	1 c	0.26
Beets, cooked, drained, whole	2	0.04
Potato, baked, medium size	1	0.07
Squash, cooked, winter, baked, mashed	1 c	0.27
Bread, white, enriched	1 sl	0.06
Oatmeal, cooked	1 c	0.05
Cornmeal, yellow, enriched	1 c	0.36
Macaroni, enriched, with cheese	1 c	0.40
Beans, dry, cooked, drained	1 c	0.13
Peanut butter	1 T	0.02
Almonds, shelled, chopped	1 c	1.20
Fats and oils	1 c	0
Sugar, brown	1 c	0.07

*Adapted from *Nutritive Value of Foods*, Home and Garden Bulletin No. 72 (Washington, D.C.: U.S. Department of Agriculture, 1981).

activity of erythrocyte glutathione reductase in the blood.

Treatment of riboflavin deficiency is simple. Symptoms heal in a few days to 2 weeks after an oral dose of 5 mg of B$_2$ has been administered two to three times per day.

Food sources

Riboflavin deficiency need not be common, for the vitamin is widely distributed in food. The best sources are muscle meats, liver, kidney, heart, milk, eggs, some leafy and/or yellow vegetables, and enriched cereals and bread. Only a few food sources, such as sugars and fats, are low in B$_2$. Food preparation and processing can deplete riboflavin, however. Cooking vegetables decreases 10% to 40% of the vitamin, and the loss can be even greater if too much water is used,

cooking is prolonged, and surface exposure is extensive (for instance, from chopping vegetables up in small pieces). Milk, a major source of B$_2$ in the American diet, can lose 50% to 80% of its vitamin content in less than 4 to 6 hours if exposed to the ultraviolet or visible rays of sunlight. Paper cartons and dark-colored containers minimize this loss. Although milling grain results in a 50% to 60% loss of riboflavin, it is believed that enrichment has corrected the problem. Table 6-12 shows the approximate contribution of riboflavin to the American diet by different categories of food. Table 6-13 lists the B$_2$ content of some representative foods.

In addition, some riboflavin can be synthesized by the bacteria in the large intestine, although not much of this is absorbed. It is known that when a large amount of cellulose, lactose, and starch is ingested, more B$_2$ is synthesized, since

TABLE 6-14 Three Chemical Forms of Vitamin B$_6$

Name of Vitamin in Food and Blood	Name of Coenzyme in Body
Pyridoxine	Pyridoxal phosphate
Pyridoxamine	Pyridoxamine phosphate
Pyridoxal	Pyridoxal phosphate

bacterial activity is increased. But whether this will increase the amount absorbed is unknown.

Vitamin B$_6$

Vitamin B$_6$ was discovered in 1934, isolated in 1938, and synthesized in 1939. It is water soluble and unstable to alkali, ultraviolet light, and oxidation, but stable to heat and acid. It exists in three different forms in food, each of which occurs mainly as a coenzyme in the body (see Table 6-14). The term *pyridoxine* is sometimes used to denote B$_6$.

The vitamin is excreted mainly in the urine as 4-pyridoxic acid, a metabolite of the different forms of B$_6$. The body stores very little B$_6$. The substance is relatively nontoxic, although a few documented cases of toxicity from consuming over 300 mg per day have been reported. Some individuals experience pain from intramuscular injection of the vitamin, but this is probably a reaction to the acid solution used.

Functions

The most important biological function of vitamin B$_6$ is to serve as a coenzyme in at least ten metabolic processes. For one, B$_6$ is involved in protein metabolism, especially in the degradation of amino acids through such processes as transamination and deamination. Second, B$_6$ is involved as a coenzyme in the transformation of tryptophan to nicotinic acid, as indicated in the following diagram:

If B$_6$ is lacking, kynurenine and xanthurenic acid will accumulate and be excreted.

Third, in certain reactions involving the central nervous system, B$_6$ is important in transforming tryptophan to serotonin. Mild B$_6$ deficiency may show up as a slight disturbance in the electroencephalogram (EEG); severe B$_6$ deficiency may lead to convulsion.

Fourth, B$_6$ is involved in the production of antibodies. If there is not enough B$_6$ in the body, skin grafts heal slowly. Presumably, there is a mild rejection of the graft because of some derangement in the immunological system due to a lack of B$_6$.

The remaining six metabolic processes in which B$_6$ is involved as a coenzyme are: (1) the formation of porphyrin from hemoglobin; (2) the synthesis of elastin; (3) the production of a nucleic acid precursor; (4) the transformation of linoleic acid to arachidonic acid; (5) the degradation of glycogen; and (6) the synthesis of sphingolipids (needed for the development of myelin sheath surrounding nerve fibers).

Deficiency

Healthy adults are rarely deficient in vitamin B$_6$ since the vitamin is widespread in nature and the body's requirements for it are small. Table 6-15 gives the 1980 RDA of B$_6$ for different age groups. Although these requirements are minimal, cases of spontaneous deficiency have been reported. In the early 1950s, infants fed autoclaved (sterilized) commercial milk formula (supplying less than 0.1 mg of B$_6$) developed deficiency symptoms that were reversible by administering the vitamin. Some infants have developed B$_6$ deficiency due to an inborn error of metabolism, and B$_6$-responsive anemia has been reported in adults. In addition, chronic alcoholism and hyperthyroidism increase the requirement for the vitamin. Because B$_6$ plays such an important role in protein metabolism, the popular practice of eating a low-carbohydrate, high-

$$\text{tryptophan} \rightarrow \text{kynurenine} \xrightarrow{\text{vitamin B}_6} \text{3-hydroxykynurenine}$$
$$\downarrow \qquad\qquad\qquad\qquad \downarrow$$
$$\text{xanthurenic acid} \qquad\qquad \text{3-hydroxyantranilic acid}$$
$$\downarrow$$
$$\text{nicotinic acid}$$

protein diet may increase the vitamin B_6 requirement. Other potential causes of B_6 deficiency include inadequate intake, intestinal malabsorption, and clinical stresses.

The usage of drugs such as penicillamine in treating cystinuria, rheumatoid arthritis, and Wilson's disease increases the body's requirement for vitamin B_6. Another drug of major importance in B_6 deficiency is the oral contraceptive pill. Its estrogen content increases the body's need for vitamin B_6, as indicated by an increased amount of tryptophan metabolites in the urine and a high incidence of depression (apparently from a lack of serotonin among the users). All of these symptoms disappear after vitamin B_6 is administered, usually at 10 to 30 mg per day.

Finally, a number of genetically caused errors in metabolism can increase the body's requirement for vitamin B_6.

Experimental human deficiency has been produced by drastically reducing the intake of B_6 and/or using an antagonist, such as INH (isonicotinic acid hydrazide) or deoxypyridoxine. The antagonist INH is chemically related to B_6 and has been used effectively in treating tuberculosis. However, there are many side effects such as skin lesions and neurological problems, which can be reversed by vitamin B_6. It is suspected that INH complexes with the vitamin and makes it unavailable for the body.

Although some patients with spontaneous B_6 deficiency lack clinical symptoms, abnormal biochemical alterations have been documented. Clinical observations of deficiency symptoms have been made only for infants. These include convulsion, irritability, and abnormal EEGs, sometimes accompanied by a macrocytic hypochromic anemia, all reversible by the administration of vitamin B_6. Such symptoms have resulted from feeding infants formulas with less than 0.1 mg of vitamin B_6. In some infants, spontaneous convulsions shortly after birth have also been reversed by B_6.

Adults put on a low-B_6 diet show nonspecific signs such as weakness, nervousness, irritability, insomnia, and difficulty in walking. Specific B_6 deficiency symptoms have been experimentally produced in adults by means of the antagonist deoxypyridoxine. The patients were irritable, depressed, and drowsy. There were distinct skin

TABLE 6-15   1980 RDA for Vitamin B_6 for Different Age Groups and During Pregnancy and Lactation

Population Group	Vitamin B_6 RDA (mg)
Infants	
0– 6 months	0.3
6–12 months	0.6
Children	
1– 3 years	0.9
7–10 years	1.6
11–14 years	1.8
Adolescents (15–18 years)	2.0
Adults (19+ years)	
Male	2.2
Female	2.0
Pregnancy	+0.6
Lactation	+0.5

lesions with seborrheic dermatitis around the eyes, nose, mouth, chin, and skin folds, extending to the face, ears, forehead, and eyebrows in some patients. Perineal and scrotal areas were affected in some. Moist areas such as folds under the breasts are susceptible to skin lesions. Angular stomatitis, glossitis, and cheilosis similar to those due to riboflavin and niacin deficiency may occur. Weight loss and increased susceptibility to infection, especially in the genitourinary tract, have also been reported. The severity of these B_6 deficiency symptoms increases when protein intake is high.

Sideroblastic anemia has been treated in some patients with vitamin B_6. It is also important to recognize that B_6 deficiency can enhance the excretion of oxalate and citrate, increasing the risk of kidney stones.

Symptoms of B_6 deficiency may be treated by 10 to 50 mg of B_6 per day. A dose of 10 to 15 mg of B_6 reverses hypochromic anemia, and a dose of 50 to 100 mg reverses the symptoms (including neurological problems) of B_6 deficiency from the use of INH in clinical therapy.

At present, diagnostic confirmation of B_6 deficiency includes the following methods: (1) the tryptophan loading test, in which the subject is given 5 to 10 g of DL-tryptophan and the urinary excretion of xanthurenic acid is determined (a normal person excretes more than 30 to 50 mg of this substance in 24 hours, whereas a pyridoxine-deficient subject excretes less); (2) enzyme assays, in which the blood levels of two enzymes, glutamic oxaloacetate transaminase and glutamic pyruvic transaminase, decrease if the person is deficient in vitamin B_6; (3) the saturation test; and (4) a test for metabolite formation (in a person deficient in B_6, urinary pyridoxic acid level is about 0.1 to 0.2 mg).

Food sources

Vitamin B_6 is widespread in nature, with good sources including muscle meats, organs (liver and kidney), egg yolk, yeast, corn, wheat, and other whole-grain cereals. By contrast, milk and many vegetables have a low B_6 content. However, despite their low B_6 content, vegetables contribute more B_6 to the American diet than many other foods because the vitamin in vegetables resists destruction during processing and storage. For example, freezing vegetables results in a 20% to 30% loss of B_6 while milling grains results in a 90% loss. The B_6 levels in most enriched grain products using refined flour are not restored, although some manufacturers do add the vitamin to their products.

Table 6-16 describes the approximate vitamin B_6 contribution to the American diet by different categories of food. Table 6-17 lists the B_6 content of representative foods.

Pharmacological doses

In clinical medicine, pharmacological doses of pyridoxine have been used in several different therapeutic regimens. A dose of 50 mg of B_6 can occasionally relieve morning sickness, although clinicians tend to avoid prescribing drugs as much as possible, especially during a patient's early pregnancy. Second, the sucking of lozenges containing 1 to 5 mg of B_6, two to four times a day, can reduce cavities, especially in pregnant women and children. It is suspected that the substance inhibits the growth of bacteria. Third, some types of dermatitis respond to topically ap-

TABLE 6-16 Approximate Contribution of Vitamin B_6 to the American Diet by Different Categories of Food

Food Group	% of Vitamin B_6 Intake
Meat, eggs	45–55
Fruits and vegetables	25–35
Dairy products	5–15
Cereal products	5–10
Dry peas, beans	0–5

plied vitamin B_6. And fourth, pyridoxine has been used successfully in treating hyperoxaluria and recurrent oxalate kidney stones.

Niacin

Niacin as a vitamin was discovered and isolated in 1936, although the substance has been known chemically since 1867. It is a white substance, moderately stable to heat, light, acid, alkali, and oxidation. As a result, very little of the vitamin is lost during food preparation except through leaching if the liquid is discarded.

The two main forms of the vitamin are *niacin* (nicotinic acid) and *niacinamide* (nicotinamide). The former is associated chiefly with plant products, and the latter with animal products. For convenience, the term *niacin* is used to denote either chemical unless stated otherwise. Under most circumstances the two substances have nearly the same biological effects, although there are differences. Niacin is absorbed readily by the body. Very little of the substance is stored, since any excess is excreted in the urine.

Functions

The biochemical functions of niacin are well known. The vitamin is required by all living cells and is the component of two important coenzymes, nicotinamide adenine dinucleotide (NAD) and nicotinamide adenine dinucleotide phosphate (NADP). As a coenzyme the vitamin can release energy from carbohydrate, fat, and protein and assist in the synthesis of protein, fat, and pentoses (for DNA formation). More specifically, as a coenzyme niacin transports electrons

TABLE 6-17 Vitamin B₆ Content of Representative Foods*

Foods	Serving Size	Amount of Pyridoxine (mg)
Cottage cheese, creamed	½ c	0.2
Milk, whole, fluid	1 c	0.1
Yogurt, regular, plain	8 fl oz	0.1
Egg, whole, cooked, large	1	0.06
Beef, hamburger, broiled, 21% fat	¼ lb	0.4
Chicken, roasted, light meat, no skin	3½ oz	0.7
Salmon, steak, broiled, average size	1	1.0
Apricots, fresh, medium size	2–3	0.07
Cantaloupe, medium size	½	0.1
Bread, cracked wheat	1 sl	0.02
Cereal, shredded wheat, spoon sized	1 c	0.1
Noodles, egg, cooked, enriched	⅔ c	0.02
Peas, split, dry, cooked	½ c	0.04
Peanuts, roasted, salted	1 oz	0.1
Asparagus, fresh, green, cooked	½ c	0.2
Brussels sprouts, fresh, boiled, large	4	0.4
Squash, summer, boiled	½ c	0.2
Fats and oils	1 c	0
Sugar, white, granulated	1 c	0
Brewer's yeast	1 T	0.1

*These data have been obtained from the results of a number of reports.

and hydrogen atoms, making oxidation possible. Along the respiratory chain, the hydrogen atoms are transported by sequential substrates until they combine with oxygen to form water. This oxidation of food releases energy, which is stored in ATP to be drawn on later for heat, mechanical work, and the like. These metabolic processes are described in greater detail in Chapter 8.

Partial synthesis by the body

Niacin is the only water-soluble vitamin that the body tissues can synthesize to a certain extent. In 1945 scientists found that the body cells can convert tryptophan to niacin. This transformation requires the presence of three water-soluble vitamins: B_1, B_6, and B_2, plus L-tryptophan. In general, about 60 units of tryptophan are converted to 1 unit of niacin. This process may proceed more efficiently during pregnancy. On the average, tryptophan contributes about 60% to 70% of the niacin metabolized in an adult. The

tryptophan available to the body is used primarily for protein synthesis; its conversion to niacin is actually a secondary function.

This unique transformation explains why milk, low in niacin, can usually cure niacin deficiency: Milk has a high tryptophan content. The term *niacin equivalent* refers to a combination of a preformed niacin and the potential amount of niacin from tryptophan in the diet.

Deficiency

Niacin deficiency causes *pellagra*. The term is derived from the Italian words *pelle* ("skin") and *agra* ("rough"). Pellagra was common in the southern United States in the early 1900s, causing many deaths, especially among prisoners, poor people, and blacks. It was and still is common in places where corn is the major cereal, especially among the very poor. At present, pellagra is a problem in Rumania, Yugoslavia, and parts of Egypt, India, and Africa. Corn is associated with pellagra because of its low content of both tryptophan and free niacin. In rice and corn, much of the niacin exists as *niacinogen* (a peptide of at least 17 amino acids), and this inactive or bound niacin is unavailable to the body. However, alkalis can release the free vitamin. For instance, in Mexico, Central America, and a few other countries, more free niacin becomes available when corn is treated with lime to make such dough products as tortillas. These people have therefore experienced a low incidence of pellagra even though they eat a large amount of corn.

In the United States, classic pellagra was the result of a dietary lack of niacin. Among Southerners, the disease occurred mainly in the spring and the fall. Niacin intake was deficient in the winter, and exposure to the sun and increased physical activities led to greater niacin demand during the summer.

Today, pellagra due to a dietary lack of niacin and/or tryptophan is uncommon in the United States. At present, pellagra in this country is usually associated with diabetes, alcoholism, liver cirrhosis, cancer, thyrotoxicosis, and prolonged intravenous feeding without niacin added. Table 6-18 shows the 1980 RDA for niacin for different age groups.

Early symptoms of pellagra include loss of appetite, lassitude, weakness, irritability, anxiety, depression, numbness, insomnia, and many gastrointestinal problems such as glossitis, stomatitis, heartburn, and abdominal pain, all of which are aggravated by highly seasoned or acidic foods. The extent of symptoms varies with the duration and degree of niacin deficiency.

The classical clinical manifestations of pellagra are frequently termed the "4 D's": dermatitis, diarrhea, depression or dementia, and, if un-

TABLE 6-18   1980 RDA for Niacin for Different Age Groups and During Pregnancy and Lactation

Population Group	Niacin Equivalent (mg)
Infants	
0– 6 months	6
6–12 months	8
Children	
1– 3 years	9
7–10 years	16
11–14 years	
Male	18
Female	15
Adolescents (15–18 years)	
Male	18
Female	14
Adults	
Male	
19–22 years	19
23–50 years	18
51+ years	16
Female	
19–22 years	14
23+ years	13
Pregnancy	+2
Lactation	+5

treated, death. The disease is also known to affect the genitourinary tract in some patients. In general, pellagra is characterized by skin lesions, problems in mucous membranes, and mental deterioration.

The early signs of skin lesions are similar to

FIGURE 6-6   Classic symptoms of pellagra. (a, b, c, d) Note symmetrical dermatitis in these South African patients. ([a] From J. G. Prinsloo et al., *Amer. J. Clin. Nutr.* 21 [1968]: 98. [b, c, d] Courtesy of Dr. J. G. Prinsloo) (e) Well demarcated erythematosquamous photodermatitis of the left arm in a Canadian patient with pellagra. (f) Symmetric erythematosquamous photodermatitis of lower legs in a Canadian patient. (e, f) Originally published in J. P. Des Groseilliers and N. J. Shiffman, *Can. Med. Assn. J.* 115 [1976]: 768. (g) Skin dermatitis in an American patient. (From S. Dreizen, *Geriatrics* 29 [1974]: 97. By permission of *Geriatrics*)

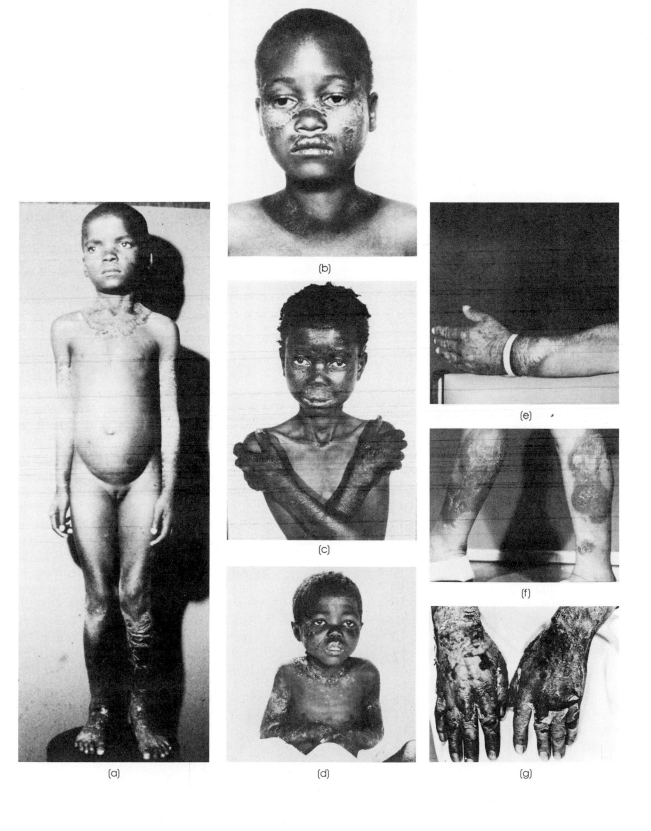

(a)

(b)

(c)

(d)

(e)

(f)

(g)

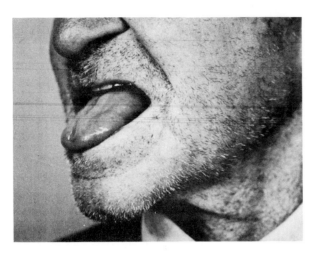

FIGURE 6-7 Glossitis. (From S. Dreizen, *Geriatrics* 29 [1974]: 97. By permission of *Geriatrics*)

ordinary sunburn, progressing to a red skin with blisters or large blebs. Infection may already have begun at this stage. The lesions progress to a severe burn with large denuded skins, and the advanced stage is characterized by skin pigmentation with infection. The lesions are located on the forearms, backs of the hands, the face, and the front surfaces of the legs, feet, and neck. Locations exposed to friction are also susceptible targets, such as the lower sides of the breasts, the groin and genital areas, the elbows, and knees. All dermatitis is symmetrical; that is, skin lesions affect both hands, arms, feet, thighs, and shoulders and both sides of the face and back. The affected areas are clearly demarcated from good skin. See Figures 6-6 and 6-7.

In addition to skin lesions, body surfaces with mucous membranes develop specific clinical problems. The tongue is swollen, red, and sore, and the victim is unable to ingest food, even fluids, because of pain in chewing and swallowing. Oral infection is not uncommon, and the esophagus, stomach, and the entire intestine may be inflamed. Common intestinal complaints include indigestion (lack of stomach acid), heartburn, abdominal pain, sore rectum, and diarrhea (watery stools sometimes containing blood). The patient loses weight from decreased nutrient absorption. Inflammation of the mucous membranes may affect the genitourinary tract, with pain accompanying urination. Female victims may suf-

fer inflammation of the vagina and cessation of menstruation.

The involvement of the central nervous system varies. Early signs are irritability, anxiety, and depression. Advanced manifestations are delusion, confusion, hallucination, and disorientation. If untreated, delirium, coma, and death may result. Overall, lethargy, apathy, stupor, fear, manic-depression, and even hyperactivity mark the behavior of the patient.

Pellagra is easily treated. The amount of oral niacin (niacinamide) given to the patient varies. Acute pellagra is managed with 300 to 500 mg daily of niacinamide divided into individual doses of 50 to 100 mg. Swallowing pain and difficulty are bypassed by the intramuscular administration of 100 mg of niacinamide for 1 to 3 days, two to three times a day. Once acute signs have disappeared, the patient is given 100 to 300 mg of oral niacinamide daily, which is divided into individual doses of 50 to 100 mg. The vitamin is given until all the symptoms have disappeared.

The patient should be confined to bed and given a liquid or soft diet if there are stomatitis (inflammation of the oral mucous tissue) and dysphagia (difficulty in swallowing). Foods such as pureed vegetables, strained cereals, eggs, and milk are appropriate, and skim milk powder may be used to increase tryptophan intake. When the patient's conditions have improved, he or she is given fruits, vegetables, and meat (especially lean organ meats).

The diagnosis of niacin deficiency may be confirmed by one or more methods. If there are no classic symptoms but the early nonspecific symptoms are present, the patient's dietary history may indicate the lack of niacin and tryptophan. One must be aware that the early skin lesions of pellagra may be confused with those of other diseases. A saturation test can be used, and urinary analysis of N'-methylniacin amide (N) and pyridone (P) is also common. If a person is deficient in niacin, the urine contains about 0.5 mg of N per gram of creatinine or less than 0.2 mg of N in the urine 6 hours after a test dose. If both P and N are analyzed, P will disappear in the urine several weeks before clinical signs appear, while N disappears at the sign of niacin deficiency symptoms. The person is first given a test dose of niacin. If N:P (per gram of creatinine) is less than 1 : 1, pellagra is present. If the ratio is 4 : 1, the person is normal. A result of 1.3 : 1.0 indicates borderline niacin adequacy.

Food sources

Analysis of food sources of niacin must take into account the levels of niacin and tryptophan, as indicated in Table 6-19. Table 6-20 describes the approximate contribution of niacin to the American diet by different categories of food. Table 6-21 lists the niacin content of various foods.

Pharmacological doses

Niacin has been used for many years in clinical medicine to lower blood cholesterol and triglyceride levels in heart patients. The dose used ranges from ½ to 4 g daily. The major complaints from the use of niacin (but not niacinamide) are pruritus, severe flushing, gastrointestinal disorders, glucose intolerance, hyperuricemia, hyperpigmentation, arrhythmias, vision disturbances, and liver toxicity. The severity of side effects varies with the dosage and duration of use.

Folic Acid

Discovered, isolated, and synthesized in 1945, folic acid exists in many forms, including folate, folic acid, and folacin (see Table 6-22). Its crystals are yellow, slightly soluble in water, and stable in acid solution. It is rapidly destroyed in neutral or alkaline solutions and can thus be lost during food preparation. The compound is essential for humans, monkeys, hamsters, chicks, other animals, and bacteria, although rabbits, dogs, and rats will survive without a dietary source. Folic acid is relatively nontoxic, and individuals given 15 mg of folic acid per day for a month do not show any adverse effects.

Absorption and activation

Folic acid is absorbed readily, mainly in the upper part of the intestine. In order to be absorbed, many of the polyglutamyl forms of folate are hydrolyzed by conjugases in the small intestine to the free form of folic acid (see Table 6-22). About 30% to 50% of ingested food folate is absorbed, while 70% to 80% of a chemical supplement is absorbed. To estimate dietary folic acid requirements, the RDA assumes a conservative 25% absorption rate. Vitamin C and some antibiotics facilitate absorption.

During and after absorption, chemical reduction and partial methylation change folic acid to a mixture of tetrahydrofolic acid and methyl tetrahydrofolic acid, the main active form in the liver and plasma. Figure 6-8 summarizes this process. Much of the folacin (the methylated form of folic acid) may recombine with glutamic

TABLE 6-19   Food Sources and Niacin and Tryptophan

Characteristic	Food
Rich in niacin	Meat (especially lean and organ meats); poultry; fish; yeasts, peanut butter
Fair content of niacin	Enriched whole-grain products (bread, cereal), especially cereal bran and germs; potatoes; some green vegetables
Low in niacin	Unenriched, refined white flour, cornmeal, grits
Low in niacin, high in tryptophan	Milk; eggs; most animal products except gelatin
High in niacin and tryptophan	Legumes (beans, peas); nuts; peanuts

TABLE 6-20   Approximate Contribution of Niacin to the American Diet by Different Categories of Food

Food Group	% of Daily Niacin Intake
Meat, poultry, fish, eggs	40–50
Cereal products, raisins, coffee	35–40
Fruits, vegetables	15–20
Dairy products	0– 5

TABLE 6-21   Niacin Content of Representative Foods*

Food	Serving Size	Amount of Niacin (mg)
Cheese, cheddar	1 oz	trace
Milk, whole, fluid	1 c	0.2
Ice cream, regular, hardened	1 c	0.33
Egg, whole, raw	1	trace
Crabmeat, canned, not pressed down	1 c	2.6
Beef, ground, broiled, lean, 10% fat	3 oz	5.1
Liver, beef, fried	3 oz	14.0
Chicken, breast, fried, bones removed	2.8 oz	17.6
Apricot, raw, no pits	3	0.6
Avocado, Florida	1	4.9
Grapefruit, raw, medium, pink or red	½	0.2
Prune juice, canned	1 c	1.0
Strawberries, whole	1 lb	2.3
Asparagus, green, cooked, drained	1 c	2.0
Beets, cooked, drained, peeled, whole	2	0.3
Corn, sweet, cooked, drained	1 ear	1.1
Potato, baked	1	2.7
Bread, French	1 sl	1.2
Cereal, rolled wheat	1 c	2.2
Rice, white, enriched, long grain, cooked	1 c	2.1
Peas, dry, cooked	1 c	1.0
Peanuts, roasted in oil, salted	1 c	24.8
Navy beans, dry, cooked	1 c	1.3
Fats and oils	1 c	trace
Honey, strained or extracted	1 T	0.1
Sugar, brown, pressed down	1 c	0.4
Sugar, white, granulated	1 c	0
Brewer's yeast, dry	1 T	3.0

*Adapted from *Nutritive Value of Foods*, Home and Garden Bulletin No. 72 (Washington, D.C.: U.S. Department of Agriculture, 1981).

acid units to form large polyglutamate molecules, which are retained instead of excreted. About 10 mg of the active vitamin can be stored in the liver. This will last a vitamin-deprived host 4 to 5 months before signs of deficiency appear. Because of the complex chemical nature of the process of folic acid activation, further exploration of this subject is beyond the scope of this book. Additional information may be obtained from references at the end of this chapter.

Folic acid absorption is decreased by drugs such as alcohol, oral contraceptive pills, and anticonvulsants. Such drugs may also interfere with the utilization and metabolism of the vitamin, further increasing the host's requirement.

Functions

Folic acid participates in many biological reactions by virtue of its coenzyme form (methyl THFA), which is important in the transfer of one-carbon (CH_3) units. Among its many responsibilities, folic acid helps to synthesize purine, which is a component of DNA (deoxyribonucleic acid). Without the vitamin, the normal turnover of cells is defective. The first biological process to show this effect is the manufacture of red blood cells. If folic acid is deficient, *megaloblastosis* (failure of red blood cells to mature) occurs in the bone marrow. However, to convert folic acid to the coenzyme form, vitamin B_{12} is needed (see

TABLE 6-22   Different Forms of Folic Acid

Form	Constituents
Pteroic acid	Pterin and paraminobenzoic acid
Folate	Pteroic acid with 1, 3, or 7 units of glutamic acid
Folic acid	Pteroic acid with 1 unit of glutamic acid
Folacin	Tetrahydrofolic acid

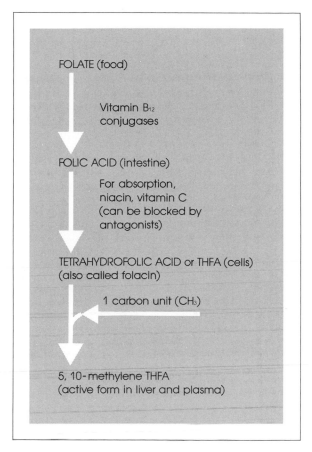

FIGURE 6-8   Absorption and activation of folate.

Figure 6-8). As a result, vitamin B_{12} deficiency also hinders DNA synthesis. Since folic acid is essential for rapid cell divisions, more of it is needed during pregnancy, hyperthyroidism, hemolytic anemia, and other stressful clinical situations.

Folic acid is also indirectly responsible for the synthesis of enzymes and other indispensable protein molecules. The following lists those chemical reactions in which folic acid plays an important role in the one-carbon-transfer process.

1. Homocystine $\longrightarrow$ methionine
2. Glycine $\longrightarrow$ serine
3. Ethanolamine $\longrightarrow$ choline (a vitamin-related substance)
4. Precursors $\longrightarrow$ histidine
5. Nicotinic Acid $\longrightarrow$ N-methylnicotinamide (for excretion)
6. Precursors $\longrightarrow$ purines (adenine and guanine), pyrimidines (thymine and methylcytosine), both of which are components of nucleic acids (DNA and RNA)
7. Phenylalanine $\longrightarrow$ tyrosine
8. Precursors $\longrightarrow$ hemoglobin

Deficiency

The classic clinical manifestation of folic acid deficiency is macrocytic and megaloblastic anemia (megaloblastosis of bone marrow), which is illustrated in a later discussion. In addition to anemia, folic acid deficiency is characterized by clinical signs such as diarrhea, glossitis, weight loss, and a red, sore tongue with atrophic pa-

pillae. Anemia and the low supply of oxygen to tissues results in fatigue, weakness, fainting, and pallor. Cardiac enlargement with occasional congestive heart failure is not uncommon. See Figure 6-9.

The causes of folic acid deficiency are many: inadequate intake, reduced absorption, increased demands and/or losses, and metabolic derangement. Deficiency of this vitamin is widespread in all parts of the world, especially the tropical zones. It is probably the most prevalent of all vitamin deficiencies, even in the United States. Most American diets provide about 200 to 250 μg of folic acid, considerably less than the RDA for adults shown in Table 6-23. Human storage of the vitamin is minimal. For a healthy adult, dietary deprivation of folic acid can cause megaloblastic anemia in about 5 months; this condition can develop in about 2 months in an infant.

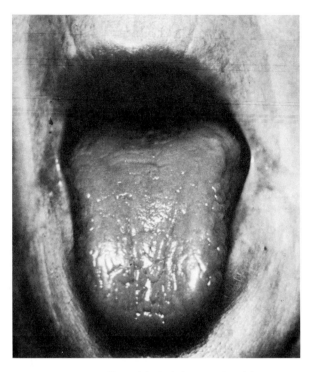

FIGURE 6-9 Folic acid deficiency glossitis. (From S. Dreizen, *Geriatrics* 29 [1974]: 97. By permission of *Geriatrics*)

TABLE 6-23 1980 RDA for Folacin for Different Age Groups and During Pregnancy and Lactation

Population Group	Folacin RDA (μg)
Infants	
0– 6 months	30
6–12 months	45
Children	
1– 3 years	100
7–10 years	200
Adolescents and adults (11+ years)	400
Pregnancy	+400
Lactation	+100

Infants, adolescents, and pregnant women are vulnerable to folic acid deficiency, since they require rapid cell divisions for growth, thus creating a large demand for DNA and, consequently, folic acid. Dietary intake is often insufficient to meet this need.

In poor countries, the percent of folic acid deficiency is high and frequently associated with vitamin B_{12} deficiency. About 20% to 30% of the populations in poor countries suffer folic acid deficiency, which accounts for up to 50% of all hospital admissions. Affected infants and children in poor countries usually suffer malabsorption, caused in part by megaloblastic anemia. The malabsorption further aggravates folic acid deficiency, which intensifies anemia further. It is a vicious cycle. In some underdeveloped countries, about 20% to 25% of pregnant women develop macrocytic anemia, with half of the anemic patients showing abnormal changes in the bone marrow. All over the world, folic acid deficiency is common among the old, the poor, and those living alone for a long period, probably because of their infrequent food preparation and imbalanced eating habits.

In the Western world, many people are prone to folic acid deficiency. More than half of the alcoholics suffer folic acid deficiency because of their imbalanced diet, defective absorption, liver failure, excess excretion, and disturbed metabolism and utilization of the vitamin. Low-income individuals, who account for 35% to 45% of the population studied, show biochemical deficiency of the vitamin, some with clinical manifestations. Folic acid deficiency is frequently reported during pregnancy, especially if toxemia is present. About 10% to 20% of women with a normal pregnancy may have folic acid deficiency, usually because of inadequate intake and increased requirements, although occasionally malabsorption causes the deficiency. Macrocytic anemia during pregnancy results mainly from folic acid deficiency rather than vitamin B_{12} deficiency.

Elderly people, especially those in nursing homes, also have a tendency to develop folic acid deficiency. Those with rheumatoid arthritis are especially susceptible. In addition, patients of all ages with various clinical problems (such as loss of appetite, infection, and scurvy) are susceptible to this vitamin deficiency.

Parasitic infection, although uncommon in this country, can cause folic acid deficiency. Some drugs—such as anticonvulsants and oral contraceptive pills—can interfere with the absorption, utilization, and metabolism of the vitamin, thus causing deficiency. The excessive use of folic acid antagonists, such as aminopterin and methotrexate, used in the treatment of psoriasis and leukemia, can cause folic acid deficiency. Patients with congenital metabolic problems such as sickle cell anemia and thalassemia major may have concomitant folic acid deficiency. Finally, protein-calorie malnutrition and malabsorption (from conditions such as sprue and gluten-sensitive enteropathy described in Chapter 24) can lead to megaloblastic anemia, which is relieved by folic acid. Extensive clinical observations have confirmed that if the patient is given vitamin C, the anemia can be prevented. It appears that ascorbic acid can enhance the absorption of folic acid.

Folic acid deficiency is usually diagnosed by analyses of blood profile and metabolite-vitamin levels. Under the microscope, abnormally large red blood cells, known as megaloblasts, are present in the blood. The popular index used is the percent normal hemoglobin level divided by the percent normal red blood cell count. A normal person has an index of 1; the figure is below 1 for a patient with folic acid or vitamin B_{12} deficiency. Another test involves the blood level of folate, which is normally 6 to 20 ng/L of blood. A decreased intake of the vitamin results in less than 3 ng folate per liter of blood in a week, a sign of low folic acid intake, which precedes any clinical signs. Third, during folic acid deficiency, certain metabolites such as formimino glutamic acid accumulate, which are useful diagnostic indicators (see Figure 6-10).

The treatment for folic acid deficiency is fairly simple. Synthetic folic acid appears to be well assimilated by the body, and a dose of 0.1 mg can prevent deficiency. For a number of years, infants with folic acid deficiency have been managed with 5 mg daily of oral folic acid; affected adults have been given 5 mg orally two to three times a day, although some clinicians currently suggest that a dose of 25 to 100 μg (0.025 to 0.1 mg) may be adequate. Patient response is rapid. Within a few days after treatment, patients have better appetites and signs of general well-being; their blood profile gradually returns to normal.

Some patients have recurrent megaloblastic anemia during certain clinical conditions, such as

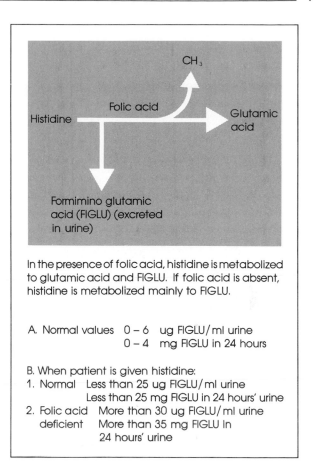

In the presence of folic acid, histidine is metabolized to glutamic acid and FIGLU. If folic acid is absent, histidine is metabolized mainly to FIGLU.

A. Normal values   0 – 6   ug FIGLU/ml urine
                   0 – 4   mg FIGLU in 24 hours

B. When patient is given histidine:
1. Normal   Less than 25 ug FIGLU/ml urine
            Less than 25 mg FIGLU in 24 hours' urine
2. Folic acid   More than 30 ug FIGLU/ml urine
   deficient   More than 35 mg FIGLU in
                24 hours' urine

FIGURE 6-10   Biochemical abnormalities during folic acid deficiency.

pregnancy. Taking 5 mg folic acid daily will again solve the problem. However, it is important to ascertain that folic acid deficiency and pernicious anemia are not simultaneously present, for pernicious anemia can be masked by a large dose of folic acid (see the discussion on vitamin B_{12}).

Food sources

The folate in food exists in two forms: free and conjugated. Conjugated folic acid must be digested by conjugase in the intestine to release free folates and polyglutamates. Free folates, which make up about 25% of the total folates in food, are easily digested. Folates are also synthesized by intestinal bacteria, contributing to the daily intake of the vitamin.

The richest food sources of folic acid are green leafy vegetables (such as spinach and beet greens), asparagus, liver, kidney, yeast, and wheat

TABLE 6-24 Approximate Contribution of Folic Acid to the American Diet by Different Categories of Food

Food Group	% of Daily Folic Acid Intake
Fruits, vegetables	40–45
Meat, fish, poultry, eggs	20–25
Dry beans, peas, nuts	15–20
Cereal products	10–15
Dairy products	0– 5
Fats, oils	0– 1

germ. Good sources are beef, whole-grain cereals, nuts, lima beans, legumes, green vegetables, and fruits such as cantaloupes, lemons, strawberries, and bananas. Although high in folic acid, foods such as liver, wheat germ, and mushrooms are usually insignificant food sources because of the small amounts typically consumed. Orange juice is a significant source, especially because the ascorbic acid present protects the vitamin. Yeast added to bread increases its folic acid content, but baking heat destroys about one-third of the vitamin. Table 6-24 shows the approximate contribution of folic acid to the American diet by different categories of food. Table 6-25 provides the folacin content of some representative foods. For additional information, refer to Table 7 in the appendix.

The actual amount of folic acid that reaches the blood varies greatly because the amount in food, the forms in food, the status of conjugase, and the extent of destruction during cooking and processing all vary. Most diets actually provide only about 200 to 250 μg of folic acid, which is less than the adult RDA of over 400 μg (see Table 6-23). Because of different individual food preferences, the average daily intake of folic acid among Americans can vary between 20 and 1,700 μg.

The folic acid in different foods is absorbed to different degrees. Less than 10% to 15% of the folic acid in most foods is absorbed, although 30% to 60% of the vitamin in yeast, egg, and liver may be absorbed. Folic acid is highly susceptible to degradation during food preparation, with 50% to 90% of the vitamin present in the food lost during cooking and processing. High temperature and excess water leaching can be responsible for nearly 100% of the losses of folic acid. Light is also responsible for some destruction.

Clinical usage

In clinical medicine, folic acid and its derivatives are used extensively. The vitamin is, of course, used to correct folic acid deficiency. Second, the vitamin is effective in relieving some of the symptoms of tropical sprue, such as anemia, glossitis, and gastrointestinal disturbance. Third, the use of folic acid antagonists can create side effects that can be managed only by folic acid. Fourth, many different forms of anemias, including those that fail to respond to vitamin B_{12}, can be corrected to various extents by folic acid. Finally, the vitamin can correct the macrocytic anemia of B_{12} deficiency, but not the neurodegeneration (see the discussion on vitamin B_{12}).

Instead of relieving the neurological degeneration caused by vitamin B_{12} deficiency, folic acid can actually worsen the symptoms. Furthermore, a large dose of folic acid can cure the anemia of B_{12} deficiency and thus mask its neurodegeneration.

Vitamin B_{12}

Vitamin B_{12} occurs as hydroxocobalamin, cyanocobalamin, nitritocobalamin, and thiocyanatecobalamin, all of which are active. *Cobalamin* is the general term for the vitamin. When the functional group is replaced by adenosine, the resulting active vitamin is cobamide coenzyme. The main form of the vitamin used is cyanocobalamin synthesized by bacteria. The chemical was discovered and isolated in 1948 and synthesized in 1973. Structurally, the vitamin contains cobalt in the core of a large, complex skeleton, the corrinoid, which resembles chlorophyll or hemoglobin. It is occasionally called the "red vitamin," since in its crystal form it is bright red.

In the body, much of the B_{12} is not free flowing. This small molecule is normally attached to a large protein molecule, which transports the vitamin from one part of the body to the next. The resulting complex makes it difficult for the kidney to excrete the vitamin. Any excess B_{12} is stored in the liver bound to a protein. Under

TABLE 6-25 Folacin Content of Representative Foods*

Food	Serving Size	Amount of Folacin (μg)
Milk, whole, fluid	1 c	10
Yogurt, low fat, plain	8 fl oz	25
Egg, whole, raw	1 large	25
Margarine	1 T	0
Beef, steak, broiled	3 oz	3
Turkey, roasted, dark meat	2 sl	7
Cod, steak, sauteed	4 oz	10
Sugar, granulated	1 T	0
Rice, white, cooked	⅔ c	1
Apple, raw, medium size	1	5
Banana, medium size	1	25
Orange juice, fresh	¾ c	65
Asparagus, fresh, green, cooked	6–7 spears	60
Potato, baked, large	1	20
Lettuce, raw, head	⅙	30
Soybeans, mature, dry, cooked	½ c	20
English walnuts, halves	1 c	45
Beer	12 oz	25
Wheat germ, raw	1 oz	80
Custard pudding	½ c	4

*These data have been obtained from the reports of a number of investigators. Also see Table 7 of the appendix.

optimal circumstances, the liver can accumulate adequate vitamin to last the host for 5 to 7 years without any intake.

Absorption

The absorption of cobalamin, which occurs mainly in the lower ileum, requires the presence of an *intrinsic factor*, unlike the absorption of other water-soluble vitamins. This factor is a mucoprotein (protein and carbohydrate) synthesized by the parietal cells of the stomach and secreted with the gastric juice. It is heat labile and species specific. The intrinsic factor combines with ingested vitamin B_{12} and transports the vitamin into the mucosal wall at the absorption site, where the vitamin is released and transferred into the blood. If the intrinsic factor is absent for any reason, little or no B_{12} is absorbed, although an experimental dose of 1,000 times the normal need will force the absorption of a moderate amount by simple diffusion. If B_{12} deficiency results from a lack of the intrinsic factor, the best

method of treatment is intramuscular administration of the vitamin.

The percent of B_{12} absorbed is inversely related to that ingested. For example, if 0.5 μg is ingested, about 60% to 80% of it is absorbed, whereas an intake of 16 μg results in only 5% to 15% absorption. The absorption is decreased by old age, iron or pyridoxine deficiency, or hypothyroidism. By contrast, vitamin B_{12} absorption may increase during pregnancy.

Functions

Vitamin B_{12} plays an important role in the metabolism of all cells, tissue growth, and the maintenance of the central nervous system. The first two functions result from the central role of B_{12} in nucleic acid (DNA) formation, while the relationship between the vitamin and the nervous system is not clear.

The biologically active form of vitamin B_{12} is *cobamide coenzyme*, which is synthesized from the vitamin with the assistance of manganese, niacin,

Hyperpigmentation of Pernicious Anemia in Blacks*

A 47-year-old black woman had several months of progressive generalized weakness, easy fatigability, poor appetite, intermittent episodes of mental confusion, generalized skin hyperpigmentation, and four weeks of bilateral diffuse palmar hyperpigmentation. She also complained of a persistent bitter taste, hoarseness, intermittent dysphagia for solids, and was easily bruised.

Her medical history revealed hypertension that responded to hydrochlorothiazide therapy. Family history revealed that just before the patient's mother died, she also had become weak and had increased skin pigmentation and "thyroid trouble."

Results of physical examination revealed a lethargic and confused obese woman who appeared chronically ill. Her temperature was 38.2 C; pulse rate was 100 beats per minute, and respiration was 24/min. Blood pressure was 130/76 mm Hg when she was in a supine position, and 104/54 mm Hg when sitting, with orthostatic symptoms. The mucous membranes were pale, and the tongue showed some bluish gray macular lesions. The thyroid gland was normal; pulmonary and cardiovascular systems were normal, and neurological examination revealed a severely ataxic gait. Axillary and pubic hairs were intact, and the skin showed deep hyperpigmentation of the face, neck, palms, and soles (Figure, top).

The anemia and the nervous system dysfunction responded to cyanocobalamin therapy, and the clearing of the hyperpigmentation was first noted two months after this therapy was started (Figure, bottom).

Top, Photograph taken before therapy with cyanocobalamin. Note hyperpigmentation of palms. Bottom, Photograph taken a few months after therapy with cyanocobalamin was started. Note clearing of hyperpigmentation of palm.

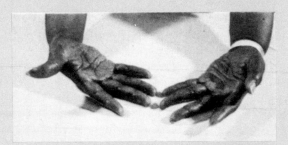

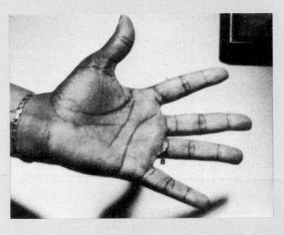

*Source: O. Ogbuawa et al., *Archives of Internal Medicine* 138 (1978):388. Copyright *1978*, American Medical Association.

and vitamin B₂. As a coenzyme, the vitamin is partially responsible for the synthesis of thymidylate, a component of DNA. Since DNA is important for all cells, vitamin B_{12} is essential to them also.

This function is especially significant in the case of red blood cells and cells of the gastrointestinal tract, all of which are constantly being broken down and replaced. A B_{12} deficiency first affects blood metabolism. As in folic acid deficiency, the development of red blood cells becomes defective, and megaloblasts form, which

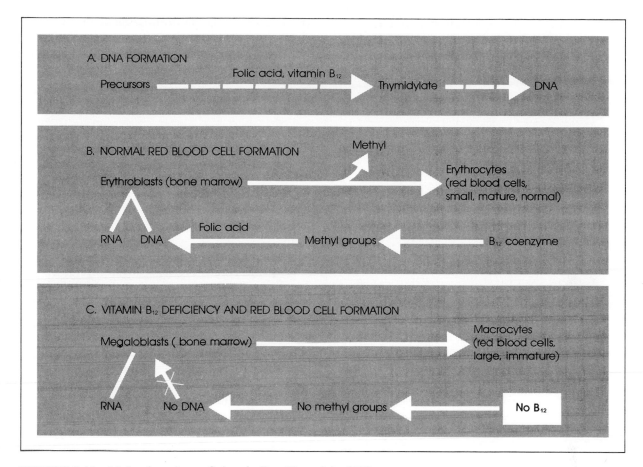

A. DNA FORMATION

Precursors — Folic acid, vitamin B_{12} → Thymidylate --→ DNA

B. NORMAL RED BLOOD CELL FORMATION

Erythroblasts (bone marrow) → Methyl → Erythrocytes (red blood cells, small, mature, normal)

RNA DNA ← Folic acid — Methyl groups ← B_{12} coenzyme

C. VITAMIN B_{12} DEFICIENCY AND RED BLOOD CELL FORMATION

Megaloblasts (bone marrow) → Macrocytes (red blood cells, large, immature)

RNA No DNA ← No methyl groups ← No B_{12}

FIGURE 6-11   Major functions of vitamin B_{12}. (Copyright 1973, American Medical Association)

are later changed to macrocytes (abnormally large red blood cells carrying a normal hemoglobin concentration). These major functions of B_{12} are depicted in Figure 6-11.

As a coenzyme, B_{12} participates in a number of single-carbon (methyl group) reactions, including the transformation of homocysteine to methionine and the synthesis of an intermediate metabolite in the metabolism of folic acid. The relationship between folic acid and vitamin B_{12} appears in several processes, two of which are given:

1. Folic acid conjugates with 3 or 7 glutamic acid molecules $\xrightarrow{\text{vitamin } B_{12}}$ folic acid conjugates with 1 glutamic acid molecule

2. Folic acid $\xrightarrow{\text{vitamin } B_{12}}$ folic acid coenzymes

In all major reactions, folates transfer single-carbon units, while vitamin B_{12} is necessary for the formation of these units.

Exactly how B_{12} affects the nervous system is not clear. Two explanations have been proposed. One is that vitamin B_{12} deficiency leads to defective carbohydrate metabolism, so the supply of glucose to the nerve cells decreases. A second is that since the vitamin is needed for myelin formation, its deficiency results in imperfect myelin sheathing on nerve cells.

Requirements and sources

Scientists do not know our exact need for vitamin B_{12}. They have recommended only 3 μg/day, of which 1 to 1.5 μg is absorbed; whereas the average diet contains about 7 to 30 μg of the vitamin. In general, a person's requirement increases during illness and hyperthyroidism. Ta-

TABLE 6-26 1980 RDA for Vitamin B₁₂ for Different Age Groups and During Pregnancy and Lactation

Population Group	Vitamin B$_{12}$ RDA (μg)
Infants	
0– 6 months	0.5
6–12 months	1.5
Children	
1– 3 years	2.0
7–10 years	3.0
Adolescents and adults (11+ years)	3.0
Pregnancy	+1.0
Lactation	+1.0

TABLE 6-27 Approximate Contribution of Vitamin B₁₂ to the American Diet by Different Categories of Foods

Food Group	% of Daily Vitamin B$_{12}$ Intake
Meat, eggs	75–80
Dairy products	20–25
Cereal products	0– 5

ble 6-26 presents the 1980 RDA for vitamin B_{12} for different age groups.

Bacterial synthesis of cobalamin is the main source of the vitamin in nature. Some vitamin B_{12} is synthesized by intestinal bacteria in the human body but in the terminal end of the colon, making absorption in the ileum (the site for B_{12} absorption) difficult. However, food-producing animals such as ruminants feed on plant products from which they synthesize cobalamin in the stomach. The absorbed vitamin is deposited in their tissues, which serve as an excellent source of B_{12} for the human diet. Edible plant foods do not contain any vitamin B_{12}, although a small amount is synthesized by bacteria in the root nodules. Sometimes if the soil contains certain kinds of bacteria, they may make some cobalamin that reaches plant parts, although this is very rare.

The best sources of vitamin B_{12} are chicken, pork, beef liver, kidney, eggs, whole milk, and fresh shrimp and oysters. Table 6-27 lists the approximate contribution of vitamin B_{12} to the American diet by different categories of food. Table 6-28 presents the vitamin B_{12} content of representative foods.

Cobalamin is stable to acid and oxidation but is destroyed by alkali. Most cooking methods do not destroy the vitamin itself, but cobamide coenzyme is very susceptible to the heat used in food preparation.

Deficiency

As indicated above, cobalamin deficiency causes megaloblastic (macrocytic) anemia and neurodegeneration. If the anemia is caused by a deficiency of the intrinsic factor needed for B_{12} absorption instead of a lack of B_{12} in the diet, the condition is called *pernicious anemia.*

Dietary deficiency of vitamin B_{12} is not common in this country. Occasionally strict vegetarians may suffer a dietary lack, but people who eat animal products rarely encounter this problem. The body stores about 2 to 4 mg, which can last the person 5 to 6 years before deficiency develops. However, deficiency caused by defective intestinal absorption is fairly common in different parts of the world, including the United States. In general, inherited pernicious anemia is common among individuals of northern European ancestry, especially women and children.

Partial or total removal of the stomach or ileum usually results in a reduced absorption of the vitamin. In addition, intestinal infection with worms or other parasites decreases the amount of B_{12} available to the host. In most of these circumstances, the patient needs folic acid in addition to B_{12}.

In addition to megaloblastic anemia, a person with B_{12} deficiency develops *glossitis,* a smooth, bright red tongue with atrophic papillae (Figure 6-12a). Other symptoms are tiredness, headache, breathing difficulty, and low-grade fever. Patients with pernicious anemia may show lemon yellow pallor, hyperpigmentation (Figure 6-12b), weight loss, and various gastrointestinal problems such as loss of appetite, nausea and vomiting, indigestion, heartburn, and diarrhea. There

TABLE 6-28 Vitamin B$_{12}$ Content of Representative Foods*

Food	Serving Size	Amount of B$_{12}$ (μg)
Dairy products		
Cottage cheese, creamed	½ c	0.7
Cream, half and half	¼ c	0.2
Ice cream, vanilla, 10% fat	½ c	0.3
Milk, whole, fluid	1 c	0.9
Milk, dried, instant, nonfat	¼ c	1.4
Yogurt, low fat, plain	8 fl oz	1.3
Eggs		
Whole, raw or hard-cooked, large	1	0.6
Egg white	1	0.02
Egg yolk	1	0.6
Fish, shellfish, meat, poultry		
Beef, hamburger, broiled, 21% fat	¼ lb raw wt	1.5
Beef, steak, broiled, round, with fat	3 oz	2.2
Chicken, roasted, light meat, no skin	3½ oz	0.4
Clams, canned, with liquid	½ c	20.0
Salmon, steak, broiled (6″ × 2″)	1	5.8
Liver, beef, fried	3 oz	68.0
Fats and oils	——	none
Fruits, vegetables, and their products	——	none
Legumes, nuts, and seeds	——	none
Sugars and sweets	——	trace to none
Grain products	——	trace to none

*These data have been obtained from published results of a number of investigators.

is a claim that female patients with pernicious anemia may have difficulty in conceiving.

A patient with a prolonged B$_{12}$ deficiency may eventually develop neurodegeneration of the spinal cord and peripheral nerves. The patient loses sensation in the hands and feet, with a loss of positional, vibratory, and coordinating movements. The muscles are weak and atrophied and lack sensation. Other signs of neurodegeneration include spasm, abnormal tendon reflexes, and mood changes such as irritability, loss of memory, and depression. Strict vegetarians who have developed B$_{12}$ deficiency may manifest these neurological symptoms with little change in the blood chemistry or profile.

Vitamin B$_{12}$ deficiency is treated mainly with hydroxocobalamin via intravenous administration. Severe deficiency is managed with 50 to 100 μg three times a week until all abnormal blood and neurological manifestations have improved or disappeared. If the deficiency is due to malabsorption of B$_{12}$ (pernicious anemia from a lack of the intrinsic factor or a defective intestine), the patient may require administration of vitamin B$_{12}$ permanently, depending on the particular situation. If so, one management procedure is the parenteral administration of 50 to 100 μg of vitamin B$_{12}$ monthly or 1,000 μg every 2 or 3 months. As discussed earlier, the lack of intrinsic factor may be overcome by a massive oral dose of B$_{12}$ (for example, 1,000 times the normal intake), although few clinicians recommend this.

In most patients undergoing treatment for B$_{12}$ deficiency, the blood profile (red blood cell count, cell size, color index, and so on) becomes normal in about several months, whereas the patient shows external improvements in only a few days: feeling better, improved appetite, normal tongue appearance and sensation, and good mental condition. However, recovery of the nervous system, if damaged, may take a long period, although complete healing is likely if the

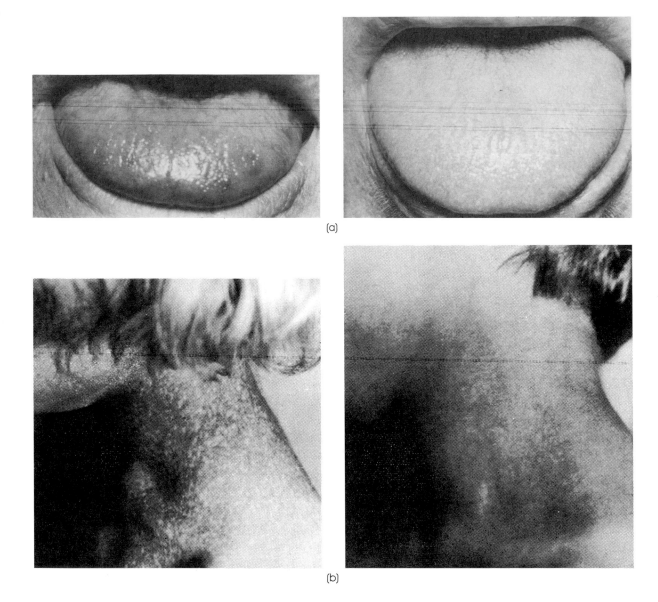

FIGURE 6-12 Some signs of vitamin B_{12} deficiency. (a) Vitamin B_{12} deficiency glossitis before (top) and after (bottom) treatment. (From S. Dreizen, *Geriatrics* 29 [1974]: 97. By permission of *Geriatrics*) (b) Left: skin before vitamin B_{12} replacement. Widespread mottled pigmentation simulated that in arsenical dermatosis. This change was most severe over back, lateral abdomen, groins, axillae, and flexor surface of the extremities. Right: striking resolution of pigmentary disturbance 14 months after vitamin B_{12} replacement. (From J. N. Gilliam and A. J. Cox, *Arch. Dermatol.* 107 [1973]: 231. Copyright 1973, American Medical Association.)

deficiency has not been prolonged. In some patients the healing process takes 1 year or more. Whatever the cause of B_{12} deficiency, it must be diagnosed early in order to prevent permanent damage to the nervous system.

Diagnosis of B_{12} deficiency is now a well-established, accurate procedure. It consists of a study of the dietary history, clinical manifestations, blood and urinary profile, and the Schilling test. The clinician looks for bone marrow megaloblastosis with macrocytic anemia (many large, nucleated red blood cells). The corpuscular volume is more than 100 to 160 μm³, with low white cell and platelet counts. Normally, one excretes about 3 mg of methylmalonic acid daily in the urine, while a patient with a B_{12} deficiency excretes about 5 mg. To confirm the presence of pernicious anemia, the Schilling test is performed. This complicated test is described in standard medical textbooks, books on laboratory medicine, and the references cited at the end of this book. The test is based on the principle that if the patient is given radioactive vitamin B_{12}, its absorption and excretion in urine and feces can be ascertained. Chapter 24 also briefly discusses the Schilling test.

Pantothenic Acid

Pantos is Greek for "everywhere," a fitting label for this vitamin, which is widely distributed in nature and known to be essential for animals, plants, bacteria, and yeast. Pantothenic acid was discovered in 1933, isolated in 1938, and synthesized in 1940. Although once termed *vitamin B_3*, it no longer carries this name. The acid is a pale yellow, oily liquid and can be crystallized in the form of calcium pantothenate, which is commercially available in nutritional supplements.

Functions

Pantothenic acid is very important for nutrient metabolism. In the body it combines with mercaptoethanol amine (a sulfur-containing substance) and phosphates to form *coenzyme A* (CoA), which is important in the metabolism of fat, protein, and carbohydrate. As discussed in Chapter 8, CoA participates in the citric acid cycle and permits the release of energy. Since CoA activity is concentrated within the cell, organs with

TABLE 6-29 Symptoms of Pantothenic Acid Deficiency in Animals

Animals	Symptoms
Chicks	Dermatitis around eyes, "spectacle eyes," lesion of thymus gland, spinal cord degeneration, fatty liver
Ducks	Anemia
Rats	Growth failure, whiskers covered with reddish pigment porphyrin, adrenal gland hemorrhage, graying of hair (in black rats)
Pigs	Changes in the sensory system

high metabolic activity—such as the liver, kidney, brain, heart, and adrenal gland—contain high levels of CoA. However, CoA is essential to all cells that require energy. Some specific functions of CoA are: (1) energy metabolism; (2) synthesis of fatty acid, cholesterol, steroids, porphyrin (a component of hemoglobin), and acetylcholine (important for body detoxification and transmission of nervous impulses); (3) formation and activation of antibodies; (4) metabolism of vitamins, amino acids, and sulfonamides; and (5) active transport of glucose through intestinal walls.

Deficiency

There are no documented cases of pantothenic acid deficiency from a natural cause. Experimental human subjects fed a pantothenic acid antagonist and a semisynthetic diet relatively free of the vitamin developed a combination of nonspecific symptoms, including fatigue, insomnia, nausea, intestinal disturbances, decreased resistance to infection (from decreased antibody formation), burning feet with tingling sensation and numbness, mood changes (mental depression), muscle cramps, loss of coordination, and upper respiratory infections. Immediately after World War II, some Americans released from Japanese prisons complained of the "electric foot syndrome" (burning feet with a tingling sensation and numbness), which was relieved by pantothenic acid. However, a cause-and-effect relationship was never established.

Table 6-29 describes the symptoms that ap-

TABLE 6-30 Pantothenic Acid Content of Representative Foods*

Food	Serving Size	Amount of Pantothenic Acid (mg)
Milk, whole, fluid	1 c	0.8
Cheese, pasteurized, processed, American	1 oz	0.1
Egg, whole, raw or cooked	1	0.9
Margarine	1 t	0
Beef, roast, chuck, braised	3 oz	trace
Salmon steak, broiled, 6" × 2"	1	1.9
Liver, beef, fried	3 oz	0.65
Dates, dried, pitted	10 dates	0.6
Watermelon, 1/16 of 2 lb melon with rind	1	1.2
Bread, whole wheat	1 sl	0.2
Cashews, roasted	1 oz	0.4
Peas, split, dry, cooked (1 oz dry)	1/2 c	0.6
Cake, angel food	1 sl	0.08
Pie, cream, pudding type with meringue	1 sl	1.4
Avocado, 4" long	1/2	1.1
Potato, baked, large	1	0.8
Pickle, dill, large	1	0.3
Yeast, brewer's, debittered	1 T	0.6

*These data have been obtained from the published results of a number of investigators.

pear in animals with pantothenic acid deficiency. These are much more specific than the symptoms observed in humans.

Requirements and sources

It is currently believed that the human body needs about 5 to 10 mg of pantothenic acid per day. We consume about 10 to 20 mg, of which about 30% to 50% consists of the free vitamin. Each day our body excretes in urine about 50% of the pantothenic acid ingested. Intestinal bacteria synthesize the vitamin, although how this contributes to body need is unknown.

The vitamin is widely distributed in nature, with the best food sources being organ meats (liver and kidney), fish, egg yolk, fresh vegetables, yeast, and wheat bran. Fair sources are lean beef, skim milk, sweet potatoes, and molasses. Table 6-30 shows the pantothenic acid content of some representative foods.

Since pantothenic acid is soluble in water, it can be leached from foods. Although stable in neutral solution, it is decomposed in acid or alkaline mediums. Pantothenic acid is stable to moist heat, and normal cooking temperatures cause only a slight loss of the vitamin. On the other hand, any dry-heat cooking or processing will cause a large loss. Canning of animal products is accompanied by a 15% to 35% loss of the vitamin, while 40% to 80% is lost when processing vegetable products. The milling of grain results in about a 50% loss of pantothenic acid.

Clinical usage

Large doses of pantothenic acid have been used to relieve the intestinal paralysis that follows surgery. Apparently, the vitamin stimulates gastrointestinal activity. If the postoperative condition is not treated, the patient suffers abdominal pain and gas accumulation. However, doses of 10 to 20 g of pantothenic acid can cause diarrhea.

Biotin

Biotin, a vitamin that occurs in many foods, is known to be essential for humans and other animal species. There are five different forms of this vitamin, which normally occurs as a white crystal. Biotin in food may be free or bound to a protein. The bound form, which occurs mainly in animal products, is fat soluble, while plants contain mainly the free form, which is water soluble. The vitamin was isolated in 1935 and synthesized in 1942.

Functions

In the human body, much biotin occurs as a coenzyme and plays a major role in adding a carbon unit to other chemicals (carbon dioxide fixation). As a coenzyme, it participates in many important biological reactions: oxidation of fatty acids and carbohydrates; deamination of aspartic acid, threonine, and serine; conversion of tryptophan to niacin; and phosphorylation of glucose.

Deficiency

Spontaneous deficiency of biotin is uncommon. However, biotin deficiency in humans has been experimentally induced by giving subjects either a low-biotin diet with 15% to 30% of raw, dried egg white as protein or a low-biotin diet with 30% of its calories from egg white (about 24 to 27 egg whites per day). This unusual diet induces biotin deficiency, for while egg yolks contain biotin, egg whites contain *avidin*. Avidin is a heat-sensitive glycoprotein that is a potent natural biotin antagonist. It can complex with biotin, which prevents the intestinal tract from absorbing the vitamin. Since heating during cooking destroys avidin, only raw egg white contains the active substance.

The so-called raw egg white injury refers to the lesions that develop in rats fed raw egg white. The animals develop eczemalike dermatitis, with hardened and scaly skins. When the skin lesions localize around the eyes, the animals appear to wear spectacles. The animals also lose hair from various parts of their bodies and develop muscular atrophy.

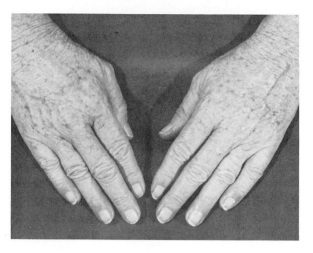

FIGURE 6-13 Shiny, dry, scaly dermatitis in a female patient with biotin deficiency induced by daily consumption of 6 raw eggs and 2 qt of skim milk for 18 months. The diet was prescribed to increase her protein intake. (From C. M. Baugh et al., *Amer. J. Clin. Nutr.* 21 [1968]: 173)

Although a normal human does not eat 24 to 27 egg whites in 1 day, a few cases of natural biotin deficiency have been documented. One boy with bulbar poliomyelitis was given 6 raw eggs a day via gastric tubing. After 18 months of treatment, he developed scaly dermatitis. A man with liver cirrhosis developed biotin-deficiency symptoms when given raw eggs. For personal reasons, another man was consuming six dozen raw egg whites per day with 4 quarts of red wine. He eventually developed severe dermatitis, which an injection of biotin methylester relieved. See Figure 6-13.

Symptoms of biotin deficiency are loss of appetite, nausea, muscle pain, depression, anemia, pallor, dermatitis, glossitis, raised blood cholesterol, abnormal sensation, increased skin sensitivity, and abnormal changes in EKG (electrocardiogram). The injection of 150 to 300 μg of biotin per day reverses these symptoms in 3 to 4 days.

Nutritional biotin deficiency also causes the seborrheic dermatitis of infants under 6 months old. A daily dose of 5 mg of biotin, given intramuscularly or intravenously, promptly relieves this condition.

Sources

Conventional mixed American diets contain about 100 to 300 μg of biotin, which is considered adequate for a healthy adult. In foods, biotin is normally associated with other B vitamins. The richest food sources of biotin are organ meats (liver and kidney), egg yolk, milk, and yeast. Fair sources are legumes, nuts, chocolate, and some vegetables (such as cauliflower). Other animal meats, dairy products, cereals, and some other vegetables are poor sources. Cow's milk contains about ten times more biotin than breast milk, and a woman's diet does not influence the level of biotin in her milk. Biotin is stable to heat used in cooking, processing, and storage, but unstable to alkali and oxidation and can be leached from food by water.

The intestinal synthesis of biotin by bacteria is believed to contribute to our daily need. Antibiotics such as sulfonamides and oxytetracycline, given to many hospitalized patients, can inhibit bacterial activity and reduce the availability of this vitamin, possibly causing human deficiency.

FAT-SOLUBLE VITAMINS

The remaining four substances classified as vitamins are known as vitamins A, D, E, and K. They are the currently known fat-soluble vitamins. As indicated in Table 6-1, they are similar in many aspects: solubility medium, body storage capacity, body disposal route, body absorption, urgency of dietary intake, rapidity of symptom appearance if deficient, and chemical constituents. However, these vitamins differ considerably in functions, sources, and other characteristics.

Vitamin A

Vitamin A was discovered in 1915, isolated in 1937, and synthesized in 1946. It exists in three main forms: *retinol* (vitamin A alcohol), *retinal* (vitamin A aldehyde), and *retinoic acid* (vitamin A acid). The first two forms are of equal biological activity and are found both in foods and body tissues. The third is a metabolite found chiefly in the body and has some biological activity. Retinol

TABLE 6-31 Conversion of β-Carotene to Vitamin A

	Initial Amount of β-Carotene	Expected Amount of Vitamin A Formed
Laboratory	2 units	4 units
Human intestinal mucosal walls	2 units	1 unit

and retinal are also called *preformed vitamin A* in foods. However, the vitamin can also be formed in the body from a group of precursors called *carotenes*. In foods, the preformed vitamin is found in animal products, while the precursor or provitamin A, carotene, is found in plant products.

Vitamin A is almost colorless or pale yellow and soluble in fat and other fat solvents. Although relatively stable, it is sensitive to ultraviolet light and destroyed by oxidation at high temperatures. Oxidation is responsible for the rancidity found in fats and oils, which can be prevented by antioxidants and/or refrigeration.

Food sources

The provitamin found in plants includes carotenes, which are also called carotenoid pigments because they are highly colored orange or yellow substances. Examples of such plant foods include carrots, peaches, sweet potatoes, and other yellow-colored vegetables and fruits. The green color of chlorophyll in most vegetables can disguise the orange-yellow color of carotene, although chlorophyll itself does not contain any vitamin A activity.

The pigments in plants include α-carotene, β-carotene, γ-carotene, and cryptoxanthine. Beta-carotene is the active precursor of vitamin A. Table 6-31 shows that the conversion of β-carotene to vitamin A in the body is less efficient than in the laboratory. About 25% to 35% of ingested carotene is converted to vitamin A, with half of that in leafy vegetables and one-fifth of that in carrots and similar root vegetables being converted. Any ingested carotene that is not con-

TABLE 6-32   Approximate Contribution of Vitamin A to the American Diet by Different Categories of Foods

Food Group	% of Daily Vitamin A Intake
Fruits, vegetables	50–55
Meat, poultry, fish, eggs	25–30
Dairy products	10–15
Fats, oils	5–10

TABLE 6-33   Vitamin A Content of Different Types of Liver

Liver Type*	IU Vitamin A	μg RE†
Calf	1,900	576
Beef	45,450	13,773
Pork	12,000	3,637
Lamb	43,000	1,303
Chicken	27,000	8,182

*90-g (3-oz) portion.
†Retinol equivalent.

verted is partially absorbed into the circulatory system, with the remaining excreted in the stool. Carotene is stored in the adrenal glands and fat.

Vitamin A in food or nutrient supplements occurs as retinyl palmitate (the salt of retinol). It is digested by pancreatic enzymes, which release the retinol for absorption by the mucosal cells. Within the mucosal walls, retinol is esterified mainly to palmitate, which becomes part of the chylomicron system (see Chapters 8 and 27) and enters the circulation via the lymphatic system and thoracic duct. After release from the chylomicrons, much of the vitamin A is stored in the liver.

Preformed vitamin A is found in organs (kidney and liver), egg yolk, and butter cream. The provitamin A is found in green and yellow vegetables and fruits, such as sweet potatoes, squash, carrots, apricots, cabbage, broccoli, spinach, collard, and other dark green vegetables. The presently accepted system of units for measuring vitamin A and carotene is as follows:

$$1 \text{ retinol equivalent (RE)} = 1 \ \mu g \text{ retinol}$$
$$= 6 \ \mu g \ \beta\text{-carotene}$$
$$= 12 \ \mu g \text{ other provitamin A carotenoids}$$
$$= 3.33 \text{ IU* vitamin activity from retinol}$$
$$= 10 \text{ IU vitamin A activity from } \beta\text{-carotene}$$

*IU = international unit

Table 6-32 lists the approximate contribution of vitamin A to the American diet by different categories of food. Table 6-33 shows the vitamin A content of different types of liver, and Table 6-34 the vitamin A content of some representative foods. Refer to the appendix for more data.

Functions

It is now believed that vitamin A has five important functions. It is essential for forming *rhodopsin*, which is responsible for night vision, and for bone growth and nervous system development. Although the process is not yet clear, vitamin A is closely associated with cell membrane metabolism and structure. In animals, vitamin A is also essential for reproduction.

Deficiency

Vitamin A deficiency is uncommon in Western countries for two reasons: dietary abundance and ample body storage. As indicated in Table 6-35 (the 1980 RDA for vitamin A), adults need about 3,000 IU of the vitamin, whereas the normal adult stores about 500,000 IU in the liver. This amount can last the person for years without an external supply, and body storage must be depleted before deficiency symptoms appear. However, vitamin A deficiency affecting the eyes is common in many underdeveloped areas of the world, such as Central and South America, parts of India, Southeast Asia, and Africa. It is the major cause of blindness in some of these areas, especially in the young who suffer protein-calorie malnutrition.

In Western societies, vitamin A deficiency re-

TABLE 6-34 Vitamin A Content of Representative Foods*

Food	Serving Size	Amount of Vitamin A (IU)
Milk, whole, fluid, 3.3% fat	1 c	310
Cottage cheese, creamed, low fat	1 c	80
Egg, whole, raw	1	300
Butter	1 T	430
Chocolate, milk, plain	1 oz	80
Sugar, brown, pressed down	1 c	none
Bread, white, enriched	1 sl	trace
Bran flakes (40% bran)	1 c	1,650
Cornmeal, yellow, degermed, enriched	1 c	610
Shad, baked with butter, bacon, or margarine	3 oz	30
Liver, beef, fried	3 oz	45,390
Beef, roast, with some visible fat	3 oz	10
Chicken, drumstick, fried, bones removed	1.3 oz	50
Apricots, canned in heavy syrup	1 c	4,490
Cherries, sour, red, pitted, canned in water	1 c	1,660
Beet greens, leaves and stems, cooked, drained	1 c	7,400
Carrots	1 c	23,250
Tomato, raw	1	1,110
Beans, navy, dry, cooked, drained	1 c	none
Lentils, whole, cooked	1 c	40
Walnuts, black, chopped kernels	1 c	380
Barbeque sauce	1 c	900
Olives, pickled, canned, green, medium-sized	4	40

*Adapted from *Nutritive Value of Foods*, Home and Garden Bulletin No. 72 (Washington, D.C.: U.S. Department of Agriculture, 1981).

sults mainly from a low-fat diet, fat malabsorption (steatorrhea), lack of bile salts and pancreatic juice, jaundice and other gall bladder diseases, intestinal mucosal damage or disorders, and increased loss or utilization of the vitamin. Another cause of deficiency is when carotene is not converted to vitamin A in the intestinal walls. Mineral oil used in low-calorie salad dressings causes some loss of fat-soluble nutrients, including vitamin A, since mineral oil is not digested. Clinical observations have also associated vitamin A deficiency with disorders such as liver cirrhosis, kidney malfunction, tuberculosis, pneumonia, urinary tract infection, cancer, and infection, most of which cause an increased excretion of the vitamin. In diabetic patients, any vitamin A deficiency may be due to a reduced conversion of carotene to the vitamin.

Vitamin A deficiency in animals can retard growth and cause abnormal bones and teeth. These symptoms have been reported in a small number of children suffering vitamin A deficiency. Also, some children have been reported to lose the senses of taste and smell. The subsequent loss of appetite and reduction of food intake in these children may lead to arrested growth. But the symptoms of classic vitamin A deficiency involve the eyes and epithelia.

Eye symptoms. A patient suffering vitamin A deficiency shows a sequence of changes in the eyes. The duration and severity of symptoms vary with the extent of the deficiency. These changes are summarized below.

1. *Night blindness (nyctalopia).* When the supply of vitamin A to the eyes decreases, the availability of rhodopsin—which is important for

TABLE 6-35 1980 RDA for Vitamin A for Different Age Groups and During Pregnancy and Lactation

Population Group	Vitamin A RDA	
	μg RE	IU
Infants		
0– 6 months	420	1,390
6–12 months	400	1,320
Children		
1– 3 years	400	1,320
7–10 years	700	2,310
Males (11+ years)	1,000	3,300
Females (11+ years)	800	2,640
Pregnancy	+200	+660
Lactation	+400	+1,320

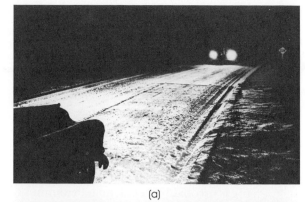

(a)

(b)

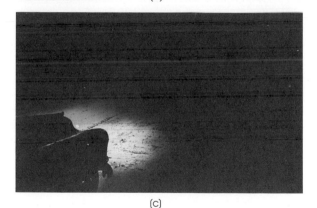

(c)

FIGURE 6-14 Night blindness caused by vitamin A deficiency. (Courtesy of the Upjohn Company) Night blindness is a useful and early diagnostic sign of vitamin A deficiency. This loss of visual acuity in dim light following exposure to bright light is illustrated here. Both the normal individual and the vitamin-A-deficient subject see the headlights of an approaching car as shown in (a). After the car has passed, the normal individual sees a wide stretch of road, as it appears in (b). The vitamin-A-deficient subject, whose view of the road is shown in (c), can barely see a few feet ahead and cannot see the road sign at all.

vision in dim light—declines, and the patient develops night blindness. The classic test is the inability to adapt to dim light when entering a dark theater or room from a lighted area. Another classic test is the inability to adapt to darkness after being temporarily blinded by the headlights of an oncoming car (see Figure 6-14). However, clinicians have experienced difficulty in detecting night blindness in infants and children of poor countries that have a high incidence of vitamin A deficiency. The usual warning signal is that the child is unable to feed himself or stumbles when the light is dim. Night blindness is easily reversed if vitamin A is administered; however, after a prolonged deficiency, structural changes of the retina may occur.

2. *Dryness of the conjunctiva (xerosis).* The conjunctiva begins to lose its luster, with dryness occurring at the thickened and wrinkled corners of the eye. The transparent structure becomes opaque because of the presence of fine, milky droplets, and the white of the eye becomes muddy and greasy. Eventually the skin around the eyes becomes thin and dry, while that between the lashes is scaly. If this condition is severe, the result is xerophthalmia (Figure 6-15).

3. *Bitot's spots.* Bitot's spots are triangular collections of peeling epithelial cells that appear on the lateral side of the equatorial region of the eye. The patch looks like a rugged area the color of aluminum paint, surrounded by smooth terrain (see Figure 6-15b, c). If these spots appear, the person is probably deficient in vitamin A. However, some clinicians question whether vitamin A deficiency can produce this lesion.

4. *Dryness of the cornea (xerosis).* As the disease progresses, the cornea is involved and becomes insensitive to touch. It becomes dry, rough, hazy, dull, and unable to reflect light. The tear ducts become blocked and the lachrymal glands unable to secrete tears.

5. *Keratomalacia.* The term *keratomalacia* refers to the softening and necrosis of the cornea. As the disease progresses, the cornea erodes, and the iris collapses and is expelled. In children, the lesion causes them to avoid light. This stage is followed by inflammation, ulceration, and perforation of the cornea with exodus of pus and hemorrhaging of the eyes. There may be a thick scar preventing the entrance of light. The patient becomes seriously ill, with fever and grossly inflamed eyes.

6. *Blindness.* Total blindness in one or both eyes may ultimately result if treatment is not administered before the advanced stage. Figures 6-15 and 6-16 show the classical eye lesions of vitamin A deficiency.

Epithelial degeneration. In addition to pathological conditions in the eyes, vitamin A deficiency causes problems in the *epithelial cells*, which form the covering of most internal surfaces and organs as well as the outer surface of the body. Vitamin A ensures the proper functioning of these cells. In its absence, the epithelial tissues show horny degeneration called *keratinization*, which shows up in the skin and mucous-membrane-lined tracts. The skin becomes dry, rough, and crackled. The base of the hair follicles thickens (folliculosis), resulting in "toad skin," especially on the buttocks and shoulders of children. There may be hypertrophy of the horny layer of the skin, especially around the eyes. For most patients, vitamin A relieves the symptoms. Vegetable oils (with polyunsaturated fatty acids) without vitamin A also benefit some patients. The skin lesions are most likely a result of combined deficiencies of vitamin A, linoleic acid, ascorbic acid, and other nutrients. Figure 6-17 shows the classic signs of skin lesions during vitamin A deficiency.

In addition to skin symptoms, the mucous membranes lining the respiratory, gastrointestinal, and genitourinary tracts are damaged by vitamin A deficiency. Many cilia are lost, and the cells do not make their normal secretions. The person becomes susceptible to respiratory infections, such as sinus trouble and sore throat. Along the gastrointestinal tract, diarrhea and

FIGURE 6-15   (a) Conjunctival xerosis in a 4-year-old child. (Courtesy of the World Health Organization and Dr. D. S. McLaren) (b) Bitot's spot in a 2-year-old child. (Courtesy of the World Health Organization and Dr. D. S. McLaren) (c) Bitot's spot with conjunctival xerosis. (Courtesy of the World Health Organization and Dr. A. Sommer) (d) Conjunctival and corneal xerosis. (Courtesy of the World Health Organization and Dr. A. Sommer) (e) Corneal ulceration with xerosis. (Courtesy of the World Health Organization and Dr. A. Sommer) (f) Keratomalacia. (Courtesy of the World Health Organization and Dr. D. S. McLaren) (From *Control of Vitamin A Xerophthalmia* [Geneva: World Health Organization, 1982])

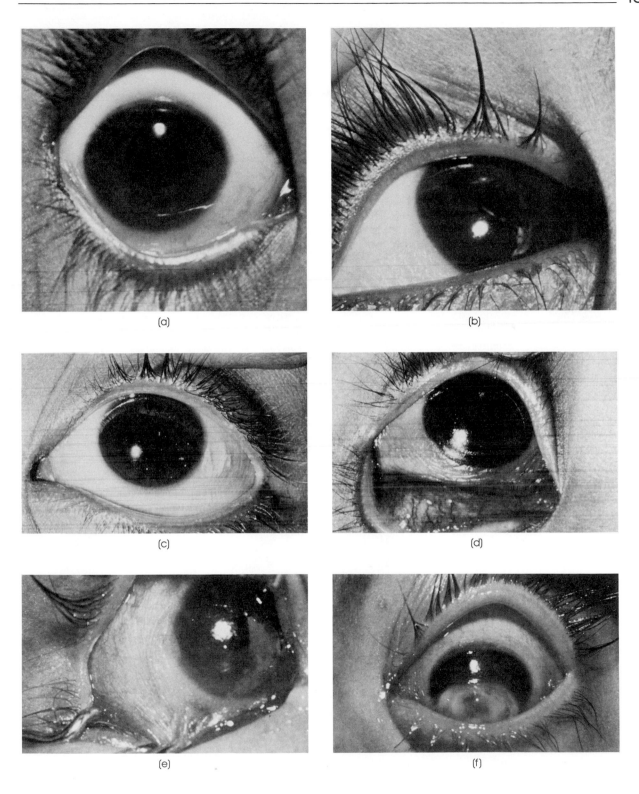

(a)

(b)

(c)

(d)

(e)

(f)

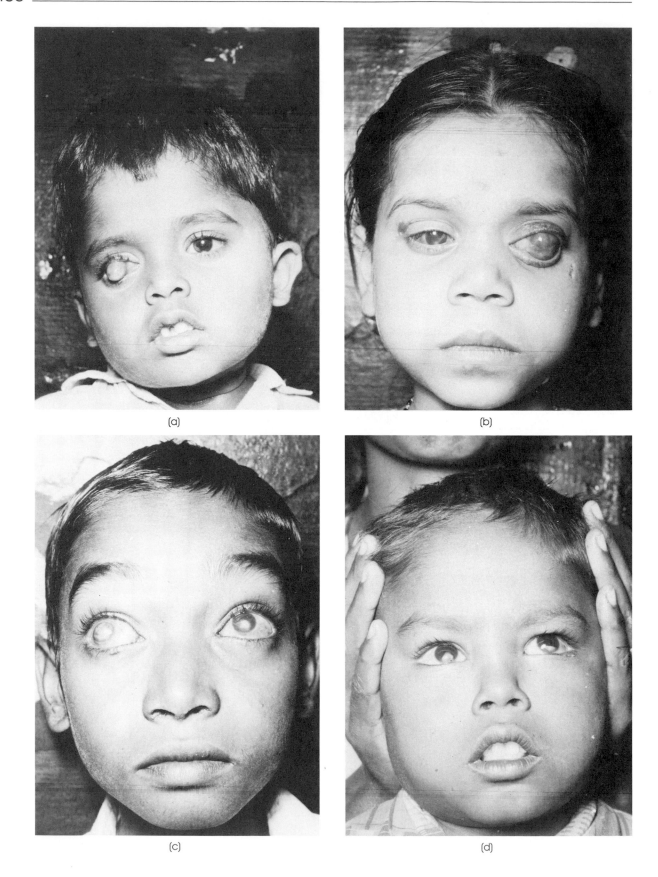

(a)

(b)

(c)

(d)

malabsorption may occur. There may be pain in urination, and infection of the genitourinary tract is likely.

Diagnosis and treatment. The earliest and easiest way to diagnose vitamin A deficiency is the dark-adaptation technique, although it is difficult to conduct with children. At present there is no foolproof biochemical test for vitamin A deficiency, but blood tests give some clues. The normal level of vitamin A in the blood is about 30 to 50 μg per 100 mL. If the level drops below 10 μg per 100 mL, the person is probably deficient. Experimental studies indicate that an increase in dietary protein consumption may produce a normal vitamin A level, while a decrease in protein will lower the blood level of vitamin A to under 10 μg per 100 mL. Another test involves the amount of carotene in the blood. The normal blood carotene level is about 50 to 150 μg per 100 mL. Since it usually takes 3 to 7 hours for an ingested dose of carotene to appear as vitamin A in the blood, blood carotene reflects the amount recently ingested and is unrelated to vitamin A storage and/or nutriture. However, this test does indicate whether the patient has eaten any carotene-rich vegetables lately.

An oral dose of 30,000 IU remedies a mild deficiency of vitamin A. In cases of severe xerophthalmia or keratomalacia, large doses of vitamin A are needed. The management procedure for children is shown in Table 6-36. If the patient has fat malabsorption, water-miscible preparations may be used. Supportive therapy includes antibiotics and a nutritious diet high in calories, protein, and vitamin A activity.

Toxicity

Large doses of vitamin A have produced toxic side effects in numerous documented cases. The general characteristics of poisoning are shown in Table 6-37.

The higher the dose, the more rapid the onset of toxicity. For adults, it is suspected that

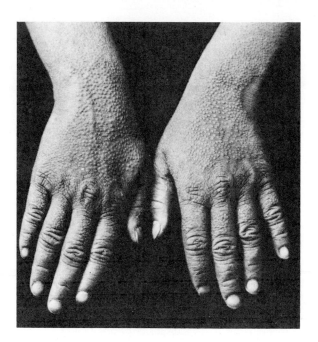

FIGURE 6-17   Classic skin lesions of follicular hyperkeratosis due to vitamin A deficiency, which resembles gooseflesh but can be distinguished from it because it does not disappear when the skin is rubbed. (From S. Dreizen, *Geriatrics* 29 [1974]: 97. By permission of *Geriatrics*)

eating more than 20,000 IU of vitamin A per day for 1 or 2 months is hazardous. Some clinicians suggest that 10 to 40 times the RDA per day for 5 to 20 months will have toxic effects. However, there are documented cases of acute toxicity precipitated by a single dose 200 times the RDA, that is, 1,000,000 IU.

Some of the earliest documented cases of vitamin A poisoning involved the accidental ingestion of the livers of large animals such as polar bears and seals. For example, just 1 oz (28 g) of polar bear liver contains 600,000 IU vitamin A.

Immediately after World War II, vitamin A poisonings increased among infants and children in the United States. The cause was even-

FIGURE 6-16   (a, b, c) Blindness in one eye due to keratomalacia. (d) Partial blindness in both eyes due to keratomalacia. (From G. Venkataswamy, *Israel J. Med. Sci.* 8 [1972]: 1190)

TABLE 6-36 Vitamin A Therapy for Children with Xerophthalmia and Keratomalacia

Day	Vitamin A Source	Dose of Vitamin A*	Route
1	Palmitate (aqueous dispersible vitamin A)	100,300 IU (= 30,000 μg retinol)	Parenteral
2–6	Same as above	50,000 IU	Oral, twice daily
7 and on	Cod liver oil	10,000 IU*	Oral, once daily

*30 ml oil gives 25,000 IU vitamin A or 7,500 μg retinol.

TABLE 6-37 Characteristics of Vitamin A Toxicity

Population Group	Documented Harmful Doses	Clinical Manifestations
Infants under 6 months old	18,500–25,000 IU/day for 1–3 months.	Scaly dermatitis, weight loss, anorexia, bone pain, bulging head, hydrocephalus, increased intracranial pressure, hyperirritability.
Adults and children	25,000–1,000,000 IU per day or per dose. If under 50,000 IU, poisoning takes effect in a few months. The effect of 1,000,000 IU may be instantaneous.	Sweating, headache, fatigue, anemia, drowsiness, nausea, loss of hair, dry skin, diarrhea, itchiness, rash, irritability, neurological signs, and enlargement of spleen and liver. Mild fever, tender long bones, periosteal elevation shown under X-rays, with calcium deposition. There are also changes in the long bones as seen by X-rays. Fingernails may be brittle. In girls and women, there may be cessation of menstruation with abnormal blood chemistry, e.g., decreased hemoglobin and RBC potassium.

tually traced to overzealous mothers who gave their children vitamin A supplements (cod liver oil) in addition to the vitamin they ingested in foods.

A third cause of vitamin A poisonings can be traced to the belief that large doses of vitamin A can cure skin problems such as acne. During the past 30 years, self-prescription for treatment has resulted in many cases of poisoning.

Fourth, many individuals have been led to believe that consuming large amounts of vitamins daily, including A, will improve health. A number of documented cases of vitamin A poisoning have stemmed from this belief. This accidental poisoning is especially dangerous among the elderly, since their age intensifies the ill effect. At present, it is also believed that consuming a large amount of the vitamin during pregnancy can harm the unborn, although there is some controversy about this.

The only therapy for vitamin A poisoning is to stop taking the vitamin, either through vitamin A–rich foods or tablets. The symptoms are reversed within 72 hours unless the poisoning is severe.

All the above poisonings are caused by preformed vitamin A and not carotene. However, excessive carotene ingestion can cause some unique problems. Hypercarotenemia refers to a high blood carotene level of 250 μg per 100 mL, versus a norm of 90. When this occurs, the person develops yellow or orange skin discoloration, especially in the groin and on the soles, palms, forehead, and base of the nose, since the carotenoids are secreted in sweat and sebum. The signs do not indicate jaundice, since the buccal

(a)

(b)

FIGURE 6-18 Prevention of vitamin A deficiency. (a) Youngster in the town of Bogra, Bangladesh, receives a high-potency vitamin A capsule to help prevent blindness. (Courtesy UNICEF, photo by Steiner) (b) A village health worker in Kijia distributes vitamin A capsules to a mother for her child. (Courtesy UNICEF, photo by Horst Max Cerni)

mucosa is not affected. The usual cause of this condition is an excessive consumption of green leafy and yellow vegetables, carrot juice, citrus fruits, and tomatoes, although the symptoms can be caused by a disturbed carotenoid metabolism due to diabetes, hypothyroidism, or hyperlipidemia.

Clinical usage

The claim that vitamin A can cure acne is not justified. However, recent research has indicated that the related chemical retinoic acid (vitamin A acid) can exert a beneficial effect on certain skin problems such as acne, lichen planus, psoriasis, keratoderma, and a certain type of skin cancer. However, retinoic acid is a drug and requires a prescription. Furthermore, its usage requires careful consideration of factors such as dosage, route of administration, duration of treatment, responses at different treatment stages, and concomitant use of other chemicals.

Vitamin D

Vitamin D is fat soluble and very stable. It exists in two main forms in food: vitamin D_3, or *cholecalciferol* (found in animal products), and vitamin D_2, or *ergosterol* (from plant products). Popularly known as the "sunshine vitamin," vitamin D was discovered in 1918, isolated in 1930, and synthesized in 1936. Rickets, the disease that results from D deficiency, has been known for more than 60 years, but only part of the mechanism has been deduced in the last 20 years.

Synthesis, activation, and absorption

With the help of sunlight, the body can transform an ordinary body precursor (metabolite) into vitamin D_3. Because of this characteristic, some scientists have suggested that the substance should be treated as a hormone instead of a vitamin. In food fortification and nutrient supplements, vitamin D is obtained from irradiation of the appropriate precursors. However, ingested vitamin D_2 or D_3 has to be activated to be of use in the body. At present, "active" vitamin D has been synthesized for special clinical investigations and is not available for prescription or nonprescription purposes.

The body process of synthesis and activation of vitamin D is shown in Figure 6-19, in which the active vitamin is represented by 1,25-DHCC. In the presence of sunlight, the body manufactures vitamin D from its precursor under the skin. In this unique biological phenomenon, vitamin D_3 (cholecalciferol) is produced from 7-dehydrocholesterol. The transformation is made possible by light of 275 to 300 nm wavelength. These are the ultraviolet (UV) rays from the sun or mercury vapor sunlamp.

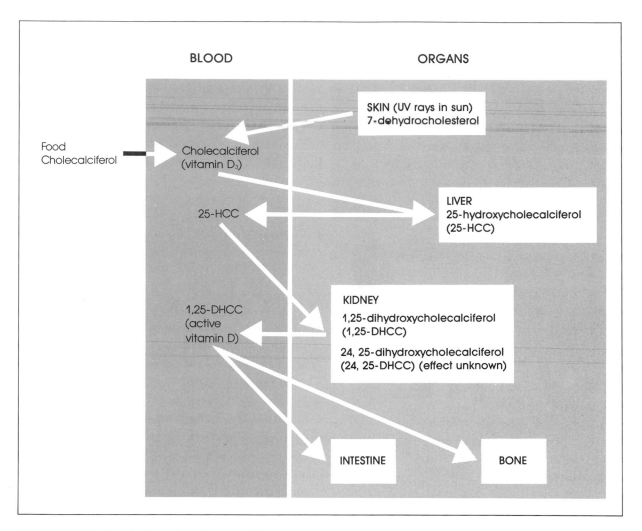

BLOOD   ORGANS

SKIN (UV rays in sun)
7-dehydrocholesterol

Food
Cholecalciferol   Cholecalciferol
                         (vitamin D₃)

                                         LIVER
25-HCC   25-hydroxycholecalciferol
                                         (25-HCC)

                                         KIDNEY
1,25-DHCC   1,25-dihydroxycholecalciferol
(active   (1,25-DHCC)
vitamin D)
                                         24, 25-dihydroxycholecalciferol
                                         (24, 25-DHCC) (effect unknown)

                         INTESTINE   BONE

FIGURE 6-19   Synthesis and activation of vitamin D.

UV rays are unable to penetrate skin pigments, regular glass, clouds, smoke, smog, or textiles. Accordingly, black people cannot make vitamin D in the presence of sunlight, unlike individuals with fair skin. Dark-skinned individuals, especially infants living in areas with little sunlight, therefore require additional amounts of vitamin D. Premature infants or infants confined to a hospital for a long period also have a high risk of rickets. One remedy still practiced by many hospitals around the world is to use mercury-quartz glass in nursery windows to permit UV light to enter. Some clinicians object to this practice because of the uncertainty of the presence of sunlight and the cost of the special glass versus the cheap, dependable administration of a chemical vitamin D supplement.

Vitamin D is absorbed mainly in the duodenum and jejunum, and the absorption is facilitated by the presence of fat and bile salts. The substance is absorbed together with chylomicrons and eventually transported via the lymphatic system to the blood. The absorption of this vitamin is severely handicapped by steatorrhea or gall bladder disease. The vitamin is excreted in the stools via the enterohepatic system (see Chapters 8 and 25).

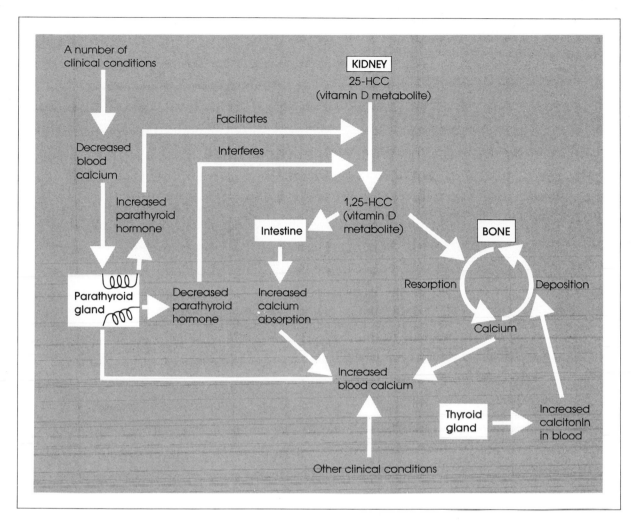

FIGURE 6-20   Vitamin D and calcium metabolism. (This figure must be studied with Figure 6-19.)

Functions and requirements

The main function of vitamin D is to regulate the calcification of bones by increasing the intestinal absorption of calcium and its deposition in bone, as shown in Figure 6-20. Note that the role of phosphorus is the same as that of calcium. Vitamin D permits 30% to 35% absorption of ingested calcium; in its absence, only 10% is absorbed.

At present, 1 IU of vitamin D is defined as the activity contained in 0.025 μg of cholecalciferol (vitamin D_3). Table 6-38 shows the 1980 RDA for vitamin D for different age groups.

Food sources

In general, only animal products—milk, eggs, butter, and cod liver oil—are acceptable food sources of vitamin D. Most other foods, especially plant products, have very little of the vitamin. However, even vitamin-D-rich foods do not provide more than 100 to 150 IU per day in a mixed American diet. This makes fortification of foods, especially milk, an essential process. In commercial homogenized and pasteurized milk, 400 IU of vitamin D are added per quart. Non-homogenized milk is generally not fortified, since most fat-soluble nutrients will accumulate

TABLE 6-38 1980 RDA for Vitamin D for Different Age Groups and During Pregnancy and Lactation

Population Group	Vitamin D RDA	
	μg	IU
Infants, children, adolescents (under 18 years old)	10	400
Adults		
19–22 years	7.5	300
23+ years	5	250
Pregnancy	+5	+250
Lactation	+5	+250

in the top cream layers. At present, the widespread addition of the vitamin to a variety of foods makes it difficult to estimate our actual vitamin D intake.

For a number of years, cod liver oil was a popular vitamin D supplement, especially for infants and children. In many European countries, this oily supplement is still in vogue, although mothers in the United States can now obtain water-soluble (miscible and dispersible) preparations. Thus the oily supplement—which has many drawbacks, such as possibly causing lipid pneumonia in infants, soiling clothes, and having a disagreeable odor—can be avoided.

The content of vitamin D in cod liver oil is about 340 IU per teaspoon or 85 IU/g. The commercial preparation Viosterol contains irradiated ergocalciferol. The potential adverse interaction between vitamin D and salts makes it inadvisable to add minerals to the vitamin preparation. Pediatricians in this country may recommend oral vitamin D supplements for infants and children, although many European physicians administer an intravenous dose of 200,000 to 300,000 IU every 1 to 3 months instead.

Deficiency

Vitamin D deficiency can cause *rickets*. The disease was once common throughout the world, mainly among infants and children, but it is now confined to underdeveloped countries. At present, rickets is prevented by various public health measures in the United States.

Epidemiology. A newborn child may suffer rickets because the mother failed to eat an adequate amount of vitamin D and calcium or suffered other conditions that interfere with calcium absorption. In many parts of the world, acute rickets at birth is endemic. In these countries, some infants not born with rickets may be predisposed to the disease later because of an imbalanced diet. In Africa, about 40% to 60% of children have some form of rickets, with about 3% to 20% having severe cases.

If the mother is in normal health, a breast-fed infant exposed to a nominal amount of sunlight will not suffer rickets, since breast milk contains a water-soluble analogue of vitamin D. However, if the child does not get enough sunlight—as may happen during bed confinement or cold weather—a vitamin supplement is needed. Most of the homogenized milk on the market has been fortified with 400 IU vitamin D per quart. Since an infant needs only 100 to 150 IU per day, a bottle-fed infant 2 to 3 months old receives more than adequate vitamin D from drinking a quart of milk each day. If a baby needs a supplement, it is usually given 400 IU per day, but the total intake of the vitamin must be considered.

Adult deficiency of vitamin D is uncommon. If a person is not exposed to much sunlight, vitamin D intake should be evaluated. Women in certain cultures suffer vitamin D deficiency because their apparel excludes sunlight; the situation is serious if the woman is pregnant.

There are other potential and documented cases of vitamin D deficiency. For one, a large reduction in fat intake decreases absorption of the vitamin. Second, some strict vegetarians risk vitamin D deficiency (see Chapter 18). Third, premature infants and elderly people are vulnerable to vitamin D deficiency because they are exposed to minimal sunlight and consume little of the vitamin. Fourth, a number of clinical stresses are known to produce adult vitamin D and calcium deficiency with the classic symptoms of osteomalacia and osteoporosis, a condition frequently called "secondary vitamin D deficiency." For example, there may be intestinal malabsorption of the vitamin from a lack of bile salts (gall bladder disease), stomach bypass surgery, obstructive jaundice, or alcoholism. Liver or kidney failure decreases "activation" of vitamin D. An inborn error of metabolism may decrease vitamin D formation or lead to vitamin D–dependent rickets. And anticonvulsants may lead to an increased vitamin D requirement.

Symptoms and treatment. Rickets is the term applied to all the clinical symptoms identified in an infant suffering from vitamin D (and thus calcium) deficiency. The early symptoms of rickets include a drop in serum-ionized calcium (hypocalcemia) characterized by tetany (see later discussion) and convulsion. The mineralization of bone is reduced, leading to eventual skeletal deformities and growth retardation. Sometimes the hypocalcemia is asymptomatic, although classic symptoms usually appear between 3 and 6 months of age.

The child shows progressive bone deformities as a result of weak bones and uneven stresses placed upon the growing bones. Part of the skull bone is soft. The parietal and frontal areas of the skull thicken and enlarge, causing "bossing" of the skull. The costochondral junctions of the ribs swell, forming the "rachitic rosary." A dip—called Harrison's groove—is formed by the retraction of the attachment between diaphragm and rib cage. The ends of growing long bones, such as those near the wrists and ankles, swell from the uneven development of calcification. Bowleggedness or knock-knee result from bending and twisting of the long bones, leading to a waddling gait. In advanced rickets, pigeon chest results from pulling in of the costal cartilages and protrusion of the sternum. Teeth erupt late and have defective enamel.

Crawling, standing, and walking all contribute to various deformities of the pelvic bones, which can pose a future reproductive problem for the female victim. Sitting may cause curvature of the spine in the child. Abnormal bone structures are easily identified by roentgenograms. Figure 6-21 shows the classic symptoms of rickets.

Infantile rickets is treated with 1,200 IU of vitamin D per day. Healing is evident in the X-ray after 3 weeks of therapy. If the rickets is severe, a safe regimen is 5,000 IU of vitamin D per day for 5 to 6 weeks. All therapies are maintained until satisfactory improvements are reached. Clinicians use the filling of bone ends as an index of healing. The regimen is then reduced to 400 IU vitamin per day.

The main form of adult rickets is *osteomalacia*, which is characterized by bone softening because of impaired mineralization. In the United States, osteomalacia due to vitamin D deficiency alone is rare. The usual cause of this disease is chronic steatorrhea, which results in a loss of vitamin D and insoluble calcium salts in the stool. A pregnant or nursing mother may suffer loss of calcium salts if her intestinal absorption system is defective. See Figure 6.21.

A patient with osteomalacia suffers pain in the legs and small of the back, most severely while walking or standing. The bones are soft and compressed with microfractures; they fail to mineralize during remodeling. The defects of bone structure occur at the sites of muscle attachment. The patient complains about muscular weakness, and bones of the ribs, thighs, and hips are highly sensitive to applied pressure. If osteomalacia is severe, bones may be bent and the patient walks with a waddling gait. Decalcification is evident in a roentgenogram. The patient may also suffer tetany. For patients with osteomalacia, treatments include 5,000 to 20,000 IU or more of vitamin D per day, plus calcium from milk, calcium gluconate, or calcium lactate (5 g per dose, dissolved in water, three times a day).

Tetany sometimes accompanies vitamin D deficiency, both in infants and adults. The nervous system is affected, with hyperirritability characterized by carpopedal spasm and convulsion, and occasionally laryngospasm. The patient demonstrates positive Chvostek's sign and Trousseau's phenomenon. The blood bound (to protein) calcium is normal in a patient with tetany, while there are 3 to 4 mg of Ca^{++} per 100 mL blood and 7 to 8 mg total calcium/100 mL blood. Acute tetany is treated by injecting calcium salt, such as about 10 to 20 mL of calcium gluconate in 10% solution (1 g of calcium gluconate provides about 90 mg of calcium). After the acute symptoms have subsided, vitamin D and/or

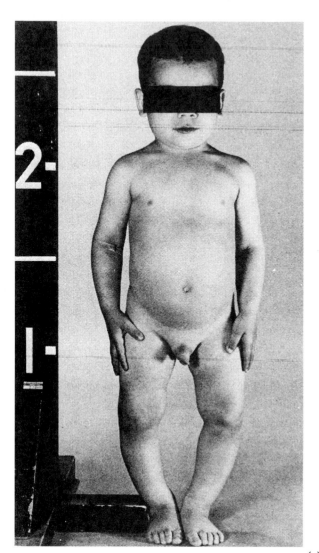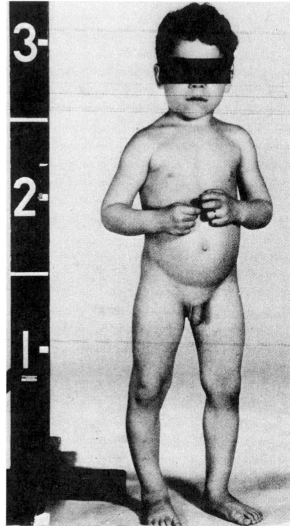

(a)

FIGURE 6-21   Classic signs of rickets. (a) Left: bowlegs in a 2½-year-old child with rickets. Right: normal bone development at 4½ years of age after treatment with vitamin D and phosphate. (Courtesy of Dr. C. R. Scriver. Reproduced with permission of *Nutrition Today* magazine, P.O. Box 1829, Annapolis, Maryland 21404 © September/October 1974) (b) A 42-year-old patient with osteomalacia (adult rickets). For many years she did not drink milk or have other adequate sources of calcium, phosphorus, and vitamin D. She had had no sunlight for 4 years before treatment. Over 5 years before treatment, her body weight fell from 140 to 110 lb and her height from 5′1″ to 4′6″. She could not stand. Most muscles were weak, but she was able to perform basic personal-care tasks. The bony skeleton was uniformly tender. She suffered from a metabolic bone disease affecting the whole skeleton. The condition was treated with vitamin D_2 and adequate dietary calcium and phosphorus. The patient recovered completely. (Courtesy of Dr. J. H. Bland and reprinted with permission of Cliggott Publishing Co., *Consultant*, vol. 16, no. 9, September 1976) (c) Left: typical enamel hypoplasia in the permanent dentition of a child with hereditary vitamin-D-dependency rickets. Hypoplasia is severe and circumferential and is present as two nar-

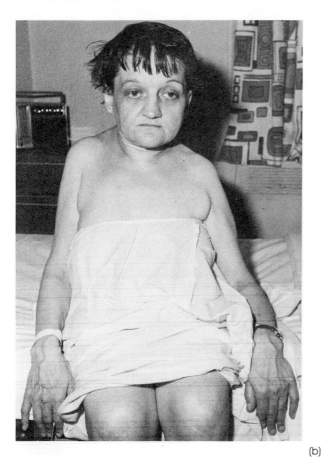

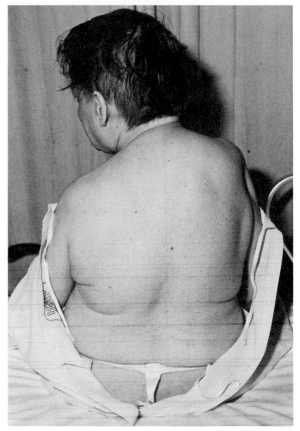

(b)

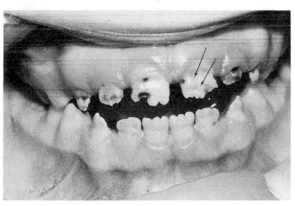

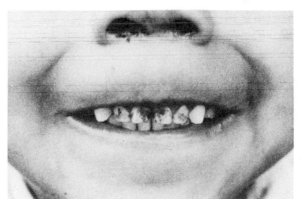

(c)

FIGURE 6-21   (continued)

row hypoplastic bands (see arrows) and some pitted areas. The incisal hypoplastic area denotes injury to the ameloblast during the latter part of the first
year of life; the gingival hypoplastic area denotes injury during the second
year of life. The intervening normal tissue was formed during a period of
effective treatment and normal plasma chemistry, after which treatment
lapsed and hypocalcemia recurred. Right: linear enamel hypoplasia in the
primary teeth of a child from Guatemala. One contributing cause is vitamin
D deficiency. (From G. Nikiforuk and D. Fraser, "The Etiology of Enamel
Hypoplasia: A Unifying Concept," *J. Pediatr.* 98 [1981]: 888)

TABLE 6-39   Doses and Duration for Vitamin D Intoxication

Population Group	Dose and Duration for Intoxication	Remarks
Adults	100,000 IU vitamin D for weeks or months	——
Infants	10,000–30,000 IU vitamin D per day	Some infants show hypersensitivity to vitamin D at low doses of 1,000 IU/day.
Children	2,500–60,000 IU/day for 1–4 months	Some cases of poisoning: 10,000 IU/day for 4 months to 200,000 IU/day for 2 weeks.

calcium are provided to manage the rickets or osteomalacia.

For information on osteoporosis, another bone disease associated partially with vitamin D and calcium metabolism, see the references at the end of this book and the discussion in Chapter 7.

Toxicity

Like vitamin A, vitamin D can cause intoxication if taken in large amounts. Table 6-39 lists the range of toxic doses.

The symptoms of poisoning are fairly specific. Among infants and children, the clinical manifestations of vitamin D toxicity are growth retardation, weight loss, loss of appetite, failure to thrive, and nausea. The classic example is the hypercalcemia which occurred among many children and infants in England during World War II. It was later decided that the excess vitamin D fortification of foods resulted in an intake of 3,000 to 4,000 IU of vitamin D per day among these children. Since then, a daily intake of less than 1,500 IU/day (from food and controlled fortification) has made spontaneous hypercalcemia in infancy uncommon.

In adults, the symptoms of vitamin D intoxication are: (1) abnormal calcium metabolism (increased calcium absorption, hypercalcemia, and hypercalciuria); (2) kidney malfunction (kidney calcium stones and renal insufficiency); and (3) other clinical signs (polyuria, polydypsia, anorexia, vomiting, nausea, constipation, and hypertension). Symptoms of severe toxicity are severe hypercalcemia, hypertensive encepha-

lopathy, calcium deposition in blood vessels and joints, and drowsiness and coma. At this state, the serum calcium level is over 12 mg/100 mL blood.

Treatment for the poisoning includes correction of fluid and electrolyte imbalance and the administration of cortisone continuously until the serum calcium level is less than 12 mg/100 mL. Also, refer to Chapter 31 for treatment of hypercalcemia.

Vitamin E

Vitamin E was discovered in 1922, isolated in 1936, and synthesized in 1937. It is called *tocopherol*, from the Greek term meaning "to bear offspring." Sometimes it is referred to as the "anti-sterility factor." This vitamin is known to be essential for about 20 animal species, including man.

In 1922, it was discovered that a lack of the vitamin caused permanent sterility in male rats; in female rats reproductive capacity was affected in a number of ways, such as difficulty in conception and delivery and a decreased number of babies per litter. The same results have been obtained for mice, rabbits, cattle, and many domestic animals. Surprisingly, since its discovery over 75 years ago, no evidence has been found that vitamin E deficiency is related to any abnormal reproductive capacity in humans. In fact, the role of vitamin E in human nutrition is still largely unknown for three reasons: (1) we have been unable to produce vitamin E deficiency in humans; (2) we know very little about the vitamin's biochemical function; and (3) deficiencies of many dietary factors, both essential and nonessential, can produce the same clinical effects as vitamin E deficiency in some but not all animals. At present, there is active research to identify the role of vitamin E in clinical nutrition and more information is expected soon.

There are many forms of vitamin E, with α-*tocopherol* the most active biologically. Since it is fat soluble, vitamin E requires bile salt for absorption and is absorbed best when fat is present. Fortunately, water-miscible or water-soluble preparations of the vitamin are now available.

The body absorbs about 20% to 30% of ingested vitamin E; the percentage absorbed is inversely related to intake. A small part of absorbed vitamin E reaches the liver via the portal vein, while the rest enters the lymphatic system and then the blood, where it is attached to a lipoprotein. The major storage sites for this vitamin are muscles, liver, and fat, although some is stored in the adrenals, testes, heart, and uterus. A newborn baby carries about 20 mg of vitamin E in its body; an adult stores about 3 to 4 g. Most of the excess vitamin E is conjugated in the liver and excreted via the bile or urine.

Functions

Vitamin E can benefit vitamin A in a number of ways. For example, in food and the intestine, vitamin E protects vitamin A from oxidation; the absorption and storage of vitamin A are also facilitated by vitamin E.

In general, vitamin E plays five major roles in animals and plants. First, it functions as an antioxidant, protecting substances such as fat, vitamins A and C, and polyunsaturated fatty acids from oxidation. As a result, fats containing vitamin E will not become rancid. Ceroid (brown lipofuscin) pigment is formed in some animals deprived of vitamin E. It is assumed that vitamin E prevents fat oxidation and the formation of ceroid pigment. Since one theory links the cause of aging to the oxidation of cells, there is much speculation that a lack of vitamin E may be related to the process of aging.

The second function of vitamin E concerns cellular respiration. Vitamin E is important in the respiratory chain, in which glucose and fatty

TABLE 6-40 1980 RDA for Vitamin E for Different Age Groups and During Pregnancy and Lactation

Population Group	Vitamin E RDA (mg α-TE)*
Infants	
0– 6 months	3
6–12 months	4
Children	
1– 3 years	5
7–10 years	7
Males (11+ years)	10
Females (11+ years)	8
Pregnancy	+2
Lactation	+3

*α-Tocopherol equivalents.

acids with the assistance of oxygen are converted to energy, water, and carbon dioxide.

Third, vitamin E is necessary for synthesizing other essential body substances. The manufacture of vitamin C in some species of animals requires the presence of vitamin E. The vitamin is also important in the synthesis of coenzyme Q and the formation of nucleic acid from pyrimidines.

Fourth, vitamin E is essential in heme synthesis, which is a component of hemoglobin. Fifth, vitamin E is necessary for the maintenance of cell membranes. Without vitamin E, cell membranes are more susceptible to hemolysis.

Requirements

The unit of measurement for vitamin E is mg α-TE (= α-tocopherol equivalents), 1 mg d-α-tocopherol = 1 α-TE. Table 6-40 lists the 1980 RDA for vitamin E for different age groups. The daily requirement increases with polyunsaturated fat intake; in the table, it is assumed that fat provides about 40% of the daily caloric need.

A newborn depends heavily on the vitamin E in milk since the vitamin does not pass easily through the placenta and thus very little is stored in the infant's body. Human milk contains four times as much vitamin E as cow's milk and can raise the infant's blood vitamin level much faster than a formula. It is important to make sure that any commercial formulation given an infant contains an appropriate level of vitamin E. Many premature infants need vitamin E supplement, since much of the vitamin is deposited in the fetus during the last two months of gestation and a baby born prematurely will have an extremely low blood level of vitamin E.

Deficiency

Deficiency of vitamin E is very uncommon in healthy adults, although clinical disorders such as malabsorption, gall bladder disease, and steatorrhea can lead to a deficiency. Premature infants tend to have a decreased blood level of vitamin E, and a formula-fed infant may be exposed to a higher risk of vitamin E deficiency than a breast-fed baby. The deficiency is unlikely to develop in bottle-fed infants, since appropriate vitamin E is added to most commercial formulas, but premature babies may need a vitamin E supplement.

In an adult, the symptoms of vitamin E deficiency from malabsorption may be increased hemolysis (destruction) of red blood cells. In premature infants, the deficiency is characterized by anemia, edema, skin lesions, increased platelet counts, and increased hemolysis. Cystic fibrosis in a child is frequently associated with vitamin E deficiency; the symptoms include increased susceptibility to hemolysis, creatinuria, and ceroid pigment in the body. The treatment of deficiency consists of 30 to 100 mg of vitamin E per day until all symptoms are cleared. The blood vitamin E level of a normal adult should be about 0.5 mg per 100 mL.

Food sources

The food products with the greatest concentration of vitamin E are probably vegetable oils, such as wheat germ oil. The level of vitamin E in the oil usually reflects the amount of polyunsaturated fatty acids present, which will be pro-

TABLE 6-41 Approximate Contribution of Vitamin E to the American Diet by Different Categories of Foods

Food Group	% of Daily Vitamin E Intake
Fats, oils: butter, margarine, shortenings and fats from meat, chicken, fish	60–70
Fruits and vegetables (especially green leafy vegetables)	10–15
Cereal products	5–10

tected from oxidation by the vitamin E. Normal cooking temperatures cause very little vitamin E loss, although deep-fat frying does destroy some of the vitamin. Frying or boiling temperatures may destroy the small amount of vitamin E in cooking oil.

In an American diet, fresh fruits and vegetables contribute little vitamin E. The same is true of grain products, because the milling of grain eliminates 90% of the vitamin E present. However, whole grains, especially wheat germ, contain a good amount of vitamin E; but it is easily destroyed by oxidation unless the product is refrigerated. Table 6-41 lists the approximate contribution of vitamin E to the American diet by different categories of food.

Toxicity

Vitamin E seems to have a low toxicity, although there are some problems associated with a large intake. A large dose of vitamin E can interfere with the utilization of at least two fat-soluble vitamins: A and K. The requirements of these two vitamins are increased when large amounts of vitamin E are ingested. The amount of vitamin A formed and stored in the liver is reduced with a high intake of vitamin E, and the patient may suffer a prolonged prothrombin time (see discussion under vitamin K), with a predisposition to bleeding. Second, a dose of more than 300 mg of vitamin E may cause mild to moderate intestinal disturbances.

TABLE 6-42 Some Characteristics of Vitamin K

Natural or Synthetic*	Name†	Solubility	Natural Analogue	Routes of Administration	Clinical Usage	Safety
Natural (from green plants, e.g., alfalfa)	Vitamin K₁ (phylloquinone)	Fat soluble	None	Oral (not recommended for infants); intravenous or subcutaneous injection	Pregnancy; surgery; countering anticoagulants. (see text)	Acceptable in appropriate doses.
Natural (from bacteria)	Vitamin K₂ (menaquinone)	Fat soluble	None	Same as above	Same as above	Same as above
Synthetic	Menadione (formerly vitamin K₃)	Fat soluble	Menaquinone	Intramuscular or subcutaneous Injection	Hemorrhage of infancy and labor; obstructive jaundice	Relatively safe for adults; safe for infants more than a few weeks old if recommended doses are complied with. Effects of large doses in infants: hemolytic anemia, hyperbilirubinemia, kernicterus.
Synthetic	Mephyton Konakion	Water miscible	Phylloquinone	Oral; intramuscular, intravenous, or subcutaneous injection	Newborn infants	Acceptable in appropriate doses.
Synthetic	Mono-Kay	Water miscible	Phylloquinone	Same as above	Same as above	Same as above

*Vitamin K is also located in purified fish meal.
†Other analogues not mentioned are Hykinone, Synkavite, and Kappadione of menaquinone and menadione.

Vitamin K

Vitamin K was discovered in 1934 and isolated and synthesized in 1939. Chemically related to coenzyme Q (see the later discussion in this chapter and in Chapter 8), vitamin K is stable to heat and reducing agents but sensitive to acid, alkali, alcohol, light, and oxidizing agents. Chemically, vitamin K is a quinone. Various forms of the vitamin are shown in Table 6-42, which also indicates their usage under different clinical conditions.

Since vitamin K is fat soluble, its absorption requires the presence of fat. About 10% of ingested vitamin K is absorbed in a normal person in the upper part of the intestinal tract. Clinical conditions such as obstructive jaundice, pancreatic disorder, and liver failure interfere with its absorption. Since mineral oil is not digested and absorbed, its usage in low-calorie salad dressings causes vitamin K to be passed with the stools. Absorbed and unused vitamin K is excreted partly in the bile and partly in the urine.

Sources

We normally obtain our required vitamin K from green and yellow vegetables and bacterial synthesis in the colon, although the contribution of the latter is usually small because of its distance from the absorption site. Drugs such as aspirin and antibiotics and other substances may inhibit or reduce intestinal synthesis of vitamin K by bacteria. No RDA has been established for this vitamin. However, the total requirement for vitamin K has been estimated by some scientists to be 70–140 μg/d for an adult. Also see Table 2 of the appendix.

Functions

Vitamin K plays an important role in blood clotting, which depends on the presence of many biological substances, such as factors IV, VII, IX, and X, prothrombin, and others. It is currently believed that vitamin K is directly or indirectly responsible for the liver synthesis of prothrombin. As a result, if there is inadequate vitamin K or a malfunctioning of the liver, there will be decreased prothrombin in the circulation, and, consequently, blood clotting will be delayed. In clinical medicine, an anticoagulant such as dicumarol works by interfering with vitamin K's role in prothrombin synthesis. This measure is extremely effective in treating thrombosis and phlebitis. However, unrestricted usage of these anticoagulants will obviously result in vitamin K deficiency and bleeding problems.

Deficiency

Formula or breast milk is low in vitamin K. Some newborn infants fed only milk without chemical supplement therefore become deficient in the vitamin. Breast milk contains only about one-fourth as much vitamin K as regular formulas. In addition, breast-fed infants receive little of the vitamin from bacterial synthesis in the intestine, since they harbor mainly *Lactobacillus*

bifidus in their digestive tracts. Breast-fed infants therefore have a higher incidence of vitamin K deficiency, resulting in bleeding or long blood-clotting time. However, infants weaned from total dependence on milk have other problems. For example, those fed baby foods using casein hydrolysate or meat base have a reduced availability of vitamin K, since these ingredients suppress bacterial synthesis of the vitamin in the intestine. Children who suffer starvation, malabsorption, diarrhea, cystic fibrosis, or exposure to antibiotics may suffer vitamin K deficiency. Chemical supplement is needed for all of these conditions.

Bleeding that is manageable by the administration of vitamin K has been reported in newborns. Although many cases of hemorrhage are a direct result of vitamin K deficiency, causes in some cases are unknown. Different types of hemorrhage among newborns may derive from the process of birth, traumatic labor, reduced oxygen supply at birth, circumcision, and obstructive jaundice. Because of the following observations or analyses, we believe that the bleeding problem of some of these infants is due to a lack of vitamin K.

1. Prothrombin levels in some affected newborns are definitely low. There will most likely be hemorrhage if the level is less than 10% to 15% of normal.
2. The newborn's liver may not be mature enough to synthesize prothrombin.
3. In the first few days of life, there may be inadequate bile salts to assist in the absorption of vitamin K.
4. Intestinal synthesis of vitamin K by bacteria may be insignificant since there are few bacteria.
5. The infant may have a low storage of vitamin K since the vitamin does not pass through the placenta easily.

Vitamin K deficiency is diagnosed by analyzing the prothrombin level in blood and the prothrombin time (time it takes for blood to clot). However, it is important to remember that if there is liver failure, prothrombin may be reduced but vitamin K nutriture may be normal.

Clinicians have suggested two procedures to avoid bleeding in newborn infants (also see Table

6-42). First, the pregnant woman may be given vitamin K immediately before delivery or for 1 or 2 weeks before term. If the doctor prescribes the vitamin for 1 to 2 weeks, the dose is usually 2 to 5 mg daily. If vitamin K is prescribed immediately before delivery, the dose is larger. To prevent indiscriminate usage, nonprescription prenatal supplements are not permitted to contain this vitamin.

Second, a dose of 1 to 2 mg of vitamin K may be given the newborn infant shortly after birth to prevent hemorrhage. However, the appropriate dose and form of vitamin K must be used. If water-miscible vitamin K is used, the dose is 0.5 to 1.0 mg. Synthetic vitamin K may cause vomiting if given orally. If the mother has received an anticoagulant during pregnancy, the baby needs a large dose of vitamin K.

In general, most clinicians prefer giving the vitamin K to the infant rather than the mother. For more information on vitamin K therapy and newborn infants, refer to references at the end of this book or standard medical textbooks.

Vitamin K deficiency in a normal adult is uncommon. However, certain standard management procedures have been established. Low blood prothrombin or long clotting time is managed by an oral dose of 2 to 5 mg of vitamin K per day. The synthetic water-miscible (soluble) vitamin K has been found to be safe and effective for adults except for pregnant women. If a patient is deficient in vitamin K because of intestinal malabsorption (due to bile lack, steatorrhea, and so on), a water-miscible preparation of vitamin K is preferred. If a fat-soluble compound such as menadione is used, the patient should be given bile salts simultaneously. Vitamin K_1 is best for delayed prothrombin time resulting from the use of anticoagulants.

Hemorrhage is common after surgery for obstructive jaundice. It usually lasts 1 to 4 days with slow bleeding at the site of surgery and from the intestinal tract, nose, and gums. The patient is given vitamin K before and after surgery. Delayed blood clotting time after any form of surgery can be prevented by a daily dose of 1 to 5 mg of vitamin K, depending on the prothrombin time.

For patients with severe hemorrhage, an instant supply of prothrombin is made possible by blood transfusion, which will reverse or prevent shock. However, this procedure is effective for only 5 to 10 hours, and vitamin K is needed to guarantee a supply of prothrombin.

Toxicity

Large doses of vitamin K are toxic under various circumstances. In infants, large amounts of vitamin K, such as 10 mg or more of the water-soluble preparation menadione sodium diphosphate may cause hyperbilirubinemia, mild hemolytic anemia, and kernicterus. If the infant is premature and deficient in vitamin E, the toxic effects of vitamin K are increased. Adults can tolerate 10 to 40 mg for several weeks without suffering ill effects, although vomiting will be precipitated if the dose is larger. Doses of one or more grams may cause increased excretion of albumin and porphyrin; in patients with severe liver disorders, the doses may actually increase prothrombin time.

NONESSENTIAL DIETARY FACTORS ASSOCIATED WITH VITAMINS

Scientists interested in the field of vitamins generally agree that certain chemicals are closely associated with vitamins, although they are not now defined as vitamins. Currently, these substances are thought to fulfill some but not all of the characteristics of a vitamin. Two important features preclude them from being considered as vitamins: They are partially or completely synthesized by the body, and their wide occurrence in foods and in the body make human deficiency unlikely. However, the possibility exists that, when more information is available, they may be labeled vitamins. These substances include choline, coenzyme Q, bioflavonoids, inositol, lipoic acid, and others.

Choline

In 1937 choline was discovered to be a cure for fatty liver in animals by mobilizing fat from the liver to other organs in the body. The body makes choline from glycine in the liver, a process that requires the assistance of methionine, folic acid, and vitamin B_{12}. Although choline is widespread in foods, it is so far considered nonessential to the human body; however, guinea pigs and fowl will not survive without a dietary source of choline.

Functionally, choline is a structural component of lecithin and sphingomyelin. The former transports fat in the body; the latter is important in the nervous tissues. Another of choline's roles involves a reaction between choline and acetyl CoA (see Chapter 8). This reaction produces acetyl choline, which is responsible for transmitting impulses at nerve endings.

We eat an estimated 0.5 to 1.0 g of choline per day. The substance is found in large amounts in any food with obvious or hidden fats: egg yolk, beef, liver, soybeans, and fish. Most fruits and vegetables do not contain choline.

Choline deficiency can be produced in animals such as rats, chickens, and turkeys, although B vitamins in general can reverse the symptoms. Although choline has been claimed to delay or prevent the formation of liver cirrhosis in alcoholics, the issue is still being debated.

Coenzyme Q

Coenzyme Q (or CoQ) resembles vitamins K and E chemically and is thus soluble in fats. The substance belongs to a class of chemicals called ubiquinones and is found in nearly all living cells. As discussed in Chapter 8, CoQ is an important component of the respiratory chain, in which energy from ingested nutrients is stored as ATP. By virtue of its chemical nature, CoQ is a perfect biological catalyst that is reduced and oxidized readily and reversibly.

In nature, CoQ is located in many foods, including meat, poultry, fish, soybeans, and vegetables. Since the human body can synthesize the substance, it is not essential. Although fat soluble, CoQ can also be excreted in the urine.

Bioflavonoids

In 1936, bioflavonoids were declared essential for humans since red pepper and lemon extracts, which contain high levels of the substances, were found to reverse the effects of vitamin C deficiency. Later, this claim was invalidated. At present, although the biological functions of this group of substances are unknown, they may have special pharmacological effects.

In the lay press, these substances are claimed to have therapeutic effects for a number of clinical problems such as strokes, joint diseases, and respiratory illness. However, positive clinical benefits have not been documented, and these substances have not been shown to be essential for humans. Natural sources of these substances include citrus fruits (and their skins) and other fruits and vegetables.

Inositol

The alcohol form of glucose is a sugar alcohol that exists in many forms, including inositol and myoinositol. Inositol is sometimes known as "muscle sugar" and is present in high concentrations in both plants and animals. In animals, inositol is a component of phospholipid, which is especially abundant in nerve and organ tissues. In grain products inositol occurs as phytic acid, which can complex with iron and calcium in the intestine. The exact function of inositol in the human body is unknown, although it can reverse fatty livers in animals and restore hair loss in mice. It is known to be essential for yeast.

Although widespread in nature, inositol occurs in higher concentration in hair and muscle (the heart and skeletal muscles). In general, meat, milk, fruits, vegetables, whole-grain cereals, and nuts are very good food sources. We eat about 1 g of inositol each day, and our bodies can also make the substance. We excrete only a small amount of inositol in urine, although diabetic patients excrete slightly more. The normal blood level of inositol is about 0.37 to 0.67 mg per 100 mL of blood.

Lipoic Acid

Lipoic acid is not an essential substance for man and other animals studied, although some bacteria require lipoic acid for growth. Lipoic acid participates in many biochemical reactions in the body, but the body seems to make enough of it for these purposes.

In the body, the conversion of pyruvic acid to acetyl CoA is accomplished by a combination of the enzyme complex pyruvic dehydrogenase (in which lipoic acid is an essential component) and the enzyme pyrophosphatase (which contains vitamin B_{12}). Chemically there are five different forms of lipoic acid, three of which are fat soluble, one a water-soluble complex, and one bound to protein. The chemical is sometimes called thioctic acid, indicating the presence of sulfur.

Although the exact role of lipoic acid in human medicine is unknown, some observations have been made. First, when animals are fed a diet to induce atherosclerosis, lipoic acid is found to regulate plasma lipid formation. Second, lipoic acid can stimulate cancer growth in animals. Third, there are suggestions that lipoic acid can benefit alcoholics, although documented evidence is lacking.

Other Factors

For a number of years, some people have claimed the existence of other vitamins, such as "vitamin B_{17}" (laetrile) and vitamin B_{15} (pangamic acid). No scientific evidence indicates that such chemicals are vitamins.

STRUCTURAL FORMULAS

Water-Soluble Vitamins

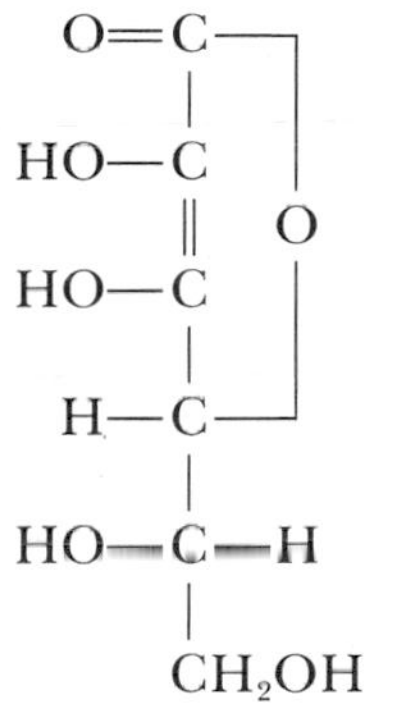

Ascorbic acid: vitamin C

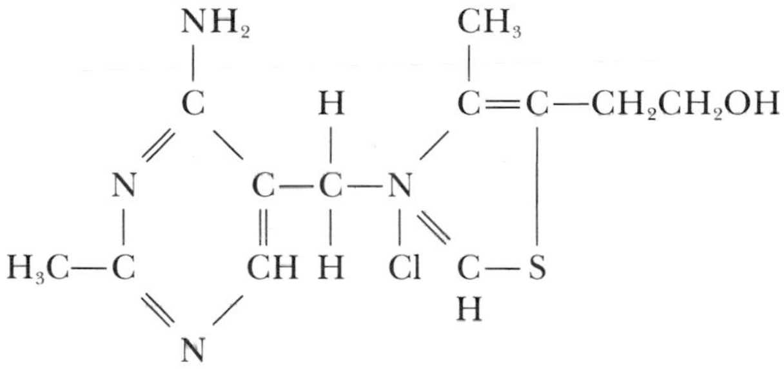

Thiamin: vitamin B_1

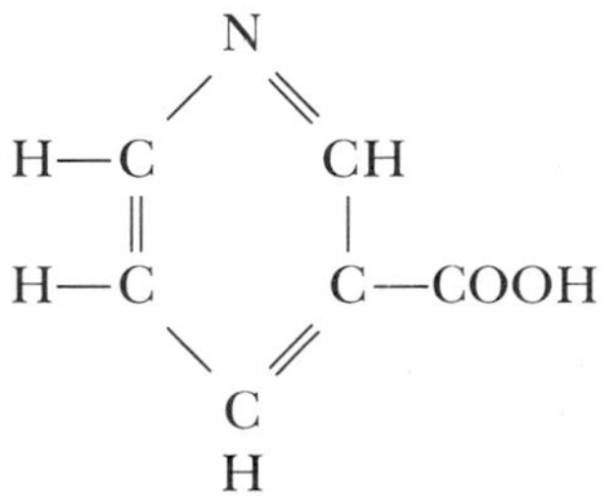

Nicotinic acid

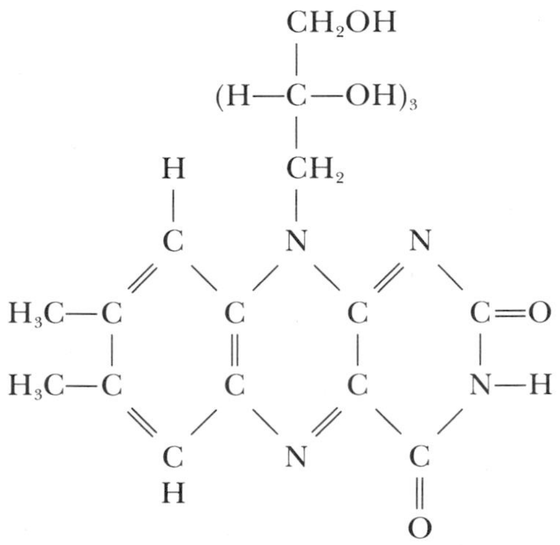

Riboflavin: vitamin B_2

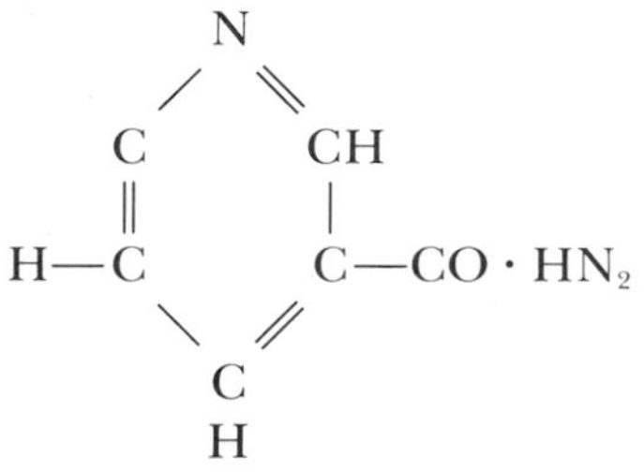

Nicotinamide

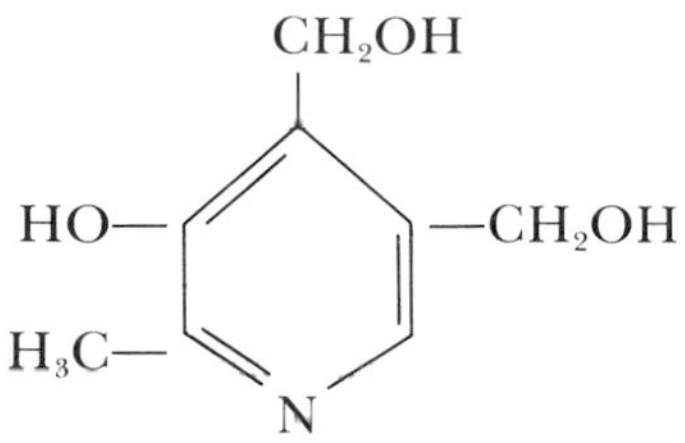

Pyridoxine

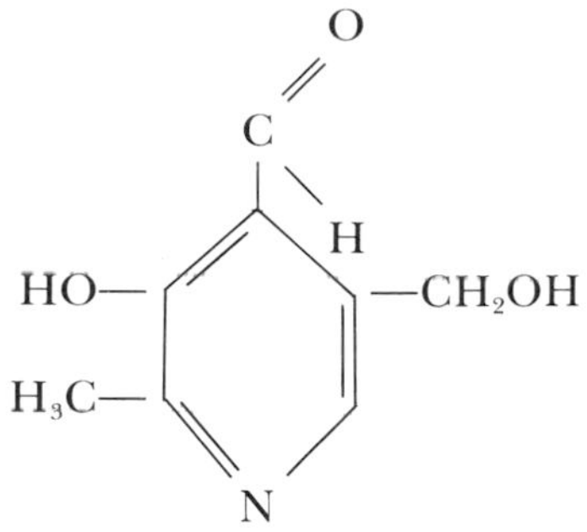

Pyridoxal

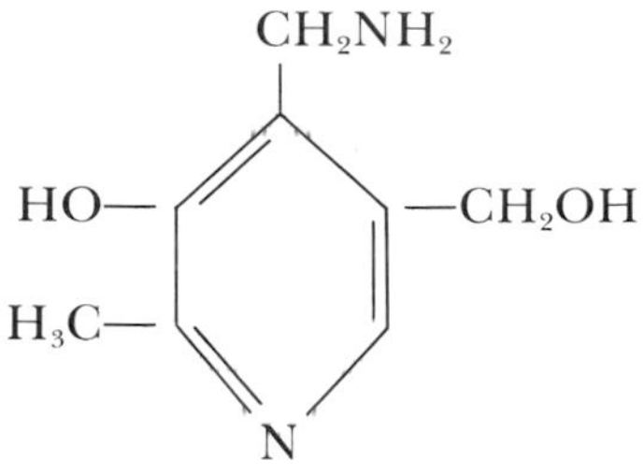

Pyridoxamine

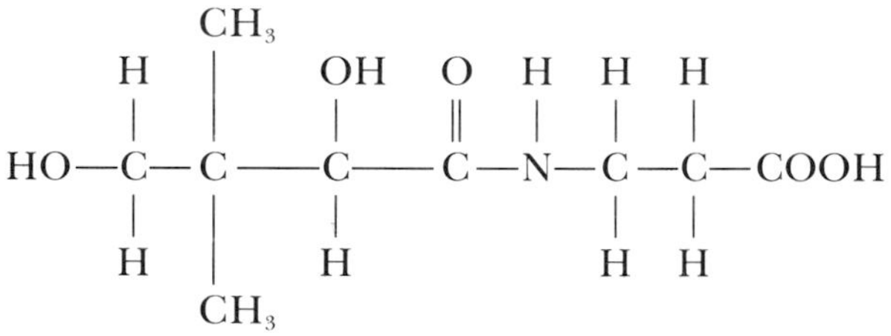

Pantothenic acid

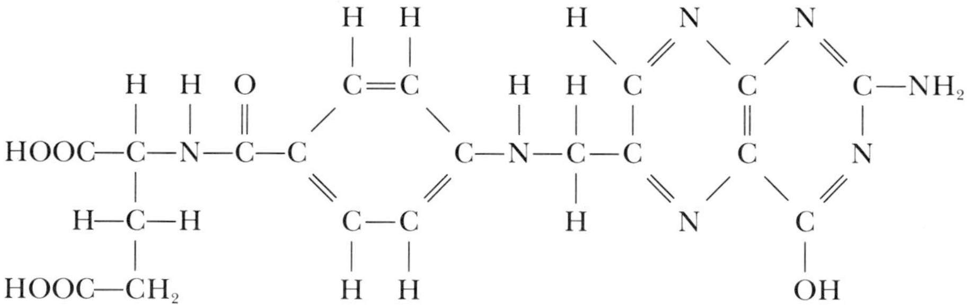

Folacin (monopteroylglutamic acid)

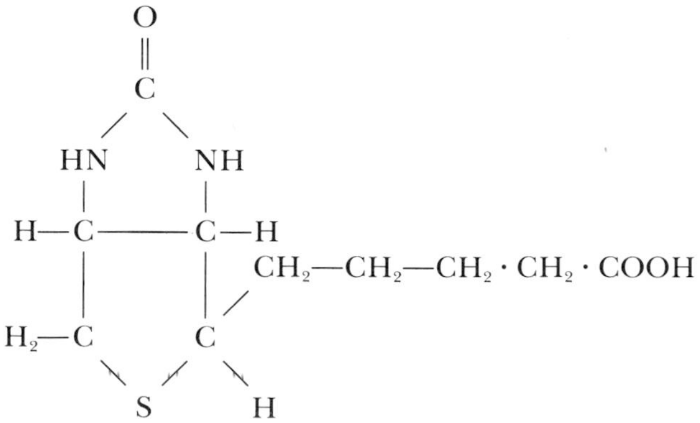

Biotin

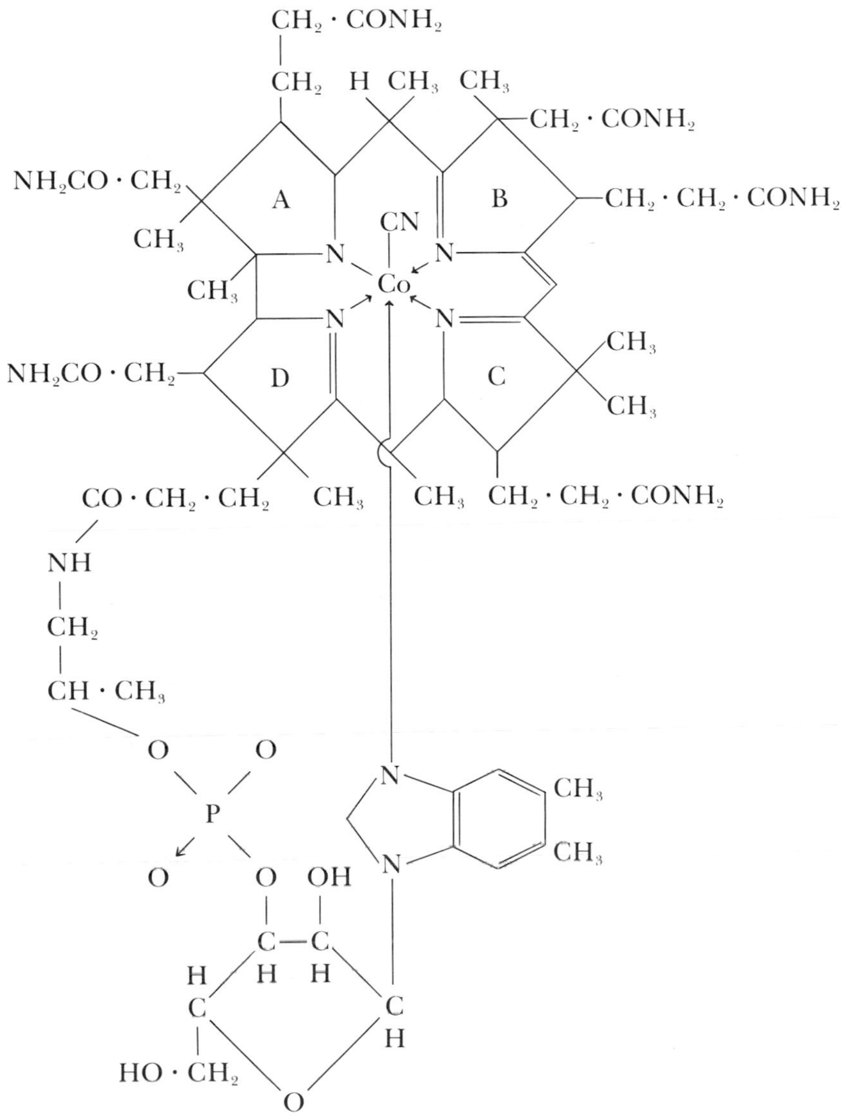

$CH_2 \cdot CONH_2$

CH_2 H CH_3 CH_3

$CH_2 \cdot CONH_2$

$NH_2CO \cdot CH_2$

A   B

CH_3

$CH_2 \cdot CH_2 \cdot CONH_2$

CN

N   N

CH_3

Co

N   N

$NH_2CO \cdot CH_2$

D   C

CH_3

CH_3

$CO \cdot CH_2 \cdot CH_2$ CH_3 CH_3 $CH_2 \cdot CH_2 \cdot CONH_2$

NH

CH_2

$CH \cdot CH_3$

O   O

P

N CH_3

O

O   OH

N CH_3

C—C

H   H   H

C   C

H

$HO \cdot CH_2$ O

Vitamin B$_{12}$ (cyanocobalamin)

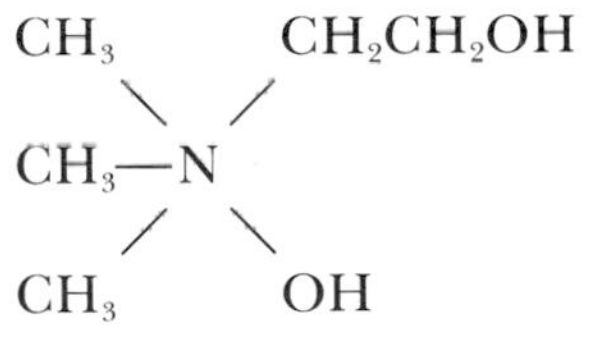

CH_3 CH_2CH_2OH

CH_3—N

CH_3 OH

Choline

Fat-Soluble Vitamins

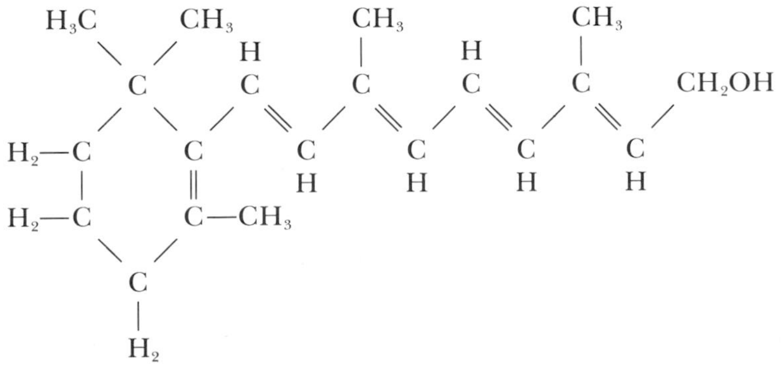

H_3C CH_3 CH_3 CH_3

H   H

C   C   C   C   C CH_2OH

H_2—C   C   C   C   C   C

H   H   H   H

H_2—C   C—CH_3

C

H_2

Vitamin A (retinol)

Vitamin D (cholecalciferol, vitamin D$_3$)

Vitamin E (α-tocopherol)

Vitamin K (phytylmenaquinone, vitamin K₁)

STUDY QUESTIONS

1. What is a vitamin? How do vitamins differ from other organic compounds?
2. Which vitamins can be synthesized by the body? Which ones must be activated by the body before they can perform their major biological functions?
3. What is a vitamin antagonist? What harm can it cause? How are vitamin antagonists used clinically?
4. What is misleading about the distinction between natural and synthetic vitamin supplements?
5. What three methods are used in diagnosing vitamin deficiency?
6. Describe the functions of vitamin C and symptoms of its deficiency. Discuss the loss of vitamin C in the handling and cooking of foods. What risks have been associated with a high intake of vitamin C?
7. What condition is associated with moderate to severe vitamin B_1 deficiency? In what groups of people has this condition been found?
8. Discuss some reasons why riboflavin deficiency may be difficult to diagnose.
9. What factors may cause vitamin B_6 deficiency? What are the nonspecific symptoms of B_6 deficiency?
10. What is the relationship of tryptophan to niacin?
11. What deficiency disease is classically characterized by the 4 D's? What are they?
12. Which B vitamins are involved in anemia? What is pernicious anemia?
13. Is pantothenic acid deficiency common? Why?
14. What characteristics do vitamins A, D, E, and K have in common?
15. Summarize the symptoms of vitamin A deficiency.
16. What is the chief function of vitamin D? Which foods contain this vitamin? What condition is created by its deficiency?
17. What is known about the role of vitamin E in human health? What are the richest food sources of this vitamin?
18. Is vitamin K deficiency more common in breast-fed or formula-fed infants? What problem may this deficiency cause?
19. Why are certain substances associated with vitamins not labeled as vitamins? What are some of these substances?

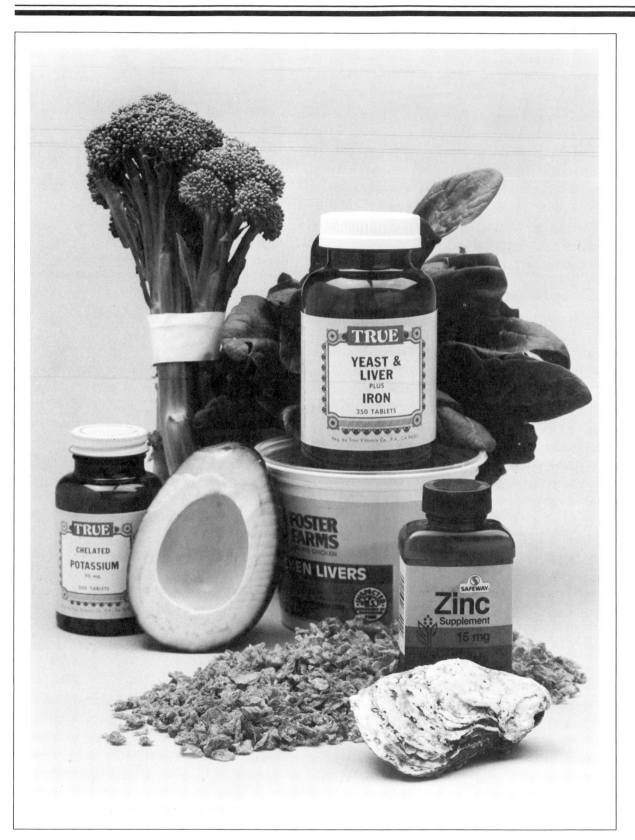

Chapter 7

Minerals

Zinc (continued)

> Sexual development, growth, and reproductive ability
>
> Wound healing and skin health
>
> Taste and smell sensation
>
> Acrodermatitis enteropathica
>
> Immunocompetence
>
> Hyperalimentation
>
> Sickle cell anemia

Fluorine

Copper

> Requirements and food sources
>
> Deficiency
>
> Excess

Other Trace Elements

ANOTHER GROUP OF essential nutrients for the body is minerals, or inorganic elements. The two terms are used interchangeably, although neither describes these nutrients accurately. The term *minerals* usually refers to substances mined from the ground, but when we eat vegetables (such as cabbage, lettuce, and spinach) and meat (beef, chicken) we take in minerals. In neither case have we actually mined the nutrients. The plants have obtained them from the soil, and the beef cattle and chicken have been fed plant feeds. The term *inorganic elements* is also imprecise, since most of the elements we consume are bound with organic substances and rarely exist as pure inorganic forms. An exception is table salt, which is mainly sodium chloride.

Another general term sometimes used for these nutrients is *ash*. In analytical chemistry and biochemistry, the term *ash* refers to the noncombustible residue left after a substance has been burnt (oxidized). The ash contains the minerals originally contained in the substance.

CLASSIFICATION AND FUNCTIONS

Approximately 4% of our body weight is made up of mineral elements. They are divided into two main groups: *macroelements* (those needed in relatively large quantity) and *microelements* (those needed in very small amounts). Table 7-1 shows their classification and approximate daily body need. Figure 7-1 shows the approximate distribution of organic and inorganic elements in the body.

Although they are far outweighed by organic elements, mineral elements are important for the body. They serve two major purposes: They

TABLE 7-1 Approximate Distribution of Mineral Elements in the Body*

Elements	% of Body Weight	Amount Needed in the Daily Diet (mg/day/ element)
Macroelements (calcium, phosphorus, potassium, sodium, sulfur, magnesium, chlorine)	3.2–3.8	100+
Microelements (iron, copper, cobalt, zinc, manganese, iodine, molybdenum, selenium, fluorine, chromium)	less than 0.1	0.05–5

*Although RDAs have not been established for sodium, potassium, chloride, copper, manganese, fluoride, chromium, selenium, and molybdenum, the National Academy of Sciences has estimated the safe and adequate daily dietary intakes of these elements.

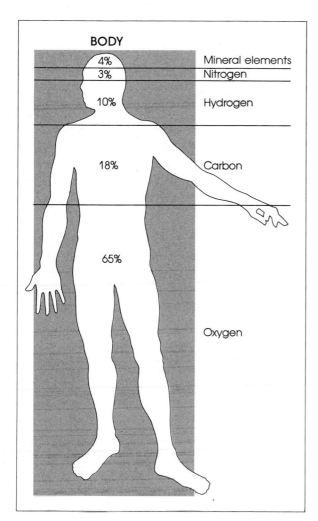

FIGURE 7-1 Approximate distribution of organic and inorganic elements in the body.

exist as structural components of parts of the body, and they regulate normal body functions. Important body substances of which some mineral elements are structural components are listed in Table 7-2. The physiological processes in which mineral elements participate include: (1) proper transmission of nervous impulses; (2) control of acid-base balance; (3) maintenance of equilibrium in fluid distribution and osmotic pressure in different compartments of the body (see Chapter 9 for details on fluid, electrolyte, and acid-base balance); (4) appropriate digestion of certain food products; (5) normal muscle contractions; and (6) a number of important chemical and biological reactions in which minerals act as catalysts.

MACROELEMENTS

The mineral elements needed in relatively large quantities by the body are sodium, potassium, calcium, phosphorus, magnesium, chlorine, and sulfur. Sodium, potassium, calcium, and magnesium are basic, or alkaline, in solution and predominate in most fruits and vegetables. Phosphorus, chlorine, and sulfur are acid in solution and predominate in protein foods (other than milk) and cereal products. Chapters 9 and 28 discuss how the intake of acid- and alkaline-forming foods can affect the acidity or alkalinity of our urine.

TABLE 7-2   Mineral Elements that are Components of Important Body Structures

Element(s)	Chemical Substance(s)	Body Structures
Calcium, phosphorus, magnesium	Hydroxyapatite	Teeth, bones
Sulfur	Cystine, cysteine, methionine	Protein of skin, hair, nails
Iron	Hemoglobin, myoglobin	Blood components
Iron, copper	Cofactors of enzymes	Enzyme complexes
Iodine	Thyroxine	Hormone of thyroid glands
Cobalt	Cobalamin	Water-soluble vitamin B_{12}

TABLE 7-3 Approximate Daily Loss of Sodium

Source of Loss	Amount (mg)
Skin	
Perspiration	15–25
Desquamation (sloughing of skin), hair loss	10–25
Urine	5–40
Stool	10–130
Menstrual fluid	trace
Approximate daily loss of sodium	40–220

Sodium

Sodium is most familiar to us as sodium chloride, or table salt, but it appears in other foods as well. Although sodium is an important element, we are still unsure how much the body needs of it daily. The body loses about 40 to 220 mg of sodium a day (Table 7-3). To provide a safety margin, a daily intake of 500 mg (½ g) should theoretically satisfy our need. However, we may be consuming 5 to 15 times more than we need. A rough estimate shows that we eat about 3 to 7 g of sodium a day. The magnitude of this quantity is apparent in the fact that 4 g of sodium is equivalent to the sodium in 2 teaspoons of table salt. However, the actual need of any individual depends on occupation, climate, and area of residence since we can lose a substantial amount of sodium when we perspire. Our personal taste for salt is determined by our childhood eating patterns, family practices, and social and cultural factors.

Figure 7-2 shows the metabolic fate of sodium in the body of a healthy person. About 3 g of sodium per liter of intestinal fluid are contributed by secretion from body compartments. However, through the enterohepatic circulation (see Chapters 9, 24, and 25), about 20 g of sodium are reabsorbed, resulting in only a small loss of sodium in the stool. The loss of sodium through perspiration varies; in tropical areas, people lose up to 5 or 6 g of sodium chloride daily. An unacclimatized person in a tropical cli-

mate can lose 2 to 4 times more sodium. Researchers have suggested that 2 g of table salt are needed to replace each liter of perspiration lost after 4 liters.

Functions

Sodium serves many functions in the body. One of its major roles is to maintain osmotic pressure and water balance, especially by protecting fluid loss from the body. Together with chloride and bicarbonate, sodium (which is basic, or alkaline, in solution) is also involved in maintaining the pH or acid-base balance of the body. One of the major causes of alkalosis (excess alkalinity) is the ingestion of excess sodium-containing antacid preparations. Third, sodium regulates the transmission of nervous impulses, cell permeability, and muscle irritability and contractibility. Fourth, sodium is important for the absorption and transportation of certain nutrients.

Deficiency or excess

Sodium deficiency is uncommon in a healthy person, because the body has a large reserve and most people love salty foods. However, a decreased intake accompanied by an increased demand can produce deficiency. Salt depletion is characterized by nausea, apathy, exhaustion, respiratory trouble, dizziness, intestinal cramps, and vomiting. Drinking salt solution reverses the symptoms (as discussed in Chapters 9, 27, and 28). If sodium loss is not replaced, the extracellular fluid becomes low in sodium, water, or both, potentially leading to dehydration, shock, and death. Excess sodium ingestion can be toxic, although severe toxic reactions are rare since an early symptom is rejection of salty food and drinks.

Sodium balance in the body is rigidly controlled by the hormonal (renin, angiotensin, and adrenal mineral corticoids) and kidney systems, which also regulate blood pressure. There is considerable genetically determined variability within these control systems, which permit the body to adapt to a wide range of sodium intake by varying the excretion of sodium to balance consumption and nonrenal losses. Figures 7-3 and 7-4 illustrate some aspects of body regulation of sodium need. Clinical conditions that may lead to

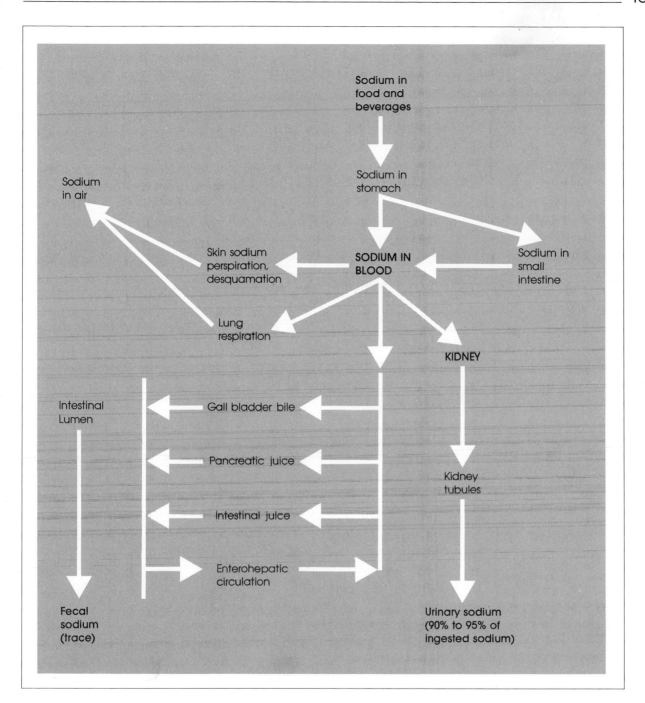

FIGURE 7-2   Metabolic fate of ingested sodium.

body sodium excess or deficiency are kidney or heart failure (see Chapters 27 and 28), adrenal insufficiency, and nonrenal losses such as diarrhea, vomiting, or fistular drainage from the intestine (Chapter 24).

Food sources

Table salt is the major source of sodium in the American diet. Sodium also occurs naturally in other foods, especially animal products. More

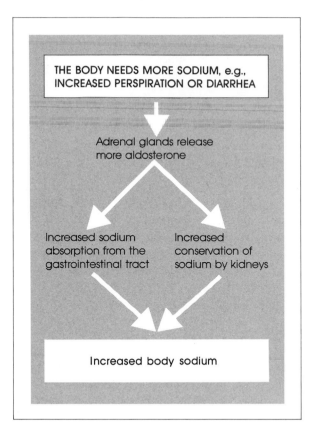

FIGURE 7-3 Regulation of body sodium need.

sodium may be added during processing. Sodium content of drinking water varies with treatment method. Soft water contains more sodium than hard water. Table 7-4 lists the sodium content of some common foods. More information on the sodium content of food is presented in Chapters 27 and 28 and the appendix.

Potassium

Potassium is also an essential element, although we do not know the exact daily need of the body. A normal American diet provides 2 to 5 g of potassium. Because of its occurrence in a wide variety of foods, the more food a person eats, the higher the intake. Any food preparation process that involves washing with water leaches some potassium from the food, as does commercial processing such as whey making. Table 7-5 presents the potassium content of some common foods.

Some major body functions in which po-

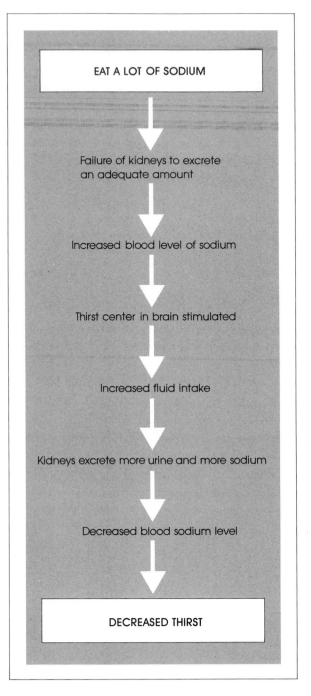

FIGURE 7-4 Relationship between sodium intake and thirst.

tassium is involved are: (1) fluid distribution and osmotic pressure balance in the different body compartments; (2) transmission of nervous impulses; (3) maintenance of body acid-base balance; (4) catalyzing of major chemical and

TABLE 7-4   Sodium Content of Representative Foods*

Food	Serving Size	Sodium (mg)
Cheese, cheddar	1 oz	168
Ice cream, 10% fat	1 c	84
Milk, whole, fluid	1 c	122
Egg, whole, raw, large	1	61
Butter or margarine	1 T	140
Beef, ground	1 c	55
Chicken, fried	1¾ oz	34
Pork, roasted	4½ oz	74
Turkey	3 oz	111
Apples	1	1
Juice, cranberry, cocktail	1 c	3
Raisins, seedless	1 c	39
Bread, white	1 sl	142
Cake, no icing	1 in³	12
Beans, dry	1 c	34
Peanut butter	1 T	97
Jam or preserves	1 T	2
Sugar, white, granulated	1 c	2
Asparagus, cooked	1 c	1
Potato, baked, no skin	1	6
Squash or zucchini, cooked, drained	1 c	2
Brewer's yeast, dried	1 T	10
Baking powder, sodium aluminum sulfate	1 T	1,205
Soy sauce	1 fl oz	2,666

*Adapted from *Nutritive Value of American Foods*, Agriculture Handbook No. 456 (Washington, D.C.: U.S. Department of Agriculture, 1975).

biological reactions in the body; (5) normal muscular relaxation (in contrast to calcium, which stimulates muscular contraction); and (6) regulation of the release of insulin from the pancreas. As a stable component of lean body mass, potassium is also useful in estimating body composition as discussed in Chapter 2.

Only a small amount of potassium (400 mg) is excreted in the sweat and stool; urine is the major disposal route. Within limits the kidney can excrete any excess intake of potassium, but it is unable to conserve potassium when the body is deficient. For example, if a person is deprived of potassium for about a week or more, the kidney still excretes between 100 and 500 mg per day.

Dietary deficiency of potassium is uncommon in a normal person. However, many clinical conditions, such as long-term intravenous feeding and malnutrition (see Chapters 9, 11, 27, and 28), can result in potassium deficiency.

Calcium

An adult body contains about 1,200 g of calcium, with 99% of it in salt forms, providing hardness to bones and teeth. Calcium exists as calcium hydroxyapatite, $Ca_{10}(PO_4)_6(OH)_2$. The remaining 1%, or 10 to 12 g, of body calcium is distributed in the various compartments of the body. Plasma calcium is kept within a narrow range. Bone serves as a reservoir that stores and releases calcium to the blood to maintain this equilibrium.

Functions

The major functions of calcium in the body are: (1) serving as a component of bone and teeth; (2) participating in the blood clotting process; (3) assisting in the transmission of messages through the nervous system; (4) regulating the contraction and relaxation of muscle fibers; (5)

TABLE 7-5 Potassium Content of Representative Foods*

Food	Serving Size	Potassium (mg)
Cottage cheese, small curd	1 c	179
Milk, fluid, whole	1 c	301
Ice cream, regular	1 c	313
Egg, raw, large	1	65
Apricots, dried, large	10 halves	470
Avocado	1	1,303
Grapefruit, raw	1	265
Mayonnaise, commercial, regular	1 T	5
Beef, round steak	3 oz	272
Ham, baked, some fat	3 oz	199
Salmon, fresh, baked	1 oz	126
Bread, cracked wheat	1 sl	34
Cashew nuts, roasted in oil	1 oz	132
Peanuts, roasted, salted	1 oz	191
Beans, navy, cooked, drained	1 c	790
Sugar, brown, packed	1 c	757
Molasses, cane, light	1 T	183
Broccoli, fresh, cooked, drained	1 c	414
Carrots, raw, whole	1	246
Potato, baked in skin	1	782
Onion, mature, raw	1 T	16
Brewer's yeast, dry, debittered	1 T	152
Soy sauce	1 T	66

*Adapted from *Nutritive Value of American Foods*, Agriculture Handbook No. 456 (Washington, D.C.: U.S. Department of Agriculture, 1975).

minimizing the absorption of the radioactive chemical, strontium-90; (6) maintaining proper heart muscle functioning by being present in the proper concentration in relation to sodium, potassium, and magnesium; (7) activating a number of enzymes; and (8) existing in the blood within a narrow range. This eighth function enables the parathyroid gland to control the homeostasis of calcium with regard to absorption, deposition in and resorption from bones, and excretion in urine.

Food sources and absorption

The RDA for calcium is highly controversial. At present, the recommended adult daily intake is 800 mg, although pregnant and nursing mothers need more. The RDA for different age groups are provided in Table 1 of the appendix.

Milk is the richest source of calcium, and cow's milk contains four times more calcium than breast milk does. Canned fish, especially those with dissolved bones, contains much calcium. Whole grains, nuts, legumes, and leafy vegetables are also good sources of calcium. Table 7-6 provides the calcium content of some common foods.

In the body, the amount of calcium available is determined largely by the amount absorbed. Factors or conditions that may increase the absorption of calcium include: (1) adequate vitamin D intake; (2) the presence of lactose; (3) dietary calcium and phosphorus in the ratio of 1 : 1; (4) conditions such as pregnancy, growing years, bone fractures, and starvation; and (5) acidic conditions that may promote the solubility of calcium. For example, ingesting ascorbic acid and amino acids (such as methionine) can increase the absorption of calcium.

On the other hand, certain factors may decrease the absorption of calcium. These include: (1) excess dietary roughage or fiber; (2) a dietary calcium to phosphorus ratio that deviates from 1 : 1; (3) excess use of laxatives; (4) diarrhea or other intestinal conditions that may exaggerate peristalsis; (5) an excess amount of magnesium, albumin, or iron, which may precipitate phosphate salts, thus decreasing the availability of calcium for absorption; (6) an alkaline intestinal medium; and (7) lack of physical activity. Clinical experience has confirmed that immobilization, such as being bedridden, can depress calcium absorption.

An eighth factor that may decrease absorption of calcium is excessive consumption of oxalic and phytic acid in the diet. *Oxalic acid* occurs in some vegetables, such as chard, rhubarb, and spinach (see Chapter 28). When present in the intestinal tract, it can chelate calcium and make it unavailable for absorption. Normally, the ingestion of a small quantity of oxalic acid poses no problems. However, the consumption of certain vegetables in considerable excess may interfere with calcium absorption. *Phytic acid*, found in the outer husks of cereals, can complex with calcium and make it unavailable for absorption. In countries where a large amount of unleavened bread is consumed, there is evidence of calcium deficiency, since the phytic acid in the flour complexes with the calcium, decreasing its absorp-

TABLE 7-6   Calcium Content of Some Common Foods*

Food	Serving Size	Calcium (mg)
Sardines	1 oz	115
Cheese, cheddar	1 oz	220
Biscuit, 2″ diam	1	40
Beans, dry, cooked	½ c	45
Milk, whole	1 c	290
Milk, skim, powdered, dry	½ c	350
Orange, medium size	1	40
Broccoli	½ c	90
Collards	½ c	190
Turnip greens	½ c	185
Artichokes	½ c	50
Kale	½ c	190
Custard, baked	⅓ c	110
Ice cream	½ c	110
Sherbet	⅓ c	25

*Adapted from *Nutritive Value of Foods*, Home and Garden Bulletin No. 72 (Washington, D.C.: U.S. Department of Agriculture, 1981).

tion. There is less phytic acid in leavened bread because the process of fermentation destroys most of the phytate through the action of the enzyme phytase.

Deficiency or excess

A number of clinical disorders may result from an imbalanced calcium metabolism. Rickets, osteoporosis, and tetany may involve calcium deficiency; hypercalcemia is a result of excess calcium in the blood.

In infancy and childhood, rickets may result from a dietary lack of calcium, although vitamin D deficiency and/or an excess or deficiency of phosphorus may produce the same disorder. Apart from bones, the growth and structure of teeth may also be affected (see Chapter 6).

In adults, nutritional *osteomalacia*, or adult rickets, is a disorder characterized by reduced mineral content in bone. The bone becomes soft, although the total amount of bone in the body remains unchanged. This condition may be caused by an inadequate calcium intake, dietary deficiency of vitamin D, or an excess or defi-

ciency of dietary phosphorus—all conditions that can reduce the absorption of calcium.

Osteoporosis is a clinical disorder characterized by a reduction in the total quantity of bone in the body. The disease is common among older Americans, especially older women. A combination of causes are thought to contribute to the disease, such as aging, hormonal imbalance, lifetime calcium deficit, overconsumption of phosphorus, and limited exercise. Treatment includes oral calcium salt, estrogen, and sodium fluoride (see Chapters 15 and 31).

In addition to the above bone disorders, which may or may not involve actual calcium deficiency, a *secondary deficiency* of calcium may result from other disorders even if dietary intake of calcium is adequate. These include renal malfunction, malabsorption, dietary magnesium deficiency, and immobilization. A secondary deficiency of calcium also results in bone disorders.

Tetany results from a decreased serum ionizable calcium level. It is characterized by increased nervous excitability, muscular twitching and contractions, instability, confusion, uncontrolled seizures, cramps, and convulsions. Skin and hair may undergo changes such as hair loss and skin dryness. This acute *hypocalcemia* (low blood calcium) may be a result of hypoproteinemia, hypoparathyroidism, vitamin D deficiency, defective calcium absorption, or magnesium deficiency.

Tetany is a clinical emergency and requires prompt diagnosis and treatment. Calcium gluconate given intravenously is the drug of choice. If the acute hypocalcemia results from hypoparathyroidism, dietary phosphorus should be restricted to the lowest possible level, and the simultaneous administration of parathyroid extract and vitamins may be necessary. A patient suffering from chronic hypocalcemia requires long-term management to increase intestinal absorption of calcium. Using parathyroid extract is part of the treatment. In some patients, increased vitamin D and calcium intake are sometimes successful.

Hypercalcemia, an excessive level of calcium in the blood, may be caused in a variety of ways: cancer, excess vitamin D intake, hyperparathyroidism, milk-alkali syndrome, immobilization, thyroidism, and hypophosphatemia. A patient with high blood calcium may suffer nausea, vomiting, anorexia, abdominal pain, constipation, increased thirst and urination, mental disorder, dullness, calcium stones, and soft-tissue calcification. Coma may occur. Hypercalcemia can be life threatening. Rehydration of the patient is the major treatment, accompanied by drugs to lower blood calcium. After the crisis is over, the patient is put on a calcium-restricted diet. However, the underlying cause should be identified and treated if feasible.

Phosphorus

There are approximately 600 to 700 g of phosphorus in the body, 80% to 90% of which is located in the bones and teeth. The rest is distributed in different compartments of the body.

Functions

The major functions of phosphorus are: (1) formation and maintenance of bones and teeth; (2) regulation of body acid-base balance; (3) control of energy [the storage and release of energy are accomplished by means of adenosine triphosphate (ATP), adenosine diphosphate (ADP), and creatine phosphate, as discussed in Chapter 8]; (4) serving as a structural component of nucleic acid, enzymes, and certain lipids in cell walls; (5) regulation of hormonal activities; and (6) participation in nutrient metabolism. Phosphorus assists in nutrient absorption, transportation, utilization, and other aspects of intermediate metabolism. One common process is phosphorylation (see Chapter 8).

Food sources and deficiency

The adult RDA for phosphorus is 800 mg/day. However, it is difficult to produce phosphorus deficiency in humans because this nutrient occurs so widely in foods. Most protein foods are rich in phosphorus, with beef, poultry, and fish being the major sources of phosphorus in the American diet. Nevertheless, individuals who consume a large amount of antacids may suffer deficiency because the drugs interfere with phosphorus absorption. Symptoms of depletion include anorexia, fatigue, and bone demineralization.

TABLE 7-7 Approximate Body Distribution of Calcium and Phosphorus

Mineral	% of Body Content		
	Bones, teeth	Soft tissues, organs	Blood, extra-cellular tissues
Calcium	99	trace	1
Phosphorus	80	19	1

TABLE 7-8 Ratios of Phosphorus to Calcium Contents of Natural Food Products

Food	Phosphorus: Calcium Ratio
Meats, poultry, fish	15–20:1
Organ meats, such as liver	25–50:1
Eggs, grains, nuts, dry beans, peas, lentils	3–10:1
Milk, natural cheese, green vegetables	0.1–0.8:1

Calcium-phosphorus relationships

Phosphorus and calcium are similar in many aspects. Both are important in bone and teeth development. Serum levels of both elements are regulated by the parathyroid gland, which also regulates the resorption of phosphorus from the kidneys. Intestinal absorption of both is increased by vitamin D, which also facilitates the resorption of phosphorus from the kidneys. Bones serve as the reservoir for the release and storage of both elements. The same factors that regulate the overall absorption of calcium also apply to phosphorus. Table 7-7 shows the body distribution of calcium and phosphorus.

In the past few years, the concept of eating the appropriate calcium:phosphorus (Ca:P) ratio has been much debated. It is suggested that a ratio of 1:1 results in the best absorption levels of both elements for an adult, although a ratio of 1.3:1 is advised for infants. The American diet

TABLE 7-9   Calcium and Phosphorus Content of Representative Foods*

Food	Serving Size	Calcium (mg)	Phosphorus (mg)
Dairy products			
Milk, whole	1 c	285	227
Milk, skim	1 c	296	233
Meat and equivalents			
Beef, rib roast	3 oz	8	158
Frankfurter	1	4	76
Luncheon meat	½ lb	25	377
Roast chicken, light meat	½ lb	25	617
Grain and equivalents			
Bread, enriched, white	1 sl	26	28
Rice, white, enriched, cooked	1 c	21	57
Potato, french fried	10 strips	5	39
Fruits			
Grapefruit, medium size	1	16	16
Apple	1	10	15
Figs dried, small	2	40	25
Vegetables			
Beans, green, cooked	½ c	63	46
Corn, sweet, yellow, fresh	½ c	2	75
Peppers, sweet, raw, green, chopped	½ c	5	15
Nuts			
Almonds, roasted	1 oz	67	143
Peanuts, roasted, salted	1 oz	20	115
Miscellaneous			
Shake, vanilla, McDonald's	1	126	105
Soft drink	8 oz	0	500
Pie, baked, sector	1	3	7
Pretzels, thin	10	13	79

*Adapted from *Nutritive Value of Foods*, Home and Garden Bulletin No. 72 (Washington, D.C.: U.S. Department of Agriculture, 1981).

may have a low Ca:P ratio for two reasons. For one, phosphorus is naturally more abundant than calcium in foods. Table 7-8 shows the calcium:phosphorus ratio in some natural, unprocessed foods. A second reason for a low calcium:phosphorus ratio is that phosphorus is used as an additive in many processed food products, increasing the intake of phosphorus. Table 7-9 shows the calcium and phosphorus content of common natural and processed foods (more examples may be obtained from Table 6 of the appendix). Despite this tendency toward a higher consumption of phosphorus, there is not yet enough scientific evidence to conclude whether Americans eat more phosphorus than is necessary and desirable.

Magnesium

Another macroelement with close relationships to calcium is magnesium. Of the 20 to 30 g of magnesium in the body, 10% is adsorbed to the bone surface, 30% is bound with phosphate, and about 50% to 60% occurs as a component of bones and teeth.

Functions

Magnesium is involved in several important functions in the body. These include: (1) muscular relaxation, a function opposite to that of calcium; (2) protein synthesis; (3) cellular respiration; and (4) catalyzing some important chemical and biological reactions involving ATP and ADP (see Chapter 8).

Food sources and absorption

According to the latest RDA, the adult requirement is 300 to 350 mg per day. The average American diet, which contains about 120 mg per 1,000 kcal, presumably satisfies the body's need. Most foods contain some magnesium, especially green leafy vegetables. Magnesium forms the "core" of chlorophyll in plants. Although milk is a poor source of magnesium for adults, it is adequate for both bottle- and breast-fed infants. Table 7-10 presents the magnesium content of some common foods.

Our consumption of magnesium is affected by a mixture of dietary factors. In general, about 40% to 50% of ingested magnesium is absorbed, but absorption decreases as the amount consumed increases. An increased intake of calcium and vitamin D can also decrease absorption of magnesium. However, calcium and magnesium absorptions are competitive and mutually exclusive. For example, if a large amount of magnesium is present, less calcium is absorbed. Furthermore, phytic and oxalic acids present in fruits and vegetables can complex with magnesium and reduce its absorption.

Deficiency

Magnesium deficiency produces characteristic symptoms. These are: (1) tetany similar to that of hypocalcemia; (2) loss of muscular control (inability to relax and contract the muscles); (3) nervousness, irritability, and tremors that may precede convulsions; (4) induction of secondary calcium deficiency leading to the release of calcium from bones and thus calcification of soft tissues; and (5) other changes affecting the cardiovascular and renal systems, such as vasodilation and skin changes.

TABLE 7-10 Magnesium Content of Some Common Foods*

Food	Serving Size	Magnesium (mg)
Dairy products		
Milk, whole, fluid	1 c	30
Milk, skim	1 c	3
Cheese, cheddar	1 oz	8
Ice cream, vanilla, plain	½ c	10
Eggs		
Whole, hard boiled, large	1	6
Grain products		
Bread, white, enriched	1 sl	5
Granola, ready-to-eat	½ c	60
Oatmeal	½ c	30
Noodle	⅔ c	25
Rice, white, cooked	⅔ c	10
Meat, fish, poultry		
Beef, chuck roast	3 oz	20
Chicken fried breast	½	10
Cod, steak, sauteed	4 oz	30
Pork chop, medium size	1	15
Lobster, Northern, meat	⅔ c	20
Fruits		
Apple, medium size	1	10
Avocado	½	55
Cherries, raw, sweet	10	10
Plum, raw, medium size	1	6
Strawberries, whole, fresh	⅔ c	12
Vegetables		
Asparagus, fresh	½ c	15
Beans, lima, boiled	½ c	55
Cauliflower, cooked	½ c	8
Mushrooms, raw	½ c	5

*Data have been adapted from published results of a number of reports.

Severe magnesium deficiency is uncommon, for the bone surface serves as a reservoir for release and storage of the element, which is at constant equilibrium with the serum level of magnesium. In addition to this reserve, the kidney tubules offer additional protection through their ability to reabsorb magnesium.

Nevertheless, nutritionists suspect that the magnesium nutriture of the average American may just barely be adequate. This may explain why magnesium deficiency is induced in some individuals when they are under stress or given medications (see discussion below). If a person is deprived of magnesium for 1 to 3 months, severe deficiency may result. The deficiency can be magnified if the person is on a diet high in calcium or fluoride, since both can increase the excretion of magnesium.

Also, a number of clinical situations can produce magnesium deficiency. One is disorders of the gastrointestinal system, such as malabsorption, steatorrhea, vomiting, nausea, and diarrhea, for there is magnesium in the fluids lost or not absorbed. Some drugs may cause magnesium deficiency; for example, diuretics can force a considerable loss of magnesium in the urine, as can many clinical disorders. Alcoholics tend to be deficient in magnesium, since alcohol can interfere with its absorption. These individuals show the classic symptoms of muscular disturbances. Kwashiorkor (a deficiency disease chiefly related to a lack of protein in severely malnourished infants and children) can induce magnesium deficiency. Finally, long-term parenteral feeding can produce magnesium deficiency if this element is not included in the intravenous solution.

Chlorine

The body contains about 100 g of chlorine, most of which exists in the form of chloride, as in sodium chloride. Extracellular fluid contains most of the chloride (Chapter 9). The functions of chloride in the body are: (1) assisting in maintaining fluid, electrolyte, acid-base, and osmotic pressure balance in the compartments of the body; (2) serving as a component of hydrochloric acid in the stomach, thus playing an important role in stomach digestion and as an acid medium; (3) regulating some enzyme activities; and (4) facilitating the transfer of carbon dioxide from blood to the lungs.

The kidney excretes and reabsorbs the chloride ion, depending on its blood level. Although chloride is an essential element, the human requirement for it is unknown. In any event, chloride deficiency is rare, since table salt contains sodium chloride. Also, all foods contain some chloride, especially fruits and vegetables. Never-

theless, some clinical conditions can produce chloride deficiency. These include vomiting, diarrhea, fistula drainage of the intestinal system, alkalosis, and excess perspiration.

Sulfur

As a component of amino acids (methionine and cystine), sulfur is found in nucleic acids and all animal protein. It is present in every cell. Methionine and cystine are especially abundant in hair, skin, and nails. When hair is burnt, the odor is caused by the release of sulfur dioxide. Sulfur also exists in the inorganic form, as sulfate in fruits and vegetables.

Some major functions of sulfur in the body are: (1) storage and release of energy; (2) serving as a structural component of nucleic acids and vitamins (thiamin, biotin, and pantothenic and lipoic acids); (3) promotion of certain enzyme reactions; (4) serving as a component of body substances needed for the detoxification process; (5) collagen synthesis; and (6) promotion of blood clotting.

The human requirement for this element is unknown, and no known deficiency symptoms have been associated with a reduced intake of sulfur.

MICROELEMENTS

The elements iron, iodine, zinc, fluorine, copper, and other trace elements exist in much smaller quantities in the human body than the macroelements. Nevertheless, their presence in these small amounts is essential to body structures and processes.

Iron

The role of iron in human nutrition has caused much concern among public health workers and the scientific and medical communities. In spite of massive research and public health efforts, iron deficiency still affects certain population groups. Because of the importance of this subject, the discussion that follows reviews the functions and distribution of iron in the body; requirements of different population groups; factors influencing the absorption of iron; food sources of iron; symptoms of and treatment for iron depletion; iron supplements; and iron toxicity.

Body functions and distribution

Iron serves two major functions in the body. First, it is involved in cellular respiration. As part of hemoglobin and myoglobin, both of which are proteins, iron makes possible the transport of oxygen and carbon dioxide to and from the cells. The iron need for this purpose varies with the person's age, sex, stage of development, and clinical conditions. Second, iron regulates many important biological and chemical reactions in the body. For instance, iron is needed to synthesize vitamins, purines, and antibodies. Many reactions would not be possible without the presence of iron.

The human body contains about 3 to 5 g of iron; 70% is in the blood, and most of the remainder is in the liver, spleen, bone marrow, and intestine. Iron is found in every living cell. In the body, most iron exists in combination with some form of protein:

Blood: for respiration purposes, *hemoglobin*
        for transport purposes, *transferrin*
Organs: for storage purposes, *ferritin*

The body cannot regulate urinary excretion of iron, and the overall body content depends on the amount absorbed. However, the body does have other very efficient release and storage mechanisms to retain iron. All iron-containing substances are recycled in the body, and all iron released from body catabolism is also recycled and mainly retained.

Requirements of different population groups

Each person needs a certain amount of iron to support a normal blood profile. For example, in the approximately 5 L of blood in the body, there are about 15 g hemoglobin/100 mL blood in the male adult and about 13.6 g in the female.

Iron is lost daily in skin, hair, feces, urine, nails, intestinal linings, and sweat. Additional iron is lost in menstrual fluids. An adult loses about 0.7 to 1 mg of iron a day, while menstruation accounts for an additional loss of 0.5 to 1 mg. In addition to replenishing daily losses, children and infants need extra iron to support their growth.

Table 7-11 gives the iron requirements of different population groups. The values here should be compared with the latest and more specific RDA presented in Table 1 of the appendix.

Absorption rate

The first part of the small intestine permits the greatest absorption of iron, although the stomach and the entire small intestine also permit absorption. The American diet provides about 10 to 20 mg of iron. Under normal circumstances, only about 2% to 10% of this ingested iron is absorbed within 5 to 24 hours. However, special needs of the body may increase this absorption rate, such as growth, iron deficiency, pregnancy, surgery, and hemorrhage. Under these stressful circumstances, about 50% to 60% of the ingested iron may be absorbed.

Some foods increase iron absorption, while others depress it. For example, meat and citrus fruits eaten together can improve iron absorption, while eggs may reduce it. About 30% to 40% of the iron in meat is absorbed, while only 5% to 10% of the iron in egg yolk is. Fruits and vegetables, because of their bulk, interfere with iron absorption.

Phytic acid in oatmeal and other whole-grain cereals may chelate iron and reduce its absorption, as can oxalic acid in vegetables such as rhubarb and spinach. However, this effect is significant only if large amounts of the two acids are present. The particular chemical form of iron in the intestinal lumen also determines the extent of iron absorption. The ferrous form is absorbed more easily than the ferric form. Any condition that favors the ferrous form therefore facilitates iron absorption. For instance, an acidic medium keeps the iron in ferrous form. The simultaneous ingestion of a large amount of ascorbic acid (vitamin C) can facilitate iron absorption. Some commercial supplements claim that their

TABLE 7-11   Approximate Iron Requirements of Certain Population Groups

| Population Group | Iron Needed Each Day (mg) | | | | |
	Obligatory loss	Loss from menstruation	Need for growth	Need for pregnancy	Total need
Postmenopausal females and adult males	0.7–1.0	0	0	0	0.7–1.0
Menstruating females	0.7–1.0	0.5–1.0	0	0	1.2–2.0
Pregnant females, over 17 years	0.7–1.0	0	0	1.0–2.0	1.7–3.0
12–17-year-old nonpregnant females	0.7–1.0	0.5–1.0	0.4–0.8	0	1.6–2.8
12–17-year-old pregnant females	0.7–1.0	0	0.4–0.8	1.0–2.0	2.1–3.8
0–3-year-olds	0.2–0.3	0	0.3–0.6	0	0.5–0.9
3–10-year-olds	0.3–0.4	0	0.4–0.5	0	0.7–0.9
10–17-year-olds*	0.5–0.8	0	0.1–0.9	0	0.6–1.7
Nursing mothers	0.7–1.0	0–1.0	0.5–1.0†	0	1.2–2.0

*Excluding 12 to 17-year-old females.
†Amount in milk for infant growth.

iron content is absorbed more easily because of the vitamin C added, but this is true only if the vitamin is present in a large dose.

Amino acids such as methionine and cystine can also maintain the ferrous form and thus facilitate iron absorption. Excess antacids may hinder absorption of iron, since the acid in the stomach will be neutralized. Iron exists mainly in the ferric form in food, but the stomach acid changes part of it to the ferrous form for absorption.

The amount of iron ingested can also influence its absorption. For example, the more iron consumed at one time, the less absorbed. A few smaller doses of iron are absorbed better than one large dose of equivalent quantity.

Foods in the stomach, or in bulk, can decrease iron absorption. Consequently, iron should be taken before the meal or on an empty stomach, although iron can produce adverse reactions if there is no food to buffer the element (see later discussion on iron supplements).

Food sources

The amount of iron needed daily to replenish losses and meet special needs is relatively small. However, because only a portion of the iron ingested is actually absorbed, iron intake must be considerably higher than iron needs.

The American diet provides about 6 mg of iron per 1,000 kcal. Most adult males with a well-balanced diet usually have no problem obtaining the iron they need daily; however, this level of intake does not give women the 15 to 20 mg iron they must consume daily unless they eat over 3,000 kcal each day.

Table 7-12 lists the iron content of some representative foods. However, it is sometimes misleading to estimate iron intake by evaluating food sources. A food containing a high level of iron will not benefit the body if only a small amount of the food is consumed. Also, an iron-rich food will not be a significant source if only a

TABLE 7-12   Iron Content of Some Representative Foods*

Foods	Serving Size	Iron (mg)
Dairy products		
Milk, whole, fluid	8 oz	0.10
Cheese, cheddar or Swiss	1 oz	0.30
Meat and alternates		
Liver, calf or lamb	2 sl	13.4
Liver, beef or chicken	¼–½ c	5.0
Beef, lamb, pork, veal; cooked	3 oz	2.5
Fish	3 oz	1.0
Grain products		
Bread, enriched or whole grain	3 sl	1.7
Cereals, enriched, ready-to-eat	1 oz	1.3
Spaghetti, noodles, macaroni, cooked	3 oz	1.0
Vegetables		
Spinach, cooked	½ c	2.0
Beet greens, cooked	½ c	1.9
Chard, cooked	½ c	1.8
Potato, white, medium size	1	0.7
Soybeans, cooked	½ c	2.5
Beans, lima, cooked	½ c	2.0
Peas, green, cooked	½ c	1.4
Fruits		
Figs, dried, small	2	0.9
Raisins	2 T	0.6
Peach, raw, medium size	1	0.6
Grapes, average size	22–24	0.4
Cherries, small	20–25	0.4

*Adapted from *Nutritive Value of Foods*, Home and Garden Bulletin No. 72 (Washington, D.C.: U.S. Department of Agriculture, 1981).

small portion of the iron in the food is available for absorption.

Many factors influence the absorption rate of iron, making it very difficult to evaluate iron intake by inspection of food sources. For example, the availability and absorption of iron in food may depend on whether the food is eaten alone or with another item.

Food preparation procedures also affect the iron content in food and thus the amount consumed. For example, using iron utensils in cooking can add a substantial amount of iron to the dishes, especially if the medium is acidic. Iron in foods leaches into the water or fluid during cooking. Thus, using a large amount of fluid in cooking and then discarding it can cause a large loss of iron, as can peeling and discarding unwanted parts.

Despite these variables, certain general statements can be made about food sources of iron. Liver is probably the richest source of iron, although the amount varies with the animal source; also, liver is not a popular food. Milk and milk products are probably the lowest food sources of iron. Vegetables in general provide two to four times more iron than fruits and juices, which are considered poor sources. Potatoes, green leaves, and stalks are good sources of iron. Peas, nuts, and beans range from poor to moderate sources of iron, depending on type. Most of the bread and flour sold in this country has a high concentration of iron because of enrichment. Some infant cereals and prepared dried cereals contain quite high levels of iron because of competition among manufacturers to increase sales through claims of high iron con-

TABLE 7-13   Progressively Reduced Body Iron Nutriture

Iron Nutriture	Clinical Observations							
	Iron storage in bone marrow	Tissue iron content	Red blood cell iron content	Iron absorption	Anemia	Transferrin* saturation (%)	Hematocrit[†] (%)	Hemoglobin[‡] (g/100 mL)
Normal body iron content	Normal	Normal	Normal	Normal	No	>16	>38	>12
Latent iron deficiency or iron depletion	Reduced	Normal	Normal	Slightly elevated	No	10–16	>38	10–12
Iron-deficient erythropoiesis or reduced red blood corpuscle formation due to iron deficiency	Empty	Normal	Slightly reduced	Greatly elevated	Maybe	10–16	31–37	10–12
Body iron deficiency anemia	Empty	Slightly reduced	Reduced by half	Greatly elevated	Microcytic hypochromic	<10	<31	<10
Body tissue iron deficiency	Empty	Reduced by half	Reduced by half	Greatly elevated	Microcytic hypochromic	<10	<30	<10

*In the presence of carbon dioxide, the iron from the plasma forms a complex with a metal-binding β-globulin known as transferrin. The extent to which transferrin is saturated with iron indicates the amount of iron (ferric) available for the bone marrow.

[†]When blood with anticoagulant is centrifuged, the cell solids settle to the bottom of the tube. A straw-colored liquid, the plasma, stays on top. Normally the cells comprise about 45% of the total volume. This reading (45%) is a normal hematocrit, or packed-cell volume, for males; for females, the figure is 41%.

[‡]The concentration of hemoglobin is usually measured by the grams of the substance per 100 mL of blood.

tent. Certain products such as raisins, blackstrap molasses, oysters, clams, and cocoa have high contents of iron, but they are usually consumed in small quantities.

Iron depletion symptoms and treatment

Although *anemia* is a household word, anemia is a severe disorder; simple iron deficiency does not necessarily produce anemia. Table 7-13 describes the different stages of iron depletion and indicates how each stage is diagnosed. In addition to these laboratory indications, there are clinical signs. When there is iron deficiency but no anemia, patients may complain of fatigue, weakness, and lassitude. It is difficult to correlate such complaints with genuine iron deficiency, because although iron therapy in these patients may eliminate the symptoms, a placebo sometimes works as well. In some asymptomatic patients, iron deficiency is detected when they are studied for other clinical conditions. Before iron depletion leads to anemia, the patient may suffer only mild effects on work and activity efficiency.

Iron deficiency with or without anemia can produce characteristic symptoms: pallor, weakness, breathing difficulty on exertion, palpitation, a sense of "dead-tiredness," and coldness and abnormal nervous sensation in the hands and feet. The lack of iron leads to a defective enzyme system, which leads to failure in converting food to energy. This failure, accompanied by a depressed blood volume, is responsible for the feeling of tiredness. In most patients, these symptoms are insidious and difficult to define when they begin.

Iron deficiency is also characterized by other symptoms. In older individuals, iron deficiency is accompanied by oral and intestinal lesions. Tongue inflammation with soreness and papillary atrophy are more common in older female patients. There is also inflammation of the corner of the mouth and oral mucosae. Intestinal disorders include fluctuating appetite, stomach pain (from inflammation of mucosa) and heartburn, flatulence, constipation, or diarrhea. Some patients, especially middle-aged women, have difficulty in swallowing. See Figure 7-5.

Long-term iron deficiency is associated with *koilonychia*, a condition in which fingernails and sometimes toenails become lusterless, thin, brittle, flattened, and then spoon-shaped. More severe clinical disturbances, which are rare, include heart trouble, spleen enlargement, headaches, edema, and visual abnormalities.

Some identifiable causes of iron deficiency are: (1) loss of blood for overt or occult (hidden) reasons, such as external or internal injuries; (2) gastrointestinal loss through diarrhea, malabsorption, and steatorrhea; (3) frequent blood donation; (4) inadequate intake, especially among the elderly, some teenage girls, and any individual with a very imbalanced diet; (5) the practice of pica—eating starch, clay, ice, and other nonfood items—especially among children; (6) drugs: laxatives, antibiotics, amphetamines, clofibrate, aspirin, and corticosteroids; and (7) the vulnerability of certain population groups to iron deficiency (Table 7-11). Premature and low-birth-weight infants have a low storage of iron, and breast and formula milk is generally low in iron. On the other hand, excess milk drinking can cause occult intestinal blood loss, especially among children. Young women of childbearing age may have excess menstrual blood loss. Women who have had more than one or two babies are likely to suffer iron lack if they do not make sure that their body storage is replenished immediately after each childbirth.

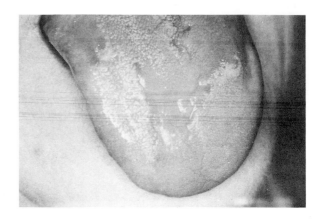

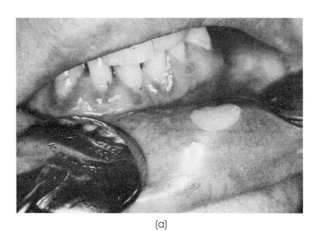

(a)

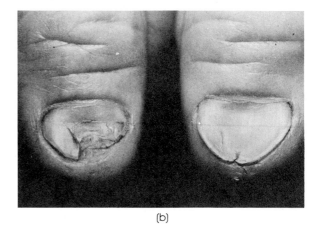

(b)

FIGURE 7-5   Signs of iron deficiency. (a) Top: patchy depapillation of tongue (latent iron deficiency). Bottom: generalized stomatitis, ulceration, and gingivitis (malabsorption syndrome). (From W. R. Tyldesley, *Brit. Dent. J.* 139 [1975]: 232) (b) Iron deficiency koilonychia. (From S. Dreizen, *Geriatrics* 29 [1974]: 97. By permission of *Geriatrics*)

Before treatment, a patient must be correctly diagnosed, and all causes of iron deficiency or anemia—especially blood loss—must be corrected. Simultaneous treatment of symptoms consists of giving the patient oral iron (50 mg per day), for example, 0.2 g of ferrous sulfate or 0.3 g of ferrous gluconate thrice daily after meals. An adequate response is indicated by a rise of at least 2 g of hemoglobin/100 mL every three weeks. The level may not increase for a week or two. Oral iron should be continued for 3 months after hemoglobin values have returned to normal in order to replenish iron values. If the response is unsatisfactory, the clinician should reconfirm the diagnostic tests and criteria, ensure that the patient has taken the tablets as prescribed, and ascertain whether the patient is losing blood faster than can be compensated.

Blood transfusion to correct the disorder is rarely indicated. The rate of patient response to parenteral iron therapy will be no faster than to oral dosages. However, acceptable indications for the use of intravenous techniques are strong patient reaction to oral iron, extensive, chronic blood loss, intestinal malabsorption of iron, and known patient noncompliance in taking prescribed oral iron. Intravenous infusion is preferred to injection. Injection may elicit responses such as pain and reaction at the site of injection, dizziness, headache, vomiting, nausea, backache, flushing, and urogenital irritation. Anaphylaxis and death have been reported. A minor but frequent reaction to intravenous iron infusion is thrombophlebitis. In general, iron dextran or iron-sorbitol-citric acid complex is the chemical compound commonly used in parenteral iron therapy.

Iron supplements

Supplemental iron is frequently taken orally in tablet, liquid, or other form, with or without prescription. Ferrous salts are better absorbed than the ferric ones. There is no difference among the different ferrous salt supplements: ferrous sulfate, ferrous gluconate, ferrous fumarate, ferrous citrate, and others are absorbed equally well. When purchased by their generic names, the label "U.S.P." (United States Pharmacopeia) guarantees purity. Some common commercial brands are Feosol, Fergon, and Ir-

con. Some tablets are time released or enteric coated.

Taking iron supplements has some side effects. The higher the dose, the more severe and frequent the side effects. If some tablets result in fewer side effects, they probably contain less iron or iron that is not in an absorbable form. Depending on the dose and the patient, about 10% to 15% of patients develop side effects. Major problems occur in the gastrointestinal tract: gastric pain, nausea, heartburn, diarrhea, constipation, and black stools. Side effects may be avoided by taking the tablets with food or starting with low doses and slowly progressing to higher ones. Sustained-release or enteric-coated preparations may decrease side effects, but again the amount of iron available is probably less. Since iron is primarily absorbed in the duodenum, any sustained-release and enteric-coated preparation may not dissolve well in the stomach and duodenal juices, and the iron may be passed in the bowel. Nevertheless, most pharmacists dispense time-released preparations unless otherwise specified. The tooth-staining effect from liquid preparations for children can be avoided by brushing the teeth or rinsing the mouth afterward or using a straw.

Ferrous sulfate is the most widely used and prescribed form of iron supplement. It is cheap and palatable, has minimal side effects, and is as effective as other, more expensive preparations. Ferrous sulfate contains about 25 mg of elemental iron per 125 mg of salt. Table 7-14 shows the appropriate form of iron supplement and the necessary number of tablets a day for a patient prescribed 200 to 250 mg of iron a day. The tablets can be taken with foods or between meals. They are best tolerated with foods, although maximal absorption occurs on an empty stomach, when there are more side effects. An oral dose of 200 to 250 mg of elemental iron generally supplies the 50 mg of iron needed for optimal bone marrow response, assuming a 20% absorption.

Vitamin C can only promote absorption if 200 to 500 mg of the vitamin is present. The small amount of vitamin C included in some supplements is therefore not worth the added expense. Preparations containing other vitamins or trace minerals offer no special advantage besides the added nutrients.

TABLE 7-14 Quantities of Elemental Iron Contained in Iron Compounds or Supplements

Iron Compound or Supplement	Iron per Tablet (mg)	No. of Tablets Daily per Adult*
Ferrous sulfate (hydrated or dehydrated)	55–65	4
Ferrous fumarate (small tablet)	65	4
Ferrous gluconate	40	5–6
Ferroglycine sulfate	40	5–6

*To provide 240 mg of iron.

Iron toxicity

Iron toxicity is associated with two clinical conditions: siderosis and hemochromatosis. *Siderosis* is an increased blood level of iron and its excess deposition in body tissues. *Hemochromatosis* is disturbed iron metabolism associated with tissue deposition of iron, skin bronze pigmentation, diabetes mellitus, and liver cirrhosis.

Iron toxicity may result from numerous causes. One is hereditary disease. There is a genetic predisposition to excess storage of iron, especially in the liver. A second cause is excess consumption. Many Bantus in South Africa suffer iron toxicity because they use rusty iron cooking utensils. In Western societies, chronic iron toxicity from long-term consumption of iron tablets has occasionally been documented. Third, iron toxicity may result from excess blood transfusion or intravenous iron therapy. Toxicity occurs when the quantity of iron administered exceeds the blood transport capacity and is deposited in the liver. Fourth, certain clinical disorders may cause increased absorption and storage of iron. For instance, as a result of diseases such as alcohol abuse and hepatitis, iron is stored in the liver because of its inability to metabolize the element.

Fifth, accidental ingestion may result in acute iron poisoning. The increasing purchase of iron supplements for home use has been accompanied by a rise in accidental iron poisonings of infants and children. Dosages of 5 to 10 tablets usually pose no problem for an adult but have proved fatal to some young children. The use of child-proof containers is expected to reduce the number of such accidents. The symptoms of acute iron poisoning are severe gastrointestinal reactions such as cramps, pain, vomiting, nausea, and blood-stained black stool; metabolic acidosis; and shock, convulsions, and coma. The patient may die within 24 hours. An overdose of iron salt in a child requires prompt treatment, which basically involves chelating the excess iron in the intestinal system and in the blood. Procedures include gastric aspiration and lavage. Chemical compounds such as sodium bicarbonate and deferoxamine may be given orally to precipitate the iron as complex or insoluble salts. Intravenous deferoxamine may be given to chelate iron in the blood system.

Iodine

Iodine is an essential element found in the thyroid gland. Tyrosine (an amino acid) combines with iodine to form the important thyroid hormone thyroxine, which regulates basal metabolic rate.

Deficiency

Simple goiter results from a lack of iodine, causing a reduction of the thyroid hormone in the circulation, which in turn stimulates the gland to make more of the hormone. This fruitless attempt results in the enlargement of the gland (Figure 7-6). In general, males are less susceptible to simple goiter than females, but during cold weather intensified body metabolism may induce iodine deficiency or goiter in both men and women.

Iodine deficiency may be particularly harmful to children. Since thyroid hormone controls metabolic rate, it regulates body growth and development. A serious deficiency of thyroid hormone from a lack of iodine may cause the clinical disorder *cretinism*, which may occur at birth or during infancy and childhood. The child is retarded in body and mental development, with apelike, coarse facial features. Because of this potential problem, the need for iodine in the

(a)

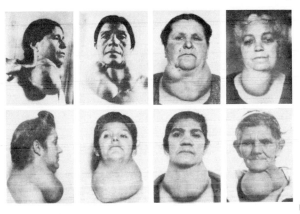

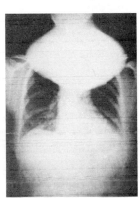

(b)

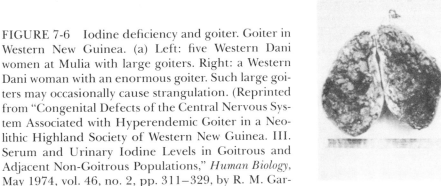
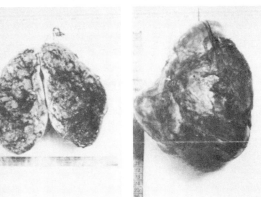

FIGURE 7-6   Iodine deficiency and goiter. Goiter in Western New Guinea. (a) Left: five Western Dani women at Mulia with large goiters. Right: a Western Dani woman with an enormous goiter. Such large goiters may occasionally cause strangulation. (Reprinted from "Congenital Defects of the Central Nervous System Associated with Hyperendemic Goiter in a Neolithic Highland Society of Western New Guinea. III. Serum and Urinary Iodine Levels in Goitrous and Adjacent Non-Goitrous Populations," *Human Biology*, May 1974, vol. 46, no. 2, pp. 311–329, by R. M. Garruto, D. C. Gajdusek, and J. ten Brink, by permission of the Wayne State University Press. © Wayne State University Press, 1974) (b) Top: severe endemic goiter in Mendoza Province, Argentina, as seen between 1930 and 1950. Right: a patient, X-ray film of chest, parts of one lobe of goiter, and the cut surface. (From H. Perinetti and L. N. Staneloni, *Environ. Res.* 3 [1970]: 463)

female population requires special attention. Teenage girls are especially susceptible to iodine deficiency and goiter because of the stress of adolescence. Sterility in a female may occur if iodine deficiency is prolonged. A lack of iodine during pregnancy may predispose the mother to goiter and the newborn to goiter and cretinism. Further, menopausal women are also susceptible to goiter if their intake of iodine falls below normal.

Iodine deficiency is particularly common in certain areas. Goiter is endemic (occurring in a relatively high percentage of the population) in areas with little iodine in the soil and drinking water. It is suspected that glacial erosion, floods, and rains leach iodine from the soil. In the United States, the Rocky Mountain states and areas around the Great Lakes (Ohio, Wisconsin, and Michigan), once called "the Goiter Belt," still have problems with iodine deficiency. A 1970 nutrition survey indicated that the incidence of goiter among children and adults in these areas was 5% to 10%. The soil and water of these locations are low in iodine, but there is some speculation that the goiter is due to something other than iodine deficiency (see Chapter 21), since iodized salt is used extensively in these regions. In general, coastal areas do not have trouble with iodine deficiency, since the air, soil, and water all have a high level of the element. But many primitive areas of the world, such as isolated spots in India and Central and South America, still have endemic goiter. Figure 7-6 provides some examples.

Requirements and food sources

The RDA for iodine is about 100 to 130 μg per day. Its level of intake in this country varies with the geography. In areas where there is a high level of iodine in the soil and animal feed, the intake of the element from plant and animal foods is large.

Iodized salt is a potent source; if it is used regularly, iodine depletion is unlikely. The next best source of iodine is seafood and seafood products. Fresh fruits, grains (especially refined flour), and pulses (certain peas) contribute little iodine to our diet. The iodine content of vegetables, milk, butter, eggs, and cheese varies with the types of soil and animal feed.

Some plant foods contain substances that can produce goiter in people. These substances, known as *goitrogens*, are discussed in Chapter 21.

Toxicity

Iodine is toxic if 1 to 50 mg per day are consumed for a long period. Doses of iodine used to treat goiter have been reported to cause poisoning in some patients. Some people eat kelp or sea salt out of personal preference or for self-treatment of clinical disorders, including goiter. This practice may result in iodine poisoning, since some of these products have a high iodine content.

Zinc

In the last few years the importance of zinc has been demonstrated by the massive amount of scientific literature written on the subject. The body contains about 1.5 to 3 g of zinc. Although it is located in almost every part of the body, bones contain the most zinc, followed by tissues such as the hair, skin, and prostate.

Requirements and food sources

According to the latest RDA, the adult requirement for zinc is about 15 to 25 mg/day; for more information, consult Table 1 of the appendix. About 15% to 35% of ingested zinc is absorbed, and the American diet provides about 10 to 15 mg of utilizable zinc per day.

Many expensive foods such as meat and oysters contain rich amounts of zinc. Since the best sources of zinc are expensive foods, low-income people may tend to have a low zinc intake. Items such as rice, noodles, fruits, and vegetables contain very little zinc. Cow's milk contains more zinc than breast milk, but the significance of this fact is unknown.

The zinc contribution of grains is somewhat complicated. In many countries grain products are refined, with loss of zinc-containing husks, and the element is not added back to flour. On the other hand, the outer husks of grains and legumes contain phytic acid, which can complex with zinc and interfere with its absorption, especially if phytic acid is consumed in excess. Un-

TABLE 7-15   Zinc Content of Some Representative Foods*

Food	Serving Size	Zinc (mg)
Dairy products		
Milk, whole	1 c	1.0
Cheese, American, pasteurized, processed	1 oz	0.8
Egg, whole, large	1	0.7
Cereals and equivalents		
Bread, white, enriched	1 sl	0.2
Bran, flakes, ready-to-eat	1 c	1.3
Grain and equivalents		
Rice, brown	⅔ c	0.8
Noodle, enriched, cooked	½ c	0.6
Potato, baked, large	1	0.4
Beans, peas, nuts		
Soybeans, cooked	½ c	0.6
Peas, split, dry, cooked	½ c	1.1
Peanut butter	1 T	0.4
Meat, fish, poultry		
Beef, roast, chuck	3 oz	3.7
Chicken, roast, light meat, no skin	3 oz	0.9
Salmon, steak, broiled	1	2.4
Oysters, Eastern, raw	6	90.0
Fruits		
Apricots, fresh, medium size	2–3	0.04
Orange, raw, medium	1	0.3
Pineapple, raw, crushed	1 c	0.3
Raisins	¼ c	0.06
Vegetables		
Broccoli, fresh, boiled	½ c	0.2
Carrot, raw	1	0.3
Onions, green, raw, bulb and top, chopped	¼ c	0.07
Tomato, raw, medium size	1	0.3

*Adapted from E. W. Murphy et al., "The Provisional Zinc Contents of Food," *J. Amer. Dietet. Assoc.* 66 (1975): 345. Also see Table 12 of the appendix.

leavened bread, used widely in many Middle Eastern countries and India, contains a large amount of phytic acid. By contrast, leavened bread has a low level of phytate because fermentation activates the enzyme phytase, which is capable of destroying phytate.

The source of drinking water and the utensils used in food preparation can also influence zinc intake. For example, galvanized utensils can leach varying amounts of zinc from foods cooked in them.

Table 7-15 describes the zinc content of some common foods. More data are provided in Table 6 of the appendix.

Functions and deficiency

Zinc deficiency is hard to diagnose, with or without clinical symptoms. Normal serum zinc level is about 6 to 13 mg per 100 mL. However, during stresses such as infection, hormonal imbalance, anemia, pregnancy, and the usage of certain drugs, the level may decrease. On the other hand, the serum zinc level may rise during tissue catabolism. A low or high urinary zinc level does not necessarily reflect body zinc nutriture. Hair zinc level reflects the chronic, rather than acute, state of zinc nutrition. Zinc levels in serum, urine, and hair may have to be analyzed simultaneously to arrive at even tentative conclusions.

Subtle signs of zinc deficiency may also show up in the body in a number of ways, since zinc is important to many body processes. It serves as a component of enzymes (such as insulin) and of DNA and RNA, and it participates in the metabolism of proteins, fats, carbohydrates, and nucleic acids (see Chapter 8). Zinc deficiencies have recently been implicated in disorders of sexual development, growth, and reproductive ability; wound healings and skin health; appetite and sensations of taste and smell; acrodermatitis enteropathica; and immunocompetence, hyperalimentation, and sickle cell anemia. These specific functions and disorders are discussed in the sections below; the following list summarizes some causes of zinc deficiency.

A. Interference with absorption.
    1. Steatorrhea and intestinal absorption.
    2. Chelating or complexing of zinc, making it unavailable for absorption, by phytate and fibers, including certain drugs, e.g., penicillamine, which can chelate metals.
B. Inborn error of metabolism.
    1. Acrodermatitis enteropathica.
C. Presence of a clinical disorder.
    1. Blood losses from trauma.
    2. Surgery, burns, injury.
    3. Liver cirrhosis and alcoholism.
    4. Sickle cell anemia.
D. Increased body zinc demand.
    1. Pregnancy and nursing.
    2. Growth and development.
    3. Tissue repair and building.
E. Low dietary supply.
    1. Imbalanced intake because of cost of foods or personal inclination.
    2. Simple starvation.

Sexual development, growth, and reproductive ability. Adequate zinc intake during the growing years is important for sexual maturation and body development. During the last 20 years, health authorities have attributed some forms of adult dwarfism in Egypt and Iran among villagers to zinc and iron deficiency. The patients show deficient zinc levels in their blood, hair, and urine. They develop symptoms such as anemia, hepatosplenomegaly, hypogonadism, growth retardation, and the absence of sexual development. The disorder is most common among male adolescents. For example, a 20-year-old man will have the physical and sexual characteristics of a 10-year-old child. Some of these patients have responded to treatment with zinc and iron and showed good recovery.

The deficiency of the elements might have been caused by several factors. First, the unleavened bread eaten by these Middle Eastern people contains a high level of phytate, which can chelate zinc and iron, making them unavailable for absorption. Second, frequent infection with schistosomiasis (infestation with tropical blood parasites) can increase the zinc and iron excreted in the urine. Third, the practice of pica among these children (eating clay, starch, and other nonfood items) can cause zinc to be complexed, rendering it less available for absorption. Fourth, excess perspiration in a hot climate increases the loss of zinc.

A number of studies have indicated that zinc supplementation may improve growth and sexual development in zinc-deficient children. In Iran, "normal" children with a marginal level of body zinc showed improvements in height, weight, bone growth, and sexual maturation when administered zinc supplements, with the males being more responsive. Before 1975, commercial infant formulas sold in the United States were not supplemented with zinc. In one study, infants on special-formula diets supplemented with zinc showed a slight increment in height and weight compared with nonsupplemented controls. Again, male infants showed a better response.

In animals, zinc deficiency in the mother during pregnancy adversely affects the newborn. Pregnant women deficient in zinc may give birth to low-birth-weight infants.

Wound healing and skin health. For many years scientists have suspected that zinc plays an important part in the healing of wounds. However, reports on this topic have been conflicting, and the information presented below must be interpreted in this light.

For damaged tissues to repair and regenerate, a large local concentration of zinc is needed. However, stresses such as trauma, crush injury, surgery, burns, and general tissue damage usually induce a large loss of zinc in the urine. Some clinical uses of supplemental zinc on wound healing have sound promising results, although there are also some negative reports. In humans, indolent wounds and chronic leg ulcers have healed spontaneously when the patients were given zinc supplementation despite being previously refractory to other treatments. Zinc supplementation has also been shown to hasten the healing of pilonidal cyst surgical wounds. In spite of conflicting reports, the rate of wound healing in patients with diagnosed zinc depletion does improve with zinc supplementation, especially during the recovery period.

The zinc nutrition of a hospitalized patient requires special considerations. Long-term borderline intake of zinc may result in poor zinc nutriture in the patient, although not necessarily a severe deficiency. Any abnormal zinc metabolism associated with an illness may increase urinary and fecal zinc loss. Also, infection and trauma may lead to a massive loss of zinc.

Thus, the clinical use of zinc supplementation may be guided by the following considerations. If wound healing in a patient is delayed, serum, urine, and hair zinc levels should be ascertained and zinc supplement used if necessary. Zinc supplementation should be considered for patients with leg, duodenal, or peptic ulcers, and bedsores, even if the plasma, urine, and hair zinc levels of these patients is adequate. In addition, clinical experience has shown that patients with malabsorption, malnutrition, malignant diseases, atherosclerosis, diabetes mellitus, and pulmonary infections heal poorly. Zinc supplementation should be considered for these patients.

In one zinc supplementation regimen, 220 mg of zinc sulfate heptahydrate (45 mg of zinc) is administered three times a day. Since a normal intake of zinc is only about 0.2 mg per day, the risks of toxicity from a supplemental dose must be considered. The clinician should be cautious of any induced copper deficiency if the patient is on a zinc supplement for more than a few months.

In addition to aiding wound healing, zinc supplementation has recently been shown to have a beneficial effect on acne. In one study, an oral dose of 135 mg of zinc (as zinc sulfate) resulted in a dramatic decrease of the acne condition within a month. In another study, the simultaneous use of zinc and tetracycline caused a 70% decrease in the acne counts. The use of low-dose zinc to reduce perspiration odor has also been suggested.

Taste and smell sensation.   Changes in taste and smell sensation, including decreased acuity and distorted perception, accompany many clinical disorders. This happens commonly in patients with cancer (Chapter 29), especially during chemo- and radiotherapy. Short-term complaints of taste and smell changes occur during acute hepatitis, early pregnancy, and infection of the upper respiratory tract. An alteration in taste and smell invariably makes the patient lose appetite and avoid food, leading to weight loss. As yet, scientists are not certain that these adverse changes are a result of zinc deficiency. However, a number of clinical reports indicate that in many of these patients the administration of zinc restores normal taste and smell sensation. Many clinicians are therefore currently testing zinc therapy with such patients, with mixed results.

In some cases, zinc deficiency itself may cause taste and smell alterations, leading people to avoid zinc-rich foods and thereby aggravating the deficiency. In the course of studying hair analyses of 132 apparently normal children, investigators noted a depressed zinc level in 8 children. Further examination indicated that these children were below standard in weight and growth. They had not been eating well and had been avoiding meat because of its "bad taste." Supplementation of 0.2 to 0.4 mg of zinc per day per kilogram of body weight improved the taste sensation in 3 of the patients in 3 months, and their weight and growth gains improved.

Acrodermatitis enteropathica.   Acrodermatitis enteropathica is a rare genetic disorder in which the victim has a severe zinc deficiency because of intestinal malabsorption. The onset of the disease, which is of autosomal recessive inheritance, occurs during infancy. The patient suffers symptoms such as diarrhea, vomiting,

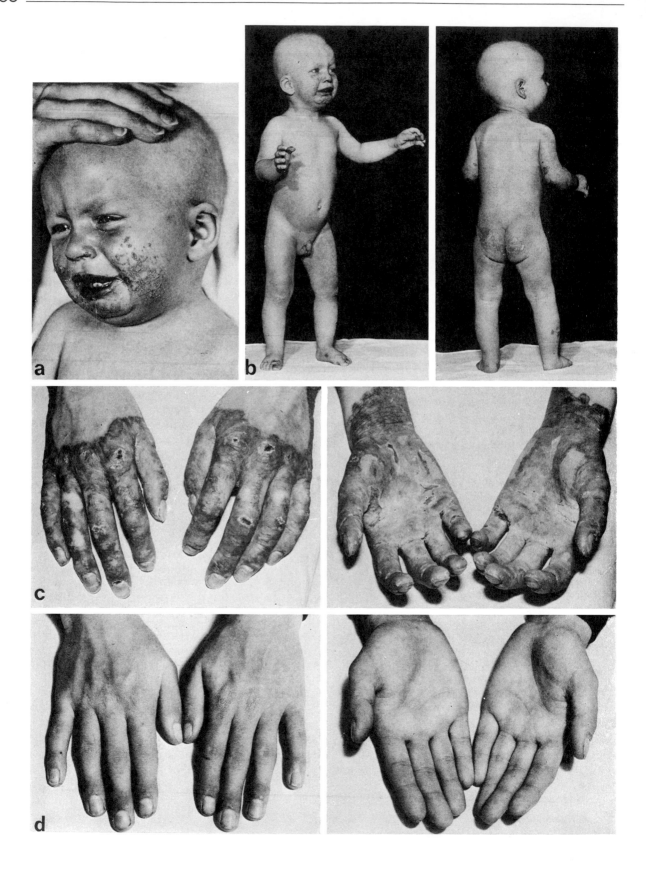

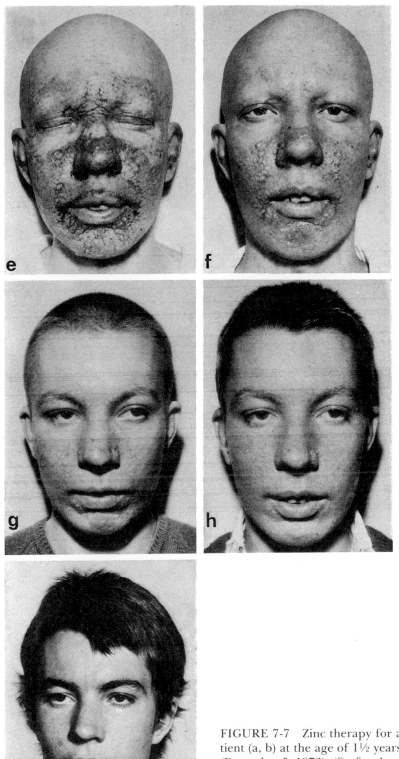

FIGURE 7-7   Zinc therapy for acrodermatitis enteropathica. The patient (a, b) at the age of 1½ years; (c, e) 20 years old, before treatment (December 5, 1973); (f) after 1 week of treatment (December 12, 1973); (g) after 6 weeks of treatment (January 17, 1974); (h) after 2½ months of treatment (February 21, 1974); (d, i) after 5 months of treatment (May 9, 1974). (From N. Thyresson, *Acta Dermato-Venereology* 54 [1974]: 383)

hair loss, growth retardation, and emotional instability. The most obvious symptom is eczematous vesicular-bullous skin lesions over many parts of the body. The time of onset depends on the presence and duration of breast feeding, with the clinical manifestations generally appearing 1 or 2 weeks after weaning. Early breast milk is unique; it has a high concentration of zinc (16 mg/L) combined with a low-molecular-weight protein that can increase the absorption of zinc. Zinc concentration in other forms of milk for infants is 0.65 mg/L in breast milk at 6 months, 3 to 4 mg/L in cow's milk, and 1.8 mg/L in formulated milk made from diluted skim milk.

We now know that acrodermatitis enteropathica can be easily managed by the daily administration of 1 to 2 mg of zinc per kilogram of body weight (Figure 7-7). The child's zinc level will return to normal and is followed by catch-up growth to a height like that of other normal children.

Immunocompetence. In a few clinical studies, zinc deficiency has been shown to cause impaired cellular immunity. It may therefore be a factor in increased susceptiblity to infections in conditions such as protein-calorie (or calorie-protein) malnutrition.

Hyperalimentation. When some patients are placed on total parenteral nutrition (see Chapter 23), they develop zinc deficiency and all the concomitant symptoms of skin lesions, diarrhea, hair loss, and severe depression. There are four possible causes: (1) insufficient zinc in the intravenous solution because of long-term feeding; (2) high zinc loss in the urine from tissue catabolism secondary to trauma or disorders that have required the total parenteral nutrition; (3) sepsis secondary to the intravenous feeding, which may result in a large loss of zinc; and (4) amino acids in high concentration in the intravenous solution that may combine with zinc in plasma and increase its excretion in the urine. Zinc supplementation in these patients results in a dramatic improvement in the skin and the patient's mood.

Sickle cell anemia. Many patients with sickle cell anemia show growth retardation, hy-

pogonadism, and poor wound healing. These patients may be suffering from zinc deficiency, since some of them excrete a large amount of zinc in the urine. The hemolytic conditions of these patients may have presented more zinc for excretion by the kidneys, which fail to retain the element. Another possibility is that the patients may not be absorbing zinc properly. In a limited number of cases, patients with sickle cell anemia have responded positively to zinc supplementation. At present, intensive research is being conducted to study the relationship between zinc and the disease.

Fluorine

Fluorine, more commonly known as fluoride (the ionized form of fluorine), has received much public attention because of its role in tooth decay, but the essential nature of fluorine has only recently been recognized. Because it is one of the most abundant elements, it is widely distributed. However, not much is known about its metabolic functions.

We do know that fluoride plays an important role in the formation and maintenance of bones and teeth. During the initial developmental stages of a tooth, systemic fluoride is incorporated into its structure in the form of calcium fluoridated apatite, $Ca_5(PO_4)_3F$. The other mineral portion of the tooth is calcium hydroxyapatite, $Ca_5(PO_4)_3OH$, which occurs in three times the quantity of the fluoride form. Fluoride is important during early childhood when the teeth are forming. After a tooth has erupted, fluoride is still important in assisting the ongoing maturation of the outer layer of enamel, for fluoride present is incorporated topically into the crystal spaces. In this manner, the tooth is subject to less decay throughout the person's life.

Since the food sources of fluoride are usually inadequate during the developmental years of a child, the practice of adding fluoride to water is common in many parts of the country. When children are brought up in areas where the drinking water contains 1 ppm of fluoride, they have up to 50% less tooth decay than children not receiving this benefit. Dietary contribution of fluoride is about 0.3 mg in nonfluoridated areas versus 3.0 mg in fluoridated localities. There is much debate over the safety of water fluoridation. However, there is no established scientific evidence that drinking water with 1 ppm of fluoride is harmful to the consumer.

In addition to its effect on the teeth, fluoride has been implicated in other clinical roles. Fluoride may also protect against magnesium deficiency, osteoporosis in later life when administered in safe doses, and certain periodontal diseases, such as jawbone fragility and loss of teeth.

Copper

The body contains about 100 mg of copper. Its major functions are: (1) synthesis of prostaglandin, an important substance claimed by some to be a hormone; (2) serving as a component of important proteins, including enzymes; (3) synthesis of connective tissues, such as elastin and collagen; and (4) maintenance of functions of the nervous system and normal blood chemistry. Nearly 90% of blood copper is complexed with ceruloplasmin (a serum protein); the rest is bound with albumin. Blood copper level is about 80 to 110 μg/mL, while about 50 μg is excreted daily in the urine.

Requirements and food sources

Although copper is an essential element, how much our bodies need of it each day is not yet known. According to a rough estimate, the American diet contributes about 2 mg of copper per day. The richest sources of dietary copper are kidney, liver, and other organ meats, shellfish, dried legumes, and raisins. Human milk contains about 0.15 to 1.0 mg of copper; the level is highest at the beginning of lactation and gradually decreases.

Deficiency

It is not easy to induce copper deficiency in adults, especially if they are eating a normal diet. But patients with severe malabsorption or long-term hyperalimentation may develop copper de-

ficiency. Copper administration can reverse any clinical manifestations.

Copper deficiency in infants can produce the following symptoms: initial reduced blood levels of copper and ceruloplasmin and decreased nonabsorption, followed by abnormal blood cell development. Bone demineralization may occur, and even death. Sometimes, taste abnormalities may also be present if there is also zinc deficiency.

There are three documented causes of copper deficiency in infants. One is long-term feeding of cow's milk, which can produce anemia in normal infants due to copper deficiency. This anemia can be corrected by a simultaneous feeding of copper and iron. Second, infants with chronic malnutrition and diarrhea may develop anemia when fed modified cow's milk (formula). The third cause is Menke's kinky hair syndrome, a sex-linked recessive defect of copper absorption. The child does not grow normally and hair develops pigment and deranged keratinization. Abnormally low body temperature, defective long-bone growth, and mental deterioration are common. When copper is given intravenously, some improvements occur.

Excess

An excess of copper in the body may produce severe acute symptoms: headache, dizziness, heartburn, weakness, vomiting, nausea, and diarrhea. Acute hemolysis with deranged kidney tubules reabsorption may occur.

High blood copper and ceruloplasmin may occur in the following circumstances: pregnancy, usage of oral contraceptive pills, acute and chronic infections, myocardial infarction, anemia of all kinds, liver diseases (biliary cirrhosis), and rheumatoid arthritis.

One well-known form of copper toxicity is Wilson's disease, or hepatolenticular degeneration. It is suspected to be the result of a genetic error in which a liver enzyme may be absent and copper accumulates in the body. Clinical signs of this disease include changes in the liver (cirrhosis) and nerve degeneration. The patient is put on a low copper diet and a chemical compound, such as penicillamine, is used to chelate or complex the copper, which is thus excreted in the urine.

TABLE 7-16 Some Relevant Information on Manganese, Chromium, Cobalt, Molybdenum, and Selenium

Mineral	Functions in the Body	Metabolism and Deficiency	Food Sources	RDA*
Manganese	Component of bone and some enzymes; major role in the intermediate metabolism of carbohydrate; protein synthesis	Not much known	Whole grains, nuts, legumes, fruit and selected vegetables	Not known
Chromium	Suspected to regulate glucose tolerance; associated with enzymes in the intermediate metabolism of carbohydrate and protein synthesis	Not much known	Whole-grain cereals, meat	None
Cobalt	Component of vitamin B_{12}, which plays a major role in body metabolism and physiology (see Chapter 6)	Assumed to be closely related to that of vitamin B_{12}	Associated with vitamin B_{12}	None unless vitamin B_{12} is considered
Molybdenum	Component of xanthine oxidase and flavoprotein, which is very important in body metabolism	Not much known	Whole grains, legumes, organ meats	None
Selenium	Component of enzyme; related to functions of vitamin E and metabolism of fat	Not much known	Grains, meats, vegetables, milk	None

*See footnote to Table 7-1.

Other Trace Elements

At present, there is much scientific interest in other essential trace elements not discussed so far, especially manganese, chromium, cobalt, molybdenum, and selenium. Table 7-16 provides a brief summary of these five elements. Additional information on these substances is beyond the scope of this book. More details on these and other trace minerals may be obtained from references at the end of this book.

STUDY QUESTIONS

1. Discuss the use of the terms *minerals*, *inorganic elements*, and *ash*.
2. In what six body processes are minerals important?
3. What distinguishes macroelements from microelements?
4. What can be said about the average person's sodium consumption?
5. What effect do calcium and potassium have on muscles?
6. How do oxalic and phytic acids influence the absorption of calcium and magnesium?
7. What three nutrients may be involved in rickets?
8. Discuss the relationships between calcium and phosphorus.

9. Under what conditions may borderline magnesium deficiency become serious?
10. Are iron deficiency and anemia inevitably linked?
11. Discuss some causes of iron toxicity.
12. Why is iodine deficiency especially damaging to children?

13. Discuss some reasons for a low intake of zinc. List at least four conditions for which zinc supplementation may be helpful.
14. What role is flouride thought to play in human health?

$$ATP + H_2O \rightarrow ADP + P + 7.5 \, Kcal$$

$$ADP + H_2O \rightarrow AMP + P + 7.5 \, Kcal$$

$$C_6H_{12}O_6 + 6O_2$$

$$\rightarrow 6CO_2 + 6H_2O + heat$$

Chapter 8

Digestion, Absorption, and Metabolism of Food

MOST OF US take the process of eating for granted, knowing that the body will take care of itself. But between eating and the cellular utilization of dietary nutrients, hundreds of thousands of metabolic processes take place. Food must first be *digested*, or broken down into particles of a size and chemical composition that the body can readily absorb. *Absorption* takes place mostly in the small intestine, where specialized cells transfer digested nutrients to the blood and lymph vessels. In some cases, special changes are needed so that the nutrients can be *transported* to the cells where they are to be used or further processed. Within the cells, the nutrients are either stored or *metabolized*—that is, broken down into simpler components for energy or excretion (*catabolism*), or used to synthesize new materials for cellular growth, maintenance, or repair (*anabolism*).

The complicated processes involved are different for each nutrient, although the paths that certain nutrients take intersect at various points. The chemical details of metabolism belong to the disciplines of biochemistry and physiology; standard texts in these subjects can be consulted for detailed information. This chapter provides a brief overview of what happens in our body to the foods we eat, with particular attention to the three major nutrients—carbohydrates, proteins, and fats.

THE ALIMENTARY SYSTEM

The *alimentary* or *digestive system* is the long tube whose parts include the mouth, the esophagus, the stomach, the small intestine, the colon, the rectum, and the anus. Some important accessory organs connected to the digestive tract are the salivary glands, the gall bladder, the pancreas, and the liver. Along this tract, foods are broken down into smaller units, both physically and chemically, and then absorbed for use by the body. Figure 8-1 shows the general outline of the entire human digestive system.

The Food Path

The food placed in our mouth is chewed, softened, and swallowed; in the stomach, it is churned, propelled into the small intestine, and mixed with the bile from the gall bladder and digestive enzymes from the intestinal walls. The products of this digestion are partly or completely absorbed into either the portal vein or the lacteal system.

In the mouth, chewing (mastication) reduces large food lumps into smaller pieces and mixes them with saliva. This wetting and homogenizing facilitates later digestion. In clinical dietetics, edentulous (toothless) patients or those with reduced saliva secretion have trouble eating dry foods and require a soft, moist diet.

Saliva facilitates swallowing and movements of the tongue and lips, keeps the mouth moist and clean, serves as a solvent for taste bud stimulants, acts as an oral buffer, provides some antibiotic activity, and inhibits loss of calcium from the teeth by maintaining a neutral pH. Saliva contains *ptyalin* (salivary amylase, a digestive enzyme) and *mucin* (a glycoprotein). Mucin lubricates food and ptyalin digests carbohydrates to a small extent. Each day the salivary gland makes about 1,500 mL of saliva (about 5½ to 6 cups).

The bolus of food is propelled forward by rhythmic contractions of the entire intestinal system. These peristaltic waves move the food from the mouth, through the esophagus, and into the stomach. Certain individuals, especially nervous people, tend to swallow air when eating. When part of the air is expelled through the mouth, belching results; the remaining air is expelled as flatus. If too much air is swallowed, there will be abdominal discomfort.

From the mouth, food travels through the esophagus, the stomach cardia, the stomach body, the greater curvature, the pylorus, and the duodenum. These are all parts of the stomach, where food is well mixed. Figure 8-2 shows the general structure of this organ and the site of specific secretions. The acid, mucus, and pepsin secreted cause partial digestion, and peristalsis mixes up the food. It is then released gradually through the pylorus into the duodenum.

The *gastrointestinal* (GI) *system*—the stomach and intestines—breaks down complex carbohydrates, proteins, and fats into absorbable units, mainly in the small intestine. Vitamins, minerals, fluids, and most nonessential nutrients are also digested and absorbed to varying degrees. Foods are digested by enzymes secreted by different

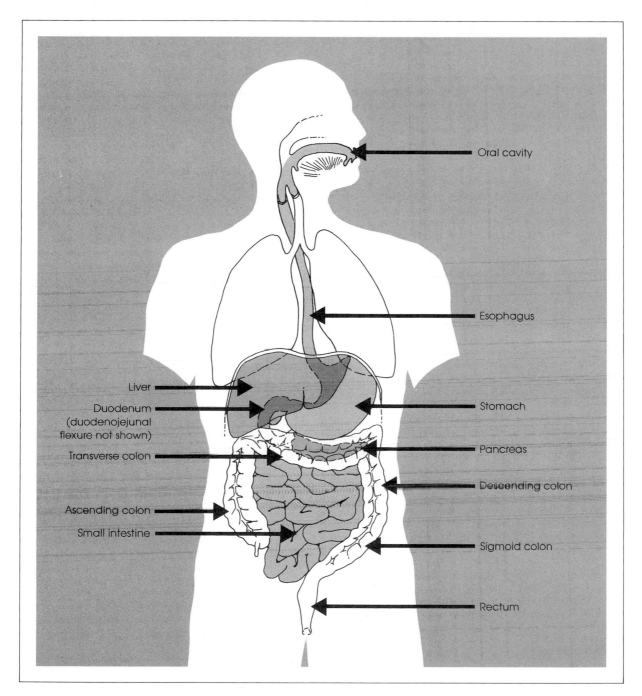

FIGURE 8-1   The digestive system of the human body.

parts of the GI system. Table 8-1 summarizes the major digestive enzymes and their actions. After the digestive process is complete, nutrients are ready for absorption, which occurs mainly at the small intestine. The absorption of each nutrient is discussed later.

After the nutrients have been absorbed, they enter the circulation in two ways. Most fat-soluble nutrients enter the *lacteal* or *lymphatic system*, which eventually joins the *systemic blood circulation* at the thoracic duct. Other nutrients enter the *hepatic portal vein* and are received by the liver, which eventually releases them to the bloodstream.

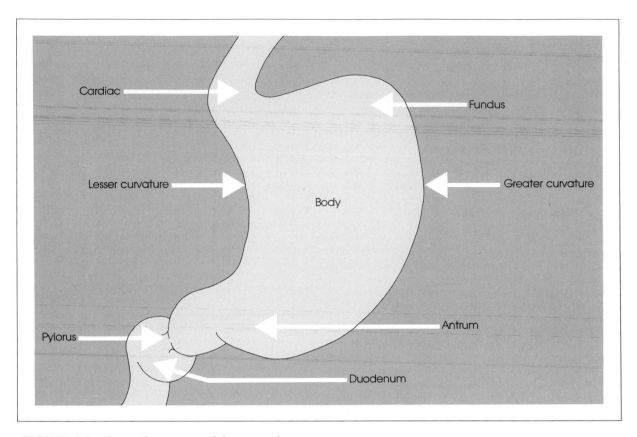

FIGURE 8-2   General structure of the stomach.

Enzymes and Coenzymes

After digestion and absorption, the nutrients exist as hexoses (mainly glucose and fructose), fatty acids, glycerols, and amino acids and are then metabolized in various fashions. Many of the metabolic processes require the presence of a *catalyst*, a substance that can facilitate a chemical reaction. Although participating in the process, it may or may not undergo physical, chemical, or other modification itself. Nonetheless, the catalyst usually returns to its original form after the reaction.

In the body, most biological reactions require a special class of catalysts—the protein catalysts or *enzymes*. Each enzyme catalyzes only one or a small number of reactions. There are many enzymes, each with a specific responsibility. Without enzymes, most biological reactions would proceed at a very slow speed.

Coenzymes are accessory substances that facilitate the working of an enzyme, mainly by acting as carriers for products of the reaction. In this case, the enzyme is composed of two parts: a protein (apoenzyme) and a nonprotein (cofactor or coenzyme). Many coenzymes contain vitamins or their slightly modified forms as the major ingredient. A coenzyme can catalyze many types of reactions. Some coenzymes transfer hydrogens; others transfer groups other than hydrogens. Table 8-2 describes the characteristics of the former; Table 8-3, those of the latter.

Because most of the metabolic reactions discussed in this chapter involve coenzymes, the biochemical role of vitamins is important. Tables 8-2 and 8-3 serve as easy references for identifying the coenzymes under discussion.

CARBOHYDRATES

As discussed in Chapter 3, starch, cellulose, and their derivatives are the only polysaccharides consumed to any extent by humans. The major

TABLE 8-1   Characteristics of the Enzymatic System of Digestion

Location	Food or Substrate	Products of Digestion	Enzyme(s) Involved for Digestion		
			Name(s)	Source(s)	Active in acid/base (pH)
Mouth	Starch	Maltose, dextrins, di-saccharides, mono-saccharides, branched oligosaccharides	Ptyalin, or salivary amylase	Salivary glands	Slightly acidic (6.7)
Stomach	Protein	Proteoses, peptones, polypeptides, di-peptides, amino acids	Pepsin	Peptic or chief cells of stomach	Acidic (1.6–2.4)
	Milk casein	Milk coagulation	Rennin	Stomach mucosa	Acidic (4.0); re-quires calcium for activity
	Fat	Triglycerides; some mono- and di-glycerides, glycerol, fatty acids	Gastric lipase	Stomach mucosa	Acidic
Small intestine (mainly duodenum and jejunum)*	Protein Proteoses, peptones, etc.	Polypeptides, di-peptides, etc.	Trypsin (activated trypsinogen)	Exocrine gland of pancreas	Alkaline (7.9)
	Proteoses, peptones, etc.	Polypeptides, di-peptides, etc.	Chymotrypsin (activated chymo-trypsinogen)	Exocrine gland of pancreas	Alkaline (8.0)
	Polypeptides with free carboxyl groups	Lower peptides, free amino acids	Carboxypeptidase	Exocrine gland of pancreas	
	Fibrous protein	Peptides, amino acids	Elastase	Exocrine gland of pancreas	
	Carbohydrate Starch, dextrins	Maltose, isomaltose, monosaccharides, dextrins	α-amylase (amylopsin)	Exocrine gland of pancreas	Slightly alkaline (7.1)
	Fat Triglycerides	Mono- and di-glycerides, glycerol, fatty acids	Lipase (steapsin)	Exocrine gland of pancreas	Alkaline (8.0)
	Cholesterol	Cholesterol esters	Cholesterol esterase	Exocrine gland of pancreas	

TABLE 8-1   (continued)

Location	Food or Substrate	Products of Digestion	Enzyme(s) Involved for Digestion Name(s)	Source(s)	Active in acid/base (pH)
Small intestine (mainly jejunum and ileum)	Nucleic acids Ribonucleic acid	Nucleotides Ribonucleotides	Ribonuclease	Exocrine gland of pancreas	
	Deoxyribonucleic acid	Deoxyribonucleotides	Deoxyribonuclease	Exocrine gland of pancreas	
	Protein Polypeptides	Amino acids	Carboxypeptidase, aminopeptidase, dipeptidase	Brush border of the small intestine	
	Carbohydrate Sucrose	Glucose, fructose	Sucrase	Brush border of the small intestine	Acidic/alkaline (5.0–7.0)
	Dextrin (isomaltose)	Glucose	α-dextrinase (isomaltase)	Brush border of the small intestine	
	Maltose	Glucose	Maltase	Brush border of the small intestine	Acidic (5.8–6.2)
	Lactose	Glucose, galactose	Lactase	Brush border of the small intestine	Acidic (5.4–6.0)
	Fat Monoglycerides	Glycerol, fatty acids	Lipase (enteric),	Brush border of the small intestine	
	Lecithin	Glycerol, fatty acids	Lecithinase	Brush border of the small intestine	
	Nucleotides	Nucleosides, phosphate	Nucleotidase	Brush border of the small intestine	
	Nucleosides	Purines, pyrimidines, pentose	Nucleosidase	Brush border of the small intestine	
	Organic phosphates	Free phosphates	Phosphatase	Brush border of the small intestine	Alkaline (8.6)

*The food is not grouped together, e.g., all fat, all proteins, etc. Instead the food is placed in an order that follows the sequence of digestion along the duodenum to jejunum. This attempts to present the digestive enzymes in their expected sequence of action.

simple sugars ingested include the monosaccharides (such as glucose and fructose in honey and fruit juices) and disaccharides (such as maltose in beer, lactose in milk, and sucrose in table sugar). Also ingested are dextrins, sugar alcohol, and tri- and tetrasaccharides, although in very small quantities. The sections that follow briefly discuss the digestion and absorption pathways of these carbohydrates, the involvement of carbohydrates in energy formation and storage, the

TABLE 8-2   Characteristics of Coenzymes That Transfer Hydrogens

Enzyme System	Coenzyme	Vitamin Component	Nonvitamin Component
Dehydrogenase	Flavin adenine dinucleotide (FAD)	Riboflavin (vitamin B_2)	Adenine, ribose, phosphate
Dehydrogenase	Nicotinamide adenine dinucleotide (NAD)	Niacin	Adenine, ribose, phosphate
Part of dehydrogenase	Lipoic acid (thiotic acid)	None	Lipoic acid
Respiratory chain	Coenzyme Q	None	Quinone (vitamin E—related substance)

TABLE 8-3   Characteristics of Coenzymes That Transfer Nonhydrogen Groups

Enzyme System	Coenzyme	Vitamin Component	Nonvitamin Component
Transaminases; decarboxylase	Pyridoxal phosphate	Vitamin B_6	None
Part of dehydrogenase	Lipoic acid (lipoamide)	None	Lipoic acid
Dehydrogenase	Coenzyme A	Pantothenic acid	β-mercaptoethylamine, adenine, ribose, phosphate
Cocarboxylase (decarboxylase, transketolase)	Thiamin pyrophosphate	Thiamin	Phosphate
Methyl transferase	5-methyltetrahydrofolate	Folic acid	None
Transmethylase	Coenzyme B_{12}	Vitamin B_{12}	Adenine, ribose
Carboxylase	Carboxyl-biotin complex	Biotin	None

specific processes by which carbohydrates are broken down or synthesized by the body, and the regulation of glucose levels in the blood.

Digestion and Absorption

Starch is partially hydrolyzed by ptyalin in the mouth (Table 8-1 and Figure 8-3). The short stay in the oral cavity permits only dextrins and small polysaccharide fragments to break off from the starch molecules, and the action of ptyalin is terminated by the acid in the stomach. In the small intestine, all digestible carbohydrates are reduced to monosaccharides, namely, glucose,

fructose, galactose, mannose, and pentoses. Currently, it is believed that the final *hydrolysis*, or digestion, of disaccharides to monosaccharides occurs in the intestinal mucosal walls. In humans, all nondigestible carbohydrates such as lignin, hemicellulose, and cellulose are passed into the colon, where they are mainly fermented to release gas. By contrast, ruminants (animals such as cattle, sheep, and goats) have the ability to digest fiber.

Most of the monosaccharides are absorbed before the food residue reaches the end of the ileum. Absorption is carried out mainly by active transport (requiring energy), although diffusion (passive movement) also occurs. Glucose and

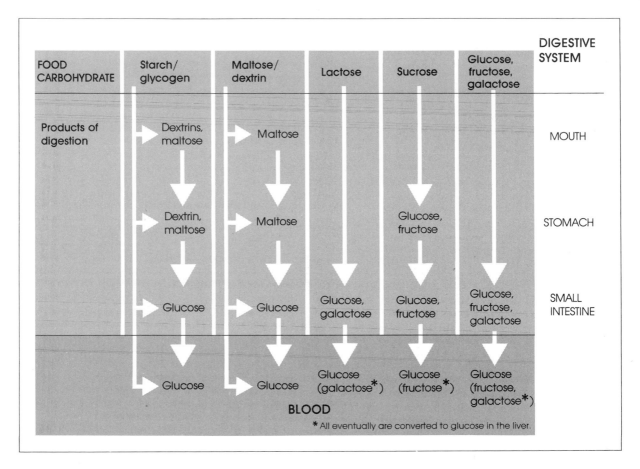

FIGURE 8-3   Carbohydrate digestion.

galactose enter the blood five times faster than mannose and pentoses, while fructose is absorbed about two to three times faster. Glucose entry into the blood may be as high as 120 g/hr.

The monosaccharides traverse the intestinal and portal veins to reach the liver, from which they may eventually be released into blood circulation. In the liver, most of the fructose and galactose are converted to glucose, which is the main simple sugar in the blood, although fructose and galactose may be present throughout the bloodstream if a person consumes a large amount of them. An actively nursing mother also has some lactose in the blood, since this disaccharide is manufactured by the active mammary tissues. In the liver, part of the glucose is released to the circulation, part converted to *glycogen* for storage, part changed to other essential substances required by the body, and part oxidized to energy. Normally, a peak plasma glucose level

of 120 to 140 mg/100 mL is reached within 60 minutes after a mixed meal.

After glucose has reached the bloodstream, some enters cells to give energy, and some is converted to glycogen in tissues such as muscle. Glycogen is found in many organs in the body, but the liver and muscle are the major storage sites. Most of the glucose is used to provide energy through a three-stage process: glycolysis, the citric acid cycle, and the respiratory chain.

Energy Formation and Storage

Everything a body does requires energy. Nature has provided the animal body with a wide spectrum of methods that permit energy either to be released or to be stored and released to satisfy its energy need. The five different energy systems known to operate in animal cells are:

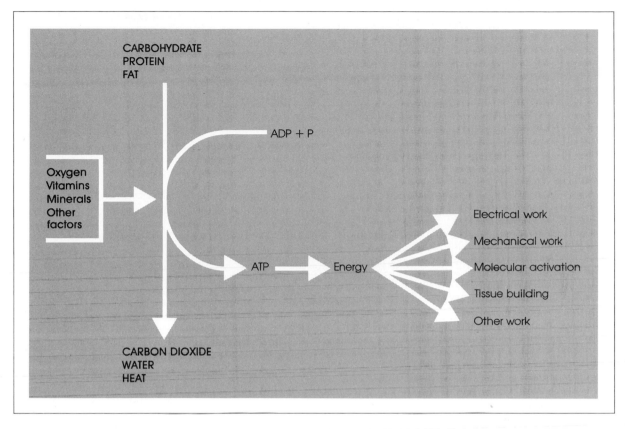

FIGURE 8-4   The role of ATP in body energy metabolism.

1. *Direct release of energy, mainly as heat:*

glucose (or fat or protein) + oxygen
$\downarrow$ oxidation
carbon + water + energy to + heat
dioxide   be stored

2. *Energy stored as adenosine triphosphate (ATP).* One technique of storing part of the energy released from the oxidation of foodstuff is incorporating it into "ester bonds" between certain organic compounds and phosphoric acid groups. The resulting substances are called high-energy phosphate compounds, the most important of which is probably *adenosine triphosphate*. This ubiquitous molecule is considered the energy powerhouse of the body. It releases its energy in the following reactions:

$$ATP + H_2O \longrightarrow ADP^* + P^\dagger + 7.5 \text{ kcal}$$

$$ADP + H_2O \longrightarrow AMP^\ddagger + P + 7.5 \text{ kcal}$$

Theoretically, the conversion of 1 mole of ATP to AMP can produce 15 kcal. However, within the body ATP is normally changed only to ADP when energy is needed. The energy released from this process can be used for such work as organ building, heartbeat, transportation across cell membranes, and muscle contraction. Sometimes these compounds are called active phosphate carriers and dischargers. Figure 8-4 summarizes the role of ATP in body energy metabolism.

_____

*ADP = adenosine diphosphate.

† P = inorganic phosphate.

‡ AMP = adenosine monophosphate.

3. *Energy stored in creatine phosphate, or phosphocreatine.* Creatine phosphate is another energy-rich phosphate compound found in muscle. It can contribute to muscle energy metabolism in two ways:

creatine + H_2O $\longrightarrow$ creatine + P + 7.5 kcal
phosphate

$$\text{creatine} + H_2O \xrightarrow{\text{ADP} \circlearrowleft \text{ATP}} \text{creatine}$$
phosphate

In the first reaction the energy is released directly. In the second the energy is transferred to ADP and later released for muscular or other work. Creatine phosphate is sometimes called an active phosphate carrier. Similar substances are 1,3-diphosphoglyceric acid and phosphoenolpyruvic acid.

4. *Energy stored in "active acetate."* The "active acetate" is the substance acetyl-CoA, which participates in intermediate metabolism. In terms of energy, formation of 1 mole of acetyl-CoA is equivalent to that of 1 mole of ATP.

5. *Low-energy phosphate compounds.* Not all organic phosphates are of the high-energy type. Examples such as glucose-6-phosphate are phosphate compounds carrying a small amount of stored energy, such as 2 to 3 kcal/mole.

If we summarize the above energy systems, the oxidation or complete metabolism of glucose will yield the following:

$C_6H_{12}O_6$ + 6 O_2 $\longrightarrow$
glucose   oxygen
6 CO_2 + 6 H_2O + heat + 38 ATP
carbon   water
dioxide

Cellular Metabolism Processes

Within the cells, a series of complex biochemical processes is needed to degrade glucose (carbohydrate) to release the energy needed by the body. Three biological processes are involved: glycolysis, the citric acid cycle, and the respiratory chain. The glucose involved derives from food and internal production, which occurs mainly in the liver. In the cells of the liver, stored glycogen may

TABLE 8-4 Definitions of Some Metabolic Terms

Term	Definition
Glycolysis	The breaking down of hexoses (six-carbon sugars), mainly glucose, into three-carbon substances (pyruvic or lactic acid). The process is sometimes termed the Embden-Meyerhof pathway.
Glycogenesis	The formation of glycogen from glucose.
Glycogenolysis	The breaking down of glycogen into glucose and its metabolites.
Gluconeogenesis	The synthesis of glucose (and thus glycogen) from noncarbohydrate sources, such as lactate, glycerol, and amino acids.
Citric acid cycle	Also termed Krebs cycle or tricarboxylic acid cycle. The process whereby carbohydrate, fat, and/or protein is completely oxidized to carbon dioxide, water, and energy. This is accomplished with the assistance of the respiratory chain.
Respiratory chain	The transport of hydrogen atoms from biological oxidation for acceptance by oxygen atoms to form water molecules.

be converted to glucose by the process of glycogenolysis; in the process of gluconeogenesis, glucose is synthesized from noncarbohydrate sources. However, as we shall see later, the muscles can also indirectly contribute the energy for cellular metabolism by participating in these processes. These processes are briefly defined in Table 8-4 and discussed in the following sections.

Glycolysis

The first step of carbohydrate metabolism is *glycolysis*, in which the six-carbon glucose is converted to a three-carbon substance (pyruvic or lactic acid), as indicated in Figure 8-5. Figure 8-6 illustrates the intermediate metabolic steps dur-

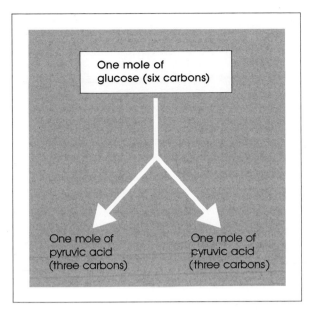

FIGURE 8-5   The overall result of glycolysis.

ing the transformation of glucose to pyruvic acid. The interconversion between pyruvic and lactic acid occurs mainly in the muscle and will be discussed later. During the process of glycolysis, the conversion of 1 mole of glucose to 2 moles of pyruvic acid generates four hydrogen atoms and 8 moles of ATP. The hydrogen atoms released are eventually converted to water; the details are discussed under the subsection "Respiratory Chain." Before the pyruvic acid can be converted to carbon dioxide, water, and energy, it must be transformed into a highly versatile metabolite, the two-carbon substance acetyl-CoA (Figure 8-6). This transformation is irreversible.

Citric acid cycle

The citric acid cycle is a series of chemical reactions that metabolizes acetyl-CoA to carbon dioxide and hydrogen atoms, as indicated in Figures 8-7 and 8-8. In each cycle, two carbon dioxide molecules and four pairs of hydrogen atoms and electrons are generated. The hydrogen atoms are put through the respiratory chain, together with the electrons, to generate 12 moles of ATP and 4 moles of water from oxygen.

This cycle is the major link, or common path, in the transformation of carbohydrate, fat, and protein to carbon dioxide and water. Metabolites of the three nutrients enter the cycle at different

strategic points. Since the cycle requires the respiratory chain to complete its work, it will not function in the absence of oxygen (anaerobically).

As indicated above, pyruvic acid may be removed from the glycolysis process by being converted to lactic acid. If so, there must be a source of hydrogen atoms, which are normally obtained from the production of phosphoglyceraldehyde (Figure 8-6 and later discussion). In this case, glucose metabolism and energy (ATP) production can continue for a while without oxygen (that is, without going through the citric acid cycle). This anaerobic respiration occurs in muscle where an occasional burst of energy is needed. The lactic acid that accumulates is converted back to pyruvic acid when the oxygen supply is restored, in which case the citric acid cycle is reactivated. The soreness of muscle from heavy work or exercise results from the presence of a large amount of lactic acid.

Respiratory chain

Biological oxidation, or the respiratory chain, is a very complicated process whereby hydrogen atoms released by substances through oxidation are transported by a number of intermediates until the hydrogen atoms are accepted by oxygen to produce water.

The respiratory chain involves both oxidation and reduction. *Oxidation* is the process whereby a substrate either takes up oxygen or loses hydrogen. The substrate is oxidized, while the source substance that provides the oxygen or accepts hydrogen is the *oxidizing agent*. *Reduction* is the reverse process, whereby a substrate loses oxygen or accepts hydrogen. This substrate is reduced and the source substance that gains oxygen or loses hydrogen is the *reducing agent*.

The respiratory chain involves coenzymes (Tables 8-2 and 8-3) and consists of the following series of events:

1. Hydrogen atoms are released from a substrate, a process requiring an energy source.
2. The coenzyme NAD accepts hydrogen (NAD to $NADH_2$).
3. The hydrogen in NAD is accepted by FAD (FAD to $FADH_2$).
4. The hydrogen in $FADH_2$ is accepted by coenzyme Q.

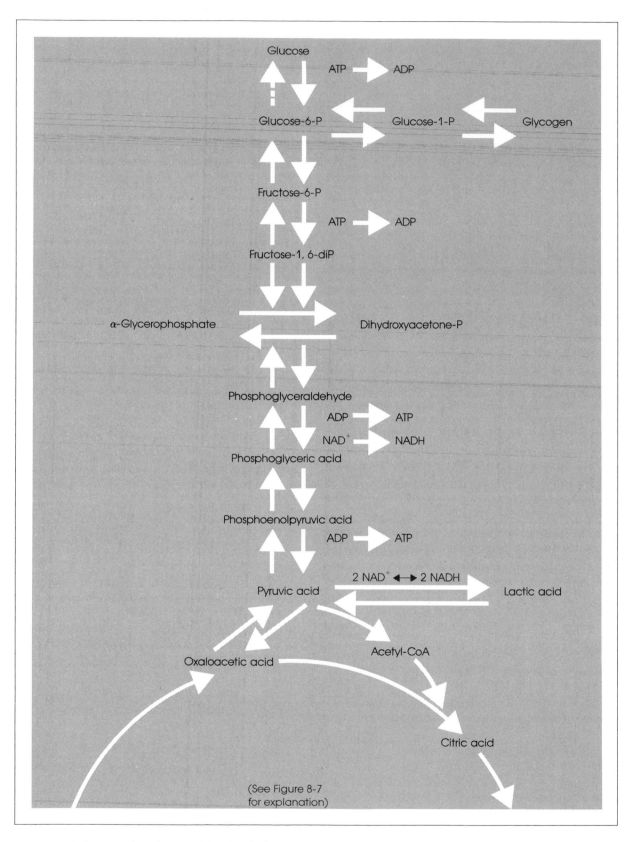

FIGURE 8-6   Reactions involved in glycolysis.

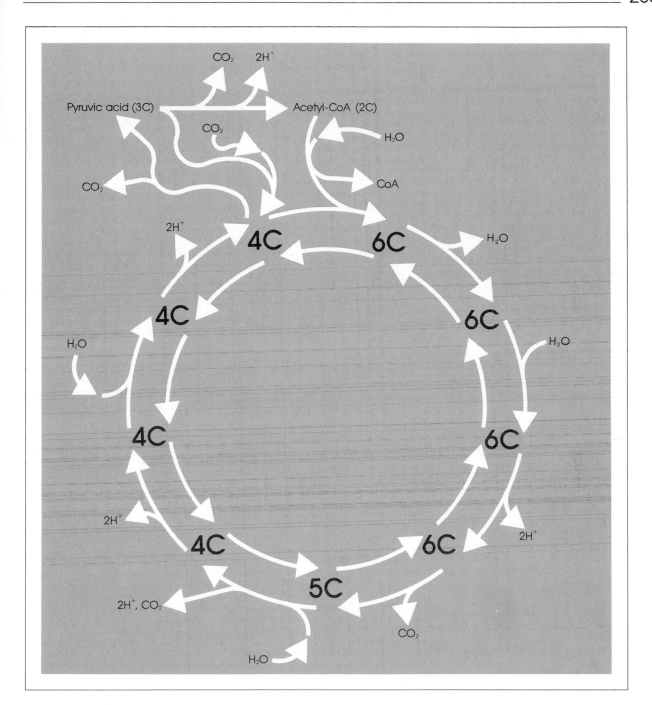

FIGURE 8-7   Outline of the citric acid cycle. ("C" refers to a carbon atom.)

5. The hydrogen in $CoQH_2$ is released as H^+ by losing an electron, and a chain of cytochromes becomes reduced by accepting the electron.

6. The electron is transferred to molecular oxygen (O_2).

7. The negatively charged oxygen (O_2) reacts with two protons (H^+) to form water.

The entire process of the respiratory chain, including the formation of ATPs, is illustrated in Figure 8-9. The complete conversion of glucose

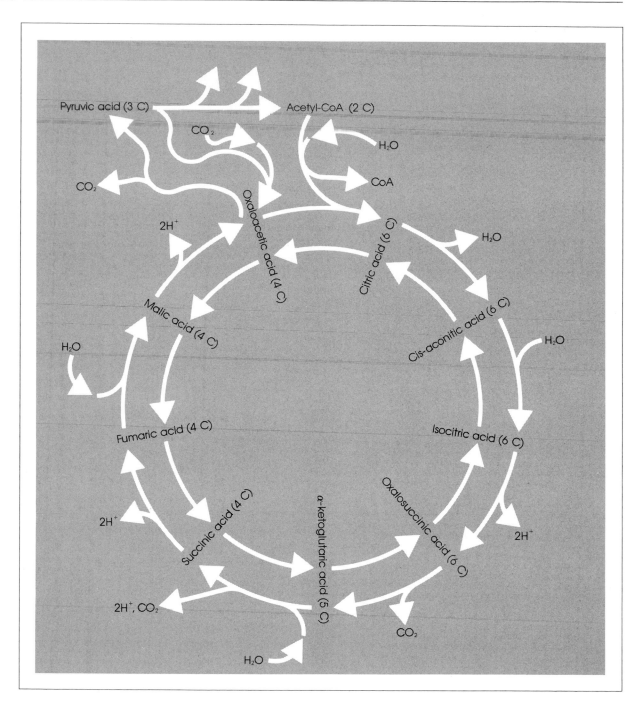

FIGURE 8-8   Components and products of the citric acid cycle. ("C" refers to a carbon atom.)

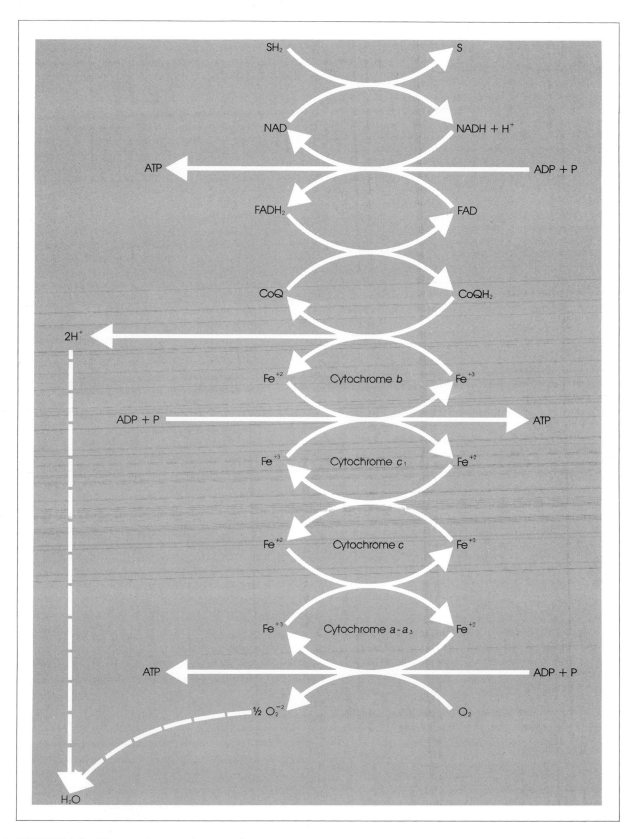

FIGURE 8-9   The respiratory chain or electron transport system. ("S" refers to substrate.)

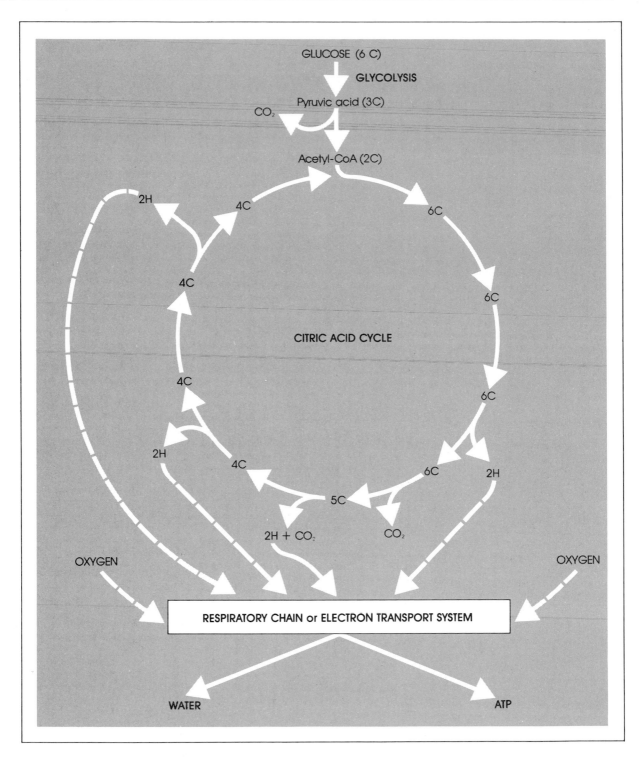

FIGURE 8-10   The three stages of converting glucose to carbon dioxide, water, and ATP. ("C" refers to a carbon atom.)

TABLE 8-5   Energy Production During the Conversion of 1 Mole of Glucose to Carbon Dioxide and Water in the Presence of Oxygen

| Sequence | Product of Specific Reaction | Phosphorylation* | | | ATP | |
		SD	SP	OP	Loss	Gain
Glycolysis	Glucose-6-P	x			1	
	Fructose-1,6-diP	x			1	
	Phosphoglyceric acid		x			2
	Phosphoglyceraldehyde			x		6
	Pyruvic acid		x			2
Citric acid cycle	Acetyl-CoA			x		6
	Oxalosuccinic acid			x		6
	Succinyl-CoA			x		6
	Succinic acid		x			2
	Fumarate			x		4
	Oxaloacetate			x		6
	Total number of ATP gained during the oxidation of 1 mole of glucose under aerobic conditions					38

*SD = substrate dephosphorylation; SP = substrate phosphorylation; OP = oxidative phosphorylation.

TABLE 8-6   Energy Production During the Conversion of 1 Mole of Glucose to Lactic Acid in the Absence of Oxygen

| Sequence | Product of Specific Reaction | Phosphorylation* | | | ATP | | Hydrogen Atoms |
		SD	SP	OP	Loss	Gain	
Glycolysis	Glucose-6-P	x			1		
	Fructose-1,6-diP	x			1		
	Phosphoglyceraldehyde			x			Released
	Phosphoglyceric acid		x			2	
	Pyruvic acid		x			2	
	Lactic acid						Accepted

*SD = substrate dephosphorylation; SP = substrate phosphorylation; OP = oxidative phosphorylation.

to carbon dioxide, water, and energy is shown in Figure 8-10. The amount of energy used or stored is shown in Tables 8-5 and 8-6.

Glycogenesis and glycogenolysis

In plants, carbohydrate is stored as starch, a polysaccharide of glucose. In animals, carbohydrate is stored in the form of glycogen, also a polysaccharide of glucose. The amount of glycogen stored in the body depends on the diet and the physiological status of the animal. In man, glycogen is produced and stored mainly in the liver and muscle. The process, known as *glycogenesis*, occurs readily when adequate glucose is present.

However, when the glucose concentration in the liver and muscle decreases, their glycogen

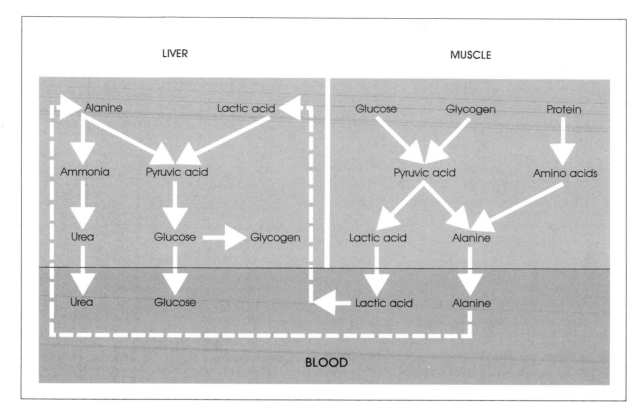

FIGURE 8-11   The role of liver and muscle in gluconeogenesis.

content must be broken down to provide glucose for energy. This reverse process of glycogenesis is *glycogenolysis*. Its occurrence in the muscle is slightly different from that in the liver. In the liver, the glycogen can be directly degraded to glucose. However, in the muscle, the enzyme for the final step is missing so that glycogen is degraded only to glucose-6-phosphate, which has to be converted to pyruvic and lactic acids instead (Figure 8-6). These can be converted to glucose via the citric acid cycle.

Gluconeogenesis

Gluconeogenesis is the synthesis of glucose (and thus glycogen) from noncarbohydrate sources such as amino acids, fatty acids, glycerol, and lactic and pyruvic acids. Figure 8-11 shows how muscle glycogen can be converted to glucose in the liver in spite of the muscle's lack of the appropriate enzyme. Figures 8-11 and 8-12 show how protein and fat can be converted to glucose. The interrelationship among the three nutrients—

carbohydrate, protein, and fat—will be discussed at length in later sections.

Regulation of Blood Glucose

Another important aspect of what happens to carbohydrates in the body is the balancing of blood glucose (or "blood sugar") levels. This subject is discussed below and also in Chapter 26 in relation to diabetes mellitus.

In a normal person, blood glucose fluctuates within narrow limits—between 70 and 100 mg/100 mL of blood. This is achieved by a balance between the supply and removal of blood glucose. If blood glucose drops below the norm, *hypoglycemia* occurs. In a healthy individual, the blood sugar is restored to normal by the provision of glucose from three sources. We may simply eat additional carbohydrates, thus increasing the absorption of monosaccharides, and the liver can then release more glucose. Second, the glycogen in liver and muscle may be degraded (glyco-

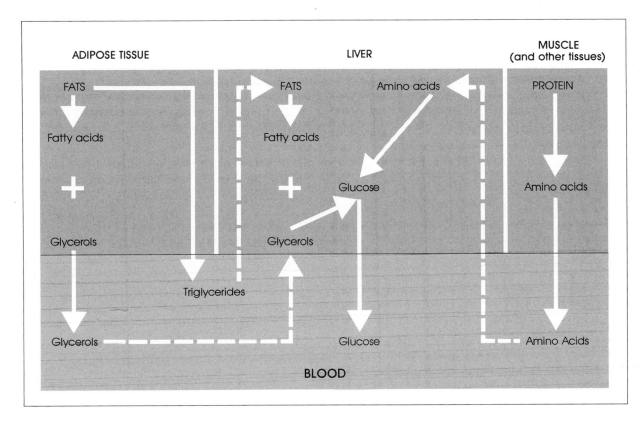

FIGURE 8-12   An overview of glucose formation from fat and protein.

genolysis) to form more glucose. Third, protein and fat may be degraded to provide glucose (gluconeogenesis).

If a person's blood glucose rises above the norm, *hyperglycemia* occurs. If the person is in normal health, then the body spontaneously lowers the blood glucose levels in one or more of the following ways: (1) More insulin is released to drive glucose into cells for oxidation; (2) more glycogen is formed (glycogenesis) in the liver and muscle; (3) more glucose is changed to fat (lipogenesis) in fat cells; and (4) more glucose is excreted in the urine (glucosuria).

PROTEINS

Dietary protein exists in three forms. The major portion is conjugated with other substances, a small fraction is associated with fats and carbohydrates, and only a very small part exists as free protein, such as that in egg white. To be used by the cells, all proteins must be broken down into their constituent amino acids. In the sections that follow, we will trace the paths of protein digestion, absorption, and metabolism.

Digestion

Digestion of protein begins in the stomach (see Table 8-1 and Figure 8-13), where acid activates the pepsinogen (an enzyme) to release pepsin (another enzyme). The pepsin cleaves peptide linkages in the protein to produce polypeptides, each with two or more amino acids. When the stomach content reaches the duodenum, the pH is raised to about 6.5 by the presence of alkaline pancreatic juice. In the small intestine, chymotrypsin and trypsin hydrolyze most of the protein molecules to form small polypeptides and dipeptides. These are further digested to form free amino acids by the pancreatic enzyme carboxypeptidase and the intestinal enzymes amino-

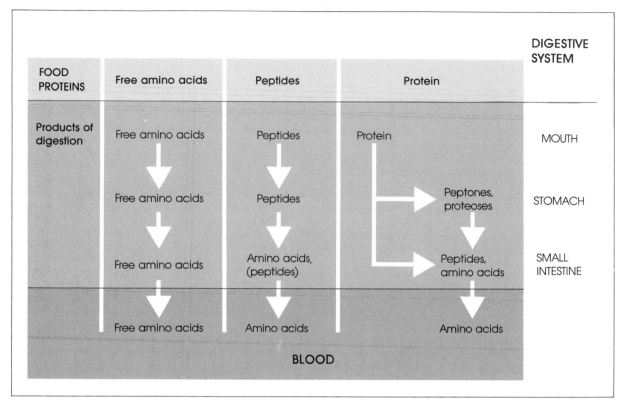

FOOD PROTEINS	Free amino acids	Peptides	Protein	DIGESTIVE SYSTEM
Products of digestion	Free amino acids	Peptides	Protein	MOUTH
	Free amino acids	Peptides	Peptones, proteoses	STOMACH
	Free amino acids	Amino acids, (peptides)	Peptides, amino acids	SMALL INTESTINE
	Free amino acids	Amino acids	Amino acids	
		BLOOD		

FIGURE 8-13   Protein digestion.

peptidase and dipeptidase. Those small peptides not split into individual amino acids may gain entry to mucosal cells to be digested later, for body tissues can utilize only amino acids.

Since protein molecules also contain non-peptide linkages, they must be denatured first (by heat or stomach acid) before the appropriate enzymes can digest them. The denaturation process exposes the protein molecules, providing more surface area for enzymatic action. On the other hand, excess heating or cooking can also re-form some other linkages, making digestion more difficult.

Absorption

Normally only amino acids (and certain small peptides) are absorbed. In the small intestine all free amino acids, whether ingested or digested products, are absorbed via the mucosal cells into the hepatic portal vein. The D-amino acids are not absorbed as well as the L forms. The L-amino acids—the biologically active ones—are absorbed by active transport (a process requiring energy). Absorption occurs along the entire small intestine, with the slowest rate along the ileum. The stomach and colon may also absorb some amino acids. About 20% to 30% of ingested proteins are unabsorbed and excreted in the stools.

Although normally only amino acids are absorbed, it is well known that in small infants some undigested proteins are also absorbed. The subsequent antigen-antibody interaction causes the child to develop an allergic reaction when ingesting the same protein foods later. This explains the high allergic incidence among infants to foods such as eggs and cereals. If adults show allergy to ingested protein foods, they are still probably capable of absorbing whole protein molecules. For the majority of the population, this ability disappears with age.

Amino acids seem to be utilized best when they are absorbed in accordance with the body need for growth and function. Any excess absorbed will not be stored but excreted in the urine or metabolized to ammonia. Studies have shown that absorption and utilization of proteins are optimized when adults evenly distribute their protein intake throughout the day.

In some cases, erratic patterns of protein absorption may be due to stomach irregularities rather than irregular protein ingestion, for the stomach regulates the emptying of the nutrient into the small intestine. In patients with partially or completely removed stomachs, the rate of protein emptying is so disturbed that much of this valuable nutrient is lost in the fecal waste or degraded by intestinal flora. When undigested amino acids are decarboxylated by intestinal bacteria, the important chemicals such as histamine, tyramine, ammonia, and similar substances are formed, many of which are absorbed. These substances are undesirable in excessive quantities. The ammonia formed by deamination plays a critical role in certain pathological conditions, for the absorbed ammonia can cause body deterioration.

The absorption of amino acids is also impaired if the intestinal mucosa is damaged, as occurs in sprue, ulcerative colitis, and resection of a moderate amount of the small intestine. With time, however, there is a functional adaptation of the intestinal mucosa.

Metabolism

The liver may release some absorbed amino acids for body metabolism. Body amino acids may be catabolized or used in body repair, building, and maintenance. The importance of protein to the body is illustrated by its numerous functions and the complexity of its metabolism. If a normal person has a regular diet, three major factors determine the direction of protein metabolism: the quality and quantity of protein consumed, the amount of calories ingested, and the physiological and nutritional status of the body.

Protein metabolism revolves around a body pool of amino acids that are continuously released by protein hydrolysis and resynthesized. The amino acids ingested are the same as those released in the body. Body tissues can utilize only amino acids, not small peptides. About 50 to 100 g of body protein turns over daily, ranging from the slowest rate in the collagen to the fastest rate in the intestinal mucosa. Any amino acids filtered through the kidneys are reabsorbed, although

certain congenital defects in the kidney tubules may interfere with this process. During pregnancy, infancy, childhood, and other conditions of growth, protein synthesis exceeds degradation. Individuals in these categories therefore require a large pool of amino acids.

Figure 8-14 illustrates the general catabolism, or degradation, of protein to amino acids and other metabolites. Figure 8-15 gives the general outline of protein formation in the body, and Figure 8-16 provides an overview of protein metabolism. The sections that follow discuss certain aspects of protein metabolism: degradation, protein synthesis, nitrogen balance, and the metabolism of creatine and creatinine.

Protein degradation

Protein is degraded to its individual amino acids in the muscle and other tissues, but the major site of actual destruction (catabolism) of each amino acid is the liver. The amino acids released from all other organs, especially the muscles, reach the blood and are diverted to the liver for degradation (Figure 8-14). Under normal circumstances, the catabolism of protein is balanced by its formation, although during stresses such as starvation and disease destruction can outstrip synthesis.

The procedure for the oxidation of an amino acid begins with *deamination*, a process in which the ammonia or amino group of the acid is removed so that only the carbon skeleton of the amino acid is left. Two metabolites are formed: the keto acids and ammonia (Figure 8-14). The ammonia is changed to urea, which is released to the blood and eventually excreted in the kidney. Normally, we excrete about 20 to 30 g of urea in the urine each day. Since urea forms exclusively in the liver, advanced liver disorders raise the blood urea nitrogen level.

The keto acids formed from deamination enter the citric acid cycle to be oxidized. The exact process whereby keto acids and ammonia are formed varies with each individual amino acid, although the goal is the same. Figure 8-17 shows the points at which each of the acids and their keto acids enter the citric acid cycle or are transformed to pyruvate to form glucose. Within the citric acid cycle, the keto acids may be made to form glucose (gluconeogenesis). The keto acids

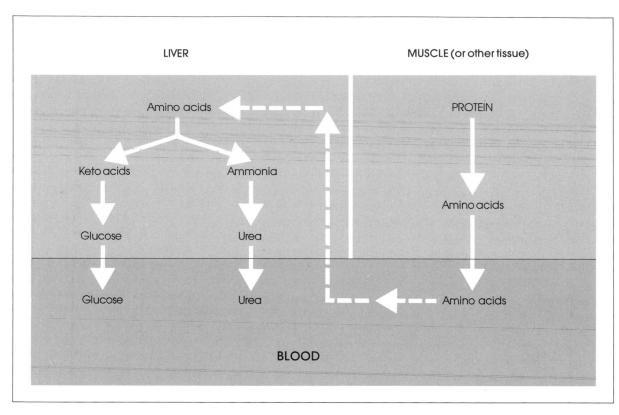

FIGURE 8-14   An overview of protein catabolism (degradation).

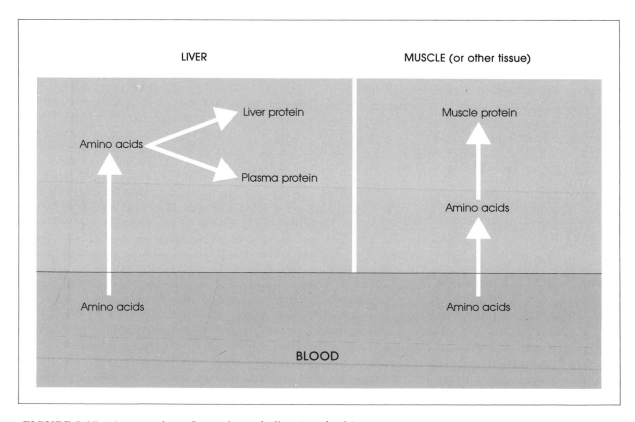

FIGURE 8-15   An overview of protein anabolism (synthesis).

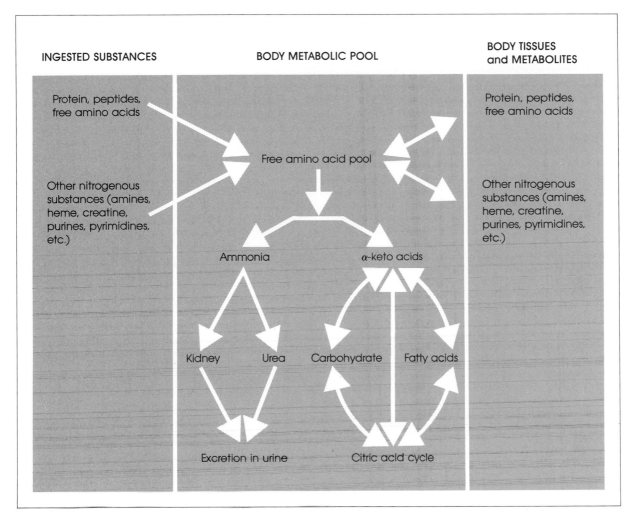

FIGURE 8-16   An overview of protein metabolism, including nonprotein nitrogenous substances.

are also tied to fat metabolism by the interconversion of keto acids and fatty acids. In sum, when protein is degraded, amino acids are formed. Some amino acids circulate, some are oxidized, some are converted to glucose, and some are directed to other paths.

Protein synthesis

Protein synthesis is the process of linking different amino acids by their amino groups (*peptide linkages*) to form a molecule of protein. This molecule must contain the right number of amino acids in the appropriate pattern and sequence needed for a specific body structure, such as hair, skin, muscle, tears, saliva, enzymes, or hormones. The nucleic acids DNA and RNA control this

process, which takes place in cell nucleus cytoplasm. The formation of each specific protein requires a highly specific genetic code, the details of which may be obtained from a standard biochemistry or molecular biology text.

Although it occurs in nearly all cells, protein synthesis in some is more frequent and intense than in others. The organs that seem to synthesize the most protein are the liver, muscle, and those cells, tissues, and organs that manufacture and/or secrete enzymes, hormones, and other protein substances. One exception is the synthesis of plasma proteins by the liver. This occurs because red blood cells have no nuclei and are thus unable to synthesize protein themselves.

For a protein to be synthesized, the appropriate type and number of amino acids must be

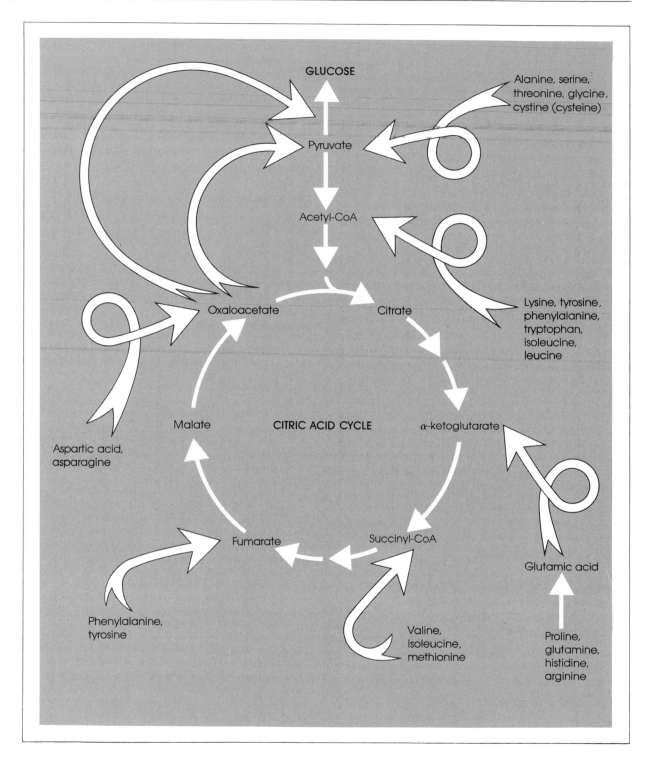

FIGURE 8-17 Introduction of the carbon structures of individual amino acids into the citric acid cycle.

available. There are 8 to 10 amino acids whose carbon skeletons cannot be synthesized or manufactured by the body. They are the essential amino acids discussed in Chapter 4, and they must be supplied in the diet. In addition, there are 10 to 15 amino acids that the body can manufacture (including their carbon skeletons), which are the nonessential amino acids. If the appropriate carbon skeleton of an amino acid is present, the body can add, subtract, and transfer the amino group until the "right" amino acid is formed. Protein synthesis is normally preceded by massive deamination, amination, and transamination to obtain the appropriate amino acids.

Nitrogen balance

Of the three major nutrients—protein, carbohydrate, and fat—protein is the most important in the sense that it makes up our lean body mass. Another factor that makes protein important is that body protein turnover is tremendous. For example, the formation of hair, skin, saliva, and sweat all involve large losses of protein that must be constantly replaced. How do we know if we are eating enough protein? One acceptable technique is to measure the ingestion and excretion of nitrogen (nitrogen balance) because all protein has a relatively constant content of this element (Chapter 4). Theoretically, if a young adult is in normal health and a proper stage of development, the amount of nitrogen consumed should be equal to the amount excreted. This is *nitrogen equilibrium*. However, depending on age, physiological condition, dietary intake, and other factors, some people are in positive nitrogen balance and others are in negative nitrogen balance. A detailed discussion of this topic is presented in Chapter 4.

Metabolism of creatine and creatinine

Body muscles perform work and may occasionally be required to provide a sudden burst of energy. They achieve this by the hydrolysis of two unique high-energy bonds. One is ATP and the other is *phosphocreatine* (or creatine phosphate), both of which were mentioned in the carbohydrates section. The body, mainly the muscles, contains about 100 to 150 g of phosphocreatine and *creatine*. Though not an amino acid, creatine is a unique nitrogenous chemical derived from three amino acids—arginine, glycine, and methionine. Creatine, which is water soluble, is found in meat and meat products (such as extracts, soups, and gravies). Food contains little or no phosphocreatine because of its easy degradation to creatine (or creatinine, another metabolite) and phosphoric acid (Figure 8-18).

Phosphocreatine is a high-energy compound that provides instant energy when the muscles need it. If it is depleted, ATP is then used. Phosphocreatine seems to help maintain the ATP levels. After exertion and after all stored energy is used, creatine is rephosphorylated to form phosphocreatine.

Though an important body constituent, creatine is usually not excreted as such. Instead, the spontaneous, nonenzymatic dephosphorylation of phosphocreatine produces creatinine, in an irreversible process. Every healthy individual excretes a constant amount of creatinine, which is thus considered to be a normal waste product. The amount in the urine also reflects the amount of active muscle mass in the host. A woman excretes about 15 to 22 mg/kg, and a man about 20 to 26 mg/kg. Because creatinine is normally excreted rapidly, any increase in its level in the blood is a sign of kidney malfunction. Physicians attempting to make sure of the proper collection of urine frequently exploit the constancy of creatinine excretion. The volume of urine collected should reflect a 24-hour excretion if the level of creatinine is within the normal range.

Although creatine is normally not excreted in the urine, children and women occasionally do dispose of the chemical in this manner. The excretion rate for women is especially high during and after pregnancy. The urinary level of creatine is also high in patients with diabetes, hyperthyroidism, and fever and those experiencing malnutrition or simple starvation. This reflects the degradation of musculature.

FATS

The digestion, absorption, transportation, and cellular metabolism of fats follow yet a third set of chemical and biological pathways in the body. However, they intersect the pathways of carbohydrates and proteins at several points. The follow-

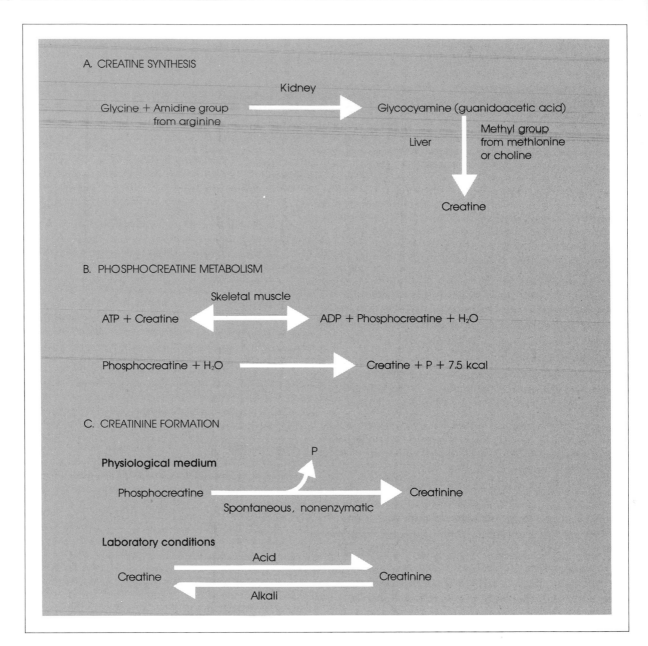

FIGURE 8-18   Metabolism of creatine and creatinine.

ing sections briefly describe the general fate of fats in the body; more details of fat metabolism are presented in Chapter 27 in the discussion of diet therapy for heart diseases.

Digestion, Absorption, and Transportation

Ingested fat meets its first significant digestive enzyme in the duodenum, where the exocrine gland of the pancreas provides the most impor-

tant lipase (Table 8-1 and Figure 8-19). The lipases in the saliva, stomach, and small intestine have only a small effect on fat digestion, as shown by the tremendous reduction in fat digestion when the pancreas is disabled. When the exocrine gland of the pancreas is not working properly, undigested and unabsorbed fat causes steatorrhea (bulky, clay-colored, fatty stools). The combined detergent actions of bile salts (from the gall bladder), fatty acids, and glycerides

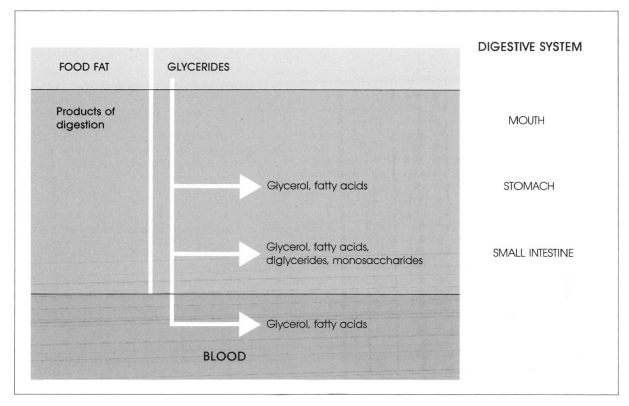

FIGURE 8-19   Triglyceride digestion.

emulsify fat, thus facilitating its digestion by lipase.

In the small intestine, half of the ingested triglycerides are hydrolyzed by lipase to form free fatty acids and glycerols. The rest are changed to monoglycerides and a small amount of diglycerides. The monoglycerides are absorbed into the intestinal mucosa, where they are further hydrolyzed to glycerols and free fatty acids.

Free fatty acids in the intestine are absorbed in two ways. Fatty acids with less than 10 to 12 carbon atoms pass directly from the intestinal lumen, through mucosal cells, into the portal vein, and to the liver. Here some are released into circulation as free fatty acids, some are converted to triglycerides for deposition, and some are circulated in the blood as glycerides or as fatty acids that reside within the complex of lipoproteins. Fatty acids with more than 10 to 21 carbon atoms are absorbed into the mucosal cells, where they are regrouped with glycerols to form triglycerides. The triglycerides attach themselves to very low density lipoproteins to form *chylomi-crons*, which enter the systemic circulation via the lymph and thoracic duct. Chylomicrons are fat globules 1 μm in diameter and visible under the microscope.

Other fatty substances are absorbed to varying degrees. For example, animal sterols are absorbed easier than plant sterols. Pancreatic secretion, fatty acids, and bile salts, which together emulsify and esterify cholesterol, are necessary for cholesterol absorption. Consequently, any disorder of the pancreas depresses the esterification and absorption of cholesterol. It is currently believed that cholesterol is absorbed mainly in the ileum. Like the triglycerides, absorbed cholesterol is incorporated into the chylomicrons, which reach the systemic circulation.

Within two to three hours after the ingestion of food containing short-chain fatty acids, the blood level of chylomicrons remains unchanged, although it may rise sharply if the meal contains long-chain fatty acids. Normally, after a mixed meal, the plasma develops a milky appearance because of the presence of chylomicrons in the blood. This is sometimes known as *lipemia*. In the presence of the enzyme lipoprotein lipase, these plasma chylomicrons are cleared and their contents diverted to the liver and *adipose tissue*.

Blood plasma therefore contains fat in the following forms: fatty acids, glycerol, glycerides, cholesterol, cholesterol esters, and phospholipids. These forms are bound to the albumin, α-globulin, and β-globulin fractions of the plasma proteins. The resulting *lipid-protein complexes* have varying densities. The highest densities occur in those with the most protein and least lipid; the lowest densities occur in those with the least protein and most lipid. Consequently, the complexes are classified into high density, low density, and very low density lipoproteins. In general, *very low density lipoproteins* carry mainly triglycerides; *low-density lipoproteins* carry mainly cholesterol; and α-*lipoproteins* carry phospholipids, albumin, and free fatty acids.

For a normal person, about 95% of ingested fat is absorbed, mainly in the duodenum and jejunum, with some absorption by the ileum. About 5% of fecal waste is fat, which comes from the diet, cell debris, and bacterial synthesis.

Although most of the fats are emptied into the lymphatic system after absorption and eventually reach the systemic circulation, the bile salts separate from the fats and travel through the portal vein into the liver. There they are reincorporated into the bile. Bile salts are thus cycled through the *enterohepatic circulation* (the liver, gall bladder, intestinal lumen, portal vein, and back to the liver). About 80% to 90% of bile salts in the intestinal lumen are reabsorbed in this way; the rest are lost in the stool.

Cellular Metabolism

The adult body distributes fats to two main locations: the membranes and other structural parts of cells (commonly called *structural fats*) and the fat cells (*neutral fats*) which are mainly white. Infants have some brown fat cells which can regulate body temperature by producing heat to support the baby's higher metabolic rate. Neutral body fat contains mainly triglycerides, plus small amounts of di- and monoglycerides which are important metabolic intermediates. Consequently, triglycerides are the main form of stored energy.

Fat degradation

Stored fat is degraded as needed to provide energy. Fat degradation occurs in two major stages: hydrolysis of glycerides and oxidation of fatty acids. In the adipose tissues, glycerides are hydrolyzed by a lipase to form fatty acids and glycerols. Both of these are released into the circulation for transport to the liver, where further hydrolysis may occur. When triglycerides are hydrolyzed, the released glycerols can be converted to phosphoglyceraldehyde in the liver (see Figures 8-6 and 8-20). This compound can in turn be converted to either carbon dioxide and water or glucose.

The process of oxidizing the fatty acids to carbon dioxide, water, and energy is called *beta-oxidation*, or alternate oxidation. It occurs mainly in the mitochondria of liver cells. The carbon chain is broken down by the successive removal of two-carbon fragments from the carboxyl end to form acetic acids. These can combine with CoA to form acetyl-CoA, which can enter the citric acid cycle to be oxidized (see Figures 8-8, 8-17, and 8-20). When the fatty acids are reduced to acetyl-CoA, hydrogen atoms are also released, which can be passed on to the respiratory chain. When fatty acids are completely oxidized, they generate more ATP than the molecular equivalent of carbohydrate because less oxygen is present. This explains why fat has a higher caloric value. However, unsaturated fatty acids generate less energy than the molecular equivalent of saturated fatty acids because less hydrogen is present in the former.

Most of the naturally occurring fatty acids are even numbered, and thus their oxidation always produces acetyl-CoA at the end. However, if the fatty acids happen to be odd chained, propionyl-CoA is formed instead. Propionyl-CoA can also enter the citric acid cycle if the coenzyme with vitamin B_{12} is available.

Fat synthesis

Fat synthesis takes place in two major stages: the formation of fatty acids and the formation of triglycerides. Fatty acid synthesis is achieved in two places: the mitochondria and the cytoplasm. Within the mitochondria, beta-oxidation is re-

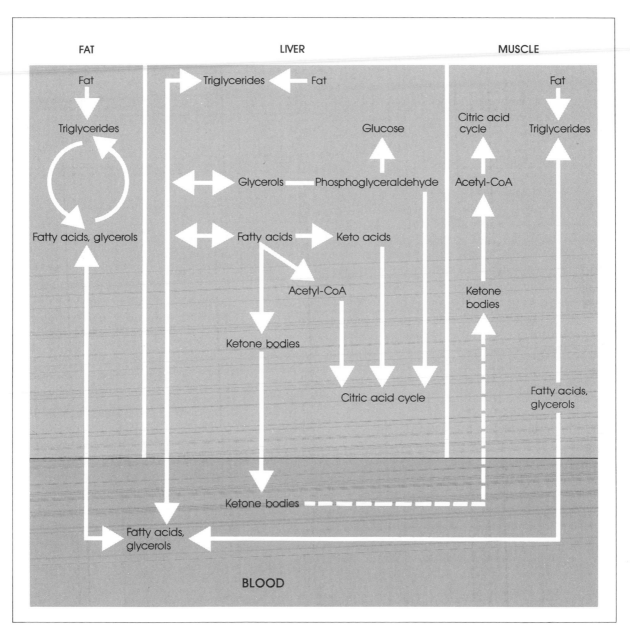

FIGURE 8-20   An overview of fat metabolism.

versed and two-carbon units are added until the appropriate fatty acids are formed. Outside the mitochondria, in the cytoplasm, another form of fatty acid synthesis occurs. Here the starting compound is acetyl-CoA, which serves as the end of the fatty acid molecule. The remaining carbons are incorporated as two-carbon units derived from the malonyl group. The incorporation is accompanied by simultaneous recarboxylation. The fatty acids formed are mainly 12 to 14 carbons long and rarely more than 16. The body can synthesize unsaturated fatty acids from the saturated ones by removing hydrogen, although it is unable to synthesize the essential ones (see Chapter 5).

In the adipose tissues, fatty acids combine with glycerol to form triglycerides, or neutral fats. This reaction occurs in the mitochondria. Figure 8-20 summarizes the information on fat synthesis.

As indicated earlier, glycerol can be converted to glucose (gluconeogenesis). However, acetyl-CoA cannot be converted to pyruvic acid (Figure 8-10). Although keto acids can enter the citric acid cycle, there is very little *net* conversion of fat to carbohydrate in the body, with the exception of the small amount of phosphoglyceraldehyde formed from glycerol.

Ketone bodies

During the normal process of beta-oxidation of fatty acids, the liver has the appropriate enzyme to remove the CoA from acetoacetyl-CoA to form acetoacetic acid. Acetones and β-hydroxybutyric acids can be formed from acetoacetic acids. The last three compounds are collectively called *ketone bodies*. The small amount of ketone bodies normally made by the liver is transported by the circulation to the muscle for conversion to acetyl-CoA, which is put through the citric acid cycle (Figure 8-20). Acetone is eliminated via urination and respiration. Because under normal circumstances the ketone bodies are metabolized as soon as they are formed, a person rarely excretes more than 1 mg of ketone each day, and blood levels are usually less than 1 mg/100 mL.

However, the ketones can accumulate under certain conditions, and the resulting clinical condition is known as *ketosis*. The main cause of ketosis is the accumulation of acetyl-CoA because the citric acid cycle in the liver is not operating at its normal or optimal efficiency. The most common cause is a sequence of events called "intracellular carbohydrate starvation." First, decreased supply of glucose leads to a reduction in pyruvic acid, acetyl-CoA, and cellular energy supply. Second, for compensation, fatty acid oxidation is increased to provide energy with an accumulation of acetyl-CoA. Third, the oversupply of acetyl-CoA leads to the formation of ketone bodies.

Glucose supply to cells is reduced during diabetes mellitus and dietary alterations such as high fat/low carbohydrate intake or simple starvation. In a diabetic patient, the lack of insulin prevents glucose from entering cells. When a person's diet is low in calories, high in fat, or low in carbohydrate, a similar metabolic pattern takes place. The inadequate intake of carbohydrate means a low supply of glucose to cells, and

ketosis may develop. However, an intravenous introduction of glucose counteracts ketosis, which is why carbohydrate is an antiketogenic agent. Chapter 26 explores this clinical condition in a diabetic patient.

Cholesterol metabolism

Body metabolism of cholesterol is of special concern to nutritional scientists. As indicated in Chapter 5, dietary cholesterol comes mainly from animal products such as fats, eggs, and organ meats. We also obtain sterols from plant foods, although they are not absorbed by our digestive system. Ingested cholesterol is readily absorbed via the lymphatic system after esterification in the intestinal mucosa (with fatty acids). The body can also synthesize cholesterol, mainly in the intestinal mucosa and liver. It is currently believed that the amount of cholesterol synthesized by the body is inversely related to the quantity consumed. However, the problem of regulating serum cholesterol level by reducing dietary intake is a much debated issue.

Synthesis and degradation of cholesterol occur simultaneously and continuously. The body removes cholesterol by conjugating it with taurine or glycine in the liver and excreting it in the bile, although the enterohepatic circulation makes sure that some cholesterol is reabsorbed. Other aspects of cholesterol metabolism are discussed in Chapters 5 and 27.

NUCLEIC ACIDS

Practically everything we eat contains nucleic acids, which occur in cell chromosomes. Nucleic acids are responsible for our heredity. During digestion, ingested nucleic acids are initially cleaved into nucleotides by pancreatic nucleases (see Figure 8-21 and Table 8-1). Next, the small intestine secretes nucleotidase, which hydrolyzes nucleotides to form phosphoric acid and nucleosides. The latter are split by intestinal nucleosidases to form sugars, purine, and pyrimidine, all of which are absorbed by active transport. Undigested large molecules of nucleic acids are excreted in the stool.

Nucleic acids can also be synthesized. In the body, purines, pyrimidines, and sugars are put

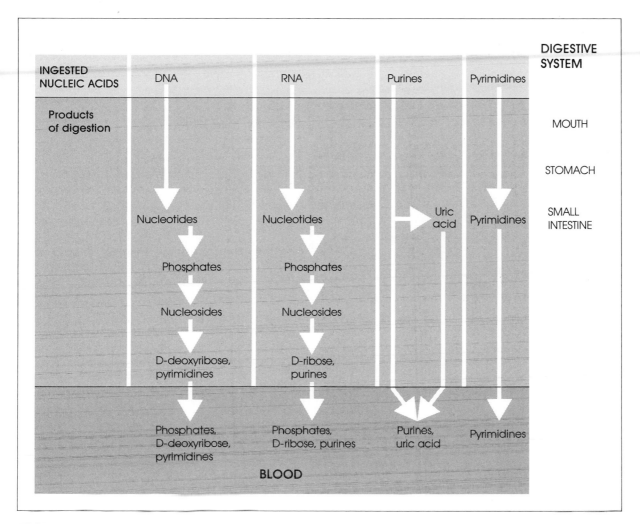

FIGURE 8-21   Digestion of nucleic acids.

together to form ribonucleic acid (RNA), deoxyribonucleic acid (DNA), nicotinamide adenine dinucleotide (NAD), and other related substances. However, the liver can also make pyrimidines and purines. Figure 8-22 shows the origins of atoms in synthesized purine, and Figure 8-23 those of pyrimidine.

Within a cell, although DNA is stable throughout life, RNA is in constant equilibrium with a metabolic pool. Purines and pyrimidines may be excreted as such in the urine or be metabolized to uric acid (purines) or carbon dioxide and ammonia (pyrimidines).

Uric acid in the body comes from two sources: synthesis from glycine and degradation of purines. In humans, uric acid is excreted in the urine, although in most other mammals it is converted to allantoin before excretion. The normal blood level of uric acid is 4 mg/100 mL. The kidney reabsorbs much of the filtered uric acid, but the body excretes about 1 g of uric acid in 24 hours. A standard reference text should be consulted for additional information on DNA, RNA, and molecular genetics.

WATER, VITAMINS, AND MINERALS

From the stomach to the colon, water passes freely and reversibly between the intestinal lumen and body compartments, although less so in the stomach than elsewhere in the gastrointestinal tract. Water moves in or out of the intestinal lumen to assure osmotic equilibrium on the two sides. In general, the osmolality (see Chapter 9)

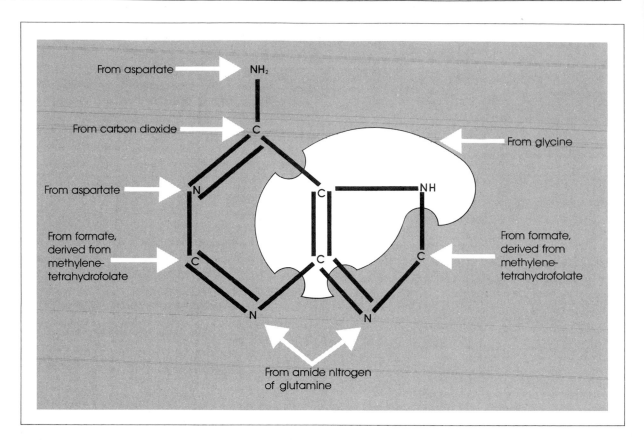

FIGURE 8-22   Origins of the atoms in purine.

of the contents of the small intestine resembles that of the plasma. After nutrients in the intestine have been absorbed, the excess water in the lumen is passed out with fecal waste in order to maintain osmotic equilibrium. Sodium moves freely according to the concentration gradient on the two sides of the mucosal cells. In the colon, sodium moves from body to lumen in accordance with the osmotic gradient. Chapter 9 discusses in detail body fluid and electrolyte balance in relation to the role of the intestine.

All water-soluble vitamins are absorbed along the small intestine. Except for vitamin B_{12}, a healthy person can absorb these vitamins rapidly. All fat-soluble vitamins require the presence of pancreatic enzyme, bile salts, glycerides, and fatty acids for absorption, as does fat itself. Chapter 6 discusses in detail the absorption and metabolism of each vitamin.

In a healthy person, all essential minerals are absorbed easily by the body, although the extent varies with individual minerals. Chapter 7 provides a detailed discussion of the absorption and metabolism of each mineral.

STUDY QUESTIONS

1. Define digestion, absorption, transportation, metabolism, catabolism, and anabolism of nutrients and their biological by-products.

2. What are the parts of the alimentary system? What general processes take place in each area?

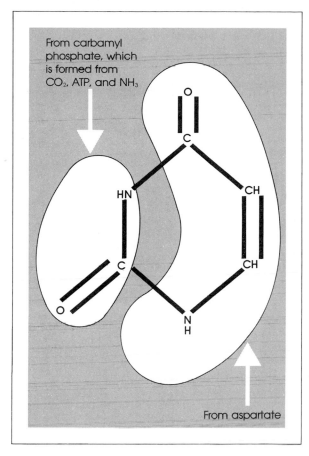

From carbamyl phosphate, which is formed from CO_2, ATP, and NH_3

From aspartate

FIGURE 8-23 Origins of the atoms in pyrimidine.

3. What is the role of enzymes? Of coenzymes?
4. To what form are all carbohydrates eventually reduced in the digestive process?
5. Discuss at least four ways in which energy is released or stored in relation to carbohydrate metabolism.
6. Discuss the three processes involved in the cellular metabolism of carbohydrates. What is gluconeogenesis?
7. How is blood sugar level usually maintained within a narrow range?
8. What is the end product of protein digestion? In what areas do protein digestion, absorption, catabolism, and synthesis take place?
9. Define nitrogen equilibrium.
10. What pancreatic enzyme is important in fat digestion? What disorder arises when the pancreas is unable to provide enough of this enzyme?
11. What forms of fat can be absorbed and are therefore found in blood plasma? To what are they bound?
12. What is the enterohepatic circulation?
13. What are the two major phases of fat degradation in the cells? Of fat synthesis?
14. Define ketosis.
15. What happens to water, vitamins, and minerals that are ingested?

Chapter 9

Fluids, Electrolytes, and Acid-Base Balance

MOST OF US are aware that water is an essential nutrient. Although humans are known to survive for weeks and even months without food, they cannot live for long without water. For all our apparent physical solidity, our bodies consist more of water than of anything else. The water within us is essential to a number of body processes and structures. One primary function of water is as a medium of transportation, carrying nutrients and wastes in and out of cells by both passive and active processes. This movement depends heavily on the levels of certain minerals or electrolytes in the intracellular and extracellular compartments. Although the levels of fluid volume and electrolyte concentration in a healthy person are subjected to a number of adjustments, they are always maintained at biological equilibrium. Similarly, the chemical conditions of acidity and alkalinity in a normal person are constantly maintained at a delicate balance despite the wide variety of foods and beverages consumed daily.

FUNCTIONS, DISTRIBUTION, AND BALANCE OF BODY WATER

As indicated in Chapter 2, water makes up more than 60% of adult body weight. Water is an important substance with many major functions in the body. It transports nutrients to the cells and waste materials through the kidney for excretion. It is the main medium in which biological and chemical reactions take place. It serves as an important substrate and reactant in chemical and biological reactions. It regulates body temperature and lubricates joints. It maintains pressure and equilibrium for certain organs and structures, such as the eyeball and fetus. It provides an emergency fluid source. Surprisingly, water is even the main structural component of the body. For example, 70% to 73% of the lean body mass is water; fat contains water as well.

Water exists both inside (*intracellular*) and outside (*extracellular*) the cells of the body. These general areas are sometimes referred to as *compartments*. As indicated in Table 9-1, the extracellular water is distributed in the blood plasma, in the spaces between cells, in bone and connective tissue, and within the gastrointestinal tract, brain, and spinal column.

We take in water daily by actually drinking water and liquids and by eating foods. The liquids we ingest include coffee, tea, alcoholic beverages, sodas, and thin soups. Practically all foods contain some water. Although some products, such as flour and nuts, contain very little water, fruits and vegetables can contain up to 95% water. Also, in a healthy person, normal metabolic processes form water inside the body.

On the other hand, we lose water daily in

TABLE 9-1   Distribution of Body Water

Body Compartment	Percent of Body Weight
Total body water (extracellular and intracellular)	60.0
Extracellular water	28.0
Plasma	4.5
Interstitial water	13.0
Bone and connective tissue*	8.0
Transcellular water*	2.5
Gastrointestinal water	
Cerebrospinal fluid	
Intracellular water	32.0

Note: About 70% to 73% of muscle cells or lean body mass is water.

*In estimating content of extracellular water, these sources are usually ignored or forgotten.

TABLE 9-2   Daily Water Balance in a Normal Adult

Factors Affecting Water Balance	Volume of Water Change (mL)
Sources of gain	
Food (meat, apples, etc.)	+500–1,000
Water, beverages, and liquid and semiliquid edible items (e.g., soups)	+1,100
Metabolic water (formed from chemical reaction, e.g., oxidation of food)*	+400
Total	+2,000–2,500
Sources of loss	
Urine	−1,000–1,300
Stools	−90–100
Perspiration, respiration	−410–500
Insensible loss	−500–600
Total	−2,000–2,500

*The oxidation of 1 g of fat, carbohydrate, and protein produces 1.1, 0.6, and 0.4 g of water, respectively.

urine, bowel movements, perspiration, respiration, and the *insensible* loss—the constant but invisible evaporation of moisture from the skin surface. In a normal person, daily losses and gains of water balance each other, as shown in Table 9-2.

Water balance in many clinical conditions deviates from those listed in Tables 9-1 and 9-2. For example, a hospitalized patient may take in more water through a special tube or through an intravenous or rectal route. On the other hand, the same patient may lose water from the body through conditions such as abnormal gastrointestinal loss (stomach suction, vomiting, colitis, intestinal suction, presence of fistula, or diarrhea), exudates (burns, ulcers, bedsores, and wounds), respiratory diseases (bronchorrhea or acute laryngotracheobronchitis), injuries, edema of damaged tissues, massive urticaria, or swellings of the skin. *Dehydration* results when water loss exceeds gain; *edema* results when more water is ingested and retained than lost (see Chapter 2). Either kind of imbalance is dangerous to body functioning and can be fatal if severe. Effects of these clinical abnormalities are discussed later.

BODY FLUIDS AND ELECTROLYTES

In general, the movement of nutrients and wastes in and out of cells is largely determined by the levels and types of electrolytes in the intracellular and extracellular body compartments. The concepts of body fluids and electrolytes have caused much confusion among students in medicine, nursing, nutrition, and dietetics. This book is not the appropriate forum to dwell at length on this topic, for it is taught in basic physiology classes. However, for easy reference, some basic definitions are provided here, followed by brief discussions of osmotic equilibrium and ways in which the gastrointestinal tract and kidney and hormonal systems help to regulate osmotic equilibrium.

Definitions

An *electrolyte* is a substance that is a charged particle or is separated into charged particles when dissolved in water or other fluids. Since such par-

TABLE 9-3   Distribution of Electrolytes in the Body

Electrolyte	Extracellular Fluid (meq/L)	Intracellular Fluid (meq/L)
Cations		
Sodium (Na$^+$)	142	10
Potassium (K$^+$)	5	150
Calcium (Ca^{++})	5	2
Magnesium (Mg^{++})	3	40
Total	155	202
Anions		
Chloride (Cl$^-$)	103	2
Bicarbonate (HCO$_3^-$)	27	10
Phosphate (HPO$_4^-$)	2	103
Sulfate (SO$_4^-$)	1	20
Organic acids ($^-$) (lactic, pyruvic)	6	10
Proteins	16	57
Total	155	202
Miscellaneous		
Glycogen nucleoproteins	trace	all
Organic phosphates (e.g., creatine)	trace	all
Glucose, urea, amino acids, creatinine	~½	~½

ticles are either positively or negatively charged, they can conduct an electric current. A positively charged particle is called a *cation*; an example is sodium. A negatively charged particle is an *anion*, such as chloride. In an electrolyte solution, the number of anions must be equal to that of cations to achieve neutrality. If practically all the particles dissociate or separate, then it is a solution of *strong electrolytes*. In a solution of *weak electrolytes*, only some of the anions and cations separate into discrete charged particles. In body fluids, which contain both cations and anions, potassium, sodium, sulfate, chloride, and bicarbonate are considered strong electrolytes; weak ones are phosphates, organic acids, carbonic acid, hemoglobin, and protein molecules. A *solute* is a substance that has dissolved in a fluid such as water to form a solution.

Diffusion is the movement of a substance from a compartment or location of higher concentration to one of lower. When two solutions of different concentrations are separated by a semipermeable membrane in a container, the dissolved molecules (solutes) move from the solution of higher concentration to the other until both concentrations are equal. This process is known as *osmosis*. *Osmotic pressure* is defined as the force per unit area applied to the side of the semipermeable membrane with the higher concentration of solute molecules just sufficient to prevent net water movement to that side. Osmotic pressure is expressed in terms of the concentration of solute molecules present.

Osmolality refers to the concentration of the solute in a solution per unit of solvent; *osmolarity* refers to the concentration of the solute in a solution per unit volume of the solution. An *osmole* is a measure of osmotically active particles. The osmolarity and osmolality of dilute aqueous solutions are fairly similar. For example, the osmolarity of a liquid diet is about 75% to 85% of its osmolality. Any solution with the same osmolarity as human body fluid is called *isotonic*. Those of higher osmolarity are *hypertonic*; those lower are *hypotonic*.

Equivalents may be used to express the electrical activity or the number of positive or negative charges present. However, because of the minuteness of such charges, the unit *milliequivalent* (meq) is used instead. For comparison pur-

TABLE 9-4   Distribution of Water, Sodium, Potassium, and Chloride in the Body

Substance	Distribution (%)	
	Extracellular	Intracellular
Water	45	55
Sodium (Na$^+$)	97–98	2–3
Potassium (K$^+$)	10–11	89–90
Chloride (Cl$^-$)	87–88	12–13

poses, *moles* express the electrolyte concentration—the number of particles per unit volume of solution. Again, *millimoles* (mmol) is the preferred unit.

Positively charged and negatively charged electrolytes are distributed both inside and outside the cells in the human body. Table 9-3 presents the distribution profile. Table 9-4 compares the distribution of water, sodium, potassium, and chloride in the human body.

The tonicity, osmolarity and osmolality, and volume of fluid in different body compartments are interrelated. Table 9-5 provides a simple illustration of these interrelationships, using some abnormal clinical conditions of water and sodium imbalances. Under normal circumstances, complex meshing of body processes prevents these imbalances from occurring. The normal condition is one of osmotic equilibrium.

Osmotic Equilibrium

As indicated in Tables 9-1 and 9-4, body fluid is distributed between two "compartments"—intracellular areas and extracellular areas. In a healthy, normal individual, this distribution must be maintained in equilibrium at all times. This equilibrium is achieved in three ways: (1) balancing of the total concentrations of salt solutes within and without the cells (that is, equalizing the number of cations and anions), (2) constant shifting of water between intracellular and extracellular compartments (such shifts are usually small and occur in both directions), and (3) excreting the appropriate electrolytes through the kidneys.

Figure 9-1 shows how water moves from the extracellular to the intracellular compartments. The movement results from either a rise in the salt concentration in the intracellular fluid or a drop in the salt concentration in the extracellular compartment. In a normal person, the net result of the movement must be a balanced equilibrium. However, some clinical conditions can produce an unbalanced movement of the fluid. Table 9-5 provides some examples, and more will be presented later. The water moves because of osmotic pressure, which attempts to equalize the concentration of the solutes on the two sides of the semipermeable cell membranes. In Figure 9-1, the extracellular fluid is hypotonic to the intracellular one; that is, the osmotic pressure of the intracellular fluid is higher than that of the extracellular fluid. The movement of water continues until equilibrium is reached.

As shown in Figure 9-2, water moves from the intracellular to the extracellular compartments when either the salt concentration in the extracellular compartment has increased or that of the intracellular compartment has decreased. In a normal person, a balanced equilibrium exists, although an unbalanced movement of the fluid occurs under some clinical conditions (Table 9-5). In Figure 9-2, the osmotic pressure of the intracellular fluid is lower than that of the extracellular fluid, and water moves out of the cells to equalize osmotic pressure on the two sides of the semipermeable membrane.

The control of fluid movement and the distribution of electrolytes is based on the following premises:

1. Because potassium predominates in the intracellular fluid, it is generally assumed that the osmotic pressure in this compartment is largely determined by the concentration of this cation. However, anions, such as phosphates, are present in this compartment, and they may play a role.

2. Because sodium predominates in the extracellular compartment, it is generally assumed that the osmotic pressure in this compartment is largely determined by the concentration of this cation. Again, it should be emphasized that anions, such as chloride, are also present in this compartment, and they, too, may affect osmotic pressure.

TABLE 9-5 Interrelationship of Tonicity, Osmolarity-Osmolality, and Volume of Fluid in Different Body Compartments

Condition of Body Water and Sodium Balances	Physiological Entity	Fluid Volume Adjustment		Osmolarity-Osmolality Adjustment
		Extracellular	Intracellular	
More sodium lost than water, e.g., impaired kidney function, adrenal hypofunction	Hypotonic dehydration	Decrease	Increase	Decrease
Loss of sodium and water in normal physiological ratio, e.g., vomiting and diarrhea	Isotonic dehydration	Decrease	No change	No change
More water lost than sodium, e.g., diabetes insipidus	Hypertonic dehydration	Decrease	Decrease	Increase

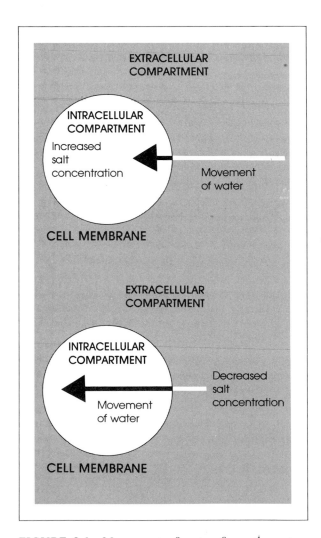

FIGURE 9-1 Movement of water from the extracellular to intracellular compartment.

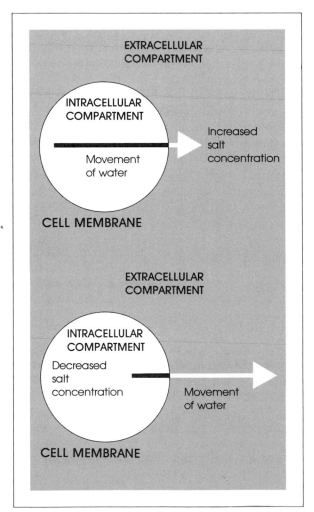

FIGURE 9-2 Movement of water from the intracellular to extracellular compartment.

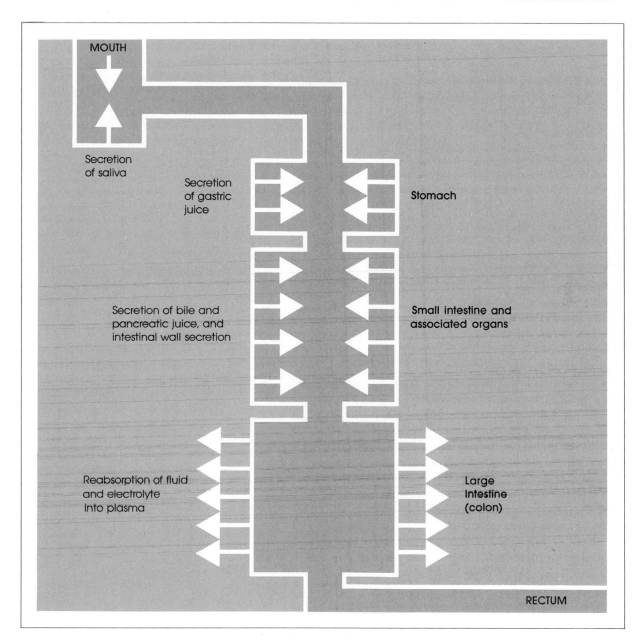

FIGURE 9-3   Exchanges of fluids and electrolytes between the extracellular compartment and the gastrointestinal system.

3. Blood plasma has a large solute load of non-diffusible proteins, such as albumin. Because these proteins cannot diffuse through cell membranes, they serve to retain a fixed amount of water inside blood vessels. Abnormally low plasma protein forces water to leak into the spaces between cells and mix with the interstitial fluids, causing edema.

Regulation by the Gastrointestinal Tract

The body fluid and electrolyte balance is related to and regulated in part by the alimentary tract. Extracellular fluids and electrolytes (for example, blood plasma) are continuously secreted into and absorbed from the digestive tract, as illustrated in Figure 9-3. During a 24-hour period, an average of 8 L of fluids circulate within the alimentary tract. In comparison, the volume of fluids in the entire body blood circulation is about 3 to 4 L. Sodium and potassium are the two major electrolytes secreted into and reabsorbed from the gastrointestinal system, although other electrolytes are also involved.

In a normal, healthy individual, the osmotic pressure is equal on both sides of the intestinal wall. This means that the fluid within the lumen of the digestive tract is isotonic to the extracellular fluid. Any major fluid-electrolyte disturbance in the body must be brought to normality by restoring isotonicity between fluids in the alimentary tract and the extracellular compartment.

Many body fluid–electrolyte disturbances result directly from abnormal fluid and electrolyte distribution within the alimentary tract. The imbalances that occur frequently due to eating and drinking are quickly corrected. For example, drinking water makes intestinal fluid hypotonic, but this imbalance draws electrolytes from the extracellular compartment. Eating food or drinking salt or sugar solution produces a hypertonic medium in the intestinal lumen. To restore isotonicity, water is secreted into the alimentary tract.

In certain clinical disturbances of the gastrointestinal tract, fluid and electrolyte imbalance is less easily corrected by the body. For instance, vomiting from pregnancy or esophageal reflux can cause loss of water, electrolytes, and hydrochloric acid. The loss of water may lead to dehydration; the loss of potassium may cause alkalosis. With diarrhea, the body loses bicarbonate, sodium, chloride, and water, and potassium may eventually be lost from the cells. Uncontrolled vomiting or diarrhea creates a metabolic disturbance in the body, which will be discussed later in this chapter.

Regulation by the Kidney and Hormonal Systems

The kidney controls body fluid and electrolyte balance in two ways. It secretes and reabsorbs water according to its level in the blood plasma, and it secretes and reabsorbs certain electrolytes, especially sodium and potassium, according to their balance in the body.

There are two major hormonal systems working in the body to maximize the effectiveness of the kidney. One involves the pituitary gland, which produces the *antidiuretic hormone* that enables the kidney to reabsorb water. Conditions such as fluid loss due to hemorrhage from a crushing injury or shifting of fluid from extracellular to intracellular volume during congestive heart failure can lower the osmotic pressure of blood plasma. This change causes the pituitary gland to make more antidiuretic hormone, which in turn causes the kidney to conserve water.

The second system comes into play when the sodium level in the intracellular fluids drops. Chemical cues trigger production of the hormone *aldosterone* by the adrenal cortex (gland). This hormone increases reabsorption of sodium and excretion of potassium in the kidney, restoring the balance of these electrolytes in body fluids.

Some Clinical Examples

To illustrate the principles of fluid-electrolyte imbalances in the body, Figure 9-4 shows how the body responds to a decrease in water intake or an increase in salt intake; Figure 9-5 illustrates fluid and electrolyte adjustments to compensate for perspiration; and Figure 9-6 shows varying fluid and electrolyte responses to an abnormally low protein intake, which is common in many underdeveloped and developing countries (see Chapter 11).

ACID-BASE BALANCE

In addition to balancing the levels of fluid and electrolyte, the body normally maintains a steady pH (acidity-alkalinity) level in its internal environment. Although many foods and metabolic processes contribute acidity and alkalinity to body fluids, the internal environment of a healthy individual is maintained at a slightly alkaline condition. Before we discuss the mechanisms responsible for this biological maintenance, the elementary principles of acids and bases are briefly reviewed below.

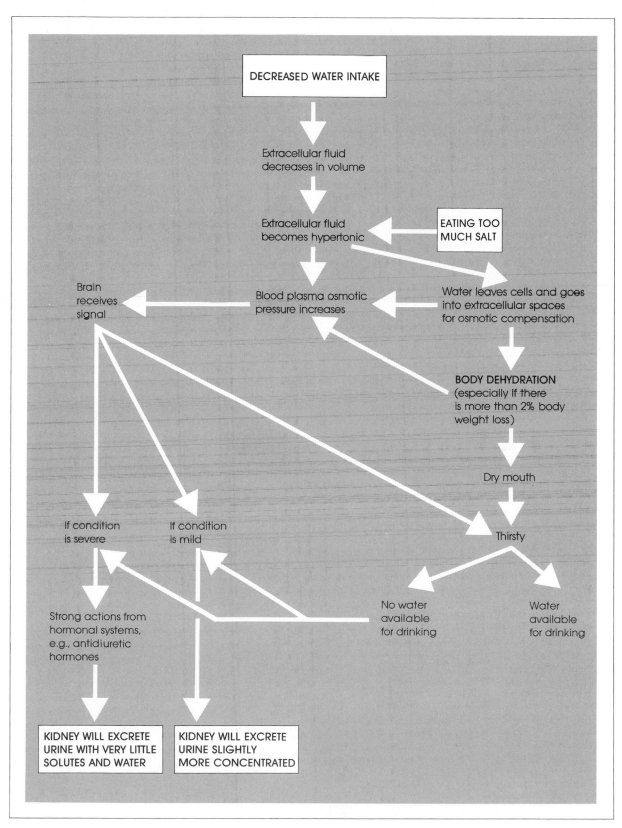

FIGURE 9-4   Body fluid and electrolyte adjustment caused by decreased
water intake or excessive salt intake.

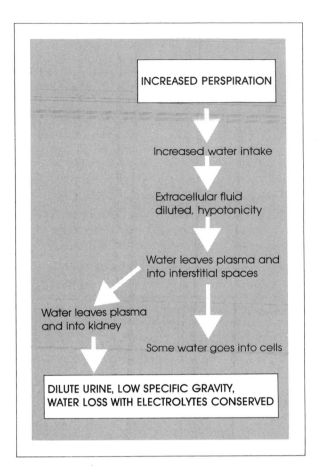

FIGURE 9-5   Body fluid and electrolyte adjustment caused by perspiration.

When an acid dissolves in a solution, it dissociates into its chemical components, hydrogen ion(s) and an anion. An acid solution is therefore an electrolyte. A base solution is also an electrolyte; it releases a hydroxide ion(s) and a cation. Hydrogen ions make a solution acidic; hydroxide ions make a solution alkaline. A salt is made from a chemical reaction between an acid and a base, with the formation of water (hydrogen ions and hydroxide ions) as a by-product. Acids and bases are considered strong if they dissociate completely in a solution; weak ones only dissociate partially.

If the conditions within human fluids are neutral, the amount of hydrogen ions is equal to that of hydroxide ions. The condition is acidic if the former exceeds the latter, and alkaline if the latter exceeds the former.

It is difficult to present the concentration of hydrogen ions in a biological fluid mathematically, because hydrogen ions usually exist in a small quantity. However, a mathematical means has been devised to quantify hydrogen ions for easy reference: the *pH scale*. The pH refers to the negative logarithm of the hydrogen ion concentration (pH = $-\log$ [H$^+$], where [H$^+$] refers to the hydrogen ion concentration). Chemically, the pH scale covers a range of 0 to 14. When a fluid has a pH of 7, it is neutral; a range of 7 to 14 is alkaline, and 0 to 7 is acidic. In a normal, healthy individual, the pH of plasma or blood is about 7.35 to 7.45. This narrow range in alkalinity is constantly maintained by three means: buffering systems of the body fluids, respiratory compensation, and renal compensation. When the systems break down, as they do in certain clinical conditions, *acidosis* (an overly acidic condition) or *alkalosis* (excessive alkalinity) may result. However, acidosis and alkalosis are usually secondary consequences of a primary disorder, and their clinical manifestations vary with the patient and the primary disorder. The symptoms of acidosis and alkalosis vary from mild to life-threatening. The following sections briefly discuss the three regulatory mechanisms that maintain body pH and some common examples of acidosis and alkalosis.

Buffering Systems in the Body Fluids

A *buffer* is defined here as a solution of a substance or substances whose hydrogen ion concentration does not change very much irrespective of how much strong acid or base is added. That is, its pH changes within only a narrow limit. A salt in a weak base or acid solution is a good buffer. Most living systems contain biological buffer systems that are made up mainly of salts and their corresponding weak acids or bases. The three important buffer systems in the human body are:

1. Sodium bicarbonate/carbonic acid: $NaHCO_3$/ H_2CO_3
2. Dibasic sodium phosphate/monobasic sodium phosphate: Na_2HPO_4/NaH_2PO_3
3. Sodium-protein/hydrogen-protein and hemoglobin/hydrogen-hemoglobin

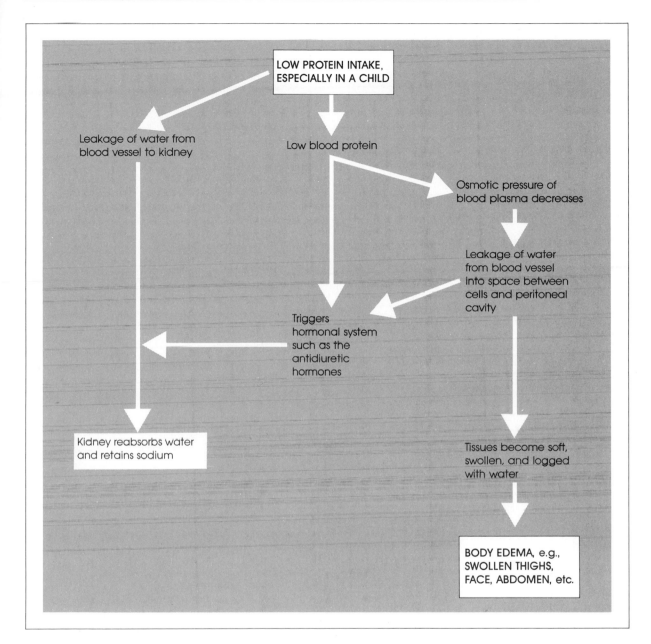

FIGURE 9-6   Body fluid and electrolyte adjustment caused by low protein intake.

In these three systems, whenever a strong base is added to a body fluid, it is buffered by a weak acid; a weak base buffers any strong acid added.

The most important of these systems is the sodium bicarbonate/carbonic acid system. A strong acid added to this buffer has the following effect:

strong + sodium $\longrightarrow$ salt + carbonic
acid   bicarbonate   acid

Most of the carbonic acid is changed to carbon dioxide and exhaled. The addition of a strong acid results in a decrease of the ratio of sodium bicarbonate to carbonic acid because of the slight increase in carbonic acid. There is a concomitant slight decrease in pH (the solution becomes slightly more acidic) because of the slight increase in hydrogen ions from the carbonic acid. However, this decrease would be much higher if the buffer was not present.

If a strong base or alkali is added to the buffer:

strong + carbonic ⟶ more bicarbonate
alkali   acid

The addition of a strong alkali increases the ratio of sodium bicarbonate to carbonic acid. Because some of the carbonic acid is used up, the hydrogen ion concentration decreases slightly with a concomitant increase in pH.

If these buffer systems fail, changes in acidity or alkalinity result in the following:

increase in acidity ⟶ decrease in pH
↓
if pH is less than 7.35
↓
acidosis*

increase in alkalinity ⟶ increase in pH
↓
if pH is greater
than 7.45
↓
alkalosis*

Respiratory Compensation

The second defense against acidosis or alkalosis involves the respiratory process. The rate and depth of respiration control the quantities of oxygen inhaled and carbon dioxide exhaled. As discussed previously, the major fluid buffer in the body is the sodium bicarbonate/carbonic acid system. When a strong acid is added to the body either externally from ingestion or internally because of altered metabolism, carbon dioxide is released to maintain the pH of the body fluid with a concomitant increase in carbonic acid (see

---

*Use the references at the back of this book to find more information on these clinical conditions. Also see "Some Examples of Imbalance" on p. 240.

the previous discussion). We can therefore eliminate excess carbon dioxide by hyperventilation both in rate and depth. The excess carbon dioxide is exhaled. If the carbon dioxide is not released, acidosis or carbon dioxide poisoning ensues.

On the other hand, if a strong base is added to the body, more bicarbonate is formed (see the previous discussion). In this case, a little extra carbon dioxide in the body restores the proper ratio of bicarbonate to carbonic acid. Hypoventilation thus releases less carbon dioxide; otherwise, there is alkalosis. These alterations in normal breathing patterns are largely involuntary and seem to be controlled by a "respiratory center" in the brain.

Renal Compensation

The kidney also helps to control body acid-base balance by two major systems. Both involve adjusting the absolute quantities of hydrogen ions and bicarbonate in the body. Because a detailed discussion of these mechanisms is beyond the scope of this book, a standard physiology textbook on kidney functions (see Chapter 28) should be consulted to augment the brief analysis below.

One system is reabsorption of bicarbonate in the proximal tubules of the kidney. When blood plasma is filtered through the kidney, a large amount of sodium bicarbonate is passed on to be excreted by the kidney tubules in the urine. However, the proximal section of the kidney tubules reabsorb about 80% to 90% of the body bicarbonate. Under normal circumstances, a healthy person's blood bicarbonate is thereby maintained at a normal level.

The second way the kidney prevents acid-base imbalance involves the handling of bicarbonate and hydrogen ions in the distal tubules of the kidney. This is achieved in three ways. First, when the urine passes through or alongside the distal tubule cells, the latter release hydrogen ions in exchange for sodium ions in the urine. When sodium ions are thus reabsorbed into the distal tubules, so are bicarbonates. This returns excreted sodium bicarbonate into the blood plasma. Second, after the distal tubules have re-

TABLE 9-6   Substances That Can Influence the Acid-Base Balance of Body Fluids

Substance	Dietary Source	Body Source
Water	Beverage, food	Metabolism of carbohydrate, protein, and fat
Sodium, potassium, magnesium (base forming)	Most fruits and vegetables	Muscle catabolism
Chloride (acid forming)	Many foods	Muscle catabolism
Phosphates, sulfates (acid forming)	Many foods, especially protein foods such as meats and cheese; soft drinks and other processed beverages	Metabolism of protein and/or fat
Calcium (base forming)	Many foods, especially milk	Mobilization of bone minerals
Organic acids, such as tartaric acid, citric acid, etc. (see Table 9-7)	Many foods, especially fruits, vegetables, and fermented foods	Metabolism of carbohydrate, protein, and fat
Carbon dioxide	Many foods, especially fruits and vegetables	Metabolism of carbohydrate, protein, and fat

leased the hydrogen ions, the latter may lower the pH of the urine too much. To guard against this, the distal tubules release ammonia at the same time. This ammonia combines with hydrogen ions and chloride or sulfate to form ammonium chloride and ammonium sulfate. These compounds raise the pH of the urine to an acceptable level. Third, if the body tends to keep all the bicarbonates, the kidney tubules simply stop giving up the hydrogen or ammonia ions. As a result, none of the bicarbonates excreted are reabsorbed by the kidney tubules. Instead, they are lost in the form of sodium or potassium bicarbonates. The distal tubules act in this way if the body is in alkalosis because of too much bicarbonate or too little carbonic acid.

Foods, Body Metabolism, and Urine Acidity

In addition to the automatic body mechanisms discussed above, a number of chemical substances in foods and from body metabolism can influence the acid-base balance of body fluids. Table 9-6 indicates what these substances are and the changes they produce. Certain foods are *acid forming* (or acid ash) foods and may produce an acid residue. Such foods can produce acidic urine. The urine's low pH is due mainly to the presence of phosphorus, sulfur, and chlorine in those foods, minerals that form acids on ashing or oxidation. Other foods are *base forming* (alkaline ash) and may produce an alkaline residue.

TABLE 9-7 Relationship Between Types of Foods and Urine Acidity-Alkalinity

Type of Food	Acidity-Alkalinity Tendency of Ingredients	Acidity-Alkalinity of Urine
Meats, fish, cheese, cereals (protein-rich foods)	Phosphates, sulfates, chlorides (acid residue)	Acidic urine
Most fruits and vegetables	Sodium, potassium, magnesium (alkaline residue)	Alkaline urine
Milk	Calcium effect surpasses protein effect (alkaline residue)	Alkaline urine
Plums, prunes, cranberries	Benzoic and quinic acids (not oxidized to carbon dioxide and water); converted in the liver to hippuric acid and tetrahydroxy hippuric acid; surpasses effect of sodium, potassium, and magnesium that are present	Acidic urine

Such foods can produce alkaline urine. The urine's high pH is due mainly to the presence of sodium, potassium, calcium, and magnesium in the foods, for these minerals form bases on ashing or oxidation. Table 9-7 indicates the types of foods that can produce an alkaline or acidic urine.

Some Examples of Imbalance

In certain clinical conditions, body systems cannot balance acid and base levels in body fluids. Acidosis accompanied by an increase in hydrogen ion concentration in the body fluids may be caused by the disappearance of base from the body due to (1) vomiting or excretion of lower intestinal contents (as in diarrhea, ileostomy, or biliary fistula) or (2) impaired bicarbonate reabsorption in the proximal tubules of the kidney (as in renal tubular acidosis).

Acidosis may also result from the addition of excess acid to the body. Some circumstances where this may happen are: (1) diabetic ketosis, (2) ingestion of acidic substances such as drugs, (3) lactic acid accumulation from strenuous exercises, (4) poisoning or intoxication with chemicals such as salicylates and others, (5) kidney malfunction so that hydrogen ions are retained, and (6) hypoventilation.

Alkalosis accompanied by a decrease in hydrogen ion concentration may be caused by the disappearance of acid in conditions such as (1) vomiting, stomach suction, and other gastrointestinal losses; (2) body potassium depletion for various reasons (for example, use of inappropriate diuretics); or (3) hyperventilation. Alkalosis may also be caused by the introduction of excess base into the body, as in (1) ingesting alkaline drugs (for example, bicarbonate), (2) drinking too much milk (milk-alkali syndrome), and (3) releasing calcium from bone for various reasons.

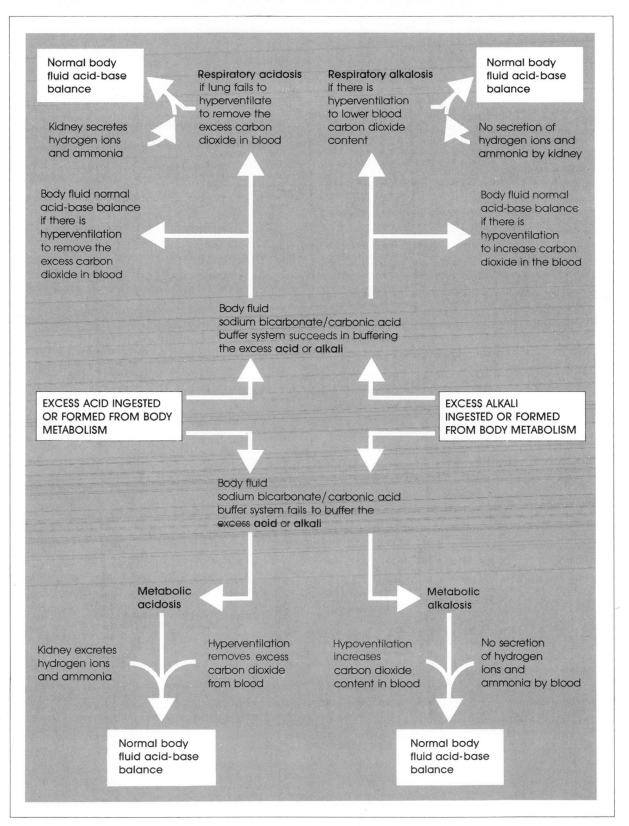

FIGURE 9-7   Relationship between body acid-base balance and changes in
acidity-alkalinity of substances ingested.

Some of the above clinical examples are discussed in different chapters of this book. The index will provide a quick identification of those discussed (under the entries *acidosis* and *alkalosis*). Information on those examples not discussed in this book may be obtained from the reference textbooks cited at the back of this book.

The sequence of events whereby the acidity and alkalinity of the human body are modified in response to the ingestion of substances (acidic or alkaline), whether food or otherwise, is best illustrated by the flow chart in Figure 9-7. The chart also applies to the formation of acidic or alkaline substances within the body under different circumstances, normal or otherwise. Whenever the topics of acidosis and alkalosis are discussed in this book, this chart should be used as a reference.

STUDY QUESTIONS

1. List at least six major functions of water in the body.
2. Where is extracellular water found?
3. Define dehydration and edema.
4. What generally determines the passage of nutrients and wastes in and out of body cells?
5. What is a negatively charged electrolyte called? A positively charged electrolyte? Give an example of each.
6. Explain osmosis. What is osmotic equilibrium and how is it achieved?

7. Use two common examples to illustrate sodium and potassium deficiencies (one for each). Make sure that your examples differ from those given in the text.
8. Which body systems help to regulate body fluid and electrolyte balance? How?
9. What is a normal acid-base balance? What body mechanisms automatically adjust acid-base balance? What are the two general forms of imbalance?

PART II

APPLIED NUTRITION

Chapter 10

Planning an Adequate Diet

UNDERSTANDING THE IMPORTANCE of various nutrients to our health is one matter; putting together daily diets with adequate quantities of all these nutrients is another. Nutritionists have devised a number of tools to meet this challenge: food composition tables, Recommended Daily Dietary Allowances, nutrient labeling, and the four food groups. Daily food guides based on the four food groups offer a simple way in which people can make sure that their diets are adequate.

In addition to examining these tools in this chapter, we shall look at other factors that meal planners should consider: the frequency and timing of meals, the effects of cooking on nutrient loss, and ways to keep food costs down without scrimping on essential nutrients. After a discussion on the latest legal requirements of nutrition labeling, we shall also look at the current techniques of determining the protein, fat, and carbohydrate content of foods.

FOOD COMPOSITION TABLES

One aspect of fitting foods into diet plans is to learn what nutrients are in the foods and in what amounts. Food composition tables are convenient sources that provide much of the information that we need. Because of the magnitude of the task of developing these tables, most have been prepared by the federal government and international organizations, although a few are published by commercial companies.

The list below shows some of the major American food composition tables.

Composition of Foods—Raw, Processed, and Prepared. USDA Agricultural Handbook No. 8. Washington, D.C.: U.S. Government Printing Office, 1963. Revised, 1980.

Nutritive Value of American Foods in Common Units. USDA Agricultural Handbook No. 456. Washington, D.C.: U.S. Government Printing Office, 1963. Revised, 1980.

Nutritive Value of Foods. USDA Home and Garden Bulletin No. 72. Washington, D.C.: U.S. Government Printing Office, 1981.

Food Values of Portions Commonly Used. 12th ed. Pennington, J. A. T., and Church, H. N. Philadelphia, Pa.: Lippincott, 1980.

Amino Acid Contents of Foods. USDA Home Economics Research Report No. 4. Washington, D.C.: U.S. Government Printing Office, 1968.

Vitamin B-6, Pantothenic Acid, and Vitamin B-12. USDA Home Economics Research Report No. 36. Washington, D.C.: U.S. Government Printing Office, 1969.

Amino Acid Content of Foods and Biological Data on Proteins. Rome: Food Agriculture Organization, 1970.

Probably the most comprehensive of these is USDA (United States Department of Agriculture) Handbook No. 8: *Composition of Foods.* The first edition, published in 1963, gives data on 16 nutrients in 2,483 food items for both 100-g edible portions or 1-lb measures as purchased.

Using USDA Handbook No. 8 as a source, the USDA developed Handbook No. 456 in 1975. It, too, provides data on 16 nutrients in 2,483 food items in household measures and market units. Home and Garden Bulletin No. 72 again used Handbook No. 8 to develop data for 16 nutrients in about 730 foods for average servings or common household units. This table is reproduced in full in Table 6 of the appendix.

Handbook No. 8 is so heavily used as a standard reference by physicians, nurses, nutritionists, and other scientists that the USDA is now massively revising it. The new edition is being released in stages. When complete, it will provide data on 61 nutrients found in about 4,000 foods. These data are presented for 100-g edible portions, common household measures, and 1 lb of the food as purchased. Sections of the revised edition released as of 1980 are listed in Table 10-1.

Another popular book of food composition tables is *Food Values of Portions Commonly Used.* Frequently updated, it is a compilation of information from various sources. These include man-

TABLE 10-1 Revised Sections of USDA Handbook No. 8 as of 1980

Section No.	Food Group	Year Issued	No. of Items
8-1	Dairy and egg products	1976	144
8-2	Spices and herbs	1977	43
8-3	Baby foods	1978	217
8-4	Fats and oils	1979	128
8-5	Poultry products	1979	304
8-6	Soups, sauces, and gravies	1980	214
8-7	Sausages and luncheon meats	1980	80

food labeling laws. In addition, foods not commonly found in the standard American diet may appear in food composition tables worked out for other areas of the world. Examples are provided in the references at the back of this book. Ethnic food compositions are also described in specialty books available at libraries and other conventional sources.

ufacturers of processed foods, the USDA, and others. These tables give data on 26 nutrients, but the data are not complete for every product. Food products tabulated include regular and basic foods, mixed varieties, and many commercially processed items.

Although food composition tables are convenient, cheap, and widely used, they have some limitations. Nutrients found in a given kind of food vary according to the soil and climate in which the food is grown, the variety, and the season; how the food is harvested, packaged, and stored; and how it is prepared, served, and consumed. Different food composition tables may therefore give different data for the same food. Some of the foods we eat may not even be in the tables—they may be too new or too uncommonly used or too complex a mixture of processed foods. The task of updating a food composition table becomes increasingly difficult since new fresh or processed foods appear continuously. The food producers may be the best source of information on the nutritional composition of these products.

Despite these drawbacks, food composition tables provide us with general guides and representative values. To minimize their limitations, the USDA is establishing a nutrient data bank to store information for revisions of the tables, for clinical applications, and for professional meal planning. These data, supplied by producers of processed foods, include information required by increasingly stringent and comprehensive

RECOMMENDED DIETARY ALLOWANCES (RDAs)

Besides knowing the essential nutrients in foods, we must know how much of each nutrient we need to consume each day. Although our understanding of the human body's minimal and optimal needs for each essential nutrient is incomplete, the National Research Council of the National Academy of Sciences in the United States has established some standard guidelines. Its Food and Nutrition Board is composed of physicians, nutritionists, and scientists highly knowledgeable in the field. This group studies and evaluates scientific data and develops the Recommended Daily Dietary Allowances (RDAs) for a number of nutrients for people in different age and sex categories.

First published in 1943, the RDAs have already been revised eight times. All editions have carried a tabulation of the daily amounts of kilocalories and selected nutrients required for different age and sex groups, a text discussion of the basis for the tabulated allowances, and a consideration of nutrients not tabulated.

The number of nutrients tabulated has grown considerably over the years. In the 1943 edition, recommended daily allowances were given only for calories, protein, vitamins A, D, B_1, B_2, and C, niacin, calcium, and iron. By contrast, the 1980 edition gives recommended daily allowances for calories, protein, vitamins A, D, E, B_1, B_2, B_6, B_{12}, and C, niacin, folacin, calcium, phosphorus, magnesium, zinc, iodine, and iron, as well as ranges of estimated safe and adequate daily dietary intakes (recommended) of vitamin

K, biotin, pantothenic acid, molybdenum, selenium, chromium, copper, manganese, fluoride, and the electrolytes sodium, potassium, and chloride. The complete 1980 RDAs are reproduced in Table 1 of the appendix.

How adequate are the RDAs? According to the latest available scientific evidence, the RDAs represent those levels of essential nutrient intakes that will adequately provide normal, healthy individuals with their known nutritional needs. Since each person has different requirements for various essential nutrients, the RDAs are intended to exceed the requirements of most normal, healthy persons and thus meet their varying needs. However, the RDAs are not considered adequate for people with clinical conditions such as hereditary diseases, illness, or trauma.

If the nutrient intakes of normal, healthy people are equal to or somewhat above the RDAs, their bodies should be nutritionally sound according to current scientific knowledge. If people are consuming the essential nutrients at levels below the RDAs, they are not necessarily deficient in those nutrients. However, their risk of becoming deficient in any particular essential nutrient is increased if such intake levels continue to drop below the RDAs for a prolonged period.

Nutritionists believe that the safest and most appropriate way to evaluate the nutritional status of a person is through a combination of methods: (1) an analysis of the person's nutrient intakes based on a record of food eaten, using the RDAs as a guide; (2) physical examination; (3) clinical evaluation; and (4) blood, urine, and other laboratory and biochemical studies.

DAILY FOOD GUIDES: THE FOUR FOOD GROUPS

Translating the RDA guidelines into daily meal plans takes time and training. Accordingly, nutritionists and home economists in the USDA have translated the scientific recommendations into specifications of the kinds and amounts of food needed for good nutrition. These translations—known as *daily food guides*—provide an easy way to make good food choices.

Scientists are not aware of any one "perfect" food that can supply all the RDAs. To meet all our nutritional needs—including those yet to be determined and incorporated into future RDAs—we must eat a variety of foods. The daily food guides thus recommend a large number of nutritious foods, grouped into four broad categories. These *four food groups* are milk and milk products, meats or meat equivalents, fruits and vegetables, and breads and cereals. Each group contributes a substantial amount of the major nutrients needed for health.

Recently, the USDA introduced a fifth food group: fats, sweets, and alcohol. Because this new group has not yet been widely adopted, this book will adhere to the four food groups previously mentioned and consider fats, sweets, and alcohol, along with a number of other items, as *supplementary foods* (see later discussion). However, the fifth food group may be used if preferred.

In addition to sorting "nutrient-dense" foods into four basic groups, the USDA has suggested an appropriate number of servings from each group to be consumed daily (Table 10-2). These recommendations are widely used by nutritionists, physicians, home economists, health agencies, government programs, and hospitals—as well as by individuals—as general guides to planning well-balanced and nutritious diets.

However, the food guides and the RDAs are neither iron-clad rules nor perfect instruments. Both criteria must be considered along with other variables in order to be applied optimally. Currently, the food guides in the United States take into account the availability of food supplies, food preferences, incomes, religious beliefs, ethnic origins, seasonal variations, and geographical distributions. In other words, the food guides tend to reflect the "standard American diet."

The foods commonly chosen in this society from each food group and the nutrients these foods provide will be examined in the following sections. We will also look at supplementary foods not included in the more nutrient-dense four food groups.

TABLE 10-2   Recommended Numbers of Servings from the Four Food Groups

Food Group	Serving Size	No. of Daily Servings
Milk and milk products Fluid milk	1 c, 8 oz, ½ pt, ¼ qt	Children under 9: 2—3 Children 9—12: ≥3 Teenagers: ≥4 Adults: ≥2 Pregnant women: ≥3 Nursing mothers: ≥4
Calcium equivalent	1 c milk 2 c cottage cheese 1 c pudding 1¾ c ice cream 1½ oz cheddar cheese	
Meat and meat equivalents	2—3 oz cooked lean meat without bone 3—4 oz raw meat without bone 2 oz luncheon meat (e.g., bologna) ¾ c canned baked beans 1 c cooked dry beans, peas, lentils 2 eggs 2 oz cheddar cheese ½ c cottage cheese 4 T peanut butter	≥2
Fruits and vegetables	Varies by item: ½ c cooked spinach 1 potato 1 orange ½ grapefruit	≥4, including 1 of citrus fruit and another fruit or vegetable that is a good source of vitamin C and 2 of a fair source 1, at least every other day, of a dark green or deep yellow vegetable for vitamin C ≥2 or more of other vegetables and fruits, including potatoes
Bread and cereals	1 slice of bread, 1 oz ready-to-eat cereal ½ to ¾ c cooked cereal, cornmeal, grits, macaroni, noodles, rice, or spaghetti	≥4

Milk and Milk Products

As indicated in the following list, we should consume at least a minimal amount of milk each day:

Fluid milk: whole, low fat, skim, fat free
Dry milk: whole, low fat, skim, fat free
Other milk: evaporated, condensed
Milk products: yogurt, cheese, cottage cheese
Milk alternates: soy milk, powdered soy milk, soy
    cheese

The recommendations range from 2 or more cups of fluid whole milk for adults and children under 9 to 4 or more cups for teenagers and nursing mothers.

The nutrient contents of cow's milk vary according to the characteristics of the cow, its lactation stage, and its diet. Milk bought at a grocery store contains a mixture of milk taken from many cows, further complicating analysis.

In general, however, milk's major contributions are calcium, protein, and vitamin B_2. Milk also contributes other nutrients, such as vitamins B_1, B_6, B_{12}, A, and D, niacin, and magnesium. Milk protein is cheap, easily digested, and of high quality; lactalbumin and casein make up about 80% of the protein in milk. The vitamin B_2 content of milk varies with the extent of light exposure. In a transparent container, the activity of the vitamin may be reduced by half. Paper cartons or opaque plastic containers help prevent this loss.

Milk is low in iron, manganese, copper, and vitamin C. A child under 6 months old will therefore receive an inadequate intake of iron if milk is the sole food source. Milk is low in vitamin C because of the heat applied during pasteurization and sometimes, in the case of infant feeding, during repeated home sterilization. However, some manufacturers do add vitamin C to their products.

Fluid whole milk

The basic form of milk is fluid whole milk. It can be consumed as a beverage, used on cereals and desserts, and added to casseroles and soups.

To safeguard the quality of the fluid whole milk—and of milk products made from it—both federal and state standards have been established. Milk is *pasteurized*—usually by heating it to 161 °F for 15 seconds—to kill bacteria. Milk may also be *homogenized*—forced through small holes at high pressure to disperse the large fat globules and distribute them evenly.

Milk products and alternates

Products derived from fluid whole milk or imitating its flavor and nutrient content may be consumed in addition to or instead of fluid whole milk. Some people cannot digest fluid whole milk. It is now well established that some individuals are deficient in the intestinal enzyme lactase. They are therefore intolerant to lactose in milk. However, many of them can tolerate fermented products such as cheese, yogurt, or buttermilk, in which the lactose has been converted to lactic acid. Some of them can also drink a small amount of milk. Many other children are actually allergic to milk (see Chapter 31), although some can become accustomed to the product if they drink gradually increasing amounts over a period of time.

When other dairy products are used in place of fluid whole milk, there are important nutritional considerations. If low-fat, skim, or nonfat milk is used, the intake of vitamins A and D and essential fatty acids may be low. If available, products fortified with these two vitamins are preferred. Also, chocolate milk has more calories than an equivalent amount of regular fluid milk.

Cheeses are popular substitutes for fluid milk. However, because cheese is manufactured from the curds of skim or whole milk, the whey is drained off. The latter contains some of the water-soluble vitamins. In the past, by-products such as whey were discarded; much research is now being conducted to find a profitable use for these products. Cottage cheese prepared by acid coagulation should not be used as a substitute for fluid whole milk, since the content of calcium in this kind of cottage cheese is low and the drainage of whey reduces the water-soluble vitamin content. Cottage cheese is nevertheless a good source of protein.

Compared with fluid whole milk, cheeses tend to have higher fat and calorie contents and lower levels of protein, calcium, and vitamin B_{12}. Otherwise, the nutrient contents of most cheeses resemble that of milk, although they vary with the method of processing.

Ice cream is made from milk, milk solids, cream, flavorings, sweeteners, and occasionally nuts and fruits. Most commercial ice cream contains food additives to improve the texture, consistency, and appearance of these mixtures. Ice cream is higher in calories than milk.

Yogurt is made by fermenting milk (whole, skim, or low fat milk or milk solids) with different strains of bacteria. Most commercial yogurts are low in fat and high (20%) in galactose. But more than half the weight of some commercial yogurts consists of added sugar and fruits.

Dairy or related products also include filled and imitation dairy products (for example, filled cheese). Most *filled* products contain milk solids and nonbutter fat; they come in many forms such as cheese and canned milk. An imitation dairy product is one that resembles real milk products, especially in flavor and cooking characteristics, but does not contain any milk solids. Instead, it contains nondairy ingredients.

How do we replace one milk product with another to derive equivalent amounts of nutrients? One cup (8 oz) of whole fluid milk is equivalent to: ¾ tablespoon butter plus 1 cup fluid buttermilk, ¾ tablespoon butter plus 1 cup fluid skim milk, ½ cup water plus ½ cup undiluted evaporated milk, ⅔ cup water plus ⅓ cup dry whole milk, or 1 cup whole milk yogurt. One cup (8 oz) fluid skim milk is equivalent to: ⅔ cup water plus ⅓ cup dry skim milk, 1 cup fluid buttermilk, or 1 cup skim milk yogurt. Table 10-3 shows the amounts of milk products that provide the same amount of protein or calcium as 1 cup of fluid whole milk.

In the last few years, the national consumption of dairy products has declined for various reasons. Technology has created a large number of nutritious beverages other than milk that cater to the taste and preference of some consumers. The threat of high blood cholesterol and obesity has also played a role; many consumers use dairy substitutes instead. In addition, many people are still ignorant about the value of milk.

TABLE 10-3   Milk Products That Contribute As Much Protein and Calcium As 1 Cup of Fluid Whole Milk

Milk Product	Amount of Product Containing Given Amount of Nutrient	
	9 g Protein	280 g Calcium
Nonfat milk	1 c	1 c
Cheddar cheese	1⅓ oz	1⅓ oz
Cottage cheese	1⅓ c	⅓ c
Ice cream	1½ c	1½ c
Cream cheese	30 T	9 T

Meats and Equivalents

According to the daily food guides (Table 10-2), we should eat two or more servings from the meat and meat equivalents group every day. In general, these two servings of meat provide approximately 50% of the protein, 25% to 50% of the iron, 25% to 30% of vitamins B_1 and B_2, and 35% of the niacin in the RDAs. Meat is not a good source of vitamins C and A or calcium. Common foods in the meat group are as follows:

Lean meat: beef, veal, lamb, pork (fresh or cured), liver
Variety meat: heart, brain, tongue, kidney
Wild meat: squirrel, rabbit, bear, deer, buffalo
Fish: shellfish, fresh and saltwater varieties (fresh, dried, frozen, canned)
Poultry: all fowl (e.g., chicken, turkey, guinea hen, duck, goose) and their giblets
Game birds: pheasant, wild duck, grouse
Miscellaneous meats: "turkey ham" (made from turkey meat but treated and smoked to look and taste like ham), "hot dogs" (made from a variety of meats including organ meats)
Dry legumes: navy beans, lima beans, lentils, peanuts, others
Nuts: nuts, nut butter
Peas: all split, dried peas, pinto beans, chick peas, pigeon peas
Meat analogues: textured vegetable proteins (TVPs), largely soy, which may be processed to simulate meat products such as sausage and bacon in shape and flavor
Meat equivalents: eggs, cheese

The contents of iron and other minerals vary according to the type of meat. Muscle meats are high in iron, and organ meats are even higher—pork liver is the richest and cheapest source of this nutrient. By contrast, chicken and fish have relatively low iron contents. In addition to iron, muscle meats contribute zinc and phosphorus.

Although meats are a major source of protein, they have varying levels of the nutrient. For example, the content varies from 12% to 13% in pork to 30% in some fish. The protein in fish is easily digestible and of good quality. Nonmeat alternates such as eggs, cheese, beans, peas, and peanut butter contain less protein, but they are cheap and provide good protein values when eaten with other protein foods. Dried beans and peas are 35% protein; nuts are 15% protein. Hard cheeses and cottage cheese may sometimes be considered as part of the meat group because of their protein contents, but cream cheese does not qualify.

The fat content of the meat group may vary from 1% to 40%, according to animal feed, slaughter weight, the cut of meat, the extent of fat trimmed, and the method of preparation. High-graded meats have a large caloric content, since they have a lot of marbled fat. Prime beef is 25% fat, standard beef is 16%, and utility beef is less than 15%. By contrast, fish has only about 1% to 7% fat. Scientists are now attempting to modify the quality of fats in some animals. For example, some animals are being fed with varying amounts of fat and carbohydrate in experimental efforts to reduce the ratio of saturated/unsaturated fatty acids in their body fats.

Fruits and Vegetables

The daily food guides recommend four or more servings of fruits and vegetables each day, since this group makes many nutritional contributions to the American diet. Fruits and vegetables are responsible for the major intakes of iron and vitamins A and C; they are also good sources of calcium, magnesium, and folic acid. They contain small amounts of trace elements, depending on the type of soil in which they are grown, and some vegetables contribute proteins. Fruits stimulate appetite, and their organic acid content helps in the absorption of iron and calcium, especially if a person does not make enough stomach acid.

Most fruits and vegetables are nutrient dense, low in calories, low in fat, and high in cellulose. Because they provide roughage, cellulose, and bulk, the products in this group assure a good intestinal environment. Some of them—such as celery, apples, and carrots—even help clean our teeth.

Although this group as a whole is a major source of vitamin A, very few vegetables and fruits contain good amounts of this vitamin. The major ones that are high in vitamin A are dark green vegetables, orange-colored vegetables, and orange-fleshed fruits, such as apricots, muskmelon, and mangoes (see Table 10-4).

Fruits and vegetables are our main sources of vitamin C. Citrus fruits are particularly high in vitamin C: a 4-oz serving of a citrus fruit juice provides 30 mg of the vitamin. Fruits such as cherries, strawberries, and cantaloupe also provide rich amounts of the vitamin. Vegetables such as spinach, cabbage, broccoli, and asparagus are good sources of vitamin C, especially when eaten raw.

The vitamin C level in many fruits and vegetables varies with the season, climate, variety of products, stage of maturity, storage period and temperature, and the plant parts utilized. Vitamin C loss after harvest, during oxidation, and in discarded parts is high. Since vitamin C is a very labile compound subject to destruction by heat, air, and light, food should be prepared in ways that minimize its loss.

We derive about one-quarter of our daily iron need from fruits and vegetables. In general, leaves contain more iron than stems, fruits, and the parts grown in the soil. Because of the roughage and phytic acid in fruits and vegetables, the iron they contain is not well absorbed (about 5% absorption). However, the absorption is increased if meat is eaten at the same time.

Fruits and vegetables contribute a small amount of calcium. However, if the person's milk consumption is low or if a large amount of fruits and vegetables is eaten, the relative contribution of calcium from this food group is magnified.

Legumes—vegetables such as soybeans, peas, and other beans—are good, acceptable sources of protein. Root tubers—such as po-

TABLE 10-4   Foods in the Fruit and Vegetable Group

Varieties Rich in Vitamin A and Carotene

Dark green leafy vegetables: beet greens, broccoli, chard, collards, watercress, kale, mustard greens, spinach, turnip tops, wild greens (dandelion and others)

Orange-colored vegetables: carrots, pumpkins, sweet potatoes, winter squash, yams

Orange-fleshed fruits: apricots, muskmelon, mangoes

Varieties Rich in Vitamin C

Citrus fruits: grapefruit, oranges, lemons, tangerines; juices of these fruits

Other good and excellent sources: muskmelon, strawberries, broccoli, several tropical fruits (including guavas), raw sweet green and red peppers

Significant sources: tomatoes, tomato juice, white potatoes, dark green leafy vegetables, other raw vegetables and fruits

Other Fruits and Vegetables

Vegetables: asparagus, lima beans, green beans, beets, cabbage, cauliflower, celery, corn, cucumber, eggplant, kohlrabi, lettuce, okra, onions, green peas, plantain, rutabagas, sauerkraut, summer squash, and turnips

Fruits: apples, avocados, bananas, berries, cherries, dates, figs, grapes, nectarines, peaches, pears, pineapple, plums, prunes, raisins, rhubarb, watermelon; juices and nectars of many fruits

tatoes—provide some protein, too. Both groups are also high in carbohydrate calories. For example, root tubers contain 2% protein and 20% carbohydrate, while legumes contain 4% protein and 13% carbohydrate.

Although many fruits and vegetables are not high in calories by themselves, they are often consumed in combination with high-caloric foods, which increases the calorie intake. Broccoli, for instance, is often eaten with a high-caloric cream sauce or butter; canned peaches usually come with high-caloric sugar syrup.

Cereals and Cereal Products

In addition to recommending servings of milk, meat, and fruits and vegetables, the daily food guides recommend four or more servings of grain products each day. The major nutrients these foods contribute are calories, iron, niacin, and vitamins B_1 and B_2.

Cereals and cereal products include all grains served in whole-grain, enriched, or fortified forms, e.g., wheat, corn, oats, buckwheat, rice, and rye. Some common items in this group are as follows:

Breads: yeast breads, rolls, quick breads, biscuits, buns, muffins, pancakes, waffles, crackers, others

Breakfast cereals: ready-to-eat types, including flaked, rolled, and puffed forms; cooked types including whole, grain, and rolled forms

Other grain foods: macaroni, spaghetti, noodles, flour, rice, cornmeal

Whole-grain products: wholewheat flour and its products, bulgur, dark rye flour, brown rice, whole ground cornmeal.

The protein in grains is incomplete. Grains can be used to provide complete proteins, however, as discussed in Chapters 4 and 18. For example, if two or three different cereals are consumed at the same time, amino acids missing in one may be supplied by the others. We also tend to combine grains with protein-rich foods—macaroni and cheese, egg noodles, buns with hamburger, rice with chicken, and milk on cereals—and thus increase our amino acid intakes. Finally, many baked goods contain liquid or dry milk, improving their protein quality.

Adding dry or liquid milk to commercial mixes for cereal products adds not only protein but also calcium and other nutrients. Many grain-related products are now enriched and fortified, an important health protection measure that will be discussed in Chapter 20.

Most nutritionists recommend eating some cereal products daily since they provide a fair amount of many nutrients at low cost. However, nutritional values of many breakfast cereals are being challenged by consumer groups. The main dispute concerns the practice of eating the cereals alone. A bowl of cereal with whole milk added is a nutritious food, but cereals by themselves contribute limited types and amounts of essential nutrients.

The Foundation Diet and Supplementary Foods

A diet consisting only of the recommended numbers of servings from the four food groups is known as a *foundation diet*. An example of such a diet is shown in Table 10-5. A foundation diet provides more than 90% of most essential nutrients and over 75% of the calories in the RDAs, as shown in Table 10-6.

We normally eat more than a foundation diet, however. We may eat extra servings of the foods in the four basic groups, and we may eat foods not included or listed in the four groups. These are called *supplementary foods*. They include spices, butter, margarine, and other fats.

TABLE 10-5   A Daily Foundation Diet for an Adult Using the Basic Foods

Food Group	No. of Servings
Milk	2 c fluid milk
Meat	3½ oz broiled round steak
	1 medium egg
Fruits and vegetables	½ c cooked asparagus
	1 medium baked potato
	½ c cooked summer squash
	6 oz orange juice
	1 pear
Bread and cereals	3 slices enriched bread
	⅔ c corn flakes

These are often ingredients in recipes or are added to other foods during preparation or at the table. Nutrient-light snacks and sweets, fabricated foods such as breakfast bars, and relatively nonnutritive beverages can also be included in this group.

Some common supplemental foods are as follows:

Beverages: coffee, tea, chocolate, soft drinks, alcoholic beverages

Fats: butter, margarine, mayonnaise, cream, oils

Sweets: sugar, jam, sweet desserts, candy, pastries, syrups

Snack items: cookies, potato chips

Spices and seasonings: all spices, seasonings, flavorings, sauces

Although fats are now classified as supplementary foods, they are essential to health (see Chapter 5). Vegetable oil should be included among the fats used. Common sources of fats are butter, margarine, shortening, cooking and salad oils, cream, most cheeses, mayonnaise, salad dressings, nuts, and bacon and other fatty meats. Meats, whole milk, eggs, and chocolate contain some fat naturally. Many popular snacks, baked goods, pastries, and other desserts are made with fat or cooked in it.

Although supplementary foods may help

TABLE 10-6   Nutrient Contribution by the Foundation Diet

Nutrient*	Amount of Nutrient Contributed†	RDA for a 25-year-old	
		Male	Female
Kilocalories	1,200–1,300	2,700	2,000
Protein	60–70 g	56	44
Vitamin A	1,100–1,400 µg RE	1,000	800
Vitamin E	1–5 mg	10	8
Vitamin C	125–135 mg	60	60
Thiamin	0.8–1.2 mg	1.4	1.0
Riboflavin	1.5–1.8 mg	1.6	1.2
Niacin	13.0–13.5 mg	18	13
Vitamin B_6	1 mg	2.2	2.0
Folacin	200–250 µg	400	400
Vitamin B_{12}	2–4 µg	3	3
Calcium	700–800 mg	800	800
Phosphorus	900–1,000 mg	800	800
Iron	10 mg	10	18
Zinc	5–8 mg	15	15

*Vitamin D and Iodine are not included. All units used comply with the RDA system. Check Table 1 in the appendix for more details.

†Because of the variation in the nutrient content of foods, only a range or an approximation is given.

round out meals and make them taste better, these foods tend to be low in nutrients. On the whole, each of the four food groups provides at least 25% of three or more nutrients to the American diet. By contrast, nutrient contributions provided by the supplementary foods are relatively insignificant except for calories and fats. For example, supplementary foods contribute 20% of the total caloric intake, 30% to 35% of the total fat intake, and 10% of the vitamin A need. The approximate nutrient contributions of the different food groups to the American diet are shown in Table 10-7. The more calories one eats from the basic four food groups, the greater the likelihood of obtaining the RDAs. On a low-calorie diet, it is even more important that most of the foods come from the basic food groups rather than the supplementary foods.

The contributions of certain supplementary foods are controversial. One such group includes condiments, spices, and herbs. Usually of plant origin, these substances have been used by all known civilizations. During this century, numer-ous claims have been made about the therapeutic effects of herbs and related substances. Many therapeutic drugs are made from plant products, and some herbs and spices may contain pharmacological compounds. However, beneficial therapeutic effects from their regular usage are not documented.

Some individuals consume a large amount of substances such as sea salt, kelp, and herbs, thinking them health giving. The safety of this practice has recently been debated. Certain adverse effects have been documented: abdominal cramps from herbs, arsenic contamination from seaweed, and lead intoxication from bone meal. It is true that items such as seaweed, iodized salt, and chili powder can provide some minerals and vitamins. However, the importance of these contributions depends on the amount consumed.

Similarly, yeast can be a good source of vitamins, protein, and minerals if consumed in large quantities. However, most people do not eat much yeast, even when it is used in the leavening of bread.

TABLE 10-7   Approximate Nutrient Contributions of the Different Food Groups

Food Group	Major Nutrient Contributed	Proportional Contribution to the American Diet
Milk	Protein	⅓
	Calcium	⅔
	Riboflavin	½
Meat	Protein	½
	Thiamin	¼
	Iron	>⅓
	Niacin	>⅓
Fruits and vegetables	Vitamin C	practically all
	Vitamin A and carotene	¾
	Iron	¼
Bread and cereals	Iron, thiamin, niacin, other B vitamins, fiber	>¼
Supplementary foods		
Fats, oils	Calories, fat-soluble vitamins	varies
Sweet products	Fluids, calories, small amount of nutrients	varies
Spices and seasonings	Iodine	varies
Alcohol	Calories	insignificant to ⅓

Another supplementary food that we consume in large amounts is beverages such as coffee, tea, and cocoa. All of these contribute some magnesium and potassium. In addition, tea provides a small amount of fluoride. However, there has been much controversy recently regarding the effects of excess coffee and tea drinking on health. Although definitive findings are not available, some facts should be noted. Caffeine is found in coffee and most cola beverages, theophylline in tea, and theobromine in cocoa. These chemicals are stimulants and can keep us awake. Caffeine is also a diuretic and may increase urination, especially at night. Tea also contains tannin, which has caused concern over the years, although not much evidence is available to substantiate claims about its adverse effects. Finally, some herb teas have been shown to cause diarrhea.

ADDITIONAL CONSIDERATIONS IN MEAL PLANNING

Familiarity with the basic four food groups allows us to plan balanced and nutritious meals. Table 10-8 suggests a meal plan for an adult, while Table 10-9 presents a sample menu of 2,400 kcal and 95 g of protein.

We all do not have to choose the same foods, however. Normal, healthy people can eat any food they like so long as they know how to combine it with other foods to provide a good diet. Life-styles, national origins, religious beliefs, individual tastes, prices, and shopping and preparation times all influence the choices. Americans are fortunate to have a wonderfully abundant and varied food supply.

TABLE 10-8 Suggested Meal Plan

Breakfast	Lunch	Dinner
Fruit/juice, ½ c/1 serving	Soup, ½ c	Soup, ½ c
Cereal: hot/6 oz; dry/1 oz	Meat (regular/substitute), 2–3 oz	Meat (regular/substitute), 3–4 oz
Egg (regular or substitute), 1 serving	Vegetable (cooked/salad), ½ c	Fruit/juice, ½ c/1 serving
Meat: 2 strips bacon; 2 sausages;	Potato (regular/substitute), ½ c	Vegetable (cooked/salad), ½ c
1 oz regular meat	Salad dressing, 1 T	Potato (regular/substitute), ½ c
Bread, 1–2 slices	Bread/roll, 1–2 servings	Salad dressing, 1–2 t
Butter/margarine, 1–3 t	Butter/margarine, 1–3 t	Bread/roll, 1–2 servings
Jelly/jam/preserves, 1–3 t	Dessert, 1 serving	Butter/margarine, 1–3 t
Milk, 1 c	Milk, 1 c	Dessert, 1 serving
Hot beverage (coffee/tea), 1–2 c	Hot beverage (coffee/tea), 1–2 c	Milk, 1 c
Cream (regular/substitute), 1–3 t	Cream (regular/substitute), 1–3 t	Hot beverage (coffee/tea), 1–2 c
Sugar, 1–3 t	Sugar, 1–3 t	Cream (regular/substitute), 1–3 t
Salt, pepper	Salt, pepper	Sugar, 1–3 t
		Salt, pepper

TABLE 10-9 Menu Plan Providing 2,400 kcal and 95 g of Protein

Breakfast	Lunch	Dinner
Orange juice, ½ c	Pea soup, ½ c	Chicken broth, ½ c
Oatmeal, 6 oz	Crackers, 2	Fried chicken, 3 oz
Egg, 1	Ham, 2 oz	Spinach, ½ c
Bread, 2 slices	Lettuce/tomato salad, ½ c	Rice, ½ c
Margarine, 2 t	Noodles, ½ c	Bread, 1 slice
Jelly, 1 t	Toast, 1 slice	Margarine, 1 t
Milk, 1 c	Margarine, 1 t	Milk, 1 c
Coffee, 1 c	Milk, 1 c	Coffee, 1 c
Cream, 1 t	Ice cream, 1 c	Cream substitute, 1 t
Sugar, 2 t	Coffee, 1 c	Sugar, 1 t
Salt, pepper	Sugar, 1 t	Salt, pepper
	Salt, pepper	

In addition to considering nutrients and the form of foods that people will happily eat, meal planners should consider some other factors. These include the frequency and timing of meals, the effects of cooking methods on nutrient loss, and ways of minimizing costs. Documents that are useful in planning an adequate diet are listed in the references at the end of this book.

Meal Frequency and Timing

For a number of years, much effort has been spent on ascertaining what meal frequency and intervals are optimal for permitting the body to utilize ingested nutrients. So far it appears that the body can adjust to any pattern of eating, be it three equal meals; five or six small meals; or one small, one moderate, and one large meal. However, some studies have confirmed that a number of small, frequent meals encourages the deposition of lean body mass, although the long-term effect of this regimen on the well-being of the body is unknown. On the other hand, other studies have shown that a nutritious breakfast raises blood glucose level and slightly increases the person's work efficiency throughout the day.

Cooking Methods and Nutrient Loss

A second concern in meal planning is trying to minimize the nutrient losses caused by home cooking and commercial food processing. These occur even while food is being stored before use. For instance, oil becomes rancid if exposed to air for a long period. In the process, unsaturated fat and vitamins E and A may be oxidized. Refrigeration helps to prevent oxidation. Cool temperatures and high humidity also help retain the nutrients in vegetables by delaying withering. But even in the freezer, the nutrients originally available in fresh foods may be slowly lost. Many frozen prepared foods continue to undergo oxidation at low temperatures.

Nutrient losses occur during precooking processing as well. A large piece of food has less surface area than the same food cut into smaller pieces, and thus fewer nutrients are lost. Most recipes, however, advise crushing, chopping, slicing, and shredding—practices that increase nutrient loss. Furthermore, trimming vegetables or removing the coarser outer leaves often results in a loss of vitamins A and C and calcium. Bruising vegetable tissues can have the same effect. Using sharp blades for trimming, cutting, or shredding fresh vegetables can avoid bruising.

High cooking temperatures may cause considerable nutrient loss. The high temperatures used in dry heat cooking—frying, roasting, baking, grilling, and broiling—may destroy any heat-sensitive nutrient. Vitamin C is unstable at dry heat cooking temperatures, and thiamin, folic acid, pyridoxine, and pantothenic acid are readily destroyed at these temperatures. Although β-carotene is stable in most cooking operations, it suffers some loss during frying. The effect of dry heat on these unstable vitamins varies with the acidity of the food and the tempera-

ture and length of cooking. Dry heat denatures, or changes the quality of, proteins, especially if heating is prolonged. Polyunsaturated fatty acids are susceptible to heat and oxidation, and they become reduced in fatty foods cooked at temperatures typically used in dry heat cookery. Only mineral salts are not affected by the temperatures of dry heat cooking.

Oriental cooking methods, such as short-term frying at high temperature, reduce nutrient loss. Nutrient losses during frying, broiling, and roasting may also be reduced by using the juices in soup or gravy. If the fat contained in the juices is of concern, it can be removed.

Moist cooking methods, such as stewing or simmering in liquid, are less likely to destroy nutrients. Although protein is denatured during any type of heat treatment, moist heat cooking generally does not alter the protein's biological value (see Chapter 4). Mild heat like that used in moist cooking generally has no detrimental effect on the biological value of meat, fish, or poultry. However, if foods are cooked in a large amount of water, minerals and water-soluble vitamins are lost, especially if the fluid is discarded. If a small amount of fluid is used, nutrient loss is minimized. Alternatively, the fluid from cooking can be reused as a soup or base. In the South, for instance, the "pot liquor" from cooking green vegetables is later used as a soup.

Not all changes in foods are undesirable. Heat treatment actually improves the digestibility and availability of certain nutrients in plant foods. Home or commercial fermentation of foods may result in the production of vitamins and other nutrients; some bacteria and molds (but not yeast) even make vitamin B_{12}.

Food Budgeting

As the economy tightens, keeping food expenses low is of increasing concern to households and institutions. There are a number of ways to keep the food budget low without cutting nutritional values.

Planning ahead

A shopper can save time, money, effort, and frustration if all needed items are listed ahead of time. It is especially helpful if foods located in the same parts of a store are listed together.

Sales, specials, and coupons

Grocery stores regularly run sales or specials on certain items. Sometimes newspapers, magazines, and other printed advertisements contain reduced price coupons. Radio and television commercials are also used to promote sales. Of course, these opportunities are useful only if one needs the sale items and does not have to go to many stores to purchase them.

Low-cost brands

In the last few years, store brands and non-brand items have become popular because they are cheaper than named brands. Savings of 5% to 10% are common.

Inexpensive- to moderate-cost items

People on fixed incomes or with low food budgets are accustomed to eating less expensive foods. However, shoppers should be sure that such items are nutritious and contribute equal amounts of nutrients as costlier products.

Products in season

Vegetables and fruits are abundant and therefore inexpensive when they are in season. Prices of such products will fluctuate. A wise shopper knows when to buy to save money. Some individuals save even more by freezing or canning seasonal products.

Wholesale or quantity purchases

If a freezer or storage space is available, purchasing a large quantity of nonperishable (or even perishable) items can save money. Of course, the wholesale store or warehouse should be within regular driving distance, and perishable items must be consumed before they spoil in order to save money.

Pricing by units

The practice of displaying cost per unit (for example, per pound, ounce, or cup) instead of per package is gaining acceptance and is common in some stores. Not yet mandatory, unit pricing makes it easier to compare the cost of goods.

Cooperatives

Some parts of the country are witnessing an increase in the number of cooperative grocery stores, in which both members and nonmembers can purchase most staple items at wholesale prices. Because cooperatives are nonprofit, most of their products are somewhat cheaper than those in other stores. However, some consumers have complained about limited selections, occasional inferior quality, and high prices for some items.

Less frequent shopping

Some consumer studies have concluded that less money is spent when visits to grocery stores are reduced from once a week to once or twice a month. Obviously, this practice does not apply to fresh produce.

Fewer fast and convenience foods

Fast and convenience foods are costly and should be avoided as much as possible. A person can usually save money by preparing a dish himself.

Despite the many aids to scientific meal planning, putting together nutritious meals that people actually like and eat is still a creative challenge. We all have our own preferences, and what a food looks, smells, tastes, and feels like is usually as important to us as how nutritious it is.

In addition to individual preferences, those who plan meals for several people are typically confronted with a range of nutritional requirements and perhaps social problems. In later chapters, we will go beyond the general concept of an adequate diet to examine the special needs of the young, elderly, pregnant, and nursing, and diet therapies for particular health problems. We will also look at diets that are either grossly inadequate or all too adequate—undernutrition and obesity. First, however, we will look at two additional concerns in planning an adequate diet: nutritional labeling and the protein, fat, and carbohydrate contents of foods.

NUTRITION LABELING

A rather new tool for planning an adequate diet is the nutrition information given on the labels of many packaged foods. In 1973, the Food and Drug Administration (FDA) completed a major rearrangement of regulations dealing with food labeling. Nutrition Labeling, the most important of these regulations, involves a whole new concept—the listing of a food's nutrient contents on its label.

This practice is still largely voluntary. Nevertheless, both large and small food producers are providing nutrient analyses for many of their food products, greatly increasing the amount of nutrient information available to both consumers and nutritionists. The milk industry, for instance, has formed a task force to update information on the nutrient content of milk according to factors such as season, geographical location, and cow species.

Nutrition labeling is regulated by the federal government and is subject to constant changes as more scientific information becomes available. Therefore, a realistic approach to studying the discussion presented below is to supplement it with the latest scientific and legal developments. Such information may be easily obtained by writing or telephoning the nearest County Extension Agent. However, if experience and time permit, the *Federal Register* may be used to identify the current legal status of food and nutrition labeling. The discussion was adapted from an article in the 1974 *Yearbook of Agriculture* (p. 62).

U.S. RDAs

To establish standards of comparison, the FDA set aside the old Minimum Daily Requirement (MDR) values listed since 1941. Instead, it developed new values based on the 1968 RDAs developed by the Food and Nutrition Board of the National Research Council of the National Academy of Sciences. The FDA used the RDAs to determine single values for the optimal intakes of different vitamins, minerals, and protein. These new values—called *U.S. RDAs*, or U.S. Recommended Daily Allowances—are used only for nutrition labeling. They give a single value for each nutrient rather than the range of values tailored to specific age and sex groups of the RDAs. In most cases, each single value is the highest value for each nutrient in the 1968 RDA for any age or sex group, excluding infants and pregnant and lactating mothers (different standards are applied to the labeling of foods for these groups). For some people, the U.S. RDA standards are therefore somewhat higher than their own RDAs.

Exceptions to this procedure for determining the U.S. RDAs are calcium and phosphorus, each set at 1.0 g, and four nutrients not tabulated in the 1968 RDAs: biotin, pantothenic acid, copper, and zinc. The U.S. RDA for protein is 45 g if the protein efficiency ratio (PER, see Chapter 4) of the total protein in the food is equal to or greater than that of casein, and 65 g if it is less. Casein, the chief protein in milk, is used as the standard in measuring the growth-supporting quality of proteins.

One should bear in mind that unlike the RDAs, the U.S. RDAs are only used to provide consumers with information about the nutrient contents of foods. The nutrient composition of a labeled food is expressed as a percentage of the U.S. RDA, as shown in Figure 10-1, a label for green beans.

In the rules and regulations for nutrition labeling, the FDA states: "It is anticipated that U.S. RDA values will be amended periodically to concur with major changes that may be made in the National Academy of Sciences–National Research Council RDA values." Consequently, the FDA is expected to decrease the U.S. RDA values for protein, ascorbic acid, vitamin E, and vitamin B_{12} to reflect the 1980 edition of the RDA. The U.S. RDA values for labeled nutrients are listed in Appendix A and should be compared with the RDAs in the same appendix.

Basic Labeling Regulations

In 1973, the FDA completed a major revision of food labeling regulations. These regulations are now being revised again. Common foods, including most of those that contain added nutrients,

NUTRITION INFORMATION
(per serving)
SERVING SIZE = 1 CUP
SERVINGS PER CONTAINER = 2

CALORIES	40
PROTEIN	2 grams
CARBOHYDRATE	7 grams
FAT	0 grams

PERCENTAGE OF U.S. RECOMMENDED
DAILY ALLOWANCES (U.S. RDA)

PROTEIN	2%
VITAMIN A	10%
VITAMIN C	8%
THIAMINE	2%
RIBOFLAVIN	4%
NIACIN	2%
CALCIUM	6%
IRON	10%

FIGURE 10-1   An example of nutrition labeling for green beans. (Reproduced from the *1974 Yearbook of Agriculture*)

can be labeled according to the "Nutrition Labeling" guidelines for the direct listing of nutrient contents of a food on the label. The "Special Dietary Foods" label is restricted to foods such as those used as the sole item in a diet (e.g., a nutrition supplement consumed to the exclusion of all other foods) or those used under a physician's supervision.

Nutrition labeling is voluntary, with the exception of foods to which nutrients are added or about which nutrition claims are made. Enriched bread, breakfast cereals, and enriched milk products are among the foods to which nutrients have been added and for which nutrition labeling is mandatory.

As shown in Figure 10-1, nutrition labeling follows a standard format. The explicit statement "per serving" is required under (or following) the heading "Nutrition Information." To avoid confusion, all values on the table refer to the amount provided per serving. The size of a serving must be listed in common household units (such as cup) or as a recognizable portion (slice). The number of servings in a container must also be listed.

Caloric content is the next item in the for-

mat. Calories are listed in 2-cal increments below 20 cal, 5-cal increments up to 50 cal, and ten-cal increments above 50 cal.

Contents of protein, carbohydrate, and fat are then listed to the nearest gram. Information on fat composition or cholesterol content may also be provided, as discussed below. The protein content provides information to aid in comparative shopping for complex food products such as pot pies. Calorie and fat content information is probably of greatest use to those interested in losing weight or in fat-modified diets.

The amounts of eight nutrients—protein, vitamin A, vitamin C, thiamin, riboflavin, niacin, calcium, and iron—are shown as "Percentage of U.S. Recommended Daily Allowances (U.S. RDA)." These seven vitamins and minerals plus protein form the lower portion of the standard format and must always be listed. If quantities of any of these nutrients are minimal, they may be replaced by an asterisk, which relates to the footnote "Contains less than 2% of the U.S. RDA of these nutrients," or the missing nutrients may be listed as a footnote: "Contains less than 2% of the U.S. RDA of [list of missing nutrients]."

Sodium content may be listed without using nutrition labeling. However, sodium content may also appear on a nutrition label as shown in the frozen main dish label (Figure 10-2). In both cases, it is listed in milligrams per 100 g, each declared to the nearest multiple of 5 mg.

The new regulations also specify details of testing compliance with the requirements, including statistical guidelines. This compliance section provides an ample range of nutrient content for indigenous nutrients in recognition of natural variations. However, its solid statistical base assures that the consumer obtains the amounts of nutrients listed on the label. Tolerances for added nutrients are considerably stricter but still provide room for reasonable variation consistent with good manufacturing practices.

Fat Composition

Final regulations have also been issued for the "Labeling of Foods in Relation to Fat, Fatty Acid, and Cholesterol."

NUTRITION INFORMATION				
(per serving)				
SERVING SIZE = 8 OZ				
SERVINGS PER CONTAINER = 1				
CALORIES	560		FAT (percent of calories 53%)	33 g
PROTEIN	23 g		*Polyunsaturated	2 g
CARBOHYDRATE	43 g		Saturated	9 g
			*CHOLESTEROL (20 mg/100 g)	45 mg
			SODIUM (300 mg/100 g)	680 mg

PERCENTAGE OF U.S. RECOMMENDED				
DAILY ALLOWANCES (U.S. RDA)				
PROTEIN	35%		RIBOFLAVIN (VITAMIN B$_2$)	15%
VITAMIN A	35%		NIACIN	25%
VITAMIN C (ASCORBIC ACID)	10%		CALCIUM	2%
THIAMINE (VITAMIN B$_1$)	15%		IRON	25%

*Information on fat and cholesterol content is provided for individuals who, on the advice of a physician, are modifying their total dietary intake of fat and cholesterol.

FIGURE 10-2   Frozen main dish label.

If a manufacturer chooses to indicate on a label the composition of the fat and/or the amount of cholesterol in a product, it must also use full nutrition labeling. This combination is shown in Figure 10-2.

In addition to stating the total grams of fat, the percentage of calories provided by fat must also be stated. Below this the grams of polyunsaturated fat and grams of saturated fat must be listed.

As indicated in Figure 10-2, the sum of saturated and polyunsaturated fats may not equal the total grams of fat. Certain unsaturated fats, short-chain fats, and some other forms of fat are not included in either "saturated" or "unsaturated." However, the data on the label provide the ratio of polyunsaturated to saturated fats and also give the actual amount of polyunsaturated fat. These are the two figures that most dietitians and nutritionists want. In addition, a conditional statement must be made as follows: "Information on fat and cholesterol content is provided for individuals who, on the advice of a physician, are modifying their total dietary intake of fat and cholesterol."

Protein Quality

Nutrition labeling also takes into account the protein quality in a food. As indicated earlier and in Chapter 4, protein quality is commonly described scientifically by the expression *protein efficiency ratio*, or PER. PER is defined as the gain in weight of a young rat divided by the weight of protein it consumes during a period of rapid growth, usually of three-week duration. A control rat consumes casein under the same conditions. The rats chosen are as nearly identical as possible. The ratio for the casein-containing diet is commonly about 2.5. If it differs from 2.5, both ratios are corrected by a factor that brings the ratio for casein-fed rat to 2.5.

Two U.S. RDA values for protein have been

set for adults. These values are 65 g if the PER of the protein is less than that of casein and 45 g if the PER is equal to or better than that of casein. This means that when a "better-than-casein" protein is consumed, less protein is needed for a person to obtain the U.S. RDA value than when a protein with a PER value below that of casein is consumed.

The former group includes the high-quality proteins from traditional sources such as meat, fish, eggs, and dairy products. Other protein products such as vegetable proteins and mixtures of cereal and animal proteins generally fall into the latter category. The protein regulation also specifies that protein with a value less than 20% of the PER of casein cannot be counted as contributing protein at all. This regulation refers to proteins such as gelatin, which contributes little quality protein.

Calorie Claims

Since the labeling regulations were established in 1973, new guidelines have been added concerning calories. These guidelines are as follows:

1. If the term *low calorie* or its equivalent appears on a label, it means that the food has a caloric density of 0.4 kcal or less per gram and provides 40 kcal or less per serving.
2. If the term *reduced calorie* appears on the label, it means that the food has a caloric reduction of at least one-third of the regular item and is not nutritionally inferior to the higher-calorie counterpart.
3. Foods can be labeled "for calorie-restricted diets" if the basis for the claim is clearly stated on the label.
4. If a food is designed for a diabetic, the label must indicate this fact and state that the food may be useful in the diet "on the advice of a physician."
5. If a food is claimed to aid in weight control, an appropriate label statement is mandatory. Terms such as *dietetic*, *diet*, and *artificially sweetened* are reserved for low-calorie, reduced-calorie, or for calorie-restriction-diet foods. If the food contains a nonnutritive ingredient, the label must state the fact and

TABLE 10-10   Approximate Relationship Between Protein and Nitrogen in Food Products

Type of Food	Percent of Nitrogen	Appropriate Conversion Factor*
Meat, eggs, corn, beans	16	6.25
Milk	15	6.67
Cereals, grains	17	5.89
Nuts	18	5.56

*Gram of protein = gram of nitrogen × conversion factor.

indicate the percentage by weight the nonnutritive ingredient represents if it is not a sweetener.

PROTEIN, FAT, AND CARBOHYDRATE CONTENTS

Accurate labeling requires an accurate measurement of nutrient contents. Of all the nutrients that we eat, we consume protein, fat, and carbohydrate in the largest quantities. Health professionals have long been concerned about the general public's overall intake of these three nutrients. Methods of ascertaining their contents in food have always played an important role in the science of nutrition. Information derived is particularly important in research and in the clinical care of patients.

The most popular and convenient method of determining the protein content of a food is to estimate its level of nitrogen by using conventional chemical analyses. Thus,

$$\text{grams of protein} = \text{grams of nitrogen} \times \text{conversion factor}$$

The conversion factor is 6.25, assuming that all proteins contain an approximately equal amount of nitrogen. This assumption is not quite accurate, as illustrated in Table 10-10 and briefly discussed in Chapter 4. Furthermore, many foods, especially seafoods and vegetables, contain some nonprotein nitrogen, which falsely inflates the content of protein in these foods when determined in this manner.

There is still no satisfactory method for determining the fat content of foods. In the solvent extraction technique commonly used, the difference in weight before and after solvent extraction of a food sample is taken to be its weight of fat. However, the organic solvent may eliminate some nonfat substances that are partially nonpolar or fail to extract fatty substances either tightly bound to other compounds or unreachable.

Determining the carbohydrate content of a food sample is still done by the old technique of weight by difference—weighing what is left after water, protein, and fat are extracted from a food:

$$
\begin{aligned}
\text{weight of carbohydrate in food} = {} & \text{weight of food} - \\
& \text{weight of water (by drying)} - \\
& \text{weight of protein (by} \\
& \quad \text{nitrogen estimation)} - \\
& \text{weight of fat (by solvent} \\
& \quad \text{extraction method)}
\end{aligned}
$$

Estimating the carbohydrate content of a food is complicated by the presence of simple sugars, starches, cellulose, organic acids, mucopolysaccharides, and other substances. Since some of these carbohydrates are neither absorbed nor metabolized to energy, their inclusion in the calculation is misleading. Like other nutrition-planning tools, these methods of measurement are subject to continual improvement as the science of human nutrition evolves.

STUDY QUESTIONS

1. What is the purpose of food composition tables? What are their drawbacks?
2. What do the RDAs represent? Which agency or organization established them? How can the RDAs be used in conjunction with other criteria to determine a person's nutritional status?
3. What are the Five Food Groups? How many servings of each are recommended by the daily food guides? What are the major nutritional contributions of each group?
4. What is a foundation diet? Discuss the role of supplementary foods.
5. How does food processing or preparation cause a loss of nutrients? How can these losses be minimized?
6. List at least seven ways of keeping food costs down without scrimping on nutritional needs.
7. What are the U.S. RDAs? For what purpose are they used?
8. What type of information about fat composition may be given in nutrition labeling? How is fat content usually measured? Is this method satisfactory?
9. Explain how protein quality is expressed. How is the protein content of a food sample usually calculated? What is the drawback of this method?
10. How is carbohydrate content estimated? Discuss the inaccuracies of this method.

Chapter 11

Undernutrition

IN COMPARISON WITH the recommendations presented in Chapter 10, many people's diets are grossly inadequate. A number of different terms are used for degrees and types of inadequacy. The terms *hunger, semistarvation, total starvation, general inanition, underfeeding,* and *undernutrition* all refer to the lack of essential nutrients in the human body caused by insufficient food intakes. The term *malnutrition* is frequently used interchangeably with undernutrition. However, it actually means "bad" (*mal-*) nutrition, which may or may not be caused by inadequate food intake.

Undernutrition exists in the United States among some population groups, such as Mexican-Americans and American Indians, but the extent and severity of this undernutrition are not comparable to its occurrence in India, the Philippines, West Africa, Ethiopia, Ghana, Guatemala, Brazil, and other underdeveloped countries. On the other hand, malnutrition from a number of causes is quite widespread in this country.

Alcoholism has caused malnutrition in many American men and women. Deficiencies of minerals and vitamins (especially thiamin), liver malfunction, neurodegeneration, and anemia are all complications from excessive alcohol consumption. Overconsumption of sugar foods causes cavities and gum diseases. Obesity predisposes people to diabetes and high blood pressure. Hospital malnutrition has recently been documented. Suspected causes include a patient's inability to adopt new eating habits, the attending physician's ignorance or underestimation of the ramifications of nutritional inadequacy, and, among other factors, a lack of communication within the medical team.

Most of these topics are explored in other chapters in this book. This chapter will focus on undernutrition: its occurrence in the United States and in underdeveloped countries, undernutrition syndromes that are all too common in these countries, ways of treating undernutrition, and current attempts to provide high-protein foods to alleviate the great suffering and ill health caused by hunger.

UNDERNUTRITION IN THE UNITED STATES

Most documented cases of undernutrition in the United States involve newborn infants, children, adolescents, college students, and the elderly. Each year, about 5% to 10% of newborns in this country are of low birth weight. Although underweight in newborns can have many causes, a major one is the mother's improper nourishment before and during pregnancy. The population groups most affected are the indigent. The pregnant mother cannot afford to purchase good protein foods and is deprived of the opportunity for good prenatal care. There is no doubt that uterine malnutrition can cause growth retardation in the fetus, although whether this has a permanent effect on mental development is still being debated.

In the United States, children of many ethnic origins (American Indians, blacks, Mexican-Americans, and Puerto Ricans) and impoverished white population groups are substandard in weight:height ratio. The causes of clinical undernourishment are many: lack of food, unsanitary living conditions, poor housing, unsafe and inadequate drinking water supplies, unemployment, lack of parental education, and other social, geographical, and cultural factors.

In addition to infants and children, high school and college students and the elderly occasionally show evidence of undernutrition. They come from different socioeconomic levels and ethnic backgrounds, and the causes of their inadequate diets vary. A teenage girl may try to lose weight to keep up with social trends, and her deliberate avoidance of food results in underfeeding. A high school student on the wrestling team may undergo semistarvation to obtain a lower weight classification; undernourishment from this practice has been documented. A college student who adheres to an ill-planned vegetarian diet may lose too much weight. Documented cases of undernutrition among senior citizens have been traced to a variety of causes including poverty, ill-fitting dentures, physical handicaps, and disinterest in cooking for themselves.

Clinical rehabilitation of undernourished in-

TABLE 11-1   A 3,000-kcal Menu Plan

Breakfast	Lunch	Dinner
6 oz unsweetened grapefruit juice	Salad:	1 c tomato soup
¾ c oatmeal, cooked with raisins	¼ head lettuce wedge	½ peach (canned)
1 sl bacon	1 sliced tomato	¼ c cottage cheese
½ English muffin, toasted	1 sliced hard-boiled egg	3 oz roast beef, chuck
1 t margarine	¼ c tuna, oil pack	1 medium baked potato
1 t jam	1 T thousand island dressing	1 t butter
¼ c whole milk	1 large hard roll	½ c cooked carrots
Coffee or tea	1 t butter	½ c tapioca pudding
	8 oz sweetened fruit yogurt	Coffee or tea
Snack	1 c whole milk	
1 medium orange	Coffee or tea	**Snack**
		2 fresh apricots
	Snack	1 c whole milk
	1 sl pecan pie	
	1 c whole milk	

TABLE 11-2   A 2,000-kcal Menu Plan

Breakfast	Lunch	Dinner
½ c oatmeal	Sandwich	1 chicken drumstick, fried
1 t sugar	1 T peanut butter	10 pieces french fried potatoes
2 T raisins	1 T jelly	½ c cooked mustard greens
1 sl whole wheat toast	2 sl white bread	1 dinner roll
1 T butter	Raw carrot sticks	1 T butter
1 T jelly	1 medium orange	1 c whole milk
1 c whole milk	1 iced brownie	
	½ c whole milk	
Snack		
1 banana	**Snack**	
	1 c apple juice	
	2 oatmeal cookies	

Note: This menu plan is acceptable for a 5- or 6-year-old who needs to gain weight.

dividuals with various medical problems requires special attention and is discussed in the third part of this book. However, if an adult or a child is simply underweight without other clinical problems, the best way to gain weight is by following a high-calorie, high-protein diet. Tables 11-1 and 11-2 provide 3,000-kcal and 2,000-kcal sample menus for an adult and child, respectively, who may need to put on weight. Refer to Chapters 10 and 22 for methods of meal planning.

UNDERNUTRITION IN UNDERDEVELOPED AND DEVELOPING COUNTRIES

Gross or classic undernutrition, which is widespread in many impoverished countries, is characterized by a number of general symptoms. They are most often seen among children of countries with minimal resources. After reviewing these general symptoms, we will examine two of the most common syndromes of gross undernutrition: marasmus and kwashiorkor.

General Symptoms

When a person is deprived of food for any reason, the body adapts to the stress, at least initially. As the lack of food continues, other more profound and overt changes take place. The functioning and physiological turnover of organ tissues slows down, and the organs' demand for nutrients declines; the individual unconsciously (or consciously) reduces physical activity in order to expend less energy. If inanition continues, a child's growth will be retarded, with the risk of permanent brain damage. As starvation progresses, victims manifest general wasting and emaciation, especially after body fat (in the buttocks, abdomen, and breasts) and part of the muscle mass have disappeared. The victims become quiet and separate themselves from activities and people. This withdrawal, together with a general apathy, is part of the body's efforts to conserve energy. Other specific changes that may take place are summarized below.

Hair

The hair becomes dry and falls out with the slightest teasing, and keratin occasionally accumulates near the hair roots.

Skin

Skin shows "color" changes because of the appearance of pigments over the different parts of the body surface, especially the face. White skin may become gray or red, although the discoloration usually appears as brown spots or patches. In cold weather the skin becomes cyanotic (blue from insufficient oxygenation); in warm weather it is pale, dry, and easily lifted, and it does not spring back when pinched because it has lost its fat and elasticity.

Body weight

Wasting and emaciation are characterized by a gradual loss of body weight, which sometimes dwindles to 50% to 60% of the original weight. Water, fat, muscle, skin, and organs such as the liver and intestine all suffer losses, as the body obtains energy by "burning" these important tissues.

Edema

The accumulation of water during inanition is observed in some but not all individuals. If present, edema is clinically identifiable. Although a depressed level of plasma protein has been suggested as one of its causes, the actual reasons are still being debated. The affected person urinates frequently in an attempt to get rid of body fluid, although there may be nothing wrong with the kidney.

Cardiovascular system

Most normal functions relating to the cardiovascular system are depressed. For example, blood pressure decreases, the output and beating of the heart slow down, and the heart shrinks in size.

Respiratory system

The rate, depth, and efficiency of the respiratory system decrease.

Basal metabolic rate

Body metabolism slows down. The body's loss of ability to adjust to cold temperatures increases the person's vulnerability to death by hypothermia.

Hormonal modifications

Hormonal changes vary. For example, growth hormone decreases, but adrenal and thyroid secretions remain within the normal range. In many females, ovaries and associated organs atrophy slightly, menstruation ceases, and sexual desire and drive are reduced. The last symptom can also be identified in some male victims.

Nervous system

The nervous system is affected if important vitamins are deficient. The person may still reason and think well, but overall personal behavior changes. For example, apathy, irritability, and failure to concentrate are evident.

Gastrointestinal system

The victim may suffer malabsorption and diarrhea. The stomach may not make enough hydrochloric acid, and the small intestine secretes fewer and less active enzymes.

Anemia

Anemia develops in some patients.

Activities

In addition, the adult victim is unable to work or move around easily because of the lack of energy and muscle, a reduced capacity of the cardiovascular system, and anemia.

The overt signs described above are easily identified in a malnourished individual. Health professionals working in the public health and community nutrition area can estimate to some extent the nutritional status of an individual by a detailed clinical examination. Chapter 19 provides more guidelines on identifying symptoms and signs of malnutrition.

Specific Forms of Undernutrition

The clinical manifestations of gross undernutrition described above are especially common among children of countries with minimal resources. These children are deficient in energy and in protein, vitamins, minerals, and other essential nutrients, although some are less severely so than others. For many years such classic undernutrition has received much attention and been given many names. One description is *protein-calorie malnutrition*, or PCM (in this case, the term *malnutrition* refers to a lack of food). Despite its name, the condition of PCM inevitably includes a deficiency of vitamins and minerals, since high calorie and protein foods that are lacking also contain the essential vitamins and minerals.

The term PCM covers a wide range of nutritional deficiency diseases. At one end of the spectrum is *nutritional marasmus*, which is characterized by a deficiency of calories and nearly all other essential substances, as in simple starva-

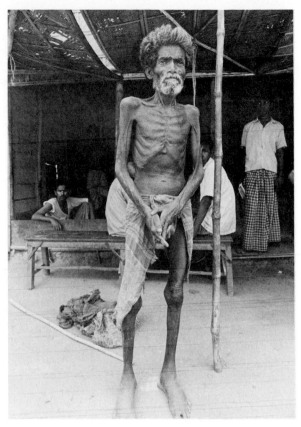

FIGURE 11-1   Undernutrition in an adult in Bangladesh. (Courtesy of the Agency for International Development)

tion. At the other end is *kwashiorkor*, characterized by a severe lack in quantity and quality (deficiency in one or more of the essential amino acids) of dietary protein,* an adequate or even excessive intake of calories, and a mild to moderate lack of other essential nutrients. However, in a clinical situation, the two diseases are not always easily distinguished. Between the two extremes are some manifestations of both conditions and varying degrees of combined energy and protein deficiencies, usually accompanied by infections and vitamin and mineral deficiencies. These are simply referred to as PCM or as marasmic-kwashiorkor.

In general, the symptoms of an adult suffer-

---

*Consult Chapters 4 and 18 on the definition of a complete protein and the planning of an adequate vegetarian diet.

TABLE 11-3 Comparison of Marasmus and Kwashiorkor Symptoms in Children

Criterion	Marasmus	Kwashiorkor
Clinical symptom		
Subcutaneous fat	Little	Some
Lean body mass	Wasted	Wasted
Edema	No	Yes
Potbelly	No	Yes
Hair	Changes common	Changes very common and severe
Skin	Occasional minor changes	Characteristic dermatosis
Liver	Frequently enlarged	Very frequently enlarged
Anemia	Usually mild	Varies from mild to severe
Symptoms from vitamin deficiencies	Yes	No
Mental status	Usually normal	Apathetic
Age of occurrence	Under 1 year old	After 1 year old
Prognosis	Fair	Good
Permanent damage		
Liver	No	No
Neurological	Yes	No
Body organs and tissues	Major	Somewhat
Some chemical and biochemical analyses		
Body potassium depletion	Mild	Severe
Fatty liver	No	Yes

ing from protein-calorie malnutrition are less defined than those of infants and children. Figure 11-1 shows an adult suffering from PCM. Malnutrition is a serious problem in many parts of the world, and marasmus and kwashiorkor in infants and children are devastating. Table 11-3 compares some characteristics of children suffering from these two conditions. Figure 11-2(a) shows drawings comparing a marasmic child with a kwashiorkor child. The following sections describe in greater detail marasmus, kwashiorkor, and the infections that frequently complicate these conditions.

Marasmus

Marasmus is derived from a Greek word meaning "to waste," and the term has been used for centuries. Nutritional marasmus refers to wasting because of a lack of food. An affected child is usually under 1 year old. The victim loses weight, fails to thrive, and is irritable. For unclear reasons, the child has no appetite, although he or she may be hungry. A marasmic infant is usually bright eyed and alert, although the face is shrunken, like that of a wizened monkey or a little old man (see Figure 11-2). Growth is retarded, and there is a loss of fat and muscle. The child is skinny and bony and may lose up to 50% or 60% of body weight, although skeletal development is usually unaffected in the beginning. The patient shows no edema. Changes in the skin, hair, mouth, mucous membranes, and liver are less noticeable than in kwashiorkor but may appear. Watery diarrhea with acid stool is common and may lead to dehydration. Because of the thinness or shrunkenness of the abdomen, one can see the movement of peristalsis, although occasionally a patient's abdomen may be distended with gas.

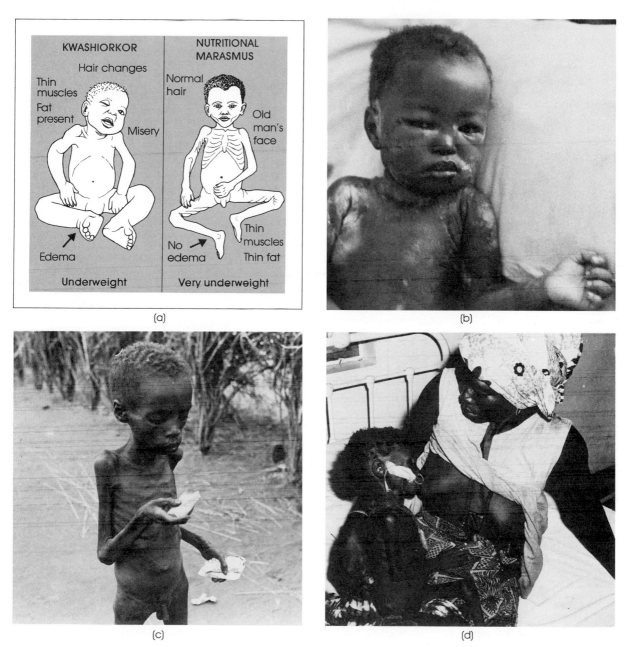

FIGURE 11-2 Children with marasmus and kwashiorkor: (a) Comparison of marasmus and kwashiorkor. (From D. B. Jelliffe, *Clinical Nutrition in Developing Countries*, 1968, U.S. Department of Health, Education and Welfare, Public Health Service) (b) A child in Chad with kwashiorkor. (UNICEF photo by Diabate) (c) A marasmic child in Uganda. (UNICEF photo by Arild Vollan) (d) A marasmic child in The Gambia. (From *The Lancet*, November 27, 1976, p. 1191; courtesy of R. G. Whitehead)

It is very rare that the patient suffers only caloric insufficiency. This nutritional marasmus may occur together with respiratory and intestinal infections, tuberculosis, and parasitic infection. Vitamin deficiencies can be very severe in some victims, and classic symptoms of these deficiencies are identifiable.

Kwashiorkor

The word *kwashiorkor* comes from the language of Ghana, an African country. The word was introduced in 1933 by Dr. Cicely Williams, who obtained it from the natives of the Ga tribe living near Accra, the capital of Ghana. The term is commonly used in two ways. Dr. Williams defined it as "the sickness the older child gets when the next baby is born." One interpretation is that the mother is unable to breast-feed two babies at once and so has to give up nourishing the first child. Many health workers who have cared for these children equate the term *kwashiorkor* to "red boy," referring to the patches of red and brown pigments that appear on the affected child's skin.

A kwashiorkor child is usually over 1 year old. The child loses weight, but this loss is less extreme than in marasmus. Apathy, irritability, diarrhea, and anorexia are all present. The child is miserable and withdrawn and sometimes has a whimpering cry that is monotonous and weak. There is muscle wasting, but some body fat remains. Edema is present, and the water and fat around the jaws gives the child a moon face (see Figure 11-2). Skeletal measurements remain unaffected, at least in the beginning. More details on each specific symptom are given below.

Edema. Edema is a characteristic diagnostic symptom of kwashiorkor. Its extent varies from slight to great and is directly related to the degree of protein deficiency and the amount of salt and water in the diet. Serum albumin level is frequently used to monitor the extent of edema; the higher the level, the more severe the disease. The edema is concentrated in the lower parts of the body, although it affects almost every part. Figure 11-3 shows the edemic condition of a kwashiorkor child; note the characteristic potbelly. Also see the swollen face of a kwashiorkor child in Figure 11-2(b).

FIGURE 11-3   Edema in a kwashiorkor child. (Courtesy of the Agency for International Development)

Hair. The hair has a fine texture, is easily plucked, and is thin, sparse, and soft. The curly hair of Africans becomes straight. The length of the hair may become pigmented, with streaks or patches of gray, blonde, or red. The color change is more common in black children than in those of other races. Among Caucasian children with straight hair, depigmentation appears as "flag" signs—alternating bands of white, black, and/or another color along the length of the hair. This unique pattern of discoloration is frequently interpreted to mean that the child has been exposed to good and bad nutrition alternately. Because it takes time for hair to grow, the hair color presumably reflects what the child has been eating for 1 to 3 months before the change takes place. Figure 11-4 shows the unique hair changes in a kwashiorkor child.

Liver. The child shows a fatty liver that is frequently enlarged.

Skin. Skin changes in a kwashiorkor child are also unique. The skin discoloration (pigmentation or depigmentation) affects every part of the body, especially the lower parts, groin, and buttocks. The changes are more frequent and severe in dark-skinned children and are characterized by patches of pigments. Because the skin

FIGURE 11-4   The flag sign in the hair of a child with kwashiorkor. (From N. S. Scrimshaw and M. Behar, *Science*, vol. 133, pp. 2039–2047, June 30, 1961. Copyright 1961 by the American Association for the Advancement of Science.)

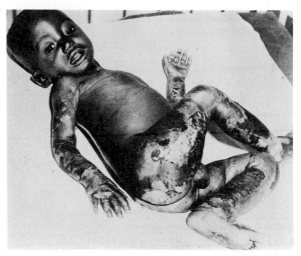

FIGURE 11-5   Skin lesions in a kwashiorkor child. (From A. J. Radford and A. J. H. Stephens, *The Lancet*, December 7, 1974, p. 1391)

is difficult to generalize about the type of anemia, since practically any form can be identified in different kwashiorkor children.

Mucous membranes. Many kwashiorkor children develop oral inflammation, lesions and cracking at the corners of the mouth, tongue atrophy, and ulcers around the anal membranes.

Infection

Cases of malnutrition such as marasmus and kwashiorkor are frequently associated with either intestinal infection caused by parasites or systemic infection brought on by agents such as virus and bacteria. Infection can deal a severe blow to the child who is suffering from malnutrition. It can intensify the negative nitrogen balance already existing, whereby less nitrogen is being absorbed and more excreted. As a result of the additional atrophy of lean body mass, more vitamins and minerals are excreted. Malnutrition and infection work together to arrest body growth and produce a subnormal weight : height ratio. The infection can also severely reduce appetite, resulting in the patient's refusal to eat solid food and further compounding the undernutrition problem. In addition, any treatment for systemic or intestinal infections can have adverse side effects. For example, antibiotics can further lower the victim's immune defense

also desquamates, it sloughs off like after a bad sunburn and has been described as looking like "flaky paint." In nonblack children, skin pigmentation affects the forehead, with desquamation and dark spots on the skin frequently described as "mosaic" or "crackled." Skin discoloration is not influenced by sunlight. Some of the affected areas may develop sores or ulcers with cracks, or bleeding and lesions in the skin folds resembling burn damage. If accompanied by infection, the skin flaking and lesion can be debilitating and even fatal (see Figures 11-2(b) and 11-5).

Anemia. The victim may develop anemia, although the degree of severity varies. The causes of anemia may be deficiencies of iron, folic acid, protein, and/or other essential nutrients. It

mechanism and simultaneously interfere with nutrient absorption.

It has been suggested that half of the world's malnourished children, especially the younger ones, may also be suffering from infection. Malnutrition and infection are often linked because the lack of dietary calories and protein impairs the body's four major immune systems, as indicated in Table 11-4. Figure 11-6 shows oral and facial lesions of a malnourished child with an oral infection.

MANAGEMENT OF PROTEIN-CALORIE MALNUTRITION

The rehabilitation of a severely undernourished adult follows the same standard clinical procedures for treating a patient under stress. Chapters 23 and 29 should be consulted for the dietary care of such patients. However, the nutritional and dietary care of a child suffering PCM requires special considerations and is conducted in two stages: immediate treatment and long-term rehabilitation.

Immediate Treatment

When a child is admitted to a hospital because of severe malnutrition or infection, the immediate treatment includes restoring fluid and electrolyte balance, antibiotics therapy, and blood transfusion. However, the measures adopted depend on the condition of the child. The next step is diet therapy.

Most such children need vitamin and mineral supplements in addition to possible electrolyte compensation. Any specific vitamin deficiency can usually be corrected, although large doses of all vitamins are given with due consideration to those likely to elicit toxic reactions. When antibiotics are considered for treating an infection, their potential interference with nutrient digestion, absorption, utilization, and metabolism are weighed against the risks of the infection itself (see Chapter 16).

Calorie and protein needs are usually supplied in the form of milk, although milk may be

TABLE 11-4   Modification of the Body Defense Mechanisms by Protein-Calorie Malnutrition

Immune System	Change
β-cell-mediated humoral immunity	
Antibody response to foreign antigens	Low to none
Circulating immunoglobulins	High to normal
Secretory IgA immunoglobulins	Reduced
Polymorphonuclear leukocytes and macrophages response	Unaffected
T-cell-mediated immunity	Depressed
Complement system	
Complement (protein components)	Reduced
Complement hemolytic activity	Reduced

inadequate for an older or a very malnourished child. In any case, too much milk should not be given in the beginning. Modern commercial nutrient supplements are an excellent source of calorie and protein. If these are unavailable, the child should be fed progressively, first with a small amount of milk, then a larger quantity, and finally a concoction of milk, potato, mash, plantain, and banana or any other combination of locally available nutrient-dense foods that are acceptable to the child. Hand feeding, holding, and touching the child give a feeling of comfort, security, and emotional and physical support. Tender care and a good diet are the best medicine.

Since hypothermia may be fatal, the child should be provided with a comfortably warm environment. The child's improved well-being, good appetite, subsiding edema, and normal reactions to environmental stimuli indicate recovery from the emergency stage. There may actually be weight reduction in some children because of water loss, but others will gain weight steadily. Satisfactory recovery may be apparent at the end of one month, with severe cases taking three to four months. Figure 11-7 shows mothers feeding their emaciated children at the Kaabong emergency center in drought-stricken Karamoja Province.

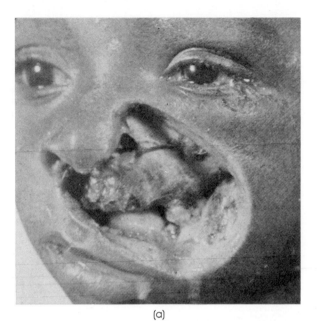
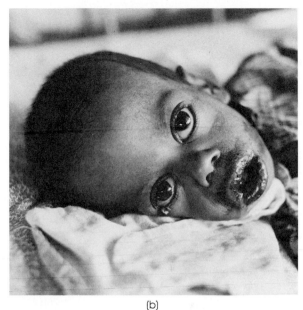

(a)   (b)

FIGURE 11-6   Oral and facial lesions in a child affected by malnutrition and infection: (a) Oro-facial gangrenous lesion (cancrum oris) in a 4-year-old malnourished Nigerian. (From C. O. Enwonwu, *Internat. Dent. J. 23*: 317, 1973) (b) Oral infection in a malnourished child. (Courtesy of the Agency for International Development)

FIGURE 11-7   Emergency feeding of malnourished children. (UNICEF photo by H. Dalrymple)

Long-term Rehabilitation

After emergency or life-saving measures have been successful, the question of the child's long-term rehabilitation remains. This is especially important in most poverty-stricken countries, where food may not be abundant. The complex and interrelated issues of food supply, population, poverty, culture, food preference, and politics have dominated history. There are many causes of malnutrition, especially in underdeveloped countries. Primary causes include natural and man-made disasters (such as accidents, sickness, drought, war, floods, and civil disorders), poverty and unequal distribution of wealth, lack of natural resources, culturally ingrained food habits, food contamination and unsanitary living conditions, malabsorption from all causes, ill-prepared pregnancy and lactation, infection, and ignorance and lack of education. For example, thousands of people died of starvation and disease in Mauritania during 1968–1973 because of the great Sahelian drought, as symbolized by the dead livestock and parched grazing grounds shown in Figure 11-8.

FIGURE 11-8 Drought in Mauritania. (UNICEF photo by Davico)

To illustrate the ecological nature of malnutrition, Doctors J. Cravioto and E. R. Delicardie of the United Nations developed a series of flow diagrams constructed with data obtained from their studies of communities in Mexico, Central America, South America, and Africa. Thus, Figures 11-9 to 11-13 illustrate how factors such as limited technology, resources, education, health knowledge, and large families in an underdeveloped or developing country can be associated with childhood undernutrition. These factors are not necessarily the causes of childhood malnutrition, but they are at least contributing factors.

Possible remedies for the multiple causes of world hunger are discussed in Chapter 1, and additional information may be obtained in the references at the back of this book. In the following sections, we shall examine ways of working directly with the victims of persistent undernutrition.

Many children are potential victims of hunger—and potential beneficiaries of programs to end malnutrition. The information in Figures 11-9 to 11-13 indicates many of the complex problems involved and the vulnerability of young children. To overcome all the causes of

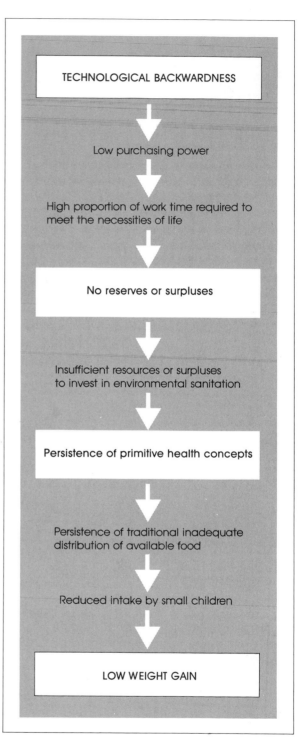

FIGURE 11-9   The association between limited technology and childhood undernutrition in a poor country. (Adapted from "Malnutrition and early childhood," J. Cravioto and E. R. Delicardie, *Food Nutrition* 2:2, 1976)

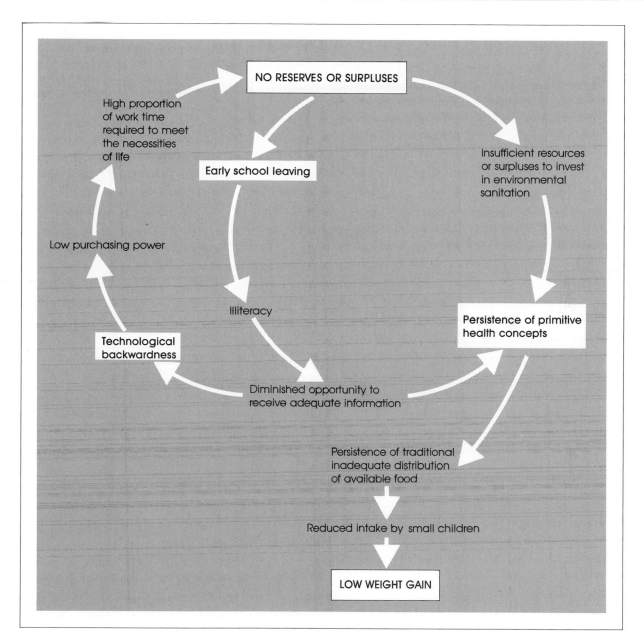

FIGURE 11-10   The association between limited resources and childhood undernutrition in a poor country. (Adapted from "Malnutrition and early childhood," J. Cravioto and E. R. Delicardie, *Food Nutrition 2 : 2,* 1976)

world hunger and the specific at-risk factors affecting the life and health of so many of the world's children will be very difficult. Underfeeding in underdeveloped countries will continue. However, health workers who care for malnourished children continue to look for ways to rehabilitate as many children as possible. The following sections describe three ways in which these workers have succeeded by using very simple and economical means.

Use of local foods

One way of combating persistent malnutrition has been to promote the use of local foods that are inexpensive but nutrient rich. This

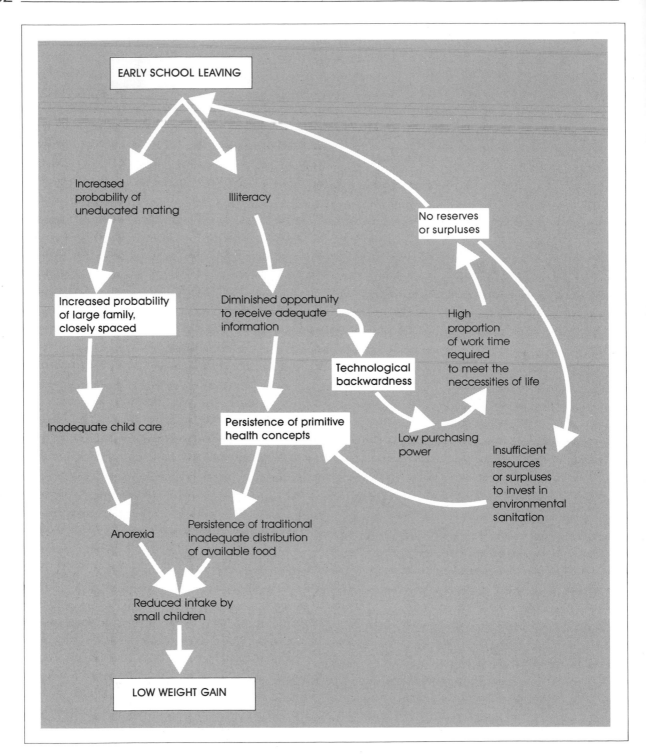

FIGURE 11-11 The association between limited education and childhood undernutrition in a poor country. (Adapted from "Malnutrition and early childhood," J. Cravioto and E. R. Delicardie, *Food Nutrition 2*:2, 1976)

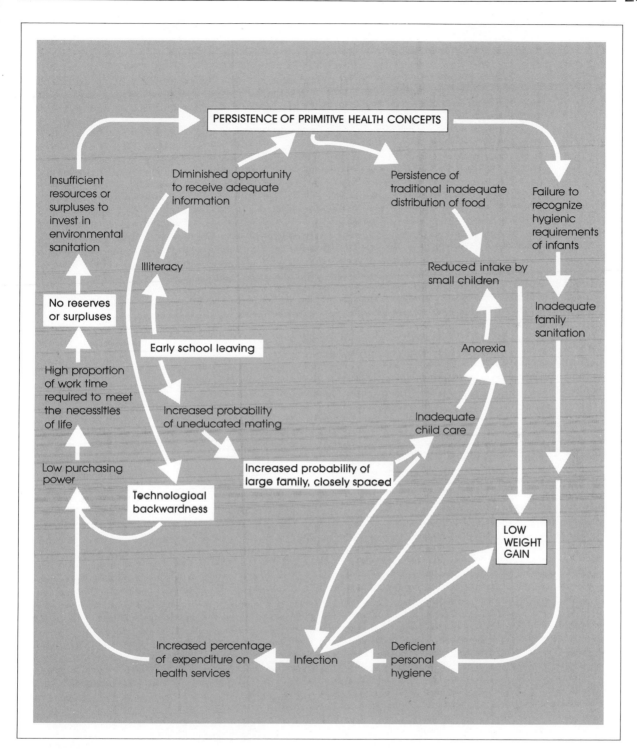

FIGURE 11-12 The association between limited health knowledge and childhood undernutrition in a poor country. (Adapted from "Malnutrition and early childhood," J. Cravioto and E. R. Delicardie, *Food Nutrition 2*:2, 1976)

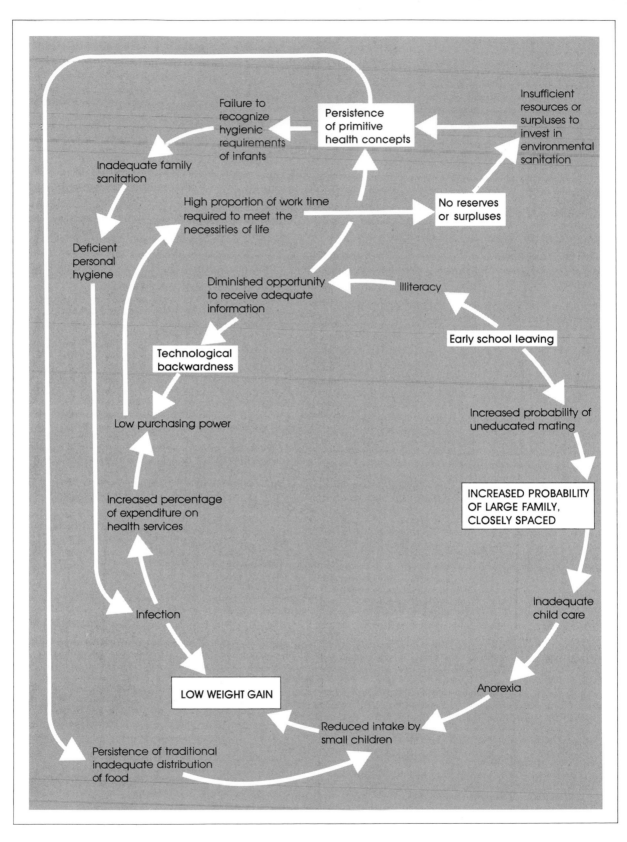

FIGURE 11-13 The association between large family and childhood undernutrition in a poor country. (Adapted from "Malnutrition and early childhood," J. Cravioto and E. R. Delicardie, *Food Nutrition 2* : 2, 1976)

method has been successful in ending moderate undernutrition among the children of Nepal. (M. R. Bomgaars, *Journal of the American Medical Association* 1976; 236:2513).

A large number of children under 4 years old in some districts of Nepal were labeled as *runche* ("the crying one") because of their miserable behavior, such as whining and refusing to eat and cooperate with family members and household activities. The natives believed that the children had been cast under a spell when they were touched by pregnant women. The local "cure" for the condition was a series of morning baths.

A nearby modern health project that provided medical care to more than 50,000 people was able to diagnose these children as being mildly to moderately underfed. The health workers carried out a very successful management program that cured the malnourishment and prevented its recurrence. Instead of spending time, money, and personnel to "scientifically" identify the affected children, the project made use of the natives' traditional recognition and isolation of those children. Treatment was then administered to the young patients. Knowledge of local food availability and dietary practices permitted the health personnel to concoct a nutritious cheap food product for the children. All activities were conducted in a way that minimally disturbed the native beliefs and practices.

For example, the local people traditionally roasted corn and soybeans for adults as a snack and served the edentulous elderly a porridge made of roasted and ground grains. Grinding stones and grains (including wheat) were thus available and cheap. The health workers instructed the local residents to prepare a high-protein, high-calorie gruel by mixing and grinding roasted corn, soybeans, and wheat. The concoction was called *sarbottam pitho* (or "super flour") and was certified to be nutritious by chemical analyses. The children ate it, and their nutriture improved. The mothers were taught to supplement their breast-fed babies with this product as a preventive measure. *Runche* children were fed the product and were eventually rehabilitated. No attempt was made to stop the baths given the children.

Promotion of relactation

A second means of combating PCM involves the promotion of relactation in some women (R. E. Brown, *Clinical Pediatrics* 1978; 17:333). The three essential factors for successful lactation in a woman are (1) a healthy baby with proper suckling reflexes, (2) an adequately nourished woman who is interested in nursing, and (3) conscientious support and encouragement from individuals close to the woman. The last criterion applies especially to women in underdeveloped countries. The same principles apply to *relactation*—stimulation of milk production in women who have not been breast-feeding. Recently, the use of relactation as a solution to PCM in young infants has received attention.

Breast-feeding by female relatives. In many underdeveloped countries and in certain modern societies, it is a custom that when a mother dies from childbirth, the surviving infant is assigned to a female relative (or even friend) for breast-feeding and care. If this woman is not making milk, she is given some local herbs and medicines and told to let the baby suckle on her as frequently as possible. It is unknown if the native medications have any physiological or psychological effects. The baby is initially given a locally available porridge as a supplement, but many babies have been able to induce an adequate flow of milk in the woman after a brief interval of suckling without receiving milk. Modern drugs may be used to induce lactation if a nurse, physician, or knowledgeable health worker is present. However, support and encouragement by family and friends play a very important role.

Interrupted breast-feeding by the mother. A second form of relactation is the renewal of breast milk in the baby's own mother. During the war in Bangladesh, many young infants suffered intestinal disorders, infection, body inflammation, diarrhea, and vomiting. These babies were given medical treatment when clinics became available. The period of treatment and recovery interrupted breast-feeding, and the mothers' milk dried up. The lack of breast milk made it necessary to feed the babies with reconstituted dry milk. Unfortunately, the contaminated water used for diluting the dry milk invariably resulted in a recurrence of gastroenteritis.

Health workers found that these mothers' breasts could easily be induced to produce a normal flow of milk by letting the baby suckle as frequently as possible, especially if relatives and friends encouraged the women. During the wartime period of uncertainty and worry, this relactation process saved many infants from infection by contaminated water and assured proper nutrient intake. In a refugee camp, after one woman was shown how lactation could be reestablished to benefit the baby, other nursing mothers were willing to follow the procedure. No drug was used to induce lactation, and the practice prevented malnutrition. Government officials in Bangladesh and India are now aware of this practice and realize the convenience and economy of feeding the mothers well instead of paying for medicine and formula milk for the infants.

Wet-nursing of orphans.   A third form of relactation involves hiring women to wet-nurse orphaned babies. At the end of the Vietnam war, South Vietnam had to deal with about 100,000 orphans, many of whom were infants. The task of feeding so many babies was very demanding, both in time and money. Health workers therefore began a large-scale employment of nearby women to wet-nurse the babies. Most of these women were not lactating. Again, interest, trials, and support enabled them to achieve a normal milk flow. Occasionally modern drugs were used to accomplish the purpose. These women benefited from this arrangement: they had an income, meals, and lodging and supportive friends. The babies definitely benefited because, in addition to breast milk, each baby also had the personal care of an adult female who served as a mother.

Relactation has served a very useful purpose in the three circumstances cited. Whether it can be applied to a whole population of malnourished infants and children is being debated. However, under certain conditions, this process is cheap, convenient, and practicable.

Nutrition rehabilitation units

In the last 30 years, the art and science of using local nutrition units to rehabilitate malnourished children has been widespread and successful in many impoverished countries (*British Medical Journal* 1975; 2:246). These units have three major functions: (1) to provide low-cost nutrition and dietary care to all individuals; (2) to rehabilitate malnourished children who have survived the emergency phase of underfeeding; and (3) to serve as major nutrition educational centers where natives (mainly women) can learn about proper dietary practices for the entire family, especially children.

These units have been organized and established according to the limitations and needs of the local people. At present, they are usually initiated by foreign and local health workers and local governments. Such units have been given many names such as mothercraft centers, family centers, nutrition rehabilitation villages, and other labels taken from local proverbs. Nutrition education is taught by a variety of methods including native songs, artwork, dances, and customs. Such units are usually started close to a hospital, health center, school, church organization, or farming area.

A number of significant health benefits have resulted from such units. The family, especially the mother, is no longer threatened by the authoritarian atmosphere of a hospital and its doctors and nurses. Thus, it is much easier to encourage the natives to follow health guidelines. The local residents accumulate a vast amount of knowledge concerning hygiene, economy, food preparation, feedings, and other nutritional information. As the underfed child becomes rehabilitated and well, the mother is especially pleased because she herself has brought about the recovery. Her attitude and behavior are influenced by her knowledge and observations. More people are willing to come and learn because satisfied mothers spread the news. The community is brought closer together and becomes exposed to some elements of medical care, education, agriculture, and community development.

TABLE 11-5   Special High-protein Products Used by Different Countries to Combat Protein-Calorie Malnutrition*

Country or Area	Product	Major Ingredients
Algeria	Superamine	Dried skim milk, chick-peas, legumes, wheat
Brazil	Incaparina	Soya, maize
Chile	Lache alim	Soya, fish protein concentrate, dried skim milk
Colombia	Duryea	Soya, dried skim milk, maize
Central America	Incaparina	Cottonseed, maize
Egypt	Weaning food	Dried skim milk, chick-peas, broad beans, wheat
Ethiopia	Faffa	Soya, dried skim milk
India	Bal-Amul	Soya, dried skim milk, legumes, wheat
Kenya	Simba	Dried skim milk, maize
Madagascar	Weaning food	Soya, dried skim milk, rice
Mexico	Conasupo products	Soya, kidney bean
Mozambique	Super Maeu	Soya, dried skim milk, maize, malt
Nigeria	Arlac	Groundnut, dried skim milk
Peru	Peruvita	Cottonseed, dried skim milk, quinoa
Senegal	Ladylac	Groundnut, dried skim milk, millet
South Africa	Pronutro	Soya, groundnut, dried skim milk, maize, yeast, wheat germ
Taiwan	Weaning food	Soya, dried skim milk, rice
Thailand	Noodles	Soya, wheat
Turkey	Weaning food	Soya, dried skim milk, chick-peas, wheat
Uganda	Soya porridge	Soya, dried skim milk, maize
United States	WSB (wheat and soy blend)	Soya, wheat
Venezuela	Incaparina	Soya, cottonseed, maize
Zambia	Milk biscuit	Soya, casein, wheat

*Though some products have existed for many years, others change constantly. Current references should be used to supplement this list.

HIGH-PROTEIN FOODS

At the national and international level, many efforts have been made to increase the availability of high-protein foods in underdeveloped countries. These include programs of supplementation and fortification and the "green revolution"—a highly technological approach to intensified food production. A simpler but perhaps more successful approach is supplying infants and children with special cheap and semisynthetic high-protein foods made of locally available food products. Many governments are issuing products that contain all the essential amino acids as well as other essential nutrients.

Table 11-5 presents a partial list of those products and their major ingredients.

Figure 11-14 shows starving Ugandan children pressing together for comfort and warmth and waiting to be fed a high-protein meal at the Kaabong emergency feeding center in Karamoja Province. Figure 11-15 shows a severely malnourished child in the Provincial Hospital in Kuito, Angola, drinking K-Mix II (a high-protein food mixture developed by UNICEF). Figure 11-16 shows children in Tchin Tabaraden (Niger) being fed a meal of milk and cooked grain. Figure 11-17 shows children in Dacca (Bangladesh) sharing a bowl of CSM (Corn-Soya-Milk plus sugar, a high-protein food supplied by UNICEF). Figure 11-18 shows Bengali women preparing CSM chapattis to serve to their fam-

FIGURE 11-14 Malnourished Ugandan children. (UNICEF photo by H. Dalrymple)

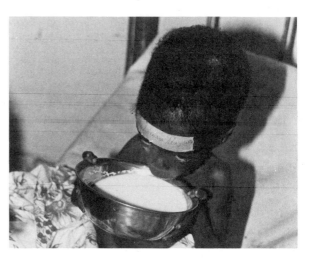

FIGURE 11-15 Rehabilitating an Angolan child. (UNICEF photo by Horst Ulax Cerni)

FIGURE 11-16 Rehabilitating children in Niger. (Courtesy of the Agency for International Development)

FIGURE 11-17   Rehabilitating children in Bangladesh. (UNICEF photo by Jacques Danois)

FIGURE 11-18 Preparing chapattis from CSM. (UNICEF photo by Jacques Danois)

ilies. The chapatti—a staple of Asian diet—is usually a flat round of unleavened bread. The women have adapted the form and now use the high-protein CSM yellow powder as the base. They mix it with water, roll the dough into a loaf, and then cut it into chapattis with a string. By serving CSM in this familiar form, acceptability has been greatly increased.

The effort to cure and prevent worldwide malnutrition is far from complete. Concerned individuals all over the world will have to continue to work toward a solution, and it is hoped that everyone will do his or her share of helping others in need.

STUDY QUESTIONS

1. Distinguish between the terms *undernutrition* and *malnutrition*.
2. In the United States, which age groups are most likely to be undernourished? Why?
3. Describe the general symptoms of gross undernutrition.
4. What is protein-calorie malnutrition? In what way is this term misleading?
5. What is the theoretical difference between kwashiorkor and marasmus? Describe some characteristic symptoms of each condition.
6. Discuss three successful approaches to rehabilitating young victims of malnutrition in some underdeveloped countries.
7. What is being done at the national and international levels to increase the supply of high-protein foods in countries at risk of widespread malnutrition?

Chapter 12

Obesity

THE ACCUMULATION OF excess body weight can affect individuals of both sexes from infancy to old age. As discussed in Chapter 2, the body contains fat, water, muscle mass, and cell solids. When a person gains (or loses) weight, any of these components may increase (or decrease) in quantity. Although obesity may or may not be a clinical disorder, there is no known cure for afflicted individuals. Only control is feasible.

This chapter begins with some basic definitions and ways of estimating desirable body weight and individual energy needs. From this information the caloric intake that will allow the person to maintain a desirable body weight can be determined. This chapter also examines the negative consequences of being obese and current speculation on the causes of this condition. The rest of the chapter deals with ways of losing weight, both scientific and unscientific, and the obstacles and hazards in doing so.

A PRIMER ON OBESITY

Although the terms *overweight* and *obesity* are used frequently, their precise meanings are not fully appreciated. When a person is overweight, he weighs more than his "ideal" or "desirable" body weight. The excess may be due to fat, muscle, water, and/or large bones. For example, a football player may be overweight, but the excess may be bone or muscle and not fat. Obesity usually means that a person weighs more than his ideal or desirable weight by 15% to 25% and that the excess is fat rather than water, muscle, or bone. Some clinicians refer to weight 15% above normal as being "mildly obese" and 25% above normal as "grossly obese." To comply with common usage, obesity and overweight are used interchangeably in this chapter, but with the understanding that the excess weight is fat.

Although there is no "cure" for obesity, some scientific observations have been made. Obesity is the consequence of a constant small accumulation of calories from overeating over a long period of time. Calories do count: this applies to all healthy individuals. Energy spent must be balanced by the amount consumed or there will be a weight change. The mathematical relationship between body fat and caloric contribution takes into account the fact that body fat includes some water and nonfat cell components, as follows:

$$1 \text{ lb pure fat} = 454 \text{ g} \times 9 \text{ kcal/g} = 4,086 \text{ kcal}$$

$$1 \text{ lb body fat} = 85\% \text{ fat} + 15\% \text{ water and cell components}$$

$$= \frac{85}{100} \times 4,086 \text{ kcal}$$

$$= 3,473 \text{ kcal (or approximately } 3,500 \text{ kcal)}$$

For simplification, we can say that there are 7.7 kcal (that is, $3,500 \div 454$) per gram of body fat.

For each 3,500 kcal we eat more than we expend as energy, we gain approximately 1 lb of weight. As an example of how easy it is to gain weight, suppose that a young woman suddenly decides that she likes to consume an extra ¾ cup of celery soup and one slice of toast as an afternoon snack, and that she does this three times a week. If her other daily meals and activities remain unchanged, this woman will gain 8 to 9 lb of body fat within 1 year.

In general, women start to gain weight after age 20, and further gain occurs during pregnancy and after menopause. Men usually gain weight between the ages of 25 and 40. Adult males can lose weight slightly more easily than females. Currently about 20% to 25% of Americans over 30 years old are 10% to 25% above their desirable body weights.

ESTIMATING DESIRABLE BODY WEIGHT

In this book, the terms *ideal* and *desirable body weight* are used interchangeably to refer to the optimal weight for good health. Four general methods for determining ideal weight are in common use: standard tables, the sex-frame-height rule of thumb, standard growth charts for children, and various popular methods.

TABLE 12-1 Desirable Weights by Height and Body Frame for Adults (Issued by the Metropolitan Life Insurance Company of New York and Derived from the Build and Blood Pressure Survey of 1959 by the Society of Actuaries)

	Desirable Weight (lb)		
	Small frame	Medium frame	Large frame
Man, 5'10" with shoes on 1" heels*	140–150	146–160	155–174
Woman, 5'7" with shoes on 2" heels*	118–127	124–139	133–150

Note: The complete tables are located in Table 18 of the appendix.

*Dressed in indoor clothing.

TABLE 12-2 Layman's Method to Determine Body Frame

A. **Encircle the wrist bone with index finger and thumb.**

If the fingers do not touch or overlap, the body frame is large.

If the fingers just touch or overlap, the body frame is medium.

If the fingers overlap, the body frame is small.

B. **Measure the circumference of the wrist bone.**

Men

If the circumference is less than 6 in., the body frame is small.

If the circumference is 6 to 7 in., the body frame is medium.

If the circumference is more than 7 in., the body frame is large.

Women

If the circumference is less than 6 in., the body frame is small.

If the circumference is between 6 and 6½ in., the body frame is medium.

If the circumference is more than 6½ in., the body frame is large.

Standard Tables

The most widely used tables of desirable body weight are those issued by the Metropolitan Life Insurance Company, Society of Actuaries, and the Association of Life Insurance Medical Directors of America, the National Academy of Sciences, and the U.S. Public Health Service. Table 12-1 provides two examples from the tables issued by the insurance company that present the desirable weights in pounds of adult males and females of different body heights and frames.

The use of standard tables to determine ideal body weight is very common in this country. However, the practice has some drawbacks. For one thing, the tables do not indicate the amount of body fat. This can be misleading, since any excess weight can be fluid, muscle, or bone and not fat. Also, some of the popular tables do not distinguish between average and desirable body weights. Most tables, especially those issued by the insurance company, exclude individuals with extreme body weights. This practice may eliminate about 5% of a statistically important population group if an average is taken. Since many individuals over 40 are overweight, it is difficult to compile real standards to begin with, since we do not know what their ideals are. Using such "standard" tables for these middle-aged individuals can create problems.

Another drawback involves the body frame classification—usually "small," "medium," and "large"—used in most standard tables. Although trained personnel with the proper facilities and equipment can determine the build and frame of an individual, the general public using these tables does not have the scientific means to ascertain one's classification. Unaccountably, adult females are more likely to select inaccurately "small" as their body frame.

In addition to guessing, the lay public has devised two methods for estimating body frame. Although not scientifically sound, they at least provide some guidance. Table 12-2 indicates how this is done.

TABLE 12-3 Ideal Body Weights Using the Height-Frame Rule

Frame Size	Height Data	Weight (lb) Men	Weight (lb) Women
Medium	First 5 feet	106	100
	Each inch above 5 feet	6	5
Large	Each inch above 5 feet	$\frac{110}{100} \times$ weight calculated for medium-frame person	
Small	Each inch above 5 feet	$\frac{90}{100} \times$ weight calculated for medium-frame person	

Sex-Frame-Height Rule of Thumb

For many years, calculations based on sex, frame, and height have been used to determine the ideal body weights for men and women. Table 12-3 describes the procedure. This rule of thumb only approximates ideal body weight, and it is subject to some of the same drawbacks as the standard tables. For instance, the rule of thumb does not distinguish between fat and other forms of extra weight, and it requires judgment of body frame, which is usually unscientific.

Growth Charts for Children

The ideal body weights for infants, children, and adolescents can be ascertained by using standard growth (height-weight) charts, such as those of Wetzel, Iowa, Stuart, or the U.S. Public Health Service. Some are reproduced in the appendix. These charts are very useful in evaluating the growth rate of children. They are considered some of the best tools available in spite of some drawbacks that are too technical to discuss here.

Popular Physical Measurements

In addition to weighing oneself and comparing that weight with one's ideal weight, there are a number of popular methods of physically determining whether one is overweight. The most ob-

vious is visual inspection, preferably in the nude. Another is the "pinch test." When areas such as the abdomen are pinched between the thumb and index fingers, the skinfold fat should be less than 1 in. If more fat is pinched, one is probably overweight. Another measurement is the "ruler test." When one lies on one's back, a ruler placed vertically between the pubic bone and the rib cage should be flat. For males, the "girth test" can also be used. The waist and chest (nipple level) circumferences should be about the same.

More information on assessing a person's nutritional status, including the extent of overweight or obesity, is given in Chapters 19 and 22.

ESTIMATING INDIVIDUAL ENERGY NEED

To calculate the number of calories needed per day to maintain the ideal body weight, we can use either a general standard or a figure for basal metabolic needs (see Chapter 2) plus the calories needed to support the individual's activity level.

Standard Caloric Approximations

The 1980 Recommended Dietary Allowance (RDA) data include recommended daily calorie allowances according to age, height, and sex. For example, for a man 23 to 50 years of age, weigh-

TABLE 12-4 American Diabetes Association Method of Calculating Daily Caloric Needs According to Basal Metabolism, Body Weight, and Activity Level

Physical Activity	Total Calories Needed Daily*
Sedentary	Basal calories + (desirable body weight × 3)
Moderate	Basal calories + (desirable body weight × 5)
Strenuous	Basal calories + (desirable body weight × 10)

*Note that only numbers are used since the units of calories and weight do not mix. This is not a mathematical formula; it is an estimation.

TABLE 12-5 One Method of Calculating Daily Caloric Needs According to Basal Metabolism and Activity Level

Physical Activity	Total Calories Needed Daily
Sedentary to light	$\frac{130}{100}$ × basal caloric need
Moderate	$\frac{150}{100}$ × basal caloric need
Strenuous	$\frac{175-200}{100}$ × basal caloric need

TABLE 12-6 Daily Caloric Needs According to Activity Level and Ideal Body Weight by Using Approximations of Caloric Expenditure per Pound Body Weight

Physical Activity	kcal/lb Ideal Body Weight
Sedentary	11–12
Light	13–14
Moderate	15–16
Strenuous	18–19

ing 154 lb (70 kg) and 5′10″ in height, the daily caloric need is 2,700 kcal. For a woman in the same age range, 120 lb (55 kg) and 5′4″, the daily caloric need is 2,000 kcal. These standards assume a moderate amount of physical activity. More information may be obtained from Table 3 of the appendix.

For children, either the RDA or the age rule can be used to estimate daily caloric need. The age rule allows 1,000 kcal per day for a 1-year-old, and 100 kcal more for each year above one. This method is used until age 13 for girls and 16 to 18 for boys.

Basal Metabolism plus Activity Level

The second general way to determine the calories needed to support ideal body weight involves adding basal metabolic needs to the calories expended in physical activity. This can be done in a number of ways.

One way to estimate basal metabolic needs is from the basal metabolic rate, which is approximately 1 kcal/kg ideal body weight/hr. Using this figure, daily basal caloric need is 70 × 24 = 1,680 kcal for the average man and 58 × 24 = 1,392 kcal for the average woman.

The American Diabetes Association and some clinicians use a different approximation: 10 kcal/lb ideal body weight. This method gives a somewhat lower daily basal caloric need: 154 × 10 = 1,540 kcal for men, and 128 × 10 = 1,280 kcal for women.

After the basal caloric need is ascertained, the actual caloric need for the amount of energy spent for activities may be estimated. This can be done in a number of ways. Table 12-4 shows the method used by the American Diabetes Association: adding the basal calories needed to the desirable body weight that has been multiplied by a factor keyed to the person's activity level. Table 12-5 gives a method using basal caloric need and degree of activity; Table 12-6 uses known caloric need per pound of ideal body weight according to activity level; and Table 12-7 gives the USDA rule of thumb for calculating daily caloric needs according to daily activity. In addition to these methods of calculation, many hospitals, clinics, organizations, and health teams have developed tables that include direct information on ideal

TABLE 12-7   USDA Rule of Thumb for Calculating Daily Caloric Needs

Physical Activity	Total Calories Needed Daily*	
	Women	Men
Sedentary	Ideal body weight × 14	Ideal body weight × 16
Moderate	Ideal body weight × 18	Ideal body weight × 21
Strenuous	Ideal body weight × 22	Ideal body weight × 26

*All ideal body weights expressed in pounds.

body weight and daily caloric needs at different activity levels.

A problem with all of these methods is defining the degree of activity. To overcome this problem, many clinicians refer to standard tables that describe the amount of calories needed for various professions. These tables are available in standard textbooks (also see the references for this chapter).

CONSEQUENCES AND CAUSES OF OBESITY

An obese person definitely has more problems, both health related and otherwise, than a person with normal weight. Medical complications that may affect people more than 15% overweight include: (1) higher morbidity and mortality; (2) respiratory difficulties, especially after exertion; (3) cardiovascular diseases (heart diseases, such as atherosclerosis, arteriosclerosis, congestive heart failure, and cardiac enlargement, and blood disorders, such as thrombosis, blood clot, and hypertension); (4) kidney diseases (nephritis); (5) diabetes mellitus (mainly the maturity-onset type); (6) increased risks during surgery and anesthesia; (7) alimentary tract disorders (hiatus hernia, gall bladder diseases, and pancreas disorders); (8) increased toxemia and prolonged labor and delivery during pregnancy; (9) arthritis in the joints; and (10) chronic illnesses.

Being overweight may also cause nonmedical complications. One is psychological maladjustment. Obese people may develop "distorted body images" and tend to blame every disappointment and failure in life on their weight. They may be preoccupied with weight, with a strong feeling of self-blame, or they may feel inferior and become passive and withdrawn.

If a person becomes obese during childhood or adolescence, he or she is more likely to face derogatory or disapproving attitudes from parents and peers at school. Some obese children are unhappy because of their inability to participate in sports and games because of their large size and ridicule from fellow classmates. In later years, discrimination in college admissions and job placements is possible. Perhaps because of these instances of social rejection, the obese person turns to eating for comfort. This further increases his or her weight, which in turn may result in more rejection, especially from the opposite sex.

The cost of living for an obese individual is higher, since the cost of clothes, food, furniture, transportation, and other expenses are affected by one's size. An obese person also suffers personal inconveniences and discomfort, such as pain in the back and feet from the added weight on the bones. In general, an obese person is more likely to be frustrated in life than a person whose weight is more nearly ideal.

Given all these disadvantages to carrying excess body fat, why do some people overeat to the point of obesity? Over the years, many theories have been put forward. As of yet, there is no satisfactory answer except for those patients whose obesity is caused by a clinical disorder. Table 12-8 summarizes some current thoughts on the possible causes of obesity.

TABLE 12-8   Some Proposed Causes of Obesity

Factor	Analysis
Genetics	
Body build by birth	All types: round, plump, thin, fragile, heavily muscular. For example, a person born thin, fragile, and linear may grow up to be a small person and underweight.
Familial traits	If parents are obese, their children have a higher chance of being obese.
Defective hunger and satiety center	Hypothalamus does not respond normally. Usually, it responds to hunger and informs the person to stop eating when full. Its failure to do so results in obesity.
Defective body metabolism	Defects in an obese person: inability to release energy efficiently (from ATP, for example), reduced lipase (enzyme) activity to mobilize fat, and overactive fat storage enzyme system.
Body fat cell type	An obese person may be born with a large number of fat cells or a special type of fat cell that can hypertrophy easily.
Anthropological factors	
Cultural acceptance	Obesity is considered good fortune or a beautiful attribute in many countries.
Food and hospitality	The expression of hospitality through food and drink makes food more available. In an affluent society like the United States, this increases food consumption.
Eating habits	
Overeating	Obese people like to eat. They eat more calories than they expend.
Meal pattern	Eating three meals a day may predispose some individuals to deposit more fat. Nibbling the same quantity of food throughout the day may enable the body enzyme system to use the calories more efficiently, and less fat is deposited.
Childhood conditioning	
Infancy eating maladjustment	Solid foods given too early, excess high-caloric density milk, and excess food consumption all may result in large weight gain. A big baby (from too much fat) is not necessarily a healthy baby.
Overeating	A fat child can grow into an obese adult.
Psychological factors	
Eating as an emotional outlet	If the person wants to stay away from food, he must be convinced to use another means of emotional support.
Eating to allay anxiety, tension, frustration, and insecurity	The greater the level of anxiety, tension, frustration, or insecurity, the more food a person eats and the more likely he is to gain weight.
Eating as a substitute or demonstration of love and affection	The relationship between family members is expressed with food. To show love and affection, one person serves more food to another. Or to replace loss of love and affection, a person eats more or is served more food.
Eating as a substitute for whatever is missing (e.g., no job)	In this context, food is similar to excess alcohol drinking and heavy smoking.
Physiological factors	
Hormones	Hypothyroidism or decreased metabolism may result in weight gain and therefore obesity.
Basal metabolic rate	BMR decreases with age, while the caloric consumption is undiminished and there is a decrease (or no increase) in daily activity.
No exercise or activity	Eating a lot of foods without a good exercise program results in obesity.
Environmental factors	
Trauma and emotion	Certain individuals are susceptible to traumatic and emotional experiences and will eat more food.
Family eating habits	One develops an overeating habit if parents and other members in the family eat too much.

TABLE 12-8   (continued)

Factor	Analysis
Sedentary job	A job requires constant sitting, with minimal movement.
Abundance of foods	Obesity is more common in affluent societies.
Advertisements	A person is conditioned to the type of foods advertised on television and in magazines, most of which are high in calories.
Living comfort	Comfortable ambient temperature, light clothing, minimal shivering, and lack of heavy work all contribute to reduced expenditure of calories.
Convenience of food preparation	Minimal preparation time and labor. Less activity, more food consumed.
Smoking or alcohol	When a person tries to stop smoking or drinking, he or she may eat more and gain weight.

LOSING WEIGHT

In 1958, Dr. A. J. Stunkard of Stanford University stated: "Most obese persons will not stay in treatment for obesity. Of those who stay in treatment, most will not lose weight and of those who do lose weight, most will regain it." Although this statement is still true, the number of obese individuals who manage to lose and maintain the ideal body weight is increasing.

Obstacles to Weight Loss

Many of us have tried to lose weight at some time. We all know how difficult it is. This is so in part because most of us like to eat, and in part because common problems are always there to interfere with a regimen of weight reduction. One is our habitual eating pattern. Complying with a low-calorie regimen is difficult because changing a lifelong eating habit is difficult. Most people have difficulty in avoiding foods. A second problem is our expectation of losing weight quickly. For a person 5 to 10 pounds overweight, adhering to a moderately low-caloric diet for 2 to 3 weeks will not produce any visible results because the empty fat cells may be temporarily filled with water. A period of at least 2 to 3 months on a diet is needed to produce any real loss. If a 50 to 100-lb overweight individual loses 1 or 2 pounds a week, it will probably take him or her 1 to 2 years to achieve the goal. Such slow results are discouraging.

A third problem involves seeking professional help. When an overweight patient goes to a doctor to seek help, the slightly protruding abdomen of an overweight, middle-aged physician may shatter the patient's confidence at the first interview. Even if the doctor is in good shape, clinical experience indicates that every obese person seeking medical assistance expects dramatic results. Often the relationship between patient and doctor results in a waste of time and money with very little weight loss. The patient blames the doctor and the other weight reduction schemes he or she has followed previously, while the doctor feels that the patient has failed to follow instructions to reduce eating and increase exercise.

Nevertheless, experience has shown that if overweight people are given *free* advice regarding a low-caloric diet, perhaps by an acquaintance who is a nutritionist or dietitian or by a professor in nutrition, they are likely not to follow the instructions. However, if they go to a clinic and are charged $15 or more per office visit by a doctor, they are likely to comply with the low-caloric diet with some enthusiasm, even if the information is nearly the same. In any event, the earlier an overweight person seeks medical advice, the easier it is to lose weight.

Finally, losing excess weight is only half of the problem; maintaining the ideal weight is the other half. The best and most reliable regimen to keep one's body weight within normal range is to eat a proper diet, comply with a good exercise program, and develop good eating habits as a child and continue them through adulthood.

General Considerations

When a person tries to lose weight without using any drastic means (such as prolonged starvation or surgery), a few basic considerations should always be remembered. First, the best and safest strategy is to lose 1 to 2 pounds a week—the person should avoid anticipating a grand weekly loss. Second, exercise or regular routine activity is an integral part of any successful weight loss regimen. Fifteen to 20 minutes of meaningful exercise or activity makes one feel better, helps to spend calories, and conditions muscular tone. Third, during the process of weight reduction, nearly every obese person is faced with a stage of stabilization when the body seems to refuse to shed any more poundage, at least for a period of time. Fourth, weight loss must be followed by weight maintenance.

A fifth consideration applies to those who seek to help a person lose weight: All overweight individuals need encouragement and support. Any negative and condescending attitudes should be avoided. Concerned health personnel (doctors, nurses, dietitians, and nutritionists) should become familiar with some pertinent psychological supports for the patient.

When an obese patient undergoes medical treatment to lose weight, it is very important that all communication between health personnel and that patient be sensitive and supportive, rather than tainted with value judgments such as "An obese person eats like a horse" or "All fat people love to eat." If patients fail to reduce eating and lose weight, they should not be made to feel bad, embarrassed, or discouraged. Rather, they should be told that even just maintaining the current weight is a bonus and encouraged to never stop trying. Although obesity increases the risks of a number of health problems, there is no need to frighten patients. The clinical implications that apply to the particular patient should be explained, and it should be emphasized that not every obese person experiences the same health problems. The patient's willingness to come to a clinic should be considered a praiseworthy preventive action.

The success of any weight reduction process is greatly enhanced if the patient is clearly apprised of the details of the regimen, including the treatment method, the ease or difficulty of any step, and the expected success rate. When the patient specifically expresses disapproval or unwillingness to go through a certain procedure, an alternative should be seriously considered.

A patient's maladjustment to social interaction such as dating, clothes, or housing should be viewed with sympathy and understanding. For example, a fat patient may feel that he is unable to rent a good apartment because he will be discriminated against. Perhaps he can be convinced that such pressure is not so important or that it may not even exist. There is no reason why a patient should suffer from other people's lack of consideration.

SCIENTIFIC METHODS OF WEIGHT REDUCTION

There are both scientific and unscientific ways of losing weight. At the present time, what is the most scientific and successful way to lose weight? Treatment methods have varying degrees of success, although none is successful all of the time. Table 12-9 summarizes the different scientific treatments for obesity and analyzes each briefly. Each of these methods is discussed below. Fad diets and other unscientific methods of losing weight are discussed in a later section.

Reduced Caloric Intake

The most obvious way to lose weight is to eat less. The sections that follow give the general characteristics of a successful weight loss diet and four methods of planning a reduced-calorie eating regimen.

Characteristics of a successful diet

Any successful weight reduction diet should have certain characteristics. The diet should be nutritionally adequate in all aspects but low in

TABLE 12-9   Some Scientific Methods of Reducing Weight

Treatment Method	Analysis
Reduced caloric Intake	If done without medical supervision, caloric intake should not be less than 1,200 kcal per day. May be accomplished with the help of a doctor, nurse, dietitian, nutritionist, or other allied health personnel.
Increased exercise	May be accomplished by oneself or with the supervision of a doctor, exercise physiologist, or other similarly trained personnel.
Behavioral modification	May be accomplished by oneself or with one-to-one or group counseling with a trained therapist, clinical psychologist, or psychiatrist.
Group program	May be accomplished by organizing one's own group weight reduction program, joining national groups, and participating in commercially supervised (nonclinical) weight reduction enterprises.
Hypnosis	May be achieved under the care of a clinical hypnotist or by learning self-hypnosis.
Jaw wiring or lock-jaw	Some success when conducted by experienced medical personnel.
Forced exercise	Some success when performed under the direct supervision of a physician.
Drug therapy	Overall effectiveness is not sure. Physician's prescription required.
Surgery	Some success, although some techniques are accompanied by severe side effects: high morbidity and mortality.
Starvation or fasting	1. Semistarvation. Reduction of dietary intake to 500–1,200 kcal per day requires the direct supervision of a physician. 2. Protein-sparing modified fast. Requires the direct supervision of a physician. 3. Total starvation. Requires the direct supervision of a physician.
Comprehensive medical weight reduction program	Some success. Must be conducted under direct medical supervision.

calories. The RDA for the particular individual is used as a guideline to plan the diet. The daily dietary allowances are best divided into three or four meals a day with some carbohydrate, protein, and fat in each meal. A minimal distribution provides at least 250 to 350 kcal per meal. The consumption of fat and carbohydrate should be small to moderate, while protein (meat, cheese, eggs, fish, poultry, and skim milk) should be served liberally. Staple and satisfying items such as potatoes, noodles, rice, and bread should not be completely eliminated because they provide satiety value. Whenever feasible, foods with maximal satiety and minimal caloric values should be provided.

Special attention and control should be exercised over the following foods: starches, pastries, alcoholic beverages, thick gravies, cream, mayonnaise, table sugar, and fats. Any foods eaten between meals must be accounted for, whether they are fruits or cocktails, doughnuts, cookies, peanuts, sodas, or ice cream. The habit of nibbling and snacking during meal preparation and cleanup must be avoided. Since practically all foods provide some calories, avoiding any quantity—a bite, a mouthful, a piece, a wedge, or a cup—contributes to weight loss.

A successful diet is also appetizing, tasty, and acceptable to the patient and does not require special preparation. This assures that the meal plans can be integrated into the entire family's eating routine and will not bore the patient, since he or she may have to stay with it for a long period.

When one is on a weight reduction program, a number of tips are important in preparing foods. Skim milk can be used when whole milk is called for. Visible fats should be removed from meat and meat products. Natural meat juices should be used rather than thick gravies. Fruits or plain desserts can be offered rather than high-calorie sweets. Artificial sweetener may be used if available. Green, yellow, and red vegetables are generally low in calories. Lemon juice, low-calorie dressings, or vinegar can be used on fruit and vegetable salads rather than high-calorie dressings. Meats should be baked, broiled, boiled, or roasted rather than fried. When meat is roasted, a rack should be used to keep it from remaining saturated with fat. In recipes that call for frying, foods can be steamed or simmered instead, and nonsticking cooking utensils can be used to avoid cooking fats.

Fat from juices, soups, stews, and casseroles can be skimmed off after cooking and refrigeration. Butter or margarine consumption can be reduced by using whipped products and very small servings. No fat should be used on vegetables after cooking. To improve flavor, bouillon cubes can be used instead. The cook should become familiar with new or gourmet cooking methods that minimize the use of fat and gravy. The attractiveness of foods can be improved by using herbs, spices, artificial sweetener, or diet dressings.

Some planning and learning processes are required on the part of the person who is trying to lose weight. People on a weight reduction regimen should learn about basic nutrition and new eating habits. They should make meal plans early and know what is to be consumed in the next meal. For example, they can plan at least one day ahead of time or even a few days. One way to do so is to cook a large amount of some specific dishes, divide them into portions, and freeze the portions in separate plastic bags. Each portion will thus provide the correct meal contribution. Once a diet plan is fixed, dieters should not skip meals. Dieters should also learn to recognize their own tendencies to binges and compulsive eating. These occurrences can be anticipated by setting aside a specific number of calories for

them, but meals should not be skipped nor basic nutritional needs skimped.

People on a weight reduction regime should make special plans for meals eaten away from home, such as restaurant dining, bag lunches, picnics, banquets, holidays, and festivals. Written instructions for such occasions should include what foods to eat, their caloric contribution, and preparation methods. Many reputable books provide easy, convenient, low-caloric diets for such occasions. They include guidelines, tips, and specific instructions that apply to eating out and at home.

Those seeking to reduce their caloric intake can make other preparations as well. They can compile a list of nutritious, tasty, and low-caloric snacks and regular foods; the list can be carried everywhere, and another copy can be posted in the kitchen. A list of commercial dietetic products that are low in calories can also be compiled, which include water-packed fruits and tuna, gums, soft drinks, margarine, pies, and canned goods.

Overweight people can carry out these preparations on their own, but many sources of help are available. Free classes are often given by adult schools, colleges, and church organizations, and there are many good publications on food preparation, dieting, menus, calories, and nutrition. If the cost of the publications is prohibitive, specific pages can be xeroxed or books borrowed from local libraries. University instructors, hospital dietitians, and public health nutritionists are all willing to provide advice as well.

Although calories do count, dieters should not overdo calorie counting. To do so will be frustrating to themselves and irritating to friends and relatives. Instead, every effort should be made to reduce dependency on foods. For example, dieters can make new friends and find activities and pleasurable tasks that will help to reduce their loneliness and opportunities to eat.

Calorie counting

Before starting a low-caloric diet, one must know how low it should be. After one has ascertained his or her ideal body weight, the daily caloric need according to routine activity level can be obtained by one of the methods described ear-

TABLE 12-10   A Core Eating Plan Providing 1,000 to 1,500 kcal Per Day

Food type	Serving	Approximate Caloric Contribution	Remarks
Milk	2–2½ c	Skim milk: 170–255 kcal Whole milk: 330–495 kcal	If interested in cheeses, ice cream, cream, and other dairy products, make calculations and replace.
Meat	4–6 oz	200–500 kcal for fish, poultry, meat (baked, boiled, roasted, broiled), all visible fat trimmed	If interested in eggs and shellfish, make calculations and replace.
Fruits	2–5	80–250 kcal, fruits or fruit juices, unsweetened	Make sure to include citrus fruits or a source of vitamin C.
Vegetables	2–5	20–250 kcal, with at least 1 serving of a dark green leafy vegetable	Many varieties have zero calories. Exclude peas, corns, beans, and potatoes.
Grain	2–4	50–350 kcal	Include potatoes, peas, beans, and corn.
Fats	1–3	100–300 kcal	
Free foods	No limit	Coffee, tea, lemon juice, celery, spice, condiments, consomme, bouillon and others. Very little calorie contribution.	

lier. Let us assume that the caloric need of a hypothetical patient is 2,100 kcal per day. For this particular person, the safest starter is a diet of 1,500 to 1,600 kcal per day. This will permit a loss of 3,000 to 4,000 kcal, or 1 pound of body fat, per week. Eating less than 1,000 to 1,200 kcal per day should be under medical supervision.

The next question is: How does one plan a 1,500-kcal-per-day diet without unnecessary inconvenience? There are four main ways: following a core eating plan, compiling a long list of menu plans, using a well-known and successful commercial weight reduction plan, and using the food exchange systems developed by the American Diabetes and Dietetic Associations. These methods are described below.

A core eating plan.   A core eating plan tells the dieter the approximate number of servings of each category of food he or she can eat daily. Table 12-10 provides a core eating plan that provides 1,000 to 1,500 kcal per day, depending on the number of servings of each food type consumed. Table 12-11 provides a few examples of food servings that give an approximately equiv-

TABLE 12-11   Examples of Food Items Included in the Core Eating Plan

Food Type	Servings Providing Equivalent Amount of Calories
Milk	1 c skim milk, ½ c whole milk, ⅔ c cheddar cheese
Meat	1 oz meat, 1 egg, ¼ c salmon, 3 sardines, 5 oysters
Fruits	½ c applesauce, 1 medium nectarine, ⅔ c blueberries, 1 small pear
Vegetables	½ c spinach, 1 medium artichoke, ½ c chard, ½ c cooked cabbage, 1 small cucumber, ½ c cooked mustard greens
Grain	1 sl bread, ½ c cooked cereal, ½ c cooked noodles or rice, 2 graham crackers, ½ c peas, ½ c cooked dried beans, ½ c mashed potato
Fats	½ T butter, margarine, or oil; 1 sl bacon; 1 T French dressing

TABLE 12-12   A 1,400-kcal Menu Plan

Breakfast	Lunch	Dinner
½ pink grapefruit	½ c cottage cheese on lettuce	3 oz breaded, baked haddock
½ c oatmeal	and carrot sticks	½ c asparagus spears
1 poached egg	1 c vegetable beef soup	1 baked potato
1 sl whole wheat toast	4 saltine crackers	1 sl French bread
1 t margarine	1 c sliced strawberries	1 t margarine
1 c skim milk	1 c skim milk	1 plum
Salt, pepper	Salt, pepper	10 grapes
Coffee or tea	Coffee or tea	1 c skim milk
		Salt, pepper
		Lemon
		Coffee or tea

alent amount of calories within the food type. By using Table 6 of the appendix, one can get many examples of each food type, thus gaining a number of choices from which to build a good daily menu plan. Table 12-12 uses the information in Tables 12-10 and 12-11 and Table 6 of the appendix to develop a daily menu plan of approximately 1,400 kcal. Menu plans of any caloric level can be developed in a similar manner.

Preplanned menus.   A second simple procedure is to use menus preplanned for a certain calorie level. These weekly menu plans can be developed by the person seeking to lose weight or obtained free from nutrition textbooks, public health clinics, nutritionists and hospital dietitians, agricultural extension agents, state and federal health agencies, the U.S. Department of Agriculture, and many reputable commercial diet publications (see references at the end of this book). The person follows the meal plans to the letter and repeats them weekly. Tables 12-13 and 12-14 provide daily menus for one week at a caloric level of 1,500 kcal. Tables 12-15 and 12-16 provide daily menus for one week at a caloric level of 1,200 kcal. Adjustments are needed if the lunches must be bag lunches. With menus like this, the person must also have emergency or specially designed meal plans for situations such as dining out, hiking, or picnics.

Diet reduction regimens by reputable commercial firms.   In the last few years, a number of reputable diet reduction plans have proven to be fairly successful in helping obese individuals to lose weight. Two popular publications include the *Wise Woman's Diet* (by Redbook Magazine) and *Weight Watchers Menu Plans* (by Weight Watchers International). An individual can purchase these diet plans and apply them conscientiously. Their menus do not differ greatly, since they are all low caloric and tasty. They do have drawbacks, however, such as high cost and time-consuming preparation.

The American Diabetes/Dietetic Food Exchange System.   Because many diabetics are obese and weight loss can eliminate some or all of their symptoms, the American Diabetes Association has developed a "Food Exchange System" that deals in part with a weight reduction regimen. According to this system, food products are divided into six lists: (1) milk; (2) vegetables; (3) fruits; (4) bread; (5) meat; and (6) fats. Within each list all foods with approximately the same caloric contents are grouped together and are thus interchangeable. Such lists are presented in detail in Chapter 26. Table 12-17 presents meal plans using the Food Exchange System for 12 different caloric levels. One exchange in the table refers to a particular serving portion of the food. Table 12-18 translates the exchanges into a sample menu for 1,200 kcal.

The regimens presented above show that there is no great difficulty in planning a low-calorie diet. The real catch is implementing a diet

TABLE 12-13 Daily 1,500-kcal Menu Plans for Monday to Friday

Monday	Tuesday	Wednesday	Thursday	Friday
Breakfast ½ c pineapple juice 1 hard-cooked egg 1 toasted bagel 2 t margarine ½ banana Salt, pepper Coffee or tea	**Breakfast** ½ c grape juice ½ c Cream of Wheat Cinnamon 2 T raisins 1 sl bacon 1 sl whole wheat bread 1 t margarine Salt, pepper Coffee or tea	**Breakfast** ½ c grapefruit juice ⅛ honeydew melon 1 poached egg 1 sl whole wheat toast 1 t margarine 2 sl bacon Salt, pepper Coffee or tea	**Breakfast** ½ c apricot nectar ¾ c shredded wheat biscuits (spoon size) ½ c skim milk ½ sliced banana 2 sausage links Salt, pepper Coffee or tea	**Breakfast** ½ c orange juice ½ c cottage cheese 2 pear halves, canned in water 1 sl toasted rye bread 1 t margarine 2 sl bacon Salt, pepper Coffee or tea
Lunch 2 oz chicken 2 sl whole wheat bread 1 t margarine 1 t mayonnaise 1 c mixed cooked carrots, broccoli, cauliflower 1 pear 1 c skim milk Salt, pepper Coffee or tea	**Lunch** 2 oz lean beef ½ c cooked mushrooms ½ c Swiss chard ½ c baked beans 1 sl rye bread 1 t margarine 1 apple 1 c skim milk Salt, pepper Coffee or tea	**Lunch** 2 oz turkey ½ c asparagus 1 t mayonnaise 3 sq. in. cornbread 1 t margarine 1 c lettuce salad with lemon juice 1 orange 1 c skim milk Salt, pepper Coffee or tea	**Lunch** 2 oz chicken ½ c green beans ½ c cooked carrots ½ c rice 2 t margarine ½ c ice milk 1 c sliced strawberries 1 c skim milk Salt, pepper Coffee or tea	**Lunch** 2 T peanut butter 2 sl French bread 6–8 carrot sticks ½ c cooked kale 1 pear 1 c skim milk Salt, pepper Coffee or tea
Dinner 3 oz lean beef ½ c cooked kale ½ c cooked beets 1 sl French bread 1 t margarine ½ c sliced strawberries 1 c skim milk Salt, pepper Coffee or tea	**Dinner** 3 oz halibut ½ c peas 2–3 carrot strips 1 hard roll 1 t margarine 1 orange 1 c skim milk Salt, pepper Coffee or tea	**Dinner** 1 c lettuce salad 1 c canned salmon 1 T French dressing ½ c green beans 1 sl French bread 1 t margarine 1 peach 1 c skim milk Salt, pepper Coffee or tea	**Dinner** 3 oz roast beef ½ c asparagus ½ c cooked summer squash 1 sl rye bread 1 t margarine 1 apple 1 c skim milk Salt, pepper Coffee or tea	**Dinner** 3 oz chicken ½ c rice 1 c cooked zucchini onion ½ c ice milk ⅔ c frozen blueberries 1 c skim milk Salt, pepper Coffee or tea

plan. Three basic problems interfere with compliance with a low-calorie regimen.

One is a lack of time. The American way of life does not give most people leisure time to indulge in extensive food preparation. For a mother of two or three children, it is no small matter to assign specific blocks of time to cooking. An overweight salesman finds it equally difficult to prepare some of the menus. It is true that some of the diet menus are easy to follow and prepare. However, it is important to remember that to lose 4 to 8 lb (4.4–8.8 kg) will take about 1 to 2 months (1 to 2 lb or 455–910 g weekly).

The second problem is that we like to eat. It is a painful task to be forced to eat only 60% to 80% of what one would normally eat over a period of 1 to 2 months. Third, to lose weight many of us who are inactive must eat relatively little. Because of technological advances, many routine tasks (such as doing laundry, home heating, and

TABLE 12-14   A 1,500-kcal Menu Plan for Saturday and Sunday

Saturday	Sunday
Breakfast	**Brunch**
½ c tomato juice	½ c orange juice
1 muffin	Omelet
1 t margarine	2 eggs
¼ medium cantaloupe	1 oz cheddar cheese
1 scrambled egg	Mushrooms
1 sausage link	Onion
Salt, pepper	1 sl French bread,
Coffee or tea	toasted
	1 t margarine
Lunch	½ grapefruit
2 sl whole wheat bread	1 sl bacon
1 sl tomato	1 c skim milk
2 oz cheddar cheese	Salt, pepper
1 t mayonnaise	Coffee or tea
½ c cooked carrots	
1 apple	**Snack**
1 c skim milk	1 pear
Salt, pepper	½ c grapefruit juice
Coffee or tea	
	Dinner
Dinner	3 oz roast pork (lean)
3 oz turkey	½ c sauerkraut
½ c green beans	½ c peas
1 small baked potato	1 sl whole wheat bread
1 T sour cream	1 t margarine
½ c green salad with	1 baked banana with
lemon juice	cinnamon
1 orange	1 t margarine
1 c skim milk	1 c skim milk
Salt, pepper	Salt, pepper
Coffee or tea	Coffee or tea

traveling) are done without much effort. Thus, few routine activities help a dieter to get rid of excess calories. This problem is addressed in the second way of losing weight: exercising more.

Increased Exercise

Most of us are aware that the more we exercise, the better the chance of losing weight. Exercise programs may be routine or systematic. All of us should participate in routine exercise, such as parking the car one or two blocks from work and then walking, using stairs instead of elevators, gardening, and mowing lawns. Every morning and evening, we should spend 10 to 15 minutes walking, bicycle riding, or jogging. Simple exercises can be performed for 10 to 15 minutes in the morning and before going to bed. During leisure time, we can enjoy vigorous sports, such as tennis, volleyball, golf, and canoeing.

We can perform many other routine activities without getting hurt, exhausted, or frustrated. On the other hand, recent trends show that many individuals—both thin and obese—are following rigid and strenuous exercise routines. When beginning such activities, a person should consult a physician, exercise physiologist, or other appropriate professional, especially if the person is middle-aged or older.

About the same amount of energy is expended in performing any of the following activities: swimming 800 yd, running 1½ miles in 15 minutes, bicycling for 6 minutes, or walking 3 miles in 35 to 40 minutes. A patient can select a preferred suitable activity and do it every day of the week or a few days weekly. A vigorous exercise program can be obtained from professionals or reputable publications.

Any strenuous exercise program involves certain considerations. One controversial relationship is between heavy exercise and hunger. In some situations, a person's appetite increases immediately after expending a moderate amount of energy. On the other hand, a person's appetite may actually decrease after strenuous work. This decrease has led to the suggestion that exhaustive exercise before a meal can actually cut down food intake. Although current thinking on this topic varies, it is generally agreed that jogging or running daily for 1 or 2 miles will not increase the appetite to the detriment of a person's dieting regimen.

Another consideration is the effect of exercise on the individual. Some people tire quickly. Some become dizzy during weight loss because of hypotension. All obese individuals must pay careful attention to their back. Backache is a common ailment among very fat people, and any slight but improper strain on the back can cause lifelong misery. The activity must be appropriate

TABLE 12-15 Daily 1,200-kcal Menu Plans for Monday to Friday

Monday	Tuesday	Wednesday	Thursday	Friday
Breakfast	**Breakfast**	**Breakfast**	**Breakfast**	**Breakfast**
½ c grapefruit juice	1 orange	1 c strawberries	2 canned peach	½ c tomato juice
1 poached egg	½ c oatmeal	4 T milk	halves (water	1 sl whole wheat
1 sl whole wheat	4 T milk	1 sl toast	packed)	toast
toast	1 3″ sausage link	2 T peanut butter	½ c cottage cheese	1 sl American
1 t margarine	Salt, pepper	Coffee or tea	1 muffin	cheese
Salt, pepper	Coffee or tea		1 t margarine	1 scrambled egg
Coffee or tea		**Lunch**	Coffee or tea	Salt, pepper
	Lunch	½ c cooked carrots		Coffee or tea
Lunch	1 c lettuce salad	½ c rice	**Lunch**	
Sandwich	with lemon juice	2 oz broiled chicken	6–8 carrot and	**Lunch**
2 sl whole wheat	½ c beet greens	10 pretzel sticks	celery sticks	½ c cauliflower
bread	1 hot dog	1 sl watermelon	1 c lettuce salad	½ c cabbage
2 oz cheddar	1 bun	1 c skim milk	½ c tuna (water	2 oz lean roast beef
cheese	1 t mayonnaise	Salt, pepper	packed)	2 sl whole wheat
1 sl tomato	½ banana	Coffee or tea	1 T French dressing	bread
⅛ avocado	1 c skim milk		5 saltine crackers	1 t mayonnaise
½ c cooked	Salt, pepper	**Dinner**	3 apricots	1 apple
broccoli	Coffee or tea	½ c turnip greens	½ c ice milk	1 c skim milk
1 apple		½ c summer squash	Salt, pepper	Salt, pepper
1 c skim milk	**Dinner**	3 oz lean beef	Coffee or tea	Coffee or tea
Salt, pepper	½ c cooked carrots	1 sl French bread		
Coffee or tea	½ c cooked	1 t margarine	**Dinner**	**Dinner**
	mushrooms	1 peach	½ c spinach	1 c green salad
Dinner	1 small baked	1 c skim milk	½ c cauliflower	½ c green beans
½ c asparagus	potato	Salt, pepper	½ c noodles	3 oz halibut with
½ c peas	3 oz chicken	Coffee or tea	3 oz turkey	lemon juice
½ c rice	3 apricots		½ c pineapple	1 cornmeal muffin
3 oz baked bluefish	1 c skim milk		chunks	1 orange
with lemon	Salt, pepper		1 c skim milk	1 c skim milk
⅔ c blueberries	Coffee or tea		Salt, pepper	Salt, pepper
1 c skim milk			Coffee or tea	Coffee or tea
Salt, pepper				
Coffee or tea				

and not harm the patient in any way. For example, a weak right hand is terribly tiring to a person engaging in tennis. Weight lifting can damage the fragile joints of many obese patients.

The role of the physician is important in tailoring the exercise program to the patient. The doctor must conduct an intensive physical examination of the patient to rule out the contraindications for strenuous exercise programs. Cardiovascular diseases such as angina, arrhythmias, and malignant (uncontrolled) hypertension are some reasons that patients should

not exert themselves. However, losing weight is important to control most hypertensive patients. Diseases such as severe anemia, varicose veins, fluid and electrolyte imbalance, and uncontrolled diabetes mellitus may prohibit the person from heavy exercise. The doctor should conduct a stress test, such as the treadmill, to determine the patient's heart condition and the types and intensities of exercise to be prescribed. Clinical experience indicates that a sustained pulse rate of 120 to 140 beats per minute is optimal. Although they may not be able, patients should be

TABLE 12-16   Daily 1,200-kcal Menu Plans for Saturday and Sunday

Saturday	Sunday
Breakfast	**Brunch**
½ c unsweetened applesauce	½ c orange juice
1 oz lean ham	1 sl whole wheat toast
2 2½ in.-square graham crackers	1 t margarine
1 T cream cheese	1 sausage link
Salt, pepper	1 sl quiche
Coffee or tea	¼ cantaloupe
	Salt, pepper
	Coffee or tea
Lunch	**Dinner**
2 oz turkey	½ c winter squash
½ c baked beans	½ c peas and mushrooms
1 c green salad	3 oz lean roast pork
1 T French dressing	1 hard roll
10 cherries	1 t margarine
1 c skim milk	1 baked apple with cinnamon
Salt, pepper	1 c skim milk
Coffee or tea	Salt, pepper
	Coffee or tea
Dinner	
½ c beets	
1 artichoke	
½ c mashed potatoes made with milk only	
3 oz chicken	
1 sl watermelon	
1 c skim milk	
Salt, pepper	
Coffee or tea	

encouraged to achieve a pulse rate as close as possible to this range.

Another very important role of the physician is serving as a model. It provides the patient with great confidence if the doctor maintains a good body weight, is physically fit, and enjoys wholesome sports. The doctor can also encourage and remind the patient of the benefits of a good exercise program. For example, the program will help the person to lose weight and eliminate many pains and aches of obesity. When fat is removed by exercise, skin will not be flabby, and the person will gain good muscle tone and a feeling of well-being.

Any exercise program must be started slowly and gingerly. Patients can and should pick the type of exercise they like and are interested in—games, competitive sports, noncompetitive activities, and so on. Patients should also decide the best time of day for routine exercise, depending on their work and life-style.

Behavioral Modification

Over the last few years, behavioral therapists have learned that obesity is the result of bad eating habits learned throughout life. Thus, if factors such as the why, how and when behind a person's overeating are identified, they can be changed. Once such "bad" behavior is modified, the person will develop new eating habits. According to these experts, the cure does not lie in a low-calorie diet but rather in the adjustment of behavior. It is assumed that after the behavior is corrected, the person will eat less. The assumptions behind this technique are described by Dr. M. J. Mahoney of Pennsylvania State University: (1) An obese individual is an overeater. (2) The obese and nonobese differ in eating style. (3) If the obese alter their eating styles, they will reduce. (4) The obese individual is stimulus bound. (5) Obesity is a learning disorder.

The procedures to reduce body weight by means of behavioral modifications are composed of five parts: (1) defining the specific problems and objectives, (2) compiling personal information relating to the problems and objectives, (3) studying and analyzing data and establishing a clear profile of problem areas, (4) developing specific modification procedures to alter undesirable behavior, and (5) continuously monitoring the progress of changes and revising the strategy, if necessary. A brief analysis of the first four steps is provided below; step (5) is self-explanatory. For more detailed information, consult the references at the end of this book.

Defining the problems and objectives

Initially, the patient's life history is obtained, including the person's body weight history—past, present, and ideal (from both personal and

TABLE 12-17 Using the Food Exchange Lists to Prepare Menu Plans at 12 Different Caloric Levels

Food type	Food Exchange List	Number of Exchanges Assigned to the Daily Permitted Number of Kilocalories											
		600	800	900	1,000	1,100	1,200	1,300	1,400	1,500	1,600	1,700	1,800
Breakfast													
Meat (medium fat)	5	1	1	1	1	1	1	1	1	1	1	1	1
Vegetables	2	0	0	0	0	0	0	0	0	0	0	0	0
Fruits	3	1	1	1	1	1	1	1	1	1	1	1	1
Bread	4	½	1	1	1	1	1	1	1	1	1	1	1
Milk (nonfat)	1	½	½	½	1	1	1	1	1	1	1	1	1
Fats	6	0	0	0	0	0	1	1	1	1	1	1	1
Lunch													
Meat (medium fat)	5	2	2	2	2	2	2	2	2	2	2	2	2
Vegetables*	2	1	1	1	1	1	1	1	1	1	1	1	1
Fruits	3	1	1	1	1	2	2	2	1	2	2	2	1
Bread	4	½	0	1	1	1	2	1	2	2	2	2	2
Milk (nonfat)	1	0	½	½	½	½	½	½	½	½	½	½	½
Fats	6	0	0	0	0	0	0	1	1	1	2	2	2
Dinner													
Meat (medium fat)	5	2	2	2	2	2	2	2	3	3	3	3	3
Vegetables*	2	1	1	1	1	1	1	1	1	1	1	1	1
Fruits	3	1	1	1	1	1	1	1	1	1	1	1	2
Bread	4	0	1	0	0	1	1	2	2	2	2	2	2
Milk (nonfat)	1	0	0	½	½	½	½	½	½	½	½	1	1
Fats	6	0	0	0	0	0	0	1	1	2	2	2	2

*One of the two daily servings of vegetables must be raw and have few calories (see the exchange lists in Chapter 26).
Adapted from A. Dean, Home and Family Series, Extension Bulletin E-782, Cooperative Extension Service, Michigan State University and the Food Exchange Lists of the American Diabetes Association. The exchange lists are based on material in the *Exchanged Lists for Meal Planning* prepared by Committees of the American Diabetes Association, Inc. and The American Dietetic Association in cooperation with the National Institute of Arthritis, Metabolism and Digestive Diseases and the National Heart and Lung Institute, National Institutes of Health, Public Health Service, U.S. Department of Health, Education and Welfare.

medical viewpoints)—and changes during major points in life (such as military service, college, marriage, after pregnancy, divorce, and changes in drinking and smoking habits). The person's feelings toward food—likes, dislikes, and favored means of preparation—are explored. The clinician then tries to determine the patient's emotional well-being or lack of it—depression, anxiety, frustration, dissatisfaction, negative or positive attitude, and so on. Patients are encouraged to explore reasons for their actions and behavior: Why are they unhappy? Why do they eat so much? Why do they move or change jobs? Why do they have trouble with women or men

friends? Why are they sexually frustrated? Finally, goals are set for the weight loss: how much to lose; and the time needed in which to lose it. The goals are also planned in association with the need for weight loss before traveling, changing jobs, getting married, or any other related conditions.

Compiling personal information

The second step is to compile personal information relating to the patient's problems and objectives. Clients are asked to provide very detailed information on practically every aspect of

**TABLE 12-18   Sample Menu for a 1,200-kcal Diet
Using the Exchanges in Table 12-17**

Breakfast	Lunch	Dinner
½ c orange juice	2 small boiled frankfurters	2 oz broiled hamburger
1 poached egg	½ c cooked green	½ c cooked summer squash
1 sl toast	beans	Sliced tomato on lettuce
1 t margarine	1 sl whole wheat toast	½ c cooked rice
1 c skim milk	1 medium tangerine	1 small apple
Salt, pepper	1 small banana	12 grapes
Coffee or tea	½ c skim milk	½ c skim milk
	Salt, pepper	Salt, pepper
	Coffee or tea	Coffee or tea

their life. For example, they are asked to compile one week's eating record, day by day, hour by hour, minute by minute: when they eat, what, how, how much, where, and with whom. Other aspects of life to be recorded include time spent working, walking, running, moving, sleeping, using the bathroom, and exercising. Clients are also asked to recall the circumstances that they think have caused their overeating problem.

In compiling this personal record, the therapist and client should refrain from making value judgments. All of the patient's answers must be honest and accurate. The therapist is especially interested in factors that suggest why an eating episode occurred and the daily routines that surrounded the occurrence.

Analyzing data and profiling problems

The third step in behavioral modification is to study the data and establish a clear profile of problem areas. Some questions the client and therapist might ask in analyzing the personal record are: Do you eat too much? How many calories do you eat? Do you get any exercise? Do you eat snacks between regular meals? Do you eat while watching television? Do you have morning and midafternoon coffee, doughnuts, or soft drinks? Do you eat snacks? At what specific times of day are these calories consumed? What starts the eating? Is any behavior repeated every time something is eaten or drunk? Usually a pattern emerges showing the times, places, occasions, and emotional states when the person is most likely to overeat.

Developing modification procedures

In developing procedures to modify a patient's undesirable eating behaviors, the therapist and client first identify and agree on the list of eating behaviors to be changed. They also identify all external environmental factors that affect the patient's eating habits.

Goals are set for modifying the behavior. A reasonable goal might be for the patient to lose 1 or 2 pounds weekly after some of the maladjusted behavior has been successfully modified. The therapist then proceeds to shape the client's behavior, one small step at a time, until the goals are reached. Any obvious, easy, and well-reinforced behavioral change should be made to improve the patient's expectations. The therapist should not suggest procedures that would be difficult or impossible for the patient to perform, especially in the long term. Fad diets and devices should definitely be discouraged.

A set of rules regarding rewards, reprimands, and negative and positive reinforcements to be used should also be established. Measures should also be chosen so that the therapist and client both know how much the client has changed and how close he or she is to reaching the goals.

For example, one major kind of modification involves controlling the stimuli to eating, such as modifying the amount of foods eaten, the types of food consumed, and the frequency of eating. A special low-calorie diet is not necessarily involved. Some techniques used to reduce stimulus control of eating are shown below.

A. Modifying the amount of food eaten
   1. Eat slowly, progressively lengthening the time allotted for the meal. For example, a meal should last 20 minutes or more. Delay tactics include such details as waiting 1 minute after sitting down before starting to eat.
   2. Eat in small bites and count each mouthful.
   3. Place food or eating utensils down between mouthfuls and chew the food completely. One suggestion is to chew each mouthful more than 10 times.
   4. Do not eat without utensils.
   5. Permit only one serving at a time.
   6. Allow intervals between servings; for example, walk off to get a glass of water or use some other pretext for leaving the table.
   7. Make servings of food look larger by using small plates and cups.
   8. Finish one food item (such as meat) before starting the next (the vegetable, for example).
   9. Leave all foods in the kitchen instead of placing them on the dining table. Another method is to place the serving plates on another table.
   10. Make sure, if feasible, that something is left over on the plate after each meal. Discard these leftovers or save them for snacks or the next meal. Have containers available for putting away the foods.
   11. Always keep foods in a covered container.
   12. Eat only difficult-to-prepare foods.

B. Modifying the types of food consumed
   1. Do not buy favorite foods that are calorie-dense and nutrient-light, such as snacks and convenience items. These foods are also difficult to fit into a carefully planned diet regimen.
   2. Avoid nibbling by preparing lunch after breakfast and dinner after lunch. It is not wise to prepare food when one is very hungry.
   3. Shop for groceries on a full stomach, e.g., immediately after breakfast, lunch, or dinner.
   4. Nibble on "harmless" foods such as carrots and celery. Have low-caloric foods nearby.
   5. Use a list when shopping and buy only the items on it.
   6. Fill the stomach partially with some low-caloric foods before going to a party or feast.
   7. Avoid eating when drinking coffee or alcohol, watching television, reading a magazine, etc.
   8. Reduce eating in restaurants, and at picnics, banquets, and parties as much as possible.
   9. Spread out eating favorite foods over the different meals of the day.

C. Modifying the frequency of eating
   1. When eating, do nothing else. Concentrate on the eating process.
   2. Confine eating to one place, preferably the same place every day.
   3. Do not eat in the kitchen if feasible.
   4. Do not eat on the working table or in front of the television.
   5. Eat sitting down.
   6. If feasible, eat at the same time each day.
   7. Permit an interval between the desire to eat and the actual eating.
   8. If feasible, arrange a complete place setting before eating, especially for breakfast and dinner.
   9. Kill the desire to eat during unplanned time by doing something that makes it impossible to eat (for example, have both hands occupied with knitting or sewing).
   10. If aware of when one wants to eat extra foods, arrange to be busy with some favorite work or activity that makes it difficult or inconvenient to eat.

A common undesirable eating behavior that should be controlled is the urge to eat when not hungry. A good example is the sometimes uncontrollable desire to eat randomly during the menstrual period. Dr. Johanna Dwyer of the New England Medical Center Hospital in Boston described the situation and provided some suggestions in "When to Diet" (*Redbook*, June, 1975, p. 120. Copyright ©, 1975 by the Redbook Publishing Company):

The premenstrual week is an especially dangerous time for many dieters because of the way the appetite ebbs and flows. One woman may experience a general increase in hunger, a number of days when she would like to eat almost anything in her line of vision; another will have a particular craving for sweets. . . .

The urge to eat more—more of one or any kind of food—at some point in the menstrual cycle may be associated with the mood fluctuations that are an inherent part of menstruation for so many women, and it can be the dieter's downfall. She feels at odds with the world; her moods are at the highest highs and the lowest lows, rather than on a nice, even plateau; and her way of coping is to reason, "Since the whole world is against me I deserve to be treated well, at least by myself." It's a fine thing to pamper oneself at such a time, but the dieter must indulge herself in some way other than eating, must provide herself with whatever nonfood creature comfort that will signal: "I am being good to me." Or she may practice "anticipatory dieting." If she can expect this behavior of herself at a particular time of the month, she can adhere rigorously to the diet beforehand, so that a small lapse won't do irreparable damage.

Weight reduction by behavioral modification may involve both positive and negative reinforcement. For example, a contract may be made between the patient and therapist to the effect that if the patient fails to alter undesirable eating behavior and lose 1 to 2 lb a week, she or he will lose $5 per week, to be placed in the therapist's trust. This $5 will be used to buy more low-calorie cookbooks for the patient's reading or for other nonpersonal purposes. Positive reinforcement consists of some pleasurable reward—such as a movie or a concert—for any success on the patient's part. More information on methods of losing weight through behavioral modification can be found in the references cited at the end of this book.

Group Programs

Many overweight people have long recognized that the best help is helping themselves. Some therefore band together and help one another to lose weight. Many self-help weight reduction group programs have developed all over the world. Some popular and fairly successful ones in this country include Weight Watchers, Tops, and Overeaters Anonymous, all of which have a few things in common. The members meet either once a week or according to some schedule. During the meetings, there may be a lecture on foods and nutrition, and the members talk to one another, exchange or study recipes and meal plans, or analyze exercise programs. To help members treat the program and its objectives more seriously, each member is required to pay a fee for attendance. Since the organizations are mostly nonprofit, the money is used for expenses such as renting space, printing literature, mailing free brochures, and various other educational activities. During each meeting, the person who has succeeded in losing the most poundage is given overwhelming support, such as a standing ovation. This kind of encouragement lifts the individual's spirit.

The overweight persons essentially follow a special low-calorie diet designed by the organization and report the results during each gathering. They are also taught how to implement a workable and effective exercise program. Although specific scientific data are lacking about the success rate of these self-help groups, scientists and physicians specializing in obesity generally agree that they probably have more success in helping people to lose weight than most physicians and other paid commercial weight reduction clinics.

In addition to these self-help groups, many industrial corporations, hospitals, clinics, universities, church organizations, and other large institutions have started their own nonprofit weight reduction programs, such as summer camps for obese children and teenagers, and physical fitness programs for firemen, policemen, and automobile workers. Again, data on the success of these efforts are lacking, but it is felt that group programs of this nature can only help and will rarely hurt obese individuals in their continuing efforts to lose weight.

Hypnotism

In the last few years, some clinical hypnotists have claimed good success in helping people lose weight by means of hypnotism, while others have

An Example of a Posthypnotic Weight Reduction Suggestion

And now I want you to have a clear mental image in your mind, of yourself standing on the scales and the scales registering the weight you wish to be. See this very, very clearly for this is the weight you will be. See yourself looking the way you would like to look with the weight off those parts of the body you want the weight to be off. See this very, very vividly and summon this image into your mind many times during the day; particularly just after waking in the morning and before going to sleep at night, also have it vividly in your mind before eating meals. And this is the way you will look, and this is the weight you will be. As you believe this, so it will happen. When you have attained this weight, you will be able to maintain it, you will find yourself eating just enough to maintain your weight at the weight you would like to be. Until you *do* attain this weight you will find you have less, and less desire to eat between meals. In fact, very, very soon, you will have no desire at all, to eat between meals. You simply will not want to. Also you will find

you will be content with smaller meals. There will be no sense of unhappiness or dissatisfaction, smaller meals will be quite satisfactory to you, and you will have no desire to eat large meals. Also you will have less, and less desire for high calorie, rich, unhealthy foods. Day by day, your desire for such foods will become less and less, until very, very soon, you will have no desire at all for rich, high calorie, unhealthy foods. Instead, day by day, you will desire low calorie, healthy foods, and these will replace the high calorie foods, the rich foods, you have eaten in the past.

As you lose weight and approach closer and closer to the weight you wish to be you will find yourself growing stronger and stronger, healthier and healthier. Your resistance to illness and disease will increase, day by day. With less weight you will feel better and better, and your health will become better and better. Remember too, that your own suggestions will be just as effective as the suggestions I give you, either personally or by tape.

Source: H. E. Stanton, *Am. J. of Clin. Hypnotists* 18[1975]:34.

reported failure. A brief description of this technique is given below; for more information, refer to the references at the end of this book.

A hypnotist may or may not be a medical doctor. However, in most states the person is required to be specially licensed. The procedure for weight reduction is very simple. The therapist first establishes a good relationship with the patient so as to earn the patient's trust, to develop his confidence that hypnotism will help, and to breed familiarity with the practice, purposes, and effects of hypnotism. During the first few sessions, hypnosis is induced, the trance is deepened, and the patient is then awakened. The therapist and patient then explore the experience. Once the therapist is convinced of the

favorable responses of the patient, specific posthypnotic suggestions are provided to the patient during the trance stage. Such suggestions, instructions, and commands vary and may be any of the following:

Substitution for overeating—The therapist suggests that the patient should chew gum or carrots instead of eating ice cream.

Transferring overeating habit—The patient is told to transfer his overeating activity to other activities such as riding a bicycle, physical exercise, or buying clothes.

Reduction of overeating—The patient is told that his or her present eating pattern is not normal and that he or she must eat less.

Aversion—The therapist suggests that the

patient think he or she is eating, smelling, hearing, or feeling something bad and unpleasant every time he or she eats or wants to eat a doughnut or toast with butter.

Reliving childhood—The patient is told that he is very young and that he should participate in more physically demanding activities, spending all the calories he has been eating.

Health incentive—The therapist suggests to the patient that he is achieving superior health when he loses weight by not eating too much.

Ego and image building—The therapist suggests how attractive the patient looks when he or she has lost weight and how there is promise of good social involvement.

After the patient has awakened from each trance, the total experience is again discussed. As the patient becomes more experienced, the hypnotic stage is made to last longer so that the suggestions can be repeated many times. Some patients are taught how to hypnotize themselves, repeating the same suggestions to themselves during the training sessions. Some physicians or therapists tape-record the suggestions so that the patient can take them home for repeated listening.

Jaw Wiring or Lock-jaw

Since December 1973, more than 100 obese patients have gone through the technique of having their jaws wired or locked in order to drastically reduce the consumption of foods. Physicians who have conducted the operation have reported some success; some patients have lost nearly 100 lb in a few months. In these clinical reports patients eligible for the procedure were specially selected—for instance, 50% overweight, free of health problems unrelated to the excess fat, and of acceptable oral and dental health. Under local anesthetic, their jaws were wired together near the canine and premolar regions. Patients resumed normal activity the next day and were able to speak normally two days later. The operation was uneventful and was described as "no worse than a tooth extraction."

The patients were sent home with the following instructions: (1) Eat a daily liquid diet of less than 1,000 kcal including milk, natural fruit juices, and vitamin and mineral supplements. (2)

Use special procedures to maintain oral hygiene. Bad breath and dryness of mouth were managed by dental aids such as washes and ointment. (3) As a precaution against aspiration and vomiting, each patient was given a wire cutter and taught how to use it in case of emergency.

All patients underwent periodic checkups with special attention to oral health, infection, respiratory functions, and weight loss. Some common complaints included sore gums and monotony of the liquid diet. Some patients admitted noncompliance by using high-caloric fluids and blended food purees. Some attempts to squeeze solid foods between the teeth were also reported.

Although not every patient had an acceptable weight loss because of such reasons as infection, refusal to continue, and illness, a substantial number did lose a large amount of body weight during the periods of jaw wiring. Aside from hair loss, there were no other ill effects on the patients.

Forced Exercises

Physicians who have tried the forced-exercise technique have also reported some success. The patient comes to the clinic weekly or at some other interval, where he or she is required to perform a specified amount of exercise under medical supervision. Typical forced exercises include running on a treadmill and riding on a bicycle ergometer. Some clinicians claim that the patient loses weight, improves muscle tone, and develops strong respiratory functions. Some patients have lost up to 100 lb. However, experienced clinicians recommend special attention to the following factors when implementing forced exercises.

There should be appropriate medical supervision. Any forced regimen with the treadmill or ergometer should be implemented slowly, carefully, and with constant evaluation.

The patient should not fast. A diet of 700 to 1,000 kcal per day is advised. The patient's appetite must be monitored; for instance, those who exercise for only 15 minutes may eat an amount of food afterwards that is equivalent to 2 hours of work.

Because coercion is involved in this technique,

TABLE 12-19   Characteristics of Drugs Used in Treating Obesity

Drug	Side Effects	Mode of Action	Effectiveness
Morpholine, imidazoline, and phenylethylamines, e.g., amphetamines (no longer available for prescription)	Addiction, insomnia, dry mouth, hypertension, cardiac arrhythmias, impotence, constipation, allergy, blood disorders, paranoid reactions	Makes the person lose appetite and thus eat less	Not sure
Cellulose: sodium carboxymethyl, hydroxymethyl, methyl ethyl, and methyl derivatives; carrageenin, sodium alginate	Occasional laxative effects	Adsorbs water and expands stomach to produce satiety; slows down the passage of foods, making the person feel full	Not sure
Diuretics	Many; see Chapters 16, 27, and 28	Loss of body water (weight loss is not fat)	None
Hormones			
Thyroid hormones	Hazardous: cardiovascular symptoms, including sweating and palpitation	Increases body metabolism	High doses and prolonged treatment effective; but effect transitory
Human chorionic gonadotropin hormone	Minimal	Unknown	Doubtful effect
Growth hormone	Increase in glucose tolerance, not enough data	Mobilizes body fat	May be effective; still being investigated
Progesterone	Not enough data	Reduces pulmonary complications of obesity	Doubtful effect

many patients undergo personality changes. These are important and should be monitored. For instance, a happy person may become quiet. Some change to an aggressive mood, while others become juvenile and refuse to exercise after they have come to the clinic. Each attending physician must decide if such patients are appropriate for forced exercise.

Injury to the patient is not uncommon. Exhaustion, backaches, and joint pain or swelling are sometimes reported, and the patient should be warned about the possibility of back problems. Some clinicians suggest the use of protective covering on ankles, knees, joints, and wrists.

Drug Therapy

Medical drugs have long been used to treat overweight individuals, although the recent attitude among the scientific community has not been encouraging. Table 12-19 summarizes those substances that have been used in treating obesity.

One major group is anorectic drugs, which supposedly depress the appetite of the patient. In 1980 the FDA banned this class of chemicals in the treatment of obesity. Both their effectiveness and side effects have been questioned. In general, it is felt that this type of drug helps the patient starting a very low caloric diet to over-

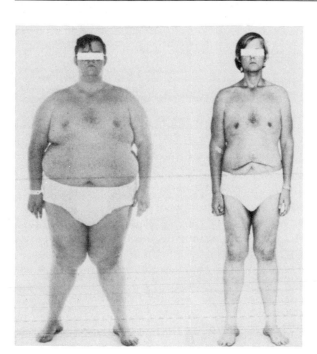

FIGURE 12-1   A 20-year-old patient before (left, at 400 lb) and 2 years after (right, at 210 lb) intestinal bypass. (From H. W. Scott et al., *South Med. J.* 69 [1976]:789)

Surgery

At present, there are two surgical approaches to treating obesity: lipectomy and gastrointestinal bypass. Both methods carry high risks of morbidity and mortality, especially the latter.

Lipectomy is a very old technique involving excision of a mass of subcutaneous adipose tissue. This technique is definitely not advised for an overall reduction in body weight, but under certain circumstances it is useful.

The other surgical approach to obesity is the gastrointestinal bypass. The technique involves either closing up the stomach partially (stomach stapling) or removing part of the small intestine. In either case, the operation reduces the amount of food digested and absorbed and thus effectively reduces caloric intake. Individuals going through this procedure may lose 100 lb within a few months to a year after the operation. Figure 12-1 shows a patient before and after intestinal bypass surgery. More details on the complications and surgical sequel are discussed in Chapter 24 and its references.

Starvation (Fasting)

Partial or total starvation—otherwise known as fasting—is one of the oldest methods of losing weight. In the last few years, it has been popular for two purposes: losing weight and achieving bodily and spiritual well-being. The following discussion concerns the former purpose.

As indicated earlier, if one reduces the caloric intake to less than 1,200 kcal per day, the person should be under a physician's supervision. Total or nearly total starvation under medical supervision has proven successful in a number of cases, although sudden death has been reported in a small number of patients. It is important to monitor liver enzyme changes, electrolyte balance (especially potassium loss), formation of ketone bodies (acetoacetic acid, β-hydroxybutyric acid, and acetones) and the ketosis they produce, dehydration, elevated blood uric acid, and psychiatric disturbances. These problems definitely require hospitalization (at least for a specified period), a generous

come the difficult transition period (the first 2 to 6 weeks of dieting). However, the effectiveness of their long-term usage is questionable.

The use of thyroid hormones to treat obesity has also been very controversial for a number of years. One major criticism concerns the catabolic effect of the hormone in both fat and muscle protein. The weight lost by using this group of hormones is more muscle protein than fat. However, it is felt that using the hormone at the beginning of a weight reduction regimen has some scientific basis. The body responds to a low-caloric diet by lowering the basal metabolic rate, which obviously interferes with weight loss. An early, small dose of thyroid hormone raises the basal metabolic rate and provides the patient with the incentive of visible weight loss. The long-term usage of this hormone is questioned by authorities because it creates a negative nitrogen balance. Recently, the FDA has issued special warnings regarding the use of this group of chemicals in weight reduction.

supply of vitamins and minerals, and an occasional dose of glucose. Slow heart rate and pulse rate, hair loss, weakness, unpleasant taste and breath, low blood pressure, disturbed menstrual cycles, and occasional gum inflammation have been observed in fasting individuals, although none of these manifestations are life threatening. Further, patients under medical supervision are rarely starved completely; most receive about 500 kcal per day.

On the other hand, prolonged unsupervised fasting may result in fluid and electrolyte imbalance, mineral and vitamin deficiency, and serious cardiovascular disorders. Individuals who fast for more than 2 months develop dry, scaly skin and arrested hair and nail growth. The longer the fast, the more hair falls out. Other observations include abnormal heart rate, renal impairment, and central nervous system damage; death may occur. At least in the beginning, the nonfatal symptoms are masked by high blood ketones, which cross the brain barriers and create transient euphoria as a prelude to mental disturbance.

The weight loss created by starvation is a mixture of water, lean muscle, and fat loss with varying proportions of each. Experienced physicians use starvation to treat individuals who are 50 to 200 lb overweight, but not those who are only 5 to 20 lb overweight. As mentioned earlier, even under medical supervision, some patients die from food deprivation.

Very recently, physicians at the Mount Sinai and New England Deaconess hospitals (Dr. Victor Vertes of Case Western Reserve University Medical School and Dr. George L. Blackburn of Harvard University Medical School, respectively) started the "modified fasting" program to lose weight. This program is based on the theory that if a fasting person is provided with essential amino acids, the body muscle protein mass will be rebuilt and maintained while the fat is being lost. Three high-quality protein mixtures have been tried by the physicians who started this technique: (1) a mixture of lean beef, chicken, skim milk, egg white, and cheese made from skim milk; (2) commercial nutrient liquid supplements made up of essential amino acids, electrolytes, minerals, vitamins, and a small amount

of defined calories normally used for surgical and kidney patients; and (3) special protein solutions containing essential amino acids, such as Optifast, which are specially prepared for and ordered by the above physicians.

All patients on the modified fasting regimen are provided with adequate amounts of essential minerals and vitamins, and they are fully informed at the beginning that they must participate in a total approach to the obesity problem. In addition to the dietary and medical regimen, there is a personalized exercise program, instruction about foods and nutrition, counseling in behavioral modifications, and maintenance of their weight loss at all costs.

Some of the side effects of the modified fasting include: (1) postural hypotension, at least at the beginning, because of diuresis (loss of water); (2) skin changes, dryness, and transient rash; (3) fatigue, diarrhea, cold intolerance, hair loss, muscle cramps, amenorrhea, decreased libido, euphoria (temporary), peroneal nerve palsy, dry mouth, and bad breath; (4) cholecystitis and pancreatitis; (5) negative psychological reactions; and (6) constipation, nausea, vomiting, and a high blood level of uric acid. However, none of these effects is life threatening.

After the modified fasting program was reported in medical literature, some commercial enterprises started selling liquid and powder protein preparations, claiming that they help one to lose weight. Unfortunately, this unscrupulous practice has resulted in death. Some deaths have followed the 1976 publication of the book *Last Chance Diet* written by an osteopath, in which the author advocated fasting supplemented by liquid protein to lose weight. Although the book warns that medical supervision is necessary for such a dietary regimen, many individuals did not follow the advice. When sales of the book rose, commercial protein supplements began to appear in the market, such as Prolinn (liquid), P-86 (powder), Ultrathin (powder), Naturslim (powder), and Slim-fast (powder). Within a short time, many individuals, from 5 to 200 lb overweight, tried the diet, some with medical supervision, others without. Since then, more than 20 individuals have died from this regimen, in spite of the fact that some were under medical supervision. At first the lack of potassium was blamed for the deaths. Later, this theory was refuted, and the reasons for death remain unknown. Almost all of those who died suffered heart abnormalities with arrhythmias.

Later the FDA (Food and Drug Administration) required a warning label on the products. Because of the adverse publicity caused by the deaths, many liquid protein products disappeared from the consumer market.

Comprehensive Medical Weight Reduction Programs

There are many well-run, authentic, reputable, and fairly successful weight reduction clinics in this country. They are staffed with physicians and nurses specializing in the treatment of or research on obesity. Some clinics also employ nutritionists, dietitians, behavioral therapists, and exercise physiologists. Well-organized programs may contain any or all of the following treatment procedures: (1) a comprehensive study of the patient's physical and mental condition and medical and weight history; (2) a carefully planned, slowly introduced diet tailored to the patient; (3) appropriate drug therapy for a defined period; (4) a well-designed exercise program that may be composed of home activities as well as occasional forced exercises in the clinic is introduced slowly and carefully; (5) intermittent or occasional fasting; and (6) systematic behavioral modifications of eating habits.

These programs can be successful if the patient is conscientious. However, these programs have a number of basic problems. One is high cost. Since the patient has to visit the clinic frequently, the cost can be very high if the treatment period is long. Most insurance carriers do not cover this type of treatment unless health hazards are involved.

A second problem is that clinic programs are time consuming. If the patient has a job, attending the clinic weekly becomes difficult and sometimes impossible. And, no matter how well organized the program, all other nagging issues connected with losing weight are still there: the patience needed to lose weight, the willpower to eat less, unwillingness to change lifelong habits, psychological frustrations, and the difficulty of maintaining normal body weight after the excess is lost.

FAD DIETS AND OTHER UNSCIENTIFIC WAYS OF LOSING WEIGHT

Dr. George V. Mann of Vanderbilt University once stated (*New England Journal of Medicine* 1974; 291:178): "An endless succession of dietary regimens appear in the media, each purporting to be the ultimate solution. These permutations of fuel mixtures range from the impossible to the ridiculous. If they have any common feature it is that they make elaborate promises of success, they understate the rigors of adherence, and they try to place the decision for dietary restriction in the hands of the dieter. . . . The other common feature of reducing regimens is their commercialism—someone stands to make money from their promotion."

Dieting is a good business for many publishers, authors, and merchants. In the United States, the fad diet market is a multi-million-dollar business. Practically all of the fad diets fall into one of the following three categories: (1) The dieter is asked to reduce the intake of one or two of the three major calorie-contributing nutrients—fat, carbohydrate, and protein. (2) The dieter is asked to consume daily the same one to three food products. (3) The dieter is asked to consume daily a nutrient (vitamin or mineral) or certain nonfood items.

The lists below give once-popular fad diets.

A. Advocating one particular type of food
   1. The Rice Diet
   2. The Banana Diet
   3. Candy Diet
   4. Grapefruit Diet
   5. Ice Cream Diet
   6. "Nova Scotia" Diet
   7. Vegetable and Fruit Diets
   8. Eating with Wine
   9. Yogurt Diet

B. Advocating a large protein intake
1. Dr. Stillman's Quick Weight Loss Diet
2. Dr. Stillman's Inches Off Diet
3. New Diet Does It
4. Lazy Lady Diet
5. Ratio Diet

C. Advocating a low carbohydrate intake
1. Carbo-Calorie Diet
2. Carbo-Cal Diet
3. Dr. Yudkin's Diet
4. Drinkingman's Diet
5. Air Force Diet
6. Airline Pilots' Diet (Astronauts' Diet)

D. Advocating a low-carbohydrate, high-fat diet
1. Dr. Atkin's Diet Revolution
2. Calories Don't Count
3. Eat, Drink and Get Thin
4. Eat and Become Slim

E. Miscellaneous
1. The Miracle Diet
2. No Will Power Diet
3. McCall's Snack Diet
4. Zen Macrobiotic Diet
5. Nine-Day Wonder Diet
6. Olympia Diet
7. Magic Formula-Plus Diet
8. Miraculous Eggnog Diet
9. Fabulous Formula Diet
10. Counterweight Diet
11. Workingman's Diet
12. Amazing "New You" Diet
13. Hambletonian Wonder-Week Diet
14. Editor's Diet
15. North Pole Slenderizing Plan
16. Melon-Berry Diet
17. Vinegar/Lecithin/B_6/Kelp Diet

The diets listed above are similar in many respects. None of them teaches a person to eat a well-balanced and nutritious diet, and practically all of them are low in calories. For the first one or two weeks of a diet, there is always some weight loss. The dieter is pleased and word starts to circulate that the diet works. Actually, two facts can explain the weight loss: The diet is low in calories, and the dieter is losing a large amount of fluid, a loss which usually accompanies a reduction in food intake.

If a person is on one of those fad diets and can lose weight immediately or over a few months, why is the diet unacceptable? Let us assume that a person loses 5 lb in one week. This rapid loss is physiologically unsound, and in fact quite difficult even if a person is on total starvation. What the person has lost is mainly water with a small amount of protein and fat. When obese people who have "lost" 10 lb after 2 weeks on a fad diet start eating regularly again, they can regain 2 to 5 lb in 3 or 4 days, as they reaccumulate a large amount of water.

If a person can faithfully adhere to a low-calorie fad diet for 6 months, there will be a substantial weight loss. In this case, the loss is due to caloric expenditure exceeding intake. Some dieters claiming to have lost weight after being on a low-calorie fad diet for a long period in fact stay on the diet only initially, for example, for 3 or 4 weeks. After becoming bored with eating the same foods all the time, they randomly eat other foods but in small quantities to insure a weight loss. Others may stay away from foods 2 or 3 days a week and eat some foods during other days. Extreme cases have been documented in which patients stay away from food completely and must be hospitalized (see references at the end of this book and the case analysis in Chapter 31 under the section "Anorexia Nervosa").

From the situations above, two conclusions can be drawn. First, the individual will be receiving less than the RDA for a number of nutrients, since the low-calorie fad diet is basically imbalanced. Second, actual weight loss depends on the length of time a person can stay on the diet. A time will come, 1 week to a few months after starting the diet, when the person can no longer withstand the monotony of eating the same foods and will return to his or her regular eating habit, soon regaining as much or more than he or she had lost by dieting. Accumulating fat is much easier than losing it.

Nutritionists and other health professionals do not recommend fad diets for a number of reasons. The diets are not well balanced and do not provide adequate amounts of all the essential nutrients. None of the diets teaches a person to develop good eating habits or to maintain normal weight over a lifetime. Some of the diets may actually be hazardous. For example, eating a large amount of fat and cholesterol ("Dr. Atkin's Diet") may not be good for individuals predisposed to heart disease. Further, semistarvation without medical supervision is hazardous. Finally, what is the use of a diet if a person gets bored with it after a few days or weeks?

Using a device to lose weight is another unscientific fad. According to the Food, Drug and Cosmetic Act, the FDA can seize a medical device if it poses human health hazards. However, the manufacturer is not required to demonstrate the effectiveness of such a device before it is marketed. Many unscrupulous merchants and organizations have advertised equipment and devices purported to aid in weight loss. Although most are not hazardous to health, some are. Special elastic clothing, tight belts, and whole-body sauna suits have been seized because there are documented cases of individuals suffering from depressed circulation because of the tightness of this apparel. If circulation is severely depressed, cardiac arrest is possible. Machines claimed to rub away fat were once popular, even though rubbing away fat is physiologically impossible. Exercise machines may help to lose weight if used conscientiously, although they cannot perform miracles by themselves.

Fad diets and weight loss devices can be detrimental in many ways: causing loss of money and time; posing health hazards; and leading to intense psychological maladjustment such as depression, disappointment, and frustration at the failure to lose weight once again.

CLINICAL PROBLEMS ASSOCIATED WITH WEIGHT LOSS

When a person is on a diet, the weight loss, especially if rapid, is usually associated with a number of clinical problems. If under medical supervision, the patient will be forewarned. However, overweight individuals trying to lose weight on their own may not be aware of potential risks. Most of the problems are not serious or life threatening if the person follows a nonhazardous or acceptable dieting regimen, including an occasional 1 or 2 days of fasting. These problems are briefly summarized below.

Hair Loss

Weight loss by reducing caloric intake or partial or total starvation is associated with hair loss. In some people, the hair falls off sparingly; in others, it falls out in chunks. The loss is usually not permanent, and hair grows back normally after dieting is stopped.

Menstrual Disorders

Dieting or weight loss in female patients frequently affects the menstrual cycle. Amenorrhea (cessation of menstruation) is most common. It is assumed that the starvation results in hypopituitarism, which in turn depresses hormone stimulation of the uterus to slough its linings. Absence of uterine bleeding also characterizes anorexia nervosa, a disorder identified in young female patients who reject foods because of psychiatric problems. When such dieting women return to regular eating habits, their menstrual periods return within a short time.

Dieting and Alcohol

Dieting and drinking alcohol are incompatible. A person on a very low caloric diet (for example, 1,000 kcal) for 2 or 3 days may develop hypoglycemia after drinking alcoholic beverages, even as little as 4 or 5 oz of whiskey. For example, within 1 hour after drinking, the person may suddenly feel tired, nervous, weak, nauseous, headachy, or ill, sweat profusely, and develop a fast pulse rate.

Peroneal Nerve Palsy

In the past few years, a number of clinical cases have been documented associating peroneal nerve palsy with weight loss. The person experiences paresthesia in the common peroneal nerve distribution of the right or left foot and leg whenever it is dragged or slapped. Apparently there is paralysis of the muscles innervated by the common peroneal nerve, resulting in foot drop and numbness. The symptoms and palsy disappear when the person returns to a normal diet.

This phenomenon has also been observed in prisoners of war who have been starved. One speculation is that the weight loss may include those subcutaneous tissues that normally cushion the nerve, making it more susceptible to injury or depression.

Syncope

A person who has not eaten for a short while, such as 1 or 2 days, faints easily in situations such as being in a hot room, standing too long, or trying to stand from a sitting position. Low blood sugar, slow circulation, and low blood pressure have all been suspected to play a part. The popular warning "Don't fly on an empty stomach" makes sense in that the person who has been fasting for a while is more sensitive to a depressed oxygen supply. The hypotension developed will make the person faint.

Other minor problems associated with weight loss are nervousness, trembling hands, coldness, and scaly and dry skin.

GENERAL ADVICE FOR WEIGHT LOSS

First, when using a diet to lose weight, check its authenticity and accuracy. Consult your physician, public health nutritionist, hospital dietitian, or academics specializing in the field.

Second, when using any over-the-counter drugs, check their effectiveness and safety. Seek medical supervision if so advised on the label. Consult *Consumer Reports*, your physician, or an academic specialist in pharmaceutics and related fields. Any prescription drug illegally obtained should not be taken without full awareness of its safety and effectiveness.

Third, do not believe any advertisement promoting a diet, drug, device, regimen, or other procedure that *guarantees* weight loss. At present, there is no known method that can guarantee weight loss with absolute safety.

Fourth, exercise, but take precautions. The exercise program must be appropriate for the individual (age, sex, and medical conditions). Proper professional advice must be sought or a professionally written manual for physical activity must be followed.

Fifth, at present, avoid most mechanical devices for losing weight, which can be harmful. Body trappings, for example, can impair circulation.

Finally, before adopting any diet or weight loss program, be sure that you are in normal health. Many diets, drugs, and exercise programs are all right for normal, healthy people. If at all feasible, inform your physician of what you are doing and ask him or her to help check your progress or check your health before beginning any program. If you are unable to consult your doctor, talk to other health professionals such as nutritionists, dietitians, and nurses. Many of the latter individuals, if they work in a health clinic, will provide advice and assistance as a public service and do not charge a fee.

The most effective way to lose weight is to combine at least a minimal amount of daily activity, learning the basics of good nutrition, retraining eating habits, and following a sensible and practical low-calorie diet.

STUDY QUESTIONS

1. What is the difference between the terms *overweight* and *obese*?
2. How many excess kilocalories (energy not spent) does it take to gain 1 lb of body fat?
3. Discuss some drawbacks of standard body weight tables.
4. What are the two basic ways of determining an individual's daily caloric need?

5. Name at least six medical problems for which people more than 15% overweight run a higher-than-normal risk. What are some nonmedical problems associated with obesity?

6. What five considerations are essential to any successful weight loss program?

7. What assumptions underlie the behavioral modification approach to weight loss? Describe some techniques for reducing stimulus control of eating.

8. Discuss the techniques and potential hazards, if any, of hypnotism, jaw wiring, forced exercise, and surgical approaches to weight loss.

9. Is fasting recommended for those who are obese or only slightly overweight? What is a modified fasting program?

10. What physical problems tend to accompany weight loss, particularly if weight is lost quickly?

11. Compile a list of diet books that were popular during the last 2 years.

12. Compile a list of diet aids that were popular during the last 2 years.

Chapter 13

Nutrition During Pregnancy and Lactation

SINCE THE BEGINNING of time, practically every ethnic and religious group on earth has offered some suggestion about what a woman should or should not eat during pregnancy. For example, the Chinese people advocate the consumption of sweet and sour pigs' feet. They claim that the vinegar used provides a "hot" characteristic, which is good for pregnancy. Nutritionally, this dish provides calories (from the fatty skin and added sugar), calcium and phosphorus (from chewing the bones), iron (leached from cooking utensils by the acid), and a small amount of protein (from the lean meat). In Western societies, milk and meats are especially encouraged for the pregnant woman because of their high nutrient contents. The phrase "eating for two," though exaggerated, is still regarded as true by laymen, and it is standard advice throughout the world.

As the fetus grows in the womb, it depends entirely on the mother for "food." The circulation, via the placenta, supplies nutrients at the beginning of the pregnancy; the amniotic fluid eventually adds to the nutrient supply. Appropriate quantities of certain nutrients are essential for the proper development of the fetus. The nutrient requirements of the fetus are superimposed on the mother's own basic needs for maintenance and repair. To insure that both she and the fetus are well nourished, the woman should be in a satisfactory nutritional status when she conceives and eat a good diet during pregnancy. For women who choose to breast-feed their infants, the need for extra nutrients continues until the baby is weaned.

NUTRITION AND PREGNANCY

What is known about the nutritional status of an American woman when she enters pregnancy? No comprehensive data provide a satisfactory answer to this question, although a few generalizations can be made.

A significant number of women entering pregnancy are unacceptably under- or overweight, especially among families with low income. Health professionals also consider the incidence of iron and folic acid deficiency among the general female population to be significant. Many women have a borderline nutriture of vitamin B_{12}. The intakes of calcium, iodine, and vitamins A and C are suspected to be low among some women, especially those under 18. Furthermore, during the adolescent years, a significant number of girls consume below the RDA in a number of nutrients. Generally, female adolescents and ethnic and low-income women have a poorer nutritional status than the rest of the female population.

The contraception method used before pregnancy has varying effects on a woman's nutritional status. Some brands of contraceptive pills regularize the menstrual period and minimize bleeding, while others may result in excess hemorrhage either during menstruation or between periods. An IUD may cause blood loss in some users, and any bleeding means iron loss.

Maternal Nutrition and Pregnancy Profile

The pregnancy profile of a well-nourished woman is clearly superior to that of a malnourished one. A well-nourished woman is most likely to be able to withstand the stresses of the 9-month period. Her appetite is good, and body changes in digestion, absorption, and metabolism are favorable. She is expected to suffer minimal complications (obstetrical risks) during pregnancy, labor, and delivery, as confirmed by the good survival record of this group of patients. She is also most likely to deliver a healthy baby who is nutritionally sound with few complications. The child is expected to show normal growth and development during the first year. The mother also experiences a successful lactation period.

By contrast, a malnourished mother, whether underweight or in an overall unsatisfactory condition, may have numerous problems. She may be exposed to pregnancy wastage: abortion during the first few weeks of conception, intrauterine death, or death after birth. Good nutritional and dietary care can probably reduce this risk. A malnourished mother may have an incompetent placenta, smaller in size and with fewer cells than that of a well-fed woman. This may affect the fetus in various ways. Malnourished women suffer more complications (high obstetrical risks) during gestation, labor, and delivery than well-nourished women. Finally, women who are malnourished are more likely to give birth to high-risk infants. Such infants may suffer from any of the following: prematurity, uteroretardation, low birth weight, small-for-gestational age, small-for-date, high morbidity and mortality, birth defects, and increased clinical problems (infection, defective thermoregulation, kidney malfunction, and the possibility of cesarean delivery). Also, the child may fail to develop normally during the first 1 or 2 years.

Of course, not all well-nourished pregnant women deliver healthy infants with minimal obstetrical risks, and not all malnourished pregnant mothers deliver high-risk infants accompanied with multiple obstetrical risks. However, *some* anthropological, epidemiological, clinical, and experimental studies have suggested that malnourished pregnancies are higher in risks. In one study, mothers in unsatisfactory nutritional status and fed a poor diet developed complications and difficulties in delivery, with a higher number of stillborns, premature births, and early infant deaths, although some well-nourished mothers were not free of these adverse effects. In some studies, malnourished mothers supplemented with nutritious foods exhibited a healthier pregnancy profile in most criteria used. Studies of this nature have been performed in the United States, Canada, India, and Guatemala. Available medical records from World War I and World War II confirm that starved pregnant women had many obstetrical problems. Finally, studies with laboratory and farm animals have confirmed that nutrient deficiency during gestation can result in adverse effects on the newborns, including birth defects.

Teenage pregnancy has long been associated with many social and medical problems. Nearly half of all American girls marry at 18 to 20 years of age, and nearly one-third of the teenage mothers are under 16. Of more than 3 million newborn babies, teenage mothers gave birth to about one-fifth. A teenage pregnant mother faces two major concerns—her own development and that of the child, both of which are expected to suffer. The young mother tends to be malnourished for a number of reasons, such as bad diet because of low income or frequent attempts to lose weight. Teenage mothers are likely to give birth to high-risk infants. Table 13-1 shows the birth rates by age of mothers in 1976 in the United States.

TABLE 13-1   Birth Rates by Age of Mother in 1976 in the United States, Excluding Nonresidents

Age of Mother (Years)	Birth Rates per 1,000 Females in the Specified Groups
10–14	1.2
15–19	53.5
20–24	112.1
25–29	108.8
30–34	54.5
35–39	19.0
40–44	4.3
45–49	0.2

Source: Facts of Life and Death (Washington, D.C.: U.S. Department of Health, Education, and Welfare, 1978), publication No. (PHS) 79-1222.

To illustrate the importance of a good diet before pregnancy, Table 13-2 presents the data from one study comparing the effects of diet before and during pregnancy on the health risk to the newborn. The data in the table suggest that a good diet before pregnancy can even lessen the risks due to a poor diet during pregnancy. The relationships between pregnancy and diet will be explored in detail in different parts of this chapter.

Determining Nutritional Risk Factors in Pregnancy

Since malnutrition may be dangerous to both the pregnant mother and the fetus, health professionals should be aware of the possibility of malnutrition when counseling pregnant women. Certain women are at particular risk of being malnourished.

Most obstetricians and gynecologists also evaluate the following physical factors on the first two visits of a woman with a confirmed pregnancy: (1) overall physical appearance; (2) body development in relation to age; (3) body weight; (4) presence of overt deficiency symptoms involving skin, hair, eyes, mouth, fingers, and nails; and (5) oral health (cavities, gum infection, glossitis, and cheilosis). The findings are then corre-

TABLE 13-2 Relation of Diet Before and During Pregnancy to Health Risk of Newborn in One Study

Diet		Risk to Infants*			
Before pregnancy	During pregnancy	Low birth weight	Still-birth	Pre-maturity	Neonatal death
Good diet	Poor diet	Moderate	Less	Less	Less
Poor diet	Poor diet	Severe	More	More	More

*Relative to known standardized national records.

lated with any applicable nutritional risk factors, as listed below.

A. Nutritional risk factors associated with reproductive history
1. Unsatisfactory reproduction history, e.g., obstetric complications.
2. Long-term breast-feeding following each pregnancy.
3. First pregnancy when mother was under 18 years old.
4. Pregnancy repeated within short intervals.
5. Multiple births.
6. Use of oral contraceptive drugs terminating less than 6 months before pregnancy.

B. Nutritional risk factors associated with current pregnancy profile
1. Age under 17.
2. Height under 5 feet.
3. Over- or underweight at conception (over: 16%–30% above normal; under: 5%–10% below normal).
4. Presence of clinical disorder, e.g., high blood pressure and viral infection.
5. On special therapeutic diet.
6. Dietary faddism, weight reduction, and pica.
7. Drug usage (cigarettes, alcohol, other drugs).
8. Other factors: low income, language and/or ethnic differences, unwanted pregnancy, emotional and psychological maladjustments.

C. Nutritional risk factors associated with clinical progress of present pregnancy
1. Restricted or excess weight gain.
2. Unsatisfactory fetal growth: more than 42

weeks of gestation, abnormal growth and/or size.
3. Obstetric complications, e.g., incompetent placenta, poor circulation, abnormal hormonal changes, hemorrhage, abnormal presentation, multiple pregnancy, toxemia, and failure of fundus to grow by fourth or fifth week.
4. Severe dependent edema.

Weight Changes

Obstetricians consider a normal weight gain to be one of the most important criteria of a healthy pregnancy. During the early part of pregnancy, the woman builds up her body tissue storage; for instance, blood volume, breast size, and uterus size all increase. By the fourth and fifth months, she starts to accumulate fat as an energy reserve, especially for lactation. During the last two months, the weight of the fetus doubles. It is extremely important that the mother eat nutritiously and adequately during this critical period. Three major considerations in evaluating the clinical course of a pregnant woman's body weight changes are the patient's concept of weight gain, the normal pattern of weight gain, and instructions given to the patient.

Patient's concept of weight gain

During the first few visits, the pregnant woman's concept of weight gain is discussed and analyzed. Clinical experience indicates that most patients are concerned about excess weight. Those who are overweight from the start of con-

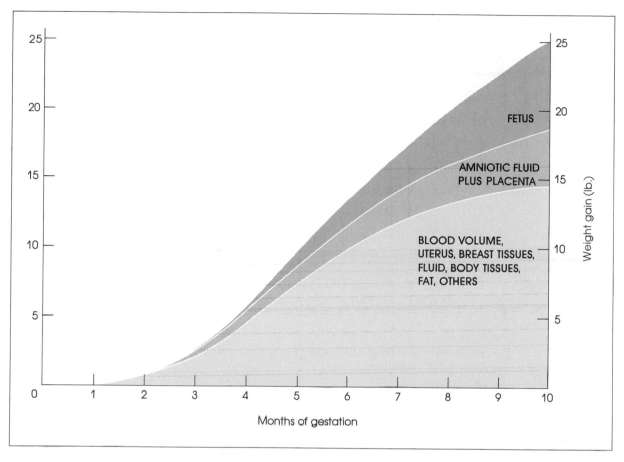

FIGURE 13-1   Weight gain during pregnancy.

ception hope that they will lose some weight so that they will be slim after delivery. Other patients express concern about the stretching of the abdominal skin, residual weight, and an undesirable distribution of body fat. However, the recent trend toward returning to nature, natural childbirth, and the avoidance of conventional medical care has decreased the undesirability of excess weight gain or the subsequent appearance. Still, physicians who care for pregnant patients should emphasize the importance of proper weight gain in a normal pregnancy.

Normal pattern of weight gain

At present, the acceptable normal pattern of pregnancy weight gain is quite different from that considered acceptable 30 to 50 years ago. The discussion below reflects the views and judgment of the National Academy of Sciences, the American College of Obstetrics and Gynecology, clinical nutritionists, and some physicians specializing in obstetrics and gynecology.

Each woman's weight gain during pregnancy should be evaluated on both absolute (weights at beginning and end of pregnancy) and progressive (rate of weight gain during the entire period of pregnancy) bases. If feasible, her ideal nonpregnant weight is determined according to the methods described in Chapter 12. At the start of pregnancy, the woman should be 95% to 120% of her ideal weight. Statistical analyses confirm that the average weight gain in a normal pregnant American woman is about 27 to 29 lb, with a standard deviation of 7 to 10 lb.

Weight gain during pregnancy should be smooth and progressive. As indicated in Figure 13-1, a little gain during the first 3 months is followed by a steady rise. Most maternal storage is deposited by midpregnancy, after which the

TABLE 13-3   Distribution of Weight Gain During Pregnancy

Component	Approximate Weight (lb)
Fetus	7½ (5–10)
Placenta	1½
Amniotic fluid	2
Uterus	2
Mother's tissue fluid	3
Blood volume	4
Breasts*	½
Fat and other reserve†	3½
Total	24

*The increase is much bigger in some women and is considered as reserve.

†In some women, fat reserve may be as high as 8 lb.

storage slows down to term. During the first 20 weeks, there should be a gain of about 9 lb in weight with a minimum of 2 lb per month. During the last 20 weeks, the person should gain about 1 lb per week, or 4 lb per month. In all, she should gain about 24 or 25 lb, with fat storage accounting for 3½ to 4½ lb (Figure 13-1). Table 13-3 indicates the approximate distribution of the weight gained during pregnancy.

An adequate fat reserve in a pregnant woman is important. The fetus draws on it, especially if the woman is not eating enough calories. During late pregnancy, she may depend on the fat herself. Fat reserve reduces health risk to both mother and child; for instance, it provides protection or cushioning from physical injury. In most women, more fat is deposited in the breast tissues.

Instructions to the patient

The patient is told that the extent of weight gain during pregnancy varies with the individual and her basic body size (frame and stature) and may be due to fat or water. For example, if nutritional and dietary care is adequate, a young woman tends to gain slightly more weight than an older one, a thin woman more than a fat one, and a first-time mother more than a mother with a previous pregnancy. The doctor, nurse, or dietitian should describe the weight gain profile.

Any concern about a swollen abdomen and an unacceptable waistline should not prompt a weight reduction regimen, since it may pose risk to the fetus. It is of paramount importance that a pregnant woman gain an appropriate amount of weight. Either excessive or restricted weight gain is undesirable.

Excessive gain or existing overweight. If a woman enters pregnancy with an ideal weight and gains more than 28 to 30 lb during the course of pregnancy, she encounters numerous clinical problems. There is an increased risk of toxemia* (including convulsion) and difficult labor and delivery. She is likely to give birth to a large baby who, according to some scientists, will have more complications in later life, especially if the baby has excess fat. If the woman shows a sudden and excessive weight gain, especially after week 20 to 24 of gestation, she, as well as the child, is exposed to higher health risks, such as increased morbidity and mortality. Also, if the woman gains excessive body weight during each consecutive pregnancy, she may become obese.

If a woman is more than 20% above her ideal weight at conception, she has special problems. Statistically, she will have three times more medical and obstetrical complications than a woman with normal weight. Nutritional deficiency is common among such patients because their excess weight is mainly fat, for they tend to eat a lot of high-caloric but nutrient-light foods. This is especially true of women 50 to 100 lb overweight.

Weight gain during pregnancy among overweight women should be carefully followed. If the woman gains 18 to 23 lb, she should be all right if she eats adequately and nutritiously. However, if she eats calories only, she must make an effort to develop new eating habits. Using recorded weight gain alone to determine nutritional adequacy may be misleading. Blood and urine analyses, daily food intakes, and past dietary history are most informative. During the entire process of weight evaluation, the patient

---

*A pathological condition in some pregnant women, which involves hyperemesis gravidarum, preeclampsia, and eclampsia. Symptoms include nausea, vomiting, liver enlargement and tenderness, raised blood pressure, edema, proteinuria, oliguria, anuria, headache, vertigo, irritability, convulsions, and coma.

should also receive a sound education in nutrition. If the woman gains 10 to 18 lb and is trying to lose weight, she should be discouraged from doing so. On the other hand, excess weight gain during pregnancy must be carefully evaluated to ascertain whether it is water or fat. When an overweight woman becomes pregnant, she tends to collect water, which accounts for some of the associated complications. Water accumulation is definitely more undesirable and dangerous than fat storage.

A doctor who decides that a pregnant patient needs to lose weight should follow certain guidelines. Weight reduction either before or after pregnancy is definitely preferable to weight loss during pregnancy, which places additional stress on the physiological demand of pregnancy. In fact, the associated tension of pregnancy may actually increase the mother's appetite. The myth that weight reduction during pregnancy results in a smaller baby and thus assists in labor and delivery is unfounded. And, when a person starves completely or partially, as in skipping meals, he or she may be predisposed to ketosis or acetonuria. The same applies if the person is eating a very low carbohydrate diet in which fat and protein are metabolized preferentially. In the case of a pregnant woman, the ketone bodies accumulated can cross the placenta and may harm the infant. A few studies have confirmed that these by-products can produce mental retardation in the child. The practice of skipping meals before regular clinical visits to minimize the apparent weight gain should be discouraged.

Despite these observations, it has been confirmed that many clinicians favor weight reduction during pregnancy and feel that the patient will be all right if she gets an adequate amount of protein, vitamins, and minerals. Caution is needed if this line of thinking is adopted.

Some very obese patients develop toxemia. To prevent such an occurrence, their physicians may attempt a weight reduction regimen. If so, the caloric intake, if reduced, should not be less than 1,500 kcal/day. Appropriate vitamin/mineral supplements should be provided. Salt and water intake should not be restricted simultaneously, and the use of diuretics must be guarded.

Inadequate gain or existing underweight. A woman may enter pregnancy at an ideal weight

TABLE 13-4 Weight Gain During Pregnancy and Infant Birth Weight According to Mother's Weight at Conception*

Mother's Weight at Conception	Mother's Weight Gain	Infant's Birth Weight
Normal	Normal	Normal
Underweight	Slightly above normal	Slightly below normal

*The data assume that the person is fed adequately throughout pregnancy.

but fail to achieve a satisfactory weight gain during the 9 to 10 months period, e.g., less than 10 to 12 lb. Her weight pattern may include a failure to gain weight during any part of the pregnancy, especially the second half. A pregnant woman with restricted weight gain may have some characteristic problems. There will be a slight increase in the risk of toxemia, especially preeclampsia, and sometimes eclampsia if her weight gain is too small. Her infant is most likely to be of low birth weight or premature. Some malnourished young women tend to give birth to fragile babies. The risk of premature separation of the placenta is increased. And, there is an overall increase in morbidity and mortality for both mother and child.

If a woman enters conception with a substandard body weight (less than 95% of the normal weight), there are again certain clinical problems. The lower the prepregnant weight, the higher the pregnancy risks. One major risk is a premature and/or low-birth-weight baby. According to the study represented in Table 13-4, the woman builds her reserve at the expense of the fetus. As indicated by the study represented in Table 13-5, a woman underweight at conception and gaining insufficient weight during pregnancy definitely experiences higher health risks than an underweight woman who gains adequate weight during pregnancy. A woman underweight at conception encounters some of the problems of a woman with an ideal weight, but the former gains less weight during gestation.

A woman underweight at conception should

TABLE 13-5   Relation Between Inadequate Weight Gain of Mothers Underweight at Conception and Incidence of Obstetric Problems

Weight Gain of Underweight Woman During Pregnancy	Incidence		
	Low birth weight	Small-for-gestational age	Severe toxemia
<12 lb	High	High	Moderate to high
20–25 lb	Low to moderate	Low to moderate	Low to moderate

be advised to gain enough weight to account for both her deficit and the pregnancy. For example, if a woman is 15 lb underweight, she should gain about 35 to 40 lb during pregnancy if the attending physician agrees that a pregnancy weight gain should be about 25 lb. It may be difficult to convince her to eat a lot of foods, for she may believe that she looks best at her present weight and that she is not underweight. Also, she will not be accustomed to eating the large amounts of food needed to gain the appropriate weight. Aggressive nutritional counseling and behavioral modifications may be needed. One popular strategy is to inform her she can lose much unwanted weight if breast-feeding is practiced later.

The question of postpartum weight loss is much debated. Available data indicate that residue weight loss in most cases follows the pattern described in Table 13-6.

Nutrient Needs

Pregnant and nursing women have heightened needs for many specific nutrients. The RDA for women at three physiological stages are described in Table 13-7. The following sections discuss a pregnant woman's increased needs for protein, calories, iron, calcium, sodium, iodine, and folic acid.

Protein

According to the latest RDA (see Table 13-7), a pregnant woman should consume about 30 g more protein daily than her prepregnancy intake. During pregnancy, she retains nitrogen twice as efficiently as usual, and she deposits about 10 g of protein daily in her tissues, placenta, and fetus. She gains about 2.2 lb (1 kg) of protein during gestation, half of which is deposited in the fetus.

Women eating an adequate amount of protein are more likely to show a satisfactory pregnancy profile. Although heredity determines the limits of the length and lean body mass of a newborn baby, the protein of the mother can influence the fetal outcomes within those limits. Many studies have confirmed that infants born to mothers with an adequate to high-protein intake are taller than those born to mothers with a restricted intake.

Some studies have shown that the clinical risks of a pregnant woman increase as her consumption of protein decreases below the RDA. The smaller babies born to mothers with a low protein intake have higher morbidity and mortality. Some claim that a baby born to a mother with deficient protein intake may suffer brain damage that is irreversible even if adequate food is provided later in life. Although this outcome has been obtained in animals, its application to humans is being debated. However, it is well known that maternal fat storage can spare some protein when protein intake is restricted and when the fetus is growing rapidly.

The mother's protein intake may also affect the child's resistance to disease, for antibodies and other immune substances in the body are synthesized from protein. If those antibodies formed in the mother's body from an exposure to a particular antigen pass through the placenta, they provide the child with passive immunity to the foreign substance.

TABLE 13-6 Residual Weight Gain After Delivery

Time Postpartum	Residual Weight Gain (lb) Over Prepregnant Weight
Immediately after birth	8–9
6 weeks	4–5
6–8 months	0

Note: These data are statistical observations. The tendency to return to prepregnant weight varies with the particular individual.

Calories

The latest RDA (see Table 13-7) indicates that a pregnant woman needs an additional 300 kcal per day. If the woman eats less than 1,800 kcal per day, she will experience a negative nitrogen balance. If so, the fetus will grow at the expense of maternal tissues. Pregnant women with a low caloric intake are more likely to have babies with low birth weight, and, according to some studies, supplementation with calories can reverse the trend.

The actual amount of calories needed to support a healthy pregnancy depends on whether the woman reduces her physical activity during the pregnancy. The entire gestation process uses about 80,000 kcal for the growth of tissues (fetus, placenta, uterus, mother's organs, fats, blood, and so on), increased caloric cost in the woman's work, and an increase in the basal metabolic rate. However, a pregnant woman may reduce her activities by a large amount, such as 50,000 to 56,000 kcal during the 9 months. For the entire period, a woman who so restricted her activities would need only an extra 24,000 to 30,000 kcal. If a woman reduced her activity even more, the caloric intake might not have to be increased by even that much. On the other hand, if a woman works full time until 1 week before delivery, she may need more than the recommended amount of calories.

Iron

The need for iron by a pregnant woman increases about 1 mg per day over the latest RDA of 18 mg per day. A woman's need for iron increases greatly during pregnancy for a number of reasons: blood loss (spotting and hemorrhage during and after delivery), increased nutrient loads to be transported, and increased oxygen demands by more tissues. During the second to eighth months of pregnancy, the woman's blood volume increases by 20% to 30%.

The lack of menstruation during gestation partially offsets the increased needs for iron. In addition, during pregnancy iron absorption increases to 25% to 30% from a normal of 10%. This increase occurs during the second half of pregnancy, when the placenta permits iron transfer to the fetus.

Iron deficiency during pregnancy may occur for a number of reasons. A woman will be deficient in iron if she fails to replenish her body after repeated pregnancies. Very few women have a bone marrow storage of iron. Those who have been on a low-flesh diet for a long time before pregnancy—for example, with 10% or less of their caloric intake from animal products—have a high incidence of iron deficiency. Many of them are anemic at the beginning of pregnancy. Those who eat 25% or more of their calories from animal sources experience less risk of iron deficiency and present a good iron nutriture at conception. The best recommendation is to eat an adequate amount of iron before pregnancy so that there is a large storage.

Even a high intake of iron may not be absorbed well, however. For example, iron is absorbed poorly from cereals and readily from animal muscles. Also, a large intake of oxalic acid or phytic acid will decrease iron absorption (see Chapter 7). And the practice of pica—eating nonfood items, such as ashes, starch, or paint—may also decrease the absorption of iron. Some women of low socioeconomic status in the southern states are known to practice pica.

Iron deficiency during pregnancy may cause anemia in both the mother and the newborn. For example, teenage mothers frequently show low blood hemoglobin—less than 10 g of hemo-

TABLE 13-7   1980 RDAs for a 25-year-old Woman at Three Physiological Stages

Nutrient	Daily Amount Needed	Additional Daily Amount Needed	
		Pregnancy	Lactation
Energy (kcal)	2,000	300	500
Protein (g)	44	30	20
Vitamin A (μg)	800	200	400
Vitamin D (IU)	200	200	200
Vitamin E (mg)	8	2	3
Vitamin C (mg)	60	20	40
Vitamin B_1 (mg)	1.0	0.4	0.5
Vitamin B_2 (mg)	1.2	0.3	0.5
Niacin (mg)	13	2	5
Vitamin B_6 (mg)	2.0	0.6	0.5
Folic acid (μg)	400	400	100
Vitamin B_{12} (μg)	3.0	1	1
Calcium (mg)	800	400	400
Phosphorus (mg)	800	400	400
Magnesium (mg)	300	150	150
Iron (mg)	18	>18*	>18*
Zinc (mg)	15	5	10
Iodine (mg)	150	25	50

*The excess need cannot be supplied by a regular diet. Supplementation is needed.

globin per 100 mL blood. This will lead to anemia (see Chapter 7). If the mother is deficient in iron, the baby will have little iron stored. This is very risky since milk is relatively low in iron, and in the first 1 to 3 months the child depends on the iron accumulated during conception.

Iron deficiency anemia is the most common form of anemia during pregnancy and puerperium. The related anemia due to moderate and acute blood loss is also common. Iron deficiency anemia occurs in 15% to 20% of pregnant women, and about 90% to 95% of pregnant women with anemia have the iron-deficient type. Although iron deficiency anemia is the most common systemic complication of iron deficiency in pregnancy, it is rarely the most severe.

Anemia during pregnancy can be microcytic (from lack of iron) and macrocytic (from lack of folic acid). The two forms of deficiency potentiate each other, so iron and folic acid supplements give better results than iron alone. If anemia from iron or folic acid deficiency is unchecked, it

can be severe and life-threatening to both mother and child. If it results from a dietary lack, appropriate corrective measures must be instituted.

The recommended dose of iron supplementation during pregnancy is 30 to 60 mg (150 to 300 mg ferrous sulfate) per day for the last 6 months of pregnancy. This builds body storage and satisfies the need of the fetus. In general, three tablets of ferrous sulfate or fumarate or six tablets of ferrous gluconate will provide about 200 mg of iron and are prescribed by some doctors. The supplementation is given not later than the second trimester and continues until the end of lactation or 1 month after delivery if the mother is not nursing. If prenatal care begins at mid-pregnancy, some clinicians recommend 300 mg of ferrous sulfate per day. Table 13-8 gives the level of iron supplementation recommended by some practitioners.

There is no evidence that controlled iron supplements given during pregnancy are harmful to the mother or child. Although iron is occa-

TABLE 13-8   Some Guidelines for Iron Supplementation During Pregnancy

Percent of Dietary Calories from Animal Sources	Body Iron Status at Beginning of Pregnancy	Daily Iron Supplement (mg)
30	Good	30
25	Below average	60
10	Deficiency prevalent, anemia	120–240

sionally injected, most clinicians avoid this practice unless clinical evaluations warrant, since some patients have adverse reactions to this procedure. However, patients with a profound depletion of body iron or who consistently fail to take prescribed tablets are likely to receive this treatment.

Calcium

Many women maintain adequate calcium levels during pregnancy without supplementation. Studies have confirmed that during the last months of pregnancy, the absorption rate of calcium is doubled and its excretion decreased. If the mother takes in an adequate amount of vitamin D and calcium, her blood calcium is maintained at an appropriate level. However, a low intake of vitamin D must be balanced by a higher intake of calcium. All other factors that regulate the absorption of this mineral also apply during pregnancy (see Chapter 7). One important note is the effect of emotional stress. If the mother is emotionally stressed, as occurs frequently in teenage pregnancy, calcium absorption may decrease without a compensating increase because of pregnancy.

The deposition of calcium increases daily during pregnancy, with 24 g deposited in the fetus in the last 3 months of gestation. This accounts for two-thirds of the total calcium in its body. An infant born deficient in calcium will suffer rickets and may also have serious and irreparable harm to the deciduous and permanent teeth. However, if the mother has a low blood calcium level, the fetus can, within limits, draw on the woman's bones. An infant 2 months premature will be grossly deficient in calcium and highly susceptible to rickets.

Since jaws and teeth are formed during the last part of gestation and the first year of infancy, the presence of appropriate amounts of calcium and phosphorus during this time is very important. Otherwise, malformed jaws and teeth may result and the teeth may also be more susceptible to decay. A disturbance in calcium and phosphorus nutrition during pregnancy or the first year of life may partly explain the poor dental conditions in many underdeveloped countries. The children may have crowded, unsymmetrical teeth of low quality.

In some women, leg cramps during pregnancy result from a low intake of calcium or a high intake of phosphorus (from milk, eggs, and meat); see Chapter 7 for the rationale. These women will benefit from calcium supplement. Some clinicians also suggest that mild to moderate calcium deficiency may cause restlessness, muscle twitching, insomnia, walking difficulty, pain in the thigh and back, and excess movement or activity of the fetus, although the cause and effect relationship has not been documented.

Other clinicians have proposed that calcium deficiency may predispose the woman to uterine inertia during labor. They feel that the weak uterus fails to mold the fetal head through the rim of the pelvis, resulting in a difficult delivery. However, direct evidence supporting this claim is not available. On the other hand, a woman may possess an unsatisfactory pelvis if she had rickets

TABLE 13-9   Water-soluble Vitamins and Pregnancy

Vitamin	Remarks
C	Requirement increases during pregnancy; can cross placenta freely. Deficiency during pregnancy may lead to easy rupture of fetal membrane and increased newborn mortality rate. Excessive intake during pregnancy is suspected to lead to a higher requirement in the newborn.
B_1	Requirement increases during pregnancy because of a higher consumption of calories; a woman can retain more B_1 in the tissues. There is a claim that a large dose of this vitamin can alleviate the symptoms of morning sickness.
B_2	Requirement increases during pregnancy. Deficiency in a pregnant animal can cause birth defects in the offspring.
B_6	Requirement increases during pregnancy. Blood level decreases when some brands of oral contraceptive pills are used. Pregnant women who used these pills may have a low storage of the vitamin. Supplementation during pregnancy has been recommended, although the practice is not common. There is a claim that a large dose of this vitamin can alleviate the symptoms of morning sickness.
B_{12}	Although absorption increases during pregnancy, the fetus uses up a large amount. An inadequate intake reduces the blood level of this vitamin, which returns to normal after pregnancy. A woman who smokes has a smaller body storage than nonsmokers. The fetus can draw from its mother's minimal storage even if she is deficient in this vitamin, and a newborn baby has a fair storage of this vitamin. There is a suggestion that the baby may be premature if the mother's body storage is very low.

as a child, although the exact form and shape of the pelvis depends on the age and development of the child when she suffers rickets. Whether the child spends time sitting, walking, or lying flat also determines how the pelvic bones are formed under an abnormal deposition of calcium.

A woman may also have an unsatisfactory pelvis because of combined gross calcium and vitamin D deficiency. Repeated pregnancy and long-term lactation without proper nutrient replenishment may also contribute to a deformed or subnormal pelvis. Though uncommon in the United States, all these undesirable conditions occur frequently in underdeveloped countries, where a normal vaginal delivery is often followed by a difficult one, which may require a cesarean.

Calcium supplementation during pregnancy may or may not be necessary, depending on the woman. If necessary, calcium gluconate or lactate four times daily (0.5 g or 1.0 g each time) is recommended.

Sodium

Sodium intake during pregnancy has long been of concern. Obstetricians are well aware that all pregnant women accumulate fluid to varying degrees. Since edema during pregnancy results partly from the retention of body sodium, many clinicians recommend that patients decrease their salt intake. However, experimental animal studies have recently concluded that a re-

TABLE 13-10   Fat-soluble Vitamins and Pregnancy

Vitamin	Remarks
A	In animals, deficiency or excess of this vitamin during pregnancy can produce adverse effects in newborns, including birth defects. In humans, a pregnant woman deficient in this vitamin may give birth to a child with arrested bone growth. It is claimed that excess intake during pregnancy may produce birth defects.
D	The intake of vitamin D during pregnancy must be carefully evaluated, since most foods are relatively low in this vitamin unless they are fortified. Deficiency or excess of this vitamin during pregnancy can be harmful to the newborn and may cause birth defects.
E	Although much is known about this vitamin concerning animal reproduction, little information is available concerning human pregnancy. By eating a well-balanced diet, the pregnant woman receives an adequate intake. Because very little vitamin E can cross the placenta, the infant has very little storage.
K	Hemorrhage in some mothers and newborns is caused by a lack of vitamin K. Vitamin K in the appropriate form and dosage can alleviate the bleeding problems. The wrong form and dosage of the vitamin can harm an infant.

duced salt intake during gestation can produce adverse effects in both mother and offspring. In the last few years, most medical and scientific authorities have therefore proposed that salt intake should not be restricted indiscriminately.

Diuretics have been used to eliminate body fluid for many years, but some diuretics are also known to pose a hazard to both mother and child (see Chapters 16, 27, and 28). At present, only a small number of diuretics are recommended for use during pregnancy, and physicians are generally advised to avoid prescribing even these drugs unless it is absolutely necessary. Further, the combined use of diuretics and salt restriction is inadvisable unless fully justified.

Iodine

The need for iodine increases during pregnancy, partly because of enhanced excretion. Iodine deficiency has been observed in pregnant mothers, especially teenage ones, and in newborn infants. In general, goiter in a mother undoubtedly increases the infant's risk of iodine deficiency. And any restriction of salt intake results in a reduced consumption of iodine. On the other hand, excess iodine intake during pregnancy is not uncommon. This includes a careless and excessive intake of substances that contain a high level of iodine, such as cough medicine, nutrient supplements, and sea salt. A high iodine intake can cause the mother's thyroid gland to enlarge as well as pose a risk to the fetus.

Folic acid

A detailed discussion of vitamin nutrition during pregnancy is not possible here. Tables 13-9 and 13-10 summarize some salient points. A brief analysis is provided below on heightened folic acid needs during gestation.

According to the 1980 RDA, a pregnant woman needs 800 μg of folic acid per day, 400 μg for maintenance and 400 μg for correction of anemia. As discussed in Chapter 6, folic acid deficiency results in megaloblastic anemia, which is

TABLE 13-11 Protective Foods for Women

Protective Food*	Recommended No. of Daily Servings		
	Nonpregnant, nonlactating	Pregnant	Lactating
Milk and milk products	3	4	5
Protein products	3	4	4
Grain products	3	3	3
Vegetables and fruits			
Rich in vitamin C	1	1	1
Green leafy vegetables	2	2	2
Others	1	1	1

*The grouping follows the basic four food groups (also see Chapter 10).

characterized by such symptoms as lethargy, depression, nausea, and progressive loss of appetite. Vomiting, diarrhea, glossitis, and gingivitis are also frequently encountered, and pallor is occasionally detected in some patients. For example, macrocytic anemia due to folic acid deficiency occurs in about 2% to 3% of pregnant women in this country. The incidence is much higher in many other countries: 2% to 6% in England and over 50% in India.

Folic acid deficiency anemia during pregnancy may be responsible for such adverse clinical effects as a small placenta, premature labor, low birth weight, abruptio placentae, and hemorrhage. Other suggestions that the woman may suffer fetal wastage or adsorption, miscarriage, or abortion or that the newborn may have birth defects have not been documented.

Folic acid deficiency anemia may occur during late pregnancy, the postpartum period, and lactation. Its occurrence in late pregnancy suggests that the person was deficient in the vitamin during the early stages of pregnancy or even before pregnancy. It is more common in pregnant women who are also deficient in iron, probably because these patients have an overall poor diet. Other susceptible individuals are multiparas over age 30, those with multiple and twin pregnancies, and those who fail to comply with doctor's instructions to take the vitamin supplement.

One major cause of folic acid deficiency is inadequate dietary intake, although it may also occur in individuals who eat a balanced diet. Individuals who eat plenty of meat, eggs, fish, and green leafy vegetables and obtain sufficient calories usually do not have trouble with folic acid nutrition. Women who do not eat animal products or adequate calories are at risk. There is speculation that women suffering megaloblastic anemia are anorexic, resulting in decreased folic acid intake. If so, periodically consuming foods rich in folic acid will probably reverse the anorexia associated with the deficiency. Hopefully, this will prevent further depletion of body folic acid.

The decision to supplement folic acid intake during pregnancy is determined by such factors as laboratory evidence of megaloblastic anemia, twin pregnancy, malaria, or other special conditions. However, many physicians who attend pregnant women routinely prescribe folic acid supplement. The supplementation should start during the second trimester and continue through lactation. The usual supplement is 5 to 10 mg of oral folic acid daily. If the anemia shows no response, parenteral vitamin administration may be needed. For some patients, providing iron simultaneously improves the absorption of folic acid. In cases of severe dietary limitation, a protein supplement can enhance the effectiveness of folic acid supplement.

Megaloblastic anemia during pregnancy is usually not severe or life-threatening unless the patient also has toxemia or systemic infection. If the condition is severe and the patient is unresponsive to folic acid treatment, blood transfusion may be necessary.

TABLE 13-12   Sample Meal Plan for a Pregnant Woman

Breakfast	Lunch	Dinner
Milk or milk products, 1 serving	Milk or milk products, 1 serving	Milk or milk products, 1 serving
Fruits or vegetables rich in vitamin C, 1 serving	Other fruits and vegetables, 1 serving	Green leafy vegetables, 2 servings
Grain products	Protein products, 1 serving	Protein products, 2 servings
	Grain products, 2 servings	
Snack*	**Snack***	
Milk or milk products, ½ serving	Milk or milk products, ½ serving	
Protein products, 1 serving		

*The snacks may be consumed at any time of the day.

TABLE 13-13   Sample Menu for a Pregnant Woman Including Protective (Basic) and Supplemental Foods

Breakfast	Lunch	Dinner
Orange juice, 4 oz	Sandwich	Roast beef, 6 oz
Oatmeal, ½ c	Whole wheat bread, 2 slices	Egg noodles, ½ c, with sauteed poppy seeds
Brown sugar, 1–2 t	Tuna fish, ½ c	Cut asparagus, ¾ c
Milk, 8 oz	Diced celery with onion	Salad
Coffee or tea	Mayonnaise	Torn spinach, 1 c
	Lettuce	Sliced mushrooms
	Banana, 1 small	Radishes
	Milk, 8 oz	Oil
	Coffee or tea	Vinegar
		Milk, 8 oz
		Coffee or tea
Snack	**Snack**	
Salted peanuts, ½ c	Oatmeal raisin cookies, 2	
Milk, 4 oz	Milk, 4 oz	

Diet

To satisfy the RDA, a pregnant woman needs a well-balanced and nutritious diet. Table 13-11 compares the recommended daily servings from the four food groups for a woman in three physiological conditions: nonpregnant, pregnant, and lactating. Table 13-12 describes a sample meal plan, and Table 13-13 a sample menu for a pregnant woman. Note that Table 13-12 includes mainly foods from the basic food guides, while Table 13-13 includes protective and supplemental foods.

According to the RDAs (see Table 13-7), a pregnant woman should eat a diet that is slightly higher in calories and greatly increased in other nutrients compared with her prepregnant diet. Most women find it difficult to fulfill these requirements. An aggressive program in nutrition education is important to convince the woman to eat low-caloric but nutrient-dense foods. Many women find it difficult to comply with this careful eating pattern over 9 or 10 months because of the physical, physiological, and emotional stresses of pregnancy.

The use of nutrient supplements during pregnancy has frequently been debated. According to the Food and Drug Administration, the intakes of five minerals and ten vitamins are permitted to be 50% to 150% above the U.S. RDAs (see Chapter 10), because a pregnant woman's need for these nutrients is greater. The supplements most frequently prescribed are iron, folic acid, and calcium. Vitamin B_{12} is also prescribed to those patients who have been vegetarians for a long period. However, it is not uncommon for a woman to react adversely to supplements, including vitamins and iron. To reduce side effects, the drugs should be taken with food.

Using nutrient supplements indiscriminately during pregnancy has been criticized for two reasons. One is that many commercial products are low in some nutrients and high in others. Nonprescribed items may therefore be unnecessary and wasteful. Second, the excessive intake of some nutrients is undesirable. For example, vitamins A and D in large doses may harm the mother and child. And as stated earlier, a newborn infant may be conditioned to a higher need of vitamin C if the pregnant woman overconsumes this nutrient.

Nutritionally Related Clinical Problems

Medical records have indicated that a pregnant woman may encounter a number of minor clinical problems that are food and nutrition related. Some examples are discussed in the following sections.

Abnormal appetite and food preferences

Many pregnant women experience changes in appetite. During the first 3 or 4 months, the appetite and thirst in a pregnant woman are likely to increase, although morning sickness will occasionally reduce her appetite for a brief period, especially during early pregnancy. How-

ever, the woman is still hungry and wants to eat; some can eat a huge amount of food. Experience shows that small, frequent meals reduce the nausea and vomiting of morning sickness as well as reduce the discomfort and distended stomach caused by frequent large meals. Although the ravenous appetite must be satisfied with foods, all pregnant women should develop good eating patterns and avoid extremes, especially in food quantity.

For reasons not yet understood, the taste preferences of a pregnant woman also change. She may develop a craving for some foods and a dislike for others. Within limits, these preferences should be respected. One exception is pica. Many pregnant women, especially those in the South, develop pica for unknown reasons. This practice should be prohibited.

Morning sickness

Morning sickness is the vomiting and nausea experienced by some pregnant women, which is usually worst on rising in the morning. It varies from mild to severe. Severe symptoms usually accompany toxemia; in this case the condition is known as pernicious vomiting of pregnancy, or hyperemesis gravidarum.

In mild to moderate conditions, morning or evening nausea and vomiting usually begin soon after the first missed menstrual period (fifth or sixth week of gestation) and cease after the fourth or fifth month. The effects of this clinical reaction are rarely severe. About three-fourths of women, most of them in their second or later pregnancy, complain of nausea and vomiting. Nutritional deficiencies because of vomiting are seldom noted.

The cause of morning sickness is unknown. Some clinicians and psychiatrists suggest that the vomiting results from a poor psychological adaptation to motherhood, emotional conflicts, resentment, and ambivalence. Nausea and vomiting during pregnancy may also result from clinical disorders such as hernias, ulcers, hepatitis, and gall bladder inflammation. Vomiting is definitely more frequent in patients with multiple or hydatidiform pregnancies.

Experienced clinicians suggest certain procedures that sometimes help to reduce mild nausea and vomiting. The patient should be assured that the symptoms are common and that severe ill effects are not expected. Simple dietary modifications are sometimes effective. Patients feel better when given dry foods at frequent intervals. The patient's aversion to certain foods must be respected. A common practice is to restrict fats, odorous foods, and spiced dishes. Some patients feel better when they drink distilled water or when they eat dry crackers in bed before rising. Some drugs are also effective, such as sedatives and antiemetics. Vitamin B_6 (50 mg per day) is effective for some patients, but the use of any drug must be carefully evaluated before prescribing.

Persistent and severe vomiting episodes during pregnancy are classified as hyperemesis gravidarum. This clinical disorder, which can be fatal if not controlled, affects about 2 in 1,000 pregnant women who have to be hospitalized. The causes are unknown. The resulting partial starvation from a loss of appetite may result in dehydration, acidosis or ketosis, weight loss, jaundice, and nutrient deficiencies. Additional complications include toxic hepatitis (jaundice), eye damage, and hemorrhage.

Medical treatment for hyperemesis gravidarum is stringent. The patient is hospitalized in a private room, confined to bed, and permitted no bathroom privileges. The patient is isolated from visitors until she stops vomiting and is able to eat and hold foods down. Abstinence from food and beverages is limited to 2 days, after which intravenous fluids with vitamins and protein supplements are given. If symptoms do not subside in 2 days, a well-balanced and formula-defined diet is given through tube-feeding via slow drip (see Chapter 23). If the patient's condition continues to deteriorate despite this medical therapy, the doctor may order a therapeutic abortion. Such a decision by the doctor depends on the urgent indications, such as jaundice, hemorrhage, blindness, and delirium.

Faintness

During early pregnancy there may be periods of faintness, a temporary and sudden loss of consciousness because of a reduced blood supply to the brain. The causes vary. One may be postural hypotension, which can cut off oxygen transiently to the brain. For example, when a woman stands or sits in a warm room for a long time, the blood is pooled in the legs, spleen, and pelvic areas. Another factor that may be responsible for fainting or light-headedness is hypoglycemia before or between meals, which is common during pregnancy.

Experienced clinicians suggest certain guidelines to reduce the risk of fainting. The patient should practice deep breathing and be constantly mobile if possible. She should move her legs vigorously and change positions slowly. If hypoglycemia is a problem, she should eat small, frequent meals, perhaps 5 to 7 meals a day. She should have food (such as candy bars or an orange) available to reduce hypoglycemia. To manage fainting due to hypotension, she should have easy access to stimulants such as coffee, tea, spirits of ammonia, or even amphetamines.

Urinary symptoms

A woman in late pregnancy may have to urinate frequently and urgently and be subject to stress incontinence. These symptoms result from pressure of the fetus on the bladder, which is already reduced in capacity. If urination is painful or bloody, there may be infection of the urinary tract. Convenient and effective bladder sedatives are available. If urinary urgency is particularly troublesome, the patient should generally avoid tea, coffee, spices, and alcoholic beverages.

Heartburn

Heartburn—also known as pyrosis or "acid indigestion"—is caused by the regurgitation of stomach contents along the gastroesophageal tract. Stomach secretion and motility are simultaneously reduced. Upward protrusion of the uterine fundus during late pregnancy can displace the stomach and further aggravate the heartburn. As a result of diaphragmatic hiatus hernia during late pregnancy, 15% of pregnant patients experience severe heartburn, which leads to nausea and vomiting. After the seventh or eighth month of pregnancy, some patients suffer "tenting" of the diaphragm and "flaring" of the lower ribs. Delivery spontaneously eliminates the hernia.

Treatment for heartburn may include several measures. Gastrointestinal motility and secretion may be stimulated by drugs. Stomach contents that are responsible for the heartburn can be "digested" by ingesting the appropriate acidifying agents. However, hydrochloric acid solutions should be avoided, since they may harm the teeth, as should antacids during early pregnancy, when the stomach acid level is already low. Some pregnant women state that hard candy, hot tea, and postural adjustments sometimes relieve the symptoms of heartburn. Finally, during late pregnancy, antacids such as aluminum hydroxide can reduce stomach irritation.

Muscle cramps

Cramping or "knotting" of the lower parts (calves, thighs, or buttocks) occurs in some women between the fourth and ninth months of gestation. For some unknown reason, the incidence decreases during the last month. The cramping occurs suddenly after sleep or recumbency. Many patients agree that the cramping may be precipitated when the legs and feet are stretched with pointed toes, a maneuver that results in a sudden shortening of the muscles.

One cause of cramping is suspected to be a high phosphorus or low calcium level (or both) in the blood. This imbalance may be due to a low dietary intake of calcium or excessive consumption of phosphorus in meat, cheese, and potatoes. A calcium supplement such as dicalcium phosphate is not recommended, since it contains excess phosphorus. Other causes of leg cramps are tiredness and slow blood circulation.

The immediate treatment for leg cramps is simple. The woman should stand barefooted on a cold surface such as a tiled bathroom floor and massage cramped muscles by rubbing or kneading the foot in the direction that will relieve the cramps. Alternatively, warm or hot compresses can be applied to the affected areas.

During early pregnancy, a woman can take preventive measures against muscle cramps, which are also useful in the long-term treatment of the problem. First, she can increase her calcium intake (for example, drinking more milk) and decrease her phosphorus intake (for instance, eating less meat). She should stop using any prescribed or over-the-counter medications that contain excess phosphorus. The blood phosphorus level can be lowered by drugs such as aluminum hydroxide, which decrease its absorption. A woman can also avoid walking on the balls of the feet. Walking on the balls of the feet causes the toes to point forward, which can precipitate cramping.

Mild edema

About two out of three women in late pregnancy develop mild edema of the lower extremities (such as the ankles) that is unrelated to toxemia. Edema of this nature results from sodium and water retention because of one or more of the following: (1) venous congestion from the presence of varicose veins; (2) increased blood levels of steroid hormones from the adrenal glands, ovaries, and placenta; (3) increased venous pressure in the legs; (4) sitting or standing for too long; or (5) the use of elastic garters.

There is no sure treatment for the edema. Therapy is largely preventive and symptomatic. Some common measures are sleeping with the legs and feet elevated, avoiding tight clothing that interferes with venous return, and providing the varicose veins with elastic supports. Although restricting salt intake is a popular procedure, salt may be used with caution. Blood hormonal levels may play a part in the edema, but they cannot be treated at present.

Constipation

Some pregnant women are plagued by constipation. Bowel sluggishness during pregnancy is caused by a reduced motility of intestinal smooth muscle, which in turn may result from the presence of too much sex steroid hormones. The enlarging uterus also displaces and applies pressure upon parts of the intestine. In some patients, constipation may cause hemorrhoids and worsen diverticular disorders.

Treatment procedures include changes in life-style and specific medical measures, as discussed in Chapter 24. For example, general measures include good bowel habits, a large intake of roughage and fluid, and a consistent exercise program. Clinical therapy includes the use of laxatives. However, strong purges must be cautiously employed since they may induce labor, and certain medications such as mineral oil may prevent absorption of fat-soluble vitamins.

Abdominal pain

A pregnant woman may suffer abdominal pain, which is separated into two categories. In one type, the pain results from increased pressure. The patient has a sagging or dragging feeling, characterized by a pelvic heaviness. The uterus is heavy and presses on the abdominal wall and other pelvic structures. The woman can relieve the pain by using a heat compress or maternity girdle, taking frequent rest periods, or sitting or lying down. The second type of abdominal pain results from gas, bloating, and bowel cramping. The swelling uterus compresses and displaces the bowel with the intestine losing tension and strength. This can result in constipation and other intestinal discomforts. Large meals, greasy foods, excess roughage, and cold beverages can also produce the reactions and should be avoided if found to be troublesome. Frequent small meals can relieve some of the symptoms; constipation is managed as indicated above. Some patients find that a frequent change of body position is also helpful.

Teeth and gum problems

Dental decay is more common in pregnant than nonpregnant women. This may be due to reduced oral hygiene and increased sugary food consumption during pregnancy. Also, some pregnant women suffer from gum infection, which may result from a combination of poor oral hygiene and hormonal imbalance. Some women develop edema of the gums, and about 50% to 70% of pregnant women have bleeding gums. The tendency to bleeding on the slightest touch is due to the high vascularity of the underlying connective tissues. In some patients, areas of inflamed gums become so large that they are termed tumors. All gingival changes are most marked in the second and third trimester. Within 2 months after delivery, the severity of the gingivitis subsides, and the gums return to normal condition given proper oral hygiene. More information on this important topic may be obtained from the references at the back of this book.

Other nutrition-related problems

Recently, it has been documented that excess alcohol consumption during pregnancy may result in the "fetal alcohol syndrome," in which the child may develop abnormal facial features, as shown in Figure 13-2. The uncontrolled use of alcoholic beverages during pregnancy is not recommended.

The current debate over the potential negative effects (including birth defects) of excess coffee drinking during pregnancy on the developing fetus is not yet settled.

NUTRITION AND LACTATION

What are the trends of breast-feeding in this country? Currently, no one knows the exact incidence of breast-feeding, even for newborns, but observers feel that more women are choosing to breast-feed their babies now than in the recent past. As an illustration, Figure 13-3 relates the incidence of breast-feeding to the mother's education between 1973 and 1975; it shows a rise for mothers at two broad educational levels. The sections that follow briefly discuss the decision of whether to breast-feed and the special nutrient needs and diet of women who do choose to nurse their babies.

The Decision to Breast-feed

Some nutritionists suggest that a woman should make a decision on breast-feeding either before or during mid-pregnancy. Individuals making the decision may be influenced by a number of factors, including the opinion of nurses and doctors and the opportunity to have physical contact with the newborn immediately after birth. The complex nutritional issues of breast versus formula feedings are discussed in the chapter on infant nutrition (Chapter 14).

The production and secretion of breast milk are influenced by many factors. To make an adequate quantity of milk, the woman must have (1) a strong desire to breast-feed; (2) plenty of support and encouragement from family, relatives, nurses, and doctors; (3) a satisfactory nutritional status; (4) a minimal knowledge of the mecha-

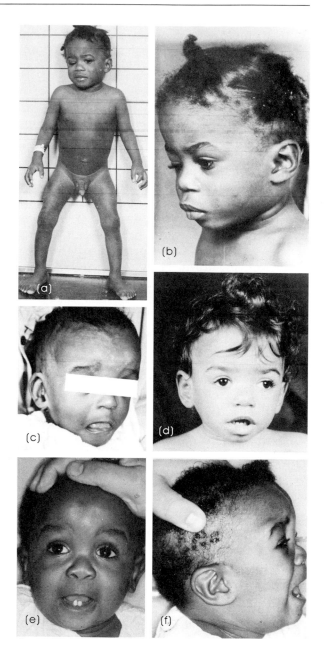

FIGURE 13-2   The fetal alcohol syndrome. (From J. J. Mulvihill et al., "Fetal Alcohol Syndrome: Seven New Cases," *Am. J. Obs. Gyn.* 125[1976]: 937) (a, b) Age 23 months, 18 lb; occipital flattening and balding, right ocular ptosis, a high-pitched cry, left cryptorchidism (inguinal testis), lack of complete extension of both knees, right transitional simian crease, and a small cafe. The mother had been an alcoholic (wine and beer) for 10 years. (c) Age 15 months, dysmorphic features, low-set ears with prominent antihelix, a 6 × 6 cm anterior fontanel, a grade 2/6 systolic murmur, delayed psychomotor development. The mother had been an alcoholic (gin and beer) for 8 years. (d) Age 20 months, with a mental age of 16 months and a motor age of 15 months; skeletal defects including a larger anterior fontanel, bilateral talipes calcaneovalgus, and, in the hands, polydactyly and hyperplasia of the second and fifth middle phalanges. The mother, an alcoholic for 10 years, during pregnancy consumed 6 cans of beer and a quarter liter of Scotch daily, smoked heavily, ate poorly, and in the first trimester, took decongestants and aspirin for a chronic cold. (e, f) Age 6 months, a 2 × 2 cm cutaneous hemangioma of the left forearm and signs of neurologic impairment (tremulousness, occasional cortical thumbs, and slight rigidity of upper limbs). The mother had been an alcoholic for 3 years.

nism of milk production, especially the process of "letdown" and suckling; (5) an adequate fluid intake; and (6) a nutritious and balanced diet, especially sufficient calories.

A woman may make more milk if she has a large body or breast size. If a woman has very little breast tissue for any reason, including severe malnourishment as a child, she may produce very little milk. A healthy mother will make more milk if nursing is frequent. If breastfeeding is constantly interfered with by formula supplements, less milk is produced because of decreased suckling. A woman also makes more milk when her breast skin temperature is high. Contrary to popular beliefs, substances such as garlic and beer have not been shown to influence milk production.

Nutrient Needs

What are the optimal nutrient requirements for a nursing mother? We know that all essential nutrients are needed for the proper storage, repair, and maintenance of her body and the produc-

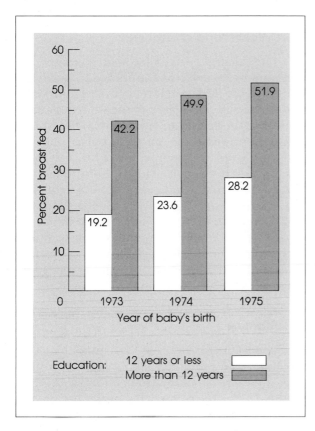

FIGURE 13-3 Trends in breast-feeding. Source: G. E. Hendershot, *Trends in Breast Feeding* (Washington, D.C.: National Center for Health Statistics, 1980), U.S. Department of Health, Education, and Welfare publication No. (PHS) 80-1250.

tion of milk that is nutritionally sound. However, there is a lack of data on the rate and volume of milk production and the variation in nutritional composition of milk formed at different times (colostrum, transitional, and mature milk). Although some nutrient levels in breast milk are fairly consistent, others vary according to the woman's physiological condition, the time of the day, and the length of time after delivery.

Information from underdeveloped countries confirms that a woman can breast-feed for a prolonged period (3 or 4 years) and the child will still receive good-quality milk. It is assumed, however, that such milk is produced at the expense of the mother's nutrient reserve, since these women do not eat adequately. It is only logical and physiologically sound that a woman breast-feeding should protect herself by eating a nutritious diet if she can afford it. It is generally

agreed that most nutrients in the milk can be derived from the mother's storage, including vitamins, minerals, calories, and protein.

The RDA values are used as a guide to determine a nursing mother's nutrient needs, as indicated in Table 13-7. A nursing mother's diet is nearly the same as that of a pregnant woman, although nutrient needs are somewhat higher since the child's demand for milk increases daily with its growth. The mother needs more protein, vitamins, minerals, and especially calories to assure that the milk has a full complement of nutrients and to rebuild her own body's nutrient storage. The woman's needs vary with her nutritional status, body size, the rate, volume, and efficiency of milk production, and infant demand.

For the first 1 to 2 weeks after childbirth, a woman is recovering and may tire easily and have a poor appetite. However, she still has to work hard to care for the infant, who frequently wakes her up at night. Under such stress, her nutritional storage before and during pregnancy will contribute substantially to the proper production of milk. However, if a woman's nutritional status is borderline and she fails to eat adequately, nursing will cause her to be deficient in nutrients. The sections below discuss the nursing mother's needs for calories, fat, iron, calcium, and vitamins, and the appearance of these nutrients in her breast milk.

Calories

An infant needs about 850 mL of milk per day; to manufacture 100 mL, the mother spends about 90 to 100 kcal. In general, the mother's ability to make milk is 60% to 80% efficient, since energy is needed to nurse and secrete the milk. The total daily caloric cost will be about 760 to 850 kcal, of which about 150 to 170 kcal are needed for making the milk and about 600 to 700 kcal are actually contained in the milk. After childbirth, the fat reserve in the woman's body provides about 200 to 400 kcal. Thus, if the woman eats an additional 500 kcal per day, she receives the total of 700 to 900 kcal needed for nursing.

About 2 to 3 months after childbirth, the nursing mother should return to her prepregnant weight, although she will typically eat 500 to 1,000 kcal more in foods. Experience has convinced many women that nursing helps them lose weight and develop a good appetite. If the food supply is adequate, the woman will usually eat well, lose weight, and maintain a trim figure even after several pregnancies.

Fat

The 1980 RDAs do not specify the fat intake needed during nursing. The fat level of her milk does not reflect the mother's intake, although the type of fat eaten is reflected in the milk. For instance, a large intake of polyunsaturated fatty acids increases their quantity in the milk. About 6% to 9% of the caloric contribution of breast milk is from linoleic acid. Fatty acids contained in breast milk are primarily of medium chain length, although small amounts of 10-carbon ones also occur.

Iron

Iron need during nursing changes. During the first 3 to 4 months of nursing, an iron supplement plus an adequate diet assures that the woman's depleted storage is replenished. Until menstruation returns, a nursing woman after the first 3 to 4 months is likely to be in good iron nutrition if she eats a nutritious and well-balanced diet, and she will not need a supplement. (Physiologically, a nursing mother is not expected to menstruate. However, some nursing mothers do have menstrual periods.) As discussed in Chapter 7, a menstruating woman often has difficulty taking in an adequate amount of iron, even when eating a satisfactory diet.

Within limits, the iron content of milk is not influenced by the woman's intake. For the first 3 months after birth, the baby should have a good storage of iron, and the intake from breast milk will be adequate.

Calcium and phosphorus

The calcium need of a woman increases during nursing, partly for the milk and partly for body storage. Calcium level in breast milk varies and is not directly related to the woman's intake. However, the secretion of calcium in breast milk is a continuous drain on the woman's calcium reserve. If it is not compensated for, a negative calcium balance will be evident. Additional complicating factors include a continuous reduction in calcium absorption months after cessation of breast-feeding, and an imbalanced intake of phosphorus. A nursing mother's dietary intakes of calcium and phosphorus must be carefully evaluated and corrected if she shows a negative balance for these two elements.

Vitamins

The RDAs for vitamins for a nursing mother are about 150% those of a nonpregnant woman (see Table 13-7). Within limits, the levels of vitamins C, B_1, B_2, B_6, and B_{12} in the breast milk reflect the person's dietary intakes. As in pregnancy, a nursing mother's folic acid nutriture requires careful monitoring. A comparison of the vitamin contents of breast and cow's milk is given in Chapter 14.

Diet

What should a nursing mother eat? Table 13-11 gives recommended amounts of protective foods for a lactating woman. Table 13-14 gives a sample meal plan, and Table 13-15 gives a sample menu. If a woman eats according to these regimens, she will receive adequate nutrients.

STUDY QUESTIONS

1. What nutritional deficiencies are common among women entering pregnancy? What health risks are greater among malnourished pregnant women than among well-nourished pregnant women?

2. Describe the currently recommended pattern and extent of weight gain during pregnancy. Why is a fat reserve important?

3. When is weight loss in an overweight woman preferable: before, during, or after pregnancy? Why?

4. What are the risks of being underweight

TABLE 13-14   Sample Meal Plan for a Lactating Woman

Breakfast	Lunch	Dinner
Milk or milk products, 1 serving	Milk or milk products, 1 serving	Milk or milk products, 1 serving
Fruits or vegetables rich in vitamin C, 1 serving	Other fruits or vegetables, 1 serving	Green leafy vegetables, 2 servings
Grain products, 1 serving	Protein products, 1 serving	Protein products, 2 servings
	Grain products, 2 servings	
Snack*	**Snack***	
Milk or milk products, 1 serving	Milk or milk products, 1 serving	
Protein products, 1 serving		

*The snacks may be consumed at any time of the day.

TABLE 13-15   Sample Menu for a Lactating Woman, Including Protective (Basic) and Supplemental Foods

Breakfast	Lunch	Dinner
Orange juice, 4 oz	Sandwich	Roast beef, 6 oz
Oatmeal, ½ c	Whole wheat bread, 2 slices	Egg noodles, ½ c, with sauteed poppy seeds
Brown sugar, 1–2 t	Tuna fish, ½ c	Cut asparagus, ¾ c
Milk, 8 oz	Diced celery	Salad
Coffee or tea	Onion	Torn spinach, 1 c
	Mayonnaise	Sliced mushrooms
	Lettuce	Radishes
	Banana, 1 small	Oil
	Milk, 8 oz	Vinegar
		Milk, 8 oz
		Coffee or tea
Snack	**Snack**	
Salted peanuts, ½ c	Oatmeal raisin cookies, 2	
Milk, 8 oz	Milk, 8 oz	

when entering pregnancy? What advice should such women be given?

5. What nutrient needs are increased during pregnancy? What can be said about the intakes of calcium, sodium, iodine, and vitamins A, D, C, and K during pregnancy?

6. What general dietary advice should be given to a pregnant woman? Plan 1 week's menus for a 25-year-old pregnant woman.

7. Name at least six minor health problems in a pregnant woman that may be related to nutrition. What dietary or related advice may be helpful in each case?

8. How does the recommended diet for a nursing mother differ from that for a pregnant woman?

Chapter 14

Nutrition and the Growing Years

PARENTS AND HEALTH professionals are understandably concerned about the diets of infants, children, and adolescents. The need for nutrients is high during the growing years, and deficiencies at this time can create health problems that persist in later life. In infancy, questions of breast versus bottle-feeding and the introduction of solid foods are important concerns. During childhood, feeding problems, snacking, obesity, food allergies, and nutrient deficiencies are the major issues. Similar problems, aggravated by emotional stress and peer pressure, continue through the adolescent years. Throughout this period, sound nutritional education is crucial for both parents and children to help them make wise food choices.

NUTRITION AND INFANTS

All newborns need an adequate amount of essential nutrients for the proper development of body organs, cells, and tissues. One major index of health for a newborn infant is its growth rate. Table 14-1 shows the weight gain from birth to 1 year old, and Tables 20–23 of the appendix contain standard growth charts for infants at different ages.

Of particular concern to health workers, nutritionists, and parents is the normal development of the child's brain in structure, size, and function. Animal experiments have confirmed that a newborn's brain development can be adversely affected by undernourishment. However, in humans, whether the effect of malnutrition during infancy on mental development and learning potential is permanent has not yet been determined.

As discussed in Chapter 13, the nutritional status of a newborn is partly determined by the health of the mother and her nutrition during pregnancy. However, it has been shown that if a child is born with nutritional problems because of a malnourished mother, there is a good chance of complete recovery if the child receives adequate nutritional care thereafter. This assumes, of course, that the nutritional insult experienced by the infant has not been extreme. High-risk

TABLE 14-1 Weight Gain from Birth to 1 Year Old

Age (mo)	Average Weight Values	
	Weight (lb)	Weight gain rate (lb/mo)
0	7½	1
4–6	15	2
10–12	22–23	3

Note: Consult the appendix for the standard growth grid.

newborns can have a multitude of nutritional problems that may or may not be correctable, as discussed in Chapter 30.

Pros and Cons of Breast-feeding

Ever since World War II, the debate over the pros and cons of the two major types of infant feeding, breast and bottle, has preoccupied the public and scientists. It is still one of the most emotional and controversial issues in nutrition. The following sections discuss the advantages, disadvantages, and techniques of breast-feeding.

Nutritional benefits

There are a number of nutritional benefits associated with breast-feeding. First, the higher level of lactose in breast milk creates a better intestinal environment, and the mild fermentation allows a better bowel movement. The child becomes hungry and eats more frequently. Sometimes lactose can complex with calcium, although synthetic lactose can now be added to commercial formulas due to technological advances. Furthermore, lactose can increase the absorption of amino acids and magnesium, and it is the major contributor of galactose for myelin formation.

Second, breast milk contains a protein-splitting enzyme that is relatively intact, whereas that in formula milk has been destroyed by pasteurization. This enzyme permits better protein digestion in a breast-fed infant. Third, the high level of polyunsaturated fatty acids in breast milk encourages easy digestion and utilization of fat by the infant. Fourth, breast milk tends to contain more vitamin C and B_1, since they are partially destroyed in cow's milk by pasteurization (however, most currently available commercial brands of formula milk are fortified with these nutrients). Finally, observations in many developing countries have confirmed that even a malnourished woman secretes milk of acceptable quality and quantity.

Few allergic incidents

Breast-fed infants tend to develop fewer allergies. Since the intestinal system of an infant just a few weeks old permits the absorption of large protein molecules, absorption of "foreign protein" from cow's milk may directly result in allergic reactions or predispose the child to life-long allergies such as milk-induced colitis.

Anti-infection properties

It has been well documented that breast-fed infants are less likely to develop intestinal infection due to *Escherichia coli*. Because this benefit of breast milk has not been duplicated by any other milk, bottle-fed infants are more likely to develop diarrhea. Clinical observations indicate that diarrhea in a bottle-fed child can be stopped by switching to breast milk from a breast-milk bank or another lactating mother. In the United States and many other countries, the greater morbidity and mortality from diarrhea among bottle-fed as compared with breast-fed infants have been documented for many years. Breast-fed babies also have fewer constipation problems than bottle-fed ones. It is suspected that the higher content of lactose in breast milk may be responsible for this difference.

What are the anti-infective factors in breast milk? No satisfactory answer is available, although there are many theories. Human milk itself is probably not sterile when it reaches the newborn. The sources of bacteria are most likely the nipples and fingers. Nevertheless, breast milk somehow protects infants from infection.

Colostrum, the yellowish fluid that comes before the white milk, is suspected to provide the child's intestinal system with passive immunity. One possibility is that certain colostrum corpuscles or particles that escape destruction by gastric juice and intestinal enzymes are able to reduce the number of intestinal bacteria. Another explanation is based on the presence of macrophages in colostrum that can digest bacteria and viruses. Some believe that colostrum contains lactoferrin, which may inhibit bacterial growth.

Like colostrum, milk may contain lactoferrin, which is suspected to prohibit the growth of bacteria. Breast milk contains the antibody immunoglobulin A (IgA), which is active against *Escherichia coli*. Milk may contain lysozymes, which have an anti-infective property. The presence of *Lactobacillus bifidus* factor in breast milk permits the growth of *Lactobacillus bifidus* (a bacterium), which can directly stop the multiplication of undesirable organisms or indirectly crowd out pathogenic bacteria such as *E. coli* or virus.

Other reports indicate that breast milk can also protect some infants against nonintestinal infection. For instance, breast-fed babies have a lower incidence of respiratory infections. It is suspected that breast milk contains an anti-staphylococcus factor.

Psychological benefits

The psychological benefits of breast-feeding are often cited. For example, many women feel that human milk is designed for human infants and is therefore the best food for them. Women who breast-feed often feel that they have established an important bond with the child. It appears that a woman's desire to breast-feed increases if she is permitted a direct and immediate contact with the child in the delivery room. Such women have a better chance of successful breast-feeding.

Oral muscles and speech development

The process of sucking milk from the breast is different from sucking milk from a bottle. An infant has to work harder to suck milk from the breast. Some suggest that this effort improves the utilization and coordination of the oral muscles, jaws, teeth, and tongue. The consequence may be the absence of overcrowded teeth and stronger oral tissues.

Some studies have claimed that breast-feeding has a beneficial effect on the speech development of the child. For example, the natural act of sucking can accelerate the development of the neuromuscular system involved in speech. Also, since the holes in an artificial nipple are slightly larger than those in the breast, the child is forced to use tongue thrusts to arrest the rapid flow of milk. Some professionals claim that this increased tongue thrusting may adversely affect the child's later speech development.

Normalization of uterus size

Clinical reports have confirmed that breast-feeding brings about a vigorous contraction of the uterus, which returns to its normal size in a shorter time than in a woman who chooses not to breast-feed. Also, bleeding of the uterus is reduced.

Miscellaneous benefits

Other benefits from breast-feeding include contraception, weight reduction, and the reduced risk of breast engorgement and trauma. Years of observation have shown that unimpaired breast-feeding is an effective contraceptive method during the first few weeks after delivery. In most mothers with successful lactation, ovulation is postponed until at least the tenth week after childbirth. The period is longer if she maintains full breast-feeding without any formula supplement. The logic is that early weaning leads to early ovulation and accelerates the possibility of another pregnancy.

Some women do not have confidence in this contraceptive explanation, since they experience menstruations 2 or 3 months after delivery. However, a possible explanation is their frequent use of supplemental feeding, which interrupts the sucking and flow of milk. Some women actually do become pregnant while breast-feeding and are understandably dissatisfied with this method of contraception. On the other hand, the hormones in some oral contraceptive pills can suppress lactation and be passed on to the infant, posing a risk. For reasons not yet clear, mechanical devices such as the IUD can increase lactation.

Many women find that breast-feeding is effective in reducing weight, although this beneficial effect does not occur in some nursing mothers. Breast-feeding is also a natural prevention for the engorgement of the breast tissues from milk. Women who choose to bottle-feed their infants find their breasts initially painful and tender from engorgement. Some suggest that this may increase their susceptibility to breast trauma and cancer. The milk supply gradually dries up if there is no sucking, but some physicians prescribe medications to arrest milk production.

Finally, as discussed later, formula feeding has a number of disadvantages, most of which can be avoided if the child is breast-fed.

Drawbacks

Contrary to the claims of many enthusiasts, breast-feeding can have some problems. One is the mother's failure to make enough milk. For breast-feeding to be successful, the mother must be able to make an adequate amount of milk. A woman who wants to nurse but is unable to make enough milk often becomes disappointed and anxious. It is important that the woman drink sufficient fluid, eat enough calories, sustain a strong desire to nurse, and provide a peaceful period for breast-feeding. Some failures are due to a negative attitude and confusion over the difference between colostrum and mature milk. Often a woman's milk production relates directly to her emotional state and degree of fatigue. Any fluctuation in the quantity of milk secreted affects the child's satiety and weight gain and may prompt excessive use of supplemental bottle-feeding. This further reduces the amount of milk formed because of a lack of stimulation of the breasts.

A second disadvantage for some women is the fear that breast-feeding may distort their physical appearance. Although most are able to lose residual pregnancy weight when breast-feeding, some are afraid that their breasts will remain enlarged for a long time, making it difficult to return to their prepregnancy weight. On the other hand, some women's breasts shrink after repeated breast-feeding.

Some women oppose breast-feeding because it restricts their freedom of movement. Obviously, nursing is difficult if a mother holds a full-time job that does not permit regular intervals for nursing.

If a woman uses drugs frequently (whether

prescription, over-the-counter, or illicit), including cigarettes and alcohol, the chemicals may appear in the milk. The risk to the infant varies with the type of drug (see Chapter 16). Any accidental ingestion or inhalation of minute amounts of pesticide and industrial chemicals can be transferred to the milk, although the clinical hazard posed by this has not been documented.

A newborn infant may have sucking difficulty for the first 2 to 3 days (or sometimes longer) if the mother was sedated because of difficult delivery and long labor. After this period, sucking improves and the difficulty rarely recurs.

Finally, some women are afraid that nursing may increase the risk of breast infection, and as discussed later, breast milk is lower than cow's milk in a number of nutrients.

The Technique of Breast-feeding

During pregnancy the breasts are prepared for lactation. Influenced by body hormones, they enlarge from the deposition of fat and a moderate collection of fluid. Hormones also prepare the secretory cells for milk production. During the last weeks of pregnancy, an amber fluid (usually thin) called colostrum is often secreted from the nipples, which also appears during the first days of breast-feeding. Colostrum is high in protein and minerals and, as mentioned earlier, may contain antibodies capable of providing the child with passive immunity. The mature milk, higher in carbohydrate and fat, is formed about the third day after birth. However, the newborn should be put to the breast within the first 24 hours of birth since its sucking will stimulate milk production. Normal white milk production is established at the end of the first week, and the woman makes about 500 mL daily.

In general, the breast-feeding woman should assume a position that is comfortable for both her and the infant. The child should be held close to the breast, whether the mother is reclining in bed or seated in a chair. A chair with low arms will give more support to the mother, although many mothers prefer a rocking chair. To initiate sucking, the nipple should be held toward the child's mouth, and brushing the baby's cheek next to the breast will cause it to turn its head in that direction as a reflex action.

TABLE 14-2 Growth Rates and Body Size of Infants by Method of Feeding

Type of Feeding	Growth Rate (mo)		Body Size at 2 Years
	0–5	5–24	
Breast	Faster	Slower	Same
Bottle	Slower	Faster	Same

The nipple should be held by the mother in such a way as to insure that both nipple and areola are in the baby's mouth; this procedure maximizes the flow of milk. If the infant is permitted to suck only the end of the nipple, milk flow is reduced and the nipple may become very tender and sore. Both breasts should be used alternately at each feeding.

Nursing time may vary from 5 minutes (for a tiny infant) at each breast to 20 minutes. When the baby is satisfied, it will stop nursing and often go to sleep. After and perhaps during the feeding, the infant should be held to the shoulder and patted on the back to help expel any swallowed air. Experienced mothers are familiar with other ways to "burp" the baby. The intervals between feeding are shorter for the newborn and gradually extend to 3 or 4 hours.

To make an adequate amount of milk, the mother should eat nutritious meals, drink an adequate amount of fluid, and be relaxed. Normal care of the breasts during nursing includes washing them with plain water and the adequate support of a properly fitted brassiere. Clean, white, cotton fabric (or nursing pads) may be placed in the brassiere cup to absorb any milk leakage. Plastic-lined brassieres are not advised because they prevent air circulation and drying of the nipple areas.

Pros and Cons of Formula Feeding

If a woman wants to breast-feed she should do so, since breast milk is nature's food for a human infant. However, in the last 50 years clinical observations have confirmed that a child grows equally well when bottle-fed, as shown in Table 14-2. If the mother and doctor have decided that the child is to be bottle-fed, the ideal is to

TABLE 14-3   Approximate Nutritional Content of Colostrum, Breast Milk, and Whole Cow's Milk*

Nutrient Per 100 mL	Colostrum	Breast Milk	Cow's Milk
Water (mL)	87	87	87
Kcal	59	75	68
Protein (g)	2.8	1.2	3.5
Lactose (g)	5.5	6.9	4.9
Fat (g)	2.8	4.4	3.7
Calcium (mg)	30	34	120
Phosphorus (mg)	15	14	94
Sodium (mg)	45	160	505
Potassium (mg)	75	407	1,360
Iron (mg)	0.1	0.13	0.1
Vitamin A (IU)	200	210	150
Vitamin D (IU)	No information	0.5	2.0
Vitamin E (mg)	1.0	0.6	0.06
Vitamin K (μg)	No information	1.4	5.8
Vitamin C (mg)	5.0	4.3	1.8
Vitamin B_1 (mg)	13	16	41
Vitamin B_2 (μg)	25	40	160
Vitamin B_6 (μg)	No information	10	50
Vitamin B_{12} (μg)	No information	0.03	0.4
Folic acid (μg)	0.05	5	5
Pantothenic acid (μg)	180	190	340
Niacin (μg)	70	170	90

*Information obtained from a number of investigators' reports. All values are averages.

modify cow's milk so that it approximates breast milk's nutrients in quality and quantity. As Tables 14-3 and 14-4 illustrate, whole cow's milk is higher in certain nutrients and lower in others than breast milk. Cow's milk can be modified in various ways to make it similar to breast milk, as indicated below.

The protein and some minerals in cow's milk must be reduced in quantity. This is accomplished by heat, acid, alkali, enzyme, bacterial action, or dilution with water. The last technique is the most common and can effectively reduce protein and calcium levels, although it also decreases the caloric density. This loss is usually compensated for by adding a carbohydrate such as sucrose, dextromaltose, or lactose to either commercial or home-prepared formulas. Because of the high content of sodium in cow's milk, the mineral is usually partially removed by dialysis to approach the concentration in breast milk, although this method again in-

volves a loss of other minerals. When whole milk is diluted, the curd formation is reduced with a flocculent, an additive that gives the milk a soft texture for easier digestion. Table 14-5 compares the protein in breast and cow's milk before the latter is modified for formula feeding.

Because of the high ratio of saturated to unsaturated fat in cow's milk, part of its butterfat is replaced by a vegetable oil such as corn oil, which has a high level of long-chain, polyunsaturated fatty acids, especially linoleic acid. To prevent oxidation, an antioxidant such as vitamin E may be added. Table 14-6 compares the quantity and quality of fat in breast and cow's milk before it is modified for bottle-feeding of infants.

Disadvantages

Although bottle-fed formulas can be made nutritionally similar to breast milk, formula feeding has a number of drawbacks. One is the possi-

TABLE 14-4 Comparison of Vitamins and Minerals in Breast and Cow's Milk

Nutrient	Breast Milk	Cow's Milk
Vitamin B_1	More	Less because of destruction due to pasteurization
Vitamin C	More	Less because of destruction due to pasteurization
Overall minerals	Fewer if distilled water is used in supplemental feeding	Varies with the type of feed and drinking water
Strontium	A specified amount	About six times more
Calcium:phosphorus	$\approx 1.9:1.0$	$\approx 1:1$

TABLE 14-5 Comparison of Protein in Breast and Cow's Milk

Protein Quality and Quantity	Breast Milk	Cow's Milk
Quantity	Standard amount	Twice as much
Type	Mainly lactalbumin	Mainly casein
Amino acid profile	Pattern resembling human protein	Pattern slightly different from human protein
	More essential amino acids	Less essential amino acids
Digestion	Soft and flocculent curd, rapid and easy digestion and absorption	Hard curd, more difficult digestion and absorption
Cysteine and methionine content	Higher, making more efficient use of methionine	Lower, making less efficient use of methionine
Proteases (enzymes)	Higher level, facilitating degradation by splitting protein to less complex forms	Mostly destroyed by pasteurization, thus making protein digestion a little more difficult

ble lack of sanitation in preparing the formula, which can result in infection. This problem is especially common among families of low socioeconomic status and in underdeveloped countries.

Underdilution of a formula may cause de-hydration and pose the major hazard of solute overload. This may happen when the mother does not pay adequate attention to the preparation instructions. Even when properly diluted, the high levels of protein and sodium in cow's milk are of major concern.

TABLE 14-6   Comparison of Fat in Breast and Cow's Milk

Fat Quantity and Quality	Breast Milk	Cow's Milk
Amount (g/100 mL)	4.4	3.7
Percent of total calories	53–55	47–49
Linoleic acid (g/100 g fat)	10–11	2–2.5
Percent of total calories	6–9	1–2
Cholesterol (mg/100 mL)	19–21	13–15
Fatty acids		
Saturation	Fewer	More
Carbon chain	Mainly 10–14	Mainly less than 10
Digestion	More effective (95%)	Less effective (60%)
Free palmitic acids	Releases very little free palmitic acid in the intestine, thus reducing interference with calcium absorption	Releases more free palmitic acid in the intestine, thus increasing interference with calcium absorption
Ratio of polyunsaturated fatty acids to saturated fatty acids	Is increasing because of general increase in unsaturated fats consumption in this country	Constant if animal feeding practices remain unchanged
Fat variation with each feeding	At the end of each feeding, level of fat in the milk increases, making the infant satisfied and thus spontaneously regulating total milk intake	Remains constant

Formula-fed babies have a higher incidence of allergy and constipation, diarrhea, and infection of the gastrointestinal and respiratory tracts than breast-fed babies. The tendency for a formula-fed infant to overfeed is also high, probably because of the easy access to the feed.

The preparation of some formula milk calls for the addition of syrup or sugar. There are documented cases of mothers using salt instead of sugar by accident, with disastrous consequences. Containers for salt and sugar must be clearly labeled.

Because of the high fat content of some formula milk, it is possible that an infant fed such milk accumulates lipids in its blood. High blood cholesterol and triglycerides may pose a risk later in life (Table 14-6).

An infant may be conditioned to prefer sweet things because of exposure to sugar, honey, or syrup in a bottle containing milk, juice, vitamin C supplement, or plain water. A higher incidence of cavities may also result as the child grows. Obviously, the effect is exaggerated if the child sucks the bottle for a prolonged period.

Dentists and physicians have recently identified a "nursing bottle syndrome" or "dummy reservoir syndrome," in which the teeth and gums of youngsters show excess rotting because as infants they were permitted to fall asleep with a bottle of sugary liquid in their mouth. The sugar solution soaks the mouth for hours and causes the decay. See Figure 14-1.

Another potential disadvantage of bottle-feeding is the option of changing formulas. Frequent changing of infant formulas (from ready-to-serve to evaporated milk, for example) is not advised, since it varies the child's caloric intake and tampers with its hunger-satiety rhythm.

Advantages

On the other hand, bottle-feeding has many advantages. First, the mother enjoys freedom of movement, especially valuable given the increasing number of women joining the work force. Second, breast milk is not necessarily cheaper than formula: the price comparison varies with the formula used and the diet of the mother. Third, breast-feeding is not recommended for women who drink and smoke excessively, use contraceptive pills and illicit drugs, receive medications, or are exposed to chemical compounds in their occupations. Fourth, some babies fed breast milk do not gain weight satisfactorily or may develop an occasional allergy. For these infants, bottle-feeding is preferred.

There is a variety of milk that can be used to feed an infant. However, the use of skim, nonfat, or low-fat milk has a number of problems. Nutritionally, the product is not appropriate as the only food for infants of any age. The child may suffer linoleic acid deficiency. The minimal requirement of an infant for this nutrient is 1% to 3% of total caloric intake. For breast milk, skim milk, and commercial formulas, the figures are about 6% to 9%, 0% to 1%, and 10% to 20%, respectively.

Some infants are susceptible to diarrhea because of low intestinal fat if fed skim milk. Because of the partial or total removal of fat, the supplies of vitamins A and D are low, and cases of their deficiency have been documented. Fortification with these nutrients does not guarantee an adequate intake, since the lack of fat decreases

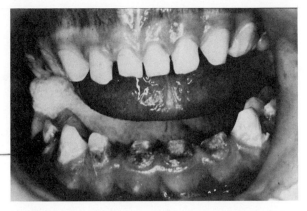

FIGURE 14-1   Rampant decay in primary dentition of 4-year-old boy with continuous history of bottle-feeding prior to sleeping. Lower anterior teeth are not carious because of protection from tongue during sucking and swallowing. (From T. E. Cone, Jr., *Journal of the American Medical Association* 245[1981]:2334. Copyright 1981, American Medical Association.)

their absorption. Some infants fail to gain weight and store very little body fat. The decreased intake of cholesterol may interfere with proper myelin formation.

The high nitrogen and sodium contents of skim milk may pose hazards, and a child given the product should be provided with enough fluid to excrete the waste in the urine. The low level of iron and copper in the product may pose a risk. Chapter 30 explains in detail how using boiled skim milk to treat diarrhea in infants is ill advised, since the dehydration caused by the diarrhea will be intensified by the large load of solute in the milk.

Feeding low-fat milk to decrease cholesterol intake and avoid obesity is a preventive measure in health care, but its actual benefits have not been substantiated. The use of condensed milk to feed an infant is not advisable, since it contains too much sugar, which may result in an overweight baby.

The Technique of Bottle-feeding

For infants under the care of a pediatrician, the formula to be used will be "prescribed" or recommended. Normally, the base of the formula is cow's milk, which is diluted with water to reduce its protein and mineral contents and supplemented with sugar, syrup, and/or lactose to raise the carbohydrate content. The form of milk used is determined by convenience, cost, and special needs. Commercial powdered or liquid formulas can be used, although some prefer fresh, evaporated, or dried milk. Nutrient supplements may or may not be needed.

Enough formula for 24 hours' feeding may be prepared at one time. Preparation is easier if some standard equipment is assembled and stored together. Some important utensils are the following:

1. 8-oz nursing bottles, usually made of heat-resistant glass or plastic that can withstand boiling temperature, plus two or three 4-oz bottles for water or orange juice. Wide-mouth bottles are easier to clean.
2. Nipples and nipple covers with plastic, glass, aluminum, or paper caps.
3. A measuring cup, marked in ounces, with a pouring lip and a standard measuring spoon.
4. A 2-qt bottle, pan, or jar for mixing the formula.
5. A small kettle or lid for boiling nipples (if the aseptic method of sterilization is used).
6. A small covered jar for keeping used nipples.
7. Tongs for handling hot bottles.
8. A spoon with a long handle for mixing formula.
9. A sturdy, well-bristled, long-handled bottle brush to aid in cleaning. It is helpful to wash out bottles with cold water after use and to rinse the nipples so that the milk does not dry on them.
10. A large kettle with a lid to be used in sterilizing the day's formula. It is convenient to have a rack to hold bottles. One may be improvised from a flat lid; or a folded, clean towel can be placed on the bottom of the kettle to prevent the bottles from breaking.
11. A funnel or a Pyrex cup with a pouring spout to help in filling of bottles.

When using new rubber nipples, it is important to test the rate of flow; the openings may have to be enlarged. A simple test is to turn a filled bottle upside down with the nipple in place; there should be a steady drip. If the holes in the nipple are too small, the infant will have to work hard to get even a small amount of milk. If the holes are too large, the rapid flow may cause choking or excessive thrusting of the tongue. The nipple hole(s) should be enlarged by carefully inserting a small needle heated in a match flame into the hole(s).

Two basic methods of formula preparation and sterilization are commonly used: terminal sterilization and the aseptic technique. The hospital nurse may instruct the new mother in either method adopted. Excellent pamphlets on the two methods are usually available at hospitals and doctor's offices.

Terminal sterilization

The terminal sterilization of bottles and formula is the simplest method and the one most commonly used. It involves preparing the formula, pouring it into clean but unsterilized bottles, and processing both bottles and formula in boiling water simultaneously.

All the articles to be used in mixing the formula, the bottles, and the nipples must be washed well and rinsed. The formula is prepared and mixed with all ingredients carefully measured. Milk bottles and the tops of evaporated milk cans should be wiped to remove dust and dirt.

The formula is then poured into the clean bottles, which should be marked in ounces, and divided for the whole day's feedings. Nipples and nipple covers should be placed on the bottles. The covers should not be screwed down tightly, since the high temperature of sterilization could blow the caps off. The formula-filled bottles and two smaller bottles of drinking water should then be placed on a rack in a large kettle. Water is added to the kettle until the bottles are halfway covered; then the kettle is covered and heated. The water should boil for 2 to 5 minutes before the heat source is turned off. The kettle should cool until the bottles can be handled before they are removed from the water. After the caps are tightened, the cooled bottles are stored in the refrigerator.

Aseptic sterilization

The aseptic method of sterilization is used with commercially prepared powdered or liquid formulas. Powders should be mixed with boiling water unless instructed otherwise. Bottles, nipples, nipple covers, a funnel, a spoon, and a mixing bowl should be thoroughly washed and rinsed. Bottles should be scrubbed with a bottle brush, and nipples should be turned inside out and scrubbed. Bottles, nipple covers, a measuring cup and spoon, a funnel, tongs, and a can opener (if used) are all placed in the sterilizing kettle. If the kettle has a tight-fitting cover, 5 or 6 in. of water are added; the steam formed will sterilize the equipment. If the cover does not fit tightly, the equipment should be completely covered with water for thorough sterilization. The water in the kettle is then brought to a boil and boiled for 5 minutes. Afterward, the equipment is left in the water until it is used. The nipples are boiled separately in a small covered kettle for 5 minutes. The water is then poured off, and the nipples are kept in the kettle until they are used. Overboiling the nipples or letting them stand in hot water will deteriorate the rubber and should be avoided. The formula is then mixed with boiling water if the powdered form is used. It is then divided into sterilized bottles and covered with nipple and nipple covers, which should be screwed down completely. The formula-filled bottles are then stored in the refrigerator until use.

At feeding time, each bottle should be removed from the refrigerator and placed in a small kettle with hot water. The formula, usually fed at body or a warm temperature, is tested by sprinkling a few drops on the inside of the wrist. Some studies have indicated that babies do not suffer any ill effect even when fed very cold formulas, although warm feedings may facilitate the digestive process, including intestinal secretions and the operation of enzymes.

Nutritional Adequacy of a Milk Diet

How adequate is an all-milk diet for an infant? The answer varies with the baby's age, milk intake, and the type of milk.

The amount of milk consumed by a baby varies from about 3 oz per pound body weight during the first 5 to 10 days of life to 1½ to 2 oz per pound during the second or third months. For example, an average infant may consume about 1 qt of milk daily during the first 2 to 4 weeks.

The exact volume of milk consumed depends on body size, growth rate, appetite, and supplemental liquids. Also, there is no fixed feeding schedule. Early feeding may be 5 to 10 times daily, decreasing to about 4 to 6 times at about 3 months.

Assume that an infant under 3 months needs and normally consumes about 800 to 900 mL of milk. For the most part this amount, especially if breast milk, satisfies the child's RDAs during the first 3 months. However, between 3 and 6 months of age, iron intake may not be adequate if the child is on a milk diet only. The remedy is using infant iron supplement or commercial formulas that have been fortified with iron. A fluoride supplement may also be needed, depending on water fluoridation, formula content, and so on.

Some formula-fed infants may need vitamin C supplementation. Liquid commercial ready-to-serve formulas with added vitamin C are acceptable. However, if the formula preparation involves commercial pasteurization or home sterilization, vitamin C supplement may be needed, since vitamin C is destroyed by heat. Such formulas include regular whole milk, evaporated milk, and other formulas requiring home sterilization. The RDA for the vitamin may be met by a liquid supplement or 1 teaspoon of orange juice per day. At the beginning, the juice is diluted with another teaspoon of water. Gradually the amount is increased to 2 teaspoons of juice a day, with proper dilution for tolerance. Some infants are allergic to the oil extract in the juice; if so, a liquid nutrient supplement may be used. Some evidence suggests that if the mother consumes an abnormally high amount of vitamin C during pregnancy, the newborn baby may be conditioned to an excessively high requirement for the vitamin.

The need for vitamin D supplementation varies under different circumstances. Because regular and evaporated milk and most commercial formulas are fortified with vitamin D, the intake should be adequate. However, breast-fed infants over 3 months old should be provided with an additional source of vitamin D. If the child's exposure to sunlight is sufficient (30 to 60 minutes daily for a clothed infant), no other measure is needed. Otherwise, the child should be provided with a supplement. The availability of water-miscible vitamin D has reduced the use of cod liver oil, which poses the risk of being aspirated into the lungs. Premature or high-risk infants tend to be deficient in vitamin D which frequently must be administered. Nevertheless, the possibility of vitamin D toxicity cannot be underestimated, especially for very young infants.

Cow's milk contains less vitamin E than breast milk. Because of the difficult passage of the vitamin through the placenta, a premature infant tends to be deficient in vitamin E because of its shorter gestation period. Most commercial formulas now have vitamin E added.

Some infants have a tendency toward hemorrhage that can be managed by an injection of vitamin K. This applies especially to the breast-fed newborn and infants consuming relatively small amounts of human milk during the first few days of life.

Two final points should be mentioned. First, goat's milk does not have enough folic acid to sustain a growing child. Second, infants of strictly vegetarian mothers may be deficient in vitamin B_{12}, especially if a supplement is not used by the mother or given to the child.

Introducing Solid Foods

People have argued over when to wean a young infant from milk and introduce solid foods for nearly a century. Table 14-7 shows some trends in the practice of introducing solid foods. Factors to be considered when introducing solid foods to an infant are: (1) the nutritional requirements of the infant; (2) the appropriate physical and physiological development, especially of the child's digestive system; (3) relative advantages and disadvantages of introducing solid foods early; and (4) the importance of establishing eating habits that will lead to good nutritional intake throughout life. Some aspects of these considerations are discussed below.

Ability to eat solid foods

One important consideration is the oral development of the child. An infant under 2 months old can perform three basic oral functions: rooting (searching for the nipple), sucking, and thrusting (extruding the tongue). Ex-

actly when the child starts to swallow is unknown, although it is generally agreed that this ability develops at about 3 months. At about 2½ to 3 months, the child can manipulate its tongue to convey liquid food particles to its throat. If solid food is fed at this young age, then the caretaker must place the food at the back of the child's mouth. The use of force here will encounter resistance, frustration, and a generally unhappy feeding atmosphere. The child may eventually develop uncooperative eating habits because of this unpleasant experience.

Another important consideration is the physiological development of the child. The child's digestive system should be able to handle foods. When the child is under 1 month old, its enzyme system is only appropriate for digesting milk protein. Salivary amylase for digesting starches is not present until 2 or 3 months, although lactose and sucrose in milk do not require salivary enzymes for hydrolysis. Only at 4 to 6 months of age do most infants acquire the appropriate enzyme system to digest nonmilk protein. Thus, too early an introduction to solid foods may result in an excess protein intake that cannot be digested properly by the child. Since the child's kidney functions are not fully developed, an excess solute load from sodium and protein may then pose a problem.

In areas with a hot climate, calorie-dense foods can cause dehydration. Because of the high concentration of nitrate and nitrite in such vegetables as celery, spinach, carrots, and lettuce, homemade baby foods with these ingredients should not be fed to babies under 6 months old to prevent methemoglobinemia.

Pros and cons of early solid food feeding

In addition to questions of whether the child is physiologically capable of swallowing and digesting solid foods at an early age, the practice of introducing solid foods early has been criticized as nutritionally unwise. For one thing, if the child can eat only a small amount of solid foods, then nutrient intake will be limited. Solid food feeding may not be worth the work, time, cost, and risk of contamination. Second, many solid foods have a higher caloric density than breast or formula milk. If the child eats solid foods and drinks a lot

TABLE 14-7 Practices in Introducing Solid Foods to Infants

Year	Pediatrician-recommended Time to Start Solid Foods
1900	>12 months old: meat and cereal supplementing milk
1920	8–12 months old: meat broth supplementing milk >12 months old: solid foods supplementing milk
1960	2–6 weeks old: cereal supplementing milk 4–5 months old: meat, eggs, vegetables, fruits, cereal
1980*	0–4 months old: milk, nutrient supplements 4–6 months old: solid foods supplementing milk

*In 1980, 90% of U.S. infants were fed solid foods before 3 months of age.

TABLE 14-8 Nutritional Aspects of Introducing Solid Foods to Infants

Food*	Some Observations
Single-grain cereals	Popularly started first; good iron content, cheap, least allergenic, easily prepared and stored
Strained vegetables and fruits	Avoid those that can cause gas and irritation to the intestine
Egg yolk	Usually introduced early; provides protein, iron, vitamins A and B$_{12}$†
Meat	Provides the RDAs of several nutrients

*Items arranged in chronological order of introduction (meat last). With each item, start with small quantities and progress to larger ones.
†A small amount should be given first to ascertain if the child is sensitive to the substance.

of milk, it may overeat and become obese. A third possible problem is that forced feeding of semisolid foods before 9 to 12 weeks of age will increase the feeding problems and food dislikes of the infant. If the child is not yet ready, it will fight back and become resentful.

Infants introduced to a variety of foods at an early age may have an increased incidence of food allergy. This is an especially important consideration if the child has a family history of allergy. For such children, feeding sensitive foods such as fruits, vegetables, and even rice cereal should be delayed. If the child is fed such foods, the exposure should be kept brief by switching to other foods.

Some claim that tongue extrusion or thrusting is a natural process. Prolonged spoon feeding due to the early introduction of solid foods may thwart this natural instinct and cause frustration in self-feeding, delay in manipulating finger foods, and even maladjustment in the childhood eating pattern.

On the other hand, some people feel that if a child eats solid foods early, this is a superior achievement. Another unconfirmed claim suggests that introducing solid foods at an early age will keep the infant sleeping through the night.

Most professionals accept the decision of the mother to feed the child solid foods early because most infants appear to tolerate the foods well. In addition, the practice is so common that nothing much can be done about it. Probably the best advice is to avoid telling the mothers to start solid foods at precisely 4 or 6 months. Rather, they should be asked to postpone the introduction of solid foods as late as possible, preferably after 4 to 6 months. Recently, nutritionists and pediatricians have adopted the term *beikost* (introduced by Dr. S. J. Fomon of the University of Iowa) for infant foods other than milk, although its use is not widespread.

Guidelines for solid food feeding

Professionals have suggested certain guidelines in introducing new foods to an infant, since the order in which solid foods are usually introduced is only semiscientific and strongly traditional. These guidelines are given in Table 14-8. It is important that the infant be made familiar with new foods one at a time. A new food should not be introduced until the child is used to the last one. Mixtures of foods should be avoided, especially if they contain a new food.

Each new food is tried for a few days to detect tolerance. The caretaker should not feed any food that the child objects to. Like adults, infants also have food preferences. Any food preferred by the child for the first few days and then genuinely disliked and rejected should not be given. As the child grows, it may come to like a food it once rejected.

Most infants are given a very small amount of a new food at first and then slightly larger portions. The texture of the food must be appropriate. The smaller the child, the less viscid the food. Initially solid foods are mashed, pureed, strained, or blended. All these processes increase the softness of a food and minimize the residue. A soft food is followed by chopped solid food or bits of solid food. The transition depends on the child's ability to chew. The initial inability to move food back with the tongue for swallowing is indicated by the frequency with which the child spits it out, although this outward tongue thrusting may also indicate a dislike for the food or some other individual factor. The child should be permitted to eat as much and as slowly as it wants unless there is a reason to suspect that the child is not eating adequately. However, the child should not be forced to eat more than it wants.

The use of sugar, salt, and other seasoning is generally avoided, although certain cultural groups may prefer to use special spices or herbs. As the child becomes increasingly used to solid foods, its preferences can be broadened by providing a large selection of items, serving a combination of foods (such as egg and formula or vegetables and milk), and not allowing the child to see an adult show any sign of dislike for food (especially nutritious ones).

The technique of solid food feeding

Solid foods are given when the child is ready; for example, when it develops the ability to move food from the front to the back of its mouth with the tongue, which usually occurs at about 4 or 5 months. Otherwise, the food is placed at the back of the mouth to avoid spitting. During the feeding process, the child sits on the lap of or in front of the caretaker. Sitting upright, the child is fed with a spoon and should be able to see the entire feeding process. The child progresses to holding its own bottle or drinking from a special cup. At 5

TABLE 14-9 Suitable Supplemental Foods for Infants During the First Year

Food	Usual Age when Supplemented
Orange juice, tomato juice (source of vitamin C)*	10 days
Well-cooked cereals	2–4 months
Strained, pureed vegetables and fruits	3–5 months
Pureed, strained meats	4–7 months
Mashed home-cooked vegetables, potatoes, carrots	6–9 months
Mashed egg yolk	6–7 months
Crackers, zwieback, dried bread	7–9 months
Regular cooked cereals, meats, eggs	10–12 months

*If vitamin C supplementation is necessary and the child cannot tolerate juices, administer liquid ascorbic acid supplement.

to 7 months of age, the child may be given family table food.

The feeding sequence of liquids, soft (pureed) foods, chopped foods, and solid foods of biting size is recommended to assure that the child learns how to coordinate the different oral structures (teeth, jaws, tongue, palate, etc.). When the child shows preference for crackers and cookies, it can bite them. A child 8 to 9 months old can swallow mashed and cut-up vegetables and chopped-up moist meat. Feeding techniques for a child between 1 and 3 years are given in references at the back of this book. Table 14-9 shows a list of suitable supplemental foods for infants during the first year.

Care and preparation of baby foods

An important aspect in infant feeding is the proper care of baby foods. All leftover foods must be handled with care to prevent spoilage. Unused portions should be placed in an appropriate storage container and stored in a refrigerator for the next feeding. Leftover food that has been handled or placed on the infant's plate should be discarded to avoid contamination and spoilage. Once a jar of baby food has been opened, the contents should be used within 2 or 3 days, even if it is refrigerated.

Homemade baby foods are becoming increasingly popular, although they may or may not be economical. Spicy and strong foods (e.g., sausages, some salad dressings) should be avoided. Plain family foods are preferred. A strainer, blender, and grinder can be used to make baby food that is frozen and used later. For example, cooked potatoes or bananas are easily mashed and then frozen for later use.

NUTRITION AND CHILDREN

The nutritional and dietary intake of children has been much debated in this country. Some major concerns are children's nutritional status, feeding problems, questions about milk's reputation as a near perfect food, snacking, obesity, anemia, cavities, and food allergies. School lunches and sound meal plans are useful ways to improve nutrition during these years.

Nutritional Status

The nutritional status of children under 6 years of age has been reported in several national surveys, including the Preschool Nutritional Survey (1968–1970) (G. Owen, *Pediatrics* 1974; 53:11 [supplement]), the Ten-State Nutrition Survey (1968–1970) (Department of Health, Education, and Welfare publication No. [HSM] 72-8132), and the Health and Nutrition Examination Survey (1971–1974) (Department of Health, Education, and Welfare publication No. [HRA] 74-1219-1).

From these surveys, it appears that the nutritional status of most children in the United States is satisfactory, although family income has an undeniable influence. For example, children from poor families have slightly arrested body growth, while those from well-to-do families tend to consume more essential nutrients.

Iron deficiency was the most prevalent nutritional disorder among American children. Anemia was reported in 7% to 12% of all children studied, especially youngsters from poor families. On the other hand, about 5% to 10% of children were overweight, many of them from families with moderate to high incomes. Protein intake was in general higher than the RDA. And one-quarter to nearly half of the preschool children were being given vitamin supplements. However, some black and Spanish-American children were receiving a substandard amount of vitamin A, and about 10% to 15% of children had a low intake of vitamin C. About 10% to 30% of children, especially blacks, did not eat an adequate amount of calcium.

Coping with Feeding Problems

Feeding children sometimes becomes a problem. Nutritionists recommend a number of pointers to avoid or manage eating problems.

One is to take the child's food preferences into account. Like adults, children have likes and dislikes about foods. Table 14-10 summarizes general attitudes of children toward foods. The caretaker should become familiar with these criteria and tailor meals to the child's preferences. Quite often, the child's eating preferences reflect those of the parents; for instance, both parents and children may dislike vegetables. Since in many families foods are prepared according to the preferences of the father, the child's attitude toward certain foods may reflect the father's behavior. If the child is known to prefer moist foods, his fluid intake should be studied, for he may not be making adequate saliva. If children prefer mildly flavored foods, they should be allowed to eat what they like at the beginning. Flavors can gradually be made more intense by adding cream, juice, sauce, and other dressings to the diet until the child accepts normal food flavors. Sometimes children may not like a food at first but may develop a taste for it after repeated exposures.

Guardians should note that a child eats better in a gay and attractive environment. Foods requiring manipulation should be slowly introduced as the child's motor development and manual dexterity allow. The care giver can help the child to relax before mealtime. Many children have a difficult time settling down to eat.

TABLE 14-10   Criteria for the Acceptance of Foods by Children

Food Characteristics	Preferred by Children	Disliked by Children
Texture	Soft, e.g., thin soup or puddings, tender beef, moist ground meat, soft mashed potatoes, soft bread	Thick, tough, stringy, dry, e.g., stringy beans, dry toast, coarse bread, thick soup, dry fish
Temperature of foods	Lukewarm, e.g., milk that is out of the refrigerator for a while, slightly melted ice cream	Very cold or hot, e.g., hot soup, cold rice, and meat
Flavor	Normal, unspoiled flavor	Any off flavors, e.g., slightly colored (e.g., very light yellow) or scorched milk, strong cabbage or onion flavor unless they are creamed to modify the flavor
Color	Colorful meal setting including the food, plate, table, and room decoration	Strange color such as blue or purple foods
Serving portion	Small portions and small utensils	Large portions and large utensils
Food shapes	Forms that they can manipulate with their hands rather than with utensils, e.g., strips of vegetables or meats	Shapes and forms that they cannot manipulate with their utensils and hands

The adult can read the child a story or have the child sit and talk for a few minutes before mealtime. The child should be discouraged from eating any food for at least an hour before a meal. If children do not eat at mealtime, they should not be allowed to fill up on snack foods later.

Refusing to eat is one way of attracting a parent's attention. Hovering over the child and fretting about her or his refusal to eat may actually reinforce this behavior. Is the child getting enough attention at other times of the day? If not, he or she may be trying to make up for it at mealtime.

It is not unusual for children suddenly to have a favorite food that they want to eat every day. Such food obsessions rarely last more than a week or two, as the child tires of having the same thing over and over. There is no need to go to great lengths to indulge the child, but it will not hurt if the child does have a favorite food every day.

Some families have a hard and fast rule that a child must eat everything on the plate before leaving the table. Nutritionists are beginning to wonder if this practice accounts for the fact that there are so many overweight people in our society. Maybe adult overeating can be traced to this "clean-plate policy" of early childhood years. Adults should let children eat until they are just satisfied, rather than using their own appetites as a guide.

If a child has a real eating problem, professional help is needed. Behavioral modification together with an aggressive program in nutrition education can improve the eating habits of many children.

Problems with Milk

Although milk is advocated by all professionals as a good food for children, it is by no means a perfect food. It has a short shelf life and deteriorates easily. Pasteurization and refrigeration are needed. Milk is low in iron and copper and some vitamins, while being high in fat and cholesterol. Some individuals have lactose intolerance or milk allergy. In some, milk causes constipation or intestinal bleeding. Milk can also be a cause of obesity if too much is consumed. Finally, the waste by-products of commercial milk production are environmental pollutants.

Snacking

Snacking among children has been one of the most controversial issues in nutrition. It is well confirmed that excess snacking, especially when it occurs close to mealtime, will decrease appetite. However, since children have small stomachs, they cannot eat a large amount of food during regular meals even if they have not been snacking. Yet, even if children consume large meals, they may still not get enough food, especially during periods of rapid growth. In this case, snacks solve part of the problem. There is no doubt that some snacks are nutritious and others are not. Aggressive nutrition education of children and parents can mold their snacking pattern in healthy ways.

Snacks are bad if a child gobbles up foods that are loaded with sugar, salt, and fat but low in protein, vitamins, and minerals. But if children use snacks to supply their bodies with nutritious foods that are lacking in their regular meals, then snacking is a great idea. For a child, a slice of cheese, a wheat cracker, or a banana eaten at mid-morning or mid-afternoon could help supply the energy needed to keep them from tiring out.

Obesity

Pediatricians find that obesity is a big problem in infancy and childhood. The major cause is too much food. To determine the extent of childhood obesity, one should ask whether the child is obese or overweight (see Chapter 12) and whether the extra weight consists of fat, bone, or muscle. The child's weight : height ratio is a more accurate indication of obesity than weight alone.

Many factors must be considered in identifying the child at risk of becoming an obese adult. Since obesity runs in a family, if one or both parents are obese, the child is more likely to become obese. The child's weight pattern between 4 and 7 years of age, the weight pattern during first 6 months of life, and the birth weight may show an emerging pattern of obesity. For example, babies that are overweight from excess fat have a higher tendency to become obese adults. The family's eating habits should also be taken into account.

To manage an obese child, care givers must first find the reasons for the obesity. They should then help the child to establish a good eating habit. Balanced diets with a variety of foods should be fed. The inclusion of foods such as gravies, pastries, pork, greasy beef, and fried foods should be reduced in the family diet. The child should reduce snacking and eat nutrient-dense items when he or she does snack. Foods should not be used as a reward or reprimand to regulate the child's conduct at home or school. Overfeeding should be avoided, and the child should be encouraged to become aware when he or she is full. Care givers should make sure that the child does not depend on food for emotional or social comforts. For example, a child may overeat because he or she is not loved or accepted by other children. As the child grows, he or she should be educated in nutrition and increasingly allowed to choose his or her own foods. The child should be taught to follow a good exercise program. Children often exercise little, watch too much television, and overconsume soft drinks, and fat babies and children are not as active as their thin counterparts.

The goal of such measures is for the child to achieve an appropriate weight : height ratio. In many cases, the child need not actually lose weight but rather maintain a constant weight while gaining height. Depending on the child's age, caloric intake should be kept about 1,200 to 1,400 kcal per day. The child does need energy to grow.

Parents can practice some preventive measures to avoid obesity in infants and children. If possible, a child should be breast-fed with minimal but adequate supplemental feeding. A fat baby should not be fed solid foods before 3 or 4 months of age, preferably at 5 or 6 months.

Anemia

A number of surveys indicate that many youngsters suffer iron deficiency anemia. The blood hemoglobin of these children is less than 10 g per 100 mL. Many of them come from poor families, and their poor diets may be the cause of their low iron intake. Some experts suggest that the children's parents do not feed them the right foods because of ignorance or cultural traditions rather than poverty. Some suggest that the children may be harboring intestinal parasites or that some may have occult bleeding from excess milk drinking.

Cavities

Dental cavities among children mainly result from consuming too much fermentable carbohydrate. Children must also have a good diet to have strong teeth and oral tissues. At present, nutritionists propose the following preventive measures:

1. Avoid foods that tend to cause cavities, mainly carbohydrate (sugar, pastries, and so on).
2. Replace snacks with tasty fruits and vegetables, cheese, nuts, and so on.
3. Reduce the consumption of sweetened carbonated beverages.
4. Avoid all forms of sticky candy and sweet gums.
5. Eat a well-balanced and nutritious diet.
6. Make sure that there is a source of fluoride and calcium.
7. Practice good oral hygiene.

Food Allergies

Food allergies are common in infants and children; Chapter 31 discusses the topic in detail. However, since milk allergy is one of the most common food allergies, a few guidelines are provided here.

Childhood allergy to cow's milk is probably the most common food allergy in this country, affecting 2% to 4% of all infants and children. It can occur in a child of any age. Milk allergy runs in the family, and pediatricians can sometimes predict likely victims. Milk allergy is frequently, though not always, associated with allergic reactions to egg white or citrus fruits. The symptoms of milk allergy are diarrhea, skin reactions (eczema), respiratory difficulties, asthma, headache, irritability, and tiredness. One must distinguish some children's intolerance for milk (due mainly to a lack of intestinal lactase) from actual milk allergy. If milk substitutes are recommended for an allergic child, careful dietary planning (see Chapter 31) is necessary to assure an adequate nutrient intake. Sometimes heating milk before serving can denature the offending protein, although the heat destroys some of the nutrients.

Children and infants are also frequently allergic to such foods as cola drinks, chocolate, eggs, peas, corn, tomatoes, citrus fruits, cinnamon, wheat, and food colors (for example, tartrazine). Since allergy tends to run in a family, doctors in general request parents to pay particular attention to such foods. Foods such as nuts, eggs, and seafood (especially fish) can produce an immediate allergic reaction, while others such as chocolate, corn, milk, and wheat may produce a delayed reaction.

School Lunches

Since children of school age may eat five meals a week at school, school lunches have been seen as a way to improve their nutrition. The U.S. Department of Agriculture administers many child nutrition programs. The following discussion has been adapted from its public announcements.

The U.S. Department of Agriculture (USDA) administers the school program at the federal level. In most states, the state educational agency operates the program through agreements with local schools or school districts. The program offers federal financial assistance for each lunch served, technical assistance and guidance, USDA-donated foods or cash, and additional financial assistance for each lunch served free or at a reduced price to eligible children.

Any public or nonprofit private primary or secondary school is eligible to enroll in the program. Also eligible are public and licensed, nonprofit, private residential child care institutes such as orphanages, homes for retarded children, and temporary shelters for runaway children. To reach as many needy children as possible, participating schools and institutions send information to parents and the news media each year to explain how families can apply for free and reduced-price lunches.

For participating schools to be reimbursed for meals served through the program, lunches must meet USDA requirements. These specify that each lunch consist of specific amounts of lean meat or meat alternate (poultry, fish, cheese, cooked dry beans or peas, eggs, or peanut butter); two or more vegetables and/or fruits; whole-grain or enriched bread or bread alternate; and fluid milk served as beverage. (Only the general requirements are stated here. More details may be obtained from the USDA.) The pattern is designed to provide about one-third of the RDAs for key nutrients established by the National Research Council of the National Academy of Sciences (see Chapter 10). This pattern also encourages serving a wide variety of conventional foods, including whole-grain breads and fresh fruits and vegetables.

Meals must be not only nutritionally adequate but also prepared and served in an attractive manner. The USDA periodically reviews and revises program meal requirements to take into account new information about eating patterns, food preferences, and the nutritional needs of children.

Meal Plans

What is a nutritious meal for a child? Tables 14-11, 14-12, and 14-13 provide meal plans and sample menus for children aged 1 to 2, 3 to 6,

TABLE 14-11   Suggested Meal Plan and Sample Menu for 1- and 2-year-olds*

Meal Plan	Sample Menu
Breakfast	**Breakfast**
Juice or fruit	Orange juice
Cereal (hot or dry) with milk	Hot oatmeal with milk
Toast or egg (soft-boiled)	Whole wheat toast
Butter or margarine	Butter
Milk	Milk
Snack	**Snack**
Milk or juice	Apple juice
Lunch	**Lunch**
Meat, cheese, egg, or alternate	Grilled cheese sandwich
Potato, bread, crackers, or alternate	Peas
Vegetable	Milk
Butter or margarine	Ice cream
Milk	
Dessert	**Snack**
	Rice pudding
Snack	
Milk, juice, pudding, or crackers with cheese or alternate	**Dinner**
	Meat loaf
	Spinach or carrots
	Roll
Dinner	Butter
Meat, cheese, poultry, or alternate	Applesauce
Vegetable or salad	Milk
Potato, bread, roll, or alternate	
Butter or margarine	
Dessert	
Milk	

*Serving size varies with the child. Other nutritious items not shown may be used, e.g., jams, oatmeal, cookies, peanut butter. Their inclusion must be integrated into the child's overall daily intake of calories and nutrients.

and 7 to 12 years old, respectively. The meal plans in these tables are based on the basic four food groups discussed in Chapter 10. When they are used to feed a child, serving sizes must be adjusted to the age, development, activity, and appetite of the child.

TABLE 14-12   Suggested Meal Plan and Sample Menu for 3 Through 6-year-olds*

Meal Plan	Sample Menu
Breakfast	**Breakfast**
Juice or fruit	Apple
Cereal (hot or dry)	Bran flakes with milk
Egg, meat, or toast	Egg (soft-boiled) with
Milk	whole wheat toast
	Milk
Snack	
Dry fruits or nutritious	**Snack**
cookies	Dates
Lunch	**Lunch**
Meat, egg, or alternate	Peanut butter and jelly
Potato, bread, or	sandwich
alternate	Vegetable soup with rice
Vegetable	Margarine
Butter or margarine	Milk
Milk	Custard pudding
Dessert	
	Snack
Snack	Orange juice
Milk or juice	Apple wedges with
Crackers, pudding, or	peanut butter
dried fruits	
	Dinner
Dinner	Fish sticks
Meat, cheese, poultry, or	Sweet corn
alternate	Baked potato
Vegetable or salad	Butter
Potato, bread, roll, or	Fruit pudding
alternate	Milk
Butter or margarine	
Dessert	
Milk	

*Serving size varies with the child. Other nutritious items not shown may be used, e.g., jams, oatmeal, cookies, peanut butter. Their inclusion must be integrated into the child's overall daily intake of calories and nutrients.

TABLE 14-13   Suggested Meal Plan and Sample Menu for 7 Through 12-year-olds*

Meal Plan	Sample Menu
Breakfast	**Breakfast**
Juice or fruit	Pear(s)
Cereal (hot or dry) with	Farina with milk
milk	Toast
Toast	Egg or sausages
Egg, meat, or alternate	Margarine
Butter or margarine	Milk
Milk	
	Lunch
Lunch	Macaroni and cheese
Meat, cheese, or	Coleslaw
alternate	Milk
Potato, bread, or	Fresh peaches
alternate	
Vegetable	**Snack**
Butter or margarine	Molasses cookies
Milk	Apple juice
Dessert	
	Dinner
Snack	Hamburger
Dried fruits or nutritious	Carrots and peas
cookies	Shredded raw cabbage
Milk or juice	salad
	Baked potato
Dinner	Bread
Meat, cheese, or	Butter
alternate	Ice cream
Vegetable	Milk
Salad	
Potato or alternate	
Bread or alternate	
Butter or margarine	
Dessert	
Milk	

*Serving size varies with the child. Other nutritious items not shown may be used, e.g., jams, oatmeal, cookies, peanut butter. Their inclusion must be integrated into the child's overall daily intake of calories and nutrients.

NUTRITION AND ADOLESCENCE

The period of pubescence and adolescence spans the years from 12 to 18 and is characterized by major body compositional and devel-opmental changes. (Chapter 2 provides a brief discussion of body compositional changes. The appendix contains growth curves for this population group. More information on developmental aspects may be obtained from the references at the end of this book.) These young adults have rapidly developing bodies and are in a highly emotional state. Each therefore has a large nutritional need with a unique process of nutrient utilization. Their special needs derive from the enlargement of body organs and tissues. These needs are probably surpassed only by those associated with pregnancy and lactation (and the special requirements of the ill).

Eating Habits

Teenagers are influenced by their family background; the combined effects of physical, physiological, and emotional development; and their changes in life-style, characterized by increased mobility and independence. Teenagers are usually relatively deficient in nutrition education. They like to eat outside the home and share meals with their peers, but when they do, their nutritional intake is frequently poor.

If a teenager's eating habits are tied significantly to social acceptance by peers, dietary habits are more likely to be unsatisfactory. On the other hand, if health and family relationships are important, the teenager may develop wise food choices.

The season also affects the eating habits of teenagers. Young adults tend to have a more regular eating pattern in winter than in summer, and so they generally have a larger selection of food during the winter.

Adolescents have a number of bad food habits: the omission of meals, especially breakfast; no time for regular meals; dislike for nutritious foods such as milk; frequent consumption of unbalanced meals outside the home; and concern for body weight (and hair and skin problems, especially acne).

There is much current concern in this country about the dietary habits of teenagers, especially as they affect their physical, physiological, and emotional development. It is claimed, but not totally substantiated, that dietary inadequacies are common among adolescents. The occurrence of tuberculosis among young adults may be the result of nutrient deficiency. Nutrient deficiencies among teenage girls are especially critical.

Teenage girls who become pregnant impose a heavy demand on their nutritional storage. A young mother's nutritional status has a profound effect on the outcome of the pregnancy and the health of the newborn.

Many young adults omit breakfast. Reasons commonly cited are being in a hurry, lacking time, having no appetite, preferring to spend more time on their personal appearance, trying to maintain their weight, and having no company to eat with. Boys eat breakfast more frequently and in greater quantity than girls. Because many homemakers also omit breakfasts, it has been suggested that young girls copy their mothers. Young adults in towns do not skip breakfast as frequently as those in cities or rural areas. Although people who skip breakfast may still eat adequately, they may not be able to satisfy their nutritional need by two meals and snacks. Because skipping breakfast is so common among teenagers, they especially need to receive a good nutrition education.

With the wide selection of fresh, processed, and convenience foods, a nutritious breakfast can be easily put together, including regular foods such as eggs, fruits, milk, juice, bacon, toast, and hot cereals and processed items such as beverages, dry cereals, and snack bars. A breakfast should contribute approximately 500 kcal and is especially important for contributing vitamins C and B_2 and calcium, maintaining a normal to high level of blood glucose, and reducing the appetite for snacks.

Snacking and Obesity

In recent years, snacking by teenagers and concern over this habit have been on the rise. According to a current estimate, daily snacks may make up one-fourth to one-third of adolescents' RDA of calories. Although girls snack more frequently than boys, they do not necessarily have more nutritional problems. Whether snacking is good or bad for a person depends on his or her dietary intake.

Some snacks contribute a significant amount of nutrients without reducing the appetite for regular meals. There is no doubt that excessive snacking on nutrient-light foods is undesirable, especially if they are eaten just before bedtime. However, if the habit of snacking persists, should several small meals a day be encouraged that include nutritious snacks?

Some nutritionists propose that nutritious foods be made available at such strategic places as home refrigerators, school lunches, vending machines, and grocery stores near schools. However, there is a strong feeling that banning nutrient-light snacks is not a key to good dietary intake. Nutrition education is still the most important step.

Fortifying popular snack foods with nutrients that are likely to be lacking in teenage diets is another suggestion, since one survey has shown that some teenagers who snack have inadequate intakes of nutrients such as calcium and iron.

In addition to inadequate nutrition, another common teenage problem is overweight: About 20% to 30% of them may be considered obese. Others have fluctuating body weights. Obese teenagers occasionally suffer respiratory problems. A young adult should be advised to engage in physical exercises and learn to stop eating when full.

Teenage girls are especially unhappy about body fat since they want to be slim and fashionable; many will starve to lose weight. Some who do so may not get adequate nutrients, and occasionally the self-starvation may lead to anorexia nervosa (see Chapter 31).

American teenagers desperately need nutrition education, and implementing this knowledge is as important as acquiring it (see Chapter 17). Good eating habits will develop if the person is motivated. A young adult pays attention to personal appearance, emotional fluctuations, and peer opinions. Health usually does not play an important part in eating choices. Thus, in addition to learning about good dietary intake, teenagers should be subjected to behavioral modification (discussed in detail in Chapter 12) to change old eating habits to positive new eating behaviors.

STUDY QUESTIONS

1. Discuss some nutritional benefits of breast milk. What are some other advantages of breast-feeding? What are the potential disadvantages?
2. What are some differences between the modified milk in most common infant formulas and regular cow's milk?
3. Discuss some advantages and disadvantages of bottle-feeding.
4. Describe two common methods for preparing and sterilizing bottle-feedings.
5. Discuss the nutritional adequacy of milk for the first 3 months and for the next 3 months. What supplements may be needed and under what circumstances?
6. What are some reasons why feeding solid foods to an infant during the first few months of life is not recommended?
7. What are some nutrition problems revealed by national surveys of American children?
8. What is the current thinking among nutritionists about the "clean-your-plate" rule often laid down by parents?
9. Does snacking have any potential benefits?
10. Using an appropriate reference source, compile a list of foods to which children are commonly allergic.
11. What is the *latest* meal pattern requirement for school lunches? (You may have to check into your nearest school lunch program.)
12. Why is it important that teenagers learn not to skip breakfast?

Chapter 15

Nutrition and the Elderly

THE LIFE SPAN of an individual has increased during the twentieth century. In the first decade of this century, life expectancy was only about 50 years; in the 1970s, the average life span was 65 to 70 years for males and 70 to 75 years for females. This older population now constitutes the fastest-growing minority group in the United States. In the early 1900s only about 3 million people were over 65 years; in 1976, there were more than 25 million. Because of the larger number of older people, many of their problems, such as housing, income, diet, and health, are now given more recognition. This recognition and studying of problems should eventually lead to a greater chance for the formulation and implementation of solutions. We will first consider their health status.

HEALTH PROBLEMS OF SENIOR CITIZENS

About 60% to 75% of people over 65 have at least one chronic illness, and 30% to 50% are chronically disabled. Seniors of low socioeconomic status have more health problems, and many of the elderly have low and fixed incomes. The health status of the elderly is also affected by the degree of independence, which is best illustrated by comparing the health of those who are institutionalized with those who are not.

Many known physical factors can affect the health of an older person. These include heredity or genetic constitution; the quality of the air and water; deleterious substances such as pesticides and harmful bacteria; tobacco in any form; alcoholic beverages; drugs; and short- and long-term nutritional intakes.

Since illness frequently accompanies old age, an older person is obviously more concerned with health. However, while many of the health problems of the elderly are real, others are imaginary. Further, some of the problems can be managed, while others cannot. Preoccupation with one's health is common, especially with the functioning of the gastrointestinal tract.

The health problems of old people can be complicated by a lack of health knowledge and a surplus of misinformation. Because older people want to be healthy, possess youthful vigor, and live long, they become very susceptible to quick cures or the unsubstantiated benefits of "patent medicines." They are more gullible than younger, healthier people.

CONSIDERATIONS IN NUTRITIONAL AND DIETARY CARE

With the understanding that health problems of the elderly are only partially related to nutrition, we look now at factors affecting older people's food intake and nutrient utilization: body changes with aging, personal factors, and specific nutrient needs.

Major Biological Changes of the Body

The mechanism of human aging is still unknown, although the types of physiological and anatomical changes associated with the aging process are well documented. Various organs show progressive changes or deteriorations, which are reflected in altered physiological functions. Some of these alterations have a direct impact on the nutritional and dietary status of the person, while others, though of clinical significance, do not. It is suspected that many changes that affect nutritional status are responsible for some of the degenerative diseases associated with aging. The major biological changes of old age are described below.

Respiratory system

As a person ages, the capacity of the lung decreases, thus decreasing the oxygen supply to various organs. This has a direct effect on the basal metabolic rate of the body.

Urinary system

The kidney eliminates waste products less efficiently. Urinary tract changes are marked by an excessive need for nighttime urination. The filtration rate of the kidney and the rate of renal blood flow are also reduced. Renal stones are more common, possibly because of a reduction in their solubility and a change in urinary pH (see Chapter 28).

Musculoskeletal system

Muscular strength, endurance, and agility decrease. The loss of the elasticity of muscles in the abdomen and pelvis contributes to problems in defecation and urination. Also, the nitrogen content in the urine increases because of atrophy of the lean body mass.

Blood system

An older person may suffer forms of anemia from a variety of causes including malnutrition, malabsorption, and chronic diseases such as infections, arthritis, and malignant diseases. Other disturbances of the intestinal system, such as bleeding from hemorrhoids, may also contribute to anemia.

Hormonal changes

Aging also involves hormonal changes. One example is that cells become less sensitive to the action of insulin in some elderly diabetics. This may increase the blood glucose level. Other hormonal changes may affect body nutrient metabolism. The atrophy of muscle or lean body mass may be partially explained by the disturbed hormonal balance.

Body thermoregulation

Temperature maintenance seems to be less reliable in the aged. This fact accounts for many of the tragic deaths of older persons who succumb to extreme heat or cold.

Cardiovascular system

The pumping action of the heart, blood flow, and heart muscle sensitivity to oxygen all decrease in old age. Such changes can slow blood flow and allow fatty chemicals to deposit on the walls of blood vessels. Blood clotting and heart disease become more likely. The smooth muscle of blood vessels is replaced by hyaline and fibrous tissue, thus reducing vascular elasticity. This causes an increase in the systolic blood pressure and pulse pressure.

Alimentary canal

In an older person, changes in the alimentary tract affect nutrient intake, digestion, and absorption. Changes occur along the entire canal—the oral cavity and the gastrointestinal system.

Elderly patients have numerous problems with the mouth: dryness, pain, a burning sensation, tongue fissures, cracking of the lips and corners of the mouth, loss of taste sensation, and difficulty in chewing and swallowing. In the oral cavity, taste, odor, and saliva all undergo changes. Taste bud and olfactory sensitivity is altered, resulting in a loss of taste sensation and the desire for food. Food becomes less appealing. Further, among many patients with artificial upper dentures, taste sensitivity for bitter and sour decreases, though remaining normal for salty and sweet. However, many elderly people with full dentures become conditioned to this loss of taste acuity for bitter and sour.

The loss of taste sensation, especially for salt, in an older person may result from a specific nutrient deficiency (such as inadequate folic acid), degeneration of nerves supplying the oral cavity, and/or epithelial keratinization (structural changes of the surface layer of cells) of the tongue.

The tongue undergoes an aging process itself; in edentulous people it loses some of its papillae and also hypertrophies. The latter may occur because the tongue now does most of the mastication and thus increases in size. However, specific nutrient deficiencies are occasionally responsible.

The aging process definitely affects the salivary glands: They make less saliva. Food becomes less palatable and the person has difficulty in masticating, which normally involves mixing with saliva and swallowing. Saliva content also changes: There is less ptyalin and more mucus, and the saliva is ropier and more viscous. The partial digestion of starch in the mouth is reduced because of insufficient ptyalin (amylase). As a result of these saliva changes, more dental plaque forms. This, together with increased sucrose intake, permits bacteria to grow that cause tooth decay. Some elderly people are reported to have a large number of cavities. Others develop a dry mouth. The oral mucosa is often translucent and pale, although it is inflamed and atrophic in some older people. In some patients, sore spots develop under the dentures because of a lack of saliva to lubricate the area. In addition, the dentures do not stay in place well because of the reduced saliva flow. This partially explains why the elderly prefer liquid and soft diets.

There are also major changes in the gastrointestinal system. The stomach has a higher pH because of a decrease in hydrochloric acid formation. Fewer digestive enzymes are formed and released, interfering with digestion. The intestinal mucosa becomes physically altered, which impairs digestion and absorption. Because of the decreased formation and release of bile, an older person has more difficulty in digesting fat. Reduced intestinal blood flow usually accompanies a decrease in motility of the stomach and intestines. Because of a decline in a number of intestinal absorptive cells, nutrient transport systems are modified. Loss of peristaltic tone increases the likelihood of constipation. Calculus formation in or calcification of the biliary system increases with advancing age. Finally, both prescription and over-the-counter drugs, which are commonly consumed by the elderly, have a profound effect on the gastrointestinal system (as discussed in the next section and in Chapter 16).

Personal Factors Affecting Nutritional Status

In addition to debilitating body changes, elderly individuals may be subject to a number of personal factors that limit the adequacy of their diets. These include food habits, financial problems, limited resources, physical handicaps, psychological problems, clinical conditions, and drug use.

Food habits

Very few people do not like foods; both young and old enjoy eating. However, the past eating habit of an older person may be bad. An unwholesome eating pattern should definitely be modified as age advances; however, this frequently proves to be very difficult. All the unavoidable changes in later years, such as limited income, solitude, and physical handicaps, affect the traditional dietary pattern, even if an elderly person has been following a wholesome diet throughout life. This person will also face some difficulties in adjusting to a new nutritional pattern.

Financial problems

While food prices keep rising, the income of a senior citizen is usually fixed. As a result, food selection is limited, and even occasional eating out may be impossible. The belief in the miraculous benefits of special foods such as supplements, yeast, and seaweed has drained some of the financial resources of the elderly, since most of these items are extremely expensive.

Scarcity of food-related resources

The lack of cooking utensils, refrigerators, adequate housing, storage, and kitchen facilities can affect the eating pattern of an older person. Purchasing food is sometimes difficult or impossible because of a lack of transportation. Other problems include the decreasing number of neighborhood grocery stores and the wide selection of foods in a modern supermarket, which can be confusing when a person is trying to select the right foods that are within one's means. Also, if a person cannot cook, walking to a distant restaurant can be tiring.

Physical handicaps

Some elderly people are very fragile, which poses numerous problems in food shopping, cooking, and eating. Teeth that are in poor condition or completely lacking is one of the major problems. Some elderly suffer from "old age" conditions of the esophagus (see Chapter 24) such as achalasia, hiatus hernia, spasm, and diverticula, all of which can affect eating and drinking. Because of the paralysis resulting from a stroke, some may be unable to feed themselves. Other physical handicaps of the aging and aged may hinder their eating and drinking ability.

Psychological problems

The emotional and psychological makeup of older people has a tremendous influence on their nutritional and dietary intakes. Some psychological factors that can affect this population group include: death of a spouse or a dear friend; lack of meaningful work or interactions because of retirement or the departure of children; loss of youthful vitality and deterioration of health; maladjustment to the changes in self-image and self-regard; uneasiness after relocating; lack of social activities and companionships, resulting in slow alienation; and constant fear of death.

These psychological problems can make an older person susceptible to depression, which may lead to either disinterest in food or overeating. Some individuals suffer a loss in interest and desire to shop and cook because it is troublesome to prepare meals for one person. Boredom, inconvenience, and lassitude can therefore lead to undesirable eating habits and patterns. Sometimes people may express their anger, resentment, and dejection by rejecting food or overeating.

Clinical conditions

As a person ages, two types of clinical entities occur. The person may be disabled or die because of *old age* or *diseases* of old age. It is generally agreed that good nutrition throughout life helps to prevent or delay the diseases of old age, although its specific impact on delaying the aging process is still unknown. Many older persons are fit and independent without any sign of old age diseases if they follow good eating and exercising patterns. On the other hand, some older people suffer from nutritionally related clinical problems. The major ones are anemia, a diabetic tendency, cardiovascular diseases, bone diseases, muscle atrophy, weight imbalance, and nutrient deficiencies.

Anemia. Old people are very susceptible to nutritional anemias because of deficiencies in dietary iron, folic acid, and vitamin B_{12}.

Diabetic tendency. For unknown reasons, as one ages, glucose tolerance is impaired. In some patients this results in clinical diabetes, although

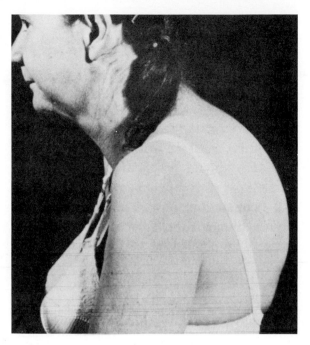

FIGURE 15-1 The "dowager's hump" in a patient with osteoporosis. Some patients with the appearance are asymptomatic. (From J. Ingham, *Drug* 8[1974]: 290)

most patients never proceed to this stage (see Chapter 26).

Cardiovascular diseases. Heart disease is recognized as a serious problem among older men. This is further complicated by the frequently high lipid blood profiles among the elderly. High blood pressure is also common in this population group. Circulatory complications from high blood pressure may be related to a high salt intake.

Bone diseases. Many older people, especially women, have osteoporosis, a disease that accounts for much bone trouble, such as fractures and back pain (see Chapter 7). Figure 15-1 shows the characteristic signs of osteoporosis. The deteriorating condition of the bones can affect teeth and is definitely related to dental problems such as periodontal diseases and cavities. Deafness can also occur as a direct result of osteoporosis of the ear cochlea. The exact cause of osteoporosis is unknown, but inadequate dietary intakes of vitamin D, calcium, and/or fluoride may play a role and should be carefully monitored.

Muscle atrophy. As discussed in Chapter 2, a decline in lean body mass or muscle atrophy becomes more evident as one ages. The resulting negative nitrogen balance is one of the fundamental signs of deteriorating nutritional status. The loss of body fat will exaggerate any protein malnutrition that may exist.

Weight imbalance. Probably the two most obvious clinical signs of nutrient imbalance are underweight and overweight. Some older people are highly susceptible to either deficient or excess caloric consumption. More details on this topic are presented later in this chapter.

Nutrient deficiencies. Deficiencies of dietary nutrients among older Americans occur in all segments of the population, although the extent varies. However, those elderly who are alcoholic or indigent make up a sizable portion of those with nutrient deficiencies. More information is presented later in this chapter.

Drugs

Because debilitating conditions are common among some elderly people, drugs are frequently prescribed. The major categories of drugs are aimed at correcting problems of the mind, the heart and circulation, blood pressure and chemistry, pain, infection, the alimentary tract, and nutritional deficiencies. Complete information on the relationship between drugs and nutrients in the body is presented in Chapter 16, but we will briefly overview the effects of drugs commonly prescribed for older people here.

Drugs prescribed for the mind include those that treat mental disorders, are antidepressant, or that produce sedation. Chlorpromazine (Thorazine) is used to treat mental disorders, especially in the elderly. Because it stimulates food intake, overconsumption and overweight can become problems. Monoamine oxidase inhibitors (for example, isocarboxazid) are antidepressants; they can interact with tyramine in such foods as cheese to produce hypertensive crisis.

Frequently, high blood pressure is already a problem in an older person. Other antidepressants may cause constipation and paralytic ileus.

Sedatives are employed by elderly people to combat anxiety, insomnia, or nocturnal restlessness. Popular prescriptions include barbiturates and benzodiazepines (Librium, Valium, and Dalmane). These chemical compounds affect the nutritional status of individuals in many ways. Barbiturates may induce vitamin deficiencies by interfering with their absorption and secretion. In some cases, because of the strong effects of these sedatives and hypnotics, an old person may become confused and take an overdose. Because of such drug-induced confusion and forgetfulness, they may also neglect their food and liquid intake, which may, in extreme form, result in dehydration and starvation.

Drugs for the heart and circulation are prescribed for a large number of elderly people. Common ones such as digitalis glycosides and quinidine can confuse the patient and precipitate nausea and vomiting. Because of this reaction, the old patient may eat less, although the nausea and vomiting may help an obese patient to lose weight. Nevertheless, using these drugs for that purpose is obviously unacceptable.

Control of high blood pressure in the elderly is a major task in geriatric medicine. However, antihypertensive chemical compounds such as hydralazine may induce vitamin deficiency and the use of diuretics to control blood pressure can create numerous problems. For example, the use of furosemide (Lasix) may increase potassium excretion and result in hypokalemia in the patient. Often the symptoms of low blood potassium, such as lethargy and muscular weakness, are passed off as signs of old age, but hypokalemia can complicate other existing clinical conditions in the patient and be fatal.

Many older patients are treated for other problems related to the blood, including such common illnesses as anemia, blood clots, and varicose veins. Some of the therapeutic chemicals used to treat these illnesses have an adverse effect on nutritional status. On the other hand, anticoagulants such as coumarin may be counteracted (negated) by the vitamin K included in some vitamin supplements when the patient uses these supplements at the same time. Long-term use of large doses of iron therapy may produce constipation or diarrhea, although the use of hematologic agents does not necessarily produce such problems.

The need to relieve pain in some older patients necessitates the use of analgesics and anti-inflammatory agents (for arthritis) such as aspirin (salicylates) and corticosteroids. The former may cause intestinal bleeding; the latter may cause ulcers. The use of antibiotics in older people, though not a common practice, can have a profound effect on body nutrients. As an example, neomycin interferes with the absorption of essential nutrients (see Chapter 16).

Probably the drugs most "abused" by older people are those that regulate intestinal functions. Older people frequently use antacids to treat indigestion and heartburn. One complication of the long-term usage of certain antacids is the excessive consumption of sodium. Laxative usage by American senior citizens has become legend, so much so that a large percentage of prime-time TV commercials are devoted to the sale of these products. Some common side effects from using laxatives frequently are prolonged constipation, dehydration, and electrolyte imbalance. Psychological and physiological dependence on laxatives occurs in many patients.

In the United States the pursuit of health has made many elderly people believe in the miracle of vitamin and mineral supplements. Sometimes they are prescribed by physicians to correct genuine nutrient deficiencies. However, indiscriminate use of these supplements can cause poisoning. The adverse effects of high doses of niacin, ascorbic acid, and vitamins A and D are discussed in Chapter 6.

Nutritional Needs

As at other ages, an elderly person must have an adequate intake of nutrients and food. It is generally agreed that the consumption, digestion, absorption, utilization, storage, and excretion of nutrients are all affected by nutrition and those physiological, psychological, social, economic, and cultural changes associated with old age.

However, there have been very few controlled studies to ascertain the appropriate nutrient intakes of the elderly. One thing is certain: There is no one single "special" or "right" food for someone who is growing old.

Although there is very little documented information to indicate the exact nutrient requirements of the elderly, experts in the field generally assume that, with the exception of calories, the RDAs of an older person are about the same as those of a 25-year-old. A brief analysis is provided below.

Calories

According to the current RDAs, the daily caloric requirement for people over 50 decreases. Some reasons for this decline include a decrease in the basal metabolic rate, atrophy of the lean body mass, and decreased activity. Retirement, a relaxed attitude, disability, or chronic illness can decrease daily activities. Many older women expend less energy because their children have left home.

Experts agree that a man between 60 and 70 uses about 75% to 90% of the calories of a 25-year-old. There is no fixed daily caloric recommendation for ages above 50, although caloric intake should correlate with the person's age, physical activity, and body condition. Being underweight or obese should be avoided.

Protein

We can study the protein need of an elderly person from a number of perspectives. According to the latest RDA, an adult needs about 0.8 g of protein per kilogram body weight. It is estimated that the senior population in this country consumes about 40 to 50 g of protein a day, less than is recommended for most of them. One study concluded that many women under 40 years of age consumed nearly twice as much meat, poultry, and fish as women over 70. However, given the many factors involved in the nutritional and dietary care of an older individual, it is difficult to conclude exactly what the most appropriate amount of protein is for an older person.

It must be emphasized that the protein consumption of an older person should not be excessive, since kidney problems increase as age advances. A large amount of ammonia and urea must be excreted if too much protein is eaten. On the other hand, many clinical problems of the elderly may be related to insufficient protein intake, including such complaints as fatigue, backache, and hair loss. Low protein consumption usually means that the intake of many essential nutrients occurring in protein-rich foods is also inadequate.

There are many possible reasons why the protein intake of an older person may be less than what is recommended. Since most protein foods are expensive, many senior citizens have few opportunities to get good and tasty protein-rich products such as meat, fish, and poultry. Another good source of protein is milk. A decline in consumption of dairy products may be due to high cost or adverse intestinal reactions such as lactose intolerance or constipation.

Another major reason for the decreased intake of good protein food among senior citizens is dental problems. Loss of teeth and poor-fitting dentures make it difficult to chew meat. Because of the decline in the total intake of food or calories among the elderly, much of the protein they consume is actually used as energy sources. The overall result is a decrease in protein intake and utilization efficiency.

Because many elderly have chronic illnesses, protein absorption and utilization and nitrogen retention may all be affected. Older people characteristically have an unusually high nitrogen content in their urine. Their ability to retain nitrogen may be decreased or become less efficient with a concomitant, slow atrophy of the lean body mass. One additional cause may be common psychiatric problems such as depression. Emotional instability has been related to decreased nitrogen retention. There is also some nitrogen loss because of reduced physical activity.

Carbohydrate

Carbohydrate should make up 50% to 55% of an older person's total daily caloric intake. Carbohydrate and protein intakes should be coordinated so that there is sufficient carbohydrate

to "spare" protein but not so much that protein intake is limited.

About 40% to 45% of carbohydrate consumption should be starch and other complex forms, with sugar intake limited to about 5% to 10%. An older person should be careful not to eat too many sugary products, for they may increase dental problems, are notoriously "empty-caloried," and can inhibit the intake of essential nutrients. Persons over 40 are susceptible to the development of diabetes. Pancreas malfunctioning, decreased cellular sensitivity to insulin, or glucose malutilization may impair glucose tolerance.

Lactose in milk products poses a difficult problem; intolerance to this disaccharide is being recognized more frequently in older people, although the reason is unknown. One should always ascertain if an elderly person can drink milk and eat dairy products without intestinal discomfort.

Fat

There is much controversy surrounding the quantity and quality of fat needed or eaten by older people. The major question is the effect of dietary fat on the cause and outcome of heart disease. It is also noted that an aging digestive system provides less pancreatic lipase for fat digestion and absorbs fat less efficiently. Currently, it is recommended that the fat intake of people over 50 should make up about 30% or less of their total caloric intake.

Vitamins and minerals

Vitamin and mineral deficiencies in old people are common. Vitamin deficiency in the elderly progresses in five stages: body storage depletion; an abnormal biochemical profile; physiological maladjustments such as general tiredness and anorexia; general clinical manifestations such as anemia, hair loss, and weight loss; and finally identifiable clinical symptoms with organs manifesting pathological conditions.

The elderly have the same stated requirement for vitamins as 25-year-olds, although old people are suspected of having a higher need. A brief analysis of the vitamin needs of senior citizens is provided below.

Vitamin C is the vitamin most likely to be low in the diet and blood of older people, especially those who are chronically ill or living alone. The body's ability to retain the vitamin appears to decline, and there is definitely a reduced level of the vitamin in tissues, blood, and cerebrospinal fluid. The low intake of this vitamin in some senior citizens is probably related to their lifelong eating habits; others limit their intake of fresh fruits and vegetables since these foods are expensive and contain undigestible cellulose. The need for vitamin C may be especially high during old age, possibly because of decreased efficiency in utilization, although the relationship between vitamin C metabolism and old age is very complex. As discussed earlier, drug use can decrease the absorption and increase the excretion of vitamins, including C.

Thiamin, or vitamin B_1, deficiency in old age can be brought about in several ways. First, old age itself may increase the need and decrease the efficiency of utilization of the vitamin. Second, certain drugs can decrease absorption, increase excretion, and distort proper metabolism of the vitamin. For example, diuretics can increase excretion. Third, excessive alcohol consumption can result in the well-known Wernicke's disease, although this syndrome is actually associated with multiple nutrient deficiencies. Fourth, because of the decreased secretion of hydrochloric acid in the stomach, thiamin can be inactivated there. Fifth, clinical circumstances such as fever, cancer, or the intravenous administration of dextrose may precipitate deficiency of the vitamin. Finally, a low-cost, starchy diet can precipitate deficiency, since the metabolism of carbohydrate requires a large amount of thiamin.

For vitamin B_2, riboflavin, an increased need because of old age is suspected. The clinical use of testosterone therapy and tissue repair from trauma such as bedsores may increase the requirement. The types and quantity of intestinal flora may adversely affect the utilization, synthesis, and secretion of the vitamin.

The need for pyridoxine, or vitamin B_6, is governed by a number of factors: generally increased need during old age; the use of drugs such as isoniazid or penicillamine, which induce deficiency; adverse effects of the intestinal flora on the absorption and synthesis of the vitamin; and decreased intestinal mucus secretion of the vitamin. Finally, urinary tract infections may be associated with vitamin B_6 deficiency.

Folic acid deficiency is common in old people. Reasons for the deficiency are an increased body need, the effects of drugs, an insufficient intake, destruction during cooking, a decreased absorption and utilization, reduced intestinal synthesis, and decreased intestinal mucus secretion.

As discussed in Chapter 6, there is a very important clinical relationship between folic acid and vitamin B_{12}. Vitamin B_{12} deficiency can be masked by a large dose of folic acid. The deficiency of vitamin B_{12} in older people may reflect decreased absorption, gastric atrophy with a decrease in intrinsic factor (see Chapter 6), or abnormal bacterial growth in the small intestine. Although serious vitamin B_{12} deficiency can result in neurodegeneration, the relationship between the psychiatric problems in the elderly and vitamin B_{12} deficiency is not clear. However, some studies have shown that when older patients are given B_{12} injections or even oral doses, the symptoms of fatigue disappear and the person's sense of disorientation and confusion can be alleviated. Other studies have reported negative results.

The two vitamins B_{12} and folic acid can be affected by iron intake: a decreased iron intake will decrease their absorption. Iron, B_{12}, and folic acid are responsible for the well-known nutritional anemia in some older Americans.

The absorption of all fat-soluble vitamins is affected by a low fat intake, insufficient secretion of bile, pancreatic failure, and extensive dependence on antibiotics and laxatives. The conversion of provitamin A to the vitamin may be affected by old age. Deficiencies of vitamin D (and thus calcium) are partially responsible for osteoporosis. For example, low milk consumption and little exposure to sunlight are major factors. Excessive consumption of vitamins A and D in supplements is always hazardous, but especially so for older people. For those older individuals who are prescribed a diet high in polyunsaturated fat, the requirement for vitamin E may be increased to preclude oxidation. Some clinicians therefore prescribe vitamin E supplement for these individuals.

Vitamin K may be deficient in some older people, but not from insufficient dietary intake. A number of clinical conditions predispose older people to this vitamin deficiency: liver and gall bladder disease, excessive use of antibiotics, too much use of aspirin or related chemicals (salicy-lates), decreased intestinal synthesis of the vitamin for various reasons, and the excessive use of mineral oil. Ecchymosis (discoloration due to extravasculation of blood) is a sign of possible vitamin K deficiency.

According to the 1980 RDAs, an older person requires the same essential minerals as a 25-year-old, including calcium, phosphorus, iodine, iron, magnesium, and zinc. However, older people may have a special need for fluoride, although this is not yet confirmed. Iron, calcium, and possibly fluoride intakes require special attention because of the incidence of nutritional anemia and osteoporosis in the older population. Since calcium absorption is related to the dietary intake of phosphorus, the latter is of obvious importance.

Calcium deficiency plays an important role in the development of osteoporosis (see Chapter 7). Low calcium intake may be due to consuming too few dairy products. However, osteoporosis has multiple etiologies. For example, many patients show clinical improvement when given sodium fluoride.

Iron deficiency among the elderly is common and may result from many causes, including a low intake. Elderly women living alone who consume only doughnuts, coffee, and a limited number of other food items are commonly affected by iron deficiency anemia. Fortunately, anemia can be easily identified in an older person. In general, iron deficiency is less common among elderly men.

The water and fiber requirements of an older person are especially important. As indicated earlier, aging is accompanied by decreased intestinal muscle tone and peristalsis. This condition usually results in constipation. To manage constipation, a person should drink 6 to 8 glasses of water daily and eat abundant whole grains, fresh fruits, and vegetables that will contribute fiber or cellulose. If desired, the liquid may be hot bouillon (not recommended if salt is not advised), coffee, tea, fruit juice, or vegetable juice to add variety. Consult Chapters 3, 22, and 24 for more information on the importance of fiber in the diet. Nutrition education may be needed if the person does not like some of the suggested foods.

PLANNING A GOOD DIET

In providing dietary care for the older population, care givers should remember that each person has unique problems and must be evaluated individually. The multiple considerations discussed in this chapter should be reviewed. The elderly, as a population group, can be aided nutritionally only when those who work with them can perceive the entire environment in which the elderly live. The nutritional and dietary care of a senior citizen must be supplemented by a complete understanding and consideration of the social, economic, psychological, environmental, and clinical factors involved.

Care givers should take into account the person's present nutritional status and eating patterns, age, lifelong eating habits, income, social standing, education, activity, illnesses, physical handicaps, psychological problems, and living arrangement (independent living versus institutionalization). Nutrition education may be needed, for although it is never too early or late to establish good eating habits, the eating habits of an older person may be more ingrained than those of a younger person. All abnormal physical and other problems that may result in poor nutritional status should be corrected as much as possible. And some elderly people may need advice on how to spend money wisely on food.

In diet planning, the total calories of an older person should be reduced, but all other essential nutrients must be provided in adequate quantities. Chapter 10 should be consulted for some basic information about planning a balanced diet. Using the basic four food groups is a good start. The foundation diet for an older person should contain about 1,100 to 1,200 kcal a day, which may be provided by serving the following:

Food Groups*	Sample Serving
Milk and equivalents, e.g., yogurt, ice cream	2 to 8 oz milk
Meat and equivalents, e.g., eggs, legumes, peas, peanut butter	2 to 4 oz cooked lean meat 1 egg
Vegetable and fruit group	½ c yellow or deep green vegetable ½ c other vegetable 1 medium cooked (baked) potato 6 oz tomato, orange, or grapefruit juice (citrus juices) 1 serving other fruit or juice, such as apple, banana
Cereal and equivalents, e.g., bread, macaroni	3 sl bread ⅔ c cereal

The above diet meets the RDAs for older people in all nutrients except calories. When one uses this foundation diet in meal planning, the foods mentioned may be combined in the cooking process and need not be consumed in the forms listed. The food items listed may not be very flavorful by themselves, since they lack the fat and sugar normally found in pastries, honey, cream, butter, and gravies. All these appetizing additions may be used, although overindulging in any of these items should be avoided.

In using the foundation diet for older people, good protein foods include meat, poultry, fish, and cheese, especially if they are cooked until tender. Many elderly individuals do not include such items in their diet for reasons such as low income, ignorance of protein value, and poor dental conditions. Many elderly people have problems with milk: it is costly, it may cause diarrhea or constipation, some older people simply do not like it, and it may not be advisable for some people because of its high saturated fat and cholesterol content. All these parameters must

be taken into consideration when planning menus with milk as a major source of calcium, vitamin B_2, and possibly protein. For some older people, low-fat or skim milk can be used as a beverage or in cooking. If fluid milk must be totally excluded, more tender meat, canned fish, cheese, and similar protein-rich foods (such as yogurt) may be used than indicated in the foundation diet. However, the calcium intake of these individuals must be monitored.

In determining how many calories should be added to the foundation diet to meet a particular older person's needs, the body weight is the major index.

It can be assumed that a person 60 years old should weigh the same as when he or she was 25. If the person is not underweight or overweight and is doing a fair amount of activity such as walking or light gardening, a daily intake of 1,600 to 1,900 kcal for a male and about 1,500 to 1,700 kcal for a female is sufficient. If the person is underweight or overweight, the caloric intake should be adjusted so that he or she will achieve the optimal weight and then maintain it.

In planning menus for older people, the foods should be those that they like, with as few restrictions as possible. This will ensure that similar foods can be found in restaurants or friends' homes. A reasonable arrangement is to use a combination of the foundation foods and a fair amount of those other items that the person likes. Foods with low-fat sauces will help those with a reduced saliva flow. The family, patient, or nursing home operator must be carefully taught how to provide the diet, with special attention to food preparation and the size of serving portions. Table 15-1 gives sample menus for 7 days for an elderly person.

UNDER- VERSUS OVERNUTRITION

An older person with an intestinal problem may have many nutritional and dietary complications. However, for healthy elderly individuals, inadequate dietary intakes and overeating are probably the most widespread problems.

Inadequate dietary nutrient intakes may re-

---

*For complete information on different food items in the food groups, consult Chapter 10.

TABLE 15-1 A Week's Sample Menus for Older People

Snacks: Some suggested items are fresh fruit; soft, dried prunes; whole wheat crackers with cheese; cheese sticks; peanut butter on toast; and yogurt. Snacks may be served in mid-morning, mid-afternoon, and/or before bedtime.

Breakfast	Lunch	Dinner
Monday		
½ c orange juice	1 c creamed tuna on noodles	1 c chicken, rice, and pea casserole
Poached eggs	Celery or carrot sticks	½ c buttered spinach
Whole wheat toast	1 c skim milk	Fresh fruit; banana, melon
2 slices bacon	1 orange	Decaffeinated coffee
Tuesday		
½ c grapefruit juice	Cottage cheese with pineapple	3 oz broiled fish
½ c cooked oatmeal, sugar, and	salad	½ c mashed potato
milk	Banana	½ c creamed peas
1 fruit or 2 sausages	Toasted raisin bread with butter	Celery sticks
	Tea or decaffeinated coffee	Gingerbread, 1 square
		Decaffeinated coffee
Wednesday		
Sliced banana and milk	1 c split pea soup	1 c beef and vegetable stew
2 bran muffins	Tomato and shredded lettuce salad	½ c cabbage coleslaw
1 baked egg with cheese	Crackers and cheese	½ c rice pudding
1 orange	Skim milk	Decaffeinated coffee
	1 pear	
Thursday		
3 stewed prunes	1 c minestrone soup	3 oz hamburger steak
2 French toast slices with butter and	Cottage cheese and peach salad	½ c mashed potatoes
syrup	2 crackers	½ c buttered broccoli
8 oz skim milk	Skim milk	1 sliced tomato with dressing
	Decaffeinated coffee	2 oatmeal cookies
		½ c gelatin
Friday		
Sliced orange	Tomato and rice soup	1 c tuna noodle casserole
1 c puffed rice with milk and sugar	⅔ c potato salad	½ c mixed vegetables
Sliced cheese	Celery or green pepper sticks	½ c lettuce salad
Hot tea	½ c strawberries	1 slice angel food cake
	Skim milk	Decaffeinated coffee
Saturday		
Melon or fresh fruit	1 c creamed chicken and	1 c spaghetti and meatballs in
3 hotcakes	mushrooms on toast	tomato sauce
2 sausages	½ c carrot and raisin salad	½ c string beans
8 oz skim milk	Fresh fruit	½ c fruit gelatin
	Skim milk	Decaffeinated coffee
Sunday		
3 stewed figs	2-egg cheese omelet	1 baked pork chop with applesauce
½ c hot cream of wheat	½ c steamed rice	½ c buttered peas
Milk	½ c asparagus	1 baked potato
2 slices crisp bacon	Celery or carrot sticks	Lettuce wedge
8 oz hot chocolate made with skim	8 oz skim milk	½ c custard
milk		Decaffeinated coffee

Note: Each day's caloric contribution is about 1,800 kcal. The amount can be increased or decreased by adjusting the serving sizes. Thus, the serving sizes of some items are not provided.

To provide the adequate RDAs, use the snacks to complete the foundation diet as discussed in Chapter 10.

If there is concern about the cholesterol in eggs, replace some egg servings with lean meat (e.g., turkey), fish, and so on.

sult from many factors, including a decreased intake of food or a selective eating habit (that is, eating the same one or two foods daily). Those who do not eat enough food may suffer from dental problems, lack of money, loneliness, or other factors discussed earlier. Many are underweight and exhibit old-age symptoms such as backache, tiredness, weakness, loss of alertness, and nutrient deficiencies or a borderline nutritional status. Some may have other pathological conditions, such as chronic illness.

Those whose diets provide plenty of calories but are lacking in nutrients will not be underweight, but they may have the other symptoms of old age, such as backache. Their main problem is eating foods that are high in calories and low in essential nutrients. This inclination may be related to physical or physiological handicaps. For example, dry mouth and ill-fitting dentures predispose them to eating processed foods such as frozen dinners, sugary pastries, and canned spaghetti. Many of these prepackaged foods are soft, require minimal cooking, and are tasty. However, they are high in cost and low in good proteins and essential vitamins and minerals.

Why are some older Americans overweight? Some health professionals believe that many of them eat too many calories and drink too many alcoholic beverages. Foods such as fatty beef, potato chips, and pastries are all fattening. Individuals who eat these foods may or may not have essential nutrient deficiencies. Inactivity is also a major cause of obesity in this population group: They often lead sedentary lives with little exercise and too much sleep (8 to 12 hours versus 6 to 10 hours for young adults). Some elderly people eat excessively because of psychiatric problems, while others have carried obesity from childhood into old age.

FOOD AND NUTRITION INTERVENTION PROGRAMS

To help improve the nutritional status of the elderly, Congress passed the Older Americans Act. In 1972, the act was amended (Public Law 92-128) by Title VII, the National Nutrition Program for the Elderly. (At the time this was writ-

ten, a proposed federal budget cut would have eliminated this program.) This legislation is currently administered by the Administration on Aging, Office of Human Development, Department of Health and Human Services. Its major responsibility is to grant money to each state for specific nutrition projects that are designed for individuals over 60. Some basic aims of the legislation are to provide the elderly with (1) nutritious and hot meals at a low cost, (2) food and nutrition education, (3) an opportunity for socialization and recreation, (4) information on other health and social assistance programs, and (5) low-cost and convenient transportation. Aggressive outreach programs and personal approaches to the elderly provide senior citizens with the incentive to use these services.

Although the federal government provides the money, private or public nonprofit organizations such as churches and women's clubs usually run the food programs. Any organization should be made up of a board consisting of local citizens and professionals. Each organization is required to have a dietitian or nutritionist on its staff to provide professional advice about the food and nutritional needs of old citizens.

At present, two special programs are common: home-delivered programs ("Meals-on-Wheels") and congregate meals programs. In the first program, meals are served to individuals at their homes for various reasons. They may be living in isolated spots far away from large meal centers, or chronic illnesses or disability may make it inconvenient or impractical to transport them to a meal center. The second program appears to be more common, although accurate statistics are lacking. Older citizens come to a central kitchen where they are served hot, nutritious meals and at the same time engage in social interaction.

The policy on the cost of the meals is simple. Older citizens who prefer to pay may do so; otherwise, the meals are free. Meals served at home may be paid for with food stamps, but not congregate meals.

The meals served should contain:

1. Milk or other source of calcium (one serving, e.g., 8 oz of milk)
2. Meat, fish, or poultry (one serving, e.g., 3 oz)
3. Bread or equivalent (e.g., 1 or 2 slices)

4. Vegetables and fruits (2 servings of green/ yellow vegetables and other fruits)
5. Desserts such as pastries, pie, or cake (one serving)

As with all meal planning for older people, these special feeding programs must take into consideration the person's situation and his or her environment.

STUDY QUESTIONS

1. Describe the health status of older people in this country according to the latest statistics.
2. Explain the effects of aging on at least five of the following body systems: respiratory, urinary, musculoskeletal, blood, hormonal, thermoregulatory, cardiovascular, and digestive.
3. What are some physical, psychological, and financial conditions that may contribute to malnutrition in elderly people?
4. What clinical problems are common among older people?
5. Name some drugs commonly used by older people, and explain their potential effects on nutritional status.
6. How do the RDAs for an old person generally compare with those for a 25-year-old?

Discuss the effects of a deficient or excessive protein intake on the elderly.
7. What vitamins are the diets of older people most likely to supply in inadequate amounts? Why? Inadequacies of what nutrients may be responsible for nutritional anemia?
8. Why is a high intake of water and fiber recommended for older people?
9. Why is milk sometimes omitted from diets planned for older people? How can its nutritional contributions be compensated for in these diets?
10. Describe the aims of the National Nutrition Program for the Elderly. What kinds of programs are currently used to meet these goals?

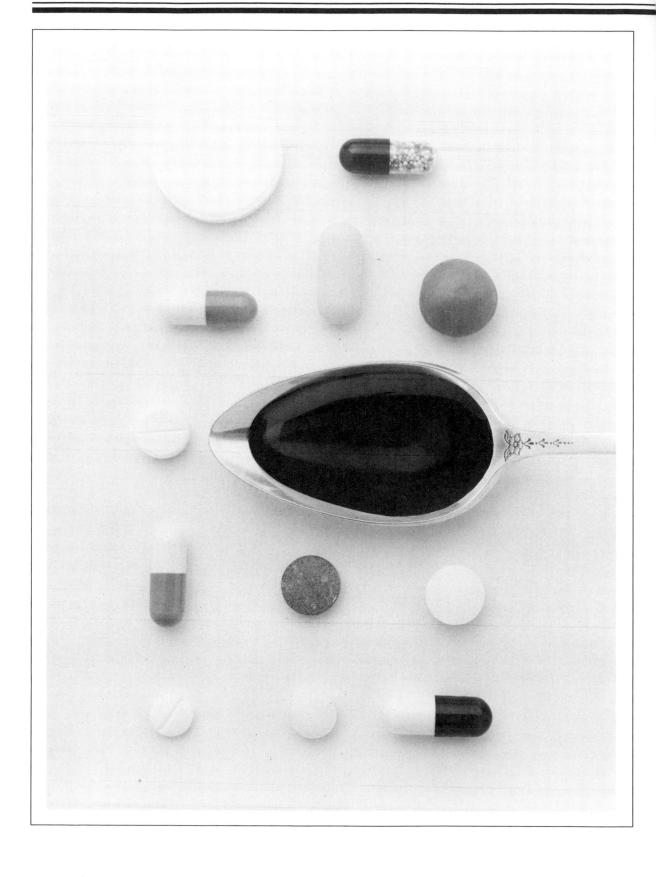

Chapter 16

Nutrition and Drugs

IN THE LAST few years, there has been a tremendous amount of concern about the relationship between drug usage and certain nutritional parameters. Much research and clinical information are now available, and many books and review articles have been written on the topic. This chapter is not intended to present a comprehensive discussion on this subject; more details may be obtained from the list of references provided at the back of this book. In this chapter, six main concerns about the interaction between drugs and nutrition are briefly discussed: the effects of drugs on the nutritional status of a person; the influence of foods and nutrients on the effectiveness of drugs; nutritional imbalances and drug metabolism; the relationship between drugs and certain active substances in food; drugs and breast milk; and preventive and corrective measures.

EFFECTS OF DRUGS ON NUTRITIONAL STATUS

The effects of drugs on a person's nutritional status vary with the type of drug. One type of drug is actually nutrients themselves. When a large dose of a nutrient is used to achieve a certain pharmaceutical effect, this nutrient will most likely be labeled a drug. For example, in clinical medicine, a large dose of vitamin C or ascorbic acid is frequently used as a drug for acidifying urine to cure bladder infections. Another example is niacin (a vitamin; see Chapter 6), which is frequently used in large doses to lower blood cholesterol.

Although some drugs can influence the nutritional status of a person, the extent of this influence is controlled by many factors. Some of these factors are related to the usage of the drugs, for example, the type, the dose, the time and frequency of intake, and so on. Another factor is the nutritional status of the patient when the drug is taken, e.g., drugs may have more profound effects on a malnourished individual. A person in good nutritional standing can handle a larger dose of a drug; a malnourished person may need a higher dose for the desired therapeutic effect. A third factor is body adaptation to drugs. Individuals differ in their abilities to handle foreign substances, such as drugs. Those who can adapt better to the consumption of drugs apparently suffer fewer nutritional problems. A fourth factor is a person's ability to absorb drugs and/or nutrients, which is controlled by factors such as age, the production of digestive juices, and so on.

Single or multiple drug therapy is known to have specific short-term and long-term effects on a person's nutritional needs and status. Specific effects on the gastrointestinal system include: pharmacological effects (such as stimulating peristalsis); alteration of intestinal mucosa (such as destruction of cells); effects on the intestinal bacteria (for instance, permitting some to grow faster than others); diarrhea and constipation; direct and indirect nausea and vomiting; and altered taste and smell sensitivity. Drugs may affect hunger, satiety, and appetite, as well as the digestion, absorption, utilization, storage, and body synthesis and metabolism of nutrients. This last category of effects is of major importance.

Many drugs cause malabsorption of nutrients, including laxatives, cathartics, cholestyramine, oral hypoglycemics, antibiotics, anticonvulsants, and antigout agents (colchicine). A drug can interfere with the absorption of a nutrient via one or more mechanisms. A drug can solubilize a nutrient. For instance, mineral oil (a major ingredient in some drugs) dissolves dietary carotene, which then is lost to the normal absorptive process and passes out in the feces. Second, drugs can absorb or interfere with the physiological activity of bile salts so that fats and fat-soluble vitamins that require bile salts for optimal absorption are not taken up efficiently from the intestinal tract. Third, drugs can induce cellular damage to the intestinal mucosa or selective blockage of and interference with nutrient transport mechanisms. Fourth, drugs can damage the exocrine pancreas, causing decreased synthesis and/or release of pancreatic enzymes with consequent maldigestion of fat, protein, and starch.

Drugs can affect nutrients in several ways. They may complex a nutrient, making it unavailable for attachment to its normal binding site on a tissue or substance, or they may simply replace the nutrient on a protein-binding site. A combination of such effects may also occur. These interactions may promote kidney excretion of the affected nutrients in free or complexed forms.

Drugs can affect fat metabolism in many ways: malabsorption, the excretion of bile salts and acids in the fecal mass instead of their normal recirculation, inefficient absorption of cholesterol, malfunctioning of lipoprotein lipase, formation of fatty liver, development of abnormal serum lipid levels, and alteration of the extent of triglyceride catabolism in the adipose tissues.

Drugs affect carbohydrate metabolism by controlling the blood glucose level in accordance with the dose, type, and route of administration of the drug. Drugs may also affect either insulin level or liver metabolism.

Drugs also influence vitamin metabolism in a number of ways. Drugs can increase catabolism of body tissue and cells, thus increasing excretion and decreasing body storage of vitamins. Some drugs can increase the breakdown of vitamins, as do anticonvulsant drugs with vitamin D. Some drugs can affect specific cells, interfering with the formation of a vitamin from a provitamin, some deter the synthesis of vitamins by the intestinal flora, and some (such as vitamin antagonists or antimetabolites) can induce vitamin deficiencies.

Below is a list of some categories of drugs that may affect a person's nutritional status.

1. Alcohol
2. Alkylating agents
3. Analgesics
4. Antacids
5. Antibiotics
6. Anticholinergics
7. Anticoagulants
8. Anticonvulsants (including sedatives)
9. Antihistamines
10. Antihyperglycemic drugs
11. Antihyperlipidemic drugs
12. Antihypertensives
13. Anti-inflammatory drugs
14. Antimaniac depression agents
15. Antimetabolites
16. Antipsychotic drugs
17. Appetite depressants
18. Bulking agents
19. Cardiovascular drugs
20. Chelating agents
21. Diuretics
22. Herbal medicines
23. Hormones
24. Purgatives
25. Miscellaneous

Table 16-1 describes the clinical usages and the specific effects on nutritional status of each category in the above list. As an illustration, Figures 16-1 and 16-2 show symptoms of folic acid deficiency in a patient who had been on long-term anticonvulsant drug therapy (refer also to Table 16-1). The patient's oral ulcerations improved and epithelialization was complete on the eighth day following the administration of sodium folate.

INFLUENCE OF FOODS AND NUTRIENTS ON THE EFFECTIVENESS OF DRUGS

Just as some drugs interfere with the body's use of nutrients, foods and nutrients may interfere with the effectiveness of drugs by affecting their absorption or their neutralizing or eliminating effects, by directly interacting with drugs, or by influencing the excretion rate of drugs or their by-products.

When a doctor prescribes a drug, he or she obviously wants its pharmacological action to exert the maximum therapeutic effect. However, it has long been assumed that the presence of food in the intestinal tract affects the absorption of most drugs, although the extent is not clear. Food substances change the pH, secretions, motility, and other conditions (e.g., osmolarity) of the intestinal lumen, all of which can influence the ionization, solubility, stability, transit time, and absorption of drugs. Additional factors that can affect drug bioavailability are preabsorptive inactivation, incomplete absorption, biotransformation, and the person's physiological status.

The direct interaction between nutrients and drug-metabolizing enzymes and the effects of pharmacologically active substances in foods

TABLE 16-1   Examples of Common Drugs, Their Clinical Usages, and Their Specific Effects on Nutritional Status

Drug	Clinical Usage	Possible Direct and Indirect Effects on Nutritional Status
Alcohol	A minor ingredient in medications[†]	Refer to Chapter 25 for nutritional status of an alcoholic. Thiamin and magnesium deficiencies most common; deficiencies of folic acid, niacin, and pyridoxine may also occur. May decrease absorption and utilization and increase excretion of affected nutrients.
Alkylating agents Cyclophosphamide (Cytoxan) Nitrogen mustard (Mustargen)	Cancer chemotherapy	Anorexia, vomiting, nausea, hemorrhagic cystitis and colitis, ulceration of intestinal mucosa. Anorexia, vomiting, nausea, diarrhea, and metallic taste.
Analgesics Aspirin	Multiple uses	May fluctuate blood glucose, deplete body folic acid and vitamin C. Stomach bleeding may result in iron-deficiency anemia. Potential hypernatremia, especially undesirable for heart or kidney patients.
Cocaine		Decreases sensitivity of taste, especially of bitterness and sweetness.
Phenylbutazone		May ulcerate stomach walls, decrease intestinal mucus secretion.
Antacids Aluminum hydroxide	Buffering stomach acids	Chronic ingestion results in hypophosphatemia, especially low phosphate intake. Also causes constipation and potential vitamin malabsorption.
Calcium carbonate or too much milk		Milk-alkali syndrome. Hypercalcemia, which can be serious.
Sodium bicarbonate		Hypernatremia, especially undesirable for kidney and heart patients.
Antibiotics	Destruction of pathogenic organisms	Most drugs can irritate intestinal walls, causing diarrhea, thus fluid and electrolyte imbalance. Causes malabsorption of various nutrients to different extents. Decreases nutrient contribution by intestinal flora, for example, vitamins such as K, folic acid, biotin, and B_{12} and amino acids.
Bleomycin (Blenoxane)	Cancer chemotherapy	May cause stomatitis, anorexia, nausea, vomiting, fever, oral ulceration.
Cycloserine	Antituberculosis; treatment of urinary tract infection	Folic acid and pyridoxine deficiencies.
Dactinomycin (actinomycin D, Cosmegen)	Cancer chemotherapy	May cause stomatitis, anorexia, nausea, vomiting, diarrhea, oral ulceration.
Griseofulvin	Controlling growth of some dermatophytes	May cause loss of taste sensitivity; nausea.
Isoniazid	Antituberculosis	Niacin and pyridoxine deficiencies.
Neomycin (and kanamycin)	Nonabsorbable; gut sterilization and prevention of coma from liver failure	May damage small intestine walls; malabsorption of various nutrients usually not significant because of short-term usage.

TABLE 16-1   (continued)

Drug	Clinical Usage	Possible Direct and Indirect Effects on Nutritional Status
Paraaminosalicylic acid (PAS)	Antituberculosis	Decreases absorption of fat and vitamin B_{12}, especially if given at high dosage.
Tetracycline	Multiple uses (systemic effect)	May specifically affect bone growth, malabsorption of various nutrients. Usually not significant because of short-term usage.
Anticholinergics	Treatment for peptic ulcer	May cause dry mouth, constipation, and urinary retention.
Belladonna		
Propantheline bromide		
Anticoagulants	Preventing blood clotting	
Coumarin		Works by counteracting the function of vitamin K, i.e., synthesis of prothrombin.
Phenindione		Steatorrhea. May bring about loss of fat-soluble vitamins and essential fatty acids in the stool.
Anticonvulsants (including sedatives) Barbituates Dilantin Diphenylhydantoin Others	Sedation, tranquilizing, control of epilepsy	Folic acid and vitamin D deficiencies; sometimes vitamin K deficiency (see Figures 16-1 and 16-2).
Antihistamines	Multiple uses, e.g., antiallergy	Dry mouth, increased appetite; intestinal problems may cause malabsorption of nutrients.
Chlorpheniramine		
Promethazine		
Antihyperglycemic drugs (oral)	Lowering blood glucose; optional treatment for diabetes	May interfere with vitamin B_{12} absorption.
Biguanides		
Metformin		
Phenformin		
Sulfonylureas		May increase appetite.
Antihyperlipidemic drugs Cholestyramine Clofibrate	Lowering blood cholesterol	Both may interfere with the absorption of fat-soluble vitamins A, D, and K, fat, iron, and vitamin B_{12}. Clofibrate may also induce nausea and abnormal muscle metabolism.
Niacin		May interfere with glucose metabolism.
Antihypertensives Hydralazine	Lowering blood pressure	Vitamin B_6 deficiency by binding with B_6 and increasing its excretion.
Propranolol		Hypoglycemia.

TABLE 16-1   (continued)

Drug	Clinical Usage	Possible Direct and Indirect Effects on Nutritional Status
Anti-inflammatory drugs Colchicine	Treatment for gout	Maldigestion and malabsorption. Diarrhea and steatorrhea. Sodium, potassium, B_{12}, lipid, nitrogen, fat-soluble vitamins may be lost in stool. Decreases disaccharidases in intestine. Lowers blood carotene concentration. Damages the intestinal walls.
Antimaniac depression agents Lithium carbonate	Treatment for mental disorders	Blocks release of thyroid hormone, which can cause hypothyroidism with possible goiter. Strange, unpleasant taste sensation. May affect renal function and fluid and electrolyte balance.

Antimetabolites
    Cytarabine (Cytosar)
 	
    5-Fluorouracil
    6-Mercaptopurine
 	
    Methotrexate
	Cancer chemotherapy	Most produce nausea, vomiting, and diarrhea. Also anorexia, megaloblastic anemia. Antagonist to pyrimidine.
		Also stomatitis, gastrointestinal ulceration and bleeding.
		Also stomatitis, fever. Antagonist to purine and pantothenic acid.
		Also stomatitis, anorexia, abnormal liver function, and gastrointestinal ulceration.

Antipsychotic drugs
 	
    Butyrophenone
    Phenothiazines
    Thioxanthenes
	Treatment of psychiatric problems	Weight gain, hyperglycemia, lactation, temperature irregularities, and paralytic ileus.

Appetite depressants
 	
    Amphetamine*
    Fenfluramine
	For losing weight	Decreased food intake results both in decreased caloric and essential nutrient intake.

Bulking agents
 	
    Guar gum
    Methylcellulose
	For losing weight	These substances take up fluid and swell in the intestine. There may be decreased caloric and essential nutrient intake.

Cardiovascular drugs
    Digitalis and its glycosides
 	
    Quinidine
    Procainamide
	Treatment of heart problems Increasing the force and velocity of cardiac contraction
	Treatment of antiarrhythmias
		Most can produce anorexia, nausea, and vomiting.

Chelating agents	Treatment of poisoning with heavy metals; sometimes used for other diseases such as arthritis and Wilson's disease	May also chelate essential minerals such as calcium and iodine.

TABLE 16-1   (continued)

Drug	Clinical Usage	Possible Direct and Indirect Effects on Nutritional Status
Deferoxamine Penicillamine		
Diuretics	Removing excess water from body	
Benzothiadiazine Thiazide Diazoxide		Diabetogenic; increased urinary excretion of potassium, hypokalemia.
Furosemide Ethacrynic acid. Spironolactone Triamterene		Increased urinary potassium, hypokalemia. Increased urinary calcium, hypocalcemia. Hyperkalemia, decreased urinary excretion of potassium. Hyperkalemia, hypocalcemia, possible folic acid deficiency.
Chlorothiazide Hydrochlorothiazide Thiazides Thiazides		Increased urinary potassium, hypokalemia. Decreased urinary calcium, hypercalcemia.
Chlorthalidone Furosemide		Increased urinary excretion of zinc.
Herbal medicines	Multiple uses in some countries[†]	Diarrhea may cause loss of fluid and electrolyte. Presence of oxalic acid in plant parts may cause some essential mineral elements to precipitate. Some plant parts, when ingested, may cause hypoglycemia.
Hormones		
Insulin	Lowering blood glucose	Increases appetite.
Oral contraceptive pills (mestranol, conjugated estrogens, ethynyl estradiol)	Contraception	Multiple and profound effects on the nutritional status of a woman. May produce vitamin B_6, B_{12}, and folic acid deficiencies. Affects the body metabolism of protein, fat, carbohydrate, calcium, phosphorus, magnesium, and zinc. Effects of the new "low-dose" contraceptive pills are unknown.
Steroids (cortico-steroids such as cortisone and prednisone)	Multiple uses	Diabetogenic; growth retardation; muscle protein catabolism; adipose tissue deposition; electrolyte imbalances, hypernatremia, hypokalemia, hypocalcemia, fluid retention; potential osteoporosis; increased excretion of zinc and iodine; peptic ulcer.
Purgatives	Laxatives (cathartics)	
Mineral oil Phenolphthalein		May result in loss of fat-soluble nutrients in the stool. May interfere with the absorption of calcium and vitamins.
Miscellaneous		
Marijuana (either smoked or ingested)		May increase appetite.

[*]Authority to prescribe this type of medication is now "limited."

[†]Clinical usage of these drugs is uncommon in the United States.

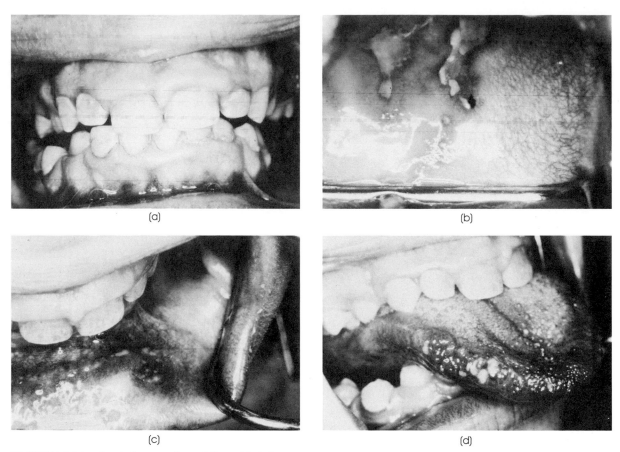

FIGURE 16-1   Oral changes in a folic-acid-deficient patient precipitated by anticonvulsant drug therapy (G. M. Stein and H. Lewis, *Journal of Periodontology*, 1973; 44:645): (a) Macrogingival pallor and gingival hyperplasia; (b) Ulcerations of buccal mucosa; (c) Ballooning and ulcerations of alveolar mucosa; (d) Ulcerative glossitis.

on therapeutic drugs will also affect the effectiveness of drugs; both of these relationships will be discussed later in this chapter.

How food chemicals or nutrients can affect the absorption of drugs is best illustrated by minerals such as iron, magnesium, calcium, and aluminum salts. These can complex with one common category of antibiotics—tetracyclines—to form an insoluble precipitate. Simultaneous ingestion of tetracyclines and foods containing these mineral elements will therefore significantly reduce the therapeutic effectiveness of the antibiotic. Consequently, a larger dose may be needed. Such interaction calls into question the common practice of ingesting drugs with some foods and/or liquids to mask the unpleasant taste

and flavor of the drugs. Doctors and all concerned health professionals should ensure that a patient adheres to instructions regarding when to take a drug and its relationship to the time, size, and type of meals.

NUTRITIONAL IMBALANCES AND DRUG METABOLISM

The body may be able to metabolize drugs, just as it metabolizes ingested foods. If the process fails, the substances may be toxic to the body. Nutritional imbalances are known to affect the metabolism of drugs.

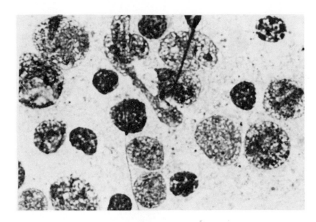

FIGURE 16-2 Megaloblastic bone marrow with granulocytic hyperplasia in the same patient as shown in Figure 16-1. (G. M. Stein and H. Lewis, *Journal of Periodontology*, 1973; 44:645)

Metabolism of Drugs

Once a drug has been absorbed, a group of enzymes located mainly in the liver handles its metabolism. The term "mixed-function oxidase" has been given to this group of enzymes. This enzyme system is made up of a number of components found in the hepatic microsomes: nicotinamide adenine, dinucleotide phosphate, flavoprotein reductase, cytochrome P-450 (heme protein), oxygen, phosphatidylcholine, and other substances. An absorbed drug interacts with this system in the liver before the substance or its metabolite achieves its intended purpose. The interaction is illustrated in Figure 16-3.

Figure 16-3 shows one way in which a drug undergoes changes in the body. In general, any ingested drug undergoes two major changes in its metabolic pathway. The first involves a chemical alteration of the drug itself, which may be reduction, oxidation, or hydrolysis. The new product may be formed directly, as shown in Figure 16-4. Then the product undergoes a second major change, in which a conjugation or synthetic product is formed. In the human body, various types of conjugation process are available. Some of the most common ones are conjugation with glucuronic acid, glycine (hippuric acid synthesis), sulfuric acid, and acetic acid.

This new conjugated product is excreted either in the bile or the urine.

If either metabolic change fails to occur, the drug may be toxic to the body. Figure 16-4 shows how the toxicity of a drug is determined by which critical point in the metabolic path fails. As the figure indicates, the body must maintain full functioning of both the mixed-function oxidase and the conjugation mechanisms.

Effects of Nutritional Status

The body's nutritional status is related to the two systems that metabolize drugs. First, for the oxidation-reduction-hydrolysis process, the mixed-function oxidase involves most of the following essential nutrients: niacin, riboflavin, pantothenic acid, ascorbic acid, protein (amino acids), iron, copper, calcium, zinc, and magnesium. Second, the conjugation system involves the following nutrients: glucose, amino acids, acetate groups from fat, carbohydrate, protein, vitamins (including pantothenic acid, folic acid, vitamin B_{12}, and niacin), and the chemical lipoic acid. If any of these nutrients are unavailable, normal drug metabolism will suffer. For example, the toxicity of a drug may be increased or decreased or its effective dosage higher or lower than planned. Much of this information has been confirmed in animal studies and been assumed to apply to humans.

In humans, extremes of nutrient deficiencies or excesses are expected to create imbalances of the two systems that regulate drug metabolism, with mixed results. For example, many children in undeveloped countries suffer from inadequate dietary protein and calories. Nutritional rehabilitation of such individuals is frequently accompanied by the usage of drugs. Their malnourished bodies can affect drug metabolism in at least two ways. Because of the lack of protein, the synthesis of enzymes, including the mixed-function oxidase, is reduced. Conjugation groups such as glucuronide, glycine, and sulfate are also deficient. Many children suffering from protein deficiency are also infested with hookworms. The drug used to destroy the hookworms in infested individuals, tetrachloroethylene, is known to be toxic in high doses.

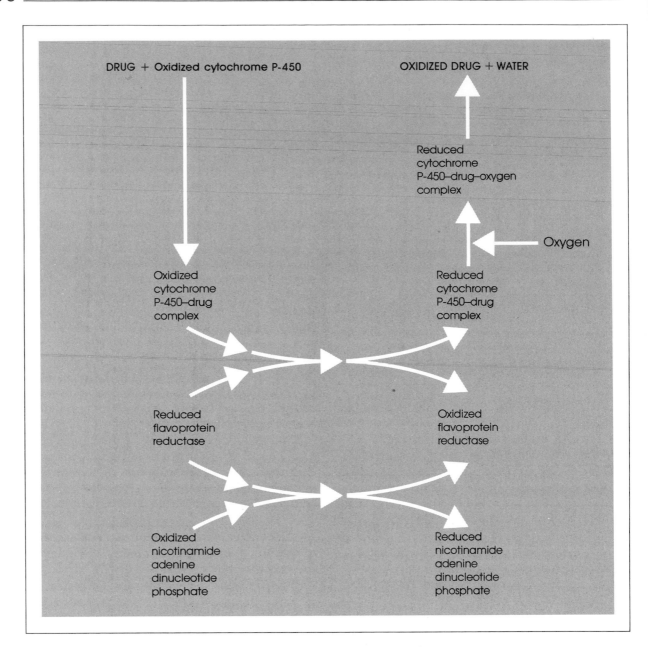

FIGURE 16-3 Interaction between an ingested drug and the mixed-function oxidase.

However, undernourished children do not exhibit toxic effects when given large doses of the drugs. It is speculated that because of the depressed quantity of the enzymes involved, the drug does not form as many of the usual toxic by-products.

Disturbed drug metabolism from a nutritional imbalance does not always have such unexpected results. For instance, heart patients are sometimes given digitalis, the toxicity of which depends on body potassium level. If the blood potassium of the patient is low because of certain medical treatments or other reasons, there is a greater risk of induced cardiac arrhythmias.

Older people have adverse reactions to many drugs, which is suspected to result from vitamin

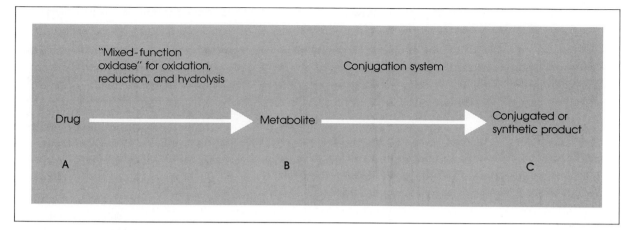

"Mixed-function oxidase" for oxidation, reduction, and hydrolysis

Conjugation system

Drug → Metabolite → Conjugated or synthetic product

A   B   C

FIGURE 16-4   Normal and disturbed metabolism of a drug. If substance **A** is toxic and the mixed-function oxidase system fails, then the drug is toxic to the body. If substance **A** is not toxic and the mixed-function oxidase system fails, then the drug is not toxic to the body. If substance **A** is not toxic but substance **B** is toxic and the conjugation system fails, then the drug is toxic to the body.

C deficiency, common among the elderly population. Normally, vitamin C participates in the regulation of drug-metabolizing enzymes.

RELATIONSHIPS BETWEEN DRUGS AND CERTAIN ACTIVE SUBSTANCES IN FOOD

For a long time, some foods and beverages have been known to contain certain pharmacologically active ingredients that are incompatible with some therapeutic drugs. The active ingredients are amines and ethyl alcohol; the drugs affected include monoamine oxidase inhibitors, disulfiram, and others. Table 16-2 summarizes these incompatible relationships, and an example is discussed below.

Tyramine and its related amines are found in cheese and other foods. Monoamine oxidase inhibitors such as procarbazine are frequently prescribed for treating depression. Clinical reports have shown that the tyramine in cheese can react with procarbazine and similar-purpose drugs to create a "hypertensive crisis" in the patient. Reac-

tion usually takes place within 30 minutes to an hour of consuming the offending food if the drug has been taken some time before eating. Some individuals show extreme symptoms, such as severe headache, subarachnoid hemorrhage, and even death. It appears that the drug raises the levels of serotonin and norepinephrine in the central nervous system and reinforces the cardiovascular effects of tyramine (phenylethylamine). The severity of the reaction depends on the total quantity of tyramine ingested (from food), the drug dosage used, patient susceptibility, and the interval between eating the food and taking the drug.

Since tyramine is produced from the amino acid tyrosine, any food containing protein is suspect if it has undergone degradation. For example, when cheeses are permitted to mature, there is increased putrefaction from bacterial action and consequently a higher content of tyramine. Thus, unmatured cheeses contain less tyramine than those with a strong (acidic and rancid) flavor and those that have been aged for a long time. Cheddar cheeses rank high on the list of tyramine-containing foods, with Roquefort, Camembert, and Stilton cheeses following.

Recently, the use of monoamine oxidase in-

TABLE 16-2   Examples of Interactions Between Drugs and Active Ingredients in Certain Food Products

Foods Involved	Pharmacologically Active Ingredients	Affected Drugs		Clinical Symptoms
		Type	Therapy	
Major types:* cheese, Marmite (a hydrolyzed yeast product), chicken liver, pickled herring, meat extract (Bovril), broad beans, beer, wine Minor types:* canned figs, sour cream, aged meats, soy sauce, raisins, caffeine, chocolate	Phenylethylamine derivatives (pressor amines): tyramine, dopamine, and norepinephrine	Monoamine oxidase inhibitors, e.g., isocarboxazid, tranylcypromine, pargyline, phenelzine, nialamide, procarbazine	Treating depression	A marked rise in blood pressure and other cardiovascular changes, such as vomiting, nausea, headache, palpitations. Cerebral hemorrhage and death may result. Sometimes termed "hypertensive crisis."
Charcoal-broiled beef	Polycyclic hydrocarbon	Phenacetin	Analgesic	May increase degradation of drugs, thus decreasing their effectiveness.
Alcoholic beverages and any foods that use wine or other form of alcohol as a preparation ingredient, e.g., wine sauce or beef in wine.	Ethyl alcohol	Disulfiram (Antabuse)	Treating alcoholics	Low blood pressure, nausea, flushing, headache, vomiting, weakness, visual problems, convulsions
		Metronidazole (Flagyl)	Treating vaginitis from *Trichomonas vaginalis*	Same as above
		Sulfonylureas	Oral antihyperglycemic agents for diabetes	Headache, blurred or double vision, fine tremors, uncontrollable yawning, mental confusion and incoordination

*"Major types" refers to those foods that are more likely to cause the interaction; "minor types" are less likely because of either infrequent consumption or a low level of the active substances.

hibitors in treating depression has declined, mainly because of the possible hypertensive reaction. However, some clinicians have questioned the wisdom of this decline. The tyramine content of food varies from sample to sample. The causes of many of the reactions reported have not been adequately substantiated. And in some patients, the benefit of monoamine oxidase inhibitors should be balanced against the limited, questionable, or even preventable risk.

DRUGS AND BREAST MILK

For centuries breast milk has been considered by some as the perfect food for an infant. In addition, there have long been jokes associating an infant's rejection of breast milk with the mother's having gorged on garlic, onion, chocolate, and other strong-flavored foods. Recent studies have provided some scientific bases for these jokes. Certain chemical ingredients in garlic, onion, and chocolate may produce an unpleasant reaction in some nursing babies. A more serious concern now is the appearance of drugs in the breast milk and their potential effects on nursing infants. Doctors are worried about numerous therapeutic drugs (and nondrug chemicals) that the nursing mother may be consuming either willingly or inadvertently.

This concern has been heightened by a number of factors. Within the last few years, breast-feeding has regained popularity and the number of mothers nursing has been steadily increasing. At the same time, drug usage in the United States has also been on the rise. A large number of new drugs are now available for prescription and over-the-counter sales, and physicians are prescribing more drugs. The American public, including nursing mothers, is spending millions of dollars on nonprescription drugs each year. There is also a large number of women who are taking oral contraceptive pills while nursing. And it is now known that there is substantial contamination of the environment by industrial and household chemicals, some of which have reached our food and drinking water supplies. Some, such as pesticides, have appeared in breast milk.

Thus, the type and quantity of drugs and environmental chemicals that a woman is ingesting during her lactation period have become very important issues. However, a lack of information has hindered our understanding of the important relationship between drugs and breast milk. The basic uncertainty concerns the passage of chemicals from the mother's blood plasma via the milk to the infant. Because of the obvious unwillingness of nursing mothers to permit a study of the passage of chemical(s) through their milk to their infants, most existing scientific literature on the subject comes from animal studies. Aside from the questionable validity of extrapolating animal results to human situations, it is not even easy to conduct animal experiments.

From available studies, we know that five factors determine the passage of drugs from blood plasma to milk: (1) the degree of ionization of the chemical, (2) the difference in pH between the two media plasma and milk, (3) the solubility of the chemical in fat (organic) and water (aqueous) media, (4) the transport mechanisms involved, and (5) the proper functioning of the mother's renal system.

In addition to these factors, we must consider the variables of concentration and time. Obviously, prolonged usage of a drug at high concentration affects the direction of the drug's flow. On the other hand, if the concentration of a drug gradually decreases in the plasma, the drug may back-diffuse from the milk to the plasma (if the mother breast-feeds very frequently during a long interval of drug ingestion). In sum, back-diffusion occurs when the drug has cleared from the plasma over a period of time. Contrary to popular belief, the quantity of milk secreted has very little to do with the amount of drug passing through.

The evaluation of drug passage into the milk involves several factors. First, the amount appearing in the milk depends on the type and concentration of the drugs consumed and the interval between drug consumption and breast-feeding. If the drug is not given orally, then the total amount injected is important. An injected dose of a drug that normally appears in the milk will appear faster than an oral one. Second, the amount of the different types of drugs appearing in the milk may be high, moderate, low, or insignificant. Third, a drug appearing in the milk may be harmless for various reasons: It may be nontoxic, the metabolite that appears in the milk or the blood of the infant may be nontoxic or ineffective, the drug may be destroyed in the infant's intestine or body system, or the drug may be inactivated or not absorbed by the infant. Certain drugs in the milk may not affect the infant at all unless the mother has consumed a large amount of them, or they may be extremely potent even in small amounts.

Fourth, toxicity of certain drugs may be heightened by the small size of the infant, the immature detoxification system of the infant, possible accumulation of the drug by the infant, or hereditary problems in the infant that can aggravate the harmfulness of the drug. Consequently, some drugs in milk may be harmless to infants; others may cause death.

The physician should take some precautions when a nursing mother needs a prescription drug. The physician should also be concerned if she is taking an over-the-counter drug or inadvertently consuming environmental chemicals. The necessity for the drug and the desire of the mother to breast-feed should be taken into account. If the woman has a specific illness such as diabetes, arthritis, high blood pressure, edema, psoriasis, or other recognizable disease that may be treated with drugs, the physician should inform the woman of the risk of the drug to a breast-fed infant and help her to decide. Physicians should have a sound knowledge of how the drugs that they prescribe operate. They should select the types that do not appear in the milk or that have minimal effects on the infant. Physicians should tightly control the type and concentration of drug used and the interval between drug consumption and breast-feeding. If feasible, the physician should advise the woman to interrupt breast-feeding while on the drug; milk flow may be maintained by manually massaging the breast. Other professionals, such as nurses, dietitians, and nutritionists, should also take note of these precautions.

Table 16-3 lists whether some drugs and chemicals pass into breast milk and produce infant reaction and whether breast-feeding is advisable. The doctor should address the question of whether a woman should breast-feed while taking a drug. In Table 16-3, the recommendation for most drugs is "monitoring needed." This means that both mother and doctor should be alert to the implications of taking the drug. The woman may have to stop breast-feeding if her doctor considers it appropriate.

PREVENTIVE AND CORRECTIVE MEASURES

Appropriate preventive and corrective measures are needed to assure that a therapeutic drug will not harm the nutritional status of a patient. Long-range programs are needed, and more clinical studies involving humans are urgently needed to add to our knowledge of the relationships between therapeutic drugs and nutrition. A coordinated monitoring program involving physicians and hospitals would yield important information. The nutritional status of women using oral contraceptive pills should be systematically studied and analyzed, since this population group takes the hormones for a long period. The same applies to older Americans, many of whom take certain drugs for prolonged periods.

Practicing physicians are encouraged to know the effects of a drug on the nutritional status of a patient; to support any public and legislative measures that may reduce the risk of drug-induced malnutrition, such as legal control of nonprescription drugs; not to prescribe drugs unnecessarily; to exercise careful control over prescribing more than one drug for any particular clinical diagnosis; and to educate patients, colleagues, and other health professionals about the effects of drugs on a patient's nutritional status. Whenever applicable, all concerned health professionals should also help to implement these suggestions.

STUDY QUESTIONS

1. Discuss at least eight ways in which drugs may alter the amount of nutrients actually available for use by the body. Give examples of specific drugs that may have these effects.

2. What is "mixed-function oxidase"? What is its relationship with drugs?
3. Under what circumstances may a drug become toxic to the body?

TABLE 16-3   Passage of Drugs and Chemicals into Breast Milk and Infant Reaction

Drug	Clinical Usage	Secreted in Breast Milk			Infant Reaction	Breast-feeding OK?		
		Yes	No	Maybe		Yes	No	Monitoring needed*
Alcohol	Not used clinically but consumed individually	x			None[†]			x
Analgesics	Multiple uses							
Salicylates (aspirin)				x	None			x
Phenylbutazone			x		No information			x
Antibiotics	Destruction of pathological organisms							
Ampicillin		x			May cause diarrhea, candidiasis			x
Erythromycin		x			No information			x
Isoniazid	Antituberculosis	x			None			x
Metronidazole (Flagyl)	Antiprotozoal agent	x			May cause vomiting, loss of appetite, blood problems			x
Nalidixic acid		x			May cause hemolytic anemia if mother is uremic			x
Nitrofurantoin				x	None	x		
Oxacillin		x			None	x		
Penicillin		x			Usually no effects when taken in very small amount; may provoke antigenic response			x
Streptomycin		x			None if mother otherwise healthy; may cause ototoxicity if mother has renal failure			x
Sulfonamides				x	May cause neonatal jaundice, hemolytic anemia			x
Tetracycline		x			None			x
Anticancer agents	Treatment of cancer				Possibility of bone marrow depression			
Cyclophosphamide		x			No information			x
Methotrexate			x		No information			x
Anticoagulants	Preventing blood clotting							
Heparin			x		Destroyed in infant's intestinal system if ingested			x
Coumarins (some)		x			May cause hemorrhage			x
Phenindione		x			Prothrombin time may increase; one case with postoperative hepatoma		x	
Warfarin		x			No information			x

TABLE 16-3 (continued)

Drug	Clinical Usage	Secreted in Breast Milk			Infant Reaction	Breast-feeding OK?		
		Yes	No	Maybe		Yes	No	Monitoring needed*
Anticonvulsants	Sedatives and control of epilepsy				May reduce effectiveness of other therapeutic drugs			
Barbiturates				x	May cause depression of central nervous system			x
Phenytoin		x			No information			x
Phenobarbitone, Phenytoin		x			May develop methemoglobinemia if large dose			x
Antihistamines	Multiple uses	x			No information			x
Antihyperglycemic drugs	Used orally to lower blood glucose				Possible hypoglycemia			
Phenformin HCl (DBI)		x			No information			x
Tolbutamide (Orinase)		x			No information			x
Antihypertensives	Lowering blood pressure							
Propranolol		x			No information, although suspected to cause cardiovascular and hypoglycemic problems			x
Anti-inflammatory drugs	Treatment of arthritis							
Colchicine		x			No information			x
Antipsychotic drugs	Treatment of psychiatric problems							
Chloral hydrate		x			Sedation			x
Chlorpromazine				x	No information			x
Diazem		x			Sedation			x
Diazepam (Valium)		x			Weight loss, lethargy			x
Dichloralphenazone		x			Sedation			x
Lithium carbonate		x			No information, suspected to cause flaccid muscles			x
Propoxyphene HCl (Darvon)		x			No information			x
Cardiovascular drugs	Treatment of heart problems							
Reserpine		x			May produce galactorrhea in the mother, diarrhea, lethargy, and sucking difficulties such as respiratory blockage			x

TABLE 16-3 (continued)

Drug	Clinical Usage	Secreted in Breast Milk			Infant Reaction	Breast-feeding OK?		
		Yes	No	Maybe		Yes	No	Monitoring needed*
Diuretics	Eliminating body water							
Cyclopenthiazide			x		No information			x
Furosemide			x		No information			x
Hydrochlorothiazide		x			No information			x
Environmental chemicals and related substances	Rare				May produce undesirable effects, depending on the substance			
Chlorobenzene		x			Multiple, extreme, adverse effects, e.g., coma, death			x
Chlorophenothane (DDT)		x			No information			x
Mercury		x			May produce adverse effects, e.g., nerve damage			x
Polychlorinated biphenyls		x			May produce adverse effects, e.g., discoloration of skin			x
Hormones and related substances	Multiple uses							
Insulin, adrenaline, corticotropin		x			Destroyed in infant's intestine	x		
Oral contraceptive pills	Contraception	x			Male infants may develop gynecomastia; female vaginal linings may proliferate; may decrease milk supply		x	
Thyroxine, corticosteroids			x		No information			x
Laxatives	Purgatives, cathartics							
Aloe		x			May be laxative			x
Anthraquinone derivatives		x			As above			x
Cascara		x			As above		x	
Phenolphthaleine (in nonprescription items)		x			No information			x
Rhubarb		x			No information			x
Senna		x			May cause diarrhea			x
Narcotics	Multiple uses							
Heroin		x			Addiction, withdrawal symptoms		x	
Methadone		x			None			x
Morphine, codeine		x			None			x

TABLE 16-3   (continued)

Drug	Clinical Usage	Secreted in Breast Milk			Infant Reaction	Breast-feeding OK?		
		Yes	No	Maybe		Yes	No	Monitoring needed*
Miscellaneous	Variable							
Allergens (milk, fish, cheese)	None	x			Destroyed in infant's intestine	x		
Minerals	As supplement							
Iodide		x			May produce thyroid goiter and cancer if large dose			x
Fluoride		x			May mottle teeth if large dose	†		x
Nicotine (smoking)	None	x			No known immediate health hazard to infants if maternal smoking is less than 1½ packs of cigarettes a day; more than this may reduce milk supply and disrupt infant feeding schedule and response		x	
Radioactive materials, e.g., ¹²⁵I, ¹³¹I	Thyroid diagnosis and therapy	x			May destroy infant thyroid		x	
Theophylline	Multiple uses	x			May cause irritability			x
Vitamins	As supplement							
D		x			May cause hyper-calcemia if large dose			x
Carotene		x			May cause yellowing of skin if large dose			x

*As a precautionary measure, monitoring is recommended even if a drug is currently known not to be secreted in milk.

†Medical texts record one known case of mild intoxication of an infant breast-fed by a woman who had consumed a few glasses of wine (reported in 1936).

4. Why is it important to monitor the foods or liquids taken with drugs? Give two examples.
5. What factors could render drugs passing into breast milk harmless to the nursing baby? What factors could exaggerate their effects?

6. Give at least five examples of drugs thought to reach infants through breast milk and their possible effects on the baby. What precautions should be taken to minimize dangers of infant reaction to chemicals in breast milk?

Chapter 17

Nutrition Education

BECAUSE OF THE increasing concern about food, nutrition, and health during the last decade, professionals and organizations in the health field have all expressed an intense interest in nutrition education. Consequently, organizations such as the American Dietetic Association, the American Diabetes Association, the American Medical Association, the Society of Nutrition Education, and the American Institute of Nutrition all have issued a definition for nutrition education. Further, prominent nutritionists, physicians, scientists, and educators have also provided their definitions for nutrition education. Some of these definitions may be obtained from the references cited at the back of this book. For the purposes of this chapter, *nutrition education* is defined as the process whereby the most basic and recent knowledge acquired in the discipline of nutritional sciences is interpreted and transmitted by experts to both professionals and the lay public, so that they can apply the information to improve human health and the quality of life.

Nutrition education is needed to counteract poor nutrition in all population groups. Well-controlled nutritional surveys have indicated that undesirable dietary practices and subnormal nutritional status can be identified among the American public at all levels of socioeconomic status and among all segments of the population. This is especially true in regard to certain high-risk groups such as alcoholics, infants, and old people. These surveys have also shown that poverty and ignorance are still two major barriers to good nutritional and dietary practices. The American public is tremendously confused about correct and authentic nutrition information because of past unsuccessful development and implementation of nutrition education programs.

Both state and federal governments have expressed concern about the lack of success in nutrition education endeavors. In 1969, the White House Conference on Food, Nutrition, and Health gave priority status to nutrition education. However, these efforts have been hampered by the difficulty in changing lifelong eating habits.

THE IMPORTANCE OF NUTRITION EDUCATION

Nutrition education is urgently needed by the lay public and professionals for many reasons. For instance, clinical and experimental evidence indicates that lifelong good nutritional practices may reduce one's risk of contracting a crippling or fatal disease. Good diet and nutritional practices also maintain body functions at healthy levels.

The general public has indicated concern and is interested in knowing more about:

1. How to eat well on less money.
2. How to avoid foods with harmful ingredients.
3. How to plan "balanced" meals.
4. Better ideas for healthful snacks.
5. How food and diet are related to one's health.
6. The availability of food for everyone in the world.
7. The safety and nutrient contents of the American food supply.

KNOWLEDGE ABOUT FOOD AND NUTRITION

In 1964 the United States Department of Agriculture (USDA) formed the Interagency Committee on Nutrition Education. This committee developed four basic concepts that were to be used in implementing nutrition education programs. In 1969 the White House Conference on Food, Nutrition, and Health used these concepts to develop a framework that included seven nutrition concepts for use in planning nutrition curricula in public school systems. The language and content of these concepts are simple to understand and applicable to all who want to be in good health. These concepts are reproduced in the list below.

I. Nutrition is the process by which food and other substances eaten become you. The food we eat enables us to live, to grow, to keep healthy and well, and to get energy for work and play.

II. Food is made up of certain chemical substances that work together and interact with body chemicals to serve the needs of the body.
   (a) Each nutrient has specific uses in the body.
   (b) For the healthy individual, the nutrients needed by the body are usually available through food.
   (c) Many kinds and combinations of food can lead to a well-balanced diet.
   (d) No natural food by itself has all the nutrients needed for full growth and health.

III. The way a food is handled influences the amount of nutrients in the food, its safety, appearance, taste, and cost; handling means everything that happens to food while it is being grown, processed, stored, and prepared for eating.

IV. All persons, throughout life, have needs for about the same nutrients but in varying amounts.
   (a) The amounts needed are influenced by age, sex, size, activity, specific conditions of growth, and state of health, altered somewhat by environmental stress.
   (b) Suggestions for kinds and needed amounts of nutrients are made by scientists who continuously revise the suggestions in the light of the findings of new research.
   (c) A daily food guide is helpful in translating the technical information into terms of everyday foods suitable for individuals and families.

V. Food use relates to the cultural, social, economic, and psychological aspects of living as well as to the physiological.
   (a) Food is culturally defined.
   (b) Food selection is an individual act, but it is usually influenced by social and cultural sanctions.
   (c) Food can be chosen so as to fulfill physiological needs and at the same time satisfy social, cultural, and psychological wants.
   (d) Attitudes toward food are a culmination of many experiences, past and present.

VI. The nutrients, singly and in combination of chemical substances simulating natural foods, are available in the market; these may vary widely in usefulness, safety of use, and economy.

VII. Food plays an important role in the physical and psychological health of a society or a nation just as it does for the individual and the family.
   (a) The maintenance of good nutrition for the larger units of society involves many matters of public concern.
   (b) Nutrition knowledge and social consciousness enable citizens to participate intelligently in the adoption of public policy affecting the nutrition of people around the world.

Consumers and professionals alike need nutrition education. For instance, with accurate nutrition information, the mother of a 3-year-old boy will understand the value of milk and its contribution to the nutritional care of the child. Thus, if he drinks little milk and eats a limited amount of meat, fish, poultry, and cheese, she will know that his intake of protein and calcium is low. If he drinks too much milk, she will know that he will not feel like eating other foods. If he eats a lot of other foods simultaneously, she will know that he may gain too much weight. If any of these situations occur, the mother should know that her child is not getting a balanced diet.

Let us consider the case where the son drinks a lot of milk. He may thus be ingesting excess butterfat and cholesterol. Overconsumption of milk may predispose him to anemia because of either the low iron content in milk or occult intestinal bleeding caused by the milk. If the child shows signs of bowel discomfort when drinking milk, he may be unable to digest lactose or have milk allergy. The mother can receive all this valuable nutrition information by reading the literature on food and nutrition, viewing educational films, or participating in an adult education workshop.

Adults also need accurate nutrition information in evaluating their own food habits. A 45-year-old salesman who likes to drink alcoholic beverages should know that excessive drinking may have an adverse effect on his nutritional status. His working schedule and drinking habits may cause him to eat a one-sided diet comprised mainly of baked potatos, steak, and wine with little consumption of fruits and vegetables. He may become overweight in addition to having deficiencies of essential nutrients. Also, the alcohol may interfere with the absorption and utilization of dietary nutrients.

Possible consequences of excess alcohol consumption are a decline in work efficiency, high blood pressure, and prolonged exhaustion from strenuous work. This salesman can receive proper nutrition information from his doctor, by paying more attention to the labels of foods, and by watching educational and documentary television shows on health, agriculture, and food-related topics. This person needs to curb his drinking and eat a balanced diet. Local self-help groups, newspaper articles, and his company's employee counselor can all give much advice and support. He can also acquire useful nutrition information from health professionals such as nurses, doctors, dentists, nutritionists, and dietitians. If circumstances permit, he should receive nutrition counseling.

Health professionals need to keep themselves constantly informed. For example, by not reading current literature or attending professional conferences, a busy practicing physician may not be aware that consuming an excessive amount of ascorbic acid or vitamin C can result in a falsely positive urine test for diabetes. For the same reason, he or she may not be aware that behavioral modification has been used with some success as a new approach to losing weight.

Many physicians need nutrition education. If a medical curriculum includes some basic information on nutritional principles, future physicians can prescribe preventive measures, especially with regard to nutritional care. For practicing physicians, the situation becomes complicated, partly because most are extremely busy with other branches of medicine and some are simply not interested in this discipline. However, some physicians are interested in nutrition and will make an effort to learn about it. To do this, they spend time reading such journals as the *Journal of the American Dietetic Association*, the *American Journal of Clinical Nutrition*, the *American Journal of Enteral and Parenteral Nutrition*, *Preventive Medicine*, and the *American Journal of Public Health*. Some physicians even enroll in courses or workshops 2 or 3 weeks a year that provide the most recent information on basic and clinical nutrition.

Lacking proper nutrition education, athletes frequently follow improper advice. For instance, a long-distance runner may practice "carbohydrate loading" before an event. Without fully realizing the implications of this action, he or she eats too much bread. This practice can actually damage athletic performance. Where can an athlete get nutrition information? An undergraduate majoring in physical education should be required to take a course in basic nutrition, especially those who want to become coaches or trainers. Qualified individuals such as dietitians and nutritionists should provide an athletic team with proper nutritional and dietary advice.

The basic policy of *most* health insurance carriers covers illness and not preventive health care. However, it is well known that malnutrition in any form, such as being underweight or overweight or having anemia or constipation can predispose a person to illness. It may benefit these insurance companies to cover preventive measures such as nutrition counseling and physical conditioning to prevent larger claims from being made against them later.

The nutritional status of a teenage girl with very unbalanced eating habits can be further imperiled if she uses oral contraceptive pills, since the hormones in the drug can interfere with the absorption and utilization of a number of essential nutrients. This girl should be provided with nutritional counseling. School districts should have nutritionists on their staff, or health and home economics teachers should have the appropriate training to pass along the information to female students.

Individuals who prefer vegetarian diets definitely need nutritional information. For example, they should know that suddenly switching to a vegetarian diet may cause weight loss because it is difficult to consume sufficient calories on a strict vegetarian diet, especially at the beginning. Prospective vegetarians should be aware that the central issue of their diet is to eat a variety of vegetables in order to obtain enough protein products. There are specific problems with certain nutrients when one consumes a totally vegetarian diet.

There are various sources for obtaining information on vegetarianism. For example, many reputable organizations interested in vegetarianism, such as the Seventh Day Adventists, provide good nutrition information at little or no cost. Vegetarian cookbooks published by reputable firms and qualified individuals are another useful source. Some university and college courses also provide valuable information, as can educational films and other audiovisual aids.

There are many foods and beverages that a 5-year-old likes to eat and drink, such as soft drinks, candies, cookies, desserts, french fries, and thick shakes. The value of these food items has been questioned, and many of them have been blamed for contributing to ill health in children. At present, many individuals and organizations in this country are concerned about television commercials aimed at children, causing them to develop a habit of eating sugary foods. Thus, it is felt that grammar school curricula should include some basic information on foods and nutrition. Television commercials should also be modified to foster good nutritional habits.

Currently, a tremendous amount of misinformation on foods and nutrition is circulating in this country. One example is the mistaken idea that vitamin supplements can cure fatal disease. Another is that aggressive human behavior is caused by eating meat and other animal products. Other poor ideas in circulation are the managing of arthritis with special diets and the numerous "miracle" diet plans for weight loss. Obviously, the public must be armed with some basic nutrition knowledge. This is probably one of the most important aspects of nutrition education.

NUTRITION EDUCATION AND THE PUBLIC SCHOOL SYSTEM

As indicated earlier, if children are taught good nutritional habits, they will likely follow healthy eating patterns throughout life. Thus, grade school is the place to begin and emphasize nutrition education.

A public school system can teach nutrition concepts in many ways. The three most acceptable ones are:

1. Utilizing the regular school curriculum, which covers grades 1 to 12.
2. Integrating nutrition education into the food service system if there is one.
3. Participation of school health services.

There are recognized procedures for implementing nutrition education in a public school system. First, the concepts should be taught at a graded level throughout primary and secondary schools. The subject matter itself may be integrated into other disciplines or taught as a discipline of its own.

Those responsible for implementing nutrition education should have basic training in teacher education, have nutritional knowledge, and have a good, organized curriculum. Ideally, all responsible school personnel must coordinate their efforts. Principals, superintendents, teacher's aides, school nurses, and all food preparation supervisors should be involved.

Teachers should meet stiffer requirements for certification to improve nutrition programs. A number of states require at least some coursework in nutrition in order to qualify for elementary school credentials. Graduates of these programs are better able to integrate nutrition education into their daily classroom routine.

Nutrition education in public schools is now an important issue. Basic nutrition facts should be taught in kindergarten and the primary grades and then reinforced and developed in the upper grades. This technique is the same as that used in teaching reading and mathematics. With younger children, it is extremely important to reinforce learning with activity. Children enjoy doing more than listening, and we must take into account their short attention span.

NUTRITION EDUCATION AND THE FEDERAL GOVERNMENT

The federal government conducts two major types of nutrition education activities: distributing nutrition information and participating in community nutrition education and counseling programs.

Nutrition information is distributed in written forms such as pamphlets, brochures, bulletins, handbooks, and mimeographed sheets. Audiovisual materials such as films, filmstrips, slides, posters, and models are also used. Both kinds of material are put together by the efforts of lay persons and professionals.

Government agencies participate in various community nutrition education and counseling activities. For example, the USDA conducts three major federal food and nutrition improvement programs in which nutrition education is an integral part. The titles of these programs are the Program for Women, Infants, and Children (WIC), the National Nutrition Program for the Elderly (NNPE), and the Expanded Food and Nutrition Education Program (EFNEP). The USDA also either conducts or participates in a number of formal education programs, such as the Head Start program. It is also involved in training and educating people who implement child nutrition programs (such as the school lunch programs). Various programs designed to introduce or improve nutrition education in the medical, dental, nursing, pharmaceutical, and public health fields and teacher education also receive USDA input.

The government's attempt to educate the public about food and nutrition has succeeded in some cases and failed in others. However, at the time of this writing, both federal and state agencies are working hard to assure that nutrition education for the American public is a top priority and that better methods are developed to convey nutrition information. However, because of cutbacks in the federal budget, there is concern about a lack of money to continue many of the above-mentioned programs.

NUTRITION EDUCATION AND THE MASS MEDIA

The best way to educate people about nutrition is on a one-to-one basis. If this is not feasible, the use of mass media is an effective and acceptable alternative. Mass media can reach almost everyone and thus broadly disseminate nutrition information. They can provide the American public with desperately needed basic nutritional knowledge, show how nutrition plays a role in health and disease, and give some sound guidelines for purchasing food. At present, mass media have not been adequately explored as a means to promote nutritional information.

Some problems arise when mass media are used to disseminate food and nutrition information. For example, television, radio, and newspapers are structured so that only two objectives are promoted—news and entertainment. To transform the media within a short time into instruments for informing the public about nutrition, food, and good eating habits would be a difficult, if not unrealistic, task. On the other hand, there are regularly broadcast programs about food and nutrition. For instance, certain news stories, educational reports, social gatherings for charity causes, children's shows, and documentaries on war, hunger, famine, childbearing, agriculture, and related topics can be used to educate the listener.

Another problem is that there is very little assurance that the person preparing the news or program is well informed and can present the scientific information accurately in easy-to-understand terms.

Additional problems include:

1. Mixing political motivation with scientific knowledge in an attempt to capture a wider audience and viewers.
2. Telling the public what they want to see and hear, for example, magnifying the importance of certain scientific information though it is about a rare situation.
3. Biased reporting.
4. Failure to interpret, evaluate, and balance certain knowledge.
5. Plain errors.

It is obvious that some of the messages distributed by mass media can do more harm than good. This is why it is important for well-informed professional people to seek opportunities to contribute information to mass media.

At present, professional nutrition educators believe that the American people are responding to the country's effort in helping them to be better informed in food, nutrition, and health. But this is only a beginning. It will take many more years of aggressive nutrition education before we will all adopt wholesome eating habits.

STUDY QUESTIONS

1. Aside from poverty, what is the major barrier to sound nutritional practices?

2. Explain at least five of the basic nutritional concepts suggested for use in public school systems.

3. Describe the problems that may develop in an adult whose diet consists largely of steak, potatoes, and wine. Discuss four other groups of people who would benefit from relevant nutritional education and why.

4. When should nutrition education in the schools begin? Why?

5. What programs sponsored by the federal government include nutrition education?

6. Which health professionals are likely to be knowledgeable about nutrition? Which health professionals frequently have little training in nutrition? Do some library research and use the references at the back of this book.

7. What are some problems that might arise in using mass media to promote nutrition education? What concern has been voiced about food commercials aimed at children?

Chapter 18

Cultural Nutrition

WHEN PEOPLE ARE asked what their favorite foods are, they will usually mention some favorite family dishes served by their mothers during their childhood. Basic food habits are difficult to change. However, in this country mobility is great, there is a wide selection of foods all year round, and we are exposed to many religious, ethnic, and regional influences. People have become especially interested in trying new recipes and experimenting with the cuisines of different cultures and countries. Perhaps the popular trend toward dining out has led to a greater willingness to sample unfamiliar and exotic menus. Any good-sized city today will host restaurants that offer Indian, Chinese, Russian, French, Swiss, German, and other foreign dishes. Nevertheless, in most cases, the food served at home still reflects the background, experience, and likes or dislikes of the parents. Where an ethnic community is established, the cultural food habits are more apparent. In certain parts of a major city, one will find stores selling groceries familiar to and well liked by their Puerto Rican, Mexican, or Italian clientele.

Personal food patterns and preferences are especially strong among the elderly and the ill. The nutritionist, dietitian, or nurse who knows what a patient's favorite foods are and prepares them in ways the patient likes has a better chance of assuring that the patient eats adequately.

Chapter 22 has more information on accommodating individual food preferences in meal planning. This chapter briefly discusses the food patterns of people in this country of different regions, ethnic origins, cultural backgrounds, religious practices, and life-styles.

REGIONAL DIFFERENCES

Regional food patterns are not as strongly defined as they once were. Advances in food technology, numerous food preservation techniques, rapid and convenient transportation, the influence of advertisements, and the tendency of Americans to move long distances has weakened traditional regional food patterns. However, in certain sections of the country, some foods are still widely preferred. This pattern often reflects foods that are locally abundant. Geographical, climatic, and other conditions may favor growing certain crops or raising certain animals for meat, eggs, or dairy products, and the abundance of seafoods in coastal diets obviously results from the nearby waters.

In California, many people's eating habits are influenced by Spanish-Mexican, Oriental, Italian, and other ethnic groups, although the state's agricultural bounty also constitutes an important factor: California supplies most of the fruits and vegetables for the nation and has popularized the salad as an important part of the meal. The extensive consumption of fruits of all varieties from apples and berries to avocados and citrus fruits has improved the diet of the nation.

In the southern states, fish, rice, and corn are frequently used. Traditionally, almost every meal here is accompanied by hot bread of some kind, such as biscuits or corn bread. Another typical dish is green leafy vegetables cooked with a piece of pork back fat; the resulting liquid or juice, known as pot liquor, is also consumed. In the past, only small amounts of milk and cheese were consumed, especially among low-income families. This was partly because of the lack of refrigeration, although the national consumption of dairy products has increased since the 1940s and 1950s.

ETHNIC, CULTURAL, AND RELIGIOUS INFLUENCES

The following sections discuss the dietary habits of some ethnic, cultural, and religious groups in the United States.

Europeans

Many of the foods we think of as typically American were brought to this country by European immigrants. Settlers from Western Europe ate many of the foods familiar to us today. Many of the Norwegian, Swedish, and Danish peoples were dairymen, thus leading to a greater use of milk, innumerable kinds of cheese, cream, and butter. Western European immigrants living near bodies of water depended on fish and shellfish. Vegetables—the same kinds we use today—were in liberal supply, although the early settlers used a few more root vegetables than we do. Popular items included potatoes, dark breads, and meats such as beef, pork, and poultry. Eggs and cheeses were plentiful favorites.

Central Europeans had a diet high in potatoes and grains, especially rye flour and wheat. Among meats, pork was a favorite, including different types of sausages; meat and sausage were often cooked with vegetables. One of the most popular green vegetables was cabbage, which is easy to grow and stores well. It was consumed raw, cooked, or salted as sauerkraut. Other common vegetables included turnips, carrots, squash, onions, beans, and greens.

Italian families in the United States have a strong liking for the foods of their ancestors. Some of these foods have become popular items in the American diet. This is substantiated by the number of Italian restaurants and the huge sale of pizza and pasta products in this country. The number of pizza stands almost equals those of hamburger stands and fried chicken houses. The basic food of an Italian meal is pasta in one of its many forms. Hard-wheat dough, which may be shaped into endless different forms, is used almost daily. Pasta can be served with a variety of sauces, tomato, cheese, peppers, onion, and meat and is usually accompanied by bread.

There are some differences between northern and southern Italian foods. The north is more industrialized, and people use more meat, dairy products, and root vegetables. The food of southern Italy includes more fish, spices, and olive oil. Adding green vegetable salads, fruits, and eggs will increase the nutritional value of the southern Italian diet. More meat and milk, especially for young children, will further improve nutrient intake.

Experienced dietitians and nurses are aware that hospitalization can be especially trying for Italian patients because of their strong feeling for family and traditional foods. Any effort to cater to their food preferences will ease their feeling of isolation.

Jewish People

Orthodox Jews follow the Biblical and rabbinical dietary laws. Conservative Jews distinguish between meals in the home and those outside. Most Reformed Jews do not observe any dietary regulations. A Jewish family's country of origin also greatly influences the foods served in the home.

The followers of kosher or kashrut regulations (foods used according to strict Jewish laws are kosher), eat only animals that are designated as clean and that are killed in the ritualistic manner. This method of slaughter minimizes pain for the animal and maximizes blood drainage. Blood, as the symbol of life, is strictly avoided. This is assured by soaking the meat in cold water and then thoroughly salting, draining, and rinsing it three times. Permitted meats are derived from quadruped animals that chew the cud and divide the hoof, poultry, and fish with fins and scales. The hindquarter of the quadruped animals is acceptable if the hip sinew of the thigh vein is removed. Kosher laws also regulate the separation of meat and milk. Milk and its products are excluded from meals containing meat, although dairy products may be consumed just before the meal. Meat and its products are excluded at milk meals and for 6 hours thereafter. Two separate sets of dishes, utensils, and cooking equipment are maintained in kosher households. Foods cooked in milk pots, such as vegetables, can only be consumed at milk meals. Generally two milk meals and one meat meal are eaten each day.

Certain foods are also designated as pareve, or neutral. These include fruits, uncooked vegetables, "clean" fish, and eggs, all of which may be consumed at meat or milk meals. Eggs with blood spots are avoided.

No food may be cooked or heated on the Sabbath, which is Saturday. The evening meal before the Sabbath is usually the most substantial of the week, at which both fish and chicken are served. Food eaten on the Sabbath is prepared the day before. On holidays symbolic food items are served. Celebrations include Rosh Hashana, the Jewish New Year; Sukkoth, the fall harvest; Hanukkah, the feast of lights; and Purim, the arrival of spring. Passover, also a spring festival, is celebrated to commemorate the flight of the

Jews from Egypt. This holiday is celebrated for 8 days and only unleavened bread, or matzo, is allowed. Another two complete sets of dishes, utensils, and cooking equipment are required in Orthodox homes in order to avoid any contact with leavening.

Mexican-Americans

People of Mexican descent comprise a large portion of the population of the Southwest, where their ties to Mexican traditions are strengthened by proximity to their mother country. Traditionally, a lack of refrigeration has limited the use of perishable foods—meat, milk, eggs, vegetables, and fruits—and these nutrient-rich but sometimes expensive foods may still be scarce in the diets of lower-income Mexican-Americans.

Staple items in the Mexican diet are dry beans (often consumed several times a day as a major source of protein), chili peppers, tomatoes, and corn, often used together in a variety of highly seasoned dishes. The corn is ground, soaked in lime water, and baked on a griddle to make tortillas. These thin, flat breads may be served plain or rolled and filled with ground beef and topped with a hot chili sauce and perhaps grated cheese and lettuce to make tacos. Tacos supply nutrients from all four food groups, but the growing practice of using wheat instead of lime-soaked corn for the tortillas is cutting down on the amount of calcium formerly furnished by the lime. Many foods are fried, and beans may be refried until they absorb all the fat in the pan.

Nutritionists now encourage Mexican-Americans who have not adopted the standard American diet to retain the basic Mexican diet, with just a few changes to increase its nutrition. To eliminate deficiencies often noted in iron, vitamin A, and calcium, increased amounts of inexpensive lean meats can be used in taco fillings, more dark green and yellow vegetables and fruits can be used, and milk (dried if the cost of fresh milk is too high) can be added to the diet, particularly for children. The traditional Mexican practice of limiting sweet desserts is recommended over changes to a diet high in candy, sweet drinks, and sweet rolls.

Orientals

The United States is also home to many people of Asian heritage. As an illustration, the diets of Chinese are discussed below.

China is a vast country with many different regional foods. In this country, most of the Chinese on the West Coast come from southern China and adhere to a Cantonese diet. This type of cookery uses little fat and subtle seasonings. Beef, pork, poultry, and all kinds of seafoods are well liked. In Chinese cooking, all parts of the animal are utilized, including organs, blood, and skin. Rice is the predominant cereal used by the Cantonese, both at home and in the United States. Northern Chinese use more bread, noodles, and dumplings, which are prepared from wheat, corn, and millet.

The Chinese diet is varied, containing eggs, fish, meat, soybeans, and a great variety of vegetables. Many green, leafy vegetables unfamiliar to Americans, such as leaves of the radish and shepherd's purse, are enjoyed. Sprouts of bamboo and beans are incorporated into some dishes, giving a distinctive flavor and texture. Many Chinese recipes call for mushrooms and nuts. Eggs from ducks, hens, and pigeons are widely used—fresh, preserved, and pickled. Soy sauce is used both in preparation and serving. It is flavorful, although its high salt content is a problem for Chinese patients whose salt intake may be restricted by the physician.

Chinese cookery is unique in many ways. Food is quickly cooked over the heat source, usually cut into small pieces so that the short cooking period is adequate. Vegetables retain their crispness, flavor, and practically all their nutrients; this method of cookery, which has been widely adopted, is quite beneficial. When vegetables are cooked in water, the liquid is also used.

Probably the greatest weakness in the Chinese diet is a low intake of milk and milk products, a consequence of lactose intolerance. However, a higher consumption of meat and the frequent use of soybeans prevents calcium and protein deficiency. In addition, Chinese children born in the United States have a higher tolerance for milk.

Information about the food habits of other

groups such as black and Native Americans, Middle-Eastern people, Puerto Ricans, and other oriental people may be obtained from the references at the back of this book.

VEGETARIANISM

Within the last decade, many young people in this country have adopted nontraditional lifestyles with nontraditional food choices. Vegetarianism has become quite common, especially among college students.

The reasons for adopting a vegetarian diet are many, including health, ethics, economics, politics, ecology, religion, metaphysical beliefs, and, lately, current fads. Vegetarianism includes different dietary practices, some nutritionally sound and others not. Anthropological, epidemiological, experimental and clinical studies have indicated that a person can enjoy good health while on a vegetarian diet, whether practiced for a short or long period, although certain vegetarian practices may promote nutritional inadequacies.

Dietary Adequacy

There are three major types of vegetarians: individuals whose diets contain no flesh (meat, poultry, or fish), called *lacto-ovo-vegetarians*; individuals whose diets contain no flesh or milk and milk products, called *ovo-vegetarians*; and individuals whose diets contain no flesh, milk and milk products, or eggs, called strict or pure vegetarians or *vegans*.

Individuals who consume dairy products with or without eggs can receive nearly the same nutrient intake as those who eat animal flesh. This diet can support the young. However, a strict vegetarian, or vegan, must exercise care and comply with certain guidelines to assure a sound diet.

The average body weight of vegetarian adults and children is below reference standards (see Chapter 12). This is because they eat fewer calories and have a low fat deposition. There are no data to indicate whether their daily activities are reduced or whether the lighter body weight poses any problem. Clinical records indicate that heart disease, gout, and diabetes are positively correlated with a higher body weight among westerners. Does that mean that vegetarians have a better chance of survival? On the other hand, an underweight person is more susceptible to infection, delayed recovery from trauma, and anemia with easy fatigue. Does this mean that vegetarians have a reduced chance of survival? Neither question can be answered from existing data.

If vegetarians eat an adequate quantity of foods, their intake of iron is equal to or higher than that of those who eat flesh. However, there are two points to be noted. First, the absorption is higher for iron from animal sources than from vegetable sources. Second, most vegetarians do not eat an adequate amount of foods, and iron deficiency is not uncommon among them. Nevertheless, its occurrence is not necessarily higher than that for nonvegetarians.

Vitamin B_{12} deficiency has been identified in strict vegetarians, since the nutrient occurs only in animal products. However, its deficiency can be easily prevented by a chemical supplement or an intake of plant foods fortified with vitamin B_{12}, such as soy or nut "milks." Such products are now widely available. It should be noted that symptoms of vitamin B_{12} deficiency may not appear, depending on many circumstances, including masking of the deficiency by a large intake of folic acid from products such as green vegetables and grains (see Chapter 6).

Specific Nutrient Considerations

The nutrient that requires the most consideration in a vegetarian diet is protein. As indicated in Chapter 4, most animal proteins are complete proteins with the exception of gelatin, which is low in lysine and tryptophan. By contrast, most vegetable proteins are incomplete proteins (low in one or more essential amino acids) with nuts most resembling a complete or animal protein (see Table 18-1).

Because of the worldwide lack of animal pro-

TABLE 18-1   Categories of Vegetable Protein Foods with the Limiting Amino Acids

Categories of Vegetable Protein Foods	Limiting, Low, or Deficient Essential Amino Acids
Most grain products	Lysine, threonine (sometimes tryptophan)
Most legumes or pulses	Methionine, tryptophan
Nuts and oil seeds	Lysine
Green leafy vegetables	Methionine
Leaves and grasses	Methionine

teins, scientists have proposed many ways to improve the protein quality of vegetable products. One common method is to add the deficient or limiting amino acids to the vegetable produce; for instance, lysine may be added to rice. A second method is to combine two or more appropriate vegetable products so that the missing or low amino acids will be mutually supplemented. There are various names for this practice, including *complementary proteins* and *protein supplementation*. For example, wheat, which is low in lysine, may be combined with corn, which is low in tryptophan. In the last decade many strict vegetarians have learned to obtain the proper amount of complete proteins by eating any of the following combinations: grains and legumes (including nuts), legumes (including nuts) and seeds, and grains and seeds. If these foods are eaten separately, the same desired effect can be achieved if the interval between them is less than 2 to 3 hours.

A third method of improving protein quality in a vegetarian diet is to supplement a vegetable protein with a small amount of an animal product. For instance, wheat, low in lysine, may be supplemented with a small amount of milk powder. In addition to using complementary vegetable proteins, lacto-ovo-vegetarians use the following combinations to obtain their share of complete proteins: grains and dairy products, legumes (including nuts) and dairy products, and seeds and dairy products.

Vegetarians must carefully consider the amount of foods they consume. Table 18-2 provides examples of various vegetable products. Those such as grains and potatoes are bulky and have a high satiety value. However, to obtain adequate calories and other nutrients, a large quantity of food has to be consumed. In some cases, part of the protein ingested is metabolized to give

TABLE 18-2   Examples of Different Groups of Vegetable Products

Grains	Legumes or Pulses	Nuts and Oilseeds	Green Leafy Vegetables
Whole rice	Black beans	Sunflower seeds	Brussels sprouts
Whole wheat	Cowpeas (black eye)	Sesame seeds	Kale
Millet	Mung beans	Sesame meal	Collards
Wheat gliadin	Broad beans	Black walnuts	Asparagus
Whole oats	Kidney beans	Brazil nuts	Turnip greens
Barley	Lima beans	Cashew nuts	Cauliflower
Whole rye	Navy beans		Mustard greens
Corn	White beans		White potatoes
	Various peas		Okra
	Chickpeas (garbanzos)		
	Lentils		
	Green peas		
	Soybeans		
	Peanuts		
	Peanut butter		

calories, thus reducing the nitrogen source and increasing the risk of protein deficiency. To increase protein intake, vegetarians must eat more legumes, or pulses.

The risk of nutrient deficiency among vegetarians cannot be overestimated. The risk of calorie, protein, vitamin, and mineral deficiencies are increased if people depend excessively on one cereal or confine themselves to a small selection of foods. The three micronutrients that may pose special problems are calcium and vitamins B_2 and B_{12}. Ordinarily, calcium and B_2 are obtained mainly from milk, while B_{12} is obtained entirely from animal products.

Food Guides

An adequate diet can be planned without using foods shunned by vegetarians. The major contributions of vegetable products are shown in Table 18-3. Table 18-4 summarizes the four food groups for lacto-ovo-vegetarians; Table 18-5 describes the four food groups for a strict vegetarian. Information for planning menus using these food guides is discussed in Chapter 10. Table 18-6 gives a sample menu for a strict vegetarian; more vegetarian menus are presented in Chapter 23.

As in the foundation diet discussed in Chapter 10, there are many miscellaneous food items not indicated in Tables 18-4 and 18-5. These foods include sugar and other sweeteners; table fats, other fats, and oils, including salad dressings; and unenriched refined breads, cereals, flours, and meals. Often, these are ingredients in a recipe or are added to other foods during preparation or at the table. Although a number of these foods provide some protein, minerals, vitamins, or essential fatty acids, their main contribution is often food energy (calories).

To assure an adequate intake of nutrients, vegetarians should be careful to follow certain guidelines. They should use a wide selection of foods based on the food groups and not limit their diets to a small number of items. An adequate amount of foods should be eaten to provide the caloric requirements and some spare protein; one way of doing this is to increase the amount consumed from each food group. Only a minimal amount of nutrient-light, caloric-dense foods such as candy, soft drinks, sugars, jams,

TABLE 18-3 Nutrient Contributions of Vegetable Products

Food Group	Nutrient Characteristics
Legumes and pulses (beans, peas, lentils), nuts, nutlike seeds	They provide, among all vegetable products, high-quality protein in good quantity. Soybean formulas that have been fortified are included in this category. The major nutrients provided are iron, niacin, vitamins B_1 and B_2, and others. Nuts and nutlike seeds provide fat, which tends to be low in a vegetarian diet.
Whole-grain or enriched cereals and breads	They provide calories, protein, iron, and some of the B vitamins.
Vegetables and fruits	They provide rich amounts of vitamins and minerals, especially vitamin C. There is a wide selection of this food group. Dark green and leafy vegetables help to supply an adequate amount of calcium and riboflavin, both of which will be lacking if the patient does not drink milk. They also provide roughage or fiber, which promotes motility and the general health of the gastrointestinal tract.

and jellies should be eaten. However, if a person is unable to maintain weight on a vegetarian diet, sugars and fats are needed to provide calories. If dairy products are not consumed, good sources of calcium and vitamin B_2 are dark green, leafy vegetables such as dandelion, kale, mustard greens, turnip greens, and collards; green vegetables such as cabbage, spinach, broccoli, and brussels sprouts; legumes such as soybeans; nuts such as almonds; and dried fruits.

The following three special requirements are important for a vegetarian:

1. Include 2 c of legumes daily to meet calcium and iron requirements.
2. Include 1 c of dark greens daily to meet iron requirements for women.

TABLE 18-4 Food Groups for Lacto-ovo-vegetarians

Food Group	Major Products	Daily Servings
Meat equivalents	Legumes, pulses, nuts; textured vegetable proteins (soy meat analogues and other formulated plant protein products and spun soy isolates)	≥2
Milk and dairy products	Milk, eggs, cheese, yogurt, many other milk products	≥2
Breads and cereals	All varieties	4–6
Fruits and vegetables	All varieties	Vegetables: 3; Fruits: 1–3

TABLE 18-5 Food Groups for Strict Vegetarians

Food Group	Major Products	Daily Servings
Meat equivalents	Legumes, pulses, nuts; textured vegetable proteins (soy meat analogues and other formulated plant protein products and spun soy isolates)	≥2
Milk equivalents	Soybean milk, preferably fortified with calcium, vitamins B_2 and B_{12} (if not fortified, supplements, especially vitamin B_{12}, may be necessary)*	≥2
Fruits and vegetables	All varieties	Vegetables: 4; Fruit: 1–4†

*Nut milks are nutritionally inadequate, especially for infants.
†Including a source of vitamin C.

3. Include at least 1 T fat daily for proper absorption of vitamins.

The use of nutrient supplements may also be necessary.

Hospitalized Vegetarians

Information on feeding hospitalized vegetarians is presented in Chapter 23. Most vegetarians need simple advice on menu planning to achieve a balanced and nutritionally adequate diet. Some are extreme in their habits. Some suffer because of a prolonged adherence to a diet that is nutritionally unsound. The extreme practice of eating only a few food items can produce scurvy, anemia, low blood calcium and protein, body wasting, and kidney malfunction. Iron and zinc deficiencies have been documented. A vegetarian may be hospitalized for nutrient deficiencies, which vary with patient nutrient requirement, food choices, and length of time on the diet.

TABLE 18-6   Sample Menu Plan for a Strict Vegetarian Diet

Breakfast	Lunch	Dinner
Orange, 1	Split pea soup, 2 c	Soybeans, 1 c
Bulgur, 1 c	Peanut butter sandwich	Brown rice, cooked, 1 c
Brewer's yeast, 1 T	Peanut butter, 2 T	Fried in oil, 2 T
Wheat-soy bread,	Whole-wheat bread,	Chestnuts, 2 T
toasted, 1 sl	2 sl	Sesame seeds, 2 T
Honey, 1 T	Honey, 1 T	Collards, 1 c
	Fruit-sunflower seed salad	Pear, medium, 1
Snack	Apple, medium, ½	Snacks, ¼ c
Shelled almonds	Banana, medium, ½	
	Sunflower seeds, ¼ c	
	Lettuce, leaf, 1	
	Snack	
	Peach, medium, 1	

Source: N. R. Raper and M. M. Hill, Vegetarian diets. *Nutrition Program News*, July–August, 1973.

Two major considerations in caring for vegetarian patients are familiarity with the patient's background and identification of those at nutritional risk. The following questions should be used in evaluating the patient's background:

1. What is the patient's history of vegetarianism?
2. Does the patient practice vegetarianism with a group?
3. What are the patient's food choices? A vegetarian belonging to a group tends to have a wider selection of foods.
4. What is the ethical and philosophical attitude of the patient?
5. How does the patient handle social interaction?
6. What is the patient's diet history?

Because the vegetarian prefers an alternative eating pattern and sometimes even an alternative life-style, some hospital staffs may have difficulty accepting the preferences of a hospitalized vegetarian. Therefore, individuals caring for this type of patient must make an effort to understand and respect their food choices. Otherwise, the health professional's chief goal of a speedy recovery for the sick may not be achieved.

STUDY QUESTIONS

1. What factors have weakened regional and ethnic food traditions?
2. Name some now-common American foods used by settlers from various parts of Europe.
3. What are some kosher food regulations? What is the significance of pareve foods in kosher meal planning?
4. How adequate is the traditional Mexican diet? Which foods are little used and why?
5. Describe Chinese cookery. What is the nutritional advantage of its food preparation methods? What food is notably lacking in the Chinese diet? Why?
6. Define *lacto-ovo-vegetarians*, *ovo-vegetarians*, and *vegans*. What nutrients are most likely to be lacking in their diets? How can these needs be met? What general guidelines should vegetarians use in meal planning?

Chapter 19

Public Health and Community Nutrition

SENATOR EDWARD M. Kennedy delivered the following opening statement on June 21, 1974, the first of the three-day National Nutrition Policy Study hearings:

"Nutrition adequacy is a prerequisite for good health. No matter what conditions the body may be forced to suffer, the provision of adequate nutrition is the most fundamental requirement for survival. No internist can substitute for proteins. No surgeon can excise iron deficiencies, and no pediatrician can replace the nutrients lost in premature birth due to poor prenatal care. . . . The delivery of good nutritional care is, in the long run, the most important medicine that each of us can and must administer to ourselves."

Items concerning good and bad nutrition are in the news almost daily. People are interested not only in the cost, convenience, and taste of foods, but also in quality, safety, and nutritional contribution. Why the sudden interest? It is increasingly evident that good health and wholesome dietary and nutritional habits are intimately related. Although what we eat is important to our body, our food choices have often been based not so much on health as on cultural background, income level, personal inclination, and social conditions. Furthermore, sophisticated technology, rapid communication, and increasing public knowledge have made the art and science of nutrition available to the general public. This chapter will describe some formal ways in which nutrition services are being provided to the public.

PREVENTIVE NUTRITION

People want preventive nutrition. They want to know what they should eat, to enjoy what they eat, and, most important, to eat so as to assure good health and a long life. The government has responded to this desire in several ways.

Dietary Goals

In recent years, intensive efforts have been made to develop a national nutrition policy that will suggest nutritional patterns that would enable every American to achieve true preventive nutrition. The *Dietary Goals of the United States* was one such national policy proposed. However, its release a few years ago started a controversy among health professionals and organizations, many of whom disagreed with the report's recommendations.

The U.S. Senate Select Committee on Nutrition and Human Needs released its second edition of *Dietary Goals for the United States* in 1977 (Washington, D.C.: Government Printing Office). The goals proposed were designed to assure the best health for the American people. Selected recommendations from this report are listed below:

1. To avoid overweight, consume only as much energy (calories) as is expended; if overweight, decrease energy intake and increase energy expenditure.
2. Increase the consumption of complex carbohydrates and naturally occurring sugars from about 28% of energy intake to about 48%.
3. Reduce the consumption of refined and processed sugars by about 45% to account for about 10% of total energy.
4. Reduce overall fat consumption from approximately 40% to about 30% of energy intake.
5. Reduce saturated fat consumption to account for about 10% of total energy intake, and balance that with polyunsaturated and monounsaturated fats, each of which should account for about 10% of energy intake.
6. Reduce cholesterol consumption to about 300 mg a day.
7. Limit the intake of sodium by reducing the intake of salt to about 5 g a day.

To meet these goals, certain changes in food selection and preparation are recommended. Consumption of fruits, vegetables, and whole grains should be increased, while consumption of refined and other processed sugars and foods high in such sugars should be decreased. The dietary goals report recommends decreased consumption of foods high in total fat and partial replacement of saturated fats, whether obtained from animal or vegetable sources, with polyunsaturated fats. Consumption of animal fat should be decreased, and meats, poultry, and fish that will reduce saturated fat intake should be eaten. Except for young children, low-fat and nonfat milk should be substituted for whole milk, and low-fat dairy products for high-fat dairy products. Consumption of butterfat, eggs, and other high cholesterol sources should be decreased. However, premenopausal women, young children, and the elderly should obtain the nutritional benefits of eggs. Finally, the report advises decreased consumption of salt and foods high in salt content.

These goals are recommendations and not laws. There are good and bad points about them, but this book is not the appropriate forum for debate. However, the recommendations do emphasize that legislators are genuinely concerned about the nutritional intakes of the American people. Such concern is expected to be translated into large-scale nutrition education and health care programs, for adequate health services are a right and a necessity, not just a luxury or a privilege. Although the medical profession considers health care and medical care to be synonymous, they are not. A disease can be cured by the appropriate treatment, but a life or a person has to be cared for by proper health services. The first is episodic; the latter is continuous.

On the other hand, each person must contribute to his or her own health care, as clearly stated by Senator Kennedy. Furthermore, according to Dr. P. B. Peacock of the American Health Foundation, "health maintenance refers to measures that will enable an individual to stay young and healthy in body and mind for as many years as possible. . . . With our present knowledge, to achieve success in the control of these (cancer and heart) diseases we must directly influence those who are being protected and require that they take positive action on their own behalf. The development and maintenance of such programs is health maintenance."

Public Health and Community Nutrition Services

Public health and community nutrition is an important component of any health service program, since it educates the public about nutrition

and at the same time delivers the proper dietary and nutritional care to those who need it. It provides cure, care, and the tools to keep oneself nutritionally sound.

The field of public health nutrition is very similar to that of community nutrition. For convenience, this chapter assumes that the two fields have so much in common that their activities largely overlap. The following definitions are provided for reference purposes.

According to Dr. Cicely D. Williams, community nutrition is "the whole of the nutritional sciences applied to the consumer as groups or as individuals. It is the interface between food and people and probably some 90 percent of all nutrition takes place in the home. Each culture has always had its special preferred food, food taboos, and food habits" (McLaren, D. J. (ed.), *Nutrition in the Community*. London, John Wiley & Sons, Inc., 1976, p. xii).

According to the *Dictionary of Occupational Titles* compiled by the U.S. Department of Labor, the public health nutritionist is defined as an individual who "organizes, plans and conducts programs concerning nutrition to assist in promotion of health and control of disease. Instructs auxiliary medical personnel and allied professional workers on food values and utilization of foods by human body. Advises health and other agencies on nutritional phases of their food programs. Conducts in-service courses pertaining to nutrition in clinics and similar institutions. Interprets and evaluates food and nutrient information designed for public acceptance and use. Studies and analyzes scientific discoveries in nutrition for public health agency and can be designated as Nutritionist, Public Health."

FOOD AND NUTRITION SURVEYS AND PLANNING

Public health and community nutritionists become involved in many types of activities and programs. One major activity of community nutritionists is to participate in or conduct food and nutrition surveys and planning. A list of such projects with examples is provided below.

TABLE 19-1 Methods of Evaluating Nutritional Status

Procedure	Purpose and Brief Description
Clinical assessment	To detect physical signs and symptoms of deviation from health due to malnutrition; to include medical history, physical examination, various anthropometric measurements such as height, weight, and subcutaneous fat, and X-ray measurement of bones.
Biochemical measurements	To obtain earliest evidence of deficient nutritional status. Depletion of body stores of nutrients is the first step in the development of nutritional-deficiency disease. Biochemical measurements of the levels of various substances in body tissue and fluids, e.g., blood and urine, can often provide preliminary information about the person's nutritional status. As the deficiency progresses, functional impairment develops, and finally the physical changes characteristic of a clinically manifest deficiency disease appear. Biochemical measurements, therefore, allow an identification of populations at risk, as well as populations with frank malnutrition.
Dental examination	To detect physical signs and symptoms of deviation from normal; to include an evaluation of dental health and the condition of the soft (periodontal) tissues of the mouth. While all dental findings cannot be claimed to result from inadequate nutrition, obvious relationship to dietary intake exists, e.g., the presence of caries may be associated with a low intake of fluoride.
Dietary evaluation	To assist in a complete interpretation of clinical and biochemical findings (see text). Information is basic to planning dietary changes, modifying existing programs, and initiating new ones that will have an influence on food habits and intake.
Collection of data on	To enable a complete assessment of possible causes underlying malnutrition to be made, and to provide a basis for future planning.
Level and distribution of income	(Monthly earnings, amount spent on food, clothes, etc.)
Income maintenance and other social service programs	(Length of period with or without a job, receiving welfare, etc.)
Government food and nutrition programs	(Participation in school lunch programs, food stamps, etc.)

TABLE 19-1   (continued)

Procedure	Purpose and Brief Description
General food availability and acceptance	(Distances from food stores, availability of ethnic foods, likes and dislikes for food purchased within short distances, etc.)
Health and educational facilities	(Hospital and colleges close by, etc.)
Socioeconomic, ethnic, and cultural characteristics	(Immigrants, Native Americans, etc.)
Overall health status and disease factors	(Frequency of family members becoming sick, genetic diseases, etc.)

Source: Adapted from *Ten-State Nutrition Survey, 1968–1970*. I. *Historical Development*. II. *Demographic Data*. U.S. Department of Health, Education and Welfare Publication No. (HSM) 72-8130. Atlanta, Center for Disease Control, 1972, p. I-3.

1. Food habits: nutrition and dietary habits of ethnic populations, the elderly, rural and urban populations, and groups of low socioeconomic status.
2. Food prices: rise in cost with reference to location, regional distribution, and other economic factors.
3. Nutritional status: the nutritional status of selected population groups including data such as weight, height, body build, and chemical analysis of blood and urine.
4. Food safety: family practices of safety in food preparation and preservation.
5. Food equipment usage: the extent of usage of some of the latest equipment including microwave ovens, electric pressure cookers, slow cookers, and freezers.
6. Oral hygiene: health care of the mouth (teeth and gums) and effects of food, alcohol, and tobacco on the mouth.

The following section discusses the role of the practitioner in one such project: using nutritional assessment to determine the nutritional status of a population group.

Table 19-1 summarizes methods of evaluating the nutritional status of an individual or individuals in a group. Nutritional assessment is probably one of the most important techniques, especially in evaluating children. The four major phases in assessing nutritional status are: anthropometric measurements, clinical examinations, biochemical data, and dietary evaluations. They are briefly discussed below.

Anthropometric Measurements

Assessment of growth and development by studying anthropometric measurements (physical measurements of the human body) provides important information about the nutritional status of infants, children, adolescents, and pregnant women. Standard measurements include weight, height, head circumference, midarm circumference, chest circumference, and skinfold thickness. These data provide developmentally significant ratios, including weight : height, midarm circumference : head circumference, chest circumference : head circumference, and midarm circumference : height. Data obtained over a period of time are especially helpful.

Although height and weight measurements are common, they are usually made improperly. For infants, the body weight should be measured to the nearest ½ oz, or 10 g; for children, ¼ lb or 100 g. Whenever feasible, a beam balance scale should be used, which should be calibrated against reference weight as frequently as possible. Zero alignment must be adjusted at every

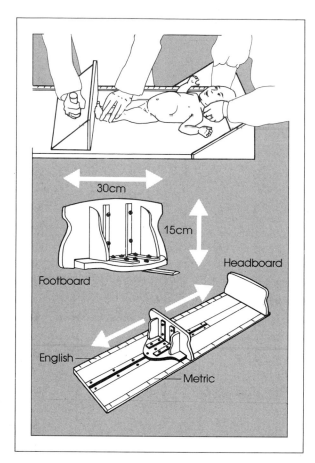

FIGURE 19-1   The proper way to measure the length of a child under 3 years old.

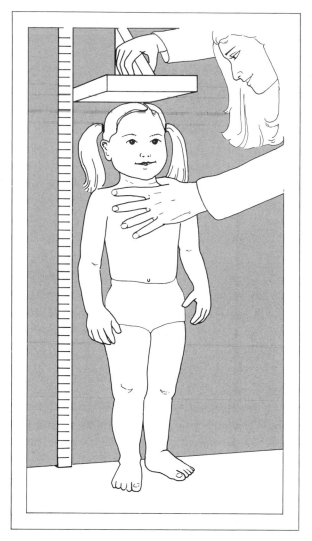

FIGURE 19-2   The proper way to measure the height of a child older than 3 years.

weighing session. The length of children under 3 years old should be measured with the child lying on its back; standing measurements of height are recommended for older children. Lengths and heights should be measured to the nearest ¼ in. or 1 cm. Figures 19-1 and 19-2 show the proper ways of measuring length and height. Head circumference is obtained by using any insertion tape; the measurement is taken as shown in Figure 19-3.

Skinfold measurements appear to be the best single determination of adiposity (degree of fat in body tissues).* This measurement reflects the amount of subcutaneous fat. Skinfold thickness can be obtained for the subscapular area, abdomen, triceps, and biceps.

The accepted national standard is a pressure of 10 g/mm² on the caliper face. The contact surface should be about 20 to 40 mm². These recommendations are satisfactorily met by the Lange calipers, which are used by most public health workers. The reading of the calipers should be checked daily; small metal blocks for this purpose are available from suppliers of anthropometric tools.

The skinfold measure obtained is the double thickness of the pinched, folded skin plus the

*The discussion has been adapted from *Ten-State Nutrition Survey, 1968–1970.* I. *Historical Development.* II. *Demographic Data.* U.S. Department of Health, Education and Welfare Publication No. (HSM) 72-8130. Atlanta, Center for Disease Control, 1972, pp. I-39, I-40.

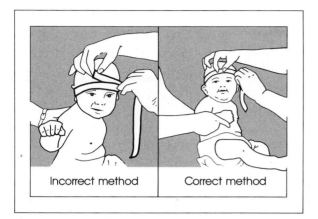

FIGURE 19-3   The proper way to measure head circumference.

subcutaneous adipose tissue. In the approved method of measuring skinfold, a full fold of skin and subcutaneous adipose tissue is pinched between the thumb and forefinger of the left hand, away from the underlying muscle, and held firmly while the measurement is being taken. The calipers are applied to the skinfold about a centimeter from (below or distal and below) the fingers and at the least depth of the fold at which the surfaces of the skin are approximately parallel. The distance of the measuring point from the fingers should be such that the pressure on the fold at this point is exerted by the faces of the caliper rather than by the fingers. The handle of the caliper is then released slowly to permit the full force of the caliper arm pressure. The dial is read to the nearest millimeter. Caliper measurement should be made at least twice to obtain a stable reading. If the skinfold is extremely thick, dial readings should be taken three seconds after the caliper pressure is applied for utmost accuracy. The two examples below underscore the importance of carefully attending to the locations of and procedures in skinfold measurements.

The triceps skinfold (Figure 19-4) is measured midway between the shoulder (tip of the acromion) and the elbow (tip of the olecranon) of the *right* arm, with the crest of the skinfold parallel to the long axis of the arm. The midpoint is critical because of the gradation of subcutaneous fat thickness from elbow to shoulder. With the subject's arm flexed at 90°, the midpoint is lo-

cated by measuring with a tape and marking with a pencil. The arm of the subject should then hang freely when the skinfold measurement is made. Care is necessary to avoid lifting the muscle tissue along with the skinfold on some subjects.

The subscapular skinfold (Figure 19-5) is taken just below the angle of the *right* scapula (with shoulder and arm relaxed) following the natural cleavage of the skin. This is often along a line about 45° from the horizontal extending medially upward.

Clinical Examinations

A second major way to study the nutritional status of people is by clinical examination, although clinical examinations are not always possible because of the number of subjects involved. However, whenever feasible, the field physician or nurse should perform a complete physical examination of each subject, examining the hair, face, eyes, lips, tongue, teeth, gums, glands, skin, nails, subcutaneous tissues, muscular and skeletal systems, cardiovascular system, gastrointestinal system, genital system, and nervous system. The extract below describes the physical signs and symptoms of malnutrition (U.S. Department of Health, Education and Welfare Publication No. (HSM) 72-8130, 1972, pp. I-44–I-47) that such an examination may reveal.

Hair

Dry staring: Dry wirelike, unkempt, stiff hair, often brittle, sometimes may exhibit some bleaching of the normal color.

Dyspigmentation (pediatric form only): Definite change from normal pigment of the hair, most usually evident distally and best seen by carefully combing hair strands upward and viewing the orderly array of hair in good light. Dyspigmentation includes both change of pigment (usually lightening of color) and depigmentation. Not to be confused with dyed or tinted hair, dyspigmentation is always bandlike in character and usually is associated with some change in texture of hair in the depigmented band. In some ethnic groups, particularly Negroid groups, the pigment may be slightly reddish in color. In others, especially among straight black-haired peoples, the bandlike depigmentation ("flag sign") is common. Only rarely observed in adults.

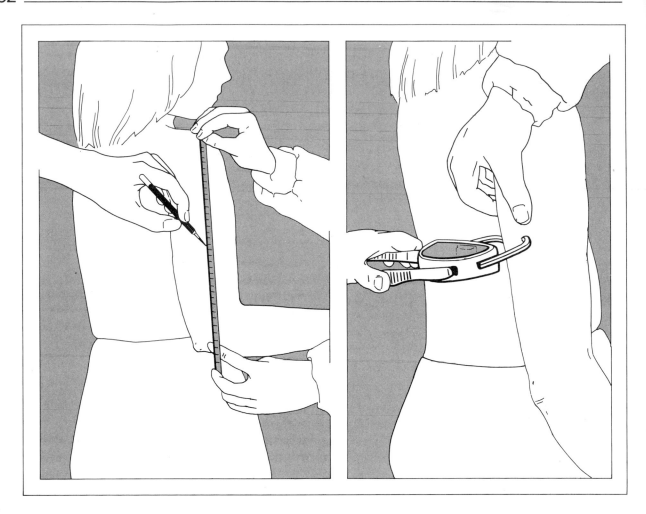

FIGURE 19-4   Measuring the triceps skinfold.

Easily pluckable (pediatric form only): Easily pluckable hair is that in which the shafts are readily removed with minimum tug when a few strands are grasped between the finger and thumb and gently pulled. In such cases there is a lack of reaction of the child, indicating a lack of pain associated with removing of the hair.

Abnormal texture or loss of curl (pediatric form only): Changes in texture of the hair to a soft, silk-like hair. Loss of curl self-explanatory.

Eyes

Thickened opaque bulbar conjunctivae (adult form only): All degrees of thickening may occur. The blueness of the sclera may disappear and the bulbar conjunctivae develop a wrinkled appearance with increase in vascularity. The thickened conjunctivae may result in a glazed, porcelain-like appearance, obscuring the vascularity. Do not confuse with pterygium.

Angular lesions of eyelids (adult form only):

Circumcorneal injection (bilateral): Increase in vascularity by new ingrowth of capillary loops, with particular concentration around the cornea in the absence of obvious infection, etc.

Conjunctival injection (bilateral): Generalized increase in the vascularity of the bulbar conjunctivae in the absence of obvious infection.

Xerosis conjunctivae: The conjunctivae, upon exposure by holding the lids open and having the subject rotate the eyes, appear dull, lusterless, and exhibit a striated or roughened surface.

Bitot's spots: Small circumscribed, grayish or yellowish-gray, dull, dry, foamy superficial lesions of the conjunctivae. Seen most often on the lateral

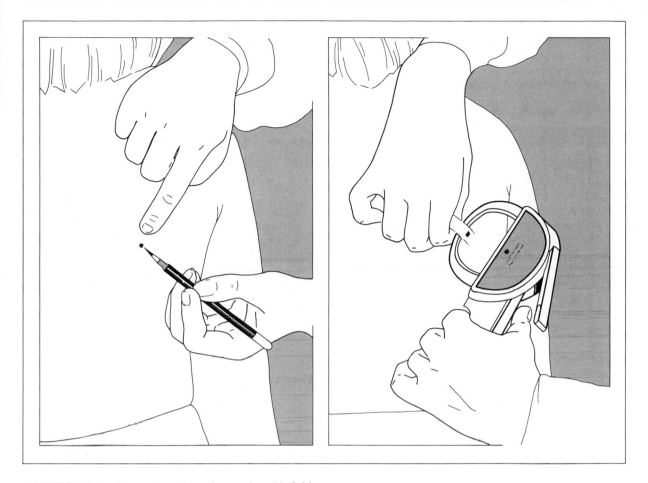

FIGURE 19-5   Measuring the subscapular skinfold.

aspect of the bulbar conjunctivae and in children. Usually bilateral. Not to be confused with pterygium.

Xerophthalmia: Xerophthalmia is recorded when the bulbar conjunctiva and cornea are dry and lusterless with a decrease in lacrimation. It is often associated with evidence of infection or, in extreme cases, keratomalacia.

Keratomalacia (pediatric form only): Corneal softening with deformity, either localized, usually central part of lower half of cornea, or total.

Lips

Angular lesions: Record only if definitely present bilaterally when mouth is held half open. May appear as pink or moist whitish macerated angular lesions which blur the mucocutaneous junction. Angular fissures are recorded only when there is definite break in continuity of epithelium at the angles of the mouth.

Angular scars: Scars at the angles, which, if recent, may be pink; if old, may appear blanched.

Cheilosis: Different from ordinary chapping. The lips are swollen or puffy and appear as if the buccal mucosa extends out onto the lip. There may be desquamation. This category may be used to include vertical fissuring of the lips. If associated with herpes labialis, note under "Remarks."

Teeth

Visible caries 4+—For the purpose of the medical examination, caries refers to lesions readily visible. (This is in contrast to the usual definition that a tooth is considered carious when the enamel yields to underlying soft material with the explorer tip.)

Debris: Calculus: Fluorosis . . .

Gums

Atrophy, recession, inflammation: Atrophy and recession refer to loss of substance of interdental papillae resulting in unfilled space between teeth at gingival line. Inflammation refers to typical gingivitis.

Marginal redness or swelling: Marginal redness refers to a definite red border along the dental margin of the gum. Marginal swelling refers to a swollen border of the gum which may be spongy or firm.

Swollen red papillae: Red, congested, spongy, swollen interdental papillae. Record whether localized to small area or diffuse throughout whole dental area.

Bleeding gums: Abnormal gums which either bleed spontaneously or bleed upon slight pressure with a swab stick.

Tongue

Filiform papillary atrophy: The filiform papillae are exceedingly low or absent, giving the tongue a smooth or "slick" appearance which remains after scraping slightly with an applicator stick. "Slight" involves less than one-fourth of the tongue (tip and lateral margins only); "moderate" involves one-fourth to three-fourths of the tongue; "severe" involves over three-fourths of the tongue.

Fungiform papillary hypertrophy or hyperemia: Can be seen and is felt when a tongue blade is drawn lightly over the anterior two thirds of the tongue. Hyperemia refers to definite red papillae which give the tongue a berrylike appearance. Record as moderate or severe if over 50 percent of papillae are hypertrophied or hyperemic.

Geographic tongue: Irregularly outlined and distributed areas of atrophy, with irregular white patches resembling leukoplakia.

Fissures: Linear lesions or cracks, with definite break in continuity of epithelium.

Serrations or swellings: Tooth impressions at sides of tip, often noted when tongue is swollen.

Red, scarlet, beefy (glossitis): Entire tongue is red, angry in appearance, with or without denudation or fissures. Not just a modification of the natural color due to the loss of papillae. Associated almost always with subjective symptoms of hypersensitivity, burning, even taste changes.

Magenta colored: The color of alkaline phenolphthalein.

Face and Neck

Malar pigmentation (adult form only): Areas of darkened, brown pigmentation over the malar eminences.

Nasolabial seborrhea: A definite greasy yellowish scaling or filiform excrescences in the nasolabial area which become more pronounced on slight scratching with the fingernail or a tongue blade.

Parotids visibly enlarged: Due to difficulties in assessing parotid enlargement, record as positive only if clearly visible and bilateral enlargement present.

Thyroid enlarged: The World Health Organization (WHO) criteria used for grading goiter are:

Grade 0: Persons without goiter. By definition these are persons whose thyroid glands are less than 4 to 5 times enlarged.

Grade I: Persons with palpable goiters. The thyroid is considered to be more than 4 to 5 times enlarged although not visible with head in normal position. Most of these will be readily visible with the head thrown back and the neck fully extended.

Grade II: Persons with visible goiters. Persons with goiters which are easily visible with the head in normal position but which are smaller than those in Grade III. Palpation may be helpful in determining the mass of the gland, but is not needed for diagnosis.

Grade III: Persons with very large goiters. The goiters of persons in this category can be recognized at a considerable distance. They are grossly disfiguring and may be of such size as to cause mechanical difficulties with respiration and in the wearing of clothes. (Perez, C., Scrimshaw, N. S., and Munos, J. A., Technique of endemic goitre surveys. In Endemic Goitre: p. 369, see esp. p. 376. World Health Organization Monograph Series No. 44. Geneva, 1960.)

Fingernails

Clubbing refers to an increase in the angle at the base of the fingernail. *Spooning* indicates concavity of the outer surfaces of the nail. *Ridging* refers to the presence of multiple longitudinal ridges in the nail. The last two signs are seen in some cases of chronic iron deficiency anemia.

Skin

Follicular hyperkeratosis: This lesion has been likened to "gooseflesh" which is seen on chilling, but it is not generalized and does not disappear with brisk rubbing of the skin. Readily felt, as it presents a "nutmeg grater" feel. Follicular hyperkeratosis is more readily detected by the sense of touch than by the eye. The skin is rough, with papillae formed by keratotic plugs which project from the hair follicles. The surrounding skin is dry and lacks the usual amount of moisture or oiliness. Differentiation from adolescent folliculosis can usually be made through recognition of the normal skin between the follicles in the adolescent disorder. It is distinguished from perifolliculosis by the ring of capillary congestion which occurs about each follicle in scorbutic perifolliculosis.

Dry or scaling skin (xerosis): Xerosis is a clinical term used to describe a dry and crinkled skin which is accentuated by pushing the skin parallel to its surface. In more pronounced cases it is often mottled and pigmented, and may appear as scaly or alligatorlike pseudoplaques, usually not greater than 0.5 cm in diameter. Nutritional significance is not established. Differential diagnosis must be made from changes due to dirt and exposure and ichthyosis.

Hyperpigmentation: Asymptomatic, with no inflammatory component. It is seen most frequently on the dorsum of the hands and lower forearms, particularly where skin hygiene is poor. The skin is rough, dry, and often has a grayish cyanotic base. There is not a sharp line of demarcation at the border of the lesion such as one sees in pellagra.

Thickened pressure points (other than elbows and knees): Look especially at belt area, ischial tuberosities, sacrum and over greater trochanters. Other sites may occur as a result of a given occupation. Do not record when found only on elbows and knees.

Perifolliculosis (adult form only): Congestion around the follicles which does not blanch upon pressure. (See discussion of follicular hyperkeratosis above.) Early ring of capillary engorgement around some hair follicles which does not disappear on pressure. It is more frequently encountered on the dependent parts such as the legs. Swelling and hypertrophy of the follicles may occur, at which time the skin becomes rough. Follicular hyperkeratosis and perifolliculosis may coexist.

Purpura or petechiae (adult form only): Small localized extravasations of blood, red or purplish in color, depending on time elapsed since formation. Usually distributed at sites of pressure, and may be perifollicular.

Crackled skin (adult form only): Definite scales larger in size than those seen in xerosis. It is often congenital and is most prominent in cool weather. It is non-nutritional in origin.

Pellagrous dermatitis (adult form only): Record when symmetrical lesions typical of acute or chronic, mild or severe pellagra are observed. Record location.

Abdomen

Potbelly (pediatric form only): Record if abdomen appears abnormally distended and enlarged, with due recognition of the usual contour of the young child.

Hepatomegaly: Record liver edges more than 2 cm below the costal margin.

Lower Extremities

Pretibial edema: Record only if bilateral.

Calf tenderness (adult form only): Record when definite bilateral evidence of painful sensation occurs upon squeezing the calf muscles firmly between the thumb and finger. Record only if moderate or severe.

Absent knee/ankle jerk (adult form only): Record only if absent bilaterally with reinforcement.

Absent vibratory sense (adult form only): Test with tuning fork at 128 vibrations per minute over the lateral malleoli. Record as positive only if absent bilaterally.

Scrotum

Scrotal dermatitis (adult form only): The scrotum usually must be rotated to see the lesions. Differentiate from fungus infections which usually extend onto the skin of the groin adjacent to the scrotum.

Pulse Rate and Blood

Pulse rate (adult form only): Count for a minimum of 30 seconds.

Blood pressure (adult form only): Take on right arm, with individual in sitting position. Make reading upon disappearance of sound. Record data to nearest even unit.

Skeletal (pediatric form only)

Beading of ribs: Record when there is definitely palpable and visible enlargement of the costochondral junctions.

Bossing of skull: Record when there is abnormal prominence or protrusion of frontal or parietal areas.

Clinical manifestations of nutrient deficiencies will only be apparent when malnutrition is in an advanced state. To diagnose the initial stages of malnutrition requires anthropometric, biochemical, and dietary data.

While signs of classical malnutrition are common in underdeveloped countries, similar overt clinical symptoms from undernourishment are encountered less frequently in the United States. On the other hand, malnutrition from excessive alcohol or calorie consumption is evident in this country (see Chapter 11). During a clinical examination, an American child with suspected or evident nutrient deficiencies should be given additional confirmatory studies. Examples of obvious poor nutrition signs in children are cavities, missing and decayed teeth, and gum hypertrophy. Overconsumption of sugary foods and poor oral hygiene are usually responsible for these clinical manifestations.

Biochemical Data

A third important set of measurements indicating nutritional status are biochemical data—the levels of specific chemicals in major body fluids such as blood, urine, feces, tears, saliva, and mucus. From this information, actual or borderline deficiency of a particular nutrient can be determined. Chemical analyses of hair and skin can also be used to determine the nutriture of a subject. Biochemical data are most valuable in identifying covert (subclinical) deficiencies before they progress to overt symptoms, thus allowing early intervention.

The chemical substances analyzed are categorized into three groups: blood components, nutrients and their metabolites, and body waste products. Blood components include proteins such as albumin, hemoglobin, and fibrinogen; minerals such as cations and hydrogen ions; and

special substances such as adenosine triphosphate and glutathione. Nutrients and their metabolites include protein (amino acids); fat (fatty acids, glycerol, phospholipids, cholesterol, and triglycerides); carbohydrate (glucose, fructose, and galactose); vitamins; minerals; hormones; pyruvate and lactate; and creatinine. Body waste products include carbon dioxide, water, bilirubin, urea, and creatinine. Table 19-2 describes the guidelines for classifying and interpreting group blood and urine data.

Dietary Evaluations

The fourth way to measure nutritional status is to determine the amount and type of foods consumed. The nutrient contribution or quality of the diet is evaluated in accordance with the latest RDAs. If anthropometric measurements, biochemical data, and clinical observations are available to supplement the dietary evaluations, the nutritional status of an individual can be determined—a dietary study by itself cannot accomplish this. However, a properly conducted dietary survey serves as a focal point for developing government food and nutrition policies; designing health services and programs with an adequate food and nutrition component; implementing more intensive nutrition education programs; and counseling individuals, who can be encouraged to modify faulty eating habits that are unrelated to food availability.

To obtain accurate results in a dietary study is difficult. At present, five methods are available.

Individual food history

One method is a qualitative analysis of a person's past dietary practices. A food history explores the patient's likes and dislikes for food, the type and quantity of food consumed, the locations and times of daily meals, the frequency of eating out, the use of alcoholic beverages, and the type and frequency of snacking. A good history can be obtained if the subject is willing and cooperative and the interviewer is skillful. However, this procedure is usually very costly because it takes time. Today, commercial computer data enterprises can analyze the nutrient intakes of an

TABLE 19-2 Guidelines for Classification and Interpretation of Group Blood and Urine Data

Substance	Classification Category		Acceptable*
	Less than acceptable		
	Deficient	Low	
Hemoglobin (g/100 mL)			
6–23 months	< 9.0	9.0–9.9	≧ 10.0
2–5 years	< 10	10.0–10.9	≧ 11.0
6–12 years	< 10	10.0–11.4	≧ 11.5
13–16 years, male	< 12	12.0–12.9	≧ 13.0
13–16 years, female	< 10	10.0–11.4	≧ 11.5
>16 years, male	< 12	12.0–13.9	≧ 14.0
>16 years, female	< 10	10.0–11.9	≧ 12.0
Pregnant, 2nd trimester	< 9.5	9.5–10.9	≧ 11.0
Pregnant, 3rd trimester	< 9.0	9.0–10.4	≧ 10.5
Hematocrit (%)			
6–23 months	< 28	28–30	≧ 31
2–5 years	< 30	30–33	≧ 34
6–12 years	< 30	30–35	≧ 36
13–16 years, male	< 37	37–39	≧ 40
13–16 years, female	< 31	31–35	≧ 36
>16 years, male	< 37	37–43	≧ 44
>16 years, female	< 31	31–37	≧ 38
Pregnant, 2nd trimester	< 30	30–34	≧ 35
Pregnant, 3rd trimester	< 30	30–32	≧ 33
Hemoglobin conc, MCHC (g/100 mL RBC)			
All ages	—	30	≧ 30
Serum iron (μg/100 mL)			
0–5 months	—	—	—
6–23 months	—	<30	≧ 30
2–5 years	—	<40	≧ 40
6–12 years	—	<50	≧ 50
>12 years, male	—	<60	≧ 60
>12 years, female	—	<40	≧ 40
Transferrin saturation (%)			
0–5 months	—	—	—
6–23 months	—	<15	≧ 15
2–12 years	—	<20	≧ 20
>12 years, male	—	<20	≧ 20
>12 years, female	—	<15	≧ 15
Red cell folacin (ng/mL)			
All ages	<140	140–159	≧160–650
Serum folacin (ng/mL)	3.0	3.0–5.9	≧ 6.0
Serum protein (g/100 mL)			
0–11 months	—	<5.0	≧ 5.0
1–5 years	—	<5.5	≧ 5.5
6–17 years	—	<6.0	≧ 6.0
Adult	< 6.0	6.0–6.4	≧ 6.5
Pregnant, 2nd and 3rd trimester	< 5.5	5.5–5.9	≧ 6.0
Serum albumin (g/100 mL)			
0–11 months	—	<2.5	≧ 2.5
1–5 years	—	<3.0	≧ 3.0

TABLE 19-2   (continued)

| Substance | Classification Category | | |
| | Less than acceptable | | |
	Deficient	Low	Acceptable*
6–17 years	—	<3.5	≥ 3.5
Adult	< 2.8	2.8–3.4	≥ 3.5
Pregnant, 1st trimester	< 3.0	3.0–3.9	≥ 4.0
Pregnant, 2nd and 3rd trimester	< 3.0	3.0–3.4	≥ 3.5
Serum vitamin C (mg/100 mL)			
0–11 months	—	—	—
≥1 years	< 0.1	0.1– 0.19	≥ 0.2
Plasma carotene (µg/100 mL)			
0–5 months	—	<10	≥ 10
6–11 months	—	<30	≥ 30
1–17 years	—	<40	≥ 40
Adult	< 20†	20–39	≥ 40
Pregnant, 2nd trimester	—	30–79	≥ 80
Pregnant, 3rd trimester	—	40–79	≥ 80
Plasma vitamin A (µg/100 mL)			
All ages	< 20	20–29	≥ 30
Urinary thiamin (µg/g creatinine)			
1–3 years	<120	120–175	≥176
4–6 years	< 85	85–120	≥121
7–9 years	< 70	70–180	≥181
10–12 years	< 60	60–180	≥181
13–15 years	< 50	50–150	≥151
Adult	< 27	27–65	≥ 66
Pregnant, 2nd trimester	< 23	23–54	≥ 55
Pregnant, 3rd trimester	< 21	21–49	≥ 50
Urinary riboflavin (µg/g creatinine)			
1–3 years	<150	150–499	≥500
4–6 years	<100	100–299	≥300
7–9 years	< 85	85–269	≥270
10–15 years	< 70	70–199	≥200
Adult	< 27	27–79	≥ 80
Pregnant, 2nd trimester	< 39	39–119	≥120
Pregnant, 3rd trimester	< 30	30–89	≥ 90
Urinary iodine (µg/g creatinine)	< 25	25–49	≥ 50

Source: *Ten-State Nutrition Survey, 1968–1970*. I. *Historical Development*. II. *Demographic Data*. U.S. Department of Health, Education and Welfare Publication No. (HSM) 72-8130. Atlanta, Center for Disease Control, 1972, pp. I-115–I-116.

*Excessively high levels may indicate abnormal clinical status or toxicity.

†May indicate unusual diet or malabsorption.

individual if the diet history is provided on a standard form. However, such computer analyses are not widespread, and they are not recommended unless a qualified person such as a nutritionist interprets the results. The information derived from a dietary history is of little signifi-cance in determining a subject's present nutritional status. However, it serves a useful purpose if it is interpreted along with other assessment data. If the patient shows overt signs of nutrient deficiencies, his or her diet history may confirm the specific nutrients involved.

Individual record of food intake

In a second method, a nutritionist, dietitian, or nurse may ask a subject to keep a food record for 1 to 7 days. The information is valuable if the person records every item eaten and accurately lists portion sizes. Unfortunately, most people fail to meet both requirements.

Individual recall of food intake

In a third method, the person is asked to recall what was eaten within the past 24 hours. Most people can recall their food intake over this time period with some accuracy. Meaningful results can be obtained if the interviewer is skillful. This method is probably the most common one used in a dietary survey.

Household recollection of food intake

In the fourth method of dietary evaluation, the food preparer in the family is requested to recollect the type and amount of foods purchased and consumed by the entire family for the previous week. Other requested data include the number of family members and their ages, the food budget, the meals eaten away from home, and the number of guests eating in the house that week and their ages. An alternative is finding the difference in the weights of food available in the household at the beginning and at the end of each week. The amount of foods discarded after each meal must be taken into account as well. At present, these two techniques are the only convenient ways to estimate the amount of foods consumed in a household, but they are not accurate.

Individual and household food weighing

The most accurate way to estimate food intake is to ask a person or household to weigh foods served immediately before a meal and then subtract the weight of the leftovers. However, this method is inconvenient and time consuming. Most dietary studies do not require this procedure because of the large number of subjects involved. However, diet weighing is used in some situations.

In a human nutrition experiment with a controlled environment, such as a metabolic study or a study of the food intake of a diabetic or kidney patient, sometimes the exact amount of food consumed must be known. This knowledge may be part of the mandatory treatment of the disease, or it may be necessary because the patient has difficulty in complying with a prescribed diet either because of eating habits or job routines.

Results and Uses of Major Nutrition Surveys

Three major national nutrition surveys have recently assessed the nutritional status of the American people. They are the Ten-State Nutrition Survey (1968 to 1970), the Preschool Nutrition Survey (1968 to 1970), and the Health and Nutrition Examination Survey (Hanes, 1971 to 1972) (see Chapter 19 references). These studies identified several problem areas. Children did not show any classical clinical manifestations of malnutrition (see Chapter 11), but some children showed growth retardation from undernutrition. Most of these children belonged to families of low socioeconomic status. Dental cavities, iron-deficient anemia, overweight, and high blood lipid profiles were common. Population groups at high risk of malnutrition included infants, children, pregnant women, the elderly, adolescents, and individuals from low-income families.

The National Center for Disease Control of the Department of Health and Human Services is conducting a continuous national nutrition surveillance program. This center makes use of existing clinics, programs, projects, and centers that compile information on the nutritional status of different population groups. The existing programs studied include Head Start; well-baby clinics; family planning clinics; Early Periodic Screening, Diagnosis, and Treatment programs; and the special supplemental food program for women, infants, and children (WIC). Data compiled by this center will be used to monitor the nutritional adequacy of the American diet.

Nutritionists, dietitians, and public health nurses participate in many other activities directly related to community and public health nutrition. They deliver the food and nutrition component of health care to individuals and families. They serve as the major nutrition and diet counselors of public health programs. For more information, consult the references at the back of this book.

STUDY QUESTIONS

1. What are at least five recommendations from the 1977 edition of *Dietary Goals for the United States*? What dietary changes are recommended to meet these goals? Are these suggestions followed by all nutritionists?

2. What four general methods are used in determining people's nutritional status? What is the best single method of determining adiposity?

3. Which areas and body systems should be examined for clues to nutritional status? Are these sufficient for diagnosing the early stages of malnutrition?

4. What is the most valuable contribution of biochemical analyses in evaluating nutritional status? What is analyzed?

5. What is a dietary study? How is it used? Describe at least three methods of conducting dietary studies, and discuss their pros and cons.

6. What nutrition-related problems have been identified by major national nutrition surveys?

Chapter 20

Food Additives and Related Chemicals

THE SAFETY OF food additives is a hot topic today. Few days now pass without the appearance of a newspaper article on the safety of chemicals used in food processing. Colleges across the nation offer courses about the issues involved. Unfortunately, it is extremely difficult to convince the general public—including college students—that there is no such thing as absolute safety in foods. The hazards and degrees of safety of food chemicals are best evaluated by considering their risks, benefits, and costs, which are currently the major components of government policy analyses. This comparison will be the primary means of evaluation until there are new scientific data.

There are numerous kinds of hazards involved in eating foods, and this book is not the proper forum to discuss all of them. This chapter examines food and color additives: what these substances are, how their use is regulated by the government, what functions they serve, and if they pose any hazards to our health.

TYPES OF FOOD HAZARDS

According to Dr. Virgin O. Wodicka, former head of the Bureau of Foods of the Food and Drug Administration (FDA), the risks posed to us by our food supply and our ways of eating are, in decreasing order of severity: (1) microbiological hazards, (2) nutritional hazards, (3) environmental pollutants, (4) natural toxicants, (5) pesticide residues, and (6) food additives.

The priority listing of Dr. Wodicka is based on four important premises. First, a hazard must be scientifically measurable and applicable to humans. Second, it is assumed that a hazard from a high-risk source occurs more frequently than that of a low-risk one. Third, a high-risk hazard is one that has been clinically documented to hurt more people than a low-risk one. Fourth, it is assumed that the usage of any food chemicals complies with *all* legally applicable regulations.

Microbiological hazards—the most dangerous risk to the safety of our food supply—will be considered in detail in Chapter 21. In brief, when people eat a food product containing a harmful number of bacteria or amount of bacterial toxin, they become ill. There may be vomiting, abdominal cramps, vision trouble, and even death, all of which are clinically measurable symptoms. Food poisoning has harmed many people and occurs frequently. Hardly a day goes by without someone in this country suffering from food poisoning.

As discussed throughout this book, there are many documented nutritional hazards among the population. For example, many alcoholics do not eat the right quantity and quality of food and may suffer severe nutritional imbalances and hazards. A middle-aged person who eats a lot of salt may be predisposed to high blood pressure. There are many other forms of nutritional hazards. Although these hazards occur frequently, their clinical manifestations are not as acute and severe as microbiological hazards, which can pose immediate danger.

Although environmental pollution is widespread, situations that severely endanger health are uncommon. Many instances of environmental contamination started years ago; such instances are expected to occur less frequently in the future because of tighter federal regulations. However, two notorious instances of accidental environmental pollution have involved human foods. One was the well-publicized mercury contamination of seafood, which resulted in the poisoning of many Japanese villagers in the 1950s. In this instance a chemical firm disposed of large quantities of mercury into a nearby river, from which many of the victims and their families fished. The accidental contamination of animal feeds with the fire retardant polybrominated biphenyl in Michigan during the early 1970s forced the government to destroy contaminated cows, cattle, beef, poultry, eggs, cheese, and milk. The risk to human health of this incident is still unknown.

The fourth most dangerous hazard in the food supply—natural toxicants—will be discussed in Chapter 21. Pesticide residues and food additives rank the lowest on the hazard list because, when used in accordance with federal regulations, they have not produced any clinical adverse effects that are *measurable*. No documented cases of poisoning due to food additives are available. However, the intake of pesticide residues and food additives is quite common. Today, some 2,800 substances are intentionally added to foods (as additives) to produce desired effects, such as keeping bread longer and improving the texture of ice cream. As many as 10,000 other compounds or combinations of compounds find their way into various foods during processing, packaging, and storage. Examples of these unintentional additives include infinitesimal residues of pesticides used to treat crops, minute amounts of drugs fed to animals, and chemical substances that migrate from plastic packaging materials.

Since small amounts of food additives, pesticide residues, and other chemicals are so common in our food supply, consumer groups and concerned citizens have questioned their safety. Some of the risks mentioned by these individuals or groups are difficult to substantiate with current scientific knowledge.

One frequently asked question is, Can pesticide residues and food additives cause such nonspecific manifestations as headache, nervousness, tiredness, depression, and irritability? Although these symptoms are important, they are very difficult to define and categorize. Unless medical science improves, it will be some time before a concrete relationship can be established between these symptoms and the usage of the chemicals.

Another common question is, Can pesticide residues and food additives be responsible for human cancer, birth defects, and mutations? Legally, if such substances are permitted in food, they are not supposed to produce such clinical problems, at least in animals. However, in humans, there is still no satisfactory way to indicate that they do not. More scientific data are needed.

A third question is, Can pesticide residues and food additives accumulate in our bodies and produce some future harm that is not apparent now, such as a shortened life span? Again, information is difficult to obtain, and there is no way to know what will happen to a person 20 years from now.

GOVERNMENT REGULATION OF FOOD AND COLOR ADDITIVES*

The federal government has long tried to protect consumers from food hazards. The 1906 Food and Drug Act and the more comprehensive Food, Drug, and Cosmetic Act of 1938 gave the federal government authority to remove adulterated and poisonous foods from the market. The enactment of the Food Additives Amendment in 1958 and the Color Additive Amendment in 1960 increased the government's authority to regulate food and color additives. In those amendments, the burden was shifted from the government, which had had to prove a food additive was unsafe, to the manufacturer, who has to prove it safe. The amendments authorized the FDA to regulate additives only on the basis of safety. The FDA was not given power to limit the number of chemicals approved or to decide whether a particular food color, thickener, or sweetener is really needed.

Defining Food Additives to Be Regulated

What is a food additive? The Food, Drug, and Cosmetic Act was amended in 1958. Specifically, this Food Additive Amendment contains four important features: (1) it defines what a food additive is; (2) it authorizes the FDA to "license" the use of food additives; (3) it permits the proposed use of a food additive if it can be proven safe when present at a certain level in food; and (4) if a food additive is a proven carcinogen (cancer-causing agent) in animals or humans, it cannot be added to food. This last feature is in a special provision of the 1958 amendment, the so-called Delaney clause.

In addition, certain substances—such as pesticides and related substances, color additives, and new animal drugs—are excluded from

---

*The information in this section has been adapted from P. Lehmann, (*FDA Consumer* 1979; 13 [April]:10–16; 13 [May]:18–23; 13 [June]:12–19).

the legal definition of a food additive. They are regulated by other provisions of the Food, Drug, and Cosmetic Act or other acts. Second, certain chemical substances, although technically food additives, are also exempt from the regulations. A chemical substance is not legally regulated as a food additive if it is "generally recognized as safe" (GRAS) under the conditions of intended use by scientists qualified by experience and training to evaluate food safety.

Also, a chemical substance is not legally regulated as a food additive if it is used in accordance with sanctions granted prior to the passage of the Food Additives Amendment. In actual practice, these "prior-sanctioned" chemicals may be divided into three categories: (1) those used in food products that have been standardized by the FDA; (2) those approved by the U.S. Department of Agriculture (USDA) for use under the Meat Inspection Act and the Poultry Products Inspection Act; and (3) those approved specifically by the FDA before the passage of the Food Additives Amendment. The approval was usually granted by a written statement, such as letters, memoranda, and other evidence of direct communication.

The idea behind what has come to be known as the "GRAS list" was to free the FDA and manufacturers from being required to prove the safety of substances already considered harmless because of past extensive use with no known harmful effects. Their efforts, it was felt, would be better spent on evaluating new additives and those compounds about which little was known. As testing methods and scientific understanding of toxicology improve, new evidence and questions may arise about the safety of old stand-bys. Cyclamates, for instance, were once on the GRAS list but have been removed because of new findings. To make sure that all substances are judged by the latest scientific standards, the FDA is now reviewing all categories of food additives.

The federal regulations governing color additives are quite similar to those for food additives, although there are three major differences: (1) there are less than 50 color additives; (2) color additives do not have a GRAS list; and (3) the safety of color additives is evaluated according to whether their sources are synthetic or natural.

Approval Procedures

If a food manufacturer wants to introduce a new chemical as a direct food additive or a new use for an old one, the company must file a petition with the FDA and request the issuance of a regulation sanctioning the proposed use of the substance.

The FDA recommends two guidelines on safety to any petitioner for a food additive. First, the petitioner should follow the principles and procedures for establishing the safety of food additives stated in current publications of the National Research Council of the National Academy of Sciences, although this is not binding. Second, the tolerance of a food additive issued by the FDA will not exceed $\frac{1}{100}$th of the maximum amount demonstrated to be without harm to experimental animals. The FDA regards this factor of 0.01 as the safety factor.

After an adequate and unbiased review of the petition, the FDA will not issue a regulation allowing the use of the food additive if the data confirm one or more of the following: (1) the safety of the proposed use is not established; (2) deception of the consumer may result from the intended use; (3) the intended technical or physical effect will not be accomplished by the proposed use; (4) it may be unsafe for a person to accumulate the substance taken in from more than one food source; or (5) the substance can cause cancer in animals.

MAJOR FUNCTIONS OF INTENTIONAL FOOD AND COLOR ADDITIVES

An additive is intentionally used in foods for one or more of the following purposes: to maintain or improve nutritional value, to maintain freshness, to help in processing or preparation, or to make food more appealing.

Table 20-1 describes the major functions of food and color additives and provides some examples. Table 20-2 describes examples and food sources of food additives according to their functions. Table 20-3 lists natural and synthetic colors legally permitted to increase the appeal of foods.

TABLE 20-1   Major Functions of Food Additives and Food Colors

Major Function	Examples	Specific Uses
To maintain or improve nutritional quality	Nutrients	Enriching (replacing vitamins and minerals lost in processing); fortifying (adding nutrients that may be lacking in the diet)
To maintain product quality	Preservatives (antimicrobials)	Preventing food spoilage from bacteria, molds, fungi, and yeast; extending shelf life; protecting natural color and flavor
	Antioxidants	Delaying or preventing rancidity or enzymatic browning
To facilitate processing or preparation	Emulsifiers	Helping to distribute evenly tiny particles of one liquid throughout another; improving homogeneity, consistency, stability, and texture
	Stabilizers, thickeners, texturizers	Imparting body or improving consistency or texture; stabilizing emulsions; affecting "mouth feel"
	pH agents	Regulating acidity or alkalinity
	Anticaking agents	Preventing caking, lumping, or clustering of a finely powdered or crystalline substance
	Dough conditioners, maturing and bleaching agents	Accelerating the aging process; improving baking qualities
	Leavening agents	Affecting cooking results such as texture and volume
	Humectants	Permitting retention of moisture
To maintain or improve appeal or sensory characteristics	Flavor enhancers	Supplementing, magnifying, or modifying the original taste and/or aroma without imparting a characteristic flavor
	Flavors	Heightening natural flavor; restoring flavors lost in processing
	Colors	Providing appetizing, desired, or characteristic color
	Sweeteners	Making the aroma or taste more agreeable or pleasurable

COLORING

Legally food colors are divided into two major categories: uncertified and certified. The former consists of those mainly from natural sources, and the latter those synthesized from organic petroleum products. Table 20-3 indicates these two groups of chemicals. The procedure for obtaining legal permission to use a new food color additive is nearly the same as that for a food additive with one additional important requirement: all legally permitted synthetic food colors must be certified. This means that each batch of the chemical sold for food processing must be sampled by the government to ensure that it complies with specifications concerning chemical purity and other qualities.

Because synthetic food colors are not derived

TABLE 20-2   Examples and Food Sources of Food Additives According to Their Functions

Function	Food Additive	Foods in Which Used	Purpose(s)
To improve or maintain nutritional value	β-carotene	Margarine	Fortification
	Iodine, potassium iodide	Salt	Fortification
	Iron	Grain products	Enrichment, fortification
	Vitamin A	Milk, margarine, cereals	Fortification
	Vitamin B$_1$, vitamin B$_2$, niacin	Flour, breads, cereals, rice, macaroni products	Enrichment
	Vitamin C	Beverages, beverage mixes, processed fruit	Fortification
	Vitamin D, vitamin D$_2$, vitamin D$_3$	Milk, cereals	Fortification
	Vitamin E	Cereals, grain products	Fortification
To maintain product quality (antioxidants)	BHA (butylated hydroxyanisole), BHT (butylated hydroxytoluene)	Bakery products, cereals, snack foods, fats and oils	Delay or prevention of undesirable changes in color, flavor, or texture, such as enzymatic browning or discoloration due to oxidation; delay or prevention of rancidity in foods with unstable oils
	Citric acid	Fruits, snack foods, cereals, instant potatoes	
	EDTA (ethylenediaminetetraacetic acid)	Dressings, sauces, margarine	
	Propyl gallate	Cereals, snack foods, pastries	
	TBHQ (tertiary butylhydroquinone)	Snack foods, fats and oils	
	Tocopherols (vitamin E)	Oils and shortening	
	Vitamin C (ascorbic acid)	Processed fruits, baked goods	
To maintain product quality (antimicrobials)	Benzoic acid, sodium benzoate	Fruit products, acidic foods, margarine	Prevention of food spoilage from bacteria, molds, fungi and yeast; extension of shelf life; protection of natural color or flavor
	Citric acid	Acidic foods	
	Lactic acid, calcium lactate	Olives, cheese, frozen desserts, some beverages	
	Parabens (butylparaben, hyptylparaben, methylparaben, propylparaben)	Beverages, caketype pastries, salad dressings, relishes	
	Propionic acid (calcium propionate, potassium propionate, sodium propionate)	Breads and other baked goods	
	Sodium diacetate	Baked goods	
	Sodium erythorbate	Cured meats	
	Sodium nitrate, sodium nitrite	Cured meats, fish, poultry	
	Sorbic acid (calcium sorbate, potassium sorbate, sodium sorbate)	Cheese, syrups, cakes, fruit products, beverages, mayonnaise, processed meats	

TABLE 20-2   (continued)

Function	Food Additive	Foods in Which Used	Purpose(s)
	Vitamin C (ascorbic acid)	Fruit products, acidic foods	
To aid in processing or preparation (emulsifiers)	Carrageenan	Chocolate milk, canned milk drinks, whipped toppings	Helping to evenly distribute tiny particles of one liquid throughout another, e.g., oil and water; modification of surface tension of liquid to establish a uniform dispersion or emulsion; improvement of homogeneity, stability, consistency, and texture
	Dioctyl sodium sulfosuccinate	Cocoa	
	Lecithin	Margarine, dressings, frozen desserts, chocolate, baked goods	
	Monoglycerides, diglycerides	Baked goods, peanut butter, cereals	
	Polysorbate 60, polysorbate 65, polysorbate 80	Gelatin and pudding desserts, ice cream, dressings, baked goods, nondairy creams	
	Sorbitan monostearate	Cakes, toppings, chocolate	
To aid in processing or preparation (stabilizers, thickeners, texturizers)	Ammonium alginate, calcium alginate, potassium alginate, sodium alginate	Dessert-type dairy products, confections	Imparting body, improving consistency, texture; stabilizing emulsions; affecting appearance and mouth feel of the food; many are natural carbohydrates that absorb water in the food
	Carrageenan	Frozen desserts, puddings, syrups, jellies	
	Cellulose derivatives	Breads, ice cream, confections, diet foods	
	Flour	Sauces, gravies, canned foods	
	Furcelleran	Frozen desserts, puddings, syrups	
	Modified food starch	Sauces, soups, pie fillings, canned meals, snack foods	
	Pectin	Jams and jellies, fruit products, frozen desserts	
	Propylene glycol	Baked goods, frozen desserts, dairy spreads	
	Vegetable gums, guar gum, gum arabic, gum ghatti, karaya gum, locust (carob) bean gum, tragacanth gum, larch gum (arabogalactan)	Chewing gum, sauces, desserts, dressings, syrups, beverages, fabricated foods, cheese, baked goods	

TABLE 20-2 (continued)

Function	Food Additive	Foods in Which Used	Purpose(s)
To aid in processing or preparation (pH control agents)	Acetic acid and sodium acetate	Candies, sauces, dressings, relishes	Controlling (changing and maintaining) acidity or alkalinity; affecting texture, taste, and wholesomeness
	Adipic acid	Beverage and gelatin bases, bottled drinks	
	Calcium lactate	Fruits and vegetables, dry and condensed milk	
	Citric acid and sodium citrate	Fruit products, candies, beverages, frozen desserts	
	Fumaric acid	Dry dessert bases, confections, powdered soft drinks	
	Lactic acid	Cheese, beverages, frozen desserts	
	Phosphoric acid and phosphates	Fruit products, beverages, oils, ices and sherbets, soft drinks, baked goods	
	Tartaric acid and tartrates	Confections, some dairy desserts, baked goods, beverages	
To aid in processing or preparation (anticaking agents)	Calcium silicate	Table salt, baking powder, other powdered foods	Helping keep salts and powders free-flowing; prevention of caking, lumping, or clustering of a finely powdered or crystalline substance
	Iron ammonium citrate	Salt	
	Silicon dioxide	Table salt, baking powder, other powdered foods	
	Yellow prussiate of soda	Salt	
To aid in processing or preparation (maturing and bleaching agents, dough conditioners)	Acetone peroxide, benzoyl peroxide, hydrogen peroxide	Flour, breads, and rolls	Acceleration of aging process (oxidation) to develop the gluten characteristics of flour; improving baking qualities
	Azodicarbonamide	Cereal flour, breads	
	Calcium bromate and potassium bromate	Breads	
	Sodium stearyl fumarate	Yeast-leavened breads, instant potatoes, processed cereals	
To aid in processing or preparation (leavening agents)	Baking powder, double-acting (sodium bicarbonate, sodium aluminum sulfate, calcium phosphate)	Quick breads, caketype baked goods	Affecting cooking results; improving texture and increasing volume; some flavor effects
	Baking soda (sodium bicarbonate)	Quick breads, caketype baked goods	
	Yeast	Breads, baked goods	

TABLE 20-2 (continued)

Function	Food Additive	Foods in Which Used	Purpose(s)
To aid in processing or preparation (humectants)	Glycerine Glycerol monostearate Propylene glycol Sorbitol	Flaked coconut Marshmallow Confections, pet foods Soft candies, gum	Retention of moisture
To affect appeal characteristics (flavor enhancers)	Disodium guanylate Disodium inosinate Hydrolyzed vegetable protein MSG (monosodium glutamate)	Canned vegetables Canned vegetables Processed meats, gravy and sauce mixes, fabricated foods Oriental foods, soups, foods with animal protein	Supplementation, enhancement, or modification of original taste and/or aroma of a food without imparting a foreign taste or aroma
To affect appeal characteristics (flavors)	Vanilla (natural) Vanillin (synthetic) Spices and other natural seasonings and flavorings	Baked goods Baked goods Many products	Making foods taste better; improvement of natural flavor; restoration of flavors lost in processing
To affect appeal characteristics (sweeteners)	Corn syrup, corn syrup solids, invert sugar Dextrose, fructose, glucose, sucrose (table sugar) Nonnutritive sweeteners (saccharin) Nutritive sweeteners (mannitol [sugar alcohol], sorbitol [sugar alcohol])	Cereals, baked goods, candies, processed foods, processed meats Cereals, baked goods, candies, processed foods, processed meats Special dietary foods, beverages Candies, gum, confections, baked goods	Making aroma or taste of a food more agreeable or pleasurable

from food sources, their long chemical names have caused some trouble. For simple identification, the colors are assigned initials, the shade, and a number, for example, FD&C red no. 2 ("FD&C" stands for Food, Drug, and Cosmetics).

The 1960 Color Additive Amendment subjected coloring agents used in foods, drugs, and cosmetics to rigorous premarket testing. Colors in use when the amendment was passed were placed on a provisional approval list pending further investigation or confirmation of their safety. Nearly 200 colors have been on the provisional approval list at one time or another. A large number have been dropped from the list for various reasons, including being potential hazards.

ADDITIVES LEGALLY PROHIBITED FROM USE IN FOOD

The FDA prohibited the use of a number of chemicals in foods for human consumption, because they either present a risk to the public health or have not been shown safe by adequate

TABLE 20-3 Colors Legally Permitted to Increase the Appeal of Foods

Color Additive	Origin		Foods in Which Color is Permitted
	Natural	Synthetic	
Annatto extract (yellow-red)	x		No restrictions
Dehydrated beets, beet powder	x		No restrictions
Ultramarine blue		x	Animal feed only, 0.5% by weight
Canthaxanthin (orange-red)	x	x	Limit = 30 mg/lb food
Caramel (brown)	x		No restrictions
β-apo-8′-carotenal (yellow-red)	x	x	Limit = 15 mg/lb food
β-carotene (yellow)	x	x	No restrictions
Citrus red no. 2		x	Orange skins of mature, green eating oranges; limit = 2 ppm
Cochineal extract, carmine (red)	x		No restrictions
Toasted, partially defatted, cooked cottonseed flour (brown shades)	x		No restrictions
FD&C blue no. 1		x	No restrictions
FD&C red no. 3		x	No restrictions
FD&C red no. 40		x	No restrictions
FD&C yellow no. 5		x	No restrictions
Ferrous gluconate (black)		x	Ripe olives
Grape skin extract (purple-red)	x		Beverages only
Iron oxide (red-brown)		x	Pet foods only, 0.25% or less by weight
Fruit juice, vegetable juice	x		No restrictions
Dried algae meal (yellow)	x		Chicken feed only
Tagetes (Aztec marigold)	x		Chicken feed only
Carrot oil (orange)	x		No restrictions
Corn endosperm (red-brown)	x		Chicken feed only
Paprika, paprika oleoresin (red-orange)	x		No restrictions
Riboflavin (yellow)	x	x	No restrictions
Saffron (orange)	x		No restrictions
Titanium dioxide (white)		x	Limit = 1% by weight
Turmeric, tumeric oleoresin (yellow)	x		No restrictions

Note: Usage of this list must be supplemented with the latest legal developments.

TABLE 20-4   Additives Prohibited from Use in Foods for Human Consumption

Food Additive	Usage
Agene (nitrogen trichloride)	Bleaching and aging substance for flour
Cobalt salts	Stabilizer in beer permitting foam formation
Coumarin	Flavoring agent
Cyclamate	Artificial sweetener
Diethyl pyrocarbonate (DEPC)	Preservative, especially for alcoholic beverages
Dulcin (p-ethoxyphenyl urea)	Artificial sweetener
Ethylene glycol	Humectant, solvent
Monochloroacetic acid	Preservative
Nordihydroguaiaretic acid (NDGA)	Antioxidant
Oil of calamus	Flavoring agent
Polyoxyethylene-8-stearate (Myrj 45)	Emulsifier
P-4000	Proposed artificial sweetener
Safrole	Flavoring agent
Thiourea	Preservative

scientific data. Table 20-4 lists the food additives that manufacturers are presently prohibited from adding to food, and prohibited synthetic food colors are listed below.

Butter yellow	FD&C green no. 1
Sudan 1	FD&C green no. 2
FD&C red no. 1	FD&C yellow no. 1
FD&C red no. 2	FD&C yellow no. 2
FD&C red no. 4	FD&C yellow no. 3
FD&C red no. 32	FD&C yellow no. 4
FD&C orange no. 1	FD&C violet no. 1
FD&C orange no. 2	orange B

For easy reference, the table and list above include only some of the substances prohibited from use in human food. In order to remove any legal substance from use, proper legal procedures must be followed.

INDIRECT FOOD ADDITIVES

In addition to the food additives discussed above, many others perform multiple functions and are difficult or impossible to classify. They are known as unintentional or indirect food additives, meaning that their presence in food is neither intentional nor for any specific technical effect. They may be used in the growing, harvesting, and processing of foods and in the protective packaging used between either processing and consumption or harvest and processing. Their usage is carefully regulated by the FDA, which prescribes the legal amount of their residues in foods for human consumption.

PUBLIC CONFIDENCE IN THE USE OF FOOD AND COLOR ADDITIVES

Public confidence in the use of chemical additives in food is currently low, mainly because of uncertainty about the health hazards that they pose. Public confidence might increase if consumers had more information about food chemicals, government regulations governing their use, and the differences between measurable and nonmeasurable health hazards. The public mistrusts the government because they believe that it is not releasing everything known about food chemicals. Unfortunately, the knowledge of scientists (in and out of government) about the safety of food additives is limited, and the public must recognize this. People should seek a balance between the relative risks and benefits of food and color additives.

As a consumer, you should become informed. Start by reading labels to find out what is in the foods you buy. Additives must be listed with the ingredients, although the law permits colors and flavors to be described in general terms like "artifically flavored" and "artificially colored." Learn what the various additives do and decide which ones are of most concern to you. If you have questions, contact the consumer affairs officer at your nearest FDA office, listed in the telephone directory under U.S. Department of Health and Human Services, or write to the manufacturer.

Exercise your right to choose. Once you are informed, you can select foods on the basis of which characteristics—convenience, appeal, storage characteristics, or ease of preparation—mean the most to you. You might want to continue buying bread with sodium propionate if you know it prevents mold, but you may not want to buy cookies that are artificially colored. The choice is yours.

Finally, make your views known. Let manufacturers and your representatives in Congress know what you want and do not want in your food. Discuss the problems with academicians in foods and nutrition.

Food additives, like most things in life, involve a trade-off. Scientists will never be able to guarantee that anything added to food is absolutely safe. Ultimately, the consumer must decide what degree of risk is acceptable for foods that keep well and are appealing, nutritious, convenient, and readily available year-round.

STUDY QUESTIONS

1. Briefly explain the potential health risks in foods. Which is thought to be the most serious hazard? What general questions about food safety are yet unanswered?
2. Who now bears the burden of proving food products safe? What does "GRAS" mean? Does the GRAS list ever change? Give some examples of GRAS substances that are not mentioned in the chapter.
3. What agency reviews petitions for the sale of new food additives or new uses for old additives? How does the government determine the level of additive permitted to be used in food?
4. What are antioxidants? Give some examples.
5. Describe at least five ways in which chemicals are used in food processing and give examples of each.
6. How many synthetic colors are legally permitted as food additives? Which ones are controversial? Why?
7. What are indirect or unintentional food additives?

Chapter 21

Food Contamination and Natural Toxicants

AS INDICATED IN Chapter 20, microbiological contamination and natural toxicants rank first and fourth, respectively, on the FDA Bureau of Food's list of health risks in our food supply. The major biological agents that may cause food and water poisoning are listed below.

A. Bacteria
   1. *Staphylococcus*
   2. *Clostridium perfringens*
   3. *Clostridium botulinum*
   4. *Escherichia coli* (some strains)
   5. *Vibrio parahaemolyticus*
   6. *Vibrio cholerae*
   7. *Shigella*
   8. *Salmonella*
   9. *Francisella tularensis*
   10. *Brucella*
B. Virus
   Infectious hepatitis
C. Fungus
   Aspergillus flavus (aflatoxin)
D. Protozoa
   1. Amebiasis (*Entamoeba histolytica*)
   2. Giardiasis (*Giardia lamblia*)
   3. Balantidiasis (*Balantidium coli*)
   4. Coccidiosis (*Isospora belli* and *Isospora hominis*)
E. Metazoa (multicellular animals, i.e., all animals except protozoa)
   1. Trematode
      a. Schistosomiasis (*Schistosoma mansoni*)
      b. Fascioliasis (*Fasciola hepatica*)
      c. Clonorchiasis (*Clonorchis sinensis*)
      d. Paragonimiasis (*Paragonimus westermani*)
   2. Cestode (tapeworms)
      a. *Taenia saginata* (beef tapeworm)
      b. *Taenia solium* (pork tapeworm)
      c. *Diphyllobothrium latum* (fish tapeworm)
      d. *Echinococcus granulosus* (echinococcosis, hydatid disease)
   3. Nematode (roundworms)
      a. *Trichinella spiralis* (trichinosis)
      b. *Trichuris trichiura* (trichuriasis)
      c. *Ascaris lumbricoides* (ascariasis)
      d. *Enterobius vermicularis* (enterobiasis)

This chapter examines food poisoning from biological agents and toxicants occurring naturally in certain foods.

BIOLOGICAL CONTAMINATION

Spoiled food may cause illness. The contamination usually results from bacteria introduced when the food is prepared, served, or stored. Since the illness is limited to individuals rather than a large number of families or households, it is not epidemic. In general, illness from eating spoiled food is usually moderate in severity and may occasionally be mild. Each of us during our lifetimes will probably suffer from food contamination to some degree.

Food poisoning by biological agents varies in severity. Some signs include abdominal pain, diarrhea, nausea, vomiting, and general discomfort and malaise. Severe symptoms are fever and nervous disorders. The instability of vital signs, tiredness, and dehydration suffered by the victim are due mainly to a loss of fluid and electrolytes. Individuals who are most susceptible to moderate and severe reactions are the sick, the very young, and the elderly. Most adults can tolerate the discomfort and intestinal upset of food poisoning.

Food poisoning by biological agents is classified into two types. *Food-borne infection* is the consumption of food containing a large number of live bacteria capable of producing enough toxin in the intestine to poison the host. Incubation for this type of poisoning is about 36 to 48 hours. *Food-borne intoxication* is consumption of a food in which the pathogenic bacteria have already released the toxin capable of poisoning the host. The incubation period for this type of poisoning is about 1 to 12 hours.

The growth of bacteria is determined by the type of food, the presence or absence of oxygen, moisture content, acidity or alkalinity, time, and temperature. However, given sufficient time, bacteria can frequently adapt to all types of foods and all conditions of moisture, acidity, oxygen,

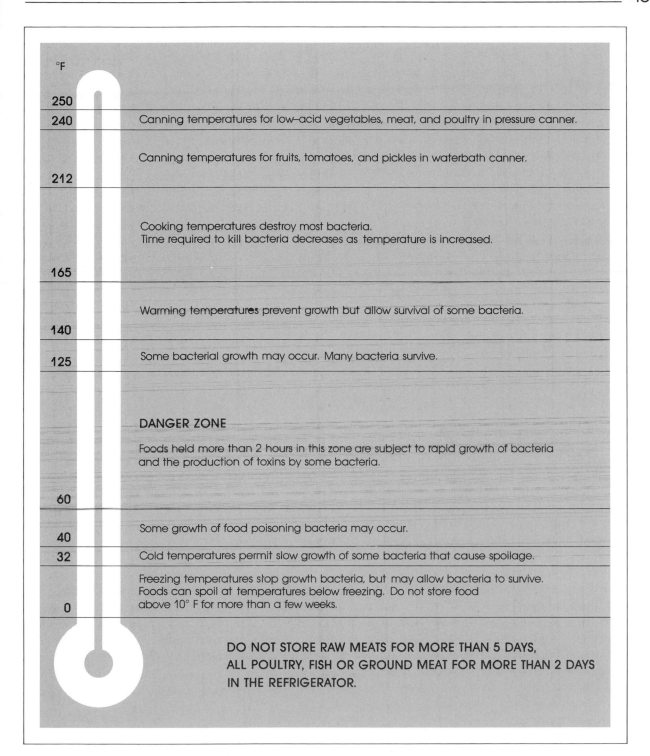

°F

250

240 Canning temperatures for low–acid vegetables, meat, and poultry in pressure canner.

Canning temperatures for fruits, tomatoes, and pickles in waterbath canner.

212

Cooking temperatures destroy most bacteria.
Time required to kill bacteria decreases as temperature is increased.

165

Warming temperatures prevent growth but allow survival of some bacteria.

140

125 Some bacterial growth may occur. Many bacteria survive.

DANGER ZONE

Foods held more than 2 hours in this zone are subject to rapid growth of bacteria
and the production of toxins by some bacteria.

60

Some growth of food poisoning bacteria may occur.

40

32 Cold temperatures permit slow growth of some bacteria that cause spoilage.

Freezing temperatures stop growth bacteria, but may allow bacteria to survive.
Foods can spoil at temperatures below freezing. Do not store food
0 above 10° F for more than a few weeks.

**DO NOT STORE RAW MEATS FOR MORE THAN 5 DAYS,
ALL POULTRY, FISH OR GROUND MEAT FOR MORE THAN 2 DAYS
IN THE REFRIGERATOR.**

FIGURE 21-1   Temperature guide to food safety. Distributed by the U.S.
Department of Agriculture.

and temperature; in fact, most bacteria can get used to a new environment within about 4 hours and start multiplying thereafter. For this reason foods should not be left at room temperature for more than 4 hours. Figure 21-1 presents a temperature guide to food safety.

Table 21-1 presents some known food-borne diseases, including the causative organisms, symptoms, and preventive methods.

SAFE FOOD PREPARATION PRACTICES

To avoid food poisoning, personal hygiene is very important. Hands should always be clean whenever food is handled. Hot water and soap should be used to wash hands after going to the bathroom, before handling cooked foods, and after handling raw foods. A person who is ill should not prepare food. During food preparation, contact between hands and the mouth, nose, or hair should be avoided, as should coughing and sneezing over foods. Tissues or handkerchiefs should be used to prevent contamination. Food tasting with fingers and cooking utensils used during preparation is not advised, even if the cooking temperature is very hot.

In addition to good personal hygiene, food preparers should take certain precautions. All kitchen equipment and utensils should be thoroughly cleaned before contact with all foods. Cooked foods should not be allowed to stand at room temperature for more than 2 to 3 hours whenever feasible. Exposure of food to temperatures between 5 and 60 °C (40 and 140 °F) should be kept to a minimum. The practice of preparing foods a day or several hours before eating should be done with care and avoided if possible.

Hot foods should never be allowed to cool slowly to room temperature before refrigerating. The slow cooling period provides an ideal growth temperature for bacteria. Foods should be refrigerated immediately after removing them from a steam table or warming oven. To cool foods rapidly for storage, a shallow pan, cold

running water, or ice bath can be used. A large amount of food in a big container requires many hours of cooling before all the contents are below 7 °C (45 °F).

When leftovers are served, the food should be heated until all parts reach a temperature of 74 °C (165 °F). This destroys all vegetative cells of bacteria. Whenever applicable, food should be chopped into small pieces and boiled to destroy any susceptible vegetative cells of the bacteria. No cooling should be permitted after preparation—the food should be served hot.

Certain popular foods—stuffed turkey, gravies, cream pies and puddings, sandwiches, and salads—are frequent culprits in food poisoning. When preparing roast turkey, do not stuff the bird but cook the stuffing separately. If turkey is stuffed with raw fillers, avoid stuffing it the night before. If stuffing is cooked separately, it should be cooked immediately after mixing, especially if in a large quantity. Stuffing is an excellent place for bacteria to grow, and if a large amount of lukewarm stuffing is permitted to stand at room temperature, the organisms will surely multiply.

Gravies and broths are quite susceptible to bacterial contamination, especially as leftovers. These foods should be placed in the refrigerator as soon as possible. Gravy or broth should not be held in the refrigerator more than 1 or 2 days, and it should be reheated or boiled for several minutes before serving. A reheated dressing should not be permitted to stay at room temperature.

Cream pies and puddings are also often involved in food poisoning. People dislike keeping these items in the refrigerator, because they can become soggy. However, leaving them at room temperature is definitely not advisable, since bacteria will multiply rapidly. Ideally, such pastries should be prepared as close to serving time as possible.

Items such as ham sandwiches, turkey and chicken salads, and deviled eggs require special attention. One good practice is to freeze the sandwiches immediately after preparation and thaw them whenever they are needed. Chicken salads may be prepared by using frozen chicken cubes, which will thaw as the salad stands; the entire salad dish should be kept cool.

TABLE 21-1   Characteristics of Different Food-Borne Diseases*

Disease and Organism That Causes It	Source of Illness	Symptoms	Prevention Methods
Salmonellosis *Salmonella* (bacteria; more than 1,700 kinds)	May be found in raw meats, poultry, eggs, fish, milk, and products made with them. Multiplies rapidly at room temperature.	Onset: 12–48 hours after eating. Nausea, fever, headache, abdominal cramps, diarrhea, and sometimes vomiting. Can be fatal in infants, the elderly, and the infirm.	Handling food in a sanitary manner Thorough cooking of foods Prompt and proper refrigeration of foods
Staphylococcal food poisoning Staphylococcal enterotoxin (produced by *Staphylococcus aureus* bacteria)	The toxin is produced when food contaminated with the bacteria is left too long at room temperature. Meats, poultry, egg products; tuna, potato, and macaroni salads; and cream-filled pastries are good environments for these bacteria to produce toxin.	Onset: 1–8 hours after eating. Diarrhea, vomiting, nausea, abdominal cramps, and prostration. Mimics flu. Lasts 24–48 hours. Rarely fatal.	Sanitary food handling practices Prompt and proper refrigeration of foods
Botulism Botulinum toxin (produced by *Clostridium botulinum* bacteria)	Bacteria are widespread in the environment. However, bacteria produce toxin only in an anaerobic (oxygenless) environment of little acidity. Types A, B, and F may result from inadequate processing of low-acid canned foods, such as green beans, mushrooms, spinach, olives, and beef. Type E normally occurs in fish.	Onset: 8–36 hours after eating. Neurotoxic symptoms, including double vision, inability to swallow, speech difficulty, and progressive paralysis of the respiratory system. **Obtain medical help immediately. Botulism can be fatal.**	Using proper methods for canning low-acid foods Avoidance of commercially canned low-acid foods with leaky seals or with bent, bulging or broken cans Toxin can be destroyed after a can is opened by boiling contents hard for 10 minutes—**not recommended**
Perfringens food poisoning *Clostridium perfringens* (rod-shaped bacteria)	Bacteria are widespread in environment. Generally found in meat and poultry and dishes made with them. Multiply rapidly when foods are left at room temperature too long. Destroyed by cooking.	Onset: 8–22 hours after eating (usually 12). Abdominal pain and diarrhea. Sometimes nausea and vomiting. Symptoms last a day or less and are usually mild. Can be more serious in older or debilitated people.	Sanitary handling of foods, especially meat and meat dishes and gravies Thorough cooking of foods Prompt and proper refrigeration

TABLE 21-1 (continued)

Disease and Organism That Causes It	Source of Illness	Symptoms	Prevention Methods
Shigellosis (bacillary dysentery) *Shigella* (bacteria)	Food becomes contaminated when a human carrier with poor sanitary habits handles liquid or moist food that is then not cooked thoroughly. Organisms multiply in food stored above room temperature. Found in milk and dairy products, poultry, and potato salad.	Onset: 1–7 days after eating. Abdominal pain, cramps, diarrhea, fever, sometimes vomiting, and blood, pus, or mucus in stools. Can be serious in infants, the elderly or debilitated people.	Handling food in a sanitary manner Proper sewage disposal Proper refrigeration of foods
Campylobacterosis *Campylobacter jejuni* (rod-shaped bacteria)	Bacteria found on poultry, cattle, and sheep and can contaminate the meat and milk of these animals. Chief food sources: raw poultry and meat and unpasteurized milk.	Onset: 2–5 days after eating. Diarrhea, abdominal cramping, fever, and sometimes bloody stools. Lasts 2–7 days.	Thorough cooking of foods Handling food in a sanitary manner Avoiding unpasteurized milk
Gastroenteritis *Yersinia enterocolitica* (nonspore-forming bacteria)	Ubiquitous in nature; carried in food and water. Bacteria multiply rapidly at room temperature, *as well as* at refrigerator temperatures (4° to 9° C). Generally found in raw vegetables, meats, water, and unpasteurized milk.	Onset: 2–5 days after eating. Fever, headache, nausea, diarrhea, and general malaise. Mimics flu. An important cause of gastroenteritis in children. Can also infect other age groups and, if not treated, can lead to other more serious diseases (such as lymphadenitis, arthritis, and Reiter's syndrome).	Thorough cooking of foods Sanitizing cutting instruments and cutting boards before preparing foods that are eaten raw Avoidance of unpasteurized milk and unchlorinated water
Cereus food poisoning *Bacillus cereus* (bacteria and possibly their toxin)	Illness may be caused by the bacteria, which are widespread in the environment, or by an enterotoxin created by the bacteria. Found in raw foods. Bacteria multiply rapidly in foods stored at room temperature.	Onset: 1–18 hours after eating. Two types of illness: (1) abdominal pain and diarrhea, and (2) nausea and vomiting. Lasts less than a day.	Sanitary handling of foods Thorough cooking of foods Prompt and adequate refrigeration
Cholera *Vibrio cholera* (bacteria)	Found in fish and shellfish harvested from waters contaminated by human sewage. (Bacteria may also occur naturally in Gulf Coast waters.) Chief food sources: seafood, especially types eaten raw (such as oysters).	Onset: 1–3 days. Can range from "subclinical" (a mild uncomplicated bout with diarrhea) to fatal (intense diarrhea with dehydration). Severe cases require hospitalization.	Sanitary handling of foods Thorough cooking of seafood
Parahaemolyticus food poisoning *Vibrio parahaemolyticus* (bacteria)	Organism lives in salt water and can contaminate fish and shellfish. Thrives in warm weather.	Onset: 15–24 hours after eating. Abdominal pain, nausea, vomiting, and diarrhea. Sometimes fever, headache, chills, and mucus and blood in the stools. Lasts 1–2 days. Rarely fatal.	Sanitary handling of foods Thorough cooking of seafood

TABLE 21-1   (continued)

Disease and Organism That Causes It	Source of Illness	Symptoms	Prevention Methods
Gastrointestinal disease Enteroviruses, rotaviruses, parvoviruses	Viruses exist in the intestinal tract of humans and are expelled in feces. Contamination of foods can occur in three ways: (1) when sewage is used to enrich garden/farm soil, (2) by direct hand-to-food contact during the preparation of meals, and (3) when shellfish-growing waters are contaminated by sewage.	Onset: After 24 hours. Severe diarrhea, nausea, and vomiting. Respiratory symptoms. Usually lasts 4–5 days but may last for weeks.	Sanitary handling of foods Use of pure drinking water Adequate sewage disposal Adequate cooking of foods
Hepatitis Hepatitis A virus	Chief food sources: shellfish harvested from contaminated areas, and foods that are handled a lot during preparation and then eaten raw (such as vegetables).	Jaundice, fatigue. May cause liver damage and death.	Sanitary handling of foods Use of pure drinking water Adequate sewage disposal Adequate cooking of foods
Mycotoxicosis Mycotoxins (from molds)	Produced in foods that are relatively high in moisture. Chief food sources: beans and grains that have been stored in a moist place.	May cause liver and/or kidney disease.	Checking foods for visible mold and discarding those that are contaminated Proper storage of susceptible foods
Giardiasis *Giardia lamblia* (flagellated protozoa)	Protozoa exist in the intestinal tract of humans and are expelled in feces. Contamination of foods can occur in two ways: (1) when sewage is used to enrich garden/farm soil, and (2) by direct hand-to-food contact during the preparation of meals. Chief food sources: foods that are handled a lot during preparation.	Diarrhea, abdominal pain, flatulence, abdominal distention, nutritional disturbances, "nervous" symptoms, anorexia, nausea, and vomiting.	Sanitary handling of foods Avoidance of raw fruits and vegetables in areas where the protozoa is endemic Proper sewage disposal
Amebiasis *Entamoeba histolytica* (amoebic protozoa)		Tenderness over the colon or liver, loose morning stools, recurrent diarrhea, change in bowel habits, "nervous" symptoms, loss of weight and fatigue. Anemia may be present.	Sanitary handling of foods Avoidance of raw fruits and vegetables in areas where the protozoa is endemic Proper sewage disposal

*Source: C. L. Ballentine and M. L. Herndon, *FDA Consumer*, July–August 1982, pp. 25–28.

TABLE 21-2   Natural Toxicants in Food

Toxicant	Food Source	Effects	Destroyed by Heat Yes	No	Unknown
Antitrypsin	Soybeans, lima beans	Destroys trypsin in digestive tract	x		
Aglycone of methylazoxy-methanol-β-glucoside	Cycad	Unknown			x
Ascorbic acid oxidase	Vegetables, fruits	Destroys vitamin C	x		
Avidin	Egg white	Antagonizes biotin	x		
Goitrogen	Cabbage, rutabagas	Goiter	x		
Hemagglutinins	Soybeans, lima beans	Retards animal growth	x		
Lipoxidase	Soybeans, lima beans	Destroys vitamin A	x		
Mushroom toxins (see Table 21-8)	Mushrooms	Many		x	
Oxalic acid	Rhubarb, spinach	Binds calcium and zinc		x	
Phytic acid	Oatmeal	Binds calcium and iron		x	
(β-N-oxal)-amino-1-alanine*	Vetches (lathyrus plants)	Lathyrism		x	
Solanine	Immature or sprouting potatoes	Vomiting, diarrhea		x	
Sterculic acid	Cottonseed oil	Interference with digestion and reproduction	x		
Thiaminase	Fern, fish, clams	Antagonizes thiamin	x		
Unknown	Fava or broad beans	Favism		x	

*This is one suspected toxin. The exact chemical compound responsible for human poisoning is still unknown.

NATURAL TOXICANTS IN FOODS

Food poisoning by natural toxicants in food is not common in this country, although it is in other countries, especially underdeveloped countries. Table 21-2 summarizes the characteristics of some common natural food toxicants. The following sections provide brief discussions of plant toxins, thiaminase, and fish poisoning. Chapter 16 describes how normally harmless foods may be rendered toxic if the person is also taking certain drugs.

Plant Toxins

Many edible plants contain natural toxic substances. Mushroom poisoning is well known. Deaths from eating mushrooms have occurred in this country, with the victims usually amateur collectors who have eaten either *Gyromitra esculenta* or *Amanita* species. Preventing mushroom poisoning is still very difficult because, in spite of all the literature on mushroom identification, classifying these fungi is still difficult.

Different individuals have highly variable responses to mushroom toxicity. Some people are very susceptible, others are not. Also, a person can become accustomed, or "conditioned," to mushroom poison. To relate symptom characteristics with a specific type of mushroom poisoning requires the expertise of a professional. Table 21-3 presents the guidelines for confirmation of mushroom poisoning issued by the Center for Disease Control to public health officials. For interested individuals, references at the back of this book provide more information.

In the United States, the major toxic mushrooms are *Amanita phalloides* and *A. muscaria*, whose toxins are cyclopeptides and alkaloidlike

TABLE 21-3 Guidelines for Confirmation of Food-borne Disease Outbreak*

Mushroom Group	Clinical Syndrome	Laboratory and/or Epidemiological Criteria
Containing ibotenic acid and muscimol	A. Incubation period 1 to 12 hours (usually less than 4 hours) B. Characteristic clinical syndrome compatible with mushroom poisoning by this group—including confusion, delirium, visual disturbances	A. Demonstration of toxic chemical in epidemiologically incriminated mushrooms *or* B. Epidemiologically incriminated mushrooms identified as a toxic type
Containing ama-toxins and phallotox-ins, or gyromitrin	A. Incubation period 5 to 18 hours B. Characteristic clinical syndrome compatible with mushroom poisoning by this group—upper and lower gastrointestinal symptoms followed by hepatic and/or renal failure	A. Demonstration of toxic chemical in epidemiologically incriminated mushrooms *or* B. Epidemiologically incriminated mushrooms identified as a toxic type
Containing mus-carine, psilocybin and psilocin, gastrointestinal irritants, disulfiramlike compounds	A. Characteristic incubation period B. Clinical symptoms compatible with mushroom poisoning by this group	A. Demonstration of toxic chemical in epidemiologically incriminated mushrooms *or* B. Epidemiologically incriminated mushrooms Identified as a toxic type

*Source: *Foodborne Disease Surveillance*, Annual Summary 1978. Atlanta, Center for Disease Control, November 1979.

compounds, respectively. *A. phalloides* have been responsible for the most serious mushroom intoxication, and the antidote currently available is not 100% effective.

In *A. phalloides* poisoning, the victim suffers diarrhea, vomiting, abdominal pain, and intense thirst. The victim often screams from the intense pain, although the pain occasionally subsides. If a large quantity of the mushroom is eaten, the victim rapidly weakens and may die within 48 hours. If poisoning is less severe, cold skin, jaundice, and cyanosis develop in 2 or 3 days, and the patient may die 6 to 8 days after eating the poison if there is no medical attention. Coma and convulsion may precede death. Autopsy of the victim usually shows a fatty liver with necrosis, kidney degeneration, and hemorrhage of some organs.

A number of plant species contain a *goitrogen*, a substance capable of inducing goiter. The poison goitrin is found in cabbage, rutabaga, turnips, and other members of the cabbage family, and it is also found in kale and winter rape. The development of goiter due to the ingestion of a goitrogen is uncommon. However, goiter occurs if a large amount of the vegetable is consumed, especially if the person has not been ingesting adequate iodine.

The *cycad* is a palmlike tree whose products can be toxic. This plant can survive even in very adverse environmental conditions such as drought. Because of the high caloric content of its seeds, the seeds are a popular food when nothing else grows. People in Guam like to use the starch kernels of the seeds to thicken soups, desserts, and tortillas. The external husk of the seed is used as a confection. However, there is a poison in the cycad that can harm various species of animals. The people in Guam soak the seeds in water repeatedly to remove most of the poison. Later the kernels are dried in the sun, ground to a powder, and then stored. Although the soaked products are claimed to be safe, they may pose a risk to the fetus of a pregnant woman.

Many common vegetables—rhubarb, spinach, Swiss chard, beet tops, lamb's-quarters, purslane, and poke—contain the chemical *oxalic acid*. The oxalates exist as insoluble calcium oxalate crystals, which can be observed under the microscope in the leaves. They can decrease calcium

TABLE 21-4   Geographical Locations of Lathyrus Plants

Common	Botanical	Area and Use
Chickling vetch	*Lathyrus sativus*	India—human consumption
Flat-podded vetch	*Lathyrus cecera*	Italy, Algeria, France—cattle feed
Spanish vetch	*Lathyrus clymenum*	Spain, North Africa, Orient—partly for human consumption

absorption from foods, thus rendering calcium, which occurs in spinach for example, unavailable. Rhubarb leaves contain three to four times as much oxalic acid as the stalks. Acute oxalic acid poisoning occurs in children who have eaten the raw leaves and stalks of rhubarb. These children develop gastroenteritis with abdominal pain, vomiting, and diarrhea. If the poisoning is severe, there can be convulsions, failure of the blood to clot, and coma. Since a number of house plants contain oxalic acid, care is needed to prevent children from accidentally ingesting them. Sheep poisoning by oxalic acid is not uncommon, since halogeton range crops contain about 35% to 40% oxalic acid by dry weight.

Favism is a clinical disorder associated with the eating of fava or broad beans by individuals with a certain inherited metabolic defect. Susceptible individuals have a deficiency of glucose-6-phosphate dehydrogenase. Such people may develop hemolytic anemia after inhaling the plant pollen or ingesting raw or cooked beans, but they recover once the hemolysis has stopped. However, death can occur. Individuals of Mediterranean and Asian origins are more likely to be deficient in that enzyme. In June 1965, more than 1,000 people in Iran developed hemolysis when broad beans were harvested.

Lathyrism refers to poisoning from eating certain plants. After eating a large quantity of these plants, the victim develops heaviness of the legs and weakness of the whole body. The gait becomes jerky; the person drags his or her feet and eventually is unable to walk. Many victims are unresponsive to heat and pain. Eventually some show spinal cord degeneration.

Table 21-4 shows the geographical distribution of lathyrus plants. Algeria has more cases of lathyrism than any other country. Because the plants grow well in very stressful climatic conditions, Asian Indians grow and eat them when faced with drought and famine. During a famine in India, the plant may account for 30% to 50% of a person's diet. Clinical observations indicate that if a person eats a large amount of the plant for 6 or more months, lathyrism will develop. Neurolathyrism seems to develop mainly in 15- to 30-year-old males.

Soybeans contain a number of natural toxicants. The best-known one is a trypsin inhibitor that is heat sensitive. Animals become sick when fed raw soybeans. Another heat-sensitive toxicant in this plant is the hemagglutinating factor. Also, phytic acid in soybeans can bind zinc, producing zinc deficiency in animals. A heat-sensitive goitrogen is also present in soybeans.

Thiaminase

In addition to natural plant toxins, certain foods contain the vitamin antagonist thiaminase (see Chapter 6), consumption of which can cause thiamin (vitamin B_1) deficiency. Thiaminase is destroyed by heat, such as cooking temperatures. It is currently believed that thiaminase occurs in 31 vegetables and 18 fruits, with especially active forms in red cabbage, black currants, blackberries, red beets, and brussels sprouts. Some Orientals often eat thiaminase-containing ferns, including brackens. After horses have eaten raw bracken ferns, they develop thiamin deficiency in about 4 weeks; the animals recover when the vitamin is administered. In most Western societies, thiaminase ingestion from bracken ferns is not a problem since the plant is rarely eaten.

Significant amounts of thiaminase occur in a number of fish species, such as carp, perch, bream, and lake trout. A classic observation was the development of thiamin deficiency in foxes who were fed frozen carp. Since the thiaminase in fish is susceptible to heat, only raw fish may pose a problem; however, the thiaminase in raw fish has never caused a documented case of vitamin B_1 deficiency in humans.

Fish Poisoning

Seafood poisoning may be caused by shellfish toxins or poisonous fish. Paralytic shellfish poisoning is a significant problem in the United States. Mussels, clams, and sometimes scallops and oysters from both seacoasts and other locations can cause poisoning in humans. The organisms responsible are dinoflagellates, which are one-celled organisms (including *Gonyaulax catanella* and perhaps *G. tamarensis* and *Pyrodinum phoneus*). These organisms grow in the water and serve as feed for the shellfish. Once consumed, a poison from the dinoflagellate—saxitoxin—is retained in the host's tissues. The shellfish themselves are not susceptible to the chemical compound. When these seafoods are ingested by a human, poisoning symptoms appear in 30 minutes to 3 hours. If poisonous dinoflagellates are suspected to be in the water, authorities can quarantine the area. However, this precaution is sometimes considered useless, since the presence of toxic shellfish in one location does not mean that its immediate neighborhood is unsafe. At present, shellfish from Alaska are under constant observation, since they are widely distributed.

Cooking can reduce the toxicity of saxitoxin but does not guarantee safety. Most toxin occurs in dark meat—very little is ever found in white meat. The symptoms of paralytic shellfish poisoning are very severe. The patient develops numbness of the fingertips and lips, and the paralysis gradually moves toward the chest. Death can result from respiratory paralysis. Although about 5% to 10% of the victims die within 3 to 20 hours after eating the shellfish, those who survive the first 24 hours are considered to have a good chance of recovery.

There are many poisonous fish, most of which are found in tropical waters in areas around coral reefs. Many poisoning outbreaks occur in Japan, where neurological symptoms occur for which there are no antidotes. For more information on poisonous fish, consult the references at the back of this book or standard textbooks on poisonous fish.

STUDY QUESTIONS

1. What are the symptoms of bacterial food poisoning? In whom are these conditions most likely to be severe?
2. Distinguish between food-borne infection and food-borne intoxication. What are the two most important kinds of food-borne intoxication discussed in the text?
3. What are some common sources of staphylococcal bacteria in foods? Under what conditions do they grow best? Give at least five foods in which they may be found. What preventive measures should the cook take?
4. What are some sources of *Clostridium perfringens*? Under what conditions do they grow best?
5. What is the main source of botulism? What are the symptoms of poisoning by *Clostridium botulinum*? How can death be averted? How can the toxin be destroyed in foods?
6. Describe at least eight measures that help prevent food poisoning.
7. Discuss at least five sources of plant toxins. Define goitrogen, vitamin antagonist, favism, and lathyrism.
8. What is thiaminase? How can it be destroyed?
9. Define saxitoxin. What are its effects on humans? What preventive measures can be taken, and how effective are they?

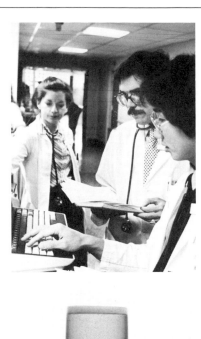
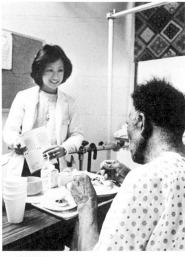

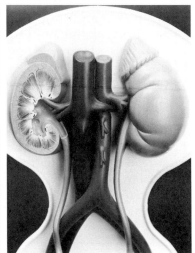

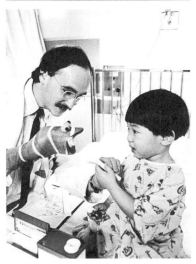

PART III

THERAPEUTIC NUTRITION

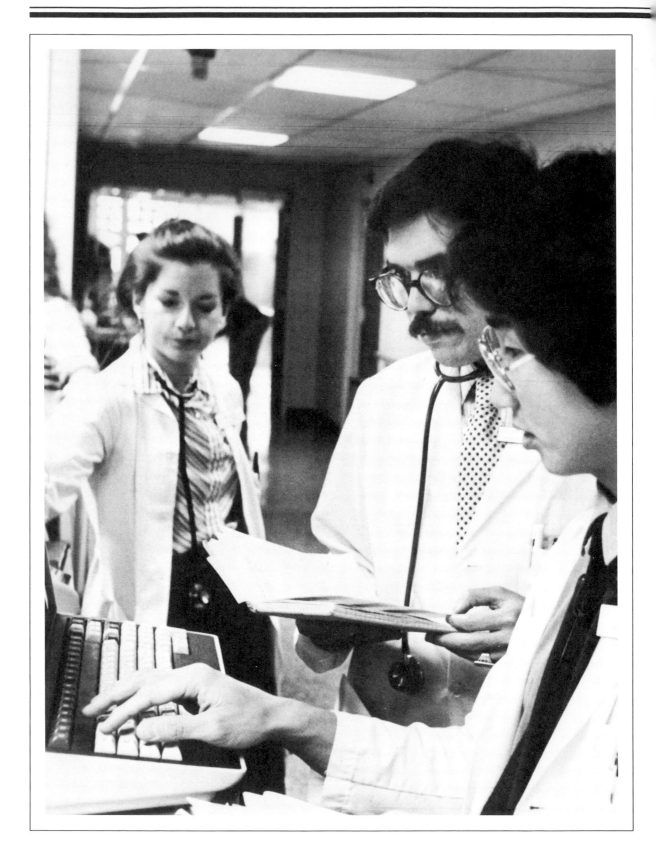

Chapter 22

Principals of Nutritional Support and Diet Therapy

THE FINAL CHAPTERS of this book will deal with the applications of basic nutritional and dietary principles in the treatment of human diseases, including a discussion of known preventive measures for particular disorders. This facet of patient care forms an important aspect of the practice of *dietetics*. According to the American Dietetic Association (*Journal of the American Dietetic Association*, Vol. 54:92, 1969), dietetics is "a profession concerned with the science and art of human nutrition care, an essential component of the health sciences. It includes the extending and imparting of knowledge concerning foods which will provide nutrients sufficient for health and during disease throughout the life cycle and the management of group feeding for these purposes." Dietitians, as discussed below, are not the only health professionals who employ nutritional and dietary principles to help treat (and prevent) diseases, however. As we will see, doctors, nurses, and others who work with sick patients all contribute to their dietary care.

BASIC CONCEPTS OF DIET THERAPY

Basically, diet and nutrition may be related to disease in two ways:

1. *Therapy*—special dietary and nutritional care and perhaps even cure for people with certain forms of illness. This is the field of therapeutic nutrition. Many questions of health care concern this field. For instance, how should a person feed a patient who is recovering from an accidental ingestion of cleansing detergent? How should a person feed a burn victim to assist in the recovery process? How should we feed a patient with a kidney problem or diabetes to control or reduce his symptoms? And, can we cure a disease through a dietary regimen or the administration of some nutrients? Can we cure mental illness with a special diet? Can we cure cancer with vitamin C?

2. *Prevention*—the use of the knowledge that certain dietary practices or substances may produce specific clinical disorders. For example, eating too much salt may cause high blood pressure. A main question in preventive nutrition is, Can specific clinical diseases be prevented by adopting certain lifelong dietary habits? For example, can we avoid hypertension by reducing our consumption of salt? Many health practitioners are now paying increasing attention to such questions and trying to impart knowledge of long-term preventive measures to their patients.

In practice, the two approaches—therapy and prevention—may be used simultaneously, depending on the patient's needs and particular disease. If a well-nourished patient has a good appetite and eats well, he is fed a regular diet to maintain his nutritional status and permit a speedy recovery. The calories and protein may be increased from the normal somewhat, but the diet does not require any special modifications. On the other hand, some patients need special diets to control a disease, to correct nutrient deficiencies, and to provide life support in the overall management plan of the attending physician.

Especially in a hospital setting, diet therapy is rarely the only component of a treatment or cure. However, diet therapy is almost always part of a coordinated clinical management program. For example, the appropriate treatment for a kidney patient on hemodialysis has many components: the proper use of the artificial kidney, a specific dietary regimen, a program of drugs including vitamin and mineral supplements, diagnostic tests, psychotherapy, and patient education and compliance.

Although diet therapy is undoubtedly a science, the practice of clinical dietetics is also an art. Because eating is important to us, there are intense human factors to be considered in translating therapeutic ideas into diets that patients will readily follow. The practitioner must be prepared to deal with the patient's emotions, cultural and socioeconomic background, and many other psychological factors.

THE HEALTH TEAM

Diet therapy usually involves the interaction of at least three care providers: the doctor, the dietitian, and the nurse. Other specialists may be called in as needed, but these three positions form the core of the nutritional health team. Under ideal circumstances, each has clearly defined responsibilities and works in close cooperation and communication with the others and with the patient for the best possible nutritional and dietary care. Ideally, if a patient needs a special diet, the doctor prescribes a diet order. The dietitian prepares the meal plan and transmits it to the food service staff for preparation. The nurse serves the meals and assures that the patient eats the foods. However, the current practice in many hospitals is less clear-cut.

The Doctor

Although the extent of a physician's participation in the nutritional and dietary care of a patient varies with the circumstances, such as the types of patients and facilities and the availability of trained personnel and nutrient formulas, only the doctor is authorized to perform some basic duties. In general, the doctor diagnoses the illness or condition of the patient and decides if special nutritional or dietary care will benefit the patient. If the doctor believes that such care would be helpful, he or she recommends a prescription for the nutritional and dietary needs of the patient. This recommendation is implemented in a number of ways, as discussed below.

The Dietitian

While the doctor suggests the general framework for a patient's dietary management, the dietitian usually develops the specific dietary plan. Circumstances where this may not be the case are discussed later.

According to the American Dietetic Association, a registered dietitian (R.D.) is "a specialist educated for a profession responsible for the nutritional care of individuals and groups. This care includes the application of the science and art of human nutrition in helping people select and obtain food for the primary purpose of nourishing their bodies in health or disease throughout the life cycle. This participation may be in single or combined functions; in food service systems management; in extending knowledge of food and nutrition principles; in teaching these principles for application according to particular situations; or in dietary counseling."*

The *clinical dietitian*, a registered dietitian, "is a member of the health care team and affects the nutritional care of individuals and groups for health maintenance. The clinical dietitian assesses nutritional needs, develops and implements nutritional care plans, and evaluates and reports these results appropriately. When functioning in an organization that provides food service, the clinical dietitian cooperates and coordinates activities with those of the department's management team."*

In practice, however, many small and under-budgeted hospitals do not have a full-time dietitian. In some cases, ordinary clinical dietetics may be planned by the attending physician and implemented by the nurse. Many of these hospitals may either employ a part-time dietitian as a consultant or contract for the services of professional dietitians in nearby larger hospitals or cities when necessary.

Many hospitals have a small dietetic department where the dietitian attends to food purchasing, storage, and preparation and personnel management as well as prescribed dietary orders. In such a situation, although the dietitian implements the doctor's diet prescription, the nurse does much of the food serving, patient monitoring, and evaluation.

In some hospitals the food service operation is divided into different departments, such as dietetics, food purchasing and planning, kitchen staff, and personnel management. Here other dietitians or dietetic aides assist the chief dietitian. Within such a setting, the dietitian assumes a large part of the practice of clinical dietetics, although the nurse still plays an important role because of his or her constant contact with the patient.

Many university teaching hospitals and large medical centers, in addition to having fully staffed dietetic departments, also employ nutritionists, some of whom provide out-patient care. A number of highly regarded hospitals and medical centers have established a sophisticated "nu-

---

*Copyright The American Dietetic Association. Reprinted by permission from *Journal of the American Dietetic Association*, Vol. 77:62, 1981.

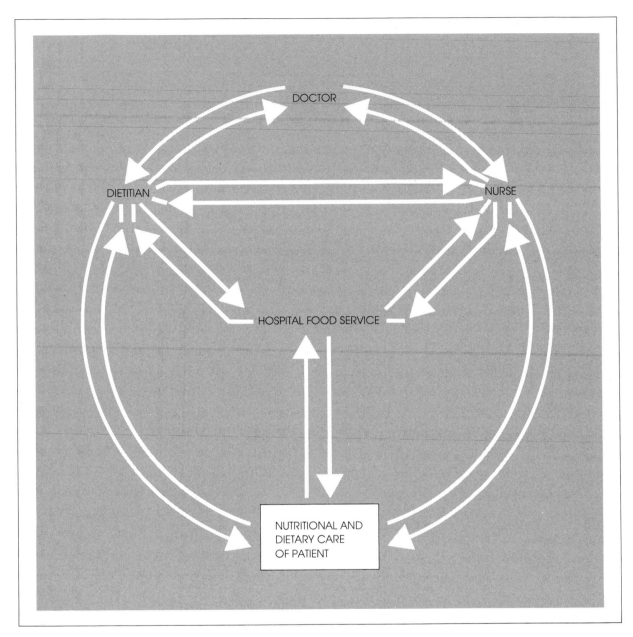

FIGURE 22-1 The clinical relationship between doctor, nurse, and dietitian.

trition support service," which integrates the activities of a number of health professionals. These health professionals give optimal nutrition and dietary care to the patient in an effort to prevent and manage any risk of morbidity and mortality caused by an unsatisfactory nutritional status.

Institutions vary in the degree of responsibility they give to dietitians who provide nutritional and dietary care to patients, although dietitians are the best-trained personnel to administer this aspect of patient care. Figure 22-1 is a simple diagram of possible clinical relationships between the doctor, dietitian, and nurse.

The Nurse

Under almost any form of personnel management, nurses play an extremely important role in clinical dietetics: They coordinate the activities of doctors, dietitians, and patients, including such concerns as the diet prescription, food service, meal serving, and patient response.

The nurse arranges the food trays, helps patients in feeding, answers questions, and provides additional beverages. The nurse can also observe patients directly, recording the amounts of fluid, food, and nutrient supplements consumed. Measuring the amount of urine voided is also an important index. Patient response to the dietary regimen is best evaluated by the nurse because of the nurse's constant presence.

Enteral and parenteral feedings (clinical practices discussed in detail in Chapter 23) are administered and monitored by the nurse. Proper administration of these feedings requires the nurse to have a good working knowledge of the nutritional bases of these commercial or hospital-prepared products. In the case of intravenous fluids and electrolytes, the doctor's prescription is implemented by the nurse only, who also monitors the patient's response. The nurse's observation and record will help the dietitian or nutritionist in planning other aspects of the patient's nutritional and dietary needs.

As discussed in Chapter 16, drugs profoundly affect a person's nutritional status. Nurses know firsthand what, how much, and when drugs are taken by the patient. If a drug causes nausea or drowsiness, the nurse may understand why a meal is not eaten.

If the patient is eating a regular diet, the dietitian or doctor will not be very concerned about the patient's nutritional and dietary need. In this circumstance, the nurse is the sole source of nutritional and dietary information or advice.

The patient's medical record is reviewed and studied by the nurse frequently. The nurse should relate all information regarding body weight, food consumption, medications administered, and overt clinical signs to the dietitian and physician at the earliest opportunity.

The nurse has the best opportunity to teach a patient principles of nutrition. In many cases, after the patient is discharged, the nurse is the only contact with the patient, especially if special feedings are part of the home care regimen.

In many small as well as large health clinics throughout the country, a nurse frequently assumes the roles of nutritionist and dietitian as well as nurse. With the increasing popularity of nurse practitioners, some nurses even assume certain aspects of the physician's role. Because of the nurse's importance in the nutritional and dietary care of the patient, some people have argued that nurses need to receive a stronger background in nutrition and dietetics. Chapter 17 provides more information on this issue.

NUTRITIONAL MAINTENANCE

Nutritional care in many hospitals has not always been satisfactory. In the last few years, a large number of cases of hospital undernutrition have been documented, especially protein and calorie deficiencies. Hospital malnutrition occurs for a variety of reasons: the patient's poor nutritional status; adverse effects from medical and drug treatment; the clinical course of the disorder, including pain, nausea, and vomiting; lack of communication between the doctor, nurse, and dietitian; inadequate hospital equipment and trained personnel; failure of the technical staff to keep up with new knowledge in clinical nutrition; and the patient's noncompliance with the dietary prescription.

Many patients admitted to the hospital are in an unsatisfactory nutritional status. Frequently the condition is unnoticed and untreated, and the patient is permitted to undergo major medical treatment and surgery. There is always some weight loss with surgery or even a simple operation, and the body wasting from treatment or an operation can produce profound malnutrition. One frequent complaint of hospital staff is that patients do not eat their food. As a result, the possibility of complications, morbidity, and mortality are increased, especially if the patient is nutritionally depleted when admitted to the hospital. The extent that unnecessary morbidity and mortality will be avoided depends on the degree of success of the diagnosis and treatment of hospital malnutrition.

Examples of circumstances that may increase a patient's susceptibility to malnutrition and complication include: extremely underweight or overweight condition; alcoholism; severe intestinal disorders; intravenous feeding with dextrose and electrolytes only for 2 or more weeks; semistarvation in a hospital for more than 10 days; and stressful conditions such as trauma, burn, fever, infancy, and pregnancy.

Knowing the Patient

A hospital and health team can do many things to prevent malnourishment in a patient. Probably one of the most important things is to know the patient and monitor his or her progress, especially regarding nutrition. Experienced practitioners emphasize the following patient factors (if the patient is very ill, most of the background information can be obtained from other sources):

1. Knowing the personal history, especially of medical matters.

The background history of a patient can best be obtained by studying his or her medical records, interviewing health personnel, and talking with the patient's family members. Relevant details include: employment factors such as type of work, present and past occupations, the location of work and transportation needed, and the daily work schedule; family history such as the number and ages of family members and their medical conditions; physical activities and living conditions; health problems such as ulcers, high blood lipids, episodes of illness, and pregnancy; and any special feeding problems relating to enteral and parenteral nutrition.

2. Knowing the lifelong eating habits and nutritional status upon entering the hospital.

Details on the patient's eating habits include: the number of meals eaten daily; the time and location of each meal, including snacks; the sizes of servings; the types and quantities of foods eaten; the extent of self-control in abstaining from certain types and quantities of foods; the ability to handle food (e.g., patient is handicapped); oral conditions (e.g., swollen gums, wearing dentures); participation in any food as-

sistance programs; use of food utensils; and food preparation habits.

To determine the general nutritional status, the patient's height, weight, and any overt signs of clinical malnutrition are assessed and recorded. However, only some hospitals and medical centers (see later discussion and Chapter 19) evaluate anthropometric measurements and other indexes of nutritional adequacy.

3. Knowing the body weight history.

The body weight history is especially important for certain disorders such as diabetes and renal diseases. A comprehensive record includes: degree of overweight or underweight condition, if any; body weight history since childhood; body weight pattern since 20 years of age, if applicable; the highest and lowest adult body weight ever experienced; weight at specific times such as marriage, periods of employment change, and periods after pregnancy; family weight history (of siblings and parents); weight at admission or initial interview; the weight most desired by the patient; the ideal body weight; the need for the patient to gain or lose weight, if any; and the distribution of fat in the buttocks, abdomen, and other areas.

4. Knowing the drug use history.

Because of the relationship between drugs and nutritional status, it is of paramount importance to have a thorough knowledge of the patient's drug use history. General information on drugs and nutrition is presented in Chapter 16. Relevant details are also presented with particular disorders discussed in the following chapters.

5. Determination of the ideal body weight and the appropriate caloric intake.

The ideal body weight of a patient may be determined from standard tables and sex-frame-height rules of thumb. A patient's appropriate caloric intake may be determined from the latest Recommended Dietary Allowances (RDAs), standard tables, the patient's basal metabolic rate, and the U.S. Department of Agriculture (USDA) rule of thumb. Detailed discussions of the ideal body weight and caloric intake determinations are presented in Chapters 12 and 26.

6. Monitoring the eating pattern during the hospital stay.

The eating pattern of a hospitalized patient is a major and useful index to monitor his nutritional status, which the nurse can greatly aid in evaluating. It is important to know how much of the foods served have been eaten, since clinical experience has clearly illustrated the importance of the correlation between the amount of food served and that eaten. Documented reports indicate that 5% to 40% of some items, such as bread, meat, vegetables, and salad, are not eaten. In general, patients eat more in a dining room setting than when served on a tray in bed. This finding applies especially to children and elderly patients.

The importance of monitoring the patient's food consumption frequently and consistently cannot be understated. Whenever feasible, the nutrient and calorie intake of a patient should be calculated daily. The overall monitoring is intensified for patients with fever, infections, weakened and debilitated conditions, or traumas such as surgery or burn, with particular attention to inadequate and marginal nutrient intake. Subnormal protein and calorie consumption is of major concern and should be corrected. If normal oral feedings do not correct unsatisfactory nutritional conditions, drastic measures such as aggressive enteral or parenteral feeding may be indicated.

7. Keeping the medical record.

The patient's medical record should provide detailed information on nutritional status; results of blood and urine analyses; medications administered; the comprehensive descriptions of hospital feeding such as the diets ordered, the nutrient intake, and use of enteral and parenteral feeding.

8. Consultation with other medical personnel.

The patient receives the best care when the doctor, nurse, and dietitian are in close communication. Certain disorders such as cancer, burns, chronic illnesses, and childhood diseases may require coordination with other professionals as well—pharmacists, oral surgeons, physical therapists, psychiatrists, social workers, school

teachers, and so on. Examples of particular disorders and the special coordination required are discussed in the chapters that follow.

Assessment by a Nutritional Support Team

Within the last few years, some major hospitals and medical centers in this country have initiated a nutritional and dietary support service. This service involves clinical and medical specialists, nurses, dietitians, nutritionists, pharmacists, physical therapists, and other professionals. The goals of this support service are: (1) to determine the patient's nutritional status and needs; (2) to identify patients suffering or likely to suffer malnourishment; (3) to consult, organize, and supervise intensive nutritional and dietary support*; and (4) to identify and manage hospital malnutrition as a team.

Within such a service, the nutritional status of a patient should be evaluated from the following criteria: height and weight; extent of edema; weight : height ratio; measurements of triceps skinfold and upper arm circumference; serum albumin and prealbumin levels; height : creatinine ratio; total serum lymphocyte count; serum transferrin levels; hair and nail growth; serum carotene levels; and nitrogen balance. Some of these measurements are discussed in Chapter 19.

Recently, identification charts such as that in Table 22-1 have been developed to screen hospitalized patients for malnourishment. Individuals identified as severely malnourished will require rigorous nutritional and dietary therapy. However, even without the sophisticated equipment and the information in Table 22-1, gross overt signs such as weight 20% to 30% below normal are obvious indications for intensive nutritional support and maintenance.

At present, most hospitals lack nutritional support teams. An inadequate hospital budget is one of the major barriers. S. J. Dudrick of the

---

*In clinical dietetics, the term *support* has broad meanings. They may include calculating nutrient requirements, planning a meal, coordinating fluid intake with amount of urine voided, relating nutritional status to medication taken, and so on.

TABLE 22-1 Some Criteria for the Identification of Nutritional Status of a Hospitalized Patient*

Criterion	Normal Nutritional Status	Mildly Undernourished	Moderately Undernourished	Severely Undernourished
Mid-arm circumference (cm)				
Male adult	23.0–29.0	21.0–22.9	17.4–20.9	≤17.5
Female adult	22.0–28.0	20.0–21.9	17.1–19.9	≤17.0
Triceps skinfold (mm)				
Male adult	11.0–13.0	10.0–10.9	7.6–10.8	≤7.5
Female adult	13.5–17.0	12.2–13.4	10.0–12.1	≤9.9
Serum albumin (g/100 mL)	≥3.5	3.0–3.5	2.1–3.0	≤2.1
Lymphocyte count/mm^3	≥1,600.	1,300–1,599	850–1,300	≤849
Number of positive "delayed hypersensitivity skin" tests out of four	≥2	1	1	0

*Data obtained from results of different investigators. Each clinic follows a different standard. References at the end of this book provide additional information. Clinical nutritionists recommend using all criteria indicated to obtain an accurate diagnosis.

medical school at the University of Texas stated in 1978, "Dietitians are in a Catch 22 situation. To do an adequate job in nutrition you must encourage patients to consume more food, and the more food they consume, the more it costs the hospital. The nutrition policy should separate the food costs so that nutrition is viewed as therapy with costs assigned just as they are for antibiotics or for use in the operating room. The American Medical Association should establish a firm nutrition policy so that hospitals would be required to have a minimal, established, effective, working nutrition program in order to be accredited."

CONSIDERATIONS IN PATIENT COMPLIANCE

A lack of well-funded nutritional support programs is not the only reason for malnourishment among hospital patients. Another problem is a patient's unwillingness or inability to eat what is provided.

To help a patient comply with dietary pre-scriptions, the dietitian, nurse, and doctor must know the patient well. All sick people experience physical and psychological trauma to some degree. Whether the patient is a chronically ill elderly person, an institutionalized middle-aged housewife, a college student with kidney failure, or a 10-year-old girl with leukemia, hospitalization can aggravate anxiety and confusion. The sterile environment and the presence of so many health personnel add to the discomfort, as do the physical interferences (bandages, feeding tubes, etc.), psychological factors, personal inclinations (preferring teacup to a mug, soft to hard bed, etc.), and gaps in health team communication listed in the box below. It is not surprising that some patients have trouble in eating; food may be the patient's last concern. Some major considerations concerning how well a patient complies with a dietary regimen are discussed below.

Food Habits

Basic eating patterns are largely determined by socioeconomic, ethnic, cultural, family, and religious factors. Eating habits acquired during the growing years, personal preferences, and con-

Taste Tray Increases Acceptance of Nutritional Supplements*

Nutritional support may be provided by hyperalimentation, tube feedings, oral feedings, or a combination of these methods. Oral feedings generally cause least discomfort for the patient and are less expensive. However, the dietitian is challenged to motivate the patient to ingest adequate amounts of the oral feedings. Many nutritional supplements taste "different" and may be refused.

When the burn and oncology units at Miami Valley Hospital were opened, we became more aware of the nutritive needs of patients in these and other units of the hospital. Thus, more patients began to receive nutritional supplements. Comments solicited from patients, nurses, foodservice assistants, and dietitians indicated that a large number of supplements were being returned untouched. The reasons varied, but a common problem was that the patient did not like the supplement the physician had prescribed or the dietitian had selected.

This continuing problem is now approached by asking the patient what kind of supplement he/she would prefer. The dietitian stresses high-calorie, high-protein products, such as milk shakes, eggnogs, puddings, and custards. If the items offered are not acceptable, a taste tray is offered to allow the patient to select the supplemental feedings he/she would prefer.

Prior to the taste trial, the dietitian discusses with the patient his/her food and flavor preferences, difficulties encountered in eating, allergies, and intolerances. Using this information, the dietitian orders six to eight nutritional supplements from Central Food Production. The samples are either commercially or institutionally prepared products. A small tray, set with tray cover, napkins, straws, water glass, and products for the trial, is sent to the floor galley. Each product is served in a 4-oz glass with a fitted lid labeled with the name of the product.

The taste test is scheduled between meals to avoid interfering with the patient's appetite for the next meal. The patient is asked to take a small sip of each product and note whether it is acceptable. When all of the products have been tested, the patient and the dietitian list acceptable and nonacceptable products. With the assistance of the nursing staff, a between-meal feeding schedule is arranged. The nurse may reschedule therapies to ensure that the patient receives supplemental feedings. The dietitian may space meals further apart so that the patient can consume all of his/her meals, as well as the supplemental feedings.

Using the taste tray has several benefits. While participating in the taste test, the patient is given information about the content of the product, its benefits, and its role in recovery. With such information, the patient realizes that the supplemental feeding is a part of therapy and influences the course of his/her hospitalization. Also, because the patient selected the nourishment, he/she is more willing to consume it.

Nursing personnel who have participated in the development of the feeding schedule feel they are a part of the team working to improve nutritional status. Information about acceptance or rejection of feedings is more frequently sent to the dietitian when the nurse has participated in the taste tray trial. Currently, a number of nurses contact the dietitian to request a taste tray for a patient they believe would benefit from nutritional supplementation.

Physicians have been supportive of the taste tray concept. Some physicians specifically order a consultation with the dietitian for supplementation of calories and expect a taste tray to be included. When a specific product is ordered, the dietitian checks the

*Copyright The American Dietetic Association. Reprinted by permission from: E. Bayless, *Journal of the American Dietetic Association*, Vol. 73:542, 1978.

patient's acceptance of the product; if there is a problem, she recommends a taste tray.

Products Developed for the Taste Tray

The taste tray has been used for two years. During that time, several recipes have been developed or adapted from recipes provided by companies producing nutritional supplements. Recipes are evaluated by the clinical and food production dietitians for nutrient content, taste, ease of preparation, and sanitation. When recipes are approved, copies are provided to Central Food Production and the offices of the clinical dietitians.

Use of a taste tray for selection of nutritional supplements by the patient requires additional time. However, greater patient acceptance of supplemental products indicates that this is time well spent. Since product and portion size are dictated, in part, by the patient, fewer items are returned partially or completely untouched, and less food is wasted.

The taste tray has proved itself a valuable tool in nutritional support for patients. While the dietitian is usually the initiator of the taste tray, other health team members see its benefits and support the concept. The patient benefits both from receiving supplemental products he/she can enjoy and from becoming a part of the team working for his/her well-being.

---

cerns about health, food, and nutrition all affect eating behavior. Since the practitioner must treat the person as well as the clinical disorders, the practitioner must also be prepared to learn about a patient's eating behavior.

Behavior and Illness

When people are sick, many facets of their living condition undergo change. Relationships with coworkers, family members, and friends may become strained. Because patients are very sensitive to any strange practice and environment, they look for familiar comforts. Some patients experience depression, fear, anxiety, frustration, and insecurity. Patients are often unhappy that they must depend on others for their well-being. Not uncommonly, patients become uncooperative, especially when asked to eat a modified diet.

Most people see food as some kind of symbol. They may associate it with personal satisfaction, a reward for daily hard work, a memory of their mothers or some other individuals, memorable events from their past life, ethnic origins, or other things they hold dear. Some patients therefore become extremely unhappy when long-time favorite foods are taken away or not served and they are asked to eat some items they do not like. For example, many people become dependent on tea, coffee, and alcohol. If a patient with a myocardial infarction is asked to abstain from these beverages, he may become anxious and reluctant. A patient may have loved to eat meals served hot before she developed cancer, but may suffer oral lesions because of chemo- or radiotherapy. Although cold foods will soothe her mouth, she may be disheartened at having to eat only cold foods for days or weeks. A bed-ridden young man with a kidney failure may feel very hopeless. There is only one way he can exert influence and attract attention: by complaining about the food, simply to have some control over his environment.

All members of a health team must understand, respect, and sympathize with what foods mean to people in general and to the patient in particular. The more they listen to their patients, the easier it will be to make them comply with recommended dietary regimens. By knowing what bothers patients, health team members can plan meals to their patients' liking as much as possible.

Conditions on Admission

Carefully noting a patient's clinical condition on admission can further facilitate dietary care. A person with physical handicaps requires standard help in self-feeding or assisted feeding. A poststroke patient who can only partially use her

Eating Problems of Hospitalized Patients

A hospitalized patient may have trouble obtaining satisfactory nutrition. Some common reasons are summarized below.

A. Inability to eat because of physical interferences
   1. Loss of mobility to eat because of IV tubes (especially if not well placed), traction, splints, casts, or motor impairment
   2. Weakness, pain, and discomfort from diagnostic tests, especially the frequent drawing of blood
   3. Incapacitated gastrointestinal system from disease
   4. Oral difficulties such as ill-fitting dentures, pain and difficulty in swallowing, or sore throat
   5. Maladjustment to regular solid foods after receiving nourishment intravenously
   6. Side effects of drugs and radiotherapy, including anorexia, cramps, stomach irritation, dry mouth, abnormal taste and flavor sensations, depression, and drowsiness (the effects of drugs are especially undesirable when the drugs are taken shortly before mealtime)
   7. Abnormal taste sensitivities related to certain clinical disorders (for example, burns decrease taste sensitivity, cystic fibrosis and hypofunctioning of the adrenal cortex increase taste sensitivity, diabetes decreases sensitivity to sweetness, kidney diseases decrease sensitivity to sour, salty, and sweet tastes, and neoplasms decrease sensitivity to sweet and salty tastes and greatly increase sensitivity to bitterness)
   8. Ill-scheduled hospital procedures or health team practices that interfere with mealtime, such as dressing changes, baths, doctor visits, and untimely delivery and/or removal of food trays
   9. Too much food (in some cases, however, the doctor may want the patient to eat more food)
   10. Lack of food (semistarvation due to long-term intravenous feeding with only fluid and glucose or lack of nutritional support because the patient is unconscious)
   11. Miscellaneous difficulties (such as patient intolerance to certain foods, too hot or too cold food, unappetizing meals, or failure of food service department to observe orders or changes requested)

B. Inability to eat for psychological or psychiatric reasons
   1. Worry, fear, and depression because of illness and its consequences, with special anxiety about money, family, and appearance
   2. Organic brain disturbance aggravating refusal to eat (disorder leads some patients to imagine that the food is poisonous)
   3. Food becoming the least important concern
   4. Rebellion against food (the patient uses food as a weapon against a hostile world that has played tricks with his health)
   5. Wanting attention
   6. Unfamiliar environment and lack of socialization

C. Inadequate food intake for personal reasons
   1. Religious beliefs about the proper types of food
   2. Ethnic preferences for certain foods
   3. Personal idiosyncrasies
   4. Unfamiliarity with the foods served
   5. Eating habits such as mealtime and size of meals (breakfast, lunch, or dinner may have been smaller or larger than hospital meals, eaten at different times, or skipped entirely)
   6. Strong beliefs about food, including rejection of processed foods

D. Inadequate food intake because of poor communication among members of the health team
   1. Unawareness of patient's past eating pattern
   2. Inappropriate diet prescription
   3. Failure to monitor patient's eating profile in hospital

left hand, a blind diabetic, a car accident victim with injured hands, and a patient with oral lesions are classic examples of patients with difficulties in self-feeding. A patient with swallowing difficulties or ill-fitting dentures may also have trouble in eating or drinking. Patients who are elderly, feeble, coughing constantly, or suffering from asthma, emphysema, or other respiratory difficulties may take longer to eat their meals. Children and adults who have been starved over a prolonged period may react adversely if suddenly provided with a large quantity of food. In this last case, progressive feeding according to the patient's tolerance is the safe practice.

One should be careful about judging another person's eating capacity. A small person may not be able to eat a standard 2,500- to 2,800-kcal diet because it simply contains too much food. Conversely, a large adult who may or may not be obese may complain that a menu of 2,500- to 2,800-kcal contains too little food. Also, a large, muscular man may consider 12 oz of beefsteak as one serving.

Diet Prescriptions

The more restricted the prescribed diet, the more difficult it is to prepare appetizing meals. This can cause problems in getting patients to eat.

When a doctor prescribes an 800-mg-sodium and 2,800-kcal diet, it is difficult to avoid using some dietetic products such as low-sodium bread, butter, and cheese. Invariably this reduces patient acceptance of the foods served. One possible remedy is for the doctor to prescribe an appropriate diuretic, thus permitting a somewhat higher sodium intake. On the other hand, prescribing a 1,500-kcal and 1,800-mg-sodium diet may actually require the patient to use the salt shaker to supplement the sodium naturally supplied by the small amounts of food eaten. The attending physician may not intend this.

If a high-potassium diet is ordered, a large quantity of certain foods may have to be consumed; if these foods are not acceptable to some patients, meal planning will be difficult. A potassium supplement or other drugs may be used to reduce the need for a food source high in potassium. If a very low potassium or low phosphorus diet is ordered, the choice of foods for meal planning will likewise be drastically reduced. Under these circumstances, the use of chemical binders or chelating agents will permit a higher intake of the forbidden nutrients and a larger selection of foods.

Overrestrictive diets can be avoided. Frequent and direct communication between the doctor and the hospital dietitian is the best way to do so. If the attending physician gives a range of modification, the dietitian is given some flexibility in drawing up the patient's meal plan. The clinician will further facilitate patient compliance if he or she carefully considers the necessity of any dietary restriction. Finally, the health team should avoid using negative-sounding terms to describe a diet in the patient's presence. Words such as *restricted*, *rigid*, *very low*, and *zero* can arouse fear and anxiety in the patient, thus influencing his or her acceptance of the meals.

Patient Education

Since the willingness of the patient to take prescribed drugs is important, some patient education is needed. The same should be true for diet prescriptions, but relatively little is usually done to educate the patient about a prescribed diet. Some clinics and hospitals provide the patient with standard instructions and diet prescription sheets without trying to educate the individual. In many cases, the patient does not comply because he or she will not or cannot follow the instructions well.

Prompt and early patient education reduces anxiety and fear and increases acceptance of the nutritional and dietary regimen. This education, which should include issues about food, nutrition, and diet therapy, should begin with admission or the first interview between the patient and nurse (or nutritionist or dietitian) and continue after discharge. The main objective is to assure not only patient compliance during the hospital stay but also the development of good eating habits in the future. During the patient's hospital stay, the doctor, dietitian, and especially the nurse should listen to, speak with, and observe the patient. Every item of information about the patient is useful in educating him or her about diet, food, nutrition, and health.

Nutritional and dietary education of a patient can be both general and specific. The former involves discussing nutrition information, issuing standard hospital pamphlets about diet and nutrition, displaying educational materials, and asking the patient to attend scheduled talks and shows. Specific patient education is individualized. Each patient should be provided with information on his or her particular disease; its causes, symptoms, and total management program; and the role of diet. Other relevant information includes: specific diet prescriptions, food selection systems (see discussion later), meal plans, preparations for emergencies, and eating strategies for dining out and special occasions.

A successful patient education program takes into consideration the patient's background knowledge. If the person has some basic idea of nutrition, food, and health, some elementary principles may be omitted. Otherwise, patient resentment may arise. For example, a school teacher may already know some basics of the four food groups and the RDAs. A chemist is likely to have some knowledge of protein, carbohydrate, and fat. A patient who has had diabetes for a number of years probably knows something about foods and nutrition.

The simple routine of providing information is not expected to be very effective alone, and some practitioners consider it to be unsound. A problem-solving approach using food models, information sharing, and relevant examples is often more effective. When a diabetic patient is served lunch, she can be reminded why she is served the particular foods. A young man with broken legs and confined to bed may appreciate an explanation of why eating particular foods in the prescribed quantities is to his advantage. For instance, he may be told that the protein in meat and milk will facilitate his tissue repair, but that if consumed in excess the calcium in milk could cause renal stones.

Before giving programmed instructions, be sure the patient can read, understand the contents, and follow directions. Complete dietary plans and strategies must be provided to patients in written form as well as verbal.

No matter how information is conveyed, a successful patient education program will involve at least one of the patient's family members. This effort assures that the family knows what the patient needs and promotes good rapport among the patient, the family, and the health team. A few joint sessions of a member of the health team, the patient, and a family member will eliminate any misunderstanding in a recommended dietary plan.

For example, a doctor may feel that a post-heart-attack patient should adopt a more wholesome life-style—reducing stress, exercising more, and eating moderately with a reduced consumption of animal fats and alcohol. A joint discussion supplemented with films and slides on the risk factors of heart disease would be interesting, educational, and easy for the family and patient to remember and understand. However, the patient must also receive some specific instructions as well.

All members of the health team should coordinate their efforts to educate the patient. Procedures should also be established to assure that the patient receives a proper dietary and nutritional education after hospital discharge.

Adjustments for Specific Problems

In addition to educating the patient about the reasons for a prescribed diet, the health team may change management procedures accordingly to help a patient accept and eat what is provided. For example, if pain is interfering with eating, a medication can be used to relieve the pain. The medication will be especially effective if given a short time before meals. The eating problems of patients with dry mouth may be managed by using moist foods such as gravies, cream sauces, extra milk or juice, lemon wedges, or soups. If a patient obviously cannot eat solid foods, liquid feedings should be used. If the patient fails to eat a regular meal, nutrient intake may be increased by giving nutritious snacks such as homemade or commercial liquid diet supplements. If a patient must consume a commercial nutrient solution several times a day, patient acceptance may be increased if the patient is told that the liquid feedings are prescribed medications that may help him or her to get well faster.

Members of the health team should learn to recognize a patient's rebellion against foods. Although it is difficult to change the patient, health practitioners can be pleasant and avoid becoming angry or talking about the patient's behavior. Food can be served casually, and the practitioner can visit and talk with the patient during mealtime. Whenever possible, the health team should comply with the patient's requests, such as serving a particular food or beverage, adjusting meal size, and using a favorite flavor or spice. The different eating patterns of children, young adults, and the elderly should also be kept in mind.

Although some hospitalized patients have feeding problems, many patients are very cooperative, have a good appetite, comply with a diet prescription, and achieve a speedy recovery.

TOOLS FOR THE PRACTITIONER

In addition to knowing and trying to accommodate the patient's personal needs, health practitioners need special diet-planning tools to provide optimal patient care. In hospitals with a dietetic staff, the therapeutic dietitian has the necessary accessories, and most practicing nurses accumulate some of the needed items throughout their careers.

Food composition tables for common American foods are very important reference sources. Chapter 10 discusses the different comprehensive food composition tables available in the United States, one of which is reproduced in the appendix. Health practitioners should also keep abreast of the latest RDAs.

Tables describing the sugar and sodium contents of medications and the caffeine contents of food are important reference sources. Also very important is information on the nutrient composition of special medical and dietary foods, such as infant formulas, supplementary nutrient solutions, amino-acid-modified therapeutic diets, lactose-free products, and low-protein bread. Many dietitians and nurses keep a list of the manufacturers and any accompanying literature describing specific products.

Some hospitals develop their own diet manuals for staff use, while others use standard ones prepared by professionals, clinics, organizations (such as the state dietetic association), or other hospitals. Most therapeutic dietitians and some nurses have at least one such diet manual. The recipes and compositions of blended diets and tube feedings used by the hospital are also important tools.

A number of important clinical disorders require the food exchange or food selection systems developed by the American Heart Association, American Diabetes Association, and the American Dietetic Association. Food exchange systems for patients with kidney diseases or phenylketonurias have been developed by a number of private and public organizations and clinics. Clinical managements for other specific disorders have been published by various professional organizations, such as the American Academy of Pediatrics, the American Cancer Society, and the American Medical Association. Practitioners may also consult state and national organizations such as the Kidney Foundation, the March of Dimes, the LaLeche League, and the Cystic Fibrosis Society and should keep these addresses on file.

For basic reference, health practitioners also need books on nutrition, diet therapy, clinical nutrition, and techniques of nutrition counseling. Other standard reference materials include growth charts of infants, children, and adolescents of both sexes; weight charts and standard methods of determining ideal weight and caloric needs; and tables of conversion factors, calories versus joules, the metric system, and sodium and potassium conversion (weight and equivalent). Food posters, slides, and pictures are also useful in nutrition education.

Other indispensable accessories include regular and special cookbooks, as well as scales, measuring devices, calipers, food models, and similar equipment. Also important is a list of food preparation equipment and serving utensils for handicapped individuals, manufacturers' addresses, and current prices.

For ethnic patients, relevant forms of some of the accessories described above may be needed.

DIETARY CARE FOR SPECIAL PATIENTS

Although the basic principles of clinical dietetics apply to all patients, some patients require special considerations because of their unique conditions. These include patients discharged from a hospital, elderly people in nursing or convalescent homes, patients undergoing rehabilitation, and immobilized patients. Information on the last three groups is presented in Chapter 31; a brief discussion of the first is presented below.

Some hospitals have established procedures for the nutritional and dietary care of patients about to be discharged. They usually assert that the nutritional status of the patient leaving the hospital should be better than or at least equal to that on admission. On leaving, a proper transition period is important for certain patients. Patients already on a regular diet pose no problems, but patients receiving a modified diet or enteral or parenteral feedings need attention. If the patient's modified diet is to be continued at home, there is no problem. However, if a person is given a soft diet in the hospital, a transition to regular foods at home should be slow and progressive, from liquid to semisolid to solid. It is not advisable to remove a nasogastric tube or intravenous fittings and then send the patient home to three full meals a day.

Special nutritional and dietary strategies for home care are needed for patients with clinical disorders that require temporary or permanent dietary modifications. Examples include diseases of the heart, kidney, and liver and disorders such as diabetes, ulcers, and cancer. Very detailed and explicit guidelines are needed; a few hours of predischarge instructions are especially worthwhile in addition to previous patient education.

The members of the health team should be in complete agreement about the kind of home dietary care needed. At least one member of the family should be familiar with the patient's condition and know what is expected of patient feeding at home. The family should also be taught to make the daily diets acceptable to the patient.

Some special points the health team should remember to discuss with the family are food costs, strategies for eating outside of the home, and the suitability of convenience foods. For a patient with temporary dietary modifications, the nurse or dietitian should also attempt to convince the patient and family to learn about food and nutrition and develop wholesome eating habits and life-styles.

In many metropolitan cities, hospitals and public health agencies provide free home visits by dietitians, nurses, nutritionists, and allied health personnel. This service is useful for checking up on patient compliance, food purchasing, food preparation, and kitchen facilities. Unfortunately, many cities cannot provide this type of service because of the time and money involved. For some patients with cancer, kidney, diabetes, or other disorders, some form of long-term monitoring and evaluation is nevertheless important. This responsibility usually becomes that of the patient's physician or the local clinic that the patient visits regularly.

STUDY QUESTIONS

1. Discuss the two basic relationships between nutrition and disease.
2. What are the roles of the doctor, the dietitian, and the nurse in the dietary management of a patient?
3. Give at least five reasons for malnutrition in hospitalized patients.
4. Discuss at least five types of information about a particular patient that are important in individualizing his or her dietary care.
5. What is a nutritional support service?

6. Give at least twelve causes of eating problems in hospitalized patients.
7. When should patient education in nutrition and diet therapy begin? What may be included?
8. What are at least ten tools needed by professional diet planners?
9. Discuss some measures to assure that a patient discharged from a hospital will receive adequate nutritional and dietary care at home.

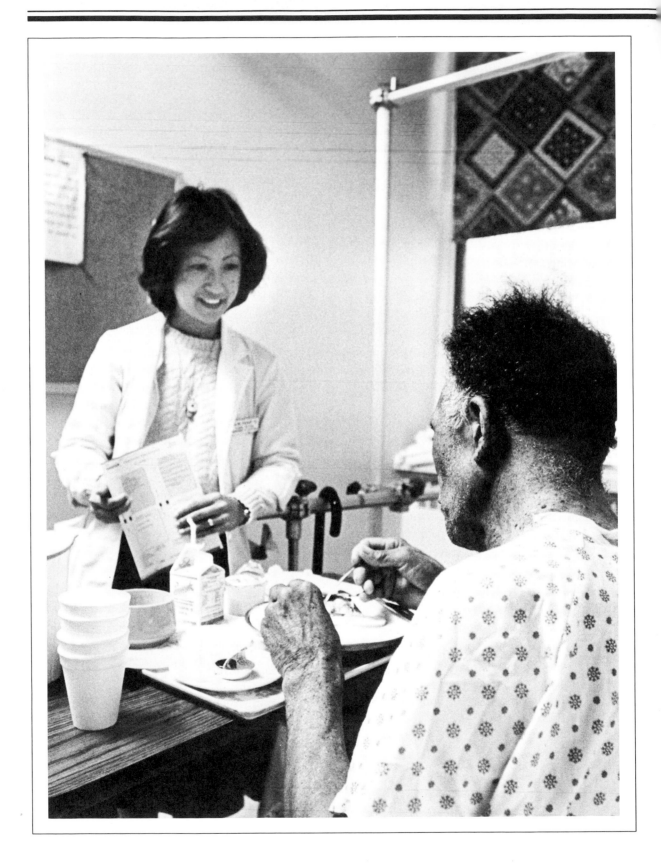

Chapter 23

Hospital Diets and Enteral and Parenteral Nutrition

IN CLINICAL DIETETICS, a therapeutic diet can be described in two ways. One refers to the name of the disorder, as in ulcer diet, kidney diet, diabetic diet, ketogenic diet, and cardiac diet. The other refers to a modification of nutrient contents: low-calorie diet, low-protein diet, high-fat diet, sodium-regulated diet, and so on. Most chapters in Part III of this book describe the diet therapy for a particular clinical disorder, giving detailed discussion of nutrient modifications. Before examining therapeutic diets for specific disorders, however, we will look at the general formats for hospital diets. These range from regular menus to artificial feedings of liquid nutrients, and may include special dietary foods.

Hospital feedings fall into six categories: (1) regular diets, (2) diets with texture and blandness modifications, (3) diets with nutritional modifications, (4) diets with miscellaneous modifications, (5) artificial feeding methods in which regular foods may or may not be employed, and (6) special test diets for clinical diagnoses and confirmation. Table 23-1 provides examples for each of these categories. Categories 1, 2, and 5 are discussed in this chapter; category 3 is discussed in the chapters that follow. Information concerning categories 4 and 6 may be located in the references provided at the end of this book.

REGULAR DIETS

Hospital diet planning uses a regular diet for a healthy person as a frame of reference. This diet contains all the essential nutrients, such as calories, protein, fat, carbohydrate, minerals, and vitamins, in adequate amounts to satisfy the RDAs. Such a diet is based on the basic four food groups and the formulation of a foundation diet, the details of which are presented in Chapter 10. Table 23-2 shows a meal plan for a regular diet for a healthy adult male that contributes 2,600 to 2,900 kcal, 95 to 105 g of protein, 95 to 125 g of fat, and 300 to 320 g of carbohydrate.

This diet must be properly adjusted according to the patient's age, sex, and activity level, as indicated in Chapter 10. If the diet is modified to treat a patient with a disease, the nutrient contents must still comply with the RDAs. Thus, in planning any regular or therapeutic diet, the major objective is nutritional adequacy.

Sometimes a regular diet need only be slightly adjusted for a hospitalized patient. For

TABLE 23-1   Examples of Different Types of Hospital Diets

Category of Diet	Examples of Diets or Descriptions of Usage
1. Regular diets	Regular foods with simple adjustments
2. Diets with texture and blandness modifications	Fluid-regulated diet Liquid diet Soft diet Fiber-regulated diet Diet for dental problems Bland diet
3. Diets with nutritional modifications	Calorie-controlled diet Protein-controlled diet Fat-controlled diet Carbohydrate-controlled diet Mineral-controlled diet (electrolyte-controlled diet)
4. Diets with miscellaneous modifications	Tyramine-controlled diet Uric-acid-controlled diet Purine-controlled diet Coal tar regimen
5. Artificial feeding methods (semi-synthetic, synthetic, and regular foods may all be used)	Enteral feedings Parenteral feedings
6. Special test diets for clinical diagnosis, confirmation, and assessment of a disorder	The diet may be a test for: Fat excretion Metabolic studies X-ray studies Stool blood Glucose tolerance Ketogenic hypoglycemia Hyperaldosteronemia Pheochromocytoma Carcinoid tumors Collagen degradation Urinary creatinine excretion

TABLE 23-2   Sample Meal Plan for a Regular Diet

Breakfast	Lunch	Dinner
Fruit or juice, ½ c	Soup, ½ c	Soup, ½ c
Cereal: hot, 6 oz; or dry, 1 oz	Meat or alternate, 2–3 oz	Meat or alternate, 3–4 oz
Egg or substitute, 1	Potato or alternate, ½ c	Potato or alternate, ½ c
Meat: regular meat, 1 oz; or bacon, 2 strips	Vegetable (cooked or in a salad), ½ c	Vegetable (cooked or in a salad), ½ c
Bread, 1–2 sl	Salad dressing, 1 T	Salad dressing, 1–2 t
Butter or margarine, 1–3 t	Bread or roll, 1	Bread or roll, 1
Jelly, jam, or preserves, 1–3 t	Butter or margarine, 1–2 t	Dessert
Milk, 1 c	Dessert	Milk, 1 c
Hot beverage, 1–2 c	Beverage (cold or hot)	Butter or margarine, 1–2 t
Cream (regular or substitute), 1 t	Cream (regular or substitute), 1 t	Hot beverage, 1–2 c
Sugar, 1–3 t	Sugar, 1–3 t	Sugar, 1–3 t
Salt, pepper	Salt, pepper	Cream (regular or substitute), 1–2 t
		Salt, pepper

TABLE 23-3   Sample Menu for a 3,500-kcal, 150-g-Protein Diet

Breakfast	Lunch	Dinner
Orange juice, ½ c	Split pea soup, 1 c	Chicken, broiled, 6 oz
Eggs, scrambled with milk, 2	Corn muffins, 2	Sweet potato, baked, 1
Ham, 3 oz	Butter, 2 pats	Broccoli, steamed, 1 stalk
Waffle, 1	Jam, 2 T	Bread, whole wheat, 1 sl
Syrup, 2 T	Cheddar cheese, 1 oz	Butter, 1–2 pats
Margarine, 1 T	Salad:	Pear poached in wine and sugar:
Banana, sliced, 1	Tomato, medium, 1	Pear, 1
Yogurt, 1 c	Raw spinach, 1 c	Wine, white, 3½ oz
Cocoa, 1 c	Celery, 1 stalk	Sugar, 1 T
Salt, pepper	Almonds, ¼ c	Milk, 1 c
	Olive oil and vinegar dressing, 2 T	Tea, 2 c
	Applesauce, sweetened, 1 c	Honey, 1 T
	Brownies, 2	Salt, pepper
	Coffee, 1 c	
	Sugar, 1 t	
	Salt, pepper	

Note: If meals are too large, they can be divided into five to seven feedings or three medium-sized meals with two to four snacks.

TABLE 23-4   Sample Menu for a 3,500-kcal Diet

Breakfast	Lunch	Dinner
Orange juice, 6 oz	Sandwich:	Split pea soup, 1 c
Bran flakes, ½ c	Bread, cracked	Fruit cocktail, ½ c
Half and half, ¼ c	wheat, 2 sl	Hamburger, ¼ lb
Poached egg, 1	Mayonnaise, 1 T	Bun, 1
Toast, whole wheat, 1 sl	Turkey, light meat,	Catsup, 1 T
Margarine, 1 t	2 sl	Mayonnaise, 1 T
Ham, 3 oz	Corn, cream style, ½ c	Tomato, ¼
Sugar, 1 t	Salad:	Cauliflower, ½ c
Coffee, 1 c	Lettuce wedge,	Cheese sauce, 1 T
Salt, pepper	¼ head	Ice cream, ½ c
	Tomato, sliced,	Sugar, 1 t
Snack	medium, 1	Coffee
Banana	Alfalfa sprouts, ½ c	Salt, pepper
	Italian dressing, 2 T	
	Milk, whole, 1 c	
	Snack	
	Iced cupcake,	
	medium, 1	
	Milk, whole, 1 c	

Note: If meals are too large, they can be divided into five to seven small feedings.

example, if a person needs a high-protein, high-calorie diet to rebuild body muscle after a minor operation, the regular diet is used with some additional foods high in protein and calories, such as cheese, meat, bread, fat, ice cream, and milk shakes. Table 23-3 provides an example of a 3,500-kcal, 150-g-protein menu. Three large meals may be divided into a number of small feedings (perhaps five to seven) or three medium-sized meals with two to four snacks.

If a person needs to gain weight, a regular diet can be supplemented with high-calorie foods such as fatty meats (beef or pork), potato, bread, and candies. Table 23-4 provides an example of a 3,500-kcal diet.

If a patient has a large appetite, he or she may need a regular diet served in one-and-a-half or double portions. On the other hand, some patients prefer smaller servings. If so, the patient can indicate this on the meal selection sheet or during the initial interview.

Even if a patient is permitted a regular diet, he or she may not be able to tolerate certain items. In this case, the doctor should prescribe a regular diet that can be tolerated, and the doctor,

dietitian, and nurse can help the patient to select foods so that the RDAs will be met. If the patient only selects those items that he or she likes, the diet may lack some of the necessary nutrients.

A post-myocardial-infarction patient may be permitted to eat a regular diet except for any stimulant that may excite the heart. Such stimulants include the caffeine in coffee, tea, and cola beverages and the theobromine in chocolate. Sometimes alcoholic beverages are considered stimulants, and foods and beverages with extreme temperatures may also excite the heart. The appendix lists the approximate caffeine content of some beverages and drugs.

There should not be any trouble in providing a nutritious diet for a vegetarian patient, although it may not be possible to provide patients having extreme eating habits, such as following the Zen macrobiotic diet, with all the essential nutrients. Some nutritional counseling may be needed in this case. Chapters 10 and 18 should be consulted for vegetarian meal planning. Table 23-5 provides a sample menu for a diet that excludes meat. Table 23-6 provides a sample menu for a diet that contains vegetable products only.

TABLE 23-5 Sample Menu for a Lacto-ovo-vegetarian, 3,000-kcal, 110-g-Protein Diet

Breakfast	Lunch	Dinner
Egg omelet:	Split pea soup, 1 c	Minestrone soup, ½ c
Eggs, 2	Sandwich:	Salad:
Swiss cheese, ¼ oz	Avocado, ½	Beets, 2
Milk or fat	Cheese, 1 oz	Tomato, ¼
Tomato, 1	Sprouts, ½ c	Lettuce leaves, 4
Toast, whole wheat, 2 sl	Mayonnaise, 1–2 t	Mushrooms, ½ c
Cranberry juice, 8 oz	Bread, whole wheat,	Parmesan cheese,
Margarine, 1 pat	2 sl	2 T
Coffee, 1 c	Margarine, 1 pat	Blue cheese dress-
Milk, 1 T	Banana, 1	ing, 1–3 t
Salt, pepper	Fig bars, 2	Spaghetti with mush-
	Prune juice, 1 c	room and tomato
	Skim milk, 1 c	sauce, 1 c
	Salt, pepper	Bread, 1 sl
		Margarine, 1 pat
		Milk, 1 c
		Sherbet, 1 c
		Salt, pepper
		Snack
		Popcorn, 1 c
		Apple juice, 1 c

Note: Reduce the amounts of food accordingly if a 2,500-kcal diet is desired.

TABLE 23-6 Sample Menu for a Strict Vegetarian, 2,800-kcal, 90-g-Protein Diet

Breakfast	Lunch	Dinner
Oatmeal, 1 c	Minestrone soup, 1 c	Stuffed peppers:
Banana, 1	Potato salad, 1 c	Peppers, 2
Orange juice, 1 c	Peanut butter, 2 T	Spinach, 1 c
Tea, 1–2 c	Apple butter, 1 T	Bulgur, 1 c
	Bread, whole wheat,	Walnuts, ¼ c
Snack	2 sl	Tomato, 1
Almonds, ¼ c	Apple juice, 1 c	Salad:
	Brownie, 1	Lettuce leaves, 2
	Salt, pepper	Carrot, 1
		Tomato, ½
		Bean sprouts, ¼ c
		Kidney beans, ½ c
		French dressing, 1 T
		Corn muffins, 2
		Margarine, 1 pat
		Melon cup:
		Cantaloupe,
		wedge, 1
		Honeydew, wedge, 1
		Grapefruit juice, 1 c
		Salt, pepper

DIETS WITH TEXTURE AND BLANDNESS MODIFICATIONS

Every hospital has diets for patients who have no need for a special modified diet but, because of their physical condition or food tolerances, are not yet ready for regular foods. Although the types of diets vary from hospital to hospital, they usually include the following: a clear-liquid diet, a full-liquid diet, a high-nutrient or modified full-liquid diet, a pureed diet, a mechanical soft diet, and a soft diet.

Many hospitals do not classify these diets rigidly; patients are fed according to their preferences and tolerances. In other hospitals, a routine progression from a clear-liquid diet, to a full-liquid diet, to a soft diet and finally to solid, regular foods is used for certain patients. A high-nutrient or modified full-liquid diet, pureed diet, and mechanical soft diet may also be introduced at appropriate stages. The following sections describe each type of blandness- and texture-modified diet.

Clear-Liquid Diet

This diet consists of fluids that are liquid at body temperature, with mono- and disaccharides as the major caloric sources. Such a diet is beneficial in the following clinical conditions: (1) before and after an operation, (2) during acute stages of a number of clinical disorders, (3) during a fever, or (4) under circumstances that require very little residue or fecal waste in the bowel.

The clear-liquid diet quenches thirst and prevents dehydration until a full-liquid diet or solid food can be tolerated. The diet provides about 600 to 1,000 kcal and 50 to 150 g of carbohydrate. It is inadequate in all essential nutrients, and in some cases it does not provide enough fluid. It should not be used for more than 24 hours unless additional nutrients are supplied. Whenever feasible, an extra intake of water and/or calorie-containing fluids should be encouraged. Commercial nutritional supplements with little residue (see later discussion) may be tolerated.

The list below describes those food and beverages permitted in a clear-liquid diet.

Soups: clear broth, bouillon, consommé
Desserts: plain or clear-flavored gelatin, Popsicles, fruit-flavored ices without pieces of fruit or milk, water ices
Sweets: honey, jelly, syrup, sugar; plain sugar candy; sugar substitutes
Fruits: all strained or clear fruit juices; apple and citrus juices only if tolerated
Vegetables: vegetable broth
Beverages: clear tea and regular coffee, decaffeinated coffee, water, strained lemonade and limeade, strained fruit punches, fruit-flavored drinks, cereal beverages, carbonated beverages and certain commercial beverages such as Gatorade, Pedialyte (for young children and infants), and Kool Aid
Miscellaneous: salt

Table 23-7 provides a sample menu plan.

Full-Liquid Diet

This diet includes certain foods and beverages that are liquid at body temperature. This diet will benefit the following clinical conditions: (1) swallowing and chewing difficulty, (2) any condition in which the patient cannot eat semisolid or solid foods, (3) postsurgical recovery, and (4) acute infections.

The full-liquid diet is inadequate in most nutrients and should be used for a minimal period of time. Again, commercial nutrient solutions should be consumed whenever the patient tolerates them. This diet provides approximately 1,500 to 2,000 kcal, 50 to 70 g of protein, and 180 to 250 g of carbohydrate. The foods and beverages permitted in a full-liquid diet are listed below.

Milk and milk products: whole milk, skim milk, chocolate, buttermilk, smooth or plain yogurt, whey, milk shakes, cocoa
Cheeses: cheese soup
Eggs: eggnog from pasteurized mix or other egg forms prepared in a beverage; scrambled or soft-cooked eggs if tolerated

TABLE 23-7 Sample Menu for a Clear-Liquid Diet

Breakfast	Lunch	Dinner
Juice, ⅔ c	Juice, ⅔ c	Juice, ⅔ c
Coffee or tea	Broth (chicken, beef, or	Broth (chicken, beef, or
Sugar	vegetable), ⅔ c	vegetable), ⅔ c
	Flavored gelatin, ½ c	Fruit ice or flavored
Snack	Coffee or tea	gelatin, ½ c
Juice, ⅔ c; or broth,	Sugar	Coffee or tea
clear, ½ c		Sugar
	Snack	
	Flavored ice, ½ c	**Snack**
		Carbonated beverage

TABLE 23-8 Sample Meal Plan for a Full-Liquid Diet

Breakfast	Lunch	Dinner
Juice, ½ c	Juice, ½ c	Juice, ½ c
Cereal, ½ c	Soup, ⅔ c	Soup, ⅔ c
Milk, ½ c	Milk, ½ c	Milk, 1 c
Beverage, 1–2 c	Dessert, ½ c	Dessert, ½ c
Cream	Beverage, 1–2 c	Beverage, 1–2 c
Sugar	Cream	Cream
Salt	Sugar	Sugar
	Salt	Salt
Snack		
Eggnog (from pas-	**Snack**	**Snack**
teurized mix), 1 c	Custard, ½ c	Milk shake, 1 c

Cereals: Cream of Rice; Cream of Wheat; cooked, refined cereals such as farina, grits, cornmeal, strained thin oatmeal and granulated rice, gruels

Meats, fish, poultry, legumes, and nuts: strained and pureed forms added to broth and cream soup

Potatoes: pureed form added to soup

Soups: any pureed or strained soup; cream soup, broth, bouillon

Fruits: all juices, including nectars

Vegetables: all juices and pureed forms used in preparing soups

Beverages: coffee (regular, decaffeinated, or substitute), tea, carbonated types, lemonade, commercial types such as Kool Aid, other tolerated varieties

Desserts: custards, plain or flavored (no fruits) gelatin, smooth ice cream, plain water ices, ice milk, puddings, sherbets, Popsicles

Sweets: honey, molasses, sugar, syrup, hard candy, jellies

Fats: margarine, butter, cream, oils

Miscellaneous: nutritious protein supplements (homemade or commercial); Instant Breakfast; salt; any finely ground herbs, spices, or flavorings tolerated by the patient

Table 23-8 is a sample meal plan for the diet, and Table 23-9 shows a sample menu.

TABLE 23-9   Sample Menu for a Full-Liquid Diet

Breakfast	Lunch	Dinner
Orange juice, ½ c	Pineapple juice, ½ c	Grapefruit juice, ½ c
Cream of Rice, ½ c	Cream soup, strained,	Vegetable soup,
Milk, ½ c	⅔ c	strained or pureed,
Coffee or tea, 1–2 c	Milk, ½ c	⅔ c
Cream	Gelatin, strawberry fla-	Milk, 1 c
Sugar	vored, ½ c	Pudding, ½ c
Salt	Coffee or tea, 1–2 c	Coffee or tea, 1–2 c
	Cream	Cream
Snack	Sugar	Sugar
Apple juice, 1 c	Salt	Salt
	Snack	**Snack**
	Ice cream, 1 c	Custard, ½ c; or nutri-
		tional supplement

High-Nutrient or Modified Full-Liquid Diet

As indicated above, a full-liquid diet is nutritionally inadequate. For long-term home and hospital use, many hospitals have developed a high-nutrient or modified full-liquid diet that is nutritionally adequate. It is made of nutritionally potent liquids and semisolid foods of a consistency that can be taken as a beverage or through a straw. The diet is appropriate for patients with broken or wired jaws, oral or throat injuries, or other clinical disorders that require prolonged liquid feedings.

The diet provides about 2,300 to 2,800 kcal, 120 to 150 g of protein, 90 to 100 g of fat, and 250 to 300 g of carbohydrate and is high in cholesterol, saturated fats, and fat-soluble vitamins. If the patient's ability to chew and swallow improves, additional foods can be given as tolerated. Those foods and beverages permitted in a high-nutrient or modified full-liquid diet are listed below.

Beverages: all types including coffee (regular or decaffeinated), milk, milk beverages, high-protein solutions, cocoa

Cereals: Cream of Wheat, Cream of Rice; cooked refined cereals diluted with milk, such as farina, grits, granulated rice; certain strainable cereals, for example, oatmeal

Cheeses: finely grated cheese in soup; blended cottage cheese; melted cheese if tolerated

Meats (beef, pork, poultry, fish): strained or baby food meats (thinned with gravy, broth, or milk)

Eggs: cooked, preferably incorporated into beverages such as eggnog; soft or scrambled eggs if tolerated

Fruits: all nectars and juices; strained or baby food fruits diluted with fruit juice

Vegetables: baby food or strained vegetables (thinned with strained vegetable juice, cream, or milk); juices

Potatoes: mashed potatoes, thinned with gravy or milk

Soups: strained, pureed, or cream soups without solids

Sweets: syrup, sugar, jelly, honey, molasses

Desserts: melted, smooth sherbet and ice cream; thin, strained puddings; thin Jello-O; custard sauce; thin yogurt

Fats: butter, margarine, cream, or plain gravy used in food preparation

Miscellaneous: salt; all finely chopped or ground herbs and spices; commercial nutrient supplement solutions

Table 23-10 provides a sample meal plan for the diet. Table 23-11 presents a sample menu for the diet.

TABLE 23-10   Sample Meal Plan for a Modified Full-Liquid or High-Nutrient Liquid Diet

Breakfast	Lunch	Dinner
Fruit juice, ½ c	Soup or broth, ½ c	Meat or broth, ½ c
Cereal, ½ c	Meat or broth, ½ c	Potato or gravy, ½ c
Milk, 1 c	Vegetable, ¼ c	Vegetable, ½ c
Butter or margarine	Fruit, ¼ c	Fruit, ¼ c
Beverage	Milk, 1 c	Milk, 1 c
Cream	Butter or margarine	Butter or margarine
Sugar	Beverage	Beverage
Salt	Sugar	Cream
	Cream	Sugar
Snack	Salt	Salt
Nutritional		
supplement*	**Snack**	**Snack**
	Nutritional	Nutritional
	supplement*	supplement*

Note: The portion sizes refer to undiluted items; the appropriate amount of fluid at the correct temperature is added to permit drinking or sucking through a straw.

*Any commercial liquid or high-nutrient diet supplement, milk shake, malted milk, or eggnog.

TABLE 23-11   Sample Menu for a Modified Full-Liquid or High-Nutrient Liquid Diet

Breakfast	Lunch	Dinner
Orange juice, strained, ½ c	Vegetable soup, strained, ½ c	Chicken, strained, thinned with broth, ½ c
Farina, cooked, refined, thinned with milk, ½ c	Beef, baby food, thinned with broth, ½ c	Potatoes, mashed, thinned with milk and gravy, ½ c
Milk, 1 c	Spinach, strained, thinned with spinach juice, ¼ c	Carrots, strained, thinned with carrot juice, ¼ c
Margarine or butter, 1 t	Peach, strained, thinned with peach juice, ¼ c	Apricots, strained, thinned with apricot juice, ¼ c
Sugar	Milk, 1 c	Milk, 1 c
Cream	Butter or margarine	Margarine or butter, 1 t
Salt	Coffee or tea	Coffee or tea
	Sugar	Sugar
Snack	Cream	Cream
Milk shake, 8 oz	Salt	Salt
	Snack	**Snack**
	Meritene liquid, 1 c	Sustacal liquid, 1 c

TABLE 23-12 Sample Meal Plan for a Pureed Diet

Breakfast	Lunch	Dinner
Fruit or juice, ½ c	Meat, poultry, or fish, 2 oz	Meat, fish, or poultry, 3–4 oz
Cereal, ½ c	Vegetable, ½ c	Potato, ½ c
Egg, 1	Cereal, ½ c; or mashed potatoes	Vegetable, ½ c
Butter or margarine, 1 t	Dessert, ½ c	Butter or margarine, 1 t
Milk, 1 c	Butter or margarine, 1 t	Dessert, ½ c
Hot beverage, 1–2 c	Milk, ½ c	Hot beverage, 1–2 c
Sugar	Hot beverage, 1–2 c	Cream
Cream	Cream	Sugar
Salt	Sugar	Salt
	Salt	

Pureed Diet

This diet is appropriate for patients who cannot chew or swallow well. It consists of food items that are easy to digest, and the food consistency is between liquid and soft. Basically, all meats and vegetables are pureed. Any additional foods that are tolerated by the patient may also be given. The diet is nutritionally adequate and provides about 1,800 to 2,500 kcal, 60 to 70 g of protein, 180 to 220 g of carbohydrate, and 60 to 80 g of fat. Those foods and beverages permitted in a pureed diet are listed below. To increase nutritional content, pureed regular foods, such as casseroles, may be served rather than commercial pureed products.

Dairy products: all types of fluid milk, including whole, skim, and chocolate and buttermilk; milk shakes, cocoa, yogurt, eggnog; cottage cheese, cream and mild cheese sauces; other tolerated melted cheeses
Eggs: poached, soft, scrambled
Meats, fish, poultry: all strained or pureed products
Cereals: cooked cereals, Cream of Wheat, Cream of Rice, grits, oatmeal (thinned); white bread and toast if tolerated
Soups: strained cream soups, broth, and pureed soups from permitted foods; broth, bouillon, consommé

Potatoes: mashed, whipped, and creamed potatoes (white and sweet)
Beverages: all types including coffee (regular or decaffeinated), tea, carbonated beverages, lemonade; other commercial beverages such as Kool Aid
Fruits: mashed, strained, and pureed fruits and juices
Vegetables: mashed, strained, and pureed vegetables and juices
Sweets: sugar, honey, jelly, syrup
Desserts: plain custard, ice cream, gelatin, sherbet, ices, puddings, fruit whip, plain or smooth desserts without any fruit
Fats: margarine, oils, sour cream, cream, butter, mayonnaise, cream cheese
Miscellaneous: salt; other flavorings such as pepper, herbs, and spices if tolerated (in moderation); cream sauces and gravies

Table 23-12 provides a sample meal plan for the diet, and Table 23-13 gives a sample menu.

Mechanical Soft Diet

This diet is a simple modification of the regular diet and is made up of foods and beverages that require little chewing. It is appropriate for a patient with chewing difficulty who can tolerate foods of a more solid texture than those for whom the pureed diet is ordered. Patients with

TABLE 23-13   Sample Menu for a Pureed Diet

Breakfast	Lunch	Dinner
Orange juice, ½ c	Chicken, pureed, 2 oz	Beef, pureed, with
Oatmeal, ½ c	Beets, pureed, ½ c	gravy, 3–4 oz
Egg, scrambled, soft, 1	Applesauce, ½ c	Potatoes, mashed, ½ c
Butter or margarine, 1 t	Sweet potato, mashed,	Asparagus, pureed,
Coffee or tea, 1–2 c	½ c	½ c
Milk, 1 c	Margarine or butter, 1 t	Butter or margarine, 1 t
Sugar	Coffee or tea, 1–2 c	Pudding, butterscotch,
Cream	Cream	½ c
Salt	Sugar	Coffee or tea, 1–2 c
	Salt	Cream
		Sugar
		Salt

few or no teeth, poor teeth, and ill-fitting dentures are candidates for this diet. It provides about 2,200 to 2,600 kcal, 85 to 95 g of protein, 100 to 110 g of fat, and 295 to 315 g of carbohydrate.

Pureed, ground, chopped, and mashed foods are served according to individual desires and needs. Individualized diet planning is essential, since it is important that the nurse and dietitian determine the patient's chewing ability before deciding on the appropriate food consistency. A diet based on the particular patient's food choices can be planned to meet all RDAs.

The foods permitted in a mechanical soft diet are listed below.

Milk: all forms
Cheeses: all forms
Eggs: any cooked form
Breads: white, rye without seeds, refined whole wheat; corn bread; any cracker not made with whole grains; French toast made from permitted breads; spoon bread; pancakes; plain soft rolls
Cereals: all cooked, soft varieties; puffed flakes and noncoarse ready-to-eat varieties
Flour: all forms
Meats, fish, poultry: small cubed and finely ground or minced forms; as ingredients in creamed dishes, soups, casseroles, and stews
Seafoods: any variety of fish without bone (canned, fresh, or frozen; packaged pre-

pared forms in cream sauces); minced, shredded, ground, and finely chopped shellfish
Legumes, nuts: fine, smooth, creamy peanut butter; legumes (if tolerated) cooked tender, finely chopped, mashed or minced
Potatoes: white potatoes: mashed, boiled, baked, creamed, scalloped, cakes, au gratin; sweet potatoes: boiled, baked, mashed
Soups: all varieties, preferably without hard solids such as nuts and seeds
Fruits: raw: avocado, banana; cooked and canned: fruit cocktail, cherries, apples, apricots, peaches, pears, sections of mandarin oranges, grapefruits, or oranges without membranes; all juices and nectars
Vegetables: all juices; all vegetables cooked tender, chopped, mashed, canned, or pureed; canned, pureed, or paste forms of tomato
Sweets: marshmallow and chocolate sauces; preserves, marmalade, jelly, jam; candy: hard, chocolate, caramels, jellybeans, marshmallows, candy corn, butterscotch, gumdrops, plain fudge, lollipops, fondant mints; syrup: sorghum, maple, corn; sugar: granulated, brown, maple, confectioner's; honey, molasses
Desserts: all plain or certain flavored varieties (permitted flavorings include liquids, such as juice; finely chopped or pureed fruits without solid pieces of fruit, seeds, nuts, etc.);

TABLE 23-14 Sample Meal Plan for a Mechanical Soft Diet

Breakfast	Lunch	Dinner
Fruit or juice, ½ c	Soup, ½ c	Soup, ½ c
Cereal, ½ c	Meat, fish, or poultry, 2–3 oz	Meat, fish, or poultry, 3–4 oz
Egg, 1	Potato, ½ c	Potato, ½ c
Bread or toast, 1 sl	Bread or toast, 1 sl	Vegetable, ½ c
Butter or margarine, 1 t	Vegetable, ½ c	Bread or toast, 1 sl
Milk, 1 c	Butter or margarine, 1 t	Butter or margarine, 1 t
Hot beverage, 1–2 c	Dessert, 1 serving	Dessert, 1 serving
Cream	Milk, 1 c	Milk, 1 c
Sugar	Hot beverage, 1–2 c	Hot beverage, 1–2 c
Salt, pepper	Cream	Cream
	Sugar	Sugar
	Salt, pepper	Salt, pepper
		Snack
		Beverage, fruit, or dessert

TABLE 23-15 Sample Menu for a Mechanical Soft Diet

Breakfast	Lunch	Dinner
Orange juice, ½ c	Clam soup, ½ c	Cream soup, ½ c
Oatmeal, ½ c	Chicken, minced and creamed, ½ c	Roast beef, chopped, with gravy, 3–4 oz
Egg, scrambled, soft, 1	Potato, baked, ½ c	Potato, mashed, ½ c
Toast, 1 sl	Toast, 1 sl	Spinach, ½ c
Butter or margarine, 1 t	Beets, diced, ½ c	Toast, 1 sl
Milk, 1 c	Butter or margarine, 1 t	Butter or margarine, 1 t
Coffee or tea	Custard, plain, ½ c	Ice cream, ½ c
Cream, 1 T	Milk, 1 c	Milk, 1 c
Sugar, 1–2 t	Coffee or tea	Coffee or tea
Salt, pepper	Cream, 1 T	Cream, 1 T
	Sugar, 1–2 t	Sugar, 1–2 t
	Salt, pepper	Salt, pepper
		Snack
		Cookies, plain, 3

gelatins, puddings; ice cream, ice milk, sherbet; water ices; cakes, cookies, cake icing; cobblers

Fats: butter, margarine, cream (or substitutes), oils and vegetable shortenings, and bacon fat; salad dressings, tartar sauce, sour cream

Seasonings: salt, pepper, soy sauce, vinegar, catsup; all other herbs, especially finely chopped or ground, that can be tolerated

Table 23-14 gives a sample meal plan for the diet, and Table 23-15 presents a sample menu.

Soft Diet

Although there is no well-founded scientific basis for the usage of such a regimen, hospitals have traditionally used a soft diet during the transition from liquid to regular foods, especially when the patient is convalescing (for example, after surgery). The consistency of the diet is easy to chew and can be adjusted to suit individual needs, preferences, and intolerances. This diet is especially appropriate for patients who are psychologically or physically unable to tolerate a general diet. In general, clinical experience indicates that fried foods, many raw fruits and vegetables, very hard or coarse breads and cereals, and highly seasoned dishes can cause abdominal discomfort (including flatulence) and are not welcomed by many patients.

The soft diet provides about 2,200 to 2,600 kcal, 90 to 100 g of protein, 90 to 110 g of fat, and 250 to 300 g of carbohydrate. Table 23-16 describes the foods permitted and prohibited in a soft diet, Table 23-17 shows a sample meal plan for the diet, and Table 23-18 gives a sample menu.

TABLE 23-16   Foods Permitted and Prohibited in a Soft Diet

Food Types	Foods Permitted	Foods Prohibited
Milk	All milk and milk products without added ingredients; condensed and evaporated milk, chocolate milk and drink; cocoa and hot chocolate; yogurt and whey	Any milk product with prohibited ingredients
Cheese	Cottage cheese, cream cheese, mild cheese, and any cheese not prohibited	Any sharp, strongly flavored cheese; any cheese with prohibited ingredients
Eggs	Poached, scrambled, soft- and hard-cooked eggs; salmonella-free egg powder (pasteurized)	Raw or fried eggs
Breads and equivalents	Breads: white, Italian, Vienna, French, refined whole wheat, corn bread, spoon bread, French toast, seedless rye; muffins, English muffins, pancakes, rolls, waffles; melba toast, rusk, zwieback; biscuits, graham crackers, saltines, and other crackers not made with whole grains	Breads: any variety with seeds or nuts Boston brown, pumpernickel, raisin, cracked wheat, buckwheat; crackers: all made with whole grain; rolls: any made with whole grain, nuts, coconut, raisins; tortillas
Cereals	Cooked and refined dry cereals	Dry, coarse cereals such as shredded wheat, all bran, and whole grain
Flours	All varieties except those prohibited	Any made with whole-grain wheat or bran
Beverages	All types	None
Meat, fish, poultry	Meats: beef, liver, pork (lean and fresh), lamb, veal; poultry: turkey, chicken, duck, Cornish game hens, chicken livers; fish: all types of fresh varieties, canned tuna and salmon*	Fried, cured, and highly seasoned products such as chitterlings, corned beef, cured and/or smoked products, most processed sausages, and cold cuts; meats with a lot of fat; geese and game birds; most shellfish; canned fish such as anchovies, herring, sardines, and any strongly flavored seafoods
Legumes, nuts	Fine, creamy, smooth peanut butter	Most legumes, nuts, and seeds

TABLE 23-16   (continued)

Food Types	Foods Permitted	Foods Prohibited
Fruits	Raw: avocado, banana; canned or cooked: apples, apricots, cherries, peaches, pears, plums, sections of oranges, grapefruits, mandarin oranges without membranes, stewed fruits (except raisins), fruit cocktail, seedless grapes; all juices and nectars	All raw fruits not specifically permitted; all dried fruits; fruits with seeds and skins
Vegetables	All juices; canned or cooked: asparagus, beets, carrots, celery, eggplant, green or wax beans, chopped kale, mushrooms, peas, spinach, squash, shredded lettuce, chopped parsley, green peas, pumpkin; tomato: stewed, pureed, juice, paste	All those not specifically permitted
Fats	Butter, margarine, cream (or substitute), oil, vegetable shortening, mayonnaise, French dressing, crisp bacon, plain gravies, sour cream	Other forms of fats and oils, salad dressings, highly seasoned gravy
Soups	Any made from permitted ingredients: bouillon (powder or cubes), consommé, cream soups; strained soups: gumbos, chowders, bisques	Soups made from prohibited ingredients; split pea and bean soups; highly seasoned soups such as onion
Potatoes	White potatoes: scalloped, boiled, baked, mashed, creamed, au gratin; sweet potatoes: mashed	White potatoes fried, caked, browned, and in salad; yams
Rice and equivalents	Rice (white or brown), macaroni, spaghetti, noodles, Yorkshire pudding	Wild rice, bulgur, fritters, bread stuffing, barley
Sweets	Sugar: granulated, brown, maple, confectioner's; candy: hard, jelly beans, mints, marshmallows, butterscotch, candy corn, chocolate, caramels, fondant, plain fudge, gumdrops; syrups: maple, sorghum, corn; jelly, marmalade, preserves, jams; honey, molasses, apple butter; marshmallow and chocolate sauces	All candies containing nuts, coconut, and prohibited fruits
Desserts	Cake, cookies, custard, pudding, gelatin, ice cream, cobblers, ice milk, sherbet, water ice, cream pie with graham cracker crust; all plain or flavored without large pieces of fruits	Any products containing nuts, coconut, or prohibited fruits
Miscellaneous	Sauces: cream, white, brown, cheese, tomato; vinegar, soy sauce, catsup; all finely ground or chopped spices and herbs served in amounts tolerated by the patient	Spices and sauces that the patient is unable to tolerate, such as red pepper, garlic, curry, mustard; pickles; olives; popcorn, potato chips; Tabasco and Worcestershire sauces

*Cooked tender—may be broiled, baked, creamed, stewed, or roasted.

TABLE 23-17 Sample Meal Plan for a Soft Diet

Breakfast	Lunch	Dinner
Fruit or juice, ½ c	Soup, ½ c	Soup, ½ c
Cereal, ½ c	Mealt, poultry, or fish,	Meat, poultry, or fish,
Egg, 1	2–3 oz	3–4 oz
Bacon, 2 strips	Rice or equivalent, ½ c	Potato, ½ c
Toast, 1 sl	Vegetable or salad,	Vegetable or salad,
Butter or margarine, 1 t	½ c	½ c
Jam, preserves, or jelly	Bread or toast, 1 sl	Bread, 1 sl
Milk, 1 c	Butter or margarine, 1 t	Butter or margarine, 1 t
Hot beverage	Dessert	Dessert
Cream	Hot beverage	Milk, 1 c
Sugar	Sugar	Hot beverage
Salt, pepper	Cream	Cream
	Salt, pepper	Sugar
		Salt, peper

TABLE 23-18 Sample Menu for a Soft Diet

Breakfast	Lunch	Dinner
Orange juice, ½ c	Chowder, strained,	Soup, creamed, ½ c
Farina, ½ c	½ c	Beef, stew meat,
Egg, soft-boiled, 1	Cod, broiled, 2–3 oz	tender, 3–4 oz
Bacon, crisp, 2 strips	White rice, ½ c	Potato, baked, me-
Toast, 1 sl	Toast, 1 sl	dium, 1
Butter or margarine, 1 t	Butter or margarine, 1 t	Asparagus, canned,
Jam, 1–3 t	Pudding, plain, ½ c	½ c
Milk, 1 c	Coffee or tea, 1–2 c	Toast, 1 sl
Coffee or tea, 1–2 c	Sugar, 1–3 t	Butter or margarine, 1 t
Sugar, 1–3 t	Cream, 1 T	Gelatin, flavored, ½ c
Cream, 1 T	Salt, pepper	Coffee or tea, 1–2 c
Salt, pepper		Cream, 1 T
		Sugar, 1–3 t
		Salt, pepper

SPECIAL DIETARY FOODS

Some hospital diets include special dietary foods. These generally satisfy particular dietary needs of patients with certain physical, physiological, or pathological conditions. Some clinicians define these foods as medical foods "intended for use solely under medical supervision for the dietary management of diseases and disorders."

Administered orally or enterally, these foods range from complete defined-formula diets to a single nutrient. These products may be in liquid or powder form, and some are modified regular foods. Though available without a prescription, special dietary foods are used under a doctor's supervision, whether within a hospital or for outpatient care. Legally all such products are considered as foods for special dietary use rather than as drugs, and the FDA is currently developing labels for them. By contrast, nutrient solutions for parenteral feeding are classified as drugs and are subject to special regulations.

Some examples of special dietary or medical foods include: (1) meal replacement items, (2) food supplements, (3) defined-formula diets, (4) low-residue foods, (5) amino-acid-restricted diets, (6) foods for treating a specific food intolerance, (7) foods for treating food allergies, (8) foods for treating diarrhea, (9) foods that are high in calories or protein, (10) foods composed of one or more nutrients, (11) foods low in sodium and/or potassium, and (12) foods low in protein.

The major considerations in using these products are safety, effectiveness, convenience, and acceptability. In particular, there is a growing interest in assuring that hospitals have trained personnel to assess the safety and efficacy of special dietary and medical foods. Furthermore, for some underbudgeted hospitals, cost can also be a factor.

ENTERAL AND PARENTERAL FEEDINGS

In spite of advancements in clinical medicine, oral ingestion and digestion of an adequate amount of regular foods and beverages still constitute the best way to assure the proper nutrient intake of a patient. However, a number of clinical conditions render the normal route of nourishment unsatisfactory or inadvisable. Recently much progress has been made in the two basic artificial methods of feeding a hospitalized patient: enteral and parenteral nutrition. *Enteral* feedings are destined for the gastrointestinal tract; *parenteral* feedings enter the body by injection directly into blood veins. Below is an outline of how such feedings are formulated and administered.

I. Enteral feeding
  A. Oral feeding
    1. Hospital-made formulas using regular foods as well as semisynthetic and synthetic nutrients
    2. Commercial nutritional supplements or formulas using regular foods as well as semisynthetic and synthetic nutrients

  B. Tube feeding
    1. Hospital-made formulas using regular foods as well as semisynthetic or synthetic nutrients
    2. Commercial nutritional supplements or formulas using regular foods as well as semisynthetic or synthetic nutrients
II. Parenteral feeding
  A. Standard intravenous (IV) therapy
  B. Simple modified intravenous feeding
  C. Hypotonic intravenous alimentation or near total parenteral nutrition
  D. Total parenteral nutrition (TPN)

A number of factors determine which of these special feeding methods is used; these factors are discussed in detail below. However, one useful index is the "five-day rule": No special nutritional support is provided if a reasonably nourished patient can eat normally within 2 days of partial or total starvation lasting for five continuous days; otherwise, the patient is protected from further cachexia by implementing aggressive nutritional therapy such as nutrient-dense solutions administered orally, by tube feeding, or parenteral nutrition.

Enteral feedings

Although some patients cannot eat regular solid foods, they can still drink and swallow liquid products. For these patients, some hospitals prepare special nutrient-dense liquid formulas; there are also many commercial liquid supplements that are highly nourishing. However, some clinical conditions render oral feeding difficult, insufficient, impossible, or impractical; these are outlined below.

I. Mechanical difficulties (oral feeding impossible)
  A. Head and neck tumor; cancer of the mouth, larynx, or esophagus
  B. Use of the mouth incapacitated by severe accident
  C. Inability to swallow due to certain neurological diseases
  D. Oral or esophageal surgery or trauma
  E. Obstruction of esophagus or pylorus
II. Intestinal diseases (oral feeding inadequate)

TABLE 23-19 Standard Hospital Tube Feeding

Ingredient	Measure	Weight (g)	Kcal	Protein (g)	Fat (g)	Carbo-hydrate (g)	Iron (mg)	Vitamin C (mg)
Milk, whole	2 c	488	318	17	17	24	0.2	4.0
Milk, instant, nonfat, dry	1 c	70	250	24	0	35	0.4	5.0
Corn syrup	4¾ T	97.4	280	0	0	71	1.3	0
Egg, powdered, pasteurized*	4 T	30	163	13	12	1	2.3	0
Salt	1 t	5.5	—	—	—	—	—	—
Vitamin preparation	5 mL	—	—	—	—	—	—	—
Total	—	—	1,011	54	29	131	4.2	9.0

Note: Nutrient compositions are adapted from USDA Home and Garden Bulletin No. 72.

Enough water is added to the total ingredients to make 1,000 mL of solution.

*To avoid salmonella contamination, do not use fresh raw eggs. One egg is equivalent to 15 g of powdered eggs.

A. Malabsorption, persistent diarrhea, chronic bowel obstruction, radiation injury, short-bowel syndrome, fistula, peritonitis, granulomatous enterocolitis

B. Intestinal cancer with or without surgery

III. Refusal to eat (eating sufficient quantities difficult)

A. Psychological reasons, such as anorexia nervosa

B. General weakness or debilitation

C. Senile dementia

D. Recovery from a stroke

E. Unconscious or semicomatose state

F. Severe burns

G. Nausea (usually accompanied by vomiting)

IV. Inadequate oral consumption of foods

Under the above circumstances, tube feedings may be necessary through the nasogastric (nasopharyngeal) route, gastrostomy, or jejunostomy. The following sections discuss hospital and commercial tube feedings in more detail.

Types of tube feedings

Tube feedings are fluid or semifluid and may be hospital prepared or commercially purchased. Commercially prepared formulas are presently favored because they reduce the risk of contamination. These products are discussed in detail in a later section.

Although tube feedings may not be completely adequate nutritionally, they should be reasonably nutritious. The formulas for preparing a tube feeding vary. Both commercial and hospital formulas usually provide about 1 kcal/mL, although the concentration may be adjusted to between ½ and 1½ kcal/mL. Hospital-prepared tube feedings are usually of two types: *standard* and *standard blenderized*. A sample recipe of a standard hospital-prepared tube feeding is shown in Table 23-19. The basic ingredients used are milk products. Table 23-20 provides an example of a standard hospital-prepared, blenderized tube feeding. The basic ingredients are regular nutrient-dense foods that have a fluid, semifluid, or very soft texture, such as items used in infant feeding.

A patient usually tolerates a standard blenderized tube feeding better than a standard (commercial) tube-feeding formula. This difference may be related to the use of ingredient ratios in the blenderized feeding that are fairly similar to the ratios in the person's regular diet.

Basic nutritional considerations

The caloric concentration in a hospital-prepared tube feeding of ½ to 1½ kcal/mL allows a wide range of caloric density within which the individual patient's tube feeding may be programmed to tolerate. Although caloric density is limited by the patient's tolerance, there should be a reasonable content of carbohydrate, fat, and protein. For example, 40 to 50 g of protein of

TABLE 23-20 Standard Blenderized Tube Feeding

Ingredient	Measure	Weight (g)	Kcal	Protein (g)	Fat (g)	Carbo-hydrate (g)	Iron (mg)	Vitamin C (mg)
Milk, evaporated	1½ c	428	517	26.4	29.8	36.6	0.4	4.5
Farina, cooked, enriched	1 c	245	108	3.2	0.2	21.3	12.3	0
Egg, powdered, pasteurized*	6 T	45	243	18.5	18.0	1.5	3.3	0
Liver, pureed	1 jar	100	94	14.0	3.1	2.4	6.8	27.4
Orange juice, fresh	½ c	123	49	0.7	0.2	11.0	0.2	64.0
Carrots, cooked	½ c	77	22	0.6	0.2	4.8	0.5	1.5
Total	—	—	1,033	63.4	51.5	77.6	23.5	97.4

Note: Nutrient compositions are adapted from USDA Home and Garden Bulletin No. 72.

Enough water is added to the total ingredients to make 1,000 mL of solution.

*To avoid salmonella contamination, do not use fresh raw eggs. One egg is equivalent to 15 g of powdered eggs. Cooked egg custard, salmonella-free frozen eggs, or egg yolks processed for infant feeding may also be used.

high biological value (such as milk casein) per 1,000 mL of formula are acceptable. A high protein concentration is not recommended, since most patients do not retain nitrogen satisfactorily at this stage of feeding. Because of the demonstrated risk of essential fatty acid deficiency in hospitalized patients (see later discussion), 40 to 60 g of fat per 1,000 mL, of which a large fraction is unsaturated fatty acids, should provide the needed linoleic or arachidonic acid. In most patients, the stomach-emptying time is slowed down by the presence of fat, which also decreases the high osmolarity of the formulas. About 90 to 110 g of carbohydrates per 1,000 mL, which contain mainly oligosaccharides such as sucrose and lactose, should suffice.

The vitamin and mineral contents of most hospital-prepared tube feedings and even some commercial ones are usually inadequate, especially in vitamin C, folic acid, and iron. The supplements may be either directly added to the feedings or given to the patient separately, depending on the circumstances. Otherwise, 2 L of a tube feeding containing 1 kcal/mL should approximately satisfy the RDAs for the patient.

Administration

Table 23-21 describes the various means of enteral feedings. The feedings are usually administered through #8 and #10 French feeding tubes. A Barron pump (or similar device)

equipped with a drip meter regulates the flow and volume delivered. To acclimate the patient, great care should be used in the initial feedings. If the patient has not had any food for a long period, the tube feedings should be started at a very low concentration. Table 23-22 lists the progressive concentrations and delivery rates for tube feedings. Some institutions even prefer to start with skim or whole milk. A denser solution may be used if the patient has been eating.

Depending on the patient, the intial diluted feedings are usually maintained for about 24 hours. Then the concentration, volume, and frequency are increased if the patient is adapting. Most practitioners first increase the concentration and then the frequency and volume, if necessary.

All tube feedings are given slowly. Some patients may regurgitate or aspire the formula, and some may retain the liquid diet in their stomach. To avoid these incidents, incline the patient's head at an angle and give the initial feeding slowly. A conscious patient who is not in severe pain usually cooperates well. An initial feeding of 150 to 200 mL in 4 to 8 hours is usually tolerated, but every patient must be monitored and evaluated. Once the patient has adapted to the formula and concentration, the feeding may be kept continuous under sanitary supervision.

A physician's prescription for tube feeding should specify the type of feeding, modifications in any of the nutrients (especially protein and

TABLE 23-21   Different Means of Enteral Feedings

Anatomical Site	Feeding Method	Technique Used
Mouth	Normal oral	No special procedure required.
Nose	Nasogastric	Tube leads through nose into stomach. Extreme caution must be exercised when used in comatose patients because of risk of regurgitation and food aspiration.
Stomach	Gastrostomy	Surgery needed to insert feeding tube into the stomach through the anterior abdominal wall. Risk of regurgitation unlikely. Same feeding formula as in nasogastric feeding.
Small intestine	Jejunostomy	Required for patients in coma or with stomach obstruction or removal. Surgery needed. Technique more complicated; caution important; special feeding formula and schedule required. For more information, check standard surgical manual or textbook.

TABLE 23-22   Tube-Feeding Regimen for Programming Patient Tolerance

Progressive Concentration (kcal/mL)	Progressive Feeding Rate (mL/h)*
¼–½	35–50
½–¾	50–75
¾–1	75–100
1	100–130†
1–1½	

*The period of feeding at each rate varies from a few hours to a few days.

†Maximum rate.

calories), and volume and number of feedings per 24 hours. The total calories to be administered within a specific period can be calculated. The order may also specify intermittent or continuous feedings. Most large hospitals prefer that brands of tube feedings not be specified since not all brands are stocked. However, certain brands are commonly available, and some physicians do specify the formula brand name.

The formula should always be shaken before using since some products may separate upon standing, and only the amount needed should be dispensed. Warm feedings are preferred, since cold ones may increase the stomach-emptying time and induce diarrhea. However, the formula should not be placed over direct heat since the ingredients may decompose.

Precautions and problems

The major precautions and problems in the use of tube feedings include the following: (1) maintaining a record, (2) avoiding contamination, (3) controlling osmolarity, (4) being alert to patient maladjustment, (5) being aware of treatments for diarrhea, and (6) considerations for long-term feeding.

Maintaining a record.   Records relating to tube feedings should be carefully kept, and they should include the type, amount, and concentration of feeding; the rate of delivery; the period of time used; and the patient's fluid intake and output. This information is especially valuable if the patient develops diarrhea and other complications. Data on the amount of protein, calories, and other nutrients consumed are also useful.

Avoiding contamination. Contamination of tube feedings is a real problem that may lead to intestinal infection and diarrhea. It may be avoided by maintaining strict sanitary conditions at all stages. Hospital-prepared formulas should be made daily and transported to the location for use under sanitary conditions. If the formula is commercially purchased or obtained from an affiliated pharmacy, the package or can should be opened under sanitary conditions and all preparations and dilutions should be performed by trained dietary or nursing personnel. Any unused feedings should be refrigerated, dated, and, if not consumed within 24 hours, discarded. Some institutions discard any unused portions immediately. Any additional dilutions should be done by the dietary and pharmacy departments or trained nursing personnel.

Controlling osmolarity. The osmolarity in the formula is related mainly to the presence of electrolytes and simple carbohydrates. The former include calcium, phosphorus, sodium, and potassium. High osmolarity may cause diarrhea and dehydration. Both can be prevented if concentrations are increased progressively and if an isotonic or hypotonic formula is used initially, if possible. About 14 mosm should be the maximum osmolarity permitted per liter of formula. To avoid excessive concentrations, practitioners should always consult the record of tube feedings and adhere to the manufacturer's directions for dilution.

Being alert to patient maladjustment. A patient receiving tube feedings should be constantly checked for certain adverse responses. One such response is diarrhea and dehydration. Although these may be due to high osmolarity, another possibility is intolerance to lactose in the formula. For this reason, patients should be screened for lactose intolerance before treatment, and lactose-free formulas should be given accordingly.

Another adverse response is constipation. Any constipation after a long period of tube feedings should be corrected by increasing the sugar concentration or administering enemas.

Some patients develop stomach retention and bloating. These may be due to an excessive volume of feeding, a situation that can be easily corrected and avoided. Certain patients may de-

velop necrosis, inflammation, and partial obstruction along some areas of the nasopharynx. In some cases, tube feeding may have to be terminated and alternative means of feeding used.

Some patients have specific clinical problems—such as coma, extensive tissue damage, or fever—that are responsible for adverse responses. A kidney patient may have special requirements for protein and electrolytes, and elderly patients are especially sensitive to high concentrations. Some patients may also require special attention to their water intake.

Being aware of treatments for diarrhea. Patients with stubborn diarrhea may require special therapy. Some treatments for uncontrolled or severe diarrhea are: the administration of drugs such as Kaopectate, diet supplementation with pectin or methylcellulose, and feeding high-fiber and semisolid foods such as applesauce. All methods of reducing diarrhea are aimed at giving bulk and/or absorbing water. For more information, consult Chapter 24.

Considerations for long-term tube feedings. If the patient is to be tube-fed for a prolonged period, special considerations include: record keeping, monitoring serum nutrient levels, adequate nutrient intake by the patient, the risk of dehydration and hyperosmolality, cost, convenience, and psychological adjustment of the patient.

Commercial nutritional formulas

Commercial liquid nutritional formulas, which are increasingly available and popular, can be used both for oral and tube feedings. In addition to being suitable for the clinical conditions outlined earlier in this chapter, commercial liquid formulas may be advisable for patients with conditions such as kidney malfunctions, genetic metabolic diseases, severe stress, and premature birth. They may also be used for preparing the bowel of a patient for an operation.

Commercial liquid nutritional formulas have many descriptions: "nutrient or dietary supplements," "enteral feedings," "elemental diets," and "defined chemical diets." Experts have questioned the accuracy of the last two names, since the ingredients of these products are neither made up of elements nor chemically

TABLE 23-23 Liquid Formulations with Protein as the Major Nutrient

| Product (manufacturer) | kcal/unit | Nutrient Content | | | Electrolyte Presence |
		Protein	Carbo-hydrate	Fat	
EMF (Control Drugs)	2.0/mL	High	None	None	Yes
DP High P.E.R. Protein (General Mills)	4.0/g	High	Some	Some	Yes (low)
Gevral* (Lederle)	0.9/mL	High	Trace	Moderate	Yes (low)
Pasteurized egg powder, salmonella-free	3.5/g	High	Trace	Some	Yes
Casec (Mead Johnson)	3.7/g	High	None	Trace	Yes (low)

*Also a calorie source.

defined. The phrase "defined formula diets for medical use" has been advocated instead.

Such nutritional formulas come in many forms and flavors and provide essential nutrients to varying extents. One group of nutritional supplements provide protein and sometimes calories as the major nutrients; some common ones are presented in Table 23-23. A second group of nutritional supplements provide carbohydrate and calories as the major nutrients. Some common brands are presented in Table 23-24. A third group of nutritional supplements provide fat and calories as the major nutrients. Two common examples are presented in Table 23-25.

The medium-chain triglycerides (MCTs) indicated in Table 23-25 serve an important purpose under some clinical conditions. MCTs are obtained mainly from coconut oil; they contain mostly fatty acids with eight or ten carbon atoms. They are better absorbed than long-chain fatty acids under three important pathological conditions: (1) when pancreatic enzymes and/or bile salts are either absent or present in very small amounts; (2) when the lymphatic system has an obstruction, especially in the branches leaving the intestinal walls; and (3) when the intestinal mucosa is defective. For example, a patient with steatorrhea can absorb MCTs much better than ordinary fat.

Despite its usefulness for certain conditions, MCTs create some problems that should be monitored. Because they are easily absorbed, any excess consumption forces their increased degradation. As a result, the formation of acetone, acetoacetic acid, and β-hydroxybutyric acid may increase and acidosis may occur. Patients susceptible to hepatic encephalopathy (see Chapter 25) may react adversely to MCTs that reach the liver directly from the gut.

In addition to formulas with protein, carbohydrates, or fat as the major nutrient, a fourth group is administered to patients with special clinical conditions, such as renal failure, carbohydrate intolerance, and phenylketonuria, and to patients requiring sodium-regulated intakes. Some common examples are presented in Table 23-26.

A fifth group of commercial formulas is considered nutritionally complete. For convenience, they will be called "complete defined-formula diets." Sometimes they are also called "meal replacements." An analysis of their protein, fat, and carbohydrate contents is provided below.

Nutrient analysis of complete defined-formula diets. The complete defined-formula diets that are available contain about 10% to 25% of their total calories from protein. The protein source

TABLE 23-24   Liquid Formulations with Carbohydrate as the Major Nutrient

Product (manufacturer)	kcal/unit	Nutrient Content			Electrolyte Presence*
		Protein	Carbo-hydrate	Fat	
CAL powder (General Mills)	2.28/mL	Trace	High	None	Yes (low)
Hycal (Beecham)	2.3/mL	Trace	High	Trace	Yes (low)
Controlyte† (Doyle)	5.0/g	Trace	High	Moderate	Yes (low)
Citrotein† (Doyle)	3.8/g	Some	High	Trace	Yes
Lytren† (Mead Johnson)	3.73/g	None	High	None	Yes (high)
Polycose‡ (Ross)	4.0/g	None	High	None	Yes (low)
Sumacal (Hospital Dietetic Products)	2.78/mL	None	High	None	Yes (low)

*Includes sodium and potassium.
†Also a calorie source.
‡The major carbohydrates are oligosaccharides.

TABLE 23-25   Liquid Formulations with Fat as the Major Nutrient

Product (manufacturer)	kcal/unit	Nutrient Content			Electrolyte Presence
		Protein	Carbohydrate	Fat	
Lipomul-Oral (Upjohn)	6.0/mL	Trace	Trace	High	Yes (low)
MCT Oil* (Mead Johnson)	8.30/mL	None	None	High	None

*Contains medium-chain triglycerides (MCTs).

may be meat (pureed), milk (whole, skim, or non-fat), casein (whole or hydrolyzed), soybean (isolates), egg white (isolates), and crystalline amino acids. The formulation may therefore contain whole or intact protein, hydrolyzed protein, amino acids, or combinations of these forms. Whole protein (such as beef and milk) is the cheapest and most palatable. Whole casein has a low viscosity and is easily digested, while hydro-lyzed casein is a good source of peptides, which are very appropriate for a patient who cannot digest and/or absorb nutrients well. It is currently believed that small peptides (comprised of two to four amino acids) are better digested than pure amino acids even in a patient with maldigestion. An appropriate protein source must be chosen for each patient individually. For example, a patient unable to eat but with a normal

TABLE 23-26 Liquid Nutrient Supplements for Patients with Special Clinical Conditions

Product (manufacturer)	kcal/unit	Nutrient Content			Electrolyte Presence*	Remark
		Protein	Carbo-hydrate	Fat		
Amin-Aid (McGaw)	4.69/g	Low	High	Some	Yes (low)	Used mainly for patients with renal failure (see Chapter 28)
Lofenalac (Mead Johnson)	0.67/mL	Some	High	Some	Yes (moderate)	Used for phenylketonuria patients (see Chapter 30)
Lonalac (Mead Johnson)	0.67/mL	Some	Some	Some	Yes (low)	Used for patients on low-sodium diets (see Chapters 27 and 28)
Pedialyte (Ross)	0.2/mL	None	High	None	Yes (high)	Used to supply electrolytes with some calories
Liprotein (Upjohn)	5.44/g	Some	Some	Some	Yes (low)	Used for patients on high-calorie, and low-sodium diets (see Chapters 27 and 28)
Probana (Mead Johnson)	0.67/mL	Some	High	Some	Yes (high)	High-protein formula (from banana powder) for patients with diarrhea and celiac diseases (see Chapter 24)

*Including sodium and potassium. Content of sodium present may be low, moderate, or high as indicated in parentheses.

functioning (or slightly defective) intestine is a candidate for a whole-protein source, which is cheaper and more palatable.

Commercial nutrient solutions that are now available contain about 40% to 90% of their total calories as carbohydrate, which serves as the main source of energy in these formula diets. The type of carbohydrate is very important in deciding which solution is best for a patient. If fat does not contribute significantly to the caloric content, a large amount of mono- and disaccharides will be used. Because of their small particle size, they can increase the osmolality of the diet. This high osmolality can cause the "dumping" syndrome (see Chapters 24 and 29) and result in diarrhea and abdominal pain. However, if fat replaces the carbohydrate as a source of calories, the osmolality will be reduced.

Formulas with polysaccharides and certain oligosaccharides as the major carbohydrates have low osmolalities. Polysaccharides include starches, which are chains of hundreds of glucose molecules; suitable oligosaccharides should contain more than five glucose molecules per chain (see Chapter 3). Because low osmolality decreases the incidence of diarrhea and intestinal

pain, a much larger quantity of the product may be used. Because of the bland flavor of this mixture of carbohydrate, a small amount of sucrose and glucose is often added to make the formula more palatable. The products currently available may contain corn syrup solids, fructose, sucrose, lactose, mashed or pureed fruits and vegetables, and juices.

At present, between 0% and 47% of the total calories of most commercial nutrient solutions come from fat. Because of their organic and nonpolar nature, fats do not dissolve in an aqueous medium and thus do not affect osmolality. Because of this, they are good sources of calories and can increase the palatability of the formulas as well. Triglycerides in the formulas come in two forms: (1) long-chain fatty acids, as in corn, soy, and safflower oil; or (2) a mixture of long-chain and medium-chain fatty acids, such as soy or corn oil plus fractionalized coconut oil (which contains MCTs).

Table 23-27 presents some common examples of complete defined-formula diets containing intact or complete protein and milk. Table 23-28 presents some examples of those formulas containing protein isolates, intact protein, and

TABLE 23-27   Complete Defined-Formula Diets Containing Intact or Complete Protein and Milk

Product (manufacturer)	kcal/mL	Protein Source	Carbohydrate Source	Fat Source	Osmolality*	Volume to Provide 100% RDA (mL)[†]
Compleat B (Doyle)	1	Nonfat milk, beef	Sucrose, maltodextrin, fruits, vegetables, orange juice, lactose	Corn oil	1.75	1,000
Formula 2 (Cutter)	1	Nonfat milk, beef	Sucrose, dextrose, farina, vegetables, orange juice, lactose	Corn oil, egg yolk	1.79	2,000
Meatbase Formula 142 (Hospital Diet Products)	1.50	Nonfat milk, soy protein isolate, beef	Fruits, vegetables, dextrose	Corn oil	2.59	1,000
C.I.B.[‡] (Carnation)	1.14	Nonfat milk, sodium caseinate, soy protein	Sucrose, corn syrup solids, lactose	Milk fat	Unknown	1,373
Meritene Liquid (Doyle)	1	Concentrated skim milk, sodium caseinate	Corn syrup solids, sucrose, lactose	Vegetable oil, mono- and diglycerides	2.59	1,200
Meritene[‡] (Doyle)	1	Nonfat milk, whole milk	Corn syrup solids, lactose	Milk fat	2.46	1,095
Nutri-1000 (Syntex)	1.04	Skim milk	Sucrose, corn syrup solids, lactose	Corn oil	1.79	1,920
Sustacal liquid (Mead Johnson)	1	Concentrated skim milk, sodium and calcium caseinate, soy protein	Sucrose, corn syrup solids, lactose	Soy oil	2.23	1,080
Sustacal[‡] (Mead Johnson)	1	Nonfat milk, whole milk	Sucrose, corn syrup solids, lactose	Milk fat	2.7	1,500
Sustagen[§] (Mead Johnson)	1.67	Nonfat milk, whole milk, calcium caseinate	Corn syrup solids, glucose, lactose	Milk fat	4.76	1,050

Note: Minerals and vitamins present in all formulations in varying degrees.

*Numbers refer to the approximate ratio of osmolality of solution to osmolality of body fluid, which is assumed to be 280 mosm.

[†]In vitamins and minerals.

[‡]Whole milk added.

[§]Water added.

TABLE 23-28 Complete Defined-Formula Diets Containing Protein Isolates and Intact Protein That Are Low in Lactose and Residue

Product (manufacturer)	kcal/mL	Protein Source	Carbohydrate Source	Fat Source	Osmolality*	Volume to Provide 100% RDAs (mL) [†]
Compleat Modified [‡] (Doyle)	1.07	Peas, green beans, beef	Hydrolyzed cereal solids, peas, green beans	Corn oil	1.07	1,500
Ensure (Ross)	1.06	Soy protein, sodium and calcium caseinate	Corn syrup solids, sucrose	Corn oil	1.61	1,920
Ensure Osmolite (Ross)	1.06	Soy protein isolates, sodium and calcium caseinate	Corn syrup solids	Corn oil, soy oil, MCTs	1.01	1,920
Ensure Plus (Ross)	1.48	Soy protein, sodium and calcium caseinate	Corn syrup solids, sucrose	Corn oil	2.14	1,920
Isocal (Mead Johnson)	1.04	Soy protein, sodium caseinate	Corn syrup solids	Soy oil, MCTs	1.25	1,920
Lolactene (Doyle)	0.8	Nonfat dry milk, sodium caseinate	Corn syrup solids, sucrose, glucose, galactose, lactose (very little)	Vegetable oil, mono- and diglycerides	2.39	1,150
Nutri-1000 LF (Cutter)	1.19	Soy protein isolates, sodium and calcium caseinate	Corn syrup solids	Soy oil (partially hydrogenated)	1.70	1,500
Precision HN (Doyle)	1.05	Egg white solids	Maltodextrin, sugar	Vegetable oil, mono- and diglycerides	1.99	2,950
Precision Isotonic (Doyle)	0.96	Egg white solids	Maltodextrin, sugar	Vegetable oil, mono- and diglycerides	1.07	1,560
Precision LR (Doyle)	1.11	Egg white solids	Maltodextrin, sugar	Vegetable oil, mono- and diglycerides	1.88	1,710
Precision MOD N (Doyle)	1.21	Egg white solids	Maltodextrin, sugar	Vegetable oil, mono- and diglycerides	1.41	1,650
Portagen (Mead Johnson)	1	Sodium caseinate	Maltodextrin, sucrose, lactose, and other substances	Corn oil, MCTs, lecithin	1.28	960

Note: Minerals and vitamins present in all formulations in varying degrees.

*Numbers refer to the approximate ratio of osmolality of solution to osmolality of body fluid, which is assumed to be 280 mosm.

[†] In vitamins and minerals.

[‡] The formula is not as low in residue as others in this table.

TABLE 23-29 Infant Formulas Containing Intact or Complete Protein and Protein Isolates That Are Low in Lactose and Residue

Product (manufacturer)	kcal/mL	Protein Source	Carbohydrate Source	Fat Source	Osmolality
Isomil (Ross)	0.67	Soy protein isolate, L-methionine	Corn syrup, sucrose	Soy oil, corn oil, coconut oil	Not known
Mull-Soy (Syntex)	0.67	Soy flour	Sucrose, invert sucrose	Soy oil	0.9
Neo-Mull-Soy (Syntex)	0.67	Soy protein isolate, L-methionine	Sucrose	Soy oil	0.98
ProSobee (Mead Johnson)	0.67	Soy protein isolate, L-methionine	Sucrose, corn syrup solids	Soy oil	0.92

Note: Minerals and vitamins present in all formulations in varying degrees.

TABLE 23-30 Complete Defined-Formula Diets Containing Hydrolyzed Proteins and/or Amino Acids That Are Low in Lactose and Residue

Product (manufacturer)	kcal/mL	Protein Source	Carbohydrate Source	Fat Source	Osmolality*	Volume to Provide 100% RDA (mL)[†]
Flexical (Mead Johnson)	1	Hydrolyzed caseinate, amino acids	Sugar, dextrin, citrate	Soy oil, MCTs	2.58	2,000
Vital (Ross)	1.18	Hydrolyzed soy, whey and meat, amino acids	Glucose oligo- and polysaccharides	Sunflower oil	1.60	1,500
Vivonex (Norwich-Eaton)	1	Crystalline amino acids	Glucose oligosaccharides	Safflower oil	1.79	1,800
Vivonex HN (Norwich-Eaton)	1	Crystalline amino acids	Glucose oligosaccharides	Safflower oil	3.04	3,000

Note: Minerals and vitamins present in all formulations in varying degrees.

*Numbers refer to the approximate ratio of osmolality of solution to osmolality of body fluid, which is assumed to be 280 mosm.

[†]In vitamins and minerals.

very little lactose and residue. Table 23-29 describes some infant formulas containing protein isolates, intact protein and/or amino acids, and little lactose and residue. These formulas can also be considered as complete defined-formula diets for adults. Table 23-30 presents some examples of formulas containing hydrolyzed proteins and/or amino acids with little lactose and residue. Table 23-31 describes infant formulas that contain hydrolyzed proteins and are low in lactose and residue. These are also suitable for adults. Figure 23-1 shows recovery of a child fed

TABLE 23-31   Infant Formulas Containing Hydrolyzed Proteins That Are Low in Lactose and Residue

Product (manufacturer)	kcal/mL	Protein Source	Carbohydrate Source	Fat Source	Osmolality
Nutramigen (Mead Johnson)	0.67	Hydrolyzed casein	Sucrose, tapioca, starch	Corn oil	1.58
Pregestimil (Mead Johnson)	0.67	Hydrolyzed casein	Glucose, tapioca, starch	Corn oil, MCTs	2.17

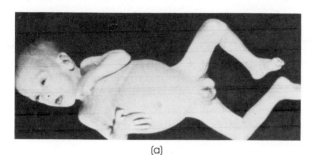

(a)

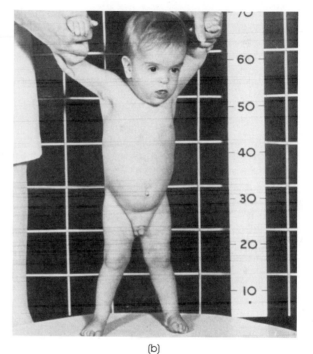

(b)

FIGURE 23-1   Use of a chemically defined fat-free liquid diet in the nutritional management of catabolic disease in infants. (From R. V. Stephens et al. *American Journal of Surgery* 1972; 123:373.) (a) Ten-month-old male infant suffering from unknown malabsorption syndrome who had gained only 960 g since birth. (b) Growth seen after 111 days of continuous chemical diet therapy supplying an average daily intake of 125 kcal/kg. Total weight gain was 3,060 g, which was accompanied by a 20-cm increase in body length and increased muscular strength, activity, coordination, alertness, and responsiveness.

a commercial chemically defined liquid via naso-gastric feeding tube.

Considerations when using commercial formulas. Commercial formulas have both advantages and drawbacks. All commercial defined-formula diets can reduce stomach acidity by increasing the pH. They also reduce the release of enzymes from the pancreas because they hardly stimulate this organ. Since they are pre-digested, they are especially helpful for individuals with minimal ability to digest and absorb foods. They are a potent source of nutrients when the patient is restricted to clear soup, tea,

water, and carbonated beverages for a prolonged period. In addition, they have been shown to permit normal growth and the attainment of ideal body weight in a patient, and they can accelerate wound healing.

The action of commercial diet formulas in the intestines can also be beneficial. In the large intestine (colon), they are responsible for extremely low residue. In addition to decreasing bulk content, they may decrease colon bacteria with little effect on the types of bacteria present. Although they can increase intestinal secretion, there is minimal peristaltic activity.

Commercial formulas can be served in many

forms—chilled, cooled, or warmed. They can also be used as ingredients in Popsicles, ice cream, snow cones, sauces, puddings, and numerous other preparations. They come in many flavors and can also be added to beverages, pastry mixes, and so on, if the patient prefers. They can be used both days and nights and be used as medicine by serving them at nonmeal times. When informed that this "medication" can improve their well-being, some patients are more willing to drink them, especially those who have been refusing foods. Many hospitals use these commercial preparations since they are easy to order, prescribe, and administer.

Although commercial liquid nutrient solutions have many advantages, they have some problems. Since the products come in a form requiring only dilution, their nutritional compositions are fixed. This situation can create mild discomfort to high risk for some patients. For example, a patient with congestive heart failure cannot use any formula containing sodium. A bedridden patient may not tolerate the high concentration of calcium in some nutrient supplements.

Another problem is that most formulas provide adequate calories only in large volumes, a situation posing obvious difficulties to people who work with these products.

Experienced practitioners in this field have suggested three ways to remedy the rigid composition of the formulas. Whenever feasible, any necessary nutrient that is low or missing may be added, while any nutrient present in excess may be reduced by a larger dilution with a concomitant addition of essential nutrients. Second, with the necessary facility and resources, some experienced health teams can make their own complete defined-formula diets. Clinical reports have indicated some success. Some manufacturers are currently experimenting with a third alternative: making a standard solution to which nutrients may be added as needed.

The increasing complexity and variety of commercial formulas pose another problem of sorts: To derive maximal benefit from the products, the health team—the doctor, the dietitian, and the nurse—must have a good working knowledge of the characteristics of available formulas so that the most appropriate one can be selected.

In deciding whether to use a commercial formula and which one, the health team should take many factors into account. The type of disorder and the patient's clinical conditions determine when to use the formula diets and whether to use oral or tube feeding. If the formula is taken orally, then palatability, acceptability, and the period of use are extremely important considerations. If tube feeding is used, the type of tube and the rate of drip are important.

Whether formulas are given orally or by tube, determining which formula to use depends on the patient's clinical condition and the known characteristics of the formula, such as osmolality; protein, carbohydrate, and fat content; and caloric density. If maldigestion or malabsorption is present, a formula with amino acids and hydrolyzed protein may be used; otherwise, the patient may be fed regular liquid and semiliquid foods. If the patient has milk intolerance, he may need a formula without lactose.

A decision must also be made regarding the cost:benefit ratio. The cheapest preparation is probably one prepared by the patient or family. Hospital-prepared formulas may or may not be cheaper than commercial products, whose costs vary widely. Economy must be weighed against possible benefits that more expensive preparations might offer the patient.

In addition to being used exclusively in treating patients with specific clinical disorders, enteral feeding may be used simultaneously with parenteral feeding or as a transition to parenteral feeding. On the other hand, it may also be used to enable the intestine to adapt slowly to regular foods after parenteral feeding is ended and before the resumption of a solid food diet.

Parenteral Feedings

Under certain circumstances, which are discussed below, a patient needs to be nourished directly through the bloodstream, bypassing the gastrointestinal system. Procedures used vary in nutritional adequacy from the very temporary standard intravenous (IV) therapy to the potentially nutritionally complete technique of total parenteral nutrition.

The patient's overt responses can be monitored to evaluate the effectiveness of parenteral feeding methods. These responses include weight gain and maintenance, complexion/perfusion, the degree of hydration, the extent of diarrhea or steatorrhea, the response to environmental routine (e.g., understanding questions and providing answers, noticing light intensity, requesting water), and a general feeling of well-being.

Standard IV therapy

In standard intravenous therapy, a supportive system of fluids and electrolytes (usually sodium, ammonium chloride, and dextrose solutions of 5% to 20%) is used. The solution is given in isotonic form to avoid any disturbance in osmolality during the infusion via peripheral veins. The nutrient contribution of this method is *minimal*. It is used for emergency situations such as the period after childbirth, the immediate postoperative period, and periods immediately after poisoning. The patient is kept on this treatment for a very short period (1 to 2 days) to avoid semistarvation.

Simple modified IV feeding

Clinicians have sometimes resorted to a simple modified IV solution (also administered through peripheral veins) that is slightly more nutritious and complicated than the standard IV solution. Additional nutrients used may include calories, vitamins, minerals, and, recently, pure amino acids and hydrolyzed proteins. The amounts of these nutrients are usually low to moderate. Theoretically, such nourishment can prevent the degradation of lean body mass or body wasting when IV therapy is administered for 3 or 4 days.

Near total parenteral nutrition

Sometimes it is advantageous to provide a patient with intravenous feedings that will provide nearly complete nutrition. Solutions used for near total parenteral nutrition (sometimes known as "hypotonic intravenous alimentation") may contain amino acids, amino acids plus dextrose, amino acids plus fat, or amino acids plus dextrose and fat. Vitamins and minerals may or may not be present. The osmolality of such solu-

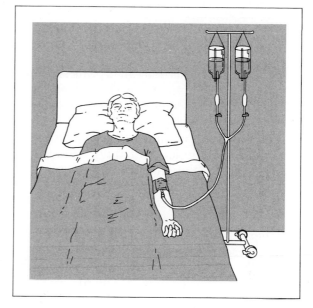

FIGURE 23-2   Conventional intravenous feeding via peripheral veins.

tions is hypotonic and especially suited for infusion through the peripheral veins.

Near total parenteral nutrition is appropriate for almost any patient who requires good temporary nutritional support. For example, it may be used during the transitional periods between nonoral and oral or oral and total parenteral nutrition. However, this approach has many disadvantages. First, the amount of nutrients that can be administered is limited because of the hazards of excess volume, especially for young and elderly patients. By itself, the infusion is therefore unable to support the patient nutritionally and weight loss continues. Second, the continuous infusion of amino acids raises the serum urea nitrogen level, posing an additional risk. And third, when the patient is experiencing a high rate of metabolism, the lack of calories for glucose production will lower the blood glucose.

Some clinical reports indicate that patients fare better when tube-fed than when given near total parenteral nutrition. Cost:benefit:risk analyses imply that this mode of feeding should not be randomly used. Nevertheless, some clinicians who have tried near total parenteral nutrition prefer it to other forms of enteral and parenteral feeding.

Figure 23-2 illustrates conventional intravenous feeding via peripheral veins.

Total parenteral nutrition

Within the last few years, many major medical centers in the country have established parenteral nutrition units that can provide partial or total intravenous nourishment to patients when indicated. Total parenteral nutrition (TPN) provides an adequate amount of calories, protein, fat, carbohydrate, vitamins, and minerals.

Because of the large quantity of nutrients involved, TPN solutions cannot be introduced subcutaneously, intramuscularly, or intraperitoneally. Furthermore, the mandatory hyperosmolality or hypertonicity of the solutions makes peripheral infusion impossible. The nutrients must instead be administered via a central venous access into an area with rapid blood flow (in an adult, the subclavian vein is used).

If feasible, TPN should be started early to prevent unnecessary starvation and to reverse deteriorating clinical conditions. TPN must be individualized, especially the nutrient requirements. Careful monitoring is necessary to make sure that the patient is fed orally as soon as his or her condition permits, at which time TPN is reduced or terminated.

Detailed analyses of this method can be found in the references listed at the end of this book. Advantages, disadvantages, individualized nutrient requirements, and the long-term use of TPN are briefly discussed in the following subsections. Below is a list of some situations where TPN might be the preferred route of feeding.

1. Oral feeding inadvisable or impossible.
2. Use of tube feeding or other forms of enteral nutrition impracticable or grossly inadequate for an extended period of time because of aspiration pneumonia, coma, intestinal bleeding, etc.
3. Need for intense nutritional therapy and support. For example, nutritional need may be heightened before and after operations and after trauma such as burns or body injuries.
4. Highly unsatisfactory nutritional status accompanied by other complications such as sepsis. An overt indication is 10% or more below normal body weight.
5. Thereapeutic adjunct for the clinical management of patients with certain chronic dis-

orders such as cancer or renal, respiratory, or hepatic failure.
6. Necessity for forced feedings because of refusal of foods for various reasons including psychiatric disturbances (such as anorexia nervosa).
7. Necessity for the intestinal system to have a prolonged rest.
8. Temporary intense nutritional support where required.

Advantages. Total parenteral nutrition is increasingly used because of its many advantages. It directly provides body organs with concentrated calories, amino acids, essential fatty acids, vitamins, and minerals. Nutrients are completely used, without the waste involved in enteral alimentation. The gastrointestinal tract is permitted to rest, a consideration that is especially important when the tract is suffering from a lesion or an operation. TPN gives the body ample opportunity to rehabilitate and replenish itself.

TPN can also lead to the speedy rehabilitation and repair of organs and tissues because of the direct availability of nutrients. It can lead to weight gain, a positive nitrogen balance, wound healing, the spontaneous closure of fistulas, and the synthesis of hormones and enzymes. Risks from TPN can be minimized through the appropriate training of administering personnel and the use of appropriate equipment. When conducted both carefully and aggressively, TPN can hasten recovery and improve the patient's recovery from the primary disorder. Since the introduction of TPN, hospital malnutrition has been diagnosed and treated more frequently and effectively than in previous years.

Disadvantages. Despite its advantages, TPN has many side effects and complications. The procedure is expensive, inconvenient, complicated, and time consuming. Nutrient deficiencies have been documented, especially in essential amino acids, fatty acids, and trace minerals. Metabolic disturbances from TPN may include: fluid and electrolyte imbalance, hyper- and hypoglycemia, abnormal hormonal profile, and hyperammonemia. An "overloading syndrome" has been reported from the infusion of fat, and sepsis can occur around the entrance of the

Intravenous Alimentation After Removal of Intestine*

At age 63, Lorene L. was nearing retirement. She had served the town as schoolteacher for almost 40 years. She had a reputation for humorlessness, but she was fair and demanding and her pupils remembered her classes with affection. She was a prototype "schoolmarm." Single (although there were rumors of a brief and unsuccessful early marriage), she lived in a small apartment in the company of three cats and a parakeet.

Medical problems had occupied much of her spare time over the last 10 to 15 years, and she saw her doctor often, complaining of vague and recurrent abdominal pain for which no cause was ever found. Indeed, only one month earlier her abdominal complaints had led to hospitalization; upper gastrointestinal and gallbladder radiographs were normal, and ultrasonogram of the pancreas showed no abnormality. As before, the diagnosis was "functional bowel disease" and she was treated, also as before, with 10 mg of dicyclomine hydrochloride and 5 mg of diazepam (Valium), three times daily.

Emergency Evaluation and Management

Therefore, the phone call on the day of admission came as a surprise to her doctor. A neighbor called to say that Lorene was in serious distress: Several days of intermittent abdominal pain had markedly worsened in the early morning. The pain (for the first time) radiated to her midback and she was vomiting almost continuously. Her doctor arranged to meet her in the hospital emergency room. On the way, her pain became so severe that the neighbor stopped at a local hospital. Meperidine had to be given before Lorene was able to continue on to the hospital to keep her appointment.

On examination, she was afebrile with a blood pressure of 150/70 mm Hg and a pulse of 76 beats/min. She complained of abdominal pain, but the abdomen was soft and not distended. Infrequent bowel sounds were present and there was no tenderness on palpation. Heart and lungs were normal. She was not jaundiced. White blood cell count was 9,700/mm³ with a normal differential. Urine was clear. Blood chemistries, including serum amylase, were normal. She was admitted for observation.

That night Lorene's temperature rose to 103 F. Her abdomen was diffusely tender but without rebound. Abdominal radiographs showed distended loops of small bowel consistent with obstruction. White blood count rose to 16,000/mm³ with 73% neutrophils and 14% band forms. She was begun on intravenous cephalexin (Keflex) with prompt defervescence, but her pains did not improve. Serum potassium fell to 2.9 mEq/l and potassium chloride was added to the intravenous infusion. Bowel sounds disappeared, and her abdomen became distended and tympanitic.

At laparotomy the small bowel was found infarcted and dead, due to a midgut volvulus. The surgeon resected 200 cm of small intestine and 12 cm of colon, leaving 28 cm of jejunum beyond Treitz' ligament. The jejunal remnant was successfully anastomosed to the ascending colon.

Postsurgical Course

After surgery Lorene's temperature again rose to 103 F and she was given cephalexin and gentamicin (Garamycin). Bowel sounds returned and she passed a spontaneous bowel movement on the third postoperative day. Within five days after surgery, her serum protein concentration had fallen from its initial value of 6.7 to 5.4 gm/dl, and serum cholesterol from 215 to 129 mg/dl. In anticipation of the need for prolonged intravenous alimentation (while her intestinal remnant "adapted"), she was transferred to the medical center.

*Source: F. A. Neelon, Drug Therapy 10 (February 1980): 121–122.

On arrival her temperature was 102.2 F, blood pressure 100/40 mm Hg, and her pulse 108 beats/min and regular. There were dullness and diminished breath sounds over the right lower thorax. Heart examination was normal. The abdomen was slightly distended and tympanitic, but good bowel sounds were present. There was no guarding, rigidity, or rebound tenderness.

Chest radiograph showed a right-sided pleural effusion and lower lobe pulmonary infiltrate. Blood gases showed a PO_2 of 78 mm Hg and PCO_2 of 33. Upper gastrointestinal series showed a normal small bowel remnant with a patent anastomosis to the colon. Abdominal ultrasound showed no subphrenic or hepatic abscess. Serum urea nitrogen was found to be elevated at 79 mg/dl and gentamicin was stopped.

Initiation of Parenteral Nutrition

The surgical consultant from the parenteral nutrition team recommended transfer to his service for prolonged intravenous alimentation. After bowel adaptation, he thought oral feeding would maintain her weight at about 80% of predicted ideal. The next day she was taken to the operating room, and under local anesthesia a feeding catheter was placed in the left superior vena cava via the left subclavian vein. Parenteral nutrition was begun with 2 liters/day of fluid containing 50 gm carbohydrate, 39 gm crystalline amino acids, and appropriate amounts of sodium, potassium, chloride, calcium, and phosphorus. Total administered calories were calculated at 1,800/day.

Lorene remained febrile with temperature spikes to 102 F. The abdominal wound was red and somewhat fluctuant; it was opened and 10 ml of foul-smelling pus removed. Culture grew *Escherichia coli*, sensitive to ampicillin, and she received intravenous ampicillin and four units of packed red blood cells. Thoracentesis yielded 50 ml of grossly bloody fluid, which proved sterile on culture. Pulmonary embolism was suspected, but the patient refused to undergo arteriography and so heparin was begun empirically.

Over the next two weeks Lorene did fairly well. She began physical therapy. Her serum urea nitrogen stabilized and urine output was good. Intravenous amino acid dose was increased to 66 gm/day. However, she remained febrile until cephalexin was substituted for ampicillin. Thereafter, her temperature became normal but she complained of weakness. A stool sample was black and gave a positive reaction for blood. Gastric aspiration yielded 200 cc of guaiac-positive black material. Heparin was stopped and she was treated with three units of packed red blood cells. Gastric lavage with iced saline controlled the bleeding. Subsequent endoscopy showed multiple gastric mucosal erosions. Cimetidine (Tagamet) and antacids were prescribed, and there was no further gastrointestinal bleeding.

Management of Fistula

Lorene maintained her weight but continued to feel "unwell." One month after her initial surgery she began to bleed from the wound. An arteriole was identified and ligated, but the next day some 20 ml of feculent material drained spontaneously from the wound. Gentle pressure on the abdomen resulted in expression of flatus through the wound, confirming the presence of an enterocutaneous fistula. The wound was packed with iodoform gauze and intravenous alimentation increased to 2,800 calories/day.

Her serum urea nitrogen began to fall and as it did, her serum calcium increased to 11 and then 12 mg/dl. Calcium was omitted from her intravenous fluids. Renal function continued to improve, and serum calcium slowly returned to normal, which was consistent with a diagnosis of transient hypercalcemia during recovery from acute renal failure. Her wound became dry, and antibiotics were stopped. The enterocutaneous fistula had closed.

Setback and Recovery

Lorene had been hospitalized nearly two months. Her weight was stable and she was taking small amounts of food by mouth with only occasional diarrhea. However, the nurses noted that she began "not to participate" in her care. She refused to see the physical therapist. She refused to dress in clothes or to try walking. She wouldn't eat. Her surgeon thought she "looked depressed" and asked for psychiatric consultation. At the suggestion of the psychiatrist,

doxepin (Adapin, Sinequan) was started at 50 mg nightly and later increased to 100 mg. Lorene became more talkative and alert. She and the psychiatrist began to discuss her plans for the future, for disability retirement, for living alone or moving to another city to live with her niece.

Ten weeks after her surgery Lorene left the hospital. It was not certain yet that she would need no further parenteral nutrition. But her renal function was normal, her strength was good, and she was hopeful for the future, and she weighed six pounds more than when she entered the hospital.

TABLE 23-32   Characteristics of Some Amino Acids/Protein Hydrolysate Injections

Product	Manufacturer	Volume (mL)	mosm/L	Amino Acids/Protein Hydrolysate Content
Amigen 5%	Travenol	500, 1,000	430	5% protein hydrolysate
Amigen 10%	Travenol	500	860	10% protein hydrolysate
Aminosol 5%	Abbott	700	292	5% protein hydrolysate
Aminosyn 3.5%M	Abbott	1,000	460	Amino acids 3.5%
Aminosyn 5%	Abbott	250, 500, 1,000	500	Amino acids 5%
CPH 5%	Cutter	1,000	528	5% protein hydrolysate
FreeAmine II 8.5%	Abbott	500	850	Amino acids 8.5%
Nephramine	McGaw	250	420	Essential amino acids 5.1%
3.5% Travasol M with Electrolyte 45	Travenol	500, 1,000	450	Amino acids 3.5%
5.5% Travasol without electrolytes	Travenol	500	520	Amino acids 5.5%
8.5% Travasol with electrolytes	Travenol	500	1,160	Amino acids 8.5%
8.5% Travasol without electrolytes	Travenol	500	860	Amino acids 8.5%
Veinamine	Cutter	500	950	Amino acids 8%

Note: This list should not be used as a direct clinical reference. A clinical practitioner should refer to standard pharmaceutical literature for a comprehensive and updated listing of such intravenous products. The information in this table provides a general idea of the products used in TPN.

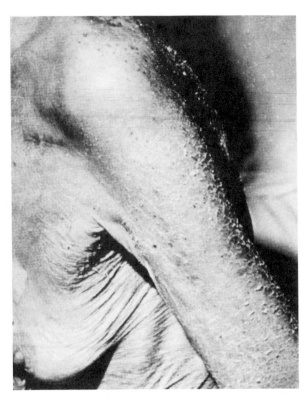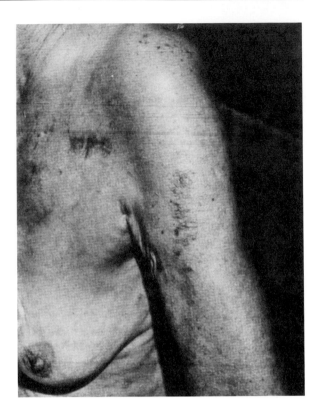

FIGURE 23-3   *Left*: Severe exfoliative dermatitis developing in patient receiving TPN. *Right*: Two weeks after daily administration of 500 mL of Intralipid. (From: M. C. Riella et al., *Annals of Internal Medicine* 83 [1975]: 786)

catheter into the subclavian or central vein. Although most patients can tolerate the feeding well, nausea and vomiting have been noted in some. Decreasing the rate of infusion can reduce these two side effects. Other side effects include an abnormal liver function and allergy.

Nutrient requirements. The specific nutrient requirements of patients vary. It is important to adjust the nutrient contents of TPN to the patient's needs, especially with regard to protein and calories. For example, a burn victim has a much higher need than a patient with kidney failure, and a child's requirements differ from those of an adult.

TPN solutions supply varying amounts of electrolytes, vitamins, and minerals. The levels have not been standardized and may vary from 50% to 150% of the RDA, depending on the particular nutrient and the patient's condition.

Protein and calories are provided in an appropriate ratio with glucose and fat as major sources of calories. L-Amino acids are better utilized than the D forms, and the addition of several nonessential amino acids improves nitrogen retention. At present, experts in this field cannot determine if any commercial amino acid solution is ideal. Table 23-32 presents some commercial protein products for intravenous infusion. In general, glucose provides 25% to 50% of the total calories, and L-amino acids provide 3% to 8%. The patient may need 25 to 50 kcal/kg body weight and 1 to 2 g protein/kg daily.

To avoid essential fatty acid deficiency (see Chapter 5 and Figure 23-3), the infusion of either Intralipid (soybean oil, glycerol, and purified egg phosphatides) or Liposyn (safflower oil, egg phospholipids, glycerine, linoleic acids and other fatty acids) is legally permitted. If the patient cannot tolerate intravenous fat, the topical application of sunflower oil has been shown to be effective.

Home use. The use of TPN has largely been confined to the hospital because of the complications and safety considerations of the technique. However, many patients are now using this means of feeding at home. Most of these patients have a nearly totally malfunctioning digestive system or a part of the intestine removed. Their home-based TPN is known as "ambulatory parenteral nutrition."

Numerous issues should be considered before the clinician permits this practice at home. These include: (1) selection of an appropriate patient (age, clinical condition, living arrangement, suitability for procedure, etc.); (2) evaluating the suitability of the home environment and family members; (3) total understanding and control over technical details by the health team; (4) evidence of successful training and self-support program for the patient; (5) development of a backup unit in case the patient's system fails; and (6) checkup and evaluation.

Figure 23-4 illustrates TPN feeding in a hospital; Figure 23-5 compares a patient before and after TPN feeding.

FIGURE 23-4 Total parenteral feeding as administered in a hospital.

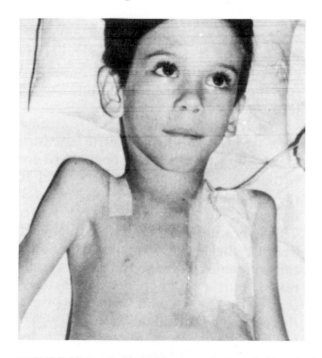
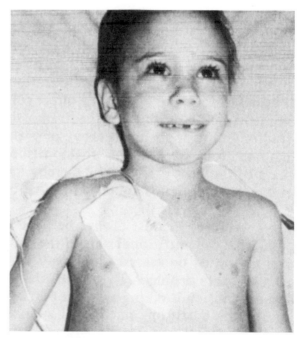

FIGURE 23-5 A child with cancer before (left) and after (right) total parenteral nutrition. (Reprinted with permission from J. van Eys, "Nutrition and Cancer in Children," *The Cancer Bulletin*, 3:[1978] 93–97. Copyright Medical Arts Publishing, Houston)

STUDY QUESTIONS

1. Around what core does hospital diet planning revolve? Give three examples of slight modifications of this basic diet.
2. What is the traditional four-stage progression from most to least easily tolerated foods? What other stages may now be added or substituted? What approach do some hospitals take instead of routine progressive feeding?
3. When is a clear-liquid diet advised? What essential nutrients does it adequately supply?
4. How does a full-liquid diet differ nutritionally from a clear-liquid diet? How adequate is a modified full-liquid diet? What is it?
5. Describe the consistency of a pureed diet, a mechanical soft diet, and a soft diet. For whom might each be prescribed?
6. Give at least seven examples of special dietary foods now available.
7. Define enteral and parenteral feedings.
8. Discuss the nutritional adequacy of tube feedings in general. What supplements may be particularly necessary?
9. How may patients be gradually accustomed to enteral feeding? Discuss the five precautions that must be taken.
10. Discuss some pros and cons of the use of MCT in commercial nutritional formulas. Give at least three advantages and two disadvantages of using commercial liquid nutritional formulas.
11. Describe the four approaches to parenteral feeding. When might each be used?
12. Give at least five advantages and five disadvantages of TPN.

Chapter 24

Diet and Diseases of the Gastrointestinal System

SINCE FOODS MUST pass directly through the gastrointestinal tract under normal conditions, the diet of a patient with intestinal disorder is frequently modified. As we will see in this chapter, some of the traditional forms of dietary management are now considered ineffective or undesirable. Nevertheless, certain diet therapies are very important in managing gastrointestinal conditions.

This chapter will examine dietary considerations in treating common diseases of the stomach, esophagus, and small and large intestines and the conditions of constipation and diarrhea. Many references will be made to medium-chain triglycerides (MCTs), defined formula diets, intravenous hyperalimentation, oral nutrient supplements, routine progressive diets (clear liquid to full liquid to soft diets), bland diets, low- and high-residue diets, and low-fat diets. Detailed information on these topics is provided in other chapters as indicated in the text or the index.

SOME BASIC PROBLEMS WITH CLINICAL MANAGEMENT

Medical practitioners have long encountered a number of fundamental problems when treating patients with gastrointestinal diseases. Anxiety, anger, worry, and other emotional states have often been blamed for the occurrences of some gastrointestinal diseases, and it is well known that they do influence the course of recovery. Also, many symptoms of gastrointestinal diseases are secondary to other specific primary clinical conditions. Therefore, a health practitioner may have to deal with a cause that has nothing to do with the gut. The primary diseases or conditions include obesity, congestive heart failure, endocrine failures, pregnancy, and pneumonia. Finally, intestinal diseases and an abnormal nutritional status are probably parts of a vicious cycle that afflict the patient. For example, the pathological condition of the gut may lead to maldigestion, malabsorption, and subsequent poor utilization of food. The resulting nutritional deficiencies further aggravate the condition of the diseased intestine, repeating the whole cycle.

The nature of intestinal diseases has generated numerous controversies. Consequently, there is no consensus on the diagnosis and treatment of certain diseases. Dietary management often varies with the practitioner and the institute. Another problem is that some practitioners impose rigid dietary regimens without duly considering their effectiveness, side effects, and acceptability to the patients. The treatment of some diseases by excluding certain foods has also come under fire. Although practiced for many years, this approach has recently been criticized for causing nutrient deficiencies, being of doubtful efficacy, creating monotonous and unattractive diets, and disregarding individual needs and conditions and thus leading the patients to stop observing the diet. Despite these controversies, it is generally agreed that, in treating any gastrointestinal disease with dietary manipulation, the physician, nurse, and dietitian should teach the patient about food and develop healthy, lifelong dietary habits.

STOMACH

A discussion of stomach diseases is useful before describing the types of diets important in treating upper gastrointestinal disorders. Refer to Figure 24-1 for names and locations of different parts of the stomach.

Peptic Ulcer

The term *peptic ulcer* is generally used to describe an ulceration found in the lower end of the esophagus or, more commonly, any part of the stomach or duodenum. The affected area is thus exposed to the erosive effect of any acid or pepsin (an enzyme) present.

Symptoms

The outstanding symptoms of a peptic ulcer are pain and discomfort. When located high in the abdomen, just below the front of the chest, the "mid-epigastric" pain is often described as steady, burning, and gnawing, like a severe hun-

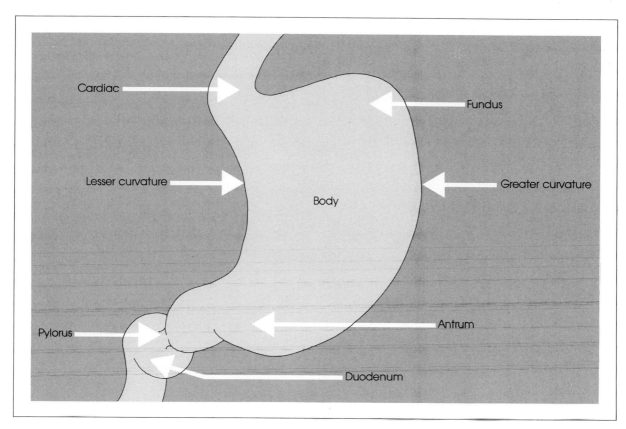

FIGURE 24-1   Parts of the stomach.

ger pain. The pain is periodic, occurring in attacks lasting a few days, weeks, or months, and is usually relieved by food. Frequently the patient is awakened at night with pain. In contrast, functional gastrointestinal discomfort unrelated to ulcers, such as gas and indigestion, rarely awakens the patient.

A number of peptic ulcer patients lose weight. Other symptoms such as vomiting, nausea, and heartburn are less common, although they tend to accompany complicated (e.g., bleeding) peptic ulcers. In these cases, the symptoms include pain radiating into the back and abdominal area. If the patient has a bleeding ulcer, other clinical manifestations include blood in the stools or vomitus.

Etiology

At present, it is generally agreed that the ulceration may be the result of either too much hydrochloric acid or an altered mucosal lining of the affected area showing lowered resistance to whatever amount of acid is present. The secretion of gastric acid is regulated in various ways, such as by drugs or protein (Figure 24-2). Figure 24-3 describes the transformation of the mucosal barrier of the stomach walls from a normal to an altered state. Much research has attempted to determine what is responsible for the increased acid production and mucosal alteration.

Increased acid secretion.   This can be caused by overresponsive or excess number of parietal cells; excess gastrin production; rapid food transit; frequent consumption of alcohol, caffeine, methyl xanthine, theobromine, and similar stimulants.

Rapid food transit may cause continuous ulceration in patients with duodenal ulcers. Food that passes too quickly from the stomach to the duodenum may cause both mechanical and chemical erosion or ulceration of the area. Thus, the ulceration is more severe and prolonged.

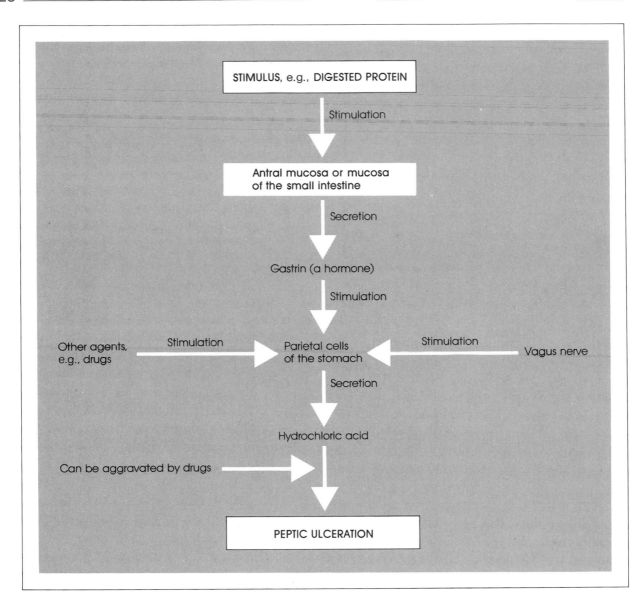

FIGURE 24-2   Secretion of hydrochloric acid by the stomach.

Loss of resistance.   Contemporary research suggests that the stomach mucosa may lose resistance to secreted acid because of several different factors.

If the mucosa exhibits local gastritis, resistance may decrease. Poor nutritional status, alcohol, smoking, drugs, other local irritants, infection, ischemia, and bile reflux are contributing factors in the development of this condition.

Various drugs can either lower the resistance of the mucosal barrier or aggravate any existing ulceration. Aspirin (salicylates), alcohol, antiar-thritis and antigout drugs (such as phenylbuta-zone), analgesics (such as cinchophen), cortico-steroids, and different sedatives and hypotensives (such as rauwolfia) are among those drugs found to lower the resistance of the stomach mucosa.

Epidemiology

Increased acid action and decreased mucosal resistance may cause ulceration. However, the basic question of what causes these changes remains to be answered. Heredity, sex differences,

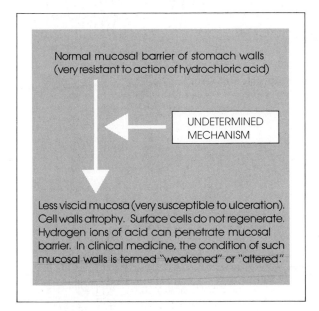

Normal mucosal barrier of stomach walls (very resistant to action of hydrochloric acid)

UNDETERMINED MECHANISM

Less viscid mucosa (very susceptible to ulceration). Cell walls atrophy. Surface cells do not regenerate. Hydrogen ions of acid can penetrate mucosal barrier. In clinical medicine, the condition of such mucosal walls is termed "weakened" or "altered."

FIGURE 24-3   Transformation of stomach mucosal walls.

and serum pepsinogen as well as drugs and smoking, occupational factors, and emotional instability have been implicated.

Heredity.   Heredity may be responsible for peptic ulcers in at least some patients. People who have parents or siblings with a history of gastric or duodenal ulcers have about three times the likelihood of developing ulcers than a control population. The type of ulcer inherited also seems to be inherited, suggesting that gastric and duodenal lesions are inherited independently. Moreover, it appears that if peptic ulcers run in a family, they develop early in life.

Sex differences.   More men have ulcers than women. The incidence of ulcers in women apparently relates to the physiological phases of their life cycle. During active reproductive years, women seem to be protected from ulcers. For example, pregnant women rarely develop active ulcers, and the prepregnancy ulcer symptoms, if they exist, usually disappear shortly after conception, although they reappear shortly after delivery. Menopausal women are more susceptible to ulcer development, symptoms, and complications.

Estrogen, the major female sex hormone, may deter ulceration of the upper gastrointesti-

nal tract. Clinical trials with this hormone did relieve symptoms in some young male patients with duodenal ulcers. However, its potential side effects have discouraged large-scale application.

Serum pepsinogen.   Present research suggests that a combination of increased serum pepsinogen (an enzyme), the presence of certain pepsinogen phenotypes, and a particular psychological profile may indicate the likelihood of a peptic ulcer in some individuals.

Emotional instability.   Emotional instability may predispose a person toward ulcers. People who are chronically anxious or depressed are definitely more prone to develop ulcers than the population in general. Demonstrated neuroses and duodenal ulcers are correlated in some female patients. Neither anxiety nor neurosis can be said to cause ulcers—they are simply seen more often in those people with ulcers. They may thus only be strong predisposing factors.

Occupational factors.   Certain professionals such as doctors, firefighters, and business executives are more likely to have ulcers. The stress and hurry associated with these professions may exacerbate existing physiological tendencies. Bolting food and inadequate chewing are also possible factors for these people.

Drugs and smoking.   For a number of years, drugs and smoking have been implicated as one cause of peptic ulcers. Some common drugs involved have already been mentioned. Heavy smoking is associated with an increased incidence of peptic ulcers, and quitting smoking contributes significantly to the healing of ulcers. However, many nonsmokers also develop ulcers.

Gastric versus duodenal ulcers.   Two common types of peptic ulcers are gastric ulcers and duodenal ulcers. Numerous clinical reports have attempted to compare the symptoms and epidemiology of these two types of ulcers. A list of comparisons is presented in Table 24-1.

Medical management

The goals of ulcer therapy are to relieve pain and discomfort, to hasten healing, to prevent complications, and to avoid recurrences. To achieve these goals, an ulcer patient is usually

TABLE 24-1   A Comparison of Gastric and Duodenal Ulcers

Criterion	Gastric Ulcer	Duodenal Ulcer
Common anatomical site	At the angulus of the stomach; adjacent to the boundary between the mucosa of the body and the antrum	Generally in the duodenal bulb or cap, i.e., the first 5 cm of the duodenum; within a centimeter of the junction between the pyloric and duodenal mucosa
Hydrochloric acid secretion	Usually normal	Usually high
Occurrence of symptoms	Usually on an empty stomach	Usually within ½ to 2 hours after a meal
Relief of symptoms	By ingesting food or antacids or vomiting	By ingesting food or antacids or vomiting
Ulcer seen by X-rays and/or endoscopy	Yes	Yes
Sex-linked factors		
Male:female incidence	2–3:1	6–12:1
Complications and mortality	Higher in men	Higher in men
Acid secretion per unit body weight	No difference between men and women	Higher in men
Female patients	More common	Less common
Percentage of total population affected	1	5–10
Annual new cases per 1,000 males at risk	1–2	3–4
Age of peak occurrence	40–60	30–50
Gastritis	Usually present, severe, and extensive	May or may not be present
Bile reflux	More frequent	Less frequent
Tendency to develop ulcer in an individual with O-type blood who lacks group AB antigen in the saliva	High	Very high

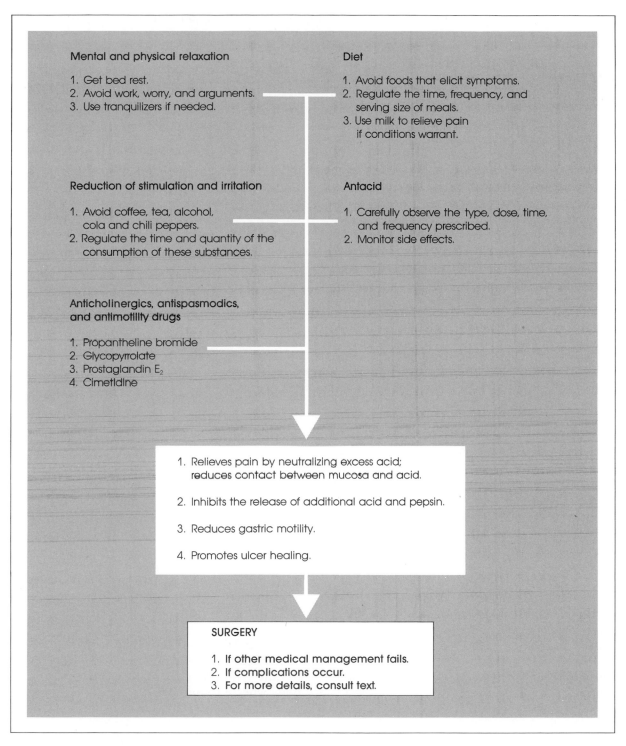

Mental and physical relaxation

1. Get bed rest.
2. Avoid work, worry, and arguments.
3. Use tranquilizers if needed.

Diet

1. Avoid foods that elicit symptoms.
2. Regulate the time, frequency, and serving size of meals.
3. Use milk to relieve pain if conditions warrant.

Reduction of stimulation and irritation

1. Avoid coffee, tea, alcohol, cola and chili peppers.
2. Regulate the time and quantity of the consumption of these substances.

Antacid

1. Carefully observe the type, dose, time, and frequency prescribed.
2. Monitor side effects.

Anticholinergics, antispasmodics, and antimotility drugs

1. Propantheline bromide
2. Glycopyrrolate
3. Prostaglandin E_2
4. Cimetidine

---

1. Relieves pain by neutralizing excess acid; reduces contact between mucosa and acid.

2. Inhibits the release of additional acid and pepsin.

3. Reduces gastric motility.

4. Promotes ulcer healing.

SURGERY

1. If other medical management fails.
2. If complications occur.
3. For more details, consult text.

FIGURE 24-4   Medical management of a peptic ulcer.

TABLE 24-2   Basic Types of Dietary Recommendations for Ulcer Patients with No Complications

Patient Condition	Strict Ulcer Diet	Liberalized Ulcer Diet	Individualized Ulcer Diet	Antacid*	Anticholinergic*
Acute phase with aggravating symptoms	Recommended	Optional	Optional	Hourly	Recommended
Convalescent with occasional symptoms	Optional	Optional	Optional	Hourly	Recommended
Ambulatory	Optional	Optional	Optional	Between meals and at bedtime	Discontinued
Recurring with symptoms	Optional	Optional	Optional	Hourly	May be resumed

Note: Dietitians, nurses, and physicians work together in planning any diet. Details of each diet are provided in the text.
*Prescribed by physicians.

instructed to obtain mental and physical rest, revise the diet, avoid potentially aggravating agents, follow an appropriate antacid treatment, use anticholinergic drugs, and, if conditions warrant, have surgery. Figure 24-4 illustrates the main points of medical management of an ulcer patient.

Diet and irritating agents. The relationship between peptic ulcers and irritating agents in the diet has been very controversial. In the past, the dietary treatment of an ulcer patient was very stringent. For example, the use of milk and bland foods and the avoidance of irritating agents were rigidly prescribed. However, such conservative diet therapy is now believed to pose a number of problems. Although milk can relieve pain, it has not been proven to heal ulcers. Furthermore, the usefulness of a bland diet for an ulcer patient has been seriously questioned. At present, no known clinical or dietary method can heal an ulcer permanently. However, it is generally accepted that certain agents such as caffeine and alcohol can irritate the ulceration.

What should the dietary care be for a patient with an ulcer? The dietary strategy of most practitioners reflects two seemingly contradictory guidelines: "No acid, no ulcer" and "Let the patient enjoy his food." At present, many diet manuals use both conservative and modern diet treatments for ulcer patients. Table 24-2 indi-

cates the different types of diet recommendations. Since antacids and drugs are usually part of clinical care, their usage is also indicated in the table. As shown in Table 24-2, during the acute phase of an ulcer, a physician will usually place a patient on a strict ulcer diet. This consists of an hourly program of 4 oz of whole milk, skim milk, or milk and cream. These feedings begin at 7 AM and continue until 9 PM. The physician might also prescribe these feedings at 2-hour intervals during the night. This is an inadequate diet nutritionally and should be given for only a brief period of time. It may be supplemented with an appropriate vitamin and mineral supplement, especially if the treatment lasts more than 2 or 3 days. In this case, the physician may prescribe other means of nutritional compensation.

Milk has been used to relieve ulcer pain for more than 50 years. Because of the high concentration of protein in milk, it is a very effective buffer (pH 6.7) and thus relieves ulcer pain by neutralizing excess acid. However, milk therapy has the following drawbacks: (1) the calcium in milk, when consumed in excess, can bring about hypercalcemia, which results in the milk-alkali syndrome. Hypercalcemia can also stimulate gastric acid secretion, further aggravating the ulcer. (2) A high consumption of milk can lead to weight gain. This is especially unacceptable for patients who are overweight. (3) Drinking a lot of whole milk can lead to an excessive intake of fat

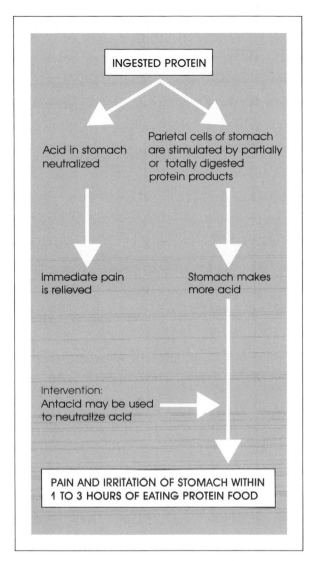

INGESTED PROTEIN

Acid in stomach neutralized

Parietal cells of stomach are stimulated by partially or totally digested protein products

Immediate pain is relieved

Stomach makes more acid

Intervention: Antacid may be used to neutralize acid

PAIN AND IRRITATION OF STOMACH WITHIN 1 TO 3 HOURS OF EATING PROTEIN FOOD

FIGURE 24-5   Contrasting effects of protein in ulcer treatment.

and cholesterol, increasing the risk of myocardial infarction and atherosclerosis. (4) The buffering capacity of milk protein is actually quite weak. Milk protein and its digested products can also eventually stimulate gastric acid secretion (acid rebound). This undesirable effect of protein in ulcer treatment is illustrated in Figure 24-5. As shown in this figure, the use of an antacid may alleviate part of the discomfort from acid rebound.

As shown in Table 24-2, a liberalized ulcer diet may also be prescribed, especially for convalescent and ambulatory patients or patients with recurring symptoms. Details of such a regimen are presented in Tables 24-3 and 24-4. The diet consists of either many small meals or three moderate meals with three snacks interspersed. This diet eliminates substances that irritate the gastric lining or increase the flow of gastric secretions. Nutritionally, the dietary regimen is adequate if the daily food guide shown in Table 24-4 is followed.

Within the last few years, many hospitals and health practitioners have advocated an individualized diet for an ulcer patient not suffering an acute attack (see Table 24-2). Experience indicates that patients enjoy the foods on such a diet and are thus more responsive to the treatment. Table 24-5 describes the details of such a dietary regimen, which has few restrictions.

The dietary management of an ulcer patient is not yet uniform. Some physicians still prescribe the milk regimen initially and then move progressively toward the liberalized diet. Sometimes this practice is called "stage feeding." The patient regulates food intake, paying special attention to blandness and the size and number of servings. On the other hand, many hospitals, especially research university ones immediately begin the individualized diet after the acute phase of the disease has passed.

Regardless of diet, the patient should adopt the following guidelines, with which the dietitian and nurse should help the patient comply: (1) Meals should be regular, frequent, and served in small portions. Four to six feedings a day are preferable. Large meals should be avoided. (2) The time of eating is important. Late evening snacks should be discouraged, since the food may stimulate nocturnal acid secretion, causing loss of sleep. (3) Chewing, eating, and drinking should be done slowly. (4) Stressful activity before and after each meal should be avoided. The patient should rest at these times if possible. (5) Cigarettes and alcohol should be avoided before meals or on an empty stomach. Patients who insist on drinking alcoholic beverages should consume them with food.

Antacid therapy.   Antacid therapy is usually part of the clinical management of an ulcer patient. The prescribing physician should coordinate its use with the dietary plan.

TABLE 24-3   Foods Permitted and Prohibited in a Liberalized Ulcer Diet

Food Group	Foods Permitted	Foods Prohibited
Milk, milk products	Whole milk; skim milk; plain yogurt; milk shakes; egg-nog; evaporated or condensed milk; related products such as chocolate milk, low-fat milk, etc.	Any not tolerated by patient
Eggs	Any type not specifically excluded	Fried and raw* if not tolerated
Meat, poultry, fish, and cheese	Tender chicken, beef, liver, lamb, turkey (meats may be ground, chopped, or pureed if so prescribed); fish, shellfish; cottage cheese, cream cheese, mild cheeses	Meat that is tough, gristly, cured, salted, or highly spiced, such as luncheon meats, sausage, sardines, anchovies, and corned beef
Potatoes or substitute	Mashed sweet or white potato; creamed potatoes and baked without skin; rice; noodles, macaroni, spaghetti	Potato skin; any rice, pasta, or potato that is fried or highly spiced
Cereals and bread	Enriched white bread; cooked refined cereals, corn flakes, Rice Krispies, Puffed Wheat, Puffed Rice; other varieties not excluded	Cereals containing bran, whole grains, nuts, seeds, or dried fruits
Fats	Margarine, butter; sour cream; oils; mayonnaise; shortening; crisp, drained bacon	All others
Soups	Cream soups (may be strained and prepared from any permitted vegetables; use mild seasonings)	Meat broth, bouillon, consommé, other soups prepared with meat extracts; no highly seasoned soups or soups containing dried beans or peas

Four clinical observations emphasize the importance of antacid treatment. First, the medical observation of "No acid, no ulcer" is still valid. Antacids can neutralize hydrochloric acid in the stomach and should theoretically reduce ulceration. Second, the neutralization of acid always reduces peptic activity, thus reducing the ulceration process. Third, the use of antacids in experimental animals has shown that antacids prevent ulcer formation. Fourth, the healing of an ulcer by surgery such as drainage, vagotomy, or pyloroplasty is simultaneously accompanied by a re-

TABLE 24-3   (continued)

Food Group	Foods Permitted	Foods Prohibited
Fruits	Canned applesauce, apricots, cherries, peaches, pears; orange, grapefruit, tomato juice (all acidic citrus juices should be consumed in limited quantities and given when tolerated; may be diluted or sieved before serving and given during a meal; ripe bananas, oranges, grapefruit (membranes removed if not tolerated); fresh, ripe, peeled peaches and pears	Fruits not permitted, especially raw and whole fruits and those with many seeds; coconut; raisins; dried fruits
Vegetables	Canned or well-cooked peas, carrots, asparagus, summer squash, spinach; any strained vegetables	All other whole vegetables, especially if raw; other green vegetables; okra; corn; eggplant
Beverages	Milk drinks, weak tea and decaffeinated coffee, Ovaltine	Alcoholic beverages; coffee, tea; cocoa; carbonated beverages
Desserts	Plain ice cream, sherbet without fruit or nuts; cookies; wafers; custard; gelatin; angel food cake; jelly; plain puddings	Those with raisins, dried fruits, coconut, nuts, etc.
Sweets	Candies, sugar, honey, syrup, marshmallows	Chocolate candy, rich candy with nuts or fruits; preserves, jams, marmalades
Spices and dressings	Sage, paprika, thyme, mace, allspice, cinnamon; salt; cream sauces	Black pepper; chili powder; olives; mustard; nutmeg; dressings with onion, garlic, or vinegar

*Most practitioners do not recommend using raw eggs because of possible salmonella contamination.

duction in acid and pepsin secretion. Some clinicians believe that judicious use of antacids can achieve the same result.

Commercially available antacids vary in potency, effectiveness, and side effects. The attending physician should be familiar with the properties of any antacid prescribed. Antacids come in liquid (suspension) and tablet forms. Tablets are less useful because their neutralizing effect varies. They are also more expensive than liquid antacids, although they are convenient to use. If tablets are used, the patient should be instructed

TABLE 24-4   Daily Food Guide and Two Sample Menus for a Liberalized Ulcer Diet

Daily Food Guide		

2 cups of milk or substitute
2 servings of meat or substitute
4 servings of fruit and vegetables with at least 1
  serving of vitamin C–rich fruit such as oranges
  and 1 serving of deep yellow or dark green
  vegetable such as spinach or squash
4 servings of cereal or bread		

Mealtime	**Menu 1**	**Menu 2**
Breakfast	½ c orange juice 1 poached egg 1 slice toast Margarine Jelly	½ c tomato juice ½ c strained oatmeal 1 c milk Sugar
Mid-morning	½ c Cream of Wheat 1 c milk Sugar	½ c plain pudding

Lunch	3 oz ground beef patty
	1 baked potato (no skin)
	½ c chopped spinach with
	  cheese sauce
	½ c Jell-O made with fruit
	  juice
	Margarine
		3 oz chicken breast
		1 c rice
		1 t butter
		½ c creamed peas
		½ c orange sections (membranes removed)

Mid-afternoon	1 piece plain cake 1 c milk	1 c eggnog

Dinner	3 oz chicken (boiled with
	  ingredients below)
	  ½ c noodles
	  ½ c mashed carrots
	½ c tomato juice
		3 oz chopped liver
		1 c noodles
		½ c asparagus tips
		1 t butter
		½ c Jell-O

Evening snack	½ c cottage cheese 4 crackers	½ c ice cream 4 plain cookies

Note: Fruit juices and other beverages may be taken halfway through each meal.

to chew them thoroughly. Most tablets containing aluminum hydroxide preparations are ineffective and should not be prescribed. The usual prescription is an hourly ingestion of an appropriate number of tablets. Since 1 T of liquid antacid is equivalent in potency to 3 or 4 tablets, the liquid is preferred for patients with an active ulcer.

Antacids containing sodium cannot be prescribed for patients with such conditions as congestive heart failure, hypertension, and ascites; these patients are usually on sodium-restricted

TABLE 24-5   General Principles and a Sample Menu for an Individualized Ulcer Diet

General Principles
Most foods in a regular diet are included that the individual can tolerate. Highly seasoned foods or those that cause excessive gastric juice secretion are eliminated (for example, pepper, chili powder, and caffeine). Whenever possible, the patient should eat three moderate meals and snacks.

Sample Menu Plan

Breakfast	Lunch	Dinner
½ c fruit or juice	2–4 oz meat, fish, etc.	3–5 oz meat, fowl, fish,
½ c cereal	½–1 c potato or	or substitute
1–2 eggs	substitute	1 c potato or alternate
1 sl bread	½ c salad or	½ c salad or
1 t margarine	vegetable	vegetable
1 c milk	1–2 sl bread	1–2 sl bread
Weak tea or decaffei-	1 t margarine	1 t margarine
nated coffee	1 c milk	Weak tea, decaffei-
	Weak tea or decaffei-	nated coffee, or
	nated coffee	other beverage tol-
		erated by patient, in-
		cluding milk and
		milk drinks

Between-meal and evening snacks: milk, ice cream, milk shakes, cookies, crackers, plain cakes, puddings, Jell-O, cottage cheese (no nuts or coconut if not tolerated); amounts served as preferred by patient.

Note: Serving sizes of all meals should be according to individual need and preference.

diets. A patient on an intensive, sodium-bearing antacid therapy may take in approximately 2 to 3 g of sodium per day. Currently the brands of antacid with low sodium contents are Riopan and Magaldrate, which contain less than 2.5 mg of sodium per 10 mL.

Depending on the type of antacid, the patient may suffer from diarrhea, constipation, and fecal impact. Calcium carbonate may lead to constipation, hypercalcemia, and the milk-alkali syndrome. Aluminum hydroxide gel may cause constipation and phosphate depletion, and mixtures of magnesium and aluminum compounds may cause diarrhea. Magnesium oxide preparations may also have laxative effects.

In the past, calcium carbonate was considered an ideal antacid. Now it is known to have two drawbacks. First, long-term ingestion causes hypercalcemia, which can increase the secretion of gastrin, which leads to more acid production. Second, hypercalcemia can cause renal malfunctions and result in the milk-alkali syndrome. Noncalcium antacids, such as liquid magnesium hydroxide, magnesium trisilicate, and aluminum hydroxide, are now preferable.

An antacid has a very short-lasting buffering capacity when ingested on an empty stomach. The buffering effect is much longer when an antacid is taken 1 to 3 hours after a meal. Thus, during the acute phase of an ulcer, a patient is usually asked to take an antacid hourly after each meal, starting at breakfast and continuing until bedtime. However, many patients are awakened by pain at night (often at regular hours). Under these circumstances, the patient should wake up 1 hour before the expected pain and take some antacid. In most patients, this alleviates the pain.

Since patients with gastric ulcers secrete either normal or low amounts of hydrochloric acid, the dose of antacid needed is usually small. One to two tablespoons of Maalox or Mylanta (15 to 30 mL), which contain a mixture of aluminum and magnesium hydroxides, will usually suffice. However, patients with duodenal ulcers tend to secrete acid copiously and therefore require higher doses (30 to 60 mL). The latter dose of Maalox or Mylanta gives the patient an excess amount of magnesium, however, and may produce diarrhea. To counter this side effect, some physicians prescribe Amphogel (40 to 80 mL), which contains only aluminum hydroxide and is as effective as the magnesium-containing antacid.

Recurrences, complications, and surgery

A patient whose ulcer has healed has no assurance that it will not recur, even though current techniques for healing an ulcer are effective. There are no statistics available on the incidence of recurrence, but it probably ranges between 25% to 50% of all ulcer patients within 2 years. Some patients may develop complications in their peptic ulcers that increase their discomfort and damage nearby tissues and organs. Treatment varies, and surgery is used in the most severe cases.

An *intractable ulcer* is one that causes persistent pain and indigestion, resulting in bed confinement and absenteeism from work in spite of intense medical therapy. An intractable ulcer must be distinguished from an intractable patient with an ulcer—one who is probably not following medical advice. Intractable patients will complicate clinical diagnosis, especially if the physician is not aware that they are not complying with the prescribed regimen.

An ulcer with complications may penetrate locally into adjacent organs such as the pancreas, which may cause acute and localized pancreatitis. Another complication may be perforation of the stomach or duodenum. Some clinicians manage this complication with nasogastric suction, intravenous fluids, and antibiotics, but this treatment may be unsuccessful. Also, gastric or duodenal obstruction, especially pylorus obstruction, may result from an active ulcer and its accompanying edema; this may cause food retention.

Some patients develop a hemorrhagic, or bleeding, ulcer. This complication is initially managed by nasogastric suction. Severe bleeding is treated by cleansing the stomach with water or iced saline, which is inserted through a large tube. Antacid and milk are administered after the bleeding has stopped. Blood transfusions and surgery are necessary in some cases.

The upper gastrointestinal tract sometimes becomes scarred from ulceration, and in some cases the ulcer and its surrounding tissue become malignant.

Occasionally complications of peptic ulcers require surgical intervention. This may include any of the following procedures: drainage, vagotomy, pyloroplasty, antrectomy and gastroduodenostomy (Billroth I), gastric resection of two-thirds of the stomach and gastrojejunostomy (Billroth II), or a combination of these procedures. For the dietary management of a patient with stomach surgery, consult Chapter 29.

Gastritis

Gastritis means inflammation of the stomach. There are three main types of gastritis: acute simple gastritis, acute corrosive gastritis, and chronic gastritis. Table 24-6 provides a description of their causes and symptoms. Because gastritis is less common than other disorders of the alimentary tract, only a brief discussion of its medical management is provided below.

In a patient with gastritis, the causal agent must be removed or treated. The patient is provided with routine hospital supportive measures: blood transfusion, antibiotics, fluids and electrolytes, sedatives, and analgesics. If the symptoms are acute and painful, oral feeding is avoided. The patient is placed on progressive diets as soon as they are tolerated. The diets consist first of clear liquids, then full liquids, and finally soft diets (see Chapter 23). Because these diets are nutritionally inadequate, patient cachexia may occur if the treatment is prolonged. Other feeding procedures mentioned in

TABLE 24-6 Causes and Symptoms of Different Types of Gastritis

Type	Causes and Occurrences	Symptoms
Acute simple gastritis	Caused by a virus (e.g., hepatitis), food allergy (e.g., fish, wheat), bacteria or their toxins (e.g., staphylococcus, pneumonia), or chemicals (e.g., aspirin, alcohol, or drugs). Usually accompanied by inflammation of the intestine.	Vomiting, nausea, stomach fullness and tension. Mild epigastric tenderness may be palpitated. If caused by biological agents, general malaise, headache, diarrhea, chills, colic, and muscle pains may be present, sometimes accompanied by dehydration and prostration. If caused by alcohol or other chemicals, bleeding may be present. Most persistent symptom is loss of appetite. All symptoms last 1 to 10 days.
Acute corrosive gastritis	Caused by attempted suicide through poisoning and accidental consumption of corrosive chemicals such as acid, alkali, mercury, and arsenic.	Stomach damage ranges from mild edema to perforation. Nausea, vomiting, diarrhea, stomach cramping, and burning pains present. Esophagus, pharynx, mouth, tongue, and lips may suffer corrosive damage. Discoloration of mucous membranes varies with the chemical ingested. Blood with other stomach contents may be vomited. Epigastric tenderness may be palpitated. Shock, thirst, and prostration may occur.
Chronic gastritis	Causes unknown. Seen in association with stomach and duodenal ulcers. Could be a mild case of acute simple gastritis.	Nonspecific. Loss of appetite and stomach fullness and pressure may be present. Heartburn, vomiting, nausea, food allergy or intolerance (may or may not be specific food), anemia, and hemorrhage may also occur.

Chapter 23 may have to be instituted. After the acute phase, the patient can be fed any of the peptic ulcer diets that can be tolerated.

ESOPHAGUS

In addition to stomach conditions, a number of diseases are directly and indirectly related to the esophagus. They include achalasia, esophageal web, peptic esophagitis, stricture, and hiatus hernia. Table 24-7 briefly describes these diseases and their symptoms. Some terms used in Table 24-7 are *dysphagia*, which means difficulty in swallowing; *odynophagia*, pain accompanying the swallowing of food; *melena*, fecal darkening by blood pigments; *melenemesis*, vomiting of black

matter due to staining by blood; and *hematemesis*, the vomiting of blood.

Lesions of the esophagus are less common than other gastrointestinal disorders. Therefore, only a brief summary of the medical management of esophageal diseases is presented in Table 24-8.

SMALL INTESTINE

The major clinical problem of the small intestine is the *malabsorption syndrome*, which involves a failure to absorb nutrients properly. Nutrient malabsorption may be due to: (1) a failure in digestion because of the lack of bile salts, digestive enzymes, and/or normal peristalsis; (2) a

TABLE 24-7 Clinical Characteristics of Selected Diseases of the Esophagus

Clinical Entity	Symptoms	Description
Achalasia or cardiospasm	Dysphagia and dilatation of esophagus	Cause unknown; lower sphincter or part of esophagus remains closed because of failure of relaxation mechanism
Esophageal webs, sideropenic dysphagia, Paterson-Kelly or Plummer-Vinson syndrome	Dysphagia, iron-deficiency anemia, splenomegaly, spoon-shaped nails, glossitis (patients mainly premenopausal women)	Produced by ulceration, local infection, hemorrhage, or mechanical trauma; most likely result from iron and possibly B vitamin deficiency
Peptic esophagitis, reflux esophagitis	Pyrosis ("heartburn") worsened by recumbency, dysphagia, odynophagia; melena and hematemesis possible as late complications; regurgitation of stomach contents into mouth during night or when bending	Cause unknown; failure of the lower sphincter of esophagus to prevent reflux of either acid or alkaline gastric juice into the esophagus; hiatus hernia, pregnancy, pernicious vomiting, and use of nasogastric intubation may contribute to reflux
Stricture	Dysphagia, odynophagia	Causes include healing from an inflammation, reflux esophagitis, ulceration, ingestion of corrosive substances, acute viral or bacterial infectious diseases
Hiatus hernia or diaphragmatic hernia	Severe pyrosis ("heartburn") initiated or accentuated by recumbency and relieved by sitting upright; pain at the lower sternal level frequently radiates into neck, jaw, or down arms; occasional dysphagia or regurgitation (There may be no symptoms.)	Some causes are aging, obesity, pregnancy, crush injuries, and poor musculature; herniation of a portion of the stomach through the diaphragm; patient may actually suffer from peptic esophagitis due to reflux of stomach contents

failure in absorption because of a deficiency of mucosal enzymes and/or inflammation (or degeneration) of part(s) of the intestinal mucosa; or (3) a failure in transportation because of the blockage of the lymphatic system and the portal veins and/or a deficiency of the blood transport protein.

Symptoms of Intestinal Malabsorption

Symptoms may manifest themselves in overt physical signs such as diarrhea, weight loss, abdominal cramps, distension, and possibly fever. Sometimes less obvious but no less important are symptoms related to vitamin, mineral, and protein deficiencies.

Vitamin K, D, and A deficiencies occur because of a malabsorption of fat (steatorrhea).

Vitamin K deficiency is indicated by purpura, discoloration, and bleeding problems. If accompanied by calcium loss and/or magnesium malabsorption, vitamin D deficiency results in bone problems such as osteoporosis and, in some cases, other disorders such as tetany. Vitamin A deficiency is indicated by a roughening of the skin.

The kind of deficiency involving water-soluble vitamins varies. A lack of folic acid and vitamin B_{12}, which are crucial nutrients, is the likeliest. These deficiencies result in macrocytic or orthochromic anemia (megaloblastic). However, vitamin C and B-group deficiencies can occur with symptoms such as stomatitis, glossitis, dermatitis, and cheilosis.

The most common mineral deficiencies in the malabsorption syndrome involve iron, calcium, and magnesium. However, levels of gen-

TABLE 24-8 Summary of the Medical Management of Esophageal Diseases

Esophageal Disease	Medical Management
Achalasia	Initial treatment: administer sedatives and antispasmodic drugs; have patient eat while standing; try ulcer-type bland diets; if no relief, try secondary treatment Secondary treatment: brusque dilatation and surgery may be indicated; may be given progressive hospital routine diets using small and frequent feedings; use other feeding methods if indicated
Esophageal web	If undernourished, use nutritional rehabilitation; give iron and vitamin supplements if indicated
Peptic esophagitis	Use antacid therapy; have patient adopt most favorable posture and avoid stooping or sitting hunched over, especially after meals; have patient sleep with head and upper trunk propped up; have patient avoid foods not tolerated; may use bland diets
Stricture	Mechanical dilatation; surgery if indicated; if undernourished, use nutritional rehabilitation
Hiatus hernia	Have patient achieve and maintain ideal weight; have patient avoid tight garments and avoid lying down immediately after meals; have patient sleep with head of bed elevated 8 to 10 in.; follow a rigid antacid treatment; permit foods tolerated by patient

eral electrolytes (sodium, potassium, and chloride) should be monitored as well.

Edema is most likely to result from hypoproteinemia or a loss of protein into the intestine caused by damage to the mucosa.

Patients with malabsorption diseases also exhibit symptoms such as increased oxalic acid absorption and lactose intolerance. The former is accompanied by inflammation of the small intestine (also called short-bowel syndrome). This condition increases the risk of developing urinary calculi. The latter is now increasingly observed in patients with malabsorption diseases, even though they may not be genetically predisposed.

Intestinal malabsorption is sometimes associated with *protein-losing enteropathy*. The small and large intestines regulate the excretion and absorption of plasma protein, especially albumin and γ-globulin. Some of the amino acids absorbed are synthesized into serum protein in the mucosal walls. Conversely, serum proteins are excreted into the gut lumen, where they are degraded into constituent amino acids, which may or may not be reabsorbed. A healthy individual has a proper balance of absorption and excretion. However, hypoproteinemia or low serum protein develops when more serum protein is excreted into the gut lumen than is created by the absorption of amino acids and their resynthesis into serum proteins. Thus, protein-losing enteropathy is a symptom secondary to any disease that results in decreased serum protein, especially albumin.

It is currently known that protein-losing enteropathy may accompany any of the following: malabsorption diseases such as Crohn's disease, ulcerative colitis, or celiac sprue; intestinal allergy; and other pathological conditions such as congestive heart failure. More details on these diseases are discussed later. Treatment usually involves treating the cause and providing supportive measures such as intravenous feeding with blood components.

Diagnosis of Malabsorption Diseases

Many techniques exist for diagnosing malabsorption diseases. The three most common ones are a fecal fat excretion test, the D-xylose absorption test, and Schilling's test. More detailed information about these techniques may be obtained from standard medical textbooks, which also discuss the new techniques of breath hydrogen analysis in certain malabsorption diseases.

Fecal fat excretion test

To quantify the amount of fat excreted, the patient should be put on an 80- to 100-g-fat diet supervised by the hospital dietitian and nurse. Fecal matter should be collected for 3 days. Excretion of less than 6 g of fat a day is considered normal. A patient consistently excreting a higher amount of fat is diagnosed as having steatorrhea. For information on low-fat menu planning, consult Chapters 10, 23, and 27.

D-xylose absorption test

Orally ingested, the five-carbon sugar D-xylose does not require digestion and is absorbed easily by the proximal intestine, provided its mucosa is undamaged. The patient is instructed to consume 25 g of D-xylose, and if 4 or more grams are excreted in the urine in the next 5 hours, the intestinal mucosa is normal. However, if a lower amount is excreted, the patient has a malabsorption problem, probably tropical sprue, celiac sprue, blind-loop syndrome, or a number of other malabsorption diseases.

Schilling's test

The patient is given about 0.5 μg of radio-cobalt-labeled vitamin B_{12} orally. After 2 hours, the patient is given a parenteral dose of 1 mg of unlabeled vitamin B_{12}. If under 5% of the radioactivity appears in the urine in 24 hours, then the patient is not absorbing vitamin B_{12}. Normally about 15% to 40% appears. However, as discussed in Chapter 6, this malabsorption can also be due to a lack of the intrinsic factor. Thus, if the simultaneous oral administration of the intrinsic factor increases the excretion of radioactive B_{12} by 500% or more, the malabsorption is diagnosed as gastric mucosal damage. However, if the use of the intrinsic factor does not change the result, then the patient probably has an incompetent intestinal mucosa, especially in the distal part of the ileum. This points to a "real" malabsorption syndrome of the small intestine.

Common Malabsorption Diseases

Table 24-9 lists some common malabsorption diseases of the small intestine. Four of these are discussed below.

Cystic fibrosis

Cystic fibrosis of the pancreas is caused by genetic factors. Inheritance of certain recessive genes results in the malfunctioning of the exocrine glands of the pancreas, sweat glands, and respiratory system. It begins in infancy and exhibits most symptoms of the malabsorption syndrome. For a detailed discussion of this topic, consult Chapter 30.

Pancreatitis

Pancreatitis may be acute or chronic. The disorder results from an inflammatory process involving pancreatic tissue and the peripancreatic bed. The exocrine glandular tissue of the pancreas may be inflamed or scarred. Because of the inflammation, pancreatic enzymes escape from the acinar cells into the surrounding tissue. Thus, the fundamental pathological factor is most likely autodigestion of the gland by its activated enzymes, caused mainly by chronic alcoholism and gallstones. Other causative factors include trauma (blunt or penetrating), hyperlipemia, pregnancy, hyperthyroidism, virus, vascular diseases, uremia, genetic factors, and perforating and penetrating ulcers.

Pain, nausea, vomiting, and an elevated body temperature are the early symptoms of pancreatitis, but they may persist throughout the course of the disease. Diarrhea with steatorrhea,

TABLE 24-9   Common Malabsorption Diseases of the Small Intestine

Cause of Small Intestine Malabsorption	Disease Entity	Precipitating Cause(s)
Absence of digestive juice from pancreas	Cystic fibrosis Pancreatitis	Genetic Many, including alcoholism
Absence of bile	Diseases of the gallbladder and liver	Many, including liver cirrhosis and gallstones
Absence of specific disaccharidases	Deficiency of lactase, maltase, sucrase, isomaltase, or trehalase	Genetic, acquired, other causes
Overpopulation of bacteria in the upper small intestine	Blind-loop syndrome	Anatomical changes because of inflammation or surgery
Specific diseases of small intestinal walls	Crohn's disease Celiac sprue Tropical sprue Radiation enteritis Malignancy	Unknown Unknown, possibly genetic Unknown X-ray exposure Unknown
Surgical resection	Short-bowel syndrome Obesity bypass	Surgical intervention secondary to a specific intestinal disease Jejunoileal shunt or stomach stapling formed by surgical intervention to treat morbid obesity

jaundice, and weight loss with muscle wasting may occur. Some patients show increased iron absorption for unknown reasons. Malabsorption occurs when 75% to 95% of the exocrine pancreas has been destroyed or when obstruction of the pancreatic duct prevents pancreatic secretions from reaching the duodenum. Fat loss in the stool ranges from 5 to 100 g per day. Steatorrhea results from the lack of pancreatic lipase and abnormal emulsification of fat by the bile. Diarrhea is probably caused by excessive active hydroxystearic acids, which stimulate the colon to secrete electrolytes and water. Absorption of vitamin B_{12} is also reduced.

Treatments for nutrition-related problems are to replace pancreatic exocrine insufficiency, increase body weight, and reduce steatorrhea. Pancreatic exocrine insufficiency is managed by prescribing pancreatic extract (enzymes). Two popular pancreatic preparations are Pancreatin (Viokase) and Pancrealipase (Cotazym). Both are available in tablet form.

Clinical experience indicates that this re-placement therapy results in weight gain, less fecal fat loss, increased fat and protein absorption, and a regaining of a sense of well-being by the patient. With the enzyme preparations given at a dose and time appropriate to the patient's food consumption pattern, digestion and absorption of food soon return to normal. Since the pancreatic preparations are not pleasant tasting, patients must be persuaded to cooperate in this therapy. However, the relief of many symptoms of pancreatitis is so pronounced that patients usually comply readily. Occasionally a patient's response is of value in diagnosis—continued refusal to take the preparation probably indicates that the patient does not have pancreatic insufficiency.

If the patient responds well to pancreatic replacement therapy, he or she should be fed a diet providing 3,000 to 6,000 kcal, including 100 to 150 g of protein and 400 or more grams of carbohydrate. If steatorrhea is already under control, the patient's diet should also provide 40 g of fat. This quantity should gradually be increased to

TABLE 24-10 Dietary Disaccharides and Intestinal Disaccharidases

Disaccharide	Type of Sugar	Monosaccharide Components	Intestinal Disaccharidase
Sucrose	Table sugar	Glucose, fructose	Sucrase
Maltose	Malt sugar	Glucose, glucose	Maltase
Isomaltose*	Malt sugar	Glucose, glucose	Isomaltase (α-dextrinase)
Trehalose*	Mushroom sugar	Glucose, glucose	Trehalase
Lactose	Milk sugar	Glucose, galactose	Lactase

*Although not discussed in Chapter 3, a few patients are deficient in the corresponding disaccharidase of this disaccharide.

200 g or until steatorrhea reappears. The use of medium-chain triglycerides (MCTs) is sometimes advocated. These may be used as a substitute for regular fatty foods or as a supplement to commercial oral feeding solutions (or formula diets). For more information on MCTs, consult Chapter 23.

Disaccharidase deficiency

By the time ingested carbohydrates reach the small intestine, they are mainly in disaccharide forms. Before the latter can be absorbed, they must be digested, split, or hydrolyzed to monosaccharides. The enzymes responsible for such hydrolysis, disaccharidases, are located in the mucosa of the duodenum, jejunum, and ileum. The enzymes are distributed from the distal portion of the duodenum to the proximal section of the ileum. The disaccharides and their respective disaccharidases are presented in Table 24-10. Deficiencies in any of these saccharidases may cause intestinal maldigestion and malabsorption.

Deficiencies of sucrase, maltase, isomaltase, and trehalase have been reported, but they are rare and easily managed by removing or avoiding the offending sugar.

At present, lactase deficiency is the most common disaccharidase deficiency. Lactase deficiency may result from an isolated lack of the enzyme or a generalized deficiency secondary to some intestinal diseases, such as celiac sprue, in which the mucosal wall is damaged. An individual with this enzyme deficiency will display a combination of symptoms such as loud bowel sounds, bloating, flatulence, cramps, and diarrhea if a certain amount of whole milk is ingested. The nonhydrolyzed and unabsorbed lactose in milk remains within the lumen of the gut and creates a high osmotic load (see Chapter 9). This draws a large amount of water from the body fluids into the lumen. Bowel distension and discomfort also occur. In addition, the bacteria in the colon metabolize and ferment the lactose to form a large amount of lactic acid, carbon dioxide, butyric acid, and other volatile substances. All of these changes are responsible for the observed symptoms.

A simple test can be used to identify individuals with lactase deficiency. A patient is given 50 g of lactose orally, and his or her plasma glucose is then measured at 15-, 30-, 60-, and 120-minute intervals. Intestinal lactase deficiency should be suspected if blood glucose levels fail to rise above the fasting level by at least 20 mg per 100 mL of blood. If the patient can absorb glucose or galactose normally, then the diagnosis is further confirmed. Another technique used in diagnosing lactase deficiency is assaying lactase activity in a piece of biopsied small intestine. However, most clinicians use only the lactase test. For information on the latest diagnostic technique of breath hydrogen analysis, consult a modern textbook.

To treat lactase deficiency, all products containing lactose, such as milk and all dairy products, are prohibited. If a patient is on a lactose-restricted diet, the physician must be careful to assure a balanced diet from the permitted foods. Proper intake of the nutrients protein, vitamin B_2, and calcium is especially important.

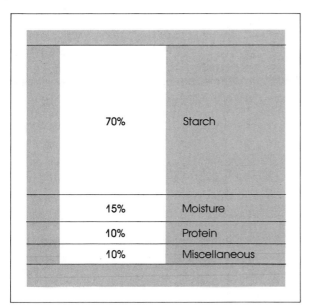

FIGURE 24-6 Composition of wheat flour. The protein contains α-gliadin, a toxic substance responsible for celiac disease.

TABLE 24-11 Types of Protein in Flour Protein

Type of Protein	Substance in Which Soluble	Protein Fraction (% content)*
Gliadins	Ethanol	α-gliadin† (30)
		β-gliadin (30)
		γ-gliadin (30)
		ω-gliadin (10)
Glutenins	Dilute alkali	—
Albumins	Water	—
Globulins	Saline solution	—

*Obtained by starch gel electrophoresis.
†Currently, this is considered responsible for celiac disease.

Celiac disease

Celiac disease results from a patient's sensitivity to flour protein (gluten). As shown in Figure 24-6, flour is made up of about 10% protein; Table 24-11 shows the general composition of this protein. Recent research indicates that the α-gliadin component of the gluten is responsible (see Table 24-11). This disease, which has several different names, tends to run in families. Names for this disease include gluten (or gluten-

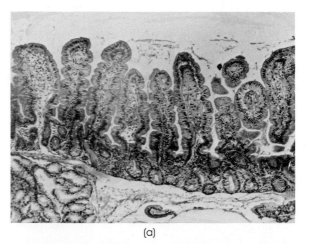

(a)

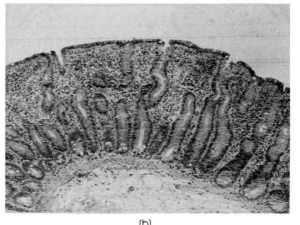

(b)

FIGURE 24-7 Mucosal surface of the small intestine of a patient with celiac sprue. (From M. R. Brown and C. B. Lillibridge, *Clinical Pediatrics* 1975; 14 : 76) (a) Normal duodenal mucosa with long, fingerlike villi, tall epithelial cells, short crypts in relation to total villous height, moderate cellularity of the lamina propria. (b) Specimen from a patient with gluten-sensitive enteropathy. Total flattening of mucosal surface, elongated deep crypts, short epithelial cells, and intense infiltration of lamina propria with mononuclear cells.

induced) enteropathy, nontropical sprue, and celiac sprue.

Jejunal biopsy of a patient with celiac disease invariably shows mucosal atrophy of the small intestine. The cells, instead of being columnar, are squamous (flat). Villi are also lacking (see Figure 24-7). These abnormal cells secrete only small amounts of digestive enzymes.

Medical records indicate that before the cause of celiac disease was identified, only children were suspected to have this disease. At present, adults with symptoms and positive identification from intestinal biopsy are also classified as having adult celiac disease, especially if they respond to gluten-free diets.

The symptoms exhibited by a patient with celiac disease are diarrhea, steatorrhea, bulky and foamy stools with very bad odor, two to four bowel movements daily, loss of appetite and weight, emaciation, and, in children, failure to thrive (such children typically have pot bellies). Children's growth is retarded because of the incompetent mucosa, causing severe malabsorption. When the fat is not absorbed, it is moved to the large intestine and becomes emulsified by bile and calcium salts. The odor of the stool is caused by large amounts of fatty acids. The unabsorbed carbohydrates are fermented by the bacteria in the large intestine, producing gas and occasional abdominal cramps. Hyperosmolality induces the colon to secrete water and electrolytes into the lumen. The patient may show many malnutrition symptoms, including bone pain and tetany, anemia, rough skin, and lowered prothrombin time. Most adult patients have iron and folic acid deficiencies, with microcytic and macrocytic anemias. Symptoms such as cheilosis and glossitis, caused by water-soluble vitamin deficiencies, may also be present.

The basic principle of diet therapy for celiac disease is to exclude all foods containing gluten—chiefly buckwheat, malt, oats, rye, barley, and wheat. The patient's response to such a regimen is dramatic. A child shows improvement in 1 to 2 weeks, while an adult takes 1 to 3 months. In either case, symptoms gradually disappear. With the child patient, there is weight gain and thriving, and diarrhea and steatorrhea clear up. The mucosal changes in Figure 24-7 will also return to normal after a gluten-free diet. The degree of improvement is directly related to the extent the patient adheres to the diet. The therapy is curing the disease if symptoms reappear when the patient returns to a regular diet. For some young patients, the treatment lasts at least 5 years before they can eat wheat and other formerly excluded products. However, some children must exclude gluten from their diet permanently. Adult patients appear to have a lesser chance of complete recovery.

After celiac disease has been diagnosed, patients should be informed about its cause and treatment. Patients who understand this illness are much likelier to follow a prescribed diet. Of course, they should know that adherence to a gluten-free or gluten-restricted diet is essential. If the patients also have lactose intolerance (as is sometimes the case), the necessity of avoiding milk and milk products must be emphasized.

Patients must be made aware of the great difficulty in following a gluten-restricted diet. Buckwheat, malt, oats, barley, rye, and wheat all contain gluten and are extensively used in different food products. It is therefore extremely important that patients read all labels on prepared and packaged foods to ascertain if they contain gluten. Gluten-free wheat products are commercially available for those on special diets. In addition, potato flour, rice, corn, soybean flour, and tapioca may be substituted.

If a patient is already malnourished when treatment begins, an aggressive nutritional rehabilitation regimen should be instituted. This includes high amounts of calories, protein, vitamins, and minerals. It should also provide fluids and electrolyte compensation (with special attention to potassium, magnesium, and calcium). MCTs should also be included. A gluten-restricted diet may be deficient in thiamin (vitamin B_1) and should include vitamin supplements.

All patients should be taught to plan their menus in accordance with some food guides to achieve their daily RDAs. Professionals should help the patient in this planning.

Table 24-12 lists those foods that are permitted or prohibited in a gluten-restricted diet. Table 24-13 provides a sample meal plan for such a diet.

LARGE INTESTINE

Diseases and disorders (including surgery) of the large intestine include the irritable bowel syndrome, ulcerative colitis, diverticular diseases, colostomy, hemorrhoidectomy, and cancer. The causes, symptoms, and dietary managements of the first three diseases are summarized in Table 24-14. Other disorders are discussed in Chapter 29. In view of the importance of intestinal resi-

TABLE 24-12   Foods Permitted and Prohibited in a Gluten-Restricted Diet

Food Group	Foods Permitted	Foods Prohibited
Meat, poultry	Those prepared without prohibited grains or their flours	All products using the prohibited flours, including swiss steak, chili con carne, commercial sausages (e.g., weiners), gravies, sauces, stews, batter, stuffings, croquettes
Fish	All fish and shellfish containing no restricted grains or their flours	Any product made with the restricted grains and flours, e.g., wheat flour breaded fish sticks and shrimp
Cheese	All not specifically prohibited	Processed cheese and cheese spread prepared with gluten as a stabilizer
Eggs	All frozen and fresh eggs and egg substitutes without restricted grains or their flours	All others
Textured vegetable proteins	All those made from soy ingredients	All others
Milk, milk products	All not specifically prohibited	Milk shakes and malted milk
Fats, oils	Butter, margarine, cream and cream substitutes; bacon; olive oil, vegetable oil, salad oil; vegetable (hydrogenated) shortening; mayonnaise	Salad dressings thickened with wheat or rye products; cream, butter, white sauce made with forbidden flour
Cereals	All cereals made from rice, corn and rice, e.g., Sugar Pops, Rice Krisples, Corn Chex, corn flakes, Puffed Rice, Frosted Flakes, Cream of Rice, grits, hominy, and cornmeal	All cereals containing prohibited grains, e.g., Cream of Wheat
Bread	Muffins, pone, and corn bread prepared without wheat flour; rolls, muffins, and breads prepared with cornmeal, cornstarch, lima bean flour, and arrowroot; rice pancakes; products made with low-gluten wheat starch	All products made from prohibited grains, e.g., sweet rolls, crackers, muffins, prepared mixes, bread crumbs, commercial yeast
Vegetables, vegetable juices	All vegetables and juices; sauces made with potato flour or cornstarch may be used	Vegetables prepared with cracker crumbs, bread, or cream sauces thickened with prohibited flours or cereals
Fruits, fruit juices	All fruits and juices	Fruit sauces thickened with prohibited grains
Potatoes or substitutes	Potatoes, rice, grits, corn, sweet potatoes, dried peas and beans	Pasta
Sweets	All unless specifically prohibited	Candies and chocolate syrup with bases made from prohibited grains
Soups	Cream or vegetable soups thickened with cornstarch or potato flour; meat stock; clear broths	Milk and cream soups; bouillon cubes or powdered soups; canned soups; soups with prohibited grain products; soups thickened with wheat flour
Beverages	Coffee, tea, cocoa, chocolate, carbonated beverages, milk, Kool Aid	Ale, beer, malted milk; instant cocoa, coffee, or tea; cereal beverages; milk shakes; others including Ovaltine, Postum

TABLE 24-12 (continued)

Food Group	Foods Permitted	Foods Prohibited
Desserts	Products made with permitted grains; plain or fruit-flavored gelatin; homemade ice, ice cream, sherbet, Popsicles; cornstarch, rice and tapioca puddings; cakes, pies, and cookies, using water, sugar, and fruits	All products made with prohibited grains, e.g., pastries (cakes), desserts (ice cream cones, sherbet), prepared mixes
Miscellaneous	Herbs, pepper, olives, salt, vinegar, catsup, pickles, relishes, spices; sauces prepared from permitted grains and their flours; peanut butter, nuts, flavoring extracts, popcorn	Creamed and scalloped foods; au gratin dishes, rarebit; fritters, timbales, malt products, prepared mixes of all kinds, condiments prepared with cereal

TABLE 24-13 Sample Meal Plan for a Gluten-Restricted Diet

Breakfast	Lunch	Dinner
Juice	Meat	Meat, fish, or poultry
Cereal, hot or dry	Potato	Potato
Scrambled egg(s)	Vegetable	Vegetable
Corn bread (special)	Salad with dressing	Juice
Margarine	Fruit or dessert	Fruit or dessert
Jelly	Corn bread	Corn bread with margarine
Milk	Margarine	Milk
Coffee or tea	Milk	Beverage
Sugar	Beverage	Cream
Cream	Cream	Sugar
Salt, pepper	Sugar	Salt, pepper
	Salt, pepper	

due with the above disorders, we shall first define a modified-residue diet and then provide detailed discussions of ulcerative colitis and diverticular diseases.

Modified-residue Diets

Though sometimes used as if they were synonyms, traditionally the terms *fiber* and *residue* have different meanings. *Fiber* (also known as *roughage* or *bulk*, see Chapter 3) includes cellulose, hemocellulose and pectins in plant foods and connective tissues of meats. It cannot be broken down by the enzymes of the human digestive system. Whereas fiber refers to ingested substances, *residue* (or *fecal mass*) refers to the contents of the large intestine—the materials that are left after completion of the digestive processes. It consists not only of indigestible fibers but also of bacterial residues and discarded mucosal cells. The fecal mass is about 75% water and 25% solids—cellulose, inorganic matter, bacteria, some fat and its breakdown products, mucous, and mucosal cells. All foods will leave some residue; if a person has eaten no food, there will still be some residue in the large intestine from normal metabolic processes.

We need fiber in our diet to maintain normal peristaltic action in the intestinal tract and removal of wastes from this tract. Fiber achieves this by absorbing moisture and providing bulk that stimulates emptying of the large intestine.

TABLE 24-14 Causes, Symptoms, and Dietary Management of Some Colon Disorders

Colon Disorder	Dietary Treatment*
Irritable bowel syndrome Also known as colon spasm and colon neurosis. Most common gastrointestinal disorders. Causes unknown. Symptoms: abdominal pain with occasional watery diarrhea. Constipation may be present.	Controversial, not used by many clinicians. If there is constipation, follow the dietary regimen for constipation discussed in text.
Ulcerative colitis Also known as idiopathic proctocolitis or inflammatory bowel disease. Causes unknown. Symptoms: diarrhea, rectal bleeding, nausea, anorexia, weight loss, loss of protein, vitamins, or minerals in the bowel, dehydration, abdominal tenderness and distension, fever and tachycardia, allergy. Symptoms sometimes absent.	All dietary procedures are supportive and nonspecific. No one diet can heal, cure, or prevent disorder. Bland or low-residue diet may be used. Food items to which patient is allergic should be identified and prohibited. Lactose intolerance corrected by eliminating dairy products. Undernourishment may be rehabilitated. Anabolic hormones may help patients gain weight. Intravenous feeding may be indicated.
Diverticular diseases Covers a range of colon disorders. A diverticulum is a blind pouch along the colon. One disorder is diverticulitis of the colon because of a perforated diverticulum. Causes are unknown. Symptoms: pain, altered bowel habit, bleeding, infection and perforation. Symptoms sometimes absent.	Some success with a high-fiber diet, although some patients still benefit from a bland and low-residue diet.

*This is usually only a component of the overall medical management plan.

How much is needed for these purposes is not precisely known. One recommendation is daily consumption of 100 mg of fiber per kg of body weight; for the average adult, about 5 to 6 g of fiber per day should be sufficient. This recommended daily allowance is easily met by one serving of whole-grain cereal or bread, two servings of vegetables, and two servings of fruits. Vegetables with long fibers, such as celery and greens, have a laxative effect. Whether cooked or uncooked, fruits and vegetables maintain the same fiber content, for cooking does not change the amount of cellulose and hemocellulose. Further-

more, the kinds of vegetables and fruits consumed is of less consequence to the production of residue than is the quantity consumed. Those who need a diet with minimum residue should therefore minimize consumption of all kinds of fruits and vegetables, including those that have been cooked or pureed.

Traditionally, patients who need a minimum-residue diet have been asked to minimize their intake of fresh milk and many milk products, for these may leave fecal residue. Clinicians who recommend this practice explain this residue formation in two ways. In the stomach, ingested

TABLE 24-15   Foods Permitted in Two Residue-Regulated Diets

	Foods and Daily Servings Permitted*	
Food Group	Low-to-moderate-residue diet (0–4 g fiber)	Minimum-residue diet (0–1 g fiber)
Meat, equivalents	Beef, veal, ham, liver, and poultry (broiled, baked, or stewed to tender); fish, fresh or salt (broiled, baked); canned tuna or salmon; shellfish, tender meat only	Beef, veal, ham, liver, and poultry (broiled, baked, or stewed to tender); fish, fresh or salt (broiled, baked); canned salmon or tuna
Milk, milk products	Whole, skim, chocolate; buttermilk, yogurt (2 c daily including amount in food preparation)	None
Cheeses	Cottage, cream, American, Muenster, and Swiss 1 c milk = 1 oz cheese	Cream, dry cottage, and American (in food preparation) Daily allowance: 1 oz American or cream cheese or ¼ c cottage cheese
Eggs	All varieties except fried	All varieties except creamed and fried
Grain, grain products	Bread (Italian, Vienna, or French); toast (French or melba); crackers (saltines or soda); rolls (plain, soft, or hard); others: biscuits, zwieback, rusk All above prepared with refined whole wheat or rye (without seeds), with no nuts or raisins	Same
	Cereals (ready-to-eat, cooked, all prepared from refined grains); oatmeal	Same, except no oatmeal
	Flours from refined grains other than graham or bran	Same
	White rice	Same
	Plain spaghetti, noodles, and macaroni	Same
Potatoes	Potatoes without skin (creamed, mashed, scalloped, boiled, baked); sweet potatoes without skin	None
Fruits	Daily allowance: 2 servings All juices and nectars; fruits, ripe and fresh (peeled, without seeds), frozen, or canned: grapes, bananas, apricots, plums, peaches, pears, cherries, avocados, citrus fruits (segments only), e.g., oranges, grapefruit, tangerine, honeydew, cantaloupe, pineapple, and nectarines	Citrus fruit juices (strained); other juices and nectars

TABLE 24-15   (continued)

Food Group	Foods and Daily Servings Permitted*	
	Low-to-moderate-residue diet (0–4 g fiber)	Minimum-residue diet (0–1 g fiber)
Vegetables	Daily allowance: 1 serving for vegetables, with no limitation on juices Vegetables, well-cooked or canned: green and waxed beans, carrots, asparagus, beets, eggplant, mushrooms, onions, cauliflower, peas, winter squash, pumpkin, cabbage Vegetables, cooked, chopped: turnip greens, broccoli, spinach, kale, collards Vegetables, raw, chopped: lettuce	Daily allowance: 1 serving Vegetable juices (fresh, cocktail); tomato juice
Beverages	Coffee (regular, decaffeinated), tea; others: soft drinks, cereal beverages All drinks may be flavored with permitted fruits.	Same
Soups	Broth and cream-based soups made from other permitted ingredients	Same
Candies, sweets	Plain candies, jelly, honey, syrup, sugar, jelly beans, mints	Plain hard candies, jelly, honey, syrup, sugar, jelly beans, mints
Fats	Cream: regular, dried substitutes, sour; dressings: mayonnaise and mayonnaise-type, all must be plain; regular smooth salad oil; butter, margarine, oils; others: crisp bacon, shortenings	Daily allowance: no limitation except heavy cream must be limited to ½ c Cream: heavy, substitutes, nondairy, sour; dressings: mayonnaise and mayonnaise-type, all must be plain; regular smooth salad oil; butter, margarine, oils; others: crisp bacon, shortenings
Desserts	All must be plain and made from permitted ingredients: pie, cakes, cookies, pudding, gelatin, sherbet, ice cream	Cookies: plain sugar or vanilla wafers, arrowroot; cakes: sponge, angel food; puddings: tapioca or cornstarch made with fruit juices; others: meringues, plain gelatin desserts, plain water ices
Miscellaneous	Spices and herbs (ground or finely chopped); flavorings: soy sauce, vinegar, salt, monosodium glutamate, chocolate, catsup, and all commercial flavoring extracts; sauces and gravies: mild and made from permitted ingredients	Flavorings: salt, vinegar, commercial flavoring extracts; spices and herbs (ground or finely chopped, in small amounts, in food preparation only); gravies and sauces: made from permitted ingredients and used in minimal quantity

*When daily number of servings is not indicated, there is no restriction on the amount consumed by the patient. Also refer to the "soft diet" discussed in Chapter 23.

milk is clotted by pepsin, which, by slightly hydrolyzing casein, renders it calcium caseinate. Pepsin can digest this clot in the presence of hydrochloric acid. However, if an excessive amount of hydrochloric acid is present, casein hydrochloride will be formed. This makes the clot so leatherlike and hard that its digestion by pepsin is difficult. As a result, considerable residue will remain. As the milk clot passes through the digestive tract it undergoes further digestion by pancreatic proteases. Any casein that remains undigested is eliminated as residue. The other explanation relates to the stimulation of pancreatic enzyme secretion by the protein in milk, thus increasing fecal weight by increasing endogenous losses. Obviously, this possibility applies also to protein foods other than milk. On the other hand, many clinical practitioners believe that milk has minimal effect on fecal weight, and they will not restrict their patients' milk intake if they need a diet with minimal residue.

Some practitioners have compromised on this issue by permitting the patient to include heated milk and certain processed milk products. When milk is heated, calcium caseinate is formed. This compound coagulates slowly, producing a clot soft enough to be digested by pepsin. In some cultured milk products, the protein is predigested by microorganisms during processing. For example, cheddar cheese, American cheese, and cottage cheese are partially digested by added rennin. The same applies to some yogurts, although it depends on the extent of fermentation. This partial digestion facilitates their more thorough digestion by pepsin in the stomach.

Table 24-15 describes the foods permitted in two residue-regulated diets: a low-to-moderate-residue diet and a minimum-residue diet. Wherever applicable, the restriction in the daily number of servings is also provided. When using this table as a reference guide, the following must be considered. Residue is used as defined above. Individual practitioners should make modifications according to their clinical experience. Meal plans based on the permitted foods must assure nutritional adequacy by complying with the RDAs. In the following discussion, residue-regulated diet plans may contain additional items not listed in the table.

At present, low-residue diets find most common application before and after colon surgery (e.g., fistula), preparation for urograph in conjunction with barium enema, and before colonoscopy. However, such diets are still used by some practitioners in the treatment for ulcerative colitis and diverticular diseases as discussed below.

Ulcerative Colitis

Although the cause of ulcerative colitis is unknown, it manifests recognizable symptoms (see Table 24-14). If acute symptoms are present, foods may be withheld and intravenous nutrition instituted. Otherwise, shortly after an attack, the patient should be provided with the routine hospital progressive diet. As soon as the patient recovers from an acute attack, regular food should be provided.

In general, the bowel may be rested by providing the patient with frequent, small feedings. Food that the patient finds unpleasant should be excluded. Most modern dietary manuals suggest a low-residue and bland diet. Table 24-16 provides a sample menu for a bland and minimum-residue diet, and Table 24-17 shows a moderately low-fiber diet. For more information on planning bland diets, consult the discussion on ulcers. Such diets take into consideration all forms of irritants, including osmotic, chemical, thermal, and mechanical irritants. Symptom-provoking foods include fruits, vegetables, juices, spices, alcohol, and hot and cold drinks and foods. If the food variety is very restricted, the meals should be attractively prepared. This enhances the desirability and thus the patient's appetite.

Whenever possible, the patient should be provided with a high-protein, high-carbohydrate (polysaccharides), and high-calorie diet and appropriate vitamin and mineral supplements. Caloric content should be about 2,000 to 3,500 kcal, while the protein contribution should be 100 to 150 g. High-quality proteins such as eggs, meat, and cheese should be used whenever permitted. The amount of fat provided should be adjusted according to the degree of steatorrhea. If advisable, MCTs (see Chapter 23) may be substituted for regular fats. Sometimes a mixture of both regular fats and MCTs proves beneficial.

TABLE 24-16 Sample Menu for a Bland and Minimum-Fiber Diet

Breakfast	Lunch	Dinner
Orange juice, strained, ½ c	Chicken, tender, 3 oz	Beef patty, well cooked, 3 oz
Farina, ½ c	Rice, ½ c	Mashed potato, ½ c
Milk, 1 c	Vegetable juice, 1 c	White bread, 1 sl
Toast, white bread, 1 sl	White bread, 1 sl	Grapefruit juice, strained, ½ c
Margarine	Ice cream, ½ c	Custard, ½ c
Sugar	Vanilla wafers, 2	Margarine
Jelly	Milk, 1 c	Coffee or tea
Coffee or tea	Coffee or tea	
	Snacks	
	Gelatin	
	Crackers	

Note: This menu contains about 1 g of fiber. Quantities of servings should be adjusted to meet the needs of the individual.

TABLE 24-17 Sample Menu for a Moderately Low-Fiber Diet

Breakfast	Lunch	Dinner
Tomato juice, ½ c	Melted cheese sandwich:	Roast beef, tender, 3 oz
Egg, poached, 1	White bread, 2 sl	Potato, mashed, 1 c
Toast, white bread, 1 sl	Cheese, mild, 2 oz	Carrots, cooked, ½ c
Bacon, 2 sl	Green beans, ½ c	Orange juice, strained, ½ c
Margarine	Apple juice, ½ c	White bread, 1 sl
Jelly	Gelatin, 1 c	Margarine
Coffee or tea	Vanilla wafers, 2	Ice cream, ½ c
	Coffee or tea	Coffee or tea
	Snacks	
	Milk, 1 c	
	Cookies, plain, 2	

Note: This menu contains about 3 to 4 g of fiber. Quantities of servings should be adjusted to meet the needs of the individual.

Lactase deficiency is currently suspected to be directly related to the severity of the disease. Patients with severe ulcerative colitis are more likely to be lactase deficient than people in normal health. Therefore, patients should be tested for lactose intolerance and, if necessary, told to avoid all products containing lactose.

Nutritionally undernourished patients must be rehabilitated (see Chapters 22 and 23), which may take 3 to 10 months. Intravenous feeding with defined-formula diets has been somewhat successful.

Diverticular Diseases

The term *diverticular diseases* describes a group of specific diseases of the large intestine. A diverticulum (plural *diverticula*) is a blind pouch along the length of the colon. Diverticulosis refers to the presence of diverticula, and diverticulitis is inflammation of the colon due to a perforated diverticulum. Diverticular diseases is an all-inclusive term covering one or more of these conditions.

Most patients with diverticulosis are asymptomatic. However, some develop pain, altered bowel habits, bleeding, infection, and perforation. Symptomatic patients complain of occasional pain originating from the lower quadrant of the abdomen. Pain can last for days and ranges from cramps to severe abdominal discomfort. Constipation alternates with diarrhea. After a bowel movement or passing flatus, symptoms subside temporarily. Some patients have blood and mucus in their stools. Massive hemorrhage may also occur with diverticulitis.

In the past, a low-residue diet was prescribed for patients with symptoms of diverticular diseases. The treatment was based on the premise that such a regimen minimizes irritation to the intestine and inhibits gas and distension of the bowel. However, it has been recently suspected that diverticula could develop from a lifetime of consuming low-fiber foods. Within the last decade, some clinicians have successfully managed diverticular diseases with high-fiber diets. Currently, such treatment is advocated in most diet manuals as well as medical textbooks on intestinal diseases.

To increase dietary fiber, many clinicians now recommend the use of unprocessed bran, a detailed discussion of which is presented later. Since the extent of fiber deficiencies varies, the amounts of bran needed will differ also. Each patient must therefore find by trial and error the correct amount of bran to use. An average of 2 t of unprocessed bran three times a day (the equivalent of 2 to 3 g of fiber) usually relieves the symptoms of the disease. The dose of bran needed to produce results may be higher for some patients. Most treated patients show decreased diverticulitis, return of normal bowel habits, and a lessening of pain. Patients who cannot tolerate bran should eat a high-fiber diet consisting of commercially available foods. However, many clinicians still advocate the use of a low-residue diet for patients with diverticular diseases in the inflammatory and bleeding stages.

CONSTIPATION

Constipation is a symptom of an underlying condition, not a disease in itself. A person suffering from constipation may have any of several complaints. Bowel movements may be infrequent. Conversely, frequent bowel movements may occur with small amounts of very hard and dry stools present. There may be difficulty in passing stools, including general abdominal discomfort or even pain during a bowel movement.

Causes

Delayed transit time in the colon and stools with abnormal structure and consistency occur under a variety of circumstances and in association with a number of pathological conditions.

Improper eating habits can easily lead to constipation. Conditions include a voluntary or imposed lack of food, insufficient dietary roughage, imposed dehydration, and insufficient water intake. Lack of water and a lack of dietary residue are the most common causes.

Constipation can also have a psychological origin. Stressful emotional states such as depression and anxiety can predispose a person to constipation. In these states the patient may fail to respond to the need to defecate.

Intestinal diseases of various types also affect constipation. They include Crohn's disease, irritable bowel syndrome, tumor, obstruction, and defective electrolyte transfer. The relationship between constipation and diverticular diseases has already been mentioned. At present, the cause and effect relationship between the two is not clearly understood.

Various other medical conditions affect constipation as well. They include hypothyroidism, hyperparathyroidism, hypercalcemia, porphyria, hypokalemia, lead intoxication, and Hirschsprung's disease. The use of such drugs as opiates, antihypertensives, calcium carbonate, aluminum hydroxide, and antacids must also be considered.

Medical Management

Finding and treating an organic cause (such as the diseases mentioned above) of constipation is the first priority in its medical management. Communication with the patient plays a very important role. The symptoms of constipation should be explained and clarified, and the adverse effects of commercially available laxatives emphasized. It is useful in this regard to suggest an easy home remedy for simple chronic constipation, as described below. Other appropriate clinical measures and obtaining a detailed medical history ensure good medical management of constipation.

Counseling the patient

Patients with constipation should know that good health does not depend on a daily bowel movement. However, if a problem exists, patients should be informed of common conditions that cause constipation. Among these are the omission of breakfast, irregular or strange dietary habits, very little activity or exercise, prolonged intake of certain drugs and laxatives, pregnancy, the use of contraceptive pills, and obesity. The connection between constipation and ignoring the urge to move the bowel should be explained. Various factors may be responsible for this inattention, such as a change in job or home environment, social activities, working routines, inconvenience, travel, increased age, convalescing from an illness, and emotional disturbances.

Older patients with constipation require special understanding. Their constipation problems may be directly related to age, and general weakness or a dental handicap can be significant factors. A lack of interest in food and its preparation may also be present. Older patients may dislike high-fiber foods such as raw fruits and vegetables or be unable to afford foods with high roughage contents, which serve as laxatives.

The use of enemas and laxatives should be clearly explained to the patient. Long-term use of such substances weakens the muscles of the colon and the abdomen. The colon muscle must work normally and respond to regular stimuli for a bowel movement to be accomplished.

In the home remedy for simple constipation, the patient's habits must be changed first. Defecation should occur at about the same time each day. An after-breakfast routine is a good beginning. Drinking hot water and lemon juice after waking will help initiate intestinal motility. Walking and regular exercise of the abdominal musculature are also beneficial. Responding to the urge to defecate is important as well. The patient should avoid straining and use handrails or a footstool if necessary. The process should be completed in less than 15 minutes. The habitual use of laxatives should be stopped, and the patient should inform the physician of the extent of their use.

Patients must also adjust their food and drink habits. They must consume adequate amounts of food and liquids; they should always include roughage in the diet and drink 5 to 8 glasses of water each day. If regular high-fiber foods are too expensive, they can use inexpensive unprocessed bran.

Increasing roughage

As indicated above, either regular high-fiber foods or unprocessed bran can be used to increase dietary roughage. If a patient chooses regular foods, an appropriate menu must be planned (see Chapter 23 for information). A high-fiber menu plan is shown in Table 24-18. See the references at the end of this book for information on fiber content of foods.

Some high-fiber foods are whole-grain cereals and bread, leafy vegetables, and raw and cooked fruits. Prunes, rhubarb, figs, dates, bananas, and applesauce are good laxatives as well as being high in fiber and residues. For those individuals who cannot tolerate lactose and have developed constipation, milk and milk products may solve the problem at least at the beginning. Older people may be served foods with soft residues, such as cooked vegetables and canned or stewed fruits.

Unfortunately, high-fiber diets can be expensive in some parts of the country. They may also be high in calories and contain too many fruits and vegetables. In addition, these diets take some time to relieve constipation.

Eating unprocessed bran can also increase

TABLE 24-18   A High-Fiber Menu Plan

Breakfast	Lunch	Dinner
Dried figs, stewed, 3	Fish, baked, 3 oz	Beef stew, with vegeta-
Oatmeal, 1 c	Potato, baked, with	bles, 1 c
100% Bran*, 2 T	skin, 1	Cole slaw, ½ c
Toast, whole wheat, 1 sl	String beans, ½ c	Beets, buttered, ½ c
Margarine	Lettuce and tomato	Muffins, bran, 2
Jam, 2 T	salad:	Margarine
Coffee or tea	Tomato, ½	Ice cream, 1 c
	Lettuce leaves, 3	Chocolate sauce, ½ c
	Bread, whole wheat,	Coffee or tea
	1 sl	
	Margarine	
	Pudding, chocolate,	
	¾ c	
	Cookies, oatmeal and	
	raisin, 2	
	Snacks	
	Strawberries, ½ c	
	Ice cream, ½ c	

Note: This menu contains approximately 12 to 13 g of undigestible fiber.

*A breakfast cereal marketed by Nabisco; it contains about 7.5% fiber.

fiber intake. Bran is inexpensive and can be obtained easily. It serves as a laxative because it cannot be digested and is able to absorb water, thus keeping the feces soft. It has been used successfully to treat constipation, irritable bowel syndrome, and diverticular diseases.

Bran is the by-product of the milling of wheat or rice. Bran from wheat contains almost 20% indigestible cellulose and is an excellent source of dietary bulk. Unprocessed bran contains about 14% fiber, in contrast to the lesser bran or fiber content of 100% Bran (7.5%), All Bran (7%), Bran Buds (7%), and Raisin Bran (3%). Since the fiber in unrefined bran is the important ingredient, natural bran flakes or whole bran should be used, not products such as 40% Bran Flakes or compressed pellets such as All Bran. Bran and other natural fiber bulk foods do not irritate a healthy intestinal mucosa, and they readily add fiber to the diet.

A patient should take 2 t of unprocessed bran two or three times a day for 1 to 2 weeks. The bran can be taken in any way the patient prefers. It can be swallowed with water or juices,

taken with cereals and milk, mixed with porridge, or added to flour in baking. The consistency of bran is like sawdust, and it is very difficult to swallow. If possible, the patient should eat it simultaneously with some other regular foods that are high in roughage. Hopefully, the addition of bran will enable the patient to have one or two bowel movements of soft stools daily without straining.

After the initial trial, the patient should progress to 2½ or 3 t of bran until bowel movements with soft stools are regular. The treatment should be discontinued after the patient has established a good daily regimen. The patient should be told that initial consumption of bran may cause flatulence; this should not cause the patient to stop taking the bran. Some patients may also have abdominal pain, distension, and discomfort initially, all of which usually disappear with time. However, some constipated patients cannot tolerate unprocessed bran. Once the bowel has returned to normal, the patient should maintain a balanced diet with adequate daily roughage.

It is important, though, to emphasize that a high-fiber intake is not without potential problems. For one thing, a high-fiber intake can interfere with the absorption of certain drugs. Second, ingested fiber can reduce the intestinal tract's ability to digest and absorb food. The physical presence of fiber reduces the time for digestion and the rate of absorption. Third, high amounts of fiber cause continuous mechanical irritation of the mucosal wall. Hence, there is some increased loss (from wear and tear) of mucosal substances. A fourth problem is that whole-grain products contain phytic acids, which may chelate trace minerals and decrease their presence in the body. Finally, the large amount of phosphorus in high-fiber foods may create problems for certain individuals, especially patients with renal problems.

Clinicians sometimes use other substances to promote defecation in a constipated patient. They may be administered orally or rectally. The common laxatives are divided into five types: lubricants, stool softeners, bulk producers, osmotically active chemicals, and irritants (stimulant purgatives). Physicians are usually careful about their usage and prescribe them only if necessary.

DIARRHEA

Diarrhea is the frequent passage of loose or watery unformed stools with or without mucus. It may be acute or chronic. Because it is a symptom and not a disease, the cause must be carefully investigated. Diarrhea may alternate with constipation and result from the irritation of the mucous membrane by impacted hard feces.

The cause of diarrhea can be psychological (such as nervousness), purely physical (such as an irritating agent, for example, intestinal bacteria), or an intestinal disease (such as Crohn's disease). Occasionally diarrhea may be a symptom of a nonintestinal disease, such as diabetes. Other etiologic factors of diarrhea are osmotic imbalance and allergy.

When diagnosing this condition, the following points should be noted: patient history, study of the stools, clinical clues, and cultures. Proctoscopic, sigmoidoscopic, radiological, and digital examination should be used. In this way, functional diarrhea can be separated from organic diarrhea.

Table 24-19 describes the relationships between clinical observations and diarrhea. These relationships are useful in diagnosing the cause of diarrhea. In a patient with diarrhea, the stool sometimes contains different undigested and unabsorbed nutrients. For example, granules of starch indicate the presence of carbohydrates. The presence of partly digested muscle fibers indicates proteins, and crystals of fatty acids and globules of fat indicate fats.

Diet therapy for diarrhea depends on whether the condition is acute or chronic. If diarrhea is acute, only clear liquids should be given exclusively for 24 to 48 hours. Fluid intake should be frequent, and intravenous hyperalimentation should be used if oral feedings are postponed. After acute symptoms have subsided, the patient can be fed a routine progressive diet. Once the progressive diet is tolerated, bland and low-residue diets can be instituted. Possible patient allergy or intolerance to the foods should be monitored.

The chronic diarrhea that some individuals develop usually follows an acute attack. Depending on the underlying cause, dietary management consists mainly of replacing lost nutrients. All secondary deficiencies, such as of minerals, vitamins, and protein (especially serum), must be corrected. In planning dietary intake, one must consider long-term nutrient losses through chronic diarrhea, especially for child patients (see Chapter 30). Diets should be adequate in protein, calories, and other essential nutrients. All irritants and stimulants should be excluded. Roughage, spices, greasy and fried foods, and temperature extremes in food and drink should be avoided. Frequent small feedings and a bland diet are recommended.

Information on planning such menus are located in Chapter 23 and later discussions. Supplements may include vitamin, mineral, and protein preparations. Each patient should be guided in the progression from a special to a normal diet. Tolerance and discomfort should be monitored in relation to the type of food consumed.

TABLE 24-19 Implications of Clinical Observations of Diarrhea in a Patient

Observation	Implication(s) or Conclusion
Recent onset	Symptoms severe enough to require patient's consultation with doctor
Nocturnal diarrhea	Organic cause (functional diarrhea rarely causes patient to defecate at night)
Cramping pain in mid-abdomen	Small bowel possibly obstructed
Passage of stools relieves cramping pain in lower abdomen	Possible disease of the colon
Undefined cramping pain	Usually functional problem
Unable to defecate in spite of straining, rectal pain, continuous anal seepage	Possible disease of the mucosal wall of the sigmoid and rectum
Loss of weight and appetite, tiredness, sweats, fever	Possible serious organic disease
Stool characteristics	
Very watery	Increased motility of small intestine
Moderate thickness	Possible colon lesion
Blood or mucus present	Disease of large bowel; ulcerated mucosa or tumor; imperative to identify cause
Pus present	Often described as "white mucus"; imperative to identify cause
Greenish or fatty	Possible disease of the small bowel
Pale brownish clay hue	Steatorrhea; if stool also oily, may be pancreatic insufficiency
Acidic and frothy	Carbohydrates not digested but fermented instead

STUDY QUESTIONS

1. What are some basic problems with the clinical management of gastrointestinal diseases? How has the controversy affected treatment?

2. Define *peptic ulcer*. What are its symptoms? Etiology? What can increase stomach acid secretion in an ulcer patient? Why does this occur?

3. Discuss three factors that may predispose a person to develop a peptic ulcer.

4. How does the dietary strategy for the treatment of an ulcer revolve around two contradictory opinions? What guidelines should be uniformly followed?

5. How do antacids help an ulcer patient? What

CASE STUDY   A Patient with Malabsorption Syndrome

H.G., a 50-year-old white woman, was admitted to the hospital because of critical illness. For a number of years, H.G. had nutritional anemia caused by a deficiency of iron and folic acid. She was also suffering from diarrhea. She had a reduced serum albumin level, and her malabsorption status was confirmed by a D-xylose tolerance test. Although her doctor had diagnosed her as gluten sensitive, she had failed to comply fully with a prescribed gluten-free diet.

When the patient was admitted to the hospital she was very sick, with severe diarrhea. During the 12 months before admission, her body weight decreased from 49.9 kg (110 lb) to 38.6 kg (85 lb). She was 5'6" (167.6 cm) tall. She had edema from a low serum protein level and ascites, and she also had a low blood level of vitamin B_{12}. The attending physician suspected she was suffering from protein-losing enteropathy. Repeated jejunal biopsy showed extreme villous atrophy, and the enterocytes had suffered heavy damage and loss.

She was required to subsist on a diet completely free of gluten with vitamin B_{12} injections and oral enzyme extract replacement therapy. However, her condition did not improve. After a careful study, the health team decided to administer prednisolone. Her response was dramatic. The edema and ascites cleared with an increase of serum protein, and jejunal biopsy indicated only partial villous atrophy. She also remained on the prescribed dietary regimen during prednisolone therapy.

To test the patient's response, the attending physician reduced the prednisolone dosage. Within 24 hours, the patient developed hypoproteinemia, accompanied by intestinal protein loss. When the dosage of prednisolone was again increased, her condition improved. After she had been in the hospital for 3 weeks, her serum proteins returned to normal. She recovered well and felt comfortable on a gluten-free diet with vitamin supplementation. At this stage, when the dose of prednisolone was cautiously reduced, her clinical conditions and laboratory results remained normal. She had 4.5 g of albumin, 2.2 g of globulin, and 14.1 g of hemoglobin per 100 mL of blood.

Review and Analysis

1. Why was the patient suffering from nutritional anemia?
2. What is the D-xylose tolerance test?
3. What was the cause of her diarrhea?
4. What does protein-losing enteropathy mean?
5. If you were the nurse assisting the attending physician, what questions would you ask the patient to determine how to improve her compliance with a gluten-free diet?
6. What is a gluten-free diet?
7. What does the oral enzyme extract usually contain? Can you name a common brand?
8. What is prednisolone? What are the general functions of this substance in clinical medicine? Do some library research and describe some possible reasons why prednisolone worked for this patient.
9. What does "villous atrophy" mean?
10. After the patient returned home, what caloric and protein levels would you have recommended to her? Assume that she was still underweight.

Mrs. K.F., a 40-year-old manager of a grocery store, had been suffering from Crohn's disease for 3½ years. Upon recommendation from her personal physician, she was admitted to a local hospital. One year earlier, doctors in the same hospital had removed about 18 in. of her ileum. Her postoperative course was stormy. The patient's reaction to the old operation took a turn for the worse 3 weeks before she was admitted to the hospital. She had developed severe symptoms, including abdominal pain, sweating, and uncontrolled diarrhea. She had also been losing weight for the past few months.

For the first 2 weeks in the hospital, Mrs. K.F. was placed on a low-residue liquid diet that was lactose free. She responded to the diet well, and most of her symptoms disappeared. However, Mrs. K.F. continued to lose weight. The health team concluded that she was not receiving sufficient nutrients from her special diet, especially since her appetite was not very good. After a careful consultation, members of the health team decided that she might benefit from a nutritious supplement if she could be encouraged to consume an acceptable amount. Flexical, a commercial formula diet, was administered to the patient in addition to her therapeutic diet. Mrs. K.F. was unable to drink more than one-third of a can of this supplement each day for the first 2 days. She vomited within 1 or 2 hours every time after drinking this supplement. However, the nurse and dietitian worked diligently to find ways to increase her consumption of the formula diet. Eventually she found the supplement to be more acceptable when there were frequent feedings and changes of flavor and concentration. She liked it best when it was ice cold.

After 11 days on this diet regimen, Mrs. K.F. slowly gained weight. However, the clinical condition of her intestine did not improve in spite of her weight gain and the subsiding of her symptoms. The attending surgeons had to remove an additional 18 in. of the terminal ileum affected by Crohn's disease. About 2 weeks after the operation, the patient's consumption of the formula increased from 1,200 to 2,300 kcal per day in addition to her regular low-residue diet. She was discharged from the hospital 3 weeks after the surgery. A few days before the discharge, Mrs. K.F. was able to eat regular food in addition to the supplement.

Mrs. K.F. preferred the supplement cold and also drank either water or ginger ale with the formula. She required only gentle persuasion by the hospital staff to overcome the unfamiliar texture and taste of the formula. Mrs. K.F. definitely did not like the formula when it was at room temperature. Mrs. K.F. also indicated that the use of a straw sometimes made it easier for her to swallow the formula.

During her first 2 weeks in the hospital, Mrs. K.F.'s body weight decreased from 48.8 kg (107.4 lb) to 47.4 kg (104.3 lb). During the first 2 weeks on Flexical, her weight increased from 47.4 kg (104.3 lb) to 49.4 kg (108.7 lb). It was calculated that during this period, her daily caloric intake was about 800 to 1,000 kcal from Flexical and about 1,200 to 1,300 kcal from low-residue foods.

Review and Analysis

1. What is Crohn's disease? Do we know what causes this intestinal disorder?
2. Why was Mrs. K.F. not receiving adequate nutrients from her prescribed diet of regular liquid foods?
3. Name other commercial formulas that can replace Flexical and indicate their manufacturers.
4. Describe as many ways as you can to improve a patient's acceptance of an unfamiliar formula diet.
5. Describe the dietary management of Mrs. K.F. for the first 3 days after her operation.
6. If Mrs. K.F. wanted to gain more weight after her discharge from the hospital, what type of diet would you recommend? What should Mrs. K.F.'s ideal weight be?

form is most effective? What precautions should be followed with different types of antacid?

6. What is the major clinical problem of the small intestine? Why does it occur? Briefly describe its symptoms, diagnosis, and treatment.

7. How does pancreatitis occur? What factors may cause it? Define *replacement therapy*.

8. What is celiac disease? Discuss the physiological abnormalities that lead to this condition. By what means can a dramatic improvement of this condition occur?

9. Define *diverticulum*. How is it related to diverticulosis? What change in the treatment of diverticulosis has taken place? Why?

Chapter 25

Diet and Diseases of the Liver and Gallbladder

THE LARGEST VISCERAL organ in the body, the adult liver weighs from 3¼ to 3½ lb (1.4 to 1.6 kg). Highly complex, it is intimately involved in the metabolism and storage of nutrients. The liver, gallbladder, and small intestine are linked by the circulation of bile salts, a system known as the enterohepatic circulation. This chapter first briefly describes the structure and functions of the liver and the enterohepatic circulation and then considers dietary measures that can be taken when these systems fail. Specific clinical conditions dealt with are viral hepatitis, liver cirrhosis, ascites and edema, hepatic encephalopathy, and gallstones.

UNIQUE FEATURES OF THE LIVER

The liver has three major and unique features: its circulatory system, its regenerative ability, and its physiological functions.

Circulatory System of the Liver

Arterial blood from the systemic circulation enters the liver from the hepatic artery (see Figure 25-1) and provides nutrition for the connective tissue of the liver, especially in the walls of the bile duct (see the later discussion). The intestine is supplied with blood by the intestinal artery and vein. The latter vein and the vein from the spleen empty jointly into the portal vein, which ends in the liver. After portal blood has entered the liver, it flows through the venous sinuses in very close contact with the cords of the liver parenchymal cells. Then it enters the central vein and leaves the liver via the hepatic vein and vena cava (see Figures 25-1 and 25-2).

Within the liver, the portal triad refers to the interwoven branches of the bile duct, the hepatic artery, and the portal vein. It forms the fibrous sheath sometimes also known as the portal tracts (see Figure 25-2). The terminal branches of the portal and hepatic venous systems are joined by a network of sinusoids, or lobules. Basically, the hepatic venous system runs through the center of the liver, while the portal system is located on its periphery. Between the sinusoids are located the one-cell-thick plates of the hepatocytes, which are very specialized glandular cells (see Figure 25-2).

Regeneration

Liver cells have a high turnover rate, and they have a unique ability to regenerate if damaged. If any trauma, infection, poisoning, or other adverse condition leaves a sufficient quantity of liver cells intact, the liver regenerates to its normal size. If one-quarter of a human liver is removed, it normally needs 1 to 2 weeks to regenerate completely. On the other hand, any unremoved dead liver cells may create fibrous tissues that are unable to perform normal functions.

Essential Functions

The liver performs many important functions. The major ones are: receiving and storing absorbed nutrients, metabolizing nutrients, synthesizing and secreting bile, detoxifying poisonous and waste substances in the blood, and storing blood.

After digestion, ingested nutrients are absorbed into the capillaries of the villi of the intestinal mucosa, from which they enter the portal vein. In the liver, the nutrients are readied for redistribution, metabolism, and storage. These nutrients include monosaccharides, amino acids, fatty acids (eventually), vitamins, minerals, and other substances.

Much of the body's metabolism occurs in the liver, and it plays a vital role in nutrient metabolism. (Detailed information on body metabolism is presented in Chapter 8.) It regulates the synthesis of amino acids into protein, especially plasma proteins such as globulin, albumin, and prothrombin. Liver disease is sometimes characterized by an abnormal blood level of these substances. In the liver, glucose may be degraded to carbon dioxide, water, and energy or transferred to glycogen. The liver also plays an important role in regulating blood glucose. In the liver, fatty acids are either metabolized to energy or incorporated into triglycerides or complex and compound lipids such as lipoproteins, phospholipids (see Chapters 5 and 27), and cholesterol.

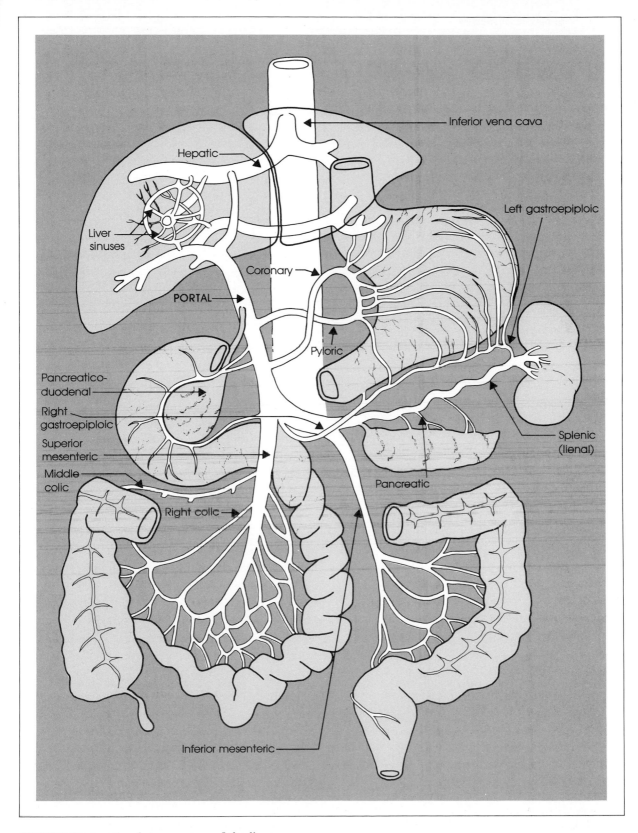

FIGURE 25-1   Circulatory system of the liver.

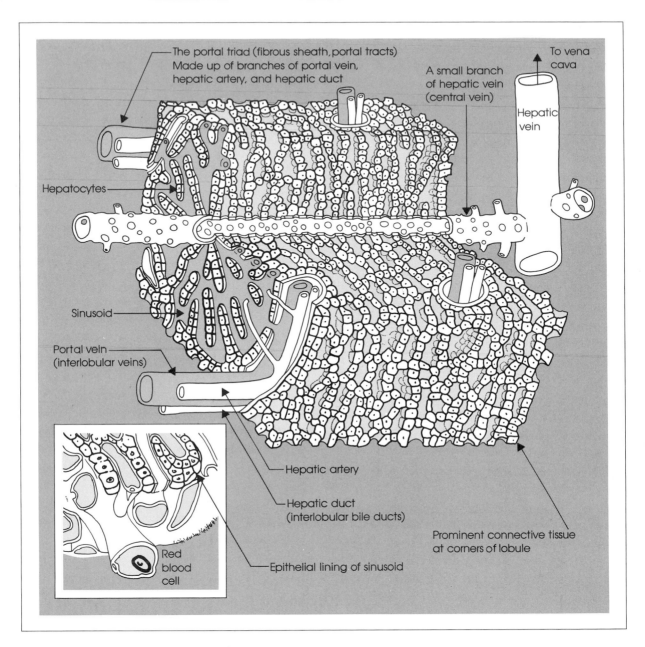

The portal triad (fibrous sheath, portal tracts)
Made up of branches of portal vein,
hepatic artery, and hepatic duct

To vena
cava

A small branch
of hepatic vein
(central vein)

Hepatic
vein

Hepatocytes

Sinusoid

Portal vein
(interlobular veins)

Hepatic artery

Hepatic duct
(interlobular bile ducts)

Prominent connective tissue
at corners of lobule

Red
blood
cell

Epithelial lining of sinusoid

FIGURE 25-2   Architecture of the liver.

The liver can also transform the cholesterol into steroid hormones and bile acids.

The liver stores some vitamin B_{12}, folic acid, and vitamin C and much larger quantities of the fat-soluble vitamins, A, D, and K. In addition, the transformation of carotene to vitamin A and of inactive vitamin D to the active form and the synthesis of prothrombin in the presence of vi-tamin K all take place in the liver. The liver is also the storage site for minerals such as copper and iron.

Bile is synthesized and secreted by the liver and contains the following components:

1. Water (more than 95%)
2. Bile salts

3. Inorganic salts
4. Bile pigments
5. Fatty acids
6. Fats
7. Lecithin
8. Cholesterol
9. Alkaline phosphatase

The bile salts are sodium and potassium salts of bile acids conjugated to glycine or taurine, a derivative of cystine.

Detoxification is another indispensable function of the liver. The liver can remove injurious or waste products, including substances occurring naturally in food, produced by intestinal bacteria, ingested or injected as drugs, or occurring as metabolites. The amino acids in protein and other nitrogenous substances (see Chapter 4) produce ammonia as a by-product or metabolite. Ammonia is toxic in excessive quantities in the blood but is normally changed to urea by the liver, which is then excreted in the urine. No other organ can do this. When the liver fails, the blood ammonia level rises. This excess is sometimes detoxified partly by other organs through incorporation into glutamine or glutamate and asparagine or aspartate, all of which are amino acids or derivatives.

Because the liver can store 500 to 1,000 mL of blood, it is sometimes referred to as a blood reservoir. If a person has hemorrhaged, the blood stored in the liver sinusoids is released into circulation to restore the amount lost. On the other hand, if blood pressure in the hepatic vein increases, a large amount of blood is forced into the sinusoids of the liver, which can swell considerably.

Consequences of Liver Failure

Because the liver performs all these important functions, liver failure may produce the following clinical consequences: (1) blockage of the portal system, which can result in many clinical problems; (2) failure to excrete bile, resulting in jaundice and defective nutrient digestion and absorption; and (3) multiple failure of liver functions, including the inadequate synthesis of prothrombin, which is essential to blood clotting.

The clinical course of any liver disorder de-

pends upon the ability of the liver to regenerate. Sometimes when there is extensive structural damage, liver cells can recover and perform most or all normal functions. Thus, the nutritional and dietary care of a patient with liver disease during the recovery stage and in the absence of hepatic coma consists mainly of providing an optimal amount of calories, protein, vitamins, and minerals for the liver cells to rebuild.

ENTEROHEPATIC CIRCULATION

Figure 25-3 shows the anatomical relationships between the liver, gallbladder, pancreas, and small intestine. The liver is closely linked to the gallbladder and small intestine by the *enterohepatic circulation* of bile salts from the liver to the gallbladder, to the intestinal lumen, to the portal vein, and back to the liver.

A small amount of bile is continually secreted by the liver cells into the bile duct (see Figures 25-2 and 25-3), which empties into the hepatic and common bile ducts, from which the bile enters either the gallbladder or the duodenum. Normally the bile is stored in the gallbladder and emptied into the duodenum only when food, especially fat, is present there. Inside the gallbladder, the bile is concentrated five- to tenfold when its water, electrolytes, and other ingredients are absorbed into the surrounding mucosa. The bile empties from the gallbladder into the duodenum when fat in the small intestine elicits the hormone cholecystokinin from the intestinal mucosa. When this hormone reaches the gallbladder via the bloodstream, the latter contracts and releases the bile.

The main function of the bile is to provide bile salts, which can emulsify fatty particles in the food (chyme) and facilitate the intestinal absorption of fatty acids and other simple lipids. Without bile salts, fats are not easily emulsified and absorbed, resulting in a loss of fat and fat-soluble vitamins in the stool (steatorrhea).

In a healthy person, after absorption, most of the fats are emptied into the lymphatic system and eventually reach the systemic circulation. However, the bile salts separate from the fats and

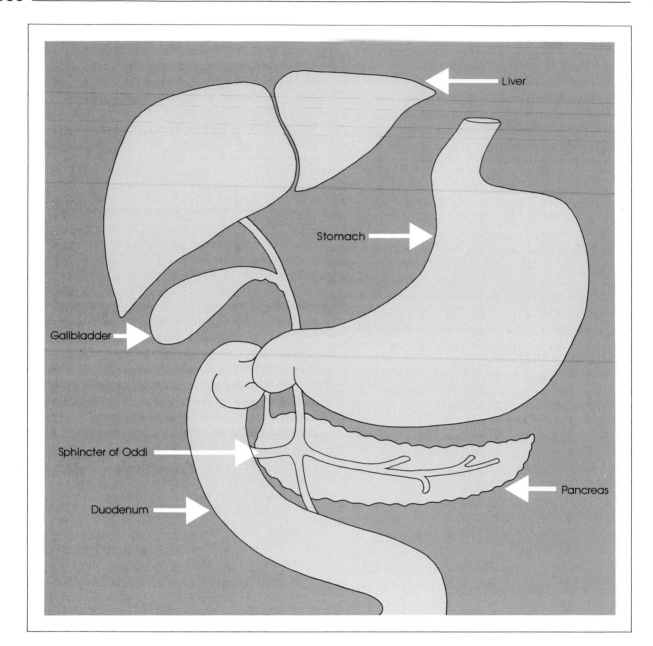

FIGURE 25-3   Anatomical relationships among the liver, pancreas, gallbladder, and duodenum.

travel through the portal vein into the liver, where they are incorporated into the bile again. Thus, bile salts complete the entire enterohepatic circulation (liver, gallbladder, intestinal lumen, portal vein, and liver again). In this way, about 80% to 90% of the bile salts in the intestinal lumen are reabsorbed; the rest are lost in the stool.

VIRAL HEPATITIS

With this background, we can now look at what happens when these organs malfunction. The first condition to be considered is viral hepatitis, a liver disease.

Types and Symptoms

There are two types of viral hepatitis. *Hepatitis type A*, previously known as infectious hepatitis, is a viral infection of the liver that may occur in epidemics or sporadically. Its onset is acute, with a 3- to 5-week incubation period. Urticarial rash and joint pain are usually absent. *Hepatitis type B*, previously known as serum hepatitis, is a viral infection of the liver, which has an insidious onset and a relatively long (more than 5 weeks) incubation period. Urticarial rash and painful joints are usually present.

Type A is the most common infection of the liver and often becomes a troublesome health problem in crowded living areas, especially among children and young adults. Mainly transmitted through food, sewage, and drinking water, this disease is contagious; during certain phases of its course, the disease can be transmitted through blood donation. Type B is commonly associated with contaminated blood from transfusions, needles and syringes used by drug addicts, sharp objects used for ear piercing, and dental equipment.

In both types of liver infection, there is necrosis of liver parenchymal cells with plasma cells and lymphocytes present in necrotic and portal areas. As indicated above, the surviving liver cells can regenerate, maintaining the basic architecture of this organ.

Symptoms of viral hepatitis range from nonspecific to very serious. In a few patients, death occurs in a few days. The disease is characterized by three phases: prodromal, icteric, and convalescent.

During the *prodromal phase*, the patient experiences muscular pain, general discomfort, frequent tiredness, and respiratory problems such as nasal discharge and inflammation of the pharynx. Severe loss of appetite is frequently accompanied by vomiting, nausea, diarrhea, or constipation. There is usually fever, which subsides with the onset of jaundice. Mild abdominal pain occurs in the right upper quadrant.

The clinical *icteric phase* may or may not occur. This jaundice stage usually occurs 2 to 5 days after the prodromal phase.

During the *convalescent phase*, the appetite and a feeling of well-being return, and symptoms (pain, tiredness, and jaundice) disappear within 1 to 5 weeks. Liver enlargement and tenderness occur in more than half the patients, and the spleen may swell.

It is important to realize that not all patients recover from viral hepatitis. A chronic situation may lead to liver cirrhosis and, in some acute and fulminating cases, death. However, overall mortality is less than 1%. The rate is higher among the elderly, especially postmenopausal women. Liver damage in an older patient may be severe and result in fatty infiltration of the liver followed by hepatic coma.

Medical Management

The medical management of a patient with viral hepatitis consists of bed rest and dietary care. Medications such as corticotropin and corticosteroids are recommended in treating fulminating hepatitis, but they should not be used in the routine, uncomplicated case of viral hepatitis.

If a patient wants bed rest during the acute symptomatic phase, he or she should have it. However, since this practice has been seriously questioned, bed rest should not be required of every patient. The patient can resume normal activity after a lengthy convalescent period.

Liquid and solid foods should be encouraged as the patient's strength returns. Frequent and small feedings may be necessary at the beginning to ensure proper caloric intake.

If oral intake is insufficient or if the patient is unable to eat because of anorexia, nausea, and vomiting, intravenous feeding may be necessary. In this case, the patient should be initially provided with 5% to 10% dextrose solution. However, if such semistarvation is maintained for long, more intense parenteral nutrition may be instituted (including the administration of amino acids, protein hydrolysates, and human plasma or albumin). Some patients need tube feedings to provide aggressive nutritional support, especially during the transitional period. More information on intravenous and tube feedings is presented in Chapter 23.

If a patient can eat regular foods (usually within a week after the onset of symptoms) and has a good appetite, he or she should be fed a high-calorie, high-protein diet that is attractive

TABLE 25-1   Sample Menu for a Diet Containing Approximately 3,000 kcal, 125 g of Protein, 300 g of Carbohydrate, and 100 g of Fat

Breakfast	Lunch	Dinner
Orange juice, 1 c	Pea soup, ½ c	Lamb chops, 2
Eggs, scrambled, 2	Tuna salad, 1 c	Carrots, cooked, 1 c
Sausages, 2 links	Lettuce leaves, 4	Cole slaw, with mustard and vinegar, 1 c
Muffin, whole wheat, 2	Tomato, 1 sl	
Margarine, 1 pat	Bread, whole wheat, 2 sl	Potato, baked, 1
Coffee, tea	Margarine, 1 pat	Margarine, 1 T
Sugar	Milk, 1 c	Sour cream, 2 T
Cream	Coffee, tea	Milk, skim, 1 c
Salt, pepper	Sugar	Ice cream, 1 c
	Cream	Coffee, tea
	Salt, pepper	Sugar
		Cream
	Snack	Salt, pepper
	Plums, canned, 1 c	
	Doughnut, 1	**Snack**
		Pudding, chocolate, 1 c
		Apple juice, 1 c

and palatable, which supplies approximately 2,800 to 3,500 kcal, 90 to 130 g of protein, and 300 to 400 g of carbohydrate. However, any item not tolerated by the patient should be avoided in the meal plan. Consult Chapters 10 and 22 for planning such diets. If the patient has no jaundice and normal bile salt secretion, he or she should be provided with 100 to 150 g of fat. However, if the patient has steatorrhea and shows fat intolerance, fat intake should be reduced to 20 to 50 g per day. Planning a low-fat diet will be discussed later. Table 25-1 provides a menu plan for a diet containing approximately 3,000 kcal, 125 g of protein, 300 g of carbohydrate, and 100 g of fat.

If any sign of impending coma is present, dietary protein intake may have to be reduced. If the clinical profile improves, the patient may eat permitted protein foods again. Vitamin supplements may be necessary, with special attention to vitamins C, B_1, B_{12}, folic acid, and vitamin K.

Patients may infect hospital equipment and personnel. Routine hospital anti-infection precautions must be followed, and all food-serving utensils should be isolated and handled with care.

LIVER CIRRHOSIS

Liver cirrhosis is a serious disease characterized by chronic hepatic insufficiency. It may or may not be preceded by a fatty liver. This degenerative chronic liver disorder has a number of features: (1) a reduced number of liver cells; (2) the derangement of the blood circulation system in the liver because of the disruption of liver lobules and the reticulin supporting network, leading to fibrosis and collapse; (3) nodular regeneration throughout the remaining liver cells; and (4) death and scarring of liver cells.

Causes and Symptoms

The causes of liver cirrhosis are not well defined, although the following factors, in decreasing order of importance, are known to be able to produce the disease: excess alcohol consumption; poisoning by toxic substances, such as plant toxins; infections; and an inborn error of metabolism, such as Wilson's disease and hemochromatosis. Severe malnutrition such as kwashiorkor can potentiate the development of liver cirrhosis. While half of the clinical cases in the United States are due to alcohol abuse, many cirrhotic patients develop the disease without a known cause. To avoid involving the cause of cirrhosis, clinicians have recently described the disease according to the size of the resultant nodules: macronodular, micronodular, and intermediate.

Symptoms in a cirrhotic patient range from none to fulminating, and while its onset is usually insidious, it is sometimes abrupt. Below is a list of symptoms at different stages, although many patients show mixed manifestations.

I. Early symptoms
   A. Weakness
   B. Tiredness
   C. Weight loss and wasting
   D. Abdominal pain from liver enlargement and possibly ascites
   E. Diarrhea with occasional constipation
   F. Amenorrhea and other menstrual irregularities
   G. Impotence, sterility, and/or loss of libido
   H. Vomiting blood
II. Intermediate symptoms
   A. Severe anorexia with nausea and vomiting
   B. Palpable and firm liver with a blunt edge
   C. Glossitis and cheilosis due to vitamin deficiency
   D. Appearance of a chronic illness
   E. Various types of skin lesions (spider nevi, palmar erythema, and telangiectases)
   F. Jaundice (usually not present at the beginning, then mild to severe signs as disease progresses, especially if the biliary tract is involved)
III. Late symptoms
   A. Ascites
   B. Pleural effusion
   C. Peripheral edema
   D. Purpuric lesions
   E. Precoma and encephalopathy or comatose state
   F. Feminization of male characteristics
      1. Enlarged breast tissues
      2. Loss of chest hair
      3. Testicular atrophy

G. Fever (especially in alcoholic hepatitis)
H. Splenomegaly
I. Dilatation of the superficial veins of the thorax and abdomen (due to blockage of portal blood circulation system)

Diet Therapy

The medical management of a cirrhotic patient consists of diet therapy, bed rest, medications, and removal of the cause of the disorder. The diet prescription varies with the condition of the patient. If the patient has difficulty in eating normally, transition to routine hospital feedings should be followed (see Chapter 23). Otherwise, feeding with regular foods is encouraged. If the patient is bedridden, an initial 1,900 to 2,000 kcal and 80 to 90 g of protein may be indicated; if sedentary, 2,400 to 2,600 kcal and 95 to 105 g of protein; if ambulatory, 3,000 kcal and 100 to 130 g of protein. However, if the patient has a good appetite and likes to eat, he or she can be provided with high-calorie, high-protein meals. About 300 to 400 g of carbohydrate (half of the caloric intake) should be given to assure that the protein will be spared for rebuilding the liver. The patient should be provided with a good supply of B vitamins (B_{12}, folic acid, and others) and vitamin C, with fat-soluble vitamins A, D, and K being supplemented if necessary. If prothrombin time is low, vitamin K may have to be injected.

In planning a diet for a cirrhotic patient, the patient's individual conditions must be considered. Obese patients should have a lower caloric prescription to permit a chance for weight loss. Fat intake is regulated by the normalcy of bile salt metabolism—by whether the patient has jaundice or steatorrhea, for instance. The presence of a fatty liver indicates fat restriction or the use of MCTs (see Chapter 23). Planning a low-fat menu is discussed later in this chapter. On the other hand, if fat metabolism is normal, the patient should be fed 65 to 100 g of fat per day. Salt and fluid intake is determined by the extent of ascites and edema. Protein intake must be restricted if the patient shows signs of hepatic coma.

Feeding a cirrhotic patient is sometimes difficult because of anorexia, nausea, and vomiting. One useful technique is to divide the meals into five to seven small ones. Planning a larger meal at a time when the patient eats well has proven effective. Chapters 22 and 23 provide more details on how to feed patients with eating problems. Good patient education and planning favorite meals will help when a patient finds eating difficult.

When the patient's nutritional status improves, clinical and laboratory results also improve. It must be emphasized that if the patient fails to eat an adequate amount of food for a prolonged period, aggressive nutritional measures are needed, such as hospital or commercial high-nutrient preparations, tube feedings, and parenteral alimentation (see Chapter 23).

Patients with liver cirrhosis are susceptible to blood diseases. Hypochromic microcytic anemia from iron deficiency is corrected by administering one enteric-coated tablet (about 300 mg) of ferrous sulfate three times a day after meals. Macrocytic anemia is corrected by giving 5 mg of folic acid daily, assuming that there is no vitamin B_{12} deficiency.

Decreased prothrombin time may be corrected by administering vitamin K, although other coagulation factors may be absent if there is severe liver disease. A fresh blood transfusion may be necessary to arrest any nonclotting or bleeding tendency. Vitamin K should be administered as 2 mg of menadione sodium bisulfite intramuscularly or intravenously or 1 to 3 mg of menadione orally, three times each day after meals.

As indicated earlier, a patient with liver failure may develop ascites, edema, or hepatic encephalopathy. These conditions are described in the following sections.

ASCITES AND EDEMA

Ascites refers to the accumulation of fluid in the peritoneal cavity. In a patient with liver failure this accumulation is caused by: (1) increased pressure in the portal vein system; (2) decreased plasma protein (usually albumin) due to decreased liver synthesis, leading to a depressed plasma osmotic pressure; (3) newly synthesized albumin being released into the peritoneal cav-

ity; and (4) increased sodium retention in the body.

Although ascites must be treated, the condition is not life threatening. Conservative and cautious management is necessary, since aggressive therapy may result in electrolyte imbalance (especially hypokalemia), and the reduced intravascular volume may lead to hepatic encephalopathy, renal crisis, and death. The treatment of ascites and edema includes the regulation of salt and fluid intakes, administering diuretics, bed rest, and paracentesis. The regulation of the patient's salt and fluid intake is briefly discussed below.

A diet of 500 mg of sodium per day is recommended. Although a 250-mg-sodium diet is more effective and sometimes prescribed, its low acceptability by the patient and inadequate nutritional content limits its usefulness. Once diuresis has started, the patient's sodium intake may be progressively increased to 1,000 mg daily. The actual need for fluid and sodium is best determined by monitoring urinary excretion. More details on this topic and the planning of sodium-restricted diets are presented in Chapters 27 and 28.

Fluids do not have to be restricted with all patients. However, an intake of 1,500 mL of water per day will prevent hyponatremia (low blood sodium) induced by excess fluid intake in those patients with an impaired ability to handle a fluid load. Again, urine volume is a good index.

HEPATIC ENCEPHALOPATHY

Hepatic or portal system encephalopathy is a disorder caused by failure of the liver to remove toxic waste. It is currently believed that toxic nitrogenous waste from protein or similar compounds can accumulate as blood ammonia.

In a normal patient the liver receives ammonia from the portal vein and the systemic circulation and metabolizes it to urea, which is then excreted by the kidney. If the liver cannot function properly, ammonia accumulating in the liver will not be converted to urea.

For example, proteins, peptides, amino acids,

TABLE 25-2   Clinical Development of Hepatic Coma

Phase	Clinical State	Mental Condition	Tremor
A	Premonitory symptoms	Mild confusion	Slight
B	Impending symptoms	Confusion	Yes
C	Stupor	Extreme confusion	Depends on patient alertness
D	Coma	Coma	No

and ammonium salts may be ingested and partly degraded to ammonia by intestinal bacteria, and any urea normally formed by the bowel can be degraded to ammonia by intestinal bacteria. Normal amino acid metabolism in the body also produces ammonia in the blood.

Causes and Symptoms

The conditions that can precipitate hepatic encephalopathy are as follows:

1. Fulminating liver failure: hepatitis, cirrhosis
2. Portacaval shunt procedure subsequence
3. Elevated amines and ammonia in the blood due to excess protein intake, bleeding in the digestive tract, or the presence of ammonium chloride from ingestion or injection (Intestinal hemorrhage can contribute blood protein to the gut, where it is degraded to form more ammonia for absorption.)
4. Drugs: sedatives, tranquilizers, and narcotics
5. Alkalosis and low blood potassium
6. Azotemia from misuse of diuretics or renal failure, creating more urea to be degraded by the bacteria (Further, kidney failure might result in the tubules reabsorbing more ammonia into the bloodstream, thus aggravating encephalopathy.)
7. Alcoholism, infection, some surgical procedures, dehydration and shock, constipation, and other conditions

Intestinal ammonia formation depends on the substances ingested, types and population of intestinal flora, and the extent of peristalsis of the large intestine. Eventually the ammonia escapes from the liver and mixes with the systemic circulation. It is suspected that when the ammonia affects the brain, the patient manifests clinical signs, showing both neurological and psychiatric adverse reactions and personality changes such as irritability, confusion, and apathy. Table 25-2 shows a simplified description of the stages of development of the disorder. "Flap" is the well-known neurological sign: Patients exhibit a flapping tremor of the hands when the fingers of their outstretched arms are spread. In addition, intestinal hemorrhage may permit gut bacteria to invade body circulation, hastening the development of hepatic coma.

Dietary Management

The medical management of hepatic encephalopathy and coma consists of controlling the bleeding in the gastrointestinal tract, removing all medications containing ammonia or its salts, administering antibiotics, correcting any electrolyte imbalance, diet therapy, and miscellaneous treatments.

The main purpose of diet therapy is to restrict the amount of nitrogenous substances, mainly ammonia, in the gastrointestinal tract and blood and to stop the catabolism of lean body mass. Depending on the particular patient and the philosophy of the doctor, the patient is permitted to ingest anywhere from 0 to 40 g of protein. A comatose patient is fed no protein. In this case, a commercial protein-free nutritional supplement is used, such as Polycose, Sumacal, and Lipomul-Oral. This may be adjusted to provide 1,500 to 2,000 kcal per day, and tube feeding may be necessary. If intravenous nutrition is preferred, the patient should be provided a dex-

TABLE 25-3 Protein Contents of Protein Exchange Food Lists

Food Group	Protein Exchange Food List	Approximate (g) Protein Content per Exchange
Milk and milk products	I	4
Grain products	II	2
Meat and equivalents	III-1	6
	III-2	8
Fruits	IV-1	0.5
	IV-2	1
Vegetables	V-1	1
	V-2	2
Free foods (see text)	VI	None to trace
Alternates	VII	None to trace

trose solution and, if necessary, essential fatty acids (for instance, Intralipid). Vitamins and minerals may have to be administered depending on the length of the nonoral feeding; if clinical conditions of the patient permit, the patient should be given protein-sparing solutions (see Chapters 23 and 29).

Chapter 23 provides details on various methods of enteral and parenteral nutrition. If the patient's fluid intake is restricted, hypertonic glucose solution may have to be used, in which case a proper catheter bore is needed for either tube or intravenous feeding.

If the patient shows clinical improvement and can eat, he or she may be fed 20 to 40 g of protein a day, with 10 g more added every 2 to 3 days. During this treatment individual protein tolerance, signs of hepatic encephalopathy, and serum ammonia must be closely monitored.

It is currently believed that if the protein intake is restricted, the patient should be given good, quality products such as milk, cheese, eggs, and meat, which contain high levels of essential amino acids. The protein should have a high biological value (see Chapters 4 and 28). This, together with a generous amount of carbohydrate and fat, will provide an acceptable diet. If the patient is not consuming adequate protein, the catabolism of the lean body mass will produce more nitrogen (ammonia) in the blood. Constipation and hypermetabolism from stress such as infection can reduce patient tolerance, intensify encephalopathy, and elevate body nitrogen con-

TABLE 25-4 Protein Exchange Food List I: Milk and Milk Products

Food	One Exchange
Milk, whole	½ c
Milk, skim or nonfat	½ c
Milk, canned, evaporated	¼ c
Milk, chocolate, commercial	⅓ c
Milk, chocolate, homemade	½ c
Milk, goat	½ c
Buttermilk	½ c
Cream cheese	3½ T
Cheddar cheese	½ oz
Ice cream, plain	⅔ c
Ice milk	⅔ c
Yogurt, from skim or whole milk	½ c

Note: One exchange contains 4 g of protein.

centration. These variables must be considered in determining appropriate feeding for the patient.

Assume that a patient eats normally and is permitted 20 to 60 g of protein a day. How should the meals be planned? One practice is to divide foods into groups of similar products and then, within each group, determine what portions of different food items supply a certain amount of protein. For example, within the group of milk and milk products, ½ c of yogurt or 3½ T of cream cheese provides about 4 g of protein. The Protein Exchange Food Lists were

TABLE 25-5 Protein Exchange Food List II: Grain Products

Food	One Exchange
Bread, cracked wheat	1 sl
Bread, raisin	1 sl
Bread, white	1 sl
Bread, whole wheat	¾ sl
Cereals, dry, ready-to-serve	
Bran flakes (40% bran)	½ c
Cheerios	¾ c
Corn flakes	1 c
Corn, puffed	2 c
Corn, shredded	1 c
Raisin bran	½ c
Rice Krispies	1 c
Wheat, puffed	1 c
Wheat, shredded	1 biscuit
Cereals, cooked	
Corn (hominy) grits, degermed	⅔ c
Cornmeal, degermed, enriched	⅔ c
Farina	½ c
Oatmeal	⅓ c
Cookies, crackers, etc.	
Brownies	2
Cookies, chocolate chip	2
Crackers, graham	3
Crackers, Ritz	8
Doughnut	2
Muffin	⅔
Saltines	6
Triscuits	5
Wheat Thins	16
Macaroni, noodles	¼ c
Melba toast	3 sl
Pancake, 4″ diameter	1
Parsnips, cooked	½ c
Popcorn, popped	1 c
Potato, baked or boiled, medium	1
Potato, mashed	½ c
Rice, cooked	½ c
Spaghetti, cooked	⅓ c
Squash, winter, cooked	½ c
Sweet potato, cooked	½ c

Note: One exchange contains 2 g of protein.

TABLE 25-6 Protein Exchange Food List III-1: Meat and Equivalents

Food	One Exchange
Beans and nuts*	
Beans, dry, cooked	¼ c
Beans, kidney, cooked	½ c
Peanut butter	1 T
Cheese and eggs	
Cheese, cheddar or brick	1 oz
Egg	1
Fish and shellfish	
Clams	5
Haddock	1 oz
Lobster	¼ c
Perch	1 oz
Salmon	¼ c
Scallops	1 oz
Shrimp, medium	5
Meat	
Hot dog†	1
Lamb	1 oz
Luncheon meat and alternates†	1 oz

Note: One exchange contains 6 g of protein.

*Use these items as protein sources only if the patient prefers them.

†Whenever possible, avoid these items if the patient is permitted less than 40 g of protein per day.

and the serving size of one exchange for each food. One can replace one serving of a food with that of another food from the same list and obtain an equivalent amount of protein.

Table 25-12 (List VI) describes "free" foods, which contain very little protein, that may be used as desired by the patient within reasonable limits. Table 25-13 (List VII) describes alternate foods, which are mainly special dietary foods such as commercial high-nutrient, low-protein solutions and low-protein bakery products. Again, the patient may use the items in List VII within reasonable limits.

Table 25-14 lists the nutrient contents of various diets containing 20 to 60 g of protein a day. Table 25-15 uses Tables 25-3 to 25-13 to prepare meal plans for the diets indicated in Table 25-14. Table 25-16 provides a sample menu supplying 20 g of protein per day, using the information in Tables 25-3 to 25-15. Similarly, Table 25-17 presents a sample menu supplying 60 g of

developed by using this technique (Table 25-3). In the example used above, ½ c yogurt or 3½ T cream cheese represents 1 exchange within List I, milk and milk products. Tables 25-4 to 25-11 describe the food products included in lists I to V

TABLE 25-7   Protein Exchange Food List III-2: Meat and Equivalents

Food	One Exchange
Cheese	
American	1 oz
Cottage	¼ c
Cream	3 oz
Edam	1 oz
Gouda	1 oz
Parmesan, grated	4 T
Swiss	1 oz
Fish, cooked	
Cod	1 oz
Crabmeat, canned	1½ oz
Oyster meat	3 oz
Tuna	¼ oz
Meat, cooked	
Bacon, cooked, medium thick	4 sl
Beef	1 oz
Chicken	1 oz
Deviled ham, canned	2 oz
Liver	1 oz
Pork	1 oz
Turkey	1 oz
Veal	1 oz

Note: One exchange contains 8 g of protein.

TABLE 25-8   Protein Exchange Food List IV-1: Fruits

Food	One Exchange
Apple, raw, medium	1
Apple butter	5 T
Apple juice	1 c
Applesauce	½ c
Apricots, canned	⅓ c
Apricots, fresh	2
Apricot nectar	½ c
Blackberries	½ c
Boysenberries	½ c
Fruit cocktail	½ c
Figs, canned	½ c
Grape juice	1 c
Grapes, raw, seedless	½ c
Grapefruit, fresh, 3½" diam.	½
Grapefruit juice	½ c
Grapefruit or orange juice	½ c
Peaches, canned	2 halves
Peach, raw, medium	½
Pear, raw, medium	½
Pears, canned, solids and liquid	1 c
Pear nectar	½ c
Pineapple, fresh or canned	½ c
Plums, canned with liquid	3
Plums, raw	¾ c

Note: One exchange contains 0.5 g of protein.

protein per day. However, in planning low-protein diets, food items in List VI (Table 25-12) and VII (Table 25-13) must be used to make sure that the patient is getting enough calories and other nonprotein essential nutrients.

Because of the limited selection of regular foods, patients may have trouble accepting the dietary regimen. Chapter 28, which provides some guidelines on how to improve patient compliance, should be consulted for additional information, especially if the patient is prescribed a low-sodium, low-protein diet. Recently some clinicians have suggested that different foods contain varying levels of ammonia and that those items with high levels of ammonia should be avoided. However, this proposal is not widely accepted since no relationship between the nitro-

TABLE 25-9   Protein Exchange Food List IV-2: Fruits

Food	One Exchange
Banana, small	1
Cantaloupe, small	¼
Cherries, canned	½ c
Cherries, raw	10
Lemon, medium	1
Orange, small	½
Orange juice	½ c
Raspberries	½ c
Strawberries	½ c
Watermelon	1 c

Note: One exchange contains 1 g of protein.

TABLE 25-10   Protein Exchange Food List V-1: Vegetables

Food	One Exchange
Beans, green, fresh or canned, cooked	½ c
Beets, cooked	½ c
Cabbage, cooked or raw	½ c
Carrots, fresh or canned, cooked	½ c
Cauliflower, fresh, cooked	½ c
Celery, raw, cooked	1 c
Chard, leaves and stalks, cooked	⅓ c
Cucumber, raw, medium	1
Escarole, raw	5–10 leaves
Lettuce	1 wedge
Onions, cooked	½ c
Onions, raw, chopped	¼ c
Parsley, chopped	2 T
Pepper (sweet, green, or red), medium	1
Pumpkin, canned	½ c
Radishes, raw, small	10
Sauerkraut	½ c
Squash, summer	½ c
Tomato, raw, canned	½ c
Tomato juice	½ c
Turnip, cooked	½ c

Note: One exchange contains 1 g of protein.

TABLE 25-11   Protein Exchange Food List V-2: Vegetables

Food	One Exchange
Asparagus, cooked	½ c
Bean sprouts, cooked	½ c
Broccoli, cooked	½ c
Brussels sprouts, cooked	⅓ c
Collards, cooked	½ c
Corn (canned, frozen, or fresh), cooked	⅓ c
Dandelion greens, cooked	½ c
Kale, cooked	½ c
Mushrooms, canned, fresh	½ c
Okra, cooked	8 pods
Peas (fresh, frozen, or canned and drained), cooked	¼ c
Spinach, cooked	¼ c
Turnip greens	½ c

Note: One exchange contains 2 g of protein.

TABLE 25-12   Protein Exchange Food List VI: Free Foods

Fats and oils*	Beverages	Sweets and candies	Condiments	Miscellaneous
Butter	Carbonated beverages	Fondant	Herbs	Cornstarch
French dressing	Coffee	Gum drops	Pepper	Marshmallows
Italian dressing	Cranberry juice	Hard candies	Salt	Popsicles
Margarine	Fruit-flavored drinks	Honey	Spices	Tapioca, dry
Mayonnaise	Lemonade	Jams	Vinegar	
Oil	Limeade	Jellies		
Oil and vinegar	Tea	Jelly beans		
Salad dressing		Lollipops		
Shortening		Sugar		
Thousand Island dressing		Syrups		

Note: All foods contain only trace amounts of protein. They should be eaten in reasonable quantities.

*Because egg is used in most salad dressings, less than 2 or 3 T should be eaten daily.

gen and ammonia contents of food has been proven.

Occasionally doctors use other treatment procedures to manage the patient with hepatic encephalopathy. One example is the drug lactulose, which is a poorly absorbed carbohydrate. It can ease the symptoms of patients receiving a moderate amount of protein. It is hypothesized that the drug increases peristalsis, lowers colon pH, promotes the movement of ammonia from blood to fecal waste, and converts ammonia to ammonium salts. It is sweet and unacceptable to some patients, although mixing it with food or

TABLE 25-13 Protein Exchange Food List VII: Alternates

Liquid Oral and Tube Feedings*	Low-Protein Bakery Products†
Cal-Power	Aproten Pasta
Hyoal	dp low protein baking mix

Note: All foods contain very little, if any, protein.

*More details are provided in Chapters 23 and 28.

†More details are provided in Chapter 28.

TABLE 25-14 Nutrient Contents of Some Restricted Protein Diets

Approximate Daily Protein Permitted (g)	Approximate Calorie, Fat, and Carbohydrate Content		
	kcal	Fat (g)	Carbohydrate (g)
20–30	2,000–2,100	60–70	350–400
30–40	2,300–2,600	70	400–450
40–50	2,300–2,600	70	400–450
50–60	2,300–2,600	70–80	400–450

TABLE 25-15 Planning Restricted-Protein Meal Plans by Using the Protein Exchange Food Lists

Food Group	Protein Exchange Food Lists	Number of Exchanges			
		20–30 g Protein diet	30–40 g Protein diet	40–50 g Protein diet	50–60 g Protein diet
Milk and milk products	I	1	2	2	3
Grain products	II	0	2	3	4
Meat and equivalents	III-1	2	2	2	2
	III-2	0	0	0	2
Fruits	IV-1	3	3	3	2
	IV-2	0	0	0	2
Vegetables	V-1	2	2	1	1
	V-2	0	0	1	2
Free foods*	VI				
Alternates†	VII				

*No restriction when used within caloric allowance and given in average-sized servings.

†Use liquid supplements and low-protein bakery products as much as possible to provide the necessary calories and obtain patient acceptance. See text.

TABLE 25-16   Sample Menu Plan Containing Approximately 20 g of Protein

Breakfast	Lunch	Dinner
Apple juice, 1 c	Cheddar cheese, 1 oz	Lamb, broiled, 1 oz
Milk, whole, ½ c	Lettuce, wedge, 1	Beets, boiled, ½ c
Free foods*	Plums, canned, 3	Peaches, canned, 2 halves
Alternates†	Free foods*	Free foods*
	Alternates†	Alternates†

*The patient should be encouraged to eat as much of the free foods in List VI as possible to increase caloric intake.

†The patient is encouraged to consume the alternate items in List VII. However, the protein in these items must be taken into consideration to assure that the limit of 20 g is not exceeded.

TABLE 25-17   Sample Menu Plan Containing Approximately 60 g of Protein

Breakfast	Lunch	Dinner
Grape juice, ½ c	Cold cuts, 2 oz	Chicken, fried, 2 oz
Figs, canned, medium, 2	Toast, 1 sl	Bread, 1 sl
Egg, fried, 1	Celery, 1 c	Rice, ½ c
Raisin bread, 1 sl	Pear, fresh, 1	Mushrooms, ½ c
Milk, whole, ½ c	Chocolate milk, ½ c	Strawberries, ½ c
Free foods*	Free foods*	Ice cream, vanilla, ⅔ c
Alternates†	Alternates†	Free foods*
		Alternates†

*The patient should be encouraged to eat as much of the free foods in List VI as possible to increase caloric intake.

†The patient is encouraged to consume the alternate items in List VII. However, the small amount of protein in these items must be taken into consideration to assure that the limit of 60 g of protein is not exceeded.

fruit juices makes it more palatable. Its use by clinicians varies. Another much debated method of treating portal-systemic encephalopathy is a portacaval shunt; however, a discussion of this procedure is beyond the scope of this book.

GALLSTONES

As indicated earlier, bile contains cholesterol, which is insoluble in pure water. However, cholesterol is soluble in a mixture of water, fatty acids, bile salts, and lecithin. Normally the cholesterol remains in solution within the gallbladder even when the bile is being concentrated there. However, a number of physiological conditions decrease the solubility of cholesterol, thus precipitating this chemical as gallstones: (1) The concentration of bile may be excessive for unknown reasons, resulting in too much water, bile salts, fatty acids, and lecithin being absorbed by the gallbladder mucosa and causing cholesterol precipitation; (2) the liver releases too much cholesterol as a component of the bile, which may be due to an excess consumption of animal fat and

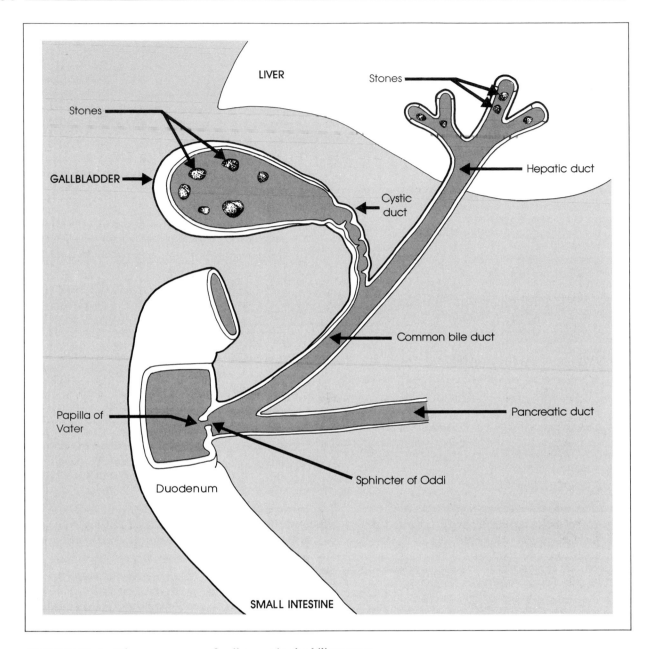

FIGURE 25-4 The occurrence of gallstones in the biliary tract.

cholesterol; or (3) the epithelium of the gallbladder becomes inflamed because of infection or other causes. As a result, the gallbladder absorbs too much water and other ingredients that help to solubilize the cholesterol, which then crystallizes as stones. Figure 25-4 shows the occurrence of gallstones in the biliary tract.

Cholelithiasis, or the formation of gallstones, develops in 10% to 20% of the Western popula-

tion, and from 80% to 90% of these stones contain cholesterol.

Included in the high-risk populations are older males and women in general. Women, especially those who have borne children, are three times more likely to have gallstones than men. In addition, American Indians are more at risk than whites.

Certain drugs can increase susceptibility,

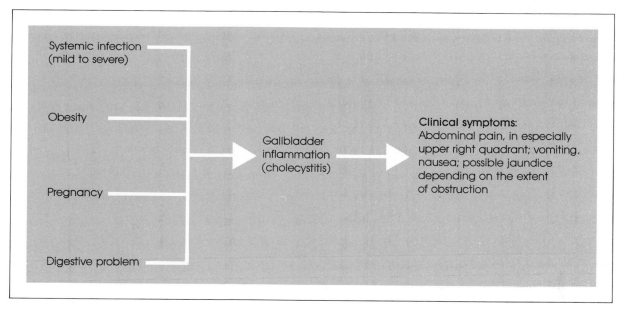

FIGURE 25-5   Gallbladder inflammation.

such as oral contraceptives or clofibrate, which is used to lower blood cholesterol. Other contributing factors include obesity and intestinal disorders involving the malabsorption of bile acids. Clinical stresses such as pregnancy occasionally cause gallstone formation, although the frequency of such occurrences among pregnant women is not known.

Symptoms and Diagnosis

While intolerance to fatty foods is a major symptom, patients with gallstones may not show any symptoms. If any duct of the biliary tract is obstructed, jaundice may develop, accompanied by a spectrum of symptoms such as severe pain of the upper right quadrant, vomiting, nausea, and fever. Uncorrected jaundice or obstruction may cause liver damage, since the bile begins to accumulate in the liver. Occasionally the stones may stay in one place and cause no pain or obstruction. Clinical experience indicates that surgical removal of the stones eliminates any symptoms. In some individuals, instead of gallstones the gallbladder is inflamed with some clinical symptoms present, as illustrated in Figure 25-5.

Gallstones are detected in two ways. Some stones contain calcium, which shows up in X rays.

For stones that do not contain any calcium, the patient is given special drugs that accumulate in the bile of the gallbladder. These agents cause the stones to appear in X rays.

Dietary Management

A low-fat diet is needed for digestive disorders involving the intestine, gallbladder, liver, or pancreas that result in the maldigestion and malabsorption of fat. To alleviate steatorrhea and occasional abdominal pains associated with the disease, the total fat intake should be restricted.

When a patient suffers acute pain because of an obstruction, no fat should be eaten that can stimulate the gallbladder or the biliary tract, which would further intensify the pain. If the patient can eat, liquid nutrient supplements are recommended for 1 or 2 days. For hospital preparations, skim milk, honey, orange or tomato juice, soft drinks, or sherbet can be used. If commercial formulas are preferred, EMP, Casec, Polycose, or Sumacal can be used. If the doctor is postponing surgery in order to evaluate the patient and is prescribing analgesics to reduce the pain, the patient needs aggressive nutritional support. If oral food consumption is normal, the patient should be provided with a nutritious diet

TABLE 25-18   Permitted and Prohibited Foods in a Fat-Restricted Diet

Food Group	Foods Permitted	Foods Prohibited
Milk and milk products	Skim milk (fortified with vitamins A and D): fluid, dry powder, and evaporated; yogurt and buttermilk made from skim milk (fortified with vitamins A and D)	Whole milk and all products made from it; low-fat and 2% milk and all products made from them; heavy cream, half and half, sour cream; cream sauces, nondairy cream substitutes
Breads and equivalents	Enriched or whole-grain bread; plain buns and rolls; crackers; graham crackers, matzo, melba toast; other varieties not specifically excluded; all cereals that are tolerated by the patient; potatoes except those specifically excluded; rice (brown or white); spaghetti, noodles, macaroni; barley; grits; wild rice; flours (all varieties)	Biscuits, dumplings, corn bread, waffles, pancakes, nut breads, doughnuts, spicy snack crackers, sweet rolls, popovers, French toast, corn chips, muffins, all items made with a large quantity of fat; cereals with nuts and 100% bran may be omitted if not well tolerated; fried potatoes, creamed potatoes, potato chips, hash-browned potatoes and potato salad, scalloped potatoes; fried rice, egg noodles, casseroles prepared with cream or cheese sauce; chow mein noodles, bread stuffing; Yorkshire pudding; Spanish rice; fritters; spaghetti with strongly seasoned sauce
Meats and equivalents	Limited to 4 to 6 oz daily; all lean fresh meat, fish, or poultry (no skin) with fat trimmed; shellfish, salmon, and tuna canned in water; foods may be pan-broiled, broiled, baked, roasted, boiled, stewed, or simmered; soybeans, peas, and meat analogues if tolerated	Fried, creamed, breaded, or sauteed items; sausage, bacon, frankfurters, ham, luncheon meats, meats with gravy, many processed and canned meats; any seafood packed in oil; nuts, peanut butter, pork and beans
Cheese and eggs	Any variety not specifically prohibited (2 oz cheese equivalent to 3 oz meat); 1 egg yolk a day, any style, with no fat used in cooking; egg whites may be used as desired; 1 egg yolk equals 1 oz meat	Any cheese made from whole milk, including cream cheese; any egg that is creamed, deviled, or fried
Beverages	Most nonalcoholic beverages except those specifically excluded	All beverages containing chocolate, cream, or whole milk, for example, milk shakes and eggnog; alcoholic beverages if not permitted by doctor
Fruits and vegetables	All varieties not excluded and tolerated by the patient	Avocado and any not tolerated by the patient; fried and creamed vegetables, vegetables with cream sauces or fat added; any variety not tolerated
Soups	Broth, bouillon, or consommé with no fat; fat-free soup stocks; all homemade soups or cream soups made with allowed ingredients; soups made with skim milk, clear soups with permitted vegetables and meats with fat skimmed off; packaged dehydrated soup varieties	Most commercial soups; any soup made with cream, fat, or whole milk

TABLE 25-18   (continued)

Food Group	Foods Permitted	Foods Prohibited
Fats	Limited to 2 to 3 t per day; all fats and oils (e.g., margarine, butter, shortening, lard); heavy cream (1 T = 1 t fat); sour cream or light cream (2 T = 1 t fat); cream substitute (4 t = 1 t fat); salad dressing (1 T = 1 t fat); low-calorie dressing in small amounts not counted in fat allowances	All fats exceeding the 2- to 3-t limit, including bacon drippings
Sweets	Plain sweets, honey, syrup, sugar, molasses, jams, jellies, plain sugar candies, chewing gum, hard candy, marshmallows, gum drops, jelly beans, sour balls, preserves, marmalade, tutti-frutti	Any candies or sweets made with nuts, coconut, chocolate, cream, whole milk, margarine, butter
Desserts	Sherbet, Jell-O, water ice, fruit-flavored Popsicles and ices; rice, bread, cornstarch, tapioca puddings; plain gelatin, gelatin with fruit added; fruit whips, puddings and custards made with skim milk and egg whites; cookies made with skim milk or egg whites; arrowroot cookies, vanilla wafers, angel food cake, sponge cake	Any products made with whole milk, cream, chocolate, butter, margarine, nuts, egg yolks
Miscellaneous	All herbs and spices tolerated and not specifically excluded; artificial sweetener, baking soda, baking powder	Any sauces made with fat, oil, cream, or milk; olives, pickles, garlic, chili sauce, chutney, horseradish, relish, Worcestershire sauce

that is low in fat, as described below. If there is intolerance to regular food, progressive hospital feeding is preferred. If the patient cannot eat regular foods, either enteral or parenteral nutrition may be administered, with special attention to the patient's fat tolerance. The feeding method depends on the clinical condition of the patient. Chapter 23 describes special hospital feeding methods and formulas.

If the gallbladder disorder is chronic and surgery is excluded for any reason, there are a number of considerations in the dietary care of the patient. An overweight patient should reduce because of the positive correlation between obesity and gallstones. Individualization of the diet is very important. Some patients develop pain when eating fat, while others exhibit abdominal discomfort when too much spice or seasoning is added. A fat-restricted diet prescribed

by the physician must be followed for a specified period. Table 25-18 lists those foods permitted in and prohibited from a fat-restricted diet. Table 25-19 provides a meal plan for a 40- to 45-g-fat diet, and Table 25-20 presents a sample menu. If the patient is permitted 25 g of fat only, the meal plan in Table 25-19 may be adjusted by reducing the consumption of meat or meat equivalents to 3 to 5 oz instead of 4 to 6 oz and omitting all servings of margarine, butter, and related dense fat.

When prescribing a fat-restricted diet, there are a number of important considerations. The patient cannot remain on the diet for long for two important reasons. First, the restriction of fat will eliminate the necessary and occasional stimulation of the biliary system. This reduces the amount of bile available for the intestinal tract, the digestion of food, and drainage of the

TABLE 25-19 Sample Meal Plan for Diet Supplying 40 to 45 g of Fat, with 80 to 90 g of Protein, 260 to 280 g of Carbohydrate, and 1,700 to 2,000 kcal

Breakfast	Lunch	Dinner
Milk or milk products, 1 c	Soup, ½ c	Soup, ½ c
Cereal, ½ c	Meat or equivalent, 2 oz	Meat or equivalent, 3 oz
Egg, 1	Vegetable or salad, ½ c	Potato or equivalent, ½ c
Bread or toast, 1 sl	Bread or toast, 1 sl	Vegetable or salad, ½ c
Jam, preserves, jelly, 1–3 t	Potato or equivalent, ½ c	Bread or toast, 1 sl
Juice or fruit, ½ c	Butter or margarine, 1 t	Butter or margarine, 1 t
Butter or margarine, 1 t	Dessert or fruit, 1 serving	Dessert or fruit, 1 serving
Sugar, 1–4 t	Sugar, 1–4 t	Milk and milk products, 1 c
Coffee or tea	Coffee or tea	Sugar, 1–4 t
Salt, pepper	Salt, pepper	Coffee or tea
		Salt, pepper

Note: Use only permitted foods. Increase caloric intake by increasing the number of servings of permitted foods.

TABLE 25-20 Sample Menu for Meal Plan Indicated in Table 25-19

Breakfast	Lunch	Dinner
Orange juice, ½ c	Beef broth and noodles, ½ c	Tomato juice, ½ c
Oatmeal, cooked, ½ c	Chicken, broiled, 2 oz	Beef, lean, broiled, 3 oz
Egg, poached, 1	Saltines, 4	Potato, baked, small, 1
Raisin toast, 1 sl	Margarine, 1 t	Green beans, ½ c
Jam, 2 t	Green salad with lemon juice, ½ c	Roll, hard, small, 1
Margarine, 1 t	Orange, 1	Butter, 1 t
Milk, skim, 1 c	Cola, 8 oz	Gelatin or fruit cocktail, ½ c
Sugar, 2 t	Sugar, 2 t	Milk, skim, 1 c
Coffee or tea	Coffee or tea	Sugar, 2 t
Salt, pepper	Salt, pepper	Coffee or tea
		Salt, pepper

biliary tract. The lack of bile salts reduces the absorption of fat-soluble vitamins. Second, since the patient's intake of fat-soluble vitamins (A, D, and K) will be low from a decrease in fat intake, some clinicians prescribe water-miscible fat-soluble vitamins. If prothrombin time is low or there is an increased bleeding tendency from a lack of vitamin K, injections of vitamin K are recommended (10 mg of phytonadione or menadione sodium bisulfite daily). Some clinicians prescribe oral or parenteral administration of bile salts. Due to the decreased intake of meat and meat products, women of child-bearing age may not obtain their iron requirement, in which case a mineral supplement is necessary.

If a patient's stones are surgically removed, maintaining a fat-restricted diet after discharge depends both on the patient and the physician. Some doctors do not institute any dietary modifications; others prefer to prescribe a low-fat diet. Eventually some part of the biliary system, usually the common bile duct, stretches to accommodate the bile.

Since 1972, the clinical management of gallstones has been supplemented by a new technique. Chenodeoxycholic acid, a normal component of human bile, has been used successfully to dissolve gallstones. The appropriate dose varies from 15 to 25 mg/kg body weight. Partial or complete dissolution of the stones occurs in 6 to 50 months. Diarrhea and intestinal discomfort are the major side effects of the drug. It is hypothesized that chenodeoxycholic acid expands the bile acid pool, returning the bile to normal so that it is no longer supersaturated with cholesterol. At present the use of this agent is still limited because of inadequate clinical trials.

STUDY QUESTIONS

1. What unique ability do liver cells have?
2. What are the main functions of the liver?
3. Describe the enterohepatic circulation. What are the two main functions of the bile salts?
4. Describe the course of viral hepatitis. If the hepatitis patient can eat regular foods, what dietary care is advisable? Under what circumstance should protein intake be reduced?
5. What are the features of liver cirrhosis? What conditions are thought to potentiate the disease? Describe the protein and calorie recommendations in diet therapy for liver cirrhosis.
6. What is ascites? What type of diet is recommended to treat this disorder? Why is aggressive diet therapy potentially dangerous in this case?
7. Define *hepatic encephalopathy*. What are the main goals of diet therapy for this disorder? What nutrient may therefore be carefully restricted in the diet? What is the danger of restricting its intake too severely?
8. What is the relationship between cholesterol and gallstones? What general dietary restriction is advised for gallstone patients? What is the disadvantage of the long-term usage of such a diet?

CASE STUDY   *An Alcoholic with Cirrhosis of the Liver*

Mr. F.M. was a 60-year-old truck driver who had been a heavy drinker for many years. In the last 10 years, his drinking had posed difficulties in his job, family life, and health. He was developing many emotional difficulties such as depression, insecurity, feelings of inadequacy, and the need to control others. When directly questioned, he denied or minimized the extent or ways in which he used alcohol. However, clinical manifestations of his alcoholism began about 1 year ago.

He began to develop a series of symptoms. He was weak, easily fatigued, and losing weight. He had a very poor appetite, sometimes abstaining completely from food, with occasional nausea and vomiting. He had frequent abdominal pain. His body showed spider nevi (upper half of the body), palmar erythema, telangiectasis (exposed areas), and glossitis and cheilosis. The patient had diarrhea and hematemesis. He also had ascites, with an enlarged liver that was palpable and firm with a blunt edge.

After admission to the hospital, the attending physician described Mr. F.M. as wasted with an appearance of chronic illness. Within 1 year, he had lost 30 lb. He was already developing mild jaundice. After less than 2 days in the hospital, Mr. F.M. was found to have pleural effusion with peripheral edema. The superficial veins of his abdomen and thorax were dilated, indicating that the portal blood flow was most likely blocked.

Laboratory findings confirmed that he had increased Bromsulphalein (BSP), anemia, low white blood cell counts, increased sedimentation rate, and proteinuria. His abnormal liver functions were confirmed by elevations of serum glutamic-oxaloacetic transaminase (SGOT), serum glutamic-pyruvic transaminase (SGPT), lactate dehydrogenase (LDH), alkaline phosphatase, and bilirubin. Liver biopsy showed a cirrhotic organ.

The patient was told to abstain from alcohol and was confined to bed with restricted movements, especially when his symptoms were acute. The initial prescribed diet contained 2,800 kcal and 75 to 100 g of protein. The nurse and dietitian were instructed to make sure that the patient ate the food.

To treat the ascites due to sodium retention, hypoproteinemia, and portal hypertension, the attending physician restricted the patient's sodium intake to 200 mg/d, with 500 mL of fluid permitted. Within a few days, the ascites had subsided and the patient's abdominal discomfort abated.

To treat the edema, a diuretic was prescribed. The patient was given 25 mg of spironolactone (Aldactone) orally four times a day, used in combination with furosemide (Lasix) at 100 mg/d.

About 1 week after hospitalization, the patient presented the major signs of precoma (asterixis, tremor, dysarthria, delirium, and drowsiness). The attending doctor decided to drastically curtail the patient's intake of protein. However, the protein-restricted diet provided the patient with an unsatisfactory amount of food. The doctor therefore ordered that the patient be put on parenteral feeding.

The intestinal bleeding was treated by magnesium sulfate (10 to 15 g) via nasogastric tube. To control the growth of intestinal flora, the patient was given 0.5 to 1.0 g of neomycin sulfate orally every 6 hours for about 1 week. To treat the hypochromic anemia, the patient was given ferrous sulfate (one 0.3 g, enteric-coated tablet after meals 3 times daily). Since the patient had a mixed type of anemia, he was also given oral folic acid at 5 mg/d. The bleeding tendency due to hypoprothrombinemia was treated with vitamin K preparation: 1 to 3 mg of menadione orally after each meal for 3 days.

Review and Analysis

1. What is liver cirrhosis?
2. Why did the patient have glossitis and cheilosis?
3. If the patient was 30 lb below ideal weight, he would need more than 2,800 kcal. Why did the doctor prescribe this caloric level?
4. Plan a diet providing 2,800 kcal, 75 to 100 g of protein, 200 mg of sodium, and 500 mL of permitted fluid. Prepare menus for 3 days and show the daily distribution of fluid.
5. To reduce the accumulation of urea nitrogen in the blood, Mr. F.M. was restricted to a daily intake of 40 g of protein. Plan a diet providing 2,800 kcal, 40 g of protein, 200 mg of sodium, and 500 mL of permitted fluid. Prepare menus for 3 days.
6. Why was it necessary to control the growth of intestinal bacteria in the patient?

Chapter 26

Diet and Diabetes Mellitus

DIABETES MELLITUS HAS been recognized as a disease for centuries. The word *diabetes* is a Greek term meaning "to draw off" or "to come through"; *mellitus* is Latin for "honey." One of the major symptoms of diabetes mellitus is the excretion of a copious amount of glucose-containing urine, hence its name. One of the earliest records of this disease dates from 1552 BC, when the disease was characterized in the Ebers Papyrus as painless, body wasting, and accompanied by increased urination. In the second century, Aretaeus provided a very good clinical description of the ailment: "Diabetes is a wonderful affection, not very frequent among men, being a melting down of the flesh and limbs into urine. . . . The course is the common one, namely, the kidneys and bladder; for the patients never stop making water, but the flow is incessant, as if from the opening of aqueducts. The nature of the disease, then, is chronic . . . but the patient is short-lived, if the constitution of the disease be completely established; for the melting is rapid, the death speedy." (Aretaeus, "On the Causes and Symptoms of Chronic Diseases," in *The Extant Works of Aretaeus, the Lappadocian*, ed. and trans. Francis Adams [London: The Sydenham Society, 1856], p. 338).

In the last two centuries, much progress has been made in understanding this disease. In the nineteenth century, it was learned that malfunctioning cells in the pancreas were responsible for diabetes. More than 50 years ago, the chemical insulin was extracted from animal pancreases and identified as a substance capable of ameliorating the clinical conditions of a diabetic patient. In the last 30 years, the concept of using diet as an adjunct to the management of a diabetic patient has become very important, sophisticated, and flexible. A study of the current literature suggests that more breakthroughs in treating this disease are expected in the near future.

Simply stated, diabetes mellitus is a disease caused by a partially malfunctioning pancreas (specifically the islets of Langerhans, discussed later) that provides little or no functional insulin to promote the entry of blood sugar (glucose) into tissues for metabolism. As a result, sugar levels in the urine and blood are higher than normal. However, this explanation for diabetes mellitus will be qualified later in this chapter since there are diabetic patients whose pancreases do secrete insulin.

OCCURRENCES AND CAUSES

The prevalence of diabetes mellitus in the United States is not known exactly. However, a broad picture may be obtained from available data. Diabetics number between 4 and 8 million people. Five to fifteen percent of these suffered onset of the disease at or before the age of 25. More women than men have the disease, although the difference is becoming smaller. Currently, the rate of occurrence of diabetes is increasing. It is estimated that between 25% and 35% of diabetic individuals are unaware that they have the disease. Individuals who exhibit prediabetic tendencies may number as high as 25 to 50 million people.

The distribution of diabetes among different age groups in this country is as follows:

Age Range (years)	Percentage of Total Age Group Population with Diabetes
Under 5	Trace
5–18	0.1–0.2
18–35	0.3–0.5
35–55	2–4
Over 60	4–6

There are a number of reasons why the incidence of diabetes in the United States is on the rise. One is most likely related to obesity. Overweight individuals are more likely to become diabetic; since the number of overweight individuals is rising in the United States, more people are becoming susceptible to the disease.

Paradoxically, progress in medicine has also increased the incidence of diabetes. Young diabetics now live longer than in the past. This greater survival rate permits diabetic individuals to marry and have children. Since the probability of intermarriage between diabetic and diabetes-prone individuals is increased, an increasing number of diabetic children are being born.

Because the mixed blessing of better medical care has also increased the average life span of Americans, the number of people over 60 has been steadily increasing. This age group has a greater tendency to become diabetic, again increasing the total number of diabetic patients in this country.

Although a diabetic patient can now live longer and in more comfort, diabetes mellitus remains one of the major contributing causes of death in the United States. A person who develops diabetes as a child tends to have a shorter life span than normal. Mortality from kidney failure in young diabetics approaches that of heart disease in adult patients. This is due to diabetic glomerulosclerosis. Onset of the disease in adulthood may not affect longevity, but other problems may manifest themselves. The incidence of coronary heart disease is two to three times higher among adult diabetics than nondiabetics. While death from diabetic coma is less likely because of medical progress, death from diabetic ketoacidosis is still common.

Ever since a malfunctioning pancreas was discovered to be directly involved in diabetes, intensive research has been directed toward identifying the exact causes of this malfunctioning. Although we do not have the answers yet, several factors have been implicated. Among these are heredity, obesity, sensitivity to insulin, and pancreatic damage.

It is known that heredity plays a role in developing the disease. Members of a family with one diabetic member are more likely to develop the disease. As discussed earlier, increased survival rates permit the propagation of diabetes.

For years, obesity has been associated with diabetes. It has been suggested that excess fat can directly cause the disease or indirectly potentiate the genetic tendency of the individual to develop the disease. However, satisfactory data for these claims are lacking. A more detailed discussion on the influence of obesity on the course of the disease is presented later in this chapter.

One obvious cause of malfunctioning of the pancreas is a direct or indirect mechanical or physiological insult to the pancreas. Another possible cause is related to an increased sensitivity of body tissues to the action of insulin so that glucose or sugar does not enter them easily. Either possibility may be brought about by a number of clinical conditions, including cancer or inflammation of the pancreas, actions of drugs or viruses, a hormonal imbalance, and such diseases as Cushing's syndrome. In addition, body injuries caused by car accidents or bullet wounds can directly cause malfunctioning of the pancreas.

BLOOD GLUCOSE, INSULIN, AND BODY METABOLISM

The pancreas contains many types of cells. Certain parts of the pancreas, known as the islets of Langerhans after their discoverer, contain three main types of cells: alpha, beta, and delta. Alpha and beta cells produce the hormones glucagon and insulin, respectively, while little is known about the role of delta cells.

Glucagon is a potent and important hormone that can stimulate the secretion of insulin. Other substances that can stimulate insulin secretion from the beta cells include amino acids, theophylline, sulfonylureas, and certain intestinal hormones. The hormone epinephrine inhibits the secretion of insulin. The most important stimulator of insulin secretion is the sugar glucose. Figure 26-1 provides a simplified description of how insulin secretion is stimulated. When the beta cells of the islets of Langerhans respond to a rise in blood glucose level by releasing their insulin, the process takes two steps. The first involves a rapid secretion of insulin from a highly concentrated pool of the hormone that can be mobilized. The second involves a slow release from a less responsive pool of the hormone, which is supplemented by insulin newly made or secreted from proinsulin.

Insulin is a protein made up of chains of amino acids. Within the beta cells insulin occurs as proinsulin. As shown in Figure 26-2, proinsulin is made up of two parts, the hormone insulin and one chain of amino acids known as a C-peptide. Each insulin molecule is made up of two chains of amino acids, A and B chains. The s-s bonds indicate bonds between sulfur amino acids.

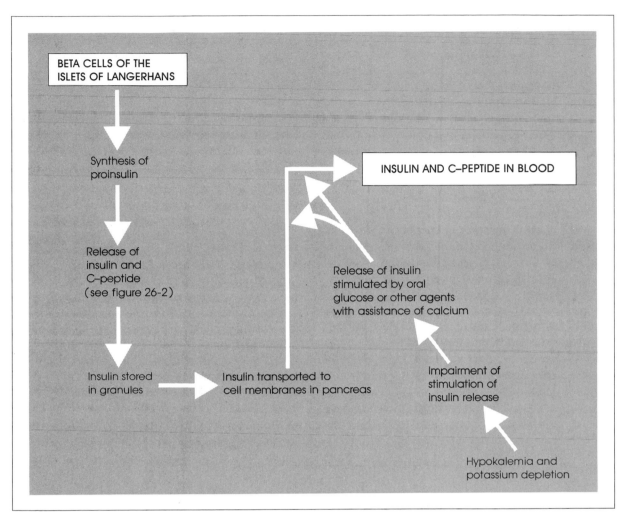

FIGURE 26-1   Stimulation of insulin secretion.

The regulation of blood glucose level by insulin and other substances is a highly sophisticated mechanism. Glucose is the only monosaccharide present at significant levels in the interstitial fluids and blood, although some fructose and galactose are present a short time after eating (especially after a mixed meal). For example, 75% to 95% of the monosaccharide mix that passes from the intestinal lumen to extracellular fluid (such as blood) of the body is glucose, while fructose and galactose make up the remaining amount. About 30 to 60 minutes after fructose and galactose have reached the bloodstream from the gut, they are changed to glucose by liver cells or participate in glycolysis, glycogenesis, or the citric acid cycle (see Chapter 8). This means that very little fructose and galactose circulate in the blood. The liver is constantly releasing glucose as well to maintain normal to high blood sugar levels, especially if the host has not ingested any carbohydrate (such as sugar or potato) for a long period of time. The blood glucose level during normal fasting is about 70 to 100 mg/100 mL.

Functionally, insulin helps blood glucose enter the cells and tissues of certain organs. These are conveniently labeled as *insulin-dependent tissues*. Conversely, some tissues and organs permit the entry of glucose molecules without the assistance of insulin. These are termed *insulin-independent tissues*. These two categories of tissues are listed below.

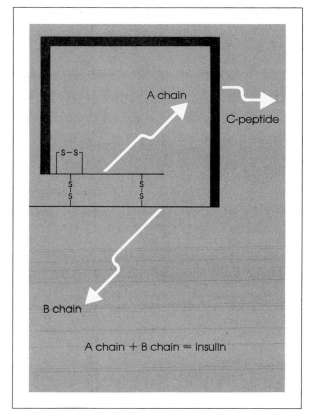

FIGURE 26-2   Simplified molecular structure of pro-insulin (pig).

Insulin-dependent Tissue	Insulin-independent Tissue
Adipose tissue	Brain and nerves
Aorta	Intestinal mucosa
Anterior pituitary	Kidney tubules
Lens (crystalline) of the eye	Liver cells
Mammary glands	Lymph nodes
Striated muscles, e.g., skeletal muscle	Red blood cells

The importance of insulin cannot be underrated. Each cell needs glucose to derive its energy and remain alive and functioning properly. For insulin-dependent tissues, any lack of the hormone will result in very little entry of glucose molecules, and the cells of these tissues will be unable to obtain energy. Two very important tissues in this category are muscle and adipose tissue.

Figure 26-3 indicates how insulin secretion increases when blood glucose levels are elevated and restores them to normal. Figure 26-4 shows how depressed blood glucose levels are normalized by the actions of different hormones, some of which operate simultaneously to directly inhibit the secretion of insulin.

The relationship between insulin and body metabolism is very complicated. Table 26-1 shows the specific metabolic effects of insulin in a healthy human body. Figure 26-5 provides an overview of the physiological distribution of body glucose, and Figure 26-6 delineates the altered metabolism of carbohydrate, protein, and fat in a diabetic patient. A detailed analysis of this relationship follows. Chapter 8 should be consulted for details on carbohydrate metabolism.

After digestion and absorption, approximately 60% to 70% of the ingested glucose is utilized by the liver. About 20% to 25% is taken up by insulin-independent tissues, and about 15% by insulin-dependent tissues. Although the entry of glucose into the liver is independent of insulin, the hormone can enhance the absorption rate of glucose into that organ. Within the liver, the presence of insulin favors the formation of glycogen and glucose-6-phosphate from glucose. Between meals the presence of insulin in the liver cells stimulates the release of glucose from glucose-6-phosphate. About 200 to 400 g of glucose are secreted daily into the bloodstream from this source. Under normal circumstances, the presence of insulin inhibits the degradation of glycogen to glucose and the formation of glucose from amino acids in the liver.

In a diabetic individual, glucose continues to enter the liver, since the latter is insulin independent. However, within the liver cells, the lack of insulin reduces the formation of glycogen and increases its degradation, releasing glucose in the form of glucose-6-phosphate. On the other hand, the liver can absorb more amino acids from the blood and use them as building blocks to form glucose. Thus, more glucose is released into the circulation. This tends to intensify the hyperglycemia (elevated blood sugar) observed in a diabetic patient.

In a healthy person, insulin promotes the entry of amino acids into muscle cells and encour-

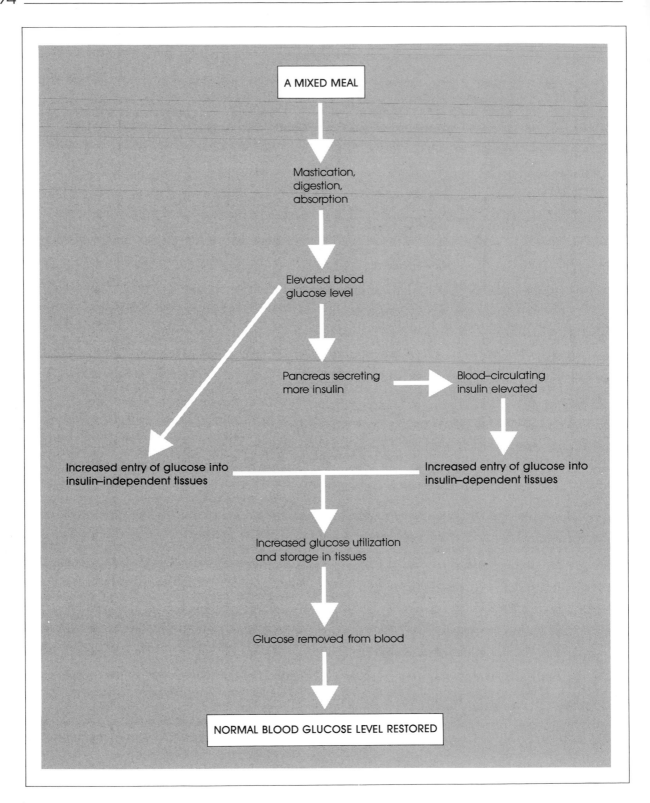

FIGURE 26-3 Insulin and elevated blood glucose levels.

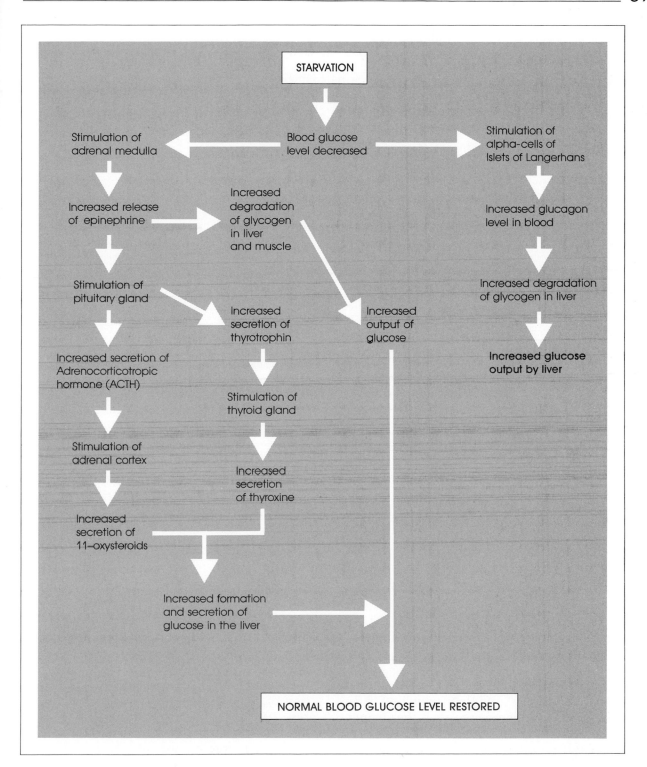

FIGURE 26-4   Insulin and decreased blood glucose levels.

TABLE 26-1 Specific Metabolic Effects of Insulin in the Healthy Human Body

Overall Action	Effect		
	Liver	Muscle	Fat
Anabolism	**Carbohydrate** Formation of more glycogen and promotion of entry of glucose	**Carbohydrate** Formation of more glycogen; glucose-permitted entry	**Carbohydrate** Glucose-permitted entry
	Fat Formation of more fatty acids; increased synthesis of fats; increased release of triglycerides as very low density lipoprotein	**Fat** None	**Fat** Formation of more fatty acids; formation of more glycerol; formation of more triglycerides (fats); promotion of entry of fatty acids
	Protein Reduced degradation	**Protein** Formation of more protein; promotion of entry of more amino acids	**Protein** None
Inhibition of catabolism of body substances	**Carbohydrate** Promotion of glucose entry; less glycogen degraded; less glucose formed from amino acids; less glucose released to blood	**Carbohydrate** Glucose-permitted entry	**Carbohydrate** Glucose-permitted entry
	Fat Less ketone bodies formed	**Fat** None	**Fat** Less fat (triglycerides) degraded
	Protein None	**Protein** Less protein degraded; less amino acids released	**Protein** None
Net effect	Net glucose stored as glycogen	Net protein synthesis	Net fat storage

ages protein formation. In a diabetic individual, the reverse is true. More protein is degraded than is formed, and the concentration of amino acids is increased in the blood. In a diabetic, more amino acids are also metabolized to form urea; complications may result if the amount of urea exceeds a certain level.

Under normal circumstances, insulin promotes the formation of needed fatty acids and glycerol molecules, and this in turn promotes the synthesis of additional glycerides. However, a dia-betic person has an increased breakdown of tri-glycerides in adipose tissue. This results in more fatty acids being released into the blood, which are eventually picked up by the liver. The deposition of some of these fatty acids in the liver is responsible for the development of a fatty liver. Since fatty acids are also metabolized mainly in the liver, a large number of ketone bodies may accumulate (β-hydroxybutyric acid, acetoacetic acid, and acetone—the first two in the ratio of $3:1$). In addition, insulin can eliminate lipopro-

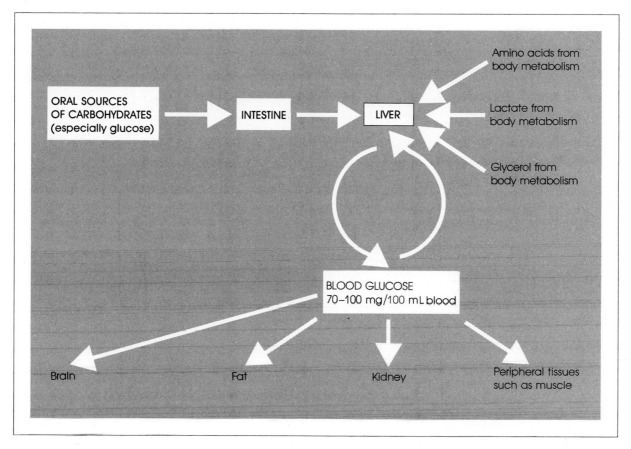

FIGURE 26-5   Physiological distribution of glucose in the body.

teins from circulation by increasing or stimulating the activity of the enzyme lipoprotein lipase. A diabetic patient lacking supplementary insulin to stimulate production of the enzyme may accumulate lipoproteins in the blood. Some fatty acids from degraded triglycerides will also attach to the accumulating lipoproteins.

Normally, insulin is needed to permit glucose to enter muscle cells. Any excess glucose can be stored in the form of glycogen. In the presence of oxygen, glucose is degraded to water, carbon dioxide, and pyruvate or lactate, which releases energy. The pyruvate or lactate is passed into the circulatory system and carried to the liver for normal metabolism. Pyruvate or lactate can be transaminated in the liver to form alanine, which may be used for glucose formation. Insulin can also promote the uptake of amino acids by the muscle cells, which in turn increases protein syn-

thesis. In a diabetic individual, the uptake of amino acids by muscle tissue is decreased, increasing the amount of amino acids in circulation.

Under normal circumstances, the liver produces small amounts of ketone bodies, most of which are metabolized by muscle cells. In an uncontrolled diabetic patient, muscle cells increase their uptake of fatty acids and ketone bodies, although a large amount of ketone bodies still accumulate in the blood. The acids (β-hydroxybutyric acid and acetoacetic acid) lower the pH of blood and cause a drop in serum bicarbonate. This condition is known as *ketoacidosis*. The accumulated acetone does not affect the acidity of blood but does cause a fruity odor on the breath. Levels of ketone bodies also increase in the urine (*ketonuria*). The kidneys increase their excretion of acids, and in the process body potassium and sodium are lost (see Chapter 9).

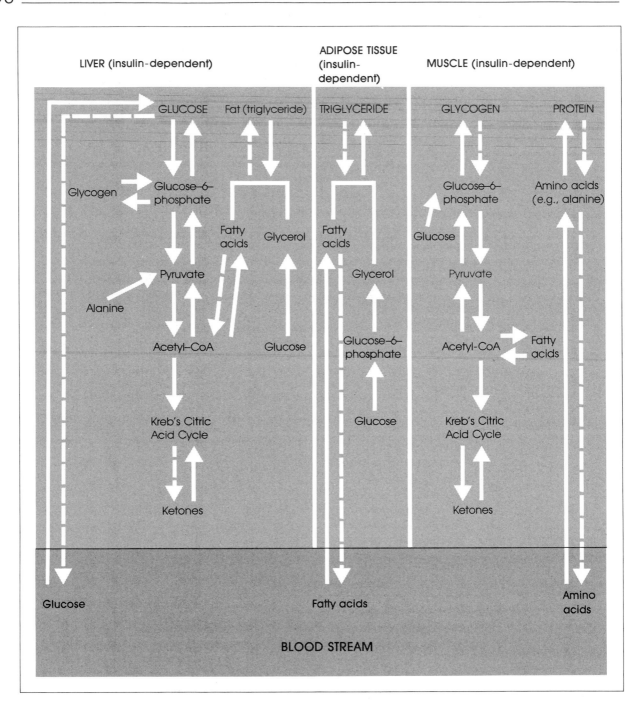

FIGURE 26-6   Body metabolism in the liver, adipose tissue, and skeletal muscle in a diabetic patient. (Broken arrows indicate the preferred direction of metabolism.)

TABLE 26-2   Effects of Six Types of Hormone on Blood Glucose Level in Relation to the Metabolism of Glucose, Glycogen, and Triglyceride

	Insulin	Growth Hormone (anterior pituitary gland)	Thyroxine (thyroid gland)	11-Oxysteroids (adrenal cortex)	Glucagon (pancreas)	Epinephrine (adrenal cortex)
Glucose						
Utilization	Increase	—	—	—	—	—
Formation	Decrease	—	Increase	Increase	—	—
Glycogen						
Synthesis	Increase	—	—	—	—	—
Degradation	Decrease	Increase	—	—	Increase	Increase
Triglyceride						
Synthesis	Increase	—	—	—	—	—
Degradation	Decrease	—	—	—	—	—
Hypoglycemia	Yes	—	—	—	—	—
Hyperglycemia	—	Yes	Yes	Yes	Yes	Yes

In addition to insulin, other hormones in the body affect blood glucose metabolism. Table 26-2 shows how different hormones can elevate blood glucose by affecting metabolism. Figure 26-7 illustrates how the metabolic defects caused by a lack of insulin can lead to all the clinical symptoms found in a diabetic patient. More information on metabolic defects is presented later in this chapter.

DIAGNOSIS OF DIABETES

Diagnostic tools to test for the presence of diabetes mellitus include studying known clinical symptoms, analyzing data on blood glucose levels, and urine testing. Together, these tools help the clinician diagnose the severity of the disease and aid the patient in choosing the correct medical treatment.

Clinical Symptoms

A diabetic presents several general clinical symptoms. Excessive thirst (polydipsia) and urination (polyuria) may exist before the patient becomes aware of them. Juvenile diabetics usually experience nocturnal urination and bedwetting. Many young diabetics also show weight loss with an increase of appetite, while many adult diabetics are obese. Itching (pruritus) is common around the groin. Other common, though not necessarily characteristic, symptoms include loose teeth, sleepiness, loss of strength, abnormal body sensations, and impotence. Perhaps the most alarming is that an untreated diabetic will become comatose after drinking alcoholic beverages.

Some diabetic patients may also present organ-specific symptoms. Blurred vision, cataracts, blood vessel hemorrhage, and retinopathy may affect the eyes. Skin may show infections at multiple sites, as well as boils. Heart and kidney problems include atherosclerosis, gangrene of the extremities, edema, and heart and kidney failure. Symptoms seen in the nervous system are neuritis of the peripheral nervous system, weakness, loss of body sensations and reflexes, and diarrhea at night. In some diabetic patients, ketoacidosis, blindness, and coma occur as culminating symptoms. Some patients may die as a result, with or without medical attention.

Blood Glucose Level

Increased blood glucose levels (*hyperglycemia*) may be discovered through laboratory analysis. Normal blood glucose level is about 70 to 100

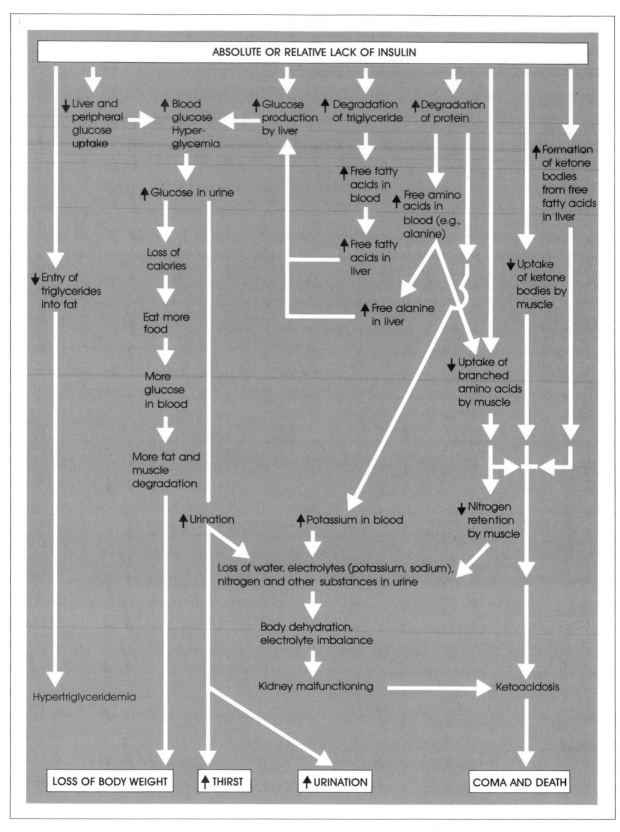

FIGURE 26-7 Metabolic aberrations from a lack of insulin leading to
clinical manifestations (↑ = increased; ↓ = decreased).

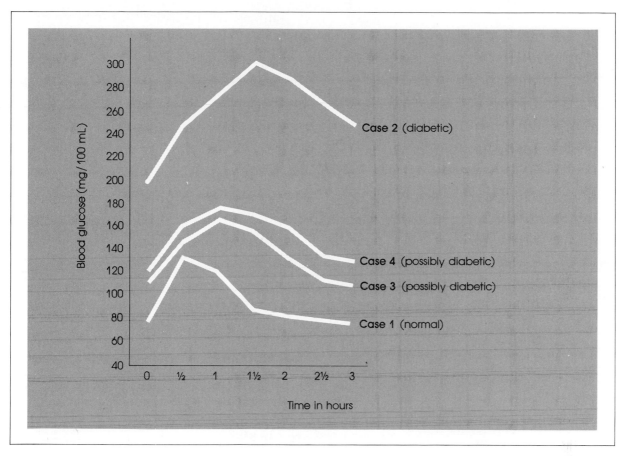

FIGURE 26-8   Four hypothetical glucose tolerance curves.

mg/100 mL of blood. A level of 200 mg or above after a 24-hour fast is fairly conclusive evidence of diabetes. If the fasting blood glucose level is above 140 mg and under 200 mg and the non-fasting level is 180 to 250 mg, the patient has hyperglycemia and should be given the glucose tolerance test (GTT) to obtain conclusive evidence of diabetes. It is important to emphasize that if the fasting blood glucose level is 200 mg or above, any GTT must be carried out under the direct supervision of a physician in anticipation of hyperglycemic coma.

The GTT is a simple test used to ascertain how well a patient tolerates an influx of glucose into the bloodstream. The rate with which glucose disappears from the blood is an indirect measure of how much circulating insulin is available to facilitate the entry of glucose into cells and tissues. The patient is asked to drink 100 g of glucose in a 25% chilled or flavored solution (usually water). Half an hour after drinking the

solution, a sample of venous blood is drawn, followed by additional blood samples at half-hour or hourly intervals for 3 to 5 hours. Most physicians prescribe a 3- to 4-hour test, although a 5-hour test is ordered if the patient is being checked for the presence of reactive hypoglycemia that is unrelated to stomach surgery (see Chapter 29). Figure 26-8 shows four hypothetical glucose tolerance curves measured at half-hour intervals. As shown in Figure 26-8, if a patient's GTT results resemble that of Case 1, the person is not a diabetic. A result similar to Case 2 means that the patient is diabetic. Unfortunately, numerous clinical cases resemble Cases 3 and 4, making diagnosis difficult.

Conducting and interpreting the GTT involves many problems and uncertainties not discussed here. Guidelines are available from the American Diabetes Association to assist physicians and dietitians with this test. Other references are also provided at the end of this book.

Urine Testing

Because the glucose level in the urine of a diabetic patient is elevated, urinary testing is another diagnostic tool. A wide variety of tests are available for this purpose. The presence of reducing sugar (e.g., glucose) may be ascertained using Benedict's reagent, although the test is not specific for glucose. A specific test for the presence of glucose involves dipping a special paper in the urine and comparing the resultant color change with colors on a standard chart. Examples of such papers are Diastix, Tes-Tape, and Clinitest, which are impregnated with glucose oxidase. The degree of color change is related to the amount of glucose present. Another test for the presence of glucose in urine or blood, Acetest, involves the use of tablets.

The presence of ketone bodies in the urine (ketonuria) may be ascertained with treated paper strips such as Ketostix. Another treated paper, Keto-Diastix, can also test for ketone bodies as well as glucose in the urine. Again, numerous problems are associated with urinary tests for glucose or ketone bodies. Some pertinent references are provided at the end of this book for further study.

TREATMENT

In clinical practice, properly classifying a diabetic patient is important because it forms the basis for devising the appropriate treatment. In 1979, the National Diabetes Data Group of the National Institutes of Health developed and published a classification of diabetes and other categories of glucose intolerance, based on contemporary knowledge of this heterogeneous syndrome. In the introduction to this work, entitled *Classification and Diagnosis of Diabetes Mellitus and Other Categories of Glucose Intolerance*, the group states, "It is proposed that this classification be used as a uniform framework in which to conduct clinical and epidemiologic research so that more meaningful and comparative data will be obtained on the scope and impact of the various forms of diabetes and other classes of glucose intolerance."

It must be emphasized that this report did not consider the medical treatment of diabetes, and the classification is not an attempt to define guidelines for the therapy of patients. Table 26-3 presents the new classification for diabetes and other categories of glucose intolerance. Because this classification is not yet widely adopted, our discussion will adhere to the conventional classification of diabetic patients. Those interested should obtain the original report for further information.

The most common types of diabetes are insulin-dependent and insulin-independent types (see Table 26-3). These were formerly known as juvenile-onset and maturity-onset diabetes, respectively. Both types of patients show an abnormal glucose tolerance curve, a high blood glucose level during fasting, and overt clinical symptoms. However, there are many differences between these two types, as shown in Table 26-4.

Insulin Therapy

In order to control their clinical instability, insulin-dependent diabetics must continually use insulin. The same applies to diabetic patients of all age groups who are prone to diabetic ketoacidosis. Insulin treatment is also considered mandatory for diabetic patients of all types who undergo surgery, experience infection, or suffer from severe illnesses, renal insufficiency, or other stresses.

Unfortunately, insulin cannot be taken orally because its polypeptide (protein) structure is susceptible to breakdown by intestinal enzymes. Consequently, this hormone is normally administered by subcutaneous injection, although an intravenous injection has a more rapid effect.

Presently, several different types of insulin preparations are available that vary in potency and duration of activity. Depending on the particular diabetic, one or more of these types of insulin may be used to regulate the disease.

Crystalline or *regular insulin* is quick acting and commonly used to treat diabetic ketoacidosis and coma. In the past 10 years, commercial preparations of regular insulin have been modified so that the insulin action can be prolonged to become intermediate or long acting. The modification includes the addition of another protein or of zinc to the preparation.

TABLE 26-3 Classification of Diabetes Mellitus and Other Categories of Glucose Intolerance

Description of Disease or Condition	Classification	Examples of Former Terminology
Diabetes mellitus (DM)	Type I, insulin-dependent type (IDDM)	Juvenile diabetes, brittle diabetes, ketosis-prone diabetes
	Type II, noninsulin-dependent type (NIDDM): 1. nonobese NIDDM 2. obese NIDDM	Maturity-onset diabetes, stable diabetes
	Other types, including diabetes mellitus associated with certain conditions and syndromes: 1. pancreatic disease 2. hormonal 3. drug or chemical induced 4. insulin receptor abnormalities 5. certain genetic syndromes 6. other types	Secondary diabetes
Impaired glucose tolerance (IGT)	Nonobese, obese IGT; IGT associated with certain conditions and syndromes which may be: 1. pancreatic disease 2. hormonal 3. drug or chemical induced 4. insulin receptor abnormalities 5. certain genetic syndromes	Chemical diabetes, latent diabetes, asymptomatic diabetes
Gestational diabetes (GDM)	Gestational diabetes (GDM)	Gestational diabetes
Previous abnormality of glucose tolerance (PrevAGT)	Previous abnormality of glucose tolerance (PrevAGT)	Prediabetes, latent diabetes
Potential abnormality of glucose tolerance (PotAGT)	Potential abnormality of glucose tolerance (PotAGT)	Prediabetes, potential diabetes

Source: Adapted from National Diabetes Data Group, "Classification and Diagnosis of Diabetes Mellitus and Other Categories of Glucose Intolerance," *Diabetes* 1979; 28:1039.

Protamine zinc insulin (PZI) is a long-acting insulin because of the addition of protamine, a protein, to the regular preparation. This hormone is released slowly from the tissues. The patient should eat something before bedtime to avoid potential hypoglycemia when this insulin is used. Many dietitians recommend a bedtime snack whether the diabetic is on insulin or oral hypoglycemic drugs.

Globin insulin and *NPH* (from "neutral," "protamine," and "Hagedorn") *insulin* or *isophane* are intermediate-acting hormones. The protein globin is added to the regular preparation, while NPH contains the protein protamine.

Semilente, *lente*, and *ultralente insulins* modify the duration of the action of regular insulin by adding a combination of an acetate buffer and zinc. This modification results in a spectrum of

TABLE 26-4 Comparison of Insulin-Dependent and Insulin-Independent Diabetes Mellitus

Criterion	Diabetes Type	
	Insulin dependent	Insulin independent
Age of onset	Under 14, not common among preschoolers; some patients over 40	Over 40, especially over 50; occasionally in children and adolescents
Percent of diabetic population	10% (5% children)	85% to 95%
Onset	Usually sudden with accompanying weight loss	Usually gradual; not diagnosed for years after onset
Disease severity	Usually very severe, especially adults	Mild to severe
Body weight at time of diagnosis	Usually lean, especially in adults	80% of patients obese
Hyperglycemia severity	Usually severe	Mild to moderate
Serum lipid profile	Usually abnormal	Usually abnormal
Insulin		
Pancreas secretion	Minimal to lacking; an occasional release of insulin	Adequate to insufficient; complete failure not common
Use in therapy	Yes	No, though long-term patients may depend on insulin
Diet therapy required	Yes	Yes
Oral hypoglycemic agents	Less common	More common
Clinical course	Unstable, high and low blood glucose, with symptoms	Usually stable except in severe cases
Proneness to ketoacidosis	Yes, from childhood to adults. More severe in adults.	No, except under unusual stress
Mortality from diabetic ketoacidosis and coma	Possible without medical attention	Not likely
Nutritional needs	Unknown and changing, especially for children	Constant and can be calculated
Physical activity	Difficult to control	Easy to plan

TABLE 26-4   (continued)

Criterion	Diabetes Type	
	Insulin dependent	Insulin independent
Role of emotional variations	Great; may influence course of disease	Less; minimal effect on course of disease
Response to infections	More likely; acidosis exhibited quickly with little warning	Acidosis less likely and more predictable
Vascular degeneration	Related to duration of disease	Common
Prognosis	Poor	Good if well controlled

TABLE 26-5   Time Action Characteristics of Commercial Insulin Preparations

Type of Insulin	Example	Onset (h)	Peak of Action (h)	Duration of Action (h)
Short acting	Regular (neutral)	½	1–3	5–10
	Semilente	1	3–5	10–15
Intermediate acting	NPH	2	7–13	24–28
	Lente	2	7–13	24–28
	Globin	2	5–7	18–24
Long acting	Ultralente	6	17–30	≥35
	Protamine zinc	6	15–20	≥35

lente insulins. There are two forms of these zinc-insulin complexes—the crystalline and the amorphous forms. The crystalline form is not as soluble as the amorphous form, which is readily soluble. The three forms of insulin—semilente (rapid), lente (intermediate), and ultralente (prolonged)—are made by varying the ratios of amorphous and crystalline components. Table 26-5 summarizes the approximate duration of action for most commercial insulin preparations.

Usually the nurse teaches the patient how to inject insulin, although the dietitian and other allied health personnel should be familiar with the procedure. In order for the hormone to act properly, it should be injected before food is consumed (i.e., shortly before a meal). Blood glucose levels should then be raised by the ingestion of food. Injections may have to be repeated several times a day, depending on how many meals the person eats. The basic techniques of injection are described in most standard nursing textbooks and other manuals on managing diabetes.

Use of Oral Hypoglycemic Drugs

Other chemical substances can lower blood glucose besides insulin. These are known as oral hypoglycemic agents, which can normalize blood glucose and are easy to take. While useful, they have marked limitations and are effective only temporarily in some patients. In the last few

TABLE 26-6   Characteristics of Sulfonylureas

| Substance | Brand Name | Duration of Activity (h) | Daily Dose | | U.S. Availability |
			Single	Divided	
Acetohexamide	Dymelor	12–18	x	x	Yes
Chlorpropamide	Diabinese	≥36	x	—	Yes
Glibenclamide (glyburide)	Daonil, Euglucon	≥ 6	x	x	No
Tolazamide	Tolinase	≥10	x	x	Yes
Tolbutamide	Orinase	6–8	—	x	Yes

years, legal controversy over the safety of these chemicals has left only one prescribable type of such agents, sulfonylureas. Table 26-6 describes their characteristics.

Sulfonylureas rarely have side effects. Reactions such as fatigue, skin rashes, and mild gastrointestinal symptoms are considered acceptable. Occasional serious reactions include water intoxication, hemolytic anemia, leukopenia, and hypoglycemia. Hypoglycemia can be prevented easily if the dosage used is the lowest effective regimen. The attending health personnel should be alerted to the few patients who may develop severe hypoglycemic reactions because of special sensitivity to the chemicals. Recent claims that the agents, if used for a long period of time, may predispose the patient to the risk of heart disease have created much controversy; however, they are not yet generally accepted.

MEDICAL MANAGEMENT OF A DIABETIC PATIENT

In treating a diabetic patient, the medical team must first establish goals, strategies, and priorities. Initial goals involve stabilizing the condition of the patient. For instance, blood glucose levels should be normalized and tolerance to glucose restored. If the patient is sensitive to insulin, steps should be taken to acclimate him or her to use of the hormone. Also important is the stabilization of body weight and control of any complication caused by the disease.

The strategies and priorities for the management of the patient should be carefully delineated by the physician with the assistance of other members of the health team. An assessment of priority is typified by the obese patient. If excess weight is a major handicap to the successful control of a patient's condition, then weight loss should be the major priority. A patient should attain ideal weight as soon as possible. If retinopathy (eye complications) is at an advanced stage, the initial effort should be to minimize further deterioration of the eyes. If the patient has no immediate problems that require attention, the strategies and priorities of most clinics are determined by whether the patient is insulin dependent or independent (or any other type of diabetic as described earlier). The treatment is then based on this determination.

Diet, insulin, and oral hypoglycemic agents all play an important role in managing a diabetic patient, although the extent to which these tools of treatment are used or are effective vary from patient to patient. If a diet is skillfully planned, professionally implemented, and faithfully adhered to, most diabetic patients can control their condition without resorting to insulin or oral drugs or both. Insulin is probably the major treatment for insulin-dependent and unstable patients and those with severe symptoms. As indicated earlier, insulin use depends on blood glucose stability. The time of use as well as the type and dose of insulin used also depends on the history and experience of the patient and the judgment of the physician. Before oral hypoglycemic agents are used, the patient's insulin secretion status and glucose tolerance should be carefully considered. Potential side effects from these medications must also be considered. Some clinicians suggest limiting the use of these drugs to insulin-independent diabetics with stable medical profiles and less severe symptoms.

In determining body weight of a diabetic patient, the terms *ideal* and *desirable* are often used interchangeably. Determining adult ideal or desirable body weights is discussed in Chapter 12. The ideal body weights of children and adolescents may be estimated by referring to standard growth charts, including those of Wetzel, Iowa, Stuart, and the U.S. Public Health Service. Appendix D provides examples of growth curves.

The health history of a patient can be obtained by studying medical records and interviewing health personnel and the patient's family members. Mandatory information for a good management program of a diabetic patient includes: general eating habits and other information related to foods, employment details, family history, physical activities and living conditions, health problems, and body weight history. The health team should study this information carefully, particularly that on body weight history. Also see Chapter 22.

Dietary Care

Diet therapy for the diabetic patient is very important, and its objectives must be clarified at the outset. The total number of calories must be regulated according to the activity level of the patient in order to achieve and maintain the desirable body weight. All essential nutrients should be provided in adequate quantities for optimal body functions for all types of diabetic patients. Food should be supplied at a rate consistent with the availability of endogenous and exogenous insulin in order to keep blood and urine glucose within acceptable limits. Any complications and existing symptoms occurring simultaneously with or because of the diabetic state should be controlled, prevented, delayed, or corrected. Once the health team has established goals, priorities, and strategies for a patient, they proceed to devise a suitable diet.

Table 26-7 describes the overall dietary care for the two major types of diabetic patients. In both situations, a rigid or strict diet is no longer advisable if the patients are cooperative, knowledgeable about the prescribed diet, and facile in exchanging one food product for another (see the later discussion). They must be willing to make adjustments for exercise, illness, work schedules, and eating out.

Caloric need

There are many ways to estimate the caloric need of a diabetic patient. The method developed by the American Diabetes Association is widely used and accepted.

If we assume that a person's daily basal caloric need is 10 kcal/lb of ideal body weight, then the basal caloric need for a man weighing 154 lb (70 kg) is $154 \times 10 = 1,540$ kcal and that for a woman weighing 128 lb (58.1 kg) is $128 \times 10 = 1,280$ kcal. After the basal caloric need is ascertained, the amount of energy expended in physical activity must be calculated (see Table 26-8). An overweight person should subtract 500 kcal from the result obtained from the above method, while an underweight person should add 500 kcal.

The caloric need for a child is determined by either the latest RDAs or the age rule. According to the age rule, 1,000 kcal/d should be allowed for a 1-year-old, with an additional 100 kcal for each year over 1. This is good up to the age of 13 for girls and 16 to 18 for boys.

For a pregnant diabetic, the American Diabetes Association recommends sustaining pre-pregnant caloric levels plus 300 kcal per day of pregnancy to achieve a weight gain of 23 lb over 9 months. For a nursing mother, 500 kcal/d should be added to the actual caloric need calculated from her ideal body weight.

Daily allowance of carbohydrate, protein, and fat

A modern diabetic diet is fairly similar to that of the general American public, especially in regard to the overall distribution of carbohydrate, protein, and fat (see Table 26-9). For instance, since Americans consume about 40% to 50% of their daily calories as *carbohydrate*, a diabetic patient is fed a similar quantity. Patients are much more comfortable with this kind of diet because

TABLE 26-7 Nutritional and Dietary Care of the Two Major Types of Diabetic Patients

Criterion	Diabetes Type	
	Insulin dependent (lean)	Insulin independent (obese)
Overall diet prescription		
Regulation	Yes	Yes
Predictability	Yes	Not so important
Rigidity	No	No
Total caloric intake	Adjusted to maintenance and activity; constant and consistent from day to day	Must be reduced; variable to achieve ideal weight
Daily intake of relative amounts of carbohydrate, protein, and fat	Constant and consistent from day to day	Usually not important
Four to six daily feedings	Highly recommended	Recommended if patient can adhere to limited caloric intake, otherwise not recommended
Coordination of meal and insulin injection times	Highly recommended	Not applicable
Dietary compensation for regular and unscheduled exercises	Very important	Not important
Dietary compensation for occasions of low blood glucose	Must eat food	Usually no measures needed
Nutritional compensation for sickness	Frequent parenteral feedings of dextrose to abort ketosis	Usually no measures needed since ketosis is unlikely

they eat what everybody else eats with a few exceptions.

Using the 40% to 60% range as a guide, the actual amount of carbohydrate prescribed should be guided by the profile of the patient's blood and urine glucose levels, the ability of the pancreas to secrete insulin, and the sensitivity of different tissues to the hormone. Given these factors, the actual quantity of carbohydrate consumed is usually between 100 and 300 g. Any amount under 100 g will produce starvation ketosis, while an amount over 300 g will exert the pancreas excessively and may produce hypertriglyceridemia.

Presently the medical community generally believes that diabetic patients should have some control over their total intake of simple sugars. About 10% to 15% of the carbohydrate calories should be simple sugars such as monosaccharides and disaccharides, with the rest from complex sources. Insulin-dependent patients are requested to restrict or eliminate their intake of simple carbohydrates more frequently than insulin-independent diabetics. Because many diabetic patients are permitted to eat a normal or high level of carbohydrate primarily from complex sources, individual needs and desires can be easily met by adjusting daily planned menus.

Protein composes 12% to 25% of the total daily calories permitted some diabetics. The actual amount varies from 0.8 to 1.5 g/kg ideal body weight/d (about 0.4 to 0.7 g/lb ideal body weight). The recommended amount for children

and pregnant or lactating women should be 1.4 to 1.6 g. For diabetic patients who have not lost much nitrogen in the urine, a daily protein intake of 0.8 to 1.0 g/kg/d is adequate. Overall, diabetic patients should not get less than 60 to 70 g of protein per day. The common practice is to provide 80 to 100 g/d, although patients usually eat more. If patients already have negative nitrogen balance, 1 to 1.5 g protein/kg/d may be appropriate.

The amount of *fat* permitted a diabetic patient has been disputed for a number of years. The central issue has been the possible detrimental effects of a high intake of fat. Saturated fat and cholesterol are especially suspect in the development and potentiation of atherosclerosis and related complications. Presently, the suggested fat intake for a diabetic is about 30% of total calories, with one-third of them consumed as saturated and two-thirds as unsaturated fats. The latter contains approximately equal amounts of polyunsaturated and monosaturated fats. It is felt that such a prescription will reduce the total amount of cholesterol consumed as well as provide the proper amount of calories from fat.

In actual practice, the physician or dietitian will have to decide for each patient the approximate amounts of carbohydrate, fat, and protein that may be consumed. Different clinics and clinicians use different methods. The American

TABLE 26-8   American Diabetes Association Method to Calculate Daily Caloric Need

Physical Activity	Total Calories Needed
Sedentary	Basal calories + (desirable body weight × 3)
Moderate	Basal calories + (desirable body weight × 5)
Strenuous	Basal calories + (desirable body weight × 10)

TABLE 26-9   Contents of a Regular Diet and Diabetic Diets for Adults and Children

Diet	Daily Permitted Caloric Intake (%)				
	Carbohydrate		Fat‡	Protein	Alcohol
	Complex*	Simple†			
Regular	20−40	25−35	35−45	10−20	0−15
Diabetic					
Adult	30−45	5−15	20−35	12−25	0−5
Children	30−40	5−15	35−40	18−23	0

Note: Ranges of values serve as a guide. Each practitioner's prescription varies.

*Includes starch and fibers.

†For nondiabetic diets, includes monosaccharides and disaccharides from all sources. For diabetic diets, includes monosaccharides and disaccharides from natural sources such as fruits, fruit juices, and milk.

‡A regular diet contains a ratio of saturated to unsaturated fats of about 2−3:1; a diabetic diet, 1:1−3.

TABLE 26-10   Relative Amounts of Nutrients by Using Approximations of Their Caloric Contributions

Daily Kilocalories Needed	Amount (g)		
	Protein	Carbohydrate	Fat
1,000	50	125	33
1,400	70	175	35
1,800	90	225	60
2,500	125	438	84
3,000	150	375	100

Note: The following percentages of total calories are obtained from each nutrient type: protein, 20%; carbohydrate, 50%; fat, 30%. An example of the calculations for a daily intake of 1,800 kcal is:

protein: 20% of total calories = 360 kcal ÷ 4 kcal/g = 90 g
carbohydrate: 50% of total calories = 900 kcal ÷ 4 kcal/g = 225 g
fat: 30% of total calories = 540 kcal ÷ 9 kcal/g = 60 g

TABLE 26-11   Relative Amounts of Nutrients by Using Approximations of Their Caloric Contributions

Daily Kilocalories Needed	Amount (g)		
	Protein	Carbohydrate	Fat
1,000	63	100	39
1,800	113	180	70
2,500	156	250	97
3,000	188	300	117

Note: The following percentages of total calories are obtained from each nutrient type: protein, 25%; carbohydrate, 40%; fat, 35%. For calculations, see Table 26-10.

Diabetes Association uses a method involving percentage approximations. This means that if a person needs a specific amount of daily calories, the assumption is that he or she will need 20% of the total calories from protein, 50% from carbohydrate, and 30% from fat. This breakdown varies with the patient and the attending health practitioner. In calculating the respective weights needed for the three nutrients, the following equivalencies are used:

1 g protein = 4 kcal
1 g fat = 9 kcal
1 g carbohydrate = 4 kcal

Tables 26-10 and 26-11 provide some examples.

Food Selection Using the Food Exchange Lists

The diet prescription for a diabetic can be easily implemented with the appropriate types of food, since we know the daily number of calories needed by the patient and the relative amounts of carbohydrate, protein, and fat permitted. There are many food selection systems available for practitioners and patients. One such system is the Food Exchange Lists developed by a joint committee of the American Diabetes Association, the American Dietetic Association, and the U.S. Public Health Service. This system is popular and used extensively in this country by health

TABLE 26-12   Outline of the 1976 American Diabetes Association Exchange Lists

Food Exchange List	Food Group	Contribution per Exchange of Food Group			
		kcal	Protein (g)	Carbohydrate (g)	Fat (g)
1	Milk	80	8	12	Trace
2	Vegetables	25	2	5	0
3	Fruits	40	0	10	0
4	Bread	70	2	15	0
5	Meat				
	Lean	55	7	0	3.0
	Medium	80	7	0	5.5
	Fat	100	7	0	8.0
6	Fat	45	0	0	5.0

practitioners. It has a number of advantages, such as flexibility of meal planning, but also contains disadvantages such as limited choices of food.

To use the Food Exchange Lists, the number of calories required by the patient and the amounts of carbohydrate, protein, and fat allowed within the daily prescribed calories must be determined. There are six exchange lists, each containing one group or category of food. Within each list are possible exchanges among the listed foods, and each exchange contributes the same or nearly the same amount of calories, carbohydrate, fat, and protein. Table 26-12 summarizes the nutrient contributions of the items in each of the six exchange lists. The different types of foods contained within each list are described in Table 26-13.* The actual exchange lists appear as Tables 26-14 to 26-21.*

According to J. S. Skyler of the University of Miami Medical Center, "utilization of the exchange system requires both literacy and above-average comprehension or intelligence." To help the student use the exchange system, step-by-step instructions for determining a patient's

*The exchange lists are based on material in the *Exchange Lists for Meal Planning* prepared by Committees of the American Diabetes Association, Inc. and The American Dietetic Association in cooperation with the National Institute of Arthritis, Metabolism and Digestive Diseases and the National Heart and Lung Institute, National Institutes of Health, Public Health Service, U.S. Department of Health, Education and Welfare.

TABLE 26-13   Types of Food Included in the Exchange Lists

Food Exchange List	Food Group	Food Types
1	Milk	Nonfat fortified milk and products; low-fat fortified milk and products; whole milk and products*
2	Vegetables	Various raw and cooked vegetables excluding starchy vegetables
3	Fruits	Various fresh, dried, canned, frozen, and cooked fruits†
4	Bread	Bread, cereal, starchy vegetables
5	Meat	Red meat, poultry, fowl, seafood, meat alternates
6	Fats	Butter, margarine, dressings, nuts, others

*Used with adjustments.

†All processed products are unsweetened.

TABLE 26-14   List 1: Milk Exchanges (Includes Nonfat, Low-fat, and Whole Milk)

Nonfat fortified milk	
Skim or nonfat milk	**1 cup**
Powdered (nonfat dry, before adding liquid)	**⅓ cup**
Canned, evaporated—skim milk	**½ cup**
Buttermilk made from skim milk	**1 cup**
Yogurt made from skim milk (plain, unflavored)	**1 cup**
Low-fat fortified milk	
1% fat fortified milk (omit ½ fat exchange)	1 cup
2% fat fortified milk (omit 1 fat exchange)	1 cup
Yogurt made from 2% fortified milk (plain, unflavored) (omit 1 fat exchange)	1 cup
Whole milk (omit 2 fat exchanges)	
Whole milk	1 cup
Canned, evaporated whole milk	½ cup
Buttermilk made from whole milk	1 cup
Yogurt made from whole milk (plain, unflavored)	1 cup

Note: One exchange of milk contains 12 g of carbohydrate, 8 g of protein, a trace of fat, and 80 kilocalories. This list shows the kinds and amounts of milk or milk products to use for one milk exchange. Those which appear in **bold type** are **nonfat**. Low-fat and whole milk contain saturated fat.

TABLE 26-15   List 2: Vegetable Exchanges

Asparagus	Greens:
Bean sprouts	Mustard
Beets	Spinach
Broccoli	Turnip
Brussels sprouts	Mushrooms
Cabbage	Okra
Carrots	Onions
Cauliflower	Rhubarb
Celery	Rutabaga
Eggplant	Sauerkraut
Green pepper	String beans, green or yellow
Greens:	Summer squash
Beet	Tomatoes
Chards	Tomato juice
Collards	Turnips
Dandelion	Vegetable juice cocktail
Kale	Zucchini

The following raw vegetables may be used as desired:

Chicory	Lettuce
Chinese cabbage	Parsley
Endive	Radishes
Escarole	Watercress

Starchy vegetables are found in the Bread Exchange List.

Note: One exchange of vegetables contains about 5 g of carbohydrate, 2 g of protein, and 25 kilocalories. This list shows the kinds of vegetables to use for one vegetable exchange. One exchange is ½ cup.

daily food needs from the Food Exchange Lists follow:

1. Determine the caloric need of the patient and the apportionment of calories contributed by protein, carbohydrate, and fat.
2. Determine the number of exchanges of nonfat milk, vegetables, and fruit needed by the patient.
3. Determine the grams of carbohydrate contributed by the nonfat milk, vegetable, and fruit exchanges.
4. Determine the number of bread exchanges permitted the patient.
5. Determine the grams of protein contributed by the nonfat milk, vegetable, fruit, and bread exchanges.
6. Determine the number of meat exchanges permitted the patient.
7. Determine the grams of fat contributed by the nonfat milk, vegetable, fruit, bread, and meat exchanges.
8. Determine the number of fat exchanges permitted the patient.

We demonstrate an example for a patient requiring 1,800 kcal daily. For Step 1 (see Table 26-10):

Number of calories needed daily   = 1,800 kcal
Nutrient contribution to caloric need:

Protein:	20% total calories =	90 g
Carbohydrate:	50% total calories =	225 g
Fat:	30% total calories =	60 g

TABLE 26-16 List 3: Fruit Exchanges

Apple	1 small	Mango	½ small
Apple juice	⅓ cup	Melon	
Applesauce (unsweetened)	½ cup	Cantaloupe	¼ small
Apricots, fresh	2 medium	Honeydew	⅛ medium
Apricots, dried	4 halves	Watermelon	1 cup
Banana	½ small	Nectarine	1 small
Berries		Orange	1 small
Blackberries	½ cup	Orange juice	½ cup
Blueberries	½ cup	Papaya	¾ cup
Raspberries	½ cup	Peach	1 medium
Strawberries	¾ cup	Pear	1 small
Cherries	10 large	Persimmon, native	1 medium
Cider	⅓ cup	Pineapple	½ cup
Dates	2	Pineapple juice	⅓ cup
Figs, fresh	1	Plums	2 medium
Figs, dried	1	Prunes	2 medium
Grapefruit	½	Prune juice	¼ cup
Grapefruit juice	½ cup	Raisins	2 T
Grapes	12	Tangerine	1 medium
Grape juice	¼ cup		

Cranberries may be used as desired if no sugar is added.

Note: One exchange of fruit contains 10 g of carbohydrate and 40 kilocalories. This list shows the kinds and amounts of fruits to use for one fruit exchange.

In Step 2 we determine the number of non-fat milk, vegetable, and fruit exchanges needed by the patient. This determination varies with the practitioner and patient. Most practitioners use the four food groups as a guide. One practitioner may decide that the patient needs 2 exchanges (servings) of nonfat milk, 2 exchanges (servings) of vegetables, and 5 exchanges (servings) of fruits. Another practitioner may decide on 4, 2, and 3 exchanges, respectively. For our hypothetical patient, we shall use the figures of 2, 2, and 5 exchanges. If the patient is not permitted excess mono- or disaccharides, fruits may have to be restricted. It needs to be emphasized that, although the serving sizes are approximations, their consistency and regularity are important. Yellow and dark green vegetables should be eaten at least every other day, and a good source of vitamin C should be consumed daily. Table 26-22 shows the protein, carbohydrate, and fat contributions of nonfat milk, vegetables, and fruits to the diet of our hypothetical patient.

In Step 3 the number of grams of carbohydrate contributed by the nonfat milk, vegetable, and fruit exchanges are totaled. In our example the total is 84 g, as shown in Table 26-22.

In Step 4 the number of bread exchanges permitted the patient is calculated. The patient is permitted 225 g of carbohydrate (Step 1), and 84 g have already been assigned (Step 3). Thus, $225 - 84$, or 141 g of carbohydrate are left to be assigned. Since meat and fat contain little carbohydrate, these 141 g can all be allocated to bread. Since 1 exchange of bread contains 15 g of carbohydrate (Table 26-12), the number of exchanges of bread permitted the patient is $141 \div 15 = 9\frac{2}{5}$, which we round off to 9. In rounding off exchanges, the practitioner does not have to follow the less-or-more-than-half rule.* The decision is made according to the practitioner's preference, the patient's condition, and the doctor's prescrip-

---

*For example, 1.4 becomes 1.0 and 1.5 or 1.6 becomes 2.0.

TABLE 26-17 List 4: Bread Exchanges (Includes Bread, Cereal, and Starchy Vegetables)

Bread			**Dried beans, peas, and lentils**		
White (including French and Italian)	1 sl		**Beans, peas, lentils (dried and cooked)**	½ cup	
Whole wheat	1 sl		**Baked beans, no pork (canned)**	¼ cup	
Rye or pumpernickel	1 sl		**Starchy vegetables**		
Raisin	1 sl		**Corn**	⅓ cup	
Bagel, small	½		**Corn on cob**	1 small	
English muffin, small	½		**Lima beans**	½ cup	
Plain roll, bread	1		**Parsnips**	⅔ cup	
Frankfurter roll	½		**Peas, green (canned or frozen)**	½ cup	
Hamburger bun	½		**Potato, white**	1 small	
Dried bread crumbs	3 T		**Potato (mashed)**	½ cup	
Tortilla, 6″	1		**Pumpkin**	¾ cup	
Cereal			**Winter squash, acorn, or butternut**	½ cup	
Bran flakes	½		**Yam or sweet potato**	¼ cup	
Other read-to-eat unsweetened cereal	¾ cup		Prepared foods		
Puffed cereal (unfrosted)	1 cup		Biscuit 2″ dia.		
Cereal (cooked)	½ cup		(omit 1 fat exchange)	1	
Grits (cooked)	½ cup		Corn bread, 2″ × 2″ × 1″		
Rice or barley (cooked)	½ cup		(omit 1 fat exchange)	1	
Pasta (cooked),	½ cup		Corn muffin, 2″ dia.		
Spaghetti, noodles, macaroni			(omit 1 fat exchange)	1	
Popcorn (popped, no fat added)	3 cups		Crackers, round butter type		
Cornmeal (dry)	2 T		(omit 1 fat exchange)	5	
Flour	2½ T		Muffin, plain small		
Wheat germ	¼ cup		(omit 1 fat exchange)	1	
Crackers			Potatoes, french fried, length 2″ to 3½″		
Arrowroot	3		(omit 1 fat exchange)	8	
Graham, 2½″ sq.	2		Potato or corn chips		
Matzoth, 4″ × 6″	½		(omit 2 fat exchanges)	15	
Oyster	20		Pancake, 5″ × ½″		
Pretzels, 3⅛″ long × ⅛″ dia.	25		(omit 1 fat exchange)	1	
Rye wafers, 2″ × 3½″	3		Waffle, 5″ × ½″		
Saltines	6		(omit 1 fat exchange)	1	
Soda, 2½″ sq.	4				

Note: One exchange of bread contains 15 g of carbohydrate, 2 g of protein, and 70 kilocalories. This list shows the kinds and amounts of **breads**, **cereals**, **starchy vegetables**, and prepared foods to use for one bread exchange. Those which appear in **bold type** are **low-fat**.

tion. The nutrient contribution of 9 exchanges of bread is shown in Table 26-23.

Step 5 calculates the number of grams of protein contributed by the nonfat milk, vegetable, fruit, and bread exchanges. The amount is 38 g, as shown in Table 26-23.

Step 6 specifies the number of meat exchanges permitted the patient. The patient is permitted 90 g of protein (Step 1), and 38 g have

already been assigned (Step 5). This patient is still left with 90 − 38, or 52 g of protein to be obtained from other foods. Since fat contains no protein, we can assign all 52 g to meat. Since 1 exchange of meat contains 7 g of protein, the number of exchanges of meat permitted the patient is 52 ÷ 7 = 7²⁄₇, which we round up to 8 exchanges. The nutrient contribution of 8 exchanges of meat is shown in Table 26-24.

TABLE 26-18   List 5: Meat Exchanges (Lean Meat)

Beef:	Baby beef (very lean), chipped beef, chuck, flank steak, tenderloin, plate ribs, plate skirt steak, round (bottom, top), all cuts rump, sirloin, tripe	1 oz
Lamb:	Leg, rib, sirloin, loin (roast and chops), shank, shoulder	1 oz
Pork:	Leg (whole rump, center shank), ham, smoked (center slices)	1 oz
Veal:	Leg, loin, rib, shank, shoulder, cutlets	1 oz
Poultry:	Meat (without skin) of chicken, turkey, Cornish hen, guinea hen, pheasant	1 oz
Fish:	Any fresh or frozen	1 oz
	Canned salmon, tuna, mackerel, crab, and lobster	¼ cup
	Clams, oysters, scallops, shrimp	5 or 1 oz
	Sardines, drained	3
Cheeses containing less than 5% butterfat		1 oz
Cottage cheese, dry and 2% butterfat		¼ cup
Dried beans and peas (omit 1 bread exchange)		½ cup

Note: One exchange of lean meat (1 oz) contains 7 g of protein, 3 g of fat, and 55 kilocalories. This list shows the kinds and amounts of **lean meat** and other protein-rich foods to use for one low-fat meat exchange. To plan a diet low in saturated fat, select only those exchanges that appear in **bold type**.

TABLE 26-19   List 5: Meat Exchanges (Medium-Fat Meat)

Beef:	Ground (15% fat), corned beef (canned), rib eye, round (ground commercial)	1 oz
Pork:	Loin (all cuts tenderloin), shoulder arm (picnic), shoulder blade, Boston butt, Canadian bacon, boiled ham	1 oz
Liver, heart, kidney, and sweetbreads (these are high in cholesterol)		1 oz
Cottage cheese, creamed		¼ cup
Cheese:	Mozzarella, Ricotta, farmer's cheese, Neufchatel,	1 oz
	Parmesan	3 T
Egg (high in cholesterol)		1
Peanut butter (omit 2 additional fat exchanges)		2 T

Note: For each exchange of medium-fat meat omit ½ fat exchange. This list shows the kinds and amounts of medium-fat meat and other protein-rich foods to use for one medium-fat meat exchange. To plan a diet low in saturated fat, select only those exchanges that appear in **bold type**.

Step 7 specifies the number of grams of fat contributed by the nonfat milk, vegetable, fruit, bread, and meat exchanges. The figure is 24 g, as shown in Table 26-24.

Step 8 specifies the number of fat exchanges permitted the patient. The patient is permitted 60 g of fat (Step 1), and 24 g have already been assigned (Step 7). Thus, the patient is still left with 60 − 24, or 36 g of fat to consume. Since 1 exchange of fat contains 5 g of fat, the number of

TABLE 26-20 List 5: Meat Exchanges (High-fat Meat)

Beef:	Brisket, corned beef (brisket), ground beef (more than 20% fat), hamburger (commercial), chuck (ground commercial), roasts (rib), steaks (club and rib)	1 oz
Lamb:	Breast	1 oz
Pork:	Spare ribs, loin (back ribs), pork (ground), country style ham, deviled ham	1 oz
Veal:	Breast	1 oz
Poultry:	Capon, duck (domestic), goose	1 oz
Cheese:	Cheddar types	1 oz
Cold cuts		4½" × ⅛" slice
Frankfurter		1 small

Note: For each exchange of high-fat meat omit 1 fat exchange. This list shows the kinds and amounts of high-fat meat and other protein-rich foods to use for one high-fat meat exchange. To plan a diet low in saturated fat, select only those exchanges that appear in **bold type**.

fat exchanges permitted the patient is 36 ÷ 5 = 7⅕, which we round off to 7. The nutrient contribution of 7 exchanges of fat is shown in Table 26-25, which summarizes the total food exchanges in a 1,800-kcal diet for our hypothetical diabetic patient.

Using the procedures discussed so far, four different methods of assigning the exchanges for a 1,800-kcal diet are shown in Table 26-26. The numbers of exchanges for Methods A and B are used to apportion the foods into breakfast, lunch, dinner, and a snack meal, as shown in Table 26-27. Two sample menus are shown for method A and method B in Tables 26-28 and 26-29, respectively.

At present, health practitioners disagree about the best food selection method. Many use the Food Exchange Lists of the American Diabetes Association. Others believe that this method is too complicated and restrictive in food choices. Many clinics and individuals have developed their own methods, many of which are discussed in the references at the end of this book.

Meal Planning

A diabetic patient's daily meal plan is regulated by his or her needs for insulin, which in turn determine the type and amount of food served at each meal. Some clinicians feel that only carbohydrates should be regulated, while others think that protein, fat, and carbohydrate should all be regulated. For convenience, the following discussion assumes that if each of the nutrients (protein, carbohydrate, and fat) is permitted a specific number of calories, then they will be distributed proportionally among each meal (breakfast, lunch, dinner, and snacks). Table 26-30 shows different ways of dividing the daily calories according to patient status.

Insulin-independent patients usually have stable blood glucose levels and do not require oral hypoglycemic agents. Most doctors and dietitians permit these patients liberal meal planning. For example, such patients may have three regular meals a day, evenly divided or with a larger dinner, or three meals interspersed with snacks. Possible caloric distributions of carbohydrate, protein, and fat are shown in Table 26-30. Exceptions include those patients with slight fluctuations of blood glucose. For example, for patients whose blood sugar level increases in the evening, the last meal of the day should be the smallest of the three. If the morning blood glucose level tends to be higher, breakfast should be the smallest.

Insulin-dependent patients require meal planning that takes into account the type of in-

TABLE 26-21 List 6: Fat Exchanges

Margarine, soft, tub, or stick*	1 t
Avocado (4" in diameter)[†]	⅛
Oil, corn, cottonseed, safflower, soy, sunflower	1 t
Oil, olive[†]	1 t
Oil, peanut[†]	1 t
Olives[†]	5 small
Almonds[†]	10 whole
Pecans[†]	2 large whole
Peanuts[†]	
Spanish	20 whole
Virginia	10 whole
Walnuts	6 small
Nuts, other[†]	6 small
Margarine, regular stick	1 t
Butter	1 t
Bacon fat	1 t
Bacon, crisp	1 strip
Cream, light	2 T
Cream, sour	2 T
Cream, heavy	1 T
Cream cheese	1 T
French dressing[‡]	1 T
Italian dressing[‡]	1 T
Lard	1 t
Mayonnaise[‡]	1 t
Salad dressing, mayonnaise type[‡]	2 t
Salt pork	¾-inch cube

Note: One exchange of fat contains 5 g of fat and 45 kilocalories. This list shows the kinds and amounts of fat-containing foods to use for one fat exchange. To plan a diet low in saturated fat, select only those exchanges which appear in **bold type**. They are **polyunsaturated**.

*Made with corn, cottonseed, safflower, soy, or sunflower oil only.

[†]Fat content is primarily monounsaturated.

[‡]If made with corn, cottonseed, safflower, soy, or sunflower oil, can be used on fat modified diet.

sulin used as well as individual habits and preferences. For instance, in the last few years, the use of regular or crystalline insulin alone by diabetics has not been common. However, if it is used, the patient should eat three equal meals, similarly to a patient not using insulin. This insulin is usually used either in combination with another type of insulin or during ketoacidosis or surgery.

If intermediate-acting insulin is used alone, the caloric distributions of ⅙, 2/6, ⅙, and 2/6, as shown in Table 26-30, are acceptable. The mid-afternoon snack prevents hypoglycemia, since the insulin is given before breakfast. If long-acting insulin is used, the caloric distributions of 2/7, 2/7, 2/7, and 1/7 are appropriate. This prevents hypoglycemia during the night and/or early morning.

Flexibility and alternatives in meal planning should also be available to insulin-dependent diabetics. For example, if patients like to eat a small,

TABLE 26-22   Amount of Carbohydrate Calculated from Milk, Vegetable, and Fruit Exchanges

Food List	No. of Exchanges	Protein (g)	Carbohydrate (g)	Fat (g)
Nonfat milk*	2	16	24	0
Vegetables†	2	4	10	0
Fruits‡	5	0	50	0
Total		—	84	—

*From Table 26-12, we see that 2 exchanges of nonfat milk provide $2 \times 8 = 16$ g of protein, $2 \times 12 = 24$ g of carbohydrate, and $2 \times$ trace $= 0$ g of fat.

†From Table 26-12, we see that 2 exchanges of vegetables provide $2 \times 2 = 4$ g of protein, $2 \times 5 = 10$ g of carbohydrate, and $2 \times 0 = 0$ g of fat.

‡From Table 26-12, we see that 5 exchanges of fruits provide $5 \times 0 = 0$ g of protein, $5 \times 10 = 50$ g of carbohydrate, and $5 \times 0 = 0$ g of fat.

TABLE 26-23   Amount of Protein Calculated from Milk, Vegetable, Fruit, and Bread Exchanges

Food List	No. of Exchanges	Protein (g)	Carbohydrate (g)	Fat (g)
Nonfat milk	2	16	24	0
Vegetables	2	4	10	0
Fruits	5	0	50	0
Bread*	9	18	135	0
Total		38	—	—

*From Table 26-12, we see that 9 exchanges of bread provide $9 \times 2 = 18$ g of protein, $9 \times 15 = 135$ g of carbohydrate, and $9 \times 0 = 0$ g of fat.

TABLE 26-24   Amount of Fat Calculated from Milk, Vegetable, Fruit, Bread, and Meat Exchanges

Food List	No. of Exchanges	Protein (g)	Carbohydrate (g)	Fat (g)
Nonfat milk	2	16	24	0
Vegetables	2	4	10	0
Fruits	5	0	50	0
Bread	9	18	135	0
Meat, lean*	8	56	0	24
Total		—	—	24

*From Table 26-12, we see that 8 exchanges of lean meat provide $8 \times 7 = 56$ g of protein, $8 \times 0 = 0$ g of carbohydrate, and $8 \times 3 = 24$ g of fat.

TABLE 26-25   Total Food Exchanges in an 1,800-kcal Diet for a Diabetic Patient

Food List	No. of Exchanges	Protein (g)	Carbohydrate (g)	Fat (g)	kcal*
Nonfat milk	2	16	24	0	160
Vegetables	2	4	10	0	50
Fruits	5	0	50	0	200
Bread	9	18	135	0	630
Meat, lean	8	56	0	24	440
Fat†	7	0	0	35	315
Total		94	219	59	1,795

*Calories are obtained by using the following equivalencies: 1 g protein = 4 kcal; 1 g of carbohydrate = 4 kcal; 1 g fat = 9 kcal.

†From Table 26-12, we see that 7 exchanges of fat provide 7 × 0 = 0 g of protein, 7 × 0 = 0 g of carbohydrate, and 7 × 5 = 35 g of fat.

TABLE 26-26   Four Ways of Assigning the Distribution of Food Exchanges in an 1,800-kcal Diet

	No. of Exchanges			
	Protein: 20% calories / Fat: 30% calories / Carbohydrate: 50% calories		Protein: 26% calories / Fat: 34% calories / Carbohydrate: 40% calories	
Food List	Method A*	Method B†	Method C‡	Method D§
Nonfat milk	2	4	2	4
Vegetables	2	2	2	2
Fruits	5	3	5	3
Bread	9	8	7	6
Meat, lean	8	6	11	9
Fat	7	10	7	9

*Figures obtained from Table 26-25.

†In this method, 4, 2, and 3 exchanges of nonfat milk, vegetables, and fruits, respectively, are assigned in Step 2 (see text).

‡In Step 1, the amounts of protein, fat, and carbohydrate are determined. Step 2 begins by assigning 2, 2, and 5 exchanges of nonfat milk, vegetables, and fruits, respectively, to the patient. See text.

§In Step 1, the amounts of protein, fat, and carbohydrate are determined. Step 2 begins by assigning 4, 2, and 3 exchanges of nonfat milk, vegetables, and fruits, respectively, to the patient. See text.

especially late breakfast, then rapid-acting (regular) insulin should be given in a small dose or not used at all. The amount of rapid-acting insulin can be adjusted if the patient prefers to eat a large breakfast. A large dose can be given before breakfast, or a regular dose 10 to 20 minutes earlier than usual. If the patient wants an afternoon snack, intermediate-acting insulin can be used so that its action time coincides with the snack time.

Considerations for Variations in Routine

Diabetics must guard against variations in routine that could cause large swings in blood glucose levels. Diabetic patients may have difficulty complying with a specific dietary plan in a number of situations. The three most common ones are exercise, eating out and meal delays, and illness.

TABLE 26-27 Distribution of Food Exchanges over Meals Using the Number of Exchanges Given in Methods A and B of Table 26-26

Exchange List	No. of Exchanges	
	Method A	Method B
Breakfast		
1 Nonfat milk	½	1
2 Vegetable	0	0
3 Fruit	1	1
4 Bread	2	2
5 Meat, lean	1	1
6 Fat	3	4
Lunch		
1 Nonfat milk	½	1
2 Vegetable	1	1
3 Fruit	1	1
4 Bread	2	2
5 Meat, lean	2	2
6 Fat	2	2
Dinner		
1 Nonfat milk	0	1
2 Vegetable	1	1
3 Fruit	1	1
4 Bread	3	2
5 Meat, lean	3	2
6 Fat	2	2
Bedtime Snack		
1 Nonfat milk	1	1
2 Vegetable	0	0
3 Fruit	2	0
4 Bread	2	2
5 Meat, lean	1	1
6 Fat	2	2

TABLE 26-28 Sample Menus for Method A Exchange Distribution of Table 26-27

Breakfast
Oatmeal, ½ c
Light cream, 4 T
Toast, whole wheat, 1 sl
Margarine, 1 t
Cantaloupe, small, ¼
Cottage cheese, ¼ c
Milk, skim, ½ c
Coffee or tea

Lunch
Turkey sandwich:
    Bread, whole wheat, 2 sl
    Margarine, 1 t
    Turkey, 2 oz
String beans, ½ c
Margarine, 1 t
Yogurt, skim milk, ½ c
Grapefruit juice, ½ c
Salt, pepper
Coffee or tea

Dinner
Tomato juice, ½ c
Green salad
    Lettuce
    Radish
    Italian dressing, 1 T
Salmon, broiled, 3 oz
Bagel, small, 1
Cream cheese, 1 t
Green peas, ½ c
Apple, small, 1
Salt, pepper, lemon
Coffee or tea

Snack
Apple juice, ⅓ c
Bran flakes, ½ c
Raisins, 2 T
Milk, skim, ½ c
Biscuit, plain, small, 1
Margarine, 1 t
Chicken, 1 oz
Milk, skim, ½ c

Breakfast
Yogurt, skim milk, ½ c
Pineapple, chunks, ½ c
Ham, 1 oz
Biscuits, 2
Butter, ½ t
Coffee or tea

Lunch
Salad:
    Lettuce wedge, 1
    Radish, sliced, 1
    Tomato, sliced, ½ c
    Crab, canned, ¼ c
    Shrimp, 1 oz
    French dressing, 1 T
Matzo, 4" × 6", 1
Butter, 1 t
Peach, 1
Buttermilk, skim, ½ c
Salt, pepper
Coffee or tea

Dinner
Beef, tenderloin, 3 oz
French fries, 8
Vegetable medley:
    Zucchini, cooked, ½ c
    Corn, cooked, ⅓ c
Bread, rye, 1 sl
Margarine, 1 t
Honeydew, ⅛
Salt, pepper
Coffee or tea

Snack
Banana, 1
Graham crackers, 2½ in. square, 4
Cream cheese, 2 T
Chicken, leg, cold, 1 oz
Milk, skim, 1 c

Exercise

Any form of exercise, whether mild or strenuous, can lower blood glucose and cause hypoglycemia. A readily available form of carbohydrate is needed to compensate for the extra blood glucose used during exercise. Mild exercise requires 5 to 10 extra grams of glucose, moderate exercise 10 to 25, and intense exercise 25 to 50. Carefully planning patient diets in regard to

TABLE 26-29   Sample Menus for Method B Exchange Distribution of Table 26-27

Breakfast	**Breakfast**
Puffed rice, 1 c	Ham, 1 oz
Banana, sliced, ½	Pancakes, 2
Light cream, 6 T	Butter, 1 t
English muffin, toasted, ½	Applesauce, un-
Margarine, 1 t	sweetened, ½ c
Ham, 1 oz	Milk, skim, 1 c
Milk, skim, 1 c	Coffee or tea
Coffee or tea	
	Lunch
Lunch	Sandwich:
Baked beans, 1 c	Bread, whole wheat,
Asparagus spears,	2 sl
cooked, ½ c	Turkey, 2 oz
Roll, plain, small, 1	Lettuce, leaf
Butter, 1 t	Mustard
Almonds, 10	Mayonnaise, 1 t
Pear, small, 1	Spinach, cooked, ½ c
Milk, skim, 1 c	Mayonnaise, 1 t
Salt, pepper	Apricots, fresh, 2
Coffee or tea	Milk, skim, 1 c
	Salt, pepper
Dinner	Coffee or tea
Pork, rump, roast, 2 oz	
Sauerkraut, ½ c	**Dinner**
Potatoes, mashed, ½ c	Veal, cutlet, 3 oz
Margarine, 1 t	Brussels sprouts, ½ c
Strawberries, sliced, ¾ c	Lima beans, ½ c
Milk, skim, 1 c	Butter, 1 t
Salt, papper	Roll, small, 1
Coffee or tea	Butter, 1 t
	Yogurt, skim milk, 1 c
Snack	Blueberries, ½ c
Tuna sandwich:	Salt, pepper
Bread, whole wheat,	Coffee or tea
2 sl	
Mayonnaise, 2 t	**Snack**
Tuna, canned, ¼ c	Chicken, 1 oz
Buttermilk, skim, 1 c	Bread, pumpernickel, 2 sl
	Margarine, 2 t
	Milk, skim, 1 c

amount of carbohydrate consumed must be considered as part of the patient's diet. This is especially important if the patient's physical exertions are unplanned. Overconsumption of carbohydrate unintentionally may eventually cause fluctuation in the blood sugar level and patient discomfort.

Eating out and meal delays

Eating in a restaurant, at a picnic, or at a friend's house poses problems for diabetic patients because the ingredients and quantities of the food consumed are unknown. The most fortunate patients are thin diabetics who require no insulin—they need only pay some attention to the amount of food eaten and whether it contains carbohydrate, protein, or fat. Occasionally eating out poses few problems for them. Overweight diabetics requiring no insulin must lose weight before eating out of the home; eating out too frequently can prevent weight from being lost. Patients who depend on insulin and are not obese should plan ahead for each occasion. For example, they should incorporate foods served at a picnic into their diet prescription. Learning to estimate the quantity and nutrient content of foods served and increasing the frequency of urine testing also reduce the risks posed by eating out.

Meal delays or a simple lack of food can create problems for diabetic patients. They should know what to do if no food is available for a certain period of time. One quick remedy is to have some form of simple carbohydrate available. For example, a soft drink will provide small amounts of sucrose and prevent hypoglycemia for ½ to 2½ hours. The amount of simple sugars consumed in these instances should be 10 to 35 g.

Illness

When a diabetic patient is ill, dietary care instantly becomes more complicated. Most hospitals are so sensitive to this problem that physicians leave specific instructions for all personnel on how to deal with sick diabetic patients. Figure 26-9 describes what to do when a diabetic is ill, especially in regard to dietary care.

insulin usage and regular exercise is important. For example, if a diabetic patient uses insulin and intends to exercise strenuously for an hour, he or she should eat some form of carbohydrate either before or during the exercise. However, the

TABLE 26-30   Distributions of Calories over Meals

| Patient Status | Daily Caloric Distribution in Proportion | | | | | |
	Breakfast	Mid-morning snack	Lunch	Mid-afternoon snack	Dinner	Bedtime snack
No insulin needed; blood glucose level stable; usually no oral hypoglycemic agents needed	3/10 1/3	— —	3/10 1/3	— —	4/10 1/3	— —
Insulin needed; blood glucose level stable; usually no oral hypoglycemic agents needed	3/10 2/7 1/6 2/7	— — — —	3/10 2/7 2/6 2/7	— 1/7 1/6 —	3/10 2/7 2/6 2/7	1/10 — — 1/7
Insulin needed; variable blood glucose level throughout the day	2/10 1.6/10	1/10 1.6/10	2/10 1.6/10	1/10 1.6/10	3/10 2/10	1/10 1.6/10

Use of Dietetic Products

Special dietetic products may help diabetics. A number of substitutes for foods and nutrients are available for diabetics that consist of special commercial dietetic foods, natural sugar substitutes, and synthetic sugar substitutes.

Special commercial dietetic foods contain little carbohydrate, especially mono- and disaccharides. However, the consumption of such substances must be carefully evaluated since most diabetic patients do not require the use of these products. A diabetic should be aware that labeling statements about calorie and carbohydrate contents may be lacking or confusing. If the doctor, dietitian, nurse, or patient prefers these products, only those that have clear instructions and a precise description of contents should be used. Food substitutes for eggs, butter, and other high-cholesterol and saturated-fat products are also available and may be useful.

Some sugar alcohols (see Chapter 3) such as sorbitol, xylitol, and levulose have been proposed for use by diabetic patients as natural sugar substitutes. They are sweet, slowly absorbed, and do not influence blood glucose levels, at least not initially. However, they contribute to caloric intake and may cause gastroenteritis, diarrhea, and abdominal pain when 50 g or more are eaten, and they are eventually converted to glucose. Whether these substances are really sweet enough to substitute for sugar has been debated. Some diabetics may find them distasteful.

For a number of years, the monosaccharide fructose has been suggested as a replacement for glucose. It is sweeter than glucose and does not raise the blood glucose level immediately after ingestion. However, fructose contributes calories, since it is eventually changed to glucose. Some clinics in Europe have given fructose to diabetic patients and found it to be a satisfactory substitute. However, its use is not advocated in this country at the present time.

Synthetic sugar substitutes are artificial sweeteners, and the controversy surrounding their use is well known. A brief discussion of saccharin, a currently available artificial sweetener, is provided in Chapter 1. Chapter 20 discusses food additives in general.

Ideally, all diabetic patients should be taught to become independent of sweeteners. However, such an attempt may prove futile in many cases. If the patient insists on sweetness, any available legal artificial sweetener should be prescribed, especially if the patient is overweight. Furthermore, some beverages containing artificial sweet-

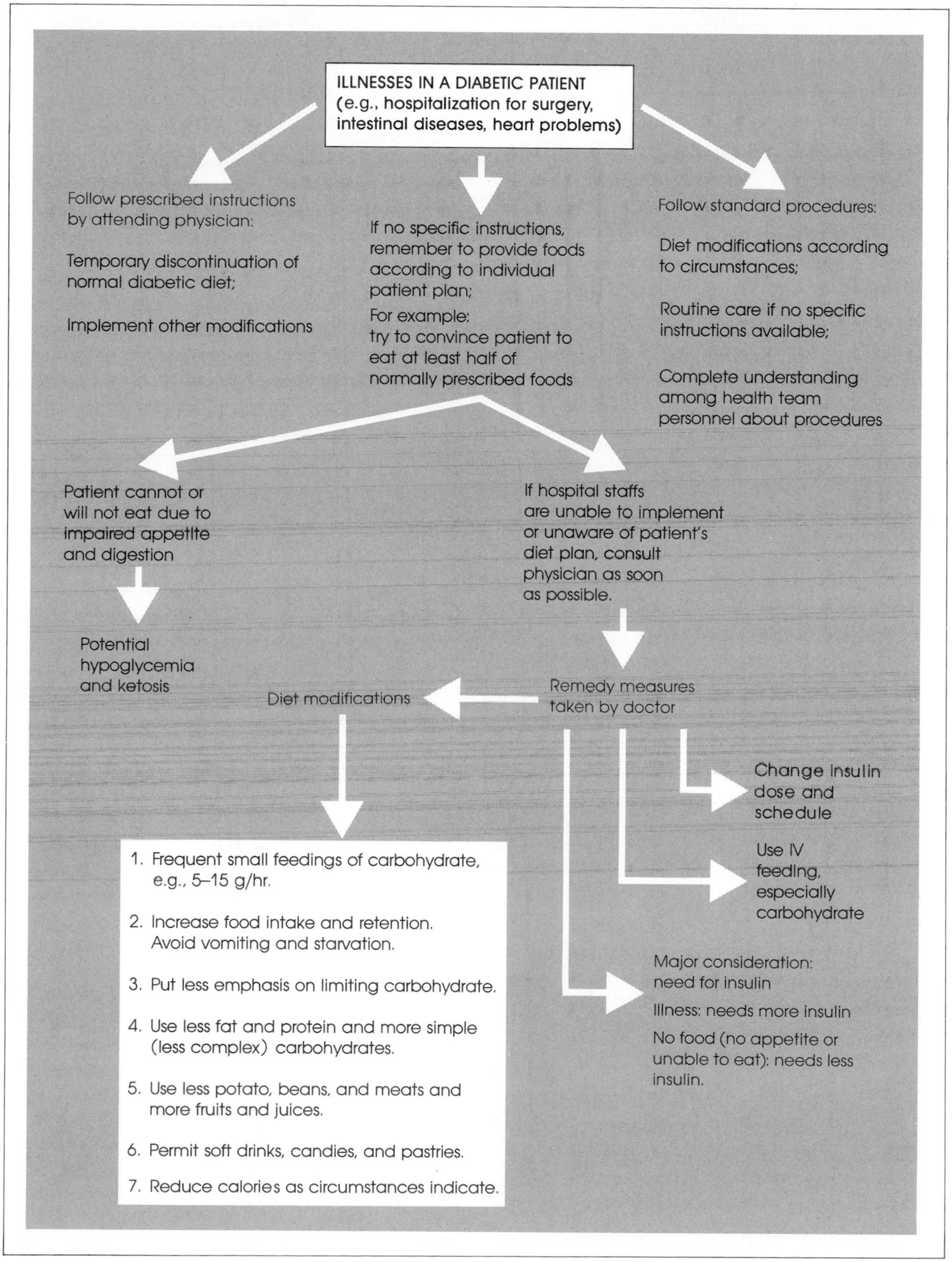

FIGURE 26-9 Dietary management of an ill diabetic patient.

eners also contain sugar and appeal to many diabetics. If it becomes necessary to use such items, it is advisable to space their usage appropriately and substitute them for the carbohydrate in a prescribed food to make meals appealing.

Consumption of Alcoholic Beverages

Alcohol usage by a diabetic patient requires careful consideration. In some patients, alcoholic beverages can cause hypoglycemia. The mechanism of the cause is unknown and the reaction is more severe in insulin-dependent diabetics, especially if they have received no food because of delayed or missed meals. Alcohol can enhance the effect of insulin and vice versa. Since alcohol is rapidly absorbed, both intoxication and hypoglycemia develop rapidly. Because hypoglycemia can result in a confused state, an observer can mistake it for drunkenness and not attempt to correct the hypoglycemia.

All alcoholic beverages should be considered by a diabetic as a source of carbohydrate and fat. The calories contained in alcoholic beverages (7 kcal/g ethyl alcohol) must also be taken into consideration, especially if the patient is obese. Obviously, if the patient drinks regularly, the extra calories should be included in the diet prescription. It is difficult to plan a proper diet for a diabetic when this variable is added to the others—patient condition, the use of insulin, the need for oral drugs, and exercise.

There is a spectrum of nonspecific symptoms occasionally observed in diabetic patients who drink alcoholic beverages. These include nervousness, sweating, slurred speech, and a staggering gait. Some patients develop hypertriglyceridemia and this, as discussed elsewhere, may predispose the patient to a higher risk of atherosclerosis.

If patients want to drink alcohol, their diabetic condition must be kept under control. One guideline is to drink moderately, preferably with or immediately after a meal. Another is to avoid alcoholic beverages with high sugar contents, such as red wines, liqueurs, mixed cocktail drinks, beer, ale, and other fermented malt drinks. It is important not to drink and exercise simultaneously. Finally, diabetic patients trying to lose weight should abstain from alcoholic drinks until they reach their ideal weight.

COMPLICATIONS

Diabetics are always faced with the possibility of complications. Complications generally result from too much or too little insulin, degenerative changes caused by diabetes, associated clinical stresses, and special problems (e.g., pregnancy).

Diabetic Coma

A number of clinical conditions can lead to coma in a diabetic patient. These are diabetic ketoacidosis, nonketotichyperosmolar hyperglycemia, lactic acidosis, alcoholic ketoacidosis, and hypoglycemia. Table 26-31 describes the characteristics of each condition. The following briefly discusses hypoglycemia from insulin.

Hypoglycemia from excess insulin or oral hypoglycemic agents is the opposite of diabetic ketoacidosis, although the two conditions are sometimes confused because of similar clinical appearances (see Table 26-31). Hypoglycemia sometimes occurs in a diabetic when food is not available to compensate for injected insulin. The insulin is then more potent, even if it is a regular dose. Other precipitating factors include unplanned exercise without ingesting extra food to prevent an excess drain of blood glucose. Symptoms of hypoglycemia are changes in mood and personality, hunger, sweating, faintness, a fast heartbeat, dilated pupils, hyperactivity, and anxiety. The patient may go into a coma if these symptoms are left unattended. A well-informed patient will recover easily through a quick oral dose of hard candy, fruit juice, a soft drink, or any form of simple sugar. If these remedies are unavailable, the unconscious patient may be restored to normal by a subcutaneous injection of glucagon. Following a hypoglycemic episode, a diabetic should have a snack if the next meal is more than an hour away. Small amounts of foods such as cheese and toast may be used for this purpose.

TABLE 26-31   Different Causes of Coma in a Diabetic Patient

Clinical Stress Leading to Coma	Characteristics
Diabetic ketoacidosis	Most frequent in patients requiring insulin; symptoms: nausea, vomiting, diarrhea, abdominal pain, polydipsia, polyuria, Kussmaul's respiration (air hunger), dehydration, confusion; blood glucose >600 mg/100 mL blood if severe, serum acetone >4 with >1 dilution if severe, pH less than 7.2 if severe, osmolarity 300–350 mosm/kg. Precipitating events include failure to inject insulin, heart attack, pregnancy, and illness
Nonketotic hyperosmolar hyperglycemia	Most frequent in patients requiring no insulin, the elderly, patients with kidney problem; can be drug induced; symptoms: constant thirst, somnolence, polyuria, dehydration, confusion, nervous disorder; blood glucose >400 mg/100 mL, serum acetone >2 with >1 dilution, pH less than 7.5, osmolarity >350 mosm/kg
Lactic acidosis	Cause unknown; most frequent in patient on oral hypoglycemic agents with liver, heart, or kidney troubles; may be drug induced; symptoms: skin flushing, air hunger
Alcoholic ketoacidosis	Caused by too much drinking without food; symptoms: enlarged liver without dehydration; blood glucose about 150 mg/100 mL (between 20 and 250 mg), serum acetone >3 with no dilution, pH 7–7.3, osmolarity 300 mosm/kg
Hypoglycemia	Caused by too much insulin, alcohol, or oral hypoglycemic agent; symptoms: sweating, fainting, mood and personality changes, hyperactivity, fast heartbeat, confusion, blood glucose less than 50 mg/100 mL

Degenerative Changes and Associated Clinical Stresses

Two other groups of diabetic patients require special attention: those with degenerative changes caused by the diabetic condition and those with other clinical conditions. These changes may be chronic, debilitating, and possibly life threatening.

The cardiovascular system often degener-ates in diabetics. The major problem is athero-sclerosis, which may lead to coronary heart dis-ease, stroke, and associated circulatory diseases (such as gangrene). Another serious cardiovas-cular problem is microangiopathy, which may cause kidney and eye diseases. Kidney failure and blindness may occur in the final stages of diabetes.

Degeneration of the nervous system may af-fect the peripheral, cranial, and autonomic nervous systems. Diabetics may have tingling or pain in the extremities as a result. Eye twitching, grimacing, diarrhea, incontinence, and male impotence can also be consequences of nervous system degeneration.

Diabetics are also highly susceptible to infection by all forms of biological agents. The infection may affect the skin, the kidney, the lungs, and other organs.

For more information on these complications in a diabetic patient, consult the references at the end of this book.

Diabetic patients often have other stresses to cope with such as pregnancy, hyperlipidemia, surgery, kidney failure, congestive heart failure, and numerous problems of the gastrointestinal system. The first two conditions are briefly described below.

Pregnant diabetic patients need only make minor adjustments. If such a patient is hyperglycemic and in negative nitrogen balance, the dietary supply of protein (refer to the protein need discussed earlier) should be very generous. Calorie amounts should be adjusted so that between 23 and 24 lb (1 to 1.1 kg) are gained in 9 months. Toxemia and accumulation of excess body and amniotic fluid may occur. To prevent this, some clinicians prescribe a moderate salt intake during the last 3 months of pregnancy.

The 1976 Food Exchange Lists of the American Diabetes Association have improved the management of diabetic patients with hyperlipidemia. Since the lists contain the levels of total fat, saturated fat, polyunsaturated fat, and cholesterol in food, they help in controlling the condition. Three major considerations are important in managing these patients. First, the serum lipid profile of many nonobese diabetic patients returns to normal after the diabetic condition is controlled. Second, diabetic patients with an abnormal serum lipid profile are usually obese and exhibit type IV hyperlipoproteinemia (see Chapter 27). Losing weight solves the two problems simultaneously. Third, in general, the abnormal serum lipid profile of almost any diabetic patient can be corrected by an appropriate combination of the following: (1) correcting the hyperglycemia, (2) ingesting suitable amounts of calories, (3) reducing the total intake of fat and cholesterol, and (4) increasing the dietary ratio of polyunsaturated to saturated fats (see Chapter 27).

PATIENT EDUCATION

The diabetic patient must be considered a member of the health team. The success of the diet and of the treatment with insulin and oral drugs largely depends on patient cooperation. Thus a comprehensive and successful diabetic management program must always include patient education. The extent of patient education, of course, depends on the individual and the seriousness of his or her condition.

Educating a diabetic patient begins with the first visit to a clinic or upon admission into a hospital. The nurse, doctor, dietitian, and nutritionist work together to decide the best way to educate the patient. The advantages and disadvantages of treatments with diet, insulin, and oral hypoglycemic agents should be stressed. When teaching a patient, some special points should be kept in mind.

1. Teaching one patient instead of a group of patients is more useful to the patient, though much more costly in time and money.
2. If group education is used, patients should be sorted by the type of diabetes, for example, young diabetics, insulin-independent diabetics, obese patients using insulin, and thin patients using insulin. This sorting reduces confusion in the teaching process. If feasible, both individualized and group education is ideal.
3. The benefits and limitations of using paraprofessionals to teach the patient should be considered.
4. The patient's history should be studied, especially the type of diet instructions he or she has received. This ensures that the patient will not receive contradictory information during an educational session. Any information presented that seems to conflict with previous instructions can be explained to a patient's satisfaction.
5. At least one close relative or the patient's caretaker should be familiar with the information presented to the patient.

The characteristics of the disease should be explained as well as the role and interrelationship of insulin, diet, drugs, and exercise. The importance of instructions for coping with variations from the usual routine should be emphasized. Major differences between a lean and overweight diabetic also should be pointed out, and it should be emphasized that a lean diabetic has more flexibility in the amount of foods permitted.

Basic principles and methods of diabetic management and their implementation should be presented. The advantages of diet modification should be pointed out, and any misunderstandings about the diet plan should be clarified. It is also important to show that a diet for diabetes varies with the patient's condition and nutritional needs, the relative distribution of protein, carbohydrate, and fat intake, and in the manner, time, and location of eating. Apart from food components, a diabetic should know that a good diet plan is characterized by its consistency, predictability, and palatability. The diet is dependable if the patient eats it.

Diet instructions must be written down. They should contain specific diet prescriptions and means of implementing them. Reasons for not eating certain foods should also be given. Instructions should include lists of the foods permitted, forbidden, and encouraged; recommended serving sizes; feeding schedules; guidelines about alcoholic beverages and the flexibility of meal planning (see discussion under "Meal planning"); and so on. If necessary, the patient should be taught at least one food selection system. When Food Exchange Lists are used, the patient should be able to make the calculations and to interchange food items. He or she should be familiar with the composition of food and the estimation of approximate contents of protein, carbohydrate, and fat.

The teaching process is always helped by fostering the right attitudes in the patients. Patients are willing to cooperate and learn if they know that the disease is controllable and if they understand that their diet can be pleasant, manageable, and not too restrictive. The better diabetic patients feel, the more likely they are to follow the diet instructions. Two conditions lead patients not to comply with dietary instructions: severe dietary restrictions and exaggeration of the adverse effects of deviating from a dietary prescription.

Some teaching aids and counseling services for diabetes are listed below.

1. Local, city, and county diabetic programs
2. Private and public diabetic (clinical) centers
3. Professional sources of materials: drug companies, American Dietetic Association, American Diabetes Association, state health agencies
4. Food models, films, and slides
5. Ethnic teaching materials
6. Demonstration kitchen and demonstration food portion sizes
7. Recipes and cookbooks

THE INSULIN PUMP

A new approach to the treatment of insulin-dependent diabetics is the *insulin pump*, a small portable device that continually delivers a measured flow of short-acting insulin. Although insulin pumps are so new that many technical problems and questions remain, they offer hope that certain diabetic patients can live normal lives, eat unrestricted diets, and carry on normal activities.

In contrast to daily injections of long-acting insulin, continual low-dosage infusion of insulin with stepped-up delivery during meals may better simulate the action of a normal pancreas in helping the liver regulate blood glucose level. Based on electronic microcircuitry, an insulin pump can be as small as a cigarette pack. It can be carried in the patient's underclothes and be remote-controlled by a programming device which permits different rates of flow depending on the patient's basal metabolic rate and meal intake.

The insulin is slowly pumped through a tube into the injection site of choice: subcutaneous, intravenous, or perhaps intraperitoneal. If the system can be sufficiently miniaturized, the pump may even be implanted in the patient's body as an artificial pancreas.

Insulin pump technology is still in its infancy, and it carries a number of potential hazards. The implantation procedure could create hypoglycemic shock and even death if a faulty device suddenly released too much insulin. Another problem, noticed in experimental implantations, is the precipitation of insulin in the implanted reservoir and tube. Acceptance of the pump materi-

CASE STUDY   *An Obese Diabetic Woman*

Mrs. S.P., a 41-year-old patient of German descent, was admitted to the hospital after experiencing for 5 weeks excessive urination (especially at night), frequent thirst, visual disturbances, and vaginal itching.

She had been hospitalized 3 years earlier when she showed a fasting blood glucose of 110 mg/100 mL and a 2-hour postprandial blood glucose of 190 mg/100 mL. A liver biopsy performed at that time showed fatty infiltration. This patient was obese as a child and had a weight history of 74.8 kg (165 lb) at age 18, 81.6 kg (180 lb) at age 21, and ranging from 86.2 kg (190 lb) to 97.5 kg (215 lb) between ages 25 and 31. Occasionally her body weight was lower during periods of dieting, although she never lost more than 11.3 kg (25 lb). Her other past clinical problems included pneumonia, frequent infections of the eyes and the genitourinary tract, back injury, vocal cord paralysis, and appendectomy. There was a family history of gout, diabetes, and coronary heart disease.

On admission, the patient was 157.5 cm (5'2") tall, weighed 99.8 kg (220 lb) (about 165% of her ideal body weight), and had a pulse of 88 and a blood pressure of 120/80 mm Hg. The patient had a slight white vaginal discharge, and she also had a erythematous perineal skin. She had a fasting blood glucose of 250 mg/100 mL. She excreted about 66 g of glucose in the urine in a 24-hour period, and her urinary glucose level was 500 mg/100 mL. She was also excreting some acetone and protein. A vaginal culture showed a mild yeast infection. Her other laboratory data were normal. After a glucose tolerance test, the attending doctors were sure that this patient had diabetes mellitus.

Three days after the patient had been admitted to the hospital, the attending health team placed her on an intensive program of weight reduction, using supplemental fasting. After 3 weeks, she had lost about 13.6 kg (30 lb) and weighed 86.2 kg (190 lb).

Her fasting blood glucose had dropped to 100 mg/100 mL, and she was excreting a normal amount of glucose in her urine. Her symptoms had disappeared. She was discharged during the fourth week and was instructed to continue the weight reduction program (including fasting) on an outpatient basis. Five months later, the patient's weight had dropped to 61.2 kg (135 lb), with a fasting blood glucose of 71 mg/100 mL. The patient was then instructed to change to a regular diet at a caloric level that would maintain her body weight.

Although this patient was paying regular visits to the doctor for follow-up, she began to eat uncontrollably and started to gain weight 1 year after her discharge. The doctor immediately placed her on supplemental fasting again. However, she did not comply with the dietary restrictions, and she regained her original weight within another year. Her fasting blood glucose was again 270 mg/100 mL, and she was excreting an excessive amount of glucose. She started having the classic symptoms of a diabetic. To control her disorder, the doctor started her on a regimen of insulin.

Review and Analysis

1. Using Mrs. S.P. as an example, is it appropriate to state that obesity can cause diabetes?

2. Discuss the current known relationships between diabetes mellitus and obesity.

3. What should be the patient's ideal weight?

4. Is Mrs. S.P.'s itching a symptom of her diabetes?

5. Set up an intensive program of weight reduction incorporating supplemental fasting. Describe in detail the protocol, meal planning, caloric levels, frequency of clinical checkups, recording of medical data, etc. Obtain an appropriate ref-

erence source for the most current information.

6. Using the available information in the case history, suggest an initial regimen of insulin administration. If you need more data, list them. Make some assumptions and develop an insulin administration plan.

7. Speculate on the cause(s) of Mrs. S.P.'s vaginal discharge.

---

als by the body, the need to replace pump batteries periodically, and the sterile procedure for adding insulin to the pump are additional concerns.

There is also the problem of where the insulin should best be directed. Under normal circumstances, insulin from the pancreas is secreted directly into the portal vein leading to the liver. Using other delivery routes for insulin may create imbalances. Both the subcutaneous and intravenous routes may create a hyperinsulin condition in the peripheral circulation. Absorption of insulin from subcutaneous injection may be too slow to prevent hypoglycemia; distribution of insulin injected intravenously may be too fast to match the digestion and absorption of carbohydrates. Intravenous injections also carry the risk of clotting and thrombosis. The speed of insulin diffusion from intraperitoneal injection is moderate, with direct absorption into the portal vein, but access is difficult and there is the chance of peritonitis. To date, only the subcutaneous route is used on a large scale.

Another major question to be studied is, "For which patients is the insulin pump appropriate?" At present, it appears that those who would most profit from an improvement in insulin delivery are those with no potential for secreting insulin on their own. Other individual biological factors may also be involved, and for some patients the initial cost of the device might be prohibitive. Nevertheless, the insulin pump may eventually simplify life for many insulin-dependent diabetics.

STUDY QUESTIONS

1. What is diabetes mellitus? Why is the incidence of this disease on the rise? What complications are often associated with it?

2. Describe the metabolic changes in a patient with diabetes mellitus.

3. What are the clinical symptoms of diabetes mellitus? Briefly describe the laboratory tests used to confirm diabetes in a patient.

4. What are the different types of insulin preparations currently available in the United States for diabetic patients?

5. Identify factors that determine the kinds and amounts of nutrients a diabetic may consume.

6. Explain briefly how a Food Exchange List works. Use specific examples from the tables in the text to illustrate your explanation. Calculate the daily exchange requirements of one of your diabetic patients. Follow the calculations in this chapter.

7. What two factors must be taken into account in meal planning for insulin-dependent diabetics? Briefly describe variations in routine that must be considered in dietary planning for diabetics. How does each of these factors alter caloric and/or nutrient intake?

8. Why is the consumption of alcoholic beverages dangerous for diabetics? Consider all relevant factors.

9. When educating a diabetic patient, what points should be especially emphasized? How can a positive attitude be encouraged?

10. What is an insulin pump? Do some library research and describe its latest scientific and legal status.

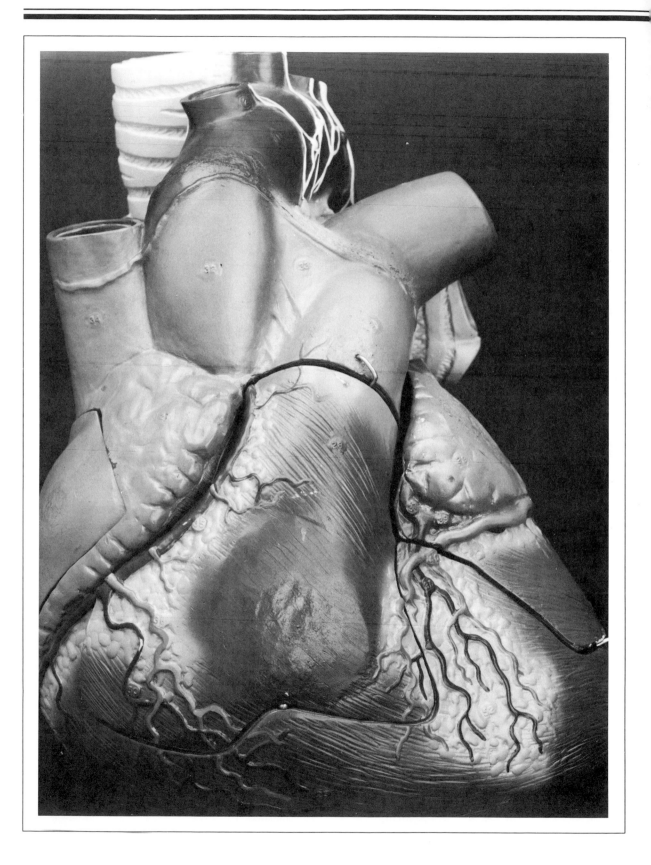

Chapter 27

Diet and Cardiovascular Diseases

THE INCIDENCE OF heart disease has reached epidemic proportions in industrialized societies. In the United States, for instance, heart disease is still the number one killer, despite recent declines in mortality rates from heart-related disorders.

Arteriosclerosis (atherosclerosis in particular) is the major pathological condition that leads to a diseased heart. Table 27-1 defines these two terms and related conditions. Scientists currently believe that both heredity and environmental conditions are involved in the development of these clinical disorders. We will begin with a discussion of atherosclerosis, emphasizing medical management and the role of diet in its development.

ATHEROSCLEROSIS

In a healthy person, the lumina of blood vessels are wide and clear, permitting blood to pass easily. If the process of *atherosclerosis* has started, the tunica intima of a blood vessel may become thickened by deposited lipid materials that become covered by fibrous connective tissues. This is the process of *plaque formation*. Blood then moves through a narrower passage, and its rate of flow is reduced. As the plaque deposition increases and severe thrombosis sets in, the ensuing blockage may completely stop the blood flow. If this occurs in a coronary artery, the heart muscle cells die from ischemia, or lack of oxygen. The resulting condition, known as atherosclerotic coronary artery disease, is triggered by a chain of events that may result in sudden death from myocardial infarction (Figure 27-1). Figure 27-2 illustrates the blockage of blood vessels by plaque and a thrombus.

Ulceration, plaque hemorrhage, and thrombosis are the major complications of the atherosclerotic process. Atherosclerosis is the main cause of heart disease (such as angina pectoris or myocardial infarction), stroke (cerebral infarction), gangrene of the extremities, and aneurysm of the abdominal aorta. Renal failure and hypertension occur less frequently but are also important complications. Disorders resulting from the atherosclerotic process are illustrated in Figure 27-3.

In industrialized societies, atherosclerotic coronary artery disease is the leading cause of death. In the United States, it is estimated that 150,000 to 200,000 people under 65 years old die from this disease annually. A comparison of the incidence of this disorder among men and women is presented in Table 27-2.

Medical and Dietary Management of the Atherosclerotic Patient

Dietary care and nutritional considerations for the atherosclerotic patient may be immediate or long-term. Patients who have suffered stroke, gangrene, or aneurysm need no specific immediate dietary therapy, especially if they are normal otherwise. Routine hospital feeding is adequate. If an operation has been performed, postsurgical dietary management is necessary (see Chapter 29). In the case of a poststroke patient who is suffering paralysis that interferes with the mechanics of eating, an occupational or physical therapist should be sought. During the recovery period, dietary care for a physically handicapped individual should be emphasized (see Chapters 22 and 31). If the nervous supply to the digestive system in an atherosclerotic patient is severely disturbed, nutritional and dietary care appropriate to the specific clinical conditions (e.g., inadequate stomach contraction or secretion) of the patient is necessary.

On the other hand, if the poststroke, gangrene, or aneurysm patients are also suffering from other clinical disorders, such as undernourishment, diabetes mellitus, or endocrine imbalances, then the dietary treatment must be specific for that particular problem. For patients also having hypertension, refer to the discussion later in this chapter.

Angina pectoris

Although proper dietary care is part of the clinical management of an angina patient, initial treatment is usually nonnutritional. It consists of using nitroglycerin to reduce myocardial oxygen demand of affected arteries by dilating other blood vessels. This relieves strain placed on the

TABLE 27-1   Medical Terms Commonly Used in Discussions of Cardiovascular Diseases

Term	Definition
Aneurysm	Blood-filled sac formed from a dilatation of an artery
Angina pectoris	Distinctive type of pain in the chest area caused by a decreased blood supply to the heart muscle
Arrhythmia	A state of rhythm that deviates from the normal, especially in the case of heart beat
Arteriosclerosis	Process whereby arterial walls become thickened because of certain inflammatory changes
Atherosclerosis	Specific form of arteriosclerosis; primarily involves the intima (innermost layer) of medium muscular and large elastic arteries; area of hardening and degeneration is characterized by the deposition of lipid, blood components, and connective tissue in the form of plaques
Cerebral infarction	Formation of an infarct in the nervous tissues of the cerebrum (brain) because of blockage of blood supply to this area
Gangrene	Death of certain body part(s) because of a lack of oxygen and other nutrients; results mainly from a failure of the blood to reach the location and is associated with postmortem changes
Infarct	Localized area of ischemic necrosis caused by blockage of arterial blood supply
Infarction	Presence or development of an infarct due to engorgement or stoppage of a blood vessel
Ischemia	Lack of oxygen
Myocardial infarction	Formation of an infarct in the heart muscle because of blockage of the blood supply to this area
Plaque	Flat, disclike body with a fibrous connective tissue cap covering a small lump of fat; located in the intima of a blood vessel
Thrombus	Deposited mass of blood components in the living heart or blood vessel(s); *thrombosis* is the process of this deposition
Xanthoma	Disease characterized by formation of yellow neoplastic nodules or smooth plates on the skin; these growths contain lipid deposits

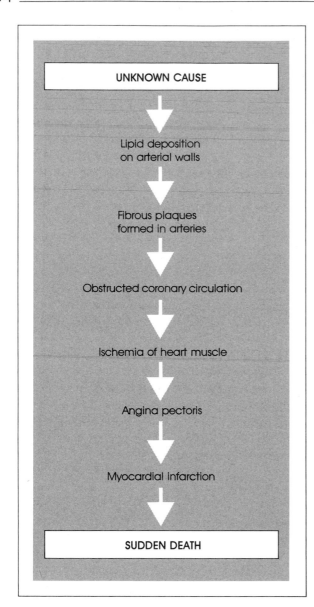

FIGURE 27-1   Clinical events leading to sudden death in atherosclerotic coronary artery disease.

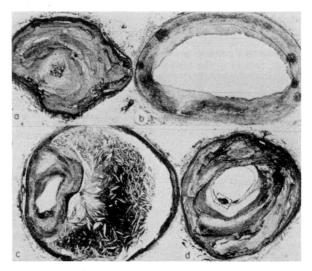

FIGURE 27-2   Coronary arteries at sites of maximal narrowing in a 65-year-old man. He died suddenly without previous symptomatic evidence of ischemic heart disease. (a) Right, (b) left main, (c) left circumflex, and (d) left anterior descending coronary arteries. The luminal narrowing in three of the vessels is severe and due to various types of complicated atherosclerotic plaques. The area in brackets in (d) is a small platelet thrombus. (Moval stain [a], elastic–van Gieson stain [b], hematooxylin-eosin stain [c, d]; each × 20, reduced by 58%.) (From W. C. Roberts et al., *Am. J. Cardiol.*, 31 [1973]: 557)

coronary vessels that have become partially occluded. In some serious cases of angina, bypass surgery is necessary.

The presence or absence of pain determines an angina patient's daily eating schedule. Pain during or after eating indicates that the patient should eat small portions slowly or not eat at all until the pain disappears. The use of nitroglycerin before eating sometimes alleviates the associated pain.

An overweight angina patient should reduce to and then maintain ideal body weight. This goal can be attained by adhering to a prescribed diet. In general, clinicians prescribe a diet low in calories, total fat, cholesterol, and carbohydrates, with a high polyunsaturated : saturated fat ratio. If hyperlipoproteinemia is present, it is managed according to the specific blood chemistry and clinical diagnosis and the clinical philosophy of the attending physician. (More information on these topics is presented later in this chapter.) All nutritionally related clinical problems such as diabetes mellitus and hypertension are managed accordingly.

Of special importance in treating the post-angina patient is alcohol use. This particular point has been a long-standing subject of medical controversy. Therefore, it is important for the dietitian and nurse to become familiar with the basic issues involved so they can better inform the patient and his or her family members.

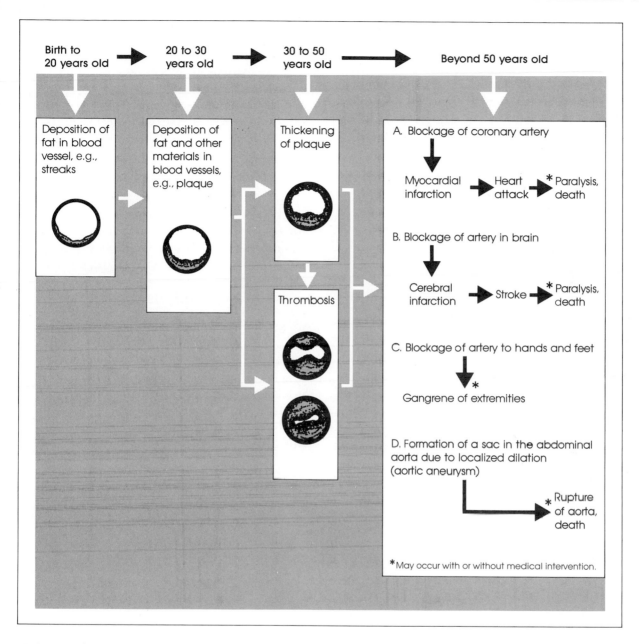

FIGURE 27-3 Clinical disorders resulting from the atherosclerotic process.

Alcohol may present some danger to an angina patient. For instance, it is generally agreed that patients having myocardial infarction or showing other signs of coronary disease should not drink alcoholic beverages. Alcohol can also potentiate or produce hyperglyceridemia in an angina patient for reasons not yet known. It oc-casionally elicits heart arrhythmias and has been suspected of causing damage to the myocar-dium, which may ultimately result in heart fail-ure. Alcohol consumed in large quantities can increase the load on the heart by increasing blood pressure. Nitroglycerin and alcohol should not be used simultaneously by an angina patient

TABLE 27-2 Comparison of the Incidence of Coronary Heart Disease among Men and Women

Age Group	Incidence Comparison
Under 45	5 to 8 times more common in men
45 to 80	2 to 3 times more common in men
Over 80	About equal among men and women

since peripheral collapse may occur. Finally, the use of alcohol interferes with dietary distribution of protein, carbohydrate, and fat since it contributes calories.

However, alcohol does have some beneficial effects. Small amounts, for instance, can decrease the load on the heart by decreasing blood pressure. This occurs because alcohol dilates the blood vessels, but the dilation occurs mainly in peripheral and not necessarily in coronary vessels. Small amounts of alcohol (about 5 mL) have successfully been used in some patients in lieu of nitroglycerin where intolerance to the latter exists. It is also generally agreed that a small amount of alcohol can produce a tranquilizing effect, resulting in relaxation and a relief of tension. Thus, alcohol reduces anxieties and has an analgesic effect.

Thus, the benefits of permitting the patient to drink alcohol must be weighted against its risks, and special consideration must be given to the exact amount permitted, if any. Only the physician can make this decision.

Myocardial infarction

Although dietary care is only a small part of the medical management of a patient confined to an intensive care unit following myocardial infarction, its mishandling can have dire consequences. Before the details of the dietary regimen are presented, a summary of three nutritionally related and controversial problems is pertinent. These involve the quantity of food served, temperature of food and drink, and restriction of sodium intake.

A health team caring for a patient in intensive care has sometimes been criticized for adopting one of two extreme practices in feeding a patient. At one end of the spectrum is the failure to feed the patient adequately, causing undernourishment. This can occur in an effort to prevent the patient from eating too much food, which can endanger the patient by increasing the blood pressure and adding an extra load onto the heart. In this case all parties involved, including the doctor, nurse, and dietitian, have adopted a conservative attitude. They are either feeding the patient a liquid diet or only a small quantity of food for a prolonged period. In some cases, patients actually suffer from malnutrition.

At the other extreme, the patient is fed too much food. G. E. Burch of Tulane University School of Medicine has stated, "These enormous meals often consist of fried eggs, bacon or ham, potatoes, cereal, fruit juice, coffee, rolls and/or toasted bread, and milk for breakfast. The noon and evening meals are even larger, each consisting of soup, potatoes, two vegetables, a portion of meat (roast beef, steak, fish or chicken), bread, coffee and/or iced tea, milk and at least a rich dessert—all in liberal servings" (G. E. Burch, Sick People's Food, *American Heart Journal*, 1973; 85:279). Some physicians have reported that patients, after eating such meals, develop symptoms such as profuse sweating, breathing difficulty, fast heartbeat, palpitations, and cardiac arrhythmia.

Overfeeding of the patient may result from a number of factors. Concern for the nutritional status of the patient may exist if he or she was malnourished when admitted to the hospital. There may be a simple unawareness or disregard for the danger of such a practice. A lack of communication among members of the health team may also be responsible.

There has been a long and sometimes strong debate over whether a patient should be fed food and drink that are very hot or cold. Cardiac arrhythmia may result from either practice. Currently, sufficient scientific data are not available to settle this issue. Each physician usually gives specific instructions as to the advisability of serving the patient hot or cold foods and drinks.

Some clinicians in the past have restricted the sodium intake of a patient with suspected or confirmed myocardial infarction. However, such a restriction is known to produce or potentiate shock. Furthermore, in the common case of a cardiac patient with renal failure, restricting dietary sodium will add to the existing problem of uncontrolled loss of sodium by the kidney. There is an additional loss in patients who vomit or have diarrhea. Thus sodium restriction is justified only in patients with obvious pulmonary edema or congestive heart failure.

Dietary considerations for a patient recovering from myocardial infarction may be divided into three phases: acute, subacute, and rehabilitative. Each phase involves its own strategy.

The *acute phase* refers to the 1- or 2-day period immediately following an attack when the patient is in the intensive care unit. At this point, apparatus necessary for intravenous feeding is usually set up. This facilitates the administration of glucose, fluids, electrolytes, and drugs if and when they are prescribed. Any food that is to be taken orally is prescribed by the physician, who ascertains the usefulness and safety of the particular food involved.

After the doctor has given instructions for a liquid diet, the patient is fed clear soup, broth, skim milk, ginger ale, fruit juices, water, weak tea, and coffee with little or no caffeine. The number of calories provided daily is about 500 to 800. The food is given to the patient throughout the day in progressive amounts according to patient tolerance. If at all feasible, patients should feed themselves. This encourages them to eat and gives the clinician a good idea of how much they are able to eat.

The degree of restriction of dietary sodium varies with the clinical condition of the patient. The doctor makes the decision after carefully studying the patient's urine and blood chemistry. As indicated earlier, caution is needed since a low sodium intake may not be compatible with a patient's electrolyte balance. Information on how to plan a sodium-restricted diet is presented later in this chapter.

During the *subacute phase*, the patient is allowed more calories and a variety of foods. The patient is provided about 750 to 1,250 kcal per day and is fed 4 to 6 small meals with a progressive increase in quantity. The approximate nutrient composition of the diet is as follows:

1. Carbohydrate: 40% to 50% of total daily permitted calories
2. Protein: 15% to 25% of total daily permitted calories
3. Fat: 25% to 35% of total daily permitted calories
4. Cholesterol: 100 to 300 mg/d
5. Polyunsaturated : saturated fat ratio: 1.5 : 1.0 to 2.0 : 1.0

Diet planning information is presented later in this chapter.

Meals should be served at the temperature prescribed by the attending physician. Generally, food at room temperature is preferred. The food should be soft and tender and contain no roughage, stimulants, or gastrointestinal irritants. Items usually included in the subacute phase are canned or cooked fruits and vegetables, light puddings, gelatin, cooked cereals, plain bread, lean meat, poultry, and fish. If desired, a patient may have one or two eggs per day or be permitted egg substitutes in more liberal amounts. If a sodium-restricted diet has been prescribed, eggs and egg substitutes may be limited or withheld.

No food to which the patient is sensitive should be served. This may include high-lactose products, sugary fruit juices, and carbonated soft drinks. Whenever feasible, the patient should be provided with similar but nonoffending products.

Foods and beverages containing methylated xanthines and their derivatives, including caffeine, theobromine, and theophylline should not be served, although some clinicians permit weak coffee and tea. Daily fluid intake is usually restricted to less than 2 c per meal, preferably 1 to 1½ c. Excess fluid intake may distend the abdomen, which may exert pressure on the heart.

Again, regulating the dietary sodium and potassium intakes varies with the clinical condition of the patient. It is very important that the attending physician leave specific instructions regarding this matter, since the patient's course of recovery may depend on serum sodium and potassium levels.

In the nutritional and dietary management of a subacute phase patient, the nurse and dietitian should pay special attention to several important matters. They should prevent pain, exertion, and sweating in the patient during eating. Arrhythmia must also be prevented at all costs, since it can seriously endanger a patient. Patients with arrhythmia should not be permitted to eat.

The nurse and dietitian must ensure that the patient complies with the dietary regimen and receives adequate nutrients. A record should be kept of the patient's food and nutrient intake, which helps in assessing the course of recovery.

Dietary care during the *rehabilitative phase* is close to a normal regimen. A wider and more attractive selection of food is provided, but the intake of calorie and fat is still controlled. Rapidly absorbed fat should be restricted, since it can dangerously increase blood lipids, occasionally leading to sudden death in this group of patients. Similar precautions should be taken with other susceptible individuals such as middle-aged males with atherosclerotic tendencies or a history of heart attacks who tend to engage in intense exercise after meals.

Several steps should be taken to assure the physical well-being of patients. They should be advised to achieve and maintain ideal body weight. This is important because bedridden patients may gain weight rapidly. The attending physician specifies the need for continuing or beginning sodium restriction and will probably prohibit alcohol consumption. Complete blood lipid analyses are repeated during the rehabilitative phase and studied carefully. If conditions warrant, some clinicians may put patients on a special diet to correct any abnormal blood lipid profile, such as high blood cholesterol or hyperlipoproteinemia.

Obviously, all members of the health team and a patient's family are interested in persuading the patient to adopt a wholesome life-style, especially if the patient's previous way of living led to the cardiac problem. Changing the attitude toward diet and a regimen of physical activity will help the patient to achieve this goal. Patient education, especially in the hospital, is beneficial. In addition to learning about good eating habits, the patient must understand the relationship between physical activity and the heart. Moderate exercise that places minimal stress on the heart is recommended.

At present, some cardiologists, nutritionists, dietitians, and other health personnel believe that special long-term "prudent" diets may benefit patients who have suffered gangrene, aneurysm, and/or stroke. More information on this is presented later.

Atherosclerosis, Risk Factors and Nutrition

As discussed earlier, the formation of plaque is a prelude to coronary heart disease. The central question here is: What causes the deposition of the lipid substances in an artery or the thickening of the intima of the blood vessel? We do not know the answer to this question yet. Presumably, if there is no thickening or deposition, atherosclerosis and its complications will not occur.

At present, it is assumed that blood contributes to the fatty components in fibrous plaque. The lipid materials in plaque are made up mainly of cholesterol, triglycerides, and lipoproteins, although minor blood components such as protein, phospholipids, fatty acids, glycerides, and calcium are also present. Chapter 5 provides more information on lipids. The possible relationship between blood lipid levels, plaque, and coronary heart disease has long been debated.

Although the exact cause of atherosclerosis is unknown, during the last 50 years medical science has identified a number of factors thought to increase a person's likelihood of developing this condition. These risk factors are listed below.

Age
Sex
Genetic makeup
Abnormal electrocardiogram
Environmental stresses
Hypertension
Cigarette smoking
Personality and behavior
Lack of physical activity
Use of alcohol (However, it is currently believed that moderate drinking may reduce the risk of atherosclerosis.)
Use of drugs such as oral contraceptive pills
High blood uric acid level
High level of blood lipid chemicals
    Cholesterol
    Triglycerides
    Fatty acids and phospholipids
    Lipoproteins
High blood insulin level
Dietary factors
    High caloric intake
    High fat intake, especially saturated fat; insufficient polyunsaturated fat intake

High cholesterol intake
High sucrose intake
High or low intake of certain minerals
Soft drinking water
High coffee intake
Low fiber intake
Nutrient deficiencies
Presence of other diseases
Diabetes mellitus
Gout
Obstructive liver disease
Hypothyroidism
Nephrosis
Pancreatitis

Some factors are more valid than others according to experts in this field; the reasons are beyond the scope of this book, although the references at the end of this book will provide additional information. However, most dietitians and nutritionists are specially concerned about two risk factors—serum lipid profile and dietary fat intake—both of which are briefly discussed below.

Scientists who believe that high serum cholesterol is a major factor in atherosclerosis use medical data to support their contention. Several important correlations have been found between high serum cholesterol and the development of atherosclerosis. (1) Since the major lipid in plaque is cholesterol, it is assumed that the logical source of the substance is the blood. (2) Many patients with coronary heart disease, especially those identified at an early age, have high levels of blood cholesterol. (3) Many, but not all, patients with a high serum cholesterol level because of heredity factors develop heart disease early. (4) Studies of selected population groups have shown that the risk of having heart disease is directly related to the level of serum cholesterol (the higher the level, the higher the risk). (5) Countries with populations having a high serum level of cholesterol have high mortality rates from heart disease. Conversely, countries with a low mortality rate from heart disease have populations with low levels of serum cholesterol. (6) Finally, many human disorders such as diabetes mellitus, renal failure, and hypothyroidism are associated with a high serum level of cholesterol. The rate of heart diseases among such patients is also higher. It must be emphasized that there are exceptions to most of the positive associations described above.

A relationship between dietary fat, serum cholesterol, and coronary heart disease is suggested by the following observations. Exceptions exist for each of them. First, in many population groups where the intake of fat is low, serum cholesterol and the incidence of heart disease are also low, and vice versa. Second, there are three types of fat: saturated fat, monounsaturated fat, and polyunsaturated fat (see Chapter 5). Their role is as follows. A high consumption of saturated fats is associated with a high serum cholesterol level and high incidence of heart disease. A high intake of polyunsaturated fats is associated with a low serum cholesterol level and low incidence of heart disease. Monounsaturated fats have no effect on serum cholesterol level. In experiments where the total amount of fat consumed by animals was held constant, an increase in polyunsaturated fats in the diet lowered the serum cholesterol level. In addition, twice the amount of dietary polyunsaturated fats is needed to restore serum cholesterol to normal after it has been raised by a specific amount of ingested saturated fats.

Finally, animal and human studies indicate that if all other variables in a diet are held constant, a low intake of cholesterol depresses serum cholesterol. However, the effect is not dramatic. But, if a diet is low in cholesterol and high in polyunsaturated fats, the serum cholesterol decreases markedly.

Lipoproteins

In the last few years, we have learned about another group of fat-related substances in the body called *lipoproteins*. These substances, which consist of fat plus protein, are currently suspected to play an important role in atherosclerosis.

In the human body, fats in different forms are distributed in the blood, fluids, adipose tissue, muscle, and organs such as the liver, kidneys, and others. The processes of fat catabolism and anabolism (see Chapter 8) require lipoproteins for efficient transportation to and from different compartments of the body. For fat to be transported by the blood, it must be made water-soluble. This is accomplished by the presence of plasma lipoproteins, which are made either by the intestinal walls or the liver. Each lipoprotein substance is composed of fat and protein. Because protein is water soluble, the entire chemical complex is also soluble in blood plasma. There are five groups of lipoproteins, which are distinguished by their behavior under different methods of laboratory analysis, as indicated in Table 27-3. A portion of the albumin (protein) in the blood also carries some fats and is considered another form of lipoprotein. The protein component of each lipoprotein indicated in Table 27-3 is manufactured mainly in the intestinal mucosa and liver, while the fat part may come from either the diet or internal production. Table 27-4 describes the chemical composition of these lipoproteins.

The rate of fat absorption after its digestion plays an important role in health. Fast absorption can be detrimental, especially to heart patients (see the beginning of this chapter). Although slowly absorbed fat can create some digestive discomfort, it stays in the alimentary tract longer, and the person does not become hungry too soon. Also, the fatty chemicals appear in the blood slowly and at a more constant level. The fate of ingested fat is illustrated in Figure 27-4.

After digestion, fat exists in the form of glycerol, fatty acids, and cholesterol, some of which combine with protein to form the lipoprotein *chylomicron* within the intestinal walls. Table 27-4 indicates the approximate lipid and protein composition of this complex. Chylomicrons are large molecules made up mainly of triglycerides with approximately 98% dry weight of fat. They have an extremely low density. What happens after chylomicrons are synthesized in the intestinal walls is illustrated in Figure 27-5. They are transported via the lymphatic system to the thoracic duct. Since they reflect light, they give the plasma a milky appearance when they are present in high concentrations. Their main function is to transport dietary fat in the body, primarily in the form of triglycerides. All medium- and long-chain fatty acids are transported as part of the triglycerides to the plasma via the thoracic duct.

The fatty chemicals carried by the chylomicrons must eventually be released. This is

TABLE 27-3 Types of Lipoproteins Analyzed by Ultracentrifuge or Electrophoresis

Type of Lipoprotein*	
According to density of the substance in an ultracentrifuge	According to the migration behavior of the substance in an electric field (electrophoresis)
Chylomicron	Chylomicron
Very low density lipoprotein	Pre-β-lipoprotein
Intermediate-density lipoprotein	None
Low-density lipoprotein	β-lipoprotein
High-density lipoprotein	α-lipoprotein

*See text for an explanation of the relationship of one type to another.

effected by the enzyme lipoprotein lipase, which clears the plasma of its milky appearance. It hydrolyzes the triglycerides and is suspected to act within or around the capillary endothelial cells. It is present in many tissues, including adipose tissue, and is capable of removing most triglycerides from the capillaries of the tissue.

Very low density lipoproteins are also very large complexes containing about 90% lipid, mostly as triglycerides (see Table 27-4). They are manufactured in the liver and serve to transport triglycerides from the liver to other tissues, particularly adipose tissue. These lipoproteins are also called pre-β-lipoproteins because of their electrophoretic mobility.

Intermediate-density lipoproteins are produced in the plasma when very low density lipoproteins are changed (by means of the lipoprotein lipase) to low-density lipoproteins. The quantities of cholesterol and triglyceride in intermediate lipoproteins are also intermediate between those of the very low and low density lipoproteins. After an overnight fast, most very low density lipoproteins have been transformed to low-density lipoproteins, and very little intermediate-density lipoprotein can be identified in the blood, although it exists in appreciable amounts when the transformation is defective. The electrophoretic mobility of the intermediate-density lipoprotein is similar to that of the low-density lipoprotein—the beta band (see Table 27-3).

Figure 27-6 shows the metabolic fate of the

TABLE 27-4   Lipid and Protein Composition of Lipoproteins

Substance	Chylomicrons	Very low density lipoprotein	Intermediate-density lipoprotein	Low-density lipoprotein	High-density lipoprotein
		Approximate Percentage			
Protein	2	10	10	25	50
Triglyceride	90	60	40	10	5
Cholesterol	5	12	30	50	20
Phospholipid	3	18	20	15	25

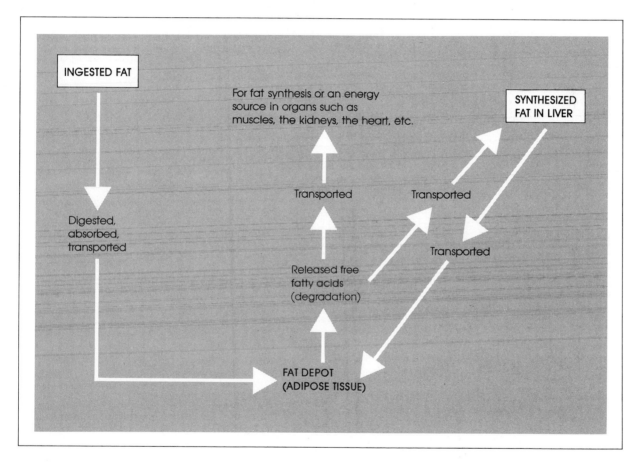

FIGURE 27-4   Ingestion, transportation, degradation, synthesis, and storage of fat.

different lipoproteins. After an overnight fast in a normal person, low-density lipoproteins are formed and become the major carrier of cholesterol (about one-third to one-half of plasma cholesterol; see Table 27-4). It is believed that most of these lipoproteins are derived from the very low density lipoproteins. If analyzed by electrophoresis, such lipoproteins are called β-lipoproteins.

High-density lipoproteins (Table 27-4) are also called α-lipoproteins. They are produced by the liver, and their exact functions are unknown. They may participate in interchanging lipid components with other lipoproteins and assisting the catabolism of very low density lipoprotein and chylomicrons. At the time of this writing, the role of high-density lipoproteins in atherosclerosis is being reconsidered, which will be discussed later.

Dietary Treatment and Prevention of Hyperlipidemia

Normally, the plasma levels of different forms of lipid exist within certain limits. However, particular individuals may deviate from such norms and develop hyperlipidemia, or an elevated level of serum lipid. Three main types of lipid are involved in this condition: cholesterol (an excess of which is called hypercholesterolemia), triglyceride (hypertriglyceridemia), and certain forms of lipoprotein (hyperlipoproteinemia). Hyperlipoproteinemia is usually associated with hypercholesterolemia or hypertriglyceridemia, or both, although the reverse is not necessarily true. Any of the hyperlipidemias is undesirable because it may potentiate atherosclerosis or cause its associated clinical symptoms.

Primary hyperlipoproteinemias are inherited. The patient normally does not show other diseases. Secondary hyperlipoproteinemias result from other diseases such as alcoholism, liver dysfunction, myxedema, kidney failure, and diabetes mellitus.

There are five types of hyperlipoproteinemia, which are distinguished by the lipoprotein and lipid component that is elevated in the blood. Table 27-5 summarizes this classification system; note that type II is divided into two subtypes. The information in Table 27-5 is more meaningful when studied with Figures 27-5 and 27-6. Tables 27-6 and 27-7 provide the diagnostic characteristics of hyperlipoproteinemias. Table 27-8 describes the suggested etiology of each type.

Typing a patient requires a number of considerations. A careful medical history and physical examination can provide much information, especially with the help of diagnostic characteristics such as those presented in Tables 27-6 to 27-8. For example, if the patient has been using certain brands of oral contraceptive pills, the blood lipid levels may be abnormally high. These levels may be high in an overweight person also, on whom the diagnostic test may not be run until

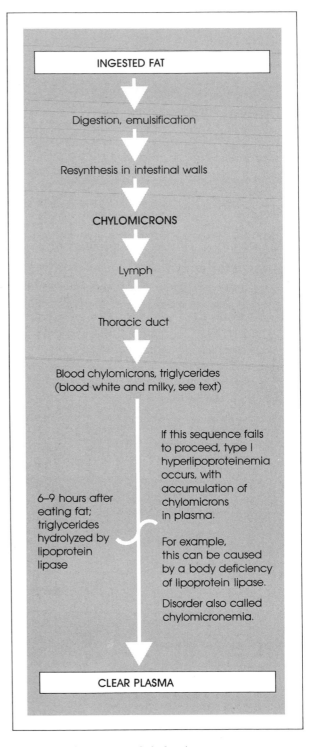

FIGURE 27-5   Fate of chylomicrons.

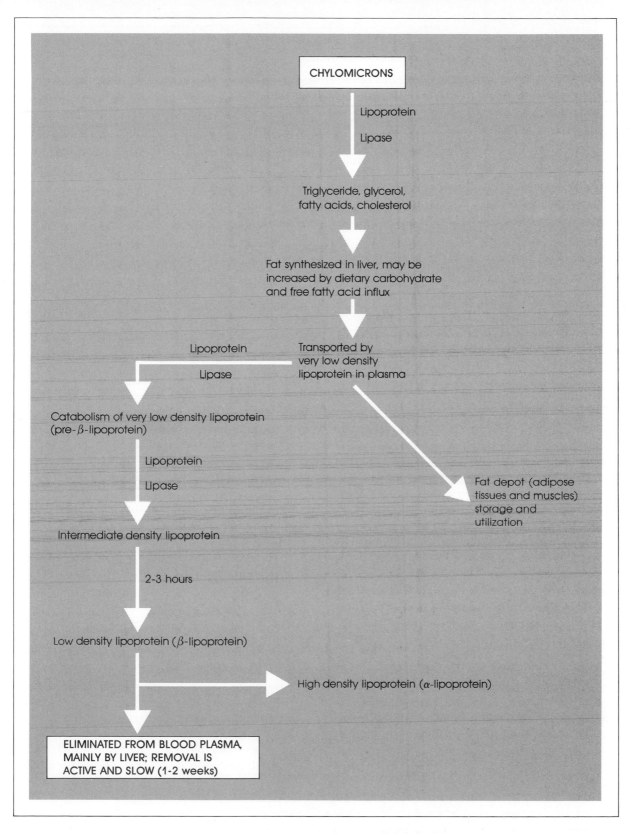

FIGURE 27-6   Metabolic fates of different types of lipoproteins in the body.

TABLE 27-5   The Five Types of Hyperlipoproteinemia

Type	Increased Plasma Lipoprotein	Increased Plasma Lipid*	Probable Metabolic Defect
I	Chylomicrons	Triglyceride	Lipoprotein lipase fails to remove chylomicrons
IIa	Low-density lipoprotein or β-lipoprotein	Cholesterol	Low-density lipoprotein not cleared from or produced excessively in the plasma
IIb	Low-density lipoprotein (β-lipoprotein); very low density lipoprotein (pre-β-lipoprotein)	Cholesterol, triglyceride	Excessive production or decreased clearance of low-density lipoprotein and very low density lipoprotein
III	Intermediate-density lipoprotein	Triglyceride, cholesterol	Accumulation of intermediate-density lipoprotein
IV	Very low density lipoprotein or pre-β-lipoprotein	Triglyceride (cholesterol)	Overproduction or decreased clearance of the very low density lipoprotein
V	Chylomicrons; very low density lipoprotein or pre-β-lipoprotein	Triglyceride (cholesterol)	Decreased chylomicron clearance; overproduction or decreased clearance of very low density lipoprotein

*Parentheses indicate minor proportion.

ideal weight is achieved. Before a diagnostic test is performed, each patient is asked to follow a regular diet consistently for a period of time. Excessive exercise or alcohol consumption is undesirable during this period. Blood levels of cholesterol and triglycerides are studied by taking a fasting serum sample every 2 hours during the 10 to 20 hours after a meal. Experienced clinicians advise repeated analyses of serum triglyceride and cholesterol levels and cold storage of the serum for observation.

Use of an ultracentrifuge and electrophoresis to determine serum lipoprotein levels is usually not necessary, since other available data can provide an acceptable diagnosis. However, if proper facilities and personnel are available, such tests will confirm the type of hyperlipoproteinemia present, especially if the serum shows abnormal levels of cholesterol and triglyceride.

It is currently believed that all five types of hyperlipoproteinemia are genetically transmitted (see Table 27-8). What is their frequency of occurrence among Americans and how should they be treated? Based on the scant data available, clinicians believe that type IV is the most common, followed by type II. In the noninstitutionalized population, about 8% to 18% may have type IV (hypertriglyceridemia) and 3% to 10% may have type II (hypercholesterolemia). Males and females of all ages can be affected. The frequency of the other three types is probably less than 1% each. It should be emphasized here that at the time of this writing, these estimates have been taken from fewer than 10 scientific screenings involving fewer than 5,000 subjects.

A patient with any of the five types of hyperlipoproteinemia may or may not have clinical symptoms (see Tables 27-6 and 27-7). The most common of these are abdominal pain, pancreatitis, and xanthomas. Without overt symptoms, the only observable abnormality is elevated serum lipid and lipoprotein levels. Some scientists and clinicians feel that hyperlipoproteinemic patients with or without clinical manifestations should be treated, while others disagree. Treatment of these patients includes dietary changes, drugs, and sometimes surgery. For patients with overt clinical symptoms such as abdominal pain and xanthoma, proper diet and drug treatments can usually eliminate the symptoms. Xanthomas can be successfully removed by surgery. Presumably diet and drug treatment for an asymptomatic patient with hyperlipoproteinemia will prevent any occurrence of symptoms. The decision to treat any asymptomatic

TABLE 27-6   Diagnostic Characteristics of the Five Types of Hyperlipoproteinemia

Criterion	Type I	Type IIa (endogenous)	Type IIb (exogenous)	Type III	Type IV	Type V
Designation	Hyperchylo-micronemia	Hypercholes-terolemia	Hypercholes-terolemia	Hypercholes-terolemia; hyperglyc-eridemia*	Hyperglyc-eridemia	Hyperglyc-eridemia
Chemistry						
Cholesterol (per 100 mL blood)	Normal, slightly elevated	300–600 mg	300–600 mg	350–800 mg	Normal, slightly ele-vated	250–350 mg
Triglyceride (per 100 mL blood)	5,000–10,000 mg	Normal	150–400 mg	400–800 mg	200–2,000 mg	500–5,000 mg
Plasma after storage at 4 °C	Creamy top layer, clear infranatant	Clear	Slightly turbid	Varies: clear, cloudy or milky	Clear, cloudy or milky	Creamy layer over turbid infranatant
Lipoprotein						
Chylomicrons	Increased	—	—	—	—	Increased
Very low density	—	—	Increased	—	Increased	Increased
Intermediate density	—	—	—	Increased	—	—
Low density	—	Increased	Increased	—	—	—
Age of onset	Under 10	Often during childhood	25–45	20–35	Over 20	Over 20
Frequency or etiology	Rare	Common	Environ-mental	Uncommon	Most common	Uncommon
Clinical features						
Xanthoma†	Yes	Yes	Yes	Yes	Yes	Yes
Hepato-splenomegaly	Yes	—	—	—	Rare	Yes
Abdominal pain	Yes	—	—	—	—	Yes
Pancreatitis	Occasionally	—	—	—	—	Yes
Lipemia retinalis	Yes	—	—	—	Yes	Yes
Paresthesia	—	—	—	—	—	Occasionally
Arcus corneae juvenilis	—	Yes	Yes	Occasionally	—	—
Other features						
Fat tolerance	Very abnormal	—	—	—	—	Abnormal
Glucose tolerance	—	—	—	Abnormal	Abnormal	Abnormal
Serum uric acid level	—	—	—	Increased	Increased	Increased
Atherosclerotic tendency	None	Very high	Very high	High risk of peripheral vascular disease	High	Unknown

Note: The symbol "—" means (1) No information is available; (2) clinical status is normal; (3) the symptom is not present.

*Hyperglyceridemia is equivalent to hypertriglyceridemia.

†See Table 27-7 for the types of xanthoma involved.

TABLE 27-7 Hyperlipoproteinemias and the Development of Xanthomas

Type of Hyperlipopro-teinemia	Eruptive Xanthoma	Tendon Xanthoma	Xanthelasma	Tuberous Xanthoma	Planar Xanthoma	Tuberoeruptive Xanthoma
I	Yes	—	—	—	—	—
IIa	—	Yes, sometimes with polyarthritis	Yes	Yes	—	—
IIb	—	Yes, sometimes with polyarthritis	Yes	Yes	—	—
III	—	Yes	Occasionally	—	Yes	Yes
IV	Occasionally	—	—	—	—	Occasionally
V	Yes	—	—	—	—	Occasionally

Note: Xanthoma is a yellow papule, nodule, or plaque in the skin due to lipid deposits; seen microscopically, the lesions show light cells with foamy protoplasm.

TABLE 27-8 Suggested Etiology of Hyperlipoproteinemias

Type	Suggested Primary Etiology	Possibly Caused by or Associated with the Following Diseases (secondary etiology)
I	Possible lipoprotein lipase deficiency, transmitted via recessive trait	Diabetes; hypothyroidism; pancreatitis and alcoholism may inhibit lipoprotein lipase activity
IIa	Detectable at birth, autosomal dominant transmission, either parent may have disorder, 50% of kindred affected	Porphyria; diseases related to liver obstruction; hypothyroidism; multiple myeloma
IIb	If environmental, excessive intake of cholesterol, saturated fat, calories; smoking	No information
III	Probable inherited autosomal recessive trait	Diabetic acidosis; multiple myeloma; hypothyroidism
IV	Inherited, 50% of kindred affected, either parent may have disorder; obesity, alcohol, and stress may exaggerate condition	Alcoholism, diabetes, hypothyroidism, pancreatitis, pregnancy, nephrotic syndrome; glycogen storage disease, use of female sex hormones
V	Inherited recessive trait	Alcoholism, pancreatitis, glycogen storage disease, hypothyroidism, nephrosis, diabetic acidosis

TABLE 27-9   Recommended Dietary Prescriptions for Different Types of Hyperlipoproteinemias

Diet Characteristics	Type I	Type IIa	Type IIb	Type III	Type IV	Type V
Nutrient(s) regulated	Fat	Fat	Protein, fat, carbo-hydrate	Protein, fat, carbo-hydrate	Protein, fat, carbo-hydrate	Protein, fat, carbohydrate
Achieve and main-tain ideal body weight	No*	No*	Yes	Yes	Yes	Yes
Protein:						
% total calories	Any	Any	20	20	15–25	15–25
Carbohydrate:						
% total calories	Any	Any	40	40	45	50
Restrictions	None	None	Sweets	Sweets	Sweets	Sweets
Fat:						
% total calories	12–20†	Any	40	40	20–35	12–30‡
Saturated fat, % total calories	Any	4–7.5	4–7.5	4–7.5	4–7.5	4–7.5
PUFA,§ % total calories	Any	8–13‖	8–13‖	8–13‖	8–13‖	8–13‖
P/S ratio¶	Any	1.5–3.0/1	1.9/1	1.2–2.4/1	1–2.4/1	0.5–1.5/1
Cholesterol per day	No limit	100–300 mg	100–300 mg	100–300 mg	300–500 mg	300–500 mg
Alcohol	Not recommended	May be used with discretion	0–2 oz hard liquor#	0–2 oz hard liquor#	0–2 oz hard liquor#	Not recommended

*No restriction on caloric intake.
†Limited to 25 to 35 g per day.
‡As low as practical.
§Polyunsaturated fatty acids.
‖High level of PUFAs is recommended.
¶PUFA/saturated fatty acids.
#Amount of liquor consumed must replace equivalent amount of carbohydrate prescribed.

and hyperlipoproteinemic patient depends entirely on the clinical philosophy of the attending physician. According to one school of thought, treating patients with hyperlipoproteinemia (especially types II and IV) will decrease their chance of developing heart diseases. However, others hold the opposite viewpoint.

In the last few years, the dietary management for hyperlipoproteinemias has received much attention. The most popular regimen was developed by the National Heart and Lung Institute of the National Institutes of Health (NIH), but other dietary systems are available. Even though the causes of abnormal serum lipid levels are unknown, diet therapy is designed to restore them to normal. How any dietary measure is able to achieve lower serum lipid levels is not known. The measures are employed on an empirical basis only. Table 27-9 summarizes the dietary modifications needed to achieve normolipoproteinemia. Much of the material discussed below has been adapted from the NIH handbook.* For

*The Dietary Management of Hyperlipoproteinemias. A Handbook for Physicians and Dietitians. Rev. ed. Department of Health, Education and Welfare Publication No. (NIH) 75-110. (Bethesda, Md.: National Heart and Lung Institute, reprinted 1974).

TABLE 27-10 Major Characteristics of Recommended Diets for Each Type of Hyperlipoproteinemia

Diet Number	Type of Hyperlipo-proteinemia	Major Characteristics
1	I	Low in fat (25–35 g)
2	IIa	Low in cholesterol, high polyunsaturated to saturated fatty acid ratio
3	IIb, III	Total carbohydrate and fat controlled, high in polyunsaturated fat, low in cholesterol, high in protein
4	IV	Controlled carbohydrate, high in polyun-saturated fat, moderately restricted cholesterol
5	V	Controlled carbohydrate, restricted total fat, polyunsaturated fat used whenever feasi-ble, moderately restricted cholesterol

TABLE 27-11 Foods Permitted and Prohibited in Diet 1

Food Group	Foods Permitted	Foods Prohibited
Beverages	Coffee, tea, carbonated beverages, fruit and vegetable juices	None unless unaccounted for fat is contained in the beverage.
Breads	Whole wheat, white, rye, and pumpernickel breads; oatmeal bread, raisin bread, Italian bread, French bread, English muffins, matzoth, saltines, graham crackers, pretzels; all baked goods containing no whole milk, egg yolk, or fat	Egg or cheese bread; biscuits, muffins, sweet rolls, corn bread, pancakes, waffles, French toast; high-fat rolls; corn chips, potato chips, cheese crackers, other flavored crackers
Grains and equivalents	All cereals; rice, noodles, macaroni, spa-ghetti, flour, other grain products; potatoes, all potato items with no fat, egg yolk, or whole milk added	None
Dairy products	Skim (nonfat) milk, skim milk powder, evapo-rated skim milk; buttermilk, cottage cheese, yogurt, specially prepared cheese contain-ing up to 1% fat; sherbet (1%–2% fat); sapsago cheese	Whole milk and whole milk products, includ-ing chocolate milk, evaporated and con-densed milk, cream (sweet or sour), ice cream, ice milk; nondairy substitutes for cream, sour cream, and whipped topping; cream cheese and all other cheese made from cream or whole milk; regular creamed cottage cheese unless substituted for meat (½ c = 1 oz meat)

TABLE 27-11   (continued)

Food Group	Foods Permitted	Foods Prohibited
Meat, poultry, fish, legumes, nuts	Limited to 5 oz per day; lean, well-trimmed meat such as beef, pork, lamb, liver, veal, chicken, turkey; fish and water-packed salmon or tuna; shellfish, dried or chipped beef, dry (no-fat) cottage cheese, and vegetarian baked beans may be used as desired	Fried meats; fried fish, fatty meats such as bacon, cold cuts, sausage, luncheon meats, hot dogs, corned beef; goose, duck, poultry skin; fish canned in oil; pork and beans; spareribs; regular ground beef or hamburger; meats canned or frozen in sauces or gravy; frozen or packaged dinners and prepared products (convenience foods) containing fat; nuts, peanut butter
Eggs	Egg white as desired; one egg yolk may be substituted for 1 oz meat; limited to 3 egg yolks per week	Egg yolk unless prescribed and accounted for
Desserts	Fruit ices (water ices), sherbet (1%–2% fat), gelatin, fruit whips, meringues, angel food cake (including the mix); cakes, pies, cookies, pudding and frostings made with allowed ingredients such as skim milk and egg whites; junket made with skim milk	Commercial cakes, pies, cookies, mixes; ice cream, ice milk; desserts containing whole milk, fat, and egg yolks
Soups	Bouillon, clear broth, fat-free vegetable soup, cream soup made with skim milk, packaged dehydrated soups (broth base)	All others
Fruits	Any fresh (except avocado), canned, frozen, or dried fruit; any fruit juice	Avocado
Vegetables	Any fresh, frozen, or canned vegetable without fat; vegetarian baked beans	Buttered, creamed, or fried vegetables; pork and beans
Sweets	Pure sugar candy, such as gumdrops, jelly beans, hard candy, marshmallows, and mints (not chocolate); jam, jelly, honey, and syrup (containing no fat)	All other candy
Fats	None unless medium-chain triglycerides are prescribed	All fats and oils; gravies and cream sauces containing fat; salad dressings and mayonnaise; whipped toppings
Miscellaneous	Pickles, salt, spices, herbs, cocoa (limited to 1 T dry cocoa per day)	Nuts, olives, peanut butter, coconut, chocolate

Note: Table adapted from *Diet 1. For Dietary Management of Hyperchylomicronemia (Type I Hyperlipoproteinemia)*. Department of Health, Education and Welfare publication No. (NIH) 77-111 (Bethesda, Md.: National Heart and Lung Institute, 1973).

more detailed information, the original source should be consulted.

For convenience, special diets for treating each type of lipoproteinemia are given numbers, as shown in Table 27-10. Major characteristics of each diet are also included. Tables 27-11 to 27-25 provide the following information: foods permitted in and prohibited from each diet, sample meal plans, and daily menus. Diets 3, 4, and 5 are *only* for patients who have achieved ideal body weights.

In addition to dietary treatment, hyper-

TABLE 27-12   Sample Meal Plans for Diet 1 for Children and Adults*

| Food Group | No. of Servings per Day | |
	Child[†]	Adult[‡]
Skim milk	4 servings	4 servings
Meat, fish, poultry, eggs, legumes, nuts	2 oz	5 oz
Breads, cereals	>4 servings	>6 servings
Potato, rice, or equivalent	>1 serving	>1 serving
Desserts, sweets, sugars	0–2 servings or as desired	0–2 servings or as desired
Fruits, vegetables	4 servings	5 servings
Fats, oils	None, unless medium-chain triglycerides are prescribed within caloric allowance	None, unless medium-chain triglycerides are prescribed within caloric allowance

*See footnote for Table 27-11.
[†]For a child aged 4 to 6 weighing 35 to 40 lb. Diet should supply 1,400 to 1,600 kcal.
[‡]Diet should supply 1,700 to 2,000 kcal.

TABLE 27-13   Sample Menu for Diet 1

Breakfast	Lunch	Dinner
Juice, pineapple, orange, ½ c	Veal, 2 oz	Salmon, broiled, 3 oz
Cream of Wheat, ½ c	Noodles, ½ c	Potato, baked, 1
Toast, whole wheat, 1 sl	Broccoli, ½ c	Brussels sprouts, ½ c
Skim milk, 1 c	Bread, French, 1 sl	Roll, hard, small, 1
Jelly	Strawberries, sliced, ½ c	Sherbet, pineapple, ½ c
Sugar	Cake, angel food, 1 sl	Skim milk, 1 c
Coffee or tea	Skim milk, 1 c	Jelly
	Jelly	Sugar
	Sugar	Coffee or tea
	Coffee or tea	
	Snack	
	Skim milk, 1 c	
	Banana, 1	
	Graham cracker, 1	
	Jelly or jam	

Note: Menu supplies 1,800 kcal, 90 g of protein, 15 g of fat, and 310 g of carbohydrate.

TABLE 27-14 Foods Permitted and Prohibited in Diet 2

Food Group	Foods Permitted	Foods Prohibited
Beverages	Coffee, tea, carbonated beverages, fruit and vegetable juices	None unless unaccounted for fat is contained in the beverage.
Breads	Whole wheat, white, rye, and pumpernickel breads; oatmeal bread, raisin bread, Italian bread, French bread, English muffins, matzoth, saltines, graham crackers, pretzels; baked goods containing no whole milk or egg yolk and made with allowed fat	Egg or cheese bread; commercial biscuits, muffins, sweet rolls, corn bread, pancakes, waffles, French toast; butter rolls; corn chips, potato chips, cheese crackers, other flavored crackers
Grains and equivalents	All cereals; rice, noodles, macaroni, spaghetti, flour, other grain products; potatoes; all potato items with no fat, egg yolk, or whole milk added	Egg noodles
Dairy products	Skim (nonfat) milk, skim milk powder, evaporated skim milk; buttermilk, cottage cheese, yogurt, specially prepared cheese containing up to 1% fat; sherbet (1%–2% fat); sapsago cheese, specially prepared cheese high in polyunsaturated fat	Whole milk and whole milk products, including chocolate milk, evaporated and condensed milk, cream (sweet or sour), ice cream, ice milk; nondairy substitutes for cream, sour cream, and whipped topping (usually contain coconut oil); cream cheese and all other cheese made from cream or whole milk; regular creamed cottage cheese unless substituted for meat (½ c = 1 oz meat)
Meat, poultry, fish, legumes, nuts	Limited to 3 oz, 3 times per week, of lean beef, lamb, ham, or pork; or 9 oz of such meat per day and 1 t polyunsaturated fat (in any form) for 1 oz cooked meat consumed. Other meals to include no more than 9 oz per day of fish, clams, scallops, oysters, crab, lobster, chicken, turkey, veal, and dried or chipped beef; allowed as desired are peanut butter, nonprohibited nuts, soy protein meat substitutes, vegetarian baked beans; 1 t polyunsaturated fat may be replaced by 3 walnut halves or 2 T sunflower seeds	Regular ground beef or hamburger; heavily marbled and fatty meats, spareribs, bacon, hot dogs, sausages, luncheon meats and cold cuts, fatty corned beef, goose, duck, poultry skin, shrimp, fish roe including caviar, all organ meats (heart, liver, brains, kidney, sweetbread), commercially fried foods, meats canned or frozen with sauces or gravies, frozen or packaged dinners, prepared products (convenience foods) containing fat not polyunsaturated; macadamia and cashew nuts; pork and beans
Eggs	Egg white and egg substitutes containing no cholesterol	Egg yolk
Desserts	Fruit ices (water ices), sherbet (1%–2% fat), gelatin, fruit whips, meringues, angel food cake (including the mix); cakes, pies, cookies, pudding and frostings made with allowed ingredients such as allowed fats, skim milk, and egg whites; junket made with skim milk	Commercial cakes, pies, cookies, mixes; ice cream, ice milk; desserts containing whole milk, saturated or hydrogenated fat, and egg yolks
Soups	Bouillon, clear broth, fat-free vegetable soup, cream soup made with skim milk, packaged dehydrated soups	All others

TABLE 27-14 (continued)

Food Group	Foods Permitted	Foods Prohibited
Fruits	Any fresh, canned, frozen, or dried fruit; all fruit juices; avocado in small amounts	None
Vegetables	Any fresh, frozen, or canned vegetable without saturated fat; vegetarian baked beans	Buttered, creamed, or fried vegetables unless prepared with allowed fat; pork and beans
Sweets	Pure sugar candy, such as gumdrops, jelly beans, hard candy, marshmallows, and mints (not chocolate); jam, jelly, honey, and syrup (containing no fat)	All other candy
Fats	For each ounce of meat eaten, use at least 1 t of one of the following: corn oil, safflower oil, soft (tub) safflower margarine; commercial mayonnaise and other salad dressings not containing sour cream or cheese; 1 t polyunsaturated fat may be replaced by 3 walnut halves or 2 T sunflower seeds	Other margarines, shortenings, and oils; butter, lard, salt pork, suet, bacon and meat drippings; foods containing coconut oil or palm oil; gravies and cream sauces unless made with allowed fat or skim milk
Miscellaneous	Olives, pickles, salt, spices, herbs, cocoa	Coconut, chocolate

Note: Table adapted from *Diet 2. For Dietary Management of Hypercholesterolemia (Type IIa Hyperlipoproteinemia)*. Department of Health, Education and Welfare publication No. (NIH) 76-112 (Bethesda, Md.: National Heart and Lung Institute, 1973).

TABLE 27-15   Sample Meal Plans for Diet 2 for Children and Adults

Food Group	No. of Servings per Day	
	Child*	Adult†
Skim milk	>4 servings	>2 servings
Meat, fish, poultry	Up to 9 oz fish, shellfish (except shrimp), poultry, and veal; beef, lamb, ham, and pork limited to 2 oz, 3 times per week; if the latter is not possible, limit all meat to no more than 9 oz cooked meat per day and consume in some fashion 2 t polyunsaturated fat for each ounce of cooked meat	Up to 9 oz fish, shellfish (except shrimp), poultry, and veal; beef, lamb, ham, and pork limited to 3 oz, 3 times per week; if the latter is not possible, limit all meat to no more than 9 oz cooked meat per day and consume in some fashion 2 t polyunsaturated fat for each ounce of cooked meat
Breads, cereals	>4 servings	>7 servings

TABLE 27-15   (continued)

Food Group	No. of Servings per Day	
	Child*	Adult†
Potato, rice, or equivalent	>1 serving	>1 serving
Fruits, vegetables	4 servings, including 1 serving citrus fruit and 1 serving dark green or deep yellow vegetable	5 servings, including 1 serving citrus fruit and 1 serving dark green or deep yellow vegetable
Desserts, sweets, sugars	Permitted items as desired	Permitted items as desired
Fats, oils	8–10 servings, for each ounce of meat consumed, take 1 t permitted oil	8–10 servings, for each ounce of meat consumed, take 1 t permitted oil

*For a child aged 4 to 6 weighing 35 to 40 lb. Diet should supply 1,400 to 1,600 kcal.
†Diet should supply 1,700 to 2,000 kcal.

TABLE 27-16   Sample Menu for Diet 2

Breakfast	Lunch	Dinner
Juice, pineapple, ½ c	Turkey, roast, cooked without skin, 4 oz	Veal, 5 oz
Cream of Wheat, ½ c		Potato, boiled, 1
Toast, whole wheat, 2 sl	Barley, cooked, ½ c	Margarine, safflower, soft (tub), 1 t
Margarine, safflower, soft (tub), 1 t	Green beans, fresh, cooked, ½ c	Salad, lettuce
Skim milk, 1 c	Margarine, safflower, soft (tub), 2 t	Dressing, Italian, commercial, 2 t
Sugar, 1 t	Carrot, sticks, raw	Bread, Italian, 1 sl
Coffee or tea	Bread, raisin, 1 sl	Margarine, safflower, soft (tub), 1 t
	Margarine, safflower, soft (tub), 2 t	Cantaloupe, wedge, 1
	Sugar, 1 t	Skim milk, 1 c
	Salt, pepper	Sugar, 1 t
	Coffee or tea	Salt, pepper
		Coffee or tea

Note: Menu supplies 1,800 kcal, 100–110 g of protein, 60–70 g of fat, and 200 g of carbohydrate.

TABLE 27-17   Foods Permitted and Prohibited in Diet 3

Food Group	Foods Permitted	Foods Prohibited
Beverages	Coffee, tea, diet soft drinks, club soda, un-sweetened vegetable and fruit juices	All beverages with unaccounted for fat and those with sugar added
Breads, grains, equivalents	Any of the following is one serving: 1 sl whole-grain or enriched bread; ¾ oz bread sticks, rye wafers, or pretzels; 2 graham crackers (2½″ sq.); 3 soda crackers (2½″ sq.); 5 saltines (2″ sq.); ½ c or 20 oyster crackers; ½ hamburger or hot dog roll; 1 small or ½ large hard roll; 1 piece matzo (6″ sq.); 4 pieces melba toast (3½ × 1½ × ⅛ in.); 3 T flour, cornmeal, or dry grated bread crumbs; ⅓ c corn or ½ large ear corn on the cob; ½ c beans, dried peas, lentils, chick-peas, lima beans (all cooked); 1 small baked or ½ c mashed white potato; ½ c spaghetti, rice, noodles (all cooked); ½ c cooked cereal; ¾ c cereal, dry, ready-to-eat; 1½ c popcorn, popped with no fat Products permitted if made with allowed ingredients and replacing 1 serving of fats and oils: 1 biscuit (2″ diam.), 1 muffin (3″ diam.), 2 pancakes (4″ diam.), ½ waffle (7″ diam.)	Butter rolls, cheese or egg breads; corn chips, potato chips, flavored crackers; soups not permitted; commercial biscuits, muffins, doughnuts, sweet rolls, pancakes, and waffles unless made as specified
Dairy products	Any of the following is one serving: 1 c skim milk or 99% fat-free milk, 1 c buttermilk made from skim milk, ⅓ c dry powdered skim milk reconstituted to 1 c liquid, ½ c undiluted evaporated skim milk, 1 c yogurt made from skim milk	Whole milk, condensed milk, dried whole milk, evaporated whole milk, whole milk drinks; commercial whipped toppings, cream (sweet or sour), cream substitutes; ice cream, ice milk
Meat, fish, poultry, cheese, eggs	Lean, well-trimmed cuts, fresh or frozen (one serving is 3 oz cooked meat); beef, lamb, pork or lean ham, veal, poultry; fish (if canned, drain oil); clams, crab, lobster, oysters, scallops; specially prepared low-fat cheese, creamed cottage cheese (½ c = 1 oz meat); egg whites and dry (nonfat) cottage cheese eaten as desired	All fatty meats; bacon, sausage; canned meat products; cheeses (including cream cheese) not permitted; corned beef; duck, goose; egg yolk or products containing egg yolk; fish roe including caviar; commercially fried meats and fried fish; frozen and packaged dinners; frozen and packaged prepared products (convenience foods); luncheon meat, cold cuts, hot dogs; meats canned or frozen in gravy or sauce; organ meat (brains, heart, kidney, liver, sweetbread); poultry skin; regular ground beef or hamburger; spareribs; shrimp
Desserts, sweets	1–2 servings per day Any of the following is one serving and may be exchanged for one serving from the bread group:	Commercial cakes, pies, and cookies, including mixes; other candies, chocolate

TABLE 27-17   (continued)

Food Group	Foods Permitted	Foods Prohibited
	1½" cube angel food cake; ⅓ c gelatin; ¼ c sherbet or fruit ice; ½ c plain pudding, prepared with skim milk If permitted by physician, only one serving of the following may be substituted for one serving of dessert: 1 T sugar, honey, syrup, molasses, jam, preserves, and jelly; ½ oz jelly beans, gumdrops, hard candy, marshmallows, and mints (not chocolate); 6 oz carbonated water, cola, ginger ale, root beer; 3 oz fruit-flavored sodas, Tom Collins mix	
Fruits, vegetables	½ c fruit, fresh, frozen and canned (unsweetened); ½ c juice, unsweetened; ½ c dried fruit, unsweetened, cooked; 1 serving citrus fruit (preferably daily); any vegetables without fat or sauces; 1 serving dark green or deep yellow vegetable recommended daily Though not restricted, the amount of vegetables eaten should be within normal limits using medium-sized servings. For beans, peas, and potatoes, see breads group.	Sweetened fruits and juices; buttered, creamed, or fried vegetables unless prepared with allowed fat
Fats, oils	Any of the following is one serving: 1 T vegetable oil (sunflower, corn, safflower, cottonseed, soybean); 1 T special margarine (with polyunsaturated fats); 1 T nuts, coarsely chopped; 1 T commercial salad dressing containing no sour cream or cheese; ⅛ avocado (4 in. diam.); 5 small olives; 2 T peanut butter	Bacon and meat drippings; butter and products made with butter; coconut, coconut oil, palm kernel oil; gravies except those containing no animal fat;* solid vegetable shortening (hydrogenated); lard, salt pork, or suet; sauces such as cream sauces unless made with allowed margarine or oil
Alcohol	0–2 servings per day if permitted; any of the following is one serving, which may be exchanged for one serving from the breads group: 1 oz gin, rum, vodka, or whiskey; 1½ oz dessert or sweet wine; 2½ oz dry table wine; 5 oz beer	
Free choices	Bouillon (no fat), clear broth; club soda, coffee, tea; plain gelatin; flavoring essences, herbs, mustard, spices, vinegar, Worcestershire sauce; rennet tablets, soy sauce	

Note: Table adapted from *Diet 3. For Dietary Management of Hypercholesterolemia with Endogenous Hyperglyceridemia (Type IIb or Type III Hyperlipoproteinemia)*. Department of Health, Education and Welfare publication No. (NIH) 76-113 (Bethesda, Md.: National Heart and Lung Institute, 1973).

*Gravies made from defatted meat drippings.

TABLE 27-18 Suggested Food Distribution for Meal Plans at Various Caloric Levels for Diet 3

	Caloric Level						
	1,500	1,800	2,000	2,200	2,400	2,600	2,800
Nutrient (g)							
Protein	75	80	90	116	120	120	125
Fat	70	80	95	100	110	120	130
Carbohydrate	135	180	195	210	225	255	285
Food group (no. of servings)							
Lean cooked meat*	2	2	2	3	3	3	3
Skim milk	2	2	3	3	3	3	3
Breads, cereals, etc.	5	8	8	9	10	12	14
Fat	10	12	15	15	17	19	21
Fruit[†]	3	3	3	3	3	3	3
Vegetables[‡]	No limit	No limit	No limit	No limit	No limit	No limit	No limit

Source: *The Dietary Management of Hyperlipoproteinemia. A Handbook for Physicians and Dietitians.* Rev. ed. Department of Health, Education and Welfare publication No. 75-110 (Bethesda, Md.: National Heart and Lung Institute, reprinted 1974).

*3 oz is one serving. Each ounce of meat, fish, or poultry is considered to contain 8 g of protein and 3 g of fat.

[†]One-half cup of any fresh or unsweetened fruit or juice is considered to have 10 g of carbohydrate.

[‡]Excluding beans, peas, and potatoes.

TABLE 27-19 Sample Menu for Diet 3

Breakfast	Lunch	Dinner
Juice, apple, un-sweetened, ½ c	Ham, lean, trimmed, 3 oz	Chicken, broiled, with-out skin, 3 oz
Cream of Rice, ½ c	Potato, baked, small, 1	Rice, cooked, ½ c
Toast, whole wheat, 1 sl	Juice, tomato, ½ c	Mustard greens, cooked, ½ c
Margarine, corn or saf-flower, 3 t	Beets, cooked, ½ c	Bread, enriched, 1 sl
Skim milk, 1 c	Roll, hard, large, 1	Gelatin, ⅓ c
Artificial sweetener	Margarine, corn or saf-flower, 4 t	Margarine, corn or saf-flower, 5 t
Coffee or tea	Orange, medium, 1	Pineapple, unsweetened, canned, ½ c
	Artificial sweetener	Skim milk, 1 c
	Salt, pepper	Artificial sweetener
	Coffee, tea, or diet cola	Salt, pepper
		Coffee or tea

Note: Menu supplies 1,800 kcal, 80 g of protein, 80 g of fat, and 180 g of carbohydrate.

TABLE 27-20   Foods Permitted and Prohibited in Diet 4

Food Group	Foods Permitted	Foods Prohibited
Beverages	Coffee, tea, diet soft drinks, club soda, unsweetened vegetable and fruit juices	All beverages with unaccounted for fat or with sugar added
Breads, grains, equivalents	Any one of the following is one serving: 1 sl whole-grain or enriched bread; ¾ oz bread sticks, rye wafers, or pretzels; 2 graham crackers (2½" sq.); 3 soda crackers (2½" sq.); 5 saltines (2" sq.); 20 oyster crackers (½ c); ½ hamburger or hot dog roll; 1 small or ½ large hard roll; 1 piece matzo (6" sq.); 4 pieces melba toast (3½ × 1½ × ⅛ in.); 3 T flour, cornmeal, or dry grated bread crumbs; ⅓ c corn or ½ large ear of corn on the cob; ½ c cooked, dried peas, beans, lentils, chick-peas, or lima beans	Butter rolls, cheese or egg breads; corn chips, potato chips, flavored crackers; soups other than those listed; commercial biscuits, muffins, doughnuts, sweet rolls, pancakes, waffles unless made as specified
Milk and related products	Any one of the following is one serving: 1 c skim milk or 99% fat-free milk; 1 c buttermilk made from skim milk; ⅓ c dry powdered skim milk, reconstituted to 1 c liquid; 1 c yogurt made from skim milk	Whole milk, condensed milk, dried whole milk, evaporated whole milk, whole milk drinks; commercial whipped toppings, cream (sweet or sour), cream substitutes; ice cream, ice milk
Meat, poultry, fish, eggs, cheese	One serving is 3 oz of cooked meat (for the calorie-controlled plan); lean, well-trimmed cuts of meat, fresh or frozen; beef, lamb, pork or lean ham, veal, poultry; fish (drained if canned in oil); clams, crab, lobster, oysters, scallops, shrimp; specially prepared low-fat cheese, creamed cottage cheese; egg whites; 3 egg yolks per week (includes egg yolks used in cooking); may substitute 2 oz liver, sweetbread, or heart for 1 egg yolk; 2 oz regular cheese, such as cheddar, per week	All fatty meats; bacon, sausage; canned meat products; corned beef; duck, goose; fish roe including caviar; commercially fried meats and fried fish; frozen and packaged dinners; frozen and packaged prepared products (convenience foods); luncheon meats, cold cuts, hot dogs; meats canned or frozen in gravy or sauce; poultry skin; regular ground beef or hamburger; spareribs; egg yolks, cheese (including cream cheese) and organ meats except as specifically permitted
Desserts, sweets	Limited to no more than two servings per day. Any one of the following is one serving and may be exchanged for one serving from the breads group: 1½" cube angel food cake; ⅓ c gelatin; ¼ c sherbet or fruit ice; ½ c plain pudding, prepared with skim milk. If permitted by physician, one serving of the following may be substituted for one serving of dessert. Limited to one serving per day. 1 T sugar, honey, molasses, syrup, jam, preserves, and jelly; ½ oz jelly beans, gumdrops, hard candy, marshmallows, and mints (not chocolate); 6 oz cola, ginger ale, root beer; 3 oz fruit-flavored sodas, Tom Collins mix	Commercial cakes, pies, and cookies, including mixes; other candies; chocolate

TABLE 27-20 (continued)

Food Group	Foods Permitted	Foods Prohibited
Fruits, vegetables	Any of the following is one serving (½ c) of any fresh, unsweetened canned or frozen fruit or unsweetened fruit juice; ½ c cooked, unsweetened dried fruit; one serving citrus fruit (recommended daily) Any fresh, frozen, or canned vegetables without added fat or sauces (one serving of dark green or deep yellow vegetable recommended daily) Though unlimited, vegetables should be eaten within normal limits, with medium-sized servings. Potatoes, corn, lima beans, dried peas, and beans are limited as described in the breads group.	Sweetened fruit and juice; buttered, creamed, or fried vegetables unless prepared with allowed fat
Fats, oils	Amount listed is one serving for the calorie-controlled plan: 1 t any vegetable oil except coconut; 1 t specially prepared margarines; 1 T commercial salad dressing containing no sour cream; ⅛ avocado (4 in. diam.); 1 T nuts except coconut; 5 small olives; 2 t peanut butter	
Alcohol	If approved by the physician, use the following exchanges. Any one of the following in the amount listed is one serving, which may be exchanged for one serving from breads group: 1 oz gin, rum, vodka, or whiskey; 1½ oz dessert or sweet wine; 2½ oz dry table wine; 5 oz beer	
Free foods	Bouillon (no fat), clear broth; club soda, coffee, tea; gelatin, unflavored; flavoring essences, herbs, mustard, spices; vinegar, Worcestershire sauce; rennet tablets, soy sauce	

Note: Table adapted from *Diet 4. For Dietary Management of Endogenous Hyperglyceridemia (Type IV Hyperlipoproteinemia)*. Department of Health, Education and Welfare publication No. (NIH) 78-114 (Bethesda, Md.: National Heart, Lung, and Blood Institute, undated).

lipoproteinemia may also be treated with drugs. Some clinicians prefer to use drugs alone. At the time of this writing, five common drugs are available (Table 27-26). They act by either increasing lipoprotein degradation or decreasing their production. However, all these drugs may have adverse effects on the nutritional status of the patient. Additional information is provided later in this chapter and in Chapter 16.

Some patients may fail to respond to the dietary and drug treatments. If their hyperlipoproteinemia poses a risk of heart disease and if other risk factors such as hypertension, obesity, and diabetes are present, an intestinal bypass can be performed. This operation restores normal blood lipid levels fairly quickly. The operation successfully reduces the absorption of ingested cholesterol as well as the secretion of cholesterol

TABLE 27-21 Suggested Food Distribution for Meal Plans at Various Caloric Levels for Diet 4

	Caloric Level						
	1,500	1,800	2,000	2,200	2,400	2,600	2,800
Nutrient (g)							
Protein	65	75	85	95	105	115	125
Fat	65	72	87	90	97	107	115
Carbohydrate	165	210	225	240	270	285	315
Food group (no. of servings)							
Lean cooked meat*	2	2	2	3	3	3	3
Skim milk	2	2	3	3	3	3	3
Breads, cereals, etc.	5	8	8	9	11	12	14
Fat†	7–9	9–11	12–14	12–14	12–14	15–17	17–19
Fruit‡	6	6	6	6	6	6	6
Vegetables	No limit	No limit	No limit	No limit	No limit	No limit	No limit

Source: *The Dietary Management of Hyperlipoproteinemia. A Handbook for Physicians and Dietitians.* Rev. ed. Department of Health, Education and Welfare publication No. (NIH) 75-110 (Bethesda, Md.: National Heart and Lung Institute, reprinted 1974).

*3 oz is one serving. Each ounce of meat is considered to contain 8 g of protein and 3 g of fat. Amount limited only to control weight.

†Fat is limited only to control weight.

‡One-half cup of any fresh or unsweetened fruit or juice is considered to have 10 g of carbohydrate.

TABLE 27-22 Sample Menu for Diet 4

Breakfast	Lunch	Dinner
Juice, grapefruit, un-sweetened, ½ c	Lamb, roast, lean, 3 oz	Turkey, cooked, without skin, 3 oz
Banana, sliced, ½	Potato, baked, small, 1	Potato, mashed, ½ c
Puffed rice, ¾ c	Mixed vegetables, frozen, cooked, ½ c	Swiss chard, cooked, ½ c
Toast, whole wheat, 1 sl	Matzo, 6″ sq., 2	Juice, tomato, ½ c
Margarine, corn or saf-flower, 2 t	Margarine, corn or saf-flower, 4 t	Bread, whole wheat, 1 sl
Skim milk, 1 c	Juice, apple, un-sweetened, ½ c	Sherbet, 1%–2% fat, ¼ c
Artificial sweetener	Peach, fresh, small, 1	Margarine, corn or saf-flower, 4 t
Coffee or tea	Artificial sweetener	Fruit cocktail, un-sweetened, ½ c
	Salt, pepper	Orange, fresh, sections, ½ c
	Coffee, tea, or diet soda	Skim milk, 1 c
		Artificial sweetener
		Salt, pepper
		Coffee or tea

Note: Menu supplies 1,800 kcal, 80 g of protein, 70 g of fat, and 210 g of carbohydrate.

TABLE 27-23 Foods Permitted and Prohibited in Diet 5

Food Group	Foods Permitted	Foods Prohibited
Beverages	Coffee, tea, diet soft drinks; club soda, unsweetened vegetable and fruit juices	All beverages with unaccounted for fat and those with sugar added; alcohol
Breads, grains, equivalents	Any one of the following is one serving: 1 sl whole-grain or enriched bread; ¾ oz bread sticks, rye wafers, or pretzels; 2 graham crackers (2½" sq.); 3 soda crackers (2½" sq.); 5 saltines (2" sq.); 20 oyster crackers (½ c); ½ hamburger or hot dog roll; 1 small or ½ large hard roll; 1 piece matzo (6" sq.); 4 pieces melba toast (3½ × 1½ × ⅛ in.); 3 T flour, cornmeal, or dry grated bread crumbs; ⅓ c corn or ½ large ear of corn on the cob; ½ c cooked, dried peas, beans, lentils, chick-peas, or lima beans; 1 small white baked potato or ½ c mashed; ½ c cooked spaghetti, rice, or noodles; ½ c cooked cereal; ¾ c ready-to-eat (dry) cereal; 1½ c popcorn, popped (no fat added); ¼ c baked beans (no pork added) The following items are allowed if made with permitted ingredients and they replace one serving of fats or oils if served: 1 biscuit (2 in. diam.); 1 muffin (3 in. diam.); ½ waffle (7 in. diam.); 2 pancakes (4 in. diam.)	Butter rolls, cheese or egg breads; corn chips, potato chips, flavored crackers; soups other than those listed; commercial biscuits, muffins, doughnuts, sweet rolls, pancakes, and waffles unless made as specified
Skim milk and related products	Any one of the following is one serving: 1 c skim milk or 99% fat-free milk; 1 c buttermilk made from skim milk; ⅓ c dry powdered skim milk reconstituted to 1 c liquid; ½ c undiluted evaporated skim milk; 1 c yogurt made from skim milk	Whole milk, condensed milk, dried whole milk, evaporated whole milk, whole milk drinks; commercial whipped toppings; cream (sweet or sour); cream substitutes; ice cream, ice milk
Meat, poultry, fish, eggs, cheese	One serving is 3 oz of cooked meat; lean, well-trimmed cuts of meat and fish, fresh or frozen; beef, lamb, pork or lean ham, veal, poultry; fish (drained if canned in oil); clams, crab, lobster, oysters, scallops, shrimp; specially prepared low-fat cheese; creamed cottage cheese (¼ c = 1 oz meat); egg whites and dry (no-fat) cottage cheese may be eaten as desired; 3 egg yolks per week (includes egg yolks used in cooking); may substitute 2 oz liver, sweetbread, or heart for 1 egg yolk	All fatty meats; bacon and sausages; canned meat products; corned beef; duck, goose; fish roe (including caviar); commercially fried meats and fried fish; frozen and packaged dinners; frozen and packaged prepared products (convenience foods); luncheon meats, cold cuts, hot dogs; meats canned or frozen in gravy or sauce; poultry skin; regular ground beef or hamburger; spareribs; egg yolks, cheese (including cream cheese) and organ meat except as specifically permitted

TABLE 27-23   (continued)

Food Group	Foods Permitted	Foods Prohibited
Desserts, sweets	Limited to no more than 2 servings per day. Any one of the following is one serving and may be exchanged for one serving from the breads group: 1½" cube angel food cake; ⅓ c gelatin; ¼ c sherbet or fruit ice; ½ c plain pudding, prepared with skim milk If permitted by the physician, one serving of the following may be substituted for one serving of dessert. Limited to one serving per day. 1 T sugar, honey, molasses, syrup, jam, preserves, and jelly; ½ oz jelly beans, gumdrops, hard candy, marshmallows, and mints (not chocolate); 6 oz cola, ginger ale, root beer; 3 oz fruit-flavored sodas, Tom Collins mix	Commercial cakes, pies, and cookies, including mixes; other candies; chocolate
Fruits, vegetables	Any of the following is one serving: ½ c of any fresh, unsweetened, canned or frozen fruit or unsweetened fruit juice; ½ c cooked, unsweetened dried fruit; one serving citrus fruit (recommended daily); any fresh, frozen or canned vegetable without added fat or sauces (one serving of dark green or deep yellow vegetable recommended daily) Though unlimited, vegetables should be eaten within normal limits, with medium-sized servings. Potatoes, corn, lima beans, dried peas, and beans are limited as described in the breads group.	Sweetened fruit and juice; buttered, creamed, or fried vegetables unless prepared with allowed fat
Fats, oils	Each of the following amounts is considered one serving: 1 T any vegetable oil (except coconut oil); 1 T specially prepared margarine; 1 T commercial mayonnaise; 1 T coarsely chopped nuts; 1 T commercial salad dressing containing no sour cream or cheese; ⅛ avocado (4 in. diam.); 5 small olives; 2 T peanut butter	Bacon and meat drippings; butter and products made with butter; coconut; coconut oil; gravies except those containing no animal fat;* solid vegetable shortening (hydrogenated); lard, salt pork, suet; sauces such as cream sauces unless made with allowed margarine or oil
Free foods	Bouillon (no fat), clear broth; club soda, coffee, tea; gelatin, unflavored; flavoring essences, herbs, mustard, spices; vinegar, Worcestershire sauce; rennet tablets, soy sauce	

Note: Table adapted from *Diet 5. For Dietary Management of Mixed Hyperglyceridemia (Type V Hyperlipoproteinemia)*. Department of Health, Education and Welfare publication No. (NIH) 77-115 (Bethesda, Md.: National Heart and Lung Institute, 1973).

*Gravies made from defatted meat drippings.

TABLE 27-24 Suggested Food Distribution for Meal Plans at Various Caloric Levels for Diet 5

	Caloric Level						
	1,500	1,800	2,000	2,200	2,400	2,600	2,800
Nutrient (g)							
Protein	90	100	105	130	135	140	145
Fat	50	50	65	70	70	85	85
Carbohydrate	180	235	250	265	310	325	370
Food group (no. of servings)							
Lean cooked meat*	2	2	2	3	3	3	3
Skim milk	3	4	4	4	4	4	4
Breads, cereals, etc.	7	10	11	12	15	16	19
Fat	6	6	9	9	9	12	12
Fruit†	3	3	3	3	3	3	3
Vegetables	No limit	No limit	No limit	No limit	No limit	No limit	No limit

Source: *The Dietary Management of Hyperlipoproteinemia. A Handbook for Physicians and Dietitians.* Rev. ed. Department of Health, Education and Welfare publication No. (NIH) 75-110 (Bethesda, Md.: National Heart and Lung Institute, reprinted 1974).

*3 oz is one serving. Each ounce of meat is considered to have 8 g of protein and 3 g of fat.

†One-half cup of any fresh or unsweetened fruit or juice is considered to have 10 g of carbohydrate.

TABLE 27-25 Sample Menu for Diet 5

Breakfast	Lunch	Dinner
Juice, orange, un-sweetened, ½ c	Shrimp, boiled, 3 oz	Turkey, cooked, without skin, 3 oz
Oatmeal, cooked, ½ c	Potato, baked, small, 1	Noodles, cooked, ½ c
Toast, whole wheat, 2 sl	Lettuce salad	Squash, winter, baked, ½ c
Margarine, safflower or corn oil, 2 t	Asparagus, spears, ½ c	Bread, whole wheat, 1 sl
Skim milk, 1 c	Roll, hard, large, 1	Gelatin, ⅓ c
Artificial sweetener	Margarine, corn or saf-flower oil, 1 t	Margarine, corn or saf-flower oil, 2 t
Coffee or tea	Salad dressing, com-mercial, 1 T	Blueberries, fresh, ½ c
	Peach, slices, canned in own juice (no sugar), ½ c	Yogurt, skim milk, 1 c
	Skim milk, 1 c	Artificial sweetener
	Artificial sweetener	Salt, pepper
	Salt, pepper	Coffee or tea
	Coffee, tea, or diet soda	
	Snack	
	Buttermilk, skim, 1 c	
	Graham crackers, 2	

Note: Menu supplies 1,800 kcal, 100 g of protein, 50 g of fat, and 230 g of carbohydrate.

TABLE 27-26   Characteristics of Some Approved Drugs Used in Lowering Serum Lipids and Lipoproteins

Drug	Type of Hyper-lipoproteinemia Treated*	Approximate Daily Dose
Nicotinic acid[†]	II, III, IV, V	0.1–3 g
Cholestyramine[‡]	II	5–15 g
Clofibrate[†]	III, IV, V	1 g
D-thyroxine[‡]	II, III	2–8 g
Sitosterol[‡]	II	30 mL

*Especially effective for those underlined.

[†]Inhibits lipoprotein synthesis.

[‡]Accelerates lipoprotein catabolism.

from the gallbladder. However, this type of operation has many potential problems (see Chapter 29 and its references).

For many years *high* blood levels of certain fat-related chemicals, such as cholesterol and triglycerides, have been considered bad for the heart. In the last decade, nutritional scientists have been speculating that the *elevated* serum level of one particular chemical substance may be good for us—*high-density lipoprotein* (HDL, see Tables 27-3 and 27-4), also known as the α-lipoprotein. Recent research suggests that this substance may protect us from heart and circulatory diseases. However, because of the scarcity of available information, the discussion presented below must be considered tentative.

Most of the cholesterol in the blood is transported by two major carriers. About 80% is transported by low-density lipoproteins (LDLs, see Tables 27-3 and 27-4), while the rest is carried by HDLs. In the early 1950s, epidemiological studies indicated that a high blood level of LDLs or total cholesterol was associated with a high risk of heart disease. However, many of the same patients showed a low blood level of HDLs. This observation did not stimulate much interest until the 1970s, when more data became available. It is now believed that HDLs are beneficial to our health. LDLs carry cholesterol and deposit it in the blood vessels, causing plaques and ultimately

heart disease to develop. Conversely, HDLs seem to remove deposited cholesterol and carry it away to the liver for excretion through the bile. It thus appears that we have two types of cholesterol circulating in the blood. The type carried by LDLs seems to be undesirable, while that carried by HDLs is beneficial. Thus, an increased serum level of HDLs is a good clinical sign. Recently additional epidemiological studies have confirmed that a high serum level of HDL is associated with a low risk of cardiovascular disease.

If high blood levels of HDL are beneficial, is it possible to induce this condition in individuals to reduce their risk of heart disease? If individuals born with a high blood HDL level are excluded from consideration, some current but tentative observations are as follows: (1) Females have higher blood HDL levels than males; (2) the more cigarettes one smokes, the lower the HDL blood level; (3) the more exercise (running in particular) one does, the higher the blood HDL level; (4) moderate alcohol drinking increases the blood HDL level; (5) obesity often produces higher blood HDL levels and weight reduction often produces low blood HDL levels; (6) lowering blood pressure reduces the blood HDL level; and (7) there is at present no information on the effect of diet on blood HDL levels.

Given the inconclusiveness of the above observations, it will certainly be some time before a specific strategy is available for raising blood HDL levels, assuming that a higher level is good for us.

In evaluating the suggestion that some types of hyperlipoproteinemia are associated with a higher incidence of atherosclerosis, one must consider a number of factors. First, the association implies a higher risk for individuals with hyperlipoproteinemia than individuals with normolipoproteinemia. Correcting hyperlipoproteinemia does not make a person immune from heart disease, but it does lessen the likelihood of such a disease developing. Second, maintaining a normolipoproteinemia requires a lifetime of good eating habits and is very demanding on an individual's life-style. For example, in some situations, a salesman may have to change his job in order to be able to modify his old eating habits. Third, as indicated earlier, only a small fraction of the entire population has inherited hyperlipoproteinemia. Fourth, the decision to treat asymptomatic patients, as indicated earlier, rests with clinical experience and philosophy of the doctor and is not mandatory. These factors determine how doctors and public health agencies treat two special groups of patients: those with normolipoproteinemia but high blood levels of cholesterol, triglyceride, or both; and those with normal blood lipid profile.

Treating patients with normolipoproteinemia who have high blood levels of cholesterol and triglyceride has been controversial for a number of years. At the center of the controversy is the timing of treatment. The National Heart and Lung Institute has issued guidelines defining "normal" levels of serum cholesterol, triglyceride, and low-density lipoprotein for population groups in different age brackets (Table 27-27). If a person's lipid profile exceeds any of these levels, treatment is needed, according to the institute. Some scientists and clinicians dispute these defined levels, but the pros and cons of this issue are too large in scope to be explored here. However, if a decision is made for treatment, a person with hypercholesterolemia will receive the same dietary treatment as one with type IIa hyperlipoproteinemia. A person with hypertriglyceridemia would use the diet for type IV. A person with both conditions would use the diet for type III hyperlipoproteinemia.

Should adults and children (especially males) with normal blood lipid levels adopt prudent eating and living habits to maintain these levels? The dietary goals proposed by the U.S. Senate (see Chapter 19) and encouraged by some health educators, doctors, dietitians, nurses, and scientists imply that there is at least no harm in eliminating as many risk factors as possible from one's diet. This adjustment begins by eating wholesome foods whose fat content is controlled. Minimizing other risk factors such as inactivity, stress, and smoking can also help (see earlier discussion).

In regard to dietary and serum lipids, the American Heart Association has specific suggestions. Obese persons should reduce and maintain ideal body weight. Fat intake should be reduced by: (1) reducing total fat intake; (2) reducing saturated fat intake; (3) increasing

TABLE 27-27 Normal Levels of Plasma Cholesterol, Triglyceride, and Low-Density Lipoprotein

Age (years)	Triglyceride (mg/100 mL plasma)	Cholesterol (mg/100 mL plasma)	Low-Density Lipoprotein (mg/100 mL plasma)
1–19	150	230	170
20–29	200	240	170
30–39	200	270	190
40–49	200	310	190
Over 50	200	330	210

Source: The Dietary Management of Hyperlipoproteinemias. A Handbook for Physicians and Dietitians. Rev. ed. Department of Health, Education and Welfare publication No. (NIH) 75-110 (Bethesda, Md.: National Heart and Lung Institute, reprinted 1974).

polyunsaturated fat intake; and (4) reducing cholesterol intake. To achieve this modification of fat intake, the American Heart Association has developed the *fat-controlled diet* (sometimes called the fat-regulated, preventive, or prudent diet). Table 27-28 lists the foods permitted and prohibited in this dietary regimen. Table 27-29 presents the meal planning for a representative 2,000-kcal diet. Table 27-30 gives a day's menu for the fat-controlled diet. The daily meal plan is low in total fat, saturated fat, and cholesterol and high in polyunsaturated fat. Caloric intake is not restricted, but if weight loss is necessary, the number of calories consumed must be reduced (also see Chapter 12).

HYPERTENSION

Hypertension refers to a sustained elevation of systolic and/or diastolic arterial blood pressure. Standard medical textbooks list the upper limits of normal blood pressure in different age groups. For reference purposes here, they are 140/90 mm Hg for 20- to 40-year-olds and 150/95 mm Hg for 50- to 60-year-olds. Despite these standard values, the clinical distinction between normal and elevated blood pressure is made by the

TABLE 27-28 Foods Permitted and Prohibited in a Fat-Controlled Preventive Diet

Food Group	Foods Permitted	Foods Prohibited
Beverages	Coffee: regular, decaffeinated Soft drinks: regular, low calorie Tea: weak, strong Miscellaneous: fruit juices, punches, flavored drinks, Postum Any dietetic low-calorie beverages with or without artificial sweeteners	All alcoholic beverages unless permitted by doctor; eggnog, milk shakes, malt drinks, chocolate drinks
Breads, grains, equivalents	No restriction on number of servings. Breads: Italian, raisin, white, whole wheat, Boston brown, French Vienna, cracked wheat, pumpernickel Rolls: all made with skim milk and very little saturated fat including plain pan, hard, and whole wheat Biscuits: homemade with skim milk and polyunsaturated fats Cereals: all ready-to-eat and cooked excluding those made with coconut and fat Flours: all varieties Crackers: pretzels, rusk, all others not containing butter and cheese Tortillas made with polyunsaturated oil, zwieback, bread sticks Miscellaneous products made with skim milk, permitted egg allowance, and polyunsaturated vegetable oil: English muffins, French toast, muffins, pancakes, quick breads, waffles, corn bread	Bread: made with egg and cheese Biscuits: all commercial varieties Crackers: made with butter and cheese All commercial products including doughnuts, muffins, puff pastry, popovers, sweet rolls, Danish pastry, spoon bread, unless they are homemade or special products made with skim milk and polyunsaturated fats and permitted egg allowance; all commercial mixes using saturated fats, whole milk, or dried eggs
Milk, milk products	Skim milk (fortified with vitamins A and D): fluid, powder Fermented skim milk: buttermilk, yogurt Other skim milk products: canned (evaporated), cocoa (with cocoa powder)	Fluid milk: whole, 2% low-fat Fermented whole milk: yogurt Canned whole milk: evaporated, condensed, powder Other whole milk products: regular hot chocolate, cocoa Cream: light, heavy, half and half, sour; non-dairy creamers and products made from them
Cheese, cheese products	Servings must replace milk allotments. All cheeses made from partially or fully skimmed milk—e.g., uncreamed cottage; baker's, farmer, or hoop; sapsago; mozzarella, and dietetic cheese low in fat and cholesterol and high in polyunsaturated fats.	All cheeses made from cream or whole milk—e.g., brick, Camembert, American, Roquefort, blue, cream, cheddar, Gouda, Edam, Parmesan, Neufchâtel, ricotta, Swiss, processed; all cheeses not specifically permitted; any commercial products made from the above cheeses
Eggs	Three whole eggs per week maximum; no limitation on egg whites and dietetic egg substitutes; prepared in any form with permitted ingredients such as skim milk and polyunsaturated fats and oils	Eggs prepared in all other forms; egg yolk limited to 3 per week

TABLE 27-28   (continued)

Food Group	Foods Permitted	Foods Prohibited
Meats and equivalents	Maximum of 9 oz daily Chicken, turkey, veal: baked, broiled, roasted, stewed; no skins Shellfish: most varieties (shrimp is low in fat and high in cholesterol; use less than 8 oz per week) (4 oz = 1 meat equivalent) Fish: most varieties Beef, lamb, pork, ham: use less frequently; use lean cuts with visible fat trimmed, fat drippings excluded; baked, broiled, roasted, stewed Beans: baked, vegetarian, all dried forms Peas: all dried forms Nuts: all varieties except walnuts and those prohibited Peanut butter Textured vegetable protein	Goose, duck; spareribs, frankfurters, sausages, cold cuts; heavily fatty and marbled meats All forms of organ meat: chicken liver, beef liver, sweetbread, heart, kidney (If liver is eaten, use once a week. If liver is totally excluded, monitor other sources of iron.); canned pork and beans Nuts: macadamia and cashew
Desserts	All homemade cakes, pies, cookies, icings, and pie crust using permitted eggs, skim milk, and polyunsaturated oils Ice milk, fruit cobblers, imitation ice cream made with polyunsaturated oil, sherbet, water ices; gelatin, plain or fruit, fruit whips, puddings; tapioca and rice products made with skim milk, permitted eggs, and polyunsaturated oils; bread, rennet, cornstarch	Most commercial desserts such as pies, cakes, cookies, puddings, ice cream, cheesecake, eclairs, strudel, turnovers, and many others prepared with whole milk, saturated fat, cream, and eggs
Sweets	Syrups, sugars, molasses, honey; preserves, jellies, jams; hard candy, candied fruits; marshmallows, marmalades	All varieties of candy made with whole milk, saturated fat, eggs, chocolate, and chocolate sauces
Potatoes, equivalents	Number of servings not limited Potatoes: boiled, baked, mashed, creamed, scalloped with polyunsaturated fat and skim milk, salad with no egg Sweet potatoes and yams: canned, mashed, boiled, baked Bread stuffing; barley; macaroni, rice, spaghetti, noodles, bulgur, wild rice; fritters, dumplings, prepared with daily permitted egg, skim milk, and polyunsaturated fats	All potatoes and equivalents prepared with whole milk, eggs, bacon, butter, cream, cheese, meat drippings, or shortening

attending physician and depends, among other factors, on the physician's experience in treating patients with high blood pressure.

In many cases, hypertension is not accompanied by symptoms until related clinical complications appear that result from damage to the kidneys, heart, and circulatory system. If these complications are evident, it may be too late to help an individual, since heart attack or stroke may soon follow, with fatal results. In such cases, linings of the blood vessels thicken to counteract the elevated blood pressure, thus curtailing blood flow to the heart and kidneys, which results in the observed complications. However, if hy-

TABLE 27-28   (continued)

Food Group	Foods Permitted	Foods Prohibited
Fruits, vegetables	All	No restrictions except those items prepared with excluded food products
Fats	No limit on permitted fats and oils; daily servings at least 2–4 T Vegetable oils: sesame, soybean, sunflower, corn, cottonseed Margarine: made with polyunsaturated oils; if hydrogenated, must contain acceptable amount of polyunsaturated oils (recommended liquid vegetable oil listed as first ingredient, and one or more partially hydrogenated vegetable oils as additional ingredients) Gravies, sauces, salad dressings (Italian, French, mayonnaise, and similar varieties) made with skim milk, polyunsaturated oils, and other permitted ingredients	All regular butter and margarine (including completely hydrogenated items); Roquefort and blue cheese salad dressings; solid shortening, lard, bacon drippings, regular gravies, meat drippings, any dressing containing cheese Oils: olive, palm, coconut, peanut (if used, limit to small amounts)
Soups	Number of servings not limited Soups: gumbos, chowders, onion, vegetable, dehydrated, packaged, bisques, and cream Broths, consommés, bouillon cubes and powder, any clear soup with no fat Only skim milk and polyunsaturated fats permitted in both commercial and homemade soups	Any commercial soup made with whole milk and saturated fats, e.g., cream soups; any commercial soup made with bacon or ham, e.g., split pea and bean soups
Miscellaneous	Spices and seasonings: soy sauce, Worcestershire sauce, all herbs and spices, cream of tartar, baking powder, sodium bicarbonate, salt, salt substitutes, monosodium glutamate, artificial sweeteners, garlic, chutney, capers, horseradish, catsup, pickles, gelatin, popcorn Sauces: chili sauce; cranberry sauce; aspic; all barbecue, creole, sweet and sour, tomato, and cocktail sauces made with skim milk and polyunsaturated oils	Most commercial snacks such as potato chips, dips; creamed dishes; olives; frozen or packaged dinners; commercial popcorn, coffee cream substitutes; any product made with saturated oil, whole milk, and eggs not within allowance

Note: Table adapted from: (1) *The Way to a Man's Heart.* American Heart Association, 1972. By permission of the American Heart Association, Inc.; (2) *Planning Fat-Controlled Meals for 1200 and 1800 Calories.* American Heart Association, 1966. By permission of the American Heart Association, Inc.

pertension itself is symptomatic, the patient may suffer dizziness, headaches, and/or palpitations. High blood pressure is a very important risk factor in the development of cardiovascular diseases. The higher the blood pressure, the greater the risk posed.

However, this hypertensive risk is influenced by the presence of other risk factors. For example, the same elevated blood pressure in two individuals may pose more danger to one than the other. At present, hypertension is easily identified, treated, and managed, especially if the patient is properly educated, provided with convenient and reasonable instructions, and not overly

TABLE 27-29 Meal Plan for a Prudent Diet

Breakfast	Lunch	Dinner
1 serving breakfast cereal	3 oz meat or equivalent	3 oz meat or equivalent
½ c fruit or fruit juice	½ c potato or 1 serving equivalent	½ c potato or equivalent
1 sl bread or toast with 2 t margarine (vegetable oil)	½ c fruit or juice	½ c fruit or juice
Jelly or equivalent	1 serving clear broth	1 serving clear broth
½ c skim milk	½ c vegetable	½ c vegetable
Coffee or tea	1 serving salad with 1 T permitted dressing	1 serving salad with 1 T permitted dressing
1 t sugar	1 sl bread or toast or equivalent (e.g., 1 roll) with 2 t margarine (vegetable oil)	1 sl bread or equivalent (e.g., 1 roll) with 2 t margarine (vegetable oil)
Salt and pepper if needed	1 serving dessert or fruit	1 c skim milk
	Coffee or tea	1 serving dessert or fruit
	1 t sugar	Coffee or tea
	Salt and pepper if needed	1 t sugar
		Salt and pepper if needed

Note: Menu supplies 2,000 kcal, 75 to 80 g of protein, 70 to 75 g of fat, and 270 to 280 g of carbohydrate. If eggs are desired, limit to three a week.

TABLE 27-30 Sample Menu for a Prudent Diet

Breakfast	Lunch	Dinner
Juice, grapefruit, ½ c	Juice, tomato, ½ c	Grape drink, canned, 1 c
Applesauce, unsweetened, 1 c	Veal, broiled, 3 oz	Soup, onion, ½ c
Oatmeal, 1 c	Potato, baked, medium, 1	Chicken, stewed, 3 oz
Toast, rye bread, 1 sl	Green salad, ½ c	Rice, ½ c
Margarine, vegetable oil, 2 t	French dressing (with polyunsaturated vegetable oil), 1 T	Broccoli, ½ c
Skim milk, ½ c	Bread, French, 1 sl	Roll, hard, small, 1
Coffee or tea	Margarine, vegetable oil, 2 t	Margarine, vegetable oil, 2 t
Sugar, 1 t	Peach, fresh, 1	Gelatin, with fruit, ½ c
Salt and pepper if needed	Coffee or tea	Skim milk, 1 c
	Sugar, 1 t	Coffee or tea
	Salt and pepper if needed	Sugar, 1 t
		Salt and pepper if needed

Note: Menu supplies 2,000 kcal, 75 to 80 g of protein, 70 to 75 g of fat, and 270 to 280 g of carbohydrate. If eggs are desired, limit to three a week.

burdened with medical costs. Still, according to a conservative estimate, there may be 25 to 30 million Americans with unidentified, untreated, or poorly controlled high blood pressure.

Prevalence

Hypertension may be primary or secondary. The latter may accompany clinical disorders such as kidney disease, heart failure, and hormonal imbalance. Also, some drugs produce secondary hypertension. Primary or essential hypertension is of unknown origin and accounts for 80% to 90% of all cases. Some important considerations in the prognosis of primary hypertension are race, age, and sex. It is seen twice as frequently in black Americans as in whites. The mortality rate of the former from related complications is also higher. For unknown reasons, as one gets older, blood pressure also increases, although hypertension occurs more commonly between the ages of 25 and 55. The disorder is more common in women than men.

Causes

Some proposed causes of primary hypertension include heredity, obesity, excess salt ingestion, stress, lack of physical activity, and an unwholesome life-style such as excess alcohol consumption and frequent, irregular meals. Any one of these alone may elevate blood pressure. If two or more of these factors are present, the likelihood of primary hypertension increases dramatically. Of all identifiable factors, obesity and excess salt ingestion are of direct interest to nutritionists and dietitians.

A person's weight is related to hypertension in many ways. In the following discussion, overweight is used synonymously with obese (see Chapter 12). In general, there is a positive relationship between obesity, high blood pressure, and cardiovascular mortality (see Table 27-31). Overweight nonhypertensive patients are more likely (sometimes twice as likely) to develop hypertension than persons of normal body weight. Clinical experience also shows that more obese than lean patients are hypertensive. An already

TABLE 27-31   Relationship between Body Weight, Hypertension, and Cardiovascular Diseases

Condition	Risk of Coronary Heart Disease and Mortality
Lean hypertensive patients	High risk
Obese normotensive patients	High risk
Obese hypertensive patients	Very high risk

hypertensive patient unfortunately also has a greater tendency to gain weight than a person with normal blood pressure. This is a vicious cycle that is difficult to break.

Among people who gain weight progressively, there is a greater tendency to develop hypertension progressively. The tendency is even stronger for individuals who are already obese or overweight. Conversely, as an overweight hypertensive patient loses weight, blood pressure tends to decline. This is more pronounced in men than women, and different patients achieve varying reductions in blood pressure for a given amount of weight loss. Blood pressure can be lowered with or without the use of drugs and/or restricting the intake of salt. Also, the relationship between weight change and blood pressure is more pronounced among black Americans.

Ingesting too much salt throughout life has been suggested as a cause of hypertension since the 1930s. The average American consumes about 10 to 15 g of salt per day, which includes about 4 to 5 g of sodium. This amount is considered too great by some experts in the field. In contrast, other population groups (especially non-Western cultures) who have had low salt intakes since childhood also show an absence of hypertension. Other relevant observations linking high salt intake with hypertension are as follows: (1) Rats with an inherited tendency toward hypertension develop elevated blood pressure and die at an early age when put on a high-salt diet. If given normal foods, they live much longer. (2) High salt consumption can increase water retention, and this accumulation of fluid consequently raises blood pressure. (3) Restricting salt intake can decrease blood pressure. The more severe the restriction, the lower the blood pressure.

Medical and Dietary Management

The current medical management of hypertension involves drug therapy, dietary and nutritional therapy, and modification of lifestyle. These methods can keep hypertension under control and reduce the risk of associated complications.

Drug therapy plays an important role in correcting hypertension. In the last 20 years, tremendous advances have been made with the development of safe and effective drugs to combat hypertension. Consequently, the practices of using a severely restricted sodium diet and the Kempner rice diet have become less common. The most common drugs used are diuretics, hydralazine, and other hypotensive agents. Diuretics eliminate sodium by reducing the amount of salt and water retained in the body and the amount of fluid in the blood. Hydralazine operates by dilating the lumina of the blood vessels. Chemicals such as propranolol, clonidine, methyldopa, reserpine, guanethidine and metoprolol, prazosine also prevent the constriction of blood vessels. However, drugs are most effective if they are used simultaneously with a proper treatment of nutritional imbalances.

Diet therapy for hypertension requires a consideration of the effects of diuretics on body functions. As indicated earlier, diuretics reduce the accumulation of water and sodium in the body. By removing sodium from the body, diuretics return blood pressure to normal and increase the effectiveness of other hypotensive drugs. Most diuretics used in treating hypertensive patients work mainly by suppressing the ability of the kidney tubules to reabsorb sodium.

Drugs that act on the loop and ascending limb of the loop of Henle in the kidneys also cause a loss of potassium in the urine. Hypokalemia or low blood potassium can be dangerous since it affects the electrolyte balance of the body, especially if the patient is also receiving other medications. All members of the health team should be alerted to the possibility of hypokalemia when using certain diuretics. Measures to guard against this condition include: (1) careful prescription of diuretics and prohibition of their continuous use; (2) greater consumption of potassium-rich foods and the use of oral potassium supplements; and (3) changing to diuretics that do not produce hypokalemia. Table 27-32 provides a list of those foods high in potassium. Refer also to Appendix B for the sodium and potassium content of a variety of foods.

Potassium loss from the use of certain diuretics usually progresses slowly, and after 2 to 3 months a total deficit of 300 mEq (about 11 to 12 g) may result. This loss is not severe for a healthy adult, but its effect may be serious in the presence of other clinical disorders. A patient using diuretics capable of producing hypokalemia may need 40 to 60 mEq (1,550 to 2,350 mg) of potassium daily. However, patients given these diuretics for long-term therapy in cases of edema may develop hypokalemia despite supplements or potassium-rich foods. Some clinicians feel that a patient's body may not be able to assimilate a large dose of potassium and that consequently the patient's normal blood potassium will not be sustained for long. Under these circumstances, the doctor may have to prescribe another type of diuretic. On the other hand, some physicians are not concerned as long as hypokalemia is asymptomatic. Refer to Chapter 28 for more information on hypokalemia.

Presently, three major types of diuretics are available for prescription. These are thiazides, loop diuretics, and potassium-sparing diuretics. Consult Table 27-33 for their proper usage.

Two major dietary considerations in managing a hypertensive patient are sodium and fluid retention and caloric intake. Because the presence of sodium causes fluid retention, which is partially responsible for high blood pressure, restriction of sodium intake is important. It is now firmly established that a moderate restriction in sodium intake definitely potentiates the effectiveness of drug therapy for hypertension. This usually means eating about 2 g of sodium daily instead of the average 5 to 6 g a day. The degree of sodium restriction is determined by the patient's clinical conditions, the drug therapy program, and the patient's response to different treatments.

TABLE 27-32 Foods High in Potassium

Food	Serving Size	Potassium (mg)
Beverages		
Apple juice, canned	1½ c	375
Coffee, brewed	1½ c	480
Grapefruit juice, canned	1 c	402
Grapefruit or orange juice, canned, sweetened	1 c	454
Milk, fluid, whole	1¼ c	433
Orange juice, from frozen concentrate	1 c	461
Pineapple juice, canned	1 c	373
Prune juice, canned	¾ c	452
Tomato juice	¾ c	401
Cereals		
Bran cereal, 100%	1½ oz	450
Bread, pumpernickel	3 oz	381
Bread pudding with raisins	¾ c	427
Buckwheat pancakes	6	398
Spoon bread	1 c	317
Rolled wheat cereal, cooked	1½ c	303
Rye wafers	10	390
Meat, fish, poultry		
Beef	4 oz	418
Chicken	4 oz	414
Halibut	3 oz	447
Lamb	6 oz	420
Liver, beef	3 oz	323
Pork	4 oz	442
Salmon	3 oz	378
Tuna, canned, water pack, solid	5 oz	395
Turkey, roasted	3 oz	312
Veal	3 oz	425
Fruits		
Apricots, fresh, medium	4	402
Avocado	¼	340
Banana, raw, medium	1	440
Cantaloupe, cut pieces	1 c	402
Casaba, cut pieces	1 c	427
Cherries, sour, canned in water	1 c	317
Dates, dried	10	518
Grapefruit, medium	1	370
Orange, large	1	400
Papaya, fresh, ½-in. cubes	1 c	328
Pineapple, raw, chunks	1½ c	339
Prunes, dried, pitted	5	354
Raisins	1½ c	328
Rhubarb, frozen, added sugar, cooked	1 c	475
Watermelon, wedge, 10 in. diam., 4 in. thick	1	426

TABLE 27-32 (continued)

Food	Serving Size	Potassium (mg)
Nuts and seeds		
Almonds, shelled, whole	½ c	503
Cashews, whole kernels, roasted in oil	¾ c	488
Filberts, shelled, whole	½ c	475
Peanuts, roasted in oil, salted	½ c	485
Peanut butter	4 T (¼ c)	400
Pecans, halves, shelled	¾ c	488
Pumpkin seeds, dry, hulled	⅓ c	462
Sunflower seeds, hulled	⅓ c	444
Walnuts, English, halves, shelled	1 c	450
Vegetables		
Asparagus, cuts and tips, cooked from frozen	1 c	396
Beet greens, cooked	¾ c	374
Blackeye peas, cooked from raw	½ c	470
Broccoli, fresh, cooked	1 c	414
Brussels sprouts, cooked	1 c	423
Carrots, cooked, sliced	1 c	344
Celery, pieces, diced	1 c	409
Collards, cooked from raw	1 c	498
Lima beans	½ c	362
Mustard greens, cooked	1 c	308
Parsnips, cooked, diced	¾ c	440
Potato, baked, medium	½	391
Pumpkin, canned	¾ c	441
Spinach, cooked	¾ c	437
Squash, winter, cooked, diced	½ c	472
Sweet potato, canned, mashed	¾ c	382
Tomato, raw, medium	1	300
Vegetables, mixed, cooked from frozen	1 c	348
Miscellaneous		
Chocolate, bitter or baking	2 oz	470
Molasses, blackstrap	1 T	586
Pickles, dill, medium	3	390
Soup, tomato, commercial condensed, prepared with equal volume milk	1 c	418
Yeast, brewer's, dry	3 T	456

The attending physician must also consider other pertinent factors when prescribing a sodium-limited diet. For example, if a 2 g sodium/d diet is tolerated well by the patient (in addition to drug therapy), blood pressure declines at a reasonable rate, and any existing clinical symptoms are relieved, then sodium intake does not have to be lowered any further. Otherwise, a reduction to 1.5 g/d may prove beneficial. It is generally agreed that the sodium intake of a hypertensive patient should not be lowered to less than 1 g/d in the absence of congestive heart failure. How-

TABLE 27-33 Characteristics of Diuretics Used in the Treatment of Hypertension

Type of Diuretic	Examples of Diuretic	Recommendations for Use	Complications
Thiazide	Chlorothiazide, hydrochlorothiazide, benzthiazide	Can reduce blood pressure moderately when given early in treating essential hypertension; no effect if edema is present without sodium excess; may enhance effectiveness of other antihypertensive drugs to prevent increase of extracellular volume	Hyperuricemia, hypercalcemia, hypokalemia, lesions of the alimentary tract, diabetogenic; can increase zinc excretion
Loop	Furosemide, ethacrynic acid	Potent; should not be used in place of thiazide unless intolerance of the latter and renal failure; dose adjusted according to patient response in chronic renal failure; can contract extracellular volume	Hypocalcemia; can increase zinc excretion
Potassium-sparing	Spironolactone, triamterene	Eliminates edema without the simultaneous loss of potassium in urine; recommended for special circumstances, for example, hyperaldosteronism and nephrotic syndrome	May produce hyperkalemia if precautions not taken to counter this effect of drug or the excess intake from potassium supplement; breast lumps in men and women; menstrual irregularities in women

ever, a major problem encountered in severely restricted sodium diets involves patient compliance. Compliance decreases proportionately as sodium intake is lowered from 2 g/d.

Severe restriction of the sodium intake of a hypertensive patient also has an inherent hazard. To conserve body sodium, the kidneys reduce their filtering capacity, thus simultaneously retaining more nitrogenous waste (urea) in the body. This may be hazardous for patients with renal failure, who require a delicately managed balance between too much and too little sodium intake.

Many patients eat more salty food than they should because diuretics deplete the body of sodium. If this increase in consumption is not monitored, the action of the diuretics will be neutralized. The diuretics administered to a hypertensive patient may also cause hypotension. When this happens, salt intake should not be increased to retain fluid for restoring a normo-

tensive state. Extra sodium is likely to be excreted because of the diuretics rather than retained. The best remedy for hypotension is either to decrease the dosages of the particular diuretic used or to lengthen the interval between drug administration.

The above discussion lists only a few of the adverse effects of the indiscriminate and careless restriction of dietary sodium intake.

In general, hypertensive patients are permitted to drink water whenever they are thirsty, although taking in an unreasonably large amount of fluid is obviously not advisable. Certain beverages such as coffee and alcohol may not be advisable since they can cause heart arrhythmia. The attending physician should determine which beverages are suitable for a patient according to the patient's heart condition.

Hypertensive patients should consume enough calories to maintain an ideal weight. There are a number of special considerations for overweight patients: (1) Every effort must be made to achieve ideal body weight. (2) If dieting is not successful, a patient should be treated simultaneously with drugs and sodium restriction if indicated. (3) Since exercise can lower blood pressure and help an overweight patient to lose weight, a good exercise program should be established. (4) Light meals are recommended, since a heavy meal is more likely to make the heart of an obese hypertensive patient work harder and to cause blood pressure to fluctuate. (5) To assure that the blood pressure reading of an obese hypertensive patient is accurate, special large blood pressure cuffs are needed.

In addition, the protein intake of hypertensive patients must also be evaluated. Protein foods contain a large amount of sodium and should obviously be regulated if the patient is on a restricted sodium diet. To plan a diet with a specified level of sodium, consult the last part of this chapter.

CONGESTIVE HEART FAILURE

More than half of all patients with organic cardiovascular disease eventually develop congestive heart failure. In these cases, the heart fails to pump sufficient blood for the physiological needs of the body. Although the right or left ventricle alone may initially be affected, both ventricles eventually fail. Symptoms include some or all of the following: labored breathing, breathing possible only in an upright position, liver enlargement, edema, and heart enlargement. In more than half of the cases there are identifiable precipitating causes such as hypertension, atherosclerosis, pregnancy, anemia, thyrotoxicosis, excess salt intake, rapid administration of parenteral fluids, and thiamin deficiency.

The most characteristic symptom of congestive heart failure is excessive retention of water and sodium, the exact cause of which is unknown. One proposed mechanism that eventually leads to edema in congestive heart failure is illustrated in Figure 27-7. The objectives of treatment are to increase the force and efficiency

of myocardial contraction and to reduce the abnormal retention of sodium and water. Patients share a significant responsibility in the management of their disease, because treatment is long-term and involves adopting a special diet, taking drugs, and following a good exercise program. Removing the cause of the disorder may cure the heart failure; otherwise, treatment includes bed rest, drugs, oxygen therapy, mechanical assistance, peritoneal dialysis, and nutritional and dietary care.

In determining the nutritional and dietary care of patients with congestive heart failure, several issues must be considered: the effects of particular drugs on nutritional status, the control of body weight, the correction of body sodium and fluid balance, and feeding routines. Drug therapy involves the use of digitalis, which increases the rate and force of cardiac contraction. Diuretics are used to eliminate water and sodium. Isoproterenol can affect cardiac muscular contraction. However, all these drugs can adversely affect the nutritional status of the patient, as discussed in Chapter 16 and later in this chapter.

Excessive fat hinders respiration and circulation, forces the diaphragm to rise, lowers the lung volume, and alters the position of the heart. Fat deposition around the heart can impair the function of the heart muscle. Since obesity can make the heart work harder, obese patients should lose weight first. Slightly malnourished persons require less oxygen and thus decrease the work the heart must perform. Patients should be provided with sufficient calories to maintain normal or slightly less than normal body weight, after taking into consideration the presence of any edema.

The abnormal retention of sodium and water may be counteracted by restricting sodium intake. The restriction ranges from severe to mild. The patient is first permitted 250 mg sodium/d and progresses to 1,000 mg. It is often difficult for a patient to eat foods included in a 250-mg-sodium diet, since most patients are accustomed to saltier foods. Some clinicians have substituted a 300 to 350 mg/d (or higher) sodium diet with the simultaneous use of diuretics. However, clinical experience has shown that patients

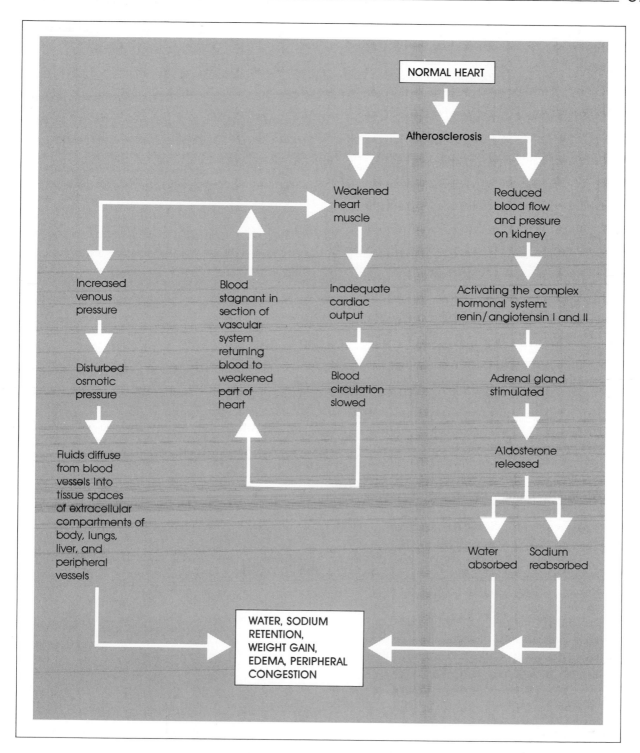

FIGURE 27-7   Proposed mechanism in the development of edema in congestive heart failure.

are more amenable to a 1-g sodium diet. Sometimes medications such as digitalis and spironolactone (a diuretic) used cautiously permit a diet higher in sodium content, which patients can observe more easily. Depending on the conditions of the patient, fluid restriction may or may not be necessary.

Sometimes a liberal fluid intake of 2,000 to 3,000 mL water/d can increase diuresis, which helps to eliminate excess sodium from the body. However, if the sodium intake of a patient is reduced to less than 250 mg, excessive fluid consumption may result in hyponatremia due to dilution of body fluid rather than sodium deficiency. The remedy in this case is to restrict fluid intake and not to increase salt consumption.

In the course of regulating body fluid and sodium, doctors, nurses, and dietitians must be alert to possible complications and side effects. For instance, sodium restriction may also result in the removal of other electrolytes from the body. In some patients, a low-sodium syndrome may occur, especially among the elderly. Unfortunately, the symptoms of this disorder resemble digitalis toxicity and may be overlooked. More on this disorder is discussed later.

Health professionals are also aware that diuretics have notorious side effects. Use of the concepts of "potassium depletion" and "potassium sparing" play a large role in taking appropriate measures for a particular patient. Refer to other sections of this chapter and Chapter 28 for more information on diuretics.

The routine feedings of a patient with congestive heart failure are very simple and should follow a few guidelines. Small, frequent feedings should be given to avoid fatigue and heavy breathing. The meal should be well balanced, nutritious, and light, composed mostly of easily digestible carbohydrates and a moderate amount of protein. High consumption of the latter nutrient increases the specific dynamic action (see Chapter 2), thus making the heart work harder. Fats and vitamins should be adequate. Salt intake should be restricted according to the severity of the particular condition. Finally, roughage and other food products that the patient may not tolerate should not be served. Consult Chapters 22 and 23 on how to plan this kind of menu.

DRUGS, VITAMINS, AND SODIUM-RESTRICTED DIETS

The medical management of patients with coronary heart disease, hypertension, and congestive heart failure can involve the administration of a number of drugs. Some of these drugs have profound effects on the nutritional status of the patient. A number of examples are listed in Table 27-34.

At present, there are some confirmed as well as suspected relationships between vitamins and cardiovascular diseases. Deficiencies of some vitamins and excesses of others can potentiate heart disease. Certain vitamins are reputed to have a prophylactic effect on heart disease, but as yet these claims are scientifically unsubstantiated. Table 27-35 provides a summary of this information.

A *sodium-restricted diet* is one in which a lower-than-normal amount of sodium is specified. Table 27-36 defines five types of sodium-restricted diet with five levels of sodium content. Some common descriptions for these diets are also included. For reference purposes, 23 mg sodium = 1 mEq sodium; mg sodium = mg sodium chloride × 0.393; and mg sodium chloride = mg sodium × 2.54.

Tables 27-37 to 27-39 indicate the nutritional composition of different types of sodium-restricted diets at three different caloric levels. The American Heart Association has developed Sodium Food Exchange Lists to assist in designing meal plans for such diets. Each exchange list is made up of various foods that contain approximately the same amounts of sodium, calories, protein, carbohydrate, and fat. Table 27-40 summarizes the approximate nutritional contents of these exchange lists. Tables 27-41 through 27-52 describe the specific food items permitted and prohibited within each exchange list. Table 27-53 indicates permitted and prohibited spices, condiments, gravies, and sauces for a patient on a sodium-restricted diet. Using these exchange lists, Tables 27-54 to 27-56 present particular meal plans (number of exchanges) for diets at different caloric and sodium levels. Tables 27-57

TABLE 27-34   Effects of Drugs Used in Treating Heart Disease on Nutritional Status

Drug	Main Purpose	Direct and Indirect Effects on Nutritional Status
Digitalis and its glycosides	Treating tachycardia	Vomiting, nausea, loss of appetite
Diuretics	Diuresis	Loss of sodium, potassium, other minerals, and vitamins
Hydralazine hydrochloride	Hypotensive	Binding vitamin B_6 and increasing its excretion
Dilantin	Treating tachycardia	Increasing serum levels of very low density lipoprotein, cholesterol, triglycerides
Doriden	Nonbarbiturate sedative	Multiple vitamin deficiencies
Clofibrate	Lowering serum lipids and lipoproteins	Nausea, diarrhea, abnormal liver function tests; potentiates hypoprothrombinemic effect of warfarin sodium; possible vitamin K deficiency and bleeding problem if drug is used at the same time as warfarin sodium
Nicotinic acid	Lowering serum lipids and lipoproteins	Nausea, diarrhea, glucose intolerance, hyperuricemia
Cholestyramine	Lowering serum lipids and lipoproteins	Hyperchloremic acidosis, biliary tract calcification, steatorrhea, constipation, nausea; promotes fecal excretion of bile acids; possible vitamins A and K deficiency
D-thyroxine	Lowering serum lipids and lipoproteins	Mild hypermetabolism, glucose intolerance, can increase caloric expenditure and vitamin requirements; increases hypoprothrombinemic effect of warfarin sodium if used together
Sitosterol	Lowering serum lipids and lipoproteins	Nausea, diarrhea
Antibiotics	Antimicrobial agents	May change intestinal flora with concomitant effect on vitamin K availability, thus complicating anticoagulant therapy

TABLE 27-35   Relationship between Vitamins and Heart Disease

Vitamin	Effects on Heart-Related Conditions	Vitamin	Effects on Heart-Related Conditions
Fat Soluble		**Water Soluble**	
Vitamin A	Any diet that significantly decreases fat intake may be deficient in this vitamin (e.g., lowered consumption of eggs, fat beef, saturated fats). That Is, dietary changes to benefit the heart may result in this vitamin's deficiency.	Thiamin	Direct effect when deficient; see Chapter 6 for more details on beriberi heart disease.
Vitamin D	Calcification of atherosclerotic plaques can be aggravated or brought about by excessive intake of vitamin D.	Nicotinic acid	As a drug in large doses, can lower serum cholesterol, triglyceride, and β-lipoprotein; all aspects of undesirable side effects must be considered when administered.
Vitamin E	Antioxidant property of this chemical prevents oxidation of fatty acids from intake of polyunsaturated fatty acids (proclaimed value of high dose of vitamin E in curing or preventing heart disease not yet substantiated).	Vitamin C	The claim about the occurrence of heart disease from its deficiency and cure from high dosage is not yet substantiated.
Vitamin K	Use of anticoagulant chemicals in treating gangrene, claudication, and other related disorders of a heart patient can induce vitamin K deficiency, causing potential bleeding problems, especially in vulnerable locations in the body.	Vitamin B_6	A current proposal is that "maternal deficiency results in imperfect crosslinking of arterial elastin as well as collagen, which may result in deposition of atherosclerotic plaques."* This claim has not yet been substantiated.

*C. I. Levene and J. C. Murray, The Aetiological Side of Maternal Vitamin-B_6 Deficiency in the Development of Atherosclerosis, *Lancet*, 19 March 1977, p. 628.

TABLE 27-36   Amount of Sodium in Sodium-Controlled Diets

Diet	Approximate Sodium Content		Approximate Equivalent of Table Salt (mg NaCl)	Common Descriptive Term
	mg	mEq		
1	250	11	625	Very low or rigid restriction sodium diet
2	500	22	1,250	Strict sodium restriction, severe sodium restriction, or low-sodium diet
3	1,000	43	2,500	Moderate sodium restriction diet
4	2,000	87	5,000	Mild restriction or mild sodium-regulated diet
5	$\geq$2,000	$\geq$87	$\geq$5,000	Regulated diet without addition of table salt

TABLE 27-37   Approximate Nutrient Composition of a 1,400- to 1,500-kcal Diet at Different Sodium Levels

Diet	Sodium (mg)	Carbohydrate (g)	Fat (g)	Protein (g)
1	250	160	60	65
2	500	160	60	65
3	1,000	160	60	65
4	2,000	160	60	65

TABLE 27-38   Approximate Nutrient Composition of a 2,000- to 2,100-kcal Diet at Different Sodium Levels

Diet	Sodium (mg)	Carbohydrate (g)	Fat (g)	Protein (g)
1	250	270	70	75
2	500	270	70	85
3	1,000	270	70	85
4	2,000	270	70	85

TABLE 27-39   Approximate Nutrient Composition of a 2,400- to 2,500-kcal Diet at Different Sodium Levels

Diet	Sodium (mg)	Carbohydrate (g)	Fat (g)	Protein (g)
1	250	290	95	90
2	500	305	90	95
3	1,000	275	95	110
4	2,000	290	95	105

to 27-61 provide sample daily menu plans for the different diets.

Using a sodium-restricted diet in treating cardiovascular disease is a common practice, but such diets must be employed with caution. When sodium intake is restricted for a prolonged period, especially if drastically reduced, the kidney glomerular filtration rate (see Chapter 28) decreases as the body attempts to conserve sodium. This decreased excretory capacity may cause the retention of urea, creatinine, and other nitrogenous wastes in the blood, all of which are harmful to the patient if the levels exceed certain limits. This adjustment by the kidneys becomes more complicated and hazardous for patients with severe kidney failure. Such patients suffer from a low-sodium syndrome.

Symptoms of sodium deficiency include vomiting, loss of appetite, lassitude, weakness, abdominal cramps, muscle aches, and mental confusion. Thus, when sodium intake must be markedly reduced, as in congestive heart failure, the diet therapy is designed mainly for a hospitalized patient, since careful monitoring is needed to prevent or control the low-sodium syndrome. The health team makes sure that the

TABLE 27-40 Approximate Nutrient Contents of the Sodium Food Exchange Lists

| Sodium Food Exchange List | Food Type | Food Group | Caloric or Nutrient Level in One Exchange | | | | |
			Sodium (mg)	kcal	Carbo-hydrate (g)	Fat (g)	Protein (g)
I	Milk	I-1	7	170	12	10	8
		I-2	120	170	12	10	8
II	Vegetables	II-1	9	0	0	0	0
		II-2	9	35	7	0	2
III	Fruits	III	2	40	10	0	0
IV	Bread, equivalents	IV-1	5	70	15	0	2
		IV-2	5	70	15	0	2
		IV-3	100–300	70	15	0	2
V	Meat, equivalents	V	25	75	0	5	7
VI	Fat	VI	0	45	0	5	0
VII	Alternates	VII*					

Adapted from (1) *Sodium Restricted Diet: 1000 Milligrams*, 1970; (2) *Your 500 Milligram Sodium Diet*, undated; (3) *Your Mild Sodium-Restricted Diet*, undated. American Heart Association. By permission of the American Heart Association, Inc.
*Nutrient contents vary.

patient adapts well to the severely restricted salt intake and monitors for any signs of sodium deficiency.

Intense patient education is needed for a patient implementing a salt-free or salt-restricted diet for a prolonged period at home. This education should include knowledge of common high-sodium foods, food preparation techniques, and miscellaneous sources of sodium. The health team should also encourage the use of dietetic products and adherence to suggestions for food preparation. Finally, the patient should also have access to accurate information on sodium restriction after he or she has left the hospital.

When a patient is put on a limited-sodium-intake diet, the common high-sodium foods listed below should be avoided.

Processed meat, fish, chicken, poultry (smoked, cured, salted, pickled)
sausage, frankfurters, salt pork, anchovies, bacon, ham, beef hash, corned beef, tongue, chipped beef

Fruits and vegetables
sauerkraut, frozen lima beans and peas, regular canned figs, applesauce, pears, regular canned vegetables (dietetic forms with no salt added are acceptable)

Grain products
baking powder, baking soda, self-rising or commercial flour, flour mixes, other bread and bakery products (acceptable if prepared without salt)

Spices and condiments
olives; catsup; Worcestershire sauce; relishes; pickles; chili pepper; celery, garlic, or onion salt; parsley and celery flakes

Gravies and sauces
meat sauces, meat gravies, meat extracts; bouillon cubes

Snack foods
popcorn, corn chips, potato chips, nuts, beef jerky, cheese balls

Miscellaneous
commercial peanut butter, cheese, butter (acceptable if prepared without salt)

TABLE 27-41   Sodium Food Exchange List I-1: Milk

Food	One Exchange	Adjustment
Low-sodium, fluid, fresh, whole milk	1 c	None
Low-sodium, reconstituted dry milk	1 c	None
Powdered low-sodium dry milk	4 T	None
Powdered low-sodium nonfat dry milk	3 T	Follow instruction on package to obtain 1 exchange. If used, must add 2 fat exchanges from List IV-1.
Reconstituted low-sodium nonfat dry milk	1 c	If used, must add 2 fat exchanges from List IV-1.
Low-sodium cocoa (low-sodium milk and cocoa powder)	⅔ c	

Foods to be avoided
1. All milk and milk products not specifically indicated.
2. All commercial milk and milk products: ice cream, sherbet, milk shakes, chocolate milk, malted milk, milk mixes, condensed milk, breakfast milk drinks, instant milk products, and others.

Note: Each exchange contains 7 mg of sodium, 170 kcal, 12 g of carbohydrate, 10 g of fat, and 8 g of protein.

Adapted from *Your 500 Milligram Sodium Diet*, undated, American Heart Association. By permission of the American Heart Association, Inc.

Although most foods contain sodium, the major source is usually the salt used in food serving, preparation, processing, and preservation. The list below indicates chemicals often added to prepared foods that should be avoided.

Baking soda and powder (leavening agents)
    sodium bicarbonate, sodium aluminum sulfate
Preservatives
    sodium propionate, sodium sulfite, sodium benzoate
Texturizers
    sodium alginate
Agents regulating pH
    disodium phosphate

Food flavors
    monosodium glutamate

Dietetic products may need to be used, since most common foods contain sodium. Patients on a markedly restricted sodium diet do not have many food choices. However, for more than two decades, the food industry has made available a wide variety of unsalted products, including cheddar and cottage cheese, butter, margarine, milk, bakery items (breads, crackers, cakes, and cookies), canned vegetables and meats, and baking powder. Not all grocery stores carry these products.

In the past, confusion has arisen concerning the terms *low salt* and *salt free*. Either term may

TABLE 27-42   Sodium Food Exchange List I-2: Milk

Food	One Exchange	Adjustment
Buttermilk, uncultured and unsalted, from whole milk	1 c	None
Buttermilk, regular, commercially cultured, from nonfat milk	½ c	If used, add 3 fat exchanges from List VI.
Chocolate milk	⅔ c	
Cocoa (powder and regular fluid milk)	⅔ c	
Ice cream	⅔ c	
Whole milk	1 c	
Whole milk dry powder	3 T	Follow instruction on package to obtain 1 exchange.
Nonfat dry milk powder	3 T	Follow instruction on package to obtain 1 exchange. If used, add 2 fat exchanges from List VI.
Reconstituted nonfat dry milk	1 c	If used, add 2 fat exchanges from List VI.
Skim milk	1 c	If used, add 2 fat exchanges from List VI.
Yogurt	1 c	

Note: Each exchange contains 120 mg of sodium, 170 kcal, 12 g of carbohydrate, 10 g of fat, and 8 g of protein.

Adapted from *Your 500 Milligram Sodium Diet*, undated, American Heart Association. By permission of the American Heart Association, Inc.

mean that the product contains less than 1 g of sodium per serving. The patient should learn to read the labels carefully or obtain information from the producers. It is important to remember that the procedures used to remove sodium from a product probably extracted other essential nutrients as well.

Two dietetic products that are of major importance are low-sodium milk and salt substitutes. Low-sodium milk has been available for more than 15 years. Although it was not well accepted in the past because of its alien flavor, recently improved products are more palatable. It comes in liquid and powdered forms and is

TABLE 27-43 Sodium Food Exchange List II-1: Vegetables

Food*				One Exchange
Asparagus	Cauliflower	Mushrooms	Tomatoes	½ c
Beans, green	Chicory	Okra	Turnip greens	
Beans, wax	Cucumber	Peppers, green	Watercress	
Broccoli	Eggplant	and red		
Brussels	Endive	Radishes		
sprouts	Escarole	Squash, summer		
Cabbage	Lettuce	Tomato juice,		
		canned, unsalted		
Carrots, raw				2–3 strips
Mustard greens				⅓ c
Parsley				⅓ c
Water chestnuts, raw				2–3 corms

Foods to be avoided

1. Artichokes, beet greens, celery, chard, dandelion greens, hominy, kale, sauerkraut, spinach, and white turnips.
2. Canned vegetables or vegetable juices except low-sodium dietetic products.
3. Frozen vegetables processed with salt (e.g., lima beans, frozen peas, and succotash) or with salt added during preparation.

Note: Each exchange contains 9 mg of sodium, few calories, and traces of carbohydrate, fat, and protein.

*All fresh or frozen products with no salt added or dietetic or low-sodium products.

Adapted from *Your 500 Milligram Sodium Diet*, undated, American Heart Association. By permission of the American Heart Association, Inc.

TABLE 27-44 Sodium Food Exchange List II-2: Vegetables

Food	One Exchange
Onions	½ c
Peas (fresh or low-sodium dietetic canned only)	
Pumpkin	
Rutabaga (yellow turnip)	
Squash, winter (acorn, Hubbard, etc.)	

Foods to be avoided

Same as for Sodium Food Exchange List II-1.

Note: Each exchange contains 9 mg of sodium, 35 kcal, 2 g of protein, no fat, and 7 g of carbohydrate. Two exchanges from List II-1 equals 1 exchange from List II-2.

Adapted from *Your 500 Milligram Sodium Diet*, undated, American Heart Association. By permission of the American Heart Association, Inc.

TABLE 27-45 Sodium Food Exchange List III: Fruits

Food	One Exchange
Apple, small	1
Apple juice or cider	⅓ c
Applesauce	½ c
Apricot nectar	¼ c
Apricots, dried, halves	4
Apricots, fresh, medium	2
Banana, small	½
Blackberries	1 c
Blueberries	⅔ c
Cantaloupe	¼ c
Cherries, large	10
Cranberries (sweetened)	1 T
Cranberries (unsweetened)	No limit
Cranberry juice (sweetened)	⅓ c
Cranberry juice (unsweetened)	No limit
Dates	2
Fig, medium	1
Fruit cup or mixed fruits	½ c
Grapefruit, small	½
Grapefruit juice	½ c
Grape Juice	¼ c
Grapes	12
Honeydew melon, medium	⅛
Lemons	No limit
Limes	No limit
Mango, small	½
Orange, small	1
Orange juice	½ c
Papaya, medium	⅓
Peach, medium	1
Pear, small	1
Pineapple, small, slices	2
diced	½ c
Pineapple juice	⅓ c
Plums, medium	2
Prunes, medium	2
Prune juice	¼ c
Raisins	2 T
Raspberries	1 c
Rhubarb (sweetened)	2 T
Rhubarb (unsweetened)	No limit
Strawberries	1 c
Tangerine, large	1
Tangerine juice	½ c
Watermelon	1 c

Foods to be avoided

1. Dried fruits and all commercial products containing sodium salts or preservatives.
2. Crystallized or glazed fruit.

Note: Each exchange contains 2 mg of sodium, 40 kcal, no protein, no fat, and 10 g of carbohydrate. If sweetened fruit or fruit canned or frozen in sugar syrup is used, the caloric content may have to be adjusted.

Adapted from *Your 500 Milligram Sodium Diet*, undated, American Heart Association. By permission of the American Heart Association, Inc.

TABLE 27-46 Sodium Food Exchange List IV-1: Bread and Equivalents

Food	One Exchange
Bread	
White bread, sl	1
Biscuit, medium	1
Bun, hamburger	1
Corn bread, 1½-in. cube	1
Crackers, 2-in. square	5
Griddle cakes, 3 in. diam.	2
Matzo, 5-in. square	1
Muffin, medium	1
Roll, plain yeast, medium	1
Waffle, 3-in. square	1
Cereals, cooked, noninstant	
Oatmeal, rolled oats, wheat meal, farina, corn, grits, Cream of Wheat, toasted wheat germ, dried cornmeal	½ c
Cereals, dry, ready-to-eat	
Enriched Puffed Rice, Puffed Wheat, shredded wheat, Sugar Smacks, other brands (check labels)	½ c
Noodles, flours, and others	
Barley, cooked	½ c
Flour	2½ T
Macaroni, noodles, spaghetti, cooked	½ c
Popcorn	1½ c
Rice, white or brown, cooked	½ c
Tapioca, uncooked	2 T

Foods to be avoided

1. Baking powder, baking soda, and commercial mixes.
2. All instant or quick-cooking cereals and enriched products.
3. Self-rising cornmeal or flour.
4. Any dry cereals not listed.
5. Commercial graham crackers or any other crackers except low-sodium dietetic products.
6. Salted popcorn, potato chips, other chips, pretzels, other salty snack items, and salt sticks.

Note: Each exchange contains 5 mg of sodium, 70 kcal, 15 g of carbohydrate, no fat, and 2 g of protein. All items are made without salt. Where necessary sodium-free baking powder or potassium bicarbonate and low-sodium dietetic mixes are used.

Adapted from *Your 500 Milligram Sodium Diet*, undated, American Heart Association. By permission of the American Heart Association, Inc.

TABLE 27-47   Sodium Food Exchange List IV-2: Bread and Equivalents

Food (starchy vegetables)	One Exchange
Beans, baked	¼ c
Beans, cooked, navy or lima, dried or fresh	½ c
Corn	⅓ c
Lentils, cooked, dried	½ c
Parsnips	⅔ c
Peas, cooked, split, fresh or dried, green or yellow	½ c
Potato, sweet, small	½
Potato, white, mashed	½ c
Potato, white, whole, small	1

Foods to be avoided

Same as those for List IV-1.

Note: Each exchange contains 5 mg of sodium, 70 kcal, 15 g of carbohydrate, no fat, and 2 g of protein. All items are prepared without salt.

Adapted from *Your 500 Milligram Sodium Diet*, undated, American Heart Association. By permission of the American Heart Association, Inc.

TABLE 27-48   Sodium Food Exchange List IV-3: Bread and Equivalents

Food*	One Exchange	Sodium (mg)
Biscuit, medium	1	255
Bread, white, sl	1	140
Bun, hamburger	1	210
Corn bread, 1½-in. cube	1	230
Crackers, 2-in. square	5	100
Griddle cakes, 3 in. diam.	2	300
Muffin, medium	1	180
Roll, plain yeast, medium	1	140
Waffle, 3-in. square	1	180

Note: Each exchange contains 100 to 300 mg of sodium, 70 kcal, 15 g of carbohydrate, no fat, and 2 g of protein.

*Prepared with salt.

Adapted from *Your 500 Milligram Sodium Diet*, undated, American Heart Association. By permission of the American Heart Association, Inc.

TABLE 27-49   Sodium Food Exchange List V: Meat and Equivalents

Food	One Exchange
Meat, poultry, fowl*	
Beef, veal, pork, lamb; chicken, turkey, duck; quail, rabbit; tongue, chicken or pork liver; beef or calf liver† (all cooked)	1 oz
Seafood*	
Bass, bluefish, catfish, cod, eels, flounder, halibut, rockfish, salmon, sole, trout, tuna (low-sodium, dietetic pack) (all cooked)	1 oz
Cheese, egg, peanut butter	
Cheese, low sodium, dietetic	1 oz
Cottage cheese, unsalted	¼ c
Egg	1
Peanut butter, low sodium, dietetic	2 T

Foods to be avoided

1. Brain, kidney.
2. All processed meat products, e.g., luncheon meat, sausages, and ham.
3. All commercially processed seafood products unless dietetic.
4. Frozen seafoods containing salt, e.g., Icelandic.
5. All shellfish such as oysters, scallops, shrimp, crab, and clams.
6. Regular peanut butter.

Note: Each exchange contains 25 mg of sodium, 75 kcal, no carbohydrate, 5 g of fat, and 7 g of protein.

*Fresh unsalted, frozen unsalted, or dietetic products.

†1 to 2 exchanges allowed in 2 weeks.

Adapted from *Your 500 Milligram Sodium Diet*, undated, American Heart Association. By permission of the American Heart Association, Inc.

available from most regional dairies. This product can be substituted for regular milk in beverages and in preparing all dishes requiring milk, such as casseroles, creams, custards, and so on. A flavoring may be used to improve the taste of low-sodium milk, such as strawberry, cinnamon, sugar, chocolate, or vanilla.

Most salt substitutes contain potassium chloride and a trace of sodium chloride. Examples are Co-salt, Adolph's salt substitute, and Morton's salt substitute. A very small percentage of the salt substitutes marketed contain calcium or aluminum chloride with a trace of sodium. Salt substitutes should be used only when prescribed by the physician. In general, potassium chloride is not very acceptable to most patients. When used in cooking, it imparts a strange flavor to the whole meal. Dietitians and nurses suggest using the chemical separately on small portions of food. The high potassium level in these substances have produced documented cases of hyperkalemia. Also, patients with renal insufficiency should be monitored when using this type of product. Refer to Chapter 28 for more information on the use of salt substitutes.

Furthermore, patients on a low-salt diet should be informed that garlic, celery, and onion salts are not salt substitutes. They are vegetable flakes with salt added and contain varying amounts of sodium. They should not be used at all. Morton's Lite salt, a "low-sodium" salt, is not a salt substitute since it contains a substantial amount of sodium and potassium. Patients on sodium-restricted diets should avoid these products completely.

Miscellaneous sources of sodium include drinking water, prescription and over-the-counter drugs, oral hygienic aids, and dishwashing agents. Most diet therapy manuals contain cautionary statements regarding these sources of sodium.

The exact sodium level in tap water must be ascertained by either inquiry to the local health department or direct chemical analysis. The sodium content of drinking water varies widely from source to source. It even varies at the same source, changing with the time of year and the origins of the water. Hence, it should be checked frequently. Deionized, distilled, or demineralized water can be used to assure a low amount of sodium.

Since dishwashing agents contain a high level of sodium, dishes and utensils must be thoroughly cleaned and rinsed with water. Many drugs contain sodium, such as sodium phenobarbital (sedative), chloromycelin sodium succinate (antibiotic), sodium salicylate (analgesic), Dilantin (antiepileptic), Alka Seltzer, and Dristan cough formula. Certain brands of toothpaste

TABLE 27-50 Sodium Food Exchange List VI-1: Fat

Food	One Exchange
Butter or margarine	1 t
Cream, heavy, sweet or sour*	1 T
Cream, light, sweet or sour*	2 T
Fat or oil, all purposes	1 t
Mayonnaise	1 t
Salad dressing	1 T
Others	
Avocado, 4 in. diam.	⅛
Nuts, small	6

Foods to be avoided
1. Bacon and bacon fat.
2. Olives.
3. Salt pork.
4. Commercial French dressing.

Note: Each exchange contains no sodium, 45 kcal, 5 g of fat, and no protein. All items are unsalted or dietetic products.

*Limited to 2 T/d.

Adapted from *Your 500 Milligram Sodium Diet*, undated, American Heart Association. By permission of the American Heart Association, Inc.

TABLE 27-51 Sodium Food Exchange List VI-2: Fat

Food	One Exchange
Butter, salted	1 t
Margarine, salted	1 t
Mayonnaise	1 t

Note: Each exchange contains 50 mg of sodium, 45 kcal, 5 g of fat, and no protein.

and mouthwash also contain large amounts of sodium.

A helpful food preparation suggestion is to use low-sodium leavening agents and avoid regular salt when making starchy foods such as bread and other bakery products. Only the prescribed

TABLE 27-52   Sodium Food Exchange List VII: Alternates

Food Type	Foods Permitted*	Foods Prohibited
Sugars, sweets	Low-sodium dietetic or homemade candies without salt, including hard candy, gumdrops, mints, and marshmallows; maple syrup and sugar (brown, granulated, and confectioner's)	All commercial products with salt or sodium compounds and/or butter added; molasses, corn syrup
Beverages	Coffee (instant, regular, substitute, or decaffeinated), tea, and Postum; selected carbonated beverages;† content of alcoholic beverages permitted by physician should be counted	Most commercial instant and quick drink mixes, e.g., fruit-flavored powders; fountain beverages and various brands of carbonated soft drinks
Desserts	Plain or flavored gelatin with permitted juices; pies or tapioca (pudding) made with permitted fruit and other ingredients; ices and Popsicles flavored with permitted juices and fruits; rennet dessert powder	Commercial gelatin made with sodium and other prohibited ingredients; commercial products made with salt; rennet dessert tablets
Miscellaneous	Any low-sodium dietetic products, e.g., soups, puddings; leavening agents: cream of tartar, potassium bicarbonate, sodium-free baking powder; cornmeal, tapioca, cornstarch, most spices (see text)	All forms of commercial soups (dehydrated, canned, or frozen) prepared with salt or sodium compounds

*These food items do not take into consideration the carbohydrate (quantity and quality) and caloric intake of the patient. They must be adjusted if the patient is on a weight-controlled or hyperlipoproteinemia-modified diet.

†Some beverages may be permitted depending on the degree of sodium restriction and the actual sodium content of the beverage.

Adapted from *Your 500 Milligram Sodium Diet*, undated, American Heart Association. By permission of the American Heart Association, Inc.

amount of high-protein foods, such as red meat, poultry, seafood, cheese, and eggs, should be used, since all are high in sodium. Avoid added salt. Vegetables may be low or high in sodium. The two types should be posted separately in the kitchen as a reminder, and of course no salt should be used in preparation. Fruits are low in sodium, fat, and calories, and the patient should be encouraged to eat them.

The omission of table salt from the diet will automatically remove a major source of iodine from the diets of many patients. The patient's

TABLE 27-53   Spices, Condiments, Gravies, and Sauces Permitted and Prohibited in a Sodium-Regulated Diet

Products Permitted		Products Prohibited
Allspice	Horseradish, prepared without salt	Broth, bouillon
Almond extract		Celery: seed, salt, dried or fresh leaves unless specifically indicated
Anise seed	Juniper	
Basil	Lemon juice or extract	Horseradish prepared with salt
Bay leaf		Meat: extracts, sauces, tenderizers
Caraway seed	Mace	MSG or sodium salt of other flavoring aids
Cardamom	Maple extract	Mustard, prepared
Carrots or celery (use sparingly)	Marjoram	Olives
	Meat extract, low-sodium dietetic	Pickles
Catsup, low-sodium dietetic		Relishes
	Meat tenderizers, low-sodium dietetic	Sugar substitute, sodium salt
Chili powder		Salt: regular, chili, garlic, onion
Chives	Mint	Sauces: barbecue, soy, Worcestershire
Cinnamon	Mustard, dry or seed	Wine: cooking, unless specifically indicated
Cloves	Nutmeg	
Cocoa (1–2 t)	Onion: fresh, juice, powder	
Coconut		
Cumin	Orange extract	
Curry	Oregano	
Dill	Paprika	
Fennel	Parsley: fresh or flakes	
Garlic: fresh, juice, powder	Pepper, fresh, green, or red	
Ginger	Pepper, black, red, or white	

(Additional Products Permitted, continued)

Peppermint extract
Pimiento peppers for garnish
Poppy seed
Poultry seasoning
Purslane
Rosemary
Saffron
Sage
Salt substitutes (if permitted by doctor)
Savory
Sesame seeds
Sorrel
Tarragon
Thyme
Turmeric
Vanilla extract
Vinegar
Walnut extract
Wine (use sparingly; more allowed if permitted by doctor)

Adapted from *Your 500 Milligram Sodium Diet*, undated, American Heart Association. By permission of the American Heart Association, Inc.

iodine need may have to be calculated and, if necessary, supplemented.

Patient compliance decreases as the amount of salt permitted falls below 1,000 mg. To improve palatability, a meal must be attractive and tasty. The use of spices and condiments should be emphasized to stimulate the patient's palate. Refer to Table 27-53 for a listing of spices permitted.

Patient education involves providing adequate information about the necessity of removing salt from the diet and the importance of complying with such a diet prescription. A salt-restricted patient should be taught progressively decreasing salt diets, exchange groups, procedures to plan menus, and the use of appropriate food items. Although some patients feel that foods without salt are not very tasty, they can be taught to make their meals more tolerable.

Learning gourmet cooking and how to use nonsalt seasonings liberally are valuable. As an example, a small amount of lemon and wine can dramatically enhance the flavor of food. Refer to Chapter 28 for more information on the use of spices in food. Also, many cookbooks contain low-sodium recipes. Local cooking classes may also be available. Many patients can be taught how to use food composition tables in addition to the exchange lists. This will open a whole new world of food choices. In addition, many items not on the exchange lists but low in sodium can be used creatively.

TABLE 27-54   Distribution of Food Exchanges in a 1,400- to 1,500-kcal Diet at Different Sodium Levels

Sodium Food Exchange List	Food Type	Food Group	No. of Exchanges			
			250 mg sodium	500 mg sodium	1,000 mg sodium	2,000 mg sodium
I	Milk	I-1	2	—	—	—
		I-2	—	2	2	2
II	Vegetables	II-1	2	2	2	2
		II-2	2	2	2	2
III	Fruits	III	3	3	3	3
IV	Bread	IV-1* or IV-2*	6	6	3	—
		IV-3	—	—	3	6
V	Meat, equivalents	V	4	4	4	4
VI	Fat	VI-1	3	3	3	—
		VI-2	—	—	—	4
VII	Alternates	VII	—	—	—	1–2

*Permitted number of exchanges may be selected from one or both groups.

TABLE 27-55   Distribution of Food Exchanges in a 2,000- to 2,100-kcal Diet at Different Sodium Levels

Sodium Food Exchange List	Food Type	Food Group	No. of Exchanges			
			250 mg sodium	500 mg sodium	1,000 mg sodium	2,000 mg sodium
I	Milk	I-1	2	—	—	—
		I-2	—	2	2	2
II	Vegetables	II-1	2	2	2	2
		II-2	2	2	2	2
III	Fruits	III	3–5	3–5	3–5	3–5
IV	Bread	IV-1* or IV-2*	6	6	3	2
		IV-3	—	—	3	4
V	Meat, equivalents	V	5	6	6	6
VI	Fat	VI-1	3–6	3–6	3–6	—
		VI-2	—	—	—	3
VII	Alternates	VII	—	—	—	1–3

*Permitted number of exchanges may be selected from one or both groups.

TABLE 27-56 Distribution of Food Exchanges in a 2,400- to 2,500-kcal Diet at Different Sodium Levels

Sodium Food Exchange List	Food Type	Food Group	No. of Exchanges			
			250 mg sodium	500 mg sodium	1,000 mg sodium	2,000 mg sodium
I	Milk	I-1	2	—	—	—
		I-2	—	2	2	2
II	Vegetables	II-1	2	2	2	2
		II-2	2	2	2	2
III	Fruits	III	3–5	3–5	3–5	3–5
IV	Bread	IV-1* or IV-2*	6	6	3	2
		IV-3	—	—	3	4
V	Meat, equivalents	V	5	6	6	6
VI	Fat	VI-1	3–6	3–6	3–6	—
		VI-2	—	—	—	3
VII	Alternates	VII	—	—	—	1–3

*Permitted number of exchanges may be selected from one or both groups.

TABLE 27-57 Sample Menu for a 250-mg-Sodium, 1,500–1,600-kcal Diet

Breakfast	Lunch	Dinner
Milk, low sodium, ½ c	Milk, low sodium, ½ c	Milk, low sodium, 1 c
Strawberries, sliced, ½ c	Brussels sprouts, ½ c	Carrot, raw, strips, 2–3
Waffles, made without salt, 3-in. square, 2	Squash, winter, ½ c	Peas, fresh, ½ c
Margarine, unsalted, 1 t	Apple, fresh, 1	Peach, canned, slices, ½ c
	Bread, low sodium, 2 sl	Roll, yeast, plain, made without salt, 1
	Mayonnaise, made without salt, 1 T	Potato, baked, small, 1
	Lamb, unsalted, 2 oz	Sour cream, unsalted, chives, 1 T
		Sole, fillet, unsalted, 2 oz

Note: The patient should be encouraged to use alternate items (List VII) that have been approved by the dietitian.

TABLE 27-58   Sample Menu for a 1,000-mg-Sodium, 1,500-kcal Diet

Breakfast	Lunch	Dinner
Juice, pineapple, ⅓ c	Juice, tangerine, ½ c	Mustard greens, ⅓ c
Cereal, wheat meal, cooked, ½ c	Carrot, raw, strips, 2–3	Squash, winter, ½ c
Milk, skim, 1 c	Peas, fresh, cooked, ½ c	Potato, mashed, ½ c
Egg, soft cooked, 1	Barley, cooked, ½ c	Bread, white, 1 sl
Toast, white bread, 1 sl	Biscuit, medium, 1	Margarine, 1 t
Margarine, 2 t	Margarine, 2 t	Pork, roast, 2 oz
	Chicken, 1 oz	Apricots, fresh, 2
		Milk, whole, 1 c

Note: The patient should be encouraged to use alternate items (List VII) that have been approved by the dietitian.

TABLE 27-59   Sample Menu for a 500-mg-Sodium, 2,000-kcal Diet

Breakfast	Lunch	Dinner
Juice, orange, ½ c	Mushrooms, ½ c	Mustard greens, ⅓ c
Puffed Rice, ½ c	Peas, fresh, ½ c	Margarine, unsalted, 1 t
Banana, sliced, ½	Corn bread, prepared without salt, 3-in. square, 1	Onion, ½ c
Toast, low-sodium bread, 1 sl	Margarine, unsalted, 2 t	Muffin, prepared without salt, medium, 1
Margarine, unsalted, 1 t	Chicken, unsalted, barbecued, without barbecue sauce, 2 oz	Margarine, unsalted, 1 t
Egg, soft cooked, 1		Barley, cooked, unsalted, ½ c
Milk, 1 c		Pork, roast, 3 oz
		Ice cream, ⅔ c
		Blueberries, frozen, ½ c

Note: The patient should be encouraged to use unsalted fat and alternate items (List VII) in order to achieve the caloric level of 2,000 kcal if so approved by the dietitian.

PREVENTING CARDIOVASCULAR DISEASES

Although heart disease remains a major killer, the actual number of Americans suffering from this disorder has declined in the last few years. It is felt that the education of the public about the risk factors and willingness of people to change their life-styles have been somewhat successful. It is to every person's advantage to adopt a life-style that will minimize this health risk. As we are all aware, intending to practice preventive medicine is different from doing so.

At present, some scientists feel that infants and children should eat less saturated fats and cholesterol in order to avoid heart diseases during adulthood. However, because of the controversy and scientific uncertainty surrounding this topic, it will not be explored here. Some addi-

TABLE 27-60 Sample Menu for a 1,000-mg-Sodium, 2,000-kcal Diet

Breakfast	Lunch	Dinner
Juice, orange, ½ c	Juice, apple, ⅓ c	Peas and onions, fresh, cooked, 1 c
Cottage cheese, un-salted, ¼ c	Mushrooms, fresh, cooked, ½ c	Potato, white, baked, small, 1
Griddle cakes, 3 in. diam., 4	Water chestnut, raw, corms, 2–3	Sour cream, 1 T
Applesauce (for top-ping), ½ c	Bread, white, low so-dium, 2 sl	Roll, yeast, without salt, 1
Margarine, 1 t	Mayonnaise, 2 t	Margarine, 1 t
Milk, whole, 1 c	Lamb, cooked, 1 oz	Halibut, 3 oz
		Ice cream, ⅔ c
		Strawberries, sliced, 1 c

Note: The patient should be encouraged to use unsalted fat and alternate items (List VII) in order to achieve the caloric level of 2,000 kcal if so approved by the dietitian.

TABLE 27-61 Sample Menu for a 2,000-mg-Sodium, 2,000-kcal Diet

Breakfast	Lunch	Dinner
Juice, cranberry, ⅓ c	Juice, tomato, canned, unsalted, ½ c	Turnip greens, ½ c
Oatmeal, ½ c	Baked beans, ¼ c	Peas, fresh, ½ c
Banana, sliced, small, ½	Biscuit, medium, 1	Corn bread, 3-in. cube, 1
Sugar, brown, 1 t	Margarine, 1 t	Margarine, 1 t
Muffin, medium, 1	Beef, roast, 2 oz	Pork, roast, 3 oz
Margarine, 1 t	Apple, small, 1	Gelatin, ½ c, made with cider and containing:
Egg, poached, 1	Pumpkin, cooked, ½ c	Fruit cocktail, ½ c
Cocoa, hot, ⅔ c	Raisins, ¼ c	Milk, whole, 1 c

Note: The patient should be encouraged to use unsalted fat and alternate items (List VII) in order to achieve the caloric level of 2,000 kcal if so approved by the dietitian.

tional information is presented in Chapters 14 and 30.

An adult can do many things to establish a wholesome life-style. Every individual should have a regular medical checkup, achieve and maintain an ideal weight, eat a nutritious and balanced diet, avoid or control high blood pressure, minimize personal and environmental stresses, follow a regular exercise program, drink moderately, and if feasible, stop smoking. Although there is no one ideal diet for every person, a little knowledge about the basic food groups will go a long way (see Chapter 10). According to Congress, Americans should follow the Dietary Guidelines (see Chapter 19). Interested people may want to follow the fat-controlled or preventive diet discussed earlier.

CASE STUDY   *Congestive Heart Failure*

For the last few months, Mr. K.T. had not been feeling very good. He tired easily from simple tasks and routine activities such as walking, going up stairs, and carrying boxes. Any exertion resulted in shortness of breath. He also urinated frequently. Although K.T. had a history of high blood pressure, his personal physician had kept it under control with medications. However, K.T. had failed to comply with a moderate sodium-restricted diet (2 to 2.5 g) simultaneously recommended by the doctor.

Mr. K.T. was 55 years old and had already had two myocardial infarctions. He had also been hospitalized three times in the last 4 years for the treatment of congestive heart failure. Apparently this clinical problem had returned. One afternoon, while attending a wedding reception, he suddenly developed respiratory difficulties. Within a few seconds he was gasping for breath. He was carried to the hospital by an ambulance.

In the hospital the attending physicians identified the characteristic symptom of congestive heart failure—dyspnea, which was also confirmed by the patient's past medical history. The patient's liver was enlarged and he had dependent edema of both legs, coolness of the extremities, and cyanosis of the nail beds. Laboratory tests indicated normal red and white blood cell counts, hemoglobin, packed cell volume, and sedimentation rate. Serum sodium, potassium, carbon dioxide, and chloride were within normal limits. However, the patient had proteinuria and elevated urine specific gravity.

The patient's immediate respiratory urgency was corrected by oxygen therapy. He was given digitalis to increase the speed and force of cardiac contraction. At this point, K.T. was resting comfortably in the hospital. The health team's other major concern was to reduce his abnormal retention of sodium and water. To achieve this goal, the major approaches were controlling sodium and fluid intake and using an appropriate diuretic.

Because of the moderate to severe edema, the doctor prescribed furosemide (Lasix) and restricted the patient's daily sodium and fluid intakes to below 1,000 mg and 1,200 mL, respectively. After K.T. had spent 2 days in the hospital, the fluid restriction was lifted and he was continued on a 2,500-kcal, 1,000-mg-sodium diet. But he had a very poor appetite and complained of abdominal pain. For the next 2 days, he was listless and drowsy. His low blood potassium confirmed that he was in negative potassium balance because of the diuretic. The doctor therefore ordered oral doses of potassium solution. On the fifth day of his hospitalization, he was feeling better and eating well. For the next 2 weeks, he gradually gained strength and the ability to perform different routine activities. During his hospital stay, he lost about 7 lb, most of which was water.

When K.T. was discharged, he was instructed to comply with a 2,000-mg-sodium diet at home. He was to continue taking his diuretic (Lasix) and oral doses of potassium chloride (K-Lyte) at specific intervals.

Review and Analysis

1. What is congestive heart failure?
2. Describe the characteristic symptoms of congestive heart failure.
3. Explain dependent edema.
4. What are the causes of cool extremities and nail bed cyanosis?
5. Describe the standard components of the medical management of a patient with congestive heart failure.
6. Describe the classic symptoms of potassium deficiency.
7. Plan a 2,500-kcal, 1,000-mg-sodium diet. Use as few dietetic foods as possible.

W.P. was a 63-year-old salesman, ready to retire in a couple of years. He was about 20 lb overweight and was smoking two packs of cigarettes daily. He had not had any serious illness in more than 15 years. He loved to eat, and his "heartland" upbringing had encouraged the consumption of many high-fat and carbohydrate-rich foods, such as beef, lamb, baked potatoes, gravies, rich pastries, and the like. W.P. had never experienced any cardiovascular complications, although his father and one aunt had died of heart diseases before they were 60.

In the last 2 years, his company had started an annual blood pressure checkup, providing free blood lipid analyses for male employees over 50 years old. W.P. was 5′10″ and weighed 200 lb. The checkup confirmed his blood pressure to be 120/80 and his serum cholesterol and triglycerides were both elevated.

To learn more about his conditions, W.P. visited his physician for his annual checkup with the data from his company. The doctor ordered another lipid determination for W.P. after an overnight fast. The patient did not exhibit any abnormal clinical signs during a complete examination. When W.P. called the doctor in a week, he was informed that his plasma cholesterol and triglycerides were 300 mg/100 mL and 360 mg/100 mL, respectively. The nurse also told W.P. that the doctor had requested urine and blood glucose tests to be taken in 3 days. However, W.P. showed an acceptable urinary glucose level and a normal glucose tolerance curve. Diabetes mellitus was ruled out.

The doctor informed W.P. that, with the exception of weight and blood lipid levels, he appeared to be healthy and normal. The doctor suggested that W.P. lose some weight, saying that if he could achieve and maintain ideal weight, the serum lipid problems might disappear. The doctor told W.P. that he would discuss his case with the local hospital dietitian and that W.P. should visit the dietitian for instructions. W.P. was instructed to return for another doctor visit in 2 months.

With the help of the nurse, the dietitian, family, and friends, W.P. followed a diet to lose weight. With great difficulty, W.P. slowly adjusted to a low-calorie diet. On his return visit, W.P. was pleased to learn that his laboratory tests had improved slightly. First, he had lost 5 lb and his serum cholesterol and triglycerides were 290 mg/100 mL and 350 mg/100 mL, respectively. The doctor believed that if W.P. continued to lose weight, his serum lipid profile should return to normal without other medical intervention. At the same time, the doctor told W.P. that stopping smoking and exercising would definitely improve his health.

Review and Analysis

1. If you were a nurse working in this doctor's office, what types of questions would you ask the patient if the doctor wanted you to find out about the body weight history of W.P.?

2. If you were the attending nurse and the patient asked you what the normal levels of serum cholesterol and triglycerides were, what range of figures would you give? If a patient insisted that he had learned different figures from a well-known newspaper, how would you answer him?

3. If you were the hospital dietitian, what would be your suggestions for an initial weight reduction diet?

4. Is it possible to classify this patient according to the type of hyperlipoproteinemia? If so, what type is this patient? If not, what other data do you need?

5. If we assume that this patient has hyperlipoproteinemia and is symptomatic, what would be the most likely clinical manifestations?

6. Do some research in the library and prepare a study exploring the relationship between alcoholic beverages and heart disease.

STUDY QUESTIONS

1. Describe the clinical events that lead to atherosclerosis and death. What complications can result from the atherosclerotic process?

2. Describe the initial treatment of an angina patient. Briefly discuss the subsequent nutritional and dietary management of an angina patient.

3. Discuss the nutritional problems that can arise in treating a postmyocardial-infarction patient. Why is it important to limit the intake of calories and fat? What is the controversy concerning drinking alcoholic beverages?

4. What correlations exist between differing levels of serum cholesterol and atherosclerosis? What is the current thinking on the relationship between ingested polyunsaturated fat and serum cholesterol level?

5. Define *lipoprotein*. What is the function of chylomicrons?

6. What are the five types of hyperlipoproteinemia? Describe their associated clinical symptoms, if any. Describe the dietary management for one type of hyperlipoproteinemia.

7. Why are HDLs considered to be beneficial? Name the conditions that favor a high blood level of HDLs.

8. What is hypertension? What accounts for complications stemming from hypertension? Differentiate between primary and secondary hypertension. What nutritional factors contribute to hypertension?

9. How should diet therapy for hypertension take into account the effect of drugs that may be used at the same time to control the condition? What is the major problem inherent in restricting the sodium intake of a hypertensive patient?

10. Name the symptoms of congestive heart failure. What is the dietary strategy in the management of congestive heart failure?

11. What preventive steps can be taken to minimize the risk of heart disease?

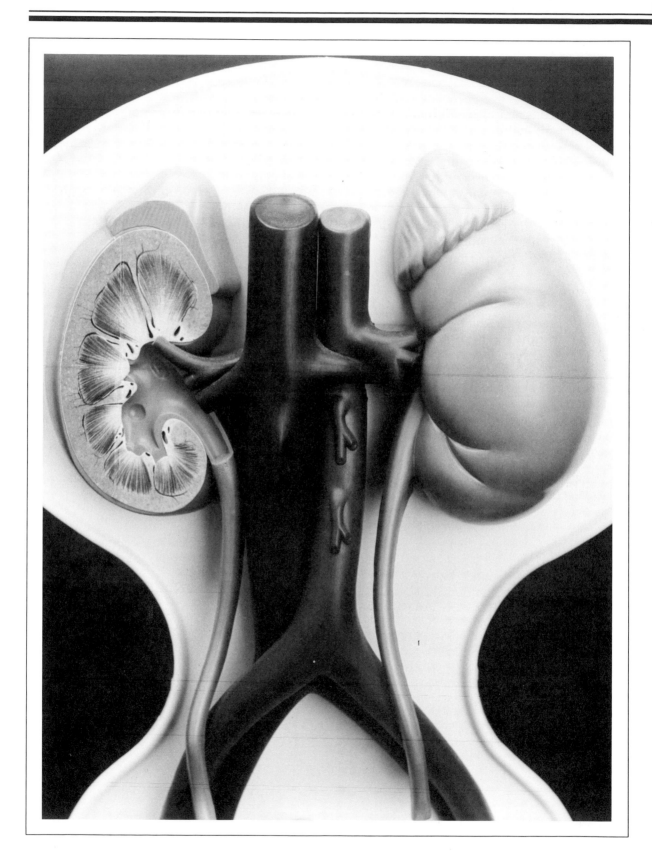

Chapter 28

Diet and Kidney Diseases

To SURVIVE, WE need at least one kidney. In patients with two diseased kidneys, a successful kidney transplant can permit a normal life. In the past, for patients with various kidney disorders, proper medical management could restore a normal life for some and permit minimal survival in others. With advances in clinical medicine, however, kidney dialysis and dietary management have improved the quality of life for many of these latter patients.

KIDNEY STRUCTURE, FUNCTIONS, AND DISORDERS

The human kidney is made up of basic structural units known as nephrons. Each kidney possesses between 1 and 1½ million nephrons. Figure 28-1 shows a longitudinal section of a kidney, and Figure 28-2 describes the different parts of a neph-

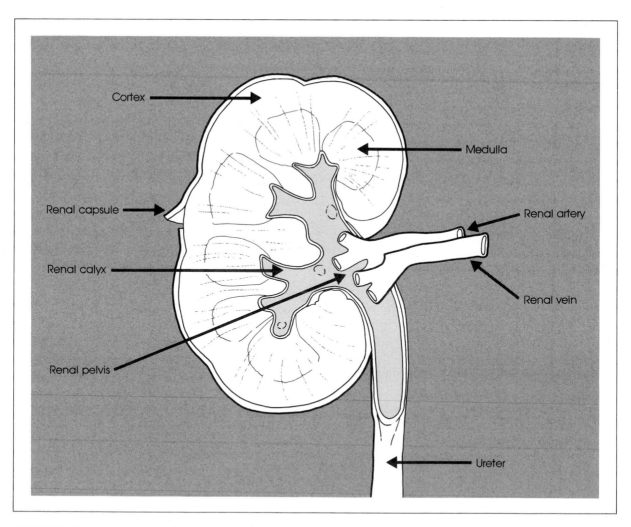

FIGURE 28-1   Section of a kidney.

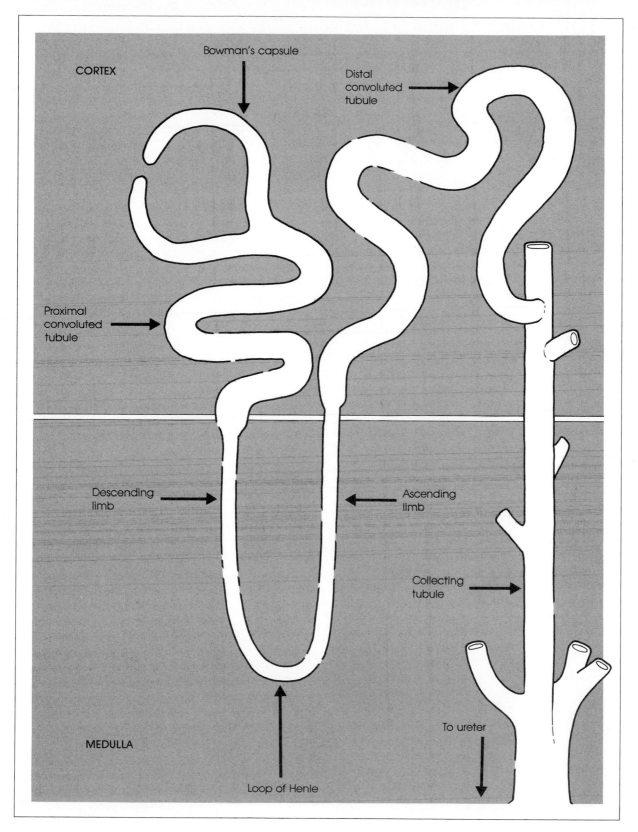

FIGURE 28-2   Parts of a nephron unit.

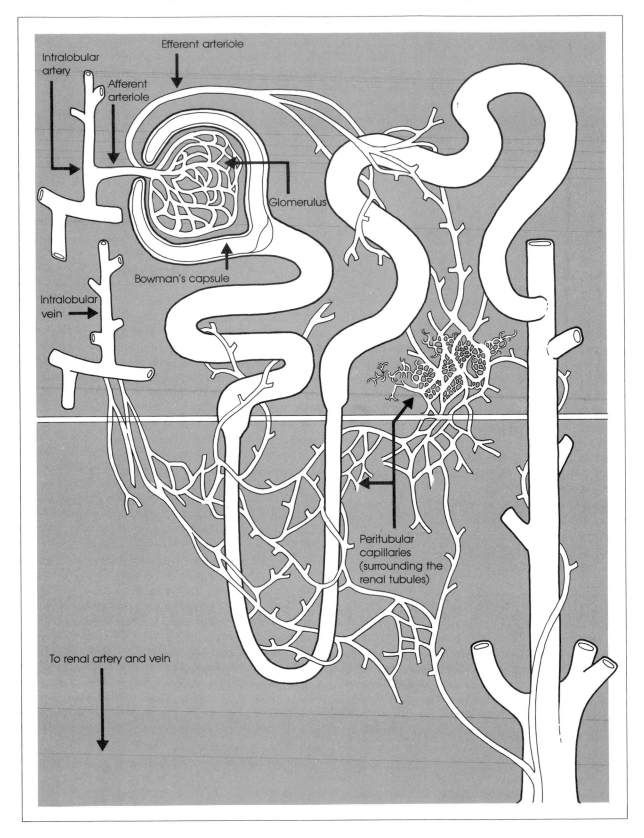

FIGURE 28-3   Blood circulation through a nephron unit.

ron. Figure 28-3 illustrates how each nephron is bathed in a "blood bed." Renal arterial blood enters the glomerulus via the afferent arteriole (see Figure 28-3). After passing through the efferent arteriole and the peritubular capillaries network, the blood moves through venules and into the intralobular veins. It finally moves through the renal veins, which leave the kidney.

Within the renal capsule (composed of the glomerulus and Bowman's capsule, see Figure 28-3), fluid is filtered from glomerular blood into Bowman's capsule. It then passes through the proximal convoluted tubule, Henle's loop, the distal convoluted tubule, and finally the collecting tubule (see Figure 28-2). Urine enters the bladder via the ureter and leaves a person at an average rate of 1,000 to 1,500 mL daily. Each part of the nephron is nourished with a blood supply that enables the tubules themselves to secrete and/or reabsorb certain substances, which can alter the final concentration of the excreted urine.

Normal kidney function is measured or diagnosed in three ways: excretory (clearance) capacity, blood analysis, and urine analysis. The kidney clearance, or glomerular filtration rate (GFR), refers to the number of milliliters of plasma completely filtered or cleared of a standard substance per minute. Blood analysis measures serum pH and levels of urea (blood urea nitrogen, or BUN, and serum urea nitrogen, or SUN) and creatinine (see Chapter 8). Urine analysis measures the pH of urine, its specific gravity, the content of casts (e.g., the amount of fat and protein and the number and types of cells), protein level, and the amount of blood. Table 28-1 summarizes the normal functions of the kidney in relation to body metabolism, waste disposal, fluid and electrolyte balance, blood pH, erythropoiesis, and vitamin D activation.

Some common terms used in describing kidney malfunctioning are *hematuria* (blood in the urine), *proteinuria* (protein in the urine), *pyuria* (pus in the urine), *albuminuria* (albumin in the urine), *oliguria* (little urine), *azotemia* (nitrogenous compounds in the blood, such as urea and creatinine), and *uremia* (presence of urinary constituents in the blood). Many of these conditions are dangerous to health. For example, abnormally high concentrations of urea or other ni-

TABLE 28-1 Major Kidney Functions

Body Substance or Process	Kidney Function
Metabolic nitrogenous waste: ammonia, urea, uric acid, creatinine	Excretion
Toxic substances ingested or formed from body metabolism	Excretion
Water	Excretion and reabsorption
Acidity	
Too acidic	Restoration of neutrality by secreting hydrogen ions
Too alkaline	Restoration of neutrality by excreting bicarbonate
Electrolytes and other substances: potassium, sodium, calcium, phosphorus, magnesium, chloride, oxalate	Excretion, secretion, and/or reabsorption
Inactive vitamin D	Conversion to active vitamin D for body metabolism; release into bloodstream and *not* excreted
Erythropoiesis	Manufacture of erythropoietin, which stimulates formation of red blood cells

trogenous wastes in the blood can poison a person.

The terms *high-biological-value* (HBV) and *low-biological-value* (LBV) *proteins* are used frequently in discussions on diet therapy for kidney diseases. Their meanings are discussed in detail in Chapter 4. Proteins of HBV are those with optimal levels of the amino acids essential for the human body. For example, those proteins found in meat, fish, poultry, cheese, and eggs are of HBV. Proteins of LBV are low or lacking in one or more of the essential amino acids. Such proteins are found in potatoes, rice, spaghetti, bread,

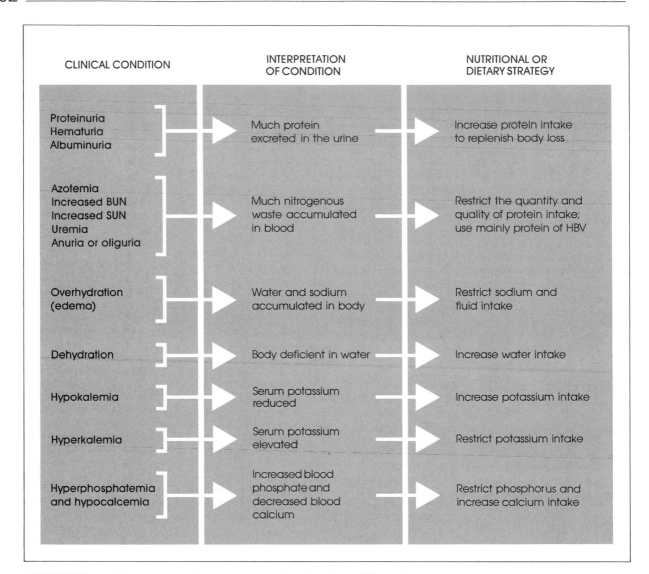

CLINICAL CONDITION	INTERPRETATION OF CONDITION	NUTRITIONAL OR DIETARY STRATEGY
Proteinuria Hematuria Albuminuria	Much protein excreted in the urine	Increase protein intake to replenish body loss
Azotemia Increased BUN Increased SUN Uremia Anuria or oliguria	Much nitrogenous waste accumulated in blood	Restrict the quantity and quality of protein intake; use mainly protein of HBV
Overhydration (edema)	Water and sodium accumulated in body	Restrict sodium and fluid intake
Dehydration	Body deficient in water	Increase water intake
Hypokalemia	Serum potassium reduced	Increase potassium intake
Hyperkalemia	Serum potassium elevated	Restrict potassium intake
Hyperphosphatemia and hypocalcemia	Increased blood phosphate and decreased blood calcium	Restrict phosphorus and increase calcium intake

FIGURE 28-4   Nutrition and dietary strategy for clinical conditions of the kidney.

and other vegetable products. For a kidney patient, soybeans, peas, and similar plant products are also considered as LBV. An LBV animal product is gelatin.

The nutritional and dietary care of kidney patients can sometimes be confusing, because they can develop reversed clinical conditions (conditions exactly opposite to those present immediately preceding prescribed dietary care), which require opposing dietary regimens. Figure 28-4 lists the different clinical conditions in kidney patients, each of which may be managed by a specific nutritional or dietary strategy. How-

ever, the information in Figure 28-4 is highly simplified and requires careful interpretation by a physician before it is implemented by a nurse or dietitian.

In discussing kidney diseases, it is helpful to classify the diseases by type. However, it is sometimes difficult to do so because some of the clinical manifestations are the same. This chapter considers four common categories of renal disorder. Their causes, symptoms, and overall dietary management are presented in Table 28-2. As indicated in the table, dietary treatment is often similar for acute nephritic syndrome and acute

TABLE 28-2   Causes, Symptoms, and Dietary Managements of Various Renal Disorders

Disorder	Causes and Symptoms	Dietary Management
Acute nephritic syndrome	An example of the syndrome is acute glomerulonephritis, caused by poststreptococcal infection of tonsils, pharynx, and skin. Most common in children and adolescents. Symptoms vary from mild to severe: fever, discomfort, headache, slight edema, decreased urine volume, mild hypertension, hematuria, proteinuria, and salt and water retention. Prognosis ranges from complete recovery to renal failure.	Controversial. Some clinicians prefer restriction of protein, fluid, and sodium intakes, while others do not. Diet therapy may be similar to the initial management of acute renal failure, e.g., 25 g of protein (70%–80% HBV) and 500 mg of sodium. Fluid permitted varies with the patient. See text.
Nephrotic syndrome	A group of symptoms resulting from certain kidney disorders (infection, chemical poisoning, etc.). Causes unknown in some patients. Symptoms: edema, proteinuria, and body wasting.	Restore fluid and electrolyte balance; reverse body wasting (malnutrition); correct hyperlipidemia if present. Details are given in text.
Acute renal failure	Abrupt renal malfunction because of infection, trauma, injury, chemical poisoning, pregnancy. Symptoms: nausea, lethargy, anorexia. Oliguria may be present at first, followed by diuresis. Azotemia may also be present.	Restore fluid and electrolyte balance, eliminate azotemia, implement nutritional rehabilitation. Dietary treatment similar to that for acute glomerulonephritis (one type of acute nephritic syndrome). Many patients need dialysis, especially if progressing to chronic renal failure.
Chronic renal failure	This results from a slow destruction of kidney tubules, which may be due to infection, hypertension, hereditary defect, drugs, etc. Symptoms develop as shown in Table 28-3. Nutritional complications are shown in Table 28-4.	Balance fluid and electrolytes, correct metabolic acidosis, minimize toxic effects of uremia, and implement nutritional rehabilitation. Details are in text.

renal failure. Following a discussion of the clinical importance and long-term implications of the nephritic syndrome and chronic renal failure, we will analyze the detailed nutritional and dietary plans prescribed for each of the four categories of renal disorder.

NEPHROTIC SYNDROME

As indicated in Table 28-2, the symptoms of nephrotic syndrome are edema, proteinuria, and body wasting. The dietary management of a nephrotic patient first involves controlling the edema. This condition can be reduced and controlled by severely restricting the sodium intake (for instance, to 250 mg). But most patients reject a diet plan containing less than 500 mg of sodium because the food lacks flavor. Thus some physicians implement a 1,000-mg-sodium diet and use a diuretic (such as spironolactone) to increase the diet's effectiveness. Detailed information on planning a low-sodium diet and the proper use of diuretics is presented later in this chapter and in Chapter 27. The nephrotic patient's wasted condition is corrected by a high-protein, high-calorie diet. The patient is fed 80 to 130 g of

TABLE 28-3   Four Stages of Chronic Renal Failure

Stage 1	Mild initial stage: hypertension, proteinuria, and hyperuricemia may be present; creatinine clearance is decreased.
Stage 2	Renal insufficiency stage: azotemia, inability to concentrate urine, nocturia, mild anemia, and creatinine clearance less than 50 mL/min for an adult.
Stage 3	Renal failure stage: creatinine clearance less than 10–15 mL/min; polyuria, hyperphosphatemia, and possibly hyperkalemia are present; calcium, chloride, and sodium blood levels are decreased; metabolic acidosis is present; hypertension may be present.
Stage 4	Terminal stage: uremias.

Characteristic symptoms

1. Classic triad: azotemia, acidosis, anemia.
2. Signs: tiredness, weakness, shortness of breath, waxy and pale complexion, abdominal pain, nausea, vomiting, diarrhea, oliguria.
3. Blood chemistry: mild to severe hyperkalemia; increased BUN, creatinine, phosphate, sulfate, chloride; decreased bicarbonate, pH (plasma).

Possible complications

1. Heart: pericardial effusion, pericarditis, and left heart failure accompanied by overt pulmonary edema.
2. Hypertension: frequently present; may produce convulsion, headache, and left heart failure.
3. Osteodystrophy: rickets and osteomalacia; may be disabling.
4. Neuropathy: incapacitated peripheral nervous system.
5. Encephalopathy: may produce convulsion.
6. Retinopathy: hemorrhage, exudate, and impairment of vision.
7. Bleeding: from mucous membranes.

protein (70% to 80% HBV) and 2,500 to 4,000 kcal per day, progressing from small to large amounts of food. Sodium may also be restricted; a typical such diet would provide 500 mg of sodium, 100 g of protein, and 3,000 kcal. Planning such a diet is discussed later in this chapter and in Chapters 23 and 27. The patient will also need vitamin and mineral supplements (except sodium), especially iron, calcium, and potassium, to relieve any existing malnourishment.

If the patient has any form of hyperlipidemia, the clinician may want to correct it by using methods discussed in Chapter 27. Some patients develop such gross edema that they are unable to eat enough or cannot eat at all. This also applies to those with mild edema but with severe anorexia and nausea. Such patients may have to be fed by tube or intravenously. A combination of enteral and parenteral feedings is not uncommon for such cases. Refer to Chapter 23 for more information on the different methods of feeding a hospitalized patient.

If a nephrotic patient develops hypertension, edema, and azotemia, the kidneys may fail. In this case, management will resemble that for treating acute or chronic renal failure. Although a low sodium intake will continue to combat edema, the high-protein prescription may have to be modified to avoid aggravating the accumulation of nitrogenous waste in the blood (azotemia).

CHRONIC RENAL FAILURE

Chronic renal failure results from a slow destruction of kidney tubules, which may be due to a variety of causes (see Table 28-2). Nutrient intakes of these patients are tightly controlled. When kidney function is impaired, it is important that nutrient amounts be adjusted to the capacity of the kidneys to filter them. However, too little of a nutrient may be as detrimental as too much for a patient with chronic renal failure. The information discussed below should be studied with Tables 28-2 to 28-4. Table 28-3 describes the four stages of chronic renal failure, and Table 28-4 outlines the nutritional complications arising during the terminal stage of chronic renal failure.

Electrolyte and Fluid Balance

The regulation of sodium intake in the patient is best illustrated in Table 28-5 and Figure 28-5. Control of water intake is illustrated in Figure 28-6. Patients are usually permitted about 1 to 3 g of sodium and 1.5 to 3.0 L of water a day, although individualized assessment and management are essential. If a patient is put on dialysis, water and sodium intake will be different (see later discussion).

An elevated level of potassium (hyperkalemia) in the serum of patients with chronic renal failure may be caused in a variety of ways (excessive intake, effects of certain medications, and so on). However, hyperkalemia is unlikely in patients passing more than 100 mL of urine a day. In general, patients should not consume more than 2.5 to 2.8 g of potassium daily. If they eat 40 or more grams of protein, they will get this amount of potassium. In spite of this assurance, hyperkalemia is a constant threat and is dangerous when it occurs. Dietary intake should be limited when the GFR of the patient is less than 5 mL/min and the patient's sodium intake is restricted. Some practitioners use a special oral cation-exchange resin with a purgative to lower blood potassium. More information on this topic is presented later in the chapter.

TABLE 28-4   Nutritional Complications during Terminal Stage of Chronic Renal Failure

1. Increased nitrogenous waste products in blood
2. Water retained and not excreted
3. Potassium, phosphorus, magnesium, and acid retained and not excreted
4. Failure to adjust to sodium intake by excretion or reabsorption
5. Decreased calcium absorption
6. Vitamin deficiencies
7. Cachexia: weight loss, loss of body fat and lean body mass, retarded growth in young patients, loss of plasma protein (especially albumin)

Protein Need

Since patients with chronic renal failure tend to accumulate nitrogen in the blood, their protein need must be very cautiously estimated. An excess intake will increase toxicity from nitrogenous wastes, while a deficiency aggravates tissue catabolism. Patients should be provided with a minimal but adequate amount of protein composed of 70% to 80% of HBV protein for maintenance and repair and a small amount of LBV protein to avoid the accumulation of urea. The two types of protein should be eaten together whenever feasible. It is now suspected that uremic patients in the terminal stage need one and one-half to two times the amount of essential amino acids required by a normal person.

When should protein intake be restricted during the course of chronic renal failure? The GFR is used as a guide, at least for the patient not on dialysis (Table 28-6). For example, a patient with GFR of 6 mL/min should be fed 40 g of protein. About 70% to 80% of this allotment should be of HBV, a level that most patients find palatable. Many patients on this level of protein intake show decreased tissue catabolism and BUN, resulting in a positive nitrogen balance. There is a concomitant reduction of uremic symptoms, such as intestinal problems, nausea, and vomiting. Patients feel better and have an improved appetite. If patients show gross proteinuria, such as 6 to 10 g/d, protein replacement

TABLE 28-5   Procedures in Monitoring Dietary Sodium Adequacy in Patients with Chronic Renal Failure and Not on Dialysis

Sodium and Water Intake	Kidney Malfunctioning	Clinical Consequences, Implications, and Symptoms	Simple Monitoring Techniques
Inadequate	Inability to conserve sodium	Salt depletion, reduction in renal blood flow; volume depletion; patient dehydration with or without overt signs; lethargy; decreased GFR*; increased uremic toxicities; patient deterioration	Observing decreased body weight and blood pressure and increased pulse rate; close monitoring of urinary output
Excessive	Inability to excrete sodium	Sodium retention, overhydration, edema (usually overt), hypertension, congestive heart failure; patient may die	Observing increased body weight and blood pressure and decreased pulse rate; close monitoring of urinary output

*GFR = glomerular filtration rate, see first part of this chapter.

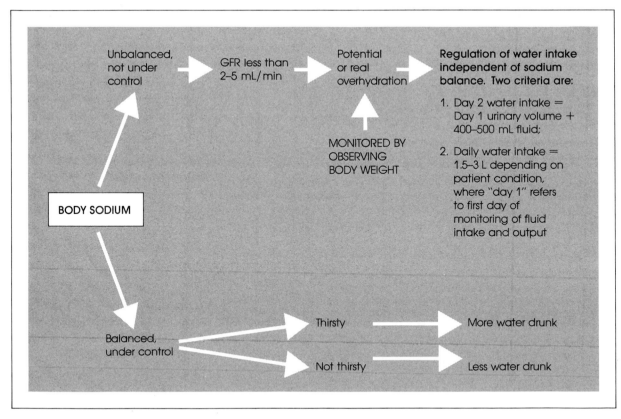

FIGURE 28-5   Regulation of sodium intake in patients with chronic renal failure not on maintenance dialysis.

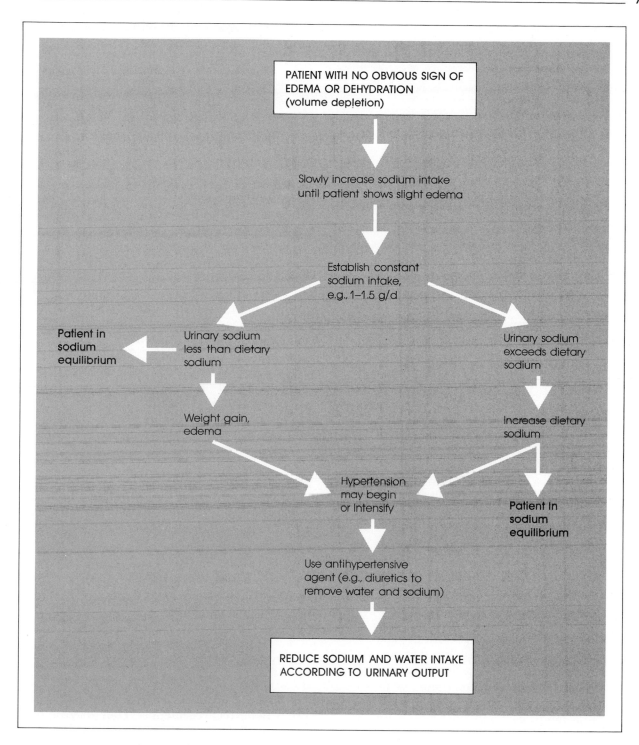

FIGURE 28-6   Water intake in relation to sodium balance in patients with chronic renal failure not on dialysis.

TABLE 28-6 Protein Need According to the GFR for Patients Not on Dialysis

GFR (mL/min)	Protein Need (g/d)
>25	No restriction
20–25	<90
15–20	<70
10–15	<50
4–10	40 (males)*
	35 (females)†

*Male patients of medium to large body frame.
†Also male patients of small body frame.

TABLE 28-7 Approximate Protein Content of Some Vegetable and Grain Products

Food	Protein (%)
Bread, white	8–10
Cereals, cooked, meal or flakes	2
Cereals, dry	7–14
Corn	3–4
Potato	2–3
Rice	2–3
Spaghetti	3–4

therapy is appropriate. Patients should have an extra quantity of protein corresponding to the amount lost in the urine, for example, one egg or 1 oz of lean beef for each 6 g of protein lost.

Caloric Need

No data can indicate the exact caloric need of patients with chronic renal failure. However, clinical experience shows that 35 to 45 kcal/kg body weight/d has proven adequate. Most practitioners use the latest RDAs as a baseline and adjust them according to the patient's condition. There are some basic problems in providing patients an adequate amount of calories. For instance, if intakes of protein, potassium, sodium, and water are restricted, the caloric consumption automatically becomes low because of the small amount of food consumed.

Because a desirable diet is high in calories, high in animal protein, and low in vegetable protein, it is unlikely to be appetizing, palatable, or tasty. This is because satisfying staple foods (see Table 28-7) are all low in good-quality protein. Excessive consumption of these foods will increase nitrogenous waste, reduce availability of essential amino acids, and increase symptoms. As a result, the needed calories must be derived from three sources: (1) fatty foods, (2) regular and/or semisynthetic high-carbohydrate foods and foods low or lacking in protein, and (3) commercial nutrient supplements high in calories

only. Protein consumed should not contribute more than 150 to 250 kcal. Every attempt should be made to prevent the protein from being used by the body as a major energy source by including enough calories in the diet. In menu planning (see later discussion), high-caloric foods that are low in protein, sodium, and potassium (either hospital-prepared or commercial products) are frequently used. Popular items include candy, honey, Popsicles, and similar products, although some patients complain about their sweetness.

For an obese patient who is 20% to 25% over ideal body weight with or without hyperlipoproteinemia, caloric intake should be reduced. For malnourished patients, 3,000 to 4,000 kcal/d may be needed to replenish body nutriture and spare dietary protein for body building and repair. However, the BUN and/or SUN must be monitored and used as guides. Various methods used to feed a patient a large amount of calories are described in Chapter 23.

Fat Intake

Some clinical reports indicate that half of the patients in the terminal stage of renal failure develop hypertriglyceridemia. They may or may not be on dialysis. Because of the potential risk of heart disease, measures to regulate serum triglycerides may be needed. Information on the dietetics of this clinical problem is presented in Chapter 27.

Anemia

When the kidneys are functioning at half their normal capacity, anemia is common. The causes are many: nutritional anemia from a dietary lack or induced deficiency of iron and/or folic acid, hemolysis of red blood cells, blood loss from the alimentary tract and open wounds, frequent blood samples, and reduced blood cell formation because of the failure of the kidney to make erythropoietin (a hormone) which stimulates red blood cell production. Most patients can tolerate the disorder and compensate for its adverse effects fairly well. In these patients, anemia is usually asymptomatic. However, whenever detected, anemia should be corrected by the most effective means available.

Oral supplementation with iron and folic acid has proven effective. However, some patients do not absorb oral iron well; they exhibit side effects, which should be identified as soon as possible. In general, a usual oral dose is 300 mg of ferrous sulfate given three times daily 30 to 60 minutes after a meal. If an oral dose is unsuccessful, injected iron dextran may be tried. Because of frequent local reactions to injections, the doses given progress from small to therapeutic levels.

Vitamin and Mineral Supplements

It has been firmly established that a uremic patient not on dialysis needs vitamin and mineral supplements. Patients without supplements show low blood levels of water-soluble vitamins. The suspected cause of this condition is either a decreased intake of vitamins and minerals or a deficiency induced by clinical conditions and the use of drugs. The recommended daily supplement of these substances is indicated in Table 28-8. Patients on a diet of less than 50 g of protein per day are especially likely to develop vitamin deficiencies and should be watched closely. The values listed in Table 28-8 are only general guidelines—some clinicians prescribe more, others less.

Deficiencies in fat-soluble vitamins A, D, E, and K in uremic patients are usually insignificant

TABLE 28-8 Water-Soluble Vitamin Needs of Patients in Terminal Stage of Chronic Renal Failure

Vitamin	Amount (mg/d)
C*	80–150
B_1 (thiamine mononitrate)	5–15
B_2 (riboflavin)	5–10
B_6 (pyridoxine hydrochloride)*	5
Niacinamide	30–50
Panthothenate, calcium	5–10
B_{12} (cobalamin)	3
Folic acid*	1

*Cases of deficiency have been reported in uremic patients.

unless there are special circumstances. For example, repeated usage of antibiotics may deprive patients of the usual contribution of vitamin K from the intestinal flora. In this case, a supplement of this vitamin may be needed. If a patient develops osteodystrophy, the need for vitamin D requires special attention, but this topic will not be discussed here (see references at the end of this book). Because some patients occasionally show decreased blood levels of vitamin E, some clinicians recommend its supplementation. The potential toxicity of vitamins A and D should be noted when considering them as supplements.

The need for sodium and potassium has already been discussed above. The calcium, phosphorus, and magnesium needs of a patient with osteodystrophy require special attention and are discussed in standard medical texts (see references at the end of this book).

KIDNEY DIALYSIS

Dialysis refers to the diffusion of dissolved particles (solutes) from one side of a semipermeable membrane to the other. Kidney dialysis was started in 1960 and has helped many uremic patients since then. Basically, there are two kinds of dialysis used to treat the end stage of renal failure: peritoneal dialysis and hemodialysis.

Peritoneal dialysis involves the insertion of a cannula (stylet catheter, for example) into the peritoneal cavity. A solution of glucose and electrolytes (dialysate) is introduced and permitted to remain in the abdominal cavity for 10 to 30 minutes. The peritoneal membrane serves as a semipermeable membrane, across which dissolved body waste substances diffuse into the dialysate. The process is repeated within a period of 8 to 22 hours, after which the fluid or dialysate is extracted and removed. This is done 3 to 5 times per week, mainly at night in the patient's home. In this procedure strict precautions must be taken against sepsis. Presently, maintenance peritoneal dialysis is suitable for use in the home by individuals who are at high risk and unable to cope with the artificial kidney, the elderly, and patients with cardiovascular disease.

Hemodialysis, sometimes known as extracorporeal dialysis, uses a machine (artificial kidney) outside the body. Blood is drawn or pumped out of the body and made to circulate through a special machine equipped with a synthetic semipermeable membrane. The dialysate in this case also contains glucose and electrolytes, resembling concentrations of blood plasma found in the body. Much nitrogenous waste from the patient's blood plasma diffuses into the dialysate. The cleansed blood is returned to the patient's body and used dialysate is replaced with fresh. The patient undergoes hemodialysis two to four times a week for 3 to 6 hours at a time in the hospital. Recently changes in government financing have permitted special profit-making private centers to provide services for maintenance dialysis. Such centers, however, are not hospitals. The pros and cons of this practice are currently under debate. In general, indications for dialysis vary with the patients and will not be discussed here. See references at the end of this book for more information.

Nutritional complications for a kidney patient on dialysis are unique. The process causes body nutrients to traverse the semipermeable membrane as nitrogenous wastes do. In many patients, cachexia (see Table 28-4) continues after dialysis is initiated. Nutrients lost in dialysis include proteins, peptides, free and bound amino acids, monosaccharides, water-soluble vitamins, and other essential substances. The extent of nutrient loss differs depending on the type of dialysis. The nutrient requirements of a patient on dialysis are summarized in Table 28-9.

POTASSIUM IN CLINICAL MEDICINE

Potassium has many important functions in the body. It regulates acid-base balance, skeletal and cardiac muscle contraction, and nervous excitation. Consumption of about 3 to 8 g/d is necessary to maintain normalcy. Both decreased (*hypokalemia*) and excess (*hyperkalemia*) serum potassium levels elicit undesirable responses from the body.

Hypokalemia may be caused by certain diuretics, a deficient intake, malabsorption, excess excretion because of renal failure, vomiting, and other factors. The clinical effects of potassium deficiency are an abnormal electrocardiogram, muscle weakness, alkaline urine, and other symptoms. The four methods of treating hypokalemia are: (1) direct potassium supplementation, (2) using potassium-sparing diuretics, (3) consumption of potassium-rich foods, and (4) using potassium-containing salt substitutes. Most clinicians favor the first method and prescribe 5 to 10 g of potassium chloride in ½ to 1 c of water flavored with orange juice, taken 2 to 3 times daily after meals.

Since hypokalemia in many kidney and heart patients is caused by the use of certain diuretics, some clinicians prefer to use potassium-sparing diuretics such as spironolactone (Aldactone) or triamterene (Dyrenium). These may be used alone or in combination with thiazide diuretics, which are very effective but cause hypokalemia as well.

Foods such as bananas and oranges are high in potassium. However, the use of potassium-rich foods has been criticized because of their cost to the patient and the resulting increase in protein, calorie, and sodium intake. Some patients may be restricted in some or all of the latter three

TABLE 28-9   Nutrient Requirements of Patients on Dialysis

Nutrient	Peritoneal Dialysis	Hemodialysis
Calories	Same as before initiation of dialysis	Same as before initiation of dialysis
Protein	110–140 g/d (1.5–2.0 g/kg/d)	70–90 g/d (1.0–1.25 g/kg/d)
Fluids	450–850 mL plus urine volume day before (monitor weight gain, limit to under ½ kg/d between dialyses)	450–850 mL plus urine volume day before (monitor weight gain, limit to under ½ kg/d between dialyses)
Sodium	450–3,000 mg/d (20–130 mEq/d)	450–3,000 mg/d (20–130 mEq/d)
Potassium	2,000–4,000 mg/d (50–80 mEq/d)	2,000–4,000 mg/d (50–80 mEq/d)

nutrients and will have problems if the amounts ingested are increased. In addition, a person with a severe potassium deficiency also has a poor appetite and is unlikely to eat enough extra food to add sufficient potassium to the body. Further, it is hard to regulate the amount of potassium consumed from food sources.

A number of salt substitutes that contain potassium instead of sodium are available for patients whose sodium intakes are restricted. Examples of such products are Morton salt substitute, Featherweight seasoned salt substitute, Adolph's salt substitute, Co-Salt, Featherweight "K" salt, Diasal, Sweet and Low brand Nu-Salt, and Neocurtasal. They are fairly uniform in composition, with each 5 g teaspoon containing about 50 to 65 mEq of potassium. These products have been found to be inexpensive, sodium-free, and successful in eliciting high patient compliance.

Hyperkalemia, or increased blood potassium, may be caused by decreased potassium excretion because of renal failure, severe dehydration, stress such as surgery, excess intake, or careless use of potassium-sparing diuretics. The symptoms of hyperkalemia are cardiac arrhythmia, abnormal EKG, abdominal distension and diarrhea, paralysis, muscular weakness and cramps, increased nervous irritability, and mental disorientation. The patient may die if the condition is not corrected. The treatment used depends on whether the hyperkalemia is mild, moderate, or life threatening. When the condition is not life threatening, patients should refrain from taking any powerful potassium-sparing diuretics (if they are the cause) and given oral drugs or an enema containing cation-exchange resins.

NUTRITIONAL AND DIETARY CARE OF KIDNEY PATIENTS

For patients with any of the kidney diseases discussed so far, dietary management involves regulation of the intake of protein, sodium, potassium, phosphorus, calcium, and/or fluid. Protein intake may be controlled both in quantity and quality (that is, HBV versus LBV). All members of the health team (doctor, nurse, and dietitian) should be fully advised of the type and extent of regulation. Because of frequent advances in this field, health personnel must be kept informed of new developments. There are three basic consid-

TABLE 28-10   Hypothetical Diet Prescriptions for Treating Different Types of Renal Diseases

Type of Disorder	Protein (g)	Sodium (mEq)	Sodium (mg)	Potassium (mEq)	Potassium (mg)	Diet Specification
Acute glomerulonephritis	25	20	460	26	1,014	A
Nephrotic syndrome	100	40	920	70	2,730	B
Acute renal failure with oliguria	25	20	460	26	1,014	C
Chronic renal failure	40	40	920	40	1,560	D
with no dialysis	60	60	1,380	60	2,340	E
Renal failure with dialysis	100	50	1,150*	80	3,120†	F

Note: In general, patients should be encouraged to eat as many calories as possible. They should be taught how to achieve a high caloric intake and simultaneously comply with the diet prescriptions. Fluid, phosphorus, and calcium intakes are discussed in the text. Acute glomerulonephritis is one form of acute nephritic syndrome.

*If the patient condition permits, a prescription of 2,000 to 3,000 mg of sodium is preferred, which improves compliance.

†This assumes that the patient excretes some potassium. If urinary potassium is very low, this may be lowered to 2,000 to 3,000 mg.

TABLE 28-11   Nutrient Contents of Foods within the Renal Food Exchange Lists

Renal Food Exchange List	Food Type	Protein (g)	Sodium (mEq)	Sodium (mg)	Potassium (mEq)	Potassium (mg)
I	Milk and milk products	4	2.6	60	4.4	170
II	Vegetables II-1	1	0.4	10	3.8	150
	Vegetables II-2	2	0.4	10	3.8	150
	Vegetables II-3	1	1.1	25	6.4	250
	Vegetables II-4	2	1.1	25	6.4	250
III	Fruits III-1	0.5	0	0	2.6	100
	Fruits III-2	0.5	0	0	3.8	150
IV	Grain products IV-1	2	0.4	10	1.3	50
	Grain products IV-2	2	5.2	120	1.3	50
V	Meat and equivalents	7	1.3	30	2.8	110
VI	Fats	0	2.2	50	0	0
VII	Alternates*					

*Nutrient contents variable and usually not significant.

erations in kidney diet therapy: (1) individualized diet prescription, (2) adoption of a food selection system and the practice of "renal" dietetics, and (3) education of the patient and his or her family.

Individualized Diet Prescription

Kidney patients show a large variation in their dietary and nutritional needs. The number of nephrons functioning normally varies as well as overall clinical conditions. Nutritional complications from drugs and the particular kidney disease, responses to diuretics, and the extent of nutrient losses through dialysis must be considered. For these reasons, diet prescriptions for kidney patients must be highly individualized.

Renal Food Exchange Lists and "Renal" Dietetics

Let us assume that for each of the renal diseases discussed above, the attending physician prescribes a specific diet after consulting with the nurse and dietitian (Table 28-10). Its implementation will be facilitated by the nurse, dietitian, doctor, and patient working together. How should each diet plan in Table 28-10 be fulfilled and implemented? In recent years, numerous organizations, hospitals, clinics, physicians, dietitians, nurses, and allied health personnel have developed different food exchange lists to assist with diet planning.

The basic aim of most lists is to arrange foods in groups, each of which contains foods with nearly the same content of protein, sodium, and potassium. Within each group, a patient can select any item or exchange one for another. The grouping is achieved by referring to the latest and most comprehensive food composition tables (for example, Pennington and Church's, *USDA Agriculture Handbook No. 8* and others; see Chapters 10 and 22) and arranging the foods according to their contents of the three nutrients.

With proper training and sufficient time, most professionals and even patients can develop exchange lists that contain as many foods as they want or can group according to the exchange formula. Such lists have been developed

TABLE 28-12   Renal Food Exchange List I: Milk and Milk Products

Food	One Exchange
Cream	
Light (20.6% fat)	⅔ c
Half and half (11.7% fat)	½ c
Heavy (37.6% fat)	¾ c
Sour	⅔ c
Ice cream and frozen custard, plain, 10% fat, may be flavored if mineral content of flavorings known	⅔ c
Ice milk, plain	⅔ c
Milk	
Whole	½ c
Skim or nonfat	½ c
Dry powder, whole, instant, high density	2 T
Dry powder, nonfat, instant, low density	2 T
Evaporated	¼ c
Condensed	2 T
Chocolate, commercial (whole, skim, or low fat), 90% milk	½ c
Yogurt, plain or flavored	½ c

Note: Each exchange contains 4 g of protein, 60 mg (2.6 mEq) of sodium, and 170 mg (4.4 mEq) of potassium.

for this chapter. Table 28-11 summarizes the seven food lists, showing the food types in each list and the approximate contents of protein, sodium, and potassium in each list exchange. Tables 28-12 to 28-22 indicate the different food items assigned to each list. Footnotes to these tables indicate the approximate contents of protein, sodium, and potassium within each exchange. In all the tables, *low sodium* refers to a dietetic product.

Table 28-23 describes the food products included under Renal Food Exchange List VII: Alternates. This list shows the types of beverages permitted with due consideration for fluid, sodium, and potassium content (if any). List VII also supplies a category of free foods that the patient may eat with no limitation. Beginning on page 714 is a list of spices that patients with kidney diseases may use (within reasonable limits) in food preparation without restriction.

TABLE 28-13 Renal Food Exchange List II-1: Vegetables

Food	One Exchange
Beans, snap, green (fresh or frozen, cooked)	½ c
Beans, wax, yellow (fresh or frozen, cooked)	½ c
Beets, canned, low sodium	½ c
Cabbage, cooked or raw, nondehydrated	½ c
Cabbage, raw, red	½ c
Carrots, low sodium	½ c
Chard, cooked	¼ c
Cucumber, raw, pared, sliced, or diced	½ c
Eggplant, fresh, cooked	½ c
Endive, raw	1 c
Escarole, raw	1 c
Kale, fresh, cooked	¼ c
Kale, frozen, cooked	½ c
Lettuce, head, raw	½ c
Onions, young, green, raw, chopped or sliced	½ c
Onions, mature, cooked or raw, chopped	½ c
Parsley, raw, chopped	⅓ c
Peppers, immature, green, raw, sweet, chopped or diced	½ c
Peppers, immature, green, sweet, strips, cooked	¾ c
Squash, summer, fresh, cooked	½ c
Zucchini, fresh, cooked	½ c
Water chestnuts	2 oz*
Watercress, whole or cut, not finely chopped	½ c

Note: Each exchange contains 1 g of protein, 10 mg (0.4 mEq) of sodium, and 150 mg (3.8 mEq) of potassium.

*Three to five medium-sized nuts.

Allspice	Chili powder
Anise seed	Chives
Bay leaf	Cinnamon
Caraway seed	Cloves
Cardamom	Cumin
Catsup (salt-free only)	Curry powder
Celery (limited to 2 T chopped)	Dill
	Fennel

TABLE 28-14 Renal Food Exchange List II-2: Vegetables

Food	One Exchange
Asparagus (fresh or frozen, cooked)	
Cut	⅓ c
Spears, large	4
Cauliflower, flower, buds, chopped (fresh or frozen, cooked)	½ c
Corn, yellow or white	
Cooked on cob, ear	1
Kernels cut off cob before cooking	½ c
Mustard greens	
Cooked leaves without stem	⅓ c
Frozen, chopped, cooked	⅔ c
Okra, sliced (fresh or frozen, cooked)	½ c
Peas (fresh or frozen, cooked)	¼ c
Turnip greens, frozen, cooked	⅓ c

Note: Each exchange contains 2 g of protein, 10 mg (0.4 mEq) of sodium, and 150 mg (3.8 mEq) of potassium.

TABLE 28-15 Renal Food Exchange List II-3: Vegetables

Food	One Exchange
Carrots	
Cooked, diced or sliced	½ c
Raw, grated or shredded	½ c
Celery, raw or cooked, diced or sliced	¼ c
Kohlrabi, raw, thickened bulblike stems, diced, cooked	1 c
Mushrooms, raw, chopped, sliced, dried	1 c
Onion, dry, flaked	¼ c
Parsnips, diced or mashed, cooked	⅓ c
Radishes, raw	
Whole, medium	10
Sliced	½ c
Rutabaga (boiled, cubed, sliced, or mashed)	½ c
Tomato	
Cooked, fresh	⅓ c
Juice, low sodium	½ c
Raw, slices, medium	2
Turnips, cooked, diced	½ c

Note: Each exchange contains 1 g of protein, 25 mg (1.1 mEq) of sodium, and 250 mg (6.4 mEq) of potassium.

TABLE 28-16   Renal Food Exchange List II-4: Vegetables

Food	One Exchange
Broccoli	
Fresh, cooked, medium	1 stalk
Frozen, chopped, cooked	⅔ c
Brussels sprouts	
Frozen, cooked	5–6
Chopped (fresh or frozen, cooked)	⅔ c
Collards	
Frozen, cooked	½ c
Leaves with or without stems, fresh, cooked in large amount of water	½ c
Dandelion greens, fresh, cooked	½ c
Mustard greens (fresh or frozen, cooked)	⅔ c
Potato	
Boiled, white, small	½
Mashed, white, no milk	½ c
Squash	
Summer, frozen	½ c
Winter, fresh, boiled, mashed	½ c

Note: Each exchange contains 2 g of protein, 25 mg (1.1 mEq) of sodium, and 250 mg (6.4 mEq) of potassium.

TABLE 28-17   Renal Food Exchange List III-1: Fruits

Food	One Exchange
Apple juice, bottled or canned	½ c
Applesauce, canned, sweetened or unsweetened	½ c
Blackberries, fresh	⅔ c
Blueberries, fresh	1 c
Boysenberries, canned (water packed) or frozen sweetened	¾ c
Cantaloupe, fresh	¼ c
Cherries	
Fresh, sour, red, whole	½ c
Fresh, sweet, whole	½ c
Cranberries, raw	1 c
Cranberry juice, cocktail	1 c
Cranberry sauce, canned	1 c
Gooseberries, fresh	½ c

TABLE 28-17   (continued)

Food	One Exchange
Grapefruit	
Fruit	¼ c
Juice (varies with different varieties)	¼ c
Grapefruit juice and orange juice, blended (varies with different varieties)	¼ c
Grape drink	1 c
Grape juice	
Canned	⅓ c
Frozen concentrate, diluted	1 c
Grapes	
American type, fresh	⅔ c
Canned, packed in water or syrup	⅓ c
European type, fresh	⅓ c
Honeydew, fresh	¼ c
Lemon, raw, peeled, large	½
Lemonade, frozen and reconstituted	1 c
Lime	1 c
Lime juice, fresh or canned	½ c
Limeade, frozen, reconstituted	1 c
Orange juice, nondehydrated	½ c
Orange juice and apricot juice drink	½ c
Peach, nectar, canned	½ c
Peaches	
Canned, sweetened or unsweetened	⅓ c
Fresh, peeled, medium	½
Frozen, sweetened	⅓ c
Pear nectar	1 c
Pears	
Canned, sweetened or unsweetened	½ c
Fresh, large	½
Pineapple	
Canned, sweetened or unsweetened	½ c
Fresh, diced	½ c
Frozen concentrate, reconstituted	2½ oz
Juice, unsweetened	2 oz
Pineapple juice and grapefruit juice	⅔ c
Pineapple juice and orange juice	½ c
Plums	
Fresh, whole, Japanese type	1
Greengage, canned in water, medium	2
Prunes, Italian, canned in water or syrup	⅓ c
Raspberries, red, raw, canned (in water) or frozen, sweetened	½ c
Raisins, uncooked, whole	1 T
Strawberries	
Canned in water	½ c
Sweetened, frozen	½ c
Tangerine, whole, fancy	1
Watermelon, fresh, diced	¾ c

Note: Each exchange contains 0.5 g of protein, no sodium, and 100 mg (2.6 mEq) of potassium.

TABLE 28-18 Renal Food Exchange List III-2: Fruits

Food	One Exchange
Apple, fresh, 2½ in. diam.	1
Apricot, nectar	⅔ c
Blackberries, canned, packed in water or syrup	⅔ c
Blueberries, frozen, sweetened or unsweetened	1 c
Cherries	
Canned, sour, red, sweet, packed in water or syrup, pitted or unpitted	½ c
Sour, red, fresh, without pits	½ c
Sweet, fresh, without pits	½ c
Figs, canned, packed in water or syrup	½ c
Fruit salad, canned, packed in water or syrup	½ c
Grapefruit	
Fruit	½
Juice (varies with varieties)	½ c
Grapefruit juice and orange juice blended (varies with varieties)	⅓ c
Grape juice, canned	½ c
Grapes	
American type, fresh	1 c
Canned, packed in water or syrup	⅓ c
European type, fresh	½ c
Lemon, raw, peeled, medium	1
Lemon juice, fresh, frozen and diluted, bottled, canned, sweetened	½ c
Lychees	10
Orange, fresh, medium	1
Peach nectar, canned	⅔ c
Peaches	
Canned, sweetened or unsweetened	½ c
Fresh, peeled, medium	⅔
Frozen, sweetened	⅓ c
Pears	
Canned, sweetened or unsweetened	⅔ c
Fresh, large	⅔
Pineapple	
Canned, sweetened or unsweetened	⅔ c
Fresh, diced	⅔ c
Frozen concentrate, reconstituted	3½ oz
Juice, unsweetened	3 oz
Pineapple juice and grapefruit juice	1 c
Pineapple juice and orange juice	⅔ c
Plums	
Fresh, whole, Damson	5
Fresh, whole, prune type	3
Purple, canned, medium, packed in water or syrup	3

TABLE 28-18 (continued)

Food	One Exchange
Prune juice	¼ c
Prunes, cooked, sugar added, medium	2
Raspberries, black, raw, canned, packed in water	½ c
Strawberries	
Fresh, medium	8–10
Sweetened, sliced, frozen	½ c
Tangerine juice, fresh, canned, sweetened or unsweetened, frozen concentrate, reconstituted	½ c

Note: Each exchange contains 0.5 g of protein, no sodium, and 150 mg (3.8 mEq) of potassium.

TABLE 28-19 Renal Food Exchange List IV-1: Grain Products

Food	One Exchange
Bread, low sodium	1 sl
Cereals	
Cooked, noninstant	
Cream of Rice, Cream of Wheat, cornmeal, pearled barley, farina, Malt-O-Meal, hominy grits, oatmeal	½ c
Dry, ready-to-eat	
Fruit Loops, Apple Jacks, Puffed Rice, Puffed Wheat, Sugar Pops	1 c
Frosted Mini Wheats, biscuits	4
Puffa Puffa Rice, Sugar Smacks, Super Sugar Crisp	½ c
Shredded wheat, biscuit	1
Grains, uncooked	
Flour, sifted	¼ c
Cornmeal	¼ c
Tortilla	1
Masa harina	⅓ c
Macaroni, noodles, spaghetti	½ c
Rice, white or brown, minute	½ c
Miscellaneous	
Piecrust	⅛ pie
Popcorn	1 c

Note: Each exchange contains 2 g of protein, 10 mg (0.4 mEq) of sodium, and 50 mg (1.3 mEq) of potassium. All products are unsalted.

TABLE 28-20   Renal Food Exchange List IV-2: Grain Products

Food	One Exchange
Breads	
Bun, hamburger or frankfurter	½
Doughnut, raised, plain	1
Melba toast	4
Muffin, English	¼
Roll, raised	1
Vienna or French	1 sl
Whole, regular	1 sl
Cereals, cooked	
All those mentioned in List IV-1, cooked regularly with salt added	½ c
Cereals, dry, ready-to-serve*	
Alpha Bits, Quangaroo's, corn flakes, Rice Krispies, Pep, Froot Loops, Special K	½ c
Miscellaneous	
Cake (angel food, yellow, spice, or white), 2-in. square or cupcake	1
Cornstick, cinnamon stick, Aunt Jemima	1
Crackers, graham	2
Muffin, honey bun, Morton's	1
Pancake	1
Wafers, vanilla	10–12

Note: Each exchange contains 2 g of protein, 120 mg (5.2 mEq) of sodium, and 50 mg (1.3 mEq) of potassium. All foods cooked regularly with salt added.

*Check labels and literature from manufacturer.

Flavoring extracts (all kinds)
Garlic and garlic juice
Ginger
Horseradish (only fresh)
Juniper
Lemon juice
Mace
Marjoram
Mayonnaise (salt-free only)
Mint

Mustard (ready-to-serve, salt-free only)
Mustard seed
Mustard (dry only)
Nutmeg
Onion (flakes, juice, or powder)
Onion, fresh (limited to 2 T chopped)
Oregano
Paprika
Pepper

TABLE 28-21   Renal Food Exchange List V: Meat and Equivalents

Food	One Exchange
Regular products*	
Egg, prepared in any way	1
Beef, lamb, veal, pork, liver, heart	1 oz
Chicken, turkey, duck, rabbit	1 oz
Clams, fresh	2 oz†
Fish, most varieties fresh‡	1 oz
Oysters, fresh	¼ c§
Squid	1 oz
Low-sodium products	
Cheese, cottage	¼ c
Cheese, hard	1 oz
Peanut butter‖	1 T
Salmon or tuna, canned	¼ c

Note: Each exchange contains 7 g of protein, 30 mg (1.3 mEq) of sodium, and 110 mg (2.8 mEq) of potassium.

*All foods are cooked and unsalted.

†Or 2 large.

‡Check food composition tables for nutrient contents.

§Or 2 to 3 small.

‖Poorer-quality protein than that of other entries in this list.

TABLE 28-22   Renal Food Exchange List VI: Fat

Food	One Exchange
Butter, salted, regular	1 t
Cream cheese	1 T
Margarine, salted, regular	1 t
Mayonnaise, salted, regular	1 t
Salad dressing (Miracle Whip)	1 t

Note: Each exchange contains no protein, 50 mg (2.2 mEq) of sodium and no potassium. All unsalted butter, margarine, and vegetable oil may be used as desired.

Poppy seed
Poultry seasoning
Rosemary
Saffron
Salad dressing (salt-free only)

Sesame seed
Tabasco
Tarragon
Thyme
Turmeric
Vinegar

TABLE 28-23 Renal Food Exchange List VII: Alternates

VII-1 Permitted beverages*

Colas: Coca, Pepsi, and RC	Hoffman sodas, regular, any flavor	Popsicles
Cranberry juice cocktail	Kool-Aid	Root beer
Faygo sodas, regular, any flavor	Lemonade, frozen, reconstituted	Schweppes mixers, all varieties
Ginger ale	Limeade, frozen, reconstituted	7-Up
Hawaiian Punch		

VII-2 Special beverages

A. Obtain doctor's permission for drinking alcoholic beverages and include their sodium and potassium content; e.g., beer has 80 mg of potassium and 25 mg of sodium in 1 c.

B. Include the potassium content in instant coffee (100 mg of potassium and no sodium in 1 t) and tea (100 mg of potassium and no sodium in one bag used to make medium strength drink).

VII-3 Foods permitted with no limitation

Arrowroot	Gumdrops	Marshmallows
Butter and margarine, unsalted	Honey	Mints, fondant, pillow
Candy, hard, clear	Instant, N-Rich	Rich's whip topping
Coffee Rich	Jams	Sago
Cool Whip	Jellies	Shortenings and oils
Cornstarch	Jelly beans	Sugar, white
Dream Whip	Life Savers	Syrup, corn or maple
Gum, chewing	Lollipops	Tapioca, granular
		Wheat starch

*The exact fluid content must be incorporated into prescribed fluid intake if the amount is regulated.

Since most kidney diets limit the amount of LBV protein, patients are usually permitted only a small amount of the grain products from List IV (because of their inferior protein content). To provide the patient with more satisfying staple foods, two different exchange measures are possible. Special semisynthetic, low-protein, starchy products (Table 28-24) and some natural ones (arrowroot, sago, and tapioca; see Table 28-23) are used frequently. A low-protein diet is also low in calories. In order to feed a patient a large amount of calories without increasing the patient's consumption of electrolytes and protein, commercial nutrient solutions and supplements (Table 28-25) and the free foods in Table 28-23 are used. Parenteral feeding of large amounts of calories is sometimes indicated for very malnourished patients.

Using the information in Table 28-11, one can assign the appropriate number of exchanges to each diet prescription listed in Table 28-10. The result is shown in Table 28-26. Using the exchange lists (Tables 28-12 to 28-23), one can translate the meal plans in Table 28-26 into sample menus (Tables 28-27 to 28-32). The process involves dividing the exchanges permitted the patient into three allotments of breakfast, lunch, and dinner.

A careful study of the sample menus brings out a number of points. For one, the patient may need to consume more sodium and potassium than prescribed (Table 28-10) or contained in the meal plans and menus (Tables 28-26 to 28-32). If so, eating more fruit will provide the extra potassium required. The patient may also be provided with a list of foods with well-known sodium

TABLE 28-24   Low-Protein Products for Kidney Patients

Manufacturer	Product
National distributors	
General Mills	Paygel-P Wheat Starch (dietetic), Paygel Baking Mix (dietetic), Paygel Low Protein Bread (dietetic, ready-to-serve), dp Low Protein Cookies with chocolate flavored chips. Aprotein products (from Carlo Erba, Milan, Italy): tagliatelle (flat noodles), rigatini (elbow macaroni), anellini (ring macaroni), porridge (semolino), rusk and hot cereals (ready-to-serve). All products contain: 0.1–0.9 g protein, 0.0–70 mg sodium, and 0–20 mg potassium in a 3- or 4-oz serving, except rusk, which contains about 400 mg of potassium. Check producer's literature.
Doyle Pharmaceuticals	Resource Baking Mix
Regional distributors*	
Chicago Dietetic Supply	Cellu: Lo/Protein baking mix, Lo/Protein pasta imitation macaroni, Lo/Na baking powder
Ener-G Foods (Seattle, WA)	Jolly Joan: low-protein baking mix and low-protein bread (ready-to-serve)
Vita-Wheat Baked Products (Ferndale, MI)	Low-protein, low-gluten bread; low-protein, low-gluten cookies

*Ask the companies and other local manufacturers about availability. Check company literature for contents of protein, sodium, and potassium. Consult the Kidney Foundation for new and additional products.

TABLE 28-25   Chemical Nutritional Solutions (Supplements) for Patients with Kidney Diseases

Product	Characteristics	Manufacturer
Cal Power	546 kcal per 8 oz; protein- and fat-free; low in electrolytes; mixed-carbohydrate solution; ready-to-eat; 8-oz carton	General Mills
Controlyte	1,000 kcal per 7 oz; protein-free; low in electrolytes; cornstarch hydrolysate, vegetable oil; in powder form	Doyle
Hycal	295 kcal per 4 oz; protein- and fat-free; no electrolytes; glucose solution; ready-to-eat; 4-oz bottle; lemon, lime, orange, and black currant flavors, with new flavors being added	Beecham
Lipomul	600 kcal per 100 mL at normal dilution; protein- and carbohydrate-free; no electrolytes; oral fat emulsion; water miscible	Upjohn
Polycose	400 kcal per 100 mL at normal dilution; protein- and fat-free; low in electrolytes; hydrolyzed products of cornstarch; in powder form; almost tasteless	Ross

TABLE 28-26   Meal Plans for Hypothetical Diet Prescriptions for Patients with Kidney Diseases

Food Group	Renal Food Exchange List	No. of Exchanges					
		Acute glomerulonephritis A	Nephrotic syndrome B	Acute renal failure with oliguria C	Chronic renal failure with no dialysis D	E	Renal failure with dialysis F
Milk and milk products	I	1	3	1	1	2	3
Vegetables	II-1	2	2	2	1	1	2
	II-2	1	2	1	1	1	1
	II-3	0	0	0	1	1	1
	II-4	0	0	0	0	1	0
Fruits	III-1	0	5	2	2	2	3
	III-2	2	0	0	1	2	2
Grain products	IV-1	1	5	1	0	0	4
	IV-2	1	2	1	1	4	3
Meat and equivalents	V	2	7	2	4	5	10
Fats	VI	4	5	4	12	11	5
Alternates*	VII						

*The patient's diet is brought up to a high caloric level by means of nutrient supplements, free foods, and low-protein bakery products. See text for more information. Alternates may be taken as desired except when otherwise instructed.

TABLE 28-27   Sample Menu Complying with the Hypothetical Dietary Prescription for Patients with Acute Glomerulonephritis

Breakfast	Lunch	Dinner
Milk, whole, ½ c	Squash, summer, fresh, cooked, ½ c	Milk, whole, ½ c
Pineapple, fresh, diced, ⅔ c	Apple, fresh, 1	Green beans, snap, fresh, cooked, ½ c
Puffed Rice, 1 c	Tuna, canned, low sodium, ¼ c	Corn, on cob, 1 ear
Cream cheese, 1 T	Mayonnaise, 1 t	Bread, French, 1 sl
Alternates, nutrient supplement, and low-protein bread*	Alternates, nutrient supplement, and low-protein bread*	Clams, fresh, 2 oz (or 2 large)
		Margarine, 2 t
		Alternates, nutrient supplement, and low-protein bread*

Note: The diet provides approximately 25 g of protein, 460 mg (20 mEq) of sodium, and 1,014 mg (26 mEq) of potassium. Without alternates, nutrient supplement, and low-protein bread, this menu contains about 1,000 to 1,050 kcal.

*The patient is encouraged to eat as many of the nonexcluded items as possible. See text for more information.

TABLE 28-28 Sample Menu Complying with the Hypothetical Dietary Prescriptions for Patients with Nephrotic Syndrome

Breakfast	Lunch	Dinner
Milk, whole, ½ c	Milk, chocolate, skim, ½ c	Milk, whole, ½ c
Juice, apple, ½ c	Chard, cooked, ½ c	Beets, canned, low sodium, ½ c
Cantaloupe, fresh, ¼ c	Cauliflower, fresh, cooked, ½ c	Peas, frozen, cooked, ¼ c
Oatmeal, ½ c	Juice, grape, from frozen concentrate, 1 c	Rice, brown, ½ c
Toast, whole wheat, 1 sl	Pear, fresh, ½	Chicken, broiled, 3 oz
Margarine, 1 t	Bread, low sodium, 1 sl	Bread, whole wheat, 1 sl
Eggs, poached, 2	Margarine, 1 t	Margarine, 2 t
Alternates, nutrient supplement, and low-protein bread*	Mayonnaise, 1 t	Juice, pineapple or grapefruit, ⅔ c
	Roast beef, 2 oz	Yogurt, skim milk, ½ c
	Alternates, nutrient supplement, and low-protein bread*	Alternates, nutrient supplement, and low-protein bread*

Note: The diet provides approximately 100 g of protein, 920 mg (40 mEq) of sodium, and 2,730 mg (70 mEq) of potassium. Without the alternates, nutrient supplement, and low-protein bread, this menu contains about 2,200 to 2,250 kcal.

*The patient is encouraged to eat as many of the nonexcluded items as possible. See text for more information.

TABLE 28-29 Sample Menu Complying with the Hypothetical Dietary Prescriptions for Patients with Acute Renal Failure with Oliguria

Breakfast	Lunch	Dinner
Milk, whole, ¾ c	Eggplant, fresh, cooked, sprinkled with nutmeg, ½ c	Milk, whole, ¼ c
Honeydew, ¼ c	Blackberries, fresh, ⅔ c	Carrots, cooked, low sodium, ½ c
Cream of Rice, ½ c	Dream Whip, ¼ c	Peas, frozen, cooked, ¼ c
Margarine, 1 t	Roast turkey, 1 oz	Bread, low sodium, 1 sl
Alternates, nutrient supplement, and low-protein bread*	Mayonnaise, 1 t	Salmon, canned, low sodium, ¼ c
	Alternates, nutrient supplement, and low-protein bread*	Margarine, 2 t
		Alternates, nutrient supplement, and low-protein bread*

Note: The diet provides approximately 25 g of protein, 460 mg (20 mEq) of sodium, and 1,014 mg (26 mEq) of potassium. Without alternates, nutrient supplement, and low-protein bread, this menu contains about 1,100 to 1,150 kcal.

*The patient is encouraged to eat as many of the nonexcluded items as possible. See text for more information.

TABLE 28-30 Sample Menu Complying with the Hypothetical Dietary Prescriptions for Patients with Chronic Renal Failure and Not on Dialysis

Breakfast	Lunch	Dinner
Corn flakes, ½ c Milk, ½ c Strawberries, sweetened (sliced, canned, or frozen), ½ c Alternates, nutrient supplement, and low-protein bread*	Juice, grape, canned, ½ c Lettuce, raw, ½ c Carrots, raw, shredded, ¼ c Tomato, raw, 1 sl Tuna, canned, low sodium, ¼ c Miracle Whip, 2 T Alternates, nutrient supplement, and low-protein bread*	Roast pork, 3 oz Corn, ear, 1 Margarine, 2 T Watermelon, fresh, diced, ¾ c Alternates, nutrient supplement, and low-protein bread*

Note: The diet provides approximately 40 g of protein, 920 mg (40 mEq) of sodium, and 1,560 mg (40 mEq) of potassium. Without alternates, nutrient supplement, and low-protein bread, this menu contains about 1,500 to 1,600 kcal.

*The patient is encouraged to eat as many of the nonexcluded items as possible. See text for more information.

TABLE 28-31 Sample Menu Complying with the Hypothetical Dietary Prescriptions for Patients with Chronic Renal Failure and Not on Dialysis

Breakfast	Lunch	Dinner
Blueberries, frozen, sweetened, 1 c Cream, heavy, 6 T Cream of Wheat, cooked, ½ c Milk, whole, ¼ c Butter, 1 t Egg, poached, 1 Butter, 1 t Alternates, nutrient supplement, and low-protein bread*	Lettuce, ½ c Celery, raw, chopped, 2 T Salmon, canned, low sodium, ¼ c Mayonnaise, 1 T Bread, whole wheat, 1 sl Margarine, 1 T Applesauce, with cinnamon, sweetened, ½ c Pudding, lemon, regular, ½ c Alternates, nutrient supplement, and low-protein bread*	Juice, grape, 1 c Chard, cooked, ¼ c Broccoli, fresh, chopped, cooked, 1 stalk Margarine, 1 t Tomato, raw, 2 sl Chicken, broiled, 3 oz Melba toast, 4 Margarine, 4 t Cantaloupe, fresh, ¼ c Milk, ½ c Alternates, nutrient supplement, and low-protein bread*

Note: The diet provides approximately 60 g of protein, 1,380 mg (60 mEq) of sodium, and 2,340 mg (60 mEq) of potassium. Without alternates, nutrient supplement, and low-protein bread, this menu contains about 2,300 to 2,400 kcal.

*The patient is encouraged to eat as many of the nonexcluded items as possible. See text for more information.

TABLE 28-32 Sample Menu Complying with the Hypothetical Dietary Prescriptions for Patients on Dialysis

Breakfast	Lunch	Dinner
Pear nectar, 1 c	Salad:	Cauliflower, fresh, cooked, ½ c
Cream of Rice (non-instant), ½ c	Lettuce, ½ c	Kale, fresh, cooked, ½ c
Margarine, 2 t	Radish, sliced, 2 T	Bread, French, 1 sl
Eggs, poached, 2	Carrots, raw, grated, ¼ c	Margarine, 2 t
Cantaloupe, fresh, ¼ c	Mushrooms, sliced, ¼ c	Chicken, fried, 4 oz
Milk, ½ c	Lemon juice, pepper	Gelatin, plain, ½ c
Alternates, nutrient supplement, and low-protein bread*	Bread, low sodium, 1 sl	Fruit salad, canned, in heavy syrup, ½ c
	Bread, whole wheat, 1 sl	Dream Whip, ¼ c
	Mayonnaise, 1 t	Milk, ½ c
	Roast beef, 4 oz	Alternates, nutrient supplement, and low-protein bread*
	Fruit salad:	
	Honeydew, fresh, ¼ c	
	Peach, fresh, sliced, ⅔	
	Milk, ½ c	
	Alternates, nutrient supplement, and low-protein bread*	

Note: The diet provides approximately 100 g of protein, 1,150 mg (50 mEq) of sodium, and 3,120 mg (80 mEq) of potassium. Without alternates, nutrient supplement, and low-protein bread, this menu contains about 2,000 to 2,100 kcal.

*The patient is encouraged to eat as many of the nonexcluded items as possible. See text for more information.

and potassium contents from which he or she can select additional items daily.

Patients must also be provided with thorough instructions on using the menus effectively. Patient response over time has indicated that most of the meal plans and menus are boring and unpalatable. The meal composition, however, is in the patient's best interest. As discussed earlier, low-protein starch products should be used as frequently as possible to improve a meal's flavor and to make up for the lack of satisfying carbohydrate products like potatoes, rice, and spaghetti, which are all restricted items. The low caloric content of some of the menus makes it very important that patients be supplied with and encouraged to eat commercial supplements and free foods.

None of the menus and diet prescriptions indicate the fluid requirement for patients or the fluid content of particular foods. Each patient's fluid need is different, and the moisture content of solid foods is quite variable. Table 28-33 presents the approximate amount of fluid in the different *categories* (not individual items) of food. The amount of water in a beverage can be easily ascertained from its label. Certain special items have varying levels of moisture; their values are given in Table 28-34.

The basic problem with diets for patients with renal problems is palatability. Because of the low-protein content and possible restriction of salt, many patients do not follow their diets. Nurses, dietitians, and doctors can follow several guidelines to minimize the inherent difficulties. One is to learn as much as possible about each patient's eating habits. Any diet planning should

TABLE 28-33   Approximate Water Contents of Nonbeverage Food Products

Food	Quantity	Water (mL)
High-protein items		
Meat, poultry, fish	1 oz	20
Oysters, fresh, medium	4	20
Clams, fresh	2 oz	20
Cottage cheese, salt-free, creamed	¼ c	40
Cheese, low sodium, dietetic	1 oz	20
Egg, medium	1	35
Vegetables excluding juices	1 serving*	70–75
Fruits excluding juices	1 serving*	80–90
Grain and equivalents		
Bread, low sodium or regular	1 sl	10
Cereals		
Dry	½ c	0–5
Cooked	½ c	100
Noodles, spaghetti	½ c	55–60
Macaroni	½ c	38–50
Grain, e.g., rice	½ c	60–75
Cupcake	1	20
Potato or sweet potato	½ c	70
Fats, salt-free or salted	1 serving*	Trace

Note: There are great variations among individual products. For more exact values, refer to food composition tables.

*The serving used here is the same as that described in the Renal Food Exchange Lists. Thus, 1 serving equals 1 exchange.

be geared to the patient's likes and dislikes. Start with a menu plan containing foods that the patient normally likes to eat and work around it to incorporate the diet requirements. If feasible, try out a new recipe on the patient. Adjust the ingredients of the recipe to cater to the patient's tastes.

Make sure that the patient divides the permitted amount of HBV protein evenly throughout the day. The HBV protein is best consumed with generous portions of fat and carbohydrate so that the protein is efficiently utilized. Though LBV protein is needed to provide palatability and flavor, it is kept to a minimum.

Plan the meals wisely and creatively so that they are tasty and varied. Information on techniques for preparing attractive meals for patients with kidney diseases may be obtained from the references listed at the end of this book.

Several other helpful suggestions are (1) to compile cookbooks, exchange lists, recipes, and menus for diets for patients with kidney problems; (2) to establish good communication with local and national organizations that provide assistance to such patients; (3) to keep a record of available dietetic products and their manufacturers and to stay abreast of new products; and (4) to be conscious of the food costs to patients.

Patient and Family Education

In most cases, the time period between the initial and terminal stages of renal failure is fairly long. Patients can thus become acquainted with the disease and diet therapy. This opportunity for education about dietary care enables patients to enjoy a better quality of life. However, a substantial number of patients are referred to a neph-

TABLE 28-34   Water Contents of Special Products

Food	Quantity	Approximate Water Content (mL)
Yogurt	½ c	120
Ice cream, 16% fat	⅔ c	90
Sherbet	½ c	120
Gelatin dessert	½ c	120
Lemon pudding, plain	½ c	120
Whip and Chill	½ c	120
Popsicle	1	100

rologist when the disease is well advanced and have never been on a therapeutic diet. Such patients are placed on dialysis early and are often difficult to help, especially in modifying their dietary habits. They need a lot of encouragement to comply with the unpalatable diets.

In educating such patients, the important topics are: (1) normal kidney functions, kidney diseases, and the stages of kidney disease development; (2) causes of symptoms and, whenever appropriate, associated behavioral and personality changes; (3) fluid and electrolyte disturbances; and (4) nutritional and dietary needs. Patients should be advised with compassion and concern that their lives depend on appropriate nutrition and diet. For patients with renal failure who are not on dialysis, compliance with diet therapy is extremely difficult. If patients have difficulty in adjusting to the dietary modifications and the disease, psychiatric assistance may be necessary. The entire health team needs family help and support to help patients comply with diet prescriptions. There is a special need in cases of patients requiring psychiatric help for someone (such as the nurse or dietitian) to listen and cater to patient desires, needs, and complaints.

Patients with kidney diseases should become familiar with many points regarding food purchasing and preparation and the Renal Food Exchange Lists. Such information can be obtained from professional literature. A few important guidelines are provided below. Patients and their families should become familiar with food measuring, food preparation terms (such as *drained*,

unsweetened, etc.), creative cooking with spices, and they should have plans to handle special occasions (Christmas dinners, picnics, etc.) and emergencies. Also important is the availability of cookbooks, alternate foods (Table 28-23), special low-protein products (Table 28-24), and nutrient supplements (Table 28-25). Hidden sources of sodium and potassium (such as preservatives, drinking water, tobacco and snuff, medications, toothpaste, and mouthwash) should also be noted.

More information on dietary sources of sodium is presented in Chapter 27. In general, it is difficult to restrict potassium in the diet, since it is found in large concentrations in meat, milk, eggs, fruits, and vegetables. The potassium in some vegetable products may be removed by a special procedure coincidentally called dialysis. This procedure is described in Table 28-35.

Some patients are advised to restrict or increase their fluid intakes. To comply, the patients must learn how to measure and record fluid amounts accurately. Conversion factors are important (for instance, ½ c = 8 T; see Appendix C). Patients must become familiar with units such as milliliters per cubic centimeter (mL/cc), teaspoon, tablespoon, cup, fluid ounce, quart, and liter.

Although kidney patients should not eat out in restaurants frequently, they may dine out occasionally. When they do, they must still follow the prescribed diet, including fluid restrictions, although substitutions may be made if they are within the allotment for given restricted nutrients. Since patients usually cannot eat all the food served in a restaurant, they may economize by taking home the uneaten portions for another meal. Table 28-36 provides some menus when eating out, and Table 28-37 presents some suggestions for a brown bag lunch.

RENAL STONES

The clinical manifestations of a patient with kidney stones range from none to an ashen pallor combined with severe flank pain. This difference in response is related to the extent of ureteral distension, which is caused by urine ac-

TABLE 28-35   Guidelines for Preparing Dialyzed Vegetables

I. **Procedure for reducing sodium and potassium content in carrots, beets, lima beans,* rutabagas, sweet potatoes, and white potatoes**
  A. Vegetables should be fresh and unpeeled.
  B. Pare the vegetables and put in cold water to avoid darkening from oxidation.
  C. Cut vegetables as thin as possible (preferably less than ⅛ in. slice).
  D. Rinse in warm water for several seconds.
  E. Let soak for at least 2½ hours in warm water, using 10 parts water to 1 part vegetable.
  F. Repeat rinsing.
  G. Cook for 5 minutes, with 5 parts water to 1 part vegetable.
  H. Individual servings can be frozen in small plastic bags.
  I. Servings may be prepared by various methods, such as boiling, mashing, scalloping, and frying.

II. **Procedure for reducing sodium and potassium in cauliflower, greens, mushrooms, and squash**
  A. Place vegetable in a colander or strainer.
  B. If frozen, let thaw and drain at room temperature.
  C. Rinse vegetable in warm water for several seconds.
  D. Let soak for at least 2½ hours in warm water, using 10 parts water to 1 part vegetable.
  E. Repeat rinsing.
  F. Prepare in customary manner, using 5 parts water to 1 part vegetable.

Source: Adapted from T. T. Tsaltas, Dietetic Management of Uremic Patients. 1. Extraction of Potassium from Foods for Uremic Patients, *American Journal of Clinical Nutrition* 22 (1969):490–493. The dialyzed vegetables will be low in certain vitamins and minerals, which should be supplied to the patient.

*For lima beans, follow steps D through I only.

cumulating behind an obstruction. Some patients may have few symptoms because the stones tend to occur in the renal calyx or pelvis, thus causing no obstruction (see Figure 28-1). In others, pain or colic is probably caused by stones blocking the pelvic-ureteric junction or creating an obstruction in the calyx.

Some stones are small enough to pass through the urinary tract and can be collected by the patient. Patients who come to the doctor because of pain or whose condition is identified by an incidental X ray are taught to collect stones by using cheesecloth, a funnel, or similar device.

Kidney stones are of various types and can be identified by a combination of visual examination, laboratory analysis, and other sophisticated techniques such as X-ray diffraction photography and polarization. Various types of stones are

listed in Table 28-38. Although kidney stones can be removed surgically, other medical measures are available for their management.

Calcium Stones

The formation of calcium stones in the kidney is likely when a patient is excreting a large amount of calcium in the urine (hypercalciuria) for any reason. Listed below are other causes of kidney stones.

I. Idiopathic or unknown causes (mainly a mixture of calcium oxalate and calcium phosphate stones)

II. Hyperplasia of the parathyroid gland (hyperparathyroidism) (mainly calcium phosphate stones)

TABLE 28-36 Restaurant Meal Suggestions for Patients with Kidney Diseases

Food Group	Breakfast Menu A	Breakfast Menu B
Protein foods (meat, milk, etc.)	Milk Egg(s), scrambled	Milk Egg(s), poached
Bread and equivalents	Toast, white bread, 1 sl Cream of Wheat, ⅓ c	Biscuit Puffed Wheat, ¾ c
Fruits and vegetables	Orange juice, ¼ c	Cantaloupe wedge
Beverage	Hot tea	Coffee
Fat	Butter or margarine	Butter or margarine
Alternates	Jelly, jam, sugar, pepper	Jelly, jam, sugar, pepper

Food Group	Lunch Menu A	Lunch Menu B
Protein foods (meat, milk, etc.)	Chicken, fried, 1 piece	Cottage cheese
Bread and equivalents	Bread, French, 1 sl	Unsalted crackers
Fruits and vegetables	Green salad	Fruit salad
Dessert	Plain Jell-O	Raspberry sherbet
Beverage	Iced tea	Lemonade
Alternates	Sugar, lemon wedge, oil, vinegar	Other free foods

Food Group	Dinner Menu A	Dinner Menu B
Protein foods (meat, milk, etc.)	Steak, charcoal-broiled	Fish, fillet, baked
Bread and equivalents	Bread, whole wheat, 1 sl	Roll, dinner, 1
Fruits and vegetables	Green salad Boiled potato	Green beans Baked potato
Dessert	Fruit salad	Peach, canned, half
Beverage	Red wine Coffee	White wine Tea
Alternates	Sugar, oil, and vinegar Cream, butter, and margarine	Choice of free foods

Note: Most serving sizes and numbers are not specified. These must be determined according to diet prescriptions.

TABLE 28-37 Brown Bag Lunch Suggestions for Patients with Kidney Problems

Menu A	Menu B
Sandwich:	Green salad, small, with
Roast beef, lean, un- salted, 1 oz	oil and vinegar
Bread, low sodium, with unsalted butter, 2 sl	Tuna, drained, ¼ c
	Bread, rye, 1 sl
	Macaroni salad, pre- pared without salt, ½ c
Mayonnaise, unsalted, 1 t	Margarine or butter, 1 T
Cole slaw, prepared without salt, ½ c	Peach pie, with Cool Whip, ½ c
Honeydew, 1 sl	Iced tea, with lemon wedge, ½ c
Lorna Doone (Nabisco), shortbread cookies, 2	Sugar
Ginger ale, ½ c	

Note: The contributions of protein, sodium, and potassium must be incorporated into the patient diet prescriptions.

III. Miscellaneous causes

  A. Drugs: diuretics such as acetazolamide; antacids

  B. Diet: excessive calcium and vitamin D intake; insufficient fluid intake

  C. Organ disorders: kidney; small intestine

  D. Secondary to other diseases: Cushing's syndrome, Paget's disease

  E. Urinary tract infection

  F. Immobilization such as bed confinement

  G. Excreting excessive amount of oxalic acid in urine

  H. Excessive urine alkalinity

Normally, a man excretes about 300 mg of calcium per day in the urine and a woman 250 mg.

Treating patients with renal calculi (stones) depends on the immediate clinical conditions. For patients with severe symptoms, the immediate concern is to relieve pain and colic. The usual procedures are bed rest, administering warm or hot compresses to the pain site, and prescribing analgesics or antispasmodic medications. Infection is controlled by antibiotics. Most patients will pass stones under this treatment. If they fail to do so in a few days, a urologist should assess whether surgery is warranted.

If pain is absent or minimal, the first order of

TABLE 28-38 Types of Kidney Stones in U.S. Patients

Type of Stone	Incidence among U.S. Patients (%)
Calcium	90
Calcium oxalate	45
Calcium phosphate	5
Calcium oxalate and phosphate	40
Magnesium ammonium phosphate	2–5
Uric acid	2–5
Cystine	1–2

business is to remove the primary cause of the stone, if known, and thus prevent future stone formation. Otherwise, the presently accepted medical management is to remove the existing stones. Table 28-39 summarizes the various approaches to managing and preventing renal calculi that are due to excess calcium in the urine from an unknown cause.

Although dietary modifications are part of the treatment for renal stones, their use has been criticized. First, they sometimes are ineffective. Second, since the stones are made up of different chemicals, dietary restriction of any one particular substance may be of no value. In addition, components of the stones can be from internal as well as external sources. However, since diet therapy has proven successful with some patients, some clinicians prefer to use a combination of medications and dietary modifications. Dietary modification may prevent the formation of future stones in some postsurgical cases, especially if the patients are prone to renal calculi.

There are some dietary modifications used to treat calcium stones of unknown origin. One very important practice is consumption of an adequate amount of fluid (Table 28-39). The main objective here is to maintain a dilute urine with a specific gravity less than 1.015 throughout each 24-hour period. To accomplish this, a patient must drink at least 12 to 16 c (3 to 4 L) of liquid daily, including at night. The latter is important because nocturnal urine is usually concentrated (especially in hot weather) and thus more alka-

TABLE 28-39 Medical Management of Patients with Renal Calculi Resulting from Excess Calcium in the Urine

Treatment	Aim of Treatment	Clinical Results
Thiazide diuretics (e.g., hydrochlorothiazide)	1. Normalize urine calcium level by tubule reabsorption of calcium 2. Increase excretion of magnesium in urine (magnesium inhibits stone formation)	Urinary calcium restored to normal; overall reduction in stone formation; reduction in rate of new stone formation
Isotonic inorganic phosphates (1.5–3.0 g phosphorus per day)	1. Increase urinary pyrophosphate, which inhibits stone formation 2. Decrease urinary calcium	Reduction of stone recurrence
Oral cellulose phosphate	Inhibit calcium absorption from gut (excessive calcium absorption causes hypercalciuria)	Reduction in excretion of calcium in urine
Decreased oral calcium intake (150–350 mg/d)	Lower calcium excretion in urine	Possible reduction in stone formation
Decreased vitamin D intake (less common treatment)	Lower calcium absorption	Possible reduction in stone formation
Increased fluid intake (3–4 L/d)	Dissolve stones	Likely elimination of stones
Increased intake of acid ash foods (see text)	Acidify urine	Possible dissolution of stones

line (the patient's urine is usually alkaline even during the day). This produces a chemical environment ideal for the precipitation of more calcium stones. More fluid should be drunk after urination, and even mild dehydration should be avoided. Daily urine should amount to approximately 3 or 4 L; less signals dehydration.

Drinking enough fluid is important. Most people are not used to consuming such a large amount of liquid, especially at night, or to the inconvenience of having to urinate so often. Compliance may be low if the patient is instructed simply to drink more fluid. The physician, nurse, or dietitian can help by giving intense support and encouragement, which aids the patient in realizing the importance of carrying out the instructions. A useful suggestion for monitoring fluid intake and urine excretion is to collect the urine in a special calibrated jar or bucket that indicates volume.

As shown in Table 28-39, acidification of urine and a low vitamin D intake are two other diet-related methods or attempts in treating calcium stones. Urine may be acidified in a number of ways (see later discussion), and a low-vitamin D diet can be planned by excluding all foods fortified with vitamin D, such as dairy products.

The use of a low-calcium diet (Table 28-39) is sometimes but not always effective in managing a patient with renal stones, although it can also serve other purposes. For example, a 200-mg-calcium diet can be ordered for treating renal calculi (or hypercalcemia) or for diagnosing hypercalciuria. For the latter purpose, the patient continues the diet for 3 days. However, this diet fails to provide the RDAs for several nutrients.

TABLE 28-40   Three Examples of Daily Meal Planning for a 200-mg-Calcium Diet

Food Group	Example 1	Example 2	Example 3	Approximate Calcium Content (mg)
Milk, cheese, eggs	None	None	None	0
Breads and equivalents	3 sl bread made without milk	3 matzoth	2 sl bread made without milk; 1 c plain popcorn	30
Cereals, flours	1 c Puffed Rice	¼ c flour	¾ c farina	7
Meat, poultry, fish	3 oz chicken; 4 oz lamb; 1½ oz shad, baked	3 oz veal roast; 3 oz chicken, boneless, canned; 2 sl bologna	2 oz liver; 3 oz pork; 3 frankfurters; 3½ oz tuna, canned, drained	30
Vegetables	½ c beets, cooked; ½ c eggplant, cooked	½ green pepper, cooked or raw; ½ c tomatoes, canned	½ c mushrooms, canned; ½ c cauliflower, cooked	30
Fruits	½ c applesauce; 2 medium nectarines; 1 medium apple	½ c nectar; ½ c peaches, canned; ½ c fresh grapes	½ c pears, canned; ½ c cranberry juice, ½ c fruit cocktail, canned	20
Fats	5–6 servings bacon fat, salad dressings, and others	5–6 servings bacon fat, salad dressings, and others	5–6 servings bacon fat, salad dressings, and others	5
Potatoes and equivalents	½ c noodles	½ c white potato	1 medium white potato, baked	15
Soup (broth of permitted meats or soups made with permitted ingredients)	No limit	No limit	No limit	0
Beverages	2–4 servings	2–4 servings	2–4 servings	10–20
Desserts	1 c flavored gelatin	1 c lemon ice	1½ oz angel food cake	5
Miscellaneous (sugar, nondairy creamer, sweets, etc.)	No limit	No limit	No limit	0

Note: Water used for cooking and drinking should not contain more than 35 mg of calcium per liter. Use distilled water if necessary.

Since the diet lacks calcium and vitamin D, it cannot support normal growth in children. Thus, it is not advised as a long-term treatment. It should also be noted that oxalate and magnesium in the diet can interfere with calcium excretion. If feasible, their intakes should also be regulated and monitored. Table 28-40 provides three examples of planning a 200-mg-calcium diet. Table 28-41 provides a sample menu.

Sometimes a 600-mg-calcium diet may be ordered for a patient, for various reasons: diagnosing hypercalciuria, treating milk-alkali syn-

TABLE 28-41   Sample Menu for a 200-mg-Calcium Diet

Breakfast	Lunch	Dinner
Juice, cranberry, ½ c	Soup, tomato, milk-free, ½ c	Fruit cocktail, canned, ½ c
Farina, ¾ c	Chicken, boneless, canned, 3 oz	Veal roast, 3 oz
Bread, made without milk, 1 sl	Mushrooms, canned, ½ c	Potato, baked, medium, 1
Margarine, 2 t	Bread, made without milk, 1 sl	Cauliflower, cooked, ½ c
Salt, pepper	Butter or margarine, 2 t	Bread, made without milk, 1 sl
Sugar	Pears, canned, ½ c	Butter or margarine, 2 t
Imitation cream, non-dairy creamer, or coffee whitener	Salt, pepper	Lemon ice, 1 c
Coffee or tea	Sugar	Imitation cream, non-dairy creamer, or coffee whitener
	Imitation cream, non-dairy creamer, or coffee whitener	Coffee or tea
	Coffee or tea	Salt, pepper
		Sugar

drome, treating hypercalcemia, counteracting excessive vitamin D ingestion, treating patients who have been bedridden for a long period, treating hyperparathyroidism or hyperthyroidism, or sometimes treating patients with renal calculi. Again, this diet is low in several nutrients. The same problems arise with reducing oxalate and magnesium in the diet (see above discussion). Table 28-42 provides three examples of planning a 600-mg-calcium diet; Table 28-43 provides a sample daily menu. To facilitate the planning of a restricted calcium diet, Table 28-44 divides foods into exchange lists, each of which includes food items with approximately equal calcium contents. By means of these exchange lists, one can easily prepare the meal plans described in Tables 28-40 to 28-43.

Calcium Phosphate Stones

When kidney stones are made up mainly of calcium phosphate, most of the management procedures in Table 28-39 also apply. However, some clinicians advocate the use of a low-phosphorus and moderately low calcium diet to treat or prevent the formation of such kidney stones, although this practice is not common for several reasons. First, the treatment is not very effective.

Second, the high amounts of citrate that may be excreted as a result of the low phosphate intake can potentiate citric acid stone formation.

The more common practice is to use aluminum hydroxide to chelate the dietary and intestinal phosphorus. (Since this is drug therapy, it will not be discussed here. See references for more information.) However the attending physician may order a low-phosphorus diet. Table 28-45 provides a sample meal for a 1,000-mg-phosphorus, 600-mg-calcium diet. Table 28-46 indicates the permitted and prohibited foods in a phosphorus-restricted diet.

Calcium Oxalate Stones

As indicated in Table 28-38, calcium oxalate is a component of a substantial portion of kidney stones. One possible cause of calcium oxalate stones is an inborn error of oxalic acid metabolism that may produce primary hyperoxaluria. Although this is not common, its occurrence can be fatal in a young patient.

Another cause may be intestinal disorders such as Crohn's disease and intestinal bypass surgery. In such cases, weight loss may increase absorption of the chemical and increase its concentration in the urine. Intestinal disorders such

TABLE 28-42 Three Examples of Daily Meal Planning for a 600-mg-Calcium Diet

Food Group	Example 1	Example 2	Example 3	Approximate Calcium Content (mg)
Milk, cheese	1 c whole milk	1 c vanilla ice cream	1 c cottage cheese	290
Eggs	1, any style	1, any style	1, any style	30
Breads and equivalents	4 sl Italian bread; 8 2-in. square saltines; 15 pretzel sticks	4 sl Vienna bread; 1 matzo; 1 c popcorn	4 sl French bread; 8 soda crackers; 8 saltines	60
Cereals, flours	1 c Kix	1 c Puffed Wheat	¾ c Malt-o-meal	7
Meat, poultry, fish	2 oz chicken drumstick; 1 lamb chop; 3 oz ham; 1 oz salami; 2 Vienna sausages	3 oz tuna; 3 oz beef heart; 4 oz luncheon meat; 3 oz pork	10 sl bologna; 3 oz roast veal; 3 breaded fish sticks	30
Vegetables	½ c beets, cooked; ½ c cucumber; ½ c summer squash; ¼ head iceberg lettuce	½ c tomato juice; ½ c corn, cooked; 1 tomato, raw; ½ c carrots, cooked	½ c mushrooms, canned; 5 spears asparagus, cooked; ½ c brussels sprouts; ½ c onions, cooked	60
Fruits	¼ grapefruit; ½ c orange juice; ½ c diced pineapple, raw; 1 c raspberries, raw	½ c strawberries; ½ wedge watermelon; 1 peach; 1 small pear	1 c pineapple, diced; 1 plum; 1 c grapefruit juice, canned	50
Fats	5–6 servings bacon fat, salad dressings, and others	5–6 servings bacon fat, salad dressings, and others	5–6 servings bacon fat, salad dressings, and others	5
Potatoes and equivalents	½ c white potato	½ c macaroni	1 medium white potato	15
Soups (broth of permitted meats or soups made with permitted ingredients, e.g., milk)	No limit	No limit	No limit	0
Beverages	2–4 servings	2–4 servings	2–4 servings	10–20
Desserts	1 c flavored gelatin	1 c lemon ice	1½ oz angel food cake	5
Miscellaneous (sugar, nondairy creamer, sweets, etc.)	No limit	No limit	No limit	

Note: Water used for cooking and drinking should not contain more than 35 mg of calcium per liter. Use distilled water if necessary.

TABLE 28-43   Sample Menu for a 600-mg-Calcium Diet

Breakfast	Lunch	Dinner
Juice, orange, ½ c	Soup, tomato, ½ c	Lettuce, iceberg, ¼ head
Grapefruit, ¼	Saltines, 2-in. square, 4	Cucumber, ½ c
Kix, 1 c	Beets, cooked, ½ c	Salad dressing, 1 T
Egg, poached, 1	Squash, summer, cooked, ½ c	Saltines, 2-in. square, 4
Ham, 3 oz	Bread, Italian, 2 sl	Potato, white, baked, ½ c
Toast, Italian bread, 1 sl	Margarine, 2 t	Bread, Italian, 1 sl
Margarine, 1 t	Salami, 1 oz	Margarine, 1 t
Jam or jelly	Chicken drumstick, 2 oz	Lamb chop, 1
Milk, whole, ½ c	Pretzel sticks, 15	Sausages, Vienna, 2
Salt, pepper	Raspberries, raw, 1 c	Milk, whole, ½ c
Sugar	Pineapple, raw, diced, ½ c	Gelatin, flavored, 1 c
Imitation cream, non-dairy creamer, or coffee whitener	Sugar	Sugar
Coffee or tea	Salt, pepper	Salt, pepper
	Coffee or tea	Nondairy creamer
		Coffee or tea

TABLE 28-44   Calcium Food Exchange Lists

Dairy products		Cereals, flours	
(1 exchange = 288 mg calcium)		(1 exchange = 7 mg calcium)	
Buttermilk, whole milk, skim milk	1 c	Cereals, cooked	
Cheese		Corn or hominy grits, farina, Malt-o-	
Cheddar	1 oz	meal, Cream of Rice	¾ c
Cottage	1 c	Oatmeal	⅓ c
Provolone	2 oz	Cereals, ready-to-eat	
Swiss	1 oz	Bran flakes	⅓ c
Cream		Corn flakes, Kix, Puffed Rice, Puffed	
Half and half	1 c	Wheat	1 c
Heavy	1½ c	Raisin bran	¼ c
Ice cream, vanilla	1 c	Shredded wheat, biscuit	¾
Yogurt, plain, low fat	⅔ c	Wheat germ	2 T
		Flours	
Breads		Cornstarch, tapioca, cornmeal,	
(1 exchange = 10 mg calcium)		wheat	¼ c
Bagel, egg or water	1		
Bread, white, rye, cracked wheat	½ sl	**Eggs**	
Bread made with no milk added, e.g.,		(1 exchange = 30 mg calcium)	
Vienna, Italian, French	1 sl	Egg	
Graham crackers, 2½-in. square	4	Fried, hard cooked, poached	1
Popcorn, popped, plain	1 c	Scrambled, milk added, in butter,	
Pretzel sticks	15	omelet	⅔
Roll, brown and serve	½	White	No limit
Saltine crackers, 2-in. square	8	Whole	1
Soda crackers, 2½-in. square	8	Yolk	1

TABLE 28-44 (continued)

Beverages
(1 exchange = 5 mg calcium)

Beer	4 oz
Coffee, tea	8 oz
Dessert wine, sherry	2 oz
Lemonade	8 oz

Meat, poultry, fish
(1 exchange = 5 mg calcium)

Beef, pork, lamb, veal, ham	1 oz
Bologna	2 sl
Deviled ham	¼ c
Dry salami	5 sl
Frankfurter	1
Heart, tongue, chicken liver, beef liver	1 oz
Turkey, chicken, duck	1 oz
Tuna, flounder, snapper, halibut, sole, fresh mackerel	1 oz

Fats, oils
(1 exchange = 1 mg calcium)

Bacon	1 strip
Bacon fat, lard, suet	1 t
Butter, margarine	1 t
Cooking fats and vegetable oils	No limit
Salad dressing (commercial):	
French, Italian, Thousand Island	1 t
Mayonnaise	1 t

Sugars, sweets
(1 exchange = 6 mg calcium)

Candy	
Jelly beans, butterscotch, fondant, hard candy, marshmallows	1 oz
Gumdrops	3 oz
Honey	2 T
Jams, preserves, jellies	1 t
Sugars	No limit
Syrup	
Table blend, corn	2 t
Thin chocolate	2 T

Grains and equivalents
(1 exchange = 15 mg calcium)

Macaroni, noodles, spaghetti	½ c
Potato	
Hashed brown, prepared from frozen	½ c
Mashed	⅓ c
White, baked or boiled, medium	1
Rice, brown or white	½ c

Vegetables (low calcium content)
(1 exchange = 15 mg calcium)

Asparagus, spears	4
Bean sprouts, raw or cooked	1 c
Beets, cauliflower, corn, eggplant, green pepper (all cooked)	½ c
Celery stalks	1
Cucumber	½ c
Green onion, bulb and white portion of top (3-in. diam.)	6
Mushrooms, tomatoes, tomato juice (all canned)	½ c
Radishes	12

Vegetables (high calcium content)
(1 exchange = 25 mg calcium)

Asparagus, brussels sprouts, carrots, green peas, onions, summer squash	½ c
Lettuce, head, medium	¼
Spinach, raw	½ c
Tomato, raw, medium	1
Turnips, raw, diced	½ c
Vegetable juice cocktail, canned	6 oz

Fruits (low calcium content)
(1 exchange = 5 mg calcium)

Applesauce	½ c
Apricot, raw	1
Cranberry juice	½ c
Cranberry sauce	⅓ c
Grape juice drink, canned	⅔ c
Nectarines, medium	2
Peach nectar, pear nectar	½ c
Peaches, canned	½ c
Pears, canned	½ c
Raisins	5–8

Fruits (high calcium content)
(1 exchange = 10 mg calcium)

Apple, medium	1
Apple juice	½ c
Apricot nectar	½ c
Avocado, medium	⅓
Banana, small	1
Cherries, sour	¼ c
Fruit cocktail, canned	½ c
Grape juice	½ c
Grapes, fresh	½ c

TABLE 28-44   (continued)

Grapes, Thompson seedless, canned	½ c	**Desserts**	
Grapefruit, medium	¼	(1 exchange = 4 mg calcium)	
Mango, small	½	Angel food cake (8-in. diam.)	1½ oz
Orange juice	½ c	Cookies	
Peach, fresh, medium	1	Chocolate chip, ginger snaps,	
Pear, fresh, medium	1	macaroons, oatmeal	1
Prune juice	½ c	Vanilla wafers	3
Pineapple juice	½ c	Fruitcake, dark (30 slices in 1 loaf)	⅓ sl
Plums, purple, canned, medium	2	Gelatin, flavored	1 c
Raisins, seedless	1 T or	Ice, lime or lemon	1 c
	35–40	Pie	
Raspberries		Apple (7 sectors in 1 pie)	½ sector
Frozen, sweetened	¼ c	Blueberry (7 sectors in 1 pie)	¼ sector
Raw	⅓ c	Peach (7 sectors in 1 pie)	⅓ sector
Strawberries, raw	⅓ c	Pound cake (17 slices in 1 loaf)	⅔ sl
Watermelon, cubed	½ c		
		Free choices	
		(trace calcium)	
Soups (trace calcium)		Carbonated beverages	No limit
Broth (e.g., chicken, beef, turkey)	No limit	Cream substitute (check label)	No limit
Soup from permitted ingredients	No limit	Spices, condiments	No limit

TABLE 28-45   A Phosphorus-Restricted Diet

Breakfast	Lunch	Dinner
Juice, orange, ½ c	Roast chicken, 2 oz	Broth, chicken, 1 c
Puffed Rice, 1 c	Rice, long grain, ½ c	Roast pork, loin, 2 oz
Egg, poached, 1	Carrots, diced,	Potato, boiled, me-
Toast, Italian bread, 1 sl	cooked, ½ c	dium, 1
Butter, 1 t	Green salad, 1 c	Asparagus, cooked,
Jelly, 1 T	French dressing, 1 T	½ c
Milk, whole, ½ c	Bread, Italian, 2 sl	Fruit cocktail, ½ c
Coffee, 1 c	Butter, 2 t	Roll, hard, 1
	Milk, ½ c	Butter, 1 t
	Gelatin, lime, ½ c	Cake, angel food,
		1 slice
		Strawberries, ½ c
		Tea

Note: This menu contains approximately 1,000 mg of phosphorus and 600 mg of calcium.

as severe diarrhea may cause the patient to pass concentrated urine, causing calcium oxalate stones to precipitate.

Finally, dietary imbalances appear to play a role in the formation of calcium oxalate stones. A lack of sufficient fluid, excessive consumption of foods that make the urine alkaline, and the ingestion of too much high-oxalate-content food (see later discussion) have been implicated as diet-related causes.

TABLE 28-46 Foods Permitted and Prohibited in a Phosphorus-Restricted Diet

Food Group	Foods Permitted	Foods Prohibited
Dairy products	1–1½ c milk daily, whole, skim, or buttermilk; 3 T dry milk; ½ oz cheddar or Swiss cheese may replace ½ c milk; one whole egg daily; no limit for egg white	Any additional servings, including cooking ingredients; all cheese and cheese spreads
Meat, fish, poultry	Beef, lamb, veal, ham, pork; turkey, chicken, duck; haddock, bluefish, cod, halibut, shad, tuna, scallops, swordfish (number of servings varies with degree of restriction)	Clams, herring, crab, lobster, mackerel, oyster, fish roe, shrimp, salmon, sardines; heart, brains, liver, kidney, sweetbread; most processed meats have added phosphate, such as cured items (check label)
Desserts	Sherbet, ices, gelatin; fruit pies, meringues (made from egg white), pudding made with permitted ingredients, fruit tapioca, fruit whip, shortbread; cookies (from white sugar), angel food cake	All forms made with milk and eggs not within daily allowance; cream-filled pies, commercial cake mixes, cakes (unless made from permitted ingredients), custard, doughnuts, junket; ice cream
Breads	Enriched commercial white bread; French or Italian bread made without milk; water rolls; soda crackers, rusks, saltines, pretzels, matzoth	Cracked wheat, brown, corn, rye, raisin, whole wheat, and any white bread made with nonfat dry milk; biscuits, pancakes, muffins, waffles, rye wafers
Beverages	Coffee, tea, fruit juices, Postum, cola, soft drinks; servings within limit since most soft drinks contain phosphate as an additive	Milk unless specifically permitted; all commercial drinks using milk powder as an ingredient; fountain beverages, cocoa, chocolate
Cereals, flours, and equivalents	Cream of Rice, Cream of Wheat, cornmeal, corn flakes, rice flakes, Puffed Rice; spaghetti, noodles, macaroni; farina, corn grits; white flour, cornstarch, tapioca	Whole-grain cereals; wheat germ, bran, corn or soy grits, bran flakes, oatmeal; shredded wheat, Puffed Wheat; flours: soybean, self-rising, whole wheat, rye
Fats, oils	Margarine, butter; French dressing; fats, lard, cooking oils, shortening	Sweet and sour cream, mayonnaise
Soups	Broth: chicken, beef, and other permitted meats; cream soups made with permitted ingredients	Cream soup made with milk and egg not within allowance; split pea, bean, lentil
Sweets	Jelly, jam, preserves; syrup; sugar, hard candy; marshmallows, clear mints (without chocolate or prohibited milk ingredients)	Molasses, brown sugar; candy made with prohibited milk or eggs, e.g., milk chocolate, fudge, caramel
Fruits	All except most commercial dried fruits (which may contain phosphate as an additive); limit consumption of commercial dates, prunes, and raisins to prescribed phosphate intake	Dried fruit unless content of phosphate specifically calculated
Vegetables	Artichokes, asparagus, brussels sprouts, cabbage, carrots, cauliflower, celery, corn, cucumber, eggplant, escarole, green and wax beans, lettuce, onions, peppers, radishes, romaine, squash, turnips; white and sweet potatoes, pumpkin	Beet greens, broccoli, chard, chick-peas, collards, dandelion greens, kale, mushrooms, okra, parsnips, peas, rutabaga, soybean sprouts, spinach, turnip greens; kidney beans, lima beans, navy beans, soybeans
Miscellaneous	Pickles, salt, seasonings, spices and condiments	Brewer's yeast, chocolate, cocoa, cream sauces, nuts, nut products, olives

The treatment for calcium oxalate stones has been quite controversial in the last few years, especially when hyperoxaluria is of unknown origin. Most clinicians use a combination of the following management procedures:

1. Prescribing an intake of 3 to 4 L of fluid daily, following the procedure discussed earlier (see text).
2. Prescribing diuretics such as thiazide.
3. Prescribing oral inorganic orthophosphate.
4. Prescribing oral cholestyramine to bind intestinal oxalate to prevent its adsorption.
5. Prescribing oral magnesium (250 mg, as the oxide).
6. Prescribing oral magnesium (200 mg, as the oxide) plus 10 mg of vitamin B_6 (pyridoxine).
7. Prescribing oral taurine (9 g/d) (in trials with patients with intestinal bypass, urinary excretion of oxalate was reduced to normal).
8. Acidifying the patient's urine with foods or drugs (see later discussion).
9. Prescribing a low-oxalate diet.

A low-oxalate diet is not always effective in curing or preventing calcium oxalate stones. It is suspected that the endogenous formation of oxalate is fairly high and that stopping the exogenous supply is of little value. However, a low-oxalate diet in combination with other treatments may be beneficial. Table 28-47, which classifies foods by oxalic acid content, can be used to plan a low-oxalate diet. People on an oxalate-restricted diet should avoid all foods with high amounts of the substance. Patients should eat low-oxalate-content foods and limited servings of foods that are moderate in oxalate content. This diet contains inadequate amounts of a few nutrients, especially vitamin C.

Magnesium Ammonium Phosphate Stones

This type of stone is sometimes called *struvite*; the stones may or may not contain calcium. Their occurrence is normally accompanied by a recurrent urinary tract infection by coliforms (*Proteus* sp. and *Staphylococcus pyogenes albus*), a neurogenic bladder, or prostate hypertrophy. The bacteria, if present, contain the enzyme urease, which can split urea to form ammonia. Ammonia increases the alkalinity of the urine, promoting the formation of magnesium ammonium phos-

phate stones. The treatment for this type of stone is prescribing antibiotics to remove the underlying infection, acidification of urine (see the later discussion), administering plenty of fluids, and surgery.

Cystine Stones

The formation of this type of stone results from an inborn error of cystine metabolism. Rather than being metabolized, the substance is excreted, namely, cystinuria. Early and accurate diagnosis of this disease is important, since it recurs frequently and can cause morbidity in young patients unless treated and the stones removed. Treatment for this type of stone includes several procedures, excluding surgery. A doctor may use any known modern method to correct an identified genetic error (for example, administering enzymes; see Chapter 30). A large intake of fluid by the patient can help to dissolve the stones. Night urine is more concentrated and acidic and thus capable of precipitating more stones if fluid intake is not maintained during the evening hours. (The patient's urine is likely to be acidic even in the daytime.) The alkalinization of the urine to a pH greater than 7.5 is also useful in this situation (see the later discussion).

A chelating, binding, or complexing agent such as D-penicillamine can be utilized (at 2 to 4 g/d) for intractable cystinuria. This chemical can form a soluble complex with cystine and thus reduce the concentration of cystine in the urine, thus inhibiting the formation of more stones. The dose of chemical given is directly related to the amount of cystine in the urine. Clinical trials have confirmed that existing stones can be dissolved, while additional ones may be prevented from precipitating. However, patients who show sensitization to the chemical should be given the substance slowly for best results.

A low-methionine diet has also been claimed to be effective. Methionine, an amino acid, is the precursor of cystine, another amino acid. By reducing methionine intake, the amount of cystine in the body may be reduced. However, this method has not been successful for two reasons. First, it is extremely difficult to construct a low-methionine diet, since practically all animal proteins contain methionine, and a commercial dietetic product low in methionine is not yet

TABLE 28-47 Oxalic Acid Content of Food

High Content of Oxalic Acid*

Almonds	Currants	Mustard greens	Rhubarb
Beet greens	Gooseberries	Okra	Sorrel
Beets	Grape juice	Orange juice	Soybeans
Cashews	Grapefruit	Oranges	Spinach
Chard	Grapefruit juice	Parsley	Sweet potatoes
Chocolate	Grapes	Parsnips	Tea, black
Cocoa	Green plantain	Peanut butter	Turnip greens
Collards	Kale	Peanuts	Turnips
Cranberries	Leeks	Pecans	Wax beans
Cranberry juice	Mushrooms	Prunes	Wheat germ

Moderate Content of Oxalic Acid†

Apples	Carrots	Onions (2–3 T)	Sweet potatoes
Asparagus	Celery (¼ stalk)	Peaches	Tea (some herb)
Bananas	Cereals	Pears	Tomato juice (4 oz)
Beer (12 oz)	Cherries	Pineapple	Tomatoes (½)
Blackberries	Coffee (2 c)	Plums	White potatoes
Bread (3–4 slices)	Green beans	Raspberries	
Brussels sprouts	Green peas	Soft drinks	
Cabbage	Lettuce	Strawberries	

Low Content of Oxalic Acid‡

Cauliflower, cheese, eggs, fish, margarine, meat, milk, radishes

Note: This classification applies to all items shown and any products made from them.

*These foods should be avoided whenever possible.

†Daily intake limited to one serving or the amount shown in parentheses.

‡There is no limit on the consumption of these foods.

available. Second, a diet relatively low in methionine is not very palatable, and therefore patient compliance is poor.

Uric Acid Stones

Normally, the amount of uric acid or urates excreted by the kidneys depends on the ability of each kidney to excrete the substance. The process also depends on the amount of uric acid produced by the body and the amount of purine consumed through food. Purine is a normal constituent of cells and is not an essential dietary substance, since the body can synthesize it; however, it is found in almost all foods. It has been estimated that we excrete an average of 700 to 800 mg of urate a day (slightly more for males than females). Patients with calcium stones usually have excess uric acid in the blood and urine.

Formation of uric acid stones may be caused by any of several factors. (1) The person may excrete excessive uric acid for unknown reasons. (2) The urine may be too acidic for a variety of reasons. Middle-aged males may have persistently high urine acidity even though they do not have clinical gout or uric acid stones. (3) A primary disorder such as glycogen storage disease can raise the blood level of uric acid and thus cause uric acid stones to form as a secondary symptom.

Uric acid stones may be treated with a number of procedures before surgery is used. Restricting the dietary intake of purine is sometimes successful in providing relief, since it is the precursor of uric acid. However, planning a low-purine diet is not easy because most foods contain purine. Using the chemical allopurinol can interfere with the formation of uric acid from hypoxanthine and xanthine in the body, thus reducing the level of uric acid in the urine. (Hypoxanthine and xanthine are intermediate metabolites formed during the conversion of purines to uric acid.) The urine can also be alkalinized to a pH of 6.0 to 6.5 (see the later discussion).

URINARY TRACT INFECTIONS

This book does not have a chapter on the role of diet in the management of patients with urological disorders (except kidney diseases). Because of the widespread occurrence of urinary tract infections, especially among females, this topic is briefly discussed below. Detailed information may be obtained from references at the end of this book.

Urinary tract infections are more common among females, partly because of the anatomical structures of their genitourinary system. Some known factors in the infection among women are as follows: (1) contamination is anatomically easier and often unavoidable because of invasion of the genitourinary tract by fecal bacteria; (2) fluid intake is insufficient; (3) voiding is habitually infrequent and hurried; (4) certain drugs, such as oral contraceptives, are used; (5) a hormonal imbalance is present, such as in elderly women, in whom the bacterial population and acidity of the vagina may change; and (6) psychological stress is present.

Infection itself is brought about by the excess growth of certain pathogenic organisms. The pH of the urine and genitourinary tract can influence the growth of these organisms. Standard gynecological and urological textbooks suggest that the clinical management of the infection should include some or all of these measures: (1) use of appropriate topical or oral antibiotics; (2) frequent voiding; (3) increased water intake (at least 1 quart a day);* (4) the use of warm water

---

*This is important especially before and after menstruation and immediately after sexual intercourse. See the previous discussion for advice on increasing fluid intake in treating calcium stones.

and mild soap in washing and avoidance of all feminine hygienic aids (perianal hygiene is also important); and (5) modification of urine pH through drugs or diet, as discussed below. If the organisms are seen to thrive in an acidic environment, the urine is made more alkaline, and vice versa.

MODIFICATION OF URINE ACIDITY AND ALKALINITY

There are basically two ways to change the pH of the urine. One is to use particular drugs, and the other is to consume certain foods. Urinary pH can be determined by using special paper (such as Nitrazine paper) that changes color according to the pH of the urine.

Drugs

Currently vitamin C (ascorbic acid) and methionine are the two drugs used most frequently to acidify urine (decrease pH). When vitamin C is used, it is important to use ascorbic acid and not sodium ascorbate, since the latter is not acidic. The dose is about 400 to 600 mg each day until the urinary pH becomes acidic. When methionine is used, the dose is about 5 to 15 g daily, given until an acidic urinary pH is obtained. However, it is important to note that metabolic acidosis may result from the large amount of acid ingested, thus increasing urinary calcium excretion. For this reason, the patient's response should be monitored.

Alkalinization of urine is best achieved by ingesting a large amount of sodium bicarbonate or citrate. Patients usually find it difficult to comply with this prescription because of the unpleasant taste. To avoid this reaction, the chemicals may be given slowly or over a period of time to habituate the patient. They should preferably be given after meals and at night, so that the patient does not lose his or her appetite for the next meal. Simultaneous administration of acetazolamide also makes it easier to increase the pH of the urine. However, a highly alkaline urine can precipitate calcium phosphate stones. To avoid this, the patient must drink more fluid.

TABLE 28-48   Classification of Foods According to their Acid-Base Reactions in the Body

Alkaline-Ash-Forming or Alkaline-Urine-Producing Foods	Acid-Ash-Forming or Acid-Urine-Producing Foods	Neutral Foods
Milk and cream, all types	Meat, poultry, fish, shellfish, cheese, eggs	Butter, margarine, fats and oils (cooking), salad oil, lard
Fruits except plums, prunes, and cranberries	Plums, prunes, cranberries	Cornstarch, arrowroot, tapioca
Carbonated beverages	Corn, lentils	Sugar, honey, syrup
All vegetables except corn and lentils	Bread (especially whole-wheat bread not containing baking soda or powder)	Nonchocolate candy
Chestnuts, coconut, almonds	Cereals, crackers	Coffee, tea
Molasses	Rice, noodles, macaroni, spaghetti	
Baking soda and baking powder	Peanuts, walnuts, peanut butter	
	Pastries, cakes, and cookies not containing baking soda or powder	
	Fats, bacon	

Diet

The pH of a patient's urine can be changed by eating certain types of food. As discussed in Chapter 9, some foods, because of their ingredients, can form an acidic or alkaline residue in the body and thus influence the pH of the urine. Table 28-48 categorizes foods according to whether they produce alkaline or acidic urine. The pH of the urine can be regulated by eating more or less of the foods indicated in Table 28-48.

STUDY QUESTIONS

1. What is the basic structural unit of the kidney?
2. How is the normal function of a kidney measured? What does GFR refer to?
3. Define chronic renal failure. How is diet related to other facets of the medical management of a patient with chronic renal failure? What problems are encountered in making this patient's diet palatable?
4. How does peritoneal dialysis differ from hemodialysis? What is the central nutritional problem with a patient undergoing dialysis?
5. How is hypokalemia treated? Why is it commonly seen in patients with kidney and heart problems? Describe the symptoms of hypokalemia.
6. What is the reason for the high variability in the nutritional needs of kidney patients? Ex-

CASE STUDY   *Chronic Renal Failure*

Mr. J.G. was a 50-year-old banker with a history of kidney disorders. Ten years ago, he was hospitalized twice for renal failure. Although he was placed on a sodium-, potassium-, and protein-controlled diet during this period, he did not comply with this diet very well.

In the last 2 months, Mr. J.G.'s conditions deteriorated and his family doctor admitted him to the hospital for diagnosis and treatment. On admission to the hospital, Mr. J.G. weighed 77.1 kg (170 lb) and was 180.3 cm (5′11″) tall. He had azotemia, acidosis, and anemia. He was tired, weak, short of breath, waxy in complexion, and vomiting. He was diagnosed as having chronic renal failure. This diagnosis was based on both his past medical history and the following supporting clinical and laboratory data: glomerular filtration rate (GFR), 7 mL/min; blood urea nitrogen (BUN), 120 μg/100 mL; blood potassium, 5 mEq/L; sodium, 120 mEq/L; and calcium, 7 mg/100 mL. He also had congestive heart failure, high blood pressure, and anemia.

The health team studied J.G.'s medical history and planned three approaches: drugs, diet, and dialysis. He was given vitamin and mineral supplements and a diuretic. He was placed on a diet of 30 to 35 g of protein, 1 to 1.5 g of sodium, and 1 to 1.5 g of potassium, with 500 to 700 mL of fluid permitted daily. He was also placed on hemodialysis.

His responses to the diet were as expected. He complained bitterly about the lack of fluid and hated the diet. He ate poorly. However, after one week of dialysis, he began to show signs of improvement. The health team increased his protein allowance to 50 to 55 g, with 1,000 to 1,200 mL of fluid permitted. He remained on the diuretics and was allowed 1.5 g of sodium daily.

Review and Analysis

1. Ascertain the ideal weight for this patient.
2. What should his vitamin and mineral supplement contain? If you are uncertain about his need for certain vitamins, make some assumptions but state the premises.
3. Plan a diet providing 2,800 kcal, 30 to 35 g of protein, 1.3 g of sodium, 1.0 g of potassium, and 600 mL of fluid.
4. Plan a diet providing 2,800 kcal, 55 g of protein, 1.5 g of sodium, 1.5 g of potassium, and 1,200 mL of fluid.
5. Describe the process of hemodialysis. Explain the types of nutrients most likely to be lost during dialysis.
6. Usually after a patient has been on dialysis for a few weeks, his or her dietary protein allowance is increased. Why? How does dialysis in a kidney patient eliminate the harmfulness of ingesting excess protein?

plain what a renal exchange list is and how it may be used. Why is the amount of LBV protein limited in the diet of a kidney patient?
7. Why is it important to educate a kidney patient in the early stages of his or her illness? What topics should be included?
8. Some patients with kidney stones have severe symptoms, while others have none. Why is this so?

9. What criticisms have been elicited by the practice of treating patients having renal stones with dietary manipulations? Which dietary treatments have met with some success?
10. Why are urinary tract infections more common in women than in men? What is the recommended course of treatment for such infections?

Chapter 29

Diet, Stress, and Trauma

A PERSON WHO SUFFERS the physical trauma and stress associated with surgery, burns, injuries, or cancer needs special nutritional attention. Without it, the recovery period may be unnecessarily prolonged, complications may occur, and, above all, human suffering may increase. The dietary and nutritional support provided by the health team plays an essential role in the healing process of a trauma patient.

NUTRITIONAL SUPPORT FOR PATIENTS WITH TRAUMA

Recent clinical reports have confirmed that a sizable number of hospital patients, both medical and surgical, suffer from varying degrees of malnutrition. This topic was briefly discussed in Chapter 22. Although vitamin and mineral deficiencies and electrolyte and fluid imbalances are more common, protein and calorie undernourishments also occur, especially among patients with trauma. Some of these patients even demonstrate clinical symptoms of nutrient deficiencies. This unpleasant situation is now being remedied by health teams working together.

This work begins when the health team makes a comprehensive nutritional assessment (whenever feasible) of a patient admitted with any form of stress or trauma, including those admitted for surgery. This assessment includes determining the following: (1) nutritional status, (2) metabolic status, (3) medical conditions of the gastrointestinal system, (4) food consumption behavior, (5) optimal nutrient needs, and (6) nutritional and dietary management alternatives (e.g., need for tube feeding). More details of this care strategy are provided in Chapter 22.

Appropriate nutritional and dietary support for patients with trauma is enhanced by an understanding of the metabolic changes that occur during surgery, burns, and body injuries. Numerous clinical studies have reported on this topic in detail; what follows is only a brief discussion that summarizes presently available knowledge. More detailed information is available in the references for this chapter. The relevant metabolic responses to trauma can be seen in three

phases—ebb, stress, and recovery—and are described in Table 29-1.

The *ebb phase* is the shortest of the three, lasting only about 24 hours. In this phase, the capacity of the body to produce heat decreases so that the body can meet the increased demands of the environment (including the trauma), and less oxygen than normal is consumed. No definitive changes have been observed in levels of hormones or body metabolites in this first stage of response to trauma.

The second, or *stress phase*, is variable and may last from 2 to 10 days. During this phase a number of dramatic changes take place in the body. In response to the trauma, whether physical, physiological, or emotional, the central nervous system sends out signals via the sympathetic nervous system to various glands (such as the adrenals, thyroid, pancreas, and pituitary), causing them to release the appropriate hormones to increase nutrient mobilization and utilization. Hormones (see Table 29-1) such as glucagon and corticosteroids from the adrenal glands break down body muscle protein, which increases nitrogen in the blood and urine in the form of urea. This breakdown of muscle protein serves two important purposes: (1) Amino acids are freed and partially converted to glucose, which provides additional fuel, and (2) the increased nitrogen is partially converted to important blood proteins, enzymes, and other structural proteins (such as albumin), which are needed to support the stresses of trauma. Because of this conversion of muscle tissue, 10 to 30 g of protein may be lost per day during the stress phase.

The relative lack of insulin action during the stress phase (see Table 29-1) to assist the entry of glucose into the fat cells triggers the breakdown of fat to provide more glucose for fuel.

In general, about the same amount of fat and muscle are lost (but protein loss through catabolism provides about 15% to 20% of the total calories needed to support a patient during the stress phase). Muscle glycogen is mobilized by hormones called *catecholamines*, which are secreted by the adrenal glands. The action of these hormones increases glucose production and can also increase the body's basal metabolic rate, resulting in higher heat production. These processes together result in hypermetabolism. It is clinically

TABLE 29-1   Description of Stages of the Body in Response to Surgery and Other Forms of Trauma

Stage	Medical Term	Duration (days)	Hormonal Changes	Variations in Body Metabolites	Body Composition and Temperature Changes
1	Ebb phase, early phase	1	Not definitive	Not definitive	Decreased heat production; decreased oxygen consumption
2	Stress phase, catabolic phase, acute phase, flow phase, hypermetabolic phase	2–10	Increased blood catecholamines, glucagon, corticosteroids, thyroid hormones; decreased blood insulin	Increased blood and urine glucose and nitrogen (in the form of urea)	Muscle protein and fat breakdown, weight loss; possible body water and electrolyte loss; possible increase in body temperature and heat production; possible skin loss; loss of potassium and retention of sodium
3	Recovery phase, anabolic phase, adaptive phase	3–10	Increased blood insulin and growth hormone; decreased blood catecholamines	Increased blood ketone bodies; decreased blood glucose; slightly elevated to normal blood and urine nitrogen (in the form of urea)	Nutrient deposition; building up of body muscle

observed as weight loss and, in some patients, fever or a mild increase in body temperature. Some of the weight loss may also be explained by water loss from blood depletion, exudates, insensible or evaporative loss, vomiting and diarrhea, and loss through urine from body muscle breakdown. The magnitude of the changes resulting from hypermetabolism depends on the type and extent of injury, the nutritional status of the patient, the immediate availability of fluid and electrolyte compensation, and the extent of anesthesia.

During the stress phase, the loss of muscle is evidenced by increases in the amounts of nitrogen, potassium, phosphorus, sulfur, magnesium, zinc, and certain vitamins (especially vitamin C) in the urine. These are all components of muscle tissue or special products released in response to the trauma. The amount of protein or nitrogen loss depends on the type and degree of trauma. Nitrogen losses from damage to skin or other tissues or organs may account for up to one-quarter of the total nitrogen loss. Also evident are water and potassium losses, which are usually accompanied by sodium retention. Figure 29-1 illustrates different types of trauma and the extent of associated nitrogen loss and hypermetabolism.

Generally, the absolute quantity of essential nutrients and metabolites in the blood increases during the stress phase. This can be seen as an attempt by the body to meet increased metabolic needs caused by trauma. The catabolic processes that increase metabolites and nutrients can be counteracted to a certain degree, but the value of such procedures has not been established. This

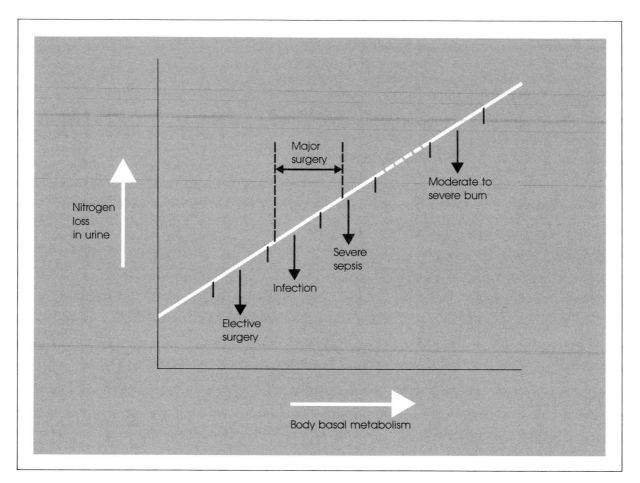

FIGURE 29-1   The interrelationship between nitrogen loss in urine, type
of trauma, and body basal metabolism.

topic has been explored in depth in numerous scientific and clinical reports, some of which are listed at the end of this book. A detailed discussion is beyond the scope of this book.

A multitude of different traumas may cause or exaggerate metabolic changes in the stress phase. The most common traumas are: (1) surgical stress, (2) systemic infection, (3) fractures, (4) blood and exudate loss, (5) crush injury, (6) burns, (7) open wounds or tissue destruction, (8) semistarvation and total starvation, (9) cold exposure, (10) prolonged inactivity such as bed rest or confinement, (11) muscle wasting, (12) inadequate nutritional status, and (13) general anesthesia. Since all these various traumas may bring about or aggravate any nutrient deficiency, the patient may die from secondary malnutrition rather than from the main injury.

The last phase of response to trauma is the *recovery* or *anabolic phase* (see Table 29-1). As the severity of the trauma decreases, the activity of the sympathetic nervous system returns to normal. This triggers an increase in insulin and growth hormone in the blood. The former ensures a steady supply of glucose to cells for fuel and repair, and the latter directs the deposition of nutrients in various parts of the body.

Transition from the stress (catabolic) to recovery (anabolic) phase depends on the type and extent of trauma, body weight loss, and related nutrient depletion. One indicator of transition is a decrease of glucose in the blood and urine. Another is that hypermetabolism abates. In some patients, the return to normal body temperature is often used as an indicator, but it may not be reliable. Most patients enter the recovery phase about 5 to 10 days after the trauma, but it is important to remember that this period is highly variable. The length of the recovery phase also varies greatly.

Identifying the transition to the recovery phase is quite important for health clinicians. For instance, if a clinical decision is premature, intravenously administered nutrients (5% dextrose and/or protein supplements) may mask the lowering of blood glucose, which characterizes the transition. Also, if the body is not yet ready to retain protein, intravenously added glucose and amino acids or peptides may exacerbate the patient's hypermetabolic condition.

However, if the patient has entered the recovery phase, he or she begins to retain administered protein. This retention assists in forming vital body cell mass, especially in depleted abdominal organs. Once protein retention begins, the body begins to respond favorably to ensuing treatment and the trauma becomes less dangerous. Nutritional factors that determine the extent of protein retention and positive nitrogen balance are: (1) body metabolic rate, (2) intake of essential amino acids and total nitrogen, and (3) calories derived from fat and carbohydrates and other nonprotein sources.

A trauma patient should receive nutritional treatment long before the recovery phase. To determine the nutritional and dietary strategy, three factors should be considered: (1) preoperative nutritional status, (2) types of pathological abnormalities, and (3) the patient's metabolic response. This aspect of general patient care is discussed in detail in Chapter 22. When diet therapy is instituted and how the patient responds depends on: (1) the duration of the trauma stages, (2) the extent of body nutrient loss, and (3) the body's metabolic rate. Careful and consistent use of these guidelines will ensure the proper care of the patient.

DIET AND THE SURGICAL PATIENT

Whether a patient undergoes elective or emergency surgery, preoperative and postoperative nutritional supports are important. The former prepares the patient for the operation, and the latter helps assure that normal body functions return as soon as possible. Together they help the entire surgical procedure be successful.

Immediate Preoperative Dietary Support

Preoperative dietary routine is fairly standard, varying somewhat with the patient and the hospital. Initially, body fluids and electrolytes are checked and maintained at proper levels. It may also be necessary to provide glucose or other nutrients intravenously.

The timing and kind of meal before surgery is also quite important. Food ingested before an operation may be aspired into the patient's lungs during recovery from anesthesia, with possibly fatal results. To prevent this, a patient should generally not be fed for 6 to 8 hours before surgery. A light evening meal with no food after midnight is recommended for patients scheduled for morning surgery. If the surgery is scheduled for early or late afternoon, a patient should have a breakfast of juice, toast, or cereal and coffee or tea. Most surgeons advise patients against ingesting food immediately before surgery. If undigested food residue is present (as it often is in emergency cases), some surgeons order that the patient's stomach be washed before the operation.

Many patients undergoing gastrointestinal surgery experience intestinal distension postoperatively. Patients who receive a preoperative fluid or low-residue diet (see Chapter 24) generally avoid this complication and tend to have a more comfortable recovery period.

Postoperative Dietary Regimen

The main goal of postoperative nutritional and dietary care is for the patient to regain a normal body weight. This is brought about by a positive nitrogen balance and the subsequent muscle formation and fat deposition. This goal can be achieved by first correcting all fluid and electrolyte imbalances and giving appropriate transfusions. The second step is to provide carefully planned dietary and nutritional support for the patient with special emphasis on those nutrients discussed at the beginning of this chapter. The third step is to make sure that the patient eats his or her food by maintaining a detailed record of what is consumed.

A postoperative dietary regimen also requires aggressive nutritional support. This is needed to maintain normal body functions and tissues. Tissue maintenance is especially important since additional losses may result from postoperative bed confinement and ensuing muscle atrophy. Nutritional supports should also attempt to replace tissue (such as muscle, bone, blood, exudate, and skin that may have been lost during the trauma or surgery). Any malnourishment should be remedied if it has not already been treated. Plasma protein should be supplied to control or prevent edema and shock. Plasma protein also provides vital components for the synthesis of albumin, antibodies, enzymes, and other necessary substances, which may have been lost through bleeding or the escape of fluids. Finally, plasma protein also accelerates the healing of wounds.

Inadequate nutritional supports may increase morbidity and mortality, delay the return of normal body functions, and retard the process of tissue rebuilding. Inadequate nutrition also prevents wounds from healing at a normal pace and may cause edema and muscular weakness. Most importantly, all of these consequences prolong convalescence and discomfort for the patient.

Since a patient usually cannot tolerate much solid food immediately after an operation, it is withheld anywhere from a few hours to 2 or 3 days. A feeding that is too early may nauseate the patient and cause him or her to vomit. This results in further fluid and electrolyte losses as well as discomfort. The outline below lists the various types of dietary support during this short part of the postoperative period.

1. No food by mouth
2. Intravenous feeding: blood transfusion, fluids and electrolytes, 5% dextrose, vitamin and mineral supplements, protein-sparing solutions (with or without intralipid), combination of above
3. Oral feeding: hospital progressive routine diet with or without supplements, liquid protein supplements with or without nonprotein calories, combination of above
4. A combination of oral and intravenous feedings.

Many clinicians feel that it is not worthwhile to provide aggressive nutritional support during such a short period of food deprivation. This decision is justified in a well-nourished individual who can afford temporary catabolic losses and would not be able to efficiently use the supplied protein or calories. The attending physician must decide if the patient is well nourished and if enteral or parenteral feedings can be tolerated. If the feedings can be tolerated, a subsequent decision must be made on benefits of these exogenous nutrients.

Blood transfusions and fluid and electrolyte compensation are administered to those patients needing them. Some doctors prescribe 5% dextrose solution in saline or water, but the amount given is limited by the patient's tolerance. Another problem is that a concentrated dextrose solution may cause thrombosis in the peripheral veins. Because of the relatively low nutrient density of dextrose solution, it should not be used as a long-term means of feeding. It is generally claimed that the infusion of dextrose spares some body protein from breakdown to provide needed calories. Recently various medical centers have experimented with the infusion of protein-sparing solutions made up mainly of essential amino acids. The preliminary trials have been very encouraging. However, if such means are used every day, it may be very costly. For more information about protein-sparing solutions, consult Chapter 23. Some hospitals use vitamin and mineral supplements as well as protein-sparing solutions.

Although solid foods are withheld from patients immediately after an operation, most hospitals provide patients with oral feedings after their intestinal functions return to normal (as early as 24 hours after the operation). The feedings consist of routine hospital progressive diets (see Chapter 23). This stepwise postoperative feeding may cover 1 to 3 days, depending on the patient's tolerance, strength, and type of operation or trauma.

Some patients may be able to start with a soft diet, while others must begin with a clear liquid diet. Occasionally progressive feedings may be supplemented with commercial formulas. Some patients are given liquid protein supplements with or without nonprotein calories if they can tolerate the feedings. Again, depending on the patient and his or her condition, a combination of feeding methods, including total parenteral nutrition (see Chapter 23), may be used. For patients requiring tube feeding, consult the detailed procedures described in Chapter 23.

At this early stage of postoperative recovery, physicians, nurses, and dietitians should work closely to determine whether dextrose solution or oral liquid diets should be continued. This is important, since both types of feeding may not be nutritionally sound without concentrated supplements. Nutritional supports, including fluids, electrolytes, protein, calories and other items should be carefully reviewed. Finally, a long-term aggressive postoperative dietary treatment should be planned and executed to combat the catabolic consequences of trauma and to bring about a speedy recovery, as discussed in the following paragraphs.

When a patient can tolerate regular hospital foods, the health team should plan and prescribe an appropriate diet. Experts in clinical nutrition have tried for a number of years to develop a postoperative diet that will provide patients with an optimal amount of nutrients. In general, the following diet prescription should satisfy most clinical conditions that involve trauma: (1) 40 to 50 kcal/kg body weight/d, (2) 12% to 15% of total calories as protein, (3) well balanced intakes of the established RDAs, and (4) carefully monitored intakes of vitamins A, K, C, B_{12}, and folic acid and the minerals iron and zinc. To illustrate the protein and calorie composition of such a diet, Table 29-2 includes two examples (40 kcal and 50 kcal/d) for a man weighing 70 kg.

If the patient has a minimal amount of tissue and blood loss, a sound preoperative nutritional status, a moderate to good appetite, and no sign of any surgical complications, a diet of 35 to 40 kcal/kg is probably sufficient. However, the diet

TABLE 29-2 Approximate Protein and Calorie Content of a Postoperative Diet for a Male Patient Weighing 70 kg

kcal/kg Body Weight	Total Daily Kilocalories	Approximate Dietary Protein (g)	Total Calories from Protein (%)
40	2,800	84	12
50	3,500	131	15

for a postoperative patient should be individualized, especially the serving sizes and the frequency of feeding. Patients usually tolerate solids better if the feedings are small and frequent.

Both carbohydrates and fats are important sources of calories, and they should be provided in about equal quantities to constitute 85% to 88% of the total calories. (If this reduces the patient's appetite, less fat should be consumed.) The calories from carbohydrates and fats used to correct hypermetabolism supply energy for all processes of rebuilding and repairing and spare protein for anabolic purposes.

If the patient is given solid food, a good quantity of fruits and vegetables should be included in meals in addition to protein, fat, and carbohydrate. Refer to Chapter 23 for planning a high-protein, high-calorie, balanced diet. The need for vitamins A, K, C, B_{12}, and folic acid in a postoperative regimen requires special attention. Vitamins A and C have been proven experimentally and clinically to assist in wound healing as well as tissue repair. Vitamin A is well known for its role in maintaining epithelial structures, and vitamin C is important for collagen synthesis. In addition, vitamin A acid (retinoic acid) has recently been shown to assist in wound healing and is currently suspected to be a possible curing agent for certain types of human cancer (see Chapter 6 for more information).

The body's ability to clot blood postoperatively depends on an adequate supply of vitamin K. Folic acid and vitamin B_{12} are necessary for the synthesis and turnover of all body cells, especially red blood cells, and should be amply provided. The postoperative use of antibiotics may inhibit

TABLE 29-3   Diet Therapy for Certain Surgical Conditions of the Gastrointestinal System

Anatomical Site	Surgical Condition	Main Concern of Diet Therapy
Stomach	Gastrectomy Gastric partitioning	Dumping syndrome Multiple complications
Gallbladder	Cholecystectomy	Possible benefit from a reduced fat intake
Jejunum and ileum	Resections	Management of the short bowel syndrome and complications from obesity bypass
Colon	Ileostomy, colostomy	Support with good patient care and education
Rectum	Hemorrhoidectomy	Support and reduction of discomfort

the formation of these three important vitamins by the intestinal flora, thus partially reducing the body's supply. Therefore, patients must be monitored for deficiencies of these nutrients and given adequate supplementation.

The importance of iron and zinc cannot be underestimated. Iron is vital for hemoglobin synthesis and is used to compensate for blood loss and possible anemia. Zinc has a definitive role in wound healing (see Chapter 7), and clinical supplementation with zinc postoperatively is now common. Zinc sulphate is the preferred form, given in dosage amounts of 25 to 250 mg.

Gastrointestinal Surgery and Nutritional Support

Some surgical or trauma patients require a specific diet therapy in addition to the overall care described above. Surgical intervention for patients with gastrointestinal diseases poses a number of diet management problems (see Table 29-3). In this section, we shall discuss diet management for patients having undergone gastrectomy, gastric partitioning, surgery of the small intestine, and ileostomy, colostomy, and hemorrhoidectomy.

Gastrectomy

Patients with stomach or duodenal ulcers may have complications requiring surgical intervention (see Chapter 24). The surgical process includes drainage, vagotomy, pyloroplasty, and partial or total removal of the stomach and/or duodenum. Complications from gastric resection vary, depending on the patient and the extent of surgery.

The dietary plan for the management of the postgastrectomy patient (see Table 29-4) begins immediately after surgery. At this time, parenteral nutrition should be considered if the condition of the patient warrants it. In this respect, postgastrectomy patients differ little from patients who undergo other surgical procedures. After this stage has passed, routine hospital progressive diets are provided. The frequency, amount, and temperature of the feedings are all important. A typical meal consists of 3 or 4 oz to 8 or 10 oz of food (30 to 60 mL) at medium temperature. When hunger is evidenced with bowel sounds and peristalsis, the patient can proceed to regular food.

Dumping syndrome.   During the transition from liquid or soft to solid food or earlier, the

TABLE 29-4   Dietary Management of Postgastrectomy Patients

Stage	Duration	Dietary Treatment
1	Days 1–2 or as tolerated	Nothing by mouth; possible parenteral feeding with nutritional support using amino acids or other nutrients
2	Days 2–5 or as tolerated	Clear liquid such as ice, water, clear broth, unsweetened gelatin and fruit drinks, tea; progressive diet with patient tolerance to low carbohydrate, small volume, 6–8 feedings; no sucrose; parenteral nutrition if indicated
3	Day 6 or as tolerated	Dumping syndrome prevention diet

dumping syndrome may occur. In this syndrome, food passes into the jejunum without undergoing normal digestion and mixing by the stomach. A series of physiological responses that constitute the dumping syndrome follow anywhere from 5 minutes to 1½ hours after eating, but is most common after 5 to 15 minutes. There are two main types of clinical manifestations. In the first, the patient experiences bloating and distension, cramping pain, and diarrhea. The second type of response is related to vasomotor disturbances. The patient shows pallor, weakness, drowsiness, warmth, fainting, palpitations, an increased pulse rate, and sweating.

This syndrome may occur in 15% to 30% of all patients undergoing gastrectomy. Most patients learn to minimize the symptoms by either avoiding foods or making postural adjustments such as lying down after eating, which tends to hold food in the stomach for a longer period and prolong the emptying of food into the small intestine. In most patients, the symptoms of the dumping syndrome are of short duration. Symptoms are alleviated as the remaining part of the stomach (if any remains) adjusts. The weight of consumed food stretches the remaining stomach tissue to form a "mini-stomach" that holds food longer and helps prevent undigested food from reaching the jejunum.

In the normal digestive process, food leaves the esophagus and enters the stomach, where it is partially digested and then slowly empties into the duodenum. The process is regulated so that the small intestine receives only small amounts of food at a time. The pyloric and peristaltic waves assure that no food is regurgitated into the stomach. The food slowly reaches the jejunum in an orderly manner. These processes together with proper mixing and digestion produce food particles of the right size and proper dilution and prevent massive, sudden changes in osmotic pressure in the intestinal lumen.

If part of the stomach and/or the duodenum is removed, food leaves the esophagus and enters what is left of the stomach, staying only for a short time. It is then emptied into the jejunum. In these circumstances, a large amount of food rapidly empties into the small intestine. The mechanical adjustment of the intestine creates the bloating and distension frequently observed after a postgastrectomy patient has eaten. Rapid hydrolysis of the nutrients, especially carbohydrates, results in a large amount of small molecules in the digestive mass. Their presence increases the osmotic load of the intestinal lumen. In response to this condition, water in the plasma is mobilized and released into the intestine to equalize the osmotic pressure. As a result of the transient and mild reduction in circulatory volume, the patient may experience sweating, palpitations, fast pulse rate, weakness, and fainting after a meal. Possible stimulation of the jejunum, change in the osmotic load, and the accumulation of a large amount of food may also result in cramping and subsequent diarrhea. However, the exact cause of the dumping syndrome has not been pinpointed.

Because protein and fat are not so easily hydrolyzed into small molecules, they do not elicit the dumping syndrome as dramatically as ingested carbohydrates. Sometimes, all the symptoms described in the above discussion are collectively referred to by some clinicians as the "early dumping syndrome."

Another problem that affects postgastrectomy patients is the "late dumping syndrome." Despite its name, it is actually a simple case of reactive hypoglycemia, in which the patient suffers symptoms typical of hypoglycemia about 1 to 3 hours after eating. This should not be confused with the real dumping syndrome. Reactive hypoglycemia is usually linked to carbohydrates present in food, especially simple sugars. The rapid absorption of glucose suddenly raises the blood level of sugar and stimulates the pancreas to produce more insulin. Blood sugar is then quickly depleted, possibly falling below 40 to 50 mg/100 mL of blood. Clinical manifestations include sweating, dizziness, fast heart beat, and others. For more information on hypoglycemia and the dietary remedy, refer to Chapter 26.

The first principle of preparing an antidumping diet involves the type of food selected. An antidumping diet should be high in fat and protein, low in carbohydrates, and nutritionally sufficient to maintain body weight. The carbohydrates used should be complex ones, such as bread and potatoes. Simple sugars (glucose and fructose) and oligosaccharides should be avoided. A high-fat diet will slow down the pace of food emptying from the stomach. In some patients, lactose may aggravate postgastrectomy reactions. Such patients should avoid milk and milk products. Diarrhea and distension after drinking milk is a positive indication that lactose should be avoided. Sweets containing simple sugars, such as candy, jams, corn syrup, pastries, and sucrose-sweetened beverages should be avoided, since they encourage food to pass rapidly through the digestive tract. However, individual tolerance to sucrose varies.

Another consideration in an antidumping diet is the size and frequency of feedings. The amount of food given per feeding should be small, and these small feedings should be frequent (for example, six feedings a day composed of three small meals and three between-meal snacks). As the patient's tolerance to food increases and the volume of food consumed becomes greater, the number of feedings may be decreased. Some protein and fat should be included with each feeding.

Food texture and consistency are also important. Dry food is preferable for use in feedings because it is devoid of solutes that can exert osmotic pressure in the small intestine. Water or some other fluid should be permitted between meals, either 1 to 2 hours before or after eating. (Depending on the patient, the period may be $\frac{1}{2}-2$ hours before or after eating.) Patients suffer an adverse dumping reaction if too much fluid is taken with meals, although most practitioners allow some fluids with meals, usually about 4 oz. The patient should also be tested for tolerance to roughage and raw foods.

In an antidumping diet, 2,000 to 3,000 kcal/d should suffice for most patients, although higher quantities may be needed if malnourishment or other kind of debilitation is present. If a patient cannot eat the amount of food provided, supplemental parenteral feeding may be necessary to provide high-density nutrients. The amount of food consumed by patients should be constantly monitored, and subsequent weight fluctuations (especially losses) noted. If there is no weight gain, the patient should be encouraged and advised to eat more food, especially after discharge from the hospital.

The use of milk and milk products has been in dispute for a number of years, but in general they should not be denied unless the patient cannot tolerate them. If milk and milk products must be avoided, they should be gradually added to the diet after the patient's condition has stabilized. Prolonged abstinence from these products should be avoided, if possible, to avoid calcium and riboflavin deficiencies. In the presence of lactose intolerance, other sources of these nutrients should be provided.

Any emergency hypoglycemic shock that a postgastrectomy patient may experience can be temporarily relieved by the ingestion of concen-

TABLE 29-5 Permitted and Prohibited Foods in an Antidumping Diet

Food Group	Foods Permitted	Foods Prohibited
Breads	All breads and crackers except those noted	Breads with nuts, jams, or dried fruits or made with bran
Fats	Margarine, butter, oil, bacon, cream, mayonnaise, French dressing	None
Cereals and equivalents	All grains, rice, spaghetti, noodles, and macaroni except those noted	Presweetened cereals
Eggs	All egg dishes	None
Meats	All tender meats, fish, poultry	Highly seasoned or smoked meats
Beverages	Tea, coffee, broth, liquid unsweetened gelatin, artificially sweetened soda ($\frac{1}{2}-1$ hour before and after meals)*	No milk or alcohol; carbonated beverages if not tolerated; beverages with meal unless symptoms begin to subside†
(The following are to be added as patient tolerance and conditions progress.)		
Vegetables	Mashed potato, all tender vegetables (peas, carrots, spinach, etc.)	None creamed; gas-forming varieties if not tolerated (cabbage, broccoli, dried beans and peas, etc.)
Fruits	Fresh or canned (unsweetened or artificially sweetened); one serving citrus fruit or juice	None canned with sugar syrup; avoid sweetened dried fruits, e.g., prunes, figs, dates
Dairy products	Milk, cheese, cottage cheese, yogurt, all in small quantities	None
Miscellaneous	Salt, catsup, mild spices, smooth peanut butter	Pickles, peppers, chili powder, nuts, olives, candy, milk gravies

Note: Check for patient tolerance and acceptability of milk and milk products.

*Some practitioners prefer 1 to 2 hours before and after meals.

†Some practitioners permit 4 oz of fluid with a meal.

trated sugar such as candy or sucrose. Second, reactive hypoglycemia can also be corrected by increasing dietary protein and fat, while decreasing ingested carbohydrates. These adjustments should be incorporated into five to six feedings daily (see Table 29-5 for permitted and prohibited food items for an antidumping diet and Table 29-6 for sample menus).

Long-term effects. Like all patients who have undergone the traumas of major surgery, postgastrectomy patients may suffer long-term effects from their operation. These include weight loss, steatorrhea, and vitamin and mineral deficiencies. Careful dietary management can help minimize these problems.

Weight loss is usually inevitable in postgastrectomy patients, although in fact only 5% to 50% of all patients are affected. Gastrectomy disturbs intestinal functions, but the long-term consequences depend on the patient and the extent of surgery. Patients may lose weight for several reasons: they may simply be avoiding food out of fear of the dumping syndrome; malabsorption of nutrients (especially fat, protein, and carbohydrates) may be taking place; or hypermetabolism

TABLE 29-6 Sample Menu Plans for an Antidumping Diet

| | Soon after Surgery | | Later after Surgery | |
	Sample 1	Sample 2	Sample 1	Sample 2
Breakfast	Egg, poached, 1 Toast, 1 sl Butter, 1 t Banana, ½	Egg, scrambled, 1 Toast, 1 sl Butter, 1 t Peaches, ½ c	Cream of Wheat, ½ c Butter, 1 t Egg, soft-cooked, 1 Cream, 1 oz	Juice, tomato, 4 oz Oatmeal, ½ c Milk, 4 oz Bacon, crisp, 2 sl Toast, 1 sl Butter, 1 t

Snack	Gelatin, fruit-flavored,
	  unsweetened, 1 c
	Cream, 1 T
		Cottage cheese, 2 oz
		Crackers, 2
			Custard, unsweetened,
			  ½ c
			Crackers, 4
				Milk, 1 c
				Crackers, 4

Lunch	Chicken breast, stewed, 3 oz Potato, mashed, ½ c Butter, 2 t	Fish, 3 oz Rice, ½ c Spinach, ½ c Butter, 2 t	Roast beef, 3 oz Rice, ½ c Peas, buttered, ½ c	Beef, patty, 3 oz Potato, ½ c Asparagus, ½ c Butter, 2 t
Snack	Cottage cheese, 2 oz Crackers, 4	Gelatin, fruit-flavored, unsweetened, 1 c	Juice, orange, ½ c Cheese, 1 oz Crackers, 2	Cottage cheese, ½ c Crackers, 4
Dinner	Meat, 3 oz Rice with grated cheese, ½ c Asparagus, tips, ½ c Margarine, 1 t	Turkey, sliced, 3 oz Potato, baked, 1 Butter, 2 t Tomato, 2 sl	Beef, 3 oz Potatoes, mashed, 1 c Carrots, ½ c Tomato, sliced, ½ Butter, 2 t	Chicken, 3 oz Noodles, 3 oz Spinach, ½ c Margarine, 1 t

Snack	Bread, 1 sl
	Meat, 2 oz
	Margarine, 1 t
		Pudding, plain, un-
		  sweetened, with
		  whipped cream,
		  ½ c
			Pudding, un-
			  sweetened, ¼ c
				Sandwich:
				  Bread, 2 sl
				  Mayonnaise, 2 t
				  Meat, 2 oz

for the repair process may be present. Clinical experience has shown that careful dietary planning along with attractive food preparation can minimize these problems, enhance the patients' appetite, and encourage weight gain.

Some postgastrectomy patients suffer from steatorrhea. For reasons not yet clear, the body does not absorb fat, which is excreted in the stools. Steatorrhea may occur because of the accumulation of bacteria at the location of the surgery, resulting in disturbed emulsification of fat by the bile salts. Fat malabsorption may also be due to the failure of pancreatic enzymes (lipase) to digest and emulsify the fat. One remedy is the use of pancreatic supplement. (For an explana-

tion and remedy of steatorrhea, refer to the discussion on the short bowel syndrome below.)

About 5% to 15% of postgastrectomy patients develop vitamin B_{12} deficiency because of loss of the intrinsic factor (see Chapter 6). Parenteral supplement of the vitamin may be necessary, or special oral extracts of the intrinsic factor may be used. Folic acid deficiency develops in about 1% of the patients. Megaloblastic anemia from this deficiency results if patients do not receive adequate supplements. Other vitamin deficiencies may also occur, especially of fat-soluble vitamins, if steatorrhea is not corrected. Calcium and iron deficiencies require special attention. Iron-deficiency anemia and metabolic bone diseases have been observed in some postgastrectomy patients a number of years after the operation. However, all vitamin and mineral deficiencies can be corrected if proper attention is paid to food intake and if patients receive periodic laboratory evaluations.

Gastric partitioning

In the gastric partitioning procedure to counteract extreme obesity, two rows of staples are applied across the upper part of the patient's stomach. This creates a pouch whose small capacity and slow rate of emptying (through a narrow gap in the stapled line) are supposed to help the patient feel full after eating a small amount of food. In theory, this effect will help obese patients decrease their food intake. At first, the pouch will hold only 1 or 2 oz of food; later it will stretch to hold 4 to 6 oz.

Candidates for stomach stapling must be strictly screened. Most practitioners require that they be extremely overweight, subject to serious obesity-related medical problems, and eager to lose weight for their own sake. Those who meet these requirements should be given preoperative interviews and counseling by the surgeon, nurse, and dietitian, stressing family support for weight loss, daily exercise, calorie counting, and behavior modification (see Chapter 12). Before the operation, extensive testing should include determination of the patient's nutritional status since it is possible to be both overweight and malnourished, which increases the risks of surgery. The nurse should emphasize the need for physical activity to stimulate circulation, teach the obese patient deep breathing, introduce behavior modification techniques, and explain the use of the nasogastric tube.

After the gastric partitioning operation, obese patients must be watched closely for pulmonary and cardiovascular complications. For the first 48 hours, a nasogastric tube is used to deliver 200 to 300 cc of fluid every 24 hours to assure drainage of both proximal pouch and distal stomach. The patient also receives electrolytes intravenously. As bowel functions begin to return (usually by the third day), the tube is removed and a gradual progression from water to clear liquids to pureed foods is offered in small medicine cups. Patients learn that if they eat too much, too fast, they cannot tolerate even those foods. Patients sip the liquid.

After 8 weeks on a liquid diet, patients can slowly switch to small portions of more solid foods, which may be put through a blender if necessary. Vitamin supplements, either liquid or chewable tablets, are prescribed to all patients. Practitioners stress that without stringent and persistent behavior modifications—such as using small dishes, eating slowly, chewing food well, and responding immediately to the feeling of being full by ceasing to eat—these patients may experience nausea and vomiting and may even fail to lose weight. Unless eating habits are changed, the pouch will eventually stretch, invalidating the operation.

Because this technique is new, not much clinical literature is available. With the few references at the end of this book, interested individuals may obtain more information from current literature in the library.

Surgery of the small intestine

Segments of the small intestine may be removed due to pathological conditions or obesity. It is generally agreed that 40% of the small intestine may be resected without malabsorption problems if the distal ileum, ileocecal valve, and the duodenum are left intact. However, surgery involving resection of 50% to 75% of the small intestine may produce severe nutritional problems.

Short bowel syndrome.   *Short bowel syndrome* occurs after the removal of a long segment of the small intestine to correct pathological conditions that include embolism or thrombosis, infarction, Crohn's disease, trauma, and malignant infiltration. It is characterized by intractable diarrhea with impaired absorption of some or many essential nutrients. Malabsorption problems from the short bowel syndrome may vary in severity depending on: (1) the length of the intestine resected, (2) the part of the intestine resected, and (3) the completeness of the resection of the diseased sections of the intestine. The short bowel syndrome can ultimately cause substantial weight loss, anemia, and other symptoms of malnutrition if there is no medical intervention.

Intestinal bypass. There are many obese individuals who have failed to lose weight in spite of exhaustive medical treatment. Intestinal bypass is based on the obvious rationale that removal of part of the digestive system will reduce the person's ability to digest and absorb food. There will be a drastic reduction in caloric intake and body weight, even if the patient is eating excessively. Both patient and doctor obtain satisfaction because the patient is losing weight and the doctor feels that something positive has been done for the patient. Though this surgical procedure is being replaced by gastric partitioning (see above discussion), its serious and sometimes fatal complications have attracted much attention and criticism. However, some physicians still use this technique.

There are two acceptable ways of "short-circuiting" the small intestine to treat massive obesity. In one, a cut is made along the jejunum and the open end of the jejunum is then drained into the distal ileum. The open end of the ileum is closed off. This is the "end-to-side" connection. The other technique cuts off a major part of the ileum and joins the open ends of the jejunum and the ileum. The bypassed small bowel is then closed at one end while the other end is drained into some point of the colon, usually the transverse section. This is the "end-to-end" connection. For either method, about 4 to 12 in. of ileum and 10 to 14 in. of jejunum are left to digest and absorb food. It has been noted that patients with the end-to-end shunt sometimes lose weight faster. This seems to imply that the blind pouch created by the end-to-side connection may permit entry of nutrients and thus negate some of the expected results.

What are the potential effects from this surgical procedure? Fat malabsorption is prominent; patients absorb only about 25% to 75% of ingested fat in contrast to the normal 95%. The defect is due mainly to reduced absorptive surface and bile salt reabsorption. Unabsorbed fatty acids and bile salts exert a cathartic effect—diarrhea. An overall malabsorption of all other nutrients is also expected, though the severity varies from patient to patient.

Renal calculi are a direct result of hyperoxaluria; the patient absorbs an increased amount of oxalic acid for reasons not yet identified. Low blood potassium, magnesium, and calcium are also observed in some patients. The most undesirable effect of the intestinal shunt operation is the high incidence of liver failure and reported death due to this complication. At present, reasons for this serious problem have not yet been ascertained.

The desirable effects of the bypass procedure are many and important. Substantial weight loss is obtained in most patients. After the operation, obese diabetic patients require less insulin and show an improved glucose tolerance curve. Some patients show lowered serum cholesterol and triglycerides; some patients' lipoprotein profile returns to normal. Blood pressure in a number of hypertensive obese patients returns to normal. The routine removal of the appendix and any discovered gallstones are always an added bonus of the operation.

Postoperative care. Postoperative medical management of patients who have had surgery of the small intestine is similar to that mentioned for other major surgery. Nutritional and diet therapy is divided into three stages, as illustrated in Table 29-7. The duration and specific treatment for each stage depends on the location and length of the resection and the speed with which the remaining gut adapts. Table 29-7 and the list of different immediate postoperative dietary managements given earlier in this chapter should be used as basic guidelines for treatment during the postoperative period.

When patients are able to consume regular food, feedings should be small, frequent, high in protein and carbohydrates, and relatively low in fat. The diet should also be low in oxalate and supplemented with vitamins, especially vitamins A, D, K, and B_{12}. If the distal ileum and ileocecal valve have been resected, about 100 μg of vitamin B_{12} must be given by injection every 3 to 4 weeks. The amount of fat given patients must be individually adjusted to patient tolerance, with MCTs occasionally used (see Chapter 23).

Ileostomy, colostomy, and hemorrhoidectomy

An *ileostomy* is a surgical procedure that creates an opening in the ileum, usually by establishing an ileal stoma on the abdominal wall.

TABLE 29-7   Dietary Management of Patients after Resection of the Small Intestine

Stage	Duration	Dietary Treatment
1*	2–4 weeks after operation	Adjustment for fluid and electrolyte imbalances; intravenous hyperalimentation†; control of gastric hyperacidity by anticholinergics, antacids, and other drugs; oral saline solutions used to determine the presence and extent of diarrhea before proceeding to stage 2
2	Several months after surgery	Intravenous hyperalimentation; oral feeding if diarrhea is less than 2 L daily; routine hospital oral progressive diet or elemental oral feeding; reduction in fat intake if necessary
3†	Convalescence (months to years)	Oral feedings; regular hospital postsurgical diets

*Most postoperative care routines apply.
†If oral feeding is used in any form, beware of diarrhea.
‡Not all patients reach this stage.

Ileostomy, usually together with partial or total colectomy, are indicated when there are perforation and massive hemorrhage of the colon. For example, such surgery may be necessary for patients with severe ulcerative colitis, Crohn's disease, or colonic cancer. Ileostomy permits defecation to occur via an alternative route.

Since the digestive process is left practically intact after an ileostomy, there is no specific kind of dietary management for the patient. The patient is reassured that a normal life is possible after the operation and is encouraged to adapt to the new physical challenges. It is extremely important that patients practice the basic principles of caring for oneself, since good sanitary care is required to prevent infection, heal the newly formed stoma, as well as hasten recovery. Patients should be given whatever food they can tolerate. Texture, irritants, fiber, fat, carbohydrate, and other aspects of the diet may be modified if patients prefer, but such changes are usually not necessary except during the immediate postoperative period. However, some patients prefer a low-residue diet since it prevents blockage of the intestine.

The nutritional status of the patient should be carefully monitored, even though malnourishment due to the operation is uncommon. However, if the ileocecal valve and part of the distal ileum are removed, the absorption of vitamin B_{12} may be inhibited. The vitamin may have to be parenterally administered. A large quantity of fluids and electrolytes may be lost initially, since a patient's colon may be partially or completely removed. The resulting imbalance may need to be remedied. In general, standard appliances specially designed for an ileostomy dispose of the digestive waste, and any extra watery material is excreted. Fluid and electrolyte loss subsides as the patient's condition improves.

Colostomy is the surgical creation of an opening between the colon and the surface of the body, mainly a stoma in the abdominal wall. This opening serves some or all of the functions of the anus. There are many variations of the procedure. The operation may be temporary or permanent, and the rectum and anus may be partially or totally removed. Although the colon is usually intact, in some cases it is partially (and even totally) removed. If the colon is completely removed, the distal ileum is joined to the stoma. The dietary considerations for ileostomy apply, but the risk of vitamin B_{12} malabsorption is less. Colostomy patients usually do not have a great number of nutritional problems after the operation, but they do have other problems associated with colostomy.

Although ostomy patients often expect that they will be unable to eat normally, most will be able to eat a regular diet. For many, this is a change from the difficulties and pain they have long associated with eating. Nevertheless, many will find that foods such as beer, nuts, onions, corn, lettuce, apples, raw carrots, and the skins of potatoes and fruits cause problems. Some are only partially digested when they reach the stoma, causing obstruction and pain in some cases; some increase the flow of wastes and therefore the frequency with which the collection bag must be emptied; and some cause the bag to swell with gas. Individuals may choose to avoid foods with these effects.

Ostomy patients soon learn to recognize their normal bowel output and to correct abnormalities by dietary alterations. Drugs are sometimes used for bowel control. Bulking agents may be used to ease constipation; drugs such as Lomotil may be used to slow motility of the gut in case of diarrhea. Both kinds are best taken before meals. Certain drugs designed to treat other conditions may affect the bowel, causing constipation, diarrhea, irritation, and excess acidity. The nausea and diarrhea often associated with radiation therapy and chemotherapy may be assuaged by an easily digested diet and drugs designed to counter bowel irritation.

General care nurses and special stoma care nurses should be readily available to help patients deal with their anxieties about eating, digestion, and elimination. They will also be needed to teach care of the stoma and appliance. Such counseling often begins before the operation and includes patients' families. With help, most patients can achieve the goal of some degree of independent self-care. However, many patients find it harder to deal with the perceived threats to their self-image. They may find it difficult to talk about their fears—of stoma spillage, of revealing the presence of the stoma bag in public situations, of noticeable odor, of childlike helpless incontinence, and of sexual inadequacy and unattractiveness—for these involve the culturally taboo subjects of elimination and sexuality. These concerns, usually strongest during the first year, can generally be met with readjustments in stoma care and attitudes.

To help patients return to a positive self-image and a productive, rewarding life, it is important that professionals and family members be sensitive to their concerns, listening as they talk about their problems. At the same time, patients should be supported in developing a positive attitude toward the stoma, and those who care for them should never speak of the stoma in negative terms.

Modern surgery textbooks emphasize three important points in caring for patients with ileostomy: physician attentiveness, availability of ostomy nurses and stoma therapists, and patient membership in the ostomy societies. Specific references on this topic are provided at the end of this book.

Hemorrhoidectomy is the excision of hemorrhoids and is considered one of the most disagreeable of all surgical experiences. Immediately after the operation, patients usually experience rectal bleeding, moderate to severe pain, and discomfort with each bowel movement. Some of these complaints can be greatly reduced if the patients are placed on a low-residue diet for a period before the operation. This diet can also benefit the patient postoperatively by reducing pain and discomfort. For information on planning low-residue diets, consult Chapter 24.

DIET AND THE BURN PATIENT

A severe burn is perhaps one of the most painful injuries a human being can receive. Burn patients undergo many of the physiological changes experienced by surgical patients. The extent of the burn injury partly determines the dietary care recommended for a burn patient. Nutritional principles for treating burn patients can also be applied to treating other forms of trauma, and vice versa.

TABLE 29-8 Description of Burns

Degree Burn	Extent of Injury	Remark
First	Superficial, only epidermis involved; erythema with no blistering	Complete healing in 5 to 10 days
Second	Corium involved; erythema with blistering	Intact hair follicles and sweat glands, both of which help in re-forming skin, especially by temporary grafting
Third	Skin completely destroyed; damage to organs and tissues below skin possible	Dead cells coagulate to form a dry tough slough, sometimes termed eschar; skin does not re-form, permanent grafting needed

TABLE 29-9 The Rule of Nines

Affected Area	Percent of Body Surface Area Burned
Head and neck	9
One arm	9
Posterior or anterior surface of upper trunk	9
Posterior or anterior surface of lower trunk	9
Posterior or anterior surface of one leg	9
Groin or perineum	1

Determining the Extent of Injury

The terms *first-*, *second-*, and *third-degree* burns are frequently used to describe the severity of a burn. A first-degree burn is the least severe and is considered only a superficial injury. Third-degree burns, on the other hand, are life threatening, since the skin is totally destroyed and internal organs adversely affected (see Table 29-8). The degree, or depth, of a burn injury differs from its area, or percentage of the body affected. In emergency medicine, the popular Rule of Nines is used to estimate the body surface area affected (see Table 29-9).

The trauma suffered by patients with burns depends on the extent (both depth and area) of the burn injury and their age. Together these factors determine the likelihood of mortality. Second- and third-degree burns of over 15% of the total body surface (10% in the elderly and children) can result in burn shock because of the quantity of fluid loss. Burns of over 50% of the body surface are frequently fatal, especially in children and the elderly.

Nutritional and Dietary Care

Badly burned patients are extremely unfortunate. They suffer great pain and sometimes face permanent maiming. In addition, they may be extremely anxious about the consequences of plastic surgery and be fearful that an altered appearance will alienate their relatives and friends.

In all major burn traumas, body tissues (and thus protein, cells, and protoplasm) are rapidly depleted, as is reserved energy, since the patients usually experience the most severe form of stress experienced by humans. The continuous loss of body tissue and energy may result in death either immediately after the burn or during the "recovery" period. Proper and aggressive dietary and nutritional therapy is critical in treating moderately to severely burned patients.

The medical team treating a burn patient should be constantly aware of: (1) fluid and electrolyte levels, (2) wounds, (3) protein loss, (4) infection and other complications, (5) weight loss, and (6) the patient's nutritional status before and after the burn. A "chronic-burn" patient usually suffers a high risk of infection and malnourishment, and management of these risks is vital in treating these patients.

Acute stress rapidly leads to nutritional deficits, which greatly impede the body's efforts to heal damaged tissue and resist bacterial invasion. Proper dietary care can make the difference between life and death. Patients in good nutritional status and with small burns recover because they can eat sufficient food for their needs. However, the survival of an undernourished person suffering a severe burn depends heavily on aggressive nutritional therapy.

The nutritional requirements of burn patients are directly related to the extent and degree of burn. In general, burn patients have more nutritional problems than patients with other kinds of trauma. Since those with large burns have the most difficulty in maintaining an adequate oral intake, they sometimes become debilitated, even in a well-organized and adequately staffed burn center. The nutritional complications of burn victims are worse than those of major surgical patients, since their nutritional therapy is much more than just supportive care.

Because of temporary grafting (xenograft) materials (biological dressings), burn patients can begin aggressive nutritional therapy sooner than was previously possible. Various modern techniques (parenteral nutrition, defined chemical diets, and tube feedings) of supplying nutrients have lessened patient malnutrition. At one time malnutrition due to the continued loss of protein from raw areas was believed inevitable until the granulating areas of the burn were completely covered with skin grafts. However, this is no longer true. Still, problems do exist during the first few days after a severe burn when adequate nutritional intake may not be possible due to extraordinary losses of nitrogen. The most essential nutrients should be restored as soon as possible and in amounts that are maximally therapeutic for the particular burn patient.

Many obvious handicaps interfere with feeding burn patients. Loss of appetite may occur for many reasons (fear, depression, drug therapy, and so on), making it difficult for patients to eat enough food to meet bodily requirements. An inability to move the head, hands, body, or feet in some patients also makes self-feeding difficult. If pain accompanies any attempt to chew, eat, or swallow, avoidance of food is common. The changing of dressings and skin grafting may also interfere with mealtime. Close supervision and encouragement of the patient are necessary to assure that as many nutrients as possible (especially calories) are ingested.

Medical Management of a Burn Patient

Medical management of a burn patient consists of a two-stage treatment program: (1) immediate treatment and (2) rehabilitation care. Immediate treatment is outlined below.

I. Nonnutritional treatment
    A. Patient evaluation (vital signs, bleeding, etc.)
    B. Pain relief and sedative administration
    C. Blood and urine analyses
    D. Writing medical and accident history
    E. Management of wound and other injuries
    F. Study of burn extent and depth
    G. Antitetanus precaution
    H. Taking photograph if feasible
    I. Antibiotics administration
    J. Blood and blood plasma transfusion
II. Nutritional treatment
    A. Establishing fluid and electrolyte balance through IV fluids; use of nasogastric tube if patient is vomiting
    B. Oral feeding not recommended*
    C. Monitoring of intake (fluid and nutrients) and output (urine and feces)
    D. Monitoring of blood and urine protein and electrolytes
    E. For severely burned patients, adequate nutrition should not be attempted during the first week after the injury

During the initial emergency, when physicians and nurses perform life support activities, the hospital dietitian or nutritionist should prepare for the eventual feeding of the patient. This includes establishing the nutrient requirements, obtaining the patient history, and formulating feeding strategies (see Chapter 22).†

---

*The attending physician may want to correct any negative nitrogen balance.

† Mild paralytic ileus (gastric distension) is common, for reasons unknown. Intestinal disturbances such as slowed peristalsis, vomiting, and nausea may prevail (2 to 10 days after burn). These affect food intake and must be considered if aggressive nutritional therapy is needed.

Initially, the fluid and electrolyte balance of a burn patient is of primary concern because these substances are lost at a remarkable rate. Immediately after the burn, the most common intravenous fluid used is Ringer's lactate followed by a dextrose solution (5%). When the patient can drink orally, plain water or glucose solution may be given. However, some physicians prefer water mixed with sodium bicarbonate (4 g/L) and sodium chloride (5.5 g/L), and the fluid may be flavored, perhaps with lemon juice. This special fluid, sometimes referred to as Haldane's solution, contains about 3 to 3.5 g of sodium per liter. It is usually well tolerated if given slowly in repeated sips.

The fluid requirement is estimated by using any of several standard formulas (for example, the Evans, Brooke, and Baxter formulas). However, fluid replacement is progressively adjusted to the patient's response. The particular formula adopted is not important, since it serves only as a convenient tool to initiate emergency fluid resuscitation. Fluid loss in the form of water depletion has been calculated to account for 15% to 25% of daily heat loss. A severe burn patient may need 6,000 to 8,000 kcal a day to compensate for this large loss from the burn area.

Following the first 2 to 4 days of recovery, the injuries and fluid and electrolyte needs should be stable. Intestinal functions may have returned to normal (shown by disappearance of ileus), and feeding by mouth may be initiated if the eating mechanism is not incapacitated.

The pace of the healing process, of course, depends on the particular injury and varies from one to many months. Once the burn wounds have been closed with skin grafts, anabolism begins. When the patient's appetite improves, it is time to rebuild the patient nutritionally. As body weight increases due to increased calories and protein, the patient will be on the road to recovery. At this point, the medical burn team should emphasize to the patient and family that recovery and future health depends on nursing care and maintaining weight, at least at the beginning. The patient must eat so as to gain weight eventually. Table 29-10 describes the feeding strategies for a burn patient.

A burn patient has a special need for calories and protein in large amounts to replace fat loss,

TABLE 29-10   Feeding Strategies for a Burn Patient

Days after Burn Injury	Feeding Strategy
0–2	Correction of fluid and electrolyte disorders by parenteral feeding of standard solutions or glucose in water
2–4	Routine hospital progressive liquid diet
4–6	Solid foods progressively fed in small, frequent feedings, providing about 25% to 50% of needed calories; remaining calories supplied by other feeding means, e.g., chemically defined diet
6–10	Solid foods progressively fed in small, frequent feedings, providing 50% to 75% of needed calories; remaining calories supplied by other chemically defined diet
Over 10	Regular meals providing needed calories

repair and deposit lean tissues, maintain body functions, and restore water loss. The calorie requirement may be as large as 6,000 to 8,000 kcal/d. This energy expenditure increases with the size of the burn and may be 30% to 300% above basal levels, and it remains at high levels until grafting is completed. Sources of body weight loss are the breakdown of fat and protein as well as water loss. Food that is consumed provides about 5,000 to 6,000 kcal/d, and the breakdown of body fat provides about 1,000 to 2,000 kcal/d. A number of formulas have been developed to calculate the caloric need of a patient with a burn injury. Two common formulas for adult patients are:

$$\begin{aligned}
\text{daily caloric need} &= 20 \text{ kcal/kg body weight} \\
&\quad + 70 \text{ kcal/\% body surface} \\
&\quad \text{with burns} \\
&\quad\quad\quad \text{or} \\
&= 25 \text{ kcal/kg body weight} \\
&\quad + 40 \text{ kcal/\% body surface} \\
&\quad \text{with burns}
\end{aligned}$$

In the following example, assume that the patient weighs 75 kg with 50% of body surface having burns. The second formula above is used.

$$
\begin{aligned}
\text{daily caloric need} &= 25 \text{ kcal/kg body weight} \times \\
&\quad 75 \text{ kg body weight} + 40 \\
&\quad \text{kcal/\% body surface with} \\
&\quad \text{burns} \times 50\% \text{ body surface} \\
&\quad \text{with burns} \\
&= (25 \times 75 + 40 \times 50) \text{ kcal} \\
&= 1{,}875 + 2{,}000 \text{ kcal} \\
&= 3{,}875 \text{ kcal} \\
&= 4{,}875 \text{ kcal (allow 1{,}000} \\
&\quad \text{kcal for margin of safety)} \\
&= 4{,}500 \text{ to } 5{,}000 \text{ kcal} \\
&\quad \text{(approximately)}
\end{aligned}
$$

A burn victim loses more nitrogen than patients who have undergone surgery, a crush injury, or other trauma. As long as the surfaces of a severe burn have not been covered by suitable grafts, such loss will continue, sometimes lasting for months. Nitrogen loss from organ catabolism and open wounds is intensified by sepsis and the inability of the body to deposit tissue in organs. Possible causes of this inability are a hormone imbalance and the patient's failure to eat sufficient protein. All these factors make recovery difficult. The nutritional status of the patient before a burn injury also plays an important role in the recovery period. A malnourished burn patient requires more protein for body rehabilitation. The therapeutic goal is to promote protein storage in order to replace the losses that occurred when the patient could not eat properly.

Another type of body protein that suffers a severe loss is plasma protein. Some patients with extensive burns lose half their normal blood protein within 12 hours of the burn. This condition increases the risk of sepsis, since a loss of plasma protein means a reduced body level of enzymes, antibodies, and hormones.

Some clinicians propose the intravenous use of amino acids with glucose to decrease the nitrogen loss and at the same time provide energy for tissue building and healing. This strategy has been successful in treating most severe burn patients, although it does fail to help some patients.

A number of formulas are used for calculating the protein need of a burn patient. A common one for adults is described below.

$$
\begin{aligned}
\text{total daily protein need} &= 1 \text{ g/kg body weight} \\
&\quad + 3 \text{ g/\% body} \\
&\quad \text{surface with burns}
\end{aligned}
$$

Assume that the patient weighs 75 kg and that 50% of the body surface has burns. The calculations are as follows:

$$
\begin{aligned}
\text{total daily protein need} &= 1 \text{ g/kg body weight} \\
&\quad \times 75 \text{ kg body weight} \\
&\quad + 3 \text{ g/\% body} \\
&\quad \text{surface with burns} \times \\
&\quad 50\% \text{ body surface} \\
&\quad \text{with burns} \\
&= 75 + 150 \text{ g protein} \\
&= 225 \text{ g protein}
\end{aligned}
$$

A common formula for estimating a child's requirement of protein is:

$$
\begin{aligned}
\text{total daily protein need} &= 3 \text{ g/kg body weight} \\
&\quad + 1 \text{ g/\% body} \\
&\quad \text{surface with burns}
\end{aligned}
$$

Assume the patient weighs 40 kg and has 50% of the body surface with burns. Then,

$$
\begin{aligned}
\text{total daily protein need} &= 3 \text{ g/kg body weight} \\
&\quad \times 40 \text{ kg body weight} \\
&\quad + 1 \text{ g/\% body} \\
&\quad \text{surface with burns} \times \\
&\quad 50\% \text{ body surface} \\
&\quad \text{with burns} \\
&= 120 + 50 \text{ g protein} \\
&= 170 \text{ g protein}
\end{aligned}
$$

A burn patient particularly needs calories and protein. However, in planning menus, fats should provide 30% to 40% of total calories, and carbohydrates 45% to 55%. A moderate amount of fat is judicious at the beginning, since a large amount of fat tends to satiate the patient and reduce the patient's appetite.

Most clinicians prescribe two to ten times the RDAs for water-soluble vitamins for burn patients. Vitamin C is given in amounts 20 to 30 times the RDA. However, fat-soluble vitamins are usually prescribed guardedly because of potential risks (see Chapter 6).

The mineral needs of burn patients require attention even after the fluids and electrolytes have been balanced. Body potassium, iron, calcium, zinc, and copper may be lowered to unacceptable levels and should be monitored accordingly.

Increased dietary protein (nitrogen) should be supplemented with oral potassium, since tissue catabolism causes a loss of nitrogen and potassium in the urine. Anemia in burn patients tends to be of mixed types, although iron-deficiency anemia is invariably present because of the loss and/or destruction of blood (red blood cells) and the frequent withdrawing of blood to perform analyses.

An increased blood calcium level is common in bedridden burn patients for two reasons. One is that attempts to increase foods high in protein, calories, and other nutrients elevate the intake of calcium. The second is that immobilization of patients causes demineralization of bone, thus raising blood calcium further. Consequently, kidney and bladder stones from calcium phosphates become a problem. Refer to Chapters 28 and 31 for more information.

The human zinc requirement is about 8 to 10 mg/d and burn patients can lose significant amounts of this element. Deficiency can be verified by analyzing the blood, urine, skin, and hair. Burned children have been shown to benefit from a zinc sulfate supplement, which facilitates the healing of wounds. Depending on the patient, zinc losses from burn injuries range from 5 to 60 mg. Thus, an oral supplement of 100 to 200 mg of zinc is appropriate. If given intravenously, the amount should be 5 to 60 mg. However, burn patients with kidney trouble should be monitored for adverse reactions to large doses of zinc.

The level of copper should also be monitored in the blood and urine of burn patients. Although the role of copper in burn patients is not known, depressed levels are occasionally noted. In such cases, some clinicians recommend the use of a copper supplement.

When a burn patient is fed orally, the amount of food progressively given should correlate with the function of the patient's gastrointestinal system (see Table 29-10 and the footnote on p. 760). Six to seven days into the postburn period, the patient should eat a high-calorie, high-protein diet, advancing from small to large meals in as many feedings as are tolerated. If the food is appealing and familiar, there should be no problems. Measures should also be taken to control or prevent Curling's ulcer, which can develop in

some burn patients. Treatment is similar to that for a gastric ulcer, that is, the use of antacids (see Chapter 24).

If the patient has inhaled fumes or flames during the burn injury, the respiratory and gastrointestinal tracts may have been damaged, making oral feeding impossible. The same applies to burns on the mouth and face. As discussed earlier, loss of appetite, body pain, and difficulty in swallowing all interfere with eating the desired quantity of food. Skin graftings and dressing changes must be timed to give the patient ample opportunity to eat.

It is almost impossible to feed patients three large meals a day. Procedures for preparing menus with 3,500 kcal with 150 g of protein and 4,000 kcal with 180 g of protein are presented in Chapters 10 and 23. The amount of foods contained in these two menus illustrate how difficult it is to feed a person 6,000 kcal with 200 g of protein. For a patient with moderate to severe burns, it is sometimes necessary to use several feeding methods to supply adequate protein and calories.

There are many ways to nourish hospitalized burn patients (see Chapter 23). Figure 29-2 is a flow sheet that indicates what method should be used to feed burn patients. It should be noted that the use of total parenteral nutrition, especially in burn patients, frequently causes infection at the site of the catheter implant. Thus, the tubes and associated equipment should be changed one to three times a week to avoid this septic thrombophlebitis.

The nutritional care of a burn patient requires efficient and conscientious teamwork. Many burn centers have established standard guidelines for dietary care. All team members should follow the individualized plans and goals for a particular patient. All parties should encourage the patient to eat and provide psychological support. A standard nutritional management record for a burn patient may be kept. Conferences should be scheduled to study the nutritional status of the patient. Many burn centers have the mother of a child burn patient participate in the conferences. The entire health team monitors the progress and status of the patient to be certain that nutritional needs are met. Weight loss and caloric intake are the two main criteria used.

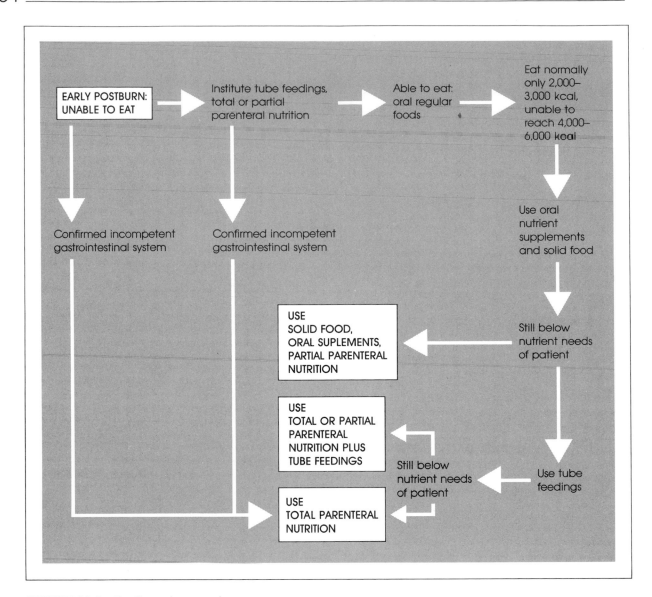

FIGURE 29-2   Feeding a burn patient.

DIET AND THE CANCER PATIENT

When cancer patients undergo treatment and rehabilitation, they face many nutritional problems. They cannot eat well because of a number of factors such as depression, pain, digestive problems, and reaction to drugs. When patients are well nourished, they respond better to treatment, survive longer, and have a greater sense of well-being. The situation is a vicious cycle. However, when people have cancer, they are usually malnourished, and because they are malnourished, they are more difficult to treat. Without sufficient treatment, the cancer can intensify its devastating effect on their nutritional status. In this section, we will discuss the nutritional and dietary treatment of this disease.

Definitions and Overview

Certain medical terms are frequently used in the discipline of nutrition and cancer. Some pertinent definitions are provided below.

1. *Cancer*: "A mass of tissue cells possessed of potentially unlimited growth that serves no useful function in the body, robs the host of nutrients necessary for survival, expands locally by invasion and systematically by transmission of cells along lymphatic and blood pathways, and unless recognized early and removed, kills the host. The disease is usually considered due to a combination of carcinogens and predisposing factors (as heredity, age, trauma, or chronic irritation). Cancer itself is never directly inherited, though a predisposition to certain forms may be hereditary" (from *Webster's Third New International Dictionary*).

2. *Neoplasm*: "A new growth of animal or plant tissue resembling more or less the tissue from which it arises but serving no physiological function. It can be benign, potentially malignant or malignant in character" (from *Webster's Third New International Dictionary*).

3. *Tumor*: "A mass of noninflammatory and independent tissue arising without obvious cause from cells of pre-existing tissue, possessing no physiologic function, and characteristically unrestrained in growth and structure" (from *Webster's Third New International Dictionary*).

Quite often, the terms *neoplasm* and *tumor* are used interchangeably. Like neoplasms, tumors may be benign or malignant. A benign tumor refers to one that is localized in one part of the body and does not spread. Such types of tumors are harmless if surgically removed or placed under medical control. *Malignant* literally means "malicious"; medically the term means that the tumor will metastasize, or spread to other parts of the body quite rapidly. Such tumors may be very harmful or even lethal with or without medical attention.

Some nutritional terms are also related to cancer. *Cachexia* is a general physical malnutrition and wasting because of the presence of a serious and chronic illness, such as tuberculosis or cancer. There is a loss of "carcass" weight and affected persons are in a very deprived state of nutrition. *Asthenia* refers to the loss of strength or energy in a person. *Anorexia* means the loss of appetite for a variety of reasons. *Hypogeusia*

means a diminished acuteness of the sense of taste. *Dysgeusia* means a perverted or distorted sense of taste.

Nutritional Disorders from Cancer Treatments

Certain metabolic and nutritional changes are characteristic of nearly all cancer patients. These include asthenia, cachexia, anorexia (hypophagia), anemia, fluid and electrolyte imbalances, hypogeusia or dysgeusia, an altered metabolic rate, a negative nitrogen balance, and edema. Infection is not uncommon.

Patients invariably suffer some form of nutritional disorder whenever they are subject to one of the three most common forms of cancer treatment. Apart from some localized impairment, their clinical situation may be aggravated by psychological and systemic physiological effects. The table below summarizes the nutritional problems produced by the three forms of cancer treatment.

Radiation Therapy (effects depend on site of irradiation)

1. Anorexia
2. Impaired taste acuity
3. Reduced food intake
4. Tooth decay and gum diseases
5. Difficulty in swallowing
6. Intestinal obstruction
7. Malabsorption
8. Diarrhea

Surgical Therapy

1. Tube feeding mandatory if food ingestion is impaired
2. Malabsorption and dumping syndrome upon removal of part of the gastrointestinal system; fluid and electrolyte imbalance
3. Low blood glucose possible after resection of part or all of the stomach
4. Insulin deficiency from resection of the pancreas

Chemotherapy

1. Multiple disturbances of nutritional status (e.g., loss of appetite) from the use of different categories of drugs
2. Body fluid and electrolyte disturbances from the use of corticosteroids and other hormones
3. Specific intestinal damage from drugs

Nutritional and Dietary Care in the Hospital

The dietary management of cancer patients in many hospitals, especially those specializing in cancer treatment, has the following features: (1) team care, (2) patient history, (3) nutritional requirements and supports, and (4) enteral and/or parenteral feedings. Chapters 22 and 23 discuss the basic principles of topics (1), (2), and (4); the following discussion analyzes topics (3) and (4) in depth.

For many years, oncologists have assumed that malnutrition in a cancer patient is a necessary evil; however, we now know that adequate nutritional support and feeding may prevent it. Many undernourished cancer patients respond to aggressive nutritional and dietary therapy. The usefulness of this diet and nutritional support is manifold. It can improve and maintain nutritional status as well as prevent weight loss. Plasma protein levels can be maintained or restored, reducing the risk of infection and thus decreasing morbidity and mortality. Aggressive dietary therapy can help the tumor to respond to treatment as well as minimize or prevent side effects of various cancer therapies, such as increasing the effectiveness of a drug while decreasing its toxicity. These supports enhance the cancer patient's sense of well-being and improve the quality of life.

The beneficial effects of intense nutritional support can be evaluated by weight gain, body measurements, and blood and urine analyses. An important controversy surrounding nutritional support involves the unavoidable consequence of permitting the tumor to grow. Tumors continue to grow when the host receives nutrients. But many experts in cancer research believe that the newly produced tumor cells are more responsive to radiation therapy. If patients with any known or suspected residual neoplastic cells undergo intensive nutritional therapy, it becomes important that treatments be instituted to destroy or at least arrest the growth of these cells.

As indicated in the first sections of this chapter and in Chapter 22, there is no reliable way of deciding the calorie and protein needs of patients. They must be evaluated according to their personal data and clinical conditions. The former includes such items as race, sex, age, and height, while the latter includes type of tumor, length of illness, laboratory studies, body weight, and others. The doctor and dietitian with inputs from the nurse decide on nutrient intakes and the means of feeding (see Chapters 22 and 23).

One method of feeding is enteral, which may be either oral or tubal. Oral feeding may include solid food, hospital or commercial nutrient supplements, or chemically defined solutions such as elemental or formula diets. Tube feeding may be nasopharyngeal or administered through an esophagostomy, gastrostomy, or jejunostomy. The substances fed the patient may be hospital prepared or commercially available. Parenteral feeding may provide an intravenous supply of simple glucose as well as highly concentrated nutrient solutions. A combination of enteral and parenteral feedings is not uncommon.

Oral feeding

If at all feasible, patients should be fed orally with solid food. The regimen should include between-meal feedings of hospital or commercial nutrient supplements. Otherwise, defined-formula diets and tube feedings may be used. Before starting oral feeding, the general problems encountered, the complications from specific therapy (e.g., drugs, radiation), and the relevant dietetic factors must be carefully considered. Below is a checklist of considerations in the oral feeding of cancer patients.

1. Patient age and type of cancer
2. Treatment side effects
3. Psychological complications: depression and lack of motivation
4. Food and eating behavior: conditioned responses, overall food acceptance
5. Anorexia
6. Taste and food aversions
7. Swallowing and saliva
8. Nausea and vomiting
9. Ulceration of buccal mucosa
10. Diarrhea
11. Weight and protein loss
12. Pain

One multifaceted problem encountered when attempting to feed cancer patients orally results from psychological complications, conditioned responses, and pain. Many cancer patients develop depressive reactions (anxiety, discomfort, and hyperactivity), especially when informed of the diagnosis or when the disease is not under control. The depression makes them avoid food. If this depression leads to suppressed intestinal activity, digestive problems also occur. If encouragement and support are provided, patients may be motivated to eat, although this does not always occur. Most clinicians disapprove of the use of antidepressive agents to improve eating. In some cancer patients, intestinal obstruction causes pain every time food is eaten. Abdominal pain when eating may continue even after surgical correction of the problem because of a conditioned response. This is a behavioral problem that requires special help. Many patients have general body pain that naturally interferes with eating. Careful use of pain killers before meals helps these patients to eat. In sum, the problem is how to make the patient eat.

Many cancer patients are permanently plagued with nausea and vomiting. The reasons are unknown, although it is generally assumed that this unpleasant pair of conditions is due to both the presence of the tumor and the side effects of drug treatment. Antiemetics can correct nausea and vomiting. The most effective of these are phenothiazine and prochlorperazine. Clinicians sometimes prescribe them ½ to 1 hour before meals, which tends to improve the appetite. Marijuana is now suspected to be effective in reducing nausea and vomiting in cancer patients. Some patients are given special permission by the federal government to smoke marijuana cigarettes as a part of medical therapy. At present, the effectiveness of this drug is not proven.

In cancer patients, the thresholds for the four taste sensations may change. Patients may complain that food is tasteless or that they have lost their sense of taste. Or they associate foods that cannot be tolerated with terrible taste sensations, stating that the foods served are either spoiled or rancid. Food texture is compared to sawdust, dry starch, and leather. Metallic, bitter, sour, or salty taste sensations are emphasized.

TABLE 29-11   Protein Food Preference in Cancer Patients with Altered Sense of Taste

Extent of Taste Alteration	Foods Liked?				
	Meat	Poultry	Fish	Cheese	Eggs
Mild	Yes	Yes	Yes	Yes	Yes
Moderate	No	Yes	Yes	Yes	Yes
Severe	No	No	No	Yes	Yes

There is also a tendency to complain about home cooking. Explaining to patients and their families that the taste sensation is altered in the patients helps alleviate strained relationships. At present, there is no scientific explanation for this change in the sense of taste.

Because of these changes in taste, patients decline to eat meat, fish, poultry, eggs, and foods fried in oil. However, for many patients the dislike for protein foods is selective. Thus, as can be seen in Table 29-11, their preference depends on the protein source and the degree of taste modification. As a consequence, some patients' diets are reduced to nonspicy items such as cottage cheese.

Taste problems can be managed in a number of ways. First, the patient, doctor, nurse, and dietitian can all provide suggestions on how to make food taste better. Seasoning can be altered to suit the patients. If a patient prefers sweet or salty flavors, these flavors can be emphasized in different foods. Other taste preferences can be satisfied by using a variety of flavorings including sugar, salt, pepper, and lemon juice.

Lunches and main dishes can include cold cuts (such as bologna and salami), cold chicken, and salads. Fresh, cold fruits should be served with the meal to improve the looks of snacks and desserts. All beverages that patients reject should not be served. Those most often liked are cold fruit juices and chocolate drinks, although individual preferences vary. Diet plans should be individualized with the single objective of getting cancer patients to consume as much protein and calories as their particular condition requires.

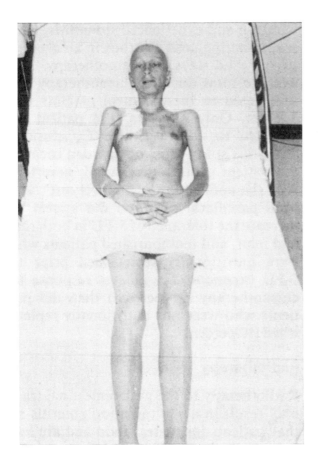
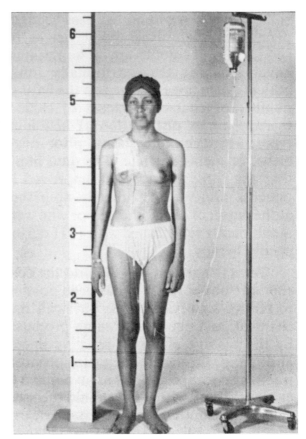

FIGURE 29-3   A 22-year-old patient with cancer before (left) and after (right) parenteral hyperalimentation. (Reprinted with permission from E. M. Copeland, "Intravenous Hyperalimentation as an Adjunct to Cancer Patient Management," *The Cancer Bulletin*, 30: [1978] 102–108. Copyright Medical Arts Publishing Foundation, Houston.)

Partial or total parenteral nutrition

If cancer patients are nutritionally depleted and all other methods of feeding have not succeeded in rehabilitating them, partial or total parenteral nutrition is indicated. Patients should not be malnourished if they are to receive any type of cancer treatment. Aggressive intravenous hyperalimentation can prepare patients for more rigorous cancer therapies. For example, intensive nutritional support via parenteral feeding can improve immunocompetency, reduce infection, accelerate wound healing, and enhance tumor response to treatment. Figure 29-3 illustrates the clinical conditions of a patient before and after parenteral hyperalimentation. Refer to Chapter 23 for more information on this means of feeding.

Nutritional and Dietary Care at Home

Before a cancer patient is sent home, the hospital team should be assured of several things: first, that the particular type of feeding care that the patient needs is available at home; second, that relevant procedures are well established so that the patient receives appropriate treatment and care at home; and last, that the patient is leaving the hospital in the same or better nutritional status than when admitted. If feasible, nutritional complications from cancer treatment should be remedied and the patient nutritionally replenished.

If patients are already eating well before discharge, there should not be any other nutritional problems. However, if patients are on tube or parenteral feeding, they need a brief period of conditioning between the termination of such feeding and leaving the hospital. Most clinicians recommend that patients be changed to convenient commercial liquid-nutrient preparations. The next step is the hospital progressive feeding routine followed by small feedings of regular food (if tolerated). These procedures are carried out to ensure that patients develop an appetite for regular food. This transition to regular food must be gradual and made with care and concern.

The doctor, nurse, dietitian, nutritionist, patient, and family members should confer to arrive at a basic understanding of the best nutritional and dietary care for the patient at home. One member of the health team should take responsibility for monitoring the nutritional well-being of the patient after hospital discharge. The particular member may be the oncologist, the radiologist, the referring or private physician, the nurse practitioner, or a private or hospital dietitian or nutritionist. This delegation of responsibility should be clear, so that there is no confusion about the monitoring work. The patient's nutritional status must not be allowed to deteriorate at home. Every reasonable effort should be made to assure that nutritional and dietary care in the home is the same as that provided in the hospital.

STUDY QUESTIONS

1. What are the three stages of metabolic response to trauma? Describe the body's hormonal responses to stress.

2. Describe the various preoperative feeding routines for a surgical patient. What complications may result if these routines are not followed?

3. What is the goal of postoperative dietary care? How is it achieved? What are the consequences of inadequate postoperative dietary support?

4. Define the *dumping syndrome*. Why does it occur? When does it occur? How can it be alleviated?

5. What nutritional problems commonly exist in the postgastrectomy patient?

6. Differentiate between ileostomy, colostomy, and hemorrhoidectomy. Aside from nutritional therapy, what is an important role of the health professional in these situations?

7. How do first-, second-, and third-degree burns differ from each other?

8. What kind of treatment should a burn patient receive? Consider both physiological and psychological factors. Discuss the dietary considerations in the management of a child with burns.

9. Can the terms *cancer*, *neoplasm*, and *tumor* be used interchangeably? Why?

10. What is the central dilemma faced by the diet therapist in attempting to help the cancer patient? What specific nutritional problems arise from the three common types of cancer treatment?

11. Briefly discuss the physiological and psychological problems that might be encountered in an attempt to provide a cancer patient with aggressive nutritional support.

12. What nutrition-related factors should be considered in helping the cancer patient make the transition from the hospital to the home?

CASE STUDY   *Total Parenteral Nutrition and Cancer*

Mr. B.K. was a 29-year-old man with mixed embryonal testicular cancer that had metastasized to the retroperitoneal nodes, liver, and kidney. Before his admission to the hospital, the patient had been receiving chemotherapy at home. On his admission, clinical examination produced the following data: weight 37 kg (81.6 lb), pulse 82 and blood pressure 95/65 mm Hg when sitting, and pulse 102 and blood pressure 90/60 mm Hg when standing. His head, nose, ears, eyes, throat, lungs, heart, and skin were all normal. The patient had an enlarged liver and showed a trace positive stool guaiac test. His reflexes were symmetrical, given a scale of 0 to 1+. B.K.'s admission prothrombin time was 14.8 seconds. Because he vomited while being admitted, the attending physician suspected obstruction of his gastric outlet.

After a careful review of B.K.'s medical history, the health team decided on two approaches: chemotherapy and adoption of aggressive nutritional procedures. The patient was given two courses of cystplatium, adriamycin, and cyclophosphamide (Cytoxan). This drug therapy cleared the gastric outlet obstruction and reduced the size of the liver lesions.

Simultaneously the patient received the hyperalimentation solution Travasol, with 25% dextrose and calculated doses of potassium, sodium, phosphate, chloride, calcium, and magnesium. Each day iodine, zinc, cobalt, manganese, and copper were added to the patient's intravenous feeding. Multivitamins (daily) and folic acid (biweekly) were also added to the intravenous solution.

During the seventh week, the patient developed a scaling, brownish, and greasy lesion of the nose, eyelids, and other facial areas. Since the patient was receiving adequate zinc, he was given topical safflower oil, which contained 80% linoleic acid.

During the course of chemotherapy and hyperalimentation, the patient gained 35 lb and his skin lesions healed completely. After about 10 weeks of treatment, the nutritional support was gradually decreased.

Review and Analysis

1. Ascertain from a hospital pharmacist the nutritional composition of Travasol.
2. List the hyperalimentation solutions legally available in the United States and provide the names and addresses of the manufacturers.
3. Why were the doctors using vitamin and trace mineral supplements?
4. Why did the patient need linoleic acid?
5. What is the preferred route of administration for a hyperosmolar solution?
6. As a nurse, describe the complications you would watch out for when a patient is receiving total parenteral nutrition in the hospital.
7. As a dietitian, what would be your major responsibilities in a team administering total parenteral nutrition to a patient?
8. Suppose that the attending physician has ordered that the patient continue to receive hyperalimentation at home for at least a short period. What are the major criteria that must be considered? What is the nurse's role? What is the dietitian's role?

CASE STUDY   *Stomach Surgery and Hypoglycemia*

Mr. S.F. was admitted to the hospital in July 1970 because of a convulsion. When this 49-year-old American Indian man had had a perforated duodenal ulcer a year before, doctors removed most of his stomach. The postoperative course was uneventful, and blood and urine analyses were normal. The patient was discharged. Follow-up visits during the next 2 months revealed that the patient was having three or four bowel movements daily compared with one a day before the operation.

Twelve months after the operation, the patient developed convulsions, and his family physician recommended admission to the hospital for diagnosis and treatment. A careful, in-depth interview with the patient by the hospital neurologist revealed some important information. Ever since the operation, the patient had experienced four to seven episodes of nervousness and sweating daily. These were relieved only by a few bites of carbohydrate-rich foods. On the day of his admission to the hospital, the sweating and nervousness had combined to produce a seizurelike reaction. His wife said that the patient had turned very blue with hyperextension of the neck and head and with eyes rolled back. The patient was nervous and hungry. This was the first time he became unconscious, which happened immediately after an evening meal.

The patient had never had any neurological problems, including epilepsy. He showed normal neurological conditions, with intact reflexes, gait, muscle movements, sensory abilities, and cranial nerves. His fasting blood glucose was 75, 85, and 80 mg/100 mL. His postprandial (2 hours) blood glucose was 75 mg in one test, and 45 mg in a standard glucose tolerance test. The neurologist suggested that the hypoglycemia was most likely caused by dumping postprandially. Additional tests confirmed the neurologist's diagnosis.

Therapeutic treatments consisted of two approaches. The patient was told to avoid carbohydrate-rich foods and eat five to eight small meals a day. He was to drink as little fluid as possible during each meal. He was also given the drug phenformin, which could reduce insulin release in response to eating. The patient improved on these two regimens.

Review and Analysis

1. Why did the patient's bowel movements change after the operation?
2. Explain postprandial hypoglycemia.
3. What is the current explanation for the hypoglycemia caused by stomach surgery, as occurred in this patient?
4. Why was the patient told to avoid carbohydrate-rich foods? Reconcile this with the fact that his symptoms could be relieved by eating carbohydrate-rich foods. Specifically, what type of carbohydrate would be preferred in this patient's meals?
5. How would five to eight small meals instead of three regular ones help the patient?
6. Why was the patient permitted only a small amount of fluid during each meal?
7. What is meant by "dumping postprandially"?

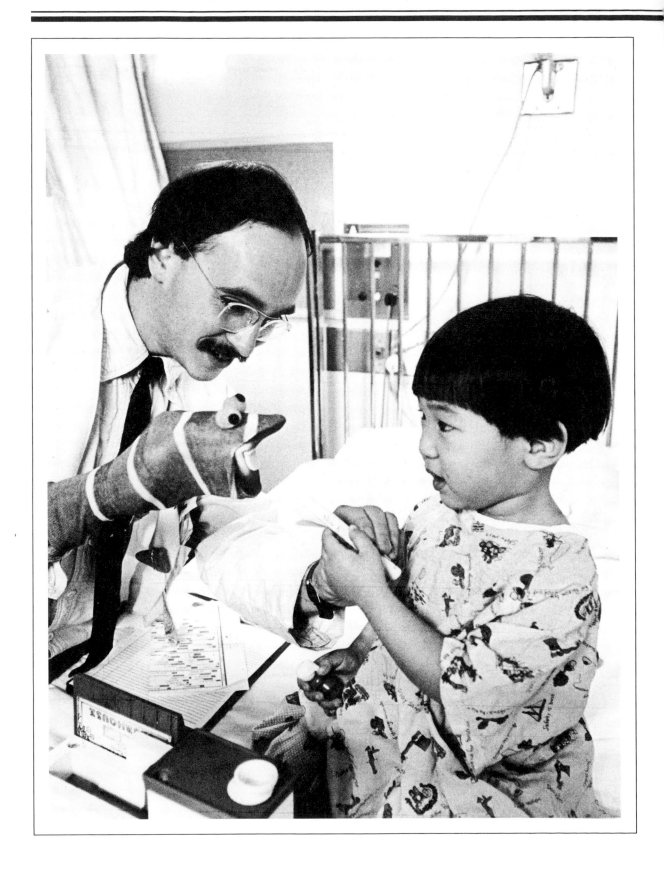

Chapter 30

Diet and Diseases of Infancy and Childhood

DISEASES OF INFANCY and childhood cause distress to all those concerned with the well-being of children. Managing these conditions requires more care than managing similar conditions in adults. Children are particularly vulnerable because their mental and physical development may depend on the proper treatment. Diet and nutritional therapy can play an important role in the full recovery of a sick child.

PRINCIPLES OF FEEDING A SICK CHILD

In spite of advances in pediatric nutrition, we cannot define the absolute nutrient requirements of a child at a particular age. The latest published RDAs serve as convenient guidelines, but they do not necessarily correspond to the optimal quantities for children. However, for practical purposes, it is generally agreed that a diet meeting the RDAs and based on the four basic food groups satisfies the nutritional needs of all growing children. This diet should also be appropriate to a child's age and stage of development. This type of diet is satisfactory for normal and sick children. Details on diet planning are presented in Chapters 10, 14, and 22.

Practically all principles of diet therapy that apply to a sick adult (see Chapters 22 and 23) also apply to a young patient. For example, pertinent factors for both groups of patients include personal eating patterns, individual likes and dislikes, and the necessity of frequent diet counseling during a hospital stay. When ill, both children and adults encounter the same difficulties in eating well—fatigue, vomiting, nausea, poor appetite, pain from the disease or treatment, drowsiness from medications, fear, anxiety, and so on. Just as with adult patients, the emotional, psychological, social, and physical needs of sick children require careful consideration. In some cases, these may be as important as the attention devoted to the clinical management of the ailment. In general, the principles of feeding a normal child apply more strictly to a sick child.

The nutritional and dietary care of a sick child depends on a number of factors: (1) the disease (its type, severity, and duration), (2) the management strategy (the onset of symptoms, the treatment method, etc.), (3) the child's age and growth pattern, (4) the nutritional status of the child before and during hospitalization, and (5) the need for rehabilitation. The major reasons why sick children do not have an adequate nutritional intake include (1) a malfunctioning gastrointestinal system; (2) high metabolic demands from stress and trauma such as fever, infection, burns, or cancer; (3) excessive vomiting and diarrhea; (4) neurological and psychological disturbances that interfere with eating, such as the inability to chew or the fear of food; and (5) specific nutritionally related diseases such as disorders of the kidney, liver, or pancreas (see Chapter 23). Sometimes a child's failure to eat cannot be traced to any specific reason.

As in the case of an adult patient, the evaluation of the nutritional status of a hospitalized child includes the following whenever feasible:

1. Anthropometric measurements: height (length), weight, head circumference, appropriate measurements of the arms, chest, and pelvis, and skinfold thickness
2. General body signs: muscle tone; activity; movement; posture; condition of the hair, mouth (teeth and gums), skin, ears, eyes
3. Laboratory studies: blood and urine analyses and bone growth assessment using X rays

Behavioral Patterns of the Hospitalized Child

Problems that adult patients have in adjusting to hospitalization are more acute among children. Children are exposed to a totally new environment without the comfort of their parents, especially the mother, and this emotional stress is superimposed upon that caused by the clinical condition. Children may also be frightened by particular treatments and anxious about their outcome. The presence of strangers may also be confusing. Hospitalized children who become psychologically maladjusted may be unable to express themselves well. They need someone whom they trust and can talk to, especially when they have eating problems. In fact, some sick children develop certain undesirable eating habits. On the other hand, for some children with adjustment problems, food is the principal enjoyment.

Quite often children readopt some elementary feeding practices that do not fit their age or stage of development. For example, an older child may ask for a bottle instead of accepting a cup and refuse to eat chopped foods, preferring liquid or pureed foods. Although fully capable of self-feeding, the child may want to be fed. Some children find reasons to reject food, even if it is their favorite item and served in a familiar manner. They may complain about the size of the portion or the flavor of the food. Some older children may either refuse to eat or eat too much. To help avoid these problems, it is helpful not to expose children to new routines and ways of eating. Old eating habits should be accommodated if at all possible.

The degree of feeding problems depends on the age of the child, the disorder, the child's past experience and nutritional status, and the child's social and emotional makeup. Many young patients are cooperative and eat well.

The Patient, Mother, and Health Team

To provide optimal nutritional and dietary care for a sick child, the health team, especially the nurse, dietitian, and nutritionist, must like children and be willing to work with them. For example, the nurse becomes familiar with a child's eating habits, preferences, reactions and remarks about food. Conveying this information to the dietetic staff helps them to prepare meals that the child will like. Of course, the parents, especially the mother, can provide much useful information about a child's eating habits. The health team must also occasionally yield to children's unreasonable demands, especially those of terminally ill children.

The nurse probably plays the most important role in ensuring that a child eats the foods that are served. When the nurse relates to the child and is considerate and attentive, the child is most likely to eat well. The nutritionist, dietitian, and doctor depend on the nurse for coordination and provision of optimal dietary care.

In hospitals where dietitians have many other responsibilities, the suggestions, observations, and opinions of the nurses are especially appreciated. A skillful and considerate nurse can help a child to recover more quickly. Apart from ensuring an adequate intake of food, the nurse monitors the fluid consumption of the child and alerts the doctor and dietitian if the intake is poor.

In caring for a sick child, the health team must be fully aware of the anxiety and concern of the parents. Whenever feasible, members of the team should grant parents' requests for additional visiting hours, thereby helping to fulfill the needs of the parents and the child. Because their child is ill, both parents have a desire to talk with someone knowledgeable. The nurse, dietitian, and nutritionist should serve as the contacts. If the parents want to help in the feeding of their child, they are usually allowed and become members of the health team. Further, the team should keep the parents well informed if they are unable to attend to their child. Parents are likely to be depressed when their child is suffering from a terminal illness, and in these instances the team should involve them in the different facets of clinical care, especially the feeding routine.

In sum, the health team shares the problems of the patient with the family and helps the family to overcome psychological and emotional distress. The parents should be taught to care for the child, and it is important that they trust the doctor and other health personnel. Under some circumstances (such as when the child suffers kidney disease, brain damage, or other special disorders), the team, especially the nurse, can assist the family in obtaining applicable financial aid.

It is very important that the child and mother are counseled together on the child's nutrition and dietary care. Sharing information and experience is important—merely instructing the mother without explanation is not sound nutritional education. During hospital feedings, the nurse can make helpful observations about the mother and child; for example, is the mother forcing the child to eat? How extensive are the child's feeding tantrums and food manipulation (see Chapter 14)? While the child is in the hospital, the mother should be fully informed of the child's progress and adjustment, especially in regard to nutrition and feeding. The mother should implement recommended changes in eating routines after the child has returned home.

Problems with Long-Term Care

A child requiring special long-term nutritional and dietary care at home because of a physical handicap or prolonged illness places many demands on all members of the family. Proper care of such children requires energy, time, and money (for foods, drugs, equipment, baby-sitters, and sometimes special health personnel). In addition, the daily routine of the entire family may be changed. Some families adjust well to these changes, while others do not. For instance, when a sick child requires a tremendous amount of time from the parents, especially the mother, other children in the family may be neglected. Siblings may thus feel resentment toward their sick brother or sister because of the special attention he or she is receiving.

Parents may encounter specific problems in providing needed care for their child. The mother (or father) may have difficulty implementing the special diet for the child for a variety of reasons, including failure to understand the diet plan itself. In some families, the mother may reach the point where she simply is unable both to *monitor* and implement the feeding of the child day after day over a period of many months. Another problem in some dietary plans involves the keeping of daily records of a child's food and fluid intake. A number of clinical reports have indicated that some parents have difficulty maintaining such records.

Children also have difficulty in complying with a prescribed dietary regimen. They may have to eat specific foods every day, including special dietetic products. Apart from a dislike for the monotonous taste, children can show a low acceptance for a diet because they see that other children can eat a variety of foods. Since many children do not want to be known as different from their peers, every effort must be made to make them feel comfortable with their diet plan. Thus, the foods they eat should differ as little as possible from those of other children.

In some families, a child's noncompliance with a dietary plan may be the result of a conflict between parent and child. If the health team becomes aware of this, they may tactfully want to recommend professional counseling for the parent. In other instances, noncompliance can be minimized if all dietary modifications are incorporated into the child's daily life-style. This will minimize interference with a child's psychological well-being. Occasions such as family gatherings, parties, and picnics may be used to implement dietary modifications and improve the child's appetite. However, some children suffering from long-term illnesses discover that eating is their only joy. Thus, some of these children overeat and become obese.

If a child's illness is lengthy, the reactions of parents can become extreme. On the one hand, they may feel guilty and anxious about their child, feeling that they are somehow to blame, and thus become overprotective. On the other hand, some parents unfortunately demonstrate shame and resentment toward their children. They may view their children as being inferior and thus reject them. Both reactions need to be watched for and avoided at all costs.

Many parents of children with inherited illnesses are unable to accept that they may have to prepare their children for genetic counseling when they mature. They must deal with the future of their children in regard to marriage, independence, and finances as well. Professional counseling may be necessary to help parents plan for these eventualities.

Special Considerations in Child Feeding

When children are required to eat a modified diet, they may have to be reeducated. To do this, the health team must first become familiar with the children's normal ways of eating, upon which the appropriate dietary changes must be based. If a child's hospital stay is long, the nutritional education program may be more aggressive and systematic. Depending on the child's age, teaching aids such as movies, slides, and skits may be used. At the beginning of diet modification, children should be given as much freedom as possible in food selection so that they can adjust to the new nutritional environment. Some children like familiar foods such as peanut butter sandwiches, hamburgers, french fries, puddings, milk, soft drinks, and cookies. If a child is expected to be hospitalized for only a short time and has neither a fluid nor electrolyte imbalance, it may be advisable for the child to eat his or her favorite foods even if they are not nutrient dense. When the child is recovering, the missing nutrients can be made up. A sick child should not be forced into new situations at mealtime, such as having to eat new foods or having to eat food cooked in an unfamiliar way. Using different utensils than the child is accustomed to and serving a combination of new and familiar foods should also be avoided. A child's attitude towards any change in dietary routine should be carefully noted.

As indicated earlier, a sick child's food preferences should be noted either by members of the health team or the parents. It is also advisable to have the list in writing. Children of ethnic origins may require special foods and food preparation. However, even when these preferences are taken into account, a child may find all food served in the hospital undesirable. The child is most likely comparing hospital food to food at home, at fast-food chains, or served in school. Although the food choices for a sick child are invariably limited, it is extremely important to try to select a diet that has familiar foods that the child will readily eat. Whenever a child does not eat, the reasons should be ascertained and new techniques or approaches found for feeding. The child may simply have a poor appetite or be too sick and anxious to eat. Different methods of food serving may be used, including tube and IV feedings. The oral feeding of a hospitalized child should never be forced. Avoid stern commands such as "Drink your milk," "Eat your fruits and vegetables," "There must be no food left on the plate," and "There will be no dessert until you have finished eating your meat and potatoes." When a child does not eat all the food on the plate, it may mean that the serving size was too large.

Regular hospital procedures such as replacing dressings, giving baths, blood drawing, IV adjustments, drainage, or blood pressure measurements should not interfere with mealtimes. The child should not be exposed to pain or physiotherapy while eating.

Whether a child is sick or well, he or she must eat appropriate amounts and kinds of food. Any nutritional problem may become severe if a child is ill for an extended period of time. Ensuring that a child with a lengthy illness eats a proper amount of food is always a problem demanding constant attention.

There are several ways to improve a child's eating and acceptance of foods. The child can become involved in the food selection process by being provided with a selective menu, cafeteria-style food service, fast-food counter food service, or a play-setting food service. Children love to get involved and will eat what they have chosen.

Children generally prefer certain eating practices. First, they like small, frequent meals (especially anorexic children). Second, they like to eat family style or in groups (especially with other sick children of the same age). Sometimes the dietetic staff can save time by serving all young sick children in one place and at one time. Third, they like to be fed by their mothers.

A child's food intake may be improved by (1) providing a cheerful eating environment (such as a room having attractive drapes, comfortable chairs and tables, and pleasing paintings), especially when meals are served in a dining room; (2) serving tasty, attractive foods, using creative menu planning and food preparation techniques for children with such preferences; (3) using occasions such as Christmas, Thanksgiving, Halloween, Easter, and birthdays to give surprise parties, which can improve appetites.

Diet Therapy and Dietetic Products

The routine house diets (liquid, soft, and so on) described in Chapter 23 are also applicable to children, as will be seen later in this chapter. Many therapeutic diets (for treating diabetes, kidney problems, heart problems, and so on) used to treat adult diseases are also used with children, although some modifications may be necessary. There are a number of home and commercial formulas and diets that are used to feed infants, children, and even adults. Table 30-1 describes some common home-prepared milk formulas for infant feeding. Table 30-2 describes a list of commercial infant formulas for

TABLE 30-1 Home-Prepared Milk Formulas for Infant Feeding

| Milk | Additional Preparation | Feeding Purpose | % of Total Calories | | | Special Nutritional Characteristics |
			Protein	Fat	Carbo-hydrate	
Breast	None	Regular	7	56	37	None
Cow's, whole	None	Regular	22	48	30	May be considered low-fat compared with breast milk
Cow's, skim (for-tified with vitamins A and D)	None	Regular	40	3	57	Usually considered as low-fat
Cow's, evaporated, with carbohydrate added	After dilution, 2 T corn syrup added	Regular	13	34	53	None
Cow's, evaporated	Dilution	Regular	20	52	26	Carbohydrate may be added
Goat's	None	Antiallergy	19	54	27	Deficient in folic acid

Note: Cow's milk is pasteurized and homogenized. For safety's sake, goat's milk should also be pasteurized.

TABLE 30-2 Commercial Infant Formulas for Regular Feeding

| Product | Manu-facturer | Preparation | kcal/100 mL | % of Total Calories | | | Basic Ingredients |
				Protein	Fat	Carbo-hydrate	
Baker's infant formula	Roerig	Must be diluted	67	13	44	42	Coconut, corn, and soy oil; cow's milk; lactose; maltose; dextrose; dex-trins; vitamins; minerals
Enfamil 13	Mead Johnson	Ready for feeding	43	9	50	41	Coconut and soy oil; cow's milk; lactose; vi-tamins; minerals
Enfamil 20	Mead Johnson	Ready for feeding	67	9	50	41	Coconut and soy oil; cow's milk; lactose; vi-tamins; minerals
Enfamil powder or liquid	Mead Johnson	Must be diluted	67	9	50	41	Coconut and soy oil; cow's milk; lactose; vi-tamins; minerals
Enfamil 20 + (iron supplemented)	Mead Johnson	Ready for feeding	67	9	50	41	Coconut and soy oil; cow's milk; lactose; vi-tamins; minerals

TABLE 30-2   (continued)

Product	Manu-facturer	Preparation	kcal/100 mL	% of Total Calories			Basic Ingredients
				Protein	Fat	Carbo-hydrate	
Enfamil 24 + (iron supplemented)	Mead Johnson	Ready for feeding	81	9	50	41	Coconut and soy oil; cow's milk; lactose; vitamins; minerals
Similac 13	Ross	Ready for feeding	44	10	47	43	Coconut and soy oil; skim milk; lactose; vitamins; minerals
Similac 20	Ross	Ready for feeding	68	9	48	43	Coconut and soy oil; cow's milk; lactose; vitamins; minerals
Similac 24	Ross	Ready for feeding	81	9	48	43	Coconut and soy oil; cow's milk; lactose; vitamins; minerals
Similac with Iron 13	Ross	Ready for feeding	44	10	47	43	Coconut and soy oil; cow's milk; lactose; vitamins; minerals
Similac with Iron 20	Ross	Ready for feeding	68	9	48	43	Coconut and soy oil; cow's milk; lactose; vitamins; minerals
Similac with Iron 24	Ross	Ready for feeding	81	10	48	42	Coconut and soy oil; cow's milk; lactose; vitamins; minerals
Similac 27	Ross	Ready for feeding	93	11	48	41	Coconut and soy oil; cow's milk; lactose; vitamins; minerals
SMA 20*	Wyeth	Ready for feeding or diluted	67	9	48	42	Coconut, safflower, soy, and oleo oil; cow's milk; lactose; vitamins; minerals
SMA 24*	Wyeth	Ready for feeding	81	9	48	42	Coconut, safflower, soy, and oleo oil; cow's milk; lactose; vitamins; minerals
Similac Advance	Ross	Ready for feeding	54	21	33	46	Corn and soy oil; cow's milk; soy protein; corn syrup solids; lactose; vitamins; minerals

*Partially demineralized; same types of fatty acids as in breast milk; casein:lactalbumin ratio = 40:60.

TABLE 30-3 Commercial Soy Formulas for Feeding Patients with Milk Allergy

Product	Manu-facturer	Preparation	kcal/100 mL	% of Total Calories			Basic Ingredients
				Protein	Fat	Carbo-hydrate	
Isomil	Ross	Ready for feeding	67	12	48	40	Coconut and corn oil; soy; sucrose; cornstarch; corn syrup; vitamins; minerals
I-Soyalac	Loma Linda	Must be diluted	68	12	49	39	Soy oil; soy protein; dextrose; maltose; sucrose; dextrins; soy; vitamins; minerals
Mull-Soy liquid*	Syntex	Must be diluted	67	19	48	31	Soy oil; soy protein; soy carbohydrate; invert sucrose; sucrose
Nursoy†	Wyeth	Ready for feeding	67	13	47	40	Coconut, safflower, soy, and oleo oil; soy protein; methionine; sucrose; corn syrup; vitamins; minerals
Neo-Mull-Soy‡	Syntex	Ready for feeding or diluted	67	12	47	38	Soy oil; soy protein; methionine; sucrose; vitamins; minerals
ProSobee	Mead Johnson	Ready for feeding or diluted	67	14	46	40	Soy oil; soy protein; methionine; sucrose; glucose; vitamins; minerals
Soyalac Liquid Concentrate	Loma Linda	Must be diluted	69	13	49	38	Soy oil; soy; methionine; dextrose; maltose; sucrose; vitamins; minerals
Soyalac Powder	Loma Linda	Must be diluted	68	12	53	35	Soy oil; protein; carbohydrate; dextrose; maltose; sucrose; dextrins; vitamins; minerals

*Made from defatted whole soybean flour; also used for adult feeding.
†Fatty acid content similar to that of breast milk.
‡Made from soy protein isolates.

regular feeding, and Table 30-3 provides a list of commercial soy formulas for infants and children who have a milk allergy. Table 30-4 lists alphabetically those commercial infant formulas with nutritional modifications for therapeutic purposes, and Table 30-5 describes the clinical indications for the use of special dietetic products.

A comprehensive discussion of diet therapy for known diseases in pediatric patients is beyond the scope of this book. The remainder of this chapter discusses a few common childhood disorders and their dietary management. Additional information on diet and pediatric patients may be obtained from the references at the end

TABLE 30-4   Commercial Infant Formulas with Nutritional Modifications for Therapeutic Purposes

Product	Manufacturer	Nutritional Modifications for Clinical Conditions Indicated in Table 30-5
Casec	Mead Johnson	Calcium or protein supplement; may be added to meats, vegetables, or formulas; calcium caseinate obtained from skim milk curd and lime water
Dextri-Maltose	Mead Johnson	Contains only carbohydrate (56% maltose, 42% dextrins)
Electrodialyzed whey	Wyeth	Complete protein, very low in electrolytes; not commercially available
Isomil	Ross	Butterfat replaced with coconut and corn oil, lactose-free, soy isolate protein; used in infants sensitive to milk protein or lactose
I-Soyalac	Loma Linda	Butterfat replaced with soy oil, soy protein, lactose-free; used in infants sensitive to milk protein or lactose
LamBase formula	Gerber	Lactose-free; used in infants with milk allergies or glycogen-storage disease
Lofenalac	Mead Johnson	Butterfat replaced by corn oil; low in phenylalanine; used in infants with phenylketonurla
Lonalac	Mead Johnson	Butterfat replaced by coconut oil; very low in sodium
Lytren	Mead Johnson	Used as an oral electrolyte and for fluid replacement; essentially consists of electrolytes and glucose
MBF (Meat Base Formula)	Gerber	Beef and sesame fat, sucrose; used in infants with nonspecific allergy, galactosemia, lactase deflciency, and mllk-induced steatorrhea
Mulsoy	Syntex	Soy protein with methionine, soy oil; lactose-free; used in infants with milk allergy
Nursoy	Wyeth	No lactose; soy protein, methionine; butterfat completely replaced by vegetable oil; used in infants with milk allergy or lactose intolerance; contains same amount of polyunsaturated fatty acids as breast milk
Neo-Mullsoy	Syntex	Soy protein with methionine, soy oils; lactose-free; used in infants with milk allergy
Nutramigen	Mead Johnson	Corn oil, hydrolyzed casein; lactose-free; used in infants with milk allergy
Pedialyte	Ross	Glucose only; no protein, no fat; used as an oral electrolyte and for fluid replacement
Polycose	Ross	No protein, no fat; glucose, hydrolyzed cornstarch; used as carbohydrate supplement for formulas
Portagen	Mead Johnson	Milk protein, butterfat replaced with coconut oil (fractionated) and corn oil (mainly MCT); lactose-free; used where MCT and lactose-free conditions are desirable
Pregestimil	Mead Johnson	Lactose-free protein, fractionated coconut oil, soy oil; used where MCT usage and lactose-free conditions are desirable
Premature formula	Mead Johnson	Skim milk, lactose, sucrose, corn oil; high in calories

TABLE 30-4 (continued)

Product	Manufacturer	Nutritional Modifications for Clinical Conditions Indicated in Table 30-5
Probana	Mead Johnson	Milk, hydrolyzed casein; low in fat; dextrose and banana powder supply carbohydrate; used for infants with celiac syndrome, diarrhea, or other conditions precipitating steatorrhea
ProSobee	Mead Johnson	Soy isolate, soy oil; lactose-free; used in infants with milk allergy
Similac PM 60/40	Ross	Corn, coconut, and olive oil; lactalbumin:casein ratio = 40:60 as in human breast milk; low in electrolytes; for renal patients
Sobee	Mead Johnson	Soy protein, soy and coconut oil; lactose-free; used in infants with milk allergy
Soyalac (liquid and powder)	Loma Linda	Soy protein, soy oil; lactose-free; used in infants intolerant to milk protein and lactose

TABLE 30-5 Clinical Indications for the Use of Special Dietetic Products

Clinical Condition	Recommended Therapeutic Products
Electrolyte and fluid replacement	
Dehydration	Pedialyte
Diarrhea	Nutramigen, Probana
Hyperallergy to milk protein	Isomil, LamBase, MBF, Mull-Soy, Nutramigen, Portagen, ProSobee, Sobee, Soyalac
Nutrient intolerance	
Fat intolerance (fat-free products containing MCTs)	Baker's Infant Formula, Enfamil, Isomil, Similac, SMA, Soyalac
Lactose intolerance or galactosemia	Isomil, LamBase, MBF, Mull-Soy, Neo-Mull Soy, Nutramigen, Pregestimil, ProSobee, Sobee, Soyalac
Sodium Deficiency	Lonalac
Electrolyte deficiency	Similac PM 60/40
Phenylketonuria	Lofenalac
Nutrient deficiency	
Protein supplement	LamBase, MBF, Mull-Soy, Probana, Sobee
High-caloric feeding for premature infants	Premature Formula
High-caloric carbohydrate source	Polycose, Dextri-Maltose

TABLE 30-6 Fecal Characteristics of Infants

Age (months)	Diet	Fecal Characteristics			
		pH	Color	Texture	Number of bowel movements daily
0–4	Home or commercial formulas	6–8	Pale yellow to light brown	Compressed, solid	2–3
	Breast milk	<6	Yellow to golden	Like cream or ointment	2–4
4–12	Regular foods and/or milk	Variable	Intensified yellow	Harder	1–3
Over 12	Regular foods and/or milk	Variable	Similar to adult, i.e., highly variable (yellow to black)	Similar to adult, i.e., highly variable (soft to very hard)	Similar to adult, i.e., highly variable (1–4)

of this book. Also, the index of this book can be used to refer to relevant information in other chapters of this book.

GASTROINTESTINAL DISEASES

Much of the information on diet therapy and gastrointestinal diseases in adults also pertains to young children (see Chapter 24). However, since children have somewhat different nutritional requirements, the adult feeding routine must be modified. In this section, we will discuss three intestinal disorders that require special diet therapy, namely, diarrhea, constipation, and cystic fibrosis.

Diarrhea

The stools of infants change with age and development, as indicated in Table 30-6. It is important for the parents to recognize a child's normal feces. Children with diarrhea have an abnormally frequent evacuation of watery (and sometimes greasy and/or bloody) stools. Diarrhea is frequent among infants and children and can be a very distressing condition. In chronic cases, it may last for weeks or months, while the child continues to grow normally. Chronic diarrhea may be a symptom of a disease. In general, one

TABLE 30-7 Possible Causes of Diarrhea in Young Patients According to Stool Profile

Stool Characteristics	Clinical Disorders
Fatty	Cystic fibrosis, celiac disease, iron deficiency anemia, intestinal allergy
Watery	Lactase deficiency, intestinal infection, intestinal allergy, diabetes mellitus
Bloody	Ulcerative colitis, amoebic dysentery, bacillary dysentery

Note: Any diagnosis made by stool analysis must be confirmed by additional tests.

classifies diarrhea (acute or chronic) according to its stool profile or cause (or site of clinical defect). There are a number of common causes of diarrhea in infants and children:

1. It can be due to a specific clinical disorder. Table 30-7 shows how a clinician may make an on-the-spot diagnosis of the cause of diarrhea by inspecting the fecal characteristics. However, other tests are needed for confirmation.
2. Bacterial contamination of formulas or foods can cause food poisoning.

TABLE 30-8 Calorie, Sodium, and Potassium Contents of Some Preparations for Treating Diarrhea

Beverage	mg Sodium/ 100 mL	mg Potassium/ 100 mL	kcal/100 mL
Milk, whole	50	144	62
Milk, skim	52	145	36
Apple juice, canned or bottled	1	101	47
Grape juice, canned or bottled	2	116	66
Orange juice, from concentrate	1	202	49
7-Up	10	Trace	40
Coca-Cola	1	52	44
Pepsi-Cola	15	3	46
Ginger ale	8	Trace	35
Root beer	13	2	41
Flavored gelatin	54	Trace	59
Pedialyte	69	78	20
Lytren	69	98	30

3. Some youngsters develop diarrhea because of intestinal reactions to certain foods such as sugars, fats (too little or too much), wheat, milk, and eggs.

The initial management of diarrhea in children involves two steps. The clinician's first and major objective is to restore fluid and electrolyte balance by oral or IV therapy, since a child is highly susceptible to dehydration. Subsequently, the clinician determines if the child can be managed adequately by oral nourishment without parenteral feeding, which requires hospitalization.

If a child's diarrhea is accompanied by mild to moderate dehydration with persistent vomiting, hospitalization for parenteral fluid therapy is indicated. In general, it is feasible to provide oral fluids and electrolytes for children with mild diarrhea or children recovering from severe diarrhea. If diarrhea is mild to moderate and the patient shows normal clinical signs otherwise and is not dehydrated, most physicians prescribe outpatient therapy consisting of an oral hypotonic solution of glucose and electrolytes.

In caring for an infant with diarrhea, the major concern is supplying an adequate supply of fluid and electrolytes. Homemade or commercial (regular and dietetic) oral solutions may be used. Below are two types of homemade solutions.

Solution A	Solution B
15–25 g glucose	1 t light corn syrup
3–4 g sodium chloride	3 oz water
2–3 g sodium bicarbonate	
1–2 g potassium chloride	
1 L water	

Although solution A is a simple mixing of chemicals, some health practitioners are still concerned about its use. If the parent makes a small error in combining the ingredients, the child may be fed a hypertonic solution that can aggravate dehydration. Home preparation can be made easier, safer, and more accurate if a defined amount of each chemical is packaged in a special paper or envelope so that final mixing is achieved by mixing the four labeled packages. Solution B, which makes a 5% glucose solution, is a little less satisfactory in electrolyte content but is safer and easier to make.

Some readily available regular and dietetic solutions are listed in Table 30-8. Because milk

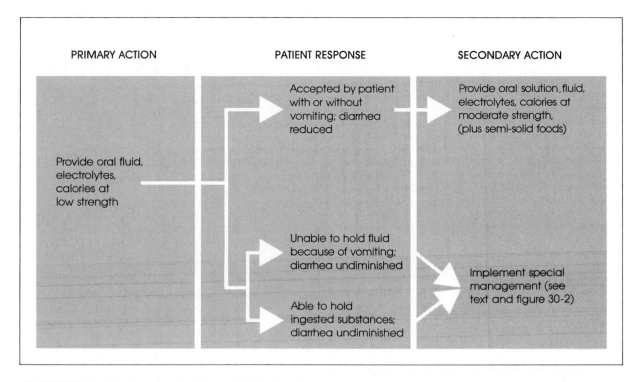

FIGURE 30-1   Strategy for feeding a child with diarrhea.

contains too many electrolytes, especially sodium, most clinicians do not recommend it at the beginning of treatment. All other solutions listed in the table may be initially fed to a child with diarrhea. To prevent gas from being trapped and the accompanying discomfort, some soda drinks can be decarbonated. The gelatin should be made in half strength to avoid aggravating dehydration. Kool-Aid and unflavored gelatin should not be used, since they contain few electrolytes.

After about 2 days of fluid and electrolyte support, as indicated above, the diarrhea should subside somewhat. At this stage, the child should be given a diluted regular infant formula, for example, one-fourth, one-third, or even one-half of normal strength. Additional calories are supplied by adding corn syrup (1 t per 3 oz of formula) or using a supplemental feeding of strained baby cereals and fruits.

Disaccharide intolerance (especially lactose intolerance) is not uncommon in infants after an episode of diarrhea (whether acute, short-term, or prolonged). The presence of lactose or milk

intolerance is confirmed by the presence of more fluid stools, a fecal pH of less than 5 or 6, and a positive Clinitest for the presence of reducing substances. Lactose intolerance may be managed by the use of lactose-free soy formulas such as Nutramigen or Pregestimil. However, they may not be suitable for long-term feeding of infants. Also, since lactose intolerance is temporary in many infants, the child should be retested frequently to check intestinal functions. Feeding with a regular formula is resumed when conditions indicate. Once a child's diarrhea has disappeared, the mother should institute a regular diet appropriate to the infant's age. Figure 30-1 is a flow diagram indicating treatment for an infant with diarrhea.

Recently concern has been expressed about the common practice of eliminating milk, eggs, and wheat to reduce diarrhea in a young patient. Although some pediatric patients benefit from this treatment, the attending physician must be alert to (1) potential undernutrition that may occur if the elimination diet is prolonged and (2) the possibility that the child has celiac disease

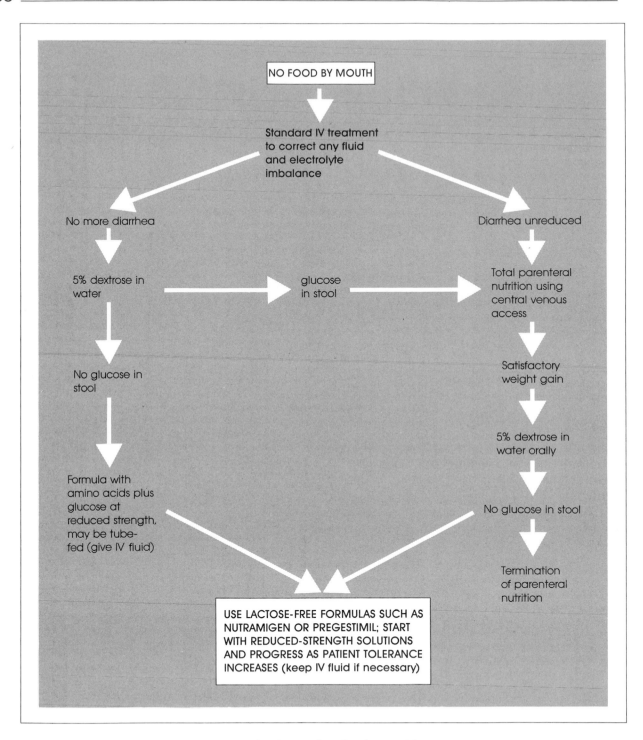

FIGURE 30-2   Strategy for treating a child with unreduced or intractable
diarrhea.

(see Chapter 24). An elimination diet may mask this disorder.

What should the management procedure be for children hospitalized with diarrhea? After obtaining all necessary data upon admission, the children should be fed a regular diet for their age unless contraindicated by the following: (1) severe diarrhea, (2) overt fluid depletion and/or electrolyte imbalance, and (3) uncertain clinical status. Estimates of food intake and weight changes since admission should be evaluated, and a daily record of the stool profile kept (including pH, frequency, amount, texture and appearance, presence of reducing substances and blood, and presence of fat and water). Stools should also be tested for the presence of biological pathogens. Standard urine and blood analyses should be made, as well as X rays of the chest and abdomen.

Children should then be treated orally with fluid and electrolytes as in the case of non-hospitalized patients. If the diarrhea is unreduced or even intractable (see Figure 30-1), the strategy outlined in Figure 30-2 should be used. Children suffering from intractable diarrhea may have changes in the mucosa of the small intestine. This can result in a vicious cycle of malnutrition (see Figure 30-3), making aggressive nutritional support necessary (see Figure 30-2). The effectiveness of drugs to treat diarrhea in infants has not been established. Such drugs include antidiarrheal agents (Lomotil, for example, diphenoxylate, pectin, and kaolin), antibiotics, and cholestyramine.

The initial treatment for diarrhea in children over 1-year-old consists of giving clear liquids such as diluted broth, fruit juices, soft drinks, gelatin dessert, and Popsicles. After the diarrhea has subsided, a low roughage diet may be used. Subsequent management is the same as that for an adult (see Chapter 24). Once the condition has stabilized, a regular diet appropriate to the child's age can be implemented.

Constipation

Patterns of bowel movements among children and infants vary. If a child is active, passes a soft to slightly compact stool, gains weight progres-

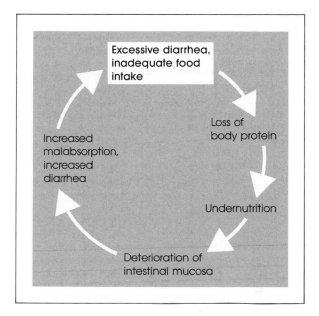

FIGURE 30-3   Relationship between diarrhea and malnutrition.

sively, shows normal development, and is free from any known clinical disorder, the mother has no reason to worry.

A newborn may have a constipation problem that is most likely the result of plugging by meconium (dark green mucilaginous material in the intestine of the full-term fetus). Constipation in an older infant is usually due to a change in the type of feeding. An anatomical defect may also be a cause, but this is rare. There are several ways to recognize the presence of constipation in a young infant:

1. A change in the stool (number, consistency, texture, appearance)
2. Pain in the infant when defecating
3. Distended abdomen with every bowel movement
4. Very black or bloody stools

The constipation of many newborns disappears shortly after discharge from hospital. If this does not occur, the mother must consult her pediatrician.

Let us examine constipation in a baby caused by a change in diet. Some babies develop constipation when breast-feeding is replaced with formula (homemade or commercial). Characteristic signs include the face turning red, strain, and the legs turned upward while defecating, even though the child may pass a soft stool. The doctor will evaluate the child after being informed of the symptoms. The doctor should first look for any obstruction that may require special medical attention. If no obstruction is found, the mother should be advised of the benign nature of the constipation and told that the child's bowel habit will return to normal after it adapts to the new formula. Actually, the stools of some infants change from soft to hard even if they are not constipated.

Other babies develop constipation when they are switched from liquid or strained food to solid food. The signs of such constipation vary. In some infants, a day with normal bowel movements is followed by one with none. In others, the passing of hard stools is accompanied by crying and intense straining. Many of these cases are of unknown origin. Some typical causes are excessive water absorption (reabsorption) by the colon, resulting in dry stools and constipation. If so, the anal passage may be stretched, causing pain and bleeding if there is an open wound. The child passes red stools, which are easily observed on toilet paper. The management of this form of constipation consists of a reduction in milk intake and an increased intake of juices, fruits, and fluids. Some clinicians may prescribe enemas, laxatives, and suppositories, such as a glycine suppository. The dosage and frequency of application of these drugs must be determined with care.

Simple home remedies have proven effective in managing constipated infants, making a visit to the doctor unnecessary. Because of the high osmotic effect of sugars, adding 1 t of table sugar to 4 or 5 oz of formula or water can help some infants to defecate. If the child can eat solid foods, the use of prune juice, apricots, and baby cereals containing bran or fiber is also beneficial, although the amount used should not be excessive, for example, under ½ oz in any one feeding. Some foods appear more likely to cause constipation than others, such as bananas, barley, and rice cereal, but this claim is presently being debated. Sick babies may also develop constipation if they do not take in an adequate amount of formula or if they have a fever.

Constipation in children under 4 or 5 years old is of two types: psychological and anatomical. The latter refers to a defect in the muscles regulating the defecation process. In some children under 2 years old, any initial sign of constipation can create a psychological barrier to defecation. When children start passing hard stools, they experience some pain, so they subsequently strain to retain the stools in order to reduce the pain. The accumulated feces become larger and harder, causing more pain in subsequent defecations. Some parents report that their children turn red in the face, strain, and arch their backs during a bowel movement. Though toilet trained, they soil their pants frequently and are reluctant to go to the bathroom. Some parents complain that these children are lazy. In this case, the parental attitudes make the constipation problem worse. This psychological barrier to bowel movement can be difficult to overcome.

On the other hand, constipation in some children results from fecal impaction, which may develop for a number of reasons. For instance, children between the ages of 5 and 8 may develop constipation because they consider visiting the bathroom a waste of time. How do we manage the older child with a constipation problem? The basic principles are similar to those for an adult and are presented in Chapter 24. If the parents consult a physician, the doctor may need to study the problem and advise the parents about what actions to take.

As a start, the parents may help the child initiate a good bowel movement by using an enema. The dose, which may be large at the beginning, may be used until a defecation pattern of 3 to 5 times a day is established. However, if a laxative such as mineral oil is used, care must be taken to avoid the potential loss of fat-soluble vitamins. Next, the child should be put on a conditioning schedule, such as 10 to 20 minutes daily on the toilet. The child should also be encouraged to have bowel movements as frequently as possible. At the same time, milk intake may be reduced to 60% to 80% of normal and the intake of fruits, juices, and bran cereals increased. Other dietary changes suggested in Chapter 24 may also be made.

Cystic Fibrosis

Among Caucasian children, cystic fibrosis is one of the more frequent and lethal of inherited diseases. It is estimated that about 1 child per 1,500 to 3,500 live births is affected. Although cystic fibrosis is most common in infants and children, it also occurs periodically in adults. Two major sites of this disease are the exocrine area of the pancreas and the mucous and sweat glands of the body. The mucous glands produce a tenacious and viscid mucous secretion, and an excessive amount of sodium chloride is found in the sweat. The patient may show any or all of the following clinical disorders:

1. Pulmonary disorder with recurrent infections and other lung trouble.
2. Pancreatic insufficiency resulting in a lack of digestive enzymes. Steatorrhea (fat in stools) and azotorrhea (nitrogen in stools) indicate malabsorption of fat and protein.
3. Excessive electrolytes in sweat.
4. Malnutrition.
5. Failure to thrive.

If the affected child is not treated, overt symptoms occurring during the first year may include any or all of the following: (1) frequent large bowel movements with foul odor, (2) substandard weight gain even with good appetite, (3) abdominal bloating, (4) moderate to severe steatorrhea, with stool fat about three to five times, normal, (5) frequent and excessive crying, (6) potential sodium deficiency and circulatory collapse resulting from an excessive salt loss in sweat (especially in hot weather), and (7) frequent episodes of pneumonia characterized by coughing and wheezing. This last symptom by itself can indicate cystic fibrosis. At present, the proper diagnosis of a child with cystic fibrosis is determined from clinical symptoms, the level of sodium chloride in sweat, and X rays of the chest.

About 8% to 12% of cystic fibrosis patients can be diagnosed at birth because of a bowel obstruction (meconium ileus) caused by a thickened meconium. This early diagnosis is helpful, since the proper nutritional and dietary care can be instituted early to prevent suffering from undernourishment. In addition, other appropriate medical treatments can be administered. At the time of this writing, improved medical management has permitted an increasing number of patients to survive to adulthood, especially males.

The nutritional needs of the cystic fibrosis patient must take into account the following considerations:

1. The problem of recurrent infection is accompanied by defective gastrointestinal functions, increasing the child's nutritional needs.
2. The child needs a working immune defense system for survival. An adequate supply of essential nutrients is necessary to assure sufficient production of antibodies and phagocytic activity of white blood cells.
3. The child suffers from severe malabsorption because of a lack of three pancreatic enzymes: lipase, trypsin, and amylase.

Children with uncontrolled cystic fibrosis have a typical profile. They have a retarded body weight for their age and height, with occasional arrested growth. They are undersized, with a bloated belly and wasted arms and legs, and they appear malnourished. Early diagnosis and management can restore body size and the deposition of muscle and fat. This allows the children to regain a normal appearance, although sexual development may be delayed. However, complete recovery is possible in some cases.

The goals of diet therapy in cases of cystic fibrosis are (1) to improve fat and protein absorption, (2) to decrease the frequency and bulk of stools, (3) to increase the body weight, (4) to control or prevent rectum prolapse, (5) to increase resistance to infection, and (6) to control, prevent, or improve associated emotional problems. General feeding techniques may be used in feeding these children.

Use of pancreatic enzymes

Pancreatic enzymes administered to children with cystic fibrosis definitely improve their condition. As the enzyme extracts are used (Viokase and Cotazym are the most common), the digestive problems abate. The children gain weight and their physical development improves.

Infants and small children should take enzymes in granule or powder form, sometimes just before a meal and sometimes mixed with food. Older children should take tablets or capsules. If too much of the enzyme is given, a child will have difficulty accepting it. There may even be psychological problems if the child is forced to take the enzymes. Therefore, prolonged usage can also cause problems.

The amount of enzyme given depends on the age of the child and the improvement in stool characteristics. A small amount is sufficient initially (for example, 1/5, 1/4, or 1/3 t or one tablet). The dosage amount can be progressively increased over 1 or 2 months. Progress is monitored by studying the child's fecal waste. If stool conditions do not improve and the child is already taking a large amount of enzyme (for example, eight tablets or 1 t per treatment), fat intake may need to be restricted. Enzyme replacement does not always work. Malabsorption may remain because of possible mucosal damage, intestinal gland malfunctioning, and viscid mucus coating the intestinal villi.

General feeding

Feeding a child with cystic fibrosis can be made easier in several ways. Menu planning should be adapted to foods that the child finds acceptable, the clinicial conditions of the child, and the child's response to enzyme treatment. Generally, the diet should be high in calorie and protein with a modified fat content. If fat intake is to be reduced, details on diet planning can be obtained from Chapter 25. However, the extent of fat restriction varies with the patient. Medium-chain triglycerides (MCTs) and essential fatty acids can be used to advantage when fat restriction is indicated. MCTs facilitate fat absorption, and essential fatty acids prevent linoleic acid deficiency. MCTs used in food preparation can increase energy intake, promote weight gain, and reduce fat malabsorption problems (also see Chapters 23 and 24).

Protein malabsorption is mild and usually presents no problem. However, in severe cases the child may lose appetite to the extent that the protein deficiency must be treated. Several procedures can increase the total calorie and protein intake.

One of these involves the addition of dry skim milk powder fortified with fat-soluble vitamins to dishes prepared for regular meals. This can be done both at home and in the hospital. It is an inexpensive, easy, and effective way to add calories and protein to the diet. Properly timed snacks at home and in the hospital are also effective, if tolerated. However, the use of pancreatic enzymes must be appropriately scheduled to improve the digestion and absorption of these items.

Apart from a high-protein and modified-fat diet, the child can be given dense nutrient and protein supplements such as the following:

1. A mixture of MCTs, oligosaccharides with four to ten glucose segments, beef serum, and protein hydrolysates
2. Commercial nutrient-protein solutions such as Pregestimil, Portagen, and Nutramigen (see beginning of this chapter and Chapter 23)
3. Fat and sugar added to foods if the child can tolerate them
4. Water-miscible vitamins A, D, and E given at 1 to 3 times the respective RDAs

If an infant is being treated, nutritional rehabilitation may require 180 to 210 kcal/kg/d (see Chapter 14 for diet planning), while the caloric need of an older child may be 80% to 110% above the norm for that age group.

Foods that are not tolerated by the child (such as raw vegetables and high-fat items) must be identified. Some cystic fibrosis patients get diarrhea when they eat rich carbohydrate foods such as fruit, ice cream, or cookies. They may be suffering a temporary carbohydrate intolerance when this occurs. Lactase deficiency, which occurs in about 1% to 10% of the patients, is to blame. Special formulas that are lactose-free (see the beginning of this chapter and Chapter 23) can be used for as long as the intolerance persists.

A high ambient temperature may cause a child with cystic fibrosis to lose electrolytes through sweating. Salty foods such as peanuts, potato chips, and other items will alleviate the problem if they are tolerated.

Since the intake of several nutrients must be tightly controlled in a child with cystic fibrosis, the child's family should become involved as soon as is feasible. Merely handing the mother a list of foods that should not be eaten by her child is not sufficient, since it could result in the child being fed a lopsided diet that omits some major food groups. Without appropriate instruction, family members cannot easily make substitutions for various foods (such as for fat) and they may not assess the nutritional intake correctly. Furthermore, concessions may have to be made to the child's demands occasionally if a restricted diet is to be implemented effectively.

Thus the dietitian, nutritionist, and nurse must work with the family (especially the mother). The essentials of the four food groups should be taught as well as techniques of substituting acceptable nutritious replacements for high-fat and poorly tolerated food items. It should be emphasized that dietary planning for a cystic fibrosis child takes into consideration: (1) the food preferences of the child, (2) the use of MCTs whenever possible so that the child can occasionally eat favorite foods (such as potato chips, doughnuts, and fried chicken), (3) learning to make foods that contain little fat (such as low-fat gravy and spreads), and (4) keeping a food record for reference so that the nutritional status of the child can be assessed and the nurse or dietitian can make suggestions.

A prescheduled procedure (weekly, monthly, during checkup, etc.) should be used to follow up on the progress of a child being treated for cystic fibrosis. An evaluation of nutritional status should be made that includes height, weight, skinfold measurement, and bone age. The information obtained should then be compared with standard values. Some practitioners recommend continuing this evaluation for 5 years. The child's dietary intake and the nutritional education of the family should also be assessed. If the condition of a child who has been feeling fine and has had a good appetite should suddenly deteriorate, immediate investigation and referral is necessary. Complications such as infection or the ineffectiveness of the diet may cause sudden changes. Arrangements can be made so that such evaluations, assessments, investigations, referrals, and emergency handling can be done by a clinic, family physician, or other health professional (nutritionist, dietitian, nurse, or public health worker).

OBESITY

Childhood obesity is a growing problem in this country. The same difficulties facing an adult trying to lose weight face a child (see Chapters 12 and 14 for details). Among children, the Prader-Willi syndrome is one of the better-known pathological conditions of obesity. Apart from obesity, a child with the Prader-Willi syndrome shows other clinical characteristics. Its cause is unknown, although some cases could be due to an insult received during pregnancy. The newborn child is usually of low weight and fails to thrive after birth. As the child grows, bone development and height are arrested while obesity becomes evident. Mental retardation may be evident in addition to undeveloped muscle tone and a lack of motor coordination. Some children have undeveloped genitals, especially males. Other outstanding physical abnormalities include small feet and hands, triangular upper lips, and Oriental-like eyes. These children also have difficult personality traits (violent reactions, hurting other children, disobedience, etc.), delayed language development, and feeding difficulties when young. A tendency to develop diabetes during adolescence is also common.

Children with Prader-Willi syndrome have some common nutrition and feeding problems. Abnormal mouth development may affect sucking ability to the extent that feeding by gavage or dropper is necessary. Affected children start to gain weight after 1 year of age and tend to become obese between the ages of 1 and 3. Their appetite is difficult to satisfy, and they eat constantly. Body fat is concentrated on the feet, hands, and lower part of the body. These children also tend to have many cavities. In view of the diabetic tendency, the caretaker may have to face the task of feeding a diabetic child.

Before a long-term dietary management program is developed for a child with this problem, feeding difficulties must be identified and corrected. If an afflicted child is not obese, an aggressive program should be implemented to prevent the child from gaining weight in the future. On the other hand, a child who is already obese must lose weight. If cavities are rampant,

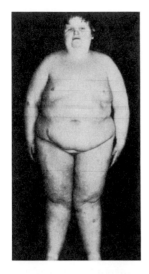
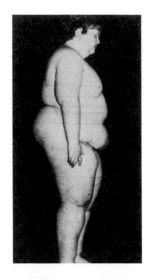

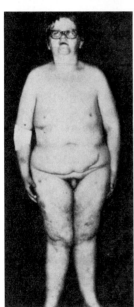
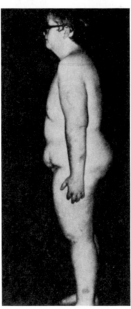

FIGURE 30-4 The Prader-Willi syndrome in a 14-year-old patient. Top: 206 lb (93.5 kg) before therapy. Bottom: 148 lb (67.45 kg) after 18 months of intensive diet therapy with an occasional dose of Fenfluramine. (From K. Widhalm and J. Deutsch, *Pädiatrie und Pädologie II*, 1976, 11:297. Courtesy of Springer-Verlag)

the child may have to learn new eating habits and avoid sugary foods. As in other instances of chronic health problems in children, the dietitian, nutritionist, nurse, parents, and child must all work together as a team.

Caloric and other nutrient needs must be determined for each child with the Prader-Willi syndrome. Early feeding training must include the conditioning of muscles involved in eating, such as those of the jaws, gums, cheek, and tongue. Daily food records should be maintained, and the child's nutritional status should be evaluated regularly. Information such as weight and height gains and problems with food intake should also be recorded.

Children with this syndrome should be conditioned to the diet and environment. For example, if their food intake must be restricted for a prolonged period, they must learn to adjust. It is definitely inadvisable for such children to eat indiscriminately. Thus, they may have to explain to friends and relatives why they must refuse certain foods.

Figure 30-4 shows a child with the Prader-Willi syndrome.

INBORN ERRORS OF METABOLISM

Advances in medical genetics have successfully identified a number of inherited diseases involving aberrations of carbohydrate, fat, protein, vitamin, and mineral metabolism. Most of these diseases are rare, and some respond to dietary management if detected early, especially during early infancy. The clinical manifestations of these disorders vary from mild signs to mental retardation, arrested growth, and even death. Most of these diseases, sometimes termed "inborn errors of metabolism," can be identified either before or during pregnancy or immediately after delivery. Genetic screening or counseling can be used to identify susceptible couples and prepare them for the well-being of their offspring. The list below and Table 30-9 describe the major inborn errors of carbohydrate metabolism.

1. Disaccharidase deficiency
2. Fructosuria
3. Fructosemia (fructose intolerance)
4. Galactosemia
5. Glucose-galactose malabsorption
6. Pentosuria
7. Abnormal glycogen metabolism

TABLE 30-9   Types of Inborn Errors of Glycogen Metabolism

Type	Name of Disorder	Enzyme Deficient	Disease Characteristic
I	Gierke's disease	Liver glucose-6-phosphatase	Excessive glycogen accumulation
II	Pompe's disease	α-1,4-glucosidase	Excessive glycogen accumulation
III	Limit dextrinosis (debrancher glycogen-storage disease)	Amylo-1,6-glucosidase	Excessive deposition of short-chain glycogen
IV	Andersen's disease (amylopectinosis)	Defective (not deficient) amylo-1,4 → 1,6-transglucosidase	Formation of abnormal glycogen
V	McArdle's disease	Muscle phosphorylase	Inability of muscle to degrade glycogen
VI	Hers' disease	Liver phosphorylase	Excessive glycogen accumulation
VII	None	Phosphofructokinase	Inability of muscle to degrade glycogen
VIII	None	Liver phosphorylase kinase	Excessive glycogen accumulation
IX	None	Liver glycogen synthetase	Inability of liver to synthesize glycogen

The errors of fat metabolism are as follows:

1. Ceramide lactoside lipidosis
2. Fabry's disease
3. Fucosidosis
4. Gaucher's disease
5. Generalized (G_{M1}) gangliosidosis
6. Globoid leukodystrophy (Krabbe's disease)
7. Metachromatic leukodystrophy
8. Niemann-Pick disease
9. Tay-Sachs disease
10. Familial hyperlipoproteinemia

Table 30-10 shows errors of amino acid metabolism. To discuss the diet therapy for all these disorders is beyond the scope of this book. Three important examples—galactosemia, disaccharidase deficiency, and phenylketonuria—are reviewed below.

Galactosemia

Galactosemia, which is one form of faulty carbohydrate metabolism, is transmitted by an autosomal recessive gene. There are two types of galactosemia. The more common one affects the enzyme galactose-1-phosphate uridyl transfer-

ase, the activity of which is either low or absent in the patient. As indicated in Figure 30-5, this enzyme deficiency makes it impossible for galactose to be metabolized. It then accumulates in the blood (galactosemia) and in the urine (galactosuria). A young child's main dietary source of galactose is milk sugar or lactose (glucose and galactose).

The onset and severity of the symptoms of galactosemia vary with the patient and may become overt immediately after birth. The classic sign is a failure to thrive, with very little weight gain. The child may have an enlarged liver and jaundice and have difficulty in sucking. Vomiting and diarrhea are common. Cataracts may develop at birth or later, and their permanence varies with the patient. In some patients, the cataracts cannot be reversed by dietary treatment and surgery is needed. Some patients show decreased blood glucose levels and increased amounts of urine protein and amino acids.

Galactosemia is diagnosed by assaying the activity level of the transferase enzyme in the red blood cells of the body. If the medical history of a pregnant woman indicates a potential occurrence of this disorder, the presence of the enzyme can be analyzed in the newborn's cord

TABLE 30-10 Types of Inborn Errors of Amino Acid Metabolism

Disorder	Location of Metabolic Defect in an Organ or Metabolic Path
Argininemia	Urea cycle
Argininosuccinicaciduria	Urea cycle
Citrullinemia	Urea cycle
Cystathioninuria	Metabolism of methionine
Cystinosis	Unknown
Cystinuria	Kidney
Histidinemia	Metabolism of histidine
Homocystinuria	Metabolism of methionine
Hyperammonemia	Urea cycle
Hyperprolinemia (type I and II)	Metabolism of proline
Hypertyrosinemia (neonatal)	Metabolism of tyrosine and phenylalanine
Hypervalinemia	Metabolism of valine
Maple syrup urine disease (branched-chain ketoaciduria)	Metabolism of valine, isoleucine, and leucine
Methylmalonic aciduria	Metabolism of isoleucine, threonine, valine, and methionine
Phenylketonuria	Metabolism of phenylalanine
Propionic acidemia (aciduria)	Metabolism of isoleucine, threonine, and methionine
Tyrosinosis	Metabolism of tyrosine, phenylalanine, and possibly methionine

blood. If the disease is then diagnosed and treated early, all overt symptoms can be eliminated, and organ and brain damage can be prevented in many cases. However, in some cases, even though the child survives, it may grow up having slightly subnormal intelligence. Some difficulties in learning and psychological adjustment may also be present. Some experts in the field propose that such "residual" effects may be a direct result of the disease or of the child's environment. A child's adverse reaction to dietary restrictions and anxiety over peer acceptance may arrest mental development. In some cases, the child's delayed physical and mental development may be accompanied by reduced motor coordination. The child can also be withdrawn, but is normal in other respects.

Recently there has been concern about exposing an unborn and susceptible child to a large amount of galactose ingested by the mother. Some clinicians place pregnant mothers who are carriers of the disorder on a low-galactose diet to eliminate any risk to the fetus. However, it is important that the mother receive an adequate amount of calcium if her milk intake is reduced or fetal development will be adversely affected.

In general, the dietary management of a child with galactosemia is simple. If feasible, the child should be fed a galactose-free diet (that is, lactose-free diet, see later discussion). Table 30-11 lists permitted and prohibited foods in such a diet. Clinical experience indicates that the child may have to be on the diet for 2 or more years. The disappearance of overt clinical signs and a favorable blood galactose level indicates improvement in the child. For example, the child's progress can be monitored by measuring the level of galactose-1-phosphate in red blood cells. A value of 30 to 50 μg/mL is considered acceptable. Table 30-12 indicates the suggested frequency of checkups.

Experience indicates that a galactose (lac-

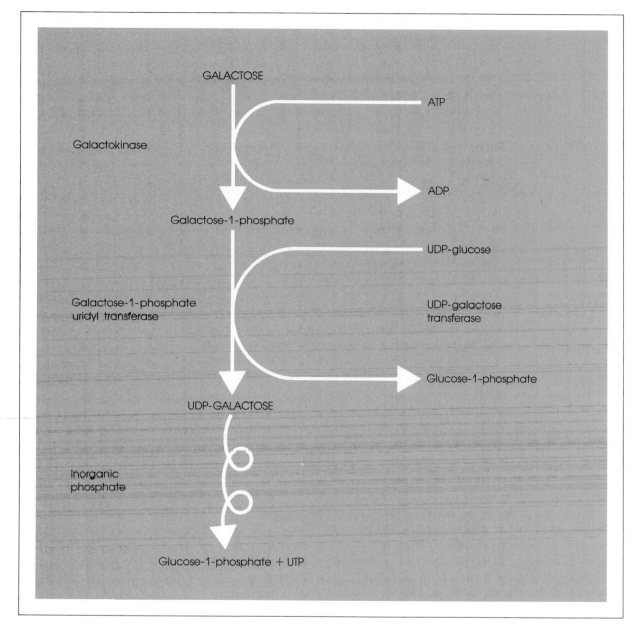

FIGURE 30-5   Metabolism of galactose.*

tose)-free diet is effective. It improves the child's
appetite, and the child gains weight and suffers
less vomiting and diarrhea. It is essential that the
permitted foods in Table 30-11 be used and that

*Note: Refer to Chapter 8.
   ATP = adenosine triphosphate
   ADP = adenosine diphosphate
   UTP = uridine triphosphate
   UDP = uridine diphosphate

a diet appropriate to the child's age and development be planned. This assures that the child gets
his or her RDAs. If the child is unable to tolerate
fat, a diet that initially has no fat or one that uses
medium-chain fatty acids may be tried until the
child's tolerance increases.

Parents must learn to study the labels of food
products carefully to make certain that the foods
given to children with galactosemia do not con-

TABLE 30-11 Foods Permitted and Prohibited in a Galactose- and Lactose-Free Diet

Food Group	Foods Permitted	Foods Prohibited
Milk, milk products, and equivalents	Milk substitutes and nondairy cream excluding those with restricted ingredients; commercial infant and dietetic formulas with lactose-free ingredients*	All forms of milk and milk products (cow's, human, goat milk); examples include yogurt, chocolate milk, cocoa, etc.
Potatoes and equivalents	White and sweet potatoes; rice, noodles, spaghetti, macaroni, pasta	All commercial and homemade potato products made with milk, cheese, butter, and margarine containing milk solids, e.g., dehydrated potato flakes, breaded, creamed, or buttered products; instant mashed potatoes
Breads and equivalents	Any of the following made without milk, milk products, whey, casein, and lactose: breads of any variety, rolls, English muffins, crackers; cooked and dry cereals; flours of all varieties	Pancakes, biscuits, waffles, doughnuts, muffins, and ready-to-use baking mixes; any bread or baked goods made with milk, milk products, whey, casein, or lactose; cereals (hot instant or high protein), e.g., Cream of Rice, Cream of Wheat
Fruits and vegetables	All fresh fruits and fruit juices; all processed (dehydrated, frozen, or canned) fruits and fruit juices containing no excluded ingredients, such as lactose and monosodium glutamate (see text); all vegetables and vegetable products not specifically excluded	All processed fruit and fruit juice (dehydrated, frozen, and canned) products containing any excluded ingredients such as lactose and monosodium glutamate (see text); all vegetables and vegetable products prepared with excluded ingredients, e.g., buttered, creamed, or breaded products; beans (dried, lima, and soy), peas, lentils
Meat and equivalents	Beef, lamb, pork, veal, poultry, fowl, fish; peanut butter and certain cold cuts (check labels for presence of prohibited ingredients); kosher frankfruters; nuts of all varieties	Any meat, fish, or poultry product prepared with a batter, stuffing, or cream sauce; any processed meats prepared with milk, milk products, casein, lactose, or monosodium glutamate (see text), e.g., sausages, nonkosher frankfurters, luncheon meats, etc.; certain shellfish and organ meats if not tolerated
Fats and equivalents	Pure mayonnaise, vegetable oils (e.g., olive and safflower), shortening, lard, bacon fat; kosher margarine (margarine without milk solids or butter added); some cream substitutes (check labels)	Any product not specifically permitted, especially all cream, butter, and margarine with added butter or milk solids; most salad dressings; certain cream substitutes
Soups	All homemade soups prepared with permitted ingredients, such as clear soup or broth; any commercial products prepared without prohibited ingredients such as milk or milk products, e.g., bouillon	All commercial soups containing milk, milk products, lactose, or monosodium glutamate, e.g., chowders and cream soups; most commercial dried soups including dehydrated powder
Sweets	Pure jam, jelly; pure hard candy, jelly beans, lollipops, gumdrops; molasses, honey, syrups, sugars	Any product with milk, milk products, or lactose added, such as caramels, toffee, and milk chocolate

TABLE 30-11   (continued)

Food Group	Foods Permitted	Foods Prohibited
Beverages	Cereal beverages; soft drinks; lemonade, limeade; beverages with fruits or added fruit flavors, including punches; tea and coffee (regular, some instant, some decaffeinated)	Malted milk, milk shakes, eggnog; some decaffeinated and instant coffees; any commercial beverages or mixes with prohibited ingredients
Cheese and eggs	Eggs prepared without milk and milk products	All varieties of cheese; eggs prepared with prohibited ingredients
Desserts	All products prepared without milk and milk products, for example, homemade cakes, cookies, and pies; Popsicles, flavored ices with or without fruits, gelatin	Any products made with prohibited ingredients such as ice cream, regular puddings and custards, and all commercial bakery products
Miscellaneous	Pepper, salt, pure spices and seasonings; popcorn prepared with permitted margarine; lemon, vinegar, pickles, olives, mustard, catsup, chili sauce, horseradish; gravies without milk and milk products	Many diabetic and dietetic preparations containing prohibited ingredients; dips for snacks; malted products; Worcestershire sauce, soy sauce; pharmaceutical agents (tablets, powders, and capsules) or packaged products using lactose or glutamate as carriers; most commercially prepared mixes; cream sauces and milk gravies

*See the discussions early in this chapter and in Chapter 23 for specific products. All formulas or nutrient supplements containing soy will contain raffinose and stachyose. These two chemicals contain galactose but are not normally digested by the alimentary tract and will be tolerated.

TABLE 30-12   Schedule for Checking Galactose-1-phosphate Levels in Red Blood Cells of a Child with Galactosemia

Number of Checkups	Months after Birth
1–5 per month	0–1
1–3 per month	1–2
1–2 per month	2–6
Once every 3 months	6–12
Annually	Over 12

tain any milk, milk products, whey, casein, or lactose. In commercial food processing, lactose may be used as a carrier or filler in such products as chewing gum, some kinds of sausage, instant cereals, instant mashed potatoes, instant soup mixes, instant coffee, and monosodium glutamate.

The lactose in casein used to make low-lactose milk substitutes is tolerated by some chil-dren but not others. Galactose from legumes (pulses) and certain organ meats may also cause tolerance problems and have to be eliminated. If these products are eliminated, the child must receive an appropriate supplement of vitamins A, D, E, K, and B_2 and calcium. If the elimination of some foods causes an insufficient caloric intake, sugar may be added to the diet. Since this may increase the child's tendency to have diarrhea, careful monitoring is needed.

As the child approaches school age, it may be advisable to relax the restrictions slowly. Galactosemia at this stage does not have any drastic symptoms, and the child's intellect is not affected. Also, a relaxation in diet will make the child feel more comfortable with his or her peers and will probably improve the child's behavior.

Disaccharidase Deficiency

Another inborn error of carbohydrate metabolism is disaccharidase deficiency. Some infants are born with a low activity of certain intestinal

TABLE 30-13 Lactose Intolerance among Different Population Groups*

Population Group	% of Population with Lactose Intolerance
Caucasians (U.S.)	2–20
Indians (U.S.)	65–70
Blacks (U.S.)	70–75
Eskimos (North America)	85–90
Orientals (worldwide)	90–100

*Figures derived from reports of a number of investigators. The ranges are approximations and serve only as a general guide.

disaccharidases and, as a result, are unable to digest particular disaccharides. Lactose deficiency or lactose intolerance is probably the most common form of this disorder, especially among non-Caucasians. Table 30-13 indicates the extent of lactase deficiency among different population groups. Some individuals in these groups have normal lactase activity immediately after birth but experience a gradual decline up to the age of 4 or 5. In others, lactase deficiency becomes apparent only during adulthood. Sometimes low lactase activity may be induced during intestinal infection, trauma, pregnancy, and other clinical conditions.

Individuals at any age with lactase deficiency may not show any overt clinical symptoms when ingesting lactose. These people have asymptomatic lactose maldigestion and malabsorption, while others exhibit the classic symptoms of flatulence, diarrhea, and abdominal pain or bloating, although the severity varies with the individual.

Since milk is the major source of lactose, many of these individuals are unable to tolerate fluid milk, although the reaction depends on the amount consumed. Many can tolerate a small quantity. Diagnosis or confirmation of lactose intolerance should first include a history of the recurrence of symptoms after drinking milk. Next the manifestation of symptoms after taking 50 to 100 g of crystalline lactose solution (equivalent to the lactose found in 1 or 2 qt of fluid milk) should be observed and noted. Blood glucose in both symptomatic and asymptomatic patients

will not rise a few hours after lactose ingestion. This is an indicator that lactase (the enzyme) activity is absent.

The treatment for a child with lactose intolerance depends on the severity of reaction to dietary lactose, which can vary from mild to violent. If a child's condition warrants a lactose-free diet, Table 30-11 should be used in meal planning. However, most young patients benefit from a lactose-restricted diet that excludes only nonfermented milk and milk products. Fermented dairy products usually contain less lactose and are tolerated well by many patients. Every patient, young or old, learns from experience what foods can be tolerated. Some patients can drink a small amount of milk over the course of a day. Table 30-14 describes those foods permitted and prohibited in a lactose-restricted diet. For a young child, such a limited diet may not have adequate amounts of some or all of the following nutrients: calcium, iron, and vitamins A, D, E, K, and B_2. Thus, meal planning must be done according to the age and physiological status of the patient, and particular attention must be paid to providing the child with his or her RDAs.

Inborn Errors of Amino Acid Metabolism—Phenylketonuria

Each of the eight to ten essential amino acids in the human body is metabolized via a unique pathway. Some infants are born with a defect in one of the enzyme systems that regulate one or more of these pathways. As a result, if the amino acid is not metabolized properly, certain products may accumulate in the blood or urine. If this occurs, an inborn error of metabolism for that particular amino acid results. Table 30-10 lists the known genetic disorders of this kind.

One example of faulty protein metabolism involves phenylalanine and tyrosine. Although both substances are essential amino acids, the body derives part of its tyrosine needs from phenylalanine. Figure 30-6 describes some aspects of phenylalanine metabolism. A newborn may have no or very low activity of the enzyme phenylalanine hydroxylase, and as a result the body is unable to change phenylalanine to tyrosine. Con-

TABLE 30-14 Foods Permitted and Prohibited in a Lactose-Restricted Diet

Food Group	Foods Permitted	Foods Prohibited
Milk and milk products	Moderate amount of fermented dairy products such as yogurt, buttermilk, acidophilus milk, and sour cream	All nonfermented milk and milk products including whole, skim, and chocolate milk and milk shakes
Potatoes and equivalents	All products not prohibited	All products made with milk or milk products, such as mashed, creamed, and scalloped potatoes, dehydrated potatoes, potato balls and cakes, and other processed potato specialties that contain lactose
Bread and equivalents	All varieties	None unless patient unable to tolerate the small amount of milk used in making bakery products
Fruits and vegetables	All products not prohibited	Any product containing cream, milk, milk products, and lactose; commercial fruit drinks with lactose added; creamed vegetables
Meat and equivalents	All products not prohibited	Meat, fish, and poultry products made with unfermented milk and milk products, such as creamed chicken, Swiss steak, cream sauces, and gravies; any commercially processed meat, fish, or poultry products in which lactose is used as a carrier or extender
Fats	All products not prohibited	All products with cream, milk, milk products, and lactose; all varieties of cream
Soups	All products not prohibited	All commercial and homemade soups prepared with cream, milk, and milk products
Sweets	Any pure candy made without lactose, cream, milk, and milk products, e.g., clear hard candy; jams, jellies; molasses, syrups, honey; sucrose, glucose, fructose, table sugar	Any product made with lactose, cream, milk, and milk products, e.g., chocolate candy
Beverages	All beverages containing no unfermented cream, milk, or milk products; regular coffee, some decaffeinated coffee, some instant coffee, some coffee substitutes; tea, cereal beverages, soft drinks; any commercial drinks made without lactose	All beverages containing unfermented cream, milk, milk products, and lactose
Cheese and eggs	Any fermented cheese or cheese aged with bacteria; eggs prepared without the use of milk and milk products	Any cheese containing unfermented milk and milk products; eggs or omelets prepared with cream, milk, or milk products

TABLE 30-14 (continued)

Food Group	Foods Permitted	Foods Prohibited
Desserts	Any product, especially homemade, prepared without unfermented milk or milk products (cream substitutes may be used); sponge, angel food, and other types of cake; fruit-flavored ices, fruit ices; gelatin, plain puddings (from fruit juice)	Commercial and homemade products containing milk and milk products, such as ice cream, custard, puddings, chocolate cake, and eclairs
Miscellaneous	All products not prohibited	All products containing lactose, cream, milk, and milk products

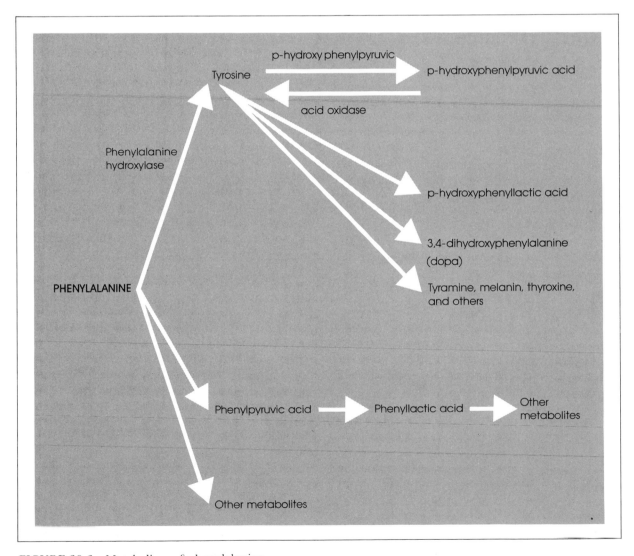

FIGURE 30-6 Metabolism of phenylalanine.

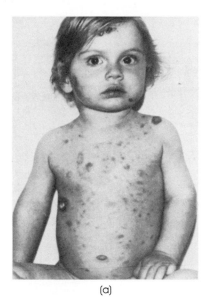
(a)

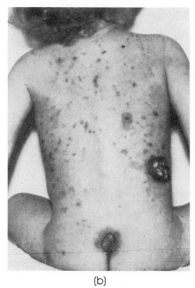
(b)

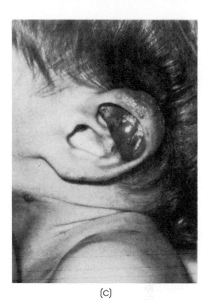
(c)

FIGURE 30-7   Reticulosarcoma-like skin lesions in phenylketonuria (PKU). Association of the lesions with PKU is indicated by their dependence on the severity of the latter and their complete healing during treatment with a diet low in phenylalanine. (From R. Exss and H. P. Weber, *Dermatologica* 148 [1974]: 382. By permission of S. Karger, AG Basel)

sequently, the chemicals phenylalanine, phenylpyruvic acid, and other metabolites accumulate (see Figure 30-6). If they exceed certain levels in the blood, they cross the brain barriers (membranes), and a child may suffer mental retardation. It is currently believed that about 1 in 10,000 newborns inherits this disorder, commonly referred to as phenylketonuria (PKU), which causes a high level of phenylpyruvic acid in the urine. Immediately after birth the body appears normal, but the child soon becomes highly irritable and hyperactive. The urine has a musty odor.

If the disorder is not diagnosed and treated, the child will develop aggressive behavior, unstable muscular and nervous systems, eczema, convulsions, and seizures. Since tyrosine is responsible for making pigments, its decreased supply results in decreased coloration, with such effects as decreased body pigmentation and blue eyes, a fair complexion, and blond hair in Caucasian patients. Some patients develop reticulosarcoma-like skin lesions (see Figure 30-7). Severe mental retardation may result. The accumulation of chemicals in the blood interferes with the normal development of the central nervous system and

the brain. Some young children show abnormal electroencephalograms. In spite of all these adverse symptoms, the child shows a normal birth weight.

Since a method of diagnosing PKU in newborns was developed in the 1960s, its use has become widespread. The method, known as the Guthrie test, involves analyzing blood drawn from the child's heel. A normal baby's blood contains about 1 to 2 mg of phenylalanine/100 mL of plasma, while that of a PKU child is about 15 to 30 mg/100 mL plasma. However, a positive Guthrie test does not necessarily indicate PKU, because transient high blood phenylalanine may occur in some infants. Thus, additional tests are required for confirmation. As of 1975, 43 states have mandated that all newborns be screened for PKU. The remaining states practice voluntary screening.

The Guthrie test is normally done before the baby is removed from the nursery, 2 to 5 days after birth. At 1 month of age the test is repeated, especially for babies that show *low* blood phenylalanine during the first blood screening. A blood level of over 4 mg phenylalanine/100 mL plasma may indicate that additional tests are

TABLE 30-15 Composition of Products for Treating PKU Patients

Product	Manufacturer	Nutrients in 100 g of Powder				
		Kilocalories	Protein (g)	Fat (g)	Carbo-hydrate (g)	Phenylalanine (g)
Lofenalac	Mead Johnson	454	15	18	60	0.08
Phenyl Free*	Mead Johnson	406	20.3	6.8	66	0
PKU Aid†	Moss	240	60	0	0	<0.07
3200-AB†	Mead Johnson	460	15	18	60	<0.08

*Formerly Product 3229.

†Experimental stage. Not yet widely used.

TABLE 30-16 Calorie, Phenylalanine, and Protein Contents of Lofenalac and Milk

Food	Amount	Kilocalories	Protein (g)	Phenylalanine (g)
Lofenalac	10 g	45.4	1.5	0.008
Milk				
Evaporated	29–30 g (1 oz)	44	2.2	106
Whole	29–30 g (1 oz)	19.7	1.1	51

needed. A level of 20 mg/100 mL definitely indicates PKU.

The dietary management of PKU children consists of rigidly restricting phenylalanine intake. For most patients, if treatment starts 1 to 2 months after birth, mental and physical development is likely to be normal. If treatment starts after retardation has already occurred, normal mental ability may not return completely, but there will be no further deterioration and no recurrence of symptoms. Although the intake of phenylalanine must be restricted, these children still need a minimal amount of the amino acid for growth and development, in addition to an adequate supply of all other essential nutrients.

A newborn child needs about 65 to 90 mg of phenylalanine per kilogram of body weight, while a 2-year-old needs 20 to 25 mg. Thus, an infant should be provided with enough phenylalanine to maintain a level of 3 to 10 mg per 100 mL of blood. If a particular level of intake raises serum levels to abnormally high concentrations, the level must be lowered. Con-versely, the serum level must not be allowed to fall below acceptable limits.

Since phenylalanine is an essential amino acid, it is found in most animal products, including milk, which is the main nutritional component of an infant's diet. Thus, milk has to be specially processed to remove part or all of the phenylalanine. For a number of years most practitioners have used the commercial powder Lofenalac (Mead Johnson). It is a special low-protein powder containing casein hydrolysate with about 95% of the phenylalanine removed. It is also supplemented with vitamins and minerals. At present, other commercial low-phenylalanine products are available, which are listed in Table 30-15.

Because Lofenalac contains less than 1% phenylalanine, it cannot support normal growth and development of a child. As a result, specified amounts of natural foods are commonly provided to increase the child's phenylalanine intake, such as evaporated or whole milk. As the child grows, additional solid foods are given.

TABLE 30-17   Suggested Phenylalanine, Energy, and Protein Intakes per Day for PKU Patients under 1 Year Old

| Age (months)* | Amount of Nutrient Needed per Kilogram Body Weight | | | Lofenalac | | Milk (oz) | |
	Phenyl-alanine (mg)	Protein (g)	Kilocalories	Protein provided by product to child's need (%)	Measures† permitted per kilogram body weight	Whole	Evaporated
0–2½	85	4.4	125	85	2½–3	2–4	1–3
2½–6½	65	3.3	115	85	2–2½	2–4	1–2½
6½–9½	45	2.5	105	90	1½–2	1½–2½	½–1½
9½–12	32	2.5	105	90	1½–2	½–1½	½–1

Note: The child may or may not need additional foods. See text.

*The separation between age groups is not exact.

†One measure equals 1 T, containing about 10 g of powder.

An example: A 1-month-old child is permitted 2 to 4 oz whole milk (or 1 to 3 oz evaporated milk) and 2½ to 3 measures of Lofenalac per kilogram body weight per day.

TABLE 30-18   Phenylalanine Exchange Food Lists

Food Group	Phenylalanine Exchange Food List	Food Type	Approximate Amount of Phenylalanine per Exchange (mg)
Vegetables	I-1	Regular table vegetables	15
	I-2	Gerber's strained and junior vegetables	15
Fruits	II-1	Regular table fruits	10
	II-2	Gerber's strained and junior fruits	10
Breads and equivalents	III-1	Regular table products	18
	III-2	Gerber's baby cereals	18
Fats and equivalents	IV	Regular table products	4–5
Free foods	V	Mainly high-calorie products	Trace

Note: In actual patient care, check the nutrient contents of commercial baby foods and make the appropriate adjustments.

Close monitoring of the child's nutrient intake is essential. Table 30-16 compares the phenylalanine content of Lofenalac with that of evaporated and whole milk. Table 30-17 describes the phenylalanine, energy, and protein intake for a PKU patient under 1 year old.

To provide the PKU child with regular food, the phenylalanine, protein, and calorie contents of regular foods must be known. As a result, young children's foods are grouped into exchange lists, each of which contains food items that contribute equivalent amounts of phenylalanine. Table 30-18 summarizes these five lists, and some examples from each list are provided

TABLE 30-19   Examples from Phenylalanine Exchange Food List I: Vegetables

Food	One Exchange
Regular table vegetables	
Asparagus, green, spears, canned	1¼
Beets, solids	½ c
Carrot, raw, small	1
Cucumber, raw, medium	⅔
Tomato, canned	¼ c
Gerber's strained and junior vegetables	
Beets	6 T
Carrots	5 T
Green beans	1¾ T
Sweet potatoes	1½ T

Note: Each exchange provides about 15 mg of phenylalanine.

TABLE 30-20   Examples from Phenylalanine Exchange Food List II: Fruits

Food	One Exchange
Regular table fruits	
Apple, raw, small	1
Apricots, raw, medium	2½
Avocado	2¼ T
Dates, dried	1½
Orange juice, frozen	3 T
Strawberries, raw, large	5
Gerber's strained and junior fruits	
Applesauce	7 T
Apricots with tapioca	8 T
Bananas with tapioca	5 T
Peaches	3 T
Orange-pineapple juice	11 T
Very low phenylalanine products*	>20 T

Note: Each exchange provides approximately 10 mg of phenylalanine.

*Examples include apple juice, orange juice, orange-apple juice and orange-apricot juice.

TABLE 30-21   Examples from Phenylalanine Exchange Food List III: Bread and Equivalents

Food	One Exchange
Regular table products	
Bran flakes	1¾ T
Rice Krispies	4 T
Farina, cooked	2¾ T
Malt-O-Meal, cooked	1½ T
Macaroni, cooked, tender	1 T
Potatoes, boiled, medium	⅕
Rice, brown, cooked	1½ T
Low-protein dietetic products*	
Anellini, uncooked (Aproten)	1 c
Paygel Low Protein Bread (General Mills)	2½ sl
Gerber's baby cereals (dry)	
Barley	1¼ T
Rice	2 T
Rice with strawberries	2¼ T
Oatmeal with applesauce-banana (in jar)	2½ T
Rice with mixed fruit (in jar)	1¾ T

Note: Each exchange provides approximately 18 mg of phenylalanine.

*See Chapter 28.

TABLE 30-22   Examples from Phenylalanine Exchange Food List IV: Fats and Equivalents

Food	One Exchange
Butter	2 t
Margarine	1 T
Mayonnaise	1 T
Salad dressing	
Italian	3 T
Thousand Island	1 T

Note: Each exchange provides 4 to 5 mg of phenylalanine.

in Tables 30-19 to 30-23. Calorie and protein contents of these foods may be obtained from the references at the end of this book. Additional exchange lists for food products are given in Table 9 of the appendix.

TABLE 30-23 Examples from Phenylalanine Exchange Food List V: Free Foods

Food
Candies
Kool-Aid
Molasses
Popsicles
Sugar, table
Syrup, corn or maple

Note: These foods contain little or no protein or phenylalanine.

How does one plan a diet for a PKU child? There are seven steps, which are indicated below.

1. Determine the age, weight, and activity of the child. In the example used here, we will assume that a patient is 6 months old, weighs 6 kg, and engages in moderate activity.

2. Determine the patient's daily requirements for phenylalanine (65 mg/kg body weight), protein (3.3 g/kg body weight), and calories (115 kcal/kg body weight) by using Table 30-17:

total daily phenylalanine needed

$= 65 \text{ mg/kg} \times 6 \text{ kg}$
$= 390 \text{ mg}$

total daily protein needed

$= 3.3 \text{ g/kg} \times 6 \text{ kg}$
$= 19.8 \text{ g}$

total daily calories needed

$= 115 \text{ kcal/kg} \times 6 \text{ kg} +$ [kilocalories for slow growth and moderate activity]
$= 690 \text{ kcal} + 300 \text{ kcal}$ (approximate)
$= 900 - 1,000 \text{ kcal}$ (approximate)

3. Determine the contributions of protein from Lofenalac ($2 \times 6 = 12$ measures needed daily) and evaporated milk ($2\frac{1}{2}$ oz needed daily) by using Tables 30-16 and 30-17:

protein in 12 measures Lofenalac

$= 12 \text{ measures} \times 10 \text{ g powder/measure} \times 15 \text{ g protein}/100 \text{ g powder}$
$= 18 \text{ g protein}$

protein in $2\frac{1}{2}$ oz evaporated milk

$= 2\frac{1}{2} \text{ oz} \times 2.2 \text{ g/oz}$
$= 5.5 \text{ g}$

total protein $= 23.5 \text{ g}$

4. Determine the contributions of calories from Lofenalac and evaporated milk by using Tables 30-16 and 30-17:

kilocalories in 12 measures Lofenalac

$= 12 \times 45.4$
$= 544.8$

kilocalories in $2\frac{1}{2}$ oz evaporated milk

$= 2\frac{1}{2} \times 44$
$= 110.0$

total kilocalories

$= 110.0 + 544.8$
$= 654.8$

5. Determine the contributions of phenylalanine from Lofenalac and evaporated milk by using Tables 30-16 and 30-17:

phenylalanine in 12 measures Lofenalac

$= 12 \times 0.008 \text{ mg}$
$= 0.096 \text{ mg}$

phenylalanine in $2\frac{1}{2}$ oz evaporated milk

$= 2\frac{1}{2} \times 106 \text{ mg}$
$= 265 \text{ mg}$

total phenylalanine $\approx 265 \text{ mg}$

6. Determine the additional amounts of phenylalanine, protein, and calories needed by the child from the information in steps 1 through 5. The patient needs about ($390 - 265$) or 125 mg of phenylalanine and ($900 - 655$) or about 245 kcal more.* The additional amounts can be obtained from natural food sources. Foods can be selected from Ta-

*The exact amount varies with the patient and the judgment of the practitioner. For example, the amount can be ($1,000 - 655$) or 345 kcal.

TABLE 30-24 Contents of Calories, Protein, and Phenylalanine in Some Selected Foods

Food	Phenyl-alanine (mg)*	Protein (g)†	Kilo-calories†
Gerber's strained and junior vegetables			
Carrots, 5 T	15	0.5	21
Sweet potatoes, 1½ T	15	0.3	15
Gerber's strained and junior fruits			
Applesauce, 7 T	10	0.2	81
Apricots with tapioca, 8 T	10	0.5	88
Orange-pineapple juice, 11 T	10	0.8	41
Peaches, 3 T	10	0.3	35
Gerber's baby cereals			
Barley cereal, 1¼ T	18	0.4	11
Rice with mixed fruit (in far), 1¾ T	18	0.3	13
Rice with strawberries, 2¼ T	18	0.5	21
Total	124	3.8	326

*Figures obtained from Tables 30-16 to 30-23.

†Obtained from standard food composition tables or exchange lists (see references at the end of this book and Table 9 of the appendix). Also, check with manufacturers of commercial products.

bles 30-18 to 30-23 so that they contribute the needed amounts of phenylalanine and calories. The information is presented in Table 30-24.

7. Develop a meal plan for the child by combining the information obtained from steps 2 to 6. A sample menu plan is presented in Table 30-25.

When feeding a patient with PKU several things should be kept in mind. First, calories and taste may be varied by using the items in Tables 30-22 and 30-23 as frequently as possible (consult references for other examples). Second, the low-protein products described in Table 30-23 can also be used to advantage. Other low-protein products are described in Chapter 28. Consult manufacturers for proper usage. Third, patients should avoid meat and dairy products (except the permitted evaporated milk). Fourth, feeding must be consistent with the age and development of the child and the food quantity and texture must be adjusted to the child's eating ability.

Fifth, the nutritional adequacy of the child's diet should be constantly evaluated, using RDA as a guide.

One of the most controversial issues in treating a child with PKU is the uncertainty about when to terminate dietary restrictions. Some children are put on a normal diet at the age of 5, when further mental progress may require additional phenylalanine. On the other hand, some clinicians keep the child on a phenylalanine-restricted diet indefinitely. For some children, these restrictions may necessitate the use of vitamin and mineral supplements. More research is needed to resolve this issue.

It should be noted that when a restrictive diet is discontinued, the child and family go through a very important transition period. The parents and child will need time and patience to adapt to this sudden exposure to meat and a whole variety of other foods.

The health team must monitor progress after a child is placed on a phenylalanine-restricted diet. During the first few weeks of the

TABLE 30-25 Sample Menu Plan for a Child with PKU

Breakfast
Lofenalac formula, 6 oz
Rice with strawberries, Gerber's baby cereal, 2¼ T
Carrots, Gerber's strained and junior vegetable, 5 T

Mid-Morning Feeding
Peaches, Gerber's strained and junior fruit, 3 T

Lunch
Lofenalac formula, 6 oz
Cereal, barley, Gerber's baby cereal, 1¼ T
Apricots with tapioca, Gerber's strained and junior fruit, 8 T
Orange-pineapple juice, Gerber's strained and junior fruit, 5 T

Mid-Afternoon Feeding
Applesauce, 7 T

Dinner
Lofenalac formula, 6 oz
Rice with mixed fruit (in Jar), Gerber's baby cereal, 1¾ T
Sweet potatoes, Gerber's strained and junior vegetable, 1½ T

Bedtime Feeding
Lofenalac formula, 6 oz
Orange-pineapple Juice, Gerber's strained and junior fruit, 6 T

diet, the child's blood should be tested twice. After the child has been on the diet for a brief period and his or her clinical condition has improved and stabilized, blood tests should be performed weekly until the child is 1 year old. Later, the toddler's blood should be tested once every 2 to 3 weeks. When all symptoms have disappeared and the child has adapted to the diet, the blood tests can be done monthly.

The dietary supply and blood levels of phenylalanine are strongly correlated with the height and weight gains of the child. If children get an insufficient amount of phenylalanine, they will become lethargic, have stunted growth, and lose their appetite. More severe effects include mental retardation, clinical deterioration (e.g., fever, coma), and even death. Also, when children with PKU become sick or have infections, blood phenylalanine may rise to unacceptable levels.

Recently, it was discovered that some babies are born with only a transient form of hyperphenylalaninemia. These children also require medical attention. These infants must be identified and treated to prevent possible mental retardation.

Another controversial issue is the management of pregnant mothers who have PKU. It has been assumed that a high level of phenylalanine in the mother's blood may be toxic to the unborn child, who may suffer arrested growth in the womb and birth defects such as mental retardation (see Figure 30-8). It has also been assumed

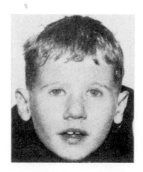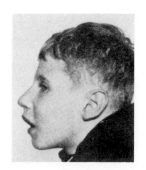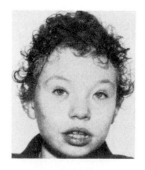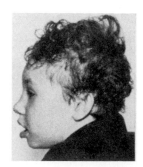

FIGURE 30-8 Mother with phenylketonuria gave birth to seven mentally retarded children, one of whom died. One brother (left, 8 years old) and one sister (right, 10 years old) also showed abnormal facies and microcephaly. (From E. Angeli et al., *Devel. Med. Child Neurol.* 16 [1974]:800)

that such women may have to decrease their intake of phenylalanine. However, normal as well as retarded babies have been born to women with PKU. If the phenylalanine intake is to be reduced, Mead Johnson's new product Phenyl Free (formerly Product 3229, see Table 30-15), which contains no phenylalanine, can be used. It has a higher concentration of protein than Lofenalac and permits a larger selection of natural foods for supplementation. This product can safely be used by pregnant women, who can also use the special low-protein foods described in Table 30-23 and Chapter 28.

In the past, the treatment of inborn errors of amino acid metabolism consisted mainly of restricting the intake of the offending amino acids. In the last few years, clinical reports have shown that large doses of specific vitamins can help in the treatment of special metabolic disorders. Table 30-26 describes those disorders that respond to vitamin therapy. In some patients, the use of particular vitamins makes any dietary restrictions unnecessary; in others it allows the restrictions to be relaxed.

HEART DISEASES

Some children are born with congenital heart disease, while others inherit the tendency to develop coronary heart disease. In recent years, arguments about preventing inherited or acquired coronary heart disease in adults have begun to involve children. However, whether to screen children for signs of atherosclerotic tendencies and how to manage their diet if signs are detected are highly controversial issues.

Congenital Heart Disease

It is currently believed that about 10 out of 100 newborns with birth defects have congenital heart disease. This disorder, which may not be identified at birth, involves a heart that is structurally defective. The causes are unknown, although the presence of German measles during pregnancy may be a factor. The disorder can re-

TABLE 30-26 Vitamins for Treating Inborn Errors of Metabolism

Disease	Vitamins That May Correct Problem
Defective sulfur amino acid metabolism	Choline*
Hartnup disease	Nicotinic acid
Homocystinuria	Vitamin B_6 or folic acid
Maple syrup urine disease	Vitamin B_1†
Methylmalonic acidemia	Vitamin B_{12}
Propionic acidemia	Biotin
Tyrosinemia	Vitamin C

*This is not a vitamin. It is grouped here for convenience. See last section in Chapter 6.
†Beneficial for at least one form of the disease.

sult in a multitude of complications, especially respiratory distress and heart failure. It is also responsible for height and weight retardation.

Congenital heart disease can retard a child's growth in a number of ways. First, it can cause the child to eat too little. The child may voluntarily reduce food intake in order to reduce the workload of the heart. Or because of rapid respiration and a lack of oxygen, the child can become listless, thus reducing the child's ability to eat an adequate amount of food. A second reason for growth retardation is a high body metabolic rate due to the increased nutrient needs of the organs and tissues and elevated body temperature and thyroid activity. A third reason is a high loss of body nutrients due to inadequate intestinal absorption, excessive urine output, and the presence of hemorrhages or open wounds. It is not known how a heart defect can cause all these clinical problems.

The only cure for congenital heart disease is successful surgery, performed during early or late infancy.

Although corrective surgery can be successful, the mortality rate is high for small children. However, if death is imminent because of heart failure, high-risk surgery is indicated. It is therefore of paramount importance that the baby get adequate nutrition so that the baby weighs 30 to 50 lb when surgery is performed. This must be accomplished despite the diminished nutrient supply to cells due to the decreased oxygen supply that results from a defective heart.

Major considerations in dietary care

There are four major considerations in feeding children with congenital heart disease. One is caloric need. Because of the expected retardation of growth caused by the clinical condition, the child's caloric need is higher than the RDAs. For example, if the RDA of calories for a normal child is 100 kcal/d, the need for a patient with congenital heart disease may be 130 to 160 kcal.

A second concern is renal load. The child may have difficulty handling any large renal load of solutes. A large renal load may be caused by excessive electrolytes or dehydration, which can result from an insufficient fluid intake.

The third consideration is food intolerance. A large amount of simple sugars may produce diarrhea, the fat in regular milk and food may cause steatorrhea, and food ingestion may cause abdominal discomfort.

The fourth major consideration is vitamin and mineral need. Vitamin and mineral deficiencies have been documented in infants with congenital heart disease. Because of the small quantity of food consumed, the child's intake of these nutrients must be carefully monitored.

Formulas and regular foods

An infant with congenital heart disease is usually fed a special formula, although regular foods are sometimes used. The formula should be high in calories but contain only the minimal amount of protein and electrolytes needed for growth without causing kidney overload. Some guidelines are as follows: 8% to 10% of the daily calories should come from protein, 35% to 65% from carbohydrate, and 35% to 50% from fat; infants under 4 months old should get 1.8 to 2.0 g of protein per 100 kcal, and infants 4 to 12 months old 1.65 to 1.75 g.

Some clinicians prefer special low-electrolyte, low-protein formulas supplemented with fat or carbohydrate solution. The preparer adds supplements to these formulas, which are commercially available. Other clinicians recommend using formulas with 25 to 30 kcal per ounce and diluting accordingly. The solute load of such preparations must be calculated, and their effects on the child carefully monitored. Sometimes the prepared formulas are supplemented with a limited amount of solid foods that is not adequate to support growth by itself. Some clinicians have good experience with Wyeth's SMA and Ross' Similac PM 60/40 (see Tables 30-2 to 30-5).

If formulas are not used, the calorie and sodium contents, digestibility, and renal solute load of the foods fed to the child must be appropriate. Carbohydrate and fat do not affect the solute load. Clinical practice has established that 1 mosm of solute is formed by 1 mEq of sodium, potassium, and chloride, and that 1 g of dietary protein provides about 4 mosm of renal solute load. If the infant is given regular food, the diet should begin with easily digestible and acceptable items such as fruit and later include cereal or unsalted vegetables.

Certain precautions are important in feeding a child with congenital heart disease. If the child is given any high caloric supplement, small amounts should be used, at least at the beginning, since large portions can produce diarrhea and reduce appetite. If the child is eating moderately to considerably less than the calculated amount, he or she is especially susceptible to folic acid deficiency. Since many nonprescription vitamin supplements for children do not contain folic acid, it is important to obtain a proper preparation. The child may also require iron and calcium supplementation.

Table foods may be introduced when the child is over 5½ to 6½ months old. Very small servings of chopped, mashed, or pureed cereal, fruits, potato, and meat with vegetables can be served, all prepared without salt. The amount of meat should be limited to less than 1 oz a day if the child's condition is poor.

The sodium intake of the child must be carefully considered. Most commercial strained baby foods, especially meat and vegetable items, contain a large amount of sodium and are usually not suitable. If they are used, their sodium contents must be ascertained and the effects monitored. Home-prepared baby foods must be prop-

TABLE 30-27 Sodium Contributed by Different Methods of Feeding

Formula*	Supplemental Food	Amount of Sodium (mEq)
Similac	1 jar strained meat, 1 jar strained vegetables	24
SMA or Similac PM 60/40	None	3–4
Enfamil[†] (Mead Johnson)	None	5–7

*Serving size of each formula is 15 oz.
[†]This is a standard infant formula.

erly selected and quantified and prepared without salt. The child's need for sodium is a delicate balance between too much, which is bad for the heart, and too little, which affects growth. For example, if the child suffers any clinical symptoms of heart failure, dietetic low-sodium formulas may be indicated. If diuretics are used to remove body sodium, all complications associated with their usage must be monitored and corrected, as discussed in Chapters 27 and 28. The child's intake of sodium should be under 8 mEq per day. Table 30-27 compares the sodium in three feeding regimens.

The fluid intake of the child should also be carefully monitored because these children can lose much water from fever, high environmental temperature, diarrhea, vomiting, and rapid respiration. Thus, children with congenital heart disease need more water than normal children of the same age. Both urine volume and solute level should be monitored to assure that patients drink enough fluid and are not overloaded with solutes. An acceptable urine solute load is 400 mosm per liter.

Managing feeding problems

Feeding children with congenital heart disease also poses problems. A child may lose appetite or become tired, thus reducing his or her food intake. Of course, food intake may be inadequate due to the regular feeding problems of normal children. For example, if the parents force a child to eat, the child may stubbornly refuse. The child may cry and become cyanotic, which can frighten some parents. If a child does not enjoy eating and the parents do not know what to do, the child's eating problems can be perpetuated.

Educating parents of children with congenital heart disease is important. The parents should become familiar with the basic eating pattern of a normal child and all associated feeding problems. They should also become familiar with managing a child with feeding problems that are psychological (see Chapter 14). For example, they can learn to anticipate the problems, to be aware of their child using food as a weapon, to avoid overconcern for their child, to be consistent in their management, and to avoid being manipulated by the child.

In addition to learning how to cope with normal feeding problems, the parents should learn about feeding difficulties related to the heart condition, such as vomiting, gagging, and regurgitation. They should learn such techniques as massaging and stimulation of the child's gums, lips, and tongue to increase the child's sucking ability. They should also learn to evaluate the child's responses such as tiredness, resting, amount of formula consumed over a fixed period, and complexion after eating. At the same time, they should seek professional help to make sure that their child is adequately nourished.

Discharge procedures

When a child with congenital heart disease is discharged from the hospital, certain procedures must be followed. The child's nutritional status must be studied periodically. The child's family background and daily routine, especially the eating pattern of the entire family, should be evaluated, and preparations should be made for meeting the child's needs (e.g., who is the caretaker, when can the child be fed, how frequent are the visits to the clinic). The mother should be completely familiar with the nutritional and dietary care of the child. If the mother is unable to cope with the different methods of combining or preparing formulas, she should be taught easier feeding methods. She can be provided a list of low-sodium, nondietetic products such as sugar, cereal, fruits, and vegetables. If diarrhea and steatorrhea occur, medium-chain triglycerides may be used and the consumption of simple sugars may be reduced.

Prevention of Coronary Heart Disease

Other forms of heart disease may appear or begin to develop during childhood. It is currently believed that type IIa hyperlipoproteinemia (see Chapter 27) affects 1 in 200 American children. Coronary heart disease can occur even in young children. At present, many of these patients are identified when overt clinical symptoms appear, such as abdominal pain and the presence of xanthomas. Since this disorder is inherited, early diagnosis and treatment are more important than prevention.

As discussed in Chapter 27, atherosclerosis and coronary heart disease in adults occurs mainly after the age of 30, especially after 60. The cause is unknown and may be related to a number of factors. At present, the much debated risk factors include an increase in blood cholesterol triglycerides and low-density lipoprotein and an increase in body weight. Two of the more widely agreed-on risk factors are high blood pressure and diabetes mellitus. Some specialists now believe that atherosclerosis begins in childhood and that the vascular lesion progresses through the adolescent period and eventually into adulthood (see Figure 27-3 in Chapter 27).

Because of this suspected origin of heart disease in childhood, there is now much debate about two issues. For one thing, should children be screened for elevated blood lipid levels? Second, if we identify children with high blood lipid levels, what should we do with them?

The screening controversy

At present, some experts feel that children should be screened for abnormal lipid profiles. They point to the hypothesis that atherosclerosis begins in childhood, and they note that children in the United States have higher blood cholesterol levels than their counterparts in countries with a very low incidence of atherosclerosis and coronary heart disease. They also cite the belief that noninherited hyperlipidemia is caused by disease, drug and nutritional excesses, and other environmental influences that can be controlled to an extent.

Other experts feel that screening is not necessary because there is no direct clinical evidence that hyperlipidemia in childhood is related to atherosclerosis and coronary heart disease in an adult. They also point out that screening is costly, time consuming, impractical, and not as important as other public health issues.

A third group of clinicians assume a middle-of-the-road position. They recommend screening children from families with known heart disease (such as atherosclerosis), stroke, or circulatory disease among members under 50 years of age; children from families with a history of gout, high blood pressure, and diabetes mellitus; and children whose parents have increased blood levels of cholesterol and/or triglycerides.

In screening children for blood lipid abnormalities, the initial study involves analyzing blood cholesterol and triglyceride levels. If the data warrant, more analyses are done. A complete blood analysis measures the levels of total plasma cholesterol, triglyceride, and high-density-lipoprotein cholesterol. The formula used is:

low-density-lipoprotein = total plasma
cholesterol   cholesterol − high-
                                          density-lipoprotein
                                          cholesterol − (⅕ ×
                                          triglyceride)

Currently, a value of 170 mg of low-density-lipoprotein cholesterol per 100 mL of plasma is considered normal for a child.

All blood tests for lipid levels must be accurate and repeated. If a child shows hyperlipidemia, the attending physician must determine if the condition is genetic or acquired. Other evaluations of the child include a physical examination; a complete drug, medical, and nutritional history; urine analysis; and blood tests for glucose and for kidney, thyroid, and liver functions.

Management of a hyperlipidemic child

If these tests indicate that a child is hyperlipidemic, some clinicians recommend that the child should first achieve an ideal body weight and then follow a prudent diet low in cholesterol, total fat, and animal fat and high in polyunsaturated fat. On the other hand, some clinicians argue that since the effectiveness of such a diet has not been proven, it is unfair to place a child on such a dietary regimen. They also argue that the indiscriminate elimination of food products by untrained parents can be risky and dangerous. For example, the complete avoidance of eggs and whole milk may result in nutritional deficiencies. Some parents indiscriminately reduce the fat intake of infants and children to a very low level. In addition to becoming deficient in essential fatty acids and fat-soluble vitamins as a result of this practice, some infants and children may develop chronic and nonspecific diarrhea. The low fat intake fails to delay gastric emptying time; the intestinal transit time is shortened, resulting in diarrhea.

Opponents of putting hyperlipidemic children on a diet low in cholesterol and saturated fats and high in polyunsaturated fats also point out that animal studies have shown that long-term feeding of polyunsaturated fats can delay the myelination of the nervous system. If this delay occurs in a child, will there be any neurological changes? If so, will they be good or bad? We do not yet know. In addition, it has been established that adults following a diet low in cholesterol and saturated fats have a higher incidence of gallstones. Opponents of putting chil-

dren on a special diet suggest that this might also occur in a child.

Diet plays only one part in the prevention of atherosclerosis and coronary heart disease; therapeutic drugs and appropriate exercise may also be needed. It is very difficult to implement all these changes in children and adolescents. The patient, parents, doctor, nurse, dietitian, nutritionist, and other professionals must all work together if preventive measures are to be taken, and the process is likely to be difficult. Details on meal planning for a child placed on a prudent diet by a doctor may be found in Chapters 10, 22, and 27.

HIGH-RISK INFANTS

There are five major types of infants considered high risk at birth: those of low birth weight, those born prematurely with complications, those delivered by diabetic mothers, those critically ill, and those with birth defects. These newborns are unable to function properly as normal infants and need special help. One of the major criteria for survival is proper nutrition, without which the child may die.

There is considerable controversy over what constitutes a low birth weight or prematurity. In this text, a *premature* infant is born before the 37th or 38th week of gestation. Standard charts show the expected infant weight at different gestational ages. If a newborn's weight is correlated with its gestational age, it is *appropriate* for the *gestational age* (AG). If the weight is unacceptably low for its gestational age, the infant is *small for date* (SFD) or *small for gestational age* (SGA). These infants have suffered intrauterine retardation but may be either full-term or premature. A *low birth weight* (LBW) infant weights 2,500 g (5½ lb) or less. These infants may be premature, small for gestational age, and/or small for date. They account for 60% to 70% of all cases of newborn mortality after birth; about 5% to 10% of live births are of low birth weight. Infants weighing less than 1,500 g (3.3 lb) at birth are considered to have *very low birth weight* (VLBW).

Nutrient Needs

The caloric need of the high-risk infant is definitely higher than that of a normal infant: about 100 to 130 kcal/kg/d. This is about three to four times that of an adult and twice that of a normal infant.

The estimated protein need of a high-risk child is 3 to 4 g/kg/d. Excessive protein is undesirable, since it can increase blood amino acids and nitrogen. However, a premature infant may require the essential amino acids tyrosine and cystine.

A high-risk infant needs a large amount of fluid for a number of reasons. It has a high body water content. Its ambient temperature may be too high, causing increased evaporation. Vomiting or diarrhea, if present, may result in a loss of intestinal fluid. The child's kidney is unable to concentrate urine, resulting in more fluid loss. If the child undergoes any form of treatment that causes body evaporation, such as photo or radiant heat therapy, its need for fluid will be further increased.

One way to assure that a child gets enough fluid is to measure the intake and output of fluid, monitor overt clinical signs of dehydration, and analyze urine osmolality, using blood sodium and nitrogen levels as guides. Extra fluid may be given orally (water, milk, or 10% glucose) or intravenously (10% glucose).

High-risk infants have special needs for calcium, iron, and vitamin K. If the intake of these nutrients is inadequate, appropriate supplementation is needed.

Initial Feedings

The first feeding should be given to a high-risk infant several hours after birth, when the child is given fluid and calories. A normal-term infant receives the first feeding 2 to 4 hours after birth, as does a baby weighing at least 1,500 g with a gestational age of 33 or 34 weeks and without any complications such as respiratory difficulty and infection. In general, this latter baby receives smaller but more frequent feedings than a normal child.

If an infant has complications, weighs less than 1,500 g, and has a gestational age of less than 33 weeks, the feeding practice is more cautious and varies with the infant and the doctor's evaluation. Depending on the practitioner, the child may be fed in one of two ways. In one, only 10% glucose is given intravenously with no other nourishment until the infant stabilizes, usually 3 days later, at which time oral or tube feedings or total parenteral nutrition is used. Some practitioners prefer direct oral feeding within the first 12 to 24 hours. If oral feeding is not feasible, total parenteral nutrition is started at the beginning of the second day.

Use of Breast Milk or Formulas

The decision of whether to nurse or formula-feed a high-risk infant depends partly on the degree of risk. Babies of nearly normal size may respond well to breast milk. Breast milk permits satisfactory growth for infants weighing more than 1,500 g, especially because of the quality of fat and protein, the solute load, and immunological protection provided. In some circumstances, breast milk produces less necrotizing enterocolitis than formulas. The mother should be actively encouraged to breast-feed if the child can suck and is over 2,000 g. If the child is unable to breast-feed, the mother can provide milk by manually squeezing her breasts. The milk is then given to the child by tube, gavage, bottle, or dropper. This procedure can also strengthen the mother's emotional attachment to the child. The milk should be fresh, unheated, and unrefrigerated and less than 8 to 10 hours old.

Although breast milk has certain advantages, it does not provide enough protein to enable some high-risk infants to grow. To supplement the low supply of protein in breast milk, a breast-fed child can be given some concentrated or standard formulas. Neither regular formulas nor breast milk is adequate for growth for most high-risk infants.

There are no readily available "standard" formulas for low-birth-weight or high-risk infants, since their requirements for nutrients are unknown. The best guide is to use the estimated nutrient needs as described earlier. However, most standard formulas are deficient in protein, calories, and calcium. The smaller the child, the more unsatisfactory these formulas are. Some clinicians propose that the formula should contain 80 to 100 kcal/100 mL and 2.6 to 3.0 g of protein/100 kcal (ideally 2.8 g).

Some formulas that approximate breast milk but contain extra protein are SMA (Wyeth) and Similac PM 60/40 (Ross), both of which have been modified from regular formulas (see Tables 30-2 to 30-5). Formulas such as Portagen and Pregestimil, which use medium-chain triglycerides, are easily absorbed by low-birth-weight infants. Some clinics and hospitals use defined-formula diets containing glucose, amino acids, minerals, vitamins, and medium-chain triglycerides (or no fat). Some infants respond favorably when fed these diets, while others do not. The major problems with these defined-formula diets are their high solute load and excessive nitrogen. Since infant response to any method of feeding varies, the high-risk baby's growth must be closely monitored. In addition to the type of formula chosen, its dilution must be carefully considered. The concentration, calories, protein, and fluid of a high-risk baby's formula should all be sufficient but within the eating and digestive capacity of the child. Whereas a normal child is usually provided about 67 kcal/100 mL (20 kcal/oz) of milk, a high-risk infant needs about 80 to 100 kcal/100 mL (25 to 30 kcal/oz) of milk. And although a normal child drinks about 100 mL milk/kg, a high-risk infant may need as much as 200 mL/kg. If the formula is too concentrated, the excessive osmotic load can be harmful to the gastrointestinal tract and the kidney.

Jaundice and Vitamin E Deficiency

Newborn infants, especially high-risk ones, may develop two nutritionally related complications: jaundice and vitamin E deficiency. Jaundice may occur because an infant's immature condition renders it unable to excrete all the bilirubin from the turnover of red blood cells. The bilirubin accumulates and may enter the brain, causing brain damage and death. The current management procedure is to use ultraviolet light (phototherapy), which can decompose the bilirubin. This practice has a number of drawbacks, however. Some decomposed products can harm the intestine when excreted and partially destroy lactose in the alimentary tract. They can also force the passage of water from body to gut, thus causing a loss of fluid. In addition, phototherapy causes a high rate of evaporation from the skin that may cause dehydration. Phototherapy can also destroy vitamin B_2, thus increasing the infant's requirement. However, in some infants, early oral feeding may reduce bilirubin reabsorption (via the enterohepatic circulation, as discussed in Chapter 25).

A premature baby is born with very little vitamin E reserve. This chemical cannot reach the baby, since most placental transfer occurs in the last weeks of gestation. When this baby is fed a formula, the vitamin E is not very well absorbed because the activity of intestinal lipase is inadequate, the intestinal absorption mechanism is not mature, and there is a relative lack of bile salts. A premature infant may thus develop hemolytic anemia, because a vitamin E deficiency can make the red blood cell membranes fragile. This happens when the baby's blood vitamin E is less than 0.9 to 1 mg per 100 mL of blood, usually occurring at 4 to 10 weeks of age.

However, whether and when hemolytic anemia occurs depends on additional factors. For one thing, the need for vitamin E increases as the baby's consumption of polyunsaturated fatty acids increases. Second, the level of vitamin E in various baby feeds—formula milk, cow's milk, evaporated milk, and breast milk—varies. In the past, breast milk offered the most vitamin E, although most commercial products are now fortified with the vitamin. Third, the level of iron consumed by a baby from different feeds is important, since an excess of iron can interfere with the absorption of vitamin E and accelerates the collapse of red blood cells.

Because of the above considerations, most premature infants are given supplemental vitamin E.

STUDY QUESTIONS

1. Compare and contrast the general dietary needs of a sick child with those of a sick adult. Why do hospitalized children sometimes develop undesirable eating habits?
2. What difficulties arise in the long-term care of a child? Why may a prescribed dietary regimen be particularly difficult for a child? List some ways these difficulties can be minimized.
3. Give some of the common causes of diarrhea in infants and children. How is it managed?
4. How can constipation be recognized and managed in a young infant?
5. What clinical disorders show that cystic fibrosis may be present? What special nutritional needs result from this disease? How is cystic fibrosis treated?
6. Aside from overeating, what can cause a pathological condition of obesity in a child?
7. What constitutes an inborn error of metabolism? Name the most common form of inborn error of carbohydrate metabolism.

What are its classic symptoms? How is it treated?
8. What is PKU? Why may it cause retardation? Briefly describe the course of treatment for this disorder. Can dietary restrictions ever be relaxed?
9. Why may a child with congenital heart disease show retarded growth? What considerations are important in feeding a child with congenital heart disease? Describe some precautions in the feeding management of this child.
10. Briefly discuss current positions of health professionals on the screening of children for abnormal lipid profiles.
11. Which infants are considered high risk at birth? Give the accepted definition for a premature infant. What does *SFD* refer to? Describe the feeding procedures for high-risk infants. Why are jaundice and vitamin E deficiency likely to occur in a high-risk infant?

CASE STUDY   *A Failure-to-Thrive Infant*

R.H., a 4-month-old infant, weighed only 4.1 kg (9 lb) and had a history of vomiting, diarrhea, and failure to thrive. Her birth weight had been 3.58 kg (7.9 lb), with an Apgar score of 3. R.H.'s pediatrician was unable to diagnose the child's illness and the reason for her failure to gain weight. The infant was admitted to a local hospital.

In the hospital, the child was studied carefully and provided with intensive care. In spite of aggressive dietary manipulations, the child gained only 1 kg (2.2 lb) after staying in the hospital for 6 months. The child had a low blood protein level (4.5 g/100 mL, of which 3.0 g was albumin). She excreted a subnormal amount of amino acids and failed to absorb an acceptable amount of a test dose

of D-xylose. During this period of hospitalization, the baby was given on separate occasions a milk-free diet, a gluten-free diet, and a Lambase diet, with no success. Pancreatic enzymes and tetracycline were also ineffective. The child was not growing properly.

Because of the patient's deteriorating conditions, the attending physicians placed her on a formula diet (Vivonex) via nasogastric feeding tube. The diet was bulk free and nearly completely fat free. The feeding was started at 0.75 kcal/mL and gradually increased to 1 kcal/mL. The increase was made in accordance with the infant's laboratory and urinary data, making sure that the patient could withstand the high osmolarity in absorption and utilization. For example, the feeding was started with 70 kcal/kg/24 hr and gradually increased to a rate of 125 kcal/kg/24 hr. Occasionally the child was able to take in 140 to 150 kcal/kg/24 hr with very little difficulty. After 2 weeks of tube-feeding, the child was able to ingest the formula from a nursing bottle.

The child was fed the formula diet for 120 days. During this period, the patient gained 3.1 kg (6.8 lb) to a weight of 7.2 kg (15.8 lb). Her blood protein increased from 5.5 to 6.3 g/100 mL, with the albumin increasing from 3.3 to 4.0 g/100 mL. Metabolic studies conducted for 65 days while the child was being fed the formula diet showed that the child was in positive nitrogen balance, excreting 1.67 to 4.08 g/24 hr. The child was also in positive potassium balance of 8.4 to 20.7 mEq/24 hr. During this same period, the child was consuming 106 to 145 kcal/kg/24 hr, with an average of 125 kcal/kg/24 hr. Her length increased from 50.8 cm (20 in.) to 70 cm (27 in.). She definitely showed more alertness, coordination, and activity.

When the child was discharged from the hospital, the diet was continued for about 1 to 2 weeks. After this period, the child was able to eat regular baby foods. She recovered completely and was doing well after 2½ years.

Review and Analysis

1. After studying the entire case history carefully, what do you think was the major reason why the child failed to thrive? Are there enough data for you to arrive at a conclusion?

2. Describe the major composition of Vivonex by obtaining the relevant information from literature or the manufacturer.

3. Use an appropriate reference source to describe the major considerations in tube-feedings with infants. Compare them with those for an adult.

4. What do negative potassium and nitrogen balances imply? In this case, what does positive potassium imply?

5. What is the caloric requirement of a 4-month-old infant? Develop a set of hypothetical values for tube-feeding, specifying the concentration of feed, flow rate, and total volume of feed consumed. This hypothetical feeding schedule should provide the child with the needed caloric requirements. If there are not enough data in the case history to establish such a hypothetical situation, assume them and state the premises.

6. After studying available commercial formulas, list other formulas that would be as effective as Vivonex.

Chapter 31

Diet and Other Clinical Disorders or Conditions

SOME PATIENTS REQUIRE special considerations in addition to standard dietary care. They include patients undergoing rehabilitation, immobilized patients, elderly patients in nursing or convalescent homes, and mental patients. The nutritional and dietary support for these groups of patients is briefly discussed. The rest of this chapter is devoted to three different types of clinical disorders that have not been presented previously: anorexia nervosa, food allergy, and infectious diseases.

PATIENTS UNDERGOING REHABILITATION

Rehabilitation is the process of restoring a patient with a physical or other disability to normal and useful activity. For instance, a patient recovering from a heart attack or stroke or a person who has lost both arms in a car accident needs rehabilitation after the critical period. In general, rehabilitation may be achieved in a hospital, at home, or in any rehabilitation center. The patient's clinical conditions determine the length and location of rehabilitation treatment.

The overall care of this group of patients constitutes a basic element of nursing and is discussed in detail in standard nursing textbooks. The nutritional and dietary care of these patients is briefly reviewed below. As in many other aspects of patient care, team efforts produce the best results. For example, the nurse, dietitian, nutritionist, therapist (physical, occupational, or recreational), home economist, social worker, and psychologist all contribute to speedy rehabilitation.

The major consideration in establishing nutritional support for the rehabilitation process is the type of physical disability. Examples include the inability to use hands, arms, or legs because of an accident, injury, surgery, arthritis, or damage to the nervous system; blindness; severe difficulty in respiration because of advanced emphysema, asthma, or nasal blockage; and lack of strength because of age or heart disease. Feeding a handicapped or confined patient requires patience and familiarity with the clinical profile. As with the nonhandicapped patient, nutritional needs, food preferences, and the importance of

food must be considered. But, there will be differences, too. For example, if the person cannot move the upper part of the body very well, eating will probably take longer than for a normal person. A person paralyzed by a stroke may not have any feeling on one side of his or her mouth. However, foods touching the other side of the mouth, especially at the back, often provide the patient with sensation and help stimulate the swallowing mechanism. If the dentures of a patient do not fit, they will have to be adjusted to facilitate eating. Spinal cord injuries may affect bladder muscle control and make the genitourinary tract more susceptible to infection. Chapter 28 gives some preventive measures for urinary tract infections. A patient with only one arm will have difficulties in feeding, peeling, and cutting vegetables and in using cooking appliances. Because many simple tasks become difficult, a handicapped homemaker needs considerable adjustment and help.

Many patients receive drugs during their rehabilitation. A typical example is the use of levodopa in treating Parkinson's disease. The adverse effects of such drugs on the patient's nutritional status must be monitored.

The caloric needs of rehabilitating patients also require special attention. On the one hand, an increased amount of energy is needed to compensate for the tremendous effort spent performing routine tasks, including eating. These patients may lose weight, especially through muscle wasting. On the other hand, a patient confined to a wheelchair may be less active and more likely to gain weight in spite of the expenditure of extra energy.

The best nutritional program is designed in accordance with not only the patient's clinical condition but also his or her emotional and psychological makeup, economic status, and family background. Cost limitations determine the type of basic care and nutritional and dietary planning. If the patient is the wage earner, the family will lose its major source of income. If the patient is the homemaker, hiring a housekeeper will be costly.

Patients undergoing rehabilitation may also suffer a multitude of psychological problems that take time and support to overcome. Any individual with a handicap, especially an inability to eat and swallow, tends to become depressed, frustrated, anxious, and frightened. To overcome any physical handicap is a very slow, difficult, and sometimes painful process, especially at the beginning. Patients suffer great emotional and physical pain and therefore need plenty of support. Even if such patients receive tremendous encouragement, they may still feel neglected, helpless, unhappy, bored, and isolated. Some patients experience shame and guilt.

Frequent communication with the patient will help. Those people involved with feeding patients should learn about each patient's likes and dislikes, plan menus together with the patient, and share mutual experiences. Keeping a record of a rehabilitating patient's food and nutrient intake is also useful.

IMMOBILIZED PATIENTS

A surgical and medical patient may be temporarily immobilized by being confined to bed. Older, chronically ill, disabled, and handicapped patients may be immobilized for many years. Some patients, such as those recovering from strokes, may be gradually rehabilitated, progressing from bed confinement to the use of a wheelchair, crutches, and a cane and finally being able to walk freely. During the immobilization period, there are four important considerations in the patient's nutritional and dietary care: nitrogen balance, calories, calcium intake, and urinary and bowel functions.

Nitrogen Balance

Long-term bed confinement causes body muscle to atrophy, even in a healthy person. This process is characterized by a negative nitrogen balance (see Chapter 4). An otherwise healthy person may lose about 2 to 3 g of nitrogen a day given an adequate calorie and protein intake. This means a loss of 13 to 20 g of protein. To compensate for that loss, the person must eat extra protein.

A chronically ill person confined to bed will also suffer skin lesions resulting from decubitus ulcers (bedsores). These ulcers may be due to prolonged pressure on some areas of the skin or an infection that aggravates the sloughing of skin cells. This skin sloughing can also contribute to the negative nitrogen balance.

During early immobilization, muscle atrophy and skin sloughing cause a nitrogen loss far exceeding protein intake; this loss cannot be arrested even by a high protein intake. However, over a long period, a high-protein diet can reverse muscle loss and partially maintain the integrity of the skin. Actual skin breakdown can be avoided only by a combination of a high-protein diet, frequent position adjustment, exercise (whenever feasible), special materials for sheets and bedding, and good hygiene. As debilitated patients stabilize, they excrete less nitrogen and can adapt to the stress of illness. However, tissue atrophy and skin lesions can continue and must be guarded against. Depending on the clinical condition, immobilized patients need 70 to 120 g of protein a day. In addition, vitamin C intake should be elevated to offset the increased stress.

Calories

The caloric intake of an immobilized patient is also very important. It must be continuously monitored and adjusted to the clinical condition of the individual patient. For example, a young athlete suffering from a bone fracture will need a high caloric intake for recovery. Some patients continue to lose weight; some reasons include catabolic and nonspecific effects of trauma and loss of appetite.

During the beginning of bed confinement, weight loss may be avoided by a high caloric intake. As the patient's weight stabilizes, the caloric intake must be adjusted to the patient's condition. Patients undergoing physical therapy work hard and may also need a high-calorie diet. But an immobilized patient who is recovering slowly, is quiet, and does very little exercise needs a normal diet or a diet that is slightly low in calories to maintain body weight.

Paralyzed patients can gain weight easily because food is their main enjoyment and they are quite inactive. Moreover, the excess weight will further limit their activity. To prepare for rehabilitation and a reasonable degree of mobility, paralyzed patients must maintain their ideal weight.

Calcium

Bedridden patients have disturbed calcium metabolism, especially patients with bone fractures. Calcium homeostasis is determined by a number of factors: bone integrity, serum calcium, intestinal function, adequacy of active vitamin D, kidney function, and parathyroid activity. Prolonged immobilization may lead to disorders related to excessive calcium: hypercalcemia, hypercalciuria, metastatic calcification of soft tissues such as muscle and kidney, and calcium stone formation in the bladder, kidney, or urinary tract.

Characteristic symptoms of hypercalcemia are nausea, vomiting, loss of appetite, excessive thirst, excessive urination, headache, constipation, abdominal pain, listlessness, malaise, dehydration, psychosis, blunting of pain sensations, and coma. If untreated, the condition can lead to kidney failure, high blood pressure, seizures, and hearing loss.

The treatment (mainly rehydration) for acute hypercalcemia is as follows: (1) intravenous fluid therapy with saline; (2) intravenous furosemide or ethacrynic acid (both diuretics, as discussed in Chapters 27 and 28) and replacement of all urinary loss of sodium, magnesium, and potassium; (3) replacement of any excessive urine loss by fluid (intravenous saline); and (4) implementation of a low-calcium diet (see Chapter 28). If there is no response, other modes of therapy are necessary.

The long-term treatment for hypercalcemia involves: (1) mobilization as soon as possible; (2) calcium intake kept at 500 to 800 mg/d (a low-calcium diet may not be effective if volume expansion has not been brought under control); and (3) phosphate supplement, which helps some, but not all, patients.

Urinary and Bowel Functions

An immobilized patient may have problems with the excretory system. The patient should drink a lot of fluid to make certain that the bladder and kidneys are kept clear. In patients with spinal cord injury, the loss of bladder control may expose the genitourinary tract to a higher risk of infection. When there is no hypercalcemia, the immobilized patient may actually have reduced thirst, and the decreased fluid intake may precipitate stone formation. Because of the importance of hydration, the patient should be monitored with some recording system either at home or in the hospital. The time and amount of water taken in both as a beverage and in food should be estimated, and the time, frequency, and volume of urination should be recorded.

Bowel movements of immobilized patients may also pose special problems. Some develop diarrhea, and others constipation. Patients must avoid foods that tend to cause gas or indigestion. They should also drink a lot of fluid, eat an adequate amount of fiber, and establish a good bowel habit to avoid constipation. Chapter 24 contains more information on dietary measures for gastrointestinal problems.

ELDERLY PATIENTS IN NURSING OR CONVALESCENT HOMES

Individuals in nursing homes and older people in general require intense nutritional and dietary care. Some details are presented in Chapter 15. Many of the disorders and disabilities of the elderly are curable or manageable, and it is especially unfortunate if ill health results from unsound dietary practices.

Malnutrition has been documented in some nursing homes and among some elderly populations. When plenty of food is available and the patient does not have any physiological disorder, malnutrition may result from any of four general causes: (1) refusal to eat; (2) eating a diet adequate in calories but inadequate in other nutrients; (3) overeating and drinking too much alcohol; and (4) physical handicaps, especially oral problems such as bad dentures, difficulty and pain in swallowing, or dry mouth.

The severity of overt clinical problems among the elderly is related to their age, mental stability, and emotional well-being, as well as to the course and extent of the specific disorders. Those in nursing homes should receive standard health care and treatment, including good nutritional care.

Nutritional care providers to the elderly

should obtain histories of each patient's eating pattern, determine the current nutritional status, and be alert to overt symptoms of nutritional deficiency, such as oral lesions, dry mouth, pallor, edema, skin lesions, hemorrhage, or bruises. The physician, nurse, and dietitian should consult with each other regularly about any change in the patient's nutritional status. Nutritious and balanced meals should be provided with attention to texture, taste, flavor, appearance, and moistness. The cessation, continuation, or initiation of a modified diet requires the attention of all health team members.

To monitor the nutritional status of elderly patients, care providers should measure their body weight at regular intervals, perhaps weekly. If patients are bedridden, special methods will be needed to weigh them. Care providers should also record daily the types and amounts of foods and liquids consumed, with special attention to the possibilities of dehydration and semistarvation.

Care providers should be sure that the elderly receive suitable dentures, spectacles, and hearing aids. Good nutritional care also means ascertaining if any drugs being taken affect nutritional status (see Chapter 16). Drug-related anorexia, nausea, vomiting, dehydration, and drowsiness are symptoms deserving special attention, for they all adversely influence the amount of foods and beverages ingested.

In general, those working with elderly patients should learn to be understanding, caring, and supportive. Problems such as refusing to eat, bad eating habits, complaints, depression, irritability, lack of memory, insomnia, delirium, and hallucinations should be anticipated. Rather than being condescending, demanding, or moralizing about such problems, care providers should know the attitudes, situations, limitations, and necessities behind the patient's behavioral adaptations.

MENTAL PATIENTS

A large number of people in this country are confined to mental institutions—half of all available hospital beds are occupied by such patients. The adequacy of care provided in a mental institution has been subject to public scrutiny for many years. Because of the complex social, political, economic, and medical issues involved, this will be a subject of controversy for many more years.

In many respects, mental patients do not differ from normal people. They need human understanding and a meaningful relationship with their environment and the people around them. They have many of the same attitudes to food as normal people, such as having food preferences and responding to the attractiveness of foods served (see Chapter 22). They need more than a well-balanced diet, however. Food and eating are especially important to them, since they are deprived of many of the other joys of life. Contrary to past belief, proper care can improve nutritional status in these patients, as evidenced by clinical studies.

In planning nutritional and dietary care of a mental patient, a well-coordinated and concerted effort is needed from every member of the health team, which may include a psychiatrist, nurse, social worker, therapist (occupational, physical, or recreational), nutritionist, dietitian, psychologist, clinical specialist, and health aides.

A patient needs total care, which requires several considerations. One is the provision of adequate health care facilities and programs. Once a patient has been admitted to an institution, financial problems, family acceptance, and negative social attitudes toward mental illness pose special problems for the patient. Regarding nutritional care, a special diet therapy may be required. The patient's nutritional status and the need for rehabilitation must therefore be evaluated. In addition, feeding a mental patient demands special procedures.

Care in mental institutions varies tremendously. Although each state establishes guidelines for public as well as private mental hospitals, numerous reports have documented substandard or plainly deficient care provided by some institutions, both private and public. Many criticisms are leveled at nutritional care.

In general, these hospitals are crowded and underbudgeted. Food budgets in particular are grossly inadequate. Facilities and equipment are out-of-date, misused, inadequate, and sometimes even decrepit. This pertains to the kitchen

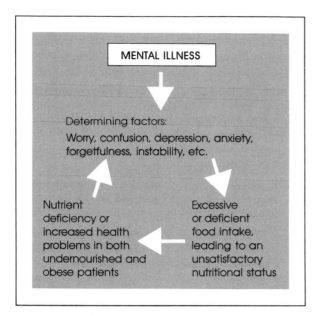

FIGURE 31-1   The vicious cycle of poor nutrition in a mental patient.

layout, equipment, and serving utensils. Dining environments are unsatisfactory. Dull dining rooms, old and displaced draperies, uncomfortable chairs, and even poor sanitation may add to an already depressing environment.

Staffs are undertrained and too small. This especially applies to dietitians, nurses, nutritionists, and food service managers. Many personnel lack the training for handling feeding difficulties. As a result, nutritional and dietary preparation, planning, and services suffer for severely handicapped patients. For instance, the food texture may be inappropriate for patients having chewing or swallowing difficulties. Cold foods, unattractive meals, over- or undersalted foods, and lack of concern and care in serving may all discourage patients from eating adequately.

Clinical reports indicate that many hospitalized mental patients have an unsatisfactory nutritional status. On one hand, there may be overall undernourishment with overt and covert signs. Emaciated patients may show a lack of interest in food because they are worried, depressed, tense, or anxious, or they may purposefully neglect it. On the other hand, some patients are grossly overweight for similar psychological reasons. They compensate for emotional turmoil by eating constantly.

Patients with an unsatisfactory nutritional status need an understanding and sympathetic staff. Some improvement will always result if they are provided a good, nutritious, balanced diet that is served in an attractive and appetizing manner. These patients need both food and emotional comforts. If they are happy, the undernourished will eat more and the obese less. The vicious cycle that produces imbalanced nutritional intake in some mental patients is illustrated in Figure 31-1.

There are some basic reasons why mental patients have nutritional and dietary problems. First, they may have eating handicaps, such as being unable to chew, lacking hand and mouth coordination, and experiencing pain in swallowing. The hospital staff may fail to correct these conditions through neglect or understaffing. Second, they may not like the foods they are served. Third, these patients may have abnormal behavioral patterns that inhibit their nutritional intake. The bizarre eating behaviors of some mental patients constitute a major challenge to nurses, dietitians, and aides. A discussion is provided below.

Confusion about Food and Eating

Patients may be uncertain about eating and unable to decide what and when to eat and with whom. In some cases, the patients forget how to eat foods such as artichokes or grapefruit. Anxiety and hesitation prolong mealtime. These patients cannot be pressured to finish meals even within a reasonable period of time. If hurried, patients may discard the foods, give them to a roommate, or try to bargain with the nurse or dietitian. If the nurse or dietitian knows the reasons behind such behavior, he or she can talk to the patient, help the patient to select menu items, and provide assistance if any difficulty in feeding arises. If a group of patients tends to take a long time to eat, the problem may be solved by letting them eat together at mealtime, thus relieving the nurses from waiting.

Mealtime Misbehavior

Mental patients may have many disrupting eating behaviors. These include throwing food and dishes, interfering with other patients' meals, playing with and discarding food, and eating others' leftovers. Patients may also ignore personal cleanliness by spitting out food and catching food thrown in the air. This behavior may result from defective mental coordination or be an expression of a whole spectrum of emotional problems. The appropriate remedy depends on whether mealtime misbehavior results from the mental derangement. If it does not, the nurse and dietitian should apply interpersonal techniques, such as ignoring the behavior. Using plastic or paper utensils reduces danger and the cost of replacing broken items.

Food Rejection

Mental patients may refuse food for many reasons, some of which are familiar and some of which are not. One familiar cause is the side effects of drugs that have been administered. Also, vomiting and food intolerance may make patients afraid to eat. The simplest reason for reduced food intake is that an overweight patient is following a self-imposed regimen of weight reduction.

Reasons for reduced food intake peculiar to mental patients include a malfunctioning hypothalamus. This problem weakens hunger reactions, making the patient want less food. A patient's mental problems may also have caused a loss of coordination, knowledge, or confidence in food acceptance. Refusing food may be a simple rejection of what food represents to or evokes in the patient (such as an event, guilt, or a lost relative). Finally, the patient may be suffering a multitude of psychological problems, such as depression, hearing voices, confusion, hallucinations, and obsession.

A nurse, dietitian, or nutritionist will find several guidelines useful in helping a patient accept food. Frequent communication is highly desirable, since talking demonstrates concern and will thus make a patient feel better. However, this communication should never include accusations of bad behavior in relation to food. Such accusations could cause the patient to reject food again.

It should be ascertained if refusal of food is related to a specific physiological disorder, since some patients may be reluctant to mention it. In some cases, the use of drugs or hormones (such as insulin) may increase a patient's appetite. In others, forced feeding or assistance in eating is required. A patient should never be made to feel guilty or uncomfortable about any extra work that the staff may have to perform to help the patient eat.

If a patient refuses food frequently, the meals missed and the quantity of food involved should be recorded (see Chapter 23). For instance, a patient may not like to eat at a certain time; so the feeding time should be adjusted, if possible. Also, an attempt must be made to replace missed meals.

In feeding mental patients, their emotional makeup must be known. Defiance, submission, self-contempt, constant demands for love and affection, and suspicion of food poisoning are some characteristics of a disturbed personality. Concerned staff and volunteers can use appropriate communication to convince patients to eat and enjoy their food, thus improving the quality of patients' lives.

The eating environment must be pleasing, clean, convenient, gay, and comfortable with attractive pictures, paintings, tables, and chairs. Group dining has proved successful in improving the eating habits of patients. They enjoy eating with other patients, relatives, and staff. Thus, arrangements should be made so that they can eat with others at regular intervals. Group dining may be enhanced by having cafeteria-style meals that provide patients with a wide variety of foods.

Other considerations in feeding mental patients are as follows: (1) If the image of a prison or institution can be transformed into that of a clinic, patients show appreciation and improvement. (2) Obesity or weight gain may be the result of extra foods given by relatives and nighttime staff. Such occurrences should be identified and corrected. (3) Keeping a weight record is important to make sure that the patient is not gaining or losing too much weight. (4) Many patients are pleased and feel needed when the hospital pays attention to their birthday and gives them special treats. The same applies to holidays and festivals.

There are some special considerations in the dietary care of elderly mental patients (see also Chapter 15 and earlier discussion). For example, the psychiatric problems of depression, confusion, anxiety, and suspicion in a mental patient are even more exaggerated when the patient is older. These patients are generally overconcerned about the functions of the alimentary tract. Their worry and concern can aggravate intestinal motility and cause cramps and even distension. Elderly mental patients also tend to need more security and more of their favorite foods. Depression and suspicion that food is poisoned may lead them to refuse food often. As a result of confusion, elderly patients may ignore food altogether.

In the last few years, psychotherapy, drugs (such as sedatives and tranquilizers) and electric shock treatment, which are now standard management programs, have helped some patients to gain a semblance of normalcy in their lives. As a result, many of these patients are no longer institutionalized. Many discharged patients who have an unsatisfactory nutritional status can be taught to nourish themselves adequately. In fact, good nutritional and dietary care with the proper vitamin and mineral supplements may improve a patient's psychological condition. However, many patients receive medications that may harm their nutritional status.

These discharged patients have the same eating problems as those living in the hospital, and they need the same remedies. Since many of these patients still attend treatment centers and clinics and need occasional hospitalization, some nurses and dietitians have succeeded in providing them with sound nutritional education programs. Included in these programs are:

1. Teaching some basic facts and skills about food budgeting, purchasing, and preparation. Many of these patients have never cooked before or have not been cooking for a while.
2. Teaching principles of nutritional needs.
3. Teaching known effects of drugs on nutritional status. Practically all mental patients receive some medications; some profound effects of these drugs on nutritional status are discussed in Chapter 16.
4. Teaching basic facts about food, such as proper sanitation and safety, meal planning, storage, freezing, use of equipment, and so on.

ANOREXIA NERVOSA

Anorexia nervosa refers to the clinical condition in which a person voluntarily eats very little food. As a result, there is a large weight loss with all its concomitant symptoms. The disorder is more common among females, especially teenage girls, although it has been identified in men and older women. Typically the teenage female patient comes from a middle- to upper-middle-class family. Before the problem occurs, the patient is usually healthy and cooperative and has made good progress in school. All indications point to a "model" student and child. Then, the child develops psychological problems leading her to resent her obesity (which may be real or imagined) and embark on a self-prescribed starvation diet. She continues to abstain from food even when she has achieved an ideal weight. After that, her health deteriorates.

Clinical Manifestations

The anorexic patient presents several clinical manifestations. No desire is present for food or drink; the patient refuses to eat, although occasionally the patient has an uncontrollable urge to gorge, which is followed by self-induced vomiting. Because of this, anorexic patients may lose 25% to 35% of their body weight and become emaciated and wasted. Electrolyte imbalances occur, and female anorexic patients develop hair over different parts of their body and cease to menstruate. Also present is decreased body metabolism, cold hands and feet, decreased blood pressure, and decreased sensitivity to insulin. Anorexic patients exhibit abnormal behavior such as frequent self-induced vomiting, excessive use of cathartics (laxatives), and overexercise (hyperactivity). In some patients, such actions may lead to death.

A number of events can spark the beginning of a voluntary, continuous reduction of food intake. A worsening mother-daughter relationship may set it off. Or a sudden, highly emotional conflict between the patient and someone else may do so. Other possible causes are an abrupt

Exercise and Urinary Nitrogen Excretion in Two Chronically Malnourished Subjects*

Twin brothers, 23 years of age, were admitted to the Mayo Clinic in September 1972 for investigation of arrested sexual development. They had been in good health and were graduate students (in different universities) where they were making satisfactory grades as Ph.D. candidates in mathematics. The onset of puberty, as evidenced by growth of pubic and axillary hair, enlargement of the penis and testes, and occurrence of erections and nocturnal emissions, occurred during the 14th year in each. Early in the 15th year, they embarked on a program of severe dietary restriction and strenuous exercise in an effort to compete in long-distance running. They soon became obsessed with the sport and spent inordinate amounts of time reading about health foods, diets, and exercise programs. Preoccupation with physical fitness and mathematics precluded their participation in social activities. They established habits of running long distances (approximately 24 km) or riding bicycles for up to 48 km in addition to a rigorous program of daily calisthenics. In spite of discomfort, they both developed bunions which required surgical correction. Both resumed running before healing was complete, and both developed traumatic arthritis of the first tarsal and metatarsal joints.

The patients had progressively lost weight since starting the program of food restriction and exercise (8.6 and 8.2 kg, respectively). Their conviction that certain foods had superior value prompted them to prepare many of their meals in their rooms. Their diets consisted principally of peanut butter, cottage cheese, Granola, fresh fruits and vegetables, and honey. Refined foods such as milled flour and sugar were excluded, and they consumed only limited amounts of meat. Meals were eaten irregularly, and excessive amounts of food were ingested on occasion. From the beginning of the dietary and exercise program, their parents were concerned about the patients but were unsuccessful in their efforts to change them.

Soon after they started this program (at age 15 years), the patients noted cessation of sexual development. Facial hair did not appear and their voices did not deepen. Nocturnal emissions and erections virtually ceased, and they were disturbed by their total lack of libido. There was no further growth of the penis or testes. They complained of feeling cold but, surprisingly, expressed no concern about their emaciated appearance.

Obsessiveness about food, desire for unusual foods, hoarding and hiding of food, irregular eating habits, bouts of excessive eating, concerns about obesity, compulsive exercising, continuous and excessive weight loss, lack of concern about their emaciated appearance, cold intolerance, and compulsive behavior—all present in these patients—are characteristics of anorexia nervosa and establish this diagnosis. . . .

*Source: R. A. Nelson et al., Mayo Clinic Proceedings 48 (1973):549–550.

---

failure in schoolwork and the emotional turmoil over beginning or continuing a sexual relationship.

In-depth studies by psychologists and psychiatrists of anorexic patients have indicated a common psychological profile. These patients show a lack of feeling for hunger, satiety, tiredness, and sometimes even physical pain. They generally have a distorted image of their physical size. Some anorexic patients think that they are 40% to 60% larger than they in fact are. Consequently, they become obsessed with dieting. In addition, these patients commonly feel inadequate in identity (role in life), competence (work or school performance), and effectiveness (in communication, controlling events, etc.). This loss of faith in personal ability leads to an attempt to control the environment by controlling body weight. Food binges, guilt about eating, and a reluctance to admit abnormal food habits are the typical attitudes of anorexic patients towards food.

Treatment for a patient with anorexia nervosa consists of psychotherapy, behavioral modification, drug therapy, and hospital feedings.

Psychotherapy, Behavioral Modification, and Drug Therapy

Anorexic patients must undergo intense psychological treatment to overcome negative perceptions of self and to normalize their food intake. Clinicians must identify the causes or initiating events of each patient's illness. All correctable family conflicts that are relevant must be resolved. However, psychotherapy is best started after a patient has gained a little body weight and then maintained even after the patient has attained normal weight. A patient may revert to abnormal eating behaviors if underlying problems have not been resolved.

Some clinicians use behavioral modification in treating anorexic patients. This consists of using rewards and reprimands to make the patient eat. For example, an agreement is reached between the patient and the practitioner that if there is any weight gain (such as 1 lb), the patient can do or receive certain things that he or she likes. If the patient fails to gain weight, activity will be restricted. Some clinicians claim reasonable success with this method, with some patients gaining 2 to 6 lb per week. Other clinicians warn against this practice, believing that a patient may feel cheated, frustrated, or despondent because of being forced into doing things he or she does not like. The insecure feelings that may ensue can thus aggravate feelings of inadequacy, which may be the source of the patient's problem.

Some clinicians use drugs such as amitriptyline and other antidepressants as treatment. This usage is based on the possibility of a brain defect. However, antidepressants have not been consistently effective in treating anorexic patients.

Hospital Feeding

Patients with anorexia nervosa are best hospitalized, because the eating environment can be controlled and family involvement is minimized. Some patients eat better in a hospital because they do not have to make any decisions about what and when to eat. In general, the dietary care requires careful planning, an experienced staff, and a tremendous amount of concern and understanding.

Once anorexia nervosa has been diagnosed, the first major responsibility of the health team is to develop a dietary and nutrition program. There should be complete understanding and communication among the health team members to avoid any inconsistency or friction. This is important, since the patient may try to manipulate the health care personnel and parents in order to avoid food intake and secure an opportunity to exercise. Most anorexic patients want to maintain a starved appearance. The nurse can coordinate all activities to assure that the program is implemented. The doctor should describe the treatment procedures to the patient, preferably in the presence of the primary nurse and the dietitian or nutritionist.

Detailed procedures for feeding a hospitalized patient with anorexia nervosa may be obtained from the references at the end of this book. The following provides a brief discussion.

The attending physician will prescribe a diet after studying the patient's condition. Most practitioners start with a diet containing 1,000 to 3,000 kcal and progressively increase the intake by 200 kcal every 3 or 4 days until a daily intake of 4,000 kcal is achieved. The intake is increased until an acceptable weight gain is achieved. To avoid any misunderstandings, any changes in caloric intake must be made by the doctor or an assigned coordinator in the form of written request. A cooperative patient can be fed three main meals and occasionally a snack. The nurse should be fully informed of the patient's conditions, including the treatment protocol. Most importantly, the attending nurse should monitor the patient's eating behavior and pay full attention to the following feeding routines:

1. Check that the foods served comply with the meal plan.

2. Pay attention to the patient's hands constantly.

3. Assume a friendly and supportive attitude so that the patient will not feel spied on.

4. Leave the room only in an emergency, since the patient may try to get rid of some foods.

5. Prevent food disposal by keeping any container (such as a facial tissue box, a wastebasket, or a flower pot) away from patient during the meal and checking the meal tray after the patient has finished eating. The patient may hide food under napkins or smear it under the bed, on the window sill, etc.

6. Permit a maximum of 1 hour for eating a meal.

7. If feasible, arrange for the patient to eat alone and be monitored by the same nurse.

8. If possible, the patient should wear a pocketless hospital gown while eating.

9. Insist that the patient rest for ½ to 1 hour after a meal and insure that he or she does not leave the bed, since she may induce vomiting.

After each meal, the dietitian should use the record obtained from the nurse and the serving tray to calculate if the patient has eaten the required calories. Any missing amount is then made up by providing a high-calorie beverage. The routine of supplemental feeding should already have been clearly explained to the patient.

Forced feeding is done only if all attempts to get the anorexic patient to eat voluntarily have failed. Obviously, if the patient resists this measure, physical restraints may be necessary. Tube feeding is tried first, before parenteral nutrition is administered. Both success and failure have been reported with the forced feeding of patients with anorexia nervosa.

Recovery is a long and difficult process that may last from 6 months to 1 year or more. About 60% to 70% of all patients may recover after several years of treatment; the remaining patients may die. Real recovery is extremely important, since most of these patients are so mentally unstable. The following guidelines should be used to determine if recovery has taken place:

1. The patient attains and maintains a normal body weight.

2. The patient shows no abnormal food behav-

ior, such as sudden food binges or self-induced vomiting.

3. The patient resumes regular menstruation and establishes a normal relationship with peers, friends, and relatives.

FOOD ALLERGY

Allergy refers to an excess sensitivity to substances or conditions such as food; hair; cloth; biological, chemical, or mechanical agents; emotional excitement; extremes of temperature; and so on. The hypersensitivity and abnormal reactions associated with allergies produce various symptoms in affected people. The substance that triggers an allergic reaction is called an *allergen* or *antigen*, and it may enter the body through ingestion, injection, respiration, or physical contact.

In food allergies, the offending substance is usually, though not always, a protein. After ingestion, it is absorbed into the circulatory system, where it encounters the body's immunological system. If this is the first exposure to the antigen, there are no overt clinical signs. Instead, the presence of an allergen causes the body to form antibodies, which are made up of four classes of immunoglobulins (Ig): IgA, IgE, IgG, and IgM. The organs, tissues, and blood of all healthy people contain antibodies that either circulate or remain attached to the cells where they are formed. When the body encounters the antigen a second time, the specific antibody will complex with it. Because the resulting complexes may or may not elicit clinical manifestations, merely identifying a specific immunoglobulin in the circulatory system will not indicate whether a person is allergic to a specific food antigen.

The human intestine is coated by the antibody IgA, which can protect a person from developing a food allergy. However, infants under 7 months old have a lower amount of intestinal IgA. The mucosa thus permits incompletely digested protein molecules to enter. These can then enter the circulation and cause antibodies to form.

Children can also develop a food allergy called the delayed allergic reaction or hyperactivity. The classic sign of this is the tension-fatigue syndrome. Children with the syndrome have a dull face, pallor, infraorbital circles, and nasal stuffiness. A delayed food allergy symptom is more difficult to diagnose than an immediate one.

Although food allergy is not age-specific, it is more prevalent during childhood. Because a reaction to food can impose stress and interfere with nutrient ingestion, absorption, and digestion, the growth and development of children with food allergies can be delayed. Half of the adult patients with food allergy claim that they had a childhood allergy as well. Apparently, a childhood food allergy rarely disappears completely in an adult. If a newborn baby develops hypersensitivity in the first 5 to 8 days of life, the pregnant mother was probably eating a large quantity of potentially offending foods, such as milk, eggs, chocolate, or wheat. The child becomes sensitized in the womb, and the allergic tendency may either continue into adult life or gradually decrease.

In clinical medicine, it is extremely important to differentiate food allergy from food intolerance. The former relates to the immunosystem of the body, while the latter is the direct result of maldigestion and malabsorption due to a lack of intestinal enzyme(s) or an indirect intestinal reaction because of psychological maladjustment.

About 2% to 8% of all Americans have some form of food allergy. The clinical management of food allergy is controversial and has many problems. For instance, a food allergy is influenced by the amount of allergen consumed, whether the allergen is cooked or raw, and the cumulative effects from successive ingestions of the allergen. A person with a food allergy also tends to be allergic to one or more of the following: pollen, mold, wool, cosmetics, dust, and other inhalable items. Because these substances are so common, they are difficult to avoid.

Other difficulties in allergy management are as follows: (1) If a person is allergic to a food, even a very small amount can produce a reaction. (2) Some patients allergic to an item at one time are not at another. (3) Some patients react to an allergen only when they are tired, frustrated, or emotionally upset. (4) Although protein is suspected to be the substance most likely to cause allergy, people can be allergic to almost any food chemical.

In managing patients with food allergy, there are two basic objectives. First, the offending substance must be identified. Patients should then be placed on a monitored antiallergic diet to assure adequate nutrient intake, especially young patients whose growth and development may be adversely affected by the allergy.

The clinical reactions of patients allergic to a food vary from relatively mild ones such as skin rash, itchy eyes, or headache to more severe ones such as abdominal cramps, diarrhea, vomiting, and loss of appetite. Other symptoms include cough, asthma, bronchitis, purpura, urticaria, dermatitis, and various problems affecting the digestive tract (vomiting, colic, ulceration of colon, etc.). In children, undernutrition and arrested development may occur.

Milk Allergy

Many individuals of all ages develop an allergy as well as an intolerance to milk and milk products. The reaction may occur when a person is sick (e.g., with infection, alcoholism, surgery, or trauma). Thus, dietitians and nurses should always check to see whether a patient can tolerate milk. If the intolerance is due to a reduced activity of lactase, the information provided in Chapters 24 and 30 should be helpful.

Someone allergic to milk must also avoid many foods containing milk products. A milk-free diet is discussed briefly in Chapters 24 and 30. Ingesting regular homogenized fresh milk can damage the digestive mucosa of some susceptible individuals, especially children. The damaged cells bleed continuously but only minute amounts of blood are lost. The result is occult blood loss in the stool and iron deficiency anemia. Professionals do not agree about whether this phenomenon is an allergic reaction. In rare cases, penicillin used in cows to prevent or control mastitis may leave a residue in milk. Consequently, some individuals who are allergic to the penicillin may have an allergic reaction to the inoculated cow's milk.

Breast milk is much preferred over cow's

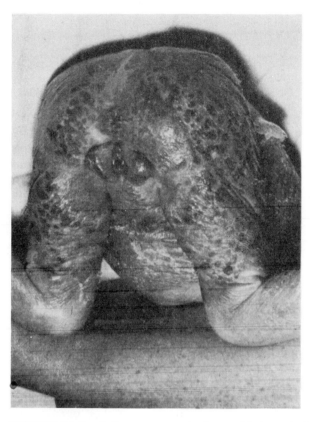
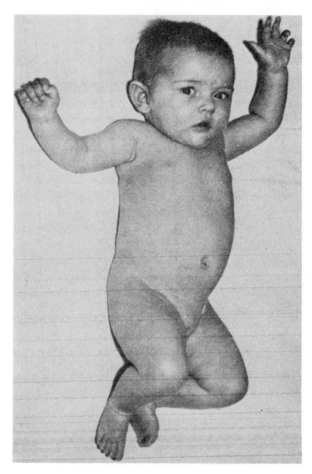

FIGURE 31-2   *Left*: severe atopic dermatitis in an infant allergic to milk. *Right*: same infant after changing to a milk free formula diet. (From A. Holzel, *Postgrad. Med. J.* 51 [1975], Suppl. 3:71)

milk for feeding a baby in a family whose members have allergies. Cow's milk contains the protein β-lactoglobulin, which may trigger an allergic reaction, while breast milk does not. If an infant has symptoms of milk allergy, special formulas with soy or another protein source as a base can be safely substituted for milk.

However, breast-feeding does have one major problem when it is used to prevent an infant from having an allergic reaction to cow's milk. If the child is also allergic to substances such as cheese, crab, or chocolate, the mother can in effect feed them to her child via breast milk if she ingests them herself. Therefore, the breast-fed child may show allergic reactions. Figure 31-2 illustrates milk allergy in an infant.

Testing and Treatment

Food allergies are difficult to test for and subsequently to diagnose and confirm. Furthermore, patients with an allergic reaction to one food may in reality be allergic to many others that contain a common ingredient. Or, when an infant is allergic to a formula, it is usually assumed that the protein is responsible. In reality, it could be the vegetable oil base.

When a patient complains about a food allergy, they should first provide the nurse, dietitian, or nutritionist with a detailed food history. A careful study of the patient's food preferences may identify the culprit. Patient reactions to food coloring and additives (which are found in many processed foods), laxatives, and salicylate-related chemicals should also be noted. Allergens are likely to be found in some of these items. Also, for a defined period, the patient should keep a complete record of food eaten.

Currently, three types of tests are available for diagnosing food allergy. None of them is guaranteed to identify an offending substance, although they can provide some information about the patient's reaction towards different foods. These three procedures are skin testing, fasting, and elimination diets.

Skin testing for food allergy involves exposing the skin to the suspected offending chemical (from a food). If the patient is allergic, local swelling and inflammation develop from within a few minutes to a day after application. However, some clinicians use this test for preliminary diagnosis while others consider it useless and unreliable. The fasting test is more reliable. After a period of fasting under medical supervision, the patient is given one food at a time to identify the offending substance. Cost and risk of nutrient deficiencies result in limited application of this test.

One method of diagnosing food allergy that has been somewhat successful is the use of progressive elimination diets. The patient is given a *basal* diet that is expected to produce no or minimal symptoms. If no reaction occurs, the patient is maintained on the diet for 2 to 4 weeks. Then other foods are added one at a time. Each new food is used for at least 5 to 10 days before another one is added. If the patient reacts to a newly added food, an offending allergen is positively identified.

If the elimination diet is short-term, there should be no concern about its nutritional adequacy, although nutrient intakes should be monitored. However, nutrient supplements, especially vitamins and minerals, may be needed if the diet is long-term. This is especially important for children.

Consultation with a nurse, dietitian, or nutritionist is important, especially when such a diet is first implemented. At least one family member should also be involved. If the diet is to succeed, the diet instructions and implementation must be completely understood. Although a progressive elimination diet does not always yield positive results, total compliance is mandatory to maximize its effectiveness. A detailed discussion of elimination diets may be obtained from the references at the end of this book.

INFECTIOUS DISEASES

Diet and infection are interrelated. Inadequate diet makes a person more vulnerable to infectious diseases, and these diseases affect the body's nutrient needs. The following section explores the relationship of nutrition to infection in general and examines the effects of infection on a person's nutritional status and the role of diet in managing infectious diseases.

Nutrition and Infection

Nutritional status affects a person's susceptibility to infection. A person with a poor nutritional status has less body resistance and is more susceptible to infection. Thus, to an extent, a good nutritional status helps protect against infection. Nevertheless, a healthy, well-nourished person can easily contract pneumonia, malaria, or infectious hepatitis. An undernourished person with an infection generally recovers more slowly than a well-nourished individual, even if the infection is of short duration. The classic example is the difficulty with which a malnourished patient recovers from pneumonia compared with the relatively rapid recovery of a well-nourished individual.

An infection, especially a severe one, has a profound effect on the nutritional status of an individual. Directly or indirectly, an infection can cause nausea, vomiting, loss of appetite, maldigestion, malabsorption, and an increased need for nutrients.

The role of nutritional therapy for a patient with an infection is mainly supportive, although it may be an important therapeutic tool in a number of situations. In a very limited number of patients, nutritional management with water, glucose, and electrolytes may determine the difference between life and death. For instance, infection in a newborn may result in life-threatening

CASE STUDY   Immobilization and Hypercalcemia

Mr. T.M. was a 25-year-old college student who suffered a fracture of his left femur because of a bicycle accident. After examining him in the emergency room, the attending physician concluded that the fractured femur was the only damage sustained by the young man, as revealed by X rays and a complete physical examination. T.M. was placed in traction. Although blood analyses were done, the serum level of calcium was not ascertained. After spending 4½ weeks in traction, T.M. was placed in a one-and-one-half left hip plaster spica. He remained in this cast for 4 months because callus failed to form.

One week after the termination of traction, T.M. complained of abdominal cramps, with occasional nausea and vomiting. For the next 2½ months, the patient had a poor appetite, demanded fluid frequently, and was constipated. He also complained of headaches. The hospital doctor requested the diagnosis of a psychiatrist, who detected no psychiatric problem. The health team felt that the patient may have been reacting negatively to the hospital environment. They believed that time and a home environment would benefit the patient and eliminate the symptoms. At the end of 3 months, T.M. was sent home. He had lost about 15 lb since the accident.

However, within 2 weeks of returning home, the parents of T.M. telephoned to inform the doctors that his clinical conditions were not improving. One month after the discharge, he was readmitted to the hospital. T.M. appeared dehydrated and weak with muscle wasting. He had lost about 10 lb during the month. This time the doctors instantly suspected that T.M. was suffering from hypercalcemia. Prompt serum calcium determination was made in addition to analyses of other blood chemicals and components. The results were as follows (per 100 mL of blood): calcium, 20 mg; phosphorus, 3 mg; potassium, 3 mEq; creatinine, 1 mg; alkaline phosphatase, 6 K-A units; uric acid, 8 mg; albumin, 3.8 g; globulin, 3.5 g; and BUN, 21 mg. The blood contained 20 mEq of CO_2 per liter. The patient excreted 200 to 300 mg of calcium in the urine in 24 hours. Tests showed that T.M.'s kidney function was greatly impaired, clearing urine with a specific gravity of less than 1.005 and clearing less than 40 mL of creatinine per minute.

A number of X-ray studies revealed that T.M. did not have renal calculi or prepyloric distension. His chest profile was normal, and there was no subperiosteal resorption of the clavicles and phalanges. However, his left femur had diffuse demineralization, and the union of the fracture was markedly delayed.

After studying all available data, the attending physicians concluded that T.M. was suffering hypercalcemia from immobilization (prolonged inactivity in the spica cast). A physical therapist was summoned to improve the patient's movement. The cast was replaced by an ischial weight-bearing spica cast on the right hip, and the patient was asked to walk 45 to 60 m three to five times each day with the assistance of the physical therapist or nurse. The patient was encouraged to implement both passive and active movements. He was given 2 L of saline solution each day via the vein, and he was also placed on a low-calcium diet.

In spite of these measures, T.M.'s serum calcium level remained consistently high (over 15 mg/100 mL). The attending physician began a series of treatments with medication. T.M. was given 10 mg of prednisone orally four times daily for 2 days. Then he received four oral doses of 5 mg of the drug daily for 1 week. During the next 10 days, the patient's serum calcium level gradually returned to normal. His clinical conditions improved dramatically at the same time. Although the serum calcium level rose slightly after administration of the drug was terminated, it eventually returned to normal. At the same time, the patient was placed on the low-calcium diet for 2 more weeks.

During the next 3 weeks, the patient's strength, appetite, and body weight continued to improve. During the same period, he was urged to move as much as possible on his own, and the physical therapist provided assistance three to four times a week. The fracture continued to heal. Urinary and blood tests confirmed normal calcium metabolism and excretion. T.M., who was 5'11", weighed 160 lb when he first had the accident. He weighed 145 lb when he was discharged from the hospital the second time. Two and a half years after the injury, the patient returned to full physical activity with complete use of his left leg. His serum calcium level remained normal. He also regained his preaccident body weight 7 months after the second discharge from the hospital.

Review and Analysis

1. Describe the symptoms of hypercalcemia. Use other references if necessary.
2. You are requested by the doctor to plan a diet providing 500 mg of calcium and 3,000 kcal. Prepare menus for 3 days.
3. The doctor requests the nurse to ascertain how much fluid the patient is consuming and excreting. Describe the protocol for the nurse to follow so that accurate measurements can be made.
4. Why should a patient confined to bed for a long period drink a lot of fluid?
5. Why was the patient given 2 L of saline solution each day?
6. What is the ideal weight for this patient? To maintain his ideal weight, what caloric level should he ingest?
7. Describe the major considerations for a patient on a low-calcium diet.
8. Aside from hypercalcemia, what other problems are likely in a patient confined to bed for a prolonged period?

hypoglycemia. In this case, early detection and intravenous glucose administration can save the child's life. Nutritional therapy is also essential in cases of infectious hepatitis, which has complications such as increased blood ammonia, hypoglycemia, and defective liver function. Proper nutritional care of these patients may be a lifesaving procedure. Patients with cholera or severe *Escherichia coli* infections can have acute, severe, or prolonged diarrhea with a loss of water, electrolytes, and nutrients. Without proper nutritional support, shock can cause death in these patients.

Patients with infections may develop fever. A patient with fever is said to be in a *febrile* condition, or suffering *pyrexia*. Human oral body temperature ranges from 35.9 to 37.2 °C, or 96.8 to 99.3 °F. Vaginal or rectal temperature averages 0.5 °C or 1 °F higher than an oral reading. Body temperature rises, producing fever, if the body cannot dissipate excess heat adequately. Once a

fever has started, body tissues and organs start to catabolize. The extent and severity of catabolism determine the overall effect of the fever on the nutritional status of the person. In general, a fever is classified by its duration (short vs. long), although some clinicians prefer to identify a third or mixed type of fever. Most fevers are short-lived with proper medical care, provided there is no severe malnutrition. However, patients with long-term fever (even under medical care) may suffer weight loss, anemia, and other symptoms of malnutrition unless aggressive nutritional support is provided.

The effects of infection on the nutritional status of the body can be considered according to anorexia, fluid and electrolyte balance, vitamins and minerals, calories, and protein.

Anorexia, or loss of appetite, is probably a major nutritionally related adverse effect that may develop in an infected patient. If anorexia is accompanied by nausea and vomiting, it is very

CASE STUDY Anorexia Nervosa

V.M. was a 15-year-old white girl from an upper-middle-class family. When she was 7, her mother died from a diabetic coma caused by excessive alcohol consumption. Her father remarried when she was 9. Her stepmother had a 10-year-old daughter and a 5-year-old son from her previous marriage. V.M.'s father worked nights 2 to 3 days a week. When she was 14 years old, the family doctor felt that this girl was immature, lacking in self-confidence, and verbally and socially inhibited. The parents sought medical help. After 10 months of psychotherapy, she showed some improvement.

When she was 15 years old, she started dieting. Although her weight was normal, she felt that her hips and thighs were fat. Within 5 months, her weight decreased from 49.9 kg (110 lb) to about 38.6 kg (85 lb) at a height of 165.1 cm (5'5"). She had practically abstained from eating, and her parents were very worried about her deteriorating conditions. The family physician placed her in the hospital for observation and treatment.

The girl had a repulsive appearance resembling the emaciated state of a concentration camp victim. The doctor conducted a complete endocrinologic workup (including studies of growth hormone, follicle-stimulating hormone, luteinizing hormone, and cortisol) and was unable to find any defects. Results of skull and upper gastrointestinal X-ray studies were also normal. The attending physicians were unable to find any cause for her weight loss. At this time V.M.'s weight was 33.2 kg (73 lb). She frequently experienced indistinct hallucinations of voices. She said that her stepmother cried repeatedly to her "Eat, eat!" and that the noises from the air-conditioning came from a crowd of people. She was depressed, had very little self-confidence and motivation, and was socially withdrawn. The doctors concluded that she was most likely suffering from anorexia nervosa. This diagnosis was confirmed by a specialist in this area.

After a careful study, the health team developed several approaches to her treatment. The doctors began giving her 200 mg/day of Elavil to control her emotional instability. She was placed on an aggressive behavioral modification program, which required her to gain weight in exchange for rewards such as cosmetics, mirrors, permission to watch her favorite television programs, etc. Apparently this program and the drug were effective, since her depression gradually disappeared and she gained 6.4 kg (14 lb) during the first 5 weeks in the hospital. However, during this period she complained frequently about everything and was manipulative, dependent, and hostile. There were many episodes of self-induced vomiting that were witnessed by the hospital staff, although she denied them when questioned. Her parents confirmed that she had frequent self-induced vomitings at home.

Because of her manipulative behavior, the therapeutic and administrative functions in caring for the patient were assigned to different groups. Among many strategies implemented by the health team, one important approach was to involve V.M. in every step of the treatment plan. She was encouraged to express how she felt and value herself as a human being.

Review and Analysis

1. If we assume that V.M.'s family background was partially responsible for her initial development of anorexia nervosa, describe some likely causes. For example, would the absence of her father 3 nights a week be a factor? Make assumptions if there are not enough data in the case history.
2. What is the ideal weight of a patient 15 years of age?
3. Why was the doctor interested in the endocrinologic status of the patient?

4. Can you provide a reason for her hallucinations?
5. Do some research and describe the pros and cons of using a reward-and-reprimand technique in treating anorexia nervosa.
6. What is the extreme method of treating anorexia nervosa?
7. Give some examples of manipulative be-

havior by the patient in dealing with the hospital staff, using V.M. as an example.
8. Plan 1 week's menus for a 15-year-old girl.
9. Develop a complete protocol for treating V.M., for example, the procedures of reward and reprimand, the menu plan, the distribution of meals, the size of meals, types of visitors, etc.

difficult for the patient to consume enough fluid, calories, and protein. Most practitioners are aware that asking such patients to eat an attractive and well-balanced meal does not always produce the desired result, even with attention and encouragement from health personnel and family. However, every attempt should be made to correct the situation. Patients should be encouraged to eat what they like, even if it is not mealtime. They may also find it easier to ingest soft and liquid foods. Some patients also appreciate nutrient-dense solutions.

The fluid and electrolyte needs of infected patients vary. Some patients may become dehydrated, while others become overhydrated. Diarrhea, extreme sweating, and nausea and vomiting predispose these patients to a loss of fluid and electrolytes. Such patients need 2,000 to 5,000 mL of fluid a day. In some severely infected patients, sodium moves from the blood to the tissue cells. If water is accumulated at the same time, the fluid and electrolyte intake of these patients should be restricted.

The body requires a number of vitamins to provide an effective defense against infection. For example, folic and ascorbic acids and other B vitamins are all needed for optimal phagocytic activity. Patients with infections may have nutritional problems involving calcium, zinc, and iron. If patients are immobilized for a long time, there will be an increasingly negative calcium balance. Infected patients show a decreased blood zinc level due to the mineral's migration to tissues and organs. The rate of zinc excretion in the urine is increased as well. Infection also has a

profound effect on iron metabolism, since infection leads to increased red blood cell destruction. Iron deficiency during an infection is common and is described as the "anemia of infection."

The caloric need of a patient suffering from infection is evaluated according to the known effects of fever and disease. Body basal metabolic rate increases proportionately with the rise in body temperature and with fever duration. There is a 10% increase in basal metabolic rate for each 1 °C increase in body temperature, or 7% for each 1 °F rise. Basic caloric need depends on the disease and fever. One formula for calculating the daily caloric need is as follows:

$$\text{RDA} \times [1 + \frac{13}{100} \times \text{rise in body temperature (°C)}]$$

The protein need of a patient is also evaluated according to well-documented effects of illness. The patient needs more protein than the RDA to cover nitrogen loss through perspiration and urine. One formula for calculating the daily protein need is as follows:

$$\text{RDA} \times [1 + \frac{10}{100} \times \text{rise in body temperature (°C)}]$$

Dietary Management

In this section, we will discuss the dietary management of a patient with fever of short duration, that is, less than 2 weeks. The main objective of such management is to help the patient eat without too much effort even if less food is con-

CASE STUDY   Food Additives and Allergy

For 5 years, Mrs. M.K., a 49-year-old white female, had intermittent episodes of slight fever, pain in the joints, and vascular purpura. Because they occurred only occasionally, she was unconcerned until the symptoms became unbearable. Unable to find the cause of this patient's illness, the doctor referred the patient to a nearby university clinic, where she was eventually diagnosed to be allergic to some substances in food. Initial studies showed that she was positive for anti-γ-globulin and antinuclear factor, and her erythrocyte sedimentation rate was about 10% above normal. Her vascular purpura was observed mainly on her lower legs. She was unable to specify the circumstances, if any, that brought about these skin changes. However, she claimed that the purpuric rashes sometimes intensified after she had consumed red wine, pears, and aspirin.

Because of her undefined clinical conditions, the attending doctor instructed her to check into the hospital for further testing. Upon admission to the hospital, her skin problems were not active and there were only old spots. When the standard thurfyl nicotinate test was applied, she did not show any purpuric reaction. The patient was then tested for her reactions to aspirin (400 mg), New Coccin (5 mg), and 4-hydroxybenzoic acid (45 mg). Her purpuric reaction appeared 5 to 7 hours after provocation, and she also showed positive thurfyl nicotinate tests. She demonstrated negative responses to placebo and other challenging chemicals such as tartrazine, Sunset Yellow, and Patent Blue V. She was instructed to remain on a diet free from chemical food additives. However, Mrs. M.K. was unable to comply with a highly restricted dietary regimen.

Although she did improve somewhat, her skin still developed purpura occasionally. It was likely that she was still ingesting some offending foods that contained the additives. The attending physician decided that she should stay on the prescribed diet and that she should be given some medications as well. She was prescribed two drugs—phenformin (50 mg) and ethylestrenol (8 mg)—for about 5 months. Her pains and skin purpura completely disappeared. However, even when she was receiving the drugs and following the special diet, she still had positive thurfyl nicotinate reactions when aspirin and New Coccin were administered. The reaction was not severe, and the patient had a completely negative reaction to 4-hydroxybenzoic acid (650 mg) when the thurfyl nicotinate was given.

Review and Analysis

1. What is vascular purpura?
2. Explain the significance of being positive for anti-γ-globulin and antinuclear factor and having an erythrocyte sedimentation rate about 10% above normal.
3. Name the food additives used in red wine.
4. List the commonly known "offending" chemicals found in red wine, pears, and aspirin.
5. Do some research and ascertain what the thurfyl nicotinate test is.
6. What are 4-hydroxybenzoic acid, tartrazine, Sunset Yellow, and Patent Blue V? In what foods are they used?
7. Use the appropriate reference to develop 1 week of menus for an additive-free diet.
8. Do some research and learn the current theories about the uses of phenformin and ethylestrenol, especially in allergy.

CASE STUDY   *A Patient with an Infection*

Mr. E.D. was a 60-year-old man who, for a month, had a fever that refused to subside in spite of all attempts by his personal physician. Mr. E.D. had infiltrates in both of his lungs. About 2 years earlier this patient had a total gastrectomy with jejunal anastomosis because of a perforated ulcer of the stomach. Over the 2-year period, E.D.'s body weight dropped from 180 to 120 lb. He had great difficulty eating. Within 1 to 2 hours after a meal, he would sweat and experience abdominal pain and diarrhea. Attempts to reduce this dumping syndrome had been unsuccessful, mainly because of his noncompliance with the dietary counseling of the nurse and dietitian. He was hospitalized twice for evaluation. Because of his severe maldigestion and malabsorption problems, his doctor gave him pancreatic enzymes and antibiotics. His condition continued to deteriorate, and he was readmitted for treatment.

Upon admission, he was weak and coughing constantly, with a fever of 38.9 °C (102 °F). Although he was a known alcoholic, he claimed that he had neither been drinking nor lost consciousness recently. Careful questionings revealed that he had not been exposed to any source of contamination such as animals, plants, or foreign travel. However, Mr. E.D. had a wasted appearance. He had pitting edema of both legs, and X-rays showed rales in both lungs. His blood pressure was 85/65 mm Hg and heart rate 100 beats per minute. His hematocrit was 25%, and his white blood cell count was 10,600/mm³, with 75% segmented neutrophils, 7% bands, and 14% lymphocytes. His serum albumin level was 2.9 g/100 mL, and his globulin level was 1.8 g/100 mL.

Other blood chemistry analyses provided the following data: glucose, 80 mg/100 mL; cholesterol, 80 mg/100 mL; iron, 9 μg/100 mL; total iron binding capacity, 300 μg/100 mL; and folic acid, 2.9 μg/100 mL. His liver functions were normal. Cultures of the patient's throat, sputum, blood, and urine and bone marrow samples were negative for bacteria, fungi, and other identifiable biological agents.

The patient was given antibiotics intravenously (cephalothin) and then orally (erythromycin). His fever persisted at 102 °F. On the sixth day of his hospital stay, a transbronchial biopsy was performed. Laboratory testing of the biopsy revealed that the patient had an infection of *Torulopsis glabrata*. At about the same time, the patient was beginning to improve and was given a high-calorie isotonic diet. His serum albumin rose to 3.8 g/100 mL, total protein to 6.5 g/100 mL, and cholesterol to 130 mg/100 mL. Since E.D. was losing a lot of fluid, he should have been losing weight. Instead, he had gained about 2 lb by the end of the second week of hospitalization. Once his appetite started to improve, he consumed a large amount of calories and protein. His nutritional status improved, with a simultaneous clearing of the pulmonary infiltrates.

He was discharged without medication, although he was instructed to eat a high-calorie diet divided into small meals and to avoid items that might elicit the dumping syndrome. When seen 3 weeks later, he was completely free from symptoms and had gained more body weight. X rays of his lungs showed complete clearing.

Review and Analysis

1. Mr. E.D. had three major problems. He had a persistent dumping syndrome, he was undernourished, and he had an infection. Discuss the current theories regarding the development of an infection from undernourishment.
2. Plan a high-caloric isotonic diet for Mr. E.D. during his hospital stay according to the data available in the case history.
3. Note that Mr. E.D. had a fever as well as edema. Assume that the patient was not

excessively thirsty at any time during his hospital stay. The case history stated that he was losing a lot of fluid. Can you estimate the daily loss of urine?

4. Can you give one possible reason why his infection slowly disappeared during the sixth to eighth days of hospitalization?

5. Imagine that this patient's wife approached you and asked you to help her convince her husband to comply with the prescribed antidumping diet. What would you tell her? Also, is it easy to prepare an isotonic diet at home? With variety? Prepare menus for 1 week.

sumed. During the first 2 or 3 days of fever, the patient should be given fluid, semifluid, and soft foods in small feedings at 2- to 3-hour intervals. Milk used may be flavored with coffee, tea, or cocoa. Occasionally a serving of milk may be replaced by eggs, fruit drinks, gruel, porridge, or a commercial or homemade high-protein nutrient solution. Fresh fruit juice should also be given liberally for calories, flavoring, and fluid intake after the attending physician has evaluated the patient's hydration status. If dehydrated, the patient may need 2,000 to 5,000 mL of fluid daily.

As the patient shows progress, a high-protein and modified full-liquid diet may be used (Chapter 23). As the body temperature subsides, the patient's appetite will improve and a bland diet may be started (see hospital routine progressive diets in Chapter 23). Two to three days after the body temperature has returned to normal, the patient can be put on a regular diet for the rest of the convalescent period. The patient should be monitored for dyspepsia, which is common in patients recovering from fever, and any intestinal disturbance caused by any medications used.

If the fever refuses to subside after a week of antibiotic therapy, special effort must be made to fulfill the nutritional needs of the patient. The major objectives of an aggressive nutritional program are to increase the chances of survival, provide adequate nutrients for the defense mechanisms, rebuild strength and reverse weight loss, and hasten convalescence.

There are several major dietary considerations in treating a patient with prolonged fever. First, the daily caloric need of such a patient is over 2,500 kcal and should be appropriate to the individual. Second, fluid intake and loss must be balanced. If the patient sweats and is unwilling to drink fluids, the fever may lead to dehydration. If vomiting and diarrhea are also present, parenteral fluid therapy may be needed. To keep fluid from being lost, the patient may need sodium chloride supplements.

Such a patient requires a good deal of protein. Vomiting, nausea, anorexia, and use of a liquid and semiliquid diet may result in a net consumption of only 70 to 90 g of protein. Generous amounts of carbohydrate are also needed to prevent ketosis, which may result from excess fat and protein metabolism. Vitamin and mineral supplements may be needed if the patient is not eating well.

The texture of food in a diet for an infected patient should progress from liquid to semiliquid. The foods should be easily digestible, well cooked, served in small portions, and given every 2 to 3 hours. As the patient's condition improves, he or she should be placed on a soft diet (which includes such items as cottage cheese, poached eggs, cooked cereals, tender beef, and stewed tomatoes—see Chapter 23). Finally, solid food may be served when tolerated. If the patient is eating well during convalescence, the following guidelines should still be adhered to: (1) The quantity of food should increase with patient tolerance. (2) High-calorie and high-protein diets should be provided. (3) Strongly spiced, seasoned, and hard-to-digest foods should be avoided.

Obviously, if the patient is not getting enough nutrients for any reason, aggressive nutritional support may be necessary. This includes tube-feeding of defined-formula diets, total parenteral nutrition, or both.

STUDY QUESTIONS

1. What is rehabilitation? Give some examples of ways in which patients undergoing rehabilitation may find eating physically challenging. What are some emotional problems they may face?

2. Discuss nitrogen balance in an immobilized patient. What dietary care will help to alleviate this condition?

3. Are immobilized patients likely to experience disorders based on hypercalcemia or hypocalcemia? What treatment is recommended in acute cases?

4. Discuss nutritional problems related to the institutional care of mental patients. What physical and psychological handicaps may prevent a mental patient from eating properly? How can these factors be dealt with constructively?

5. What basic nutritional guidelines should a mental patient be made aware of when he or she is released?

6. Define *anorexia nervosa*. Why could its occurrence be considered unusual in the type of person commonly affected?

7. Describe the clinical manifestations of anorexia nervosa. What is a possible relationship between refusing food and subsequent clinical manifestations?

8. What guidelines should be followed in the feeding routine of an anorexic? Use the references at the end of this book.

9. Why is good nutritional status important in recovering from an infection?

10. Develop a diet for a patient with a short-term fever (lasting less than 2 weeks). Be specific in your recommendations.

11. Why are infants particularly susceptible to developing food-related allergies? Why are food-related allergies in children difficult to diagnose?

12. Distinguish between food allergy and food intolerance.

13. What factors influence the manifestation of food allergy? Why do these factors present difficulties in allergy management?

Appendices

TABLES, REFERENCES, AND GLOSSARY

TABLE 1 Recommended Daily Dietary Allowances (RDAs) for the United States

Age (years)	Weight (kg)	Weight (lb)	Height (cm)	Height (in)	Protein (g)	Fat-Soluble Vitamins: Vitamin A (μg RE)*	Fat-Soluble Vitamins: Vitamin D (μg)[†]	Fat-Soluble Vitamins: Vitamin E (mg α-TE)[‡]
Infants								
0.0–0.5	6	13	60	24	kg × 2.2	420	10	3
0.5–1.0	9	20	71	28	kg × 2.0	400	10	4
Children								
1–3	13	29	90	35	23	400	10	5
4–6	20	44	112	44	30	500	10	6
7–10	28	62	132	52	34	700	10	7
Males								
11–14	45	99	157	62	45	1,000	10	8
15–18	66	145	176	69	56	1,000	10	10
19–22	70	154	177	70	56	1,000	7.5	10
23–50	70	154	178	70	56	1,000	5	10
>51	70	154	178	70	56	1,000	5	10
Females								
11–14	46	101	157	62	46	800	10	8
15–18	55	120	163	64	46	800	10	8
19–22	55	120	163	64	44	800	7.5	8
23–50	55	120	163	64	44	800	5	8
>51	55	120	163	64	44	800	5	8
Pregnant						+30	+200	+5	+2
Lactating						+20	+400	+5	+3

Source: Recommended Dietary Allowances, 9th ed. (Washington, D.C.: National Academy of Sciences, 1980).

Note: The allowances are intended to provide for individual variations among most normal persons as they live in the United States under usual environmental stresses. Diets should be based on a variety of common foods in order to provide other nutrients for which human requirements have been less well defined. See text for detailed discussion of allowances and of nutrients not tabulated.

*Retinol equivalents. 1 retinol equivalent = 1 μg of retinol or 6 μg of β-carotene.

[†] As cholecalciferol. 10 μg of cholecalciferol = 400 IU of vitamin D.

[‡] α-tocopherol equivalents. 1 mg of *d*-α-tocopherol = 1 α-TE.

[§] 1 NE (niacin equivalent) is equal to 1 mg of niacin or 60 mg of dietary tryptophan.

Water-Soluble Vitamins							Minerals					
Vitamin C (mg)	Thiamin (mg)	Ribo-flavin (mg)	Niacin (mg NE)[§]	Vitamin B_6 (mg)	Folacin[‖] (μg)	Vitamin B_{12} (μg)	Calcium (mg)	Phos-phorus (mg)	Mag-nesium (mg)	Iron (mg)	Zinc (mg)	Iodine (μg)
35	0.3	0.4	6	0.3	30	0.5[¶]	360	240	50	10	3	40
35	0.5	0.6	8	0.6	45	1.5	540	360	70	15	5	50
45	0.7	0.8	9	0.9	100	2.0	800	800	150	15	10	70
45	0.9	1.0	11	1.3	200	2.5	800	800	200	10	10	90
45	1.2	1.4	16	1.6	300	3.0	800	800	250	10	10	120
50	1.4	1.6	18	1.8	400	3.0	1,200	1,200	350	18	15	150
60	1.4	1.7	18	2.0	400	3.0	1,200	1,200	400	18	15	150
60	1.5	1.7	19	2.2	400	3.0	800	800	350	10	15	150
60	1.4	1.6	18	2.2	400	3.0	800	800	350	10	15	150
60	1.2	1.4	16	2.2	400	3.0	800	800	350	10	15	150
50	1.1	1.3	15	1.8	400	3.0	1,200	1,200	300	18	15	150
60	1.1	1.3	14	2.0	400	3.0	1,200	1,200	300	18	15	150
60	1.1	1.3	14	2.0	400	3.0	800	800	300	18	15	150
60	1.0	1.2	13	2.0	400	3.0	800	800	300	18	15	150
60	1.0	1.2	13	2.0	400	3.0	800	800	300	10	15	150
+20	+0.4	+0.3	+2	+0.6	+400	+1.0	+400	+400	+150	#	+5	+25
+40	+0.5	+0.5	+5	+0.5	+100	+1.0	+400	+400	+150	#	+10	+50

[‖] The folacin allowances refer to dietary sources as determined by *Lactobacillus casei* assay after treatment with enzymes (conjugases) to make polyglutamyl forms of the vitamin available to the test organism.

[¶] The recommended dietary allowance for vitamin B_{12} in infants is based on average concentration of the vitamin in human milk. The allowances after weaning are based on energy intake (as recommended by the American Academy of Pediatrics) and consideration of other factors, such as intestinal absorption.

The increased requirement during pregnancy cannot be met by the iron content of habitual American diets nor by the existing iron stores of many women; therefore the use of 30 to 60 mg of supplemental iron is recommended. Iron needs during lactation are not substantially different from those of nonpregnant women, but continued supplementation of the mother for 2 to 3 months after parturition is advisable in order to replenish stores depleted by pregnancy.

TABLE 2   Estimated Safe and Adequate Daily Dietary Intakes of Additional Selected Vitamins and Minerals for the United States, 1980

		Vitamins		
	Age (years)	Vitamin K (μg)	Biotin (μg)	Pantothenic Acid (mg)
Infants	0–0.5	12	35	2
	0.5–1	10–20	50	3
Children and adolescents	1–3	15–30	65	3
	4–6	20–40	85	3–4
	7–10	30–60	120	4–5
	>11	50–100	100–200	4–7
Adults		70–140	100–200	4–7

Source: *Recommended Dietary Allowances*, 9th ed. (Washington, D.C.: National Academy of Sciences, 1980).

Note: Because there is less information on which to base allowances, these figures are not given in the main table of the RDAs and are provided here in the form of ranges of recommended intakes.

Trace Elements*						Electrolytes		
Copper (mg)	Manganese (mg)	Fluoride (mg)	Chromium (mg)	Selenium (mg)	Molybdenum (mg)	Sodium (mg)	Potassium (mg)	Chloride (mg)
0.5–0.7	0.5–0.7	0.1–0.5	0.01–0.04	0.01–0.04	0.03–0.06	115–350	350–925	275–700
0.7–1.0	0.7–1.0	0.2–1.0	0.02–0.06	0.02–0.06	0.04–0.08	250–750	425–1,275	400–1,200
1.0–1.5	1.0–1.5	0.5–1.5	0.02–0.08	0.02–0.08	0.05–0.1	325–975	550–1,650	500–1,500
1.5–2.0	1.5–2.0	1.0–2.5	0.03–0.12	0.03–0.12	0.06–0.15	450–1,350	775–2,325	700–2,100
2.0–2.5	2.0–3.0	1.5–2.5	0.05–0.2	0.05–0.2	0.1–0.3	600–1,800	1,000–3,000	925–2,775
2.0–3.0	2.5–5.0	1.5–2.5	0.05–0.2	0.05–0.2	0.15–0.5	900–2,700	1,525–4,575	1,400–4,200
2.0–3.0	2.5–5.0	1.5–4.0	0.05–0.2	0.05–0.2	0.15–0.5	1,100–3,300	1,875–5,625	1,700–5,100

*Since the toxic levels for many trace elements may be only several times usual intakes, the upper levels for the trace elements given in this table should not be habitually exceeded.

TABLE 3   Mean Heights and Weights and Recommended Energy Intakes for the United States, 1980

Category	Age (years)	Weight (kg)	Weight (lb)	Height (cm)	Height (in.)	Energy Needs (with range) (kcal)	Energy Needs (with range) (MJ)
Infants	0.0–0.5	6	13	60	24	kg × 115 (95–145)	kg × .48
	0.5–1.0	9	20	71	28	kg × 105 (80–135)	kg × .44
Children	1–3	13	29	90	35	1,300 (900–1,800)	5.5
	4–6	20	44	112	44	1,700 (1,300–2,300)	7.1
	7–10	28	62	132	52	2,400 (1,650–3,300)	10.1
Males	11–14	45	99	157	62	2,700 (2,000–3,700)	11.3
	15–18	66	145	176	69	2,800 (2,100–3,900)	11.8
	19–22	70	154	177	70	2,900 (2,500–3,300)	12.2
	23–50	70	154	178	70	2,700 (2,300–3,100)	11.3
	51–75	70	154	178	70	2,400 (2,000–2,800)	10.1
	>76	70	154	178	70	2,050 (1,650–2,450)	8.6
Females	11–14	46	101	157	62	2,200 (1,500–3,000)	9.2
	15–18	55	120	163	64	2,100 (1,200–3,000)	8.8
	19–22	55	120	163	64	2,100 (1,700–2,500)	8.8
	23–50	55	120	163	64	2,000 (1,600–2,400)	8.4
	51–75	55	120	163	64	1,800 (1,400–2,200)	7.6
	>76	55	120	163	64	1,600 (1,200–2,000)	6.7
Pregnancy						+300	
Lactation						+500	

Source: Recommended Dietary Allowances, 9th ed. (Washington, D.C.: National Academy of Sciences, 1980).

Notes: The data in this table have been assembled from the observed median heights and weights of children together with desirable weights for adults for the mean heights of men (70 in.) and women (64 in.) between the ages of 18 and 34 years as surveyed in the U.S. population (Health, Education and Welfare/National Center for Health Statistics data).

The energy allowances for the young adults are for men and women doing light work. The allowances for the two older age groups represent mean energy needs over these age spans, allowing for a 2% decrease in basal (resting) metabolic rate per decade and a reduction in activity of 200 kcal/d for men and women between 51 and 75 years, 500 kcal for men over 75 years, and 400 kcal for women over 75. The customary range of daily energy output is shown for adults in parentheses, and is based on a variation in energy needs of ±400 kcal at any one age emphasizing the wide range of energy intakes appropriate for any group of people.

Energy allowances for children through age 18 are based on median energy intakes of children these ages followed in longitudinal growth studies. The values in parentheses are 10th and 90th percentiles of energy intake, to indicate the range of energy consumption among children of these ages.

TABLE 4   U.S. Recommended Daily Allowances (U.S. RDAs)

Nutrient	Adults and Children (4 years or older)	Infants (Birth to 1 year)	Children (Under 4 years)	Pregnant or Lactating Women
Required				
Protein (g)	45 or 65*	18 or 25*	20 or 28*	45 or 65*
Vitamin A (IU)	5,000	1,500	2,500	8,000
Vitamin C (mg)	60	35	40	60
Thiamin (mg)	1.5	0.5	0.7	1.7
Riboflavin (mg)	1.7	0.6	0.8	2.0
Niacin (mg)	20	8	9	20
Calcium (mg)	1,000	600	800	1,300
Iron (mg)	18	15	10	18
Optional				
Vitamin D (IU)	400	400	400	400
Vitamin E (IU)	30	5	10	30
Vitamin B_6 (mg)	2.0	0.4	0.7	2.5
Folic acid (mg)	0.4	0.1	0.2	0.8
Vitamin B_{12} (μg)	6	2	3	8
Phosphorus (mg)	1,000	500	800	1,300
Iodine (μg)	150	45	70	150
Magnesium (mg)	400	70	200	450
Zinc (mg)	15	5	8	15
Copper (mg)	2	0.6	1	2
Biotin (mg)	0.3	0.05	0.15	0.3
Pantothenic acid (mg)	10	3	5	10

Source: Food and Drug Administration, Washington, D.C.

*Lower value if protein efficiency ratio is equal to or greater than that of casein; higher value if protein efficiency ratio is less than that of casein, but greater than 20%.

TABLE 5 Dietary Standards for Canada

					Water-Soluble Vitamins						
Age	Weight (kg)	Height (cm)	Energy (kcal)	Protein (g)	Thiamin (mg)	Niacin (mg equiv)	Ribo-flavin (mg)	Vitamin B₆ (mg)	Folate (μg)	Vitamin B₁₂ (μg)	Vitamin C (mg)
0–6 mo	6	—	kg × 117	kg × 2.2(2.0)‡	0.3	5	0.4	0.3	40	0.3	20§
7–11 mo	9	—	kg × 108	kg × 1.4	0.5	6	0.6	0.4	60	0.3	20
1–3 yr	13	90	1,400	22	0.7	9	0.8	0.8	100	0.9	20
4–6 yr	19	110	1,800	27	0.9	12	1.1	1.3	100	1.5	20
7–9 yr											
Male	27	129	2,200	33	1.1	14	1.3	1.6	100	1.5	30
Female	27	128	2,000	33	1.0	13	1.2	1.4	100	1.5	30
10–12 yr											
Male	36	144	2,500	41	1.2	17	1.5	1.8	100	3.0	30
Female	38	145	2,300	40	1.1	15	1.4	1.5	100	3.0	30
13–15 yr											
Male	51	162	2,800	52	1.4	19	1.7	2.0	200	3.0	30
Female	49	159	2,200	43	1.1	15	1.4	1.5	200	3.0	30
16–18 yr											
Male	64	172	3,200	54	1.6	21	2.0	2.0	200	3.0	30
Female	54	161	2,100	43	1.1	14	1.3	1.5	200	3.0	30
19–35 yr											
Male	70	176	3,000	56	1.5	20	1.8	2.0	200	3.0	30
Female	56	161	2,100	41	1.1	14	1.3	1.5	200	3.0	30
36–50 yr											
Male	70	176	2,700	56	1.4	18	1.7	2.0	200	3.0	30
Female	56	161	1,900	41	1.0	13	1.2	1.5	200	3.0	30
51 + yr											
Male	70	176	2,300#	56	1.4	18	1.7	2.0	200	3.0	30
Female	56	161	1,800#	41	1.0	13	1.2	1.5	200	3.0	30
Pregnancy			+300**	+20	+0.2	+2	+0.3	+0.5	+50	+1.0	+20
Lactation			+500	+24	+0.4	+7	+0.6	+0.6	+50	+0.5	+30

From Bureau of Nutritional Sciences, Food Directorate, Health Protection Branch, *Dietary Standards for Canada* (Ottawa: Minister of National Health and Welfare, 1975). Reproduced by permission of the Minister of Supply and Services, Canada, and the Bureau of Nutritional Sciences, Health Protection Branch, Department of National Health and Welfare, Canada. A new edition of *Dietary Standards for Canada* is being issued, but revised data is not available at the time of this printing.

Note: Recommendations are based on estimated average daily protein intake of Canadians.

* RE = retinol equivalent.

† One microgram of cholecalciferol equals 1 μg ergocalciferol (40 IU vitamin D activity).

‡ Recommended protein intake of 2.2 g per kilogram body weight for infants age 0 to 2 months and 2.0 g per kilogram body weight for those age 3 to 5 months. Protein recommendation for infants 0 to 11 months assumes consumption of breast milk or protein of equivalent quality.

Fat-Soluble Vitamins			Minerals					
Vitamin A (RE)*	Vitamin D (μg cholecal-ciferol)†	Vitamin E (mg d-α-tocopherol)	Calcium (mg)	Phosphorus (mg)	Magnesium (mg)	Iodine (μg)	Iron (mg)	Zinc (mg)
400	10	3	500‖	250‖	50‖	35‖	7‖	4‖
400	10	3	500	400	50	50	7	5
400	10	4	500	500	75	70	8	5
500	5	5	500	500	100	90	9	6
700	2.5¶	6	700	700	150	110	10	7
700	2.5¶	6	700	700	150	100	10	7
800	2.5¶	7	900	900	175	130	11	8
800	2.5¶	7	1,000	1,000	200	120	11	9
1,000	2.5¶	9	1,200	1,200	250	140	13	10
800	2.5¶	7	800	800	250	110	14	10
1,000	2.5¶	10	1,000	1,000	300	160	14	12
800		6	700	700	250	110	14	11
1,000	2.5¶	9	800	800	300	150	10	10
800	2.5¶	6	700	700	250	110	14	9
1,000	2.5¶	8	800	800	300	140	10	10
800	2.5¶	6	700	700	250	100	14	9
1,000	2.5¶	8	800	800	300	140	10	10
800	2.5¶	6	700	700	250	100	9	9
+100	+2.5¶	+1	+500	+500	+25	+15	+1††	+3
+400	+2.5¶	+2	+500	+500	+75	+25	+1††	+7

§ Considerably higher levels may be prudent for infants during the first week of life.

Recommended energy intake for 66 years and over reduce to 2,000 kcal for men and 1,500 kcal for women.

‖ The intake of breast-fed infants may be less than the recommendation but is considered adequate.

¶ Most older children and adults receive vitamin D from the sun, but 2.5 μg daily is recommended. This intake should be increased to 5.0 μg daily during pregnancy and lactation and for those confined indoors or otherwise deprived of sunlight for extended periods.

** Increased energy intake recommended during second and third trimesters. An increase of 100 kcal per day is recommended during the first trimester.

†† A recommended total intake of 15 mg daily during pregnancy and lactation assumes the presence of adequate stores of iron. If stores are suspected of being inadequate, additional iron as a supplement is recommended.

NUTRITIVE VALUES OF THE EDIBLE PART OF FOODS

Table 6 shows the food values in 730 common foods. Foods are grouped under the following headings: dairy products; eggs; fats and oils; fish, shellfish, meat, and poultry; fruits and fruit products; grain products; legumes (dry), nuts, and seeds; sugars and sweets; vegetables and vegetable products; and miscellaneous items.

Most of the foods listed are in ready-to-eat form. Some are basic products widely used in food preparation, such as flour, fat, and cornmeal. The weight in grams for an approximate measure of each food is shown. A footnote indicates if inedible parts are included in the description and the weight. All table notes appear on pages A58–A59.

The values for food energy (kcal) and nutrients shown are the amounts present in the edible part of the item, that is, that portion customarily eaten—corn without the cob, meat without bone, potatoes without skins, and European-type grapes without seeds. If additional parts are eaten—the potato skin, for example—the amounts obtained of some nutrients will be somewhat greater than those shown.

Values for thiamin, riboflavin, and niacin in white flours and white bread and rolls are based on the increased enrichment levels put into effect for those products by the Food and Drug Administration in 1974. Iron values for those products and the values for enriched cornmeal, pasta, farina, and rice (except the value of riboflavin) represent the minimum levels of enrichment promulgated under the Federal Food, Drug, and Cosmetic Act of 1955. Riboflavin values of rice are for unenriched rice, as the levels for added

TABLE 6 Nutritive Values of the Edible Part of Foods

Food	Approximate Measures, Units, or Weight (edible part unless footnotes indicate otherwise)	Weight (g)	Water (%)	Food Energy (kcal)	Protein (g)	Fat (g)
Dairy Products (Cheese, Cream, Imitation Cream, Milk; Related Products)						
Butter. See Fats, oils; related products.						
Cheese:						
Natural:						
Blue	1 oz	28	42	100	6	8
Camembert (3 wedges per 4-oz container)	1 wedge	38	52	115	8	9
Cheddar:						
Cut pieces	1 oz	28	37	115	7	9
	1 cu. in.	17.2	37	70	4	6
Shredded	1 c	113	37	455	28	37
Cottage (curd not pressed down):						
Creamed (cottage cheese, 4% fat):						
Large curd	1 c	225	79	235	28	10
Small curd	1 c	210	79	220	26	9
Low fat (2%)	1 c	226	79	205	31	4
Low fat (1%)	1 c	226	82	165	28	2
Uncreamed (dry curd, less than ½% fat)	1 c	145	80	125	25	1
Cream	1 oz	28	54	100	2	10
Mozzarella, made with—						
Whole milk	1 oz	28	48	90	6	7
Part skim milk	1 oz	28	49	80	8	5

Dashes (—) denote lack of reliable data for a constituent believed to be present in measurable amount

riboflavin have not been approved. Thiamin, riboflavin, and niacin values for products prepared with white flour represent the use of flour enriched at the 1974 levels; values for iron for such products represent the use of flour enriched at the 1955 level.

Niacin values are for preformed niacin occurring naturally in foods. The values do not include additional niacin that the body may form from tryptophan, an essential amino acid in the protein of most foods. Among the better sources of tryptophan are milk, meats, eggs, legumes, and nuts.

Values have been calculated from the ingredients called for in typical recipes for many of the prepared items, such as biscuits, corn muffins, macaroni and cheese, custard, and many desserts. Values for toast and cooked vegetables are without fat added, either during preparation or at the table. Some vitamins, especially ascorbic acid, may be destroyed when vegetables are cut or shredded. Since such losses vary, no deduction has been made. For meat, values are for meat cooked and drained of the drippings.

A variety of manufactured items—some of the milk products, ready-to-eat breakfast cereals, imitation cream products, fruit drinks, and various mixes—are included. Frequently those foods are fortified with one or more nutrients. If nutrients are added, this information is on the label. Values shown here for those foods are usually based on products from several manufacturers and may differ somewhat from the values provided by any one source.

Table 6 has been adapted from Table 2 of Science and Education Administration, U.S. Department of Agriculture, *Nutritive Value of Foods*, Home and Garden Bulletin no. 72, rev. (Washington, D.C., April 1981).

**Nutrients in Indicated Quantity**													

| | **Fatty Acids** | | | | | | | **Vitamin A** | | | | | |
| | **Unsaturated** | | | | | | | | | | | | |
Saturated (total) (g)	**Oleic (g)**	**Linoleic (g)**	**Carbo-hydrate (g)**	**Calcium (mg)**	**Phos-phorus (mg)**	**Iron (mg)**	**Potassium (mg)**	**Value (IU)**	**Thiamin (mg)**	**Riboflavin (mg)**	**Niacin (mg)**	**Ascorbic Acid (mg)**
5.3	1.9	0.2	1	150	110	0.1	73	200	0.01	0.11	0.3	0
5.8	2.2	0.2	Trace	147	132	0.1	71	350	0.01	0.19	0.2	0
6.1	2.1	0.2	Trace	204	145	0.2	28	300	0.01	0.11	Trace	0
3.7	1.3	0.1	Trace	124	88	0.1	17	180	Trace	0.06	Trace	0
24.2	8.5	0.7	1	815	579	0.8	111	1,200	0.03	0.42	0.1	0
6.4	2.4	0.2	6	135	297	0.3	190	370	0.05	0.37	0.3	Trace
6.0	2.2	0.2	6	126	277	0.3	177	340	0.04	0.34	0.3	Trace
2.8	1.0	0.1	8	155	340	0.4	217	160	0.05	0.42	0.3	Trace
1.5	0.5	0.1	6	138	302	0.3	193	80	0.05	0.37	0.3	Trace
0.4	0.1	Trace	3	46	151	0.3	47	40	0.04	0.21	0.2	0
6.2	2.4	0.2	1	23	30	0.3	34	400	Trace	0.06	Trace	0
4.4	1.7	0.2	1	163	117	0.1	21	260	Trace	0.08	Trace	0
3.1	1.2	0.1	1	207	149	0.1	27	180	0.01	0.10	Trace	0

TABLE 6   (continued)

Food	Approximate Measures, Units, or Weight (edible part unless footnotes indicate otherwise)	Weight (g)	Water (%)	Food Energy (kcal)	Protein (g)	Fat (g)
Parmesan, grated						
Cup, not pressed down	1 c	100	18	455	42	30
Tablespoon	1 T	5	18	25	2	2
Ounce	1 oz	28	18	130	12	9
Provolone	1 oz	28	41	100	7	8
Ricotta, made with—						
Whole milk	1 c	246	72	430	28	32
Part skim milk	1 c	246	74	340	28	19
Romano	1 oz	28	31	110	9	8
Swiss	1 oz	28	37	105	8	8
Pasteurized process cheese:						
American	1 oz	28	39	105	6	9
Swiss	1 oz	28	42	95	7	7
Pasteurized process cheese food, American	1 oz	28	43	95	6	7
Pasteurized process cheese spread, American	1 oz	28	48	80	5	6
Cream, sour	1 c	230	71	495	7	48
	1 T	12	71	25	Trace	3
Cream, sweet:						
Half-and-half (cream and milk)	1 c	242	81	315	7	28
	1 T	15	81	20	Trace	2
Light, coffee, or table	1 c	240	74	470	6	46
	1 T	15	74	30	Trace	3
Whipped topping (pressurized)	1 c	60	61	155	2	13
	1 T	3	61	10	Trace	1
Whipping, unwhipped (volume about double when whipped):						
Heavy	1 c	238	58	820	5	88
	1 T	15	58	80	Trace	6
Light	1 c	239	64	700	5	74
	1 T	15	64	45	Trace	5
Cream products, imitation (made with vegetable fat):						
Sour dressing (imitation sour cream) made with nonfat dry milk	1 c	235	75	415	8	39
	1 T	12	75	20	Trace	2
Sweet:						
Creamers:						
Liquid (frozen)	1 c	245	77	335	2	24
	1 T	15	77	20	Trace	1
Powdered	1 c	94	2	515	5	33
	1 t	2	2	10	Trace	1
Whipped topping:						
Frozen	1 c	75	50	240	1	19
	1 T	4	50	15	Trace	1
Powdered, made with whole milk	1 c	80	67	150	3	10
	1 T	4	67	10	Trace	Trace
Pressurized	1 c	70	60	185	1	16
	1 T	4	60	10	Trace	1

Ice cream. See Milk desserts, frozen.
Ice milk. See Milk desserts, frozen.

						Nutrients in Indicated Quantity						
Fatty Acids												
Saturated (total) (g)	**Unsaturated**		Carbo-hydrate (g)	Calcium (mg)	Phos-phorus (mg)	Iron (mg)	Potassium (mg)	**Vitamin A** Value (IU)	Thiamin (mg)	Riboflavin (mg)	Niacin (mg)	Ascorbic Acid (mg)
	Oleic (g)	Linoleic (g)										
19.1	7.7	0.3	4	1,376	807	1.0	107	700	0.05	0.39	0.3	0
1.0	0.4	Trace	Trace	69	40	Trace	5	40	Trace	0.02	Trace	0
5.4	2.2	0.1	1	390	229	0.3	30	200	0.01	0.11	0.1	0
4.8	1.7	0.1	1	214	141	0.1	39	230	0.01	0.09	Trace	0
20.4	7.1	0.7	7	509	389	0.9	257	1,210	0.03	0.48	0.3	0
12.1	4.7	0.5	13	669	449	1.1	308	1,060	0.05	0.46	0.2	0
—	—	—	1	302	215	—	—	160	—	0.11	Trace	0
5.0	1.7	0.2	1	272	171	Trace	31	240	0.01	0.10	Trace	0
5.6	2.1	0.2	Trace	174	211	0.1	46	340	0.01	0.10	Trace	0
4.5	1.7	0.1	1	219	216	0.2	61	230	Trace	0.08	Trace	0
4.4	1.7	0.1	2	163	130	0.2	79	260	0.01	0.13	Trace	0
3.8	1.5	0.1	2	159	202	0.1	69	220	0.01	0.12	Trace	0
30.0	12.1	1.1	10	268	195	0.1	331	1,820	0.08	0.34	0.2	2
1.6	0.6	0.1	1	14	10	Trace	17	90	Trace	0.02	Trace	Trace
17.3	7.0	0.6	10	254	230	0.2	314	260	0.08	0.36	0.2	2
1.1	0.4	Trace	1	16	14	Trace	19	20	0.01	0.02	Trace	Trace
28.8	11.7	1.0	9	231	192	0.1	292	1,730	0.08	0.36	0.1	2
1.8	0.7	0.1	1	14	12	Trace	18	110	Trace	0.02	Trace	Trace
8.3	3.4	0.3	7	61	54	Trace	88	550	0.02	0.04	Trace	0
0.4	0.2	Trace	Trace	3	3	Trace	4	30	Trace	Trace	Trace	0
54.8	22.2	2.0	7	154	149	0.1	179	3,500	0.05	0.26	0.1	1
3.5	1.4	0.1	Trace	10	9	Trace	11	220	Trace	0.02	Trace	Trace
46.2	18.3	1.5	7	166	146	0.1	231	2,690	0.06	0.30	0.1	1
2.9	1.1	0.1	Trace	10	9	Trace	15	170	Trace	0.02	Trace	Trace
31.2	4.4	1.1	11	266	205	0.1	380	20[1]	0.09	0.38	0.2	2
1.6	0.2	0.1	1	14	10	Trace	19	Trace[1]	0.01	0.02	Trace	Trace
22.8	0.3	Trace	28	23	157	0.1	467	220[1]	0	0	0	0
1.4	Trace	0	2	1	10	Trace	29	10[1]	0	0	0	0
30.6	0.9	Trace	52	21	397	0.1	763	190[1]	0	0.16[1]	0	0
0.7	Trace	0	1	Trace	8	Trace	16	Trace[1]	0	Trace[1]	0	0
16.3	1.0	0.2	17	5	6	0.1	14	650[1]	0	0	0	0
0.9	0.1	Trace	1	Trace	Trace	Trace	1	30[1]	0	0	0	0
8.5	0.6	0.1	13	72	69	Trace	121	290[1]	0.02	0.09	Trace	1
0.4	Trace	Trace	1	4	3	Trace	6	10[1]	Trace	Trace	Trace	Trace
13.2	1.4	0.2	11	4	13	Trace	13	330[1]	0	0	0	0
0.8	0.1	Trace	1	Trace	1	Trace	1	20[1]	0	0	0	0

TABLE 6   (continued)

Food	Approximate Measures, Units, or Weight (edible part unless footnotes indicate otherwise)	Weight (g)	Water (%)	Food Energy (kcal)	Protein (g)	Fat (g)
Milk:						
Fluid:						
Whole (3.3% fat)	1 c	244	88	150	8	8
Lowfat (2%):						
No milk solids added	1 c	244	89	120	8	5
Milk solids added:						
Label claim less than 10 g of protein per cup	1 c	245	89	125	9	5
Label claim 10 or more grams of protein per cup (protein fortified)	1 c	246	88	135	10	5
Lowfat (1%):						
Milk solids added:						
Label claim less than 10 g of protein per cup	1 c	245	90	105	9	2
Label claim 10 or more grams of protein per cup (protein fortified)	1 c	246	89	120	10	3
No milk solids added	1 c	244	90	100	8	3
Nonfat (skim):						
Milk solids added:						
Label claim less than 10 g of protein per cup	1 c	245	90	90	9	1
Label claim 10 or more grams of protein per cup (protein fortified)	1 c	246	89	100	10	1
No milk solids added	1 c	245	91	85	8	Trace
Buttermilk	1 c	245	90	100	8	2
Canned:						
Evaporated, unsweetened:						
Whole milk	1 c	252	74	340	17	19
Skim milk	1 c	255	79	200	19	1
Sweetened, condensed	1 c	306	27	980	24	27
Dried:						
Buttermilk	1 c	120	3	465	41	7
Nonfat instant:						
Envelope[5]	3.2 oz (net weight)	91	4	325	32	1
Cup	1 c	68[7]	4	245	24	Trace
Milk beverages:						
Chocolate milk (commercial):						
Regular	1 c	250	82	210	8	8
Lowfat (2%)	1 c	250	84	180	8	5
Lowfat (1%)	1 c	250	85	160	8	3
Eggnog (commercial)	1 c	254	74	340	10	19
Malted milk, home-prepared with 1 c of whole milk and 2 to 3 heaping teaspoons of malted milk powder (about ¾ oz)						
Chocolate	1 c of milk plus ¾ oz of powder	265	81	235	9	9
Natural	1 c of milk plus ¾ oz of powder	265	81	235	11	10
Shakes, thick:[8]						
Chocolate, container	10.6 oz	300	72	355	9	8
Vanilla, container	11 oz	313	74	350	12	9

								Nutrients in Indicated Quantity				
Fatty Acids												
Saturated (total) (g)	Unsaturated		Carbo-hydrate (g)	Calcium (mg)	Phos-phorus (mg)	Iron (mg)	Potassium (mg)	Vitamin A Value (IU)	Thiamin (mg)	Riboflavin (mg)	Niacin (mg)	Ascorbic Acid (mg)
	Oleic (g)	Linoleic (g)										
5.1	2.1	0.2	11	291	228	0.1	370	310[2]	0.09	0.40	0.2	2
2.9	1.2	0.1	12	297	232	0.1	377	500	0.10	0.40	0.2	2
2.9	1.2	0.1	12	313	245	0.1	397	500	0.10	0.42	0.2	2
3.0	1.2	0.1	14	352	276	0.1	447	500	0.11	0.48	0.2	3
1.5	0.6	0.1	12	313	245	0.1	397	500	0.10	0.42	0.2	2
1.8	0.7	0.1	14	349	273	0.1	444	500	0.11	0.47	0.2	3
1.6	0.7	0.1	12	300	235	0.1	381	500	0.10	0.41	0.2	2
0.4	0.1	Trace	12	316	255	0.1	418	500	0.10	0.43	0.2	2
0.4	0.1	Trace	14	352	275	0.1	446	500	0.11	0.48	0.2	3
0.3	0.1	Trace	12	302	247	0.1	406	500	0.09	0.34	0.2	2
1.3	0.5	Trace	12	285	219	0.1	371	80[3]	0.08	0.38	0.1	2
11.6	5.3	0.4	25	657	510	0.5	764	610[3]	0.12	0.80	0.5	5
0.3	0.1	Trace	29	738	497	0.7	845	1,000[3]	0.11	0.79	0.4	3
16.8	6.7	0.7	166	868	775	0.6	1,136	1,000[3]	0.28	1.27	0.6	8
4.3	1.7	0.2	59	1,421	1,119	0.4	1,910	260[3]	0.47	1.90	1.1	7
0.4	0.1	Trace	47	1,120	896	0.3	1,552	2,160[6]	0.38	1.59	0.8	5
0.3	0.1	Trace	35	837	670	0.2	1,160	1,610[6]	0.28	1.19	0.6	4
5.3	2.2	0.2	26	280	251	0.6	417	300[3]	0.09	0.41	0.3	2
3.1	1.3	0.1	26	284	254	0.6	422	500	0.10	0.42	0.3	2
1.5	0.7	0.1	26	287	257	0.6	426	500	0.10	0.40	0.2	2
11.3	5.0	0.6	34	330	278	0.5	420	890	0.09	0.48	0.3	4
5.5	—	—	29	304	265	0.5	500	330	0.14	0.43	0.7	2
6.0	—	—	27	347	307	0.3	529	380	0.20	0.54	1.3	2
5.0	2.0	0.2	63	396	378	0.9	672	260	0.14	0.67	0.4	0
5.9	2.4	0.2	56	457	361	0.3	572	360	0.09	0.61	0.5	0

TABLE 6   (continued)

Food	Approximate Measures, Units, or Weight (edible part unless footnotes indicate otherwise)	Weight (g)	Water (%)	Food Energy (kcal)	Protein (g)	Fat (g)
Milk desserts, frozen:						
Ice cream:						
Regular (about 11% fat):						
Hardened	½ gal	1,064	61	2,155	38	115
	1 c	133	61	270	5	14
	3-fl-oz container	50	61	100	2	5
Soft serve (frozen custard)	1 c	173	60	375	7	23
Rich (about 16% fat), hardened	½ gal	1,188	59	2,805	33	190
	1 c	148	59	350	4	24
Ice milk:						
Hardened (about 4.3% fat)	½ gal	1,048	69	1,470	41	45
	1 c	131	69	185	5	6
Soft serve (about 2.6% fat)	1 c	175	70	225	8	5
Sherbet (about 2% fat)	½ gal	1,542	66	2,160	17	31
	1 c	193	66	270	2	4
Milk desserts, other:						
Custard, baked	1 c	265	77	305	14	15
Puddings:						
From home recipe:						
Starch base:						
Chocolate	1 c	260	66	385	8	12
Vanilla (blancmange)	1 c	255	76	285	9	10
Tapioca cream	1 c	165	72	220	8	8
From mix (chocolate) and milk:						
Regular (cooked)	1 c	260	70	320	9	8
Instant	1 c	260	69	325	8	7
Yogurt:						
With added milk solids:						
Made with lowfat milk:						
Fruit-flavored[9]	8 oz	227	75	230	10	3
Plain	8 oz	227	85	145	12	4
Made with nonfat milk	8 oz	227	85	125	13	Trace
Without added milk solids:						
Made with whole milk	8 oz	227	88	140	8	7
Eggs						
Eggs, large (24 oz per dozen):						
Raw:						
Whole, without shell	1	50	75	80	6	6
White	1	33	88	15	3	Trace
Yolk	1	17	49	65	3	6
Cooked, whole:						
Fried in butter	1	46	72	85	5	6
Hard-cooked, shell removed	1	50	75	80	6	6
Poached	1	50	74	80	6	6
Scrambled (milk added) in butter (also omelet)	1	64	76	95	6	7
Fats, Oils; Related Products						
Butter:						
Regular (1 brick or 4 sticks per pound)						
Stick (½ c)	1 stick	113	16	815	1	92
Tablespoon (about ⅛ stick)	1 T	14	16	100	Trace	12
Pat (1-in. square, ⅓ in. high; 90 per pound)	1 pat	5	16	35	Trace	4

								Nutrients in Indicated Quantity					
	Fatty Acids												
Saturated (total) (g)	Unsaturated		Carbo-hydrate (g)	Calcium (mg)	Phos-phorus (mg)	Iron (mg)	Potassium (mg)	Vitamin A Value (IU)	Thiamin (mg)	Riboflavin (mg)	Niacin (mg)	Ascorbic Acid (mg)
	Oleic (g)	Linoleic (g)										
71.3	28.8	2.6	254	1,406	1,075	1.0	2,052	4,340	0.42	2.63	1.1	6
8.9	3.6	0.3	32	176	134	0.1	257	540	0.05	0.33	0.1	1
3.4	1.4	0.1	12	66	51	Trace	96	200	0.02	0.12	0.1	Trace
13.5	5.9	0.6	38	236	199	0.4	338	790	0.08	0.45	0.2	1
118.3	47.8	4.3	256	1,213	927	0.8	1,771	7,200	0.36	2.27	0.9	5
14.7	6.0	0.5	32	151	115	0.1	221	900	0.04	0.28	0.1	1
28.1	11.3	1.0	232	1,409	1,035	1.5	2,117	1,710	0.61	2.78	0.9	6
3.5	1.4	0.1	29	176	129	0.1	265	210	0.08	0.35	0.1	1
2.9	1.2	0.1	38	274	202	0.3	412	180	0.12	0.54	0.2	1
19.0	7.7	0.7	469	827	594	2.5	1,585	1,480	0.26	0.71	1.0	31
2.4	1.0	0.1	59	103	74	0.3	198	190	0.03	0.09	0.1	4
6.8	5.4	0.7	29	297	310	1.1	387	930	0.11	0.50	0.3	1
7.6	3.3	0.3	67	250	255	1.3	445	390	0.05	0.36	0.3	1
6.2	2.5	0.2	41	298	232	Trace	352	410	0.08	0.41	0.3	2
4.1	2.5	0.5	28	173	180	0.7	223	480	0.07	0.30	0.2	2
4.3	2.6	0.2	59	265	247	0.8	354	340	0.05	0.39	0.3	2
3.6	2.2	0.3	63	374	237	1.3	335	340	0.08	0.39	0.3	2
1.8	0.6	0.1	42	343	269	0.2	439	120[10]	0.08	0.40	0.2	1
2.3	0.8	0.1	16	415	326	0.2	531	150[10]	0.10	0.49	0.3	2
0.3	0.1	Trace	17	452	355	0.2	579	20[10]	0.11	0.53	0.3	2
4.8	1.7	0.1	11	274	215	0.1	351	280	0.07	0.32	0.2	1
1.7	2.0	0.6	1	28	90	1.0	65	260	0.04	0.15	Trace	0
0	0	0	Trace	4	4	Trace	45	0	Trace	0.09	Trace	0
1.7	2.1	0.6	Trace	26	86	0.9	15	310	0.04	0.07	Trace	0
2.4	2.2	0.6	1	26	80	0.9	58	290	0.03	0.13	Trace	0
1.7	2.0	0.6	1	28	90	1.0	65	260	0.04	0.14	Trace	0
1.7	2.0	0.6	1	28	90	1.0	65	260	0.04	0.13	Trace	0
2.8	2.3	0.6	1	47	97	0.9	85	310	0.04	0.16	Trace	0
57.3	23.1	2.1	Trace	27	26	0.2	29	3,470[11]	0.01	0.04	Trace	0
7.2	2.9	0.3	Trace	3	3	Trace	4	430[11]	Trace	Trace	Trace	0
2.5	1.0	0.1	Trace	1	1	Trace	1	150[11]	Trace	Trace	Trace	0

TABLE 6 (continued)

Food	Approximate Measures, Units, or Weight (edible part unless footnotes indicate otherwise)	Weight (g)	Water (%)	Food Energy (kcal)	Protein (g)	Fat (g)
Whipped (6 sticks or two 8-oz containers per pound)						
Stick (½ c)	1 stick	76	16	540	1	61
Tablespoon (about ⅛ stick)	1 T	9	16	65	Trace	8
Pat (1¼-in. square, ⅓ in. high; 120 per pound)	1 pat	4	16	25	Trace	3
Fats, cooking (vegetable shortenings)	1 c	200	0	1,770	0	200
	1 T	13	0	110	0	13
Lard	1 c	205	0	1,850	0	205
	1 T	13	0	115	0	13
Margarine:						
Regular (1 brick or 4 sticks per pound):						
Stick (½ c)	1 stick	113	16	815	1	92
Tablespoon (about ⅛ stick)	1 T	14	16	100	Trace	12
Pat (1-in. square, ⅓ in. high; 90 per pound)	1 pat	5	16	35	Trace	4
Soft, two 8-oz containers per pound	8 oz	227	16	1,635	1	184
	1 T	14	16	100	Trace	12
Whipped (6 sticks per pound):						
Stick (½ c)	1 stick	76	16	545	Trace	61
Tablespoon (about ⅛ stick)	1 T	9	16	70	Trace	8
Oils, salad or cooking:						
Corn	1 c	218	0	1,925	0	218
	1 T	14	0	120	0	14
Olive	1 c	216	0	1,910	0	216
	1 T	14	0	120	0	14
Peanut	1 c	216	0	1,910	0	216
	1 T	14	0	120	0	14
Safflower	1 c	218	0	1,925	0	218
	1 T	14	0	120	0	14
Soybean oil, hydrogenated (partially hardened)	1 c	218	0	1,925	0	218
	1 T	14	0	120	0	14
Soybean-cottonseed oil blend, hydrogenated	1 c	218	0	1,925	0	218
	1 T	14	0	120	0	14
Salad dressings:						
Commercial:						
Blue cheese:						
Regular	1 T	15	32	75	1	8
Low calorie (5 kcal per teaspoon)	1 T	16	84	10	Trace	1
French:						
Regular	1 T	16	39	65	Trace	6
Low calorie (5 kcal per teaspoon)	1 T	16	77	15	Trace	1
Italian:						
Regular	1 T	15	28	85	Trace	9
Low calorie (2 kcal per teaspoon)	1 T	15	90	10	Trace	1
Mayonnaise	1 T	14	15	100	Trace	11
Mayonnaise type:						
Regular	1 T	15	41	65	Trace	6
Low calorie (8 kcal per teaspoon)	1 T	16	81	20	Trace	2
Tartar sauce, regular	1 T	14	34	75	Trace	8
Thousand Island:						
Regular	1 T	16	32	80	Trace	8
Low calorie (10 kcal per teaspoon)	1 T	15	68	25	Trace	2

								Nutrients in Indicated Quantity					
Fatty Acids													
Saturated (total) (g)	Unsaturated		Carbo-hydrate (g)	Calcium (mg)	Phos-phorus (mg)	Iron (mg)	Potassium (mg)	Vitamin A	Thiamin (mg)	Riboflavin (mg)	Niacin (mg)	Ascorbic Acid (mg)
	Oleic (g)	Linoleic (g)						Value (IU)				
38.2	15.4	1.4	Trace	18	17	0.1	20	2,310[11]	Trace	0.03	Trace	0
4.7	1.9	0.2	Trace	2	2	Trace	2	290[11]	Trace	Trace	Trace	0
1.9	0.8	0.1	Trace	1	1	Trace	1	120[11]	0	Trace	Trace	0
48.8	88.2	48.4	0	0	0	0	0	—	0	0	0	0
3.2	5.7	3.1	0	0	0	0	0	—	0	0	0	0
81.0	83.8	20.5	0	0	0	0	0	0	0	0	0	0
5.1	5.3	1.3	0	0	0	0	0	0	0	0	0	0
16.7	42.9	24.9	Trace	27	26	0.2	29	3,750[12]	0.01	0.04	Trace	0
2.1	5.3	3.1	Trace	3	3	Trace	4	470[12]	Trace	Trace	Trace	0
0.7	1.9	1.1	Trace	1	1	Trace	1	170[12]	Trace	Trace	Trace	0
32.5	71.5	65.4	Trace	53	52	0.4	59	7,500[12]	0.01	0.08	0.1	0
2.0	4.5	4.1	Trace	3	3	Trace	4	470[12]	Trace	Trace	Trace	0
11.2	28.7	16.7	Trace	18	17	0.1	20	2,500[12]	Trace	0.03	Trace	0
1.4	3.6	2.1	Trace	2	2	Trace	2	310[12]	Trace	Trace	Trace	0
27.7	53.6	125.1	0	0	0	0	0	—	0	0	0	0
1.7	3.3	7.8	0	0	0	0	0	—	0	0	0	0
30.7	154.4	17.7	0	0	0	0	0	—	0	0	0	0
1.9	9.7	1.1	0	0	0	0	0	—	0	0	0	0
37.4	98.5	67.0	0	0	0	0	0	—	0	0	0	0
2.3	6.2	4.2	0	0	0	0	0	—	0	0	0	0
20.5	25.9	159.8	0	0	0	0	0	—	0	0	0	0
1.3	1.6	10.0	0	0	0	0	0	—	0	0	0	0
31.8	93.1	75.6	0	0	0	0	0	—	0	0	0	0
2.0	5.8	4.7	0	0	0	0	0	—	0	0	0	0
38.2	63.0	99.6	0	0	0	0	0	—	0	0	0	0
2.4	3.9	6.2	0	0	0	0	0	—	0	0	0	0
1.6	1.7	3.8	1	12	11	Trace	6	30	Trace	0.02	Trace	Trace
0.5	0.3	Trace	1	10	8	Trace	5	30	Trace	0.01	Trace	Trace
1.1	1.3	3.2	3	2	2	0.1	13	—	—	—	—	—
0.1	0.1	0.4	2	2	2	0.1	13	—	—	—	—	—
1.6	1.9	4.7	1	2	1	Trace	2	Trace	Trace	Trace	Trace	—
0.1	0.1	0.4	Trace	Trace	1	Trace	2	Trace	Trace	Trace	Trace	—
2.0	2.4	5.6	Trace	3	4	0.1	5	40	Trace	0.01	Trace	—
1.1	1.4	3.2	2	2	4	Trace	1	30	Trace	Trace	Trace	—
0.4	0.4	1.0	2	3	4	Trace	1	40	Trace	Trace	Trace	—
1.5	1.8	4.1	1	3	4	0.1	11	30	Trace	Trace	Trace	Trace
1.4	1.7	4.0	2	2	3	0.1	18	50	Trace	Trace	Trace	Trace
0.4	0.4	1.0	2	2	3	0.1	17	50	Trace	Trace	Trace	Trace

TABLE 6   (continued)

Food	Approximate Measures, Units, or Weight (edible part unless footnotes indicate otherwise)	Weight (g)	Water (%)	Food Energy (kcal)	Protein (g)	Fat (g)
Homemade:						
Cooked type [13]	1 T	16	68	25	1	2
Fish, Shellfish, Meat, Poultry; Related Products						
Fish and shellfish:						
Bluefish, baked with butter or margarine	3 oz	85	68	135	22	4
Clams:						
Raw, meat only	3 oz	85	82	65	11	1
Canned, solids and liquid	3 oz	85	86	45	7	1
Crabmeat (white or king), canned, not pressed down	1 c	135	77	135	24	3
Fish stick, breaded, cooked, frozen (4 × 1 × ½ in.)	1 fish stick or 1 oz	28	66	50	5	3
Haddock, breaded, fried [14]	3 oz	85	66	140	17	5
Ocean perch, breaded, fried [14]	1 fillet	85	59	195	16	11
Oysters, raw, meat only (13–19 medium selects)	1 c	240	85	160	20	4
Salmon, pink, canned, solids and liquid	3 oz	85	71	120	17	5
Sardines, Atlantic, canned in oil, drained solids	3 oz	85	62	175	20	9
Scallops, frozen, breaded, fried, reheated	6	90	60	175	16	8
Shad, baked with butter or margarine and bacon	3 oz	85	64	170	20	10
Shrimp:						
Canned meat	3 oz	85	70	100	21	1
French fried [16]	3 oz	85	57	190	17	9
Tuna, canned in oil, drained solids	3 oz	85	61	170	24	7
Tuna salad [17]	1 c	205	70	350	30	22
Meat and meat products:						
Bacon (20 slices per pound, raw), broiled or fried, crisp	2 slices	15	8	85	4	8
Beef, canned:						
Corned beef	3 oz	85	59	185	22	10
Corned beef hash	1 c	220	67	400	19	25
Beef,[18] cooked:						
Cuts braised, simmered, or pot-roasted:						
Lean and fat (piece, 2½ × 2½ × ¾ in.)	3 oz	85	53	245	23	16
Lean only	2.5 oz	72	62	140	22	5
Ground beef, broiled:						
Lean with 10% fat patty	3 oz	85	60	185	23	10
Lean with 21% fat patty	2.9 oz	82	54	235	20	17
Roast, oven-cooked, no liquid added:						
Relatively fat, such as rib:						
Lean and fat (2 pieces, 4⅛ × 2¼ × ¼ in.)	3 oz	85	40	375	17	33
Lean only	1.8 oz	51	57	125	14	7
Relatively lean, such as heel of round:						
Lean and fat (2 pieces, 4⅛ × 2¼ × ¼ in.)	3 oz	85	62	165	25	7
Lean only	2.8 oz	78	65	125	24	3
Steak:						
Relatively fat, such as sirloin, broiled:						
Lean and fat (piece, 2½ × 2½ × ¾ in.)	3 oz	85	44	330	20	27
Lean only	2.0 oz	56	59	115	18	4

| Fatty Acids | | | | | | | | Vitamin A | | | | Ascorbic |
Saturated (total) (g)	Unsaturated Oleic (g)	Linoleic (g)	Carbohydrate (g)	Calcium (mg)	Phosphorus (mg)	Iron (mg)	Potassium (mg)	Value (IU)	Thiamin (mg)	Riboflavin (mg)	Niacin (mg)	Acid (mg)
0.5	0.6	0.3	2	14	15	0.1	19	80	0.01	0.03	Trace	Trace
—	—	—	0	25	244	0.6	—	40	0.09	0.08	1.6	—
—	—	—	2	59	138	5.2	154	90	0.08	0.15	1.1	8
0.2	Trace	Trace	2	47	116	3.5	119	—	0.01	0.09	0.9	—
0.6	0.4	0.1	1	61	246	1.1	149	—	0.11	0.11	2.6	—
—	—	—	2	3	47	0.1	—	0	0.01	0.02	0.5	—
1.4	2.2	1.2	5	34	210	1.0	296	—	0.03	0.06	2.7	2
2.7	4.4	2.3	6	28	192	1.1	242	—	0.10	0.10	1.6	—
1.3	0.2	0.1	8	226	343	13.2	290	740	0.34	0.43	6.0	—
0.9	0.8	0.1	0	167[15]	243	0.7	307	60	0.03	0.16	6.8	—
3.0	2.5	0.5	0	372	424	2.5	502	190	0.02	0.17	4.6	—
—	—	—	9	—	—	—	—	—	—	—	—	—
—	—	—	0	20	266	0.5	320	30	0.11	0.22	7.3	—
0.1	0.1	Trace	1	98	224	2.6	104	50	0.01	0.03	1.5	—
2.3	3.7	2.0	9	61	162	1.7	195	—	0.03	0.07	2.3	—
1.7	1.7	0.7	0	7	199	1.6	—	70	0.04	0.10	10.1	—
4.3	6.3	6.7	7	41	291	2.7	—	590	0.08	0.23	10.3	2
2.5	3.7	0.7	Trace	2	34	0.5	35	0	0.08	0.05	0.8	—
4.9	4.5	0.2	0	17	90	3.7	—	—	0.01	0.20	2.9	—
11.9	10.9	0.5	24	29	147	4.4	440	—	0.02	0.20	4.6	—
6.8	6.5	0.4	0	10	114	2.9	184	30	0.04	0.18	3.6	—
2.1	1.8	0.2	0	10	108	2.7	176	10	0.04	0.17	3.3	—
4.0	3.9	0.3	0	10	196	3.0	261	20	0.08	0.20	5.1	—
7.0	6.7	0.4	0	9	159	2.6	221	30	0.07	0.17	4.4	—
14.0	13.6	0.8	0	8	158	2.2	189	70	0.05	0.13	3.1	—
3.0	2.5	0.3	0	6	131	1.8	161	10	0.04	0.11	2.6	—
2.8	2.7	0.2	0	11	208	3.2	279	10	0.06	0.19	4.5	—
1.2	1.0	0.1	0	10	199	3.0	268	Trace	0.06	0.18	4.3	—
11.3	11.1	0.6	0	9	162	2.5	220	50	0.05	0.15	4.0	—
1.8	1.6	0.2	0	7	146	2.2	202	10	0.05	0.14	3.6	—

Nutrients in Indicated Quantity

TABLE 6 (continued)

Food	Approximate Measures, Units, or Weight (edible part unless footnotes indicate otherwise)	Weight (g)	Water (%)	Food Energy (kcal)	Protein (g)	Fat (g)
Relatively lean, such as round, braised:						
Lean and fat (piece, 4⅛ × 2¼ × ½ in.)	3 oz	85	55	220	24	13
Lean only	2.4 oz	68	61	130	21	4
Beef, dried, chipped	2½-oz	71	48	145	24	4
Beef and vegetable stew	1 c	245	82	220	16	11
Beef potpie (homemade), baked[19] (piece, ⅓ of 9-in.-diam. pie)	1 piece	210	55	515	21	30
Chili con carne with beans, canned	1 c	255	72	340	19	16
Chop suey with beef and pork (homemade)	1 c	250	75	300	26	17
Heart, beef, lean, braised	3 oz	85	61	160	27	5
Lamb, cooked:						
Chop, rib (cut 3 per pound with bone), broiled:						
Lean and fat	3.1 oz	89	43	360	18	32
Lean only	2 oz	57	60	120	16	6
Leg, roasted:						
Lean and fat (2 pieces, 4⅛ × 2¼ × ¼ in.)	3 oz	85	54	235	22	16
Lean only	2.5 oz	71	62	130	20	5
Shoulder, roasted:						
Lean and fat (3 pieces, 2½ × 2½ × ¼ in.)	3 oz	85	50	285	18	23
Lean only	2.3 oz	64	61	130	17	6
Liver, beef, fried[20] (slice, 6½ × 2⅜ × ⅜ in.)	3 oz	85	56	195	22	9
Pork, cured, cooked:						
Ham, light cure, lean and fat, roasted (2 pieces, 4⅛ × 2¼ × ¼ in.)[22]	3 oz	85	54	245	18	19
Luncheon meat:						
Boiled ham, slice	1 oz	28	59	65	5	5
Canned, spiced or unspiced:						
Slice, 3 × 2 × ½ in.	1 slice	60	55	175	9	15
Pork, fresh, cooked:[18]						
Chop, loin (cut 3 per pound with bone), broiled:						
Lean and fat	2.7 oz	78	42	305	19	25
Lean only	2 oz	56	53	150	17	9
Roast, oven-cooked, no liquid added:						
Lean and fat (piece, 2½ × 2½ × ¾ in.)	3 oz	85	46	310	21	24
Lean only	2.4 oz	68	55	175	20	10
Shoulder cut, simmered:						
Lean and fat (3 pieces, 2½ × 2½ × ¼ in.)	3 oz	85	46	320	20	26
Lean only	2.2 oz	63	60	135	18	6
Sausages (see also Luncheon meat):						
Bologna, slice	1 oz	28	56	85	3	8
Braunschweiger, slice	1 oz	28	53	90	4	8
Brown-and-serve (10 to 11 per 8-oz package), browned	1 link	17	40	70	3	6
Deviled ham, canned	1 T	13	51	45	2	4
Frankfurter (8 per 1-lb package), cooked (reheated)	1	56	57	170	7	15

| | Nutrients in Indicated Quantity | | | | | | | | | | | |
| Fatty Acids | | | | | | | | | | | | |
Saturated (total) (g)	Unsaturated Oleic (g)	Unsaturated Linoleic (g)	Carbo-hydrate (g)	Calcium (mg)	Phos-phorus (mg)	Iron (mg)	Potassium (mg)	Vitamin A Value (IU)	Thiamin (mg)	Riboflavin (mg)	Niacin (mg)	Ascorbic Acid (mg)
5.5	5.2	0.4	0	10	213	3.0	272	20	0.07	0.19	4.8	—
1.7	1.5	0.2	0	9	182	2.5	238	10	0.05	0.16	4.1	—
2.1	2.0	0.1	0	14	287	3.6	142	—	0.05	0.23	2.7	0
4.9	4.5	0.2	15	29	184	2.9	613	2,400	0.15	0.17	4.7	17
7.9	12.8	6.7	39	29	149	3.8	334	1,720	0.30	0.30	5.5	6
7.5	6.8	0.3	31	82	321	4.3	594	150	0.08	0.18	3.3	—
8.5	6.2	0.7	13	60	248	4.8	425	600	0.28	0.38	5.0	33
1.5	1.1	0.6	1	5	154	5.0	197	20	0.21	1.04	6.5	1
14.8	12.1	1.2	0	8	139	1.0	200	—	0.11	0.19	4.1	—
2.5	2.1	0.2	0	6	121	1.1	174	—	0.09	0.15	3.4	—
7.3	6.0	0.6	0	9	177	1.4	241	—	0.13	0.23	4.7	—
2.1	1.8	0.2	0	9	169	1.4	227	—	0.12	0.21	4.4	—
10.8	8.8	0.9	0	9	146	1.0	206	—	0.11	0.20	4.0	—
3.6	2.3	0.2	0	8	140	1.0	193	—	0.10	0.18	3.7	—
2.5	3.5	0.9	5	9	405	7.5	323	45,390[21]	0.22	3.56	14.0	23
6.8	7.9	1.7	0	8	146	2.2	199	0	0.40	0.15	3.1	—
1.7	2.0	0.4	0	3	47	0.8	—	0	0.12	0.04	0.7	—
5.4	6.7	1.0	1	5	65	1.3	133	0	0.19	0.13	1.8	—
8.9	10.4	2.2	0	9	209	2.7	216	0	0.75	0.22	4.5	—
3.1	3.6	0.8	0	7	181	2.2	192	0	0.63	0.18	3.8	—
8.7	10.2	2.2	0	9	218	2.7	233	0	0.78	0.22	4.8	—
3.5	4.1	0.8	0	9	211	2.6	224	0	0.73	0.21	4.4	—
9.3	10.9	2.3	0	9	118	2.6	158	0	0.46	0.21	4.1	—
2.2	2.6	0.6	0	8	111	2.3	146	0	0.42	0.19	3.7	—
3.0	3.4	0.5	Trace	2	36	0.5	65	—	0.05	0.06	0.7	—
2.6	3.4	0.8	1	3	69	1.7	—	1,850	0.05	0.41	2.3	—
2.3	2.8	0.7	Trace	—	—	—	—	—	—	—	—	—
1.5	1.8	0.4	0	1	12	0.3	—	0	0.02	0.01	0.2	—
5.6	6.5	1.2	1	3	57	0.8	—	—	0.08	0.11	1.4	—

TABLE 6 (continued)

Food	Approximate Measures, Units, or Weight (edible part unless footnotes indicate otherwise)	Weight (g)	Water (%)	Food Energy (kcal)	Protein (g)	Fat (g)
Meat, potted (beef, chicken, turkey), canned	1 T	13	61	30	2	2
Pork link (16 per 1-lb package), cooked	1 link	13	35	60	2	6
Salami:						
Dry type, slice (12 per 4-oz package)	1 slice	10	30	45	2	4
Cooked type, slice (8 per 8-oz package)	1 slice	28	51	90	5	7
Vienna sausage (7 per 4-oz can)	1	16	63	40	2	3
Veal, medium fat, cooked, bone removed:						
Cutlet (4⅛ × 2¼ × ½ in.), braised or broiled	3 oz	85	60	185	23	9
Rib (2 pieces, 4⅛ × 2¼ × ¼ in.), roasted	3 oz	85	55	230	23	14
Poultry and poultry products:						
Chicken, cooked:						
Breast, fried,[23] bones removed, ½ breast (3.3 oz with bones)	2.8 oz	79	58	160	26	5
Drumstick, fried,[23] bones removed (2 oz with bones)	1.3 oz	38	55	90	12	4
Half broiler, broiled, bones removed (10.4 oz with bones)	6.2 oz	176	71	240	42	7
Chicken, canned, boneless	3 oz	85	65	170	18	10
Chicken a la king, cooked (homemade)	1 c	245	68	470	27	34
Chicken and noodles, cooked (homemade)	1 c	240	71	365	22	18
Chicken chow mein:						
Canned	1 c	250	89	95	7	Trace
Homemade	1 c	250	78	255	31	10
Chicken potpie (homemade), baked,[19] piece (⅓ of 9-in.-diam. pie)	1 piece	232	57	545	23	31
Turkey, roasted, flesh without skin:						
Dark meat, piece, 2½ × 1⅝ × ¼ in.	4 pieces	85	61	175	26	7
Light and dark meat:						
Chopped or diced	1 c	140	61	265	44	9
Pieces (1 slice white meat, 4 × 2 × ¼ in., and 2 slices dark meat, 2½ × 1⅝ × ¼ in.)	3 pieces	85	61	160	27	5
Light meat, piece, 4 × 2 × ¼ in.	2 pieces	85	62	150	28	3
Fruits and Fruit Products						
Apples, raw, unpeeled, without cores:						
2¾-in. diam. (about 3 per pound with cores)	1	138	84	80	Trace	1
3¼-in. diam. (about 2 per pound with cores)	1	212	84	125	Trace	1
Apple juice, bottled or canned[24]	1 c	248	88	120	Trace	Trace
Applesauce, canned:						
Sweetened	1 c	255	76	230	1	Trace
Unsweetened	1 c	244	89	100	Trace	Trace
Apricots:						
Raw, without pits (about 12 per pound with pits)	3	107	85	55	1	Trace
Canned in heavy syrup (halves and syrup)	1 c	258	77	220	2	Trace
Dried:						
Uncooked (28 large or 37 medium halves per cup)	1 c	130	25	340	7	1
Cooked, unsweetened, fruit and liquid	1 c	250	76	215	4	1
Apricot nectar, canned	1 c	251	85	145	1	Trace

Nutrients in Indicated Quantity												
Fatty Acids												
Saturated (total) (g)	Unsaturated Oleic (g)	Unsaturated Linoleic (g)	Carbo-hydrate (g)	Calcium (mg)	Phos-phorus (mg)	Iron (mg)	Potassium (mg)	Vitamin A Value (IU)	Thiamin (mg)	Riboflavin (mg)	Niacin (mg)	Ascorbic Acid (mg)
—	—	—	0	—	—	—	—	—	Trace	0.03	0.2	—
2.1	2.4	0.5	Trace	1	21	0.3	35	0	0.10	0.04	0.5	—
1.6	1.6	0.1	Trace	1	28	0.4	—	—	0.04	0.03	0.5	—
3.1	3.0	0.2	Trace	3	57	0.7	—	—	0.07	0.07	1.2	—
1.2	1.4	0.2	Trace	1	24	0.3	—	—	0.01	0.02	0.4	—
4.0	3.4	0.4	0	9	196	2.7	258	—	0.06	0.21	4.6	—
6.1	5.1	0.6	0	10	211	2.9	259	—	0.11	0.26	6.6	—
1.4	1.8	1.1	1	9	218	1.3	—	70	0.04	0.17	11.6	—
1.1	1.3	0.9	Trace	6	89	0.9	—	50	0.03	0.15	2.7	—
2.2	2.5	1.3	0	16	355	3.0	483	160	0.09	0.34	15.5	—
3.2	3.8	2.0	0	18	210	1.3	117	200	0.03	0.11	3.7	3
12.7	14.3	3.3	12	127	358	2.5	404	1,130	0.10	0.42	5.4	12
5.9	7.1	3.5	26	26	247	2.2	149	430	0.05	0.17	4.3	Trace
—	—	—	18	45	35	1.3	418	150	0.05	0.10	1.0	13
2.4	3.4	3.1	10	58	293	2.5	473	280	0.08	0.23	4.3	10
11.3	10.9	5.6	42	70	232	3.0	343	3,090	0.34	0.31	5.5	5
2.1	1.5	1.5	0	—	—	2.0	338	—	0.03	0.20	3.6	—
2.5	1.7	1.8	0	11	351	2.5	514	—	0.07	0.25	10.8	—
1.5	1.0	1.1	0	7	213	1.5	312	—	0.04	0.15	6.5	—
0.9	0.6	0.7	0	—	—	1.0	349	—	0.04	0.12	9.4	—
—	—	—	20	10	14	0.4	152	120	0.04	0.03	0.1	6
—	—	—	31	15	21	0.6	233	190	0.06	0.04	0.2	8
—	—	—	30	15	22	1.5	250	—	0.02	0.05	0.2	2[25]
—	—	—	61	10	13	1.3	166	100	0.05	0.03	0.1	3[25]
—	—	—	26	10	12	1.2	190	100	0.05	0.02	0.1	2[25]
—	—	—	14	18	25	0.5	301	2,890	0.03	0.04	0.6	11
—	—	—	57	28	39	0.8	604	4,490	0.05	0.05	1.0	10
—	—	—	86	87	140	7.2	1,273	14,170	0.01	0.21	4.3	16
—	—	—	54	55	88	4.5	795	7,500	0.01	0.13	2.5	8
—	—	—	37	23	30	0.5	379	2,380	0.03	0.03	0.5	36[26]

TABLE 6 (continued)

Food	Approximate Measures, Units, or Weight (edible part unless footnotes indicate otherwise)	Weight (g)	Water (%)	Food Energy (kcal)	Protein (g)	Fat (g)
Avocados, raw, whole, without skins and seeds:						
California, mid- and late-winter (with skin and seed, 3⅛-in. diam.; 10 oz)	1	216	74	370	5	37
Florida, late summer and fall (with skin and seed, 3⅝-in. diam.; 1 lb)	1	304	78	390	4	33
Banana, without peel (about 2.6 per pound with peel)	1	119	76	100	1	Trace
Banana flakes	1 T	6	3	20	Trace	Trace
Blackberries, raw	1 c	144	85	85	2	1
Blueberries, raw	1 c	145	83	90	1	1
Cantaloupe. See Muskmelons.						
Cherries:						
Sour (tart), red, pitted, canned, water pack	1 c	244	88	105	2	Trace
Sweet, raw, without pits and stems	10	68	80	45	1	Trace
Cranberry juice cocktail, bottled, sweetened	1 c	253	83	165	Trace	Trace
Cranberry sauce, sweetened, canned, strained	1 c	277	62	405	Trace	1
Dates:						
Whole, without pits	10	80	23	220	2	Trace
Chopped	1 c	178	23	490	4	1
Fruit cocktail, canned, in heavy syrup	1 c	255	80	195	1	Trace
Grapefruit:						
Raw, medium, 3¾-in. diam. (about 1 lb 1 oz):						
Pink or red, with peel	½	241[28]	89	50	1	Trace
White, with peel	½	241[28]	89	45	1	Trace
Canned, sections with syrup	1 c	254	81	180	2	Trace
Grapefruit juice:						
Raw, pink, red, or white	1 c	246	90	95	1	Trace
Canned, white:						
Unsweetened	1 c	247	89	100	1	Trace
Sweetened	1 c	250	86	135	1	Trace
Frozen, concentrate, unsweetened:						
Undiluted	6 fl oz	207	62	300	4	1
Diluted with 3 parts water by volume	1 c	247	89	100	1	Trace
Dehydrated crystals, prepared with water (1 lb yields about 1 gal)	1 c	247	90	100	1	Trace
Grapes, European type (adherent skin), raw:						
Thompson seedless	10	50	81	35	Trace	Trace
Tokay and Emperor (seeded)	10	60[30]	81	40	Trace	Trace
Grape juice:						
Canned or bottled	1 c	253	83	165	1	Trace
Frozen concentrate, sweetened:						
Undiluted	6 fl oz	216	53	395	1	Trace
Diluted with 3 parts water by volume	1 c	250	86	135	1	Trace
Grape drink, canned	1 c	250	86	135	Trace	Trace
Lemon, raw, size 165, without peel and seeds (about 4 per pound with peels and seeds)	1	74	90	20	1	Trace
Lemonade concentrate, frozen:						
Undiluted	6 fl oz	219	49	425	Trace	Trace
Diluted with 4⅓ parts water by volume	1 c	248	89	105	Trace	Trace
Lemon juice:						
Raw	1 c	244	91	60	1	Trace

Nutrients in Indicated Quantity												
Fatty Acids												
Saturated (total) (g)	**Unsaturated**		Carbo-hydrate (g)	Calcium (mg)	Phos-phorus (mg)	Iron (mg)	Potassium (mg)	Vitamin A Value (IU)	Thiamin (mg)	Riboflavin (mg)	Niacin (mg)	Ascorbic Acid (mg)
	Oleic (g)	Linoleic (g)										
5.5	22.0	3.7	13	22	91	1.3	1,303	630	0.24	0.43	3.5	30
6.7	15.7	5.3	27	30	128	1.8	1,836	880	0.33	0.61	4.9	43
—	—	—	26	10	31	0.8	440	230	0.06	0.07	0.8	12
—	—	—	5	2	6	0.2	92	50	0.01	0.01	0.2	Trace
—	—	—	19	46	27	1.3	245	290	0.04	0.06	0.6	30
—	—	—	22	22	19	1.5	117	150	0.04	0.09	0.7	20
—	—	—	26	37	32	0.7	317	1,660	0.07	0.05	0.5	12
—	—	—	12	15	13	0.3	129	70	0.03	0.04	0.3	7
—	—	—	42	13	8	0.8	25	Trace	0.03	0.03	0.1	81[27]
—	—	—	104	17	11	0.6	83	60	0.03	0.03	0.1	6
—	—	—	58	47	50	2.4	518	40	0.07	0.08	1.8	0
—	—	—	130	105	112	5.3	1,153	90	0.16	0.18	3.9	0
—	—	—	50	23	31	1.0	411	360	0.05	0.03	1.0	5
—	—	—	13	20	20	0.5	166	540	0.05	0.02	0.2	44
—	—	—	12	19	19	0.5	159	10	0.05	0.02	0.2	44
—	—	—	45	33	36	0.8	343	30	0.08	0.05	0.5	76
—	—	—	23	22	37	0.5	399	[29]	0.10	0.05	0.5	93
—	—	—	24	20	35	1.0	400	20	0.07	0.05	0.5	84
—	—	—	32	20	35	1.0	405	30	0.08	0.05	0.5	78
—	—	—	72	70	124	0.8	1,250	60	0.29	0.12	1.4	286
—	—	—	24	25	42	0.2	420	20	0.10	0.04	0.5	96
—	—	—	24	22	40	0.2	412	20	0.10	0.05	0.5	91
—	—	—	9	6	10	0.2	87	50	0.03	0.02	0.2	2
—	—	—	10	7	11	0.2	99	60	0.03	0.02	0.2	2
—	—	—	42	28	30	0.8	293	—	0.10	0.05	0.5	Trace[25]
—	—	—	100	22	32	0.9	255	40	0.13	0.22	1.5	32[31]
—	—	—	33	8	10	0.3	85	10	0.05	0.08	0.5	10[31]
—	—	—	35	8	10	0.3	88	—	0.03[32]	0.03[32]	0.3	[32]
—	—	—	6	19	12	0.4	102	10	0.03	0.01	0.1	39
—	—	—	112	9	13	0.4	153	40	0.05	0.06	0.7	66
—	—	—	28	2	3	0.1	40	10	0.01	0.02	0.2	17
—	—	—	20	17	24	0.5	344	50	0.07	0.02	0.2	112

TABLE 6   (continued)

Food	Approximate Measures, Units, or Weight (edible part unless footnotes indicate otherwise)	Weight (g)	Water (%)	Food Energy (kcal)	Protein (g)	Fat (g)
Canned or bottled, unsweetened	1 c	244	92	55	1	Trace
Frozen, single strength, unsweetened	6 oz	183	92	40	1	Trace
Limeade concentrate, frozen:						
Undiluted	6 fl oz	218	50	410	Trace	Trace
Diluted with 4⅓ parts water by volume	1 c	247	89	100	Trace	Trace
Lime juice:						
Raw	1 c	246	90	65	1	Trace
Canned, unsweetened	1 c	246	90	65	1	Trace
Muskmelons, raw, with rind, without seed cavity:						
Cantaloupe, orange-fleshed (with rind and seed cavity, 5-in. diam., 2⅓ lb), with rind	½	477[33]	91	80	2	Trace
Honeydew (with rind and seed cavity, 6½-in. diam., 5¼ lb), with rind	¹/₁₀	226[33]	91	50	1	Trace
Oranges, all commercial varieties, raw:						
Whole, 2⅝-in. diam., without peel and seeds (about 2½ per pound with peel and seeds)	1	131	86	65	1	Trace
Sections without membranes	1 c	180	86	90	2	Trace
Orange juice:						
Raw, all varieties	1 c	248	88	110	2	Trace
Canned, unsweetened	1 c	249	87	120	2	Trace
Frozen concentrate:						
Undiluted	6 fl oz	213	55	360	5	Trace
Diluted with 3 parts water by volume	1 c	249	87	120	2	Trace
Dehydrated crystals, prepared with water (1 lb yields about 1 gal)	1 c	248	88	115	1	Trace
Orange and grapefruit juice:						
Frozen concentrate:						
Undiluted	6 fl oz	210	59	330	4	1
Diluted with 3 parts water by volume	1 c	248	88	110	1	Trace
Papayas, raw, ½-in. cubes	1 c	140	89	55	1	Trace
Peaches:						
Raw:						
Whole, 2½-in. diam., peeled, pitted (about 4 per pound with peels and pits)	1	100	89	40	1	Trace
Sliced	1 c	170	89	65	1	Trace
Canned, yellow-fleshed, solids and liquid (halves or slices):						
Syrup pack	1 c	256	79	200	1	Trace
Water pack	1 c	244	91	75	1	Trace
Dried:						
Uncooked	1 c	160	25	420	5	1
Cooked, unsweetened, halves and juice	1 c	250	77	205	3	1
Frozen, sliced, sweetened:						
10-oz container	1 container	284	77	250	1	Trace
Cup	1 c	250	77	220	1	Trace
Pears:						
Raw, with skin, cored:						
Anjou, 3-in. diam. (about 2 per pound with cores and stems)	1	200	83	120	1	1
Bartlett, 2½-in. diam. (about 2½ per pound with cores and stems)	1	164	83	100	1	1

	Nutrients in Indicated Quantity											
Fatty Acids												
Saturated (total) (g)	Unsaturated		Carbo-hydrate (g)	Calcium (mg)	Phos-phorus (mg)	Iron (mg)	Potassium (mg)	Vitamin A Value (IU)	Thiamin (mg)	Riboflavin (mg)	Niacin (mg)	Ascorbic Acid (mg)
	Oleic (g)	Linoleic (g)										
—	—	—	19	17	24	0.5	344	50	0.07	0.02	0.2	102
—	—	—	13	13	16	0.5	258	40	0.05	0.02	0.2	81
—	—	—	108	11	13	0.2	129	Trace	0.02	0.02	0.2	26
—	—	—	27	3	3	Trace	32	Trace	Trace	Trace	Trace	6
—	—	—	22	22	27	0.5	256	20	0.05	0.02	0.2	79
—	—	—	22	22	27	0.5	256	20	0.05	0.02	0.2	52
—	—	—	20	38	44	1.1	682	9,240	0.11	0.08	1.6	90
—	—	—	11	21	24	0.6	374	60	0.06	0.04	0.9	34
—	—	—	16	54	26	0.5	263	260	0.13	0.05	0.5	66
—	—	—	22	74	36	0.7	360	360	0.18	0.07	0.7	90
—	—	—	26	27	42	0.5	496	500	0.22	0.07	1.0	124
—	—	—	28	25	45	1.0	496	500	0.17	0.05	0.7	100
—	—	—	87	75	126	0.9	1,500	1,620	0.68	0.11	2.8	360
—	—	—	29	25	42	0.2	503	540	0.23	0.03	0.9	120
—	—	—	27	25	40	0.5	518	500	0.20	0.07	1.0	109
—	—	—	78	61	99	0.8	1,308	800	0.48	0.06	2.3	302
—	—	—	26	20	32	0.2	439	270	0.15	0.02	0.7	102
—	—	—	14	28	22	0.4	328	2,450	0.06	0.06	0.4	78
—	—	—	10	9	19	0.5	202	1,330[34]	0.02	0.05	1.0	7
—	—	—	16	15	32	0.9	343	2,260[34]	0.03	0.09	1.7	12
—	—	—	51	10	31	0.8	333	1,100	0.03	0.05	1.5	8
—	—	—	20	10	32	0.7	334	1,100	0.02	0.07	1.5	7
—	—	—	109	77	187	9.6	1,520	6,240	0.02	0.30	8.5	29
—	—	—	54	38	93	4.8	743	3,050	0.01	0.15	3.8	5
—	—	—	64	11	37	1.4	352	1,850	0.03	0.11	2.0	116[35]
—	—	—	57	10	33	1.3	310	1,630	0.03	0.10	1.8	103[35]
—	—	—	31	16	22	0.6	260	40	0.04	0.08	0.2	8
—	—	—	25	13	18	0.5	213	30	0.03	0.07	0.2	7

TABLE 6 (continued)

Food	Approximate Measures, Units, or Weight (edible part unless footnotes indicate otherwise)	Weight (g)	Water (%)	Food Energy (kcal)	Protein (g)	Fat (g)
Bosc, 2½-in. diam. (about 3 per pound with cores and stems)	1	141	83	85	1	1
Canned, solids and liquid, syrup pack, heavy (halves or slices)	1 c	255	80	195	1	1
Pineapple:						
Raw, diced	1 c	155	85	80	1	Trace
Canned, heavy syrup pack, solids and liquid:						
Crushed, chunks, tidbits	1 c	255	80	190	1	Trace
Slices and liquid:						
Large	1 slice; 2¼ T liquid	105	80	80	Trace	Trace
Medium	1 slice; 1¼ T liquid	58	80	45	Trace	Trace
Pineapple juice, unsweetened, canned	1 c	250	86	140	1	Trace
Plums:						
Raw, without pits:						
Japanese and hybrid (2⅛-in. diam., about 6½ per pound with pits)	1	66	87	30	Trace	Trace
Prune-type (1½-in. diam., about 15 per pound with pits)	1	28	79	20	Trace	Trace
Canned, heavy syrup pack (Italian prunes), with pits and liquid:						
Cup	1 c[36]	272	77	215	1	Trace
Portion	3; 2¾ T liquid[36]	140	77	110	1	Trace
Prunes, dried, "softenized," with pits:						
Uncooked	4 extra large or 5 large	49[36]	28	110	1	Trace
Cooked, unsweetened, all sizes, fruit and liquid	1 c	250[36]	66	255	2	1
Prune juice, canned or bottles	1 c	256	80	195	1	Trace
Raisins, seedless:						
Cup, not pressed down	1 c	145	18	420	4	Trace
Packet, ½ oz (1½ T)	1 packet	14	18	40	Trace	Trace
Raspberries, red:						
Raw, capped, whole	1 c	123	84	70	1	1
Frozen, sweetened	10 oz	284	74	280	2	1
Rhubarb, cooked, added sugar:						
From raw	1 c	270	63	380	1	Trace
From frozen, sweetened	1 c	270	63	385	1	1
Strawberries:						
Raw, whole berries, capped	1 c	149	90	55	1	1
Frozen, sweetened:						
Sliced	10 oz	284	71	310	1	1
Whole	1 lb (about 1¾ c)	454	76	415	2	1
Tangerine, raw, 2⅜-in. diam., size 176, without peel (about 4 per pound with peels and seeds)	1	86	87	40	1	Trace
Tangerine juice, canned, sweetened	1 c	249	87	125	1	Trace
Watermelon, raw, 4 × 8 in. wedge with rind and seeds (1/16 of 32⅔-lb melon, 10 × 16 in.),	1	926[37]	93	110	2	1
Grain Products						
Bagel, 3-in. diam.:						
Egg	1	55	32	165	6	2
Water	1	55	29	165	6	1
Barley, pearled, light, uncooked	1 c	200	11	700	16	2

	Fatty Acids		Carbo-hydrate (g)	Calcium (mg)	Phos-phorus (mg)	Iron (mg)	Potassium (mg)	Vitamin A Value (IU)	Thiamin (mg)	Riboflavin (mg)	Niacin (mg)	Ascorbic Acid (mg)
Saturated (total) (g)	Unsaturated											
	Oleic (g)	Linoleic (g)										
—	—	—	22	11	16	0.4	83	30	0.03	0.06	0.1	6
—	—	—	50	13	18	0.5	214	10	0.03	0.05	0.3	3
—	—	—	21	26	12	0.8	226	110	0.14	0.05	0.3	26
—	—	—	49	28	13	0.8	245	130	0.20	0.05	0.5	18
—	—	—	20	12	5	0.3	101	50	0.08	0.02	0.2	7
—	—	—	11	6	3	0.2	56	30	0.05	0.01	0.1	4
—	—	—	34	38	23	0.8	373	130	0.13	0.05	0.5	80[27]
—	—	—	8	8	12	0.3	112	160	0.02	0.02	0.3	4
—	—	—	6	3	5	0.1	48	80	0.01	0.01	0.1	1
—	—	—	56	23	26	2.3	367	3,130	0.05	0.05	1.0	5
—	—	—	29	12	13	1.2	189	1,610	0.03	0.03	0.5	3
—	—	—	29	22	34	1.7	298	690	0.04	0.07	0.7	1
—	—	—	67	51	79	3.8	695	1,590	0.07	0.15	1.5	2
—	—	—	49	36	51	1.8	602	—	0.03	0.03	1.0	5
—	—	—	112	90	146	5.1	1,106	30	0.16	0.12	0.7	1
—	—	—	11	9	14	0.5	107	Trace	0.02	0.01	0.1	Trace
—	—	—	17	27	27	1.1	207	160	0.04	0.11	1.1	31
—	—	—	70	37	48	1.7	284	200	0.06	0.17	1.7	60
—	—	—	97	211	41	1.6	548	220	0.05	0.14	0.8	16
—	—	—	98	211	32	1.9	475	190	0.05	0.11	0.5	16
—	—	—	13	31	31	1.5	244	90	0.04	0.10	0.9	88
—	—	—	79	40	48	2.0	318	90	0.06	0.17	1.4	151
—	—	—	107	59	73	2.7	472	140	0.09	0.27	2.3	249
—	—	—	10	34	15	0.3	108	360	0.05	0.02	0.1	27
—	—	—	30	44	35	0.5	440	1,040	0.15	0.05	0.2	54
—	—	—	27	30	43	2.1	426	2,510	0.13	0.13	0.9	30
0.5	0.9	0.8	28	9	43	1.2	41	30	0.14	0.10	1.2	0
0.2	0.4	0.6	30	8	41	1.2	42	0	0.15	0.11	1.4	0
0.3	0.2	0.8	158	32	378	4.0	320	0	0.24	0.10	6.2	0

TABLE 6 (continued)

Food	Approximate Measures, Units, or Weight (edible part unless footnotes indicate otherwise)	Weight (g)	Water (%)	Food Energy (kcal)	Protein (g)	Fat (g)
Biscuits, baking powder, 2-in. diam. (enriched flour, vegetable shortening):						
Homemade	1	28	27	105	2	5
From mix	1	28	29	90	2	3
Bread crumbs (enriched):[38]						
Dry, grated	1 c	100	7	390	13	5
Soft. See Bread, White.						
Bread:						
Boston brown bread, canned, slice, 3¼ × ½ in.[38]	1 sl	45	45	95	2	1
Cracked wheat (¾ enriched wheat flour, ¼ cracked wheat):[38]						
Loaf	1 lb	454	35	1,195	39	10
Slice (18 per loaf)	1 sl	25	35	65	2	1
French or Vienna, enriched:[38]						
Loaf	1 lb	454	31	1,315	41	14
Slice:						
French (5 × 2½ × 1 in.)	1 sl	35	31	100	3	1
Vienna (4¾ × 4 × ½ in.)	1 sl	25	31	75	2	1
Italian, enriched:						
Loaf	1 lb	454	32	1,250	41	4
Slice, 4½ × 3¼ × ¾ in.	1 sl	30	32	85	3	Trace
Raisin, enriched:[38]						
Loaf	1 lb	454	35	1,190	30	13
Slice (18 per loaf)	1 sl	25	35	65	2	1
Rye:						
American, light (⅔ enriched wheat flour, ⅓ rye flour):						
Loaf	1 lb	454	36	1,100	41	5
Slice (4¾ × 3¾ × 7/16 in.)	1 sl	25	36	60	2	Trace
Pumpernickel (⅔ rye flour, ⅓ enriched wheat flour):						
Loaf	1 lb	454	34	1,115	41	5
Slice (5 × 4 × ⅜ in.)	1 sl	32	34	80	3	Trace
White, enriched:[38]						
Soft-crumb type:						
Loaf	1 lb	454	36	1,225	39	15
Slice (18 per loaf)	1 sl	25	36	70	2	1
Toast	1 sl	22	25	70	2	1
Slice (22 per loaf)	1 sl	20	36	55	2	1
Toast	1 sl	17	25	55	2	1
Loaf	1½ lb	680	36	1,835	59	22
Slice (24 per loaf)	1 sl	28	36	75	2	1
Toast	1 sl	24	25	75	2	1
Slice (28 per loaf)	1 sl	24	36	65	2	1
Toast	1 sl	21	25	65	2	1
Crumbs	1 c	45	36	120	4	1
Cubes	1 c	30	36	80	3	1
Firm-crumb type:						
Loaf	1 lb	454	35	1,245	41	17
Slice (20 per loaf)	1 sl	23	35	65	2	1
Toast	1 sl	20	24	65	2	1

Nutrients in Indicated Quantity												
Fatty Acids												
Saturated (total) (g)	**Unsaturated**		Carbo-hydrate (g)	Calcium (mg)	Phos-phorus (mg)	Iron (mg)	Potassium (mg)	Vitamin A Value (IU)	Thiamin (mg)	Riboflavin (mg)	Niacin (mg)	Ascorbic Acid (mg)
	Oleic (g)	Linoleic (g)										
1.2	2.0	1.2	13	34	49	0.4	33	Trace	0.08	0.08	0.7	Trace
0.6	1.1	0.7	15	19	65	0.6	32	Trace	0.09	0.08	0.8	Trace
1.0	1.6	1.4	73	122	141	3.6	152	Trace	0.35	0.35	4.8	Trace
0.1	0.2	0.2	21	41	72	0.9	131	0[39]	0.06	0.04	0.7	0
2.2	3.0	3.9	236	399	581	9.5	608	Trace	1.52	1.13	14.4	Trace
0.1	0.2	0.2	13	22	32	0.5	34	Trace	0.08	0.06	0.8	Trace
3.2	4.7	4.6	251	195	386	10.0	408	Trace	1.80	1.10	15.0	Trace
0.2	0.4	0.4	19	15	30	0.8	32	Trace	0.14	0.08	1.2	Trace
0.2	0.3	0.3	14	11	21	0.6	23	Trace	0.10	0.06	0.8	Trace
0.6	0.3	1.5	256	77	349	10.0	336	0	1.80	1.10	15.0	0
Trace	Trace	0.1	17	5	23	0.7	22	0	0.12	0.07	1.0	0
3.0	4.7	3.9	243	322	395	10.0	1,057	Trace	1.70	1.07	10.7	Trace
0.2	0.3	0.2	13	18	22	0.6	58	Trace	0.09	0.06	0.6	Trace
0.7	0.5	2.2	236	340	667	9.1	658	0	1.35	0.98	12.9	0
Trace	Trace	0.1	13	19	37	0.5	36	0	0.07	0.05	0.7	0
0.7	0.5	2.4	241	381	1,039	11.8	2,059	0	1.30	0.93	8.5	0
0.1	Trace	0.2	17	27	73	0.8	145	0	0.09	0.07	0.6	0
3.4	5.3	4.6	229	381	440	11.3	476	Trace	1.80	1.10	15.0	Trace
0.2	0.3	0.3	13	21	24	0.6	26	Trace	0.10	0.06	0.8	Trace
0.2	0.3	0.3	13	21	24	0.6	26	Trace	0.08	0.06	0.8	Trace
0.2	0.2	0.2	10	17	19	0.5	21	Trace	0.08	0.05	0.7	Trace
0.2	0.2	0.2	10	17	19	0.5	21	Trace	0.06	0.05	0.7	Trace
5.2	7.9	6.9	343	571	660	17.0	714	Trace	2.70	1.65	22.5	Trace
0.2	0.3	0.3	14	24	27	0.7	29	Trace	0.11	0.07	0.9	Trace
0.2	0.3	0.3	14	24	27	0.7	29	Trace	0.09	0.07	0.9	Trace
0.2	0.3	0.2	12	20	23	0.6	25	Trace	0.10	0.06	0.8	Trace
0.2	0.3	0.2	12	20	23	0.6	25	Trace	0.08	0.06	0.8	Trace
0.3	0.5	0.5	23	38	44	1.1	47	Trace	0.18	0.11	1.5	Trace
0.2	0.3	0.3	15	25	29	0.8	32	Trace	0.12	0.07	1.0	Trace
3.9	5.9	5.2	228	435	463	11.3	549	Trace	1.80	1.10	15.0	Trace
0.2	0.3	0.3	12	22	23	0.6	28	Trace	0.09	0.06	0.8	Trace
0.2	0.3	0.3	12	22	23	0.6	28	Trace	0.07	0.06	0.8	Trace

TABLE 6   (continued)

Food	Approximate Measures, Units, or Weight (edible part unless footnotes indicate otherwise)	Weight (g)	Water (%)	Food Energy (kcal)	Protein (g)	Fat (g)
Loaf	2 lb	907	35	2,495	82	34
Slice (34 per loaf)	1 sl	27	35	75	2	1
Toast	1 sl	23	24	75	2	1
Whole wheat:						
Soft-crumb type: [38]						
Loaf	1 lb	454	36	1,095	41	12
Slice (16 per loaf)	1 sl	28	36	65	3	1
Toast	1 sl	24	24	65	3	1
Firm-crumb type: [38]						
Loaf	1 lb	454	36	1,100	48	14
Slice (18 per loaf)	1 sl	25	36	60	3	1
Toast	1 sl	21	24	60	3	1
Breakfast cereals:						
Hot type, cooked:						
Corn (hominy) grits, degermed:						
Enriched	1 c	245	87	125	3	Trace
Unenriched	1 c	245	87	125	3	Trace
Farina, quick-cooking, enriched	1 c	245	89	105	3	Trace
Oatmeal or rolled oats	1 c	240	87	130	5	2
Wheat, rolled	1 c	240	80	180	5	1
Wheat, whole meal	1 c	245	88	110	4	1
Ready-to-eat:						
Bran flakes (40% bran), added sugar, salt, iron, vitamins	1 c	35	3	105	4	1
Bran flakes with raisins, added sugar, salt, iron, vitamins	1 c	50	7	145	4	1
Corn flakes:						
Plain, added sugar, salt, iron, vitamins	1 c	25	4	95	2	Trace
Sugar-coated, added salt, iron, vitamins	1 c	40	2	155	2	Trace
Corn, oat flour, puffed, added sugar, salt, iron, vitamins	1 c	20	4	80	2	1
Corn, shredded, added sugar, salt, iron, thiamin, niacin	1 c	25	3	95	2	Trace
Oats, puffed, added sugar, salt, minerals, vitamins	1 c	25	3	100	3	1
Rice, puffed:						
Plain, added iron, thiamin, niacin	1 c	15	4	60	1	Trace
Presweetened, added salt, iron, vitamins	1 c	28	3	115	1	0
Wheat flakes, added sugar, salt, iron, vitamins	1 c	30	4	105	3	Trace
Wheat, puffed:						
Plain, added iron, thiamin, niacin	1 c	15	3	55	2	Trace
Presweetened, added salt, iron, vitamins	1 c	38	3	140	3	Trace
Wheat, shredded, plain	1 oblong biscuit or ½ c spoon-size biscuits	25	7	90	2	1
Wheat germ, without salt and sugar, toasted	1 T	6	4	25	2	1
Buckwheat flour, light, sifted	1 c	98	12	340	6	1
Bulgur, canned, seasoned	1 c	135	56	245	8	4
Cake icings. See Sugars and Sweets.						
Cakes made from cake mixes with enriched flour: [46]						
Angel food:						
Whole cake (9¾-in. diam. tube cake)	1	635	34	1,645	36	1
Piece, 1/12 of cake	1	53	34	135	3	Trace

	**Nutrients in Indicated Quantity**
Fatty Acids												
Saturated (total) (g)		**Unsaturated**	**Carbo-hydrate (g)**	**Calcium (mg)**	**Phos-phorus (mg)**	**Iron (mg)**	**Potassium (mg)**	**Vitamin A Value (IU)**	**Thiamin (mg)**	**Riboflavin (mg)**	**Niacin (mg)**	**Ascorbic Acid (mg)**
	Oleic (g)	**Linoleic (g)**										
7.7	11.8	10.4	455	871	925	22.7	1,097	Trace	3.60	2.20	30.0	Trace
0.2	0.3	0.3	14	26	28	0.7	33	Trace	0.11	0.06	0.9	Trace
0.2	0.3	0.3	14	26	28	0.7	33	Trace	0.09	0.06	0.9	Trace
2.2	2.9	4.2	224	381	1,152	13.6	1,161	Trace	1.37	0.45	12.7	Trace
0.1	0.2	0.2	14	24	71	0.8	72	Trace	0.09	0.03	0.8	Trace
0.1	0.2	0.2	14	24	71	0.8	72	Trace	0.07	0.03	0.8	Trace
2.5	3.3	4.9	216	449	1,034	13.6	1,238	Trace	1.17	0.54	12.7	Trace
0.1	0.2	0.3	12	25	57	0.8	68	Trace	0.06	0.03	0.7	Trace
0.1	0.2	0.3	12	25	57	0.8	68	Trace	0.05	0.03	0.7	Trace
Trace	Trace	0.1	27	2	25	0.7	27	Trace[40]	0.10	0.07	1.0	0
Trace	Trace	0.1	27	2	25	0.2	27	Trace[40]	0.05	0.02	0.5	0
Trace	Trace	0.1	22	147	113[41]	[42]	25	0	0.12	0.07	1.0	0
0.4	0.8	0.9	23	22	137	1.4	146	0	0.19	0.05	0.2	0
—	—	—	41	19	182	1.7	202	0	0.17	0.07	2.2	0
—	—	—	23	17	127	1.2	118	0	0.15	0.05	1.5	0
—	—	—	28	19	125	5.6	137	1,540	0.46	0.52	6.2	0
—	—	—	40	28	146	7.9	154	2,200[43]	[44]	[44]	[44]	0
—	—	—	21	44[44]	9	[44]	30	[44]	[44]	[44]	[44]	13[45]
—	—	—	37	1	10	[44]	27	1,760	0.53	0.60	7.1	21[45]
—	—	—	16	4	18	5.7	—	880	0.26	0.30	3.5	11
—	—	—	22	1	10	0.6	—	0	0.33	0.05	4.4	13
—	—	—	19	44	102	4.0	—	1,100	0.33	0.38	4.4	13
—	—	—	13	3	14	0.3	15	0	0.07	0.01	0.7	0
—	—	—	26	3	14	[44]	43	1,240[45]	[44]	[44]	[44]	15[45]
—	—	—	24	12	83	4.8	81	1,320	0.40	0.45	5.3	16
—	—	—	12	4	48	0.6	51	0	0.08	0.03	1.2	0
—	—	—	33	7	52	[44]	63	1,680	0.50	0.57	6.7	20[45]
—	—	—	20	11	97	0.9	87	0	0.06	0.03	1.1	0
—	—	—	3	3	70	0.5	57	10	0.11	0.05	0.3	1
0.2	0.4	0.4	78	11	86	1.0	314	0	0.08	0.04	0.4	0
—	—	—	44	27	263	1.9	151	0	0.08	0.05	4.1	0
—	—	—	377	603	756	2.5	381	0	0.37	0.95	3.6	0
—	—	—	32	50	63	0.2	32	0	0.03	0.08	0.3	0

TABLE 6 (continued)

Food	Approximate Measures, Units, or Weight (edible part unless footnotes indicate otherwise)	Weight (g)	Water (%)	Food Energy (kcal)	Protein (g)	Fat (g)
Coffee cake:						
Whole cake (7¾ × 5⅝ × 1¼ in.)	1	430	30	1,385	27	41
Piece, ⅙ of cake	1	72	30	230	5	4
Cupcake, made with egg, milk, 2½-in. diam.:						
Without icing	1	25	26	90	1	3
With chocolate icing	1	36	22	130	2	5
Devil's food with chocolate icing:						
Whole, 2-layer cake (8- or 9-in. diam.)	1	1,107	24	3,755	49	136
Piece, ¹⁄₁₆ of cake	1	69	24	235	3	8
Cupcake, 2½-in. diam.	1	35	24	120	2	4
Gingerbread:						
Whole cake (8-in. square)	1	570	37	1,575	18	39
Piece, ⅑ of cake	1	63	37	175	2	4
White, 2-layer with chocolate icing:						
Whole cake (8- or 9-in. diam.)	1	1,140	21	4,000	44	122
Piece, ¹⁄₁₆ of cake	1	71	21	250	3	8
Yellow, 2-layer with chocolate icing:						
Whole cake (8- or 9-in. diam.)	1	1,108	26	3,735	45	125
Piece, ¹⁄₁₆ of cake	1	69	26	235	3	8
Cakes made from home recipies using enriched flour:[47]						
Boston cream pie with custard filling:						
Whole cake (8-in. diam.)	1	825	35	2,490	41	78
Piece, ¹⁄₁₂ of cake	1	69	35	210	3	6
Fruitcake, dark:						
Loaf, 1 lb (7½ × 2 × 1½ in.)	1 lb	454	18	1,720	22	69
Slice, ¹⁄₃₀ of loaf	1 slice	15	18	55	1	2
Plain, sheet cake:						
Without icing:						
Whole cake (9-in. square)	1	777	25	2,830	35	108
Piece, ⅑ of cake	1	86	25	315	4	12
With uncooked white icing:						
Whole cake (9-in. square)	1	1,096	21	4,020	37	129
Piece, ⅑ of cake	1	121	21	445	4	14
Pound:[49]						
Loaf, 8½ × 3½ × 3¼ in.	1	565	16	2,725	31	170
Slice, ¹⁄₁₇ of loaf	1	33	16	160	2	10
Sponge cake:						
Whole cake (9¾-in. diam. tube cake)	1	790	32	2,345	60	45
Piece, ¹⁄₁₂ of cake	1	66	32	195	5	4
Cookies made with enriched flour:[50] [51]						
Brownie with nuts:						
Homemade, 1¾ × 1¾ × ⅞ in.:						
From home recipe	1	20	10	95	1	6
From commercial recipe	1	20	11	85	1	4
Frozen, with chocolate icing,[52] 1½ × 1¾ × ⅞ in.	1	25	13	105	1	5
Chocolate chip:						
Commercial, 2¼-in. diam., ⅜ in. thick	4	42	3	200	2	9
Homemade, 2⅓-in. diam.	4	40	3	205	2	12

| | Fatty Acids | | | | | | | Vitamin A | | | | |
| Saturated (total) (g) | Unsaturated | | Carbo-hydrate (g) | Calcium (mg) | Phos-phorus (mg) | Iron (mg) | Potassium (mg) | Value (IU) | Thiamin (mg) | Riboflavin (mg) | Niacin (mg) | Ascorbic Acid (mg) |
	Oleic (g)	Linoleic (g)										
11.7	16.3	8.8	225	262	748	6.9	469	690	0.82	0.91	7.7	1
2.0	2.7	1.5	38	44	125	1.2	78	120	0.14	0.15	1.3	Trace
0.8	1.2	0.7	14	40	59	0.3	21	40	0.05	0.05	0.4	Trace
2.0	1.6	0.6	21	47	71	0.4	42	60	0.05	0.06	0.4	Trace
50.0	44.9	17.0	645	653	1,162	16.6	1,439	1,660	1.06	1.65	10.1	1
3.1	2.8	1.1	40	41	72	1.0	90	100	0.07	0.10	0.6	Trace
1.6	1.4	0.5	20	21	37	0.5	46	50	0.03	0.05	0.3	Trace
9.7	16.6	10.0	291	513	570	8.6	1,562	Trace	0.84	1.00	7.4	Trace
1.1	1.8	1.1	32	57	63	0.9	173	Trace	0.09	0.11	0.8	Trace
48.2	46.4	20.0	716	1,129	2,041	11.4	1,322	680	1.50	1.77	12.5	2
3.0	2.9	1.2	45	70	127	0.7	82	40	0.09	0.11	0.8	Trace
47.8	47.8	20.3	638	1,008	2,017	12.2	1,208	1,550	1.24	1.67	10.6	2
3.0	3.0	1.3	40	63	126	0.8	75	100	0.08	0.10	0.7	Trace
23.0	30.1	15.2	412	553	833	8.2	734[48]	1,730	1.04	1.27	9.6	2
1.9	2.5	1.3	34	46	70	0.7	61[48]	140	0.09	0.11	0.8	Trace
14.4	33.5	14.8	271	327	513	11.8	2,250	540	0.72	0.73	4.9	2
0.5	1.1	0.5	9	11	17	0.4	74	20	0.02	0.02	0.2	Trace
29.5	44.4	23.9	434	497	793	8.5	614[48]	1,320	1.21	1.40	10.2	2
3.3	4.9	2.6	48	55	88	0.9	68[48]	150	0.13	0.15	1.1	Trace
42.2	49.5	24.4	694	548	822	8.2	669[48]	2,190	1.22	1.47	10.2	2
4.7	5.5	2.7	77	61	91	0.8	74[48]	240	0.14	0.16	1.1	Trace
42.9	73.1	39.6	273	107	418	7.9	345	1,410	0.90	0.99	7.3	0
2.5	4.3	2.3	16	6	24	0.5	20	80	0.05	0.06	0.4	0
13.1	15.8	5.7	427	237	885	13.4	687	3,560	1.10	1.64	7.4	Trace
1.1	1.3	0.5	36	20	74	1.1	57	300	0.09	0.14	0.6	Trace
1.5	3.0	1.2	10	8	30	0.4	38	40	0.04	0.03	0.2	Trace
0.9	1.4	1.3	13	9	27	0.4	34	20	0.03	0.02	0.2	Trace
2.0	2.2	0.7	15	10	31	0.4	44	50	0.03	0.03	0.2	Trace
2.8	2.9	2.2	29	16	48	1.0	56	50	0.10	0.17	0.9	Trace
3.5	4.5	2.9	24	14	40	0.8	47	40	0.06	0.06	0.5	Trace

TABLE 6 (continued)

Food	Approximate Measures, Units, or Weight (edible part unless footnotes indicate otherwise)	Weight (g)	Water (%)	Food Energy (kcal)	Protein (g)	Fat (g)
Fig bars, square (1⅝ × 1⅝ × ⅜ in.) or rectangular (1½ × 1¾ × ½ in.)	4	56	14	200	2	3
Gingersnaps, 2-in. diam., ¼ in. thick	4	28	3	90	2	2
Macaroons, 2¾-in. diam., ¼ in. thick	2	38	4	180	2	9
Oatmeal with raisins, 2⅝-in. diam., ¼ in. thick	4	52	3	235	3	8
Plain, prepared from commercial chilled dough, 2½-in. diam., ¼ in. thick	4	48	5	240	2	12
Sandwich type (chocolate or vanilla), 1¾-in. diam., ⅜ in. thick	4	40	2	200	2	9
Vanilla wafers, 1¾-in. diam., ¼ in. thick	10	40	3	185	2	6
Cornmeal:						
Whole-grain, unbolted, dry form	1 c	122	12	435	11	5
Bolted (nearly whole grain), dry form	1 c	122	12	440	11	4
Degermed, enriched:						
Dry form	1 c	138	12	500	11	2
Cooked	1 c	240	88	120	3	Trace
Degermed, unenriched:						
Dry form	1 c	138	12	500	11	2
Cooked	1 c	240	88	120	3	Trace
Crackers:[38]						
Graham, plain, 2½-in. square	2	14	6	55	1	1
Rye wafers, whole grain, 1⅞ × 3½ in.	2	13	6	45	2	Trace
Saltines, made with enriched flour	4 crackers	11	4	50	1	1
Danish pastry (enriched flour), plain without fruit or nuts:[54]						
Ounce	1 oz	28	22	120	2	7
Packaged ring, 12 oz	1	340	22	1,435	25	80
Round piece, about 4¼-in. diam. × 1 in.	1 pastry	65	22	275	5	15
Doughnut, made with enriched flour:[38]						
Cake type, plain, 2½-in. diam., 1 in. high	1	25	24	100	1	5
Yeast-leavened, glazed, 3¾-in. diam., 1¼ in. high	1	50	26	205	3	11
Macaroni, enriched, cooked (cut lengths, elbows, shells):						
Firm stage (hot)	1 c	130	64	190	7	1
Tender stage:						
Cold	1 c	105	73	115	4	Trace
Hot	1 c	140	73	155	5	1
Macaroni (enriched) and cheese:						
Canned[55]	1 c	240	80	230	9	10
Homemade (served hot)[56]	1 c	200	58	430	17	22
Muffin made with enriched flour:[38]						
Homemade:						
Blueberry, 2⅜-in. diam., 1½ in. high	1	40	39	110	3	4
Bran	1	40	35	105	3	4
Corn (enriched, degermed cornmeal and flour), 2⅜-in. diam., 1½ in. high	1	40	33	125	3	4
Plain, 3-in. diam., 1½ in. high	1	40	38	120	3	4
From mix, egg, milk:						
Corn, 2⅜-in. diam., 1½ in. high[58]	1	40	30	130	3	4

								Nutrients in Indicated Quantity				
	Fatty Acids											
Saturated	Unsaturated		Carbo-		Phos-			Vitamin A				Ascorbic
(total) (g)	Oleic (g)	Linoleic (g)	hydrate (g)	Calcium (mg)	phorus (mg)	Iron (mg)	Potassium (mg)	Value (IU)	Thiamin (mg)	Riboflavin (mg)	Niacin (mg)	Acid (mg)
0.8	1.2	0.7	42	44	34	1.0	111	60	0.04	0.14	0.9	Trace
0.7	1.0	0.6	22	20	13	0.7	129	20	0.08	0.06	0.7	0
—	—	—	25	10	32	0.3	176	0	0.02	0.05	0.2	0
2.0	3.3	2.0	38	11	53	1.4	192	30	0.15	0.10	1.0	Trace
3.0	5.2	2.9	31	17	35	0.6	23	30	0.10	0.08	0.9	0
2.2	3.9	2.2	28	10	96	0.7	15	0	0.06	0.10	0.7	0
—	—	—	30	16	25	0.6	29	50	0.10	0.09	0.8	0
0.5	1.0	2.5	90	24	312	2.9	346	620[53]	0.46	0.13	2.4	0
0.5	0.9	2.1	91	21	272	2.2	303	590[53]	0.37	0.10	2.3	0
0.2	0.4	0.9	108	8	137	4.0	166	610[53]	0.61	0.36	4.8	0
Trace	0.1	0.2	26	2	34	1.0	38	140[53]	0.14	0.10	1.2	0
0.2	0.4	0.9	108	8	137	1.5	166	610[53]	0.19	0.07	1.4	0
Trace	0.1	0.2	26	2	34	0.5	38	140[63]	0.05	0.02	0.2	0
0.3	0.5	0.3	10	6	21	0.5	55	0	0.02	0.08	0.5	0
—	—	—	10	7	50	0.5	78	0	0.04	0.03	0.2	0
0.3	0.5	0.4	8	2	10	0.5	13	0	0.05	0.05	0.4	0
2.0	2.7	1.4	13	14	31	0.5	32	90	0.08	0.08	0.7	Trace
24.3	31.7	16.5	155	170	371	6.1	381	1,050	0.97	1.01	8.6	Trace
4.7	6.1	3.2	30	33	71	1.2	73	200	0.18	0.19	1.7	Trace
1.2	2.0	1.1	13	10	48	0.4	23	20	0.05	0.05	0.4	Trace
3.3	5.8	3.3	22	16	33	0.6	34	25	0.10	0.10	0.8	0
—	—	—	39	14	85	1.4	103	0	0.23	0.13	1.8	0
—	—	—	24	8	53	0.9	64	0	0.15	0.08	1.2	0
—	—	—	32	11	70	1.3	85	0	0.20	0.11	1.5	0
4.2	3.1	1.4	26	199	182	1.0	139	260	0.12	0.24	1.0	Trace
8.9	8.8	2.9	40	362	322	1.8	240	860	0.20	0.40	1.8	Trace
1.1	1.4	0.7	17	34	53	0.6	46	90	0.09	0.10	0.7	Trace
1.2	1.4	0.8	17	57	162	1.5	172	90	0.07	0.10	1.7	Trace
1.2	1.6	0.9	19	42	68	0.7	54	120[57]	0.10	0.10	0.7	Trace
1.0	1.7	1.0	17	42	60	0.6	50	40	0.09	0.12	0.9	Trace
1.2	1.7	0.9	20	96	152	0.6	44	100[57]	0.08	0.09	0.7	Trace

TABLE 6 (continued)

Food	Approximate Measures, Units, or Weight (edible part unless footnotes indicate otherwise)	Weight (g)	Water (%)	Food Energy (kcal)	Protein (g)	Fat (g)
Noodles, chow mein, canned	1 c	45	1	220	6	11
Noodles (egg noodles), enriched, cooked	1 c	160	71	200	7	2
Pancakes, (4-in. diam.):[38]						
Buckwheat, made from mix (with buckwheat and enriched flours), egg and milk added	1 cake	27	58	55	2	2
Plain:						
Homemade with enriched flour	1 cake	27	50	60	2	2
Made from mix with enriched flour; egg and milk added	1 cake	27	51	60	2	2
Pies, piecrust made with enriched flour and vegetable shortening (9-in. diam.):						
Apple:						
Whole	1 pie	945	48	2,420	21	105
Sector, 1/7 of pie	1 sector	135	48	345	3	15
Banana cream:						
Whole	1 pie	910	54	2,010	41	85
Sector, 1/7 of pie	1 sector	130	54	285	6	12
Blueberry:						
Whole	1 pie	945	51	2,285	23	102
Sector, 1/7 of pie	1 sector	135	51	325	3	15
Cherry:						
Whole	1 pie	945	47	2,465	25	107
Sector, 1/7 of pie	1 sector	135	47	350	4	15
Custard:						
Whole	1 pie	910	58	1,985	56	101
Sector, 1/7 of pie	1 sector	130	58	285	8	14
Lemon meringue:						
Whole	1 pie	840	47	2,140	31	86
Sector, 1/7 of pie	1 sector	120	47	305	4	12
Mince:						
Whole	1 pie	945	43	2,560	24	109
Sector, 1/7 of pie	1 sector	135	43	365	3	16
Peach:						
Whole	1 pie	945	48	2,410	24	101
Sector, 1/7 of pie	1 sector	135	48	345	3	14
Pecan:						
Whole	1 pie	825	20	3,450	42	189
Sector, 1/7 of pie	1 sector	118	20	495	6	27
Pumpkin:						
Whole	1 pie	910	59	1,920	36	102
Sector, 1/7 of pie	1 sector	130	59	275	5	15
Piecrust (homemade) made with enriched flour and vegetable shortening, baked, 9-in. diam.	1 shell	180	15	900	11	60
Piecrust mix with enriched flour and vegetable shortening, 10-oz. package prepared and baked, 9-in. diam.	1 shell (2-crust pie)	320	19	1,485	20	93
Pizza (cheese) baked, 4¾-in. sector; 1/8 of 12-in.-diam. pie[19]	1 sector	60	45	145	6	4
Popcorn, popped:						
Plain, large kernel	1 c	6	4	25	1	Trace
With oil (coconut) and salt added, large kernel	1 c	9	3	40	1	2

								Nutrients in Indicated Quantity				
Fatty Acids												
	Unsaturated											
Saturated (total) (g)	Oleic (g)	Linoleic (g)	Carbo-hydrate (g)	Calcium (mg)	Phos-phorus (mg)	Iron (mg)	Potassium (mg)	Vitamin A Value (IU)	Thiamin (mg)	Riboflavin (mg)	Niacin (mg)	Ascorbic Acid (mg)
—	—	—	26	—	—	—	—	—	—	—	—	—
—	—	—	37	16	94	1.4	70	110	0.22	0.13	1.9	0
0.8	0.9	0.4	6	59	91	0.4	66	60	0.04	0.05	0.2	Trace
0.5	0.8	0.5	9	27	38	0.4	33	30	0.06	0.07	0.5	Trace
0.7	0.7	0.3	9	58	70	0.3	42	70	0.04	0.06	0.2	Trace
27.0	44.5	25.2	360	76	208	6.6	756	280	1.06	0.79	9.3	9
3.9	6.4	3.6	51	11	30	0.9	108	40	0.15	0.11	1.3	2
26.7	33.2	16.2	279	601	746	7.3	1,847	2,280	0.77	1.51	7.0	9
3.8	4.7	2.3	40	86	107	1.0	264	330	0.11	0.22	1.0	1
24.8	43.7	25.1	330	104	217	9.5	614	280	1.03	0.80	10.0	28
3.5	6.2	3.6	47	15	31	1.4	88	40	0.15	0.11	1.4	4
28.2	45.0	25.3	363	132	236	6.6	992	4,160	1.09	0.84	9.8	Trace
4.0	6.4	3.6	52	19	34	0.9	142	590	0.16	0.12	1.4	Trace
33.9	38.5	17.5	213	874	1,028	8.2	1,247	2,090	0.79	1.92	5.6	0
4.8	5.5	2.5	30	125	147	1.2	178	300	0.11	0.27	0.8	0
26.1	33.8	16.4	317	118	412	6.7	420	1,430	0.61	0.84	5.2	25
3.7	4.8	2.3	45	17	59	1.0	60	200	0.09	0.12	0.7	4
28.0	45.9	25.2	389	265	359	13.3	1,682	20	0.96	0.86	9.8	9
4.0	6.6	3.6	56	38	51	1.9	240	Trace	0.14	0.12	1.4	1
24.8	43.7	25.1	361	95	274	8.5	1,408	6,900	1.04	0.97	14.0	28
3.5	6.2	3.6	52	14	39	1.2	201	990	0.15	0.14	2.0	4
27.8	101.0	44.2	423	388	850	25.6	1,015	1,320	1.80	0.95	6.9	Trace
4.0	14.4	6.3	61	55	122	3.7	145	190	0.26	0.14	1.0	Trace
37.4	37.5	16.6	223	464	628	7.3	1,456	22,480	0.78	1.27	7.0	Trace
5.4	5.4	2.4	32	66	90	1.0	208	3,210	0.11	0.18	1.0	Trace
14.8	26.1	14.9	79	25	90	3.1	89	0	0.47	0.40	5.0	0
22.7	39.7	23.4	141	131	272	6.1	179	0	1.07	0.79	9.9	0
1.7	1.5	0.6	22	86	89	1.1	67	230	0.16	0.18	1.6	4
Trace	0.1	0.2	5	1	17	0.2	—	—	—	0.01	0.1	0
1.5	0.2	0.2	5	1	19	0.2	—	—	—	0.01	0.2	0

TABLE 6 (continued)

Food	Approximate Measures, Units, or Weight (edible part unless footnotes indicate otherwise)	Weight (g)	Water (%)	Food Energy (kcal)	Protein (g)	Fat (g)
Sugar coated	1 c	35	4	135	2	1
Pretzels, made with enriched flour:						
Dutch, twisted, 2¾ × 2⅝ in.	1	16	5	60	2	1
Thin, twisted, 3¼ × 2¼ × ¼ in.	10	60	5	235	6	3
Stick, 2¼ in. long	10	3	5	10	Trace	Trace
Rice, white, enriched:						
Instant, ready-to-serve, hot	1 c	165	73	180	4	Trace
Long grain:						
Raw	1 c	185	12	670	12	1
Cooked, served hot	1 c	205	73	225	4	Trace
Parboiled:						
Raw	1 c	185	10	685	14	1
Cooked, served hot	1 c	175	73	185	4	Trace
Roll, enriched:[38]						
Commercial:						
Brown-and-serve (1 oz), browned	1	26	27	85	2	2
Cloverleaf or pan, 2½-in. diam., 2 in. high	1	28	31	85	2	2
Frankfurter and hamburger (8 per 11½-oz package)	1	40	31	120	3	2
Hard, 3¾-in. diam., 2 in. high	1	50	25	155	5	2
Hoagie or submarine, 11½ × 3 × 2½ in.	1	135	31	390	12	4
Homemade:						
Cloverleaf, 2½-in. diam., 2 in. high	1	35	26	120	3	3
Spaghetti, enriched, cooked:						
Firm stage, *al dente*, served hot	1 c	130	64	190	7	1
Tender stage, served hot	1 c	140	73	155	5	1
Spaghetti (enriched) in tomato sauce with cheese:						
Canned	1 c	250	80	190	6	2
Homemade	1 c	250	77	260	9	9
Spaghetti (enriched) with meat balls and tomato sauce:						
Canned	1 c	250	78	260	12	10
Homemade	1 c	248	70	330	19	12
Toaster pastry	1	50	12	200	3	6
Waffles, made with enriched flour, 7-in. diam.:[38]						
Homemade	1	75	41	210	7	7
From mix, egg and milk added	1	75	42	205	7	8
Wheat flour:						
All-purpose or family flour, enriched:						
Sifted, spooned	1 c	115	12	420	12	1
Unsifted, spooned	1 c	125	12	455	13	1
Cake or pastry flour, enriched, sifted, spooned	1 c	96	12	350	7	1
Self-rising, enriched, unsifted, spooned	1 c	125	12	440	12	1
Whole wheat, from hard wheats, stirred	1 c	120	12	400	16	2
Legumes (dry), Nuts, Seeds; Related Products						
Almonds, shelled:						
Chopped (about 130 almonds)	1 c	130	5	775	24	70
Slivered, not pressed down (about 115 almonds)	1 c	115	5	690	21	62

Nutrients in Indicated Quantity												
Fatty Acids												
Saturated	**Unsaturated**		Carbo-		Phos-			**Vitamin A**				Ascorbic
(total) (g)	Oleic (g)	Linoleic (g)	hydrate (g)	Calcium (mg)	phorus (mg)	Iron (mg)	Potassium (mg)	Value (IU)	Thiamin (mg)	Riboflavin (mg)	Niacin (mg)	Acid (mg)
0.5	0.2	0.4	30	2	47	0.5	—	—	—	0.02	0.4	0
—	—	—	12	4	21	0.2	21	0	0.05	0.04	0.7	0
—	—	—	46	13	79	0.9	78	0	0.20	0.15	2.5	0
—	—	—	2	1	4	Trace	4	0	0.01	0.01	0.1	0
Trace	Trace	Trace	40	5	31	1.3	—	0	0.21	[59]	1.7	0
0.2	0.2	0.2	149	44	174	5.4	170	0	0.81	0.06	6.5	0
0.1	0.1	0.1	50	21	57	1.8	57	0	0.23	0.02	2.1	0
0.2	0.1	0.2	150	111	370	5.4	278	0	0.81	0.07	6.5	0
0.1	0.1	0.1	41	33	100	1.4	75	0	0.19	0.02	2.1	0
0.4	0.7	0.5	14	20	23	0.5	25	Trace	0.10	0.06	0.9	Trace
0.4	0.6	0.4	15	21	24	0.5	27	Trace	0.11	0.07	0.9	Trace
0.5	0.8	0.6	21	30	34	0.8	38	Trace	0.16	0.10	1.3	Trace
0.4	0.6	0.5	30	24	46	1.2	49	Trace	0.20	0.12	1.7	Trace
0.9	1.4	1.4	75	58	115	3.0	122	Trace	0.54	0.32	4.5	Trace
0.8	1.1	0.7	20	16	36	0.7	41	30	0.12	0.12	1.2	Trace
—	—	—	39	14	85	1.4	103	0	0.23	0.13	1.8	0
—	—	—	32	11	70	1.3	85	0	0.20	0.11	1.5	0
0.5	0.3	0.4	39	40	88	2.8	303	930	0.35	0.28	4.5	10
2.0	5.4	0.7	37	80	135	2.3	408	1,080	0.25	0.18	2.3	13
2.2	3.3	3.9	29	53	113	3.3	245	1,000	0.15	0.18	2.3	5
3.3	6.3	0.9	39	124	236	3.7	665	1,590	0.25	0.30	4.0	22
—	—	—	36	54[60]	67[60]	1.9	74[60]	500	0.16	0.17	2.1	[60]
2.3	2.8	1.4	28	85	130	1.3	109	250	0.17	0.23	1.4	Trace
2.8	2.9	1.2	27	179	257	1.0	146	170	0.14	0.22	0.9	Trace
0.2	0.1	0.5	88	18	100	3.3	109	0	0.74	0.46	6.1	0
0.2	0.1	0.5	95	20	109	3.6	119	0	0.80	0.50	6.6	0
0.1	0.1	0.3	76	16	70	2.8	91	0	0.61	0.38	5.1	0
0.2	0.1	0.5	93	331	583	3.6	—	0	0.80	0.50	6.6	0
0.4	0.2	1.0	85	49	446	4.0	444	0	0.66	0.14	5.2	0
5.6	47.7	12.8	25	304	655	6.1	1,005	0	0.31	1.20	4.6	Trace
5.0	42.2	11.3	22	269	580	5.4	889	0	0.28	1.06	4.0	Trace

TABLE 6   (continued)

Food	Approximate Measures, Units, or Weight (edible part unless footnotes indicate otherwise)	Weight (g)	Water (%)	Food Energy (kcal)	Protein (g)	Fat (g)
Beans, dry:						
Common varieties as Great Northern, navy, and others:						
Canned, solids and liquid:						
White with—						
Frankfurters (sliced)	1 c	255	71	365	19	18
Pork and sweet sauce	1 c	255	66	385	16	12
Pork and tomato sauce	1 c	255	71	310	16	7
Red kidney	1 c	255	76	230	15	1
Cooked, drained:						
Great Northern	1 c	180	69	210	14	1
Pea (navy)	1 c	190	69	225	15	1
Lima, cooked, drained	1 c	190	64	260	16	1
Black-eyed peas, dry, cooked (with residual cooking liquid)	1 c	250	80	190	13	1
Brazil nuts, shelled (6–8 large kernels)	1 oz	28	5	185	4	19
Cashew nuts, roasted in oil	1 c	140	5	785	24	64
Coconut meat, fresh:						
Piece, about 2 × 2 × ½ in.	1	45	51	155	2	16
Shredded or grated, not pressed down	1 c	80	51	275	3	28
Filberts (hazelnuts), chopped (about 80 kernels)	1 c	115	6	730	14	72
Lentils, whole, cooked	1 c	200	72	210	16	Trace
Peanuts, roasted in oil, salted (whole, halves, chopped)	1 c	144	2	840	37	72
Peanut butter	1 T	16	2	95	4	8
Peas, split, dry, cooked	1 c	200	70	230	16	1
Pecans, chopped or pieces (about 120 large halves)	1 c	118	3	810	11	84
Pumpkin and squash kernels, dry, hulled	1 c	140	4	775	41	65
Sunflower seeds, dry, hulled	1 c	145	5	810	35	69
Walnuts:						
Black:						
Chopped or broken kernels	1 c	125	3	785	26	74
Ground (finely)	1 c	80	3	500	16	47
Persian or English, chopped (about 60 halves)	1 c	120	4	780	18	77
Sugars and Sweets						
Cake icings:						
Boiled, white:						
Plain	1 c	94	18	295	1	0
With coconut	1 c	166	15	605	3	13
Uncooked:						
Chocolate made with milk and butter	1 c	275	14	1,035	9	38
Creamy fudge from mix and water	1 c	245	15	830	7	16
White	1 c	319	11	1,200	2	21
Candy:						
Caramels, plain or chocolate	1 oz	28	8	115	1	3
Chocolate:						
Milk, plain	1 oz	28	1	145	2	9
Semisweet, small pieces (60 per ounce)	1 c or 6 oz	170	1	860	7	61
Chocolate-covered peanuts	1 oz	28	1	160	5	12
Fondant, uncoated (mints, candy corn, other)	1 oz	28	8	105	Trace	1

								Nutrients in Indicated Quantity					
	Fatty Acids												
Saturated	Unsaturated		Carbo-		Phos-			Vitamin A					Ascorbic
(total)	Oleic	Linoleic	hydrate	Calcium	phorus	Iron	Potassium	Value	Thiamin	Riboflavin	Niacin		Acid
(g)	(g)	(g)	(g)	(mg)	(mg)	(mg)	(mg)	(IU)	(mg)	(mg)	(mg)		(mg)
—	—	—	32	94	303	4.8	668	330	0.18	0.15	3.3		Trace
4.3	5.0	1.1	54	161	291	5.9	—	—	0.15	0.10	1.3		—
2.4	2.8	0.6	48	138	235	4.6	536	330	0.20	0.08	1.5		5
—	—	—	42	74	278	4.6	673	10	0.13	0.10	1.5		—
—	—	—	38	90	266	4.9	749	0	0.25	0.13	1.3		0
—	—	—	40	95	281	5.1	790	0	0.27	0.13	1.3		0
—	—	—	49	55	293	5.9	1,163	—	0.25	0.11	1.3		—
—	—	—	35	43	238	3.3	573	30	0.40	0.10	1.0		—
4.8	6.2	7.1	3	53	196	1.0	203	Trace	0.27	0.03	0.5		—
12.9	36.8	10.2	41	53	522	5.3	650	140	0.60	0.35	2.5		—
14.0	0.9	0.3	4	6	43	0.8	115	0	0.02	0.01	0.2		1
24.8	1.6	0.5	8	10	76	1.4	205	0	0.04	0.02	0.4		2
5.1	55.2	7.3	19	240	388	3.9	810	—	0.53	—	1.0		Trace
—	—	—	39	50	238	4.2	498	40	0.14	0.12	1.2		0
13.7	33.0	20.7	27	107	577	3.0	971	—	0.46	0.19	24.8		0
1.5	3.7	2.3	3	9	61	0.3	100	—	0.02	0.02	2.4		0
—	—	—	42	22	178	3.4	592	80	0.30	0.18	1.8		—
7.2	50.5	20.0	17	86	341	2.8	712	150	1.01	0.15	1.1		2
11.8	23.5	27.5	21	71	1,602	15.7	1,386	100	0.34	0.27	3.4		—
8.2	13.7	43.2	29	174	1,214	10.3	1,334	70	2.84	0.33	7.8		—
6.3	13.3	45.7	19	Trace	713	7.5	575	380	0.28	0.14	0.9		—
4.0	8.5	29.2	12	Trace	456	4.8	368	240	0.18	0.09	0.6		—
8.4	11.8	42.2	19	119	456	3.7	540	40	0.40	0.16	1.1		2
0	0	0	75	2	2	Trace	17	0	Trace	0.03	Trace		0
11.0	0.9	Trace	124	10	50	0.8	277	0	0.02	0.07	0.3		0
23.4	11.7	1.0	185	165	305	3.3	536	580	0.06	0.28	0.6		1
5.1	6.7	3.1	183	96	218	2.7	238	Trace	0.05	0.20	0.7		Trace
12.7	5.1	0.5	260	48	38	Trace	57	860	Trace	0.06	Trace		Trace
1.6	1.1	0.1	22	42	35	0.4	54	Trace	0.01	0.05	0.1		Trace
5.5	3.0	0.3	16	65	65	0.3	109	80	0.02	0.10	0.1		Trace
36.2	19.8	1.7	97	51	255	4.4	553	30	0.02	0.14	0.9		0
4.0	4.7	2.1	11	33	84	0.4	143	Trace	0.10	0.05	2.1		Trace
0.1	0.3	0.1	25	4	2	0.3	1	0	Trace	Trace	Trace		0

TABLE 6   (continued)

Food	Approximate Measures, Units, or Weight (edible part unless footnotes indicate otherwise)	Weight (g)	Water (%)	Food Energy (kcal)	Protein (g)	Fat (g)
Fudge, chocolate, plain	1 oz	28	8	115	1	3
Gumdrops	1 oz	28	12	100	Trace	Trace
Hard	1 oz	28	1	110	0	Trace
Marshmallows	1 oz	28	17	90	1	Trace
Chocolate-flavored beverage powders (about 4 heaping teaspoons per ounce):						
With nonfat dry milk	1 oz	28	2	100	5	1
Without milk	1 oz	28	1	100	1	1
Honey, strained or extracted	1 T	21	17	65	Trace	0
Jams and preserves	1 T	20	29	55	Trace	Trace
	1 packet	14	29	40	Trace	Trace
Jellies	1 T	18	29	50	Trace	Trace
	1 packet	14	29	40	Trace	Trace
Syrups:						
Chocolate-flavored syrup or topping:						
Fudge type	1 fl oz or 2 T	38	25	125	2	5
Thin type	1 fl oz or 2 T	38	32	90	1	1
Molasses, cane:						
Light (first extraction)	1 T	20	24	50	—	—
Blackstrap (third extraction)	1 T	20	24	45	—	—
Sorghum	1 T	21	23	55	—	—
Table blends, chiefly corn, light and dark	1 T	21	24	60	0	0
Sugar:						
Brown, pressed down	1 c	220	2	820	0	0
White:						
Granulated	1 c	200	1	770	0	0
	1 T	12	1	45	0	0
	1 packet	6	1	23	0	0
Powdered, sifted, spooned into cup	1 c	100	1	385	0	0
Vegetables and Vegetable Products						
Asparagus, green:						
Cooked, drained:						
Cuts and tips, 1½- to 2-in. lengths:						
From raw	1 c	145	94	30	3	Trace
From frozen	1 c	180	93	40	6	Trace
Spears, ½-in. diam. at base:						
From raw	4	60	94	10	1	Trace
From frozen	4	60	92	15	2	Trace
Canned, spears, ½-in. diam. at base	4	80	93	15	2	Trace
Beans:						
Lima, immature seeds, frozen, cooked, drained:						
Thick-seeded types (Fordhooks)	1 c	170	74	170	10	Trace
Thin-seeded types (baby limas)	1 c	180	69	210	13	Trace
Snap:						
Green:						
Canned, drained solids (cuts)	1 c	135	92	30	2	Trace
Cooked, drained:						
From raw (cuts and French style)	1 c	125	92	30	2	Trace
From frozen:						
Cuts	1 c	135	92	35	2	Trace
French style	1 c	130	92	35	2	Trace

						Nutrients in Indicated Quantity						
Fatty Acids												
Saturated	Unsaturated		Carbo-		Phos-			Vitamin A				Ascorbic
(total)	Oleic	Linoleic	hydrate	Calcium	phorus	Iron	Potassium	Value	Thiamin	Riboflavin	Niacin	Acid
(g)	(g)	(g)	(g)	(mg)	(mg)	(mg)	(mg)	(IU)	(mg)	(mg)	(mg)	(mg)
1.3	1.4	0.6	21	22	24	0.3	42	Trace	0.01	0.03	0.1	Trace
—	—	—	25	2	Trace	0.1	1	0	0	Trace	Trace	0
—	—	—	28	6	2	0.5	1	0	0	0	0	0
—	—	—	23	5	2	0.5	2	0	0	Trace	Trace	0
0.5	0.3	Trace	20	167	155	0.5	227	10	0.04	0.21	0.2	1
0.4	0.2	Trace	25	9	48	0.6	142	—	0.01	0.03	0.1	0
0	0	0	17	1	1	0.1	11	0	Trace	0.01	0.1	Trace
—	—	—	14	4	2	0.2	18	Trace	Trace	0.01	Trace	Trace
—	—	—	10	3	1	0.1	12	Trace	Trace	Trace	Trace	Trace
—	—	—	13	4	1	0.3	14	Trace	Trace	0.01	Trace	1
—	—	—	10	3	1	0.2	11	Trace	Trace	Trace	Trace	1
3.1	1.6	0.1	20	48	60	0.5	107	60	0.02	0.08	0.2	Trace
0.5	0.3	Trace	24	6	35	0.6	106	Trace	0.01	0.03	0.2	0
—	—	—	13	33	9	0.9	183	—	0.01	0.01	Trace	—
—	—	—	11	137	17	3.2	585	—	0.02	0.04	0.4	—
—	—	—	14	35	5	2.6	—	—	—	0.02	Trace	—
0	0	0	15	9	3	0.8	1	0	0	0	0	0
0	0	0	212	187	42	7.5	757	0	0.02	0.07	0.4	0
0	0	0	199	0	0	0.2	6	0	0	0	0	0
0	0	0	12	0	0	Trace	Trace	0	0	0	0	0
0	0	0	6	0	0	Trace	Trace	0	0	0	0	0
0	0	0	100	0	0	0.1	3	0	0	0	0	0
—	—	—	5	30	73	0.9	265	1,310	0.23	0.26	2.0	38
—	—	—	6	40	115	2.2	396	1,530	0.25	0.23	1.8	41
—	—	—	2	13	30	0.4	110	540	0.10	0.11	0.8	16
—	—	—	2	13	40	0.7	143	470	0.10	0.08	0.7	16
—	—	—	3	15	42	1.5	133	640	0.05	0.08	0.6	12
—	—	—	32	34	153	2.9	724	390	0.12	0.09	1.7	29
—	—	—	40	63	227	4.7	709	400	0.16	0.09	2.2	22
—	—	—	7	61	34	2.0	128	630	0.04	0.07	0.4	5
—	—	—	7	63	46	0.8	189	680	0.09	0.11	0.4	15
—	—	—	8	54	43	0.9	205	780	0.09	0.12	0.5	7
—	—	—	8	49	39	1.2	177	690	0.08	0.10	0.4	9

TABLE 6   (continued)

Food	Approximate Measures, Units, or Weight (edible part unless footnotes indicate otherwise)	Weight (g)	Water (%)	Food Energy (kcal)	Protein (g)	Fat (g)
Yellow or wax:						
Cooked, drained:						
From raw (cuts and French style)	1 c	125	93	30	2	Trace
From frozen (cuts)	1 c	135	92	35	2	Trace
Canned, drained solids (cuts)	1 c	135	92	30	2	Trace
Beans, mature. See Beans, dry, and Black-eyed peas, dry.						
Bean sprouts (mung):						
Raw	1 c	105	89	35	4	Trace
Cooked, drained	1 c	125	91	35	4	Trace
Beets:						
Canned, drained, solids:						
Whole, small	1 c	160	89	60	2	Trace
Diced or sliced	1 c	170	89	65	2	Trace
Cooked, drained, peeled:						
Whole, 2-in. diam.	2	100	91	30	1	Trace
Diced or sliced	1 c	170	91	55	1	Trace
Beet greens, leaves and stems, cooked, drained	1 c	145	94	25	2	Trace
Black-eyed peas, immature seeds, cooked and drained:						
From raw	1 c	165	72	180	13	1
From frozen	1 c	170	66	220	15	1
Broccoli, cooked, drained:						
From raw:						
Stalk, medium size	1	180	91	45	6	1
Stalks cut into ½-in. pieces	1 c	155	91	40	5	Trace
From frozen:						
Chopped	1 c	185	92	50	5	1
Stalk, 4½ to 5 in. long	1	30	91	10	1	Trace
Brussels sprouts, cooked, drained:						
From raw, 7–8 sprouts (1¼- to 1½-in. diam.)	1 c	155	88	55	7	1
From frozen	1 c	155	89	50	5	Trace
Cabbage:						
Common varieties:						
Raw:						
Coarsely shredded or sliced	1 c	70	92	15	1	Trace
Finely shredded or chopped	1 c	90	92	20	1	Trace
Cooked, drained	1 c	145	94	30	2	Trace
Red, raw, coarsely shredded or sliced	1 c	70	90	20	1	Trace
Savoy, raw, coarsely shredded or sliced	1 c	70	92	15	2	Trace
Cabbage, celery (also called pe-tsai or wongbok), raw, 1-in. pieces	1 c	75	95	10	1	Trace
Cabbage, white mustard (also called bokchoy or pakchoy), cooked, drained	1 c	170	95	25	2	Trace
Carrots:						
Raw, without crowns and tips, scraped:						
Grated	1 c	110	88	45	1	Trace
Whole, 7½ by 1⅛ in. or strips, 2½ to 3 in. long	1 carrot or 18 strips	72	88	30	1	Trace
Canned:						
Sliced, drained solids	1 c	155	91	45	1	Trace

	Fatty Acids											
Nutrients in Indicated Quantity												
Saturated (total) (g)	Unsaturated		Carbo-hydrate (g)	Calcium (mg)	Phos-phorus (mg)	Iron (mg)	Potassium (mg)	Vitamin A Value (IU)	Thiamin (mg)	Riboflavin (mg)	Niacin (mg)	Ascorbic Acid (mg)
	Oleic (g)	Linoleic (g)										
—	—	—	6	63	46	0.8	189	290	0.09	0.11	0.6	16
—	—	—	8	47	42	0.9	221	140	0.09	0.11	0.5	8
—	—	—	7	61	34	2.0	128	140	0.04	0.07	0.4	7
—	—	—	7	20	67	1.4	234	20	0.14	0.14	0.8	20
—	—	—	7	21	60	1.1	195	30	0.11	0.13	0.9	8
—	—	—	14	30	29	1.1	267	30	0.02	0.05	0.2	5
—	—	—	15	32	31	1.2	284	30	0.02	0.05	0.2	5
—	—	—	7	14	23	0.5	208	20	0.03	0.04	0.3	6
—	—	—	12	24	39	0.9	354	30	0.05	0.07	0.5	10
—	—	—	5	144	36	2.8	481	7,400	0.10	0.22	0.4	22
—	—	—	30	40	241	3.5	625	580	0.50	0.18	2.3	28
—	—	—	40	43	286	4.8	573	290	0.68	0.19	2.4	15
—	—	—	8	158	112	1.4	481	4,500	0.16	0.36	1.4	162
—	—	—	7	136	96	1.2	414	3,880	0.14	0.31	1.2	140
—	—	—	9	100	104	1.3	392	4,810	0.11	0.22	0.9	105
—	—	—	1	12	17	0.2	66	570	0.02	0.03	0.2	22
—	—	—	10	50	112	1.7	423	810	0.12	0.22	1.2	135
—	—	—	10	33	95	1.2	457	880	0.12	0.16	0.9	126
—	—	—	4	34	20	0.3	163	90	0.04	0.04	0.2	33
—	—	—	5	44	26	0.4	210	120	0.05	0.05	0.3	42
—	—	—	6	64	29	0.4	236	190	0.06	0.06	0.4	48
—	—	—	5	29	25	0.6	188	30	0.06	0.04	0.3	43
—	—	—	3	47	38	0.6	188	140	0.04	0.06	0.2	39
—	—	—	2	32	30	0.5	190	110	0.04	0.03	0.5	19
—	—	—	4	252	56	1.0	364	5,270	0.07	0.14	1.2	26
—	—	—	11	41	40	0.8	375	12,100	0.07	0.06	0.7	9
—	—	—	7	27	26	0.5	246	7,930	0.04	0.04	0.4	6
—	—	—	10	47	34	1.1	186	23,250	0.03	0.05	0.6	3

TABLE 6 (continued)

Food	Approximate Measures, Units, or Weight (edible part unless footnotes indicate otherwise)	Weight (g)	Water (%)	Food Energy (kcal)	Protein (g)	Fat (g)
Strained or junior (baby food)	1 oz (1¾ to 2 T)	28	92	10	Trace	Trace
Cooked (crosswise cuts), drained	1 c	155	91	50	1	Trace
Cauliflower:						
Raw, chopped	1 c	115	91	31	3	Trace
Cooked, drained:						
From raw (flower buds)	1 c	125	93	30	3	Trace
From frozen (flowerets)	1 c	180	94	30	3	Trace
Celery, Pascal type, raw:						
Pieces, diced	1 c	120	94	20	1	Trace
Stalk, large outer, 8 by 1½ in. at root end	1	40	94	5	Trace	Trace
Collards, cooked, drained:						
From raw (leaves without stems)	1 c	190	90	65	7	1
From frozen (chopped)	1 c	170	90	50	5	1
Corn, sweet:						
Cooked, drained:						
From raw, ear, 5 by 1¾ in.	1	140[61]	74	70	2	1
From frozen:						
Ear, 5 in. long	1	229[61]	73	120	4	1
Kernels	1 c	165	77	130	5	1
Canned:						
Cream style	1 c	256	76	210	5	2
Whole kernel:						
Vacuum pack	1 c	210	76	175	5	1
Wet pack, drained solids	1 c	165	76	140	4	1
Cowpeas. See Black-eyed peas.						
Cucumber slices, ⅛ in. thick (large, 2⅛-in. diam.; small, 1¾-in. diam.):						
With peel	6 large or 8 small	28	95	5	Trace	Trace
Without peel	6½ large or 9 small pieces	28	96	5	Trace	Trace
Dandelion greens, cooked, drained	1 c	105	90	35	2	1
Endive, curly (including escarole), raw, small pieces	1 c	50	93	10	1	Trace
Kale, cooked, drained:						
From raw (leaves without stems and midribs)	1 c	110	88	45	5	1
From frozen (leaf style)	1 c	130	91	40	4	1
Lettuce, raw:						
Butter head, as Boston types:						
Head, 5-in. diam.	1	220[63]	95	25	2	Trace
Leaves	1 outer, 2 inner, or 3 heart leaves	15	95	Trace	Trace	Trace
Crisp head, as iceberg:						
Head, 6-in. diam.	1	567[64]	96	70	5	1
Wedge, ¼ of head	1	135	96	20	1	Trace
Pieces, chopped or shredded	1 c	55	96	5	Trace	Trace
Loose leaf (bunching varieties including romaine), chopped or shredded pieces	1 c	55	94	10	1	Trace
Mushrooms, raw, sliced, or chopped	1 c	70	90	20	2	Trace
Mustard greens, without stems and midribs, cooked, drained	1 c	140	93	30	3	1
Okra pods, 3 by ⅝ in., cooked	10	106	91	30	2	Trace

	Fatty Acids											
		Unsaturated	Carbo-		Phos-			Vitamin A				Ascorbic
Saturated (total) (g)	Oleic (g)	Linoleic (g)	hydrate (g)	Calcium (mg)	phorus (mg)	Iron (mg)	Potassium (mg)	Value (IU)	Thiamin (mg)	Riboflavin (mg)	Niacin (mg)	Acid (mg)
—	—	—	2	7	·6	0.1	51	3,690	0.01	0.01	0.1	1
—	—	—	11	51	48	0.9	344	16,280	0.08	0.08	0.8	9
—	—	—	6	29	64	1.3	339	70	0.13	0.12	0.8	90
—	—	—	5	26	53	0.9	258	80	0.11	0.10	0.8	69
—	—	—	6	31	68	0.9	373	50	0.07	0.09	0.7	74
—	—	—	5	47	34	0.4	409	320	0.04	0.04	0.4	11
—	—	—	2	16	11	0.1	136	110	0.01	0.01	0.1	4
—	—	—	10	357	99	1.5	498	14,820	0.21	0.38	2.3	144
—	—	—	10	299	87	1.7	401	11,560	0.10	0.24	1.0	56
—	—	—	16	2	69	0.5	151	310[62]	0.09	0.08	1.1	7
—	—	—	27	4	121	1.0	291	440[62]	0.18	0.10	2.1	9
—	—	—	31	5	120	1.3	304	580[62]	0.15	0.10	2.5	8
—	—	—	51	8	143	1.5	248	840[62]	0.08	0.13	2.6	13
—	—	—	43	6	153	1.1	204	740[62]	0.06	0.13	2.3	11
—	—	—	33	8	81	0.8	160	580[62]	0.05	0.08	1.5	7
—	—	—	1	7	8	0.3	45	70	0.01	0.01	0.1	3
—	—	—	1	5	5	0.1	45	Trace	0.01	0.01	0.1	3
—	—	—	7	147	44	1.9	244	12,290	0.14	0.17	—	19
—	—	—	2	41	27	0.9	147	1,650	0.04	0.07	0.3	5
—	—	—	7	206	64	1.8	243	9,130	0.11	0.20	1.8	102
—	—	—	7	157	62	1.3	251	10,660	0.08	0.20	0.9	49
—	—	—	4	57	42	3.3	430	1,580	0.10	0.10	0.5	13
—	—	—	Trace	5	4	0.3	40	150	0.01	0.01	Trace	1
—	—	—	16	108	118	2.7	943	1,780	0.32	0.32	1.6	32
—	—	—	4	27	30	0.7	236	450	0.08	0.08	0.4	8
—	—	—	2	11	12	0.3	96	180	0.03	0.03	0.2	3
—	—	—	2	37	14	0.8	145	1,050	0.03	0.04	0.2	10
—	—	—	3	4	81	0.6	290	Trace	0.07	0.32	2.9	2
—	—	—	6	193	45	2.5	308	8,120	0.11	0.20	0.8	67
—	—	—	6	98	43	0.5	184	520	0.14	0.19	1.0	21

TABLE 6   (continued)

Food	Approximate Measures, Units, or Weight (edible part unless footnotes indicate otherwise)	Weight (g)	Water (%)	Food Energy (kcal)	Protein (g)	Fat (g)
Onions:						
Mature:						
Raw:						
Chopped	1 c	170	89	65	3	Trace
Sliced	1 c	115	89	45	2	Trace
Cooked (whole or sliced) drained	1 c	210	92	60	3	Trace
Young green, bulb (⅜-in. diam.) and white						
portion of top	6 onions	30	88	15	Trace	Trace
Parsley, raw, chopped	1 T	4	85	Trace	Trace	Trace
Parsnips, cooked (diced or 2-in. lengths)	1 c	155	82	100	2	1
Peas, green:						
Canned:						
Whole, drained solids	1 c	170	77	150	8	1
Strained (baby food)	1 oz (1¾–2 T)	28	86	15	1	Trace
Frozen, cooked, drained	1 c	160	82	110	8	Trace
Peppers, hot, red, without seeds, dried (ground						
chili powder, added seasonings)	1 t	2	9	5	Trace	Trace
Peppers, sweet (about 5 per pound, whole),						
stem and seeds removed:						
Raw	1 pod	74	93	15	1	Trace
Cooked, boiled, drained	1 pod	73	95	15	1	Trace
Potatoes, cooked:						
Baked, peeled after baking (about 2 per						
pound, raw)	1	156	75	145	4	Trace
Boiled (about 3 per pound, raw):						
Peeled after boiling	1	137	80	105	3	Trace
Peeled before boiling	1	135	83	90	3	Trace
French-fries, 2 to 3½ in. long:						
Prepared from raw	10	50	45	135	2	7
Frozen, oven heated	10	50	53	110	2	4
Hashed brown, prepared from frozen	1 c	155	56	345	3	18
Mashed, prepared from—						
Raw:						
Milk added	1 c	210	83	135	4	2
Milk and butter added	1 c	210	80	195	4	9
Dehydrated flakes (without milk), water, milk,						
butter, and salt added	1 c	210	79	195	4	7
Potato chips, 1¾ by 2½ in. oval cross section	10	20	2	115	1	8
Potato salad, made with cooked salad dressing	1 c	250	76	250	7	7
Pumpkin, canned	1 c	245	90	80	2	1
Radishes, raw (prepackaged) stem ends,						
rootlets cut off	4	18	95	5	Trace	Trace
Sauerkraut, canned, solids, and liquid	1 c	235	93	40	2	Trace
Southern peas. See Black-eyed peas.						
Spinach:						
Raw, chopped	1 c	55	91	15	2	Trace
Canned, drained solids	1 c	205	91	50	6	1
Cooked, drained:						
From raw	1 c	180	92	40	5	1
From frozen:						
Chopped	1 c	205	92	45	6	1
Leaf	1 c	190	92	45	6	1

								Nutrients in Indicated Quantity				
Fatty Acids												
Saturated (total) (g)	Unsaturated		Carbo-hydrate (g)	Calcium (mg)	Phos-phorus (mg)	Iron (mg)	Potassium (mg)	Vitamin A Value (IU)	Thiamin (mg)	Riboflavin (mg)	Niacin (mg)	Ascorbic Acid (mg)
	Oleic (g)	Linoleic (g)										
—	—	—	15	46	61	0.9	267	Trace[65]	0.05	0.07	0.3	17
—	—	—	10	31	41	0.6	181	Trace[65]	0.03	0.05	0.2	12
—	—	—	14	50	61	0.8	231	Trace[65]	0.06	0.06	0.4	15
—	—	—	3	12	12	0.2	69	Trace	0.02	0.01	0.1	8
—	—	—	Trace	7	2	0.2	25	300	Trace	0.01	Trace	6
—	—	—	23	70	96	0.9	587	50	0.11	0.12	0.2	16
—	—	—	29	44	129	3.2	163	1,170	0.15	0.10	1.4	14
—	—	—	3	3	18	0.3	28	140	0.02	0.03	0.3	3
—	—	—	19	30	138	3.0	216	960	0.43	0.14	2.7	21
—	—	—	1	5	4	0.3	20	1,300	Trace	0.02	0.2	Trace
—	—	—	4	7	16	0.5	157	310	0.06	0.06	0.4	94
—	—	—	3	7	12	0.4	109	310	0.05	0.05	0.4	70
—	—	—	33	14	101	1.1	782	Trace	0.15	0.07	2.7	31
—	—	—	23	10	72	0.8	556	Trace	0.12	0.05	2.0	22
—	—	—	20	8	57	0.7	385	Trace	0.12	0.05	1.6	22
1.7	1.2	3.3	18	8	56	0.7	427	Trace	0.07	0.04	1.6	11
1.1	.8	2.1	17	5	43	0.9	326	Trace	0.07	0.01	1.3	11
4.6	3.2	9.0	45	28	78	1.9	439	Trace	0.11	0.03	1.6	12
0.7	0.4	Trace	27	50	103	0.8	548	40	0.17	0.11	2.1	21
5.6	2.3	0.2	26	50	101	0.8	525	360	0.17	0.11	2.1	19
3.6	2.1	0.2	30	65	99	0.6	601	270	0.08	0.08	1.9	11
2.1	1.4	4.0	10	8	28	0.4	226	Trace	0.04	0.01	1.0	3
2.0	2.7	1.3	41	80	160	1.5	798	350	0.20	0.18	2.8	28
—	—	—	19	61	64	1.0	588	15,680	0.07	0.12	1.5	12
—	—	—	1	5	6	0.2	58	Trace	0.01	0.01	0.1	5
—	—	—	9	85	42	1.2	329	120	0.07	0.09	0.5	33
—	—	—	2	51	28	1.7	259	4,460	0.06	0.11	0.3	28
—	—	—	7	242	53	5.3	513	16,400	0.04	0.25	0.6	29
—	—	—	6	167	68	4.0	583	14,580	0.13	0.25	0.9	50
—	—	—	8	232	90	4.3	683	16,200	0.14	0.31	0.8	39
—	—	—	7	200	84	4.8	688	15,390	0.15	0.27	1.0	53

TABLE 6 (continued)

Food	Approximate Measures, Units, or Weight (edible part unless footnotes indicate otherwise)	Weight (g)	Water (%)	Food Energy (kcal)	Protein (g)	Fat (g)
Squash, cooked:						
Summer (all varieties), diced, drained	1 c	210	96	30	2	Trace
Winter (all varieties), baked, mashed	1 c	205	81	130	4	1
Sweet potatoes:						
Candied, 2½ × 2 in. piece	1 piece	105	60	175	1	2
Canned:						
Solid pack (mashed)	1 c	255	72	275	5	1
Vacuum pack, 2¾ × 1 in. piece	1 piece	40	72	45	1	Trace
Cooked (raw, 5 × 2 in.; about 2½ per pound):						
Baked in skin, peeled	1	114	64	160	2	1
Boiled in skin, peeled	1	151	71	170	3	1
Tomatoes:						
Raw, 2⅗-in. diam. (3 per 12-oz package)	1	135[66]	94	25	1	Trace
Canned, solids and liquid	1 c	241	94	50	2	Trace
Tomato catsup	1 c	273	69	290	5	1
	1 T	15	69	15	Trace	Trace
Tomato juice, canned:						
Cup	1 c	243	94	45	2	Trace
Glass	6 fl oz	182	94	35	2	Trace
Turnips, cooked, diced	1 c	155	94	35	1	Trace
Turnip greens, cooked, drained:						
From raw (leaves and stems)	1 c	145	94	30	3	Trace
From frozen (chopped)	1 c	165	93	40	4	Trace
Vegetables, mixed, frozen, cooked	1 c	182	83	115	6	1
Miscellaneous Items						
Baking powders for home use:						
Sodium aluminum sulfate:						
With monocalcium phosphate monohydrate	1 t	3.0	2	5	Trace	Trace
With monocalcium phosphate monohydrate, calcium sulfate	1 t	2.9	1	5	Trace	Trace
Straight phosphate	1 t	3.8	2	5	Trace	Trace
Low sodium	1 t	4.3	2	5	Trace	Trace
Barbecue sauce	1 c	250	81	230	4	17
Beverages, alcoholic:						
Beer	12 fl oz	360	92	150	1	0
Gin, rum, vodka, whisky:						
80 proof	1½-fl oz (jigger)	42	67	95	—	—
86 proof	1½-fl oz (jigger)	42	64	105	—	—
90 proof	1½-fl oz (jigger)	42	62	110	—	—
Wines:						
Dessert	3½ fl oz	103	77	140	Trace	0
Table	3½ fl oz	102	86	85	Trace	0
Beverages, carbonated, sweetened, nonalcoholic:						
Carbonated water	12 fl oz	366	92	115	0	0
Cola type	12 fl oz	369	90	145	0	0
Fruit-flavored sodas and Tom Collins mixer	12 fl oz	372	88	170	0	0
Ginger ale	12 fl oz	366	92	115	0	0
Root beer	12 fl oz	370	90	150	0	0
Chili powder. See Peppers, hot, red.						
Chocolate:						
Bitter or baking	1 oz	28	2	145	3	15
Semisweet, see Candy: Chocolate.						

								Nutrients in Indicated Quantity				
Fatty Acids												
Saturated (total) (g)	Unsaturated		Carbo-hydrate (g)	Calcium (mg)	Phos-phorus (mg)	Iron (mg)	Potassium (mg)	Vitamin A Value (IU)	Thiamin (mg)	Riboflavin (mg)	Niacin (mg)	Ascorbic Acid (mg)
	Oleic (g)	Linoleic (g)										
—	—	—	7	53	53	0.8	296	820	0.11	0.17	1.7	21
—	—	—	32	57	98	1.6	945	8,610	0.10	0.27	1.4	27
2.0	0.8	0.1	36	39	45	0.9	200	6,620	0.06	0.04	0.4	11
—	—	—	63	64	105	2.0	510	19,890	0.13	0.10	1.5	36
—	—	—	10	10	16	0.3	80	3,120	0.02	0.02	0.2	6
—	—	—	37	46	66	1.0	342	9,230	0.10	0.08	0.8	25
—	—	—	40	48	71	1.1	367	11,940	0.14	0.09	0.9	26
—	—	—	6	16	33	0.6	300	1,110	0.07	0.05	0.9	28[67]
—	—	—	10	14[68]	46	1.2	523	2,170	0.12	0.07	1.7	41
—	—	—	69	60	137	2.2	991	3,820	0.25	0.19	4.4	41
—	—	—	4	3	8	0.1	54	210	0.01	0.01	0.2	2
—	—	—	10	17	44	2.2	552	1,940	0.12	0.07	1.9	39
—	—	—	8	13	33	1.6	413	1,460	0.09	0.05	1.5	29
—	—	—	8	54	37	0.6	291	Trace	0.06	0.08	0.5	34
—	—	—	5	252	49	1.5	—	8,270	0.15	0.33	0.7	68
—	—	—	6	195	64	2.6	246	11,390	0.08	0.15	0.7	31
—	—	—	24	46	115	2.4	348	9,010	0.22	0.13	2.0	15
0	0	0	1	58	87	—	5	0	0	0	0	0
0	0	0	1	183	45	—	—	0	0	0	0	0
0	0	0	1	239	359	—	6	0	0	0	0	0
0	0	0	2	207	314	—	471	0	0	0	0	0
2.2	4.3	10.0	20	53	50	2.0	435	900	0.03	0.03	0.8	13
0	0	0	14	18	108	Trace	90	—	0.01	0.11	2.2	—
0	0	0	Trace	—	—	—	1	—	—	—	—	—
0	0	0	Trace	—	—	—	1	—	—	—	—	—
0	0	0	Trace	—	—	—	1	—	—	—	—	—
0	0	0	8	8	—	—	77	—	0.01	0.02	0.2	—
0	0	0	4	9	10	0.4	94	—	Trace	0.01	0.1	—
0	0	0	29	—	—	—	—	0	0	0	0	0
0	0	0	37	—	—	—	—	0	0	0	0	0
0	0	0	45	—	—	—	—	0	0	0	0	0
0	0	0	29	—	—	—	0	0	0	0	0	0
0	0	0	39	—	—	—	0	0	0	0	0	0
8.9	4.9	0.4	8	22	109	1.9	235	20	0.01	0.07	0.4	0

TABLE 6   (continued)

Food	Approximate Measures, Units, or Weight (edible part unless footnotes indicate otherwise)	Weight (g)	Water (%)	Food Energy (kcal)	Protein (g)	Fat (g)
Gelatin, dry	7 g	7	13	25	6	Trace
Gelatin dessert prepared with gelatin dessert powder and water	1 c	240	84	140	4	0
Mustard, prepared, yellow	1 t or individual serving pouch or cup	5	80	5	Trace	Trace
Olives, pickled, canned:						
Green	4 medium, 3 extra large, or 2 giant	16[69]	78	15	Trace	2
Ripe, Mission	3 small or 2 large	10[69]	73	15	Trace	2
Pickles, cucumber:						
Dill, medium, whole, 3¾ in. long, 1¼-in. diam.	1 pickle	65	93	5	Trace	Trace
Fresh pack, slices 1½-in. diam., ¼ in. thick	2 slices	15	79	10	Trace	Trace
Sweet, gherkin, small, whole, about 2½ in. long, ¾-in. diam.	1 pickle	15	61	20	Trace	Trace
Relish, finely chopped, sweet	1 T	15	63	20	Trace	Trace
Popcorn. See page A40.						
Popsicle	3 fl oz	95	80	70	0	0
Soups:						
Canned, condensed:						
Prepared with equal volume of milk:						
Cream of chicken	1 c	245	85	180	7	10
Cream of mushroom	1 c	245	83	215	7	14
Tomato	1 c	250	84	175	7	7
Prepared with equal volume of water:						
Bean with pork	1 c	250	84	170	8	6
Beef broth, bouillon, consommé	1 c	240	96	30	5	0
Beef noodle	1 c	240	93	65	4	3
Clam chowder, Manhattan type (with tomatoes, without milk)	1 c	245	92	80	2	3
Cream of chicken	1 c	240	92	95	3	6
Cream of mushroom	1 c	240	90	135	2	10
Minestrone	1 c	245	90	105	5	3
Split pea	1 c	245	85	145	9	3
Tomato	1 c	245	91	90	2	3
Vegetable beef	1 c	245	92	80	5	2
Vegetarian	1 c	245	92	80	2	2
Dehydrated:						
Bouillon cube, ½ in.	1 cube	4	4	5	1	Trace
Mixes:						
Unprepared:						
Onion	1½ oz	43	3	150	6	5
Prepared with water:						
Chicken noodle	1 c	240	95	55	2	1
Onion	1 c	240	96	35	1	1
Tomato vegetable with noodles	1 c	240	93	65	1	1
Vinegar, cider	1 T	15	94	Trace	Trace	0
White sauce, medium, with enriched flour	1 c	250	73	405	10	31
Yeast:						
Baker's, dry, active	1 package	7	5	20	3	Trace
Brewer's, dry	1 T	8	5	25	3	Trace

Nutrients in Indicated Quantity												
Fatty Acids												
	Unsaturated							**Vitamin A**				
Saturated (total) (g)	Oleic (g)	Linoleic (g)	Carbohydrate (g)	Calcium (mg)	Phosphorus (mg)	Iron (mg)	Potassium (mg)	Value (IU)	Thiamin (mg)	Riboflavin (mg)	Niacin (mg)	Ascorbic Acid (mg)
0	0	0	0	—	—	—	—	—	—	—	—	—
0	0	0	34	—	—	—	—	—	—	—	—	—
—	—	—	Trace	4	4	0.1	7	—	—	—	—	—
0.2	1.2	0.1	Trace	8	2	0.2	7	40	—	—	—	—
0.2	1.2	0.1	Trace	9	1	0.1	2	10	Trace	Trace	—	—
—	—	—	1	17	14	0.7	130	70	Trace	0.01	Trace	4
—	—	—	3	5	4	0.3	—	20	Trace	Trace	Trace	1
—	—	—	5	2	2	0.2	—	10	Trace	Trace	Trace	1
—	—	—	5	3	2	0.1	—	—	—	—	—	—
0	0	0	18	0	—	Trace	—	0	0	0	0	0
4.2	3.6	1.3	15	172	152	0.5	260	610	0.05	0.27	0.7	2
5.4	2.9	4.6	16	191	169	0.5	279	250	0.05	0.34	0.7	1
3.4	1.7	1.0	23	168	155	0.8	418	1,200	0.10	0.25	1.3	15
1.2	1.8	2.4	22	63	128	2.3	395	650	0.13	0.08	1.0	3
0	0	0	3	Trace	31	0.5	130	Trace	Trace	0.02	1.2	—
0.6	0.7	0.8	7	7	48	1.0	77	50	0.05	0.07	1.0	Trace
0.5	0.4	1.3	12	34	47	1.0	184	880	0.02	0.02	1.0	—
1.6	2.3	1.1	8	24	34	0.5	79	410	0.02	0.05	0.5	Trace
2.6	1.7	4.5	10	41	50	0.5	98	70	0.02	0.12	0.7	Trace
0.7	0.9	1.3	14	37	59	1.0	314	2,350	0.07	0.05	1.0	—
1.1	1.2	0.4	21	29	149	1.5	270	440	0.25	0.15	1.5	1
0.5	0.5	1.0	16	15	34	0.7	230	1,000	0.05	0.05	1.2	12
—	—	—	10	12	49	0.7	162	2,700	0.05	0.05	1.0	—
—	—	—	13	20	39	1.0	172	2,940	0.05	0.05	1.0	—
—	—	—	Trace	—	—	—	4	—	—	—	—	—
1.1	2.3	1.0	23	42	49	0.6	238	30	0.05	0.03	0.3	6
—	—	—	8	7	19	0.2	19	50	0.07	0.05	0.5	Trace
—	—	—	6	10	12	0.2	58	Trace	Trace	Trace	Trace	2
—	—	—	12	7	19	0.2	29	480	0.05	0.02	0.5	5
0	0	0	1	1	1	0.1	15	—	—	—	—	—
19.3	7.8	0.8	22	288	233	0.5	348	1,150	0.12	0.43	0.7	2
—	—	—	3	3	90	1.1	140	Trace	0.16	0.38	2.6	Trace
—	—	—	3	17[70]	140	1.4	152	Trace	1.25	0.34	3.0	Trace

[1]Vitamin A value is largely from β-carotene used for coloring. Riboflavin value for powdered creamers apply to products with added riboflavin.

[2]Applies to product without added vitamin A. With added vitamin A, value is 500 IU.

[3]Applies to product without vitamin A added.

[4]Applies to product with added vitamin A. Without added vitamin A, value is 20 IU.

[5]Yields 1 qt of fluid milk when reconstituted according to package directions.

[6]Applies to product with added vitamin A.

[7]Weight applies to product with label claim of 1⅓ cups equal 3.2 oz.

[8]Applies to products made from thick shake mixes with no added ice cream. Products made from milk shake mixes are higher in fat and usually contain added ice cream.

[9]Content of fat, vitamin A, and carbohydrate varies. Consult the label when precise values are needed for special diets.

[10]Applies to product made with milk containing no added vitamin A.

[11]Based on year-round average.

[12]Based on average vitamin A content of fortified margarine. Federal specifications for fortified margarine require a minimum of 15,000 IU of vitamin A per pound.

[13]Fatty acid values apply to product made with regular margarine.

[14]Dipped in egg, milk or water, and bread crumbs; fried in vegetable shortening.

[15]If bones are discarded, value for calcium will be greatly reduced.

[16]Dipped in egg, bread crumbs, and flour or batter.

[17]Prepared with tuna, celery, salad dressing (mayonnaise type), pickle, onion, and egg.

[18]Outer layer of fat on the cut removed to within approximately ½ in. of the lean. Deposits of fat within the cut not removed.

[19]Crust made with vegetable shortening and enriched flour.

[20]Regular margarine used.

[21]Value varies widely.

[22]About one-fourth of the outer layer of fat on the cut removed. Deposits of fat within the cut not removed.

[23]Vegetable shortening used.

[24]Also applies to pasteurized apple cider.

[25]Applies to product without added ascorbic acid. For value of product with added ascorbic acid, refer to label.

[26]Based on product with label claim of 45% of U.S. RDA in 6 fl oz.

[27]Based on product with label claim of 100% of U.S. RDA in 6 fl oz.

[28]Weight includes peel and membranes between sections. Without these parts, the weight of the edible portion is 123 g for pink or red grapefruit and 118 g for white.

[29]For white-fleshed varieties, value is about 20 IU per cup; for red-fleshed varieties, 1,080 IU.

[30]Weight includes seeds. Without seeds, weight of the edible portion is 57 g.

[31]Applies to product without added ascorbic acid. With added ascorbic acid, based on claim that 6 fl oz of reconstituted juice contain 45% or 50% of the U.S. RDA, value is 108 or 120 mg for a 6-fl-oz can and 36 or 40 mg for 1 c of diluted juice.

[32]For products with added thiamin and riboflavin but without added ascorbic acid, values in milligrams would be 0.60 for thiamin, 0.80 for riboflavin, and a trace for ascorbic acid. For products with only ascorbic acid added, value varies with the brand. Consult the label.

[33]Weight includes rind. Without rind, the weight of the edible portion is 272 g for cantaloupe and 149 g for honeydew.

[34]Represents yellow-fleshed varieties. For white-fleshed varieties, value is 50 IU for 1 peach and 90 IU for 1 c of slices.

[35]Value represents products with added ascorbic acid. For products without added ascorbic acid, the values are highly variable; e.g., 10–25 mg for a 10-oz container, and 15–35 mg for 1 c.

[36] Weight includes pits. After removal of the pits, the weight of the edible portion is 258 g for a cup and 133 g for a portion, 43 g for uncooked prunes, and 213 g for cooked prunes.

[37] Weight includes rind and seeds. Without rind and seeds, weight of the edible portion is 426 g.

[38] Made with vegetable shortening.

[39] Applies to product made with white cornmeal. With yellow cornmeal, value is 30 IU.

[40] Applies to white varieties. For yellow varieties, value is 150 IU.

[41] Applies to products that do not contain disodium phosphate. If disodium phosphate is an ingredient, value is 162 mg.

[42] Value may range from less than 1 mg to about 8 mg, depending on the brand. Consult the label.

[43] Applies to product with added nutrient. Without added nutrient, value is trace.

[44] Value varies with the brand. Consult the label.

[45] Applies to product with added nutrient. Without added nutrient, value is trace.

[46] Except for angel food cake, cakes were made from mixes containing vegetable shortening; icings made from butter.

[47] Except for sponge cake, vegetable shortening used for cake portion; butter, for icing. If butter or margarine used for cake portion, vitamin A values are higher.

[48] Applies to product made with a sodium-aluminum-sulfate-type baking powder. With a low-sodium baking powder containing potassium, value would be about twice the amount shown.

[49] Equal weights of flour, sugar, eggs, and vegetable shortening.

[50] Products are commercial unless otherwise specified.

[51] Made with enriched flour and vegetable shortening except for macaroons, which do not contain flour or shortening.

[52] Icing made with butter.

[53] Applies to yellow varieties; white varieties contain only a trace.

[54] Contains vegetable shortening and butter.

[55] Made with corn oil.

[56] Made with regular margarine.

[57] Applies to product made with yellow cornmeal.

[58] Made with enriched degermed cornmeal and enriched flour.

[59] Product may or may not be enriched with riboflavin. Consult the label.

[60] Value varies with the brand. Consult the label.

[61] Weight includes cob. Without cob, weight is 77 g for a raw ear and 126 g for a frozen ear.

[62] Based on yellow varieties. For white varieties, value is trace.

[63] Weight includes refuse of outer leaves and core. Without these parts, weight is 163 g.

[64] Weight includes core. Without core, weight is 539 g.

[65] Value based on white-fleshed varieties. For yellow-fleshed varieties, value is 70 IU for chopped raw onions, 50 IU for sliced raw onions, and 80 IU for cooked onions.

[66] Weight includes cores and stem ends. Without these parts, weight is 123 g.

[67] Based on year-round average. For tomatoes marketed from November through May, value is about 12 mg; from June through October, 32 mg.

[68] Applies to product without calcium salts added. Value for products with calcium salts added may be as much as 63 mg for whole tomatoes, 241 mg for cut forms.

[69] Weight includes pits. Without pits, weight is 13 g for green olives and 9 g for Mission ripe olives.

[70] Value may vary from 6 to 60 mg.

TABLE 7   Folacin in Selected Foods

Food and Description	Approximate Measure	Weight (g)	Free Folacin (µg)	Total Folacin (µg)
Cereal grains and their products				
Barley, pot	1 c	200	18	40
Cornmeal, degermed	1 c	122	11	29
Macaroni, dry form	8 oz	227	9	27
Rice				
Brown	1 c	185	22	30
White	1 c	185	—	18
Parboiled	1 c	185	17	20
Rye flour, sifted	1 c	88	27	69
Spaghetti, dry form	8 oz	227	9	27
Wheat flour, whole, patent	1 c	120	48	65
All purpose, sifted	1 c	115	21	24
Bread, sifted	1 c	115	22	29
Breakfast cereals, dry				
Farina	1 c	180	—	43
Farina, wheat germ added	1 c	180	31	61
Oatmeal	1 c	80	13	42
Breakfast cereals, ready-to-eat; not fortified with folacin				
Corn flakes	1 oz	28	3	3
Oats, with added wheat gluten	1 oz	28	2	6
Rice, puffed	1 oz	28	2	6
Rice, with added protein concentrate and wheat gluten	1 oz	28	4	9
Wheat, shredded	1 oz	28	3	14
Wheat and malted barley granules	1 oz	28	4	15
Wheat germ, toasted	1 oz	28	35	118
Bakery products				
Bread				
Rye	1 slice	25	2	6
White	1 slice	25	3	10
Whole wheat	1 slice	28	8	16
Cakes				
Chocolate with icing	1 slice (3 in. high; 2⅜ in. arc)	99	4	6
Sponge	1 slice (3 in. high; 2¼ in. arc)	44	1	3
Cookies				
Chocolate chip	1	10	<0.5	1
Shortbread	1	8	<0.5	1
Doughnuts				
Cake type	1	32	2	3
Yeast leavened	1	35	2	8
Pie, apple	⅙	158	3	6
Leguminous seeds and their products				
Beans, common, mature seeds				
White				
Raw, dry	1 c	205	51	264
Canned, baked with tomato sauce	1 c	255	20	61
Pinto, mature seeds, dry				
Raw, dry	1 c	190	108	410
Cooked	1 c	190	—	112
Canned, drained	1 c	190	—	97
Red				
Raw, dry	1 c	185	44	246
Cooked	1 c	185	—	68

Food and Description	Approximate Measure	Weight (g)	Free Folacin (μg)	Total Folacin (μg)
Beans, lima, mature seeds				
Raw, dry	1 c	190	48	215
Cooked	1 c	190	—	82
Beans, mung, mature seeds, dry	1 c	210	55	279
Chick-peas (garbanzos), mature seeds				
Raw, dry	1 c	200	64	398
Cowpeas, mature seeds				
Raw, dry	6 c	170	117	226
canned, drained	1 c	165	—	132
Lentils, mature seeds, dry	1 c	190	36	68
Peanuts, roasted	1 c	144	35	153
Peanut butter	1 T	16	3	13
Soybeans, mature seeds, dry	1 c	210	158	359
Soy sauce	1 T	18	1	5
Nuts and seeds (other than leguminous seeds)				
Almonds	1 c	142	47	136
Brazil nuts, shelled	1 c	140	1	6
Cashew nuts, roasted	1 c	140	11	95
Coconut, shredded	1 c	130	13	31
Filberts (hazelnuts), shelled	1 c	135	31	97
Pecans, shelled	1 c	108	14	26
Sesame seeds	1 T	8	4	8
Walnuts, English, shelled	1 c	100	52	66
Vegetables				
Asparagus, raw	1 c	135	78	86
Beans, lima, frozen	1 c	160	14	50
Beans, snap				
Green				
Raw	1 c	110	36	48
Cooked, drained	1 c	125	—	50
Frozen	1 c	125	10	41
Yellow or wax				
Raw	1 c	110	35	44
Frozen	1 c	125	10	42
Bean sprouts, canned	1 c	125	9	12
Beets, common, red				
Raw	1 c	135	93	126
Cooked	1 c	170	65	133
Broccoli				
Spears				
Raw	3 medium	354	181	244
Cooked	1 medium	180	49	101
Flower, raw	3.5 oz	100	102	105
Stem, raw	3.5 oz	100	35	59
Brussels sprouts				
Raw	6 medium	114	63	89
Cooked	1 c	155	9	56
Cabbage				
Common varieties				
Raw	1 c	90	30	59
Cooked	1 c	145	3	26
Red, raw	1 c	90	21	31
Cabbage, Chinese (also called celery cabbage or petsai)				
Raw	1 c	75	32	62

TABLE 7 (continued)

Food and Description	Approximate Measure	Weight (g)	Free Folacin (μg)	Total Folacin (μg)
Carrots				
Raw	1 medium	59	8	19
Cooked	1 c	155	3	37
Cauliflower				
Raw	1 c	100	31	55
Cooked	1 c	125	2	42
Celery, raw	1 c	100	6	12
Collards, raw	1 c	55	—	56
Corn, sweet				
Raw, whole kernel	1 c	165	45	54
Frozen	1 c	162	3	35
Cucumber, raw, pared	1 small	128	15	19
Eggplant, cooked	1 c	200	4	32
Endive, raw	1 c	50	—	24
Kale, raw	1 c	110	48	66
Lettuce, raw				
Leaf or head	1 c	55	19	20
Romaine	1 c	55	33	98
Mushrooms, raw	1 c	68	14	16
Okra, raw	1 c	100	10	24
Onion, mature, chopped	1 c	170	17	42
	1 T	10	1	2
Onion, young green, raw				
Bulbs and white portion of top	1 c	100	40	36
	1 T	6	2	2
Tops only (green portion), chopped	1 c	100	52	80
	1 T	6	3	5
Parsnips, raw	1 c	130	74	87
Parsley, raw	1 T	4	2	5
Peas, green, frozen	1 c	145	25	77
Peppers, sweet, immature, green, raw	1 medium	164	13	31
Potatoes				
Raw	1 medium	122	13	23
Cooked				
French fried	10 pieces	50	4	11
Hashed brown	1 c	155	5	26
Mashed	1 c	210	10	21
Pumpkin, cooked	1 c	245	5	47
Radishes, common, raw	4 small	36	6	9
Rutabagas				
Raw	1 c	140	32	38
Cooked, cubed	1 c	170	15	36
Cooked, mashed	1 c	240	22	50
Spinach				
Raw	1 c	55	65	106
Cooked	1 c	180	108	164
Squash, summer				
Raw	1 c	130	30	40
Frozen, cooked	1 c	210	4	21
Sweet potatoes				
Raw	1 medium	146	48	73
Cooked	1 medium	146	10	26
Tomatoes, raw	1 medium	135	28	53
Tomato juice, canned	1 c	243	24	63
	6 oz	182	18	47

Food and Description	Approximate Measure	Weight (g)	Free Folacin (µg)	Total Folacin (µg)
Turnips, raw	1 c	130	22	26
Turnip greens, raw	1 c	55	—	52
Fruits				
Apples, raw	1 medium	166	5	13
Applesauce, sweetened	1 c	255	3	3
Apricots, dried	10 halves	35	4	5
	1 c	130	13	18
Avocados, raw	½ medium	115	36	59
Bananas, raw	1 medium	119	26	33
Blueberries, raw	1 c	145	3	9
Cantaloupe, see Muskmelon				
Cherries, raw	1 c	117	7	9
	10	68	4	5
Cranberries, raw	1 c	91	1	2
Dates, dried	1 c	178	25	37
	10	80	11	17
Figs, dried	1 large	21	1	2
Grapefruit, raw	½ medium	98	8	11
Grapefruit juice, fresh or frozen reconstituted	1 c	247	20	52
	6 oz	185	15	39
Grapes, red or white, raw	1 c	152	6	11
Grape juice, canned or frozen reconstituted	1 c	253	5	5
Lemon, raw	1 medium	74	9	9
Lemonade	1 c	248	5	12
	6 oz	185	4	9
Limes, raw	1 lime	67	4	3
Muskmelon or cantaloupe	½ medium	272	82	82
Nectarines, raw	1 medium	138	10	7
Oranges, raw	1 medium	141	45	65
Orange juice, fresh or frozen reconstituted	1 c	248	84	136
	6 oz	185	63	102
Peaches, raw	1 medium	100	2	8
Pears, raw	1 medium	164	8	23
Pineapple, raw	1 c	155	14	17
Plantain (baking banana), raw	1 medium	263	5	42
Plums, raw	1 medium	55	2	3
Prunes, dried, softenized, raw	1 medium	26	<0.5	1
Raisins, natural (unbleached), raw	1 c	145	4	6
Rhubarb, raw	1 c	122	11	9
Strawberries, raw	1 c	149	22	24
Tangerines, raw	1 medium	86	16	18
Watermelon, raw	1 wedge, 4 × 8 in.	426	9	34
Meat				
Beef, separable lean				
Raw	3.5 oz	100	4	7
Cooked	3 oz	85	—	3
Beef, ground				
Raw	3.5 oz	100	3	7
Cooked	3 oz	85	—	3
Kidney, lamb, cooked	3 oz	85	—	27
Lamb, cooked	3 oz	85	—	3
Liver				
Beef, lamb, or pork, cooked	3 oz	85	—	123
Pork, separable lean				
Cooked	3 oz	85	—	4

TABLE 7 (continued)

Food and Description	Approximate Measure	Weight (g)	Free Folacin (µg)	Total Folacin (µg)
Ham, smoked	3 oz	85	—	9
Veal, cooked	3 oz	85	—	3
Sausages, cold cuts, and luncheon meats				
Beerwurst	1 slice (1 oz)	28	<0.5	1
Bologna	1 slice (1 oz)	28	1	1
Frankfurters, unheated	1 (5 in. long, ¾ in. diam.)	45	1	2
Head cheese	1 slice (1 oz)	28	<0.5	1
Liverwurst	1 slice (1 oz)	28	6	8
Luncheon meats				
Boiled ham	1 slice (1 oz)	28	<0.5	1
Pork, spiced	1 slice (1 oz)	28	<0.5	1
Sausage, pork, raw	3 oz	85	—	12
Poultry				
Chicken, without skin				
Dark meat, cooked	3 oz	85	—	6
Light meat, cooked	3 oz	85	—	3
Liver, chicken, cooked	3 oz	85	—	204
Turkey, without skin				
Dark meat, cooked	3 oz	85	—	6
Light meat, cooked	3 oz	85	—	4
Fish and shellfish				
Cod, frozen	3 oz	85	5	15
Crab, frozen	3 oz	85	2	17
Haddock, frozen	3 oz	85	3	8
Halibut, frozen	3 oz	85	3	10
Lobster, canned	3 oz	85	7	14
Ocean perch, frozen	3 oz	85	4	8
Salmon				
Canned	3 oz	85	8	17
Frozen	3 oz	85	3	22
Sardines, canned	1 fish	12	2	2
Scallops, frozen	3 oz	85	15	14
Shrimp				
Canned	3 oz	85	7	13
Frozen	3 oz	85	7	9
Smelt, frozen	3 oz	85	5	14
Sole, frozen	3 oz	85	4	9
Tuna, canned	3 oz	85	7	13
Eggs and egg products				
Eggs				
Whole				
Raw	1 medium	44	20	29
Hard-cooked	1 medium	44	—	22
White, raw	1 medium	29	1	5
Yolk, raw	1 medium	15	18	23
Eggnog	½ c	128	—	1
Dairy products				
Butter	1 T	14	<0.5	<0.5
	1 c	227	2	7
Cheeses, natural				
Cheddar	1 c shredded	113	1	20
	1 oz	28	<0.5	5
Cottage	1 c, packed	245	—	29
Cream	8 oz	227	—	30
	3 oz	85	—	11
	1-in. cube	16	—	2

Food and Description	Approximate Measure	Weight (g)	Free Folacin (μg)	Total Folacin (μg)
Cheese spread, pasteurized process cream, fluid				
Half and half	1 c	242	5	5
	1 T	15	<0.5	<0.5
Light coffee or table	1 c	240	2	5
	1 T	15	<0.5	<0.5
Sour, cultured	1 c	230	—	25
	1 T	12	—	1
Whipping, light	1 c	239	5	10
	1 T	15	<0.5	1
Ice cream, vanilla	1 c	133	3	3
Milk, cow, fluid				
Whole, pasteurized	1 c	244	12	12
Skim, raw	1 c	245	7	—
Evaporated	1 c	252	10	20
Milk, goat	1 c	244	2	2
Milk, human	1 fl oz	31	1	2
Yogurt	1 c	245	—	27
Mixed dishes, frozen				
Beef with one vegetable	1 package	254	5	13
Beef with two vegetables, soup, dessert	1 package	456	23	55
Beef with three vegetables	1 package	327	26	78
Chicken, fried, with one vegetable	1 package	205	12	25
Chicken, fried, with two vegetables, dessert	1 package	315	19	57
Haddock with one vegetable	1 package	273	16	49
Ham with two vegetables, dessert	1 package	314	16	47
Lasagna	10 oz	280	—	62
Pizza, 13¾-in. diam.				
Cheese	⅛ pie	65	—	24
Pepperoni	⅛ pie	67	—	25
Sausage	⅛ pie	67	—	23
Pork with one vegetable, one fruit, dessert	1 package	303	6	21
Poultry, Oriental style with rice, vegetables	1 package	415	8	17
Shrimp, Oriental style with rice, vegetables	1 package	388	16	50
Shrimp with one vegetable	1 package	264	21	37
Shrimp with two vegetables	1 package	234	21	51
Spaghetti with meatballs, one vegetable, dessert	1 package	354	21	64
Turkey with one vegetable	1 package	264	11	29
Turkey with two vegetables, dessert	1 package	346	21	48
Baby foods—strained, canned				
Applesauce	1 jar	134	—	1
	1 oz	28	—	<0.5
Apricots	1 jar	134	—	1
	1 oz	28	—	<0.5
Bananas	1 jar	134	1	3
	1 oz	28	<0.5	1
Beans, green or wax	1 jar	128	1	8
	1 oz	28	<0.5	2
Beef with broth	1 jar	99	1	6
	1 oz	28	<0.5	2
Beets	1 jar	128	3	13
	1 oz	28	1	3
Carrots	1 jar	128	1	3
	1 oz	28	<0.5	1
Chicken with broth	1 jar	99	1	2
	1 oz	28	<0.5	1

TABLE 7   (continued)

Food and Description	Approximate Measure	Weight (g)	Free Folacin (μg)	Total Folacin (μg)
Corn, creamed	1 jar	128	1	4
	1 oz	28	<0.5	1
Egg yolk	1 jar	94	8	19
	1 oz	28	2	6
Fruit, mixed	1 jar	134	1	1
	1 oz	28	<0.5	<0.5
Ham with broth	1 jar	99	<0.5	6
	1 oz	28	<0.5	2
Lamb with vegetables	1 jar	99	1	8
	1 oz	28	<0.5	2
Oatmeal	1 jar	135	—	5
	1 oz	28	—	1
Peas	1 jar	128	1	9
	1 oz	28	<0.5	2
Spinach, creamed	1 jar	128	3	5
	1 oz	28	1	1
Squash	1 jar	128	1	8
	1 oz	28	<0.5	2
Sweet potatoes	1 jar	128	1	4
	1 oz	28	<0.5	1
Turkey with broth	1 jar	99	2	4
	1 oz	28	1	1
Veal with broth	1 jar	99	2	7
	1 oz	28	1	2
Vegetables, mixed	1 jar	128	1	5
	1 oz	28	<0.5	1
Miscellaneous				
Barbecue sauce	1 c	250	8	10
	1 T	16	<0.5	1
Candy, milk chocolate, plain	1 oz	28	1	2
Catsup	1 c	273	5	14
	1 T	15	<0.5	1
Margarine	1 c	227	5	5
	1 T	14	<0.5	<0.5
Mayonnaise	1 T	14	<0.5	<0.5
Rice pudding	1 c	255	13	—
	½ c	128	6	—
Soups, commercial, canned				
Asparagus, cream of	1 c	245	12	47
Beef broth	1 c	240	2	10
Clam chowder	1 c	250	8	18
Mushroom, cream of	1 c	245	2	7
Vegetable beef	1 c	250	5	15
Strawberry jam	1 T	20	1	2
Tapioca, dry	1 c	152	3	12
	1 T	8	<0.5	1
Tapioca pudding	1 c	255	5	—
Yeast				
Baker's dry, active	1 package	7	10	286
Brewer's, debittered	1 T	8	14	313

Source: Adapted from B. P. Perloff and R. R. Butrum, "Folacin in Selected Foods," *Journal of The American Dietetic Association*, 70 (1977):163–170.

Note: A dash denotes that the value is not available.

TABLE 8   Vitamin E Content of Foods

Food and Description	Alpha Tocopherols (mg/100 g food)	Food and Description	Alpha Tocopherols (mg/100 g food)
Meat (mammalian)		Whale	
Beef		Meat, frozen, raw	0.28
Muscle, skeletal, raw	0.41	Liver, frozen, raw	0.81
Ground		Sausage and luncheon meats	
Raw	0.79	Bologna	0.06
Fried	0.37	Liverwurst	0.35
Canned	0.60	Salami	0.11
Roast, cooked	0.14	Sausage	
Steak		Pork, fried	0.16
Raw	0.47	Beef, fried	0.15
Broiled	0.13		
Heart, raw	0.60	**Poultry**	
Liver		Chicken	
Raw	0.67	Meat	
Broiled	0.63	Raw	0.29
Veal		Cooked	0.35
Muscle, skeletal		Frozen fried, not heated	0.25
Very young, raw	0.08	Frozen fried, oven heated	0.19
Cutlet		Frozen raw	0.42
Pan-fried	0.05	Cooked, canned	0.28
Heart, raw	0.33	Heart, raw	1.19
Liver, raw	0.33	Pigeon	
Lamb		Breast, raw	0.06
Chop		Liver, raw	1.54
Raw	0.62	Turkey, raw	
Broiled	0.16	Breast	0.09
Cutlet, broiled	0.22	Thigh	0.64
Roast, leg, precooked, reheated	0.05	Skin	0.40
Mutton		Heart	0.16
Muscle, skeletal, raw	0.43		
Pork		**Eggs**	
Muscle, skeletal, raw	0.08	Chicken	
Chop		Yolk, raw	2.05
Pan-fried	0.16	Whole large, raw	0.70
Loin		Whole, cooked	0.77
Raw	0.40	Pheasant, yolk, raw	4.86
Canned	0.29	**Dairy products**	
Ham, fried	0.28	Butter	
Bacon		United States	1.58
Raw	0.48	Foreign	2.40
Fried	0.53	Cheese, various	0.64
Rabbit		Ice cream, chocolate	0.37
Muscle, skeletal		Ice cream, vanilla	0.06
Mature, raw	0.40	Milk, cow—fluid, whole	
Liver		U.S. commercial	0.06
Mature, raw	1.69	Foreign, commercial	0.16
Caribou, muscle, raw	0.02	Chocolate	0.09
Polar bear, meat, raw	0.04	Skim	tr
Seal, meat, raw	0.15	Milk, human, fluid	0.88

TABLE 8   (continued)

Food and Description	Alpha Tocopherols (mg/100 g food)	Food and Description	Alpha Tocopherols (mg/100 g food)
Finfish		Haddock	
Fillet		Raw	6.25
Carp (*Cyprinus carpio*)		Halibut, bastard, raw	0.34
Raw	0.63	Herring, raw	5.97
Cod, Atlantic (*Gadus morrhua*)		Mackerel, Atlantic, raw	3.10
Raw	0.23	Mackerel, jack, raw	1.21
Dark meat, raw	1.16	Ocean perch, raw	16.5
White meat, frozen	0.24	Pollock, raw	8.40
Flounder, winter		Tuna (*Thunnus thynnus*), raw	5.0
(*Pseudopleuronectes*		Turbot (*Rhombus lupus*), raw	3.0
americanus), frozen	0.36	Wolffish, Atlantic, raw	29.50
Haddock (*Melanogrammus*		Wrasse, European, raw	14.40
aeglefinus)		Yellowtail	
Raw	0.39	Raw	0.94
Broiled	0.60	Frozen, 60 days	0.64
Halibut, Atlantic (*Hippoglossus*		**Shellfish**	
hippoglossus), raw	0.85	Mollusks	
Halibut, bastard (*Paralichthys*		Limpet (*Patella vulgata*), raw	14.00
olivaceus), raw	0.14	Mussel, common (*Mytilus edulis*)	
Herring (*Clupea harengus*)		Fresh, raw	0.74
Raw	1.07	Frozen	2.5
Light meat, frozen 4–5 months	2.00	Mussel, horse (*Volsella modiolus*),	
Dark meat, frozen 4–5 months	2.30	fresh, raw	0.58
Ling (*Molva molva*), raw	0.30	Mussel, ribbed (*Volsella demissa*),	
Mackerel, Atlantic (*Scomber*		fresh, raw	0.50
scombrus)		Oyster (*Crassostrea virginica*),	
Dark meat, raw	1.52	fresh, raw	0.85
Mackerel, jack (*Trachurus*		Oyster, Australian, raw	0.26
japonicus)		Periwinkle, common (*Littorina*	
Raw	0.36	*litorea*), fresh, raw	3.90
Ocean perch (*Sebastes marinus*),		Squid (*Ommastrephes todarus*),	
raw	1.25	raw	1.2
Pollock (*Pollachius virens*), raw	0.31	Whelk (*Buccinum undatum*), raw	0.8
Sablefish (*Anoplopoma fimbria*),		Crustaceans	
frozen	4.35	Lobster (*Homarus americanus*),	
Salmon, unspecified, steak,		muscle, raw	1.47
broiled	1.35	Prawn (*Pandalus borealis*), raw	2.85
Wolffish, Atlantic (*Anarhichas lupus*),		**Fats and oils**	
raw	2.1	Mammalian	
Wrasse, European (*Labrus*		Beef tallow	2.65
bergylta), raw	0.60	Butter oil, cow	
Yellowtail (*Seriola quinque-*		Japanese	2.48
radiata),		Caribou tallow	0.37
raw	0.18	Pork lard, commercial	1.20
Frozen, 60 days	0.11	Seal oil	8.9
Liver		Whale, commercial oil	4.53
Carp, raw	0.84	Finfish, commercial oil	
Cod, Atlantic		Anchovy (*Engraulis ringens*)	29.08
Raw	15.85	Capelin (*Mallotus villosus*)	14.0
Canned	2.45	Cod, Atlantic, liver	21.96

Food and Description	Alpha Tocopherols (mg/100 g food)	Food and Description	Alpha Tocopherols (mg/100 g food)
Herring	9.22	**Cocoa products**	
Menhaden, Atlantic (*Brevoortia*		Butter, natural and Dutch	1.79
tyrannus)	7.5	Powder, natural and Dutch	0.2
Dogfish, spiny, liver	25.0	Chocolate	
Shark, Greenland (*Somniosus*		Dark, sweet	0.7
microcephalus), liver	50.0	Milk	
Finfish, noncommercial oil		12%, milk	0.7
Anchovy	74.55	20%, milk	0.7
Haddock	0.6	Bar	1.1
Haddock, liver	18.0	**Fruits**	
Salmon, chinook (*Oncorhynchus*		Apple (*Pyrus* sp.)	
tshawytscha)	19.15	Whole, raw	0.59
Wolffish, Atlantic		Flesh only, raw	0.27
Liver	185.5	Stewed with sugar	0.05
Meat	35.5	Juice, canned	0.01
Wrasse, European, liver	250.67	Apricot (*Prunus armeniaca*), canned,	
Shellfish oil		sweetened	0.89
Limpet	150.0	Avocado (*Persea americana*)	
Prawn	95.0	California Fuerte, raw	1.61
Squid, commercial oil	21.0	California Haas, raw	1.07
		Banana (*Musa sapientum*), raw	0.27
Beans and peas		Blackberry (*Rubus* sp.)	
Beans		Wild, raw	3.5
Broad (*Vicia faba*)		Cultivated, raw	0.6
Raw	0.05	Cherry (*Prunus avium*), raw	0.13
Flour, dry	1.00	Currant	
French (*Phaseolus vulgaris*), raw	<0.10	Black (*Ribes nigrum*), raw	1.0
Green (*P. vulgaris*)		Red (*R. rubrum*), raw	0.1
Fresh	0.02	Damson (*Prunus insititia*), raw	0.7
Canned	0.03	Gooseberry (*Ribes grossularia, R.*	
Freeze-dried	6.25	*uvacrispa*), raw	0.37
Frozen, not cooked	0.09	Grapefruit (*Citrus paradisi*)	
Frozen, cooked	0.13	Raw	0.25
Kidney (*P. vulgaris*)		Juice, canned	0.04
Dry	tr	Mango (*Mangifera indica*), raw	1.12
Lima (*P. lunatus*)		Muskmelon (*Cucumis melo*), raw	0.14
Dry	tr	Orange (*Citrus sinensis*)	
Navy (*P. vulgaris*)		Raw	0.24
Dry	0.34	Juice, fresh	0.04
Wax (*P. vulgaris*), canned, boiled	0.29	Pear (*Pyrus communis*)	
Scarlet runner (*P. coccineus*)		Flesh and skin, raw	0.5
Raw	<0.1	Flesh, raw	<0.1
Soy (*Glycine max*)		Pineapple (*Ananas comosus*), flesh	0.10
Dry	0.85	Raspberry (*Rubus idaeus*), raw	0.3
Peas (*Pisum sativum*)		Strawberry (*Fragaria* sp.)	
Fresh	0.13	Raw	0.12
Dry	0.09	Frozen, sliced	0.21
Frozen,		Tomato (*Lycopersicum esculentum*)	
Not cooked	0.12	Raw	0.34
Cooked	0.12	Juice, canned	0.22

TABLE 8 (continued)

Food and Description	Alpha Tocopherols (mg/100 g food)	Food and Description	Alpha Tocopherols (mg/100 g food)
Cereal grains and their products		Cake	0.04
Barley (*Hordeum vulgare*)		Cracker	0.65
Whole grain	0.57	Whole wheat	0.82
Pearled	0.02	Low grade	1.08
Buckwheat (*Fagopyrum* sp.), flour	0.32	Germ	14.07
Bulgur	0.06	Breakfast cereals	
Corn (*Zea mays*)		Flakes	0.42
Whole	0.49	Puffed	0.67
Flour	0.12	Shredded	0.36
Grits	0.12	Whole wheat	1.06
Meal	0.15	Wheat, durum (*T. durum*)	
Meal, cooked	0.08	Whole grain	0.89
Processed products		Flour	0.26
Flakes	0.10	**Nuts, peanuts, and seeds**	
Puffed	0.09	Almond (*Prunus amygdalus*)	
Shredded	0.08	Shelled, raw	23.96
Hominy grits, cooked	0.04	Meal	31.7
Millet, unspecified	0.05	Brazil nut (*Bertholletia excelsa*), raw	6.5
Oats (*Avena sativa*)		Cashew (*Anacardium occidentale*)	
Whole grain	1.09	Shelled, raw	0.19
Dry cereal	0.60	Chestnut (*Castanea sativa*), raw	0.5[†]
Granular	0.09	Coconut (*Cocos nucifera*), raw	0.7
Meal	1.51	Filbert (*Corylus* sp.), raw	23.75
Shredded	0.08	Peanut (*Arachis hypogaea*)	
Rice (*Oryza sativa*)		Shelled, raw	8.33
Brown, dehulled	0.68	Oil roasted	6.94
White, milled	0.11	Dry roasted	7.80
Grits	0.04	Pecan (*Carya illinoensis*)	
Meal	0.10	Shelled, raw	1.24
Processed cereal, dry	0.04	Pistachio (*Pistacia vera*), shelled,	
Puffed or expanded	0.06	raw	5.21
Shredded	0.02	Poppy seed (*Papaver somniferum*),	
Rye (*Secale cereale*)		raw	1.8
Whole grain	1.28	Sunflower seed (*Helianthus annuus*),	
Flour		hulled, raw	49.45
Dark	1.41	Walnut, English (*Juglans regia*),	
Light	0.43	shelled, raw	0.84
Medium	0.79	**Vegetables**	
Semolina, boiled	0.06	Artichoke, Jerusalem (*Helianthus tu-*	
Triticale (*Triticum aestivum* × *Secale*		*berosus*), tuber, raw	0.19
cereale)		Asparagus (*Asparagus officinalis*)	
Whole grain	0.90	Fresh, raw	1.98
Flour	0.20	Canned	0.38
Wheat (*Triticum aestivum*)		Frozen	1.40
Whole grain	1.01	Beet (*Beta vulgaris*)	
Bran	1.49	Root, raw	<0.03
Flour		Root, canned	0.03
Unbleached	0.25	Leaf, raw	1.5
Bleached	0.03	Broccoli (*Brassica oleracea*), fresh	0.46

Food and Description	Alpha Tocopherols (mg/100 g food)	Food and Description	Alpha Tocopherols (mg/100 g food)
Brussels sprouts (*B. oleracea*)		Baked	0.03
Fresh, raw	0.88	Boiled	0.04
Cooked	0.85	Chips	4.27
Cabbage, common (*B. oleracea*),		French fried	0.19
raw	1.67	Potato, sweet (*Ipomoea batatas*),	
Cabbage, Chinese (*B. chinensis*),		raw	4.56
raw	0.12	Pumpkin (*Cucurbita pepo*), raw	1.02
Carrot (*Daucus carota*)		Radish (*Raphanus sativus*)	
Raw	0.44	Leaf, raw	3.06
Cooked	0.42	Raisin, Sultana (*Vitis vinifera*), raw	0.7
Cauliflower (*B. oleracea*), fresh	0.03	Rhubarb (*Rheum hybridum*), raw	0.2
Celery (*Apium graveolens*), stalk and		Rutabaga (*Brassica napus*)	
pale leaf, raw	0.36	Raw	<0.03
Corn, sweet (*Zea mays*)		Steamed	0.15
Canned	0.04	Shallots (*Allium ascalonicum*),	
Frozen	0.03	green, raw	0.21
Cress (*Lepidium sativum*), raw	0.7	Spinach (*Spinacia oleracea*)	
Cucumber (*Cucumis sativus*),		Fresh, raw	1.88
whole, raw	0.15	Leaf, canned	0.02
Dandelion leaf (*Taraxacum*		Squash, marrow type (*Cucurbita*	
officinale), raw	2.5	*pepo*), steamed	0.12
Eggplant (*Solanum melongena*),		Tea leaf (*Camellia sinsensis*)	25.90
raw	0.03	Turnip (*Brassica rapa*)	
Garlic (*Allium sativum*), raw	0.01	Root, raw	<0.03
Leek (*A. porrum*), white, raw	0.92	Greens, raw	2.24
Lettuce (*Lactuca sativa*), raw	0.40	Watercress (*Nasturtium officinale*),	
Mint (*Mentha spioata*), leaf, raw	5.0	leaf and stalk, raw	1.0
Mushroom (*Agaricus bisporus*), raw	0.08	**Vegetable oils**	
Boletus, edible yellow (steinpilz),		Almond	39.17
raw	0.04	Apricot kernel	3.99
Chanterelle (pfifferling), raw	0.03	Avocado	12.55
Lorchel, raw	0.03	Barley	25.77
Morel, raw	0.05	Brazil nut	7.10
Mustard greens (*Sinapis alba*), raw	2.01	Castor bean (*Ricinus communis*),	
Nasturtium (*Tropaeolum majus*),		refined	1.91
leaf, raw	2.5	Cherry seed (*Prunus* sp.)	6.5
Nettle (*Urtica dioica*), leaf, raw	14.5	Coconut, refined	0.35
Onion (*Allium cepa*)		Corn, refined	
Raw	0.12	Commercial	14.26
Frozen		Crude commercial	13.71
French fried rings, not heated	0.56	Partially hydrogenated	
Oven heated	0.69	commercial	17.30
White, pickled in vinegar	0.19	Cottonseed (*Gossypium* sp.)	
Parsley (*Petroselinum hortense*),		Refined	35.26
raw	1.74	Crude	51.34
Parsnip (*Pastinaca sativa*), raw	1.0	Filbert	47.24
Pepper, sweet (*Capsicum* sp.), raw	0.68	Grapefruit	26.5
Potato, white (*Solanum tuberosum*)		Grape-seed (*Vitis vinifera*)	28.82
Raw	0.06	Oat (*Avena sativa*)	9.54

TABLE 8 (continued)

Food and Description	Alpha Tocopherols (mg/100 g food)	Food and Description	Alpha Tocopherols (mg/100 g food)
Olive (*Olea europaea*)	11.92	Safflower, soybean, cottonseed oils, stick	16.43
Orange flavedo	390	Soybean oil	
Palm (*Elaeis guineensis*)		Stick	3.14
Refined	18.32	Tub	2.3
Nonhydrogenated	19.12	Diet imitation tub	0.8
Hydrogenated	5.58	Soybean, cottonseed oils	
Crude	16.72	Stick	11.15
Peach kernel (*Amygdalus persica*)	13.35	Tub	8.60
Peanut		Liquid	2.53
Refined	11.62	Diet	5.62
Crude	14.41	**Other oil products**	
Hydrogenated	10.04	Mayonnaise	20.74
Pecan	0.89	Shortening, vegetable, soybean	13.97
Rapeseed (*Brassica* sp.)		**Baked products**	
Refined	17.65	Bread	
Crude	25.79	White, U.S.	0.12
Hydrogenated	16.24	Whole wheat, U.S.	0.10
Rice		Biscuit mix, dry	0.27
Bran	36.39	Cake—from soft wheat flour	0.85
Germ	103.12	Various, unfrosted	2.69
Rye	71.42	Cookies, various	2.57
Safflower seed (*Carthamus tinctorius*)		Crackers from soft wheat flour	0.37
Refined	34.05	Cupcakes, chocolate	0.14
Crude	38.25	Doughnuts	0.72
Hydrogenated	18.8	Pies—apple, blueberry, and lemon cream	1.59
Sesame		Pie shell	0.49
Refined	1.38	Pretzel sticks	0.15
Crude	28.82	Rolls	
Soybean (*Glycine* sp.)		Hamburger	0.04
Refined	10.99	From white patent flour	0.78
Crude	10.47	Dough before baking from white patent flour	0.66
Hydrogenated	9.58	**Infant and baby foods**	
Sunflower seed		Infant formulas, normal dilution	
Refined	59.50	Milk fat based, unfortified	0.03
Crude	62.26	Vitamin E fortified	0.70
Tomato seed	3.8	Non-milk-fat based; made with soybean oil, unfortified	0.46
Walnut (*Juglans* sp.)	0.44	Soybean oil, vitamin E fortified	0.55
Wheat germ	149.44	Corn oil, unfortified	0.28
Margarine		Corn, coconut, and olive oils, unfortified	0.20
Coconut, sunflower, palm oils—stick	8.8	Soybean, corn, and coconut oils, vitamin E fortified	0.51
Corn oil—stick	12.89	Coconut, corn, and soybean oils, vitamin E fortified	0.44
Corn oil—tub	10.91	Assorted fat based	0.32
Corn, soybean, cottonseed oils—stick	11.38		
Safflower, soybean oils			
Stick	17.75		
Tub	11.7		

Food and Description	Alpha Tocopherols (mg/100 g food)	Food and Description	Alpha Tocopherols (mg/100 g food)
Infant cereals		Scallops, deep-fried	0.6
Barley	0.10	Shrimp, deep-fried	0.4
High protein	0.27	Home prepared foods	
Mixed	0.16	Beans	
Oat flakes	0.90	Baked	0.22
Oatmeal	0.19	Lima with ham	0.20
Rice	0.26	Beef and vegetable stew	0.21
Baby foods, strained		Chicken and dumplings	0.08
Breakfast, cereal with fruit or egg	0.25	Sandwiches	
Desserts	0.23	Beef	0.07
Fruits	0.58	Beef and cheese	0.05
Meats	0.39	Egg salad	0.09
Dinners, meat and vegetable		Ham	
mixtures	0.22	Plain	0.88
Egg yolk	0.60	Salad	tr
Vegetables	0.45	With cheese	0.04
Mixed dishes*		Pork, hot dog	0.14
Canned convenience foods		Tuna salad	tr
Beans		Turkey	0.04
Lima, with ham	0	**Miscellaneous**	
Refried	0	Candy, toffee	0.17
Beef		Coffee, instant	0
Corned, hash	0.03	Jam and jelly	0.09
Mexican	0.06	Molasses, cane	0.41
Sloppy Joe	0.13	Mustard, prepared	1.75
Stew	0.15	Pasta	
Chicken with dumplings	tr	Macaroni	0.02
Ravioli	0.16	Peanut butter	7.0
Chow mein and meat	tr	Seaweed (dry)	
Frozen convenience foods		Kelp (*Laminaria* sp.)	0.87
Beef and vegetables	0.56	Dulse (*Rhodymenia palmata*)	3.5
Chicken and vegetables	0.38	Laver (*Porphyra umbilicalis*)	<1.0
Pasta and cheese or beef	0.16	Yeast, baker's (*Saccharomyces* sp.),	
Pork or ham and vegetables	0.43	dried or compressed	0.08

Source: Adapted from P. J. McLaughlin and J. L. Weihrauch, "Vitamin E Content of Foods," *Journal of the American Dietetic Association* 75 (1979):647–665.

*Listed by type and main ingredients.

[†] Approximately.

TABLE 9 Food Exchange Lists for Phenylalanine

Food	Amount	Phenyl-alanine (mg)	Protein (g)	Kilo-calories
Vegetables (Each serving as listed contains 15 mg of phenylalanine.)				
Baby and junior				
Beets	7 T	15	1.1	35
Carrots	7 T	15	0.7	28
Creamed spinach	1 T	16	0.4	6
Green beans	2 T	15	0.3	7
Squash	4 T	14	0.4	14
Table vegetables				
Asparagus, cooked	1 stalk	12	0.6	4
Beans, green, cooked	4 T (¼ c)	14	0.6	9
Beans, yellow, wax, cooked	4 T (¼ c)	15	0.6	9
Bean sprouts, mung, cooked	2 T	18	0.6	5
Beets, cooked	8 T (½ c)	14	0.8	34
Beet greens, cooked	1 T	14	0.2	3
Broccoli, cooked	1 T	11	0.3	3
Brussels sprouts, cooked	1 medium	16	0.6	5
Cabbage, raw, shredded	8 T (½ c)	15	0.7	12
Cabbage, cooked	5 T (⅓ c)	16	0.8	12
Carrots, raw	⅙ large (¼ c)	16	0.5	16
Carrots, cooked	8 T (½ c)	17	0.5	23
Cauliflower, cooked	3 T	18	0.6	6
Celery, cooked, diced*	4 T (¼ c)	15	0.4	6
Celery, raw*	8-in. stalk	16	0.5	7
Chard leaves, cooked	2 T	19	0.6	6
Collards, cooked	1 T	16	0.5	5
Cucumber slices, raw	8 sl, ⅛ in. thick	16	0.7	12
Eggplant, diced, raw	3 T	18	0.4	9
Kale, cooked	2 T	20	0.5	5
Lettuce*	3 small leaves	13	0.4	5
Mushrooms, cooked*	2 T	14	0.4	35
Mushrooms, fresh*	2 small	16	0.5	3
Mustard greens, cooked	2 T	18	0.6	6
Okra, cooked*	2 3-in. pods	13	0.4	7
Onion, raw, chopped	5 T (⅓ c)	14	0.5	20
Onion, cooked	4 T (¼ c)	14	0.5	19
Onion, young scallion	5 (5 in. long)	14	0.5	23
Parsley, raw, chopped*	3 T	13	0.4	5
Parsnips, cooked, diced*	3 T	13	0.3	18
Peppers, raw, chopped*	4 T	13	0.4	12
Pickles, dill	8 slices ⅛ in. thick	16	0.7	12
Pumpkin, cooked	4 T (¼ c)	14	0.5	16
Radishes, red, small*	4	13	0.4	8
Rutabagas, cooked	2 T	16	0.3	10
Soups				
Beef broth (Campbell's condensed)	1 T	14	0.5	3
Celery (Campbell's condensed)	2 T	18	0.4	19
Minestrone (Campbell's condensed)	1 T	17	1.5	25

Food	Amount	Phenyl-alanine (mg)	Protein (g)	Kilo-calories
Mushroom (Campbell's condensed)	1 T	11	0.2	17
Onion (Campbell's condensed)	1 T	14	0.6	8
Tomato (Campbell's condensed)	1 T	11	0.2	11
Vegetarian vegetable (Campbell's condensed)	1½ T	17	0.4	14
Spinach, cooked	1 T	15	0.4	3
Squash, summer, cooked	8 T (½ c)	16	0.6	16
Squash, winter, cooked	3 T	16	0.6	14
Tomato, raw	½ small	14	0.5	10
Tomato, cooked	4 T (¼ c)	15	0.6	10
Tomato juice	4 T (¼ c)	17	0.6	12
Tomato catsup	2 T	17	0.6	34
Turnip greens, cooked	1 T	18	0.4	4
Turnips, diced, cooked	5 T (⅓ c)	16	0.4	12
Fruits (Each serving as listed contains 15 mg of phenylalanine.)				
Baby and junior				
Applesauce and apricots	16 T (1 c)	15	0.6	205
Applesauce and pineapple	16 T (1 c)	11	0.5	176
Apricots with tapioca	16 T (1 c)	16	0.6	187
Bananas	8 T (½ c)	14	0.6	97
Bananas and pineapple	16 T (1 c)	18	0.6	187
Peaches	10 T	15	0.7	124
Pears	12 T (¾ c)	16	0.5	106
Pears and pineapple	16 T (1 c)	17	1.0	166
Plums with tapioca	12 T (¾ c)	16	0.5	163
Prunes with tapioca	12 T (¾ c)	16	0.5	152
Fruit juices				
Apricot nectar	6 oz (¾ c)	14	0.6	102
Cranberry juice	12 oz (1½ c)	15	0.6	39
Grape juice	4 oz (½ c)	14	0.5	80
Grapefruit juice	8 oz (1 c)	16	1.2	104
Orange juice	6 oz (¾ c)	16	1.2	84
Peach nectar	5 oz (⅔ c)	15	0.5	75
Pineapple juice	6 oz (¾ c)	16	0.6	90
Prune juice	4 oz (½ c)	16	0.5	84
Table fruits				
Apple, raw	4 2½-in. diam.	16	0.8	176
Applesauce	16 T (1 c)	12	0.6	192
Apricots, raw	1 medium	12	0.5	25
Apricots, canned	2 medium with 2 T syrup	14	0.6	80
Avocado, cubed or mashed[†]	5 T (⅓ c)	16	0.6	80
Banana, raw, sliced	4 T (¼ c)	15	0.4	32
Blackberries, raw[†]	5 T (⅓ c)	14	0.6	25
Blackberries, canned in syrup[†]	5 T (⅓ c)	13	0.5	55
Blueberries, raw or frozen[†]	12 T (¾ c)	16	0.6	60
Blueberries, canned, in syrup[†]	10 T	16	0.6	140
Boysenberries, frozen, sweet[†]	8 T (½ c)	16	0.6	72
Cantaloupe	5 T (⅓ c)	16	0.4	15

TABLE 9 (continued)

Food	Amount	Phenyl-alanine (mg)	Protein (g)	Kilo-calories
Cherries, sweet, canned in syrup[†]	8 T (½ c)	16	0.6	104
Dates, pitted, chopped	3 T	18	0.7	96
Figs, raw[†]	1 large	18	0.7	40
Figs, canned in syrup[†]	2 figs with 4 t syrup	16	0.6	90
Figs, dried[†]	1 small	16	0.6	40
Fruit cocktail[†]	12 T (¾ c)	16	0.6	120
Grapes, American type	8 grapes	14	0.5	24
Grapes, American slipskin	5 T (⅓ c)	16	0.6	25
Grapes, Thompson seedless	8 T (½ c)	13	0.8	64
Guava, raw[†]	½ medium	13	0.5	35
Honeydew melon[†]	¼ 5-in. melon	13	0.5	32
Mango, raw[†]	1 small	18	0.7	66
Nectarines, raw	1 2 in. high, 2-in. diam.	15	0.4	45
Oranges, raw	1 3-in. diam. or ⅔ c sections	15	1.1	60
Papayas, raw[†]	¼ medium or ½ c	14	0.6	36
Peaches, raw	1 medium	15	0.5	46
Peaches, canned in syrup	2 medium halves	18	0.6	88
Pears, raw	1 3 × 2½ in.	14	1.3	100
Pears, canned in syrup	2 medium halves with 2 T syrup	14	1.3	78
Pineapple, raw[†]	16 T (1 c)	16	0.6	80
Pineapple, canned in syrup[†]	2 small slices	13	0.5	93
Plums, raw	½ 2-in. plum	12	0.3	15
Plums, canned in syrup	3 plums with 2 T syrup	16	0.5	91
Prunes, dried	2 large	14	0.4	54
Raisins, dried seedless	2 T	14	0.5	54
Raspberries, raw[†]	5 T (⅓ c)	13	0.5	25
Raspberries, canned in syrup[†]	6 T	14	0.5	78
Strawberries, raw[†]	8 large	16	0.6	32
Strawberries, frozen[†]	6 T	14	0.5	108
Tangerines	1½ large	15	1.2	66
Watermelon[†]	½ c cubes	13	0.5	28
Breads and cereals (Each serving as listed contains 30 mg of phenylalanine.)				
Baby and junior				
Cereals, ready to serve				
Barley	3 T	32	0.8	24
Oatmeal	2 T	34	0.8	16
Rice	5 T (⅓ c)	30	0.6	40
Wheat	2 T	30	0.6	17
Creamed corn	3 T	30	0.5	27
Sweet potatoes (Gerber's)	3 T	32	0.5	31
Table foods				
Cereals, cooked				
Cornmeal	4 T (¼ c)	29	0.6	29
Cream of Rice	4 T (¼ c)	35	0.7	34
Cream of Wheat	2 T	27	0.6	16
Farina	2 T	25	0.5	18
Malt-o-Meal	2 T	27	0.5	17

Food	Amount	Phenyl-alanine (mg)	Protein (g)	Kilo-calories
Oatmeal	2 T	32	0.7	18
Pettijohns	2 T	24	0.5	19
Ralstons	2 T	34	0.7	18
Rice, brown or white	4 T (¼ c)	35	0.7	34
Wheatena	2 T	27	0.5	19
Cereals, ready-to-serve				
Alpha bits	4 T (¼ c)	32	0.6	28
Cheerios	3 T	32	0.6	20
Corn chex	4 T (¼ c)	29	0.6	32
Cornfetti	5 T (⅓ c)	31	0.6	46
Cornflakes	5 T (⅓ c)	29	0.6	30
Crispy critters	4 T (¼ c)	30	0.6	28
Kix	5 T (⅓ c)	31	0.6	31
Krumbles	3 T	32	0.7	26
Rice chex	6 T	32	0.7	49
Rice flakes	5 T (⅓ c)	33	0.6	32
Rice krispies	6 T	30	0.6	40
Rice, puffed	12 T (¾ c)	30	0.6	38
Sugar Crisp puffed wheat	4 T (¼ c)	30	0.6	46
Sugar sparkled flakes	5 T (⅓ c)	29	0.6	55
Wheat chex	10 biscuits	30	0.6	22
Wheaties	3 T	26	0.5	20
Wheat, puffed	6 T	30	0.6	16
Crackers				
Barnum Animal	5	30	0.6	45
Graham (65/lb)	1	26	0.5	30
Ritz (no cheese)	2	24	0.5	34
Saltines (140/lb)	2	29	0.6	28
Soda (63/lb)	1	36	0.7	30
Wheat thins (248/lb)	5	30	0.6	45
Corn, cooked	2 T	32	0.7	17
Hominy	2 T	32	0.7	17
Macaroni, cooked	1½ T	31	0.7	20
Noodles, cooked	3 T	32	0.7	20
Popcorn, popped	5 T (⅓ c)	31	0.6	17
Potato chips	4 2-in. diam.	30	0.6	44
Potato, Irish, cooked	3 T	33	0.8	31
Spaghetti, cooked	1 T	24	0.5	14
Sweet potato, cooked	2 T	25	0.4	31
Tortilla, corn	1½ 6-in. diam.	30	0.8	31
Fats (Each serving as listed contains 5 mg of phenylalanine.)				
Butter	1 T	5	0.1	100
French dressing, commercial	1 T	5	0.1	59
Margarine	1 T	5	0.1	100
Mayonnaise, commercial	½ T	5	0.1	30
Olives, green or ripe	1 medium	5	0.1	12

TABLE 9   (continued)

Food	Amount
Desserts (Each serving as listed contains 30 mg of phenylalanine.)	
Cake[‡]	1/12
Cookies	
Rice flour[‡]	2
Corn starch[‡]	2
Arrowroot	1½
Ice cream	
Chocolate[‡]	⅔ c
Pineapple[‡]	⅔ c
Strawberry[‡]	⅔ c
Jello	⅓ c
Puddings[‡]	½ c
Sauce, Hershey	2 T
Wafers, sugar, Nabisco	5

Free foods (Contain little or no phenylalanine. May be used as desired.)

Apple juice	Jellies
Beverages, carbonated	Kool-aid
Gingerbread[§]	Lemonade
Guava Butter	Molasses
Candy	Oil
Butterscotch	Pepper, black, ground
Cream mints	Popsicles, with artificial fruit flavor
Fondant	Rich's Topping
Gum drops	Salt
Hard	Shortening, vegetable
Jelly beans	Soy sauce
Lollipops	Sugar, brown, white, or confectioner's
Cherries, maraschino	Syrups, corn or maple
Fruit ices (if no more than ½ c used daily)	Tang
Cornstarch	Tapioca
Jell-quik	

Source: A Diet Guide for Parents of Children with Phenylketonuria, California Department of Public Health (Berkeley, 1966), pp. 7–11.

[*] Phenylalanine calculated as 3.3% of total protein.

[†] Phenylalanine calculated as 2.6% of total protein.

[‡] Low-phenylalanine recipes in *Phenylalanine-Restricted Diet Recipe Book*.

[§] Special recipe must be used; see *Phenylalanine-Restricted Diet Recipe Book*.

TABLE 10   Cholesterol Content of Foods

Food and Description	Household Measure Weight and/or Unit	Cholesterol (mg)
Beef, composite of retail cuts		
Total edible, cooked, bone removed	85 g (3 oz)	(80)
Lean, trimmed of separable fat		
Raw		
Cooked	85 g (3 oz)	(77)
Beef and vegetable stew		
Cooked (homemade, with lean beef chuck)	245 g (1 c)	63
Canned	245 g (1 c)	36
Beef, dried, chipped, creamed	245 g (1 c)	65
Beef potpie		
Homemade, baked	210 g	44
Commercial, frozen, unheated	216 g	38
Bread pudding with raisins	265 g (1 c)	170
Butter		
Regular (4 sticks/lb)	14 g (1 T or ⅛ stick)	35
	113 g (½ c or 1 stick)	282
Whipped (6 sticks/lb or in containers)	9 g (1 T or ⅛ stick)	22
	76 g (½ c or 1 stick)	190
Buttermilk, fluid, cultured, made from nonfat fluid milk	245 g (1 c)	5
Cakes		
Baked, from home recipes		
Chocolate (devil's food), 2-layer, with chocolate frosting	75 g (1 sl)	32
Fruitcake, dark	15 g (1 sl)	7
Sponge	66 g (1 sl)	162
Yellow, 2-layer, with chocolate frosting	75 g (1 sl)	33
Baked, from mixes		
Angel food, made with water and flavorings	53 g (1 sl)	0
Chocolate (devil's food), 2-layer, made with eggs, water, chocolate frosting	Piece (69 g) (1 sl)	33
	Cupcake (36 g)	17
Gingerbread, made with water	63 g (1 sl)	Trace
White, 2-layer, made with egg whites, water, chocolate frosting	71 g (1 sl)	1
Yellow, 2-layer, made with eggs, water, chocolate frosting	75 g (1 sl)	36
Caviar, sturgeon, granular	16 g (1 T)	>48
Cheeses, natural and processed; cheese foods; cheese spreads		
Natural cheeses		
Blue	28 g (1 oz)	(24)
	135 g (1 c)	(117)
Brick	28 g (1 oz)	(25)
Camembert	28 g (1 oz)	(26)
	38 g (1⅓ oz)	(35)
Cheddar, mild or sharp	28 g (1 oz)	28
	113 g (1 c shredded)	112
Colby	28 g (1 oz)	(27)
Cottage (large or small curd)		
Creamed		
1% fat	267 g (1 c packed)	23
4% fat	245 g (1 c packed)	48
Uncreamed	200 g (1 c packed)	13

TABLE 10   (continued)

Food and Description	Household Measure Weight and/or Unit	Cholesterol (mg)
Cream cheese	14 g (1 T)	16
	85 g (3 oz)	94
Edam	28 g (1 oz)	(29)
Limburger	28 g (1 oz)	(28)
Mozzarella, low moisture, part skim	28 g (1 oz)	18
Muenster	28 g (1 oz)	(25)
Neufchâtel	85 g (3 oz)	(64)
Parmesan	28 g (1 oz)	(27)
Grated	100 g (1 c not packed)	(113)
Provolone	28 g (1 oz)	(28)
Ricotta	28 g (1 oz)	(14)
Part skim	28 g (1 oz)	(9)
Swiss	35 g (1¼ oz)	35
Pasteurized process cheese		
American	28 g (1 oz)	(25)
Swiss	28 g (1 oz)	(26)
Pasteurized process cheese food, American	14 g (1 T)	(10)
	28 g (1 oz)	(20)
Pasteurized process cheese spread, American	14 g (1 T)	(9)
	28 g (1 oz)	(18)
	113 g (1 c shredded, packed)	(73)
Cheese sauce	250 g (1 c)	44
Cheese soufflé, homemade	110 g	184
Cheese straws	60 g	19
Chicken, all classes		
Whole, cooked, flesh and skin only	624 g	542
Cut-up parts		
Breast		
Cooked		
Total edible	92 g	74
Meat only	80 g	63
Drumstick		
Cooked		
Total edible	52 g	47
Meat only	43 g	39
Chicken à la king, cooked, homemade	245 g (1 c)	185
Chicken fricassee, cooked, homemade	240 g (1 c)	96
Chicken potpie		
Homemade, baked	232 g	71
Commercial, frozen, unheated	227 g	29
Chicken and noodles, cooked, homemade	240 g (1 c)	96
Chop suey, with meat		
Cooked, homemade	250 g (1 c)	64
Canned	85 g (3 oz)	10
Chow mein, chicken (without noodles)		
Cooked, homemade	250 g (1 c)	77
Canned	250 g (1 c)	7
Clams[1]		
Raw		
In shell		
Soft (refuse: shell and liquid, 65%)	143 g (5 oz)	72

Food and Description	Household Measure Weight and/or Unit	Cholesterol (mg)
Hard or round (refuse: shell and liquid, 83%)	389 g (13.7 oz)	194
Meat only	227 g (1 c)	114
Canned, drained solids	80 g (½ c)	(50)
Fritters[1]	1 (40 g)	51
Cod, dried, salted	80 g	(66)
Cookies		
Brownies with nuts, baked, homemade	1 (20 g)	17
Ladyfingers	4 (44 g)	157
Corn pudding	245 g (1 c)	102
Cornbread		
Baked, homemade, made with degermed cornmeal	83 g	58
Baked, from mix, made with egg and milk	Muffin (40 g)	28
	Piece (55 g)	38
Crab, all kinds		
Steamed, meat only	125 g (1 c)	125
Canned, meat only	160 g (1 c packed)	(161)
Crab, deviled[2]	240 g (1 c)	244
Crab imperial[3]	220 g (1 c)	308
Cream		
Half and half (cream and milk)	15 g (1 T)	6
	242 g (1 c)	105
Light, coffee, or table	15 g (1 T)	10
	240 g (1 c)	158
Sour	12 g (1 T)	8
	230 g (1 c)	152
Whipped topping (pressurized)	60 g (1 c)	51
Whipping, heavy	15 g (1 T)	20
	238 g (2 c)	316
Cream puffs with custard filling	130 g (1 cream puff)	188
Custard, baked	265 g (1 c)	278
Eggs, chicken		
Whole		
Raw or cooked with nothing added (refuse: shell, 11%)	1 large (50 g)	252
Scrambled or omelet with milk and fat	1 large (64 g)	263
Yolks, raw or cooked with nothing added	From large egg (17 g)	252
Gizzard		
Chicken, all classes, cooked	354 g (12½ oz)	(690)
Turkey, all classes, cooked	361 g (12¾ oz)	827
Halibut, cooked, flesh only, broiled with vegetable shortening	125 g	(75)
Heart		
Beef, cooked	145 g (1 c chopped or diced pieces)	(398)
Chicken, all classes, cooked	145 g (1 c chopped or diced pieces)	(335)
Turkey, all classes, cooked	145 g (1 c chopped or diced pieces)	345
Herring, canned, plain, solids and liquid	425 g (15 oz)	(412)
Ice cream		
Regular, approx. 10% fat	133 g (1 c)	53
	1,064 g (½ gal)	426
Rich, approx. 16% fat	148 g (1 c)	85
	1,188 g (½ gal)	682
Frozen custard or French ice cream	133 g (1 c)	97
	1,064 g (½ gal)	777

TABLE 10 (continued)

Food and Description	Household Measure Weight and/or Unit	Cholesterol (mg)
Ice milk		
Hardened	131 g (1 c)	26
	1,048 g (½ gal)	213
Soft-serve	175 g (1 c)	36
Kidneys, all kinds (beef, calf, hog, lamb), cooked	140 g (1 sl)	(1,125)
Lamb		
Composite of retail cuts		
Total edible, cooked, bone removed	85 g (3 oz)	(83)
Lean, trimmed of separable fat, cooked	85 g (3 oz)	(85)
Lard	205 g (1 c)	195
Liver		
Beef, calf, hog, or lamb; cooked	85 g (3 oz)	(372)
Chicken, all classes, cooked	25 g (1 oz)	(187)
Turkey, all classes, cooked	140 g (1 c chopped)	839
Lobster, cooked, meat only	145 g	123
Lobster Newburg[4]	250 g (1 c)	456
Macaroni and cheese, baked, homemade	200 g (1 c)	42
Mackerel		
Canned, solids and liquid	425 g (15 oz)	(399)
Cooked, flesh only, broiled with vegetable shortening	105 g (3.8 oz)	(106)
Margarine		
All vegetable fat		
⅔ animal fat, ⅓ vegetable fat	14 g (1 T or ⅛ stick)	7
	113 g (½ c or 1 stick)	56
Milk		
Fluid		
Whole	244 g (1 c)	34
Low-fat		
1% fat with 1% to 2% nonfat milk solids added	246 g (1 c)	14
2% fat with 1% to 2% nonfat milk solids added	246 g (1 c)	22
Nonfat (skim)	245 g (1 c)	5
Canned, concentrated, undiluted		
Evaporated, unsweetened	252 g (1 c)	79
Condensed, sweetened	306 g (1 c)	105
Dry		
Whole, instant	120 g (1¾ c)[5]	131
Nonfat, instant	91 g (1⅓ c low-density or ⅞ c high-density)[5]	20
Chocolate beverages		
Commercial		
Chocolate-flavored milk drink with 2% added butterfat	250 g (1 c)	20
Chocolate-flavored milk	250 g (1 c)	32
Homemade		
Hot chocolate	250 g (1 c)	31
Hot cocoa	250 g (1 c)	35
Muffins, plain, homemade	1 (40 g)	21
Noodles		
Whole egg		
Dry form	227 g (8 oz)	213
Cooked	160 g (1 c)	50

Food and Description	Household Measure Weight and/or Unit	Cholesterol (mg)
Chow mein, canned	45 g (1 c)	5
Oysters[6]		
Raw		
In shell, Eastern, select (medium) size (refuse: shell and liquid, 90%)	180 g (6⅓ oz)	90
Meat only, Eastern and Pacific	240 g (1 c)	120
Canned, solids and liquid	85 g (3 oz)	(38)
Oyster stew, home prepared[6]		
1 part oysters to 2 parts milk by volume	240 g (1 c)	63
1 part oysters to 3 parts milk by volume	240 g (1 c)	57
Pancakes, baked from mix, made with egg and milk	73 g	54
Pepper, sweet, stuffed with beef and crumbs	1 with 1⅛ c stuffing (185 g)	56
Pies, baked		
Custard	114 g (4 oz)	120
Lemon chiffon	81 g (3 oz)	137
Lemon meringue	105 g (3.8 oz)	98
Pumpkin	114 g (4 oz)	70
Popovers, baked from home recipe	1 (40 g)	59
Pork, composite of lean retail cuts, total edible		
Cooked, bone removed	85 g (3 oz)	(76)
Lean, trimmed of separable fat, cooked	85 g (3 oz)	(75)
Potatoes		
Au gratin, made with milk and cheese	245 g (1 c)	36
Scalloped, made with milk	245 g (1 c)	14
Potato salad, homemade, with mayonnaise and hard-cooked eggs	250 g (1 c)	162
Puddings, cooked		
Chocolate, made from mix	260 g (1 c)	30
Vanilla (blanc mange), homemade	255 g (1 c)	35
Rabbit, domesticated, flesh only, cooked	140 g (1 c chopped or diced)	(127)
Rice pudding with raisins	265 g (1 c)	29
Roe, salmon, raw	28 g (1 oz)	101
Salad dressings		
Mayonnaise, commercial	14 g (1 T)	10
	220 g (1 c)	154
Salad dressing		
Cooked, homemade	16 g (1 T)	12
	255 g (1 c)	190
Mayonnaise-type, commercial	15 g (1 T)	8
	235 g (1 c)	118
Salmon, sockeye or red		
Cooked, broiled with vegetable shortening, steak (refuse: bone, 12%)	145 g (5 oz)	(59)
Canned, solids and liquid	454 g (16 oz)	159
Sardines, canned in oil		
Solids and liquid	106 g (3¾ oz)	(127)
Drained solids	92 g (3¼ oz)	129
Sausage, frankfurter, all meat, cooked	1 (56 g)	(34)
Scallops, muscle only, steamed[7]	85 g (3 oz)	(45)
Shrimp, canned, drained solids	128 g (1 c)	192

TABLE 10   (continued)

Food and Description	Household Measure Weight and/or Unit	Cholesterol (mg)
Spaghetti with meat balls in tomato sauce		
Homemade	248 g (1 c)	75
Canned	250 g (1 c)	39
Sweetbreads (thymus), cooked	85 g (3 oz)	(396)
Tapioca cream pudding	165 g (1 c)	159
Tartar sauce, regular	14 g (1 T)	7
	230 g (1 c)	118
Tuna		
Canned in oil		
Solids and liquid	184 g (6½ oz)	(100)
Drained solids	157 g (5½ oz)	102
Canned in water, solids and liquid	184 g (6½ oz)	(116)
Turkey, all classes		
Whole, cooked		
Flesh, skin, and giblets	3,680 g (8.1 lb)	3,864
Flesh and skin only	3,530 g (7.8 lb)	3,283
Light meat without skin, cooked	85 g (3 oz)	65
Dark meat without skin, cooked	85 g (3 oz)	86
Turkey potpie		
Homemade, baked	232 g	71
Commercial, frozen, unheated	227 g (8 oz)	20
Veal		
Composite of retail cuts		
Total edible, cooked, bone removed	85 g (3 oz)	(86)
Lean, trimmed of separable fat, cooked	85 g (3 oz)	(84)
Waffles, baked from mix, made with egg and milk	1 (200 g)	119
Welsh rarebit	232 g (1 c)	71
White sauce		
Thin	250 g (1 c)	36
Medium	250 g (1 c)	33
Thick	250 g (1 c)	30
Yogurt, made from fluid and dry milk		
Plain or vanilla	227 g (8 oz)	17
Fruit flavored (all kinds)	227 g (8 oz)	15

Source: R. M. Feeley, "Cholesterol Contents of Foods," *Journal of The American Dietetic Association* 61 (1972): 136–146.

Note: Numbers in parentheses denote imputed values.

[1] Cholesterol accounts for about 40% of the total sterol content of clams.

[2] Prepared with bread cubes, margarine, parsley, eggs, lemon juice, and catsup.

[3] Prepared with margarine, flour, milk, onion, green pepper, eggs, and lemon juice.

[4] Prepared with butter, egg yolks, sherry, and cream.

[5] Amount needed for reconstitution to 1 qt.

[6] Cholesterol accounts for about 40% of total sterol of oysters.

[7] Cholesterol accounts for about 30% of total sterol of scallops.

TABLE 11   Sodium and Potassium Content of Foods

Food	Unit	Weight (g)	Sodium (mg)	Potassium (mg)
Dairy and Egg Products				
Butter, regular	1 T	14.2	140	3
Buttermilk	1 c	245	319	343
Cheese, blue or roquefort	1 c	135	380	70
Cheese, cheddar or American	1 oz	28	197	23
Cheese, cottage, uncreamed	1 c	226	918	194
Cheese, parmesan, grated	1 T	5	93	5
Cream, coffee	1 c	240	103	293
Cream, half-and-half	1 c	242	111	312
Cream, heavy	1 c	238	76	212
Eggs	1	50	54	57
Ice cream	1 c	133	84	241
Margarine	1 T	9.4	93	2
Milk, dry, nonfat, instant	1 envelope	91	479	1,570
Milk, dry, nonfat, regular	1 c	120	638	2,094
Milk, dry, whole, regular, instant	1 lb	454	1,837	6,033
Milk, low-fat	1 c	246	150	431
Milk, skim	1 c	245	127	355
Milk, whole	1 c	244	122	351
Yogurt, skim milk	8 oz	226	115	323
Meat and Meat Products				
Bacon, Canadian	1 slice	21	537	91
Beef, chuck, braised	3½ oz	100	60	370
Beef, corned, cooked	1 lb	454	4,277	272
Beef, hamburger, lean	1 patty	86	41	480
Beef, rib roast	2 slices	41	17	169
Beef, round, stew	¼ lb	113	68	563
Beef, sirloin tip	1 slice	44	19	199
Chicken, canned	1 c	205	—	283
Chicken, dark meat	1 c	140	120	449
Chicken, light meat	1 c	140	90	575
Gizzard, chicken	1 c	145	83	306
Heart, beef	1 c	145	151	336
Kidney, beef	1 c	140	354	454
Lamb, chop	3.4 oz	95	51	234
Lamb, leg	1 c	140	87	396
Liver, beef	1 slice	85	156	323
Pork, chops	8.6 oz	244	147	670
Pork, spareribs	6.3 oz	180	65	299
Pork, ham	10.9 oz	308	173	793
Rabbit, meat	1 c	140	57	515
Sausages, frankfurter	1	50	550	110
Sausages, Italian	1 slice	28	161	81
Sausages, knockwurst	3½ oz	100	—	—
Sausages, Polish	1 slice	30	—	—
Sausages, pork link	3½ oz	100	740	140
Sausages, salami	1 slice	30	—	—
Sausages, Vienna	1	18	590	150
Tongue, beef	1 slice	20	12	33

TABLE 11   (continued)

Food	Unit	Weight (g)	Sodium (mg)	Potassium (mg)
Turkey, meat	1 c	140	115	575
Veal	9.5 oz	269	174	795
Seafood				
Bluefish	1 lb	454	662	722
Caviar, sturgeon	1 T	16	352	29
Clams	1 pt (1 lb)	454	163	1,066
Cod, cooked with margarine	1 fillet	65	72	265
Crab, canned	1 c	135	1,350	149
Flounder, baked with margarine	1 oz	28	67	166
Haddock, fried	1 fillet	110	195	383
Halibut, broiled with butter	1 fillet	125	168	656
Lobster, northern	1 c	145	305	261
Lobster, Newburg	1 c	250	573	428
Ocean perch, Atlantic	1 oz	28	43	81
Oysters	1 c	240	175	210
Rockfish	1 fillet	115	78	513
Salmon, broiled with butter	1 steak	145	148	565
Sardines, Atlantic, canned, oil	1 lb	454	3,733	2,676
Scallops	1 lb	454	1,202	2,159
Shad, baked	12.8 oz	365	288	1,376
Shrimp	1 lb	454	844	1,039
Sturgeon	1 lb	454	490	1,066
Tuna, canned in oil	1 can	198	1,584	596
Tuna, canned in water	1 can	99	41	276
Whitefish, lake	1 oz	28	55	82
Grain and Grain Products				
Barley, pearl	1 c	200	—	592
Biscuits, from mix	1	28	272	32
Biscuits, with baking powder	1	28	175	33
Boston brown bread	1 piece	45	113	131
Bran	1 c	60	493	466
Bread, French	1 slice	35	203	32
Bread, raisin	1 slice	25	91	58
Bread, white, enriched	1 slice	28	142	29
Bread, whole wheat	1 slice	25	132	68
Cereals, hot				
Ralston	⅔ c	28	4	107
Cream of wheat, instant	1 c	38	96	—
Cream of rice	1 c	245	0	64
Oats and wheat	1 c	245	412	—
Malt-O-Meal	¾ c	28	1	16
Farina, instant	1 c	245	461	32
Oatmeal with raisins and spices, dry, instant	½ c	40	214	133
Oatmeal, rolled oats	1 c	236	1	130
Cereals, ready-to-eat				
Natural, 100% Quaker	1 oz	28	18	146
Wheaties, General Mills	1 c	28	315	—
Shredded wheat	1 biscuit	25	1	87

Food	Unit	Weight (g)	Sodium (mg)	Potassium (mg)
Puffed Rice, Quaker	1 c	14	1	15
Corn Flakes, Kellogg	1 c	22	216	26
Cheerios, General Mills	1 c	25	260	83
Bran flakes, 40%	1 c	35	207	137
All Bran, Kellogg	1 c	56	567	517
Cookies, assorted	1 lb	454	1,656	304
Cookies, butter	10	50	209	30
Cookies, chocolate chip	10	105	421	141
Cookies, molasses	1	32.5	125	45
Cookies, oatmeal with raisins	4	52	84	192
Cookies, peanut	4	49	85	86
Cookies, sugar	10	80	254	61
Cornbread	1 piece	83	491	130
Corn grits	1 c	245	502	27
Crackers, animal	10	26	79	25
Crackers, cheese	10	31	325	34
Crackers, graham	1 piece	14	95	55
Crackers, soda	10	28	312	34
Doughnut	1	42	99	34
Muffin	1	40	176	50
Noodles, egg	1 c	160	3	70
Pancake	1	73	412	112
Popcorn, buttered, salted	1 c	9	175	—
Rice, brown	1 c	195	550	137
Rice, white, enriched	1 c	205	767	57
Rolls, brown-and-serve	1	28	157	28
Rolls, dinner	1	17	83	—
Rolls, hamburger	1	30	152	28
Rolls, hard	1	35	219	34
Spaghetti	1 c	130	1	103
Waffles, baked	1	75	356	109
Wheat flour	1 c	137	3	130
Wheat flour, self-rising	1 c	115	1,241	—
Wild rice	1 c	160	11	352
Zwieback	1 package	170	425	255
Nuts and Nut Products				
Almonds, shelled	1 c	142	1	241
Brazil nuts, shelled	1 c	140	1	1,001
Cashew nuts	1 c	140	21	650
Filberts, hazelnuts	1 c	115	2	810
Peanut butter	1 T	16	97	100
Peanuts, roasted, salted	1 c	144	602	971
Pecans, halves	1 c	108	Trace	651
Walnuts, black, shelled	1 c	125	4	575
Vegetables and Juices				
Artichokes	1 bud	300	36	361
Asparagus	4 spears	60	1	110
Beans, lima	1 c	170	5	1,914

TABLE 11   (continued)

Food	Unit	Weight (g)	Sodium (mg)	Potassium (mg)
Beans, mung	1 c	125	5	195
Beans, navy	1 c	190	13	790
Beans, red, kidney	1 c	185	6	629
Beans, snap, green	1 c	125	5	189
Beans, snap, yellow or wax	1 c	110	4	189
Beets, red	1 c	170	73	354
Beet greens	1 c	145	110	481
Broccoli, stalks	1	180	18	481
Brussels sprouts	1 c	155	16	423
Cabbage, Chinese	1 c	75	17	190
Cabbage, common	1 c	90	18	210
Carrots	1	81	34	246
Cauliflower	1 c	100	13	295
Celery, stalks	1	40	50	136
Chard, Swiss	1 c	145	125	465
Corn, sweet	1 c	165	Trace	272
Coleslaw, with mayonnaise	1 c	120	144	239
Cowpeas	1 c	165	2	625
Cress	1 lb	454	64	2,749
Cucumbers	1 c	105	6	168
Dandelion greens	1 c	105	46	244
Eggplant	1 c	200	2	300
Kale, leaves	1 c	110	195	1,002
Kohlrabi	1 c	165	10	429
Lentils	1 c	200	—	498
Lettuce	1 wedge	135	12	236
Mushrooms	1 c	70	11	290
Okra	1 c	160	3	278
Onions	1 c	170	17	267
Onions, young green	1 c	100	5	231
Parsley	1 c	60	27	436
Parsnips	1 c	155	12	587
Peas, green, frozen	1 c	145	187	218
Peas, split	1 c	200	26	592
Peas and carrots	1 c	160	134	251
Peppers, sweet	1 c	100	13	213
Potato, baked	1	202	6	782
Potato, french fries	10	78	5	665
Potato chips	10	20	—	226
Pumpkin, canned	1 c	245	5	588
Rhubarb	1 c	270	5	548
Rutabaga	1	170	7	284
Sauerkraut, canned	1 c	235	1,755	329
Squash, summer	1 c	180	2	254
Spinach	1 c	55	39	259
Squash, crookneck and straight neck	1 c	180	2	254
Squash, zucchini and cocozelle	1 c	180	2	254
Soybeans	1 c	180	4	972

Food	Unit	Weight (g)	Sodium (mg)	Potassium (mg)
Soybean curd (tofu)	1 piece	120	8	50
Succotash, frozen	1 c	170	65	418
Sweet potato, baked	1	146	14	342
Tomato, ripe	1	135	4	300
Tomato juice, canned	1 c	243	486	552
Tomato juice cocktail, canned	1 c	243	486	537
Tomato paste, canned	1 c	262	100	2,237
Tomato puree, canned	1 can	822	3,280	3,502
Vegetables, mixed	1 c	182	96	348
Vegetable juice, cocktail, canned	1 can	182	364	402
Yam, tuber	1 lb	454	—	2,341
Watercress	1 c	35	18	99
Water chestnuts, Chinese	1 lb	454	70	1,747
Fruits and Juices				
Apple	1	230	2	218
Apple, dehydrated	1 c	255	3	270
Apple butter	1 c	282	6	711
Apple juice, canned	1 c	248	2	250
Applesauce, canned	1 c	255	5	166
Apricots	3	114	1	301
Apricots, canned	1 c	254	3	604
Apricots, dehydrated	1 c	300	24	897
Apricot nectar	1 c	251	Trace	379
Avocado	½	125	5	680
Banana	1	175	1	440
Blackberries, canned	1 c	244	2	281
Blueberries	1 c	145	1	117
Cherries	1 c	130	2	223
Cherries, canned	1 c	244	5	317
Coconut cream	1 c	240	203	185
Coconut meat	1 piece	45	10	115
Cranberries	1 c	110	2	90
Dates	10	92	1	518
Fig	1	50	1	97
Fruit salad, canned	1 lb	454	5	631
Grape juice, canned	1 c	253	5	293
Grapes, American	1 c	153	3	160
Grapefruit	½	184	1	132
Grapefruit juice, frozen concentrate	1 c	247	2	420
Grapefruit juice and orange juice, blended	1 c	248	Trace	439
Lemonade concentrate, frozen	1 c	248	1	40
Lemon juice	1 T	15.2	Trace	21
Lime juice	1 c	246	2	256
Mangos	1 c	165	12	312
Marmalade, citrus	1 T	20	37	—
Muskmelon	½	477	33	682
Nectarine	1	150	8	406
Orange	1	180	1	263

TABLE 11   (continued)

Food	Unit	Weight (g)	Sodium (mg)	Potassium (mg)
Orange juice	1 c	247	2	509
Orange juice concentrate, frozen	1 can	213	4	1,500
Papaya	1	454	9	711
Peach nectar	1 c	249	2	194
Peach	1	175	2	308
Pear	1	180	3	213
Persimmon	1	200	10	292
Pineapple	1 c	155	2	226
Pineapple juice, canned	1 c	250	3	373
Pineapple juice and grapefruit juice drink	1 c	250	Trace	155
Plums	10	110	2	299
Prunes, dehydrated	1 c	100	11	940
Prune juice, canned	1 c	256	5	602
Raisins	1 c	145	39	1,106
Raspberries	1 c	123	1	207
Strawberries	1 c	149	1	244
Tangerine	1	136	2	127
Tangerine juice, canned	1 can	185	2	329
Watermelon	1 piece	926	4	426
Soups				
Bean with pork, canned	1 c	265	2,136	837
Beef broth, bouillon, consommé	1 c	245	1,872	157
Beef noodle, condensed	1 c	245	1,872	157
Clam chowder, canned	1 c	250	1,915	375
Cream of asparagus, canned	1 c	245	2,009	245
Cream of celery, canned	1 c	245	1,950	221
Cream of chicken	1 c	245	1,982	162
Cream of mushroom, canned	1 c	245	1,948	201
Minestrone, canned	1 c	250	2,033	638
Tomato, canned	1 c	250	1,980	470
Vegetable beef, canned	1 c	250	2,135	328
Beverages				
Beer	12 fl oz	360	25	90
Beverages, alcoholic (gin, rum, vodka, whiskey)	1 jigger	42	Trace	1
Cocoa and chocolate-flavored powder	1 oz or 4 t	28	149	227
Coffee, instant	1 T	3.5	3	114
Soft drinks (cola, cream soda, ginger ale, root beer)	12 fl oz	369	—	—
Wine	1 gallon	103	4	77
Candy				
Caramel	1 oz	28	64	54
Chocolate, milk	1 oz	28	27	109
Fondant, mints	1 piece	8.8	19	Trace
Fudge, chocolate	1 oz	28	54	42
Gumdrops	1 oz	28	10	1
Jelly beans	1 oz	28	26	2
Marshmallow	1	7.2	3	Trace
Peanut brittle	1 oz	28	9	43
Desserts				
Cake, angel food	1 piece	60	170	53

Food	Unit	Weight (g)	Sodium (mg)	Potassium (mg)
Cake, coffee	1 piece	108	465	118
Cake, fruitcake	1 sl	15	24	74
Cake, plain	1 cupcake	33	99	26
Cake, sponge	1 piece	66	110	57
Custard	1 c	265	209	387
Gelatin dessert, from powder	1 c	240	122	—
Jellies	1 T	18	3	14
Pie, apple	1 sl	158	476	126
Pie, custard	1 sl	152	436	208
Pie, lemon	1 sl	140	395	70
Pie, mince	1 sl	158	708	281
Pie, pumpkin	1 sl	152	325	243
Pudding	1 c	260	335	354
Sherbet, orange	1 c	193	19	42
Tapioca cream pudding	1 c	165	257	223
Condiments				
Horseradish	1 T	15	14	44
Mustard	1 t	5	65	7
Pickle, cucumber, dill	1	135	1,928	270
Radishes	10	90	15	261
Relish, pickle, sweet	1 c	245	1,744	—
Salt, table	1 t	5.5	2,132	Trace
Soy sauce	1 T	18	1,319	66
Tartar sauce, regular	1 c	230	1,626	179
Tomato catsup, canned	1 can (12 oz)	340	3,543	1,234
Tomato chili sauce	1 c	273	3,653	1,010
Miscellaneous				
Baking chocolate	1 oz	28	1	235
Baking powder, phosphate	1 t	3.8	312	6
Barbecue sauce	1 c	250	2,038	435
Bouillon cube	1	4	960	4
Cornstarch	1 T	8	Trace	Trace
Fats	1 c	200	0	0
Molasses, blackstrap	1 c	328	315	9,601
French salad dressing	1 T	16	219	13
Honey, strained or extracted	1 c	339	17	173
Jams and preserves	1 T	20	2	18
Mayonnaise	1 T	14	84	5
Pretzel, twisted	1	16	269	21
Sugar, brown	1 c	145	44	499
Sugar, granulated	1 c	200	2	6
Syrup, corn	1 bottle (1½ lb)	657	447	26
Vinegar, cider	1 c	240	2	240
Yeast, brewer's, debittered	1 T	8	10	152

Source: Adapted from *Composition of Foods—Raw, Processed, Prepared*, Agriculture Handbook no. 8, U.S. Department of Agriculture (Washington, D.C., 1963).

Note: A dash means the level varies with the product.

TABLE 12   Zinc Content of Foods

Food	Approximate Measure	Weight (g)	Zinc (mg)
Apples, raw	1 medium	180	0.08
Applesauce, unsweetened	1 c	244	0.3
Bananas, raw	1 medium	119	0.3
Beans, common, mature, dry			
Raw	1 c	190	5.3
Boiled, drained	1 c	185	1.8
Beans, lima, mature, dry			
Raw	1 c	180	5.0
Boiled, drained	1 c	190	1.7
Beans, snap, green			
Raw, cut into 1- to 2-in. lengths	1 c	110	0.4
Boiled, drained, cut and French style	1 c	125	0.4
Canned, solids and liquid	1 c	239	0.6
Canned, drained solids	1 c	135	0.4
Beef, separable lean			
Cooked, dry heat	3 oz	85	4.9
Cooked, moist heat	3 oz	85	5.3
Beef, ground, cooked	3 oz	85	3.8
Beverages, carbonated, nonalcoholic			
Bottled	12 fl oz	367	0.01
Canned	12 fl oz	367	0.3
Breads			
Rye	1 slice	25	0.4
White	1 slice	28	0.2
Whole wheat	1 slice	28	0.5
Butter, 4 sticks/lb	1 c	227	0.2
	1 T	14	0.01
Cabbage, common			
Raw, shredded finely	1 c	90	0.3
Shredded, boiled, drained	1 c	145	0.6
Cake, white, without icing	1 piece (3 × 3 × 2 in.)	86	0.2
Carrots			
Raw	1 medium	72	0.3
Cooked or canned, drained solids	1 c	155	0.5
Cheese, Cheddar type	1 slice	13	0.5
Chicken, broiler-fryer, cooked, dry heat			
Breast, cooked			
Meat only	½	85	0.7
Meat and skin	½	96	0.9
Drumstick, cooked			
Meat only	1	45	1.3
Meat and skin	1	54	1.4
Drumstick, thigh, back, meat only, cooked	3 oz	85	2.4
Chick-peas or garbanzos, mature, dry			
Raw	1 c	200	5.4
Boiled, drained	1 c	146	2.0
Chocolate syrup	1 fl oz or 2 T	38	0.3
Clams			
Soft shell, cooked	3 oz	85	1.4

Food	Approximate Measure	Weight (g)	Zinc (mg)
Hard shell			
Raw	4 cherrystones or		
	5 littlenecks	70	1.1
Cooked	4 or 5	62	1.0
Surf, canned, solids and liquids, can size 211 × 300	1 can	220	2.7
Cocoa, dry powder	1 oz	28	1.6
	1 T	5	0.3
Coffee			
Dry, instant	1 T	2.5	0.02
Fluid beverage, 6 fl oz	1 c	180	0.05
Cookies (1⅜ × ¼ in.)	10	30	0.08
Corn, sweet, yellow			
Boiled, drained	1 c	165	0.7
Canned, vacuum pack, solids and liquid	1 c	210	0.8
Corn chips	1 oz	28	0.4
Corn grits, dry form	1 c	160	0.7
Corn flakes	1 oz	28	0.08
Cornmeal, white or yellow			
Bolted, dry form	1 c	122	2.1
Degermed			
Dry form	1 c	138	1.2
Cooked	1 c	240	0.3
Cowpeas			
Raw	1 c	170	4.9
Boiled, drained	1 c	250	3.0
Crabs, steamed, pieces	1 c	155	6.6
Crackers			
Graham (2½ × 2½ in.)	2	14	0.2
Saltines	10	28	0.1
Doughnuts (3¼-in. diam.)	1	42	0.2
Eggs, fresh			
White	1 large	33	0.01
Yolk	1 large	17	0.5
Whole	1 large	50	0.5
Farina, regular			
Dry form	1 c	180	1.0
Cooked	1 c	245	0.2
Fish, white varieties, flesh only			
Fillet, cooked	3 oz	85	0.9
Steak, cooked	3 oz	85	0.7
Gizzard, cooked, drained, diced			
Chicken	1 c	145	6.2
Turkey	1 c	145	6.0
Granola	1 oz	28	0.6
Heart, cooked, drained, diced			
Chicken	1 c	145	6.9
Turkey	1 c	145	7.0
Ice cream	1 c	133	0.6

TABLE 12   (continued)

Food	Approximate Measure	Weight (g)	Zinc (mg)
Lamb, separable lean			
Cooked, dry heat	3 oz	85	3.7
Cooked, moist heat	3 oz	85	4.2
Lard	1 c	205	0.4
	1 T	13	0.03
Lentils, mature, dry			
Raw	1 c	190	5.9
Boiled, drained	1 c	200	2.0
Lettuce, head or leaf	⅙ head	90	0.4
Loose leaf, chopped	1 c	55	0.2
Liver, cooked			
Beef	2 oz	57	2.9
Calf	2 oz	57	3.5
Chicken, chopped	1 c	140	4.7
Turkey, chopped	1 c	140	4.7
Lobster, cooked, cubed	1 c	145	3.1
Macaroni, cooked tender			
Measured hot	1 c	140	0.7
Measured cold	1 c	105	0.5
Margarine	1 c	227	0.5
	1 T	14	0.03
Milk			
Fluid	1 c	244	0.9
Canned, evaporated	1 c	252	1.9
Dry, nonfat	1 c	68	3.1
Oat cereal, puffed	1 oz	28	0.8
Oatmeal or rolled oats			
Dry form	1 c	80	2.7
	1 oz	28	1.0
Cooked	1 c	240	1.2
Oil, salad or cooking	1 c	218	0.4
Onions			
Mature, chopped	1 c	170	0.6
Young green, chopped	1 c	100	0.3
Oranges, raw (2⅝-in. diam.)	1	131	0.2
Orange juice			
Canned, unsweetened	1 c	249	0.2
Fresh or frozen	1 c	248	0.05
Oysters			
Atlantic			
Raw, drained, 12-fl-oz can, 18–27 select or 27–44 standard oysters	1 can	340	254.3
Frozen, solids and liquid, 12-fl-oz can	1 can	360	268.9
Pacific			
Raw, drained, 12-fl-oz can, 6–9 medium or 9–13 small oysters	1 can	340	30.6
Frozen, solids and liquid, 12-fl-oz can	1 can	360	32.4
Peaches			
Raw, peeled (2½-in. diam.)	1 medium	100	0.2
Canned, drained slices	1 c	220	0.3

Food	Approximate Measure	Weight (g)	Zinc (mg)
Peanuts, roasted	1 T	9	0.3
Peanut butter	1 T	16	0.5
Peas, green, immature			
Raw or frozen	1 c	145	1.2
Boiled, drained	1 c	160	1.2
Canned, drained solids	1 c	170	1.3
Peas, green, mature seeds, dry			
Raw	1 c	200	6.4
Boiled, drained	1 c	200	2.1
Popcorn			
Unpopped	1 c	205	7.9
Popped			
Plain, large kernel	1 c	6	0.2
Oil and salt added	1 c	9	0.3
Pork, cooked, dry heat, separable lean			
Trimmed lean cuts	3 oz	85	3.2
Boston butt	3 oz	85	3.8
Ham or picnic	3 oz	85	3.4
Loin	3 oz	85	2.6
Potatoes			
Raw, peeled (2½-in. diam.)	1 medium	112	0.4
Pared before cooking, boiled, drained	1 medium	112	0.3
Boiled in skin, drained, pared	1 medium	136	0.4
Rice			
Brown			
Dry form	1 c	185	3.4
Cooked, measured hot	1 c	195	1.2
White, regular, long grain			
Dry form	1 c	185	2.5
Cooked			
Measured hot	1 c	205	0.8
Measured cold	1 c	145	0.6
White, parboiled			
Dry form	1 c	185	2.1
Cooked			
Measured hot	1 c	175	0.6
Measured cold	1 c	145	0.5
White, precooked, quick			
Dry form	1 c	95	0.7
Cooked			
Measured hot	1 c	165	0.4
Measured cold	1 c	130	0.3
Cereal, ready-to-eat, puffed or flakes	1 oz	28	0.4
Rolls, hamburger (3½-in. diam.)	1	40	0.2
Salad dressing	1 T	15	0.03
Salmon, canned, solids and liquid	1 c	220	2.1
Sausages and cold cuts			
Bologna, beef (4½-in. diam.)	1 oz	28	0.5
Braunschweiger	1 oz	28	0.8

TABLE 12 (continued)

Food	Approximate Measure	Weight (g)	Zinc (mg)
Frankfurters			
Made with beef, 10/lb	1	45	0.9
Made with beef and pork, 10/lb	1	45	0.7
Shrimp			
Boiled, peeled, deveined, 33/lb	6	84	1.7
Canned, drained, solids	1 c	128	2.7
Spinach			
Raw, chopped	1 c	55	0.5
Boiled, drained, canned	1 c	180	1.3
Solids and liquid	1 c	232	1.5
Drained solids	1 c	205	1.6
Sugar, white, granulated	1 c	200	0.1
Tea, fluid beverage, 6 fl oz	1 c	177	0.04
Tomatoes, ripe			
Raw (2⅗-in. diam.)	1 medium	123	0.2
Boiled	1 c	241	0.5
Canned, solids and liquid	1 c	241	0.5
Tuna fish, canned in oil			
Chunk style, solids and liquid, can size 307 × 133, 6½ oz	1 can	184	1.7
Drained solids, can size 307 × 133, 6½ oz	1 can	157	1.8
Drained solids	1 c	160	1.8
Turkey, cooked, dry heat, meat only			
Light meat	3 oz	85	1.8
Dark meat	3 oz	85	3.7
Veal, separable lean			
Cooked, dry heat	3 oz	85	3.5
Cooked, moist heat	3 oz	85	3.6
Wheat flour			
Whole, stirred, spooned into cup	1 c	120	2.9
All-purpose, sifted, spooned into cup, standard granulation	1 c	115	0.8
Bread flour, sifted, spooned into cup, standard granulation	1 c	115	0.9
Cake flour, sifted, spooned into cup	1 c	96	0.3
Wheat cereal, whole meal			
Dry form	1 c	125	4.5
	1 oz	28	1.0
Cooked	1 c	245	1.2
Cooked from 1 oz dry		216	1.0
Wheat cereals, ready-to-eat			
Bran flakes, 40%	1 oz	28	1.0
Flakes	1 oz	28	0.6
Germ, toasted	1 T	6	0.9
Puffed	1 oz	28	0.7
Shredded	1 oz	28	0.8

Source: E. W. Murphy, B. W. Willis, and B. K. Watt, "Provisional Tables on the Zinc Content of Foods," *Journal of The American Dietetic Association* 66 (1975): 350–352.

Note: Measure and weight apply to edible part of food only. Data given to two decimal places if food contains less than 0.1 mg of zinc.

TABLE 13   Carbohydrate, Alcohol, and Calorie Content of Alcoholic Beverages

Alcoholic Beverage	Weight (g)	Serving Size	Carbohydrate (g)	Alcohol (g)	Kilocalories
Cocktails					
Daiquiri	100	1 cocktail glass	5.2	15.2	126
Highball	240	8 oz	Unknown	20–30	139–208
Manhattan	100	1 cocktail glass	8.0	19.1	164
Martini	100	1 cocktail glass	0.3	18.5	140
Mint julep	300	10 oz	2.8	29.0	212
Old-fashioned	100	4 oz	3.4	23.9	179
Rum sour	100	4 oz	4.0	22.0	168
Tom Collins	300	10 oz	9.1	21.0	182
Whiskey sour	75	1 cocktail glass	7.6	15.0	134
Wines					
Champagne	120	1 wine glass	3.0	11.0	85
Madeira	100	1 wine glass	1.0	15.0	105
Sauterne, California	100	1 wine glass	4.0	10.5	85
Sherry, dry	60	1 wine glass	4.8	9.0	85
Vermouth, dry	100	1 wine glass	1.0	15.0	105
Wine, red, California	100	1 wine glass	3.9	10.0	85
Wine, table	100	1 wine glass	4.2	10.5	90
American malt liquors					
Ale, mild	345	12 oz	12.2	13.0	139
Beer	360	12 oz	15.0	14.0	157
Beer, Budweiser	360	12 oz	14.0	17.6	150
Beer, Lite	360	12 oz	2.8	12.1	96
Beer, Michelob	360	12 oz	16.0	18.0	160
Beer, Natural Light	360	12 oz	6.0	14.4	100
Distilled spirits					
Liqueurs					
Benedictine	20	1 cordial glass	6.6	6.6	70
Cognac brandy	30	1 brandy glass	0.0	10.5	73
Creme de menthe	20	1 cordial glass	6.0	7.0	67
Curacao	20	1 cordial glass	6.0	6.0	55
Others (vodka, rum, gin)					
80 proof	45	1 jigger	0.0	15.0	104
86 proof	45	1 jigger	0.0	16.2	112
100 proof	45	1 jigger	0.0	19.1	133

Note: Data obtained by direct calculation from beverage label and other literature. In the body, 1 g of carbohydrate supplies 4 kcal, and 1 g of alcohol supplies 6.93 kcal. Volume contents of glassware for alcoholic beverages: 1 cordial glass = 20 mL; 1 brandy glass = 30 mL; 1 sherry glass = 60 mL; 1 cocktail glass = 90 mL; 1 burgandy glass = 120 mL; 1 champagne glass = 150 mL; 1 tumbler = 240–360 mL; 1 mixing glass = 360 mL; 1 jigger = 45 mL.

TABLE 14   Caffeine Content of Beverages and Some Nonprescription Drugs

Item	Caffeine Content (mg)	Item	Caffeine Content (mg)
Beverages		**Nonprescription drugs**	
Coffee		Aspirin-containing preparations	30–35/tablet
Decaffeinated	2–70/cup	Excedrin	60/tablet
Ground	85–200/cup	Stimulants, nonprescription	80–150/tablet
Instant	30–80/cup		
Cola	40–60/glass		
Tea	20–150/cup		

TABLE 15   Common Weights and Measures

Measure	Equivalent	Measure	Equivalent
3 t	1 T	1 fl oz	30 g
2 T	1 oz	½ c	120 g
4 T	¼ c	1 c	240 g
8 T	½ c	1 lb	454 g
16 T	1 c		
		1 g	1 mL
2 c	1 pt	1 t	5 mL
4 c	1 qt	1 T	15 mL
4 qt	1 gal	1 fl oz	30 mL
		1 c	240 mL
1 t	5 g	1 pt	480 mL
1 T	15 g	1 qt	960 mL
1 oz	28.35 g	1 L	1,000 mL

TABLE 16   Weights and Measures Conversions

U.S. System to Metric		Metric to U.S. System	
U.S. Measure	**Metric Measure**	**Metric Measure**	**U.S. Measure**
Length		**Length**	
1 in.	25.0 mm	1 mm	0.04 in.
1 ft	0.3 m	1 m	3.3 ft
Mass		**Mass**	
1 gr	64.8 mg	1 mg	0.015 gr
1 oz	28.0 g	1 g	0.035 oz
1 lb	0.45 kg	1 kg	2.2 lb
1 short ton	907.1 kg	1 metric ton	1.102 short tons
Volume		**Volume**	
1 cu. in.	16.0 cm^3	1 cm^3	0.06 $in.^3$
1 t	5.0 mL	1 mL	0.2 t
1 T	15.0 mL	1 mL	0.07 T
1 fl oz	30.0 mL	1 mL	0.03 oz
1 c	0.24 L	1 L	4.2 c
1 pt	0.47 L	1 L	2.1 pt
1 qt (liq)	0.95 L	1 L	1.1 qt
1 gal	0.004 m^3	1 m^3	264.0 gal
1 pk	0.009 m^3	1 m^3	113.0 pk
1 bu	0.04 m^3	1 m^3	28.0 bu
Energy		**Energy**	
1 cal	4.18 J	1 J	0.24 cal

Temperature

To convert Celsius degrees into Fahrenheit, multiply by ⅘ and add 32.

To convert Fahrenheit degrees into Celsius, subtract 32 and multiply by ⅝. For example:

$$30\ ^\circ C = \left(30 \times \frac{9}{5} + 32 \right)\ ^\circ F$$

$$= (54 + 32)\ ^\circ F = 86\ ^\circ F$$

$$90\ ^\circ F = (90 - 32) \times \frac{5}{9}\ ^\circ C$$

$$= 58 \times \frac{5}{9}\ ^\circ C = 32.2\ ^\circ C$$

TABLE 16   (continued)

Pounds to Kilograms (for Weight Reference)

Pounds	Kilo-grams	Pounds	Kilo-grams	Pounds	Kilo-grams	Pounds	Kilo-grams	Pounds	Kilo-grams
5	2.3	50	22.7	95	43.1	140	63.5	185	83.9
10	4.5	55	25.0	100	45.4	145	65.8	190	86.2
15	6.8	60	27.2	105	47.6	150	68.0	195	88.5
20	9.1	65	29.5	110	49.9	155	70.3	200	90.7
25	11.3	70	31.7	115	52.2	160	72.6	205	93.0
30	13.6	75	34.0	120	54.4	165	74.8	210	95.3
35	15.9	80	36.3	125	56.7	170	77.1	215	97.5
40	18.1	85	38.6	130	58.9	175	79.4	220	99.8
45	20.4	90	40.8	135	61.2	180	81.6		

Feet and Inches to Centimeters (for Height Reference)

Feet and Inches		Centi-meters	Feet and Inches		Centi-meters	Feet and Inches		Centi-meters	Feet and Inches		Centi-meters	Feet and Inches		Centi-meters
0	6	15.2	2	4	71.1	3	4	101.6	4	4	132.0	5	4	162.6
1	0	30.5	2	5	73.6	3	5	104.1	4	5	134.6	5	5	165.1
1	6	45.7	2	6	76.1	3	6	106.6	4	6	137.1	5	6	167.6
1	7	48.3	2	7	78.7	3	7	109.2	4	7	139.6	5	7	170.2
1	8	50.8	2	8	81.2	3	8	111.7	4	8	142.2	5	8	172.7
1	9	53.3	2	9	83.8	3	9	114.2	4	9	144.7	5	9	175.3
1	10	55.9	2	10	86.3	3	10	116.8	4	10	147.3	5	10	177.8
1	11	58.4	2	11	88.8	3	11	119.3	4	11	149.8	5	11	180.3
2	0	61.0	3	0	91.4	4	0	121.9	5	0	152.4	6	0	182.9
2	1	63.5	3	1	93.9	4	1	124.4	5	1	154.9	6	1	185.4
2	2	66.0	3	2	96.4	4	2	127.0	5	2	157.5	6	2	188.0
2	3	68.6	3	3	99.0	4	3	129.5	5	3	160.0	6	3	190.5

TABLE 17   **Milligrams and Milliequivalents Conversion**

Sodium (Equivalent Weight 23)		Potassium (Equivalent Weight 39)		
Milligrams	**Grams**	**Milligrams**	**Grams**	**Milliequivalents**
230	0.23	390	0.39	10
460	0.46	780	0.78	20
—	—	1,000	1.00	25.6
690	0.69	1,170	1.17	30
920	0.92	1,560	1.56	40
1,000	1.00	—	—	43.5
1,150	1.15	1,950	1.95	50
1,380	1.38	2,340	2.34	60
1,610	1.61	2,730	2.73	70
1,840	1.84	3,170	3.17	80
2,170	2.17	3,510	3.51	90
2,300	2.30	3,900	3.9	100
—	—	5,000	5.0	128
5,000	5.00	—	—	217.5
—	—	10,000	10.0	256
10,000	10.00	—	—	435

Note: To convert milligrams to milliequivalents:

$$\text{milliequivalents of sodium or potassium} = \frac{\text{milligrams of sodium or potassium}}{\text{equivalent weight in milligrams}}$$

To convert milliequivalents to milligrams:

milligrams of sodium or potassium = milliequivalents of sodium or potassium × equivalent weight in milligrams

TABLE 18 Weights in Relation to Height, Age, and Frame According to the Society of Actuaries and the Metropolitan Life Insurance Company

A. Average Weights of Men by Height and Age Group: 1959 and 1979 Build and Blood Pressure Studies*
(graduated weight in shoes and indoor clothing in pounds)

| Height | Men By Age Group: 1959 and 1979 Studies | | | | | | | | | | | |
| | 15–16 Years | | | 17–19 Years | | | 20–24 Years | | | 25–29 Years | | |
	1959 Study	1979 Study	Weight Change	1959 Study	1979 Study	Weight Change	1959 Study	1979 Study	Weight Change	1959 Study	1979 Study	Weight Change
5′ 2″	107	112	+5	119	128	+ 9	128	137	+ 9	134	140	+ 6
3″	112	116	+5	123	129	+ 6	132	136	+ 4	138	141	+ 3
4″	117	121	+4	127	132	+ 5	136	139	+ 3	141	143	+ 2
5″	122	127	+5	131	137	+ 6	139	143	+ 4	144	147	+ 3
6″	127	133	+6	135	141	+ 6	142	148	+ 6	148	152	+ 4
7″	132	137	+5	139	145	+ 6	145	153	+ 8	151	156	+ 5
8″	137	143	+6	143	150	+ 7	149	157	+ 8	155	161	+ 6
9″	142	148	+6	147	155	+ 8	153	163	+10	159	166	+ 7
10″	146	153	+7	151	159	+ 8	157	167	+10	163	171	+ 8
11″	150	159	+9	155	164	+ 9	161	171	+10	167	175	+ 8
6′ 0″	154	162	+8	160	168	+ 8	166	176	+10	172	181	+ 9
1″	159	168	+9	164	174	+10	170	182	+12	177	186	+ 9
2″	164	173	+9	168	179	+ 9	174	187	+13	182	191	+ 9
3″	169	178	+9	172	185	+13	178	193	+15	186	197	+11
4″	175	184	+9	176	190	+14	181	198	+17	190	202	+12

B. Average Weights of Women by Height and Age Group: 1959 and 1979 Build and Blood Pressure Studies*
(graduated weight in shoes and indoor clothing in pounds)

| Height | Women By Age Group: 1959 and 1979 Studies | | | | | | | | | | | |
| | 15–16 Years | | | 17–19 Years | | | 20–24 Years | | | 25–29 Years | | |
	1959 Study	1979 Study	Weight Change	1959 Study	1979 Study	Weight Change	1959 Study	1979 Study	Weight Change	1959 Study	1979 Study	Weight Change
4′10″	97	101	+4	99	103	+ 4	102	105	+ 3	107	110	+ 3
11″	100	105	+5	102	108	+ 6	105	110	+ 5	110	112	+ 2
5′. 0″	103	109	+6	105	111	+ 6	108	112	+ 4	113	114	+ 1
1″	107	112	+5	109	115	+ 6	112	116	+ 4	116	119	+ 3
2″	111	117	+6	113	119	+ 6	115	120	+ 5	119	121	+ 2
3″	114	121	+7	116	123	+ 7	118	124	+ 6	122	125	+ 3
4″	117	123	+6	120	126	+ 6	121	127	+ 6	125	128	+ 3
5″	121	128	+7	124	129	+ 5	125	130	+ 5	129	132	+ 3
6″	125	131	+6	127	132	+ 5	129	133	+ 4	133	134	+ 1
7″	128	135	+7	130	136	+ 6	132	137	+ 5	136	138	+ 2
8″	132	138	+6	134	140	+ 6	136	141	+ 5	140	142	+ 2
9″	136	142	+6	138	145	+ 7	140	146	+ 6	144	148	+ 4
10″	*	146	—	142	148	+ 6	144	149	+ 5	148	150	+ 2
11″	*	149	—	147	150	+ 3	149	155	+ 6	153	156	+ 3
6′ 0″	*	152	—	152	154	+ 2	154	157	+ 3	158	159	+ 1

*The 1959 Build and Blood Pressure Study reflects data collected during the years 1935 through 1954. The 1979 Build and Blood Pressure Study reflects data collected during the years 1954 through 1972.

†Average weights omitted in classes with too few cases for analysis.

A. Average Weights of Men by Height and Age Group: 1959 and 1979
Build and Blood Pressure Studies*
(graduated weight in shoes and indoor clothing in pounds)

Men By Age Group: 1959 and 1979 Studies

30–39 Years			40–49 Years			50–59 Years			60–69 Years		
1959 Study	1979 Study	Weight Change	1959 Study	1979 Study	Weight Change	1959 Study	1979 Study	Weight Change	1959 Study	1979 Study	Weight Change
137	142	+5	140	142	+2	142	141	−1	139	140	+1
141	143	+2	144	144	0	145	145	0	142	144	+2
145	147	+2	148	149	+1	149	150	+1	146	149	+3
149	151	+5	152	154	+2	153	155	+2	150	153	+3
153	156	+3	156	158	+2	157	159	+2	154	158	+4
157	160	+3	161	163	+2	162	164	+2	159	163	+4
161	165	+4	165	167	+2	166	168	+2	163	167	+4
165	170	+5	169	172	+3	170	173	+3	168	172	+4
170	174	+4	174	176	+2	175	177	+2	173	176	+3
174	179	+5	178	181	+3	180	182	+2	178	181	+3
179	184	+5	183	186	+3	185	187	+2	183	186	+3
183	190	+7	187	192	+5	189	193	+4	188	191	+3
188	195	+7	192	197	+5	194	198	+4	193	196	+3
193	201	+8	197	203	+6	199	204	+5	198	200	+2
199	206	+7	203	208	+5	205	209	+4	204	207	+3

B. Average Weights of Women by Height and Age Group: 1959 and 1979
Build and Blood Pressure Studies*
(graduated weight in shoes and indoor clothing in pounds)

Women By Age Group: 1959 and 1979 Studies

30–39 Years			40–49 Years			50–59 Years			60–69 Years		
1959 Study	1979 Study	Weight Change	1959 Study	1979 Study	Weight Change	1959 Study	1979 Study	Weight Change	1959 Study	1979 Study	Weight Change
115	113	−2	122	118	−4	125	121	−4	127	123	−4
117	115	−2	124	121	−3	127	125	−2	129	127	−2
120	118	−2	127	123	−4	130	127	−3	131	130	−1
123	121	−2	130	127	−3	133	131	−2	134	133	−1
126	124	−2	133	129	−4	136	133	−3	137	136	−1
129	128	−1	136	133	−3	140	137	−3	141	140	−1
132	131	−1	140	136	−4	144	141	−3	145	143	−2
135	134	−1	143	139	−4	148	144	−4	149	147	−2
139	137	−2	147	143	−4	152	147	−5	153	150	−3
142	141	−1	151	147	−4	156	152	−4	157	155	−2
146	145	−1	155	150	−5	160	156	−4	161	158	−3
150	150	0	159	155	−4	164	159	−5	165	161	−4
154	153	−1	164	158	−6	169	162	−7	†	163	—
159	159	0	169	162	−7	174	166	−8	†	167	—
164	164	0	174	168	−6	180	171	−9	†	172	—

Source: Ad Hoc Committee of the New Build and Blood Pressure Study, Association of Life Insurance Medical Directors of America and Society of Actuaries.

TABLE 18   (continued)

		Frame		
C. Desirable Weights in Pounds According to Height and Frame (in Indoor Clothing)				
	Height*	Small	Medium	Large
Men age 25 and over	5′ 2″	112–120	118–129	126–141
	5′ 3″	115–123	121–133	129–144
	5′ 4″	118–126	124–136	132–148
	5′ 5″	121–129	127–139	135–152
	5′ 6″	124–133	130–143	138–156
	5′ 7″	128–137	134–147	142–161
	5′ 8″	132–141	138–152	147–166
	5′ 9″	136–145	142–156	151–170
	5′10″	140–150	146–160	155–174
	5′11″	144–154	150–165	159–179
	6′ 0″	148–158	154–170	164–184
	6′ 1″	152–162	158–175	168–189
	6′ 2″	156–167	162–180	173–194
	6′ 3″	160–171	167–185	178–199
	6′ 4″	164–175	172–190	182–204

Source: Metropolitan Life Insurance Company, New York. Data derived from *Build and Blood Pressure Study*, Society of Actuaries, October 1959 (see Tables 18A, B). Data derived from the 1979 study (see Tables 18A and B) were not available at the time of this printing, so the 1959 figures have been given.

C. Desirable Weights in Pounds According to Height and Frame (in Indoor Clothing)

	Height*	Frame		
		Small	Medium	Large
Women age 25 and over[†]	4′10″	92–98	96–107	104–119
	4′11″	94–101	98–110	106–122
	5′ 0″	96–104	101–113	109–125
	5′ 1″	99–107	104–116	112–128
	5′ 2″	102–110	107–119	115–131
	5′ 3″	105–113	110–122	118–134
	5′ 4″	108–116	113–126	121–138
	5′ 5″	111–119	116–130	125–142
	5′ 6″	114–123	120–135	129–146
	5′ 7″	118–127	124–139	133–150
	5′ 8″	122–131	128–143	137–154
	5′ 9″	126–135	132–147	141–158
	5′10″	130–140	136–151	145–163
	5′11″	134–144	140–155	149–168
	6′ 0″	138–148	144–159	153–173

*Includes shoes with 1-in. heels for men and 2-in. heels for women.
[†]For girls between 18 and 25, subtract 1 lb for each year under 25.

TABLE 19　Guidelines for Body Weight According to the National Institutes of Health

	Metric							Nonmetric					
	Men Weight (kg)*			Women Weight (kg)*				Men Weight (lb)*			Women Weight (lb)*		
Height* (m)	Average	Acceptable weight		Average	Acceptable weight		Height* (ft in)	Average	Acceptable weight		Average	Acceptable weight	
1.45				46.0	42	53	4 10				102	92	119
1.48				46.5	42	54	4 11				104	94	122
1.50				47.0	43	55	5 0				107	96	125
1.52				48.5	44	57	5 1				110	99	128
1.54				49.5	44	58	5 2	123	112	141	113	102	131
1.56				50.4	45	58	5 3	127	115	144	116	105	134
1.58	55.8	51	64	51.3	46	59	5 4	130	118	148	120	108	138
1.60	57.6	52	65	52.6	48	61	5 5	133	121	152	123	111	142
1.62	58.6	53	66	54.0	49	62	5 6	136	124	156	128	114	146
1.64	59.6	54	67	55.4	50	64	5 7	140	128	161	132	118	150
1.66	60.6	55	69	56.8	51	65	5 8	145	132	166	136	122	154
1.68	61.7	56	71	58.1	52	66	5 9	149	136	170	140	126	158
1.70	63.5	58	73	60.0	53	67	5 10	153	140	174	144	130	163
1.72	65.0	59	74	61.3	55	69	5 11	158	144	179	148	134	168
1.74	66.5	60	75	62.6	56	70	6 0	162	148	184	152	138	173
1.76	68.0	62	77	64.0	58	72	6 1	166	152	189			
1.78	69.4	64	79	65.3	59	74	6 2	171	156	194			
1.80	71.0	65	80				6 3	176	160	199			
1.82	72.6	66	82				6 4	181	164	204			
1.84	74.2	67	84										
1.86	75.8	69	86										
1.88	77.6	71	88										
1.90	79.3	73	90										
1.92	81.0	75	93										

Source: "Obesity in America," edited by G. A. Bray, U.S. Department of Health, Education, and Welfare, Public Health Service, National Institutes of Health, NIH Publication No. 80-359, 1980, page 7.

*Height without shoes, weight without clothes.

**TABLE 20   Growth Charts with Reference Percentiles for Girls
Birth to 36 Months of Age**

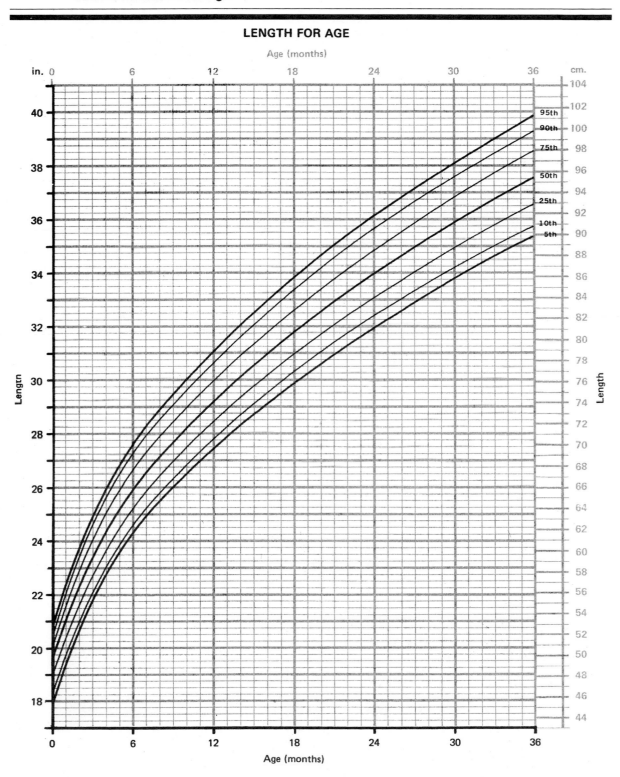

LENGTH FOR AGE

TABLE 20   (continued)

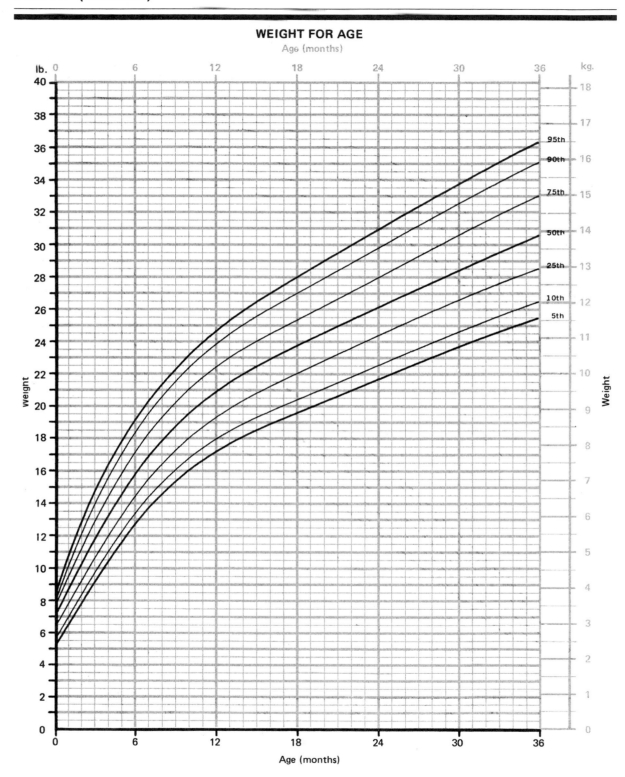

WEIGHT FOR AGE

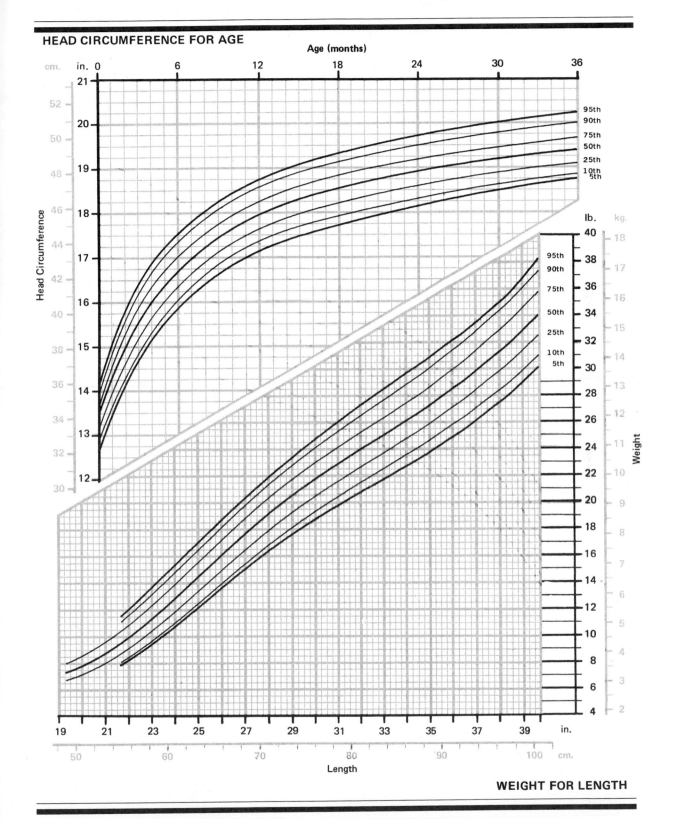

HEAD CIRCUMFERENCE FOR AGE

WEIGHT FOR LENGTH

Source: Centers for Disease Control, Atlanta, Georgia.

**TABLE 21   Growth Charts with Reference Percentiles for Boys
Birth to 36 Months of Age**

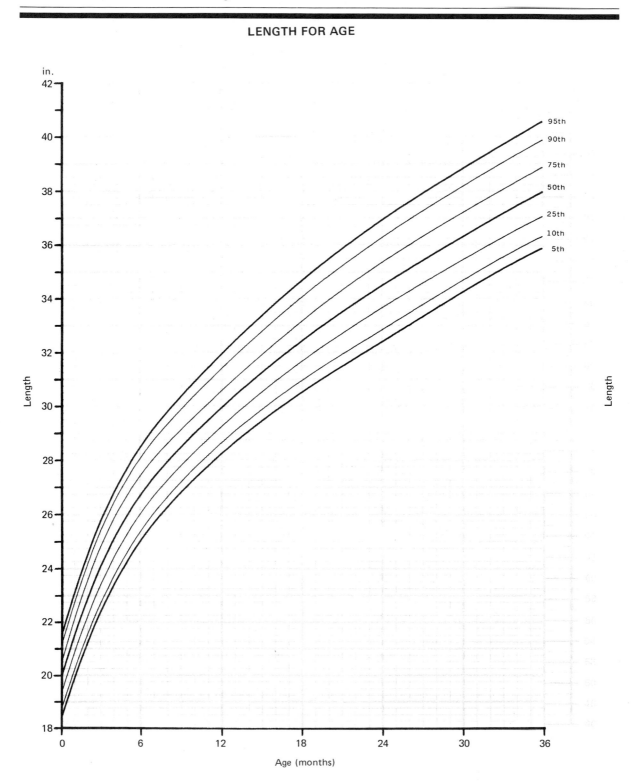

LENGTH FOR AGE

WEIGHT FOR AGE

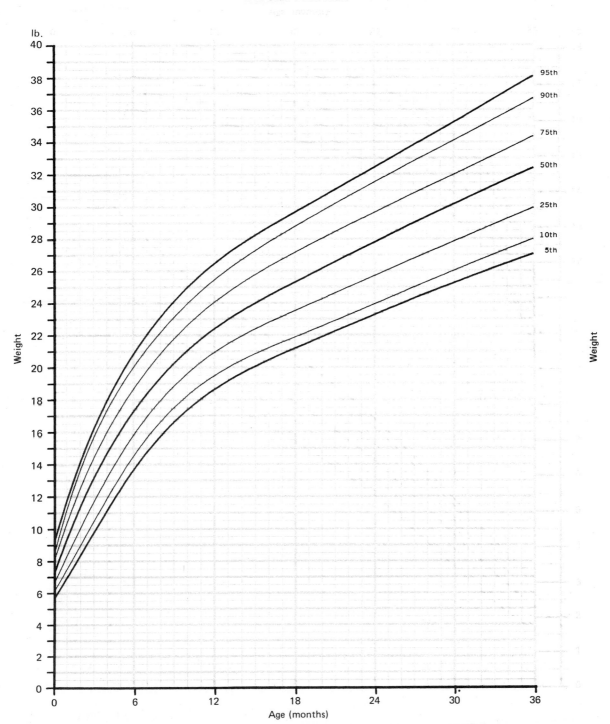

TABLE 21   (continued)

HEAD CIRCUMFERENCE FOR AGE

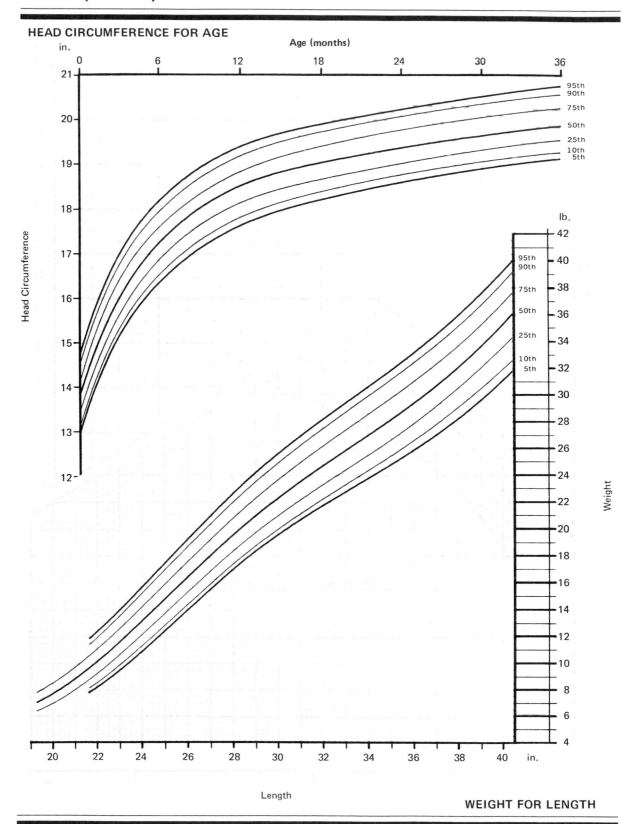

Length

WEIGHT FOR LENGTH

Source: Centers for Disease Control, Atlanta, Georgia.

TABLE 22   Growth Charts with Reference Percentiles for Girls 2 to 18 Years of Age

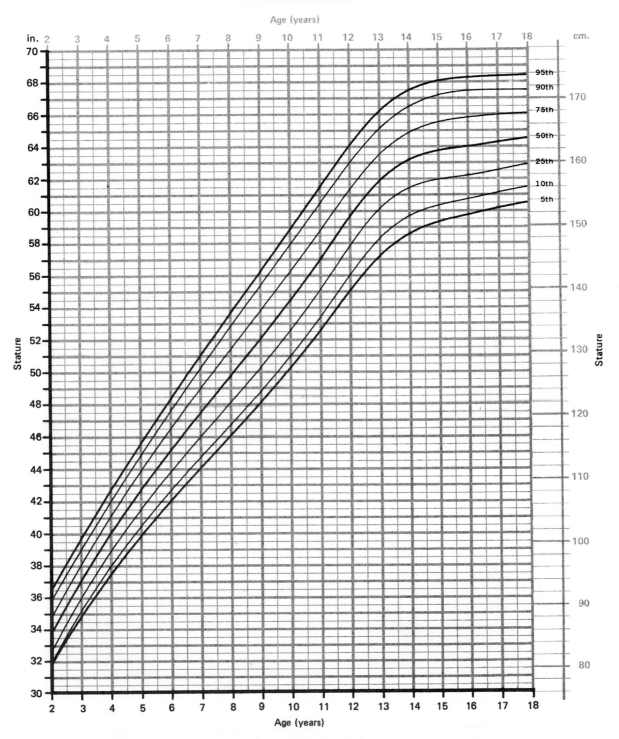

STATURE FOR AGE

TABLE 22   (continued)

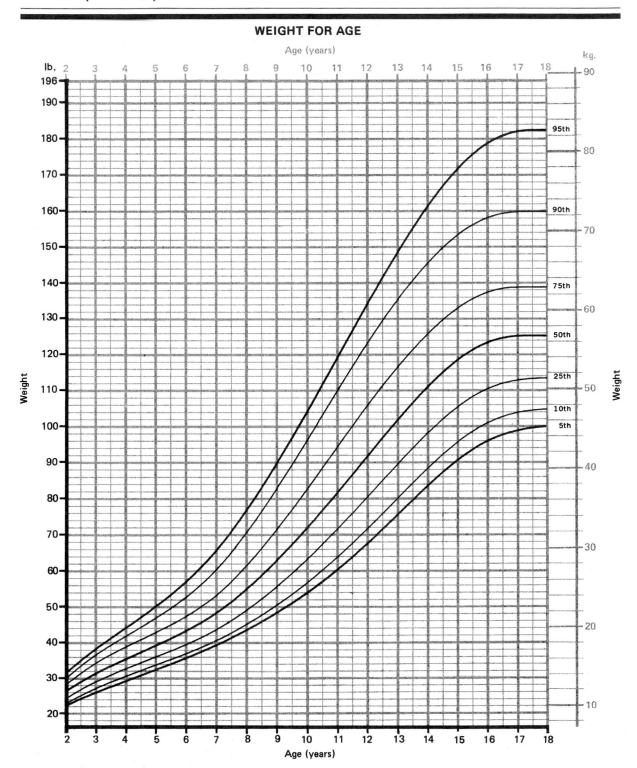

WEIGHT FOR AGE

WEIGHT FOR STATURE

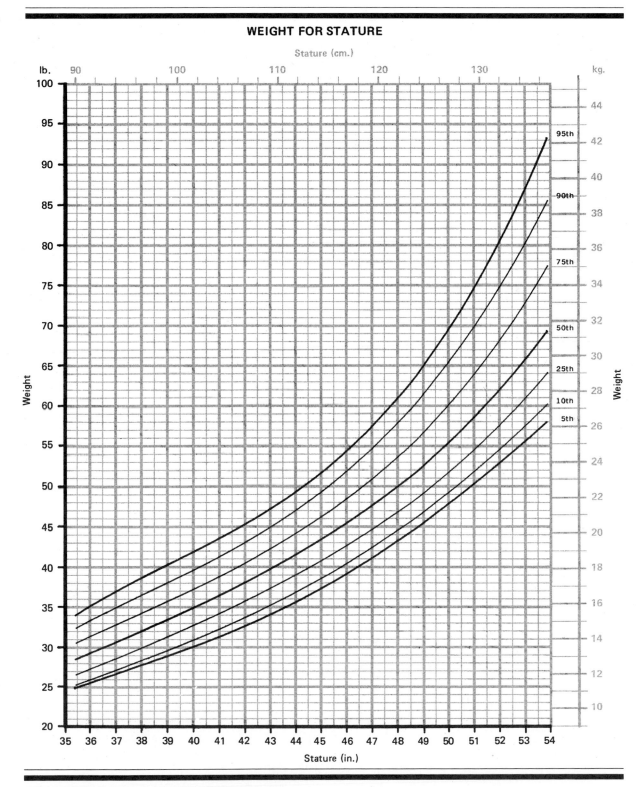

Source: Centers for Disease Control, Atlanta, Georgia.

TABLE 23   **Growth Charts with Reference Percentiles for Boys 2 to 18 Years of Age**

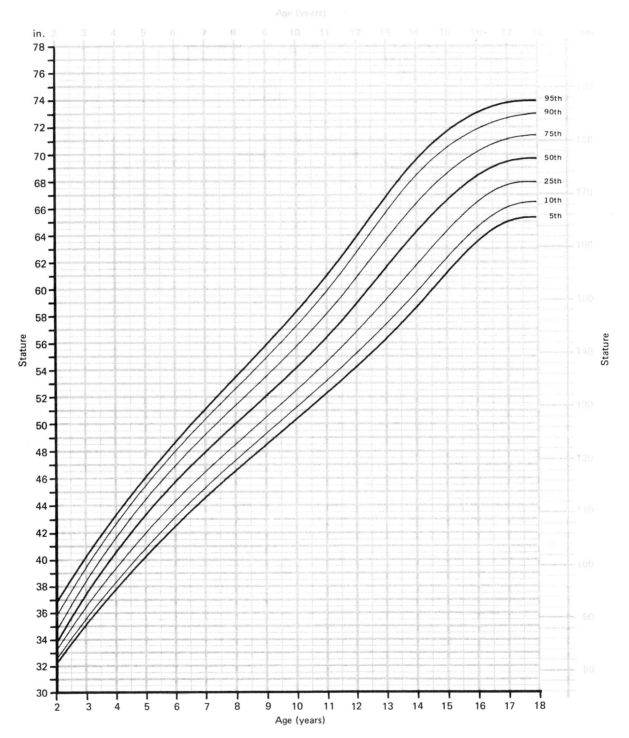

STATURE FOR AGE

WEIGHT FOR AGE

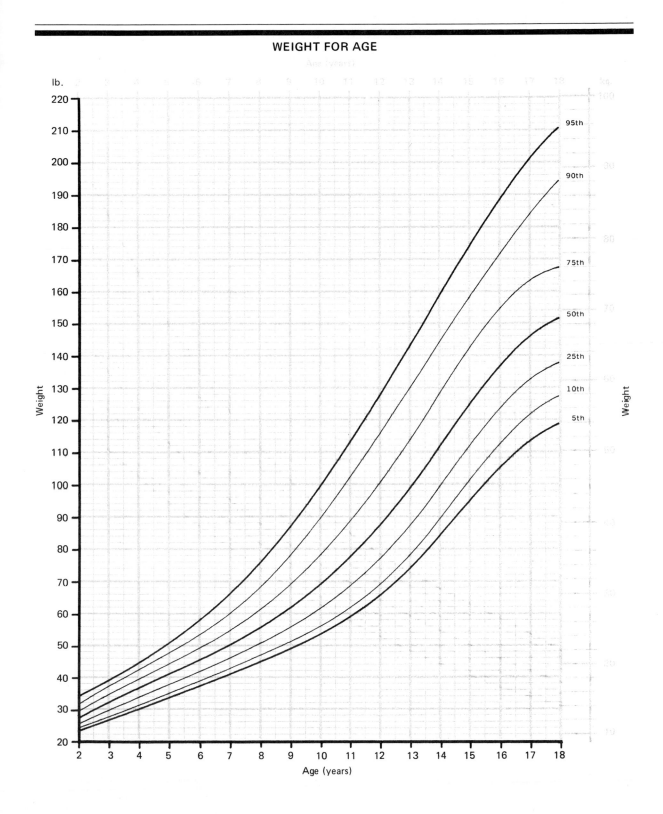

Age (years)

TABLE 23 (continued)

WEIGHT FOR STATURE

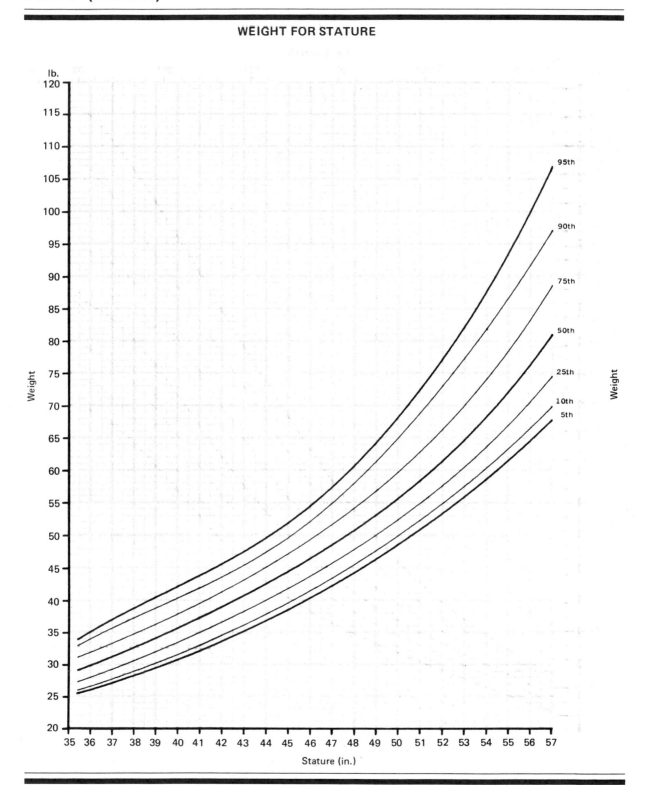

Source: Centers for Disease Control, Atlanta, Georgia.

TABLE 24   Standard Values for Constituents in the Blood of an Adult

Constituent	Normal Range	Constituent	Normal Range
Physical Measurements		**Nitrogenous Substances**	
pH	7.37–7.45	Amino acid nitrogen, blood	4–8 mg/100 mL
Capillary bleeding time	1–4 min	Ammonia, blood	40–70 μg/100 mL
Plasma prothrombin time		Creatine	0.2–0.9 mg/100 mL
(quick method)	11–19 sec	Creatinine	0.7–1.8 mg/100 mL
Sedimentation rate		Nonprotein nitrogen, blood	
(Wintrobe method)	Men: 0–9 mm/h	(NPN)	20–35 mg/100 mL
	Women: 0–20 mm/h	Blood urea nitrogen (BUN)	8–20 mg/100 mL
Specific gravity	1.025–1.030	Urea, blood	20–35 mg/100 mL
Viscosity (H_2O = 1)	4.5–5.0	Uric acid, blood	2.5–6 mg/100 mL
Protein		**Minerals**	
Albumin, serum	3.5–5.5 g/100 mL	Base, serum (total)	143–155 mEq/L
Globulin, serum	1.3–3.0 mg/100 mL	Calcium, serum	9–11 mg/100 mL
Albumin/globulin ratio	1.2–2.5		4.5–5.5 mEq/L
Ceruloplasmin, plasma	15–30 mg/100 mL	Chlorides, serum	340–372 mg/100 mL
Fibrinogen, plasma	0.2–0.4 g/100 mL		96–105 mEq/L
Total protein, serum	6–8 g/100 mL	Copper	100–240 μg/100 mL
Hematology		Iodine	Total: 7–16 mEq/L
Cell volume	39%–50%		Protein bound: 3–9 μg/
Coagulation time,			100 mL
venous blood (Lee-		Iron, serum	Men: 80–165 μg/100 mL
White method)	At 37 °C: 6–12 min		Women: 65–130 μg/
	At room temperature:		100 mL
	10–18 min	Magnesium, serum	2–3 mg/100 mL
Erythrocytes (RBCs)	Men: 4.5–6.2 × 10⁶/mm³		1.65–2.5 mEq/L
	Women: 4.0–5.5 ×	Phosphate	1.5–2.8 mEq/L
	10⁶/mm³	Phosphorus, inorganic,	
Hematocrit (vol% red		serum	Child:
cells, or PCV)	Men: 40%–52%		4.0–6.5 mg/100 mL
	Women: 37%–47%		Adult:
Hemoglobin	Adult:		2.5–4.5 mg/100 mL
	Men: 14–18 g/100 mL	Potassium, serum	16–22 mg/100 mL
	Women: 12–16 g/100 mL		4.1–5.6 mEq/L
	Children:	Sodium, serum	320–335 mg/100 mL
	10–18 g/100 mL		139–146 mEq/L
	(varies with age)	Sulfates, inorganic, serum	2.5–5.0 mg/100 mL
Leukocytes (WBCs)	5,000–10,000/mm³		0.5–1.0 mEq/L
Platelets (thrombocytes)	125,000–400,000/mm³	Zinc(s)	100–140 μg/100 mL
Reticulocytes	0.5%–2% of red cells	**Amino acids**	
Whole blood volume	70–100 mL/kg	Amino acids, total	30–70 mg/100 mL
White blood count		Alanine	3.0–3.7 mg/100 mL
(WBC) and differential		Arginine	1.2–2.0 mg/100 mL
= 5–10 × 10³/mm³	Basophils	Asparagine	0.4–0.8 mg/100 mL
	0%–1.5%	Aspartic acid	1.01–0.08 mg/100 mL
	Eosinophils	Cysteine and cystine	1.0–1.4 mg/100 mL
	0.5%–4%	Glutamine	5–14 mg/100 mL
	Lymphocytes	Glutamic acid	0.5–12 mg/100 mL
	20%–40%	Glycine	1.2–1.6 mg/100 mL
	Monocytes	Histidine	0.9–1.6 mg/100 mL
	4%–10%	Isoleucine	0.7–1.3 mg/100 mL
	Neutrophils	Leucine	1.4–2.3 mg/100 mL
	50%–65%	Lysine	2.5–3.0 mg/100 mL

TABLE 24   (continued)

Constituent	Normal Range	Constituent	Normal Range
Methionine	0.2–0.4 mg/100 mL	**Vitamins**	
Ornithine	0.5–0.9 mg/100 mL	Ascorbic acid	Serum: 0.3–1.4 mg/
Phenylalanine	0.7–1.0 mg/100 mL		100 mL
Proline	1.8–3.5 mg/100 mL		White blood cells: 25–
Serine	1.0–1.2 mg/100 mL		40 mg/100 mL
Threonine	1.2–1.8 mg/100 mL	Folic acid	2–5 μg/100 mL
Tryptophan	1.0–1.2 mg/100 mL	Riboflavin	15–25 μg/100 mL
Tyrosine	0.8–1.5 mg/100 mL	Thiamin	2–5 μg/100 mL
Valine	0.5–3.8 mg/100 mL	Vitamin A	50–100 IU/100 mL
Carbohydrates		Vitamin B_{12}	300–800 μg/100 mL
Fructose	5–9 mg/100 mL	Vitamin K, prothrombin time	
Glucose	Nelson-Somogyi:	(quick method)	10–15 s
	70–100 mg/100 mL		10–20 s
	Folin-Wu: 80–120 mg/	**Blood Gases**	
	100 mL	O_2 capacity, whole blood	16–27 vol%
Glycogen	5–7 mg/100 mL	CO_2 content	Serum:
Hexoses	70–110 mg/100 mL		45–70 vol%
Pentose, total	2–5 mg/100 mL		20.3–31.5 mM/L
Liquids			Whole blood:
Fats, neutral	140–300 mg/100 mL		40–60 vol%
Fatty acids, free	8–31 mg/100 mL		18–27 mM/L
Fatty acids, serum (total)	350–450 mg/100 mL	O_2 saturation	Arterial blood: 94%–
Triglyceride(s)	30–140 mg/100 mL		96%
Cholesterol, serum	Total: 125–240 mg/		Venous blood: 60%–
	100 mL		85%
	Esters: 90–180 mg/		
	100 mL		
Cholesterol, free	50–60 mg/100 mL		

TABLE 25   Standard Values for Constituents in the Urine of an Adult

Constituent	Normal Range	Constituent	Normal Range
Physical Measurements		**Acetone (Ketone) Bodies,**	
pH	5.5–8.0	**continued**	
Specific gravity	1.009–1.030	Glucose	0–0.002 g
Daily volume	900–1,600 mL	Iron	0.001–0.006 g
Total Solid Constituents in Daily		Magnesium (as MgO)	0.14–0.31 g
Volume	50–70 g	Nitrogen	9–18 g
Acetone (Ketone) Bodies		Phosphate (as $PO_4^=$)	2.0–3.5 g
Albumin	0–0.01 g	Potassium	1.5–3.0 g
Ammonia	0.3–1.0 g	Purine bases	0.009–0.05 g
Bile	0	Sodium	3.0–5.5 g
Calcium	0.1–0.4 g	Sulfate (as $SO_4^=$)	1.5–3.0
Chloride (as NaCl)	10–15 g	Urea	20–35 g
Creatine	0–0.1 g	Uric acid	0.5–0.7 g
Creatinine	0.9–1.6 g		

Appendix F

References

CHAPTER 1

Berg, A. 1981. *Malnourished people, a policy view*. Washington, D.C.: World Bank.

Blaxter, K., ed. 1980. *Food chains and human nutrition*. Barking, Great Britain: Applied Science Publications.

Brewster, L., and Jacobson, M. F. 1978. *The changing American diet*. Washington, D.C.: Center for Science in the Public Interest.

Callaway, C. W. 1981. Bridging the gaps in human nutrition. *Nutr. News* 44:1.

Connor, W. E. 1979. Too little or too much: the case for preventive nutrition. *Amer. J. Clin. Nutr.* 32:1975.

Davidson, S., et al. 1979. *Human nutrition and dietetics*. 7th ed. New York: Churchill Livingstone.

Ducanis, A. J., and Golin, A. K. 1979. *The interdisciplinary health care team: a handbook*. Rockville, Md.: Aspen Systems.

Eckstein, E. G. 1980. *Food, people and nutrition*. Westport, Conn.: AVI Publishing.

Ellenbogen, L., ed. 1981. *Contemporary issues in clinical nutrition. Controversies in nutrition*, vol. 2. New York: Churchill Livingstone.

Gifft, H. H., et al. 1972. *Nutrition, behavior, and change*. Englewood Cliffs, N.J.: Prentice-Hall.

Goodhart, R. S., and Shils, M. E., eds. 1980. *Modern nutrition in health and disease*. 6th ed. Philadelphia: Lea & Febiger.

Graham, H. D. 1980. *The safety of foods*. 2nd ed. Westport, Ct.: AVI Publishing.

Guggenheim, K. Y. 1981. *Nutrition and nutritional diseases: the evolution of concepts*. Lexington, Mass.: Callamore Press.

Hodges, R. E. 1979. *Human nutrition, a comprehensive treatise*, vol. 4. New York: Plenum Press.

J.A.M.A. 1980. Nutrition in the 1970s. 243:2220.

Katch, F. I., and McArdle, W. D. 1977. *Nutrition, weight control and exercise*. Boston: Houghton Mifflin.

Krentler, P. A. 1980. *Nutrition in perspective*. Englewood Cliffs, N.J.: Prentice-Hall.

Lowenberg, M. E., et al. 1979. *Food and people*. 3rd ed. New York: Wiley.

Mayer, J., and Dwyer, J. T., eds. 1979. *Food and nutrition policy in a changing world*. New York: Oxford University Press.

Page, L., and Friend, B. 1978. The changing United States diet. *Bioscience* 28:192.

Pike, R. L., and Brown, M. L. 1975. *Nutrition: an integrated approach*. New York: Wiley.

Reed, P. B. 1980. *Nutrition: an applied science*. St. Paul, Minn.: West Publishing.

Sipple, H., and McNutt, K., eds. 1976. *Nutrition Reviews' present knowledge in nutrition*. 4th ed. New York: The Nutrition Foundation.

Time-Life Books. 1981. *Wholesome diet*. Alexandria, Va.: Time-Life Books.

U.S. Department of Health, Education and Welfare. 1979. *Healthy people: the Surgeon General's report on health promotion and disease prevention*. PHS publ. no. 79-55071.

U.S. Senate. 1977. *Dietary goals for the United States*. 2nd ed. Select Committee on Nutrition and Human Needs.

CHAPTER 2

Body Composition

Brozek, J. 1965. *Human body composition*. Oxford: Pergamon Press.

Cheek, D. B. 1968. *Human growth*. Philadelphia: Lea & Febiger.

Forbes, G. B., and Reina, J. D. 1970. Adult lean body mass declines with age: some longitudinal observations. *Metabolism* 19:653.

Johnston, F. E., et al., eds. 1980. *Human physical growth and maturation: methodologies and factors*. New York: Plenum Press.

Owens, G. M., and Brozek, J. 1966. Influence of age, sex and nutrition on body composition during childhood and adolescence. In *Human Development*, ed. F. Falkner. Philadelphia: Saunders.

Parizkova, J. 1977. *Body fat and physical fitness. Body composition and lipid metabolism in different regimes of physical activity*. Littleton, Mass.: PSG Publishing.

Society of Actuaries and Association of Life Insurance Medical Directors of America. 1980. *Build Study, 1979*, vol. 1–2. Chicago.

Tanner, J. M., et al. 1976. *Assessment of skeletal maturity and predictions of adult height (TW2 method)*. London: Academic Press.

Widdlosson, E. M., and Dickerson, J. W. T. 1963. Chemical composition of the body. In *Mineral metabolism*, vol. 2, pt. A, ed. C. L. Comar and F. Bronner. New York: Academic Press.

Energy

Amer. J. Clin. Nutr. 1975. Physical growth of ethnic groups comprising the United States populations. 28:1071.

Ames, S. R. 1970. The joule-unit of energy. *J. Amer. Dietet. Assoc.* 57:415.

Bradfield, R. B., ed. 1971. Symposium: assessment of typical daily energy expenditure. *Amer. J. Clin. Nutr.* 24:1111, 1405.

Buskirk, E. R., et al. 1960. Human energy expenditure studies. I. Interaction of cold environment and specific dynamic effect. II. Sleep. *Amer. J. Clin. Nutr.* 8:601.

Calloway, D. H. 1971. Dietary components that yield energy. *Env. Biol. Med.* 1:175.

Calloway, D. H., and Zanni, E. 1981. Energy requirements and energy expenditure of elderly men. *Amer. J. Clin. Nutr.* 33:2088.

Dairy Council Digest. 1980. Energy balance throughout the life cycle. 51:19.

Dauncey, M. J. 1979. Energy metabolism in man and the influence of diet and temperature: a review. *J. Human Nutr.* 33:259.

Flodin, N. W. 1977. The energetic joule. *Amer. J. Clin. Nutr.* 30:302.

Fulton, D. E. 1972. Basal metabolic rate of women. *J. Amer. Dietet. Assoc.* 61:516.

Garrow, J. S., and Hawes, S. F. 1972. The role of amino acid oxidation in causing "specific dynamic action" in man. *Brit. J. Nutr.* 27:211.

Griffith, W. H., and Dyer, H. M. 1967. Present knowledge of specific dynamic action. In *Present knowledge in nutrition*, 3rd ed., chap. 7. New York: The Nutrition Foundation.

Grisola, S., and Kennedy, J. 1966. On specific dynamic action, turnover and protein synthesis. *Perspect. Biol. Med.* 9:578.

Hegsted, D. M. 1974. Energy needs and energy utilization. *Nutr. Rev.* 32:33.

Klieber, M. 1972. Joules vs. calories in nutrition. *J. Nutr.* 102:309.

Konishi, F. 1965. Food energy equivalents of various activities. *J. Amer. Dietet. Assoc.* 46:186.

Mahalko, J. R., and Johnson, L. K. 1980. Accuracy of predictions of long-term energy needs. *J. Amer. Dietet. Assoc.* 77:557.

McGandy, R. B., et al. 1966. Nutrient intakes and energy expenditures in men of different ages. *J. Gerontol.* 21:581.

Moore, T. 1971. The calorie versus the joule. *J. Amer. Dietet. Assoc.* 59:327.

National Academy of Sciences, National Research

Council. 1966. *Biological energy interrelationships and glossary of energy terms*. Publication no. 1411. Washington, D.C.

Proc. Nutr. Soc. 1978. The application of human and animal calorimetry. 37:1.

Richardson, M., and McCraken, E. C. 1960. *Energy expenditures and women performing selected activities*. U.S. Department of Agriculture Home Economics Research Report no. 11. Washington, D.C.: Government Printing Office.

U.S. Department of Agriculture, Agricultural Research Service. 1961. *An evaluation of basal metabolic data for children and youth in the United States*. Home Economics Research Report no. 14. Washington, D.C.: Government Printing Office.

CHAPTER 3

Carbohydrates in Nutrition

American Medical Association. 1975. *Nutrients in processed foods. Fats and carbohydrates*, vol. 3. Acton, Mass.: Publishing Science Group.

Birch, G. G., and Green, L. F., eds. 1973. *Molecular structure and function of food carbohydrate*. New York: Halsted.

Connor, O. W., and Connor, S. 1976. Sucrose and carbohydrate. In *Present knowledge in nutrition*, 4th ed. Washington, D.C.: The Nutrition Foundation.

Hodges, R. E. 1966. Present knowledge of carbohydrates. *Nutr. Rev.* 24:65.

Macdonald, I. ed. 1967. Symposium on dietary carbohydrates in man. *Amer. J. Clin. Nutr.* 20:65.

Nissenson, A. R., et al. 1979. Mannitol. *West. J. Med.* 131:277.

Sharon, N. 1980. Carbohydrates. *Sci. Amer.* 243:90.

Sipple, H. L., and McNutt, K. W., eds. 1974. *Sugars in nutrition*. New York: Academic Press.

Southgate, D. A. T., et al. 1978. Free sugars in foods. *J. Human Nutr.* 32:335.

Spiller, G. A., and Amen, R. J. 1978. *Fiber in human nutrition*. New York: Plenum.

Stare, F. J. 1975. Sugar in the diet of man. *World Rev. Nutr. Dietet.* 22:237.

U.S. Department of Agriculture. 1972. *Sugar report*. Agricultural Stabilization and Conservation Service, publ. no. 241. Washington, D.C.: Government Printing Office.

Fiber

Bing, F. C. 1976. Dietary fiber—in historical perspective. *J. Amer. Dietet. Assoc.* 69:498.

Dairy Council Digest. 1975. The role of fiber in the diet. 46:1.

Heaton, K. W. 1979. The real value of fiber. *Consultant*. 19:23.

Institute of Food Technologists' Expert Panel in Food Safety and Nutrition. 1979. *Dietary fiber: a scientific status summary*. Chicago.

Kelsay, J. L. 1978. A review in effects of fiber intake on man. *Amer. J. Clin. Nutr.* 31:142.

Mendeloff, A. I. 1975. Dietary fiber. *Nutr. Rev.* 33:321.

Nachbar, M.S., and Oppenheim, J.D. 1980. Lectins in the United States diet: a survey of lectins in commonly consumed foods and a review of the literature. *Amer. J. Clin. Nutr.* 33:2338.

Southgate, D. A. T. 1978. Dietary fiber: analysis and food sources. *Amer. J. Clin. Nutr.* 31:5107.

Spiller, G. A., and Freeman, H. J. 1981. Recent advances in dietary fiber and colorectal diseases. *Amer. J. Clin. Nutr.* 34:1145.

Health and Diseases

Bierman, E. L. 1979. Carbohydrates, sucrose and human disease. *Amer. J. Clin. Nutr.* 32:2712.

Bierman, E. L., and Nelson, R. 1975. Carbohydrates, diabetes and blood lipids. *World Rev. Nutr. Dietet.* 22:280.

Costill, D. L. 1978. Sports nutrition: the role of carbohydrates. *Nutr. News* 41:1.

Dairy Council Digest. 1974. The role of lactose in the diet. 45:26.

Forgac, M. T. 1979. Carbohydrate loading—a review. *J. Amer. Dietet. Assoc.* 75:42.

Grande, F. 1975. Sugar and cardiovascular disease. *World Rev. Nutr. Dietet.* 22:248.

Life Sciences Research Office, Federation of American Societies for Experimental Biology. N.d. *Dietary sugars in health and disease*. Bethesda, Md.

MacDonald, I. 1974. Dietary carbohydrates: their indications and contraindications in clinical medicine. *The Practitioner* 212:448.

Mayson, J. S., et al. 1972. False negative tests for urinary glucose in the presence of ascorbic acid. *Am. J. Clin. Path.* 58:297.

Page, D. M., and Bayless, T. M., eds. 1981. *Lactose digestion: clinical and nutritional implications*. Baltimore, Md.: Johns Hopkins University Press.

Yudkin, J. 1972. Sugar and disease. *Nature* 239:197.

CHAPTER 4

Protein in Nutrition

Alais, C., and Blanc, B. 1975. Milk proteins: biochemical and biological aspects. *World Rev. Nutr. Dietet.* 20:66.

Briskey, E., et al., eds. 1970. *The physiology and biochemistry of muscle as a food.* Madison, Wis.: University of Wisconsin Press.

Chopra, J. G., et al. 1978. Protein in the U.S. diet. *J. Amer. Dietet. Assoc.* 72:253.

Palombo, J. D., and Blackburn, G. L. 1980. Human protein requirements. *Contemp. Nutr.* 5 (January):1.

Porter, J. W. G., and Rolls, B. A. 1973. *Proteins in human nutrition.* New York: Academic Press.

Nitrogen Balance

Calloway, D. H. 1975. Nitrogen balance of men with marginal intakes of protein and energy. *J. Nutr.* 105:914.

Clark, H. E., et al. 1975. Nitrogen retention and plasma amino acids of men who consumed isonitrogenous diets containing egg albumin or mixtures of amino acids. *Amer. J. Clin. Nutr.* 28:316.

Hegsted, D. M. 1976. Balance studies. *J. Nutr.* 106:307.

MacLean, W. C., and Graham, G. G. 1976. Growth and nitrogen retention of children consuming all of the day's protein intake in one meal. *Amer. J. Clin. Nutr.* 29:78.

Prothro, J., et al. 1973. Utilization of nitrogen, energy, and sulfur by adolescent boys fed three levels of protein. *J. Nutr.* 103:786.

Ziegler, E. E., et al. 1977. Nitrogen balance studies with normal children. *Amer. J. Clin. Nutr.* 30:939.

Protein Needs and Requirements

Arroyave, G. 1970. Comparative sensitivity of specific amino acid ratios versus "essential to nonessential" amino acid ratio. *Amer. J. Clin. Nutr.* 23:703.

Harper, A. E., et al. 1973. Human protein needs. *Lancet* 1:1518.

Hegsted, D. M. 1965. Variation in requirements of nutrients—amino acids. *Fed. Proc.* 22:1424.

———. 1976. Protein needs and possible modifications of the American diet. *J. Amer. Dietet. Assoc.* 68:317.

Irwin, M. I., and Hegsted, D. M. 1971. A conspectus of research on amino acid requirements of man. *J. Nutr.* 101:539.

Nutr. Rev. 1975. Adaptation to low protein intakes. 33:180.

———. 1976. Protein sparing produced by proteins and amino acids. 34:174.

Pohlandt, F. 1974. Cystine: a semi-essential amino acid in the newborn infant. *Acta Paediatr. Scand.* 63:801.

Scrimshaw, N. S. 1976a. An analysis of past and present recommended dietary allowances for protein in health and disease. Part one. *N. Engl. J. Med.* 294:136.

———. 1976b. An analysis of past and present recommended dietary allowances for protein in health and disease. Part two. *N. Engl. J. Med.* 294:198.

Snyderman, S. E., et al. 1963. The histidine requirement of the infant. *Pediatrics* 31:786.

CHAPTER 5

Fat in Nutrition

American Medical Association. 1975. *Nutrients in processed foods. Fats and carbohydrates*, vol. 3. Acton, Mass.: Publishing Science Group.

Brisson, G. J. 1981. *Lipids in human nutrition.* Englewood Cliffs, N.J.: Jack K. Burgess.

Rice, E. E. 1974. Symposium: status of fat in food and nutrition. *J. Amer. Oil Chem. Soc.* 51:244.

U.S. Department of Agriculture. Revised 1976. *Fats in food and diet.* USDA Bulletin no. 361. Washington, D.C.

Vergroesen, A. J., ed. 1975. *The role of fats in human nutrition.* New York: Academic Press.

Essential Fatty Acids

Coniglio, J. G., et al. 1972. Symposium: essential fatty acids. *Fed. Proc.* 31:1429.

Cuthbertson, W. F. J. 1976. Essential fatty acid requirements in infancy. *Amer. J. Clin. Nutr.* 29:559.

Fleming, C. R., et al. 1976. Essential fatty acid deficiency in adults receiving parenteral nutrition. *Amer. J. Clin. Nutr.* 29:976.

Friedman, Z., et al. 1976. Rapid onset of essential fatty acid deficiency in the newborn. *Pediatrics* 58:640.

Hirono, H., et al. 1977. Essential fatty acid deficiency induced by total parenteral nutrition and by medium-chain triglyceride feeding. *Amer. J. Clin. Nutr.* 30:1670.

Prottey, C., et al. 1975. Correction of the cutaneous manifestations of essential fatty acid deficiency in man by application of sunflower-seed oil to the skin. *J. Invest. Dermatol.* 64:228.

Richardson, T. J., and Sgoutas, D. 1975. Essential fatty acid deficiency in four adult patients during total parenteral nutrition. *Amer. J. Clin. Nutr.* 28:258.

Vergroesen, A. J. 1977. Physiological effects of dietary linoleic acid. *Nutr. Rev.* 35:1.

Fats and Food

Carpenter, D. L., et al. 1976. Lipid composition of selected vegetable oils. *J. Amer. Oil Chem. Soc.* 53:713.

Feeley, R. M., et al. 1972. Cholesterol content of foods. *J. Amer. Dietet. Assoc.* 61:134.

———. 1975. Major fatty acids and proximate composition of dairy products. *J. Amer. Dietet. Assoc.* 66:140.

Itoh, T., et al. 1973. Sterol composition of 19 vegetable oils. *J. Amer. Oil Chem. Soc.* 50:122.

Lacroix, D. E., et al. 1973. Cholesterol, fat, and protein in dairy products. *J. Amer. Dietet. Assoc.* 62:275.

National Academy of Sciences. 1976. *Fat content and composition of animal products.* Washington, D.C.

Fats and Health

Hausman, P. 1981. *J. Sprat's legacy: the science and politics of fat and cholesterol.* New York: Richard Marek Publishers.

Levy, R. I., et al. 1979. *Nutrition, lipids, and coronary heart disease: a global view.* New York: Raven Press.

Nutr. Rev. 1978. Some present concepts concerning diet and prevention of coronary heart disease. 36:194.

Rapaport, E., ed. 1980. *Current controversies in cardiovascular disease.* Philadelphia: Saunders.

Truswell, A. S. 1978. Diet and plasma lipids—a reappraisal. *Amer. J. Clin. Nutr.* 31:977.

Walker, W. J. 1977. Changing United States life-style and declining vascular mortality: cause or coincidence? *N. Engl. J. Med.* 297:163.

Wright, I. S. 1976. Correct levels of serum cholesterol: average vs. normal vs. optimal. *J.A.M.A.* 236:261.

CHAPTER 6

Vitamins in Nutrition

Barker, B. M., and Bender, D. A. 1980. *Vitamins in medicine,* vol. I. Chicago: Year Book.

Carmel, R. 1978. The laboratory diagnosis of megaloblastic anemias. *West. J. Med.* 128:294.

Consumer Guide. 1979. *The vitamin book.* New York: Simon & Schuster.

DeLuca, H. F. 1975. Function of the fat soluble vitamins. *Amer. J. Clin. Nutr.* 28:339.

European Nutrition Conference. 1973. Recent advances in the assessment of vitamin status in man. *Proc. Nutr. Soc.* 32:237.

Grollman, A. 1975. How drugs work: vitamins. *Consultant* 15:170.

György, P. 1976. Reminiscences on the discovery and significance of the B vitamins. *Nutr. Rev.* 34:141.

Kutsky, R. J. 1973. *Handbook of vitamins and hormones.* Van Nostrand Reinhold.

Marks, J. 1975. *A guide to the vitamins: their role in health and disease.* Baltimore: University Park Press.

Orr, J. L. 1969. *Pantothenic acid, vitamin B_6 and vitamin B_{12} in foods.* Home Economics Research Report no. 36. Washington, D.C.: U.S. Department of Agriculture.

Plaut, G. W. E., et al. 1974. Biosynthesis of water-soluble vitamins. *Ann. Rev. Biochem.* 43:899.

Scriver, C. R. 1973. Vitamin-responsive inborn errors of metabolism. *Metabolism* 16:30.

Sebrell, W. H., Jr., and Harris, R. S., eds. 1967–1972. *The vitamins.* 7 vols. New York: Academic Press.

Vitamin C—General

Ann. N.Y. Acad. Sci. 1975. Second conference on vitamin C. Part IV. Ascorbic acid and respiratory illness. 258:498.

Cameron, E., and Pauling, L. 1979. *Cancer and vitamin C: a discussion of the nature, causes, prevention, and treatment of cancer with special reference to the value of vitamin C.* Menlo Park, Calif.: Linus Pauling Institute of Science and Medicine.

Cone, T. E. 1976. History of infantile scurvy in America. In *200 years of feeding infants in America.* Columbus, Ohio: Ross Laboratories.

Counsell, J. N., and Horning, D. H. 1982. *Vitamin C (ascorbic acid).* Englewood, N.J.: Applied Science Publishers.

Hanck, A., and Ritzel, G., eds. 1977. Re-evaluation of vitamin C. *Internat. J. Vit. Nutr. Res.* 47 (Suppl. 16):1.

Harper, A. E. 1975. The recommended dietary allowances for ascorbic acid. *Ann. N.Y. Acad. Sci.* 258:491.

Hughes, R. E. 1976. Vitamin C and cholesterol metabolism. *J. Human Nutr.* 30:315.

Irwin, M. I., and Hutchins, B. K. 1976. A conspectus of research on vitamin C requirements of man. *J. Nutr.* 106:821.

King, C. G., and Burns, J. J., eds. 1975. Second conference on vitamin C. *Ann. N.Y. Acad. Sci.* 258:5.

Nutr. Rev. 1976. Vitamin C toxicity. 34:236.

Vilter, R. W. 1981. Nutritional aspects of ascorbic acid: uses and abuses. *West. J. Med.* 133:485.

Zannoni, V. G., and Lynch, M. M. 1973. The role of ascorbic acid in drug metabolism. *Drug Metab. Rev.* 2:57.

Vitamin C—the Common Cold

Anderson, R., et al. 1980. The effects of increasing weekly doses of ascorbate on certain cellular and humeral immune functions in normal volunteers. *Amer. J. Clin. Nutr.* 33:71.

Ann. N.Y. Acad. Sci. 1975. Second conference on vitamin C. Part IV. Ascorbic acid and respiratory illness. 258:498.

Clegg, K. M., and Macdonald, J. M. 1975. L-ascorbic acid and D-isoascorbic acid in a common cold survey. *Amer. J. Clin. Nutr.* 28:973.

Destro, R. L., and Sharma, V. 1977. An appraisal of vitamin C in adjunct therapy of bacterial and viral meningitis. *Clin. Pediatr.* 16:936.

Dykes, M. H. M., and Meier, P. 1975. Ascorbic acid and the common cold. *J.A.M.A.* 231:1073.

Gormly, P. J. 1977. Megadosage of ascorbic acid in an Antarctic expedition. *Brit. J. Nutr.* 37:269.

Holdborow, P. L. 1980. Ascorbic acid, dietary restriction, and upper respiratory tract infection. *Pediatrics* 65:1191.

Miller, J. Z., et al. 1977. Therapeutic effect of vitamin C. *J.A.M.A.* 237:248.

Nutr. Rev. 1973. Vitamin C and the common cold. 31:303.

Shilotri, P. G., and Bhat, K. S. 1977. Effect of megadoses of vitamin C on bactericidal activity of leukocytes. *Amer. J. Clin. Nutr.* 30:1077.

Vitamin B₁

Evans, W. C. 1975. Thiaminases and their effects in animals. *Vit. Horm.* 33:467.

Fujiwara, M., and Somogyi, J. C., eds. 1976. Nutritional and clinical problems of thiamine. *J. Nutr. Sci. Vita.* 22:1.

Gubler, C. J., et al., eds. 1976. *Thiamine.* New York: Wiley-Interscience.

Hotzel, D., and Bitsch, R. 1976. Thiamine status of human subjects, estimated by biochemical methods. *J. Nutr. Sci. Vita.* 22:S41.

Krampitz, L. O. 1969. Catalytic function of thiamin diphosphate. *Ann. Rev. Biochem.* 38:213.

Loew, F. M., and Austin, R. J. 1975. Case report: thiamin status of foxes with Chastek's paralysis. *Can. Vet. J.* 16:50.

Nadel, A. M. 1976. Wernicke encephalopathy following prolonged intravenous therapy. *J.A.M.A.* 235:2403.

Peters, R. A. 1973. The neglect of nutrition and its perils. *Amer. J. Clin. Nutr.* 26:750.

Sauberlich, H. E., et al. 1979. Thiamin requirement of the adult human. *Amer. J. Clin. Nutr.* 32:2237.

Somogyi, J. C. 1976. Early signs of thiamine deficiency. *J. Nutr. Sci. Vita.* 22:S29.

Vimokesant, S. L., et al. 1976. Food habits causing thiamine deficiency in humans. *J. Nutr. Sci. Vita.* 22:S1.

Williams, R. R. 1961. *Toward the conquest of beriberi.* Cambridge, Mass.: Harvard University Press.

Vitamin B₂

Buzina, R., et al. 1973. Epidemiology of angular stomatitis and bleeding gums. *Internat. J. Vit. Nutr. Res.* 43:401.

McCormick, D. B. 1972. The fate of riboflavin in the mammal. *Nutr. Rev.* 30:75. (*See also* 31[1973]:104.)

Rivlin, R. S. 1973. Riboflavin and cancer: a review. *Cancer Res.* 33:1977.

———, ed. 1975. *Riboflavin.* New York: Plenum Press.

Skalka, H. W., and Pachal, J. T. 1981. Cataracts and riboflavin deficiency. *Amer. J. Clin. Nutr.* 34:861.

Sterner, R. T., and Price, W. R. 1973. Restricted riboflavin: within-subject behavioral effects in humans. *Amer. J. Clin. Nutr.* 26:150.

Vitamin B₆

Bapurao, S., and Krishnaswamy, K. 1978. Vitamin B-6 nutritional status of pellagrins and their leucine tolerance. *Amer. J. Clin. Nutr.* 31:819.

Gyorgy, P. 1964. The history of vitamin B-6. *Vit. Horm.* 22:361.

————. 1971. Developments leading to the metabolic role of vitamin B-6. *Amer. J. Clin. Nutr.* 24:1250.

Holtz, P., and Palm, D. 1974. Pharmacological aspects of vitamin B-6. *Pharmacol. Rev.* 16:113.

Munro, H. N. chairman. 1978. *Human vitamin B-6 requirements.* Washington, D.C.: Food Nutrition Board/National Research Council, National Academy of Sciences.

Tryfiates, G. R., ed. 1980. *Vitamin B_6 metabolism and role in growth.* Westport, Conn.: Food and Nutrition Press, Inc.

Niacin

Darby, W. J., et al. 1975. Niacin. *Nutr. Rev.* 33:289. (*See also* 33[1975]:310.)

Etheridge, E. W. 1972. *The butterfly caste: A social history of pellagra in the South.* Westport, Conn.: Greenwood Publishing.

Gopalan, C., and Kamala, S. J. R. 1975. Pellagra and amino acid imbalance. *Vit. Horm.* 33:505.

Miller, D. F. 1978. Pellagra deaths in the United States. *Amer. J. Clin. Nutr.* 31:558.

Morchek, J. E., et al. 1976. Metabolic response of humans to ingestion of nicotinic acid and nicotinamide. *Clin. Chem.* 22:1821.

Nakagawa, I., et al. 1973. Efficiency of conversion of tryptophan to niacin in humans. *J. Nutr.* 103:1195.

Roe, D. A. 1973. *A plague of corn: the social history of pellagra.* Ithaca, N.Y.: Cornell University Press.

Sydenstricker, V. P. 1958. The history of pellagra; its recognition as a disorder of nutrition and its conquest. *Amer. J. Clin. Nutr.* 6:409.

Folic Acid

Babu, S., and Srikantia, S. G. 1976. Availability of folates from some foods. *Amer. J. Clin. Nutr.* 29:376.

Batra, K. K., et al. 1977. Folic acid compounds in romaine lettuce. *Can. J. Biochem.* 55:865.

Botez, M. I., et al. 1978. Polyneuropathy and folate deficiency. *Arch. Neurol.* 35:581.

Butterfield, S., and Calloway, D. H. 1972. Folacin in wheat and selected foods. *J. Amer. Dietet. Assoc.* 60:310.

Food Nutrition Board/National Research Council, National Academy of Sciences. 1977. Folic acid: biochemistry and physiology in relation to the human nutrition requirement. Washington, D.C.: National Academy of Sciences.

————. 1978. Folic acid: biochemistry and physiology in relation to the human nutrition requirement: a review. Washington, D.C.: National Academy of Sciences.

Herbert, V. 1968. Folic acid deficiency in man: A review. *Vit. Horm.* 26:525.

————. 1973. The five possible causes of all nutrient deficiency: Illustrated by deficiencies of vitamin B-12 and folic acid. *Amer. J. Clin. Nutr.* 26:77.

Herbert, V., et al. 1970. Symposium: folic acid deficiency: A review. *Amer. J. Clin. Nutr.* 23:841.

Malin, J. D. 1975. Folic acid. *World Rev. Nutr. Dietet.* 21:198.

Norris, J. W., and Pratt, R. F. 1974. Folic acid deficiency and epilepsy. *Drugs* 8:366.

Parker, S. L., and Bowering, J. 1976. Folacin in diets of Puerto Rican and black women in relation to food practices. 8:73.

Rosenberg, I. H. 1975. Folate absorption and malabsorption. *N. Engl. J. Med.* 293:1303.

Stokstad, E. L. R., and Koch, J. 1967. Folic acid metabolism: A review. *Physiol. Rev.* 47:83.

Tamura, T., and Stokstad, E. L. R. 1973. The availabililty of food folate in man. *Brit. J. Haematol.* 25:513.

Tamura, T., et al. 1976. The availability of folates in man: effect of orange juice supplement on intestinal conjugase. *Brit. J. Haematol.* 32:123.

Vitalie, J. J. 1966. Present knowledge of folacin. *Nutr. Rev.* 24:289.

Vitamin B_{12}—General

Babior, B., ed. 1975. *Cobalamin: biochemistry and pathophysiology.* New York: Wiley-Interscience.

Baker, S. J. 1967. Human vitamin B_{12} deficiency. *World Rev. Nutr. Dietet.* 8:62.

Herbert, V. 1973. The five possible causes of all nutrient deficiency: illustrated by deficiencies of vitamin B_{12} and folic acid. *Amer. J. Clin. Nutr.* 26:77.

Herbert, V., and Das, K. G. 1976. The role of vitamin B_{12} and folic acid in hemato- and other cellpoiesis. *Vit. Horm.* 34:1.

Nutr. Today. 1973. Report: discovery and synthesis of vitamin B_{12} celebrated. 8:24.

Smith, E. L. 1965. *Vitamin B_{12}.* New York: Wiley.

Weissbach, H., and Taylor, R. T. 1968. Metabolic role of vitamin B_{12}. *Vit. Horm.* 26:395.

Vitamin B_{12}—Experimental and Clinical Studies

Adams, J. F., et al. 1973. The vitamin B-12 content of meals and items of diet. *Brit. J. Nutr.* 29:65.

Armstrong, B. K., et al. 1974. Hematological, vitamin B_{12}, and folate studies on Seventh-Day Adventist vegetarians. *Amer. J. Clin. Nutr.* 27:712.

Crosby, W. H. 1980. Improvisation revisited. Oral cyanocobalamin without intrinsic factor for pernicious anemia. *Arch. Intern. Med.* 140:1582.

Doscherholmen, A., et al. 1978. Vitamin B_{12} assimilation from chicken meat. *Amer. J. Clin. Nutr.* 31:825.

Ellis, F. R., and Nasser, S. 1973. A pilot study of vitamin B_{12} in the treatment of tiredness. *Brit. J. Nutr.* 30:277.

Farquharson, J., and Adams, J. F. 1976. The forms of vitamin B-12 in foods. *Brit. J. Nutr.* 36:127.

McCurdy, P. R. 1974. B_{12} shots. *J.A.M.A.* 229:703. (*See also* 231[1975]:289.)

Nutr. Rev. 1978. Vegetarian diet and vitamin B-12 deficiency. 36:24.

Reynolds, E. H. 1976. The neurology of vitamin B_{12} deficiency: metabolic mechanisms. *Lancet* 2:832.

Pantothenic Acid

Calloway, D. H., and Gibbs, J. C. 1976. Food patterns and food assistance programs in the Cocopah Indian community (a study of pantothenic acid and other vitamins at risk). *Ecol. Food Nutr.* 5:183.

Cohenour, S. H., and Calloway, D. H. 1972. Blood, urine, and dietary pantothenic acid levels of pregnant teenagers. *Amer. J. Clin. Nutr.* 25:512.

Fry, P. C., et al. 1976. Metabolic response to a pantothenic acid deficient diet in humans. *J. Nutr. Sci. Vita.* 22:339.

Hoppner, K., and Lampi, B. 1977. Total pantothenic acid in strained baby foods. *Nutr. Rpt. Internat.* 15:627.

Krehl, W. A. 1953. Pantothenic acid in nutrition: a review. *Nutr. Rev.* 11:225.

Novelli, G. D. 1953. Metabolic functions of pantothenic acid. *Physiol. Rev.* 33:525.

Pietrzik, K., and Hotzel, D. 1977. Studies for the evolution of pantothenic acid requirement. *Nutr. and Metab.* 21(Suppl. 1):23.

Srinivasan, V., and Belavady, B. 1976. Nutritional status of pantothenic acid in Indian pregnant and nursing women. *Internat. J. Vit. Nutr. Res.* 46:433.

Tao, H. G., and Fox, H. M. 1976. Measurements of urinary pantothenic acid excretions of alcoholic patients. *J. Nutr. Sci. Vita.* 22:333.

Walsh, J. H., et al. 1981. Pantothenic acid contents of 75 processed and cooked foods. *J. Amer. Dietet. Assoc.* 78:140.

Warden, W. K. 1973. Pantothenic acid in nutrition. *Frontiers in Nutrition*, April/May (Suppl. 252).

Biotin

Balnave, D. 1977. Clinical symptoms of biotin deficiency in animals. *Amer. J. Clin. Nutr.* 30:1408.

Bonjour, J. P. 1977. Biotin in man's nutrition and therapy: a review. *Internat. J. Vit. Nutr. Res.* 47:107.

Bridges, W. F. 1967. Present knowledge of biotin. *Nutr. Rev.* 25:65.

Klevay, L. M. 1976. The biotin requirement of rats fed 20 percent egg white. *J. Nutr.* 106:1643.

Knappe, J. 1970. Mechanism of biotin action. *Ann. Rev. Biochem.* 39:757.

McCormick, D. B. 1975. Biotin. *Nutr. Rev.* 33:97.

Wood, H. G., and Barden, R. E. 1977. Biotin enzymes. *Ann. Rev. Biochem.* 46:385.

Vitamin A

American Academy of Pediatrics Committee on Drugs and Nutrition. 1971. The use and abuse of vitamin A. *Pediatrics* 48:655.

Basu, T. K. 1979. Vitamin A and cancer of epithelial origin. *J. Human Nutr.* 33:24.

Furman, K. I. 1973. Acute hypervitaminosis A in an adult. *Amer. J. Clin. Nutr.* 26:575.

Hussaini, G., et al. 1978. Cure for night blindness. *Amer. J. Clin. Nutr.* 31:1489.

Oomen, H. A. P. C. 1974. Vitamin A deficiency, xerophthalmia and blindness. *Nutr. Rev.* 32:161.

Ott, D. B., and Lachance, P. A. 1979. Retinoic acid: a review. *Amer. J. Clin. Nutr.* 32:2522.

Rodriguez, M. S., and Irwin, M. I. 1972. A conspectus of research on vitamin A requirements of man. *J. Nutr.* 102:909.

Roels, O. A. 1970. Vitamin A physiology. *J.A.M.A.* 214:1097.

Smith, J. E., and Goodman, D. S. 1976. Vitamin A metabolism and transport. In *Present knowledge in nutrition*, 4th ed., ed. D. M. Hegsted. Washington, D.C.: Nutrition Foundation.

Solomons, N. W., and Russell, R. M. 1980. The interaction of vitamin A and zinc: implications for human nutrition. *Amer. J. Clin. Nutr.* 33:2031.

Sommer, A., et al. 1980. History of night blindness: a simple tool for xerophthalmia screening. *Amer. J. Clin. Nutr.* 33:887.

Srikantia, S. G. 1975. Human vitamin A deficiency. *World Rev. Nutr. Dietet.* 20:184.

Underwood, B. A. 1978. Hypovitaminosis A and its control. *Bull. WHO* 86:525.

————. 1980. Strategies for the prevention of vitamin A deficiency. *Food Nutr. Bull.* 2 (October):11.

W.H.O. Chronicle. 1976*a.* The prevention of blindness. 30:391.

———. 1976*b.* Vitamin A deficiency and xerophthalmia. 30:117.

Wolbach, S. B., and Howe, P. R. 1978. Tissue changes following deprivation of fat-soluble A vitamin. *Nutr. Rev.* 36:16.

Wolf, G. International symposium on the metabolic function of vitamin A. *Amer. J. Clin. Nutr.* 22:897.

Vitamin D

American Academy of Pediatrics Committee on Nutrition. 1967. The relation between infantile hypercalcemia and vitamin D—public health implications in North America. *Pediatrics* 40:1050.

Avioli, L. V., ed. 1978. Vitamin D metabolites: their clinical importance (11 papers). *Arch. Intern. Med.* 138:835.

Bergstrom, W. H. 1975. Calciferol deficiency here and now. *Am. J. Dis. Child.* 129:1137.

Bogdonoff, M. D. 1980. On vitamin D, rickets and comprehensive medical care. *Drug Therapy* 10:31.

Bronner, F., ed. 1976. Symposium: clinical implications of recent advances in vitamin D. *Amer. J. Clin. Nutr.* 29:1253.

Dairy Council Digest. 1976. Recent developments in vitamin D. 47:13.

DeLuca, H. F. 1976. Vitamin D endocrinology. 1976. *Ann. Intern. Med.* 85:367.

DeLuca, H. F., and Schnoes, H. K. 1976. Metabolism and mechanism of action of vitamin D. *Ann. Rev. Biochem.* 45:631.

Finberg, L. 1981. Human feeding and vitamin D supplementations. *J. Pediatr.* 99:228.

Food and Nutrition Board. 1975. Hazards of overuse of vitamin D. *Nutr. Rev.* 33:61.

Haussler, M. R. 1974. Vitamin D: mode of action and biomedical applications. *Nutr. Rev.* 32:257.

Holick, M. F., et al. 1981. Regulation of cutaneous previtamin D_3 photosynthesis in man: skin pigment is not an essential regulator. *Science* 211:590.

Jacobs, M. D. 1979. Vitamin D deficient states: pathophysiology and treatment. *West. J. Med.* 131:305.

Kumar, R. 1980. Vitamin D deficiencies correcting disorders of vitamin D metabolism. *Drug Therapy* 10:118.

Lakdawala, D. R., and Widdowson, E. M. 1977. Vitamin D in human milk. *Lancet* 1:167.

Lapatsanis, P., et al. 1976. Two types of nutritional rickets in infants. *Amer. J. Clin. Nutr.* 29:1222.

Lawson, D. E. M. 1981. Comment: dietary vitamin D: is it necessary? *J. Human Nutr.* 35:61.

Lovinger, R. D. 1980. Rickets. *Pediatrics* 66:359.

Moncrieff, M. W. 1974. Rickets. *Nutrition* 29:221.

Neer, R. M. 1975. The evolutionary significance of vitamin D, skin pigment, and ultra violet light. *Am. J. Phys. Anthropology* 43:409.

Norman, A. W. 1979. *Vitamin D.* New York: Academic Press.

O'Connor, P. 1977. Vitamin D-deficiency rickets in two breast-fed infants who were not receiving vitamin D supplementation. *Clin. Pediatr.* 16:361.

Schneider, J. A., et al. 1976. Rickets. *West. J. Med.* 125:203.

Shetty, K. R. 1975. Protracted vitamin D intoxication. *Arch. Intern. Med.* 135:986.

Tulloch, A. L. 1974. Rickets in the premature. *Med. J. Aust.* 1:137.

Walton, J. W. 1976. Familial hypophosphatemic rickets: a delineation of its subdivisions and pathogenesis. *Clin. Pediatr.* 15:1007.

Weick, M. T., Sr. 1967. A history of rickets in the United States. *Amer. J. Clin. Nutr.* 20:1234.

West. J. Med. 1976. Rickets. 125:223.

Wolf, G. A. 1978. A historical note on the mode of administration of vitamin A for the cure of night blindness. *Amer. J. Clin. Nutr.* 31:290.

Wurtman, R. J. 1975. The effects of light on the human body. *Sci. Amer.* 233:68.

Vitamin E

Bieri, J. G. 1975. Vitamin E. *Nutr. Rev.* 33:161.

Bieri, J. G., and Evarts, R. P. 1975. Vitamin E adequacy in vegetable oils. *J. Amer. Dietet. Assoc.* 66:134.

Bieri, J. G., and Farrell, P. M. 1976. Vitamin E. *Vit. Horm.* 34:31.

Bunnell, R. H., et al. 1965. Alpha-tocopherol content of foods. *Amer. J. Clin. Nutr.* 17:1.

Committee on Nutritional Misinformation, Food and Nutrition Board, National Research Council, National Academy of Science. 1974. Who needs vitamin E? *J. Amer. Dietet. Assoc.* 64:365.

Dallman, P. R. 1976. Vitamin E deficiency in premature infants: interactions with iron. *West. J. Med.* 124:49.

Drake, J. R. 1980. Status of vitamin E as an erythropoietic factor. *Amer. J. Clin. Nutr.* 33:2386.

Ehrenkranz, R. A., et al. 1978. Amelioration of bronchopulmonary dysplasia after vitamin E administration: a preliminary report. *N. Engl. J. Med.* 299:564.

Farrell, P. M. 1979. Vitamin E deficiency in premature infants. *J. Pediatr.* 95:869.

Farrell, P. M., and Bieri, J. G. 1975. Megavitamin E supplementation in man. *Amer. J. Clin. Nutr.* 28:1381.

Food Tech. 1977. Vitamin E. 31:77.

Fried, J. J. 1975. The glamour vitamin: E for excess? *Family Health* 7:26.

Hodges, R. H. 1973. Vitamin E and coronary heart disease. *J. Amer. Dietet. Assoc.* 62:638.

Horwitt, M. K. 1974. Status of human requirements for vitamin E. *Amer. J. Clin. Nutr.* 27:1182.

———. 1976. Vitamin E: a reexamination. *Amer. J. Clin. Nutr.* 29:569.

Horwitt, M. K., ed. 1974. Symposium: vitamin E biochemistry, nutritional requirements and clinical studies. *Amer. J. Clin. Nutr.* 27:939.

McLaughlin, P. J. 1979. Vitamin E content of foods. *J. Amer. Dietet. Assoc.* 75:647.

Mason, K. E. 1977. The first two decades of vitamin E. *Fed. Proc.* 36:1906.

Northway, W. H. 1978. Bronchopulmonary dysplasia and vitamin E. *N. Engl. J. Med.* 299:599.

Nutr. Rev. 1974. Supplementations of human diets with vitamin E. July (Suppl.).

———. 1977. Vitamin E. 35:57.

Phelps, D. L. 1979. Vitamin E: where do we stand? *Pediatrics* 63:933.

Roed-Petersen, J., and Hjorth, N. 1975. Patch test sensitizations from D,L-alphatocopherol (vitamin E). *Contact Dermatitis* 1:391.

Roels, O. A. 1967. Present knowledge of vitamin E. *Nutr. Rev.* 25:33.

Steiner, M., and Anastasi, J. 1976. Vitamin E, an inhibitor of the platelet release reaction. *J. Clin. Invest.* 57:732.

Witting, L. A. 1975. Vitamin E as a food additive. *J. Amer. Oil Chem. Soc.* 52:64.

Vitamin K—General

Almquist, H. J. 1975. The early history of vitamin K. *Amer. J. Clin. Nutr.* 28:656.

Dam, H. 1966. Historical survey and introduction. *Vit. Horm.* 24:295.

Fernlund, P., et al. 1975. Vitamin K and the biosynthesis of prothrombin. *J. Biol. Chem.* 250:6125.

Johnson, B. C. 1964. Dietary factors and vitamin K. *Nutr. Rev.* 22:225.

Mayo Clin. Proc. 1974. Symposium on vitamin K. 49:911.

Nutr. Rev. 1974. Vitamin K and prothrombin structure. 32:279.

———. 1976. The functional significance of vitamin K action. 34:182.

Olson, R. 1976. Present knowledge of vitamin K. In *Present knowledge of nutrition*, 3rd ed., ed. H. Sipple and K. McNutt. New York: Nutrition Foundation.

Shearer, M. J., et al. 1974. Studies on the absorption and metabolism of phylloquinone (vitamin K_1) in man. *Vit. Horm.* 32:513.

Suttie, J. W. 1973. Vitamin K and prothrombin synthesis. *Nutr. Rev.* 31:105.

Suttie, J. W., and Jackson, C. M. 1977. Prothrombin structure, activation and biosynthesis. *Am. Physiol. Soc.* 57:1.

Vitamin K—Obstetrics and Pediatrics

Aballi, A. J. 1977. Vitamin K deficiency in the newborn. *Lancet* 2:559.

Brit. Med. J. 1977. Bleeding in the newborn. 2:915.

Goldman, H. I., and Amader, P. 1969. Vitamin K deficiency after the newborn period. *Pediatrics* 44:745.

Owen, G. M., et al. 1967. Use of vitamin K_1 in pregnancy. *Am. J. Obst. Gyn.* 99:368.

Pediatrics. 1961. Committee on nutrition: vitamin K compounds and the water-soluble analogues. 28:501.

Wefring, K. W. 1963. Hemorrhage in the newborn and vitamin K prophylaxis. *J. Pediatr.* 63:663.

Nonessential Dietary Factors

Barak, A. J., et al. 1973. Relationship of ethanol to choline metabolism in the liver. A review. *Amer. J. Clin. Nutr.* 26:1234.

Clements, R. S., Jr., and Darnell, B. 1980. Myoinositol content of common foods: development of a high-myoinositol diet. *Amer. J. Clin. Nutr.* 33:1954.

Fernstrom, J. R. 1977. Effects of the diet on brain neurotransmitters. *Metabolism* 26:207.

Kuksis, A., and Mookerjea, S. 1978. Inositol. *Nutr. Rev.* 36:233.

CHAPTER 7

Minerals—General

Feeley, R. M., et al. 1972. Major mineral elements in dairy products. *J. Amer. Dietet. Assoc.* 61:505.

Gallagher, J. C., and Riggs, B. L. 1978. Current concepts in nutrition: nutrition and bone disease. *N. Engl. J. Med.* 298:193.

Karcioglu, Z. A., and Sarper, R. M. 1980. *Zinc and copper in medicine.* Springfield, Ill.: Thomas.

Lutwak, L., et al. 1974. Current concepts of bone metabolism. *Ann. Intern. Med.* 80:630.

Massry, S. G., et al., eds. 1980. *Phosphates and minerals in health and disease*. New York: Plenum.

Mertz, W. 1980. Mineral elements; new perspectives. *J. Amer. Dietet. Assoc.* 77:258.

Nordin, B. E. C., ed. 1976. *Calcium, phosphate and magnesium metabolism*. Edinburgh: Churchill Livingstone.

Randolph, P. M. 1981. The role of diet and nutrition in dental health and disease. *Nutr. News* 44:1.

Randolph, P. M., and Dennison, C. 1980. *Diet, nutrition and dentistry*. St. Louis, Mo.: Mosby.

Solomons, N. W. 1979. On the assessment of zinc and copper nutriture in man. *Amer. J. Clin. Nutr.* 32:856.

Steward, R. J. C. 1975. Bone pathology in experimental malnutrition. *World Rev. Nutr. Dietet.* 21:1.

Urist, M. R. 1980. *Fundamental and clinical bone physiology*. Philadelphia: Lippincott.

Sodium and Potassium

Dahl, L. K. 1972. Salt and hypertension. *Amer. J. Clin. Nutr.* 25:232.

Darby, W. J. 1980. Why salt? How much. *Contemp. Nutr.* 5 (June):1.

Earley, L. E., and Daugharty, T. M. 1969. Sodium metabolism. *N. Engl. J. Med.* 281:72.

Ellis, K. J., et al. 1976. Total body sodium and chloride in normal adults. *Metabolism* 25:645.

Freis, E. E. 1976. Salt, volume and the prevention of hypertension. *Circulation* 53:589.

Krehl, W. A. 1966a. The potassium depletion syndrome. *Nutr. Today* 1:20.

———. 1966b. Sodium: a most extraordinary dietary essential. *Nutr. Today* 1:16.

Meneely, G. R., and Battarbee, H. D. 1976. Sodium and potassium. *Nutr. Rev.* 34:225.

Taclob, L. T. 1973. Hyponatremic syndromes. *Med. Clin. N.A.* 57:1425.

Calcium and Phosphorus

Allen, L. H. 1979. Protein-induced hypercalcemia: a longer term study. *Amer. J. Clin. Nutr.* 32:741.

Anand, C. R., and Linkswiler, H. M. 1974. Effect of protein intake on calcium balance of young men given 500 mg calcium daily. *J. Nutr.* 104:695.

Baylink, D. J. 1980. Sodium fluoride for osteoporosis—some unanswered questions. *J.A.M.A.* 243:463.

Chu, J., et al. 1975. Studies in calcium metabolism. II. Effects of low calcium and variable protein intake on human calcium metabolism. *Amer. J. Clin. Nutr.* 28:1028. (*See also Nutr. Rpt. Internat.* 17 [1978]:503.)

Dairy Council Digest. 1976. Calcium in bone health. 47:31.

Heaney, R. P.; Recker, R. R.; and Saville, P. D. 1977. Calcium balance and calcium requirements in middle-aged women. *Amer. J. Clin. Nutr.* 30:1603.

Irwin, M. I., and Kienholz, E. W. 1973. A conspectus of research on calcium requirements of man. *J. Nutr.* 103:1019.

Juan, D. 1979. Hypocalcemia: differential diagnosis and mechanisms. *Arch. Intern. Med.* 139:1166.

Kooh, S. W., et al. 1977. Rickets due to calcium deficiency. *N. Engl. J. Med.* 297:1264.

Margen, S., et al. 1974. Studies in calcium metabolism. I. The calciuretic effect of dietary protein. *Amer. J. Clin. Nutr.* 27:584.

Polanska, N., and Wills, M. R. 1976. Factors contributing to osteomalacia in the elderly and in Asian communities. *J. Human Nutr.* 30:371.

Schneider, A. B., and Sherwood, L. M. 1974. Calcium homeostasis and the pathogenesis and management of hypercalcemic disorders. *Metabolism* 23:975.

Schwartz, M. K. 1975. Recent advances in calcium and phosphorus metabolism. *Ann. Clin. Lab. Sci.* 5:176.

Magnesium

Anderson, T. W., et al. 1975. Ischemic heart disease, water hardness and myocardial magnesium. *Can. Med. Assn. J.* 113:199.

Horn, B. 1981. Magnesium—it's about time. *West. J. Med.* 134:72.

Seelig, M. S. 1980. *Magnesium deficiency in pathogenesis of disease: early roots of cardiovascular, skeletal, and renal abnormalities*. New York: Plenum.

Seelig, M. S., and Heggtveti, H. A. 1974. Magnesium interrelationships in ischemic heart disease: a review. *Amer. J. Clin. Nutr.* 27:59.

Wacker, W. E. C. 1980. *Magnesium and man*. Cambridge, Mass.: Harvard University Press.

Iron

Block, M. H. 1976. *Text-atlas of hematology*. Philadelphia: Lea & Febiger.

Bowering, J., et al. 1976. A conspectus of research on iron requirements of man. *J. Nutr.* 106:985.

Conrad, M. E. 1976. Anemia: a symptom of disease. *Alabama J. Med. Sci.* 13:107.

Crosby, W. H. 1979. Iron deficiency anemia in a nutritionally complex situation. *Amer. J. Clin. Nutr.* 32:715.

Dallman, P. R. 1981. Iron deficiency: diagnosis and treatment. *West. J. Med.* 134:496.

Fairbanks, V. F., et al. 1971. *Clinical disorders of iron metabolism.* New York: Grune & Stratton.

Feiner, A. S., and Mahmood, T. 1979. Iron deficiency anemia. *Postgrad. Med.* 66:119.

Finch, C. 1969. Iron metabolism. *Nutr. Today* 4:6.

————. 1976. Iron metabolism. In *Present knowledge in nutrition*, 4th ed. New York: Nutrition Foundation.

————. 1981. Iron nutrition. *West. J. Med.* 134:532.

Fritz, J. 1970. *Measures to increase iron in foods and diets.* Washington, D.C.: Food and Nutrition Board, National Research Council, National Academy of Sciences.

Lynch, S. R. 1980. Ascorbic acid and iron nutrition. *Contemp. Nutr.* 5:1.

Peterson, C. M. 1979. Problems of iron imbalance: chronic overload syndromes. *Drug Therapy* 9:128.

U.S. Department of Health, Education and Welfare. 1976. *Iron nutriture in adolescence.* Committee on Nutrition of the Mother and Preschool Child, Food and Nutrition Board, National Research Council, National Academy of Sciences. Publication no. (HSA) 77-5100. Washington, D.C.

Wintrobe, M. 1975. *Clinical hematology.* 7th ed. Philadelphia: Lea & Febiger.

Iodine

Cullen, R. W., and Oace, S. M. 1976. Iodine: current status. *J. Nutr. Edu.* 8:101.

DeMaeyer, E. M., et al. 1979. *Control of endemic goitre.* Geneva: World Health Organization.

Fierro, B. R., et al. 1974. The clinical pattern of cretinism as seen in highland Ecuador. *Amer. J. Clin. Nutr.* 27:531.

Kidd, P. S., et al. 1974. Sources of dietary iodine. *J. Amer. Dietet. Assoc.* 65:420.

Kohn, L. A. 1976. The midwestern American "epidemic" of iodine-induced hyperthyroidism in the 1920s. *Bull. N.Y. Acad. Med.* 52:770.

Taylor, R. 1981. Iodine: going from hypo to hyper. *FDA Consumer* 15:15.

Trowbridge, F. L., et al. 1975a. Findings relating to goiter and iodine in the Ten-State Nutrition Survey. *Amer. J. Clin. Nutr.* 28:712.

————. 1975b. Iodine and goiter in children. *Pediatrics.* 56:82.

Wayne, E. J., et al. 1964. *Clinical aspects of iodine metabolism.* Oxford: Blackwell.

Zinc

Brewer, G. J., and Prasad, A. S., eds. 1977. *Zinc metabolism: current aspects in health and disease.* New York: Alan R. Liss.

Freeland, J. H., and Cousins, R. J. 1976. Zinc content of selected foods. *J. Amer. Dietet. Assoc.* 68:S26.

Gordon, E. F., et al. 1981. Zinc metabolism: basic, clinical, and behavioral aspects. *J. Pediatr.* 99:341.

Greeley, S., and Sandstead, H. H. 1980. Zinc in human nutrition. *Contemp. Nutr.* 5:1.

Haeflein, K. A., and Rasmussen, A. I. 1977. Zinc content of selected foods. *J. Amer. Dietet. Assoc.* 70:610.

Halsted, J. A., et al. 1974. A conspectus of research on zinc requirements of man. *J. Nutr.* 104:345.

Hambidge, K. M. 1974. Zinc deficiency in children. In *Trace element metabolism in animals–2*, ed. W. G. Hoekstra et al. Baltimore: University Park Press.

————. 1977. The role of zinc and other trace metals in pediatric nutrition and health. *Ped. Clin. N.A.* 24:95.

Johnson, P. E., and Evans, G. W. 1978. Relative zinc availability in human breast milk, infant formulas, and cow's milk. *Amer. J. Clin. Nutr.* 31:416.

The Medical Letter. 1978. Zinc. 20:57.

Murphy, E. W., et al. 1975. Provisional tables on the zinc content of foods. *J. Amer. Dietet. Assoc.* 66:345.

O'Dell, B. L., et al. 1972. Evaluation of zinc availability in foodstuffs of plant and animal origin. *J. Nutr.* 102:653.

Osis, D., et al. 1972. Dietary zinc intake in man. *Amer. J. Clin. Nutr.* 25:582.

Pediatrics. 1978. Zinc. 62:408.

Pores, W. J., et al. 1974. *Clinical application of zinc metabolism.* Springfield, Ill.: Thomas.

Sandstead, H. H. 1973. Zinc nutrition in the United States. *Amer. J. Clin. Nutr.* 26:1251.

Fluoride

Ericsson, Y., ed. 1970. *Fluorides and human health.* WHO Monograph Series, no. 59. Geneva: World Health Organization.

Hodge, H. C., and Smith, F. A. 1968. Fluorides and man. *Ann. Rev. Pharmacol.* 8:395.

Horowitz, H. S. 1973. Fluoride: research on clinical and public health applications. *J. Am. Dent. Assoc.* 87:1013.

Kramer, L., et al. 1974. Dietary fluoride in different areas in the United States. *Amer. J. Clin. Nutr.* 27:590.

Med. World News. 1974. Using fluoride to curb osteoporosis. 15:58.

Newbrun, E. 1977. The safety of water fluoridation. *J. Am. Dent. Assoc.* 94:301.

Osis, D., et al. 1974. Dietary fluoride intake in man. *J. Nutr.* 104:1313.

Simons, J. H., ed. 1965. *Fluorine chemistry. IV. Biological properties of inorganic fluorides and effects of fluorides on bones and teeth.* New York: Academic Press.

Taves, D. R. 1978. Fluoridation and mortality due to heart disease. *Nature* 272:361.

Copper

Baker, D. E. 1974. Copper: soil, water, plant relationships. *Fed. Proc.* 33:1188.

Evans, G. W. 1973. Copper homeostasis in the mammalian system. *Physiol. Rev.* 53:535.

Holtzman, N. A. 1976. Menkes' kinky hair syndrome: a genetic disease involving copper. *Fed. Proc.* 35:2276.

Klevay, L. M. 1975. The ratio of zinc to copper of diets in the United States. *Nutr. Rpt. Internat.* 11:237.

Mayo Clin. Proc. 1974. Symposium on copper metabolism and Wilson's disease. 49:361.

Owen, C. A., Jr. 1982. *Biochemical aspects of copper.* Park Ridge, N.J.: Noyes Publications.

Pennington, J. T., and Calloway, D. H. 1973. Copper content of foods. Factors affecting reported values. *J. Amer. Dietet. Assoc.* 63:143.

Trace Elements

Burch, R. E., et al. 1975. Newer aspects of the roles of zinc, manganese, and copper in human nutrition. *Clin. Chem.* 21:501.

Carlisle, E. M. 1975. Silicon. *Nutr. Rev.* 33:257.

Chesters, J. K. 1976. Trace elements: adventitious yet essential dietary ingredients. *Proc. Nutr. Soc.* 35:15.

Dairy Council Digest. 1982. Trace elements in human nutrition. 53:1.

Fed. Proc. 1975. Symposium: biochemical function of selenium and its interrelationship with other trace elements and vitamin E. 34:2082.

Hoekstra, W. G., et al., eds. 1974. *Trace element metabolism in animals–2.* Baltimore: University Park Press.

Kay, R. G. 1981. Zinc and copper in human nutrition. *J. Human Nutr.* 35:25.

Klevay, L. M. 1975. Coronary heart disease: the zinc/copper hypothesis. *Amer. J. Clin. Nutr.* 28:764.

Lynch, S. R. 1980. Ascorbic acid and iron nutrition. *Contemp. Nutr.* 5 (September):1.

Mertz, W. 1982. Chromium: an essential micronutrient. *Contemp. Nutr.* 7 (March):1.

Prasad, A. S., ed. 1976. *Trace elements in human health and disease,* vol. 1. *Zinc and copper,* vol. 2. *Essential and toxic elements.* New York: Academic Press.

Prasad, A., and Oberleas, D. 1974. Trace elements in maternal and fetal nutrition. In *Birth defects and fetal development,* ed. K. S. Moghissi. Springfield, Ill.: Thomas.

Saner, G. 1980. *Chromium in nutrition and disease.* New York: Alan R. Liss.

Taylor, A., and Marks, V. 1978. Cobalt—a review. *J. Human Nutr.* 32:165.

Underwood, E. J. 1975. Cobalt. *Nutr. Rev.* 33:65.

———. 1977. *Trace elements in human and animal nutrition.* 4th ed. New York: Academic Press.

———. 1981. Trace metals in human and animal health. *J. Human Nutr.* 35:37.

Utter, M. F. 1976. The biochemistry of manganese. *Med. Clin. N.A.* 60:713.

Young, V. R. 1981. Selenium: a case for its essentiality in man. *N. Engl. J. Med.* 304:1228.

CHAPTER 8

Metabolism and Physiology

Bayless, T. M., ed. 1971. Symposium: structure and function of the gut. *Amer. J. Clin. Nutr.* 24:44.

Bessman, S. P., and Geiger, P. J. 1981. Transport of energy in muscle: the phosphoryl-creatine shuttle. *Science* 211:448.

Dairy Council Digest. 1971. Diet as a regulator of metabolism. 42:25.

Edholm, O. H., and Weiner, J. S. 1981. *The principles and practice of human physiology.* New York: Academic Press.

Eisenstein, A. B., ed. 1970. Gluconeogenesis: a symposium. *Amer. J. Clin. Nutr.* 23:971.

Guyton, A. G. 1981. *Textbook of medical physiology.* 6th ed. Philadelphia: Saunders.

Johnson, L. R. 1977. Symposium: gastrointestinal hormones: physiological implications. *Fed. Proc.* 36:1929.

Montgomery, R., et al. 1977. *Biochemistry: a case-oriented approach.* 2nd ed. St. Louis: Mosby.

White, A., et al. 1978. *Principles of biochemistry.* 6th ed. McGraw-Hill.

Carbohydrate

Berdanier, C. D., ed. 1976. *Carbohydrate metabolism: regulation and physiological role.* New York: Halsted Press.

Danowski, T. S., et al. 1975. Hypoglycemia. *World Rev. Nutr. Dietet.* 22:288.

Gray, G. M. 1970. Carbohydrate digestion and absorption. *Gastroenterology* 58:96.

Hers, H. G. 1976. The control of glycogen metabolism in the liver. *Ann. Rev. Biochem.* 45:167.

Hultman, E., and Nilsson, L. H. 1975. Factors influencing carbohydrate metabolism in man. *Nutr. and Metab.* 18 (Suppl. 1):45.

Mansford, K. R. L. 1971. Problems in carbohydrate absorption and metabolism. *Proc. Nutr. Soc.* 30:230.

Protein

Adibi, S. A. 1976. Intestinal phase of protein assimilation in men. *Amer. J. Clin. Nutr.* 29:205.

Broquist, H. P. 1976. Amino acid metabolism. *Nutr. Rev.* 34:289.

Flatt, J. P., and Blackburn, G. L. 1974. The metabolic fuel regulatory system: implications for protein-sparing therapies during caloric deprivations and disease. *Amer. J. Clin. Nutr.* 27:175.

Gray, G. M., and Cooper, H. L. 1971. Protein digestion and absorption. *Gastroenterology* 61:535.

Lowenstein, J. M. 1972. Ammonia production in muscle and other tissues: the purine nucleotide cycle. *Physiol. Rev.* 52:382.

Munro, H. N. 1976. Regulation of body protein metabolism. *Proc. Nutr. Soc.* 35:297.

Proc. Nutr. Soc. 1972. Symposium: protein metabolism and hormones. 31:171.

Fat

Clement, J. 1975. Nature and importance of endogenous fatty acids during intestinal absorption of fats. *World Rev. Nutr. Dietet.* 21:281.

Grundy, S. M. 1978. Cholesterol metabolism in man. *West. J. Med.* 128:13.

Hofmann, A. F., et al. 1970. Symposium: gastroenterology: physical events in lipid digestion and absorption. *Fed. Proc.* 29:1317.

Holt, P. R. 1972. The roles of bile acids during the process of normal fat and cholesterol absorption. *Arch. Intern. Med.* 130:574.

Mansbach, C. M. 1976. Conditions affecting the biosynthesis of lipids in the small intestine. *Amer. J. Clin. Nutr.* 29:295.

McIntyre, N., and Isselbacher, K. J. 1973. Role of the small intestine in cholesterol metabolism. *Amer. J. Clin. Nutr.* 26:647.

Ockner, R. K., et al. 1972. Differences in the intestinal absorption of saturated and unsaturated long chain fatty acids. *Gastroenterology* 62:981.

Schmitt, M. G., et al. 1976. Absorption of short chain fatty acids from the human jejunum. *Gastroenterology* 70:211.

Volpe, J. J., and Vagelos, P. R. 1976. Mechanisms and regulation of biosynthesis of saturated fatty acids. *Physiol. Rev.* 56:339.

CHAPTER 9

Fluids and Electrolytes

Abbey, J. C. 1968. Nursing observation of fluid imbalance. *Nurs. Clin. N.A.* 3:77.

Camien, M. N., et al. 1969. A critical reappraisal of 'acid-base' balance. *Amer. J. Clin. Nutr.* 22:786.

Fenton, M. 1969. What to do about thirst. *Am. J. Nurs.* 69:1014.

Fitzsimmons, J. T. 1972. Thirst. *Physiol. Rev.* 52:468.

Grant, M. M., and Kubo, W. M. 1975. Assessing the patient's hydration status. *Am. J. Nurs.* 75:1306.

Grollman, A. 1976. Body fluids and electrolytes. *Consultant* 16:134.

Kassirer, J. P. 1974. Serious acid-base disorders. *N. Engl. J. Med.* 291:773.

Klahr, S., et al. 1972. Acid-base disorders in health and disease. *J.A.M.A.* 222:567.

Lee, C. A., et al. 1974. Extracellular volume imbalance. *Am. J. Nurs.* 74:888.

Lehmann, J., Jr., and Lennon, E. J. 1972. Role of diet, gastrointestinal tract and bone in acid-base homeostasis. *Kidney Int.* 1:275.

Lit, A. K. C., et al. 1980. *Fluid, electrolytes, acid-base and nutrition.* New York: Academic Press.

Patrick, J. 1978. Interactions between the physiology of sodium, potassium and water, and nutrition. *J. Human Nutr.* 32:405.

Share, L., and Claybaugh, J. R. 1972. Regulation of body fluids. *Ann. Rev. Physiol.* 34:235.

Sharer, J. E. 1975. Reviewing acid-base balance. *Am. J. Nurs.* 75:980.

Snively, W. D., and Roberts, K. T. 1973. The clinical picture as an aid to understanding body fluid disturbances. *Nurs. Forum* 12:132.

Weldy, N. J. 1980. *Body fluids and electrolytes: a programmed presentation.* 3rd ed. St. Louis: Mosby.

Water

Baker, E. M., et al. 1963. Water requirements of men as related to salt intake. *Amer. J. Clin. Nutr.* 12:394.

Culpepper, R. M., and Andreoli, T. E. 1979. Water homeostasis—facts and uncertainties. *West. J. Med.* 131:436.

Robinson, J. 1970. Water, the indispensable nutrient. *Nutr. Today* 5:16.

Stillinger, F. H. 1980. Water revisited. *Science* 209:451.

Walker, J. S., et al. 1963. Water intake of normal children. *Science* 140:890.

Weitzman, R. A., and Kleeman, C.R. 1980. The clinical physiology of water metabolism. Part III: The water depletion (hyperosmolar) and water excess (hyposmolar) syndromes. *West. J. Med.* 132:16.

Sodium and Potassium

Earley, L. E., and Daugharty, T. M. 1969. Sodium metabolism. *N. Engl. J. Med.* 281:72.

Ellis, K. J., et al. 1976. Total body sodium and chlorine in normal adults. *Metabolism* 25:645.

Fitzsimons, J. T. 1979. *The physiology of thirst and sodium appetite.* New York: Cambridge University Press.

Frazier, H. S. 1968. Renal regulation of sodium balance. *N. Engl. J. Med.* 279:868.

Krehl, W. A. 1966*a*. The potassium depletion syndrome. *Nutr. Today* 1:20.

———. 1966*b*. Sodium: a most extraordinary dietary essential. *Nutr. Today* 1:16.

Meneely, G. R., and Battarbee, H. D. 1976. Sodium and potassium. *Nutr. Rev.* 14:225.

Taclob, L. T. 1973. Hyponatremic syndromes. *Med. Clin. N.A.* 57:1425.

Whittier, F. C. 1981. Hypernatremia: misunderstood and dangerous. *Consultant* 21:206.

CHAPTER 10

Recommended Daily Allowances

Bieri, J. G. 1980. An overview of the RDAs for vitamins. *J. Amer. Dietet. Assoc.* 76:134.

Harper, A. E. 1978. Meeting recommended dietary allowances. *J. Florida Med. Assoc.* 66:419.

———. 1980. Recommended dietary allowances—1980. *Nutr. Rev.* 38:290.

Hegsted, D. M. 1976. On dietary standards. *Nutr. Rev.* 36:33.

Leveille, G. A., et al. 1979. *Nutrition and the food you eat away from home.* Chicago: International Foodservice Manufacturers Association.

Leverton, R. M. 1975. The RDAs are not for amateurs. *J. Amer. Dietet. Assoc.* 66:9.

Mertz, W. 1980. The new RDAs: estimated adequate and safe intake of trace elements and calculation of available iron. *J. Amer. Dietet. Assoc.* 76:128.

Munro, H. N. 1977. How well recommended are the recommended dietary allowances? *J. Amer. Dietet. Assoc.* 71:490.

———. 1980. Major gaps in nutrient allowance. *J. Amer. Dietet. Assoc.* 76:137.

National Academy of Sciences, National Research Council, Food and Nutrition Board. 1980. *Recommended dietary allowances.*

Nutrition Foundation. 1980. *Nutritional requirements of man: a conspectus of research.* Washington, D.C.

Food Guides

Dodds, J. M. 1981. The handy five food guide. *J. Nutr. Edu.* 13:50.

Guthrie, H. A., and Scheer, J. C. 1981. Nutritional adequacy of self-selected diets that satisfy the four food groups guide. *J. Nutr. Edu.* 13:46.

King, J. C., et al. 1978. Evaluation and modification of the basic four food guide. *J. Nutr. Edu.* 10:27.

Lachance, P. A. 1981. A suggestion in food guides and dietary guidelines. *J. Nutr. Edu.* 13:56.

Light, L., and Cronin, R. J. 1981. Food guides revisited. *J. Nutr. Edu.* 13:57.

Oace, S. M. 1981. From the editor—perspectives on food guidance. *J. Nutr. Edu.* 13:46.

Pennington, J. A. T. 1981. Considerations for a new food guide. *J. Nutr. Edu.* 13:53.

Food Composition

Appledorf, H., and Kelly, L. S. 1979. Proximate and mineral content of fast foods. Pizza, Mexican-American–style foods and submarine sandwiches. *J. Amer. Dietet. Assoc.* 74:35.

Bunker, M. L., and McWilliams, M. 1979. Caffeine content of common beverages. *J. Amer. Dietet. Assoc.* 74:28.

Deeming, S. B., and Weber, C. W. 1979. Trace minerals in commercially prepared baby foods. *J. Amer. Dietet. Assoc.* 75:149.

Dong, M. H., et al. 1980. Thiamin, riboflavin, and vitamin B_6 contents of selected foods as served. *J. Amer. Dietet. Assoc.* 76:156.

Groisser, D. S. 1978. A study of caffeine in tea. I. A new spectrophotometric micromethod. II. Concentration of caffeine in various strengths, brands, blends and types of tea. *Amer. J. Clin. Nutr.* 31:1727.

Hanson, J. M., and Kinsella, J. E. 1981. Fatty acid content and composition of infant formulas and cereals. *J. Amer. Dietet. Assoc.* 78:250.

Hawley, L. E., et al. 1978. Fatty acid composition of prepared infant formulas. *J. Amer. Dietet. Assoc.* 72:170.

Kinsella, J. E., et al. 1977. Fatty acid content and composition of freshwater finfish. *J. Amer. Oil Chem. Soc.* 54:424.

Korsrud, G. O., and Truk, K. D. 1979. Sucrose, fructose, and glucose contents of infant cereals. *J. Can. Diet. Assoc.* 40:56.

Matthews, R. H., and Workman, M. Y. 1978. Nutrient content of selected baby foods. *J. Amer. Dietet. Assoc.* 72:27.

McLaughlin, P. J., and Weihrauch, J. L. 1979. Vitamin E content of foods. *J. Amer. Dietet. Assoc.* 75:647.

Murphy, E. W., et al. 1978. Nutrient content of spices and herbs. *J. Amer. Dietet. Assoc.* 72:174.

Rezabek, K. 1979. *Nutritive Value of Convenience Foods.* Hines, Ill: West Suburban Dietetic Association.

Shannon, B. M., and Parks, S. C. 1980. Fast foods: a perspective on their nutritional impact. *J. Amer. Dietet. Asoc.* 76:242.

Southgate, D. A. T., et al. 1978. Free sugars in foods. *J. Human Nutr.* 32:335.

Walsh, J. H., et al. 1981. Pantothenic acid content of 75 processed and cooked foods. *J. Amer. Dietet. Assoc.* 78:140.

Wong, N. A., et al. 1978. Mineral content of dairy products. I. Milk and milk products. II. Cheeses. *J. Amer. Dietet. Assoc.* 72:288, 608.

Processing and Nutrient Contents

Erdman, J. W. 1979. Effect of preparation and service of food on nutrient value. *Food Tech.* 33:38.

Goodenough, P. W., and Atkin, R. K., eds. 1981. *Quality in stored and processed vegetables and fruit.* London: Academic Press.

Hurt, H. D. 1979. Effect of canning on the nutritive value of vegetables. *Food Tech.* 33:62.

Karel, M. 1979. Effect of storage on nutrient retention of foods. *Food Tech.* 33:36.

Kramer, A. 1979. Effects of freezing and frozen storage on the nutrient retention of fruits and vegetables. *Food Tech.* 33:58.

Lund, D. B. 1979. Effect of commercial processing on nutrients. *Food Tech.* 33:28.

Taub, I. A., et al. 1979. Effect of irradiation on meat proteins. *Food Tech.* 33:184.

Nutrition Labeling

Federal Register. 1982. *Food labeling: declaration of sodium content of foods and label claims for foods on the basis of sodium content and GRAS safety review of sodium chloride.* June 18, 1982, p. 26580.

National Nutrition Consortium. 1978. *Nutrition labeling: how it can work for you.* Washington, D.C.

Meal Planning

Lane, S., and Vermeersch, V. 1979. Evaluation of thrifty food plan. *J. Nutr. Edu.* 11:96.

McWilliams, M. 1979. *Food fundamentals.* 3rd ed. New York: Wiley.

Peckham, G. C., and Freeland-Graves, J. H. 1979. *Foundations of food preparation.* 4th ed. New York: Macmillan.

U.S. Department of Agriculture, Science and Education Administration. 1979. *Family food budgeting for good meals and good nutrition.* Home & Garden Bulletin, no. 94, revised.

U.S. Department of Agriculture. 1982. *Your money's worth in foods.* Home & Garden Bulletin, no. 183.

White, A., and the Society for Nutrition Education. 1980. *The family health cookbook*. New York: McKay.

CHAPTER 11

World Nutrition and Hunger

Austin, J. E. 1981. *Nutrition programs in the third world*. Cambridge, Mass.: Oelgeschlager, Gunn, and Hain.

Brown, R. E. 1977. *Starving children: the tyranny of hunger*. New York: Springer.

Caliendo, M. A. 1979. *Nutrition and the world food crisis*. New York: Macmillan.

Hensley, E. S. 1981. *Basic concepts of world nutrition*. Springfield, Ill.: Thomas.

Jelliffe, D. B., and Jelliffe, E. F. P., eds. 1979. *A good nutritional start: improving the nutrition of mothers and young children*. New York: IYC Secretariat, Technical Division.

Kutzner, P. L., and Sullivan, T. X. 1976. *Who's involved with hunger. An organization guide*. Washington, D.C.: American Freedom from Hunger Foundation and World Hunger Education Service.

Latham, M. C. 1979. *Human nutrition in tropical Africa*. Rome: Food and Agriculture Organization.

McLaren, D. S. 1976. *Nutrition in the community*. New York: Wiley.

Morley, D., and Woodland, M. 1980. *See how they grow: monitoring child growth for appropriate health care in developing countries*. New York: Oxford University Press.

Presidential Commission on World Hunger. 1979. *Overcoming world hunger: the challenge ahead, presidential commission on world hunger, final report*. Washington, D.C.: Government Printing Office.

Protein Calorie Malnutrition

Ashworth, A. 1980. Practical aspects of dietary management during rehabilitation from severe protein-energy malnutrition. *J. Human Nutr.* 34:360.

Cameron, M., and Hofvander, Y. 1971. *Manual on feeding infants and young children*. Protein Advisory Group, United Nations.

Food Nutr. Bull. 1979. Protein energy requirements under conditions prevailing in developing countries: current knowledge and research needs. (Suppl. 1), July 1979.

Olson, R. E., ed. 1975. *Protein-calorie malnutrition*. New York: Academic Press.

Waterlow, J. C. 1972. Classification and definition of protein-calorie malnutrition. *Brit. Med. J.* 3:566.

Work, T. H. 1973. Tropical problems in nutrition. *Ann. Intern. Med.* 79:701.

Immunity

Amer. J. Clin. Nutr. 1977. Symposium. Impact of infection on nutritional status. 30:1203.

Beisel, W. R. 1980. Effects of infection on nutritional status and immunity. *Fed. Proc.* 39:3105.

Chandra, R. K., and Newberne, P. M. 1977. *Nutrition, immunity and infection: mechanisms of interactions*. New York: Plenum.

Chandra, R. K., and Scrimshaw, N. S. 1980. Immunocompetence in nutritional assessment. *Amer. J. Clin. Nutr.* 33:2694.

Good, R. A., et al. 1980. Nutritional modulation of immune responses. *Fed. Proc.* 39:3098.

Gunby, P. 1980. Closing in on the nutrition-immunity link. *J.A.M.A.* 244:2715.

Latham, M. C. 1975. Nutrition and infection in national development. *Science* 188:561.

Growth, Intelligence, Behavior

Birch, H. G. 1972. Malnutrition, learning and intelligence. *Am. J. Public Health* 62:773.

Brozek, J., ed. 1979. *Behavioral effects of energy and protein deficits*. National Institute of Arthritis, Metabolism and Digestive Diseases, NIH pub. no. 79-1906. Washington, D.C.

Cheek, D. B. 1968. *Human growth, body composition, cell growth, energy, and intelligence*. Philadelphia: Lea & Febiger.

Dobbing, J. 1970. Undernutrition and the developing brain. *Am. J. Dis. Child.* 120:411.

Greene, L. S., ed. 1977. *Malnutrition, behavior, and social organization*. New York: Academic Press.

Jelliffe, D. B., and Jelliffe, E. F. P., eds. 1979. *Nutrition and growth*. In *Human nutrition, a comprehensive treatise*, vol. 2. New York: Plenum.

Mora, J. O., et al. 1974. Nutrition, health, and social factors related to intellectual performance. *World Rev. Nutr. Dietet.* 19:205.

Nutr. Rev. 1980. Review: special report: energy-protein malnutrition and behavior. 38:164.

CHAPTER 12

Obesity

Berg, F. M. 1980a. *How to lose weight the action way.* Hettinger, N. Dak.: Flying Diamond Books.

———. 1980b. *How to lose weight the action way: young adult/teen edition.* Hettinger, N. Dak.: Flying Diamond Books.

Better Homes & Gardens. 1980. *Eat and stay slim.* Des Moines, Iowa: Meredith, Consumer Book Division.

Bray, G. A. , ed. 1980a. *Obesity: comparative methods of weight control.* Westport, Conn.: Technomic Publishing.

———. 1980b. *Obesity in America.* U.S. Department of Health, Education, and Welfare/National Institutes of Health, pub. no. 80–359. Washington, D.C.

Bruch, H. 1973. *Eating disorders: obesity, anorexia nervosa and the person within.* New York: Basic Books.

Craddock, D. 1978. *Obesity and its management.* 3rd ed. New York: Longman.

Edelstein, B. 1980. *The woman doctor's diet for teen-age girls.* Englewood Cliffs, N.J.: Prentice-Hall.

Kornguth, M. L. 1981. Nursing management. *Am. J. Nurs.* 81:553.

Langford, R. W. 1981. Teenagers and obesity. *Am. J. Nurs.* 81:556.

Powers, P. S. 1980. *Obesity, the regulation of weight.* Baltimore: Williams & Wilkins.

Rapp, C. E., Jr. 1979. Treating obese adolescents. *Consultant* 19:116.

Rivlin, R. S. 1981. Obesity: dispelling some hormonal and nutritional myths. *Consultant* 21:125.

Schemmel, R., ed. 1980. *Nutrition, physiology and obesity.* Boca Raton, Fla.: CRC Press.

Sebrell, W. H. 1978. *A rational approach to weight control.* New York: Weight Watchers International.

Smith, A. 1980. *Obesity: a bibliography 1974–1979.* New York: IRL Press.

Stern, J. S., and Denenberg, R. V. 1980. *How to stay slim and healthy on the fast food diet.* Englewood Cliffs, N.J.: Prentice-Hall.

Stone, N. J., et al. 1980. *Fat chance: a diet workbook for cholesterol and calorie control.* Chicago: Year Book.

Stunkard, A. J., ed. 1980. *Obesity.* Philadelphia: Saunders.

Thompson, C. I. 1980. *Controls of eating.* Jamaica, N.Y.: Spectrum Publications.

Weintraub, M. 1981. A new look at obesity. *Drug Therapy* 11:141.

White, J. H., and Schroeder, M. A. 1981. Nursing assessment. *Am. J. Nurs.* 81:550.

Behavioral Modification

Ferguson, J. M. 1975. *Learning to eat: behavior modification for weight control.* Palo Alto, Calif.: Bull Publishing.

LeBow, M. D. 1981. *Weight control: the behavioral strategies.* New York: Wiley.

Levitz, L. S. 1973. Behavior therapy in treating obesity. *J. Amer. Dietet. Assoc.* 62:22.

Pomerlau, O., et al. 1975. Role of behavior modification in preventative medicine. *N. Engl. J. Med.* 292:1277.

Exercise

Jones, J., and Kientzler, K. 1980. *Fitness first: a 14-day diet and exercise program.* San Francisco: 101 Productions.

Katch, F. I., and McArdle, W. D. 1977. *Nutrition, weight control and exercise.* Boston: Houghton Mifflin.

Konishi, R., et al. 1979. *Eat anything exercise diet: how to be slim and fit for life.* New York: Morrow.

Pariskova, J., and Rogozkin, V. A. 1978. *Nutrition, physical fitness, and health,* vol. 7. In *International series on sport sciences.* Baltimore: University Park Press.

Vodak, P. 1980. *Exercise: the why and the how.* Palo Alto, Calif.: Bull Publishing.

Fad Diets

Berland, T., et al. 1980. *Rating the diets.* New York: Beekman House.

CHAPTER 13

Pregnancy and Lactation

Aebi, H. and Whitehead, R. 1980. *Maternal nutrition during pregnancy and lactation.* Bern, Switzerland: Hans Huber Publishers.

American Dietetic Association. 1978. *Assessment of maternal nutrition.* Chicago.

Anderson, G. D. 1979. Nutrition in pregnancy—1978. *South. Med. J.* 72:1304.

Aubry, R. H., et al. 1975. The assessment of maternal

nutrition. In *Clinics in perinatology, symposium on nutrition*, eds. L. A. Barnes and R. M. Pitkin. Philadelphia: Saunders.

Burrow, G. N., and Ferris, T. F. 1975. *Medical complications during pregnancy*. Philadelphia: Saunders.

California Department of Health. 1975. *Nutrition during pregnancy and lactation*. Sacramento, Calif.

Cowrie, A. T., et al. 1980. *Hormonal control of lactation*. New York: Springer-Verlag.

Dobbing, J., ed. 1981. *Maternal nutrition in pregnancy*. New York: Academic Press.

Filer, L. J. 1975. Maternal nutrition in lactation. *Clin. Perinatol.* 2:353.

Fuchs, F. 1980. Medicine in the '80s: obstetrics and gynecology. *Drug Therapy* 10:87.

Larson, B. L., ed. 1978. In *Lactation: a comprehensive treatise*, vol. 4. *The mammary gland, human lactation, milk synthesis*. New York: Academic Press.

Luke, B. 1979. *Maternal nutrition*. Boston: Little, Brown.

National Academy of Sciences, National Research Council, Committee on Maternal Nutrition, Food and Nutrition Board. 1970. *Maternal nutrition and the course of pregnancy*. Washington, D.C.

Pitkin, R. M., et al. 1972. Maternal nutrition: a selective review of clinical topics. *Obstet. Gyn.* 40:773.

Roberts, J. M. 1981. Preeclampsia and eclampsia. *West. J. Med.* 135:34.

Rush, D., et al. 1980. *Diet in pregnancy*. New York: Alan R. Liss.

Shanplin, D. R., and Hodin, J. 1979. *Maternal nutrition and child health*. Chicago: Thomas.

Slattery, J. S., et al., eds. 1979. *Maternal and child nutrition: assessment and counseling*. New York: Appleton-Century-Crofts.

Society for Nutrition Education. 1975. *Pregnancy and nutrition*. Nutrition Education Resource Series, no. 2. Berkeley, Calif.

Winick, M., ed. 1979. *Nutrition, pre- and postnatal development: human nutrition, a comprehensive treatise*, vol. 1. New York: Plenum.

Teenage Pregnancy

American Academy of Pediatrics, Committee on Adolescence. 1979. Statement on teenage pregnancy. *Pediatrics* 63:795.

Carruth, B. R. 1980. Adolescent pregnancy and nutrition. *Contemp. Nutr.* 5:1.

Jacobson, H. N. 1981. Nutrition—crucial factor in adolescent pregnancy. *Food Nutri. News* 52:1.

Morse, S. H., et al. 1975. Comparison of the nutritional status of pregnant adolescents with adult pregnant women. I. Biochemical findings. II. Anthropometric and dietary findings. *Amer. J. Clin. Nutr.* 38:1000 and 38:1422.

Zackler, J., and Brandstadt, W., eds. 1975. *The teenage pregnant girl*. Springfield, Ill.: Thomas.

Drugs

Berkowitz, R. L., et al., eds. 1981a. *Drugs in pregnancy*. Boston: Little, Brown.

———. 1981b. *Handbook for prescribing medications during pregnancy*. Boston: Little, Brown.

California Department of Health Services, Maternal and Child Health Branch. 1980. *Dangers of drinking alcohol during pregnancy*. Sacramento, Calif.

Clarren, S. K. 1981. Recognition of fetal alcohol syndrome. *J.A.M.A.* 245:2436.

Enloe, C. F. 1980. How alcohol affects the developing fetus. *Nutr. Today* 15:12.

Goplerud, C. P. 1981. Prescribing practices during pregnancy: some suggestions. *Consultant* 21:29.

Iber, F. L. 1980. Fetal alcohol syndrome. *Nutr. Today* 15:4.

Qazi, Q., et al. 1979. Renal anomalies in fetal alcohol syndrome. *Pediatrics* 63:886.

Rosett, H. L. 1976. Effects of maternal drinking on child development: an introductory review. *Ann. N.Y. Acad. Sci.* 273:115.

Streissguth, A. P., et al. 1980. Teratogenic effects of alcohol in humans and laboratory animals. *Science* 209:353.

Weathersbee, P. A., and Lodge, J. R. 1979. Alcohol, caffeine, and nicotine as factors in pregnancy. *Postgrad. Med.* 66:165.

CHAPTER 14

Pediatric Nutrition

American Academy of Pediatrics. 1976. Commentary on breast feeding and infant formulas, including standards for formulas. *Pediatrics* 57:278.

———. 1979. *Pediatric nutrition handbook*. Evanston, Ill.

Beal, V. A. 1980. *Nutrition in the life span*. New York: Wiley.

Endres, J. B., and Rockwell, R. E. 1980. *Food, nutrition, and the young child*. St. Louis: Mosby.

Foman, S. 1974. *Infant nutrition*. Philadelphia: Saunders.

Gifft, H. H., et al. 1972. *Nutrition, behavior, and change.* Englewood Cliffs, N.J.: Prentice-Hall.

McWilliams, M. 1980. *Nutrition for the growing years.* 3rd ed. New York: Wiley.

Nutrition Foundation. 1979. *Iron deficiency in infancy and childhood.* Washington, D.C.

Oliver, K., et al., eds. 1979. *Development nutrition.* Columbus, Ohio: Ross Laboratories.

Pipes, P. L., ed. 1981. *Nutrition in infancy and childhood.* 2nd ed. St. Louis: Mosby.

Roberts, F. B. 1977. *Prenatal nursing: the care of newborns and their families.* New York: McGraw-Hill.

Vaden, A. G., ed. 1979. *Nutrition and the school age child.* Denver: American School Food Service Association.

Wharton, B. 1980. *Topics in paediatrics 2, nutrition in childhood.* Tunbridge Wells, Kent, England: Pitman Medical Ltd.

Wilkinson, J. F. 1980. *Don't raise your child to be a fat adult.* Indianapolis: Bobbs-Merrill.

Wood, C. B. S., and Walker-Smith, J. A. 1981. *MacKeith's infant feeding and feeding difficulties.* New York: Churchill Livingstone.

World Health Organization. 1979a. *Joint WHO/UNICEF meeting on infant and young child feeding.* Geneva, Switzerland.

———. 1979b. *Meeting on infant and young child feeding: background paper prepared by WHO and UNICEF.* Parts I and II. Geneva, Switzerland.

Human Milk and Breast Feeding

American Academy of Pediatrics, Committee on Drugs. 1981. Breast-feeding and contraception. *Pediatrics* 68:138.

Gibson, R. A., and Kneebone, G. M. 1981. Fatty acid composition of human colostrum and mature breast milk. *Amer. J. Clin. Nutr.* 34:252.

Goldfarb, J., and Tibbetts, E. 1980. *Breastfeeding handbook: a practical reference for physicians, nurses, and other health professionals.* Hillside, N.J.: Enslow Publishers.

Jansson, L., et al. 1981. Vitamin E and fatty acid composition of human milk. *Amer. J. Clin. Nutr.* 34:8.

Jelliffe, D. B., and Jelliffe, E. F. P., eds. 1971. Symposium: the uniqueness of human milk. *Amer. J. Clin. Nutr.* 24:968.

J. Human Nutr. 1976. Symposium on breast feeding. 30:223.

Kitzinger, S. 1980. *Experience of breastfeeding.* New York: Penguin Books.

Lawrence, R. A. 1980. *Breast-feeding: a guide for the medical profession.* St. Louis: Mosby.

McDonald, L. 1979. *The joy of breastfeeding.* Pasadena, Calif.: Oaklawn Press.

Palma, P. A., and Adcock, E. W. III. 1981. Human milk and breastfeeding. *Am. Family Physician* 24:173.

Psiaki, D., et al. 1980. *Current knowledge on breastfeeding: a review for medical practitioners.* Ithaca, N.Y.: Division of Nutritional Sciences, Cornell University.

Rogan, W. J., et al. 1980. Pollutants in breast milk. *N. Engl. J. Med.* 302:1450.

Salmon, M. B. 1979. *The joy of breastfeeding.* 2nd ed. Demarest, N.J.: Techkits.

U.S. Department of Health, Education and Welfare. 1979. *Trends in breast feeding among American mothers.* Vital and Health Statistics: Series 23. Data from National Survey of Family Growth, no. 3. USDHEW pub. no. (PHS) 79-1979. Hyattsville, Md.: National Center for Health Statistics.

World Health Organization. 1979. *WHO collaborative study on breastfeeding.* Geneva, Switzerland.

Composition of Formulas and Baby Foods

Deeming, S. B., and Weber, C. W. 1979. Trace minerals in commercially prepared baby foods. *J. Amer. Dietet. Assoc.* 75:149.

Hanson, J. M., and Kinsella, J. E. 1981. Fatty acid content and composition of infant formulas and cereals. *J. Amer. Dietet. Assoc.* 78:250.

Hawley, L. E. 1978. Fatty acid composition of prepared infant formulas. *J. Amer. Dietet. Assoc.* 72:170.

Korsrud, G. O., and Truk, K. D. 1979. Sucrose, fructose, and glucose contents of infant cereals. *J. Can. Diet. Assoc.* 40:56.

Matthews, R. H., and Workman, M. Y. 1978. Nutrient content of selected baby foods. *J. Amer. Dietet. Assoc.* 72:27.

Dental Problems

American Dental Association Health Foundation. 1977. Symposium: cariostatic mechanism of fluorides. *Caries Res.* 11(5):1.

Dent. Clin. N.A. 1976. Symposium on nutrition. 20:441.

Dunning, J. M. 1970. *Principles of dental public health.* Cambridge, Mass.: Harvard University Press.

———. 1976. *Dental care for everyone: problems and pro-*

posals. Cambridge, Mass.: Harvard University Press.

Gibbons, R. J., and Van Houte, J. 1975. Dental caries. *Ann. Rev. Med.* 26:7136.

Hartles, R. L., and Leach, S. A. 1975. Effect of diet on dental caries. *Brit. Med. Bull.* 31:137.

Morrey, L. W., and Nelson, R. J., eds. 1970. *Dental science handbook*. Washington, D.C.: Superintendent of Documents.

Newburn, E. 1974. Diet and dental caries relationships. *Adv. Caries Res.* 2:xv.

————. 1975. Water fluoridation and dietary fluoride. In *Fluorides and dental caries*. 2nd ed. Springfield, Ill.: Thomas.

Nizel, A. E. 1973. Nutrition and oral problems. *World Rev. Nutr. Dietet.* 16:226.

Adolescence

Dairy Council Digest. 1981. Nutritional concerns during adolescence. 52:7.

Huenemann, R. L. 1973. A review of teenage nutrition in the United States. In *Proceedings of the national nutrition education conference*. U.S. Department of Agriculture, misc. pub. no. 1254. Washington, D.C.

Huenemann, R. L., et al. 1968. Food and eating practices of teenagers. *J. Amer. Dietet. Assoc.* 53:17.

————. 1974. *Teenage nutrition and physique*. Springfield, Ill.: Thomas.

Kaufmann, N., et al. 1975. Eating habits and opinions of teenagers on nutrition and obesity. *J. Amer. Dietet. Assoc.* 66:264.

Kolasa, K. 1974. Foodways of selected mothers and their adult daughters in upper east Tennessee. Ph.D. dissertation, University of Tennessee (Knoxville).

McKigney, J. I., and Munro, H. N., eds. 1975. *Nutrient requirements in adolescence*. Cambridge, Mass.: MIT Press.

Mellin, L. 1980. *Shapedown: weight management program for adolescents*. San Francisco: Balboa Publishing.

Nutr. Rev. 1973. Growth after adolescence. 31:314.

Schoor, B. C., et al. 1972. Teen-age food habits. *J. Amer. Dietet. Assoc.* 61:415.

Schwartz, N. E. 1975. Nutritional knowledge, attitudes and practices of high school graduates. *J. Amer. Dietet. Assoc.* 66:28.

Thomas, J. A., and Call, D. L. 1973. Eating between meals: a nutrition problem among teenagers? *Nutr. Rev.* 31:137.

Wyman, J. R. 1972. Teenagers and food: their eating habits. *Food Nutr.* 2(1):3.

CHAPTER 15

Gerontology and Geriatrics

Brickner, P. W. 1978. *Home health care for the aged: how to help older people stay in their own homes and out of institutions*. New York: Appleton-Century-Crofts.

Eisdorfer, C., ed. 1980. *Annual review of gerontology and geriatrics*. New York: Springer.

George, L. K., and Bearon, L. B. 1980. *Quality of life in older persons: meaning and measurement*. New York: Human Sciences Press.

Holmes, M. B., and Holmes, D. 1979. *Handbook of human services for older persons*. New York: Human Sciences Press.

Lesnoff-Caravaglia, G., ed. 1980. *Health care of the elderly: strategies for prevention and intervention. Frontiers in aging*, vol. 1. New York: Human Sciences Press.

Pieroni, R. E. 1981. *Geriatrics review*. Lexington, Mass.: D. C. Heath.

Somers, A. R., and Fabian, D. R., eds. 1981. *The geriatric imperative: an introduction to gerontology and clinical geriatrics*. New York: Appleton-Century-Crofts.

Nutrition

Gupta, C. P. 1980. Nutrition in geriatrics. *J. Indian Med. Assoc.* 74:91.

Masoro, E. J., et al. 1980. Nutritional probe of the aging process. *Fed. Proc.* 39:3178.

Mayer, J., ed. 1974. Symposium: aging and nutrition. *Geriatrics* 29:57.

Metress, S. P., and Kart, C. S. 1979. *Nutrition and aging: a bibliographic survey*. Monticello, Ill.: Vance Bibliographies.

Natow, A. B., and Heslin, J. 1980. *Geriatric nutrition*. Boston: CBI Publishing.

Posner, B. M. 1979. *Nutrition and the elderly*. Lexington, Mass.: Lexington Books.

Rockstein, M., and Sussman, M. L., eds. 1976. *Nutrition, longevity and aging*. New York: Academic Press.

Winick, M., ed. 1976. *Nutrition and aging*. New York: Wiley.

Food Preparation

Harlow, J., et al. 1979. *Good age cookbook: recipes from the institute for creative aging.* Boston: Houghton Mifflin.

Ryder, V. P. 1980. *Easy meals for senior citizens, weary workers, single sophisticates.* Laguna Beach, Calif.: Amigo Books.

Drugs

Lamy, P. P. 1980. *Prescribing for the elderly.* Littleton, Mass.: PSG Publishing.

Petersen, D. M., et al., eds. 1979. *Drugs and the elderly: social and pharmacological issues.* Springfield, Ill.: Thomas.

Programs

Buchholtz, F. 1971. *A Home-delivered meals program for the elderly.* U.S. Department of Health, Education, and Welfare, Administration on Aging. Washington, D.C.: Government Printing Office.

Committee on Guidelines for Home Delivered Meals, National Council on the Aging, Inc. 1965. Report. *Amer. J. Public Health* (Suppl.)

Greene, J. M. 1981. Coordination of older Americans act programs. *J. Amer. Dietet. Assoc.* 78:617.

Hudson, G. 1971. *A co-op approach to food for the elderly.* U.S. Department of Health, Education, and Welfare, Social Rehab. Service, Administration on Aging. Washington, D.C.: Government Printing Office.

Kohrs, M. B. 1976. *Influence of the congregate meal program in central Missouri on dietary practices on nutritional status of participants.* Jefferson City, Mo.: Lincoln University, Human Nutrition Research Program.

———. 1979. The nutrition program for older Americans. Evaluation and recommendations. *J. Amer. Dietet. Assoc.* 75:543.

Kohrs, M. B., et al. 1979. Title VII—nutrition program for the elderly. II. Relationship of socioeconomic factors to one day's nutrient intake. *J. Amer. Dietet. Assoc.* 75:537.

———. 1980. Association of participation in a nutritional program for the elderly with nutritional status. *Amer. J. Clin. Nutr.* 33:2643.

Schecter, I. 1980. *1980 chartbook of federal programs in aging.* Washington, D.C.: Care Reports, Inc.

Wells, C. 1973. Nutrition programs under the Older American Act. *Amer. J. Clin. Nutr.* 26(10):1127.

CHAPTER 16

Faloon, W. W., ed. 1973. Symposium: drug-nutrient relationships. *Amer. J. Clin. Nutr.* 26:103.

Gilman, A., et al., eds. 1980. *Goodman and Gilman's the pharmacological basis of therapeutics.* New York: Macmillan.

Hartshorn, E. A. 1977. Food and drug interactions. *J. Amer. Dietet. Assoc.* 70:15.

Hathcock, J. N., and Coon, J., eds. 1978. *Nutrition and drug interactions.* New York: Academic Press.

Hethcox, J. M., and Stanaszek, W. K. 1974. Interactions of drugs and diet. *Hosp. Pharmacy* 9:373.

Ioannides, C., and Parke, D. V. 1979. Effect of diet on the metabolism and toxicity of drugs. *J. Human Nutr.* 33:357.

Lamy, P. P. 1980. How your patient's diet can affect drug response. *Drug Therapy* 10:82.

March, D. C. 1976. *Handbook: Interactions of selected drugs with nutritional status in man.* Chicago: American Dietetic Association.

Physicians' desk reference. 1983, 37th ed. Oradell, N.J.: Medical Economics.

Pierpaoli, P. G. 1972. Drug therapy and diet. *Drug Intel. Clin. Pharm.* 6:89.

Roe, D. A. 1976. *Drug-induced nutritional deficiencies.* Westport, Conn.: AVI Publishing.

———. 1979. Interactions between drugs and nutrients. *Med. Clin. N.A.* 53:985.

Seixas, F. A. 1975. Alcohol and its drug interactions. *Ann. Intern. Med.* 83:86.

Spiller, G. A., ed. 1981. Nutritional pharmacology. In *Current Topics in Nutrition and Disease,* vol. 4. New York: Alan R. Liss.

Visconti, J. A. 1977. *Drug-food interaction.* Columbus, Ohio: Ross Laboratories.

CHAPTER 17

Children

Adler, R. P., et al. 1980. *Effects of television advertising on children: review and recommendations.* Lexington, Mass.: D. C. Heath.

Barcus, F. E. 1975. *Weekend commercial children's television—1975.* Newtonville, Mass.: Action for Children's Television.

Birch, L. L. 1979. Dimensions of preschool children's food preferences. *J. Nutr. Edu.* 11:77.

Burt, J. V., and Hertzler, A. A. 1978. Parental influence on the child's food preference. *J. Nutr. Edu.* 10:127.

Cook, C. B., et al. 1977. How much nutrition education in grades K−6? *J. Nutr. Edu.* 9:131.

Feshbach, N. D., et al. 1978. A demonstration of the use of graphics in teaching children nutrition. *J. Nutr. Edu.* 10:124.

Juhas, L. 1973. Nutrition education in day care programs. *J. Amer. Dietet. Assoc.* 63:134.

Kershner, M. H., and Storz, N. S. 1976. Nutrition education for preschoolers at the shopping mall. *J. Nutr. Edu.* 8:168.

Lowenberg, R. 1978. Nutrition education in a reading enrichment program. *J. Nutr. Edu.* 10(1):22.

Phillips, D. E., et al. 1978. Use of food and nutrition knowledge by mothers of preschool children. *J. Nutr. Edu.* 10:73.

Robinson, L. G., et al. 1976. Nutrition counseling and children's dental health. *J. Nutr. Edu.* 8(1):33.

Schwartzberg, L., et al. 1977. Issues in food advertising—the nutrition educator's viewpoint. *J. Nutr. Edu.* 9:60.

Shannon, B., et al. 1979. Foodsense: a pilot T.V. show on nutrition issues. *J. Nutr. Edu.* 11:15.

Smith, H. M., and Justice, C. L. 1979. Effects of nutrition programs on third grade students. *J. Nutr. Edu.* 11:92.

Yperman, A. M., and Vermeersch, J. A. 1979. Factors associated with children's food habits. *J. Nutr. Edu.* 11:72.

Adolescence

Axelson, J. M., and Del Campo, D. S. 1978. Improving teenagers' nutrition knowledge through the mass media. *J. Nutr. Edu.* 10:30.

Dwyer, J. T., Feldman, J. J., and Mayer, J. 1970. Nutritional literacy of high school students. *J. Nutr. Edu.* 2:59.

Frankle, R. T., and Huessenstamm, F. K. 1974. Food zealotry and youth. *Am. J. Public Health* 64:11.

Heald, F. 1973. Health status of youth. In *Proceedings of the national nutrition education conference.* U.S. Department of Agriculture, misc. publ. no. 1254. Washington, D.C.

Mapes, M. C. 1977. Gulp—an alternate method for reaching teens. *J. Nutr. Edu.* 9:12−16.

McCarthy, M. E., and Sabry, J. H. 1973. Canadian university students' nutrition misconceptions. *J. Nutr. Edu.* 5:193.

Reeder, W. W. 1973. The attitudes, values and lifestyles of youth. In *Proceedings of the national nutrition education conference.* U.S. Department of Agriculture, misc. pub. no. 1254. Washington, D.C.

Schwartz, N. E. 1975. Nutritional knowledge, attitudes, and practices of high school graduates. *J. Amer. Dietet. Assoc.* 66:28.

Singleton, N. C. 1974. Adequacy of the diets of pregnant teenagers: educational, nutritional, and socionomic factors. Ph.D. dissertation, Louisiana State University (Baton Rouge).

Society for Nutrition Education. 1976. *Nutrition education, K−12 teacher references: concepts, theories, and guides.* Berkeley, Calif.

Spitze, H. T. 1976. Curriculum materials and nutrition learning at the high school level. *J. Nutr. Edu.* 8:59.

Professionals

Barnum, H. J. 1975. Mass media and health communications. *J. Med. Educ.* 50:24.

Cyborski, C. K. 1977. Nutrition content in medical curricula. *J. Nutr. Edu.* 9:17.

DePaola, D. P., et al. 1978. An integrated nutrition program for dental students. *J. Nutr. Edu.* 10:160.

Dunphy, M. K. 1980. Effective nutrition education program for medical students. *J. Amer. Dietet. Assoc.* 76:372.

Garverick, C. M., et al. 1978. Nutrition interests of dental students. *J. Nutr. Edu.* 10:167.

Henneman, A., et al. 1976. A nutrition workshop for home economics teachers. *J. Nutr. Edu.* 8:25.

Holme, D. S., and Kim, S. 1981. Nutrition education program for nursing home staff. *J. Amer. Dietet. Assoc.* 78:366.

Kolasa, K., et al. 1979. Home-based learning—implications for nutrition educators. *J. Nutr. Edu.* 11:19.

Olson, R. E. 1980. Integrating nutrition into medical and public health programs. *Food Tech.* 34:58.

Wardlaw, J. M. 1981. Preparing the nutrition education professional for the 1980s. *J. Nutr. Edu.* 13:6.

Witteman, J. K., et al. 1978. A strategy for evaluating nutrition counseling skills of dental students. *J. Nutr. Edu.* 10:164.

Misinformation

Bruch, H. 1970. The allure of food cults and nutritional quackery. *J. Amer. Dietet. Assoc.* 57:316.

Council on Foods and Nutrition. 1971. Zen macrobiotic diets. *J.A.M.A.* 218:397.

Henderson, L. M. 1974. Programs to combat nutritional quackery. *Nutr. Rev.* 32:67 (Suppl.).

Herbert, V. 1980. *Nutrition cultism: facts and fictions.* Philadelphia: George F. Stickly.

Rynearson, E. B. 1974. Americans love hogwash. *Nutr. Rev.* 32:1 (Suppl. 1).

Swedish Nutrition Foundation. 1969. Food cultism and quackery. 8th Symposium. Uppsala, Sweden.

CHAPTER 18

Food and Culture

American Academy of Pediatrics. 1977. Nutritional aspects of vegetarianism, health foods and fad diets. *Pediatrics* 59:460.

Farb, P., and Armelagos, G. 1980. *Consuming passions: the anthropology of eating.* Boston: Houghton Mifflin.

Fitzgerald, T. K. 1977. *Nutrition and anthropology in action.* Assen, Amsterdam: Van Gorcum.

Jerome, N., et al., eds. 1980. *Nutritional anthropology.* Pleasantville, N.Y.: Redgrave Publishing.

Larsen, E. 1978. *Food: past, present and future.* New York: Crane, Russack.

Lowenberg, M. E., et al. 1979. *Food and people.* 3rd ed. New York: Wiley.

Mead, M. 1964. Food habits research: problems of the '60s. National Academy of Sciences, National Research Council, pub. no. 1225. WAS-NRC. Washington, D.C.

National Academy of Sciences, National Research Council. 1981. *Assessing changing food consumption patterns.* Washington, D.C.

Robson, J. K. R. 1980. *Food, ecology and culture: readings in the anthropology of dietary practices.* New York: Gordon and Breach.

Root, W. 1980. *Food: an authoritative and visual history and directory of the foods of the world.* New York: Simon & Schuster.

Sanjier, D. 1982. *Social and cultural perspectives in nutrition.* Englewood Cliffs, N.J.: Prentice-Hall.

Turner, M., ed. 1980. *Nutrition and lifestyles.* Essex, England: Applied Science.

U.S. Department of Agriculture, Food and Nutrition Service. 1980. *Southeast Asian American education materials.*

U.S. Department of Health, Education, and Welfare. 1972. *Nutrition, growth and development of North American Indian children.* USDHEW pub. no. (NIH) 72–26. Washington, D.C.

Walcher, D. N., et al., eds. 1976. *Food, man and society.* New York: Plenum.

Wilson, C. 1979. *Food—custom and nurture: an annotated bibliography on sociocultural and biocultural aspects of nutrition.* Berkeley, Calif.: Society of Nutrition Education.

Vegetarians

Anderson, J. J. B., ed. 1981. *Nutrition and vegetarianism.* Chapel Hill: University of North Carolina Press.

Armstrong, B., et al. 1979. Urinary sodium and blood pressure in vegetarians. *Amer. J. Clin. Nutr.* 32:2472.

Brown, P. T., and Bergan, J. G. 1975. The dietary status of "new" vegetarians. *J. Amer. Dietet. Assoc.* 67:455.

Dwyer, J. T., et al. 1974. The new vegetarians: group affiliation and dietary strictures related to attitudes and life style. *J. Amer. Dietet. Assoc.* 64:376.

Freeland-Graves, J. H., et al. 1980. Zinc and copper content of foods used in vegetarian diets. *J. Amer. Dietet. Assoc.* 77:648.

Lappe, F. M. 1971. *Diet for a small planet.* New York: Ballantine.

Moore, S. T., and Byers, M. P. 1978. *A vegetarian diet.* Santa Rosa, Calif.: Woodbridge Press.

Register, U. D., and Sonnenberg, L. M. 1973. The vegetarian diet. *J. Amer. Dietet. Assoc.* 62:253.

Sacks, F. M., et al. 1975. Plasma lipids and lipoproteins in vegetarians and controls. *N. Engl. J. Med.* 292:1148.

Schwartz, D. 1978. *Vegetable cookery: a selected annotated bibliography.* New York: Council on Botanical and Horticultural Libraries, New York Botanical Garden.

Shulman, M. R. 1979. *The vegetarian feast.* New York: Harper & Row.

Worstman, G. 1980. *The whole grain bake book.* Seattle: Pacific Search Press.

CHAPTER 19

Community Nutrition and Health

Christakis, G. 1973. Nutritional assessment in health programs. *Am. J. Public Health* 63:80.

Falkner, F., ed. 1980. *Prevention in childhood of health problems in adult life.* Geneva, Switzerland: World Health Organization.

Frankle, R. T., and Owen, A. Y. 1978. *Nutrition in the community, the art of delivering services.* St. Louis: Mosby.

Greene, L. S., and Johnston, F. E., eds. 1980. *Social and biological predictors of nutritional status, physical growth, and neurological development.* New York: Academic Press.

U.S. Department of Health, Education, and Welfare. 1979*a*. *Federal and Non-Federal Resources for Nutritional Information and Services—A Selected List.* Bureau of Community Health Services. USDHEW pub. no. (HSA) 78-5103. Supplement. Rockville, Md.

———. 1979*b*. *Healthy people: the surgeon general's report on health promotion and disease prevention.* Public Health Service, Office of the Assistant Secretary for Health and Surgeon General. USDHEW pub. no. 79-55071. Washington, D.C.

Wrights, H. S., and Sims, L. S. 1981. *Community nutrition: people, policies and programs.* Monterey, Calif.: Wadsworth Health Sciences.

Nutritional Assessment Techniques

Burk, M. C., and Pao, E. M. 1976. *Methodology for large-scale surveys of household and individual diets.* U.S. Department of Agriculture, Home Economics Resources Report no. 40. Washington, D.C.

Gray, G. E., and Gray, L. K. 1980. Anthropometric measurements and their interpretation: principles, practices and problems. *J. Amer. Dietet. Assoc.* 77:534.

Madden, J. P., et al. 1976. Validity of the 24-hour recall. *J. Amer. Dietet. Assoc.* 68:143.

Nichaman, M. Z. 1974. Developing a nutritional surveillance system. *J. Amer. Dietet. Assoc.* 65:15.

Surveys

American Academy of Pediatrics, Committee to Review the Ten-State Nutrition Survey. 1975. Nutrition, growth, development and maturation: findings from the ten-state nutrition survey from 1968–1970. *Pediatrics* 56:306.

Lopez, R., et al. 1975. Riboflavin deficiency in pediatric population of low socioeconomic status in New York City. *J. Pediatr.* 87:420.

Owen, G. M., et al. 1974. A study of nutritional status of preschool children in the United States, 1968–1970. *Pediatrics* 53:597.

Pao, E. M., and Cronin, F. J. 1980. USDA's food consumption survey: nutritional implications. *Nutr. News.* 43:5.

Sabry, Z. I. 1973. *Nutrition Canada: national survey.* Information Canada, Cat. no. H58-36.

Sabry, Z. I., et al. 1974. Nutrition Canada. *Nutr. Today* 9:5.

Trowbridge, F. L., et al. 1975. Findings relating to goiter and iodine in the ten-state nutrition survey. *Amer. J. Clin. Nutr.* 28:712.

U.S. Department of Agriculture, Agricultural Research Service. 1969. *Dietary levels of households in the United States, Spring, 1965.* Household Food Consumption Survey 1965–66. ARS Report no. 6. Washington, D.C.: Government Printing Office.

———. 1975. *Food intake and nutritive value of diets of men, women, and children in the U.S., Spring, 1975: a preliminary report.* ARS 62–18. Washington, D.C.: Government Printing Office.

U.S. Department of Health, Education, and Welfare. 1972. *Highlights, ten-state nutrition survey, 1968–1970.* USDHEW pub. no. (HSM) 72-8134. Washington, D.C.

———. 1971. *Screening children for nutritional status: suggestions for child health programs.* USDHEW pub. no. (PHS) 2158. Washington, D.C.

———. 1972*a*. *Ten-state nutrition survey: 1968–1970.* USHEW pub. no. 72-8131. Washington, D.C.

———. 1972*b*. *Ten-state nutrition survey, 1968–1970, vol. V.* Dietary Department of Health, Education, and Welfare pub. no. (HSM) 72-8133.

———. 1974*a*. *Preliminary findings of the first health and nutrition examination survey, United States, 1971–72.* I. *Anthropometric and clinical findings.* USDHEW pub. no. (HRA) 75-1229. II. *Dietary intake and biochemical findings.* USDHEW pub. no. (HRA) 76-1219-1.

———. 1974*b*. *Preliminary findings of the first health and nutrition examination survey, United States, 1971–72: dietary intake and biochemical findings.* USDHEW pub. no. (HRA)74-1219-1.

Dietary Goals

American Heart Association. 1980. *Heartbook: a guide to prevention and treatment of cardiovascular diseases.* New York: Dutton.

Connor, W. E. 1979. Too little or too much: the case for preventive nutrition. *Amer. J. Clin. Nutr.* 32:1975.

Cullen, R. W., et al. 1978. Sodium, hypertension, and the U.S. dietary goals. *J. Nutr. Edu.* 10:59–60.

Editors of Time-Life Books. 1981. *Wholesome Diet.* Chicago: Time-Life Books.

Food Tech. 1978. Symposium. Nutrition, diet, and disease. I. The case for dietary change. 32:38. II. Implementation of dietary improvements. 32:74.

Freeman, T. M., and Gregg, V. W. 1982. *Sodium intake—dietary concerns*. St. Paul, Minn.: American Association of Cereal Chemists.

Gresham, G. A. 1980. *Reversing atherosclerosis*. Springfield, Ill.: Thomas.

Jencks, T. 1980. *In good taste*. Berkeley, Calif.: Lancaster-Miller.

Livingston, G. E., et al, eds. 1982. *The role of food product development in implementing dietary guidelines*. Westport, Conn.: Food & Nutrition Press.

McNutt, K. 1978. An analysis of dietary goals for the United States, 2nd ed. *J. Nutr. Edu.* 10(2):61.

Peterkin, B. B., et al. 1978. Diets that meet the dietary goals. *J. Nutr. Edu.* 10(1):15.

———. 1981. Changes in dietary patterns: one approach to meeting standards. *J. Amer. Dietet. Assoc.* 78:453.

Shaw, S. H., and Miller, D. 1979. Preventive medicine through nutrition. *J. Amer. Dietet. Assoc.* 75:49.

CHAPTER 20

Bernarde, M. A. 1971. *The chemicals we eat*. New York: American Heritage.

Fondu, M. N.d. *Food additives tables, classes I–IV (updated ed.)*. New York: Elsevier Scientific Publishing.

Food Tech. 1978a. Symposium. Benefit/risk: consideration of direct food additives. 32:54.

———. 1978b. Symposium. Food science and public policy. 32:74.

———. 1979a. Symposium. Developing public policy for food safety. 33:42.

———. 1979b. Symposium. Migration of indirect additives to food—scientific and regulatory aspects. 33:54.

———. 1980a. Principles and processes for making food safety decisions. 34:81.

———. 1980b. Sweeteners—a scientific and regulatory update. 34:64.

———. 1981. Food ingredient safety review programs. 35:68.

Graham, H. D. 1980. *The safety of foods*. 2nd ed. Westport, Conn.: AVI Publishing.

Hui, Y. H. 1979. *United States food laws, regulations and standards*. New York: Wiley-Interscience.

Johnson, P. E. 1977. Misuse in foods of useful chemicals. *Nutr. Rev.* 35:225.

Nutr. Rev. 1973. Special report: the use of chemicals in food production, processing, storage, and distribution. 31:191.

———. 1979. Special report: perspectives in food safety. 37:29.

———. 1980. Symposium: risk versus benefits: the future of food safety. 38:35.

Taylor, R. J. 1980. *Food additives*. New York: Wiley-Interscience.

U.S. Congress, Senate, Committee on Agriculture, Nutrition, and Forestry. 1979. *Food safety: where are we?* Washington, D.C.: Government Printing Office.

CHAPTER 21

Food Safety

Ballentine, C. L., and Herndon, M. L. 1982. Who, why, when and where of food poisons (and what to do about them). *FDA Consumer* 16:25.

Betz, N. L. 1974. Prevention of food poisoning. *Cereal Science Today* 19:531.

Bryan, F. L. 1980. Epidemiology of foodborne diseases transmitted by fish, shellfish, and marine crustaceans in the United States. *J. Food Protect.* 43:859.

Economic Research Service. 1974. *Consumers' knowledge, opinions, and attitudes toward safety in selected food items*. U.S. Department of Agriculture pub. no. 582. Washington, D.C.

Gilchrist, A. 1981. *Foodborne disease and food safety*. Chicago: American Medical Association.

Guthrie, R. K. 1980. *Food sanitation*. 2nd ed. Westport, Conn.: AVI Publishing.

Riemann, H., and Bryan, F. L., eds. 1979. *Food-borne infections and intoxications*. 2nd ed. New York: Academic Press.

Tartakow, I., and Vorperian, J. H. 1980. *Food borne and waterborne diseases: their epidemiologic characteristics*. Westport, Conn.: AVI Publishing.

Woodburn, M. J. 1978. Education to prevent foodborne illness. *Food Tech.* 32:56.

Natural Toxicants

National Academy of Sciences, National Research Council. 1973. *Toxicants occurring naturally in foods*. 2nd ed. Washington, D.C.

Rodricks, J. V. 1978. Food hazards of natural origin. *Fed. Proc.* 37:2587.

Wilson, B. J. 1979. Naturally occurring toxicants in foods. *Nutr. Rev.* 37:305.

CHAPTER 22

The Team

American Hospital Association. 1976. *Recording nutritional information in medical records*. Chicago.

Ducanis, A. J., and Golin, A. K. 1979. *The interdisciplinary health care team: a handbook*. Rockville, Md.: Aspen Systems Corporation.

Hardy, M. E., and Conway, M. E. 1978. *Role theory: perspectives for health professionals*. New York: Appleton-Century-Crofts.

Modrow, C. L., et al. 1980. Survey of physician and patient nutrition education needs. *J. Amer. Dietet. Assoc.* 77:686.

Newton, M. E., et al. 1967. Nutritional aspects of nursing care. *Nurs. Res.* 16:46.

Reed, M. L., et al. 1978. Height and weight data in the patient's medical record. *J. Amer. Dietet. Assoc.* 72:409.

Roberts, R. D. 1980. An educational experience in team leadership. *J. Amer. Dietet. Assoc.* 76:487.

Rodgers, T. V., and Clark, M. E. 1973. Sharing information by means of the patient's medical record. *J. Amer. Dietet. Assoc.* 63:42.

Voytovich, A. E., et al. 1973. The dietitian/nutritionist and the problem-oriented medical record. *J. Amer. Dietet. Assoc.* 63:639.

Interview

Aronson, V., and Fitzgerald, B. D. 1980. *Guidebook for nutrition counselors*. North Quincy, Mass.: Christopher Publishing House.

Bernstein, L., and Bernstein, R. S. 1980. *Interviewing: a guide for health professionals*. New York: Appleton-Century-Crofts.

Reiser, D. E., and Schroder, A. K. 1980. *Patient interviewing: the human dimension*. Baltimore: Williams and Wilkins.

The Patient

Chewning, B., and Betz, E. 1980. Staff manuals for teaching patients. *J. Amer. Dietet. Assoc.* 77:460.

Cousins, N. 1976. Anatomy of an illness (as perceived by the patient). *N. Engl. J. Med.* 295:1458.

Fleming, F. 1980. Feeding the terminally ill patient. *J. N. Z. Diet. Assoc.* 34:22.

Hashim, A. 1962. The difficult patient: how do you feed him? *Nutr. Rev.* 20:1.

Huttman, B. 1981. *The patient's advocate: the complete handbook of patient's rights*. New York: Viking Press.

Narrow, B. W. 1979. *Patient teaching in nursing practice: a patient and family-centered approach*. New York: Wiley.

Selye, H. 1970. On just being sick. *Nutr. Today* 5:2.

Tarnower, W. 1965. Psychological needs of the hospitalized patient. *Nurs. Outlook* 13:28.

Hospital Malnutrition

Blackburn, G. L., and Thornton, P. A. 1979. Nutritional assessment of the hospitalized patient. *Med. Clin. N.A.* 63:1103.

Bushman, L., et al. 1980. Malnutrition among patients in an acute-care veterans facility. *J. Amer. Dietet. Assoc.* 77:462.

Butterworth, C. E., and Blackburn, G. L. 1975. Hospital malnutrition. *Nutr. Today* 10(2):8.

Driver, A. G., and LeBrun, M. 1980. Iatrogenic malnutrition in patients receiving ventilatory support. *J.A.M.A.* 244:2195.

Long, C. L., and Blakemore, W. S. 1979. Energy and protein requirements in the hospitalized patient. *J. Parent. Ent. Nutr.* 3:69.

Steffee, W. P. 1980. Malnutrition in hospitalized patients. *J.A.M.A.* 244:2630.

Tobias, A. L., and Van Itallie, T. B. 1977. Nutritional problems of hospitalized patients. *J. Amer. Dietet. Assoc.* 71:253.

Nutrition Support

Abbott Laboratories. 1980. *Establishing a nutritional support service*. North Chicago.

American Dietetic Association. 1979. *Costs and benefits of nutritional care: phase I*. Chicago.

Amer. J. Clin. Nutr. 1981. Workshop. Nutritional support of the patient: research directions for the 1980s. 34(S):1.

Drexler, L., and Caliendo, M. A. 1980. Developing and implementing a nutritional care audit. *J. Amer. Dietet. Assoc.* 76:374.

Goodhue, P. J., et al. 1976. Continuing nutritional care for the discharged patient. *Diet. Currents* 3(1):1.

Hooley, R. A. 1980. Clinical nutritional assessment: a perspective. *J. Amer. Dietet. Assoc.* 77:682.

Salmond, S. W. 1980. How to assess the nutritional status of acutely ill patients. *Am. J. Nurs.* 80:922.

Shapiro, L. R. 1979. Streamlining and implementing

nutritional assessment: the dietary approach. *J. Amer. Dietet. Assoc.* 75:230.

Sneider, H., ed. 1980. *Nutritional support in medical practice.* New York: Harper & Row.

Vickery, C. E., and Boylan, L. M. 1981. Development and evaluation of a new nutritional care plan model. *J. Amer. Dietet. Assoc.* 78:356.

Wade, J. E. 1977. Role of a clinical dietitian specialist on a nutrition support service. *J. Amer. Dietet. Assoc.* 70:185.

Walters, F. M., Crumley, S. J., eds. 1978. *Patient care audit: a quality assurance procedure manual for dietitians.* Chicago: American Dietetic Association.

Winborn, A. L., et al. 1981. A protocol for nutritional assessment in a community hospital. *J. Amer. Dietet. Assoc.* 78:129.

CHAPTER 23

Food Service & Meal Planning

Abiaka, M. H. 1973. Japanese-American food equivalents for calculating exchange diets. *J. Amer. Dietet. Assoc.* 62:173.

Arbogast, K. K. 1980. *Exchange lists and diet patterns.* New York: Van Nostrand Reinhold.

Cichy, R. E. 1980. Nutrition—an emerging trend in foodservice operations. *The Consultant* 13:21.

Cummings, G. W. 1979. *Quantity vegetarian recipes: entrees, gravies, accompaniments.* Vol. 1. Berrien Spring, Mich.: Andrews University Foodservice.

Illinois Nutrition Educators. 1979. *Diet counselor's supplement for expanded guide to meal planning.* Evanston, Ill.

James, S. M. 1978. When your patient is black West Indian. *Am. J. Nurs.* 78:1908.

Lutheran General Hospital. 1980. *Convenience foods update for calculated diets.* Park Ridge, Ill.

Enteral Feedings

Bayless, E. 1978. Taste tray increases acceptance of nutritional supplements. *J. Amer. Dietet. Assoc.* 73:543.

Blackburn, G. L., et al. 1975. Restoration of the visceral component of protein malnutrition during hypocaloric feedings. *Clin. Res.* 23:315A.

Bondy, R. A., et al. 1979. Comparison of two commercial low residue diets and a low residue diet of common foods. *J. Parent. Ent. Nutr.* 3:226.

Cha, C. J. M., and Randall, H. T. 1981. Osmolality of liquid and defined formula diets: the effect of hydrolysis by pancreatic enzymes. *J. Parent. Ent. Nutr.* 5:7.

Chernoff, R., and Bloch, A. S. 1977. Liquid feedings: considerations and alterations. *J. Amer. Dietet. Assoc.* 70:389.

Cortot, A., et al. 1981. Gastric emptying of lipids after ingestion of a solid-liquid meal in humans. *Gastroenterology* 80:922.

Fagawa-Busby, K. S., et al. 1980. Effects of diet temperature on tolerance of enteral feedings. *Nurs. Res.* 29:276.

Fairclough, P. D., et al. 1979. Major differences in intestinal assimilation of two protein hydrolysates: potential importance for formulation of elemental diets. *Gastroenterology* 76:1129.

———. 1980. Comparison of the absorption of two protein hydrolysates and their effects on water and electrolyte movements in the human jejunum. *Gut* 21:829.

Fairfull-Smith, R. J., et al. 1979. Superiority of nonelemental diets for enteral nutrition in surgical patients. *J. Parent. Ent. Nutr.* 3:297.

Gormican, A., and Liddy, E. 1973. Nasogastric tube feedings. *Postgrad. Med.* 53:71.

Hanson, R. L. 1979. Predictive criteria for length of nasogastric tube insertion for tube feeding. *J. Parent. Ent. Nutr.* 3:160.

Heymsfield, S. B., et al. 1979. Enteral hyperalimentation: alternative to central venous hyperalimentation. *Ann. Intern. Med.* 90:63.

Hoover, H. C., Jr., et al. 1980. Nutritional benefits of immediate postoperative jejunal feeding of an elemental diet. *Am. J. Surg.* 139:153.

Huxley, E. J., et al. 1978. Pharyngeal aspiration in normal adults and patients with depressed consciousness. *Am. J. Med.* 64:564.

Jones, A. O. L., et al. 1980. Elemental content of predigested liquid protein products. *Amer. J. Clin. Nutr.* 33:2545.

Jones, B. J. M., et al. 1979. Pump assisted enteral feeding system. *J. Parent. Ent. Nutr.* 3:297.

Kaminski, M. V. 1976. Enteral hyperalimentation. *Surg. Gynecol. Obstet.* 143:12.

Koretz, R. L., and Meyer, J. H. 1980. Elemental diets—facts and fallacies. *Gastroenterology* 78:393.

Kubo, W., et al. 1976. Fluid and electrolyte problems of tube-fed patients. *Am. J. Nurs.* 76:912.

Metz, G., et al. 1978. Simple technique for naso-enteric feeding. *Lancet* 2:454.

Newmark, S. R., et al. 1981. Home tube feeding for a long-term nutritional support. *J. Parent. Ent. Nutr.* 5:76.

Padilla, G. V., et al. 1979. Subjective distress of nasogastric tube feeding. *J. Parent. Ent. Nutr.* 3:53.

Page, C. P., et al. 1979. Safe, cost-effective postoperative nutrition: defined formula diet via needle-catheter jejunostomy. *Am. J. Surg.* 138:939.

Ruppin, H., et al. 1981. Effects of liquid formula diets on proximal gastrointestinal function. *Dig. Dis. Sci.* 26:202.

Shils, M. E., et al. 1976. Liquid formulas for oral and tube feeding. *Clin. Bull.* 6:151.

Silk, D. B. A., et al. 1980. Use of a peptide rather than free amino acid nitrogen source in chemically defined "elemental" diets. *J. Parent. Ent. Nutr.* 4:548.

Timmons, K. N., et al. 1981. Protein quality and the cost of selected commercial protein supplements. *J. Amer. Dietet. Assoc.* 78:606.

Young, C. K., et al. 1979. Effect of an elemental diet on body composition: a comparison with intravenous nutrition. *Gastroenterology* 77:652.

Total Parenteral Nutrition

Borgen, L. 1978. Total parenteral nutrition in adults. *Am. J. Nurs.* 78:224.

Bryne, W. J., et al. 1979. Home parenteral nutrition: an alternative approach to the management of complicated gastrointestinal fistulas not responding to conventional medical or surgical therapy. *J. Parent. Ent. Nutr.* 3:355.

Colley, R., and Phillips, K. 1973. Helping the patient with hyperalimentation. *Nursing '73* 3:6.

Dudrick, S. J., et al. 1979. New concept of ambulatory home hyperalimentation. *J. Parent. Ent. Nutr.* 3:72.

Ghadimi, H., ed. 1975. *Total parenteral nutrition: premises and promises.* New York: Wiley.

Goodgame, J. R., Jr. 1980. A critical assessment of the indications for total parenteral nutrition. *Surg. Gynecol. Obstet.* 151:433.

Grant, J. P. 1980. *Handbook of total parenteral nutrition.* Philadelphia: Saunders.

Grundfest, S. 1980. Home parenteral nutrition. *J.A.M.A.* 244:1701.

Herlihy, P., et al. 1977. Total parenteral nutrition. *J. Amer. Dietet. Assoc.* 70:279.

Hickey, M. M., et al. 1979. Parenteral nutrition utilization: evaluation of an educational protocol and consult service. *J. Parent. Ent. Nutr.* 3:433.

Hill, G. L., et al. 1979. Changes in body weight and body protein with intravenous nutrition. *J. Parent. Ent. Nutr.* 3:215.

Howard, L., et al. 1978. A comparison of administering protein alone and protein plus glucose on nitrogen balance. *Amer. J. Clin. Nutr.* 31:226.

Irvin, T. T. 1978. Effects of malnutrition and hyperalimentation on wound healing. *Surg. Gynecol. Obstet.* 146:33.

Johnson, R. A., et al. 1981. An accidental case of cardiomyopathy and selenium deficiency. *N. Engl. J. Med.* 304:1210.

Jonsea, A. R. 1979. Ethical problems in home total parenteral nutrition. *J. Parent. Ent. Nutr.* 3:169.

J. Parent. Ent. Nutr. 1979a. Guidelines for essential trace element preparations for parenteral use: a statement of the nutrition advisory group. 3:263.

———. 1979b. Multivitamin preparations for parenteral use: a statement by the nutrition advisory group. 3:258.

Mascioli, E. A., et al. 1979. Effect of total parenteral nutrition with cycling on essential fatty acid deficiency. *J. Parent. Ent. Nutr.* 3:171.

Page, C. P., and Clibon, U. 1980. Man the meal-eater and his interaction with parenteral nutrition. *J.A.M.A.* 244:1950.

Paradis, C., et al. 1978. Total parenteral nutrition with lipids. *Am. J. Surg.* 135:164.

Price, B. S., and Levine, E. L. 1979. Permanent total parenteral nutrition: psychological and social responses of the early stage. *J. Parent. Ent. Nutr.* 3:48.

Scribner, B. H., and Cole, J. J. 1979. Evaluation of the technique of home parenteral nutrition. *J. Parent. Ent. Nutr.* 3:58.

Wateska, L. P., et al. 1980. Cost of a home parenteral nutrition program. *J.A.M.A.* 244:2303.

Wolman, S. L., et al. 1979. Zinc in total parenteral nutrition: requirements and metabolic effects. *Gastroenterology* 76:458.

Clinical Dietetics

American Dietetic Association. 1981. *Handbook of clinical dietetics.* New Haven, Conn.: Yale University Press.

Dadd, D. L., et al. 1982. *Nutritional analysis system: a physician's manual for evaluation of therapeutic diets.* Springfield, Ill: Thomas.

Davidson, S., et al. 1979. *Human nutrition and dietetics.* New York: Churchill Livingstone.

Goodhart, R. S., and Shils, M. E., eds. 1980. *Modern nutrition in health and disease.* 6th ed. Philadelphia: Lea & Febiger.

CHAPTER 24

Gastroenterology

Arvanitakis, C. 1979. Diet therapy in gastrointestinal disease: a commentary. *J. Amer. Dietet. Assoc.* 75:449.

Berk, J. E., ed. 1980. *Developments in digestive diseases.* Philadelphia: Lea & Febiger.

Johnson, L. R. 1981. *Gastrointestinal physiology.* 2nd ed. St. Louis: Mosby.

Kurtz, R. C., ed. 1981. *Contemporary issues in clinical nutrition,* vol. 1: *nutrition in gastrointestinal disease.* New York: Churchill Livingstone.

Lebenthal, E. 1981. *Gastrointestinal disease and nutritional inadequacies,* vol 2. New York: Raven Press.

Schizas, A. A. 1967. Medium-chain triglycerides—use in food preparation. *J. Amer. Dietet. Assoc.* 51:228.

Sleisenger, M. H., and Fordtran, J. S. 1978. *Gastrointestinal disease.* 2nd ed. 2 vol. Philadelphia: Saunders.

Winick, M., ed. 1980. *Nutrition and gastroenterology: current concepts in nutrition, vol. 9.* New York: Wiley.

Ulcer

Feinberg, L. E. 1980. Recurrent duodenal ulcer—a new, nonsurgical alternative. *Drug Therapy* 10:45.

Grossman, M. I. 1980. New medical and surgical treatments for peptic ulcer disease. *Am. J. Med.* 69:647.

———. 1981. *Peptic ulcer: a guide for the practicing physician.* Chicago: Year Book.

Mayo Clinic Proceedings. 1980. Symposium on duodenal peptic ulceration—1980. 55:1.

Winans, C. S. 1980. A drug therapy patient guide: living with a duodenal ulcer. *Drug Therapy* 10:55.

Celiac Disease

Dodge, J. A. 1980. Gluten intolerance, gluten enteropathy, and coeliac disease. *Arch. Dis. Child.* 55:143.

Falchuk, Z. M. 1979. Update on gluten-sensitive enteropathy. *Am. J. Med.* 67:1085.

Katz, A. J., and Falchuk, Z. M. 1975. Current concepts in gluten sensitive enteropathy. *Ped. Clin. N.A.* 22:767.

McNeish, A. S. 1980. Coeliac disease: duration of gluten-free diet. *Arch. Dis. Child.* 55:110.

Lactose Intolerance

Newcomer, A. D. 1973. Disaccharidase deficiencies. *Mayo Clinic Proceedings* 48:648.

Page, D. M., and Bayless, T. M., eds. 1981. *Lactose digestion: clinical and nutritional implications.* Baltimore: Johns Hopkins University Press.

Welsh, J. D. 1978. Diet therapy in adult lactose malabsorption: present practice. *Amer. J. Clin. Nutr.* 31:592.

Dietary Residues

Achord, J. A. 1979. Irritable bowel syndrome and dietary fiber. *J. Amer. Dietet. Assoc.* 75:452.

Anderson, N. E., and Clydesdale, F. M. 1980. Effects of processing on the dietary fiber content of wheat bran, pureed green beans, and carrots. *J. Food Sci.* 45:1533.

Bingham, S. 1979. Low-residue diets: a reappraisal of their meaning and content. *J. Human Nutr.* 33:5.

Eastwood, M. A., and Kay, R. M. 1979. A hypothesis for the action of dietary fiber along the gastrointestinal tract. *Amer. J. Clin. Nutr.* 32:364.

Heaton, K. W., et al. 1979. Treatment of Crohn's disease with an unrefined carbohydrate, fibre-rich diet. *Brit. Med. J.* 2:764.

Levin, B., and Horwitz, D. 1979. Dietary fiber. *Med. Clin. N.A.* 63:1043.

Sandstead, H. H. 1978. Influence of dietary fiber on trace element balance. *Amer. J. Clin. Nutr.* 31:S180.

Spiller, G.A., and Kay, R. M. 1979. Recommendations and conclusions of the dietary fiber workshop of the XI International Congress of Nutrition, Rio de Janeiro, 1978. *Amer. J. Clin. Nutr.* 32:2102.

Westlake, C. A. 1980. Appendectomy and dietary fibre. *J. Human Nutr.* 34:267.

Colon

Kirsner, J. B., and Shorter, R. G., eds. 1980. *Inflammatory bowel disease.* 2nd ed. Philadelphia: Lea & Febiger.

Kroner, K. 1980. Are you prepared for your ulcerative colitis patient? *Nursing* 10:43.

Rickham, P. P., et al., eds. 1978. *Ulcerative colitis and Crohn's disease, and other diseases of the alimentary system in childhood.* Baltimore: Urban & Schwarzenberg.

Schachter, H., and Kirsner, J. B. 1980. *Crohn's disease of the gastrointestinal tract.* New York: Wiley.

Constipation and Diarrhea

Aman, R. A. 1980. Treating the patient, not the constipation. *Am. J. Nurs.* 80:1634.

Babb, R. R. 1975. Constipation and laxative abuse. *West. J. Med.* 122:93.

Benson, J. A. 1975. Simple chronic constipation: pathophysiology and management. *Postgrad. Med.* 57:55.

Chernoff, R., and Dean, J. A. 1980. Medical and nutritional aspects of intractable diarrhea. *J. Amer. Dietet. Assoc.* 76:161.

Coale, M. S., and Robson, J. R. K. 1980. Dietary management of intractable diarrhea in malnourished patients. *J. Amer. Dietet. Assoc.* 76:444.

Dhar, G. J., and Soergel, K. H. 1979. Principles of diarrhea therapy. *Am. Family Physician* 19:165.

Hardison, W. G. M. 1976. Managing diarrhea: fit the workup to the patient. *Consultant* 16:147.

Kanin, H. J. 1976. Laxatives—a last resort in chronic constipation. *Consultant* 16:25.

Kauvar, A. J. 1975. The diarrhea syndrome. *Drug Therapy* 5:192.

McCaffery, T. D. 1975. Regulating the constipated patient. *Drug Therapy* 5:41.

CHAPTER 25

Liver Diseases

Altschuler, A., and Hilden, D. 1977. The patient with portal hypertension. *Nurs. Clin. N.A.* 12:317.

Baker, A. L. 1979. Amino acids in liver disease: cause of hepatic encephalopathy? *J.A.M.A.* 242:355.

Berk, P. D. 1981. Fulminating hepatic failure can be life-threatening. *Consultant* 21:182.

Bryan, J. A. 1980. Viral heptatitis. 1. Clinical and laboratory aspects and epidemiology. 2. Prevention and control. *Postgrad. Med.* 68:66.

Fischer, J. E. 1976. Amino acid infusion in hepatic encephalopathy. *Diet. Currents* 3(2):1.

Gabuzda, G. J. 1967. Ammonium metabolism and hepatic coma. *Gastroenterology* 53:806.

Greenberger, N. J. 1977. Effect of vegetable and animal protein diets in chronic hepatic encephalopathy. *Am. J. Digest. Dis.* 22:845.

Hoyumpa, A., et al. 1979. Hepatic encephalopathy. *Gastroenterology* 76:184.

Maddrey, W. C., and Weber, F. L. 1975. Chronic hepatic encephalopathy. *Med. Clin. N.A.* 59:937.

Steigmann, F. 1979. Preventing portal systemic encephalopathy in the patient with cirrhosis. *Postgrad. Med.* 65:118.

Warren, S. E., et al. 1980. Hypernatremia in hepatic failure. *J.A.M.A.* 243:1257.

Dietetics

Amer. J. Clin. Nutr. 1970. Symposium on nutrition and liver injury. Parts I and II. 23:445, 579.

Davidson, C. 1976. Dietary treatment of hepatic disease. *J. Amer. Dietet. Assoc.* 68:617.

Freund, H. 1979. Chronic hepatic encephalopathy: Longterm therapy with a branched-chain amino-acid–enriched elemental diet. *J.A.M.A.* 242:347.

Gabuzda, G. J., and Shear, L. 1970. Metabolism of dietary protein in hepatic cirrhosis. Nutritional and clinical considerations. *Amer. J. Clin. Nutr.* 23:479.

Rudman, D., et al. 1973. Ammonia content of food. *Amer. J. Clin. Nutr.* 26:487.

Shenkin, A. 1979. Assessment of nutritional status: the biochemical approach and its problems in liver disease. *J. Human Nutr.* 33:341.

Alcohol

Amer. J. Clin. Nutr. 1980. Symposium: alcoholism and malnutrition. 33:2705.

Baraona, E., et al. 1975. Alcoholic hepatomegaly: accumulation of protein in the liver. *Science* 190:794.

Lieber, C. S. 1976. The metabolism of alcohol. *Sci. Amer.* 234:25.

Lieber, C. S., ed. 1977. *Metabolic aspects of alcoholism.* Cambridge, Mass.: MIT Press.

Mezey, E. 1980. Alcoholic liver disease: role of alcohol malnutrition. *Amer. J. Clin. Nutr.* 33:2709.

Roe, D. A. 1979. *Alcohol and the diet.* Westport, Conn.: AVI Publishing.

———. 1981. Nutritional concerns in the alcoholic. *J. Amer. Dietet. Assoc.* 78:17.

Williamson, D., and Turl, M. 1975. Nutrition in the treatment of the alcoholic. *Diet. Currents* 2(1).

Gallbladder

Carey, M. C. 1975. Editorial: cheno and urso: what the goose and the bear have in common. *N. Engl. J. Med.* 293:1255.

Hanson, R. E., and Pries, J. M. 1977. Synthesis and

enterohepatic circulation of bile salts. *Gastroenterology* 73:611.

Ratner, J. T., and Rosenberg, G. M. 1975. Management of gallstones in the aged. *J. Am. Geriatrics Soc.* 23:258.

Sedaghat, A., and Grundy, S. M. 1980. Cholesterol crystals and the formation of cholesterol gallstones. *N. Engl. J. Med.* 302:1274.

Tangedahl, T. 1979. Dissolution of gallstones—when and how. *Surg. Clin. N.A.* 59:797.

Thorpe, C. J., and Caprini, J. A. 1980. Gallbladder disease: current trends and treatments. *Am. J. Nurs.* 80:2181.

Tucker, L. 1979. Identification of gallstone disease. *Postgrad. Med.* 66:163.

Tucker, L., and Tangedahl, T. N. 1979. Manifestations of gallstone disease. *Postgrad. Med.* 66:179.

CHAPTER 26

Diabetes Mellitus

Arky, R. A. 1978. Current principles of dietary therapy of diabetes mellitus. *Med. Clin. N.A.* 62:655.

Brownlee, M. 1981. Achieving better blood glucose control. *Drug Therapy* 11:59.

Brownlee, M., ed. 1981. *Handbook of diabetes mellitus.* Vol. 1. *Etiology/hormone physiology.* Vol. 2. *Islet cell function/insulin action.* Vol. 3. *Intermediary metabolism and its regulation.* Vol. 4. *Biochemical pathology.* New York: Garland STPM Press.

Burke, M. D. 1979. Diabetes mellitus: test strategies for diagnosis and management. *Postgrad. Med.* 66:213.

Cohen, S. 1980. Programmed instruction: controlling diabetes mellitus. *Am. J. Nurs.* 80:1827.

Craig, O. 1981. *Childhood diabetes and its management.* 2nd ed. Boston: Butterworths.

Craighead, J. E. 1978. Current views on the etiology of insulin dependent diabetes mellitus. *N. Engl. J. Med.* 299:1439.

Crofford, O. 1975. *Report of the national commission on diabetes to the Congress of the United States.* USDHEW pub. no. (NIH) 76-1018. Washington, D.C.: Government Printing Office.

Drash, A. L. 1979. The etiology of diabetes mellitus. *N. Engl. J. Med.* 300:1211.

Drug Therapy. 1981. On the present status of the treatment of diabetes. 11:41.

Ellenberg, M. 1980. Oral hypoglycemic agents: a status report. *Consultant* 20:223.

Felig, P. 1980. Diabetes. *Drug Therapy* 10:93.

Goldstein, S., and Podolsky, S. 1978. The genetics of diabetes mellitus. *Med. Clin. N.A.* 62:639.

Grave, G. D., ed. 1979. *Early detection of potential diabetics: the problems and the promise.* New York: Raven Press.

Greydanus, D. F., and Hofman, A. D. 1979. Psychological factors in diabetes mellitus. *Am. J. Dis. Child.* 133:1061.

J. Amer. Dietet. Assoc. 1979. Principles of nutrition and dietary recommendations for individuals with diabetes mellitus: 1979. 75:527.

Khachadurian, A. K., et al. 1980. Management of non-insulin-dependent diabetes mellitus. *Am. Family Physician* 21:154.

Krall, L. P., and Chabot, V. A. 1978. Oral hypoglycemic agent update. *Med. Clin. N.A.* 62:681.

Lundin, D. L. 1978. Reporting urine test results: switch from + to %. *Am. J. Nurs.* 78:878.

Mahler, R. J. 1980. Maturity-onset diabetes: current basis for treatment. *Consultant* 20:23.

Meinick, D. E. 1979. Future management of diabetes mellitus. *Postgrad. Med.* 66:101.

Miller, L. V. 1979. Keeping your diabetic patients out of the hospital. *Consultant* 16:47.

Notkins, A. L. 1976. The causes of diabetes. *Sci. Amer.* 241:62.

Rifkin, H., et al., eds. 1981. *Diabetes mellitus,* vol. V., Bowie, MD.: R. J. Brady.

Rosenthal, H., and Rosenthal, J. 1969. *Diabetic care in pictures.* 4th ed. Philadelphia: Lippincott.

Rotter, J. I., and Rimoin, D. L. 1981. The genetics of glucose intolerance disorders. *Am. J. Med.* 70:116.

Schulman, P. K. 1980. Diabetes in pregnancy: nutritional aspect of care. *J. Amer. Dietet. Assoc.* 76:585.

Shagan, B. P. 1976. Diabetes in the elderly patient. *Med. Clin. N.A.* 60:1191.

Sims, D. F., ed. 1980. *Diabetes: Reach for Health and Freedom.* St. Louis: C. V. Mosby.

Traisman, H. S. 1980. *Management of juvenile diabetes mellitus.* 3rd ed. St. Louis: Mosby.

U.S. Department of Health, Education, and Welfare. 1979. *Educational material for and about young people with diabetes.* USDHEW/NIH pub. no. 80-1871.

Whitehouse, F. W. 1978. The diagnosis of diabetes—how to determine which patients to treat. *Med. Clin. N.A.* 62:627.

World Health Organization. 1980. *WHO expert committee on diabetes mellitus.* 2nd Report. WHO Technical Report Series, no. 646. Geneva, Switzerland.

Insulin

Drug Therapy. 1980. New purified pork insulin from Lilly. 10:31.

Farese, R. V. 1980. A rational approach for using insulin. *Consultant* 20:201.

Galloway, J. A. 1980. Insulin treatment for the early '80s: facts and questions about old and new insulins and their usage. *Diab. Care* 5:615.

Gunby, P. 1978. Bacteria directed to produce insulin in test application of genetic code. *J.A.M.A.* 240:1697.

Pfeifer, M. A., et al. 1981. Insulin secretion in diabetes mellitus. *Am. J. Med.* 70:579.

Sun, M. 1980. Insulin wars: new advances may throw market into turbulence. *Science* 210:1225.

Meal Planning

American Diabetes Association. 1976. *American Diabetes Association and American Dietetic Association: exchange lists for meal planning.*

————. 1977. *American Diabetes Association and American Dietetic Association: a guide for professionals: the effective application of "exchange lists for meal planning."*

Arbogast, K. K. 1980. *Exchange lists and diet patterns.* New York: Wiley.

Corvi, P., et al. 1980. *Meal planning, diabetes melllitus.* Ann Arbor: University of Michigan, University Hospital, Department of Dietetics.

Diabetes Education Center. 1979. *Exchange value of fast food restaurants.* Minneapolis.

Wheeler, M. L., and Wheeler, L. A. 1980. Computer-planned menus for patients with diabetes mellitus. *Diab. Care* 3:663.

Wyse, B. W. 1979. Nutrient analysis of exchange lists for meal planning. *J. Amer. Dietet. Assoc.* 75:238.

Dietetic Products

Brunzell, J. D. 1978. Use of fructose, sorbitol, or xylitol as a sweetener in diabetes mellitus. *J. Amer. Dietet. Assoc.* 73:499.

Koivisto, V. A. 1978. Fructose as a dietary sweetener in diabetes mellitus. *Diab. Care* 1:24.

Lenner, R. A. 1976. Specially designed sweeteners and food for diabetics—a real need? *Amer. J. Clin. Nutr.* 29:726.

Sestoft, L. 1979. Fructose and dietary therapy of diabetes mellitus. *Diabetologia* 17:1.

Exercises

Boshell, B. R. 1979. *Diabetic at work and play.* 2nd ed. Springfield, Ill.: Charles C Thomas.

Gonzalez, E. R. 1979. Exercise therapy "rediscovered" for diabetes, but what does it do? *J.A.M.A.* 242:1591.

Koivisto, V. A., and Sherwin, R. S. 1979. Exercise in diabetes: therapeutic implications. *Postgrad. Med.* 66:87.

Richter, E. A., et al. 1981. Diabetes and exercise. *Am. J. Med.* 70:201.

Vranic, M., et al., eds. 1979. Proceedings of a conference on diabetes and exercise. *Diabetes* 285:1.

Zinman, B. 1979. Diabetes and exercise. *Postgrad. Med.* 66:81.

Complications

Edwards, J. E., et al. 1979. Infection and diabetes mellitus. *West. J. Med.* 130:515.

Katzen, H. M., and Mahler, E. J., eds. 1978. *Diabetes, obesity and vascular disease: metabolic and molecular interrelationships.* Parts 1 and 2. New York: Wiley.

Kissebah, A. H. 1979. Management of hyperlipidemia in diabetes. *Am. Family Physician* 19:144.

Kolata, G. B. 1979. Blood sugar and the complications of diabetes. *Science* 203:1098.

L'Esperance, F. A., Jr. 1978. Diabetic retinopathy. *Med. Clin. N.A.* 62:767.

Scarpello, J. H. D., and Sladen, G. E. 1978. Diabetes and the gut. *Gut* 19:1153.

Ventura, E. 1978. Foot care for diabetics. *Am. J. Nurs.* 78:886.

West, K. M. 1978. *Epidemiology of diabetes and its vascular lesions.* New York: Elsevier Scientific Publishing.

Winegrad, A. I., and Greene, D. A. 1978. The complications of diabetes mellitus. *N. Engl. J. Med.* 298:1250.

Patient Education

Bowen, A. 1980. *The diabetic gourmet.* Revised edition. New York: Barnes & Noble Books.

Etzwiler, D. D. 1978. Education of the patient with diabetes. *Med. Clin. N.A.* 62:857.

Finsand, M. J. 1980. *The complete diabetic cookbook.* New York: Sterling Publishing.

Fonville, A. M. 1978. Teaching patients to rotate injection sites. *Am. J. Nurs.* 78:880.

Jackson, R. L. 1980. Education of the parents of a child with diabetes. *Nutr. Today*: May–June, p. 30.

Jorgensen, C. D., and Lewis, J. E. 1979. *The ABC of diabetes*. New York: Crown.

Lovette, B. J. 1980. *Diabetes . . . self-care acts for good control*. Asheville, N.C.: Proctor Enterprises.

MacRae, N. 1975. *How to have your cake and eat it too*. Anchorage: Alaska Northwest Publishing.

Small, D. 1978. A patient education program. *Am. J. Nurs.* 78:888.

Wishner, W. J., and O'Brien, M. D. 1978. Diabetes and the family. *Med. Clin. N.A.* 62:849.

Advances

Crapo, P. A., and Olefsky, J. M. 1980. Fructose—its characteristics, physiology, and metabolism. *Nutr. Today* 15:10.

Maugh, T. H. 1979. Virus isolated from juvenile diabetic. *Science* 204:1187.

National Diabetes Data Group. 1979. Classification and diagnosis of diabetes mellitus and other categories of glucose intolerance. *Diabetes* 28:1039.

Rizza, R. A., et al. 1980. Control of blood sugar in insulin-dependent diabetes: comparison of an artificial endocrine pancreas, continuous subcutaneous infusion and intensified conventional insulin therapy. *N. Engl. J. Med.* 303:1313.

Schade, D. S. 1981. Insulin delivery—today's systems, tomorrow's prospects. *Drug Therapy* 11:47.

Schade, D. S., et al. 1981. Implantation of an artificial pancreas. Commentary. *J.A.M.A.* 245:709.

Tamborlane, W. V., et al. 1979. Reduction to normal of plasma glucose in juvenile diabetes by subcutaneous administration of insulin with a portable infusion pump. *N. Engl. J. Med.* 300:573.

Yoon, J. W., et al. 1979. Virus-induced diabetes mellitus. *N. Engl. J. Med.* 300:1173.

CHAPTER 27

Cardiovascular Diseases

Alexander, S. 1980. *Running healthy: a guide to cardiovascular fitness*. Brattleboro, Vt.: The Stephen Greene Press.

Am. J. Nurs. 1981. New concepts in understanding congestive heart failure. Part 2. How the therapeutic approaches work. 81:357.

Braunwald, E., ed. 1980. *Heart disease: a textbook of cardiovascular medicine*. Philadelphia: Saunders.

Brisson, G. J. 1981. *Lipids in human nutrition*. Englewood, N.J.: Jack K. Burgess.

Feldman, E. B. 1976. *Nutrition and cardiovascular disease*. New York: Appleton-Century-Crofts.

Frye, R. L. 1981. Chronic congestive heart failure: eight steps in management. *Postgrad. Med.* 69:165.

Goldberger, A. L. 1981. Congestive heart failure in adults: six considerations in systematic diagnosis. *Postgrad. Med.* 69:151.

Gordon, M. S. 1981. Cardiovascular disease: a three-article symposium. *Postgrad. Med.* 69:118.

Harker, L. A., et al. 1981. Thrombosis: its role and prevention in cardiovascular events. Parts I. and II. *West. J. Med.* 134:234, 315.

Kruppand, M. A., and Chatton, M. J. 1982. *Current medical diagnosis and treatment*. Los Altos, Calif.: Lange Medical Publications.

Lequime, J., ed. 1980. *Prevention and treatment of coronary heart disease and its complications*. Amsterdam, Holland: Excerpta Medica.

Long, C., ed. 1980. *Prevention and rehabilitation in ischemic heart disease*. Baltimore: Williams & Wilkins.

Missri, J. 1979. Hematologic toxicity of drugs used in cardiovascular disease. *Postgrad. Med.* 65:165.

Acute Care

Jones, R. J. 1977. Dietary management in the coronary care unit. *J.A.M.A.* 237:2645.

Olesen, K. H., and Faergeman, O. 1980. Metabolic response to acute myocardial infarction. *J. Parent. Ent. Nutr.* 4:157.

Stegemann, N. 1977. Dietary management in the coronary care unit. *J.A.M.A.* 238:1913.

Tanner, G. 1977. Heart failure in the MI patient. *Am. J. Nurs.* 77:230.

Warren, S. E., et al. 1978. Diet in the coronary care unit. *Am. Heart J.* 95:130.

Wenger, N. K. 1979a. Guidelines for dietary management after myocardial infarction. *Geriatrics* 34:75.

———. 1979b. Rehabilitation after myocardial infarction. *Postgrad. Med.* 66:128.

Risk Factors

Bortz, W. M. 1974. The pathogenesis of hypercholesterolemia. *Ann. Intern. Med.* 80:738.

Glueck, C. J. 1979. Dietary fat and atherosclerosis. *Amer. J. Clin. Nutr.* 32:2703.

Hulley, S. B., et al. 1980. Epidemiology as a guide to clinical decisions. The association between triglyceride and coronary heart disease. *N. Engl. J. Med.* 302:1383.

Kannel, W. B., et al. 1979. Cholesterol in the prediction of atherosclerotic disease. *Ann. Intern. Med.* 90:85.

Kritchevsky, D., and Czarnecki, S. K. 1980. Lipoproteins. *Contemp. Nutr.* 5:1.

McGill, H. C. 1979. The relationship of dietary cholesterol to serum cholesterol concentration and to atherosclerosis in man. *Amer. J. Clin. Nutr.* 32:2664.

Controversies and Heart Diseases

American Heart Association Committee on Nutrition, Diet, and Coronary Heart Disease. 1978. *A statement for physicians and other health professionals.*

Hausman, P. 1981. *J. Sprat's legacy: the science and politics of fat and cholesterol.* New York: Richard Marek Publishers.

Rapaport, E., ed. 1980. *Current controversies in cardiovascular disease.* Philadelphia: Saunders.

Reiser, R. 1973. Saturated fat in the diet and serum cholesterol concentration: a critical examination of the literature. *Amer. J. Clin. Nutr.* 26:524.

Epidemiology

Dawber, T. R. 1980. *The Framingham study: the epidemiology of atherosclerotic disease.* Cambridge, Mass.: Harvard University Press.

Keys, A. 1980. *Seven countries: a multivariate analysis of death and coronary heart disease.* Cambridge, Mass.: Harvard University Press.

Levy, R. I., et al., eds. 1979. *Nutrition in health and disease.* Vol. 1. *Nutrition, lipids and coronary heart disease: a global view.* New York: Raven Press.

Treatment

American Heart Association. 1973. *A maximal approach to the dietary treatment of the hyperlipidemias: physician's handbook.* New York.

Eshleman, R., and Winston, M. 1979. *The American Heart Association cookbook.* 3rd ed. New York: McKay.

Margolis, S. 1978. Treatment of hyperlipidemia. *J.A.M.A.* 239:2696.

National Institute of Health, National Heart and Lung Institute. 1973. *Dietary management of hyperlipoproteinemia, a handbook for physicians and dietitians.* Revised edition. Bethesda, Md.

Noseda, G., et al., eds. 1980. *Diet and drugs in atherosclerosis.* New York: Raven Press.

Rifkind, B. M., and Levy, R. I., eds. 1977. *Hyperlipidemia: diagnosis and therapy.* New York: Grune & Stratton.

Sodium and Diet

Cech, I., et al. 1979. Excessive sodium in drinking water. *South. Med. J.* 72:639.

Gonzales, E. A., et al. 1979. Sodium in drinking water: Information for clinical application. *South. Med. J.* 72:753.

Marsh, A. C., et al. 1980. *The sodium content of your food.* U.S. Department of Agriculture, Science and Education Administration, Home & Garden Bulletin, no. 233. Washington, D.C.

Moses, C., ed. 1980. *Sodium in medicine and health.* Baltimore: Reese Press.

National Academy of Sciences, National Research Council. 1979. *Sodium-restricted diets and the use of diuretics: rationale, complications, and practical aspects of their use.* Washington, D.C.

Oexmann-Wannamaker, M. J. 1976. Salt substitutes. *Amer. J. Clin. Nutr.* 29:599.

Hypertension

Arch. Intern. Med. 1980. The 1980 report of the Joint National Committee on detection, evaluation, and treatment of high blood pressure. 140:1280.

DeFronzo, R. A., and Thier, S. O. 1980. Pathophysiologic approach to hyponatremia. *Arch. Intern. Med.* 140:879.

Freis, E. D. 1976. Salt, volume and the prevention of hypertension. *Circulation* 53:589.

Fujita, T., et al. 1980. Factors influencing blood pressure in salt-sensitive patients with hypertension. *Am. J. Med.* 69:334.

Gerber, J. G., et al. 1980. Antihypertensive pharmacology. *West. J. Med.* 132:430.

Gifford, R. W. 1980. The hypertension detection and follow-up program, the Joint National Committee, and non-pharmacologic management of hypertension. *Mayo Clinic Proceedings* 55:651.

Haddy, F. J. 1980. Mechanism, prevention and therapy of sodium-dependent hypertension. *Am. J. Med.* 69:746.

Hill, M. 1979. Helping the hypertensive patient control sodium intake. *Am. J. Nurs.* 79:906.

Kostas, G. 1980a. A hypertension diet education program for public health nurses. *J. Amer. Dietet. Assoc.* 77:570.

————. 1980b. Evaluation and follow-up of a hypertension diet education program. *J. Amer. Dietet. Assoc.* 77:574.

Laragh, J. H., ed. 1980. *Topics in hypertension.* New York: Yorke Medical Books.

Pleuss, J., and Kochar, M. S. 1981. Dietary considerations in hypertension. *Postgrad. Med.* 69:34.

Silverberg, D. S. 1980. Treating hypertension with diet. *Consultant* 20:115.

Stamler, J. 1980. Prevention and control of hypertension by nutritional-hygienic means. *J.A.M.A.* 243:1819.

Taylor, A. A. 1981. Diagnosis and management of mild hypertension. *Consultant* 21:225.

Tobian, L. 1979. The relationship of salt to hypertension. *Amer. J. Clin. Nutr.* 32:2739.

U.S. Congress, Senate. 1977. *Dietary goals for the United States.* Washington, D.C.

U.S. Department of Health and Human Services. 1980. *Statement on the role of dietary management in hypertension control.* PHS/NIH, pub. no. 0-311-201/3129. Washington, D.C.

CHAPTER 28

Renal Physiology and Diseases

Border, W. A., and Glassock, R. J. 1981. Progress in treating glomerulonephritis. *Drug Therapy* 11:97.

Gonick, H. C., ed. 1979. *Current nephrology.* Boston: Houghton Mifflin.

Kopple, J. D., et al., eds. 1980. Symposium. Nutrition in renal disease. *Amer. J. Clin. Nutr.* 33:1337.

Lassiter, W. E. 1975. Kidney. *Ann. Rev. Physiol.* 37:1135.

Leaf, A., and Cotran, R. S. 1980. *Renal pathophysiology.* New York: Oxford University Press.

Martinez-Maldonado, M., and Garcia, A. 1981. A practical approach to the nephrotic syndrome. *Drug Therapy* 11:79.

McDonald, F. D. 1980. *Progress in clinical kidney disease and hypertension.* Vol. 1. New York: Thieme-Stratton.

Strauss, J. 1978. *Renal failure: current concepts in diagnosis and management.* Vol. 4. In *Pediatric nephrology.* New York: Garland STPM Press.

Vander, A. J. 1975. *Renal physiology.* New York: McGraw-Hill.

Dialysis

Chambers, J. K. 1981. Assessing the dialysis patient at home. *Am. J. Nurs.* 81:750.

Kluthe, R. 1978. Protein requirements in maintenance hemodialysis. *Amer. J. Clin. Nutr.* 31:1812.

Kurtzman, N. A. 1981. Beyond dialysis. *Drug Therapy* 11:41.

Lake, B. 1979. Nutrition in renal disease: the adult on dialysis. *Am. J. Nurs.* 79:2155.

Rubin, J., et al. 1981. Total body potassium—a guide to nutritional health in patients undergoing continuous ambulatory peritoneal dialysis. *Amer. J. Clin. Nutr.* 34:94.

Sargent, J. A. 1979. Mass balance: a quantitative guide to clinical nutritional therapy. II. The dialyzed patient. *J. Amer. Dietet. Assoc.* 75:551.

Sargent, J. A., and Gotch, F. A. 1979. Mass balance: a quantitative guide to clinical nutritional therapy. I. The predialysis patient with renal disease. *J. Amer. Dietet. Assoc.* 75:547.

Wiegand, C. E., et al. 1981. Severe hypokalemia induced by hemodialysis. *Arch. Intern. Med.* 141:167.

Renal Dietetics

Blumenkrantz, M. J., et al. 1980. Methods for assessing nutritional status of patients with renal failure. *Amer. J. Clin. Nutr.* 33:1567.

Chantler, C., et al. 1980. Nutritional therapy in children with chronic renal failure. *Amer. J. Clin. Nutr.* 33:1682.

Eisinger, R. P. 1979. Office management of chronic renal disease. *Am. Family Physician* 20:109.

Furst, P., et al. 1978. Principles of essential amino acid therapy in uremia. *Amer. J. Clin. Nutr.* 31:1744.

Guarnien, G., et al. 1980. Simple methods for nutritional assessment in hemodialyzed patients. *Amer. J. Clin. Nutr.* 33:1598.

Harvey, K. B. 1980. Nutritional assessment and treatment of chronic renal failure. *Amer. J. Clin. Nutr.* 33:1586.

Hetrick, A., et al. 1979. Nutrition in renal disease: when the patient is a child. *Am. J. Nurs.* 79:2152.

Kolata, G. B. 1980. Dialysis after nearly a decade. *Science* 208:473.

Kopple, J. D. 1979. Nutrition and the kidney. Vol 4. In *Human nutrition: a comprehensive treatise*. In Metabolic and clinical applications, ed. R. E. Hodges, p. 409. New York: Plenum.

Oestreich, S. J. K. 1979. Rational nursing care in chronic renal disease. *Am. J. Nurs.* 79:1096.

Ritz, E., et al. 1978. Protein restriction in the conservative management of uremia. *Amer. J. Clin. Nutr.* 31:1703.

Vaamonde, C. A. 1979. Diet *does* make a difference for patients with chronic uremia. *Consultant* 19:156.

Walser, M. 1980. Does dietary therapy have a role in the predialysis patient? *Amer. J. Clin. Nutr.* 33:1629.

Diuretics

Drug Therapy 1981. A drug therapy patient guide: what you should know about diuretics. 11:95.

Eknoyan, G. 1981. Understanding diuretic therapy. *Drug Therapy* 11:47.

Medical Letter on Drugs and Therapeutics. 1979. *Drugs of choice from the medical letter for asthma, cancer, cardiac arrhythmias, epilepsy, hypertension, psychiatry disorders, drug abuse emergencies, and a table of drug interactions.*

Porter, G. A. 1980. The role of diuretics in the treatment of heart failure. *J.A.M.A.* 244:1614.

Tucker, R. M., et al. 1980. Series on pharmacology in practice. 7. Diuretics: role of sodium balance. *Mayo Clinic Proceedings* 55:261.

Potassium

Chojnacki, R. E. 1980. Practical potassium replacement. *Consultant* 20:241.

Knochel, J. P. 1980. Potassium deficiency: causes, complications, and treatment. *Consultant* 20:139.

Sorkin, M. I. 1980. Hyperkalemia—causes, management, and prevention. *Consultant* 20:25.

Food Preparation and Patient Instruction

Cost, J. S. 1975. *Dietary management of renal disease.* Thorfare, N.J.: Charles B. Slack.

Doyle Pharmaceutical Company. N.d. *Recipes for protein-restricted diets.* Minneapolis.

Greene, M. C. 1980. *Gourmet renal nutrition cookbook.* New York: Lennox Hill Hospital.

Johnson, J. J., and Penfield, M. P. 1976. A home-baked, yeast-leavened, low-protein bread. *J. Amer. Dietet. Assoc.* 69:653.

Margie, J. D., et al. 1975. *The Mayo Clinic renal diet cookbook.* New York: Golden Press, (distributed by the National Kidney Foundation).

National Institute of Arthritis, Metabolism and Digestive Diseases. 1975. *Diet guide for patients on chronic dialysis.* Bethesda, Md.

Urinary Stones

Chadwick, V. S., et al. 1973. Mechanism for hyperoxaluria in patients with ileal dysfunction. *N. Engl. J. Med.* 289:172.

Coe, F. L., ed. 1980. *Nephrolithiasis.* New York: Churchill Livingstone.

Derrick, F. C., Jr., and Carter, W. C. III. 1979. Kidney stone disease: evaluation and medical management. *Postgrad. Med.* 66:115.

Juan, D. 1979. Differential dignosis of hypercalcemia: a mechanistic approach. *Postgrad. Med.* 66:72.

Kleeman, C. R., et al. 1980. Kidney stones. *West. J. Med.* 132:313.

Williams, H. E. 1974. Nephrolithiasis: physiology in medicine. *N. Engl. J. Med.* 290:33.

Wilson, D. M. 1979. Medical treatment of urolithiasis. *Geriatrics* 34:65.

Zawada, E. T., Jr., et al. 1979. I. Causes of hypercalcemia. II. Management of hypercalcemia. *Postgrad. Med.* 66:91, 105.

CHAPTER 29

Trauma Patients: Metabolism and Care

Alberti, K. G. M. M., et al. 1980. Relative role of various hormones in mediating the metabolic response to injury. *J. Parent. Ent. Nutr.* 4:141.

Blackburn, G. L., and Bistrian, B. R. 1976. Nutritional care of the injured or septic patient. *Surg. Clin. N.A.* 56:1195.

Chernoff, R. 1979. The team concept: the dietitian's responsibility. *J. Parent. Ent. Nutr.* 3:89.

Clowes, G. H. A., ed. 1976. Response to infection and injury. II. Metabolism. *Surg. Clin. N.A.* 56(5).

Cuthbertson, D. P. 1979. The metabolic response to injury and its nutritional implications. Retrospect and prospect. *J. Parent. Ent. Nutr.* 3:108.

Daniel, P. M. 1977. The metabolic homeostasis role of muscle and its function as a store of protein. *Lancet* 2:446.

Doyle Pharmaceutical Company. N.d. *Nutrition in trauma and stress: reference manual.* Minneapolis.

Hoover-Plow, J. L., et al. 1980. The effects of surgical trauma on plasma amino acid levels in humans. *Surg. Gynecol. Obstet.* 150:161.

Powanda, M. C. 1977. Changes in body balances of nitrogen and other key nutrients: description and underlying mechanisms. *Amer. J. Clin. Nutr.* 30:1254.

Seltzer, M. H., et al. 1981. Instant nutritional assessment in the intensive care unit. *J. Parent. Ent. Nutr.* 5:70.

Shenkin, A., et al. 1980. Biochemical changes associated with severe trauma. *Amer. J. Clin. Nutr.* 33:2119.

Tweedle, D. E. 1980. Metabolism of amino acids after trauma. *J. Parent. Ent. Nutr.* 4:165.

Surgery

American College of Surgeons, Committee on Pre- and Postoperative Care. 1975. *Manual of surgical nutrition.* Philadelphia: Saunders.

Amer. J. Clin. Nutr. 1980. Symposium on surgical treatment of morbid obesity. 33:353.

Becker, H. D., and Caspary, W. F. 1980. *Postgastrectomy and postvagotomy syndromes.* New York: Springer.

Bingham, S. 1977. Diet for the ileostomist. *J. Human Nutr.* 31:365.

Bingham, S., et al. 1982. Diet and health of people with an ileostomy. 1. Dietary assessment. *Brit. J. Nutr.* 47:399.

Breckman, B. E. 1979. Role of the nurse specialist in stoma care. *J. Human Nutr.* 33:383.

Bromley, B. 1980. Applying Orem's self-care theory in enterostomal therapy. *Am. J. Nurs.* 80:245.

Bush, J. 1979. Cervical esophagostomy to provide nutrition. *Am. J. Nurs.* 79:107.

Buzby, G. P., et al. 1980. Prognostic nutritional index in gastrointestinal surgery. *Am. J. Surg.* 139:160.

Calam, J., et al. 1980. Elemental diets in the management of Crohn's perianal fistulae. *J. Parent. Ent. Nutr.* 4:4.

Deitel, M., ed. 1980. *Nutrition in clinical surgery.* Baltimore: Williams and Wilkins.

Gordon, P. H. 1976. The chemically defined diet and anorectal procedures. *Can. J. Surg.* 19:511.

Greenberg, G. R., and Jeejeebhoy, K. N. 1979. Intravenous protein-sparing therapy in patients with gastrointestinal disease. *J. Parent. Ent. Nutr.* 3:427.

Gurry, J. F., and Ellis-Pegler, R. B. 1976. An elemental diet as preoperative preparation of the colon. *Brit. J. Surg.* 63:979.

Hickman, D. M., et al. 1980. Serum albumin and body weight as predictors of postoperative course in colorectal cancer. *J. Parent. Ent. Nutr.* 4:314.

Hill, G. L. 1976. *Ileostomy: surgery, physiology, and management.* New York: Grune & Stratton.

Hoover, H. G., Jr., et al. 1980. Nutritional benefits of immediate postoperative jejunal feeding of an elemental diet. *Am. J. Surg.* 139:153.

Keith, R. L., et al. 1977. *Looking forward: a guidebook for the laryngectomee.* Rochester, Minn.: Mayo Foundation.

McCawley, A., et al. 1975. The psychological problems of ostomates. *Connecticut Med.* 39:151.

McNeil, N. I., et al. 1982. Diet and health of people with an ileostomy. 2. Ileostomy function and nutritional state. *Brit. J. Nutr.* 47:407.

Miller, B. K. 1981. Jejunoileal bypass: a drastic weight control measure. *Am. J. Nurs.* 81:564.

Mojzisk, C. M., and Martin, E. W. 1981. Gastric partitioning: the latest surgical means to control morbid obesity. *Am. J. Nurs.* 81:569.

Mullen, B. D., and McGinn, K. A. 1980. *The ostomy book—living comfortably with colostomies, ileostomies, and urostomies.* Palo Alto, Calif.: Bull Publishing.

Mullen, J. L., et al. 1979. Implications of malnutrition in the surgical patient. *Arch. Surg.* 114:121.

Rault, R. M. J., and Scribner, B. H. 1977. Treatment of Crohn's disease with home parenteral nutrition. *Gastroenterology* 72:1249.

Schrock, T. R., and Way, L. W. 1978. Total gastrectomy. *Am. J. Surg.* 135:348.

Sitrin, M. D., et al. 1980. Nutritional and metabolic complications in a patient with Crohn's disease and ileal resection. *Gastroenterology* 78:1069.

Strauss, R. J., and Wise, L. 1978. Operative risks of obesity. *Surg. Gynecol. Obstet.* 146:286.

Trunkey, D., et al. 1973. *Nutrition and trauma. Intake: perspectives in nutrition.* Norwich, New York: Eaton Laboratories.

Webster, M.W., and Corey, L. C. 1976. Fistulae of the intestinal tract. *Curr. Probl. Surg.* 13(6).

Woods, J. H., et al. 1978. Postoperative ileus: a colonic problem? *Surgery* 84:527.

Wright, H. K., and Tilson, M. D. 1973. *Postoperative disorders of the gastrointestinal tract.* New York: Grune & Stratton.

Yarborough, M. F., ed. 1981. *Contemporary issues in clinical nutrition.* Vol. 3. In *Surgical nutrition.* New York: Churchill Livingstone.

Burns

Artz, C. P. 1977. Guide to assessment and management of burns. *Hosp. Med.* 13:105.

Artz, C. P., et al. 1979. *Burns: a team approach.* Philadelphia: Saunders.

Campbell, L. 1976. Special behavioral problems of the burned child. *Amer. J. Nurs.* 76:220.

Crenshaw, C. 1973. *Nutritional support for burn patients.* Norwich, New York: Eaton Laboratories.

Curreri, P. W., and Luterman, A. 1978. Nutritional support of the burned patient. *Surg. Clin. N.A.* 58:1151.

Feller, I., et al. 1973. The team approach to total rehabilitation of the severely burned patient. *Heart Lung* 2:701.

Holli, B., and Oaks, J. 1975. Feeding the burned child. *J. Amer. Dietet. Assoc.* 67:240.

Larkin, J. M., and Moylon, J. A. 1976. Complete enteral support of thermally injured patients. *Am. J. Surg.* 131:722.

Liljedahl, S. O., and Birke, G. 1972. The nutrition of patients with extensive burns. *Nutr. and Metab.* 14 (Suppl.):110.

Long, J., and Pruitt, B. A. 1974. Nutritional care of the burn patient. *Diet. Currents* 1(1):1.

Long, J. C. 1979. Energy expenditure of major burns. *J. Trauma* 10S:904.

Newsome, T. W., et al. 1973. Weight loss following thermal injury. *Ann. Surg.* 178:215.

Pennisi, V. M. 1976. Monitoring the nutritional care of burned patients. *J. Amer. Dietet. Assoc.* 69:531.

Wagner, M. M., ed. 1981. *Care of the burned-injured patient.* Littleton, Mass.: Publishing Science Group.

Wilmore, D. W., and Aulick, L. H. 1980. Systemic responses to injury and the healing wound. *J. Parent. Ent. Nutr.* 4:147.

Cancer

Aker, S. N. 1979. Oral feeding in the cancer patient. *Cancer* 43:2103.

Aker, S. N., and Lenssen, P. N.d. *A guide to good nutrition during and after chemotherapy and radiation.* 2nd ed. Seattle: Fred Hutchinson Cancer Research Center.

Bernstein, I. L., and Sigmundi, R. A. 1980. Tumor anorexia: a learned food aversion? *Science* 209:416.

Brennan, M. F. 1977. Uncomplicated starvation versus cancer cachexia. *Cancer Res.* 37:2359.

Carson, J. A. S., and Gormican, A. 1977. Taste acuity and food attitudes of selected patients with cancer. *J. Amer. Dietet. Assoc.* 70:361.

Cooper-Stephenson, C., and Theologides, A. 1981. Nutrition in cancer: physicians' knowledge, opinions, and educational needs. *J. Amer. Dietet. Assoc.* 78:472.

Copeland, E. M., III, and Dudrick, S. 1975. Cancer: nutritional concepts. *Seminars in Oncology* 2:329.

Copeland, E. M., III, et al. 1977a. Intravenous hyperalimentation as an adjunct to radiation therapy. *Cancer* 39:609.

———. 1977b. Nutrition as an adjunct to cancer treatment in the adult. *Cancer Res.* 37:2451.

———. 1981. Nutrition, cancer and intravenous hyperalimentation. *Cancer* 43:2108.

Costa, G. 1977. Determination of nutritional needs. *Cancer Res.* 37:2419.

Costa, G., and Donaldson, S. S. 1979. Current concepts in cancer: effects of cancer and cancer treatment on nutrition of the host. *N. Engl. J. Med.* 300:1471.

DeWys, W. D. 1980. Nutritional care of the cancer patient. *J.A.M.A.* 244:374.

DeWys, W. D., and Herbst, S. H. 1977. Oral feeding in the nutritional management of the cancer patient. *Cancer Res.* 37:2429.

Donaldson, S. S., and Lenon, R. A. 1979. Alterations of nutritional status: impact of chemotherapy and radiation therapy. *Cancer* 43:2036.

Dreizen, S., et al. 1977. Oral complications of cancer radiotherapy. *Postgrad. Med.* 61:85.

Dwyer, J. T. 1979. Dietetic assessment of ambulatory cancer patients. *Cancer* 43:2077.

Eriksson, B., and Douglass, H. O., Jr. 1980. Intravenous hyperalimentation. An adjunct to treatment of malignant disease of upper gastrointestinal tract. *J.A.M.A.* 243:2049.

Gale, R. P. 1979. Advances in the treatment of acute myelogenous leukemia. *N. Engl. J. Med.* 300:1189.

Lucas, V. S., Jr., and Laszlo, J. 1980. Δ^9—tetrahydrocannabinol for refractory vomiting induced by cancer chemotherapy. *J.A.M.A.* 243:1241.

Marino, L. B. 1981. *Cancer nursing.* St. Louis: Mosby.

National Institute of Health. 1979. *Diet and nutrition: a resource for parents of children with cancer.* NIH pub. no. 80-2036.

———. 1980. *Eating hints: recipes and tips for better nutrition during treatment.* NIH pub. no. 80-2079.

Newell, G. R., and Ellison, N. M. 1981. Nutrition and cancer: etiology and treatment. Vol. 17. In *Progress in cancer research and therapy.* New York: Raven Press.

Nielsen, S. S., et al. 1980. Influence of food odors on

food aversions and preferences in patients with cancer. *Amer. J. Clin. Nutr.* 33:2253.

Regezi, J. A., et al. 1976. Dental management of patients irradiated for oral cancer. *Cancer* 38:994.

Remington, J. S., and Schimpff, S. C. 1981. Occasional notes: please don't eat the salads. *N. Engl. J. Med.* 304:433.

Rickard, K. A., et al. 1980. Effectiveness of enteral and parenteral nutrition in the nutritional management of children with Wilms' tumors. *Amer. J. Clin. Nutr.* 33:2622.

Rosenbaum, E. H., and Rosenbaum, I. R. 1980. Principles of home care for the patient with advanced cancer. *J.A.M.A.* 244:1484.

Rosenbaum, E. H., et al. 1980. *Nutrition for the cancer patient.* Palo Alto, Calif.: Bull Publishing.

Schreier, A. M., and Lavenia, J. 1977. The nurse's role in nutritional management of radiotherapy patients. *Nurs. Clin. N.A.* 12:173.

Segaloff, A. 1981. Managing endocrine and metabolic problems in the patient with advanced cancer. *J.A.M.A.* 245:177.

Silberman, J. 1980. Hyperalimentation in patients with cancer. *Gyn. Obs.* 150:755.

Sloan, G. M., et al. 1981. Nutritional effects of surgery, radiation therapy, and adjuvant chemotherapy for soft tissue sarcomas. *Amer. J. Clin. Nutr.* 34:1094.

Theologides, A. 1977. Nutritional management of the patient with advanced cancer. *Postgrad. Med.* 61:97.

———. 1979. Cancer cachexia. *Cancer* 43:2004.

Theologides, A., et al. 1976. Food intake of patients with advanced cancer. *Minn. Med.* 59:526.

Van Eys, J., et al., eds. 1979. *Nutrition and cancer: monographs of the American College of Nutrition.* Vol. 3. New York: SP Medical and Scientific Books.

Welch, D. 1981. Nutrition consequences of carcinogenesis and radiation therapy. *J. Amer. Dietet. Assoc.* 78:467.

CHAPTER 30

Pediatrics

Authasen, T. R., and Lesh, D. 1973. Parents need TLC too. *Hospitals* 47:88.

Farrel, E., Sr. and Kierhan, B. S. 1977. A positive approach to nutrition for hospitalized children. *Am. J. Matern. Child Nurs.* 2:113.

Glany, K. 1979. Strategies for nutritional counseling. *J. Amer. Dietet. Assoc.* 74:431.

Hoekelman, R. A., et al. 1978. *Principles of pediatrics: health care of the young.* New York: McGraw-Hill.

Magrath, H. L. 1981. Nursing pediatric burns from a growth and development perspective. In *Care of the burned-injured patient,* ed. M. M. Wagner. Littleton, Mass.: Publishing Science Group.

McFarlane, et al. 1980. *Contemporary pediatric nursing: a conceptual approach.* New York: Wiley.

Mead, J. 1973. The lemonade party. *Nurs. Outlook* 21:104.

Parsons, H. G., et al. 1980. The nutritional status of hospitalized children. *Amer. J. Clin. Nutr.* 33:1140.

Petrillo, M., and Sanger, S. 1980. *Emotional care of hospitalized children: an environmental approach.* Philadelphia: Lippincott.

Pediatric Nutrition

American Academy of Pediatrics. 1979. *Pediatric nutrition handbook.* Evanston, Ill.

Foman, S. J. 1974. *Infant nutrition.* 2nd ed. Philadelphia: Saunders.

Lebenthal, E., ed. 1981. *Textbook of gastroenterology and nutrition in infancy.* New York: Raven Press.

Suskind, R. M., ed. 1981. *Textbook of pediatric nutrition.* New York: Raven Press.

Wood, C. B. S., and Walker-Smith, J. A. 1981. *MacKeith's infant feeding and feeding difficulties.* New York: Churchill Livingstone.

Obesity (see also References for Chapter 14)

Copeland, E. T., Jr., and Copeland, S. B. 1981. Childhood obesity: a family systems view. *Am. Family Physician* 24:153.

Crnic, K. A., et al. 1980. Preventing mental retardation associated with gross obesity in the Prader-Willi syndrome. *Pediatrics* 66:787.

Feig, B. K. 1980. *The parents' guide to weight control for children ages 5 to 13 years.* Springfield, Ill.: Thomas.

Holm, V. A., et al. 1980. *The Prader-Willi syndrome.* Baltimore: University Park Press.

Winick, M., ed. 1975. *Childhood obesity.* New York: Wiley.

Allergy (see also References for Chapter 31)

Bahna, S. L. 1978. Control of milk allergy: a challenge for physicians, mothers and industry. *Ann. Allergy* 41:1.

Hill, D. J., et al. 1979. The spectrum of cow's milk allergy in childhood. *Acta Paediatr. Scand.* 68:847.

Iyngkaran, N., et al. 1979. Acquired carbohydrate intolerance and cow milk–sensitive enteropathy in young infants. *J. Pediatr.* 95:373.

Johnstone, D. E., and Dutton, A. M. 1966. Dietary prophylaxis of allergic disease in children. *N. Engl. J. Med.* 274:715.

Nutr. Rev. 1978. Breast feeding and avoidance of food allergens in the prevention and management of allergic disease. 36:181.

Total Parenteral Nutrition

Candy, D. C. A. 1980. Parenteral nutrition in pediatric practice: a review. *J. Human Nutr.* 34:287.

James, B. E. 1979. Total parenteral nutrition of premature infants. 1. Requirements for macronutritional elements. 2. Requirements for micronutritional elements. *Aust. Paed. J.* 15:67.

Levy, J. S., et al. 1980. Total parenteral nutrition in pediatric patients. *Ped. in Rev.* 2:99.

Smith, L. 1981. The use of intravenous fat emulsions in the critically ill neonate. *Nutr. Sup. Serv.* 1, No. 3:17.

Diabetes (see References for Chapter 26)

High-Risk and Chronically Ill Infants

American Academy of Pediatrics. 1977. Nutritional needs of low-birth-weight infants. *Pediatrics* 60:519.

Barness, L. A. 1975. Nutrition for the low birth-weight infant. *Clin. Perinatol.* 2:349.

Hack, M., et al. 1979. The low birth weight infant. Evaluation of a changing outlook. *N. Engl. J. Med.* 301:1152.

Heird, W. C., and Driscoll, J. M. 1975. Newer methods for feeding low birth-weight infants. *Clin. Perinatol.* 2:323.

Klaus, M. H., and Fanaroff, A. A. 1979. *Care of the high-risk neonate.* 2nd ed. Philadelphia: Saunders.

Richard, K. 1977. Nutritional management of the chronically ill child. *Ped. Clin. N.A.* 24:157.

Richard, K., et al. 1976. Care of children with conditions characterized by high nutritional risks. *J. Amer. Dietet. Assoc.* 68:546.

Richard, K., and Gresham, E. 1975. Nutritional considerations for the newborn requiring intensive care. *J. Amer. Dietet. Assoc.* 66:594.

Shaw, J. C. L. 1974. Malnutrition in the very low-birth-weight, pre-term infants. *Proc. Nutr. Soc.* 33:103.

U.S. Department of Health, Education, and Welfare. 1980. *Factors associated with low birth weight, United States, 1976.* USDHEW pub. no. (PHS) 80-1915, Series 21, no. 37. Washington, D.C. Public Health Service.

Warshaw, J. B., and Uauy, R. 1975. Identification of nutritional deficiency and failure to thrive in the newborn. *Clin. Perinatol.* 2:328.

Gastroenterology

Frantz, I. D. 1975. Necrotizing enterocolitis. *J. Pediatr.* 86:259–63.

Herbst, J. J. 1976. CHO malabsorption in NEC. *Pediatriacs* 57:201.

Kraut, J. R., and Lloyd-Still, J. D. 1980. The l-hr. blood xylose test in the evaluation of malabsorption in infants and children. *Amer. J. Clin. Nutr.* 33:2328.

Liebman, W. 1980. *Pediatric gastroenterology.* Garden City, N. Y.: Medical Examination Publishing.

Cardiovascular Diseases

Berenson, G. S. 1980. *Cardiovascular risk factors in children: the early history of atherosclerosis and essential hypertension.* New York: Oxford University Press.

Berwick, D. M., et al. 1980. *Cholesterol, children and heart disease, an analysis of alternatives.* New York: Oxford University Press.

Cystic Fibrosis

Barry, M. M. 1979. Cystic fibrosis. *J. Amer. Dietet. Assoc.* 75:446.

Chase, H. P., and Lavin, M. H. 1979. Cystic fibrosis and malnutrition. *J. Pediatr.* 95:337.

Dann, L. G., and Blau, K. 1978. Exocrine-gland function and the basic biochemical defect in cystic fibrosis. *Lancet* 2:405.

Gurwitz, D. 1979. Perspectives in cystic fibrosis. *Ped. Clin. N.A.* 26:603.

Lloyd-Still, J. D., et al. 1981. Essential fatty acid status in cystic fibrosis and the effects of safflower oil supplementation. *Amer. J. Clin. Nutr.* 34:1.

Shwachman, H., et al. 1977. Cystic fibrosis: a new outlook. *Medicine* 56:129.

Wood, R. E. 1979. Cystic fibrosis: diagnosis, treatment, and prognosis. *South. Med. J.* 72:189.

Kidney

Chantler, C., and Holliday, M. A. 1975. Growth in children with renal disease with particular reference to the effects of calorie malnutrition: a review. *Clin. Nephrol.* 1:230–42.

Chantler, C., et al. 1980. Ten years experience with regular haemodialysis and renal transplantation. *Arch. Dis. Child.* 55:435.

Fine, R. N. 1981. Treatment of end stage renal disease in children. *Ped. Ann.* 10:15.

Hetrick, A., et al. 1979. Nutrition in renal disease when the patient is a child. *Am. J. Nurs.* 79:2152.

Holliday, M. A., and Chantler, C. 1978. Metabolic and nutritional factors in children with renal insufficiency. *Kidney Int.* 14:306.

Munro, H. N. 1980. Nutritional requirements for health: their relevance to tissue function in renal failure. *Amer. J. Clin. Nutr.* 33:1555.

Spinozzi, N. S., and Grupe, W. E. 1977. Nutritional implications of renal disease. *J. Amer. Dietet. Assoc.* 70:493.

Diarrhea

Chernoff, R., and Dean, J. A. 1980. Medical and nutritional aspects of intractable diarrhea. *J. Amer. Dietet. Assoc.* 76:161.

Eastham, E. J., and Walker, W. A. 1979. Adverse effect of milk formula ingestion on the gastrointestinal tract: an update. *Gastroenterology* 76:365.

Fisher, S. E., et al. 1981. Chronic protracted diarrhea: intolerance to dietary glucose polymers. *Pediatrics* 67:271.

Lloyd-Still, J. B. 1979. Chronic diarrhea of childhood and the misuse of elimination diets. *J. Pediatr.* 95:10.

MacLean, W. C., et al. 1980. Nutritional management of chronic diarrhea and malnutrition: primary reliance of oral feeding. *J. Pediatr.* 97:316.

McGrath, B. J. 1980. Fluid, electrolyte and replacement therapy in pediatric nursing. *Am. J. Matern. Child Nurs.* 5:58.

Inborn Errors of Metabolism

Acosta, P. B., and Elsas, L. J. 1976. *Dietary management of inherited metabolic disease.* Atlanta, Ga.: ACELMU Publ.

American Academy of Pediatrics, Committee on Nutrition. 1976. Special diets for infants with inborn errors of metabolism. *Pediatrics* 57:783.

Desnick, R. J. 1980. *Enzyme therapy in genetic disease: 2.* New York: Alan R. Liss.

National Academy of Sciences, National Research Council, Committee for the Study of Inborn Errors of Metabolism. 1975. *Genetic screening: programs, principles, and research.* p. 293. Washington, D.C.

Nyham, W. L., ed. 1974. *Heritable disorders of amino acid metabolism.* New York: Wiley.

Prader, A. 1973. Inborn errors of metabolism. *Biblio. Nutri. et Dieta*, no. 18.

Raine, N., ed. 1975. *The treatment of inherited metabolic disease.* New York: American Elsevier Publishing.

Stanbury, J. B., et al., eds. 1978. *The metabolic basis of inherited disease.* 4th ed. New York: McGraw-Hill.

Thompson, J. S., and Thompson, M. W. 1973. *Genetics in medicine.* 2nd ed. Philadelphia: Saunders.

Winick, M., ed. 1979. *Nutritional management of genetic disorders.* New York: Wiley.

Phenylketonuria

American Academy of Pediatrics. 1980. New developments in hyperphenylalaninemia. *Pediatrics* 65:844.

Lenke, R. R., and Levy, H. L. 1980. Maternal phenylketonuria and hyperphenylalaninemia: an international survey of the outcomes of untreated and treated pregnancies. *N. Engl. J. Med.* 303:1202.

Marino, M. A. 1980. Developing and testing a programmed instruction unit on PKU. *J. Amer. Dietet. Assoc.* 76:29.

Meryash, D. L., et al. 1981. Prospective study of early neonatal screening for phenylketonuria. *N. Engl. J. Med.* 304:294.

Pueschel, S. M., et al. 1977. Nutritional management of the female with phenylketonuria during pregnancy. *Amer. J. Clin. Nutr.* 30:1153.

Reyzer, N. 1978. Diagnosis: PKU. *Am. J. Nurs.* 78:1895.

Scriver, C. R., and Clow, C. L. 1980. Phenylketonuria: epitome of human biochemical genetics. Parts 1 and 2. *N. Engl. J. Med.* 303:1336, 1394.

Mental and Developmental Disorders

Amary, I. B. 1979. *Effective meal planning and food preparation for the mentally retarded/developmentally disabled.* Springfield, Ill.: Thomas.

American Dietetic Association. 1981. Infant and child nutrition: concerns regarding the developmentally disabled. *J. Amer. Dietet. Assoc.* 78:443.

California Department of Health, Developmental Disabilities Program. 1974. *Nutrition and feeding techniques for handicapped children.* Sacramento, Calif.

Dufton-Gross, N. A. 1979. Nutrition intervention in a preschool for handicapped children. *J. Amer. Dietet. Assoc.* 75:154.

John F. Kennedy Institute for Handicapped Children, Nutrition Division. 1982. *Eating for good health.* Baltimore.

Palmer, S., and Ekvall, S., eds. 1978. *Pediatric nutrition in developmental disorders.* Springfield, Ill.: Thomas.

Scheiner, A. P., and Abroms, I. F. 1980. *The practical management of the developmentally disabled child.* St. Louis: Mosby.

Wood, C. B. S., and Walker-Smith, J. A. 1981. *MacKeith's infant feeding and feeding difficulties.* New York: Churchill Livingstone.

CHAPTER 31

Rehabilitation and Handicaps

American Heart Association. N.d. *Do it yourself again—self-help devices for the stroke patient.* Dallas.

Am. J. Nurs. 1979. The brain-damaged patient: approaches to assessment, care, and rehabilitation. 79:2117.

Bennett, A. 1980. Weight therapy as part of rehabilitation. *Health Soc. Work.* 5:44.

Blakeslee, M. 1981. *The wheelchair gourmet: a cookbook for the handicapped.* Ontario, Canada: General Publishing, Don Mills.

Cornelius, M. S. 1975. Feeding handicapped patients. *J. Amer. Dietet. Assoc.* 67:136.

Dehn, M. M. 1980. Rehabilitation of the cardiac patient: the effects of exercise. *Am. J. Nurs.* 80:435.

Devney, A. M. 1980. Rehabilitation of the cardiac patient: bridging the gap between in-hospital and outpatient care. *Am. J. Nurs.* 80:446.

Fleming, W. C. 1980. Guidelines for rehabilitation after paralytic stroke. *Consultant* 20:234.

Hoepfel-Harris, J. A. 1980. Rehabilitation of the cardiac patient: improving compliance with an exercise program. *Am. J. Nurs.* 80:449.

Peiffer, S. C., et al. 1981. Nutritional assessment of the spinal cord injured patient. *J. Amer. Dietet. Assoc.* 78:501.

Pershe, R., et al., eds. 1977. *Mealtimes for severely and profoundly handicapped persons.* Baltimore: University Park Press.

Ryerson Polytechnical Institute. 1981. *Food and nutrition for the disabled.* Toronto, Canada: Library Publications.

Sister Kenny Institute. N.d. *Adaptations and techniques for the disabled homemaker.* Minneapolis.

Immobilization

Claus-Walker, J., et al. 1975. Hypercalcemia in early traumatic quadriplegia. *J. Chronic Dis.* 28:81.

Hyman, L. R., et al. 1972. Immobilization hypercalcemia. *Am. J. Dis. Child.* 124:723.

Nutr. Rev. 1972. Effect of bed rest on bone mineral loss. 30:11.

Winslow, E. H., and Weber, T. M. 1980. Rehabilitation of the cardiac patient: progressive exercise to combat the hazards of bed rest. *Am. J. Nurs.* 80:440.

Elderly and Chronically Ill Patients

Allington, J. K., et al. 1980. A short method to ensure nutritional adequacy of food served in nursing homes. I. Identification of need. II. Development of a model food plan. *J. Amer. Dietet. Assoc.* 76:458.

Burnside, I. M., ed. 1980. *Nursing and the aged.* New York: McGraw-Hill.

Denham, M. J., ed. 1980. In *The treatment of medical problems in the elderly. Current status of modern therapy.* Vol. 3. Baltimore: University Park Press.

Goldberg, P. Z. 1980. *So what if you can't chew, eat hearty!* Springfield, Ill.: Thomas.

Good, S. R., and Rodgers, S. S. 1980. *Analysis for action: nursing care of the elderly.* Englewood Cliffs, N.J.: Prentice-Hall.

Green, K. B. 1978. Coping daily with the handicapped and the elderly. *J. Home Econ.* 70:15.

Klinger, J. L., et al. 1978. *Mealtime manual for people with disabilities and the aging.* Camden, N.J.: Campbell Soup Company.

Kocher, R. E. 1975. Monitoring nutritional care of the long-term patient. I. Policies and systems that support the on-going evaluation of care. *J. Amer. Dietet. Assoc.* 67:45.

Manning, A. M., and Means, J. G. 1975. A self-feeding program for geriatric patients in a skilled nursing facility. *J. Amer. Dietet. Assoc.* 66:275.

O'Hara-Devereaux, et al., eds. 1981. *Eldercare: a practical guide to clinical geriatrics.* New York: Grune & Stratton.

Owen, L. J., et al. 1979. *Dietary lesson plans for health care facilities.* Rochester, Minn.: Rochester Methodist Hospital, Learning Resources Department.

Pearson, L. J., and Kotthoff, M. E. 1979. *Geriatric clinical protocols.* Philadelphia: Lippincott.

Poleman, C. M. 1975. Monitoring nutritional care of the long-term patient. II. Experiences at the Mercy Health and Rehabilitation Center, Auburn, New York. *J. Amer. Dietet. Assoc.* 67:47.

Reichel, W., ed. 1981. *Topics in aging and long-term care.* Baltimore: Williams & Wilkins.

Robbins, A. S., et al. 1981. *Geriatric medicine: an education resource guide.* Cambridge, Mass.: Ballinger.

Schwartz, D. 1960. Nursing needs of chronically ill ambulatory patients. *Nurs. Res.* 9:185.

Schwartz, D., et al. 1964. *The elderly ambulatory patient: nursing and psychosocial needs.* New York: Macmillan.

Wainwright, H. 1978. Feeding problems in elderly disabled patients. *Nurs. Times* 34:542.

Weber, H. I. 1980. *Nursing care of the elderly.* Reston, Va: Reston Publishing.

Anorexia Nervosa

Bruch, H. 1973. *Eating disorders: obesity, anorexia nervosa and the person within.* New York: Basic Books.

Crisp, A. H. 1980. *Anorexia nervosa: let me be.* London: Academic Press.

Dally, P., and Gomez, J. 1979. *Anorexia nervosa.* London: William Heinemann Medical Books.

Day, S. 1974. Dietary management of anorexia nervosa. *Nutrition* 28:289.

Gull, W. W. 1974. Anorexia nervosa. *Trans. Clin. Soc.* (London) 7:22.

Lucas, A. R. 1981. Bulimia and vomiting syndrome. *Contemp. Nutr.* 6:1.

Olson, D., et al. 1981. Self-inflicted weight loss and subsequent refeeding. *J. Amer. Dietet. Assoc.* 78:505.

Vigersky, R. A., ed. 1977. *Anorexia nervosa.* New York: Raven Press.

Food Allergy

American Dietetic Association. N.d. *Allergy recipes.* Chicago, Ill.

Bahna, S. I., and Heiner, D. C. 1980. *Allergies to milk.* New York: Grune & Stratton.

Chicago Dietetic Supply, Inc. N.d. *Dietary information for allergy patients.* LaGrange, Ill.

Criep, L. H. 1976. *Allergy and clinical immunology.* New York: Grune & Stratton.

Douglas, J. M. 1980. Psoriasis and diet. *West. J. Med.* 133:450.

Finn, R., and Cohen, H. N. 1978. "Food allergy": fact or fiction. *Lancet* 1:426.

Frazier, C. A. 1974. *Coping with food allergy.* New York: Quadrangle Books, New York Times Company.

Gerrard, J. W., ed. 1980. *Food allergy: new perspectives.* Springfield, Ill.: Thomas.

Good Housekeeping. 125 great recipes for allergy diets. New York.

May, C. D. 1980. Food allergy: perspective, principles, practical management. *Nutr. Today* 15:28.

Middleton, E., Jr., et al., eds. 1978. *Allergy, principles and practice.* Vol. 2. St. Louis: Mosby.

Parker, C. 1980. Food allergies. *Am. J. Nurs.* 80:262.

Randolph, T. G. 1974. Dynamics, diagnosis, and treatment of food allergy. *Otolaryngol. Clin. N.A.* 7:617.

Rudoff, C. 1980. *The allergy baker.* Menlo Park, Calif.: Prologue Publications.

Sly, R. M. 1981. *Pediatric allergy.* New York: Medical Examination Publishing.

Thomas, L. L. 1980. *Caring and cooking for the allergic child.* New York: Sterling Publishing.

U.S. Department of Agriculture. N.d. *Baking for people with food allergies.* Home & Garden Bulletin, no. 147.

Infectious Diseases

Beisel, W. R. 1980. Effects of infection on nutritional status and immunity. *Fed. Proc.* 39:3105.

Beisel, W. R., and Wannemacher, J. R. 1980. Gluconeogenesis, ureagenesis, and ketogenesis during sepsis. *J. Parent. Ent. Nutr.* 4:277.

Beisel, W. R., et al. 1981. Single-nutrient effects on immunologic functions. *J.A.M.A.* 245:53.

Bistrian, B. R. 1977. Interaction of nutrition and infection in the hospital setting. *Amer. J. Clin. Nutr.* 30:1226.

———. 1981. The metabolic response to yellow fever immunization—protein-sparing modified fast. *Amer. J. Clin. Nutr.* 34:229.

Bistrian, B. R., et al. 1975. Effect of mild infectious illness on nitrogen metabolism in patients on a modified fast. *Amer. J. Clin. Nutr.* 28:1044.

———. 1980. Cellular immunity in semistarved states in hospitalized patients. *Amer. J. Clin. Nutr.* 33:2211.

Chandra, R. K. 1980. Cell-mediated immunity in nutritional imbalance. *Fed. Proc.* 39:3088.

Chandra, R. K., and Scrimshaw, N. S. 1980. Immunocompetence in nutritional assessment. *Amer. J. Clin. Nutr.* 33:2694.

Christou, N. V., and Meakins, J. L. 1979. Delayed hypersensitivity, a mechanism for energy in surgical patients. *Surgery* 86:78.

Christou, N. V., et al. 1981. The predictive role of delayed hypersensitivity in preoperative patients. *Surg. Gynecol. Obstet.* 152:297.

Clowes, G. H. A., et al. 1978. Blood insulin responses to blood glucose levels in high output sepsis and septic shock. *Am. J. Surg.* 135:577.

———. 1980. Amino acid and energy metabolism in septic and traumatized patients. *J. Parent. Ent. Nutr.* 4:195.

Dionigi, R., et al. 1979. Nutrition and infection. *J. Parent. Ent. Nutr.* 3:62.

Freund, H. R., et al. 1978. Amino acid derangements in patients with sepsis: treatment with branched chain amino acid rich infusions. *Ann. Surg.* 188:423.

Good, R. A., et al. 1980. Nutritional modulation of immune responses. *Fed. Proc.* 39:3098.

Gunby, P. 1980. Closing in on the nutrition-immunity link. *J.A.M.A.* 244:2715.

Koster, F., et al. 1981. Recovery of cellular immune competence during treatment of protein-calorie malnutrition. 34:887.

Long, C. L. 1977a. Whole body protein synthesis and catabolism in septic man. *Amer. J. Clin. Nutr.* 30:1341.

———. 1977b. Energy balance and carbohydrate metabolism in infection and sepsis. *Amer. J. Clin. Nutr.* 30:1301.

McMurray, D. N., et al. 1981. Development of impaired cell-mediated immunity in mild and moderate malnutrition. *Amer. J. Clin. Nutr.* 34:68.

Meakins, J. L., et al. 1977. Indicator of acquired failure of host defense in sepsis and trauma. *Ann. Surg.* 186:241.

Newman, C. G. 1977. Interaction of malnutrition and infection—a neglected clinical concept. *Arch. Intern. Med.* 137:1364.

Nichols, B. L., et al. 1981. Electrolyte metabolism in rhesus monkeys with experimental salmonella sepsis. *Amer. J. Clin. Nutr.* 34:1362.

Oill, P. A., et al. 1976. Infectious disease emergencies. Part III: Patients presenting with respiratory distress syndromes. *West. J. Med.* 125:452.

Rhoads, J. E. 1980. The impact of nutrition on infection. *Surg. Clin. N.A.* 60:41.

Stiehm, E. R. 1980. Humoral immunity in malnutrition. *Fed. Proc.* 39:3093.

Wannemacher, R. W., Jr. 1977. Key role of various individual amino acids in host response to infection. *Amer. J. Clin. Nutr.* 30:1269.

Appendix G

Glossary

acid/base balance The relationship of acidity to alkalinity in the body fluids, normally slightly alkaline

acidosis High acidity in body fluids

acrodermatitis enteropathica A rare genetic disorder involving a severe zinc deficiency (from malabsorption?)

adenosine triphosphate The high-energy phosphate molecule which is the major form of stored energy in the human body. Abbreviated "ATP"

alanine A nonessential amino acid

albumin An important blood protein, also found in egg white, milk, etc.

alimentary canal The mucous-membrane lined tube of the digestive system, from mouth to the anus

alkalosis Excess alkalinity of body fluids

allergen The substance that triggers an allergic reaction. Also called "antigen"

allergy An altered immunological state in which pathological reactions are induced by an antigen

Amanita The major family of toxic mushrooms in the United States

amino acids The structural units of protein molecules

amylopectin A constituent of starch, composed of many glucose units joined in branching patterns

amylose A constituent of starch, consisting of many glucose units joined linearly without branching

anabolism The metabolic process within the cells whereby metabolites (e.g., nutrients) are used to synthesize new materials for cellular growth, maintenance, or repair

anemia Pathological deficiency of oxygen-carrying material in the blood

anion A negatively charged electrolyte

anorexia The loss of appetite

anorexia nervosa A disorder in which a person refuses food and loses a lot of weight

anthropometric The physical measurements of parts of the body, e.g., height, weight, head circumference, chest circumference, etc.

antioxidant A chemical that can prevent oxidation

arachidic acid A saturated fatty acid

arachidonic acid An essential polyunsaturated fatty acid

arginine An amino acid known to be essential for infants and children

aseptic sterilization One method of sterilizing infant formulas

ash The non-combustible mineral residue left after a substance has been oxidized

asparagine A nonessential amino acid

aspartic acid A nonessential amino acid

atherosclerosis Thickening of the lining of blood vessels as lipid materials are deposited and covered by fibrous connective tissues

atrophy The wasting of tissues

avidin A heat-sensitive glycoprotein found in raw egg

white, which can complex with biotin, rendering it unavailable for absorption

basal metabolic rate The least amount of energy required by an individual's body at rest to keep the essential life processes functioning; abbreviated "BMR"

behenic acid A saturated fatty acid

beriberi A syndrome describing vitamin B_1 deficiency

BHA Butylated hydroxyanisole, a controversial antioxidant used commercially to prevent rancidity in fats

BHT Butylated hydroxytoluene, a controversial antioxidant used commercially to prevent rancidity in fats

bile The substance stored in the gallbladder and is especially important in fat digestion

bilirubin A bile pigment that is produced when hemoglobin is broken down in the turnover of red blood cells

bioflavonoids Substances in fruits and vegetables for which certain therapeutic effects have been claimed but not substantiated

biological value The degree to which a protein contains all essential amino acids in the proportions needed by the body

biotin A water-soluble vitamin and part of the B vitamin complex

bomb calorimeter A device in which food samples are oxidized to determine their energy content

botulism Food poisoning caused by ingestion of *Clostridium botulinum*, a bacterium found mainly in improperly home-canned foods. Can be fatal

butyric acid A saturated fatty acid

cachexia General wasting of the body, especially during chronic disease

calorie The amount of heat energy that will raise the temperature of 1 gm of water from 15 °C to 16 °C

capric acid A saturated fatty acid

caproic acid A saturated fatty acid

caprylic acid A saturated fatty acid

carbohydrate An organic compound containing carbon, hydrogen, and oxygen, with a ratio of carbon to hydrogen to oxygen atoms of $1:2:1$

carcinogenic Cancer-causing

cardiovascular Involving the heart and blood vessels

carotene The precursor of vitamin A, found in plant products

casein Major protein in milk, cheese, and eggs

catabolism Conversion of larger (organized) substances in body into smaller (simpler) ones. The destructive part of metabolism (= catabolism + anabolism)

cation A positively charged electrolyte

celiac disease A syndrome resulting from intestinal (small) sensitivity to gluten, a protein in flour

cellulose A polysaccharide made of many glucose molecules and not digestible by man

cheilosis Cracks at the corners of the mouth with yellow crusts, a symptom of deficiency of vitamin B_2, folic acid, vitamin B_{12}, or niacin

chemically defined diet See defined-formula diet

cholecalciferol One chemical form of vitamin D

cholesterol One chemical form of fat, found only in animal products and suspected to play a role in heart disease

choline A substance normally synthesized in the body, important in the biochemistry of metabolism and closely associated with the physiology of vitamins

chylomicron A large, low-density molecule consisting mostly of triglycerides. Its main function is to transport fat in the body, primarily in the form of triglycerides

citric acid cycle The series of chemical reactions whereby carbohydrate, fat, and/or protein are completely oxidized to carbon dioxide, water, and energy. Also called the "Krebs cycle"

clear liquid diet A diet consisting of fluids that are liquid at body temperature, with mono- and disaccharides as the major sources of calories

Clostridium perfringens A bacterium which, when present in great numbers in food, may cause nausea, diarrhea, and acute inflammation of the stomach and intestines

cobalamin Vitamin B_{12}, important in all cell metabolism, tissue growth, and maintenance of the central nervous system

cobamide coenzyme The biologically active form of vitamin B_{12}

coenzyme An accessory substance that facilitates the working of an enzyme, largely by acting as a carrier for products of the chemical reaction

coenzyme A A critical substance in the metabolism of fat, protein, and carbohydrate (it participates in the citric acid cycle and permits the release of energy) which also has other essential functions in the body. Abbreviated CoA. Also see CoQ or Coenzyme Q

coenzyme Q A fat-soluble vitamin-like substance found in most living cells. A perfect biological catalyst, it is an important component of the respiratory chain. Abbreviated CoQ

collagen An insoluble protein that holds together the cells and tissues of skin, cartilage, tendons, ligaments, bones, teeth, and blood vessels

colostomy Surgical creation of an opening between the colon and the surface of the body, usually by establishing a stoma in the abdominal wall

colostrum The thick yellowish fluid that precedes white breast milk, suspected to provide infant with passive immunity

complementary proteins Protein foods which are individually incomplete but which when combined correct each other's deficiencies in essential amino acids

core eating plan On a weight loss diet, specification of the approximate number of servings of each category of food to be consumed daily

creatine A nitrogenous chemical derived from three amino acids. In its phosphorylated form, it supplies energy for muscle contraction

creatine phosphate An energy-rich phosphate compound in muscle tissue

creatinine A nitrogenous substance in the urine derived from the catabolism of creatine

cretinism Retardation of infants and children in physical and mental development, associated with a lack of iodine

cysteine A nonessential amino acid

cystic fibrosis An inherited disease of the mucous glands which usually develops during childhood, creating pancreatic insufficiency and lung problems

cystine Though classified as a nonessential amino acid, a substance derived from the essential amino acid methionine

daily food guide A translation of Recommended Daily Allowances into simple-to-follow recommendations of the kinds and amounts of food needed for good nutrition

defined formula diet A commercially-prepared formula for artificial feeding which is considered nutritionally complete. Also called chemically defined diet or elemental diet

dehydration Excessive loss of water from the body; also called "underhydration"

dextran A polysaccharide made of many glucose molecules, with potential clinical usages. Does not occur naturally in food

dextrin A small polysaccharide of five to six glucose units, found in the leaves of starch-forming plants and in the human alimentary canal as a product of starch digestion

diabetes mellitus A disease characterized by excess blood sugar and urine sugar. Caused mostly by a malfunctioning pancreas

dialysis Diffusion of dissolved particles from one side of a semipermeable membrane to the other

dietetics The science and art of human nutrition care

diffusion Movement of a substance from a location of higher concentration to one of lower concentration

digestion The breaking down of ingested foods into particles of a size and chemical composition that the body can readily absorb

digestive system The long tube including the mouth, esophagus, stomach, small intestine, colon, rectum, and associated organs such as pancreas. These structural units and their secretions break food down into units absorbable by the body

diglyceride A glyceride with two molecules of fatty acids

dipeptide Two amino acids chemically joined

disaccharide A carbohydrate composed of two monosaccharides

disaccharidase An enzyme responsible for hydrolysis of disaccharides to monosaccharides in the duodenum, jejunum, and ileum

diuretic A substance that increases urine excretion

diverticulum A blind pouch in the colon, usually developed from some clinical disorders

dumping syndrome A set of symptoms occurring when food passes into the jejunum without first undergoing normal digestion and mixing by the stomach because of partial or complete surgical removal of stomach

dysphagia Difficulty in swallowing

edema The presence of an abnormally high amount of fluid in the intercellular spaces; also called "overhydration"

edentulous Lacking teeth previously present

electrolyte A substance that is a charged particle or is separated into charged particles when dissolved in fluid

elimination diet In attempts to diagnose food allergy, the progression from a basal diet that is expected to be nonallergenic through the gradual addition of foods one at a time. Each food added that does not cause an allergic reaction is eliminated from consideration as a possible allergen

-emia A suffix indicating the blood

emulsifier A substance that helps foods to mix

energy The capacity to do work

enrichment The addition of nutrients to foods; for example, to restore what has been lost through processing

enter- A prefix indicating intestine

enteral feeding Feeding in which nutrients are delivered to the body via the gastrointestinal tract. May be accomplished by various means including tube-feeding

enterohepatic circulation The cycling of bile salts through the liver, gallbladder, intestinal lumen, portal vein, and liver again

enzyme A protein that catalyzes a specific chemical reaction or a few specific reactions in the body

epidemiology The study of the incidence, distribution, and control of a certain disease or pathogen in a population

ergosterol The form of vitamin D found in plant products

erucic acid A monounsaturated fatty acid

Escherichia coli A pathogenic bacterium which can cause intestinal infection

essential Referring to a nutrient that the body needs but is unable to synthesize from ordinary foods

essential amino acid One of the 8 to 10 amino acids that the human body cannot manufacture and that must therefore be consumed in foods

essential fatty acids The polyunsaturated fatty acids lineoleic acid and linolenic acid, which cannot be synthesized by the body and must therefore be consumed in the diet

extracellular Located outside a cell or cells

fat An organic compound whose molecules contain glycerol and fatty acids. Also used in referring to adipose tissue

fatty acid A constituent of fat, a simple lipid containing only carbon, hydrogen, and oxygen

favism A clinical disorder associated with the eating of fava or broad beans by people with an inherited deficiency of glucose-6-phosphate dehydrogenase

fiber Indigestible carbohydrate found in plant foods and connective tissues of meats. Also known as "roughage" or "bulk"

flavor enhancer A substance that can modify or magnify the flavor of foods without contributing any flavor of its own, such as MSG

folic acid Part of the B vitamin complex, a substance which participates in many essential biological reactions in its coenzyme form; also called "folacin"

Food Exchange Lists Groups of food in which each group or list contains selected foods, each of which contributes approximately equal amounts of certain nutrients and calories. The American Diabetes Association and the American Dietetic Association originated the Food Exchange Lists for diabetic patients

foodborne infection The consumption of food containing enough live bacteria to produce sufficient toxin in the intestine to poison the person who has eaten it

foodborne intoxication The consumption of a food in which pathogenic bacteria have released toxins capable of poisoning the person who eats the food

fortification The addition of nutrients to foods to improve their nutritional value

foundation diet A diet consisting only of the recommended numbers of servings from the Four Food Groups

the Four Food Groups Milk and milk products, meats or meat equivalents, fruits and vegetables, and breads and cereals—the main groups of food now recommended for daily consumption

free amino acid An amino acid existing singly or in free form

fructose A simple carbohydrate found in many fruits, honey, and plant saps. One of the two monosaccharides forming sucrose (table sugar); also called "fruit sugar" or "levulose"

full liquid diet A liquid diet including certain foods and beverages that are liquid at body temperature

galactose A six-carbon monosaccharide usually occurring as one of the two components of lactose, or milk sugar

galactosemia An inherited form of faulty carbohydrate metabolism in which deficiency of a certain enzyme makes it impossible for galactose to be metabolized

gallstones An abnormal formation or precipitation of cholesterol crystals in the gallbladder. Can cause pain and maldigestion

gastritis Inflammation of the stomach, either chronic or acute

gastrointestinal bypass Surgical stapling of a portion of the stomach or removal of part of the intestine to reduce the amount of food eaten and/or absorbed and thus reduce caloric intake

gastrointestinal system See digestive system

globulin A form of protein occurring in blood plasma. Important in body's defense against infection

glossitis A smooth red tongue with flat, swollen or pebbled papillae, associated with deficiencies of vitamin B_2, folic acid, vitamin B_{12}, or niacin

glucagon A hormone that can stimulate insulin secretion

glucose A six-carbon monosaccharide found mostly in the blood in the human body, where it provides fuel for immediate energy when oxidized; also called "D-glucose," "fruit sugar," "corn sugar," and "dextrose"

glucose tolerance test A test used to ascertain how well a person tolerates an influx of glucose into the bloodstream, used to determine the presence of hyperglycemia or hypoglycemia. Abbreviated "GTT"

glutamic acid A nonessential amino acid

glutamine A nonessential amino acid

glyceride A simple lipid, an ester of fatty acids and glycerol

glycine A nonessential amino acid

glycogen The polysaccharide form in which energy is stored in an animal; sometimes called "animal starch"

glycolysis The degradation of glucose to pyruvate and/or lactate

goiter A lack of iodine, resulting in enlargement of the thyroid gland

goitrogen A substance capable of inducing goiter

hematuria Blood in the urine

hemocellulose A form of indigestible carbohydrate found in plant foods

hemoglobin The iron-containing protein in red blood cells which carries oxygen to the tissues

hemolytic Causing blood elements (e.g., red blood cells) to disintegrate

heparin A polysaccharide used as a blood anti-coagulant

hepatic Pertaining to the liver

hepatic encephalopathy A disorder caused by failure of the liver to remove toxic waste. Also called "portal system encephalopathy"

hexoses Six-carbon sugars, such as glucose, fructose, galactose, and mannose

high density lipoprotein One type of cholesterol carrier in the blood: that which removes deposited cholesterol and carries it away for excretion

high nutrient diet A diet made of nutritionally potent liquids and semi-solid foods of a consistency that can be taken as a beverage or through a straw. Also called "modified full liquid diet"

histidine An amino acid known to be essential for infants and children, and perhaps essential for adults as well

humectant A substance that helps food products maintain moistness

hydrogenation The commercial process by which oils with a high level of unsaturated fatty acids are turned into fats with soft to hard texture

hydrolyze To break down a chemical compound by adding water

hyper- A prefix indicating an abnormal excess

hyperalimentation An aggressive feeding process whereby a large amount of nutrients is provided the patient through intravenous feeding

hypercalcemia An excess of calcium in the blood

hypercalciuria Excretion of a large amount of calcium in the urine

hyperglycemia A high blood "sugar" (glucose) level

hyperkalemia An elevated serum level of potassium

hyperlipidemia An elevated level of lipids in the blood serum

hyperlipoproteinemia An elevated level of certain lipoproteins in the blood

hypertension Sustained elevation of systolic and/or diastolic arterial blood pressure

hypertonic Referring to a solution with higher osmolarity than human body fluid

hypo- A prefix indicating an abnormal insufficiency

hypocalcemia A low level of calcium in the blood

hypoglycemia A low blood "sugar" (glucose) level

hypokalemia A decreased serum potassium level

hypoproteinemia An abnormal decrease of protein in the blood

hypotonic Referring to a solution with lower osmolarity than human body fluid

ileostomy Surgical creation of an opening into the ileum, usually by establishing an ileal stoma on the abdominal wall

incomplete protein A protein in which one or more of the essential amino acids is missing or occurs in limited quantity

inorganic Composed of material other than plant or animal in origin

inositol An alcohol form of glucose sometimes called "muscle sugar" because of its high concentration in hair and muscle tissues. Its exact function in the human body is unknown

insensible loss The constant but invisible evaporation of moisture from the skin surface

insulin A pancreatic hormone which controls the body's use of glucose

insulin pump A small portable device which continually delivers a measured flow of short-acting insulin to an insulin-dependent diabetic

intra- A prefix meaning within or inside of

intracellular Located inside a cell or cells

intravenous Within a blood vein or veins

intrinsic factor A mucoprotein in the gastric juice which combines with vitamin B_{12} and makes its absorption possible; lack of this substance results in pernicious anemia

inulin A polysaccharide made of many fructose units, which may not be digested by the human intestinal tract

isoleucine An essential amino acid

isotonic Referring to a solution with the same osmolarity as human body fluid

Joule One thousand joules: the amount of mechanical energy required when a force of 1 Newton moves 1 kilogram by a distance of 1 meter; preferred by some professionals over the heat energy measurements of the calorie system for calculating food energy. Sometimes referred to as "kilojoule," "Kilojoule," "kJ," or "KJ"

keratinization Degeneration of the epithelial cells (which cover most internal surfaces and organs and the outer surface of the body), a condition associated with vitamin A deficiency

ketone body Describes the three chemicals, acetone, acetoacetic acid, and β-hydroxybutyric acid

ketonuria The presence of ketone bodies in the urine

ketosis A condition in which fatty acids are incompletely oxidized, with resulting accumulation of ketone bodies

kilocalorie The preferred unit of measurement for food energy, equivalent to one thousand calories. Referred to as "Kilocalorie," "Calorie," "Kcal," or "Cal."

Kilojoule See *Joule*

koilonchia A condition in which fingernails and perhaps toenails become thin, flattened, lusterless, and spoon-shaped; associated with long-term iron deficiency

kwashiorkor The syndrome resulting from a severe deficiency in dietary protein, mild to moderate lack of other essential nutrients, but an adequate or even excessive intake of calories

lact-, lacto- A prefix indicating milk

lactase The enzyme that digests lactose in the intestine

lactation Milk secretion; child suckling; period of milk secretion

lacteal system Tiny lymph-carrying vessels that convey finely emulsified fat from the intestine to the thoracic duct

lacto-ovo-vegetarian An individual whose diet contains no meat, poultry, or fish, but does include milk and eggs

lactose The disaccharide made of glucose and galactose; often called "milk sugar"

L-ascorbic acid The chemically active form of vitamin C, a monosaccharide-like six-carbon substance

lathyrism Food poisoning from eating certain peas of the lathyrus family

lauric acid A saturated fatty acid

lean body mass In determining body composition, what is left after body fat is subtracted from the total body weight. Also referred to as the "fat-free body" or "body cell mass"

leavening agent A substance that helps dough to rise when baked

leucine An essential amino acid

lignins Certain forms of indigestible carbohydrate found in plant foods

limiting amino acids The amino acids that are deficient or missing in vegetable proteins, determining the extent to which the other amino acids present can be used by the body

linoleic acid An essential polyunsaturated fatty acid

linolenic acid An essential polyunsaturated fatty acid

lipectomy Surgical excision of a mass of subcutaneous fat tissue

lipids A term for fats

lipoic acid A substance not now classified as an essential vitamin for humans. Although it is a participant in many biochemical reactions, it can be synthesized in apparently adequate amounts by the body

lipoprotein A fat combined with a protein, forming a compound which transports both in the blood circulation

liver cirrhosis A serious disease characterized by reduction and death of liver cells, derangement of blood circulation in the liver, and scarring of remaining tissues in the liver

low density lipoprotein One type of cholesterol carrier in the blood: that which carries cholesterol and deposits it in the blood vessels

lumen The open inner space of a tubular organ, such as an intestine or blood vessel

lymphatic system The system of vessels and spaces between organs and tissues through which lymph is circulated in the body

lysine An essential amino acid

macrocytic anemia A form of anemia involving immature red bood cells, resulting from lack of folic acid and/or vitamin B_{12}

macroelements Minerals needed by the body in relatively large quantity: sodium, potassium, calcium, phosphorus, magnesium, chlorine, and sulfur

malabsorption syndrome Failure of the small intestine to absorb nutrients properly

malnutrition Refers to bad (= mal) nutrition. For example: lack of food or eating too much

maltose The disaccharide whose units are each composed of two molecules of glucose; also called "malt sugar"

mannose A six-carbon monosaccharide which sometimes occurs as a free sugar

marasmus The syndrome resulting from a deficiency of calories and nearly all other essential nutrients

mechanical soft diet A diet consisting of foods and beverages that require little chewing

medium chain triglyceride A lipid fractionated from coconut oil, containing only fatty acids with 6 to 12 carbon atoms. Important in diet therapy because these compounds are liquid at room temperature, more water soluble than natural fats, and easily digested and absorbed by the body. Abbreviated "MCT"

megaloblastosis Failure of red blood cells to mature, resulting in a form of anemia which may be associated with deficiency of folic acid and/or vitamin B_{12}

metabolism The complex of processes which food nutrients undergo after absorption, including both their breaking down for energy or excretion or their use in synthesizing new materials for cellular growth, maintenance, or repair

methionine An essential amino acid

microcytic anemia Anemia resulting from a lack of iron and/or other nutrients

microelements Minerals needed by the body in very small amounts; iron, iodine, zinc, fluorine, copper, and other trace elements

mixed function oxidase A group of enzymes located mainly in the liver that metabolize drugs

mono- A prefix meaning "one"

monoglyceride A glyceride with only one molecule of fatty acid

monosaccharide One of the simplest carbohydrate

molecules, for it cannot be split into simpler forms

monosodium glutamate An amino acid used as a flavor enhancer. Abbreviated "MSG"

monounsaturated fatty acid An unsaturated fatty acid with one double bond

mucin A component of saliva that lubricates food

mucosa The mucous membrane that lines the tubes and body cavities which open to the outside of the body

mutagen A substance that alters genetic materials so that the change is passed on to the offspring, usually with adverse effects

myelomeningocele The medical condition in which a baby is born with a defect in the vertebral column, allowing the spinal cord and its covering to protrude through the opening

myristic acid A saturated fatty acid

negative nitrogen balance The condition in which nitrogen losses from the body exceed nitrogen intake

niacin (nicotinic acid) A water-soluble B vitamin that can be synthesized in limited amounts in the body if the amino acid tryptophan is present in an adequate amount

niacinamide The amide of nicotinic acid (niacin)

nitrogen equilibrium The normal condition in which nitrogen intake is equal to nitrogen loss from the body

nonessential amino acid One of the amino acids that can be manufactured in the human body if the proper building blocks are available. These compounds are nonetheless necessary in the diet, in a certain relationship to the "essential" amino acids

normoglycemia A normal level of blood "sugar" (glucose)

nutrient A nourishing organic or inorganic substance in food that can be digested, absorbed, and metabolized by the body

nutrition (1) The sum of the processes by which an animal or plant takes in and utilizes food substances: ingestion, digestion, absorption, and assimilation (2) The scientific study of these processes

obesity The condition of weighing 15% to 25% more than one's ideal body weight, with the excess consisting of fat rather than water, muscle, or bones

oleic acid A monounsaturated fatty acid

oligosaccharide A carbohydrate containing many units, each made of two to ten chemically joined monosaccharides

oliguria Abnormally low excretion of urine

organic Derived from living organisms

osmolality The concentration of a solute in a solution per unit of solvent

osmolarity The concentration of a solute in a solution per unit volume of the solution

osmosis Passage of dissolved molecules through a semipermeable membrane from an area of higher concentration to an area of lower concentration until the concentration is equal on both sides of the membrane

osteomalacia Bone softening because of impaired mineralization

osteoporosis A clinical disorder characterized by a reduction in the total quantity of bone in the body

overweight The body weighs more than an accepted norm. The excess can be fat, bone, muscle, water, etc.

ovo-vegetarian An individual whose diet contains no meat, poultry, fish, milk, or milk products, but does include eggs

oxalic acid A substance occurring naturally in vegetables such as chard, rhubarb, and spinach which can chelate calcium in the intestinal tract, rendering it unavailable for absorption

oxidation The process in which a substrate takes up oxygen or loses hydrogen

palmitic acid A saturated fatty acid, usually solid at room temperature

palmitoleic acid A monounsaturated fatty acid

pantothenic acid A B vitamin

parenteral feeding Artificial feeding in which nutrients are injected directly into blood veins

parietal cell A cell of a gastric gland which secretes hydrochloric acid and intrinsic factor

pellagra The niacin (a vitamin) deficiency syndrome, characterized by dermatitis, diarrhea, and dementia

pentoses Five-carbon sugars that play an important role in energy release and formation but are not themselves sources of energy

pepsin A protein-digesting enzyme in the gastric juice of the stomach

peptic ulcer An inflammatory lesion found in the lower end of the esophagus, or in any part of the stomach or duodenum

peptide A compound composed of two or more amino acids joined to each other

peritoneum The membrane that lines the walls of the abdominal cavity and encloses the internal organs

pernicious anemia One form of anemia caused by vitamin B_{12} deficiency, due to a lack of intrinsic factor to facilitate its absorption

phenylalanine An essential amino acid

phosphocreatine A high-energy compound that supplies instant energy when needed by the muscles

phospholipid A fat containing glycerol, two fatty acids, phosphate, and a variable chemical, which serves as a structural component of cell membranes

phytic acid A substance found in the outer husks of cereals that can complex with certain minerals including calcium and zinc, making them unavailable for absorption

plaque (1) A deposit of fat and/or fibrous matter in the wall of a blood vessel
(2) a mucus film providing a home for bacteria on a tooth

poly- A prefix meaning "many"

polypeptide 50 to 100 amino acids chemically joined

polysaccharide A carbohydrate containing many units, each made of hundreds to thousands of chemically joined monosaccharides

polyunsaturated fatty acid An unsaturated fatty acid in which two or more carbon atoms have formed double bonds, with each holding only one hydrogen atom; abbreviated "PUFA"

polyuria Excessive urination

positive nitrogen balance The condition in which nitrogen intake exceeds nitrogen losses from the body

precursor A substance from which another substance is derived. Niacin (a vitamin), for instance, can be made from the precursor tryptophan (an amino acid)

preformed vitamins One form of a group of vitamins that the body can synthesize partially. This term applies to niacin and vitamins A and D. Preformed refers to the presence of these vitamins in readily utilizable forms, e.g., in food

proline A nonessential amino acid

protein Any of the large nitrogen-containing organic compounds built of amino acids and found in the cells of all living organisms

protein efficiency ratio In determining protein quality, the gram of body weight gained by experimental animals per gram of a particular protein food eaten; abbreviated "PER"

proteinuria The abnormal presence of protein in the urine

prothrombin A protein important to blood clotting; synthesized in the liver, requiring the presence of vitamin K

provitamins One form of a group of vitamins that the body can synthesize partially. The vitamins include niacin and vitamins A and D. For example, the body can make vitamin A from carotene (found in carrot). Carotene is the provitamin A

ptyalin A digestive enzyme in saliva

pulses The edible seeds of certain pod-bearing plants, such as beans and peas

pureed diet A diet consisting of foods that are easy to digest, with a consistency between liquid and soft

purine A nitrogen-containing structural component of all cells

pyridoxine A term used for vitamin B_6, most important for serving as a coenzyme in many metabolic processes

RDA Recommended Dietary Allowances—the amounts of specific nutrients established by the National Research Council of the National Academy of Sciences as appropriate for daily consumption by people of specific age and sex groups

reduction The process by which a substrate loses oxygen or accepts hydrogen

relactation Stimulation of milk production in women who have not been breastfeeding

renal Referring to the kidney

residue One definition: the contents of the large intestine; the materials that are left after completion of the digestive processes; also known as "fecal mass." The term has other meanings in relation to food and nutrition

respiratory chain The process in which glucose and fatty acids with the assistance of oxygen are converted to energy, water, and carbon dioxide

rhodopsin The red light sensitive pigment in the retinal rods of the eyes, whose formation requires vitamin A. Also called "visual purple," it is responsible for the ability to see at night

riboflavin Vitamin B_2, important in facilitating many biological reactions

rickets The syndrome caused by vitamin D and/or calcium deficiency, characterized by bone deformities

routine progressive diet The progression from clear liquid, to full liquid, to soft, to solid regular foods traditionally used for certain hospitalized patients

saccharin A controversial artificial sweetener

Salmonella A bacterium capable of causing food poisoning, with symptoms ranging from severe headache, vomiting, diarrhea, abdominal cramps, and fever, to death

satiety The satisfying feeling of being full

saturated fatty acid A fatty acid in which each carbon is joined with four other atoms, thus tying up all potential carbon/hydrogen linkages except the carbons at the "carboxyl" end of the chain

scurvy The vitamin C deficiency syndrome characterized by bleeding gums, pain in joints, bone malformation in childhood, and other problems

serine A nonessential amino acid

serum The clear, yellowish fluid within blood, obtained when whole blood is separated into its solid and liquid constituents

soft diet A diet consisting of foods that are easy to chew

sorbitol A six-carbon sugar alcohol, often used to sweeten "diabetic" products because it has little immediate effect on blood glucose level

Staphylococcus aureus A bacterium capable of causing foodborne intoxication

starch A polysaccharide of many units, each containing hundreds or thousands of glucose molecules; the major form in which energy is stored in plants

stearic acid A saturated fatty acid, usually solid at room temperature

steatorrhea The condition in which the fecal waste is bulky, clay-colored, and fatty because fat has not been properly digested and absorbed

sterol Solid alcohol of the steroid group, found in animals and plants

stoma A small opening or pore. In gastroenterology it refers to a surgical opening in the abdominal wall, leading to a part of the small or large intestine

stomatitis Inflammation of the oral mucous tissue

subcutaneous Beneath the skin

sucrose The disaccharide composed of glucose and fructose, often called "table sugar"

systemic blood circulation The vessels carrying blood between the heart and the body tissues with the exception of the lungs

teratogen A substance with the potential of causing birth defects

terminal sterilization In bottle-feeding of infants, the sterilizing of both formula and bottles together in boiling water

tetany A syndrome resulting from a decreased serum ionizable calcium level, characterized by symptoms such as uncontrolled muscular contractions, seizures, confusion, and increased nervous excitability

thiamin(e) The original chemical name for vitamin B_1, especially important in carbohydrate metabolism

thiaminase An enzyme antagonist of the vitamin thiamin, occurring in some vegetables

threonine An essential amino acid

tocopherol One chemical form of vitamin E. The term implies "antisterile"

tonicity Normal condition of tone or tension

total parenteral nutrition Intravenous feeding which provides a large amount of calories, protein, fat, carbohydrate, vitamins, and minerals. The quality and quantity of nutrients delivered are safe and optimal. Abbreviated "TPN"

toxemia A pathological condition that develops in some pregnant women, characterized by raised blood pressure, edema, nausea, vomiting, liver enlargement and tenderness, headache, the presence of protein in the urine, reduced urine excretion, dizziness, irritability, and sometimes convulsions and coma

triglyceride A fat made of glycerol and three fatty acids; sometimes called a "neutral fat"

trypsin A pancreatic enzyme that breaks down protein molecules

tryptophan An essential amino acid and a precursor of niacin

tyrosine Although classified as a nonessential amino acid, it must be derived from the essential amino acid phenylalanine

undernutrition The lack of essential nutrients in the human body as a result of insufficient food

unsaturated fatty acid A fatty acid in which two or more carbon atoms are not joined with all the hydrogen atoms they can hold. If so, the bond between any two such carbons is called a double bond

urea A nonprotein nitrogen-containing substance produced when protein is metabolized in the liver; the main nitrogenous component of urine

uremia The presence of urinary constituents in the blood

-uria A suffix indicating the abnormal presence of a specified substance in the urine

uric acid A nitrogenous substance formed when purines are metabolized, excreted in urine

USRDA The highest level of recommended intakes for population groups excluding pregnant and nursing mothers, described in the 1968 Recommended Dietary Allowances. Used by the Food & Drug Administration in food labeling

valine An essential amino acid

vegan An individual whose diet contains no meat, poultry, fish, milk, milk products, or eggs: a "strict vegetarian"

viral hepatitis A liver disease involving pathologic death of liver cells and caused by a virus

vitamin An organic compound the body requires in very small amounts to perform its essential functions

vitamin antagonist A substance which can destroy or replace a specific vitamin in the body; also called "antivitamin," "antimetabolite," or "pseudovitamin"

vitamin B complex All known water-soluble vitamins except vitamin C: B_1, B_2, B_6, niacin, folic acid, B_{12}, pantothenic acid, and biotin

Wernicke-Korsakoff syndrome The neurological problems from vitamin B_1 deficiency that develop in alcoholics, pregnant women experiencing excessive vomiting, and patients deficient in thiamin who are given glucose intravenously

xylitol A five-carbon sugar with potential clinical applications such as use as a sweetener for diabetic patients

Index

Page numbers in italics refer to figures; t = table; A = appendix.

NOTES

NOTES

NOTES

NOTES

NOTES

NOTES

NOTES

NOTES

NOTES

NOTES

NOTES

NOTES

NOTES

NOTES

NOTES

NOTES

NOTES

NOTES

NOTES

NOTES

NOTES

NOTES

NOTES

NOTES

NOTES

NOTES

NOTES

NOTES

NOTES

NOTES

NOTES

Estimated Safe and Adequate Daily Dietary Intakes of Additional Selected Vitamins and Minerals for the United States, 1980

	Age (years)	Vitamins		
		Vitamin K (μg)	Biotin (μg)	Pantothenic Acid (mg)
Infants	0–0.5	12	35	2
	0.5–1	10–20	50	3
Children and adolescents	1–3	15–30	65	3
	4–6	20–40	85	3–4
	7–10	30–60	120	4–5
	>11	50–100	100–200	4–7
Adults		70–140	100–200	4–7

Source: *Recommended Dietary Allowances*, 9th ed. (Washington, D.C.: National Academy of Sciences, 1980).

Note: Because there is less information on which to base allowances, these figures are not given in the main table of the RDAs and are provided here in the form of ranges of recommended intakes.